# *Quangos & Quangocrats*

The Shelgate Directory of
Public Bodies,
Executive Agencies,
Nationalised Industries,
Public Corporations
& Regulators

Editors
Klaus Boehm and Bill Garlick

Shelgate

This edition is published in 1998 by The Shelgate Publishing Co Ltd, 36 Shelgate Road, London SW11 1BG.

ISBN: 1 871096 00 6

A CIP catalogue record for this book is available from the British Library.

**Publisher's note**

The information in this book was correct to the best of the Editors' knowledge and the Publisher's belief at the time of going to press. While no responsibility can be accepted for errors and omissions, the Editors and Publisher would welcome corrections and suggestions for material to include in subsequent editions of this book

***Quangos & Quangocrats*** is jointly owned by Klaus Boehm Publications Ltd and The Shelgate Publishing Company Ltd. This directory and its databases are an integral part of their joint public sector information project which will provide briefings, reports, mailing lists, advice and consultancy services. Project contact: Manager, Public Service Information Project, The Shelgate Publishing Co Ltd, 36 Shelgate Road, London SW11 1BG. (tel 0171 924 2707; fax 0171 924 3357).

Typeset and printed by Wyvern 21, Bath Road, Bristol

Cover designed by Daniel Duke

# Contents

## About the Editors

**Klaus Boehm** lives and works in London, developing reference books from scratch with a variety of British publishers. He has been closely involved in definitive titles ranging from *British Archives* to the *Macmillan Nautical Almanac* (both Macmillan) and in annual educational reference books - notably *The Equitable Schools Book* (Bloomsbury in association with *The Sunday Times)* and the *NatWest Student Book* (Trotman). He is a keen believer in institutional accessibility and transparency - and the demystification of bureaucracy and bureaucrats. Hence *Quangos & Quangocrats.*

In the field of business and professional reference books, he developed *Who's Who in the City* and has worked together with Brian Morris on a number of European titles, including *The European Community* which won the ASLIB Economic and Business Group's directory award.

**Bill Garlick** worked in both the computer and traditional book publishing industries before establishing the Shelgate Publishing Co Ltd in 1985. His and Shelgate's expertise lies in the application of computing and database techniques to the publication of business information.

Shelgate has published a number of business books in association with banks, building societies, insurance companies, accountants and solicitors. It also publishes *Who's New,* a database of recent business appointments. Bill Garlick lives and works in London.

## Acknowledgements

We are very grateful for the tremendous help and encouragement we have received from a large number of people and from very many quangos.

At the planning stage, two people made critical contributions. Wing Commander Basil D' Oliveira OBE showed us how to harness modern information technology to the printing of this directory. David Barrows OBE, then Assistant Director of the Public Appointments Unit (Office of Public Service) at the Cabinet Office, pin-pointed the limitations of central government data and led us to rely solely on primary sources. We are greatly indebted to both.

The preparation of a first edition of any annual business directory - from the drawing board to bound books - requires strong editorial and publishing management and team effort. Without the key contribution of our editorial co-ordinator, Jenny Lees-Spalding, *Quangos & Quangocrats* would never have seen the light of day. We are indebted to the astonishing efforts of the research and editorial team: Anne Greenshield made a unique contribution in researching and drafting the profiles; further invaluable research was undertaken by Brian Morris and Steve Hinchley; Renata Di Grazia Carialho, Carmen Peres and Aline Stürmer put in extraordinary hours in checking and data inputting; and Liz Murray copy-edited the book in record time. The project would not be the same without the help of Barry Ashby and Mike Baggallay; the design from Daniel Duke; or the help from Simon Baker in keeping computers up to the job.

# FOREWORD

## Introduction

Quangos are news. Judging by the *Today* programme (broadcast by the BBC - one of the better known quangos) they seem to be undergoing a process of violent change - launching, merging, winding up or locked in combat with one vested interest or another, every day of the week.

But the daily news is not the real story. Since the late eighties a quiet revolution has been taking place in the machinery of government . Quangos - unelected public bodies, including nationalised industries and public corporations - were already managing much of the public sector. But enormous slabs of work which were previously undertaken by Whitehall, such as social security payments, began to be hived off into Next Steps agencies; and quangos have continued to extend their remit into almost every managerial aspect of government to the point where, today, over 75% of the civil service works in executive agencies or government departments operating on Next Steps lines (i).

While the national role of quangos grows and grows, another largely un-noticed revolution is taking place. Quangos old and new are being required to manage themselves like businesses. There is continuous managerial review and reform of quangos, with the understanding that public money is paid for performance and efficiency. The pace is very uneven but in the long run each quango responds or goes down.

All quangos are asked to work within a business ethos in which measurable productivity and efficiency gains and targeted performance have pride of place. Private sector partnership are actively encouraged, especially where private sector finance can play a part. Where possible, work is out-sourced to the private sector. Income must be earned where possible. Today's quangocrats talk about outputs, service delivery, bearing down on costs, productivity gains allied to investment in IT or IS, and last but not least about customers and customer satisfaction, rather than public service. Managements are equipped with corporate plans, business plans, five year framework documents, clear and published annual accounts - like a commercial company. Their joint turnover is measured in £ billions.

This directory is not concerned with the political philosophy or public administration underlying the current debate about what is and what is not a quango. The fact is that there is a spectrum of executive organisations within the public sector, all at different stages of development. Some were launched so recently that they have not yet published their first Report and Accounts; others are mature bodies with the experience of half a century behind them. Our aim is simply to open up the opaque world of quangos to business for business.

## What's Covered in *Quangos and Quangocrats*?

**Quangos**. Only executive quangos are included. There are hundreds of others, depending on the definition employed (ii), but this directory concentrates exclusively on quangos with executive functions operating at the national level in England, Wales, Scotland, Northern Ireland (and in various combinations) and within the United Kingdom. It profiles over 420 executive quangos individually, some of which may not be best pleased to be described as quangos at all - and their common thread is that every one of them operates at arms length from Ministers. We summarise what they do, what they are for, what they spend and who runs them. The quangos selected for profiling are drawn almost exclusively from two documents published by the Cabinet Office (iii), together with a number of Regulators.

To be crystal clear about our selection, they comprise:

- Executive bodies (Non-Departmental Public Bodies, or NDPBs)
- Executive agencies, including Defence agencies (Next Steps agencies).
- Nationalised industries
- Public corporations
- Regulators
- and four Government departments working on Next Steps lines.

A complete alphabetical list of the quangos can be found at the start of the PROFILES section.

**Quangocrats**. Key decision makers in each executive quango. We have identified some 7,000 quangocrats involved in the management who work at supervisory or management board levels, or are senior executives or heads of department. Some quangos have no management board, only a supervisory board or a board of trustees, and a handful (eg many regulators) work without any board at all. A complete alphabetical list of all the quangocrats we have identified can be found in the PEOPLE section.

## *Modus Operandi* and Sources

This is a business directory designed to put business in touch with executive quangos. The selected quangos were asked for their annual report and accounts, business and corporate plans and any other briefing materials they cared to share with us. Our profiles were drafted from these publicly available documents. The most up-to-date Reports and Accounts were 1996/97 and this is broadly our datum point, although we have had to rely on some earlier reports and have included some later data. Finally we sent the draft profile to each quango for comment and correction. We met with a very generous response and much good advice; although to our surprise, at this vetting stage, one or two asked where we had found information which they had thought confidential. There are no secrets to be found in this directory.

## Accessing Quangos

We provide easy access to quangos - by region, by area of business activity and by level of expenditure.

**Regional Index**. Each quango's main address and branch addresses are listed under one of 14 regions. In England they are listed under the ten Government Office Regions (GORs); for the rest of the UK, they are under the country - Northern Ireland, Scotland and Wales; and a separate heading for overseas addresses.

**Professional Advisers.** Where known to us, we note the auditors, bankers, solicitors and public relations advisers on each quango's profile. We also list which qaungos are advised by each adviser in the Professional Advisers section.

**Business Index.** Executive quangos are involved in a variety of activities - giving and taxing, issuing passports and keeping people in prison, conserving works of art and protecting the natural environment.

Their spectrum of activities is almost as wide as those of national government itself. To help business access which quangos operate in a particular area of business we have placed each quango in one or more business categories eg accounting & finance, tourism, agriculture.

**Expenditure Listings**. Quangos' expenditure varies greatly - from a few hundred thousand pounds to £2 billion and more. To get a feel of a quango's business potential, we have placed each into broad expenditure categories (iv).

# Next Edition

Comments and suggestions for the next edition would, of course, be most welcome.

**Klaus Boehm and Bill Garlick**
**March 1998**

## Footnotes

*(i) The Next Steps programme aims to deliver government services more efficiently and effectively within available resources. It starts from the premise that the Civil Service is too big and its activities too diverse to be managed as one unit. It is a dynamic programme, moving quangos towards becoming customer-focused organisations. It aims to benefit taxpayers, customers and staff.*

*(ii) Many bodies which fall into the broader definitions of quango have not been selected eg advisory bodies, almost all police authorities, and other bodies described by Nolan as local public spending bodies. These include institutions of further and higher education including universities, Grant-Maintained Schools, Registered Social Landlords and Registered Housing Associations (Scotland). We exclude all bodies which form a part of the NHS, such as local trusts, which are described definitively in the IHSM Health and Social Services Year Book. There is also a seemingly endless list of advisory bodies, tribunals, boards of prison visitors etc with no executive role which we exclude. What constitutes a quango is the subject of deep feeling and intense debate. We regard the matter simply as one of branding a group of executive organisations which make a real contribution to the UK. It needs first an acceptable brand name and then to improve its image.*

*(iii) Public Bodies 1997 and Next Steps Briefing Note October 1997, both produced by the Cabinet Office, Office of Public Service.*

*(iv) Our summary income and expenditure accounts do not support detailed comparison of one quango with another. There are no summary balance sheets. There are real difficulties in refining our summary income and expenditure accounts to the point at which a true league table might emerge. Our summary accounts are intended to help business identify quangos for their own business purposes.*

*Profiles*

## List of Quango Profiles

Accounts Commission for Scotland
Advisory, Conciliation & Arbitration Service
Agricultural Research Institute of Northern Ireland
Agricultural Wages Board for England & Wales
Agricultural Wages Board for Northern Ireland
Alcohol Education & Research Council
Apple & Pear Research Council
Armed Forces Personnel Administration Agency
Army Base Repair Organisation
Army Base Storage & Distribution Agency
Army Personnel Centre
Army Technical Support Agency
Army Training & Recruitment Agency
Arts Council of England
Arts Council of Northern Ireland
Arts Council of Wales
Audit Commission
Bank of England
Benefits Agency
Biotechnology & Biological Sciences Research Council
Britain-Russia Centre
British Association for Central & Eastern Europe
British Board of Agrément
British Broadcasting Corporation
British Council
British Educational Communications & Technology Agency
British Film Institute
British Hallmarking Council
British Library
British Museum
British Nuclear Fuels plc
British Railways Board
British Shipbuilders
British Tourist Authority
British Waterways
Broadcasting Standards Commission
Business Development Service
Buying Agency
Cadw
Caledonian MacBrayne Ltd
Cardiff Bay Development Corporation
Castle Vale Housing Action Trust
Central Computer & Telecommunications Agency
Central Council for Education & Training in Social Work
Central Office of Information
Central Rail Users Consultative Committee
Central Science Laboratory
Centre for Environment, Fisheries & Aquaculture Science
Centre for Information on Language Teaching & Research
Channel Four Television Corporation
Child Support Agency
Civil Aviation Authority
Civil Service College

Coal Authority
Coastguard
Commission for the New Towns
Commission for Racial Equality
Commissioner for Protection Against Unlawful Industrial Action
Commissioner for the Rights of Trade Union Members
Commonwealth Development Corporation
Commonwealth Institute
Commonwealth Scholarship Commission
Community Development Foundation
Companies House
Compensation Agency
Construction Industry Training Board
Construction Industry Training Board (NI)
Construction Service
Contributions Agency
Council for Catholic Maintained Schools
Council for the Central Laboratory of the Research Councils
Countryside Commission
Countryside Council for Wales
Court Service
Covent Garden Market Authority
Crafts Council
Criminal Cases Review Commission
Criminal Injuries Compensation Authority
Crofters' Commission
Crown Agents Foundation
Crown Prosecution Service
Defence Analytical Services Agency
Defence Animal Centre
Defence Bills Agency
Defence Clothing & Textiles Agency
Defence Codification Agency
Defence Dental Agency
Defence Estates Organisation
Defence Evaluation & Research Agency
Defence Intelligence & Security Centre
Defence Medical Training Organisation
Defence Postal & Courier Services Agency
Defence Secondary Care Agency
Defence Transport & Movements Executive
Defence Vetting Agency
Design Council
Disposal Sales Agency
Driver & Vehicle Licensing Agency
Driver & Vehicle Licensing Northern Ireland
Driver & Vehicle Testing Agency
Driving Standards Agency
Duke of York's Royal Military School
East of Scotland Water Authority
Economic & Social Research Council
Education Assets Board
Employment Service
Employment Tribunals Service
Engineering Construction Industry Training Board
Engineering & Physical Sciences Research Council
English Heritage
English National Board for Nursing, Midwifery & Health Visiting
English Nature
English Partnerships

English Sports Council
English Tourist Board
Enterprise Ulster
Environment Agency
Environment & Heritage Service
Equal Opportunities Commission
Equal Opportunities Commission for Northern Ireland
Fair Employment Commission for Northern Ireland
Farming & Rural Conservation Agency
Financial Services Authority
Fire Service College
Fisheries Conservancy Board for Northern Ireland
Fisheries Research Services
Fleet Air Arm Museum
Food from Britain
Food Standards Agency
Football Licensing Authority
Forensic Science Agency of Northern Ireland
Forensic Science Service
Forest Enterprise
Forest Research
Foyle Fisheries Commission
Funding Agency for Schools
Further Education Funding Council
Further Education Funding Council for Wales
Gaming Board for Great Britain
Gas Consumers' Council
Geffrye Museum
General Consumer Council for Northern Ireland
Government Car & Despatch Agency
Government Property Lawyers
Government Purchasing Agency
Great Britain-China Centre
Hannah Research Institute
Health Estates
Health & Safety Commission
Health & Safety Executive
Higher Education Funding Council for England
Higher Education Funding Council for Wales
Highlands & Islands Airports
Highlands & Islands Enterprise
Highways Agency
Historic Royal Palaces
Historic Scotland
HM Customs & Excise
HM Land Registry
HM Prison Service
Home-Grown Cereals Authority
Horniman Museum
Horserace Betting Levy Board
Horserace Totalisator Board
Horticultural Development Council
Horticulture Research International
Housing Corporation
Human Fertilisation & Embryology Authority
Imperial War Museum
Independent Commission for Police Complaints for Northern Ireland
Independent Television Commission
Industrial Research & Technology Unit
Information Technology Services Agency

Inland Revenue
Insolvency Service
Intervention Board
Investors in People UK
Joint Air Reconnaissance Intelligence Centre
Joint Nature Conservation Committee
Labour Relations Agency
Laganside Corporation
Land Registers of Northern Ireland
Legal Aid Board
Liverpool Housing Action Trust
Livestock & Meat Commission for Northern Ireland
Local Enterprise Development Unit
Logistic Information Systems Agency
London Pensions Fund Authority
London Regional Passengers Committee
London Transport
Macaulay Land Use Research Institute
Marine Safety Agency
Marshall Aid Commemoration Commission
Meat Hygiene Service
Meat & Livestock Commission
Medical Devices Agency
Medical Practices Committee
Medical Research Council
Medical Supplies Agency
Medicines Control Agency
Mental Health Commission for Northern Ireland
Met Office
Military Survey
Milk Development Council
Millennium Commission
Ministry of Defence Police
Monopolies & Mergers Commission
Museum of London
Museum of Science & Industry, Manchester
Museums & Galleries Commission
National Army Museum
National Biological Standards Board
National Board for Nursing, Midwifery & Health Visiting for Northern Ireland
National Board for Nursing, Midwifery & Health Visiting for Scotland
National Consumer Council
National Film & Television School
National Forest Company
National Galleries of Scotland
National Gallery
National Heritage Memorial Fund
National Library of Scotland
National Library of Wales
National Lottery Charities Board
National Maritime Museum
National Museum of Science & Industry
National Museums & Galleries, Merseyside
National Museums & Galleries of Wales
National Museums of Scotland
National Portrait Gallery
National Radiological Protection Board
National Savings
National Weights & Measures Laboratory
Natural Environment Research Council
Natural History Museum
Naval Aircraft Repair Organisation

Naval Bases & Supply Agency
Naval Manning Agency
Naval Recruiting & Training Agency
New Millennium Experience Co Ltd
NHS Estates
NHS Pensions Agency
North of Scotland Water Authority
Northern Ireland Child Support Agency
Northern Ireland Commissioner for Protection Against Unlawful Industrial Action
Northern Ireland Commissioner for the Rights of Trade Union Members
Northern Ireland Council for the Curriculum, Examinations & Assessment
Northern Ireland Council for Postgraduate Medical & Dental Education
Northern Ireland Fishery Harbour Authority
Northern Ireland Local Government Officers' Superannuation Committee
Northern Ireland Museums' Council
Northern Ireland Prison Service
Northern Ireland Statistics & Research Agency
Northern Ireland Tourist Board
Northern Ireland Transport Holding Company
Northern Lighthouse Board
Occupational Pensions Regulatory Authority
Office of the Data Protection Registrar
Office of Electricity Regulation
Office of Fair Trading
Office of Gas Supply
Office of the National Lottery
Office for National Statistics
Office of Passenger Rail Franchising
Office of the Rail Regulator
Office for the Regulation of Electricity & Gas
Office for Standards in Education
Office of Telecommunications
Office of Water Services
Ofwat Central Customer Service Committee
Ofwat Eastern Customer Service Committee
Ofwat National Customer Council
Ofwat North West Customer Service Committee
Ofwat Northumbria Customer Service Committee
Ofwat South West Customer Service Committee
Ofwat Southern Customer Service Committee
Ofwat Thames Customer Service Committee
Ofwat Wales Customer Service Committee
Ofwat Wessex Customer Service Committee
Ofwat Yorkshire Customer Service Committee
Oil & Pipelines Agency
Ordnance Survey
Ordnance Survey of Northern Ireland
Parole Board

Parole Board for Scotland
Particle Physics & Astronomy Research Council
Patent Office
Pay & Personnel Agency
Pensions Compensation Board
Pesticides Safety Directorate
Planning Inspectorate
Planning Service
Police Authority for Northern Ireland
Police Complaints Authority
Policyholders' Protection Board
Post Office
Post Office Users' Council for Northern Ireland
Post Office Users' Council for Scotland
Post Office Users' Council for Wales
Post Office Users' National Council
Probation Board for Northern Ireland
Property Advisers to the Civil Estate
Public Health Laboratory Services Board
Public Record Office
Public Record Office of Northern Ireland
Public Trust Office
Qualifications & Curriculum Authority
Qualifications, Curriculum & Assessment Authority for Wales
Queen Elizabeth II Conference Centre
Queen Victoria School
Radio Authority
Radiocommunications Agency
RAF Logistics Support Services
RAF Maintenance Group Defence Agency
RAF Personnel Management Agency
RAF Signals Engineering Establishment
RAF Training Group Defence Agency
Rail Users Consultative Committee for Eastern England
Rail Users Consultative Committee for the Midlands
Rail Users Consultative Committee for North Eastern England
Rail Users Consultative Committee for North Western England
Rail Users Consultative Committee for Scotland
Rail Users Consultative Committee for Southern England
Rail Users Consultative Committee for Wales
Rail Users Consultative Committee for Western England
Rate Collection Agency
Registers of Scotland
Registrar of Public Lending Right
Remploy
Residuary Body for Wales
Rivers Agency
Roads Service
Rowett Research Institute
Royal Air Force Museum
Royal Armouries
Royal Botanic Garden Edinburgh
Royal Botanic Gardens Kew
Royal Commission on Ancient & Historical Monuments of Scotland
Royal Commission on Ancient & Historical Monuments in Wales
Royal Commission on Historical

Manuscripts
Royal Commission on Historical
Monuments of England
Royal Marines Museum
Royal Mint
Royal Naval Museum
Royal Navy Submarine Museum
Royal Parks Agency
Rural Development Commission
S4C
Scottish Agricultural Science Agency
Scottish Agricultural Wages Board
Scottish Arts Council
Scottish Children's Reporter
Administration
Scottish Community Education Council
Scottish Conveyancing & Executry
Services Board
Scottish Council for Educational
Technology
Scottish Court Service
Scottish Crop Research Institute
Scottish Enterprise
Scottish Environment Protection Agency
Scottish Fisheries Protection Agency
Scottish Further Education Unit
Scottish Higher Education Funding
Council
Scottish Homes
Scottish Hospital Endowments Research

Trust
Scottish Legal Aid Board
Scottish Medical Practices Committee
Scottish Natural Heritage
Scottish Office Pensions Agency
Scottish Prison Service
Scottish Qualifications Authority
Scottish Record Office
Scottish Screen
Scottish Sports Council
Scottish Tourist Board
Scottish Water & Sewerage Customers
Council
Sea Fish Industry Authority
Security Facilities Executive
Serious Fraud Office
Service Children's Education
Ships Support Agency
Simpler Trade Procedures Board
Sir John Soane's Museum
Social Security Agency (Northern Ireland)
Specialist Procurement Services
Sports Council for Northern Ireland
Sports Council for Wales
Stonebridge Housing Action Trust
Student Awards Agency for Scotland
Student Loans Company
Tai Cymru
Tate Gallery
Teacher Training Agency

Tower Hamlets Housing Action Trust
Traffic Director for London
Training & Employment Agency (NI)
Treasury Solicitor's Department
Trinity House Lighthouse Service
UK Atomic Energy Authority
UK Ecolabelling Board
UK Hydrographic Office
UK Passport Agency
UK Register of Organic Food Standards
UK Sports Council
Ulster Museum
Valuation & Lands Agency
Valuation Office Agency
Vehicle Certification Agency
Vehicle Inspectorate
Veterinary Laboratories Agency
Veterinary Medicines Directorate
Victoria & Albert Museum
Wales Tourist Board
Wallace Collection
Waltham Forest Housing Action Trust
War Pensions Agency
Water Service
Welsh Development Agency
Welsh Language Board
Welsh National Board for Nursing,
Midwifery & Health Visiting
West of Scotland Water Authority
Westminster Foundation for Democracy
Wilton Park Executive Agency
Wine Standards Board
Youth Council for Northern Ireland

### Editorial Note

Our information on quangos was gathered under standard definitions and where possible is presented in the same form. The headings normally indicate the following:

**Status** - eg executive body (NDPB), executive agency (Next Steps agency), government department operating on Next Steps lines etc.

**Founded** - year established as a public body (also year originally founded if different).

**Sponsor** - name of government department with ministerial responsibility.

**Powers** - name and date of main relevant Act of Parliament or Royal Charter. Also Framework Document, Memorandum and Articles of Association etc.

**Mission** - main purpose of quango.

**Tasks** - main activities undertaken.

**Operations** - Management: ownership and reporting structure, management boards , divisional organisation etc. Policy: new initiatives, search for private or National Lottery funds etc. Trends: growth or decline in demand, decrease in government funding etc.

**Performance** - 1996/97 targets met or not met.

**Board** - Members of supervisory and executive boards; who appoints them and from which sectors of the community.

**Staff** - average number employed 1996/97; names of senior executives, heads of departments etc.

**Financial** - where possible, income and expenditure accounts for 1996/97, and the previous two years; also designated accounting officer.

**Publications** - current corporate publications; some significant examples from the publications list.

# Accounts Commission for Scotland

18 George Street
Edinburgh EH2 2QU

**Tel** 0131 447 1234
**Fax** 0131 477 4567          **Web** http://www.scot-ac.gov.uk

| | |
|---|---|
| *status* | Executive body |
| *founded* | 1975 |
| *sponsor* | Scottish Office |
| *powers* | Local Government (Scotland) Act 1973, NHS and Community Care Act 1990 |
| *mission* | To oversee the external audit of local authorities and the health service in Scotland and through the audit process to assist them to achieve the highest standards of financial stewardship and economic, efficient and effective use of resources. |
| *tasks* | Arranges the independent external audit of some £12 billion expenditure in Scotland by the health service and local government bodies (including police and fire authorities); investigates frauds or irregularity in accounts; undertakes value-for-money studies to improve economy and efficiency; reviewing the management arrangements which the bodies have in place; setting out the performance information which local authorities have to publish annually. |
| *operations* | Management: Controller of Audit reports to the Commission and is supported by a management team of the heads of the five departments and the Secretary. The Secretary works closely with the Controller of Audit but acts independently as a legal adviser to the Commission. Recovers full costs each year from audited bodies.

Policy: Half of audits are conducted by private accountancy firms and half by Commission staff.

Trends: Scotland's unique public audit system is being considered for use elsewhere. |
| *board* | Members are appointed by the Secretary of State from a wide range of backgrounds and experience. |

| Chairman | Prof JP Percy CBE | |
|---|---|---|
| Deputy Chairman | Malcolm McIver | |
| Members | Mrs M Campbell | Donald McNeil OBE |
| | Mrs W Goldstraw | Bruce A Merchant OBE |
| | Frank Kirwan | Geoffrey T Millar |
| | Robert M Maiden | John G Mullin |
| | Ms R Marshall | John C (Ian) Stewart OBE |
| | B McGhee | Miss Margaret C Thomson |
| | Miss Elizabeth K McLean OBE | |
| *Accounting Officer* | *Controller of Audit* | |

*staff* 157

| | |
|---|---|
| Controller of Audit | Robert Black |
| Secretary to the Commission | Bill Magee |
| Director of Value for Money Studies (Local Government) | Steve Evans |
| Director of Health & Social Work Studies | Caroline Gardner |
| Director of Audit Services | Bill Hay |
| Head of Management Studies | Alan Neilson |
| Director of Audit Strategy | Harris Wells |

*financial*

**INCOME & EXPENDITURE**

| Year end: 31 March | 1997 £000 | 1996 £000 | 1995 £000 |
|---|---|---|---|
| **INCOME** | | | |
| Contributions from local authorities | 5,449 | 5,527 | 5,731 |
| Contributions from NHS | 3,649 | 1,391 | - |
| Revenue grant from NHS Management Executive | 60 | 1,142 | - |
| Bank interest | 113 | 54 | 62 |
| | **9,271** | **8,114** | **5,793** |
| **EXPENDITURE** | | | |
| Staff and Commission Members | 4,197 | 3,549 | 2,779 |
| Approved Auditors fees and expenses, local authorities | 2,063 | 2,393 | 2,433 |
| Approved Auditors fees and expenses, NHS | 1,776 | 863 | - |
| Other operating charges | 1,067 | 1,157 | 581 |
| Depreciation | 168 | 152 | - |
| | **9,271** | **8,114** | **5,793** |

| *advisers* | **Auditors** | National Audit Office | 157-197 Buckingham Palace Road |
| | | | London SW1W 9SP |

*publications*  Annual Report, Range of value-for-money reports

| *audit firms* | Coopers & Lybrand | Henderson Loggie |
| | Glasgow | Dundee |
| | Deloitte & Touche | KPMG |
| | Edinburgh | Edinburgh |
| | Deloitte & Touche | KPMG |
| | Glasgow | Glasgow |
| | Ernst & Young | Price Waterhouse |
| | Aberdeen | Glasgow |
| | Ernst & Young | Scott-Moncrieff Downie Wilson |
| | Inverness | Edinburgh |
| | Ernst & Young | Scott Oswald |
| | Glasgow | Inverness |

# Advisory, Conciliation & Arbitration Service (ACAS)

Brandon House
180 Borough High Street
London SE1 1LW

**Tel** 0171 210 3613
**Fax** 0171 210 3645

**Contact** Head of Information

| *status* | Executive body |
| *founded* | 1974 |
| *sponsor* | Department of Trade and Industry (DTI) |
| *powers* | Trade Union and Labour Relations (Consolidation) Act 1992 |
| *mission* | To improve the performance and effectiveness of organisations by providing an independent and impartial service to prevent and resolve disputes and to build harmonious relationships at work. |
| *tasks* | Preventing and resolving industrial disputes; conciliating in actual and potential complaints to industrial tribunals; providing impartial information and advice on employment matters; promoting good practice and improving the understanding of industrial relations. |
| *operations* | Management: Council members direct policy and review financial matters. The Chairman reports to the Council. Each region run by a Director. |
| | Trends: Record number of claims to industrial tribunals in 1996. Collective conciliations steady at around 1300 pa. Some indications in 1996 of worsening workplace relations. New European directives influencing working practices. 70% more conciliation cases resulted in a withdrawal or settlement without the need to go to an industrial tribunal. |
| *board* | Members of Council are appointed by the Secretary of State. |

| Chairman | JW Hougham CBE | |
| Members | B Barber | |
| | J Edmonds | Mrs SG Monk |
| | Mrs JM Gaymer | W Morris |
| | R Gilbert | Prof AJ Pointon |
| | Prof JFB Goodman CBE | BM Warman |
| | WJ Knox | Ms C Wells OBE |
| *Accounting Officer* | Chairman | |

*staff*  597

| | |
|---|---|
| Chairman | John Hougham CBE |
| Chief Conciliator | Derek Evans |
| Director, Operational Policy | Francis Noonan |
| Director, Strategy | Peter Syson |
| Director, Scotland | Frank Blair |
| Director, Resources | Hazel Canter |
| Director, South & West Region | Frank Coley |
| Director, Midlands Region | Carol Davenport |
| Director, Northern Region | Steve Fletcher |
| Director, London, Eastern & Southern Areas | Bill Greenaway |
| Director, North West Region | Paul Oliver |
| Director, Wales | Peter Richards |

*advisers*  **Bankers**  HM Treasury

**Auditors**  National Audit Office  157-197 Buckingham Palace Road
London SW1W 9SP

*publications*  *Annual Report, Codes of Practice, Advisory Handbooks, Advisory Booklets, Guides for Small Firms, occasional papers, etc.*

*branches*

Warwick House
6 Highland Road
Birmingham B15 3ED
Tel 0121 456 5856

Anderson House
Clinton Avenue
Nottingham NG5 1AW
Tel 0115 969 3355

Commerce House
St Alban's Place
Leeds LS2 8HH
Tel 0113 243 1371

Westgate House
Westgate Road
Newcastle upon Tyne NE1 1TJ
Tel 0191 261 2191

Boulton House
17-21 Chorlton Street
Manchester M1 3HY
Tel 0161 228 3222

39 King Street
Thetford
Norfolk IP24 2AU

Suites 3-5
Business Centre
1-7 Commercial Road
Paddock Wood
Kent TN12 6EN

Westminster House
Fleet Road
Fleet
Hants GU13 8PD
Tel 01252 811868

Clifton House
83-117 Euston Road
London NW1 2RB
Tel 0171 396 5100

249 St Mary's Road
Garston
Liverpool L19 0NF
Tel 0151 427 8881

Regent House
27a Regent Street
St Clifton
Bristol BS8 4HR
Tel 0117 974 4066

Franborough House
123-157 Bothwell Street
Glasgow G2 7JR
Tel 0141 204 2677

3 Purbeck House
Lambourne Crescent
Llanishen
Cardiff CF4 5GJ
Tel 01222 761126

# Agricultural Research Institute of Northern Ireland

Hillsborough
Co Down BT26 6DR

**Tel** 01846 682484
**Fax** 01846 689594

| | |
|---|---|
| *status* | Executive body |
| *founded* | 1925 |
| *sponsor* | Northern Ireland Office, Department of Agriculture for NI (DANI) |
| *powers* | Agricultural Research Station Act (Northern Ireland) 1927 |
| *mission* | To undertake research in crop and animal production to ensure a more competitive NI agri-food business. |
| *tasks* | Provides staff and facilities for research programmes undertaken within research divisions of DANI (primarily Agricultural and Environmental Science Division). Provides farm demonstration facilities and staff for students at Queen's University, Belfast. Provides specialist advice for DANI on development of people and businesses within the NI agri-food business. |
| *operations* | Management: Director responsible for day-to-day running of Institute. Some income from produce and research contracts. |
| | Policy: Computer model predicting cattle growth now used across Ireland and Great Britain. Developing linkages with farms for co-operative research programmes. |
| | Trends: Hoping to attract funding from new NI producers' research levy. |
| *board* | Trustees: three appointed by Department of Agriculture, four by Ulster Farmers' Union, one by Ulster Agricultural Organisation Society, two represent the Queen's University of Belfast, one NI Agricultural Producers' Association. |

| | | |
|---|---|---|
| Chairman | WG Smyth OBE | |
| Members | Prof MK Garrett | |
| | Prof FJ Gordon | JB Mulvenna |
| | HR Kirkpatrick | IC Murray |
| | J Mallon | JA Patton CBE |
| | CH McMurray | JA Rankin |
| Secretary | GWC Troughton | |
| *Accounting Officer* | *Permanent Under Secretary* | |

*staff* 95

| | |
|---|---|
| Director | Prof FJ Gordon |
| Sheep Production & Heifer Rearing | AF Carson |
| Crop Production | DL Easson |
| Farm Mechanisation | JP Frost |
| Milk & Beef Production | RWJ Steen |

*financial*

**INCOME & EXPENDITURE**
Year end: 31 March

| | 1997 £ | 1996 £ | 1995 £ |
|---|---|---|---|
| **INCOME** | | | |
| Department of Agriculture - Running Expenses Grant | 2,280,000 | 2,333,000 | 2,285,000 |
| Income from activities | 1,172,557 | 1,145,867 | 1,100,512 |
| | **3,452,557** | **3,478,867** | **3,385,512** |
| **EXPENDITURE** | | | |
| Staff costs | 1,763,715 | 1,734,859 | 1,657,630 |
| Depreciation | 157,552 | 157,878 | 135,370 |
| Other operating charges | 1,784,248 | 1,827,081 | 1,595,878 |
| | **3,705,515** | **3,719,818** | **3,388,878** |
| **OPERATING (DEFICIT) SURPLUS** | **(252,958)** | **(240,951)** | **(3,366)** |
| Investment income | 19,981 | 20,320 | 19,566 |
| **SURPLUS (DEFICIT) ON ORDINARY ACTIVITIES** | **(232,977)** | **(220,631)** | **16,200** |
| Transfer (to) from Capital Assets Reserve | 232,977 | 220,631 | (16,200) |
| **SURPLUS (DEFICIT) FOR FINANCIAL YEAR** | - | - | - |
| Retained surplus brought forward | - | - | - |
| **RETAINED SURPLUS CARRIED FORWARD** | - | - | - |

| | | | |
|---|---|---|---|
| *advisers* | **Bankers** | Northern Bank | Ballynahinch Street, Hillsborough |
| | **Auditors** | Johnston Graham & Co | 87 Wellington Park, Belfast |
| | **Solicitors** | Cleaver Fulton & Rankin | 50 Bedford Street, Belfast |
| *publications* | *Annual Report* | | |

# *Agricultural Wages Board for England & Wales (AWB)*

Nobel House
17 Smith Square
London SW1P 3JR

**Tel** 0171 238 6540
**Fax** 0171 238 6553

*status*  Executive body

*founded*  1948

*sponsor*  Ministry of Agriculture, Fisheries and Food (MAFF). Welsh Office

*powers*  Agricultural Wages Act 1948

*mission*  Fair wages and conditions of employment for agricultural workers in England and Wales.

*tasks*  Negotiating and deciding minimum rates of pay and terms and conditions of employment and issuing legally enforceable Orders specifying rates and terms.

*operations*  Management: The Chairman reports to the Secretaries of State. The Secretary is the Chief Executive and Orders are issued by him. AWB is financed and staffed by MAFF and the WO. MAFF and the WO may prosecute employers breaching AWB Orders. Agricultural Wages Inspectors are located in the nine MAFF Regional Service Centres in England and in the three Welsh Office Agriculture Department's Divisional Offices in Wales

*board*  Eight representatives of agricultural workers, nominated by the Transport and General Workers' Union; eight representatives of agricultural employers, nominated by the National Farmers' Union and five independent members, including the Chairman, appointed by the two Secretaries of State.

*branches*

Government Buildings
Burghill Road
Westbury-on-Trym
Bristol BS10 6NJ
Tel 0117 591000

Eden Bridge House
Lowther Street
Carlisle
Cumbria CA3 8DX
Tel 01228 234000

Alphington Road
Exeter EX2 8NQ
Tel 01392 277951

Government Buildings
Crosby Road
Northallerton
North Yorkshire DL6 1AD
Tel 01609 773751

Block 7
Government Buildings
Chalfont Drive
Nottingham NG8 3SN
Tel 01602 291191

Coley Park
Reading
Berkshire RG1 6DT
Tel 01734 581222

Block B
Government Buildings
Brooklands Avenue
Cambridge CB2 2DR
Tel 01223 462727

Berkeley Towers
Nantwich Road
Crewe
Cheshire CW2 6 PT
Tel 01270 69211

Government Buildings
Whittington Road
Worcester WR5 2LQ
Tel 01905 763355

Penrallt
Caernarfon
Gwynedd LL55 1EP
Tel 01286 674144

Government Buildings
Picton Terrace
Carmarthen SA31 3BT
Tel 01267 234545

Spa Road East
Llandrindod Wells
Powys LD1 5HA
Tel 01597 823777

# Agricultural Wages Board for Northern Ireland

Room 22A
Dundonald House
Upper Newtownards Road
Belfast BT4 3SB

**Tel** 01232 524521
**Fax** 01232 524634

| | |
|---|---|
| *status* | Executive body |
| *founded* | 1948 |
| *sponsor* | Northern Ireland Office, Department of Agriculture NI (DANI) |
| *powers* | Act 1948 |
| *mission* | Fair wages and conditions of employment for agricultural workers in Northern Ireland. |
| *tasks* | Negotiating and deciding minimum rates of pay and terms and conditions of employment for agricultural workers in Northern Ireland, and issuing legally enforceable Orders specifying rates and terms. |
| *operations* | Management: The Chairman reports to the Secretary of State. The Board is financed and staffed by DANI. The Secretary is Chief Executive and Orders are issued by him. DANI inspects employers and enforces the Board's Orders in the courts. Employees who consider their employers are in breach of the Board's Orders complain directly to the Secretary of the Board. |
| *board* | Three Board members, including the Chairman, are appointed by the Head of DANI; six are appointed by the Ulster Farmers' Union; and seven by the Transport and General Workers' Union. |

| | |
|---|---|
| Secretary | M McKillen |

# Alcohol Education & Research Council (AERC)

Room 520
Clive House
Petty France
London SW1H 9HD

**Tel** 0171 271 8379/8337
**Fax** 0171 271 8877

| | |
|---|---|
| *status* | Executive body |
| *founded* | 1981 |
| *sponsor* | Home Office |
| *powers* | Licensing (Alcohol Education and Research) Act 1981 |
| *mission* | To administer the Alcohol Education and Research Fund. |
| *tasks* | Administers charitable foundation which finances projects within the UK for education and research into alcohol and for novel forms of help to those with drinking problems including offenders. |
| *operations* | Management:  Part-time administrative staff.  Council meets four times a year to consider applications for grants and reports from grant holders.  Committees are appointed to administer the studentship scheme and to determine research priorities. |
| | Policy: Quality of research applications improving. |
| | Trends: Fewer projects being funded due to cost of research. |
| *board* | Council members appointed by the Home Secretary from a variety of professional service and business backgrounds. |

| Chairman | Baroness Flather JP |
|----------|---------------------|
| Members | AG Eadie |
| | Dr E Gilvarry |
| | Mrs G Mackenzie |
| | I Mackenzie |
| | Prof P Parsloe |
| | Dr B Ritson |

**staff** Two

| Secretary | Leonard Hay |
|-----------|-------------|
| Scientific Officer | Prof R Hodgson |

**financial**

### INCOME & EXPENDITURE
**Year end: 31 March**

| | 1996 £ | 1995 £ |
|---|---|---|
| **INCOMING RESOURCES** | | |
| Investment income | 559,187 | 498,493 |
| Requests and donations | 150,000 | - |
| Final distribution from liquidator of Licensing Compensation Authorities | - | 32,000 |
| | **709,187** | **530,493** |
| **RESOURCES EXPENDED** | | |
| Direct charitable expenditure | | |
| Grants paid | 345,936 | 458,088 |
| Studentship couse fees and expenses | 28,434 | 71,702 |
| | **374,370** | **529,790** |
| Other expenditure: management and administration of the charity | | |
| Brokers' management fee | 25,198 | 24,743 |
| Rent and service charges | 12,071 | 13,047 |
| Secretary's remuneration and national insurance | 18,192 | 16,088 |
| Secretarial expenses | 7,418 | 3,951 |
| Secretarial assistance | 7,887 | 8,442 |
| Members' travel expenses | 11,870 | 9,032 |
| Cost of council meetings | 2,269 | 2,306 |
| Auditor's remuneration | 1,939 | 2,068 |
| Accountancy fees | 3,408 | 3,290 |
| | **90,252** | **82,967** |
| | **464,622** | **612,757** |
| **NET INCOMING/(OUTGOING) RESOURCES** | **244,565** | **(82,264)** |
| Gains/(losses) on investments | | |
| Realised | 671,120 | 351,942 |
| Unrealised | (10,766) | (831,201) |
| **NET MOVEMENT IN FUND** | **904,919** | **(561,523)** |
| Fund balance brought forward | 7,626,349 | 8,187,872 |
| **FUND BALANCE CARRIED FORWARD** | **8,531,268** | **7,626,349** |

**advisers** **Auditors** Saffery Champness London

**publications** *Annual Report*

# Apple & Pear Research Council

Bradbourne House Stable Block
East Malling Research Station
East Malling
West Malling
Kent ME19 6DZ

**Tel** 01732 845115
**Fax** 01732 844828

**Contact** Malcolm Ronald, Secretary

**status** Executive body

**founded** 1989

**sponsor** Ministry of Agriculture, Fisheries and Food (MAFF). Welsh Office

| | |
|---|---|
| **powers** | Industrial Organisation and Development Act 1947. Apple and Pear Research Council Order 1989 |
| **mission** | To increase efficiency and productivity of the industry in England and Wales. |
| **tasks** | Collecting the levy from growers. Promoting or undertaking scientific research; promoting or undertaking enquiries into materials and equipment, methods of production, labour utilisation etc; running experimental establishments; collecting statistics; supplying information; promoting better UK public knowledge of technical matters, products and their use. |
| **operations** | Management: All growers in England and Wales, with two hectares or more planted with 50 or more apple or pear trees, are registered by the Council. Subject to the approval of the Minister, the Council can impose an annual charge not exceeding £25 per hectare of land planted to pay for its work. |
| **board** | Council appointed by the Minister to include five members capable of representing the interests of growers, one capable of representing employees, two independent members with no financial interest in the industry and one with special knowledge of marketing and distribution in the industry. |

| | | |
|---|---|---|
| Chairman | Prof Ian Swingland | |
| Members | Clive Baxter | Mrs Teresa Mackay |
| | Jeremy Boxall | Robert Mitchell |
| | Alan Burbridge | Simon Thirkell |
| | Balram Gidoomal CBE | Andrew Wheldon |
| Secretary | Malcolm Ronald | |
| *Accounting Officer* | *Secretary* | |

**financial**

**INCOME & EXPENDITURE**

| Year end: 31 March | 1997 | 1996 | 1995 |
|---|---|---|---|
| | £ | £ | £ |
| **GROSS INCOME** | | | |
| Levies | 300,499 | 294,419 | 331,009 |
| Corporate sponsorship contributions | 5,000 | 5,000 | 5,000 |
| Eurofru grants | 62,198 | 56,296 | 73,532 |
| | 367,697 | 355,715 | 409,541 |
| **EXPENDITURE** | | | |
| Horticultural research | 332,004 | 370,672 | 315,545 |
| Administration expenses | 34,540 | 19,659 | 16,902 |
| Staff costs | 75,495 | 54,855 | 50,643 |
| Council expenses | 7,106 | 8,758 | 8,461 |
| | (449,145) | (453,944) | (391,551) |
| **OPERATING (DEFICIT)/SURPLUS** | (81,448) | (98,229) | 17,990 |
| Interest receivable | 11,086 | 13,071 | 10,631 |
| **(DEFICIT)/SURPLUS FOR THE YEAR** | (70,362) | (85,158) | 28,621 |
| Surplus Brought Forward | 102,837 | 187,995 | 159,374 |
| **SURPLUS CARRIED FORWARD** | 32,475 | 102,837 | 187,995 |

| **advisers** | | | |
|---|---|---|---|
| **Bankers** | Barclays Bank | 40/46 High Street, Maidstone, Kent ME14 1SS |
| **Auditors** | Day, Smith & Hunter | Star House, Maidstone, Kent ME14 1LT |
| **Solicitors** | MacDonald Oates | Square House, The Square Petersfield, Hampshire GU32 3HT |

# Armed Forces Personnel Administration Agency (AFPAA)

Building 182
RAF Innsworth
Gloucester GL3 1EZ

**Tel** 01452 712612
**Fax** 01452 510814

| | |
|---|---|
| **status** | Defence agency |
| **founded** | 1997 |
| **sponsor** | Ministry of Defence (MOD) |

| | |
|---|---|
| **powers** | Framework Document |
| **mission** | Providing, on a tri-Service basis, cost effective data and systems for the payment of military personnel and to support the personnel management function - in peace, crisis, transition to war and war. |
| **tasks** | Collecting data and maintaining Records of Service for all full-time, part-time and reserve Service personnel. Providing data to personnel managers to enable them to make decisions on recruiting, training and development, manning and career management, deployment and retirement. Providing information for policy makers, statisticians and planners. Paying the correct amounts, including pensions, to individuals through bank transfers etc. Offering personnel information systems and support to the three Services. |
| **operations** | Management: AFPAA's Owner is the Deputy Chief of Defence Staff (Programmes and Personnel), who is responsible for the strategic direction, and for approving AFPAA's corporate and business plans, targets and monitoring performance. He is advised by the Owner's Advisory Board, whose main members are the Chiefs of Staff of the three Services' Principal Personnel Officers. The Chief Executive is responsible for the day-to-day management. He is advised by a Customer Advisory Group comprising senior representatives of AFPAA customers. A commercial partner will be appointed under the government's Private Finance Initiative (PFI) to provide services on behalf of the Agency and for the development and operation of an integrated computer system. Some staff may be transferred to the partner when appointed. The Headquarters is located initially at RAF Innsworth.There are separate operational locations at Worthy Down (Army), Gosport (Royal Navy) and Innsworth (RAF) and these will probably be reduced after the partnership contract is completed. The current staff is mainly civilian (960 civil servants). The 200 Service staff are almost all from the Royal Navy and RAF personnel functions; elements of the Army Personnel Centre in Glasgow will become part of the Agency. |
| | Policy: Tri-Service approach requires smooth transition to a new corporate cuture; single-Service staff will have to work with a tri-Service perspective. Civilian staff will work in a private sector environment. AFPAA, and the three Services will have much less control over methods of service delivery. |
| | Trends: Encouraging commercial partners to apply private sector innovation and skills to the harmonisation of the three Service's personnel administration. |

| **board** | *Accounting Officer* | *Permanent Under Secretary* |
|---|---|---|

| **staff** | 1160 |
|---|---|

| | |
|---|---|
| Chief Executive | Air Commodore Chris Winsland |
| Directors | Commodore KRG Bailey |
| | Group Captain I F Hendley |
| | Brigadier ML Ward |
| Assistant Director, Partnering | Colonel D Aitken |
| Director of Personnel & Finance | CJ Boyle |
| Assistant Director, Service Requirements | Group Captain JA Upham |
| Assistant Director, Personnel & Secretariat | PA Clarke |

# *Army Base Repair Organisation (ABRO)*

Building 200
Monxton Road
Andover
Hants SP11 8HT

**Tel** 01264 383295
**Fax** 01264 383144

**Contact** 01264 383295

| | |
|---|---|
| **status** | Defence agency |
| **founded** | 1993 |
| **sponsor** | Ministry of Defence (MOD) |
| **powers** | Framework document |
| **mission** | To be the preferred repair support agency for the UK armed forces. |
| **tasks** | To deliver a comprehensive repair support service to the British army in all operational readiness states - from routine training through to general war - and to support the other armed services and government departments. |

ABRO repairs and re-manufactures anything from the smallest item of individual equipment to complete weapons systems, all to exacting customer standards.

**operations** Management: ABRO is owned by the Director General of Equipment Support (Army) within the Quartermaster General's area. It is managed by the Chief Executive and his management board from the corporate headquarters in Andover. It is organised in business units focusing on delivering a quality service to customers, whether through in-house repairs or under contract with industry. They are ABRO Bovington, ABRO Donington, and LABRO Land Command Support Group. In 1997, the headquarters was restructured into two business units: the Corporate Operations Group and the Procurement Group.

Policy: The corporate plan reflects government defence planning assumptions. ABRO's strategy is to maintain and build on its position as the Army's preferred supplier and to become customer-oriented, to build a flexible team to meet changing customer requirements and to expose operations to competition in the marketplace.

Trends: ABRO's services are driven by customer requirements, primarily those of the Army's equipment support managers, army field units and individual training organisations.

**board** Executive Management Board, principally drawn from senior management.

| | |
|---|---|
| Chief Executive | JR Drew CBE |
| Corporate Operations Director & Deputy Chief Executive | Dr A Byrne |
| Procurement Director | G Burt |
| Military Director (ABRO Land Command Support) | Colonel MD Lemon |
| Contracts Director | A Lewis |
| Finance Director | J Rogers |
| Director, ABRO Land Command Support Group | G Benjamin |
| Director, ABRO Bovington | BJ Hunt OBE |
| Director, ABRO Donnington | RL Nunn |
| *Accounting Officer* | *Chief Executive* |

**staff** 3103

**financial**

| INCOME & EXPENDITURE Year end: 31 March | 1997 £000 | 1996 £000 | 1995 £000 |
|---|---|---|---|
| **INCOME** | | | |
| Income from sales & services | 592 | 555 | 1,751 |
| **EXPENDITURE** | | | |
| Staff Costs | 56,515 | 58,137 | 56,408 |
| Supplies and services consumed | 233,479 | 190,291 | 195,137 |
| Accommodation | 8,267 | 4,896 | 8,723 |
| Other administration charges | 3,117 | 1,933 | 4,884 |
| Interest charge on capital | 8,064 | 6,034 | - |
| | 309,442 | 261,291 | 265,152 |
| **NET EXPENDITURE before exceptional items** | 308,850 | 260,736 | 263,401 |
| Loss on Disposal of Discontinued Operations | 10,358 | - | - |
| **NET EXPENDITURE after exceptional items** | 319,208 | 260,736 | 263,401 |

# Army Base Storage & Distribution Agency (ABSDA)

Building 202/203
HQ QMG
Portway
Monxton Road
Andover
Hampshire SP11 8HT

**Tel** 01264 383633
**Fax** 01264 383342

**status** Defence agency
**founded** 1995
**sponsor** Ministry of Defence (MOD)
**powers** Framework Document

| | |
|---|---|
| *mission* | To operate the Army storage and distribution base, cost-effectively and worldwide, to agreed standards while sustaining the Army's technical skills in these functions for crisis and war - eg supporting all three armed services in the former Yugoslavia. |
| *tasks* | Functional command and control over Army base storage and distribution. Receiving, inspecting, storing, servicing, issuing and delivering stocks of commodities within specified levels of service for peace, crisis and war. Formal and practical training on storage-related functions for military personnel. Maintaining and modifying ammunition and associated packaging. |
| *operations* | Management: ABSDA brings together the Army's Base Depots in Great Britain and Germany and provides the vital link between equipment suppliers, managers and end users. Its Owner is the Director General of Logistics Support (Army). The Chief Executive reports to the Owner and is responsible for ABSDA's strategic direction, the achievement of key targets and resources. He is supported by the Management Board. ABSDA's services are provided through a network of seven main Base Depots in the UK and two in Germany, with a further 12 UK Distribution Outlets. Internally, ABSDA is organised into seven divisions. Four - Operations, Finance, Personnel and Secretariat - are at Andover with the Chief Executive. The other three commodity division headquarters, which are the main service providers, are colocated with main Base Depots: Stores Division at Bicester, Ammunition Division at Kineton, and Vehicles and Fuels Division at Ashchurch. The total inventory is about 600,000 items valued at around £5 billion pounds. |

Policy: Rationalisation of vehicle storage and development of a strategic information system.

Trends: Rationalisation of organisation resulted in closure of secondary storage depots. Disposal of £5 million fixed assets. Defence review may affect ABSDA.

| | |
|---|---|
| *board* | Management Board appointed by the Owner. |

| Chief Executive | Brigadier KJW Goad |
|---|---|
| *Accounting Officer* | *Chief Executive* |

| | |
|---|---|
| *staff* | 5842 (5250 civilians, 592 Army) |

| | |
|---|---|
| *financial* | |

**INCOME & EXPENDITURE**
Year end: 31 March

| | 1996 |
|---|---|
| | £000 |
| **EXPENDITURE** | |
| Staff costs | 98,187 |
| Supplies and services | 38,266 |
| Accommodation costs | 39,520 |
| Other administration costs | 20,223 |
| Depreciation of assets | 11,782 |
| | 207,978 |
| Loss on disposal of fixed assets | 5,162 |
| Interest charge on capital | 19,290 |
| **INCOME** | (1,529) |
| **NET EXPENDITURE** | 230,901 |

# *Army Personnel Centre (APC)*

Kentigern House
65 Brown Street
Glasgow G2 8EX

**Tel** 0141 224 2070
**Fax** 0141 224 2144

| | |
|---|---|
| *status* | Defence agency |
| *founded* | 1996 |
| *sponsor* | Ministry of Defence (MOD) |
| *powers* | Framework Document 1996 |
| *mission* | To provide the Army with an effective, integrated personnel management and administration services to maximise its operational capability throughout the spectrum of conflict, from peace through to war. |
| *tasks* | Manpower planning - to fill established and temporary posts, to the Army's satisfaction and where possible |

meeting the aspirations of individuals; individual officer and soldier career management, including counselling and promotion selection boards; Army personnel, pay and pension administration - creating the Record of Service from enlistment to discharge procedures.

**operations** Management: The Adjutant General is the Owner and reports to the Secretary of State. He sets the strategic operating framework. The Chief Executive is also the Military Secretary and in that capacity reports to the Chief of the General Staff. All APC functions are being collocated in Glasgow.

Policy: Building on the Army's traditional strengths to develop an integrated service supported by comprehensive IT systems.

**board**

| | |
|---|---|
| Chief Executive | Major General DL Burden CB CBE |

# Army Technical Support Agency (ATSA)

HQ QMG
Monxton Road
Andover
Hants SP11 8HT

**Tel** 01264 383753
**Fax** 01264 383294

**E-mail** all.atsa@gtnet.gov.uk
**Web** http//www.army.mod.uk/atsa/atsa.htm

**Contact** Lt Col A Phipps, Cos/Planner 01264 383 004

**status** Defence agency

**founded** 1995

**sponsor** Ministry of Defence (MOD)

**powers** Owned by the Director General of Equipment Support (Army)

**mission** To be a dynamic organisation recognised as a centre of engineering excellence and the first point of reference for technical support to the Army.

**tasks** To enhance the Army's operational capability by providing an effective and efficient technical support service to the Field Army, military and civilian workshops, contractors, the (MOD) Procurement Executive and the QMG Equipment Support Organisation and to industry.

**operations** Management: Formed from a number of existing technical branches and authorities, ATSA unites a unique range of technical support expertise under a Chief Executive. Customers can now tap this technical resource through a single organisation. The Chief Executive reports to the Director General of Equipment Support (Army) and, since its formation, the organisation has been restructured and consolidated into the Executive Management Board. Most ATSA effort is concentrated onto five main sites, but the staff is dispersed to some 23 sites and some are deployed in Germany and Bosnia.

Policy: To complete the collocation of its Land Systems Groups onto a single site from the current five main sites under a Private Finance Initiative contract by the year 2000.

Trends: Agreements with all principal customers have been reviewed and ATSA has set about ensuring that it is accessible to its customers - helplines are in place and teams are available to deploy with the Field Army. It is hoping to play a greater role within the Integrated Logistic Support Planning for equipments entering service with the Army

**board** Appointed by the Director General of Equipment Support (Army).

| | |
|---|---|
| Chief Executive | Brigadier AD Ball CBE |
| Director Engineering | Colonel M Capper |
| Director Technical Services | JR Denyer |
| Director Business Development | P Gowing |
| Director Administration | C Knapman |
| Director Aircraft Branch | Lieutenant Colonel T Mathew |
| Chief of Staff/Planner | Lieutenant Colonel A Phipps |
| Director PFI | M Stockbridge |
| *Accounting Officer* | *Director Administration* |

**staff** 1200 (civilian and military)

| financial | INCOME & EXPENDITURE | |
|---|---|---|
| | Year end: 31 March | **1997** |
| | | **£000** |
| | **EXPENDITURE** | |
| | Staff costs | 28,848 |
| | Supplies and services consumed | 11,360 |
| | Accommodation costs | 3,005 |
| | Other admin expenses | 4,891 |
| | | **48,104** |
| | **INCOME** | |
| | Less: Income from non MOD Customers | (122) |
| | **NET OPERATING EXPENDITURE** | **47,982** |
| | Interest charge on capital | 1,428 |
| | Loss on disposal of fixed assets | 136 |
| | **NET EXPENDITURE** | **49,546** |

| advisers | **Auditors** | National Audit Office | 157-197 Buckingham Palace Road London SW1W 9SP |
|---|---|---|---|
| | **Public Relations** | Leslie Sharman | 01344 635 521 |

# Army Training & Recruiting Agency (ATRA)

Trenchard Lines
Upavon
Pewsey
Wiltshire SN9 6BE

**Tel** 01980 615010
**Fax** 01980 615305

**Contact** WO1 Rigby (Tom) 0198 615033

| | |
|---|---|
| status | Defence agency |
| founded | 1996 (as Army Individual Training Organisation - AITO). Defence agency in 1997 |
| sponsor | Ministry of Defence (MOD) |
| powers | Framework document |
| mission | To recruit and train young people to become the best soldiers in the world. To provide the appropriate numbers of well-trained and motivated soldiers to meet the operational requirements of the Army. |
| tasks | Attract, select and enlist appropriate soldier recruits and officer cadets; train recruits and officer cadets in basic military skills; train personnel in specialist skills appropriate to their individual Arm or Service; provide progressive career training to enhance individual professional development; provide training for personnel from other Services, civilians and foreign nationals, as authorised; provide ATRA personnel and resources for authorised external operational and administrative tasks - both in war and the transition to war; instill the ethos of the British Army. |
| operations | Management: An integral part of the Adjutant General's Training and Personnel Command, within the Army chain of command. A flat command and management structure with training conducted by 18 Operating Divisions eg Royal Military Academy Sandhurst. Training is conducted at some 38 schools on 42 sites; recruitment at 123 towns throughout the UK. Command is vested in a Director General who is advised by a Headquarters Management Board, and is exercised through the Agency Management Board which guides strategy, reviews each Operating Division's plans and performance and deals with pan-agency issues such as validation. It is chaired by the Director General and comprises the commanders of the Operating Divisions and some non-executive members and headquarters staff. The Director General handles week-to-week management through the Headquarters Management Board which monitors performance against targets, reviews finance etc. It comprises the Heads of Branches of Headquarters. Operating Divisions have a great deal of autonomy within ATRA policy and best practice. |
| | Policy: Strategic Private Sector Involvement (SPSI) aims to embrace all areas where an alliance with the private sector may be possible - assets, future plans, and untapped opportunities. |
| | Trends: ATRA is working towards full control of its estates to make best use of its capital and revenue, particu- |

larly rationalising the estate to concentrate training on the best sites; capital works expenditure will be exposed to the Private Finance Initiative (PFI). An equipment husbandry programme uses the most cost-effective mix of internal and external equipment. A service contract was awarded to EDS Defence to provide an effective management information system (TAFMIS). ATRA wants to attract a single private sector partner (company or consortium) for each Operating Division.

**board**

| | |
|---|---|
| Director General Training & Recruiting | Major General Christopher Elliott |
| Deputy Chief Executive | Charles Gordon |
| Commandant Defence School of Transport | Brigadier Tom Blyth |
| Commandant Royal School of Military Engineering | Brigadier Robbie Burns |
| Head of Plans and Resources | Bill Clark |
| Commander Recruiting Brigadier | Andy Craig |
| Commander Initial Training Group | Brigadier Andrew Cumming |
| Commander Royal Logistic Corps Training Group | Brigadier Tony Dalby-Walsh |
| Commander Royal Armoured Corps Centre | Colonel Chris Day |
| Commandant Royal Military Academy Sandhurst | Major General Arthur Denaro |
| Non-Executive Member | Dr Roger Gilbert |
| Commandant Infantry Training Centre Warminster | Colonel David Glyn-Owen |
| Officer Commanding Defence Explosive Ordnance | |
| Disposal School | Lieutenant Commander Stuart Harper |
| Head of Corporate Strategy | Colonel Shane Hearn |
| Commander Royal School of Signals | Colonel Charles Le Gallais |
| Commandant Physical & Adventurous Training Group | Lieutenant Colonel Barry Lillywhite |
| Commandant Infantry Training Centre Catterick | Colonel Nigel Lithgow |
| Commandant Royal School of Artillery | Colonel Jim Longfield |
| Commandant Defence Nuclear Biological & Chemical Centre | Group Captain Ian McPhee |
| Commandant Adjutant General's Corps Training Group | Colonel Maurice Nugent |
| Head of Management Information Systems | Lieutenant Colonel John Richards |
| Head of Operations | Colonel Tom Richardson |
| Head of Personnel | Miss Sue Scott-Curtis |
| Commandant School of Army Aviation | Colonel Nigel Thursby |
| Commander Royal Electrical & Mechanical Engineers | |
| Training Group | Brigadier Tim Tyler |
| Commandant Infantry Training Centre Wales | Colonel Tim Weeks |
| Agency Secretary | Peter Wilson |
| *Accounting Officer* | *Chief Executive* |

**staff**   In 1997/98 11,074; 6124 military, 4950 civilian

**publications**   Framework Document, Forward Plan, Annual Report and Accounts, Guide to the ATRA, ATRA NEWS.

# *Arts Council of England*

14 Great Peter Street
London SW1P 3NQ
**Tel** 0171 333 0100
**Fax** 0171 973 6590

**E-mail** information@artscouncil.org.uk
**Web** www.artscouncil.org.uk

**Contact** Stephen Chappel, Information Officer

**status**   Executive body

**founded**   1946 as Arts Council of Great Britain. Executive body in 1994

**sponsor**   Department of Culture, Media and Sport (DCMS)

**powers**   Royal Charter 1994. National Lottery Act 1993

**mission**   To fund and support the arts.

**tasks**   To distribute government and Lottery funds to the arts in England in conjunction with the Regional Arts Boards (RABs). To develop and improve the knowledge, understanding and practice of the arts. To increase the accessibility of the arts to the public. To advise and co-operate with departments of government, local authorities and the Arts Councils of Scotland, Wales and Northern Ireland.

**operations**   Management: There is a Secretary General and a Senior Management team. The Arts Council receives a grant-in-aid from the DCMS but works at arm's length from government. It also distributes some Lottery funds. There is a comprehensive advisory structure which assists in policy formulation. Members are normally specialists (eg working artists, scholars and critics) and are appointed by the Council from nominations which are open to the public. The ten RABs are independent companies and Arts Council grants to them are subject to Arts Council conditions. Working relationships between the RABs and the Arts Council continue to strengthen. The Council is not allowed to solicit applications for Lottery awards and the RABs play a vital role in identifying regional priorities, and encouraging and helping applicants. New Lottery programmes run by the Council include a stabilisation programme to break the spiral of decline in under-funded organisations; working with cultural industries to develop the relationship between the subsidised and commercial sectors; and Arts for Everyone which awards grants for specific projects from £500 to £500,000.

Policy: Devolution is set to continue. The ten RAB Chairmen are already full members of the Council in their own right, appointed after local consultation. New Lottery rules will enable the Council to start using Lottery money to fund people as well as buildings.

Trends: The grant-in-aid has fallen by about £20 million in real terms over the last four years and is likely to continue falling, leaving some companies struggling or close to bankruptcy. Lottery funds have increased, enabling the Council to make more money than before available for buildings and facilities.

***board***    Appointed by the Secretary of State and always includes Chairmen of the ten RABs.

| | | |
|---|---|---|
| Chairman | Gerry Robinson | |
| Deputy Chairman | David Reid | |
| Members | David Brierley | |
| | Richard Cork | Prof Andrew Motion |
| | Prof Ray Cowell | Rod Natkiel |
| | Prof Brian Cox CBE | Stephen Phillips |
| | Charles Denton | Trevor Phillips |
| | Prof Christopher Frayling | Christopher Price |
| | Sir David Harrison CBE | Roger Reed |
| | Gavin Henderson | Stella Robinson |
| | Thelma Holt CBE | Prudence Skene |
| | Lady MacMillan | John Spearman |
| Observer | Denys Hodson CBE | |
| *Accounting Officer* | *Secretary-General* | |

***staff***    231 in the Arts Council and 345 in the RABs

| | |
|---|---|
| Secretary-General | Peter Hewitt |
| Deputy Secretary-General | Graham Devlin |
| Head of Secretariat | Lawrence Mackintosh |
| Head of Press & Public Affairs | Sue Rose |
| Director of Finance & Resources | Nigel Copeland |
| Financial Controller | Jennifer Oakley |
| Information Services Manager | Annie Thackeray |
| Property & Services Manager | Sam Turner |
| Director, Human Resources | Heather Daley |
| Director, Combined Arts | Iain Reid |
| Director, Dance | Hilary Carty |
| Director, Drama | Anna Stapleton |
| Director, Film, Video & Broadcasting | Rodney Wilson |
| Director, Literature | Gary McKeane |
| Director, Music | Kathryn McDowell |
| Director, Touring | Kate Devey |
| Director, Visual Arts | Marjorie Allthorpe-Guyton |
| Director, Education & Training | Pauline Tambling |
| Director, Policy, Research & Planning | Graham Hitchen |
| Director, National Lottery | Jeremy Newton |
| Director of Operations, Lottery Operations | Moss Cooper |
| Director, Lottery Film Unit | Carolyn Lambert |
| Director, Lottery Projects | Nicole Penn-Symons |
| Head of Unit, Lottery Interim Unit | Carol Stone |

*financial*

| FINANCIAL ACTIVITIES | | |
|---|---|---|
| Year end: 31 March | **1997** | **1996** |
| | **£000** | **£000** |
| **INCOMING RESOURCES** | | |
| Parliamentary grant-in-aid | 185,133 | 191,133 |
| Interest receivable | 224 | 291 |
| Other income | 1,559 | 1,517 |
| | **186,916** | **192,941** |
| **RESOURCES EXPENDED** | | |
| Grants | 180,525 | 182,711 |
| Support costs | 7,374 | 7,916 |
| | **187,899** | **190,627** |
| Management and administration | 1,703 | 3,277 |
| Resources expended before costs apportioned to Lottery | 189,602 | 193,904 |
| Less costs apportioned to the Lottery | (3,914) | (3,052) |
| | **185,688** | **190,852** |
| **NOTIONAL COSTS** | | |
| Cost of capital | (512) | (413) |
| Insurance | (10) | (9) |
| **NET INCOMING RESOURCES AFTER NOTIONAL COSTS** | **706** | **1,667** |
| Reversal of notional costs | 522 | 422 |
| **NET INCOMING/(OUTGOING) RESOURCES FOR THE YEAR** | **1,228** | **2,089** |
| Gains on investments assets | 6 | 4 |
| **NET MOVEMENT IN FUNDS** | **1,234** | **2,093** |
| Balance brought forward | 7,924 | 5,795 |
| Prior year adjustment | 0 | 36 |
| Adjusted value brought forward | 7,924 | 5,831 |
| **BALANCE CARRIED FORWARD** | **9,158** | **7,924** |

| LOTTERY DISTRIBUTION ACCOUNT | | |
|---|---|---|
| Year end: 31 March | **1997** | **1996** |
| | **£000** | **£000** |
| **INCOME** | | |
| Share of proceeds from the National Lottery | 240,880 | 244,194 |
| Investment returns on the distribution fund | 21,229 | 10,910 |
| Commitments written back | 107 | - |
| Interest receivable | 541 | 248 |
| Other Income | 45 | 8 |
| | **262,802** | **255,360** |
| **EXPENDITURE** | | |
| Grants | 344,450 | 229,918 |
| Staff costs | 1,036 | 568 |
| Other operating costs | 9,593 | 3,215 |
| Depreciation | 176 | 29 |
| Costs apportioned by grant-in-aid | 3,914 | 3,052 |
| Total operating costs | 14,719 | 6,864 |
| | **359,169** | **236,782** |
| **NET RESOURCES EXPENDED BEFORE NOTIONAL COSTS** | **(96,367)** | **18,578** |
| Cost of capital | 258 | 66 |
| Insurance | 10 | 9 |
| | **(268)** | **(75)** |
| **NET RESOURCES EXPENDED AFTER NOTIONAL COSTS** | **(96,635)** | **18,503** |
| Reversal of notional costs | 268 | 75 |
| **INCREASE/(DECREASE) IN LOTTERY FUNDS** | **(96,367)** | **18,578** |
| Accumulated funds brought forward | 66,067 | 47,489 |
| **ACCUMULATED FUNDS CARRIED FORWARD** | **(30,300)** | **66,067** |

*advisers*

| | | |
|---|---|---|
| **Bankers** | Coutts & Co | 440 Strand, London WC2R 0QS |
| **Auditors** | National Audit Office | 157-197 Buckingham Palace Road London SW1W 9SP |
| **Solicitors** | Bird & Bird | 90 Fetter Lane, London EC4A 1JP |

*publications* *Policy for Dance of the English Arts Funding System, The Regional Dance Agencies, Policy for Drama of the English Arts Funding System, Arts Networking in Europe, A Poetry Survey for the Arts Council of England: Key Findings, Writers Available for Tour Bulletin, Architectural Competitions: A Handbook for Promoters, Capital Grants for the Arts, Arts Council of England Strategy for the Support and Development of Orchestras and their Audiences, Jazz, Economics of Artists' Labour Markets, Local Authority Expenditure on the Arts in England 1995/6, Annual Report & Accounts, Arts Council News, A Guide to Audience Development*

# Arts Council of Northern Ireland

77 Malone Road
Belfast BT9 6AQ

**Tel** 01232 385200
**Fax** 01232 661715

| | |
|---|---|
| *status* | Executive body |
| *founded* | 1995 |
| *sponsor* | Northern Ireland Office, Department of Education NI (DENI) |
| *powers* | Arts Council (NI) Order 1995 |
| *mission* | To develop the arts in Northern Ireland so that as many people as possible can enjoy as many forms of art as possible to as high a standard as possible. |
| *tasks* | Grant aids individuals, events, projects, organisations and establishments in literature, traditional arts, visual arts, music, opera, drama and dance. Some direct management functions eg running Belfast Print Workshop, organising the annual touring programme of recent acquisitions. Distributes lottery funds for the arts. |
| *operations* | Management: The Chief Executive is responsible for the day-to-day management. Organised in four departments: Creative Arts, Performing Arts, Strategic Development, and Finance, Personnel & Administration (first three have Advisory Panels); and two units (Public Affairs and Lottery). DENI operates on an 'arm's length principle' in making grants to the Council, ie it may not interfere in the Council's artistic judgement. |
| | Policy: Strategic partnerships with funding agencies. District councils forming plans and targets for delivery of arts in their areas. |
| | Trends: Lottery funding exceeds revenue funding. |
| *board* | Council appointed by the Secretary of State. |

| | | |
|---|---|---|
| Chairman | Donnel Deeny QC | |
| Vice-Chairman | Sir Charles Brett CBE | |
| Members | Cllr Martin Bradley | Ms Marnie O'Neill |
| | William Burns | Glenn Patterson |
| | Sam Burnside | Richard Pierce |
| | Cllr Fred Cobain | Ms Chrissie Poulter |
| | Patrick Donnelly | Miss Irene Sandford |
| | Dr Tess Hurson | Aidan Shortt |
| | Mrs Rosaleen McMullan | Dr Brian Walker |

*staff*  44

| | |
|---|---|
| Chief Executive | Brian Ferran |
| Lottery Officer | Tanya Greenfield |
| Director, Performing Arts Department | Philip Hammond |
| Director, Strategic Development Department | Nick Livingston |
| Director, Finance, Personnel & Administration Department | Billy Lyttle |
| Director, Creative Arts Department | Noirin McKinney |
| Public Affairs Officer | Damian Smyth |

*financial*

**INCOME & EXPENDITURE**
Year end: 31 March

| | 1996 £ |
|---|---|
| **INCOME** | |
| Department of Education | |
| Basic grant | 6,964,516 |
| Cultural traditions funding | 300,000 |
| Other income | 102,958 |
| | **7,367,474** |
| **EXPENDITURE** | |
| Visual Art & Film | 811,073 |
| Literature | 249,019 |
| Traditional Arts | 107,347 |
| Music & Opera | 1,902,316 |
| Drama & Dance | 1,624,099 |
| Community Arts | 549,202 |
| Education & Youth | 155,333 |
| Development | 270,764 |

| | |
|---|---:|
| Cultural Management Training Programme | 13,271 |
| Cultural Traditions | 300,000 |
| Strategy | 19,282 |
| Purchase of Works of Art | 14,915 |
| Central Art Services | 110,101 |
| Staff costs | 708,375 |
| Other operating costs | 402,783 |
| | **7,237,880** |
| **SURPLUS/(DEFICIT) FOR YEAR** | **129,594** |
| Surplus/(Deficit) brought forward | (147,218) |
| **SURPLUS/(DEFICIT) CARRIED FORWARD** | **(17,624)** |

# Arts Council of Wales (ACW)

Museum Place
Cardiff CF1 3NX

**Tel** 01222 336500
**Fax** 01222 221447

| | |
|---|---|
| *status* | Executive body |
| *founded* | 1994 |
| *sponsor* | Welsh Office |
| *powers* | Royal Charter 1994 |
| *mission* | Responsible for funding and developing the arts (crafts, drama, dance, literature, music, visual arts) in Wales through the media of both Welsh and English. |
| *tasks* | Developing opportunities for artists within Wales and internationally. Increasing opportunities and improving facilities for the public. Supporting, through grants, the production of art including new work. Attracting new rescues and developing the arts economy. Providing advice to artists, arts groups and other organisations. Distributing Lottery money to arts organisations in Wales and monitoring projects. |
| *operations* | Management: Restructured in 1997: new management and broadening of unpaid advisory committees and panels. Chief Executive heads five new divisions: Planning & Public Affairs; Access Development; Lottery; Artform Development; Finance & Resources. Committees and panels review and recommend policy, advise and make grant decisions and are staffed by volunteers. |
| | Policy: Plans to manage arts residencies and community touring externally. |
| *board* | Council members appointed by the Secretary of State. |

| *Accounting Officer* | *Chief Executive* |
|---|---|

| | |
|---|---|
| *staff* | 78 |

| | |
|---|---|
| Chief Executive | Joanna Weston |
| Director, Artform Development Division | Michael Baker |
| Acting Director, Lottery Division | Robert Edge |
| Director, Finance & Resources Division | Andrew Malin |
| Director, Planning & Public Affairs Division | Michael Trickey |
| Director, Access Development Division | Sandra Wynne |
| Head of Mid & West Wales Office/Planning Officer | Mererid Hopwood |
| Head of North Wales Office/Planning Officer | Clifford Jones |
| Senior Literature Officer | Tony Bianchi |
| Craft Officer | Sandra Bosanquet |
| Arts Officer | Richard Cox |
| Senior Officer: Music | Lyn Davies |
| Literature Officer | Nia Gruffydd |
| Visual Arts Officer | John Hambley |
| Development Officer | Sarah Harman |
| Senior Development Officer | Diane Hebb |
| Senior Visual Arts & Craft Officer | Isabel Hitchman |
| Senior Officer: Dance & Drama | Anna Holmes |
| 'Arts for All' Officer | Catrin Jones |
| Development Officer | Amanda Loosemore |

| Development Officer | Bob Mole |
| Capital Officer | Lisa Morris |
| Capital Officer | Marion Morris |
| Community Touring Manager | John Prior |
| Senior Capital Officer | Sian Tomos |
| Senior 'Arts for All' Officer | Richard Turner |
| International Manager | Yvette Vaughan Jones |
| Dance & Drama Officer | Betsan Williams |
| 'Arts for All' Officer | Diana Woodward |

*financial*

## INCOME & EXPENDITURE
**Year end: 31 March**

| | 1997 £000 | 1996 £000 | 1995 £000 |
|---|---|---|---|
| **INCOME** | | | |
| Grants receivable | | | |
| Welsh Office | 15,489 | 14,189 | 13,541 |
| Local authorities | 247 | 229 | 233 |
| Crafts Council | 104 | 104 | 101 |
| Other | 118 | 192 | 194 |
| | 15,958 | 14,714 | 14,069 |
| Other income | 373 | 282 | 642 |
| Interest receivable | 63 | 46 | 38 |
| | 16,394 | 15,042 | 14,749 |
| **EXPENDITURE** | | | |
| Direct arts expenditure | | | |
| Grants and guarantees | 13,333 | 12,023 | 11,071 |
| Services and direct provision | 978 | 984 | 1,830 |
| | 14,311 | 13,007 | 12,901 |
| Management | 1,910 | 1,802 | 1,708 |
| | 16,221 | 14,809 | 14,609 |
| **SURPLUS FOR PERIOD** | **173** | **233** | **140** |

## NATIONAL LOTTERY INCOME & EXPENDITURE
**Year end: 31 March**

| | 1997 £000 | 1996 £000 | 1995 £000 |
|---|---|---|---|
| **INCOME** | | | |
| National Lottery | | | |
| Share of proceeds | 14,459 | 14,657 | 2,905 |
| National Lottery Distribution Fund investment income | 1,232 | 623 | 28 |
| | 15,691 | 15,280 | 2,933 |
| Interest receivable | 31 | 23 | 1 |
| | 15,722 | 15,303 | 2,934 |
| **EXPENDITURE** | | | |
| Grants commitments made | 12,018 | 10,323 | - |
| Management | 844 | 493 | 183 |
| | 12,862 | 10,816 | 183 |
| **SURPLUS FOR PERIOD** | **2,860** | **4,487** | **2,751** |

*advisers*

**Bankers** Co-operative Bank
National Westminster Bank

**Auditors** National Audit Office    157-197 Buckingham Palace Road
London SW1W 9SP

**Solicitors** Edwards Geward

*publications* Annual Report, Newsletter, Guide to Grants

*branches*
36 Princes Drive
Colwyn Bay LL29 8LA
Tel 01492 533440
Fax 01492 533677

6 Gardd Llydaw
Jackson Lane
Carmarthen SA31 1QD
Tel 01267 234248
Fax 01267 233084

# Audit Commission

1 Vincent Square
London SW1P 2PN

**Tel** 0171 396 1428
**Fax** 0171 828 5295

| | |
|---|---|
| *status* | Executive body |
| *founded* | 1982 |
| *sponsor* | Department of the Environment, Transport and the Regions (DETR). Welsh Office |
| *powers* | Local Government Finance Act 1982 and 1990 |
| *mission* | To provide independent, value-for-money audits of all local authorities and health service bodies in England and Wales. |
| *tasks* | To appoint auditors and determine their fees; regulate and control the quality of audits; identify good practice; report on the national implications of value-for-money studies and local audits; prevent and attack fraud. |

*operations*  Management: Entirely self-financing, with income from fees charged for audit work. The Commission meets monthly and has four standing panels which discuss detailed issues. Controller runs day-to-day management and his appointment is approved by the Secretaries of State for Environment, Wales and Health. Five departments; plus District Audit, which operates as an arm's length agency carrying out the audits - headed by its own Chief Executive and organised geographically in five regions. The Commission appoints external auditors - either the District Audit or one of eight private firms of auditors which meet their standards.

Policy: The basic Audit Commission's three principles were endorsed by the Nolan Committee: external auditors should be independent of the bodies being audited; local audits should include a mandatory value-for-money element in addition to probity and regularity; auditors should be entitled to publish reports about significant problems where they believe it would be in the public interest to do so.

Trends: Publishing year-on-year comparisons of the performance of councils, police forces and fire brigades. Huge changes on local government's work eg increasing influence of Europe, changes to capital financing.

*performance*  Indicators were met for 1996/97

*board*  Commission members are appointed by the Secretaries of State for the Environment, for Health and for Wales, from a wide range of interests including industry, local government, health, accountants and trade unions.

| Chairman | Roger Brooke | |
|---|---|---|
| Deputy Chairman | Jeremy Orme | |
| Members | Richard Arthur | Sue Richards |
| | Sir Terence English | Hilary Rowland |
| | John Foster | Helena Shovelton |
| | Adrienne Fresko | Peter Soulsby |
| | Kate Jenkins | Iris Tarry |
| | Sir Peter Kemp | Sir Ron Watson |
| | Rosalynde Lowe | David Williams |
| *Accounting Officer* | *Controller of Audit* | |

*staff*  1280

| Controller | Andrew Foster |
|---|---|

*financial*

**INCOME & EXPENDITURE**

| Year end: 31 March | 1996 £000 | 1995 £000 |
|---|---|---|
| **OPERATING INCOME** | | |
| Gross fee income | 90,551 | 86,972 |
| Other operating income | 1,844 | 1,909 |
| | **92,395** | **88,881** |
| **OPERATING COSTS** | | |
| Staff and members' costs | 52,346 | 51,230 |
| Bought-in services | 27,893 | 26,725 |
| Other operating costs | 12,270 | 11,024 |
| | **92,509** | **88,979** |
| **OPERATING DEFICIT** | **(114)** | **(98)** |
| Net interest receivable | 236 | 303 |
| (Net costs)/recoveries arising from litigation | (83) | 19 |
| **SURPLUS FOR THE YEAR** | **39** | **224** |

| | | | |
|---|---|---|---|
| *advisers* | **Bankers** | Lloyds Bank | 55 Corn Street, Bristol  BS99 7LE |
| | **Auditors** | National Audit Office | 157-197 Buckingham Palace Road<br>London SW1W |

*publications*  Annual Report

*branches*

| | |
|---|---|
| 4th Floor<br>Millbank Tower<br>Millbank<br>London SW1P 4QP | 2nd Floor<br>Nickalls House<br>Metro Centre<br>Gateshead NE11 9NH |
| 1st Floor<br>Sheffield House<br>Lytton Way<br>Stevenage SG1 3HB | 3rd Floor<br>Sumner House<br>St Thomas Road<br>Chorley PR7  1HP |
| Lake House<br>Acorn Business Park<br>Woodseats Close<br>Sheffield S8 0TB | 20 St Peter Street<br>Winchester SO23 8BP |
| 2nd Floor<br>1 Friarsgate<br>1011 Stratford Road<br>Solihull B90 4BN | 10 Blenheim Court<br>Matford Business Park<br>Lustleigh Close<br>Exeter EX2 8PW |
| Deacon House<br>Seacroft Avenue<br>Seacroft<br>Leeds LS14 6JD | 2nd Floor<br>2-4 Park Grove<br>Cardiff CF1  3PA |

# Bank of England

Threadneedle Street
London EC2R 8AH

**Tel** 0171 601 4444
**Fax** 0171 601 4771

**E-mail** enquiries@bankofengland.co.uk
**Web** http://www.bankofengland.co.uk

| | |
|---|---|
| *status* | Public corporation |
| *founded* | Nationalised 1946 |
| *sponsor* | HM Treasury |
| *powers* | Bank of England Act 1946.  Banking Act 1987.  These are to be amended in 1998, and meanwhile the Bank is working, *de facto*, under new monetary policy procedures set out in a letter to the Governor from the Chancellor of the Exchequer (6 May 1997). |
| *mission* | Act as UK Central Bank. Primarily to deliver price stability, as defined in the government's inflation targets, confirmed in each Budget Statement. Also, and without prejudice to price stability, to support the government's economic policies, especially for growth and employment. |
| *tasks* | Responsibility for setting interest rates; quarterly publication of *Inflation Report* analysing the economy in relation to the Bank's mission; market intervention in support of the government's exchange rate policy with its own foreign currency reserves; overall responsibility for the UK financial system; printing bank notes. |
| *operations* | Management: The Bank is accountable to the House of Commons through regular public reports and evidence to the Treasury Select Committee. Transparency and accountability in monetary decision-making are now the dominant operational characteristics of the Bank. Operational  decisions on interest rates are made by the Monetary Policy Committee, which comprises the Governor, two Deputy Governors and six appointed members. Two of the six members are appointed by the Governor and take responsibility for monetary policy and market operations respectively; and four are appointed by the Chancellor for three-year terms. Decisions are by vote with the Governor having the casting vote; minutes are published within six weeks. |
| | Day-to-day management is the responsibility of the Governor and two Deputy Governors; one Deputy supporting the Governor on monetary stability and the other on financial stability. Under the Court, the Bank's senior |

policy-making body is the Governor's Committee, comprising the Governors and four Executive Directors. Detailed implementation of policy and internal administration is the responsibility of the Management Committee. The Court reviews the performance of the Bank as a whole, including the Monetary Policy Committee, and has particular regard to the collection of regional and sectoral information for monetary policy formation. In 1997, the Bank was organised in the following divisions: Monetary Analysis; Monetary and Financial Statistics; Market Operations, including Foreign Exchange and preparations for EMU; Banking and Market Services; Bank Note Printing; Registration Services; Supervision and Surveillance; Financial Structure; and the Centre for Banking Studies.

Policy: If inflation is 1% above or below the government's target, the Governor must write an open letter to the Chancellor on behalf of the Monetary Policy Committee, explaining the reason for the variance, the policy action being taken to deal with it, the period within which inflation is expected to return to target and how all this meets the Bank's objectives as set out by the government.

Trends: In 1998, responsibility for banking supervision will be transferred to the Financial Services Authority; responsibility for government debt management and the sale of gilts will pass to HM Treasury.

**board**  The Court has been reformed and expanded and now comprises 19 members: the Governor and two Deputy Governors, and 16 non-executive members. Non-executives are appointed by the Chancellor for their expertise and drawn widely from industry, commerce and finance.

On 1 March 1998 the Members of the Court were:

| | | |
|---|---|---|
| Governor | Eddie George | |
| Deputy Governor | David Clementi | |
| Members of Court | Christopher Allsopp | Sir David Lees |
| | Roy Bailie | Dame Sheila Masters, DBE |
| | Andrew Buxton | Sheila McKechnie |
| | Sir David Cooksey | Bill Morris |
| | Howard Davies | John Neill, CBE |
| | Graham Hawker | Sir Neville Simms |
| | Frances Heaton | Sir Colin Southgate |
| | Sir Chips Keswick | Jim Stretton |
| | Mervyn King | |

Under the Court, the Bank's senior policy-making body is the Governor's Committee, comprising the Governors and four Executive Directors:

| | |
|---|---|
| Governor | Eddie George |
| Deputy Governor | David Clementi |
| Executive Director, Financial Stability | Alistair Clark |
| Executive Director, Financial Stability | Michael Foot |
| Executive Director, Monetary Stability | Mervyn King |
| Executive Director, Monetary Stability | Ian Plenderleith |

Detailed implementation of policy and internal administration is the responsibility of the Management Committee:

| | |
|---|---|
| Head, Legal Unit | Len Berkowitz |
| Head, Special Investigations Unit | Martin Foster |
| European and Parliamentary Affairs | Sir Peter Petrie |
| Deputy Governor | David Clementi |
| Deputy Director, Monetary Analysis | Bill Allen |
| Deputy Director, Financial Structure | John Footman |
| Deputy Director, Banking and Market Services | Graham Kentfield |
| Personnel Director | Merlyn Lowther |
| Deputy Director, Finance and Resources | Gordon Midgley |
| Deputy Director, Supervision and Surveillance | Oliver Page |
| Deputy Director, Market Operations | John Townend |

**staff**  On 28 February 1997 the Bank employed 3320 full-time and 215 part-time staff

**financial**

| PROFIT & LOSS Year end: 28/29 February | 1997 £m | 1996 £m | 1995 £m |
|---|---|---|---|
| **PROFIT AFTER PROVISIONS AND BEFORE TAX** | 121.3 | 214.4 | 225.9 |
| Payment to HM Treasury under Section 1(4) of The Bank of England Act 1946 | (48.7) | (88.0) | (102.2) |
| Tax on profit on ordinary activities | (23.8) | (38.1) | (32.7) |
| **RETAINED PROFIT FOR THE YEAR** | **48.8** | **88.3** | **91.0** |

**advisers**

| **Auditors** | Coopers & Lybrand |
|---|---|
| **Solicitors** | Freshfields |

# *Benefits Agency (BA)*

Quarry House
Quarry Hill
Leeds LS2 7UA

**Tel** 0113 2324000

| | |
|---|---|
| *status* | Executive agency |
| *founded* | 1991 |
| *sponsor* | Department of Social Security (DSS) |
| *powers* | Framework Document |
| *mission* | To pay the right money to the right person, at the right time - every time - in Great Britain. |
| *tasks* | The administration and payment of social security benefits, including jobseeker's allowance, income support, child maintenance bonus, incapacity benefit and industrial injury benefit. Other key tasks are security and the prevention of fraud. |

*operations* Management: The largest executive agency, with a spend of £8 billion pa, it was radically reoganised in 1996/ 97. The Chief Executive reports to the Secretary of State. Ministers and the Permanent Secretary meet regularly with the Chief Executive to assess BA's performance. There is a Board of Management, which has two non-executive directors but is otherwise entirely composed of line management. Management is the responsibility of the Chief Executive, supported by the Benefits Agency Management Team (BAMT) of eight executive directors. For field operations there are two territorial directorates, one covering Scotland and the North and the second Wales, the Midlands and the South. There are 13 area directorates containing 148 districts, and another four directorates handling centrally administered benefits, and six central services directorates managing eg accounts and security.

Policy: To encourage customers to take more responsibility for supplying information in support of their benefit claims.

Trends: In 1996/97 savings of £1.5 billion were made under the BA's Security and Control Plan and a series of local campaigns backed by a media campaign produced savings of another £86 million. Another £400 million efficiency savings have been achieved since the foundation of BA.

*performance* All four Milestone targets achieved 1996/97.

*board* Members of the Board of Management are appointed by the Secretary of State.

| *Accounting Officer* | *Chief Executive* |
|---|---|

*staff* 64,000 full-time; 15,000 part-time.

| | |
|---|---|
| Chief Executive | Peter Mathison |
| Change Management Director | Ursula Brennan |
| Operations Support Director | Alexis Cleveland |
| Director of Field Operations (Wales, Midlands & South) | Tony Edge |
| Director of Field Operations (Scotland & North) | John Lutton |
| Non-Executive Director | Alistair Lyons |
| Projects Director | George McCorkell |
| Personnel & Communications Director | Paul Murphy |
| Finance Director | David Riggs |
| Non-Executive Director | Michael Wemms |

*financial*

**INCOME & EXPENDITURE**

| Year end: 31 March | 1997 £000 | 1996 £000 | 1995 £000 |
|---|---|---|---|
| **INCOME** | | | |
| Miscellaneous income | 11,381 | 10,651 | 18,488 |
| **EXPENDITURE** | | | |
| Staff costs | (1,302,488) | (1,207,202) | (1,168,246) |
| Other operating costs | (1,295,949) | (1,273,491) | (1,204,316) |
| | **(2,598,437)** | **(2,480,693)** | **(2,372,562)** |
| **NET COST OF OPERATIONS BEFORE INTEREST** | **(2,587,056)** | **(2,470,042)** | **(2,354,074)** |
| Interest receivable and similar income | 407 | 209 | 238 |
| Interest on capital | (7,621) | (6,821) | (4,982) |
| **NET COST OF OPERATIONS** | **(2,594,270)** | **(2,476,654)** | **(2,358,818)** |

| advisers | Auditors | National Audit Office | 157-197 Buckingham Palace Road<br>London SW1W 9SP |
|----------|----------|----------------------|---------------------------------------------------|

# Biotechnology & Biological Sciences Research Council (BBSRC)

Polaris House
North Star Avenue
Swindon SN2 1UH

**Tel** 01793 413253
**Fax** 01793 413382        **Web** http://www.bbsrc.ac.uk/opennet

| | |
|---|---|
| *status* | Executive body |
| *founded* | 1994 |
| *sponsor* | Department of Trade and Industry (DTI), Office of Science and Technology |
| *powers* | Royal Charter |
| *mission* | To sustain a broad base of interdisciplinary research and training to help industry, commerce and government, create wealth and improve the quality of life. |
| *tasks* | To promote and support high-quality basic, strategic and applied research and related postgraduate training relating to the understanding and exploitation of biological systems. To advance knowledge and technology, and provide trained scientists and engineers, who meet the needs of users and beneficiaries. To provide advice, disseminate knowledge and promote public understanding in the fields of biotechnology and the biological sciences. |
| *operations* | Council is responsible for determining policy and strategy after receiving recommendations and advice from its boards and committees and the Chief Executive. There are seven research committees: Agri-Food, Animal Sciences, Biochemistry and Cell Biology, Biomolecular Sciences, Engineering and Biological Systems, Genes and Development Biology, Plant & Microbial Sciences. BBSRC supports over 7,000 scientists, postgraduate students and support staff in universities and research institutes. |
| | Policy: Maintaining the widest possible vision for the research funded, both in terms of its contribution to human knowledge and for potential application and commercialisation. |
| | Trends: Continuing debate about in**Tel**lectual property and the public and private funding of research. Supports 14 LINK programmes to catalyse collaboration between research and industry. |
| *board* | Council appointed by Secretary of State. |

| Deputy Chairman<br>& Chief Executive | | |
|---|---|---|
| Members | Prof Raymond Baker | |
| | Prof Bernard Atkinson | Mrs Judy MacArthur Clark |
| | Martyn Baker | Prof Enid MacRobbie |
| | Dr EC Dart CBE | Prof N Murray |
| | Prof Sir Brian Follett | Sir Brian Richards CBE |
| | Prof Julia Goodfellow | Muir Russel |
| | Prof Chris Higgins | Dr David Shannon |
| | Dr KW Humphreys CBE | Guy Walker CBE |
| *Accounting Officer* | *Chief Executive* | |

| | |
|---|---|
| *staff* | 2541 |

| Chief Executive | Prof Raymond Baker |
|---|---|
| Director of Science Policy, Scientific Audit & International Group | Dr Victoria Harrison |
| Director of Human & Corporate Resources Group | Bob Price |
| Director of Finance Group | SH Visscher |
| Director of Science & Technology Group | Prof David White |
| Director of Business, Innovation & International Group | Dr Doug Yarrow |

| financial | INCOME & EXPENDITURE | | |
|---|---|---|---|
| | **Year end: 31 March** | **1997** | **1996** |
| | | **£000** | **£000** |
| | **INCOME** | | |
| | Parliamentary grant-in-aid | 173,937 | 172,703 |
| | Release of deferred grant-in-aid | | |
| | On ordinary activities | 2,218 | 1,851 |
| | On net tangible assets transferred to grant-aided institutes | - | 8,656 |
| | Other income | 7,620 | 5,134 |
| | | **183,775** | **188,344** |
| | **EXPENDITURE** | | |
| | Research grants | 162,577 | 158,166 |
| | Staff costs | 6,130 | 5,553 |
| | Other operating costs | | |
| | On ordinary activities | 6,406 | 6,186 |
| | On net current assets transferred to grant-aided institutes | - | 1,314 |
| | Staff restructuring | 8,875 | 5,572 |
| | Depreciation | 3,626 | 3,116 |
| | Notional insurance costs | 134 | 120 |
| | Notional cost of capital employed | 8,441 | 7,869 |
| | | **(196,189)** | **(188,036)** |
| | **OPERATING (DEFICIT)/ SURPLUS FOR THE YEAR** | **(12,414)** | **308** |
| | Net book value of fixed assets transferred to grant-aided institutes | - | (8,948) |
| | Interest receivable | 71 | 21 |
| | (Loss)/gain on sale of fixed assets | (1,222) | 1,440 |
| | Amounts payable to the Office of Science & Technology | (11) | (2,264) |
| | Transferred from reserves | 1,541 | 1,767 |
| | Reversal of notional cost of capital employed | 8,441 | 7,869 |
| | **RETAINED (DEFICIT)/SURPLUS FOR THE YEAR** | **(3,594)** | **193** |
| | Retained deficit brought forward | (1,310) | (2,963) |
| | Transfers between reserves on sale of fixed assets | 1,573 | 1,460 |
| | **RETAINED DEFICIT CARRIED FORWARD** | **(3,331)** | **(1,310)** |

| advisers | **Auditors** | National Audit Office | 157-197 Buckingham Palace Road |
|---|---|---|---|
| | | | London SW1W 9SP |

*publications*    Annual Report, Corporate Plan

# Britain-Russia Centre

14 Grosvenor Place
London SW1X 7HW

**Tel** 0171 235 2116
**Fax** 0171 259 6254

| status | Executive body |
|---|---|
| **founded** | 1959 as the Great Britain-USSR Association. Renamed after the passing of the Soviet Union in 1991 |
| **sponsor** | Foreign and Commonwealth Office (FCO) |
| **mission** | Together with the British East-West Centre, to promote understanding through personal and professional contacts between the UK and the nations of the old USSR. |
| **tasks** | The Britain-Russia Centre promotes understanding with Russia; the British East-West Centre develops links with Ukraine, Belarus, Moldova, Kazakhstan, and the countries of Central Asia and Transcaucasia. Their joint tasks are: to run the Centre's library and information service (principally English and Russian but also other languages) and *The British East-West Journal*; to make introductions through their broad network of contacts; to co-operate on projects with many of the emerging democratic institutions in Russia and the republics (eg British observer mission to cover Russian presidential election) and their London embassies; to run seminars, receptions and exhibitions. |
| **operations** | Management: Legally the Centre is two limited companies (limited by guarantee). Managerially, it is a single unit which receives grant-in-aid from the FCO. There is a single Council of management, executive committee, Director and staff. The London headquarters houses both Centres, with all facilities jointly run. Facilities for |

seminars, receptions and exhibitions are being expanded. There are branches in Scotland, Wales and Northern Ireland which organise project work, membership events and hosting visitors. There are representatives in major UK cities.

Policy: Membership is either individual or corporate and not confined to specialists.

Trends: Project funding from the FCO, from the Know-How Fund, the Westminster Foundation for Democracy and from TACIS has allowed the Centre to expand its project activities well beyond previous levels. Membership is increasing. Library acquisitions increased at an unprecedented level.

**board**

Council members are appointed from British organisations representing most fields of national life.

| | |
|---|---|
| President | Baroness Williams of Crosby |
| Vice-Presidents | Sir Curtis Keeble GCMG |
| | Sir John Lawrence Bt OBE |
| | Sir Frank Roberts GCMG GCVO |
| | Rt Rev & Rt Hon Lord Runcie MC |
| Chairman | Sir Rodric Braithwaite GCMG |
| Vice-Chairmen | Sir Russell Johnston MP |
| | George Robertson MP |
| | Peter Temple-Morris MP |
| Hon Treasurer | Ralph French OBE |

**staff**

Six

| | |
|---|---|
| Director | Dr Iain Elliott |
| Projects Manager | Muir Brown |
| Accountant | Gerald Dorman |
| Projects Assistant | Nicola Hickman |
| Membership Secretary | Adèle Nicholson |
| Librarian and Editor of *British East-West Journal* | Helen O'Connor |

**financial**

**INCOME & EXPENDITURE**

| Year end: 31 March | 1997 £ | 1996 £ | 1995 £ |
|---|---|---|---|
| **INCOME** | | | |
| Grant-in-aid | 237,000 | 237,000 | 218,000 |
| Project income | 215,051 | 135,175 | 60,917 |
| Subscriptions and other income | 30,328 | 32,047 | 27,086 |
| Bank interest less tax | 1,892 | 1,696 | 1,119 |
| | **484,271** | **405,918** | **307,122** |
| **RUNNING COSTS** | | | |
| Salaries and pension scheme | 153,439 | 138,657 | 130,203 |
| Rent and establishment costs | 58,656 | 58,434 | 57,498 |
| Repairs and maintenance | 1,998 | 1,616 | 2,905 |
| Office expenses | 18,916 | 19,478 | 16,903 |
| Professional charges | - | 2,350 | - |
| Audit fee | 1,450 | 1,300 | 1,150 |
| Fitting-out costs | 2,836 | 5,857 | 4,148 |
| Depreciation | 2,509 | 2,625 | 6,020 |
| | **239,804** | **230,317** | **218,827** |
| **PROJECT EXPENDITURE** | | | |
| Externally funded projects | 209,049 | 127,275 | 61,507 |
| Other (branches, entertaining, events, library, publishing, etc) | 28,178 | 29,514 | 26,076 |
| | **237,227** | **156,789** | **87,583** |
| **TOTAL EXPENDITURE** | **477,031** | **387,106** | **306,410** |
| **EXCESS OF INCOME OVER EXPENDITURE FOR YEAR** | **7,240** | **18,812** | **712** |

# British Association for Central & Eastern Europe

Fourth Floor
50 Hans Crescent
London SW1X 0NA

**Tel** 0171 584 0766
**Fax** 0171 584 8831

| | |
|---|---|
| *status* | Executive body |
| *founded* | 1967 |
| *sponsor* | Foreign and Commonwealth Office (FCO) |
| *powers* | Memorandum and Articles of Association |
| *mission* | Promoting closer understanding between the British people and the peoples of the countries of Central and Eastern Europe. Since 1989, also encouraging and assisting the transformation of those countries into free and democratic societies with market-based economies. |
| *tasks* | Fostering cultural, economic, education and social contacts with, originally, people in Bulgaria, Czechoslovakia, Hungary and Romania. It expanded its activities to include Albania, Bosnia and Herzegovina, Croatia, the Czech Republic, Estonia, Latvia, Lithuania, Macedonia, Poland, the Slovak Republic and Federal Republic of Yugoslavia. Administering Know-How Fund projects in those countries. Organising seminars in Britain and abroad (covering eg Parliament, elections, the judicial system), larger conferences (eg on reconciliation in Bosnia) and Round Table Conferences (eg British/Polish) on behalf of the FCO. |
| *operations* | Management: Founded as the Great Britain/East Europe Centre, it adopted the present name in 1992. It is a company limited by guarantee, mainly financed by FCO grant-in-aid. Also funds from Parliament to transfer know-how to Central and Eastern European countries and to fulfil the purpose of the Helsinki Final Act on Security and Co-operation in Europe 1975. It seeks matching funds from grant-giving bodies to support its projects. Membership subscriptions help support its activities within the UK. The Director reports to the governing body. |
| *board* | The governing body is composed of 19 members, including five from Parliament, and representatives of the FCO, the Department of Trade and Industry and the British Council; other members are from industry, business, the media and academic life. They are elected by the membership. |

| | |
|---|---|
| Director | Sir John Birch |
| Deputy Director | Joyce McLellan |

| | |
|---|---|
| *staff* | Four |

*financial*

**INCOME & EXPENDITURE**

| Year end: 31 March | 1996 £ | 1995 £ |
|---|---:|---:|
| **INCOME** | | |
| Grant-in-aid | 197,000 | 208,000 |
| EWCF funding | 21,692 | 37,541 |
| Project-related income | 152,750 | 182,526 |
| Subscriptions and donations | 2,860 | 3,446 |
| Bank interest | 1,489 | 1,856 |
| | **375,791** | **433,369** |
| **RUNNING COSTS** | | |
| Salaries | 112,040 | 109,858 |
| Rent, rates, insurance and service charge | 38,106 | 20,089 |
| Printing, postage, stationery and telephone | 9,749 | 11,747 |
| Lighting and cleaning | 2,983 | 3,426 |
| Professional charges | 176 | 3,487 |
| Repairs and renewals | 3,728 | 1,052 |
| Recruitment | - | 8,672 |
| General expenses | 3,549 | 1,818 |
| Audit and accountancy | 4,881 | 4,729 |
| Depreciation | 8,223 | 5,518 |
| | **183,435** | **170,396** |
| Projects | 188,587 | 211,712 |
| | **372,022** | **382,108** |
| **SURPLUS BEFORE TAXATION** | **3,769** | **51,261** |
| Corporation tax | (372) | (464) |
| **SURPLUS AFTER TAXATION** | **3,397** | **50,797** |

| advisers | Auditors | BM May & Co | 41 Salisbury Road, Carshalton Surrey SM5 3HA |
| --- | --- | --- | --- |

**publications** *Annual Report and Accounts*

# British Board of Agrément (BBA)

PO Box 195
Bucknalls Lane
Garston
Watford
Herts WD2 7NG

**Tel** 01923 670844
**Fax** 01923 662133

**E-mail** bba@btinternet.com
**Web** http://www.bbacerts.co.uk

| | |
| --- | --- |
| **status** | Executive body |
| **founded** | 1966 |
| **sponsor** | Department of the Environment, Transport and the Regions (DETR) |
| **powers** | Memorandum and Articles of Association |
| **mission** | To provide independent assessment and approval of products and processes for the construction industry throughout Europe. |
| **tasks** | Provides Agrément Certificates for building products after they have successfully passed a full assessment, involving laboratory testing, on-site evaluations and inspections of production. Provides comprehensive data on product performance. Continual monitoring throughout the life of a Certificate. The Agrément process evaluates the extent to which the product complies with relevant Building Regulations and other statutory requirements. |
| **operations** | Management: Council takes decisions impartially and has three sub-committees, responsible for finance, technical advice and promotional matters. Day-to-day administration is carried out by Board of Management, composed of the Director, Commercial Manager, Sales and Marketing Manager, Technical Manager and Company Secretary. |
| | Policy: Increasing number of products approved each year (over 3000 in total). Enhancing value of BBA approval at national level eg new agreement with British Standards Institution (BSI). |
| | Trends: Seeking to achieve harmonised technical specifications across the EC. |
| **performance** | Financial self-sufficiency. Effective operation. |
| **board** | Council appointed by the Secretary of State from representatives of different sectors of the construction industry. |

| Accounting Officer | Director |
| --- | --- |

| | |
| --- | --- |
| **staff** | 95 |

| Director | PC Hewlett |
| --- | --- |

| advisers | **Bankers** | National Westminster Bank |
| --- | --- | --- |
| | **Auditors** | BDO Binder Hamlyn |
| | **Solicitors** | Stephenson Harwood |

**publications** *Agrément Certificates, Methods of Assessment and Testing*

# British Broadcasting Corporation (BBC)

Broadcasting House
Portland Place
London W1A 1AA

**Tel** 0171 580 4468/0181 743 8000      **Web** http://www.bbc.co.uk

| | |
|---|---|
| **status** | Public corporation |
| **founded** | 1922 |
| **sponsor** | Department for Culture, Media and Sport (DCMS) |

**powers**    Royal Charter 1996. But the BBC has a unique constitution contained principally in three separate documents: the new Royal Charter, which outlines the BBC's purpose and defines its constitution for a ten- year term (ending 31 December 2006); the Agreement between the BBC and the Secretary of State (accompanying the Royal Charter), which describes the services and standards expected of the BBC; and the Statement of Promises to Viewers and Listeners which details the BBC's commitment to its audiences. The BBC also has obligations under various statutes, eg the requirement to publish findings of the Broadcasting Standards Commission, and to commission 25% of non-news television programmes from independent producers.

**mission**    Public service broadcasting - providing a comprehensive range of distinctive TV and radio programmes and associated services (often with private sector creative and commercial partners). Making and broadcasting the best TV and radio programmes which inform, educate and entertain.

**tasks**    The BBC is independent of government in relation to the content, scheduling and management of its programmes and affairs. Its tasks include: BBC Home Services - Television: BBC1 and BBC 2. Radio: Radio I, 2, 3, 4 and 5 Live; Regional Broadcasting for Scotland, Wales and Northern Ireland and the English regions; Local Radio in England; BBC Education. BBC radio invests in drama, comedy, news and current affairs and music, unlike commercial radio broadcasters. BBC public service digital development. BBC Worldwide Services - BBC commercial and international activities including commercial digital services, publishing, films and video. BBC World Service - although independent of government, the Agreement requires the BBC to broadcast programmes in languages approved by the Foreign and Commonwealth Office (FCO) and consult over objectives and programme standards. Open University Production Centre. Licence enforcement.

**operations**    Management: The Governors appoint the Director-General (DG), set strategy and objectives, monitor performance and are responsible for compliance with programme standards and specific, regulatory functions (eg Acts of Parliament, EU directives and DCMS approval of commercial ventures). Day-to-day management is the task of the DG and Executive Committee, whose members also sit on the broader-based Board of Management. The Corporation comprises the Home Services Group; its subsidiary, BBC Worldwide Ltd which brings together all international and commercial activities; the Open University Production Centre; and the World Service. 1996/97 was the first year of operating within the BBC's ten- year strategy for the digital age; the organisation and management were restructured along functional and bi-media lines, separating the activities of commissioning and scheduling from the production process itself. Traditional boundaries were swept away to enable the BBC to respond to digital challenges but the World Service was excepted (with FCO co-operation). The BBC is funded mainly by an obligatory annual TV licence. The Open University Production Centre receives a grant from the Open University. The World Service is separately funded by grant-in-aid. There are National Broadcasting Councils to advise the Governors on programmes and services in Scotland, Wales and Northern Ireland. There are English Regional Advisory Councils for the North, the South and the Midlands & East. A World Service Consultative Group advises on World Service output and on audience perceptions of the Service.

Policy: The BBC will remain a public service broadcaster, making the best use of its programme assets and commercial ventures for benefit of licence fee payers.

Trends: BBC has been encouraged by the government to take a leading role in developing UK digital broadcasting. (Several digital services occupy the frequency previously occupied by one conventional analogue service.) The BBC's proposals include an extended BBC1 and BBC2 in widescreen, a 24-hour television news channel, more regional programming and an education service. A strong core of public, licence fee funded, digital services is proposed. Subscription channels are being developed by BBC Worldwide Ltd in partnership with an outside company. In December 1996, the Government agreed a new five-year licence formula which gave the first real increase in a decade.

**board**    The 12 Governors of the BBC are appointed by the Queen on the recommendation of Ministers.

# Q&Q

| Chairman | Sir Christopher Bland | |
|---|---|---|
| Vice-Chairman | Lord Cocks of Hartcliffe | |
| Governors | Sir Kenneth Bloomfield KCB | Bill Jordan CBE |
| | Janet Cohen | Lord Nicholas Gordon Lennox KCMG KCVO |
| | The Rev Norman Drummond | Sir David Scholey CBE |
| | Sir Richard Eyre CBE | Margaret Spurr OBE |
| | Roger Jones OBE | Adrian White CBE |

*staff*    20,734

| Director-General | John Birt |
|---|---|
| Deputy Director-General | Bob Phillis |
| Director of Finance | John Smith |
| Director of Corporate Affairs | Colin Browne |
| Chief Executive, BBC News | Tony Hall |
| Director of Policy & Planning | Patricia Hodgson |
| Chief Executive, BBC Resources | Rob Lynch |
| Chief Executive, BBC Production | Ronald Neil |
| Director of Personnel | Margaret Salmon |
| Chief Executive, BBC Broadcast | Will Wyatt |

*financial*

## HOME SERVICES GROUP: INCOME & EXPENDITURE

| Year end: 31 March | 1997 £m | 1996 £m |
|---|---|---|
| **INCOME** | | |
| Licence fee | 1,915.2 | 1,819.7 |
| Open University Production Centre | 9.8 | 11.9 |
| Commercial turnover | 353.8 | 338.4 |
| Other income | 55.7 | 56.9 |
| | **2,334.5** | **2,226.9** |
| **OPERATING EXPENDITURE** | | |
| **Home Services** | | |
| Funded from the licence fee: | | |
| Television | 1,160.4 | 1,130.3 |
| Radio | 388.5 | 381.0 |
| Licence fee collection costs | 96.9 | 95.0 |
| Restructuring costs | 81.7 | 35.2 |
| Other | 127.2 | 115.0 |
| Funded from external income | 55.7 | 56.6 |
| **BBC Worldwide Commercial Activities** | | |
| Cost of Sales | 198.6 | 198.5 |
| Distribution costs | 75.0 | 63.3 |
| Administrative and other costs | 28.1 | 33.7 |
| Amortisation of programme investment | 44.6 | 31.4 |
| Other activities | 9.8 | 11.6 |
| | **2,266.5** | **2,151.6** |
| Income from interests in associated undertakings | 1.1 | 1.2 |
| **OPERATING SURPLUS** | **69.1** | **76.5** |
| Profit on sale of transmission business | 25.6 | - |
| **SURPLUS BEFORE INTEREST AND TAXATION** | **94.7** | **76.5** |
| Net interest | 11.6 | 3.4 |
| **SURPLUS BEFORE TAXATION** | **106.3** | **79.9** |
| Taxation | (12.2) | (7.1) |
| **SURPLUS FOR THE FINANCIAL YEAR** | **94.1** | **72.8** |
| Transfer from/(to) capital reserve: Sale of transmission business | 187.0 | - |
| Other | 31.3 | (17.1) |
| **SURPLUS FOR THE YEAR TRANSFERRED TO OPERATING RESERVE** | **312.4** | **55.7** |

| WORLD SERVICE: INCOME & EXPENDITURE Year end: 31 March | 1997 £m | 1996 £m |
|---|---|---|
| **INCOME** | | |
| Grants-in-aid | 174.6 | 180.6 |
| Other income | 11.6 | 11.9 |
| | 186.2 | 192.5 |
| **OPERATING EXPENDITURE** | **(179.4)** | **(189.9)** |
| **OPERATING SURPLUS** | **6.8** | **2.6** |
| Sale of transmission business | (13.4) | - |
| **(DEFICIT)/SURPLUS BEFORE INTEREST AND TAXATION** | **(6.6)** | **2.6** |
| Interest receivable | 0.3 | 0.3 |
| **(DEFICIT)/SURPLUS BEFORE TAXATION** | **(6.3)** | **2.9** |
| Taxation | (0.6) | (0.4) |
| **(DEFICIT)/SURPLUS FOR THE FINANCIAL YEAR** | **(6.9)** | **2.5** |
| Transfer to HM Treasury | (16.7) | - |
| Transfer from/(to) capital reserve: Sale of transmission business | 29.6 | - |
| Other | (1.2) | (5.9) |
| **SURPLUS/(DEFICIT) FOR THE YEAR TRANSFERRED TO OPERATING RESERVE** | **4.8** | **(3.4)** |

**advisers**   Auditors          KPMG

**publications**   *Annual Report and Accounts*

# British Council

10 Spring Gardens
London SW1A 2BN

**Tel** 0171 930 8466
**Fax** 0171 839 6347

**E-mail** firstname.lastname@britcoun.org
**Web** http://www.britcoun.org/

**status**      Executive body

**founded**     1934. Incorporated by Royal Charter 1940

**sponsor**     Foreign and Commonwealth Office (FCO), through its Diplomatic Wing and the Department for International Development (DFID)

**powers**      An integral part of the UK's overall diplomatic and aid effort

**mission**     To promote Britain as a modern, dynamic nation which, by exploiting its intellectual capital and creativity, contributes to the international community. More specifically, to promote a wider knowledge of the UK and the English language and to encourage cultural, scientific, technological and educational co-operation between the UK and other countries.

**tasks**       Cultural relations overseas and the provision of development assistance.

It aims to extend the use, and improve the teaching, of English worldwide through its network of teaching centres. It supports Britain's share of the international education and training market by education export missions, overseas fairs, exhibitions and seminars - working closely with the Department of Trade and Industry and the Department for Education and Employment. Science, scientific and technical training, exchanges and research collaboration account for a quarter of its work. It supports Britain's overseas development policies through projects which include a strong commitment to human resource development, skills transfer and strengthening local institutions. It promotes innovative, contemporary British art overseas - drama, dance, music, writing, films and television and visual arts. It has 209 libraries worldwide.

**operations**  Management: As the UK's international network for education, culture and development services, it operates in 109 countries, each with at least one British Council office. The complex departmental structure reflects the different Council operations and geographical regions. Advisory committees are organised by subject eg health, law, publishing. Headquarters are in London and Manchester and there is a network of some 25 UK offices.

Policy: During the past five years the Council has strengthened its contribution to British international interests, despite cuts in funding, through a rigorous regime of efficiency and restructuring, intense concentration on priorities, and the growth of non-grant income.

Trends: It remains the Council's central proposition that, for Britain to make its way successfully in the world, traditional government-to-government links must be complemented society-to-society and people-to-people, through a wide network of institutional and individual links.

*board* Appointed under rules set out in its Royal Charter. With the exception of two members nominated by the Secretary of State for Foreign Affairs, members are appointed by the Board itself from British citizens occupying positions of recognised eminence in British educational, professional and cultural life. Appointment to the offices of Chairman, Deputy Chairman and Vice-Chairman requires prior approval from the Foreign Secretary.

| | | |
|---|---|---|
| Chairman | Sir Martin Jacomb | |
| Deputy Chairman | Lord Chorley | |
| Vice-Chairmen | Hilary Armstrong MP | |
| | Lord Renton | |
| Members | Lesley Abdela MBE | |
| | Michael Bichard | Sir Tim Lankester KCB |
| | Sir Christopher Bland | Dr Janet P Morgan |
| | Prof Robert Boucher | Timothy Rix CBE |
| | Mrs AS Byatt CBE | Dr John Roberts CBE |
| | Sir John Coles GCMG | Emma Rothschild |
| | Prof David Crystal OBE | Dennis Stevenson CBE |
| | Sir Roger Elliott | Prof Eric Sunderland |
| | Arthur Green | John Vereker CB |
| | Dr John Hemming CMG | Lord Wilson of Tillyorn GCMG |

*staff* 6000 (worldwide)

| | |
|---|---|
| Director-General | David Drewry |
| Director Educational Enterprises | Piers Pendred |
| Director Corporate Policy | Edmund Marsden |
| Director Corporate Personnel | Helena Molyneux |
| Director Finance | David Turnbull |
| Director Development and Training Services | Alen Webster |
| Secretary of the Council | Paul Docherty |
| *Accounting Officer* | *Director-General* |

*financial*

**FINANCIAL ACTIVITIES**

| Year end: 31 March | 1997 | 1996 |
|---|---|---|
| | £000 | £000 |
| **INCOMING RESOURCES** | | |
| Grants | 144,822 | 144,488 |
| Fees and income from services and other income | 157,427 | 144,555 |
| Agency activity | 129,358 | 132,058 |
| Investment income | 2,257 | 1,546 |
| | 433,864 | 422,647 |
| **RESOURCES EXPENDED** | | |
| Direct charitable expenditure | 287,636 | 284,169 |
| Agency activity | 129,358 | 132,058 |
| Other expenditure | 6,447 | 5,608 |
| | (423,441) | (421,835) |
| **NET INCOMING RESOURCES FOR THE YEAR** | 10,423 | 812 |
| Notional costs and current cost adjustment | (6,695) | - |
| **NET INCOMING RESOURCES AFTER NOTIONAL COSTS** | 3,728 | 812 |
| Reversal of notional costs | 6,896 | - |
| Transfer from/(to) capital account | 2,058 | (2,914) |
| **NET MOVEMENT IN FUNDS** | 12,682 | (2,102) |
| Fund balances brought forward at 1 April | (17,786) | (15,684) |
| **FUND BALANCES CARRIED FORWARD** | (5,104) | (17,786) |

*advisers*

| | | |
|---|---|---|
| Bankers | Midland Bank | 129 New Bond Street, London W1Y 2AA |
| Auditors | National Audit Office | 157-197 Buckingham Palace Road London SW1W 9SP |

# British Educational Communications & Technology Agency (BECTA)

Milburn Hill Road
Science Park
Coventry CV4 7JJ

**Tel** 01203 416994
**Fax** 01203 411418

**E-mail** Enquiry_desk@ncet.org.uk
**Web** http://www.ncet.org.uk

| | |
|---|---|
| *status* | Executive body |
| *founded* | 1988 |
| *sponsor* | Department for Education and Employment (DfEE) |
| *powers* | Memorandum and Articles of Association |
| *mission* | To support the Government's priorities for Information and Communications Technology (ICT). |
| *tasks* | To ensure that technology supports the DfEE's objectives to drive up standards; in particular to provide the professional expertise the DfEE needs to support the future development of the national grid for learning. BECTA also has a role in the FE sector's developing use of ICT; in the identification of ICT opportunities for special educational needs; and in the evaluation of new technologies as they come on- stream. |
| *operations* | Management: Known as the National Council for Educational Technology until April 1998. Run by Chief Executive. A government-funded charity - additional income from contracts with other bodies and publications income. |
| | Policy: Developing partnerships with national agencies working in education to develop strategic planning to ensure a systemic approach to increasing the effective use of IT in learning. |
| | Trends: Private sector showing increasing interest in investing in IT and education. |
| *board* | Members of BECTA are appointed by the Secretaries of State of Education and Employment, Scotland and Northern Ireland. |

| Chairman | Heather Du Quesnay CBE | |
|---|---|---|
| Members | Prof Kenneth Gregory | |
| | Pat Lowrie | Peter Nicholls |
| | Mary Marsh | Dominic Savage |
| | Tom McMullan | Prof Alison Wolf |
| *Accounting Officer* | *Chief Executive* | |

*staff*    125

| Chief Executive | Margaret Bell |
|---|---|
| Directors | Peter Avis |
| | Jean Beck |
| | John Brown |
| | Fred Daly |
| | Mike Littlewood |
| | Jeff Morgan |

*financial*

**INCOME & EXPENDITURE**

| Year end: 31 March | 1997 £ | 1996 £ | 1995 £ |
|---|---|---|---|
| **TURNOVER** | | | |
| Grants and other income receivable | 10,339,032 | 12,686,377 | 13,039,680 |
| Less: grants to meet the cost of fixed assets | - | (83,483) | (192,935) |
| | **10,339,032** | **12,602,894** | **12,846,745** |
| **EXPENDITURE** | | | |
| Staff costs | (2,865,721) | (2,742,641) | (2,486,800) |
| Depreciation | (142,542) | (1,428) | (947) |
| Other operating charges | (7,274,953) | (9,869,649) | (10,467,930) |
| | **(10,283,216)** | **(12,613,718)** | **(12,955,677)** |
| **OPERATING (DEFICIT)** | **55,816** | **(10,824)** | **(108,932)** |
| Investment income | 31,403 | 30,454 | 26,169 |
| **SURPLUS/(DEFICIT) BEFORE TAXATION** | **87,219** | **19,630** | **(82,763)** |
| Taxation | - | - | 88,000 |
| **SURPLUS AFTER TAXATION** | **87,219** | **19,630** | **5,237** |

| advisers | Bankers | Midland Bank |
|---|---|---|
| | Auditors | Kidsons Impey |
| | | Grant Thornton |
| | Solicitors | Radcliffes |

# British Film Institute (BFI)

21 Stephen Street
London W1P 2LN

**Tel** 0171 255 1444
**Fax** 0171 436 7950

| | |
|---|---|
| *status* | Executive body |
| *founded* | 1933 |
| *sponsor* | Department for Culture, Media and Sport (DCMS) |
| *powers* | Royal Charter |
| *mission* | UK national agency with responsibility for encouraging the arts of film and television and conserving them in the national interest. |
| *tasks* | Activities include the National Film Theatre, London Film Festival and Museum of the Moving Image. Conservation of National Film and Television Archives. Distributes grants to regional film theatres and arts bodies; research and education; production and distribution of film and video; campaigns extensively on behalf of the British film industry. |
| *operations* | Management: The Directorate is responsible for the implementation of policy, as approved by the Board of Governors. The Governors are the Trustees of the charity. Situated at five sites (three in London, one in Hertfordshire and one in Warwickshire). 40% of funding from membership and sponsorship. |
| | Policy: Implementing BFI 2000, a new vision for the organisation. |
| | Trends: Cuts in government funding but substantial Lottery grants. New tax relief for film-makers. |
| *board* | Board of Governors appointed by the Secretary of State. |

| Chairman | Alan Parker | |
|---|---|---|
| Governors | Joan Bakewell | |
| | Dame Jocelyn Barrow | Stephen Moore |
| | Ray Deahl | Steve Morrison |
| | Charles Denton | Barry Norman |
| | Sir Anthony Durant MP | Rodney Payne |
| | Matthew Evans | Sarah Radclyffe |
| | Terry Gilliam | Simon Relph |
| | Dr John Hill | Allan Shiach |
| | Geoff Hoon MP | Brian Winston |
| | Alan Howden | Jean Young |

*staff*  494

| Director | Wilf Stevenson |
|---|---|
| Assistant Director | Michael Prescott |
| Head of Personnel | Davina Boakye |
| Senior Administrative Officer | Stephen Dell |
| Head of Finance | Ian Nelson |
| Head of Computing | Peter Rutland |
| Controller | Adrian Wootton |
| Head of Programme Planning | Mark Adams |
| Complex Services Manager | Martin Harvey |
| Head of Technical Services | Stephen Herbert |
| Head of Marketing | Ian Temple |

*financial*

| FINANCIAL ACTIVITIES<br>Year end: 31 March | 1997<br>£000 | 1996<br>£000 |
|---|---|---|
| **INCOMING RESOURCES** | | |
| Grant-in-aid | 16,473 | 16,973 |
| Other grants | 1,299 | 818 |
| Lottery funding | 475 | 356 |
| Investment income | 434 | 438 |
| Income from activities | 11,681 | 12,520 |
| Fundraising activities | 939 | 1,200 |
| | 31,301 | 32,305 |
| **RESOURCES EXPENDED** | | |
| Direct charitable expenditure | 29,963 | 30,424 |
| Lottery applications | 247 | 321 |
| Fundraising and publicity | 466 | 37 |
| Management and administration | 1,341 | 1,400 |
| | 32,017 | 32,182 |
| **NET INCOMING (OUTGOING) RESOURCES** | **(716)** | **122** |
| Less notional costs: Costs of capital | 1,713 | 1,731 |
| **NET INCOMING (OUTGOING) RESOURCES AFTER NOTIONAL COSTS** | **(2,429)** | **(1609)** |
| Unrealised gains on investments | 482 | 612 |
| Reversal of notional costs | 1,713 | 1,731 |
| **NET INCOMING (OUTGOING) RESOURCES** | **(234)** | **734** |
| Fund balances brought forward as previously stated | - | 26,379 |
| Prior year adjustment | - | 2,126 |
| Fund balances brought forward as restated | 29,239 | 28,505 |
| **FUND BALANCES CARRIED FORWARD** | **29,005** | **29,239** |

*advisers*

| **Bankers** | Lloyds Bank | |
|---|---|---|
| **Auditors** | BDO Stoy Hayward | London |
| **Solicitors** | Nicholson Graham & Jones | |

*publications*   Annual Review

# British Hallmarking Council

St Philips House
St Philips Place
Birmingham B3 2PP

**Tel** 0121 200 3300
**Fax** 0121 200 3330

**Contact** MR Winwood

*status*       Executive body

*founded*      1973

*sponsor*      Department of Trade and Industry (DTI)

*powers*       Hallmarking Act 1973

*mission*      Ensuring that precious metal articles are what they claim to be.

*tasks*        To ensure that, in the UK, there are adequate facilities for the assaying and hallmarking of precious metal articles; to ensure that the law is enforced; to advise the government on the due execution of the Hallmarking Act 1973 and to fix maximum charges for assaying and hallmarking articles of precious metals.

*operations*   Management: There are four assay offices in London, Birmingham, Sheffield and Edinburgh, supervised by the Council. They are inspected annually by the Royal Mint. Responsibility for enforcement is, in the main, with the local authority trading standards officers throughout the UK.

Policy: The Council welcomes the main thrust if the DTI's draft regulations to implement the Houtwipper decision but wants amendments to the Hallmarking Act and is meanwhile working on new guidelines which will be available when the regulations become law.

Trends: A special mark was authorised to commemorate the millennium. The total number of articles hall-marked rose in 1996/97 - gold modestly, silver by 8% to 5.5 million articles. Imports rose by 31%. Work on the EU Directive has produced a consensus, now that Holland has withdrawn its objections.

**board**    Ten Council Members appointed by the President of the Board of Trade and six by the Assay Office.

| Members | M Allchin | |
|---|---|---|
| | PD Atkinson | |
| | SL Batiste | PEM Fuller |
| | JR Bettinson | J Goodall |
| | RD Buchanan-Dunlop | TK Murray |
| | RS Burman | Mrs SP Payne |
| | Sir Adam Butler | JS Pyke |
| | GR Carr | Miss ZC Simpson |
| | JG Evans | GM Smith |
| Secretary | MR Winwood | |

**financial**

| INCOME & EXPENDITURE Year end: 31 December | 1996 £ | 1995 £ |
|---|---|---|
| **INCOME** | | |
| Sales of notices | 7,053 | 5,161 |
| Less: distribution expenses | (2,450) | (2,315) |
| **Surplus on Sale of Notices** | **4,603** | **2,846** |
| **Administration Expenses** | | |
| Chairman's salary and social security costs | 10,701 | 10,700 |
| Secretarial costs and expenses | 8,418 | 11,284 |
| Printing, stationery and incidentals | 3,550 | 906 |
| Council members' expenses | 1,305 | 911 |
| Professional charges: | | |
| J Kohle litigation | - | 260 |
| EEC harmonisation | 5,435 | 9,040 |
| Auditors | 1,100 | 1,095 |
| | (30,509) | (34,196) |
| **DEFICIT ON OPERATIONS** | **(25,906)** | **(31,350)** |
| Interest received net of taxation | 177 | 230 |
| **DEFICIT BEFORE ALLOCATION FROM ASSAY OFFICES** | **(25,729)** | **(31,120)** |
| **Allocation from Assay Offices** | | |
| London | 6,635 | 8,353 |
| Birmingham | 11,434 | 13,752 |
| Sheffield | 7,042 | 8,346 |
| Edinburgh | 618 | 669 |
| | **25,729** | **31,120** |
| **DEFICIT FOR THE YEAR** | **-** | **-** |

**advisers**

| **Bankers** | Lloyds Bank | 125 Colmore Row, Birmingham B3 3AD |
|---|---|---|
| **Auditors** | Deloitte & Touche | Colmore Gate, 2 Colmore Row Birmingham B3 2BN |
| **Solicitors** | Mastineau Johnson | St Phillips House, St Phillips Place Birmingham B3 2PP |

**publications**    *Annual Reports*

# *British Library*

96 Euston Road
London NW1 2DB

**Tel** 0171 412 7111
**Fax** 0171 412 7268

| | |
|---|---|
| *status* | Executive body |
| *sponsor* | Department for Culture, Media and Sport (DCMS) |
| *powers* | British Library Act 1972 |
| *mission* | Outstanding collection of more than 150 million items representing every age of written civilisation, every written language and every aspect of human thought. |
| *tasks* | To provide: internationally important reading room and enquiry services; document supply services; specialist information services in key subject areas; National Bibliographic Service; education service, events, exhibitions and publications. Development, management and conservation of collection. |
| *operations* | Management: The British Library Board meets monthly and is ultimately responsible for the development of Library policy and the overseeing of its execution by management. The Management Committee is responsible for day-to-day management and comprises the Chief Executive, Deputy Chief Executive, the Director General (Collections and Services) and the Director (Planning and Resources). The Advisory Council advises on major areas of policy affecting the whole library, and meets three times a year. Advisory Committees provide focused guidance in the key areas of activity. Document Supply Centre is based in Boston Spa, Yorkshire. |
| | Policy: General reading room open in new building at St Pancras, rest to open over next two years. Huge investment in IT systems. Digital technologies being expanded for remote access. |
| | Trends: Huge cuts in funding (reductions in acquisitions etc). Visitor demands at record levels. |

*board*

| | | |
|---|---|---|
| Chairman | Dr JM Ashworth | |
| Deputy Chairman & Chief Executive | Dr BA Lang | |
| Members | The Hon Edward Adeane CVO | CGR Leach |
| | Prof M Anderson | PM Lively |
| | A Bloom | B Naylor |
| | DAG Bradbury | J Ritblat |
| | Sir Matthew Farrer | D Russon |
| | The Rt Hon Sir Peter Hordern MP | P Scherer |
| Secretary | D Gesua | |
| *Advisory Council* | | |
| Members | P Mathias CBE | |
| | JDE Beynon | Prof AGJ MacFarlane CBE |
| | Sir Cecil Clothier KCB QC | JL Madden |
| | C Coates | Prof CNJ Mann |
| | J Cropley | ID McGowan |
| | N Crouch | RA McKee |
| | JM Ducker | G Pachent |
| | G Ford | J Richardson |
| | O Freeman | NJ Russel |
| | Prof RL Gregory CBE | R Shimmon |
| | J Hyde | Prof J Stallworthy |
| | N Kershaw | M Warner |
| | CJ Koster | Prof F Willet |
| | F Lines | WG Williams |
| Secretary | M Taylor | |
| *Accounting Officer* | *Chief Executive* | |

*staff*     2598

| | |
|---|---|
| Chief Executive | Dr BA Lang |
| Director General, Collections & Services | DAG Bradbury |
| Director, Planning & Resources | D Gesua |
| Deputy Chief Executive | D Russon |
| Director, Public Affairs | Jane Carr |
| Director, St Pancras Operations & Estates | Ruth Coman |
| Director, Reader Services & Collection Development | Mike Crump |
| Director, Acquisitions Processing & Cataloguing | Stuart Ede |
| Director, Collections & Preservation | Mirjam Foot |

| Director, Science Reference & Information Service | Alan Gomersall |
| Director, Research & Innovation Centre | Nigel Macartney |
| Director, Information Systems | John Mahoney |
| Director, Special Collections | Alice Prochaska |
| Director, Bibliographic Services & Document Supply | Malcolm Smith |

*financial*

| FINANCIAL ACTIVITIES Year end: 31 March | 1997 £000 | 1996 £000 |
|---|---|---|
| **INCOMING RESOURCES** | | |
| Grant-in-aid | 84,324 | 80,364 |
| Trading | 29,317 | 29,462 |
| Donations | 2,640 | 3,686 |
| Interest receivable | 324 | 417 |
| | 116,605 | 113,929 |
| **RESOURCES EXPENDED** | | |
| Acquisitions | 14,035 | 15,640 |
| Research and other grants | 1,828 | 2,037 |
| Bibliographic Services & Document Supply | 25,619 | 23,069 |
| Reader Services & Collection Development | 12,527 | 10,929 |
| Science Reference & Information Service | 9,030 | 10,948 |
| Special Collections | 8,563 | 7,695 |
| Acquisitions Processing & Cataloguing | 4,016 | 3,495 |
| Collections & Preservation | 12,527 | 11,354 |
| Research & Innovation Centre | 1,819 | 1,463 |
| Public Affairs | 3,277 | 2,413 |
| Management & Administration | 15,796 | 16,510 |
| St Pancras project | 7,641 | 5,028 |
| | 116,258 | 110,071 |
| **NOTIONAL COSTS** | | |
| Cost of capital | 2,986 | 0 |
| Insurance | 117 | 0 |
| | 3,103 | 0 |
| **NET INCOMING/(OUTGOING) RESOURCES AFTER NOTIONAL COSTS** | (2,756) | 3,858 |
| Reversal of cost of capital | 2,986 | 0 |
| **NET MOVEMENT IN FUNDS** | 230 | 3,858 |
| Fund balances brought forward | 49,885 | 45,797 |
| **FUND BALANCES CARRIED FORWARD** | 49,885 | 49,655 |

# British Museum

Great Russell Street
London WC1B 3DG

**Tel** 0171 638 1555
**Fax** 0171 323 8118

**E-mail** info@british_museum.ac.uk
**Web** http://www.british_museum.ac.uk

*status* Executive body

*founded* 1753

*sponsor* Department for Culture, Media and Sport (DCMS)

*powers* British Museum Act 1963

*mission* To promote the knowledge of the cultural history of mankind from prehistoric times to the present day.

*tasks* Curatorial custody and preservation of the collections; making them available to the scholarly and the public by study, publication and exhibition; development of the collections so that they are as comprehensive as possible. Continuing development of educational facilities. Carries out excavations and fieldwork in UK and overseas.

*operations* Management: The Director is responsible for the direction and management of the Museum and is responsible to the Trustees. Ten curatorial departments, each headed by a Keeper. British Museum Development Trust spearheads fundraising for major capital development plans. British Museum Company Ltd is an independent company owned by the Trustees that undertakes the production and sale of publications and gifts, and the organisation of specialised travel tours.

Policy: Expansion plans include the Great Court project utilising space vacated by the British Library and a new Study Centre opening early in the new millennium.

**performance** Renowned for its scholarship.

**board** Trustees are appointed by: HM the Queen (1), the Prime Minister (15), nominated by learned societies (4), elected by the Trustees themselves (5).

**staff** 1000+

| Director | Dr RGW Anderson |
| Director of Finance & Resources | A Blackstock |
| Keeper, Scientific Research | Dr SGE Bowman |
| Keeper, Coins & Medals | Dr AM Burnett |
| Keeper, Medieval & Later Antiquities | J Cherry |
| Keeper, Western Asiatic Antiquities | Dr JE Curtis |
| Keeper, Egyptian Antiquities | WV Davies |
| Keeper, Prints & Drawings | AV Griffiths |
| Head of Press & Public Relations | AE Hamilton |
| Keeper, Japanese Antiquities | VT Harris |
| Head, Public Services | GAL House |
| Head of Administration | CEI Jones |
| Keeper, Oriental Antiquities | JR Knox |
| Keeper, Ethnography | Dr BJ Mack |
| Keeper, Conservation | Dr WA Oddy |
| Secretary | Mrs CN Parker |
| Keeper, Prehistoric & Romano-British Antiquities | Dr TW Potter |
| Keeper, Greek & Roman Antiquities | Dr DJR Williams |

**financial**

**INCOME & EXPENDITURE**

| Year end: 31 March | 1996 £m | 1995 £m |
|---|---|---|
| **INCOME** | | |
| Grant-in-aid | 33.4 | 34.3 |
| Other income | 23.2 | 9.9 |
| | **56.6** | **44.2** |
| **EXPENDITURE** | | |
| Salaries and superannuation | 24.6 | 24.1 |
| Buildings | 23.6 | 12.7 |
| Purchases for the Collection | 2.9 | 1.8 |
| Other expenditure | 5.5 | 5.5 |
| | **56.6** | **44.1** |

# British Nuclear Fuels plc (BNFL)

Risley
Warrington
Cheshire WA3 6AS

**Tel** 01925 832242
**Fax** 01925 835619

| | |
|---|---|
| *status* | Nationalised industry |
| *sponsor* | Department of Trade and Industry (DTI) |
| *mission* | To provide high-quality, cost-effective integrated nuclear products and services to UK and overseas customers. |
| *tasks* | To supply nuclear fuel services: conversion of uranium; manufacture and supply of uranium and plutonium based fuels; provision of fuel cycle services for nuclear power stations; reprocessing used nuclear fuel and waste treatment and storage; electricity generation: supplying electricity from Calder Hall and Chapelcross power stations; research, development, design and construction of plant and equipment. |

*operations*

Management: BNFL business groups are organised to reflect its expertise which spans uranium procurement, fuel manufacture, recycling used fuels, transporting radioactive materials, engineering, waste management and decommissioning. Thorp Business Group (provides spent fuel management services to UK and overseas power utilities); Magnox Business Group (embodies reprocessing and electricity generation, including the Calder Hall and Chapelcross reactors); Fuel Business Group; Waste Management and Decommissioning Group; Exports (international nuclear services, nuclear waste management and decommissioning - are organised in North America under the wholly owned BNFL Inc and elsewhere in the BNFL offices located in Japan, Germany, China, South Korea, Belgium and France). In April 1997 a memorandum of understanding relating to the proposed integration of BNLF and Magnox Electric plc was signed. BNLF and the government are discussing financial terms for integration.

Policy: Decommissioning of BNFL radioactive facilities - to protect the health and safety of the workforce, the public and the environment - to conform with all BNLF health, safety and environmental protection standards. Disposal of the resulting radioactive waste to conform with all regulations laid down by the appropriate authorities. Timing: the initial stage of decommissioning begins as soon as it is reasonably practicable after the end of the plant's useful life and involves the decontamination of plant and the immobilisation of radioactivity. Subsequent stages are undertaken on a different timescale which reflects, for example, utilisation of waste treatment facilities, manpower, equipment and re-use of buildings and structures.

Trends: Fundamental strategic review, *Beyond 2000*, sets a clear context for future decision-making. Its aim is to make BNFL a leading supplier of nuclear services in its selected product and geographic areas which means BNFL must be world-class and cost-effective in everything it does. If the Magnox Electric integration proceeds, it is expected that the first step towards full integration would be for Magnox to become a wholly owned subsidiary of BNFL.

*board*

Appointed by the Secretary of State.

| | |
|---|---|
| Chairman | John Guinness CB |
| Deputy Chairman | Neville Chamberlain CBE |
| Chief Executive | John Taylor |
| Non-Executive Director | Sir John Boyd KCMG |
| Group Finance Director | Ross Chiese |
| Non-Executive Director | Professor Alistair MacFarlane CBE |
| Non-Executive Director | Miss Kate Mortimer |
| Non-Executive Director | John Roques |
| Non-Executive Director | Lady Shuttleworth |
| Director Magnox Group | Grahame Smith |
| Commercial Director | Graham Watts |
| Non-Executive Director | Sir Norman Wooding CBE |
| Secretary | AJ Shuttleworth |

*staff*    12,977

*financial*

| PROFIT & LOSS | | | |
|---|---|---|---|
| Year end: 31 March | **1997** | **1996** | **1995** |
| | **£m** | **£m** | **£m** |
| **TURNOVER - Continuing operations** | | | |
| Fuel and related materials | 234 | | 232 |
| Enrichment | 6 | | 14 |
| Engineering | 10 | | 5 |
| Transport | 35 | | 51 |
| Waste disposal | 10 | | 7 |
| Waste management & decommissioning | 271 | | 199 |
| Magnox reprocessing | 117 | | 197 |
| Thorp | 440 | | 484 |
| Electricity | 111 | | 107 |
| Other | 28 | | 8 |
| | **1,262** | **1,549** | **1,304** |
| **LESS NET OPERATING COSTS AND EXPENSES** | | | |
| Raw materials and consumables | 236 | 241 | 186 |
| Employee costs | 410 | 404 | 417 |
| Depreciation | 274 | 331 | 314 |
| Provisions for liabilities and charges | 106 | 187 | 222 |
| Research and development not specifically recoverable directly from customers | 50 | 44 | 42 |
| Other external and operating charges | 231 | 220 | 189 |
| | **1307** | **1427** | **1370** |
| **Less:** | | | |
| Changes in stocks of finished goods and work in progress | 13 | (47) | (33) |
| Own work capitalised | 126 | 119 | 110 |
| Own work on manufacture of components | 14 | 20 | 20 |
| Regional development grants released | 3 | 11 | 14 |
| Other operating income | 5 | 8 | 41 |
| | **1,146** | **1,316** | **1,218** |
| **OPERATING PROFIT FROM CONTINUING OPERATIONS** | **116** | **233** | **86** |
| Income from interests in associated undertakings | 13 | 14 | 11 |
| | **129** | **247** | **97** |
| Investment income | 155 | 141 | - |
| Less interest payable and similar charges | (68) | (72) | 23 |
| **PROFIT ON ORDINARY ACTIVITIES BEFORE TAX** | **216** | **316** | **74** |
| Tax on profit on ordinary activities: | | | |
| - normal | (91) | (48) | (29) |
| - exceptional | - | (356) | - |
| **PROFIT (LOSS) ON ORDINARY ACTIVITIES AFTER TAX** | **125** | **(88)** | **45** |
| Profit attributable to minority interests | (1) | - | - |
| **PROFIT (LOSS) FOR THE FINANCIAL YEAR** | **124** | **(88)** | **45** |
| Dividends | (46) | (93) | 45 |
| **RETAINED PROFIT (LOSS) FOR THE YEAR** | **78** | **(181)** | **-** |

*advisers*

| | | |
|---|---|---|
| **Bankers** | National Westminster Bank | 55 King Street, Manchester M60 2DB |
| **Auditors** | Ernst & Young | Becket House, 1 Lambeth Palace Road London SE1 7EU |
| **Solicitors** | Freshfields | Whitefriars, 65 Fleet Street, London EC4Y 1HT |

## British Railways Board

Whittles House
14 Pentonville Road
London N1 9HF

**Tel** 0171 904 5008
**Fax** 0171 904 5018

**Contact** Peter Trewin

| | |
|---|---|
| *status* | Nationalised industry |
| *founded* | 1962 |
| *sponsor* | Department of the Environment, Transport and the Regions (DETR) |
| *powers* | Transport Acts 1962 and 1968. Railway Acts 1974 and 1993 |
| *mission* | Advising the Secretary of State on rail matters. Overall responsibility for British Transport Police Force, policing the railways and the London Underground. Managing residual activities in the interests of taxpayers and employees. |
| *tasks* | Advising government on how the passenger and freight railway can serve modern transport needs and how it can best be integrated with other transport modes, taking into account wider government policy and regional development and devolution. Residual Tasks. Property - retained land and buildings to be sold by subsidiary company, Rail Property Limited, as quickly as is consistent with best value for taxpayer. BT Police - the BT Police Committee is planning legislation to create a new independent railway police authority to take over policing of the railways and the London Underground. Debt management - debts not transferred with assets to new owners (except Railtrack) therefore Board had net liabilities March 1997; government providing necessary funding. Past liabilities - BR retains responsibility for industrial injuries liabilities over 50 years for major workforce (750,000 strong at one time) and for Eurotunnel's freight traffic toll liabilities to Channel Tunnel. Privatisation liabilities - warranties or indemnities to new private owners. Railway Heritage Committee - BR has statutory responsibility for funding its administration. |
| *operations* | Management: 1996/97 all remaining rail operations transferred from BR with the exception of Railfreight Distribution Limited (sold subsequently). In the context of its new advisory role, four individuals with experience in various facets of rail transport were appointed as non-execuitve members to replace the four members whose terms of appointment ran out in 1997. The Chairman is also Chief Executive and reports the Secretary of State. |
| | Policy: Providing a strategic focus on rail's contribution to the government's integrated transport policy. |
| | Trends: The Secretary of State wants BRB to maintain a cadre of expertise to advise him on rail matters. |
| *performance* | 1996/97 all financial targets exceeded. |
| *board* | Appointed by the Secretary of State from among persons who appear to have had wide experience of, and to have shown capacity in, transport, industrial, commercial or financial matters; administration, appied service, or the organisation of workers. |

| | |
|---|---|
| Chairman | John Welsby CBE |
| Vice-Chairman | James Jerram CBE |
| Members | Prof David Begg |
| | John Hughes |
| | Kazimiera Kantor |
| | Ron Kennedy |
| | Tony Roche |
| | Nicholas Wakefield |
| | Paul Watkinson |

| | |
|---|---|
| *staff* | 4300 |

| | |
|---|---|
| Secretary | Peter Trewin |
| Solicitor | Andrew Sim |

*financial*

| PROFIT & LOSS Year end: 31 March | 1997 £m | 1996 £m | 1995 £m |
|---|---|---|---|
| **TURNOVER** | | | |
| Trading income | 1,758.4 | 3,158.9 | 2,944.0 |
| Income from Railtrack | 131.5 | 1,260.6 | 1,237.5 |
| Revenue grant | 1,506.9 | 1,983.0 | 2,060.1 |
| | 3,396.8 | 6,402.5 | 6,241.6 |
| **OPERATING EXPENDITURE** | (3,266.5) | (5,888.8) | (5,670.5) |
| Channel Tunnel freight provision | (38.8) | (500.0) | - |
| **OPERATING PROFIT** | 91.5 | 13.7 | 571.1 |
| Loss on disposal of fixed assets | (2.0) | (3.0) | (1.4) |
| Profit on disposal of businesses | 186.8 | 152.8 | - |
| Utilisation of prior year provision | 13.3 | 30.6 | - |
| Provision for loss on disposal of businesses | (129.9) | (3.9) | (40.0) |
| Costs of fundamental restructuring incurred in 1996/97 | (16.2) | (51.6) | (61.6) |
| Provision for future costs of fundamental restructuring | (132.1) | - | - |
| **PROFIT/(LOSS) ON ORDINARY ACTIVITIES BEFORE INTEREST** | 11.4 | 138.6 | 468.1 |
| Interest receivable | 56.3 | 19.9 | 2.8 |
| Interest payable and similar charges | (104.0) | (100.6) | (108.8) |
| **PROFIT/(LOSS) ON ORDINARY ACTIVITIES BEFORE TAXATION** | (36.3) | 57.9 | 362.1 |
| Taxation | - | - | - |
| **PROFIT/(LOSS) FOR THE YEAR** | (36.3) | 57.9 | 362.1 |
| Transfers to separate Government ownership | - | (624.3) | (697.9) |
| **RETAINED PROFIT/(LOSS) FOR THE YEAR** | (36.3) | (566.4) | (335.8) |

*advisers*

| **Bankers** | Royal Bank of Scotland |
|---|---|
| **Auditors** | Price Waterhouse |
| **Solicitors** | Andrew Sim |
| **Public Relations** | Peter Trewin |

*publications*     *Annual Report*

# *British Shipbuilders*

89 Sandyford Road
Newcastle upon Tyne NE99 1PL

**Tel** 0191 232 8493

*status*  Nationalised industry

*founded*  1977

*sponsor*  Department of Trade and Industry (DTI)

*powers*  Aircraft and Shipbuilding Industries Act 1977

*mission*  To finish winding up the Corporation.

*tasks*  With the help of consultants, it is engaged in residual activities such as litigation, insurance claims and other contractual matters.

*operations*  Management: The Chairman is the only employee.

Policy: During 1996/97 it successfully settled all outstanding matters relating to the sales of subsidiary companies, resulting in significant additional profit.

Trends: Some activities will continue for many years.

*board*  Members of Corporation appointed by the Secretary of State.

*staff*  One

*financial*

| PROFIT & LOSS Year end: 31 March | 1997 £000 | 1996 £000 | 1995 £000 |
|---|---|---|---|
| Net operating expenditure - operating loss | (338) | (647) | (682) |
| Deferred consideration in respect of previous year's sale of subsidiary | 20,000 | - | - |
| Release of provision for loss on discontinued operations | 464 | 511 | (39) |
| **PROFIT (LOSS) ON ORDINARY ACTIVITIES** | | | |
| **BEFORE INTEREST** | **20,126** | **(136)** | **(721)** |
| Interest receivable (net) | 7,669 | 1,743 | 1539 |
| **PROFIT FOR YEAR BEFORE TAX** | **27,795** | **1,607** | **818** |
| Taxation | (1,760) | - | - |
| **PROFIT FOR THE YEAR AFTER TAX** | **26,035** | **1,607** | **818** |
| Adverse balance brought forward | (1,578,366) | (1,579,973) | (1,580,791) |
| **ADVERSE BALANCE CARRIED FORWARD** | **(1,552,331)** | **(1,578,366)** | **(1,579,973)** |

*advisers*

| | | |
|---|---|---|
| **Bankers** | National Westminster Bank | 1 Princes' Street, London EC2R 8BA |
| **Auditors** | Price Waterhouse | Southwark Towers, 32 London Bridge Street London SE1 9SY |
| **Solicitors** | Eversheds | Milburn House, Dean Street Newcastle upon Tyne NE1 1NP |

# *British Tourist Authority (BTA)*

Thames Tower
Black's Road
London W6 9EL

**Tel** 0181 846 9000
**Fax** 0181 563 0302          **Web** http://www.visitbritain.com

**Contact** Sandie Dawe, Director of Press & PR

*status*      Executive body

*founded*     1969

*sponsor*     Department of Culture, Media and Sport (DCMS)

*powers*      Development of Tourism Act 1969

*mission*     To promote British tourism from overseas. To advise government on tourism matters affecting Britain as a whole. To encourage the provision and improvement of tourist amenities and facilities in Britain.

*tasks*       To provide marketing leadership to the British tourism industry - particularly in respect of market segmentation; to co-ordinate overseas marketing of Britain by the national and regional tourist boards and to brand England, Scotland, Wales, London, and Britain as a whole; to develop key market intelligence for its own planning and for trade partners in Britain and overseas; to promote Britain in overseas markets, eg by opening offices in developing markets from which the industry can build and by raising potential customer awareness in 62 market segments in Europe and 18 in North America; to encourage the seasonal and regional spread of visits and tourist spending.

*operations*  Management: A public body operating in a commercial manner, BTA is funded primarily by grant-in-aid (with a special London component) and also by joint activities with the trade and related interests. Key financial and programme targets are expressed annually in a Funding Agreement. The Chief Executive is supported by a management board comprising five directors. Operationally, BTA is organised into three geographical areas: Europe; The Americas; APMEA - Asia Pacific, Middle East and Africa. Each is the responsibility of an Executive Director. There are nearly 50 overseas offices which employ the majority of staff. They also generate their own revenue (£18 million in 1996/97).

Policy: Market segmentation. Regional branding. Commercial partnerships - pivotal in reaching potential visitors cost-effectively (eg with BA, P&O Ferries, Marks & Spencer).

Trends: Thematic approach to promoting Britain continues, eg highly successful Style & Design campaign 1996/97.

*performance* As expressed in Funding Agreement.

**board**  Six non-executive members are appointed by the Secretary of State for Culture, Media & Sport  who also appoints the Chairman.  The Chairman of the Northern Ireland Tourist Board attends by invitation.

| | |
|---|---|
| Chairman | David Quarmby |
| Members | Robert Ayling |
| | Roy Bailie OBE |
| | Ian D Grant CBE |
| | John F Jarvis CBE |
| | Tony Lewis DL |
| | Patrick McKenna |
| | The Lord Rathcavan |
| *Accounting Officer* | *Chief Executive* |

**staff**  378 (210 overseas, 168 London)

| | |
|---|---|
| Chief Executive | Anthony Sell |
| Director, Press & PR | Sandi Dawe |
| General Manager, Asia, Pacific, Middle East & Africa | Robert Franklin |
| Director, Policy & Legal, Secretary to the Board | Sue Garland |
| Director, Marketing Services | Jonathan Griffin |
| General Manager, The Americas | Jeff Hamblin |
| Director, Financial Management & Information Management Services | Chris Howard |
| General Manager, Europe | Roger Johnson |

**financial**

| INCOME & EXPENDITURE | | | |
|---|---|---|---|
| **Year end: 31 March** | **1997** | **1996** | **1995** |
| | **£000** | **£000** | **£000** |
| **INCOME** | | | |
| Grant-in-aid | 35,500 | 34,560 | 33,200 |
| Income from activities | 18,009 | 16,165 | 15,493 |
| | **53,509** | **50,725** | **48,693** |
| Other operating income | 580 | 390 | 438 |
| | **54,089** | **51,115** | **49,131** |
| **EXPENDITURE** | | | |
| Staff costs | 10,777 | 10,184 | 10,756 |
| Depreciation & amortisation | 615 | 486 | 443 |
| London Tourist Board grant | 923 | 650 | - |
| Other operating charges | 43,338 | 39,806 | 37,443 |
| Notional costs | 220 | 271 | - |
| | **55,873** | **51,397** | **48,642** |
| **OPERATING (DEFICIT) SURPLUS BEFORE TAXATION** | **(1,784)** | **(282)** | **489** |
| Add notional costs | 220 | 271 | - |
| Less provision for tax | (63) | (65) | (50) |
| **(DEFICIT) FOR THE YEAR** | **(1,627)** | **(76)** | **439** |
| Retained surplus brought forward | 3,754 | 3,830 | 3,391 |
| **RETAINED SURPLUS CARRIED FORWARD** | **2,127** | **3,754** | **3,830** |

**advisers**

| **Bankers** | National Westmisnter Bank | King Street, Hammersmith W6 0QD |
|---|---|---|
| **Auditors** | National Audit Office | 157-197 Buckingham Palace Road London SW1W 9SP |

**publications**  *A Grand Tour of Britain's Hidden Treasures, Jewels of Britain, Rock & Pop Map*

**branches**  43 offices in 36 overseas countries

# British Waterways (BW)

Willow Grange
Church Road
Watford WD1 3QA

**Tel** 01923 226422
**Fax** 01923 201300

| | |
|---|---|
| *status* | Nationalised industry |
| *founded* | 1962 |
| *sponsor* | Department of the Environment, Transport and the Regions (DETR) |
| *powers* | Transport Act 1962 |
| *mission* | To manage the inland waterway system efficiently for the benefit of the UK. To provide a safe and high-quality environment and to conserve and improve the waterways for future generations. |
| *tasks* | To manage 2000 miles of canals and river navigation in England, Scotland and Wales. To manage associated reservoirs, docks, repair yards and workshops. |
| *operations* | Management: BW is run on a commercial basis and the principal difference between it and listed companies is the structure of the Board and the appointment of Board Members. BW is controlled by a Board appointed by the Secretary of State and maintains overall control over financial, strategic, budgetary and organisational issues. Reporting to it is a Chief Executive and an executive group which has responsibility for day-to-day management. |
| | Policy: To seek greater commercial and organisational independence from government. To continue adapting the canal network to modern needs ie leisure, recreation and tourism. To become financially more self-sufficient. To implement a long-term preventative maintenance programme. To develop linear networks linking major centres eg Fibreway joint venture with GPT laying fibre optic cables under towpaths and the use of canals to move surplus water between water companies. |
| | Trends: 1996/97 was a turning point for BW. After the Board warned the government that the grant projected was insufficient and would put at risk the safety and integrity of the waterway network, another £5 million was allocated, making the 1997/98 projected grant £50.89 million plus a further £2.8 million from the Scottish Office. The serious maintenance backlog will now be tackled but to eliminate it, an additional £7-8 million pa is required over eight years. The Millennium Commission pledged £32 million towards the scheme to link Edinburgh to Glasgow again and the Heritage Lottery Fund committed £25 million towards the Kennet & Avon Canal local regeneration project. A joint study with the Environment Agency (the regulator) and BW (the operator) on unlocking the River Ouse and Nene in East Anglia is under way. |
| *performance* | Financial performance met the targets set by the Transport Act 1968 (ie not to make a loss on revenue account). |
| *board* | Appointed by the Secretary of State. |

| | |
|---|---|
| Chairman | Bernard Henderson CBE |
| Vice Chairman | Sir Peter Hutchison Bt CBE |
| Members | Michael Cairns |
| | Sir Neil Cossons OBE |
| | Jane Elvy |
| | John Gordon |
| | Janet Lewis-Jones |
| | David Yorke CBE |

*staff* 1647

| | |
|---|---|
| Chief Executive | Dr David Fletcher |
| Director of Corporate Services | Jeremy Duffy |
| Finance Director | Christopher Neale |
| Director of Operations | Stewart Sim |
| Commercial Director | Ian Valder |

**financial**

| PROFIT & LOSS | | | |
|---|---|---|---|
| Year end: 31 March | **1997** | **1996** | **1995** |
| | **£000** | **£000** | **£000** |
| **REVENUE** | | | |
| Direct income | 46,829 | 41,492 | 36,632 |
| DETR grant | 51,829 | 51,377 | 48,907 |
| | **98,658** | **92,869** | **85,539** |
| **EXPENDITURE** | | | |
| Staff costs | (35,157) | (33,716) | (33,635) |
| Major repairs and renovations | (25,399) | (18,514) | (13,887) |
| Depreciation | (3,816) | (3,622) | (3,407) |
| Other operating charges | (33,981) | (37,237) | (35,055) |
| Own work capitalised or charged to major works | 64 | 486 | 628 |
| | **(98,289)** | **(92,603)** | **(85,356)** |
| **OPERATING PROFIT** | **369** | **266** | **183** |
| Profit on sale of investment properties | 1,799 | 1,258 | 1,050 |
| Interest payable net of receivable | (1,734) | (1,475) | (1,202) |
| **PROFIT FOR THE FINANCIAL YEAR** | **434** | **49** | **122** |
| Transfer of profits on sale of properties to realised capital reserve | (355) | (2) | 42 |
| **REVENUE PROFIT RETAINED** | **79** | **47** | **164** |

**advisers**

**Auditors**      Binder Hamlyn                    20 Old Bailey, London EC4M 7BH

**branches**

*Scotland*
Canal House
1 Applecross Street
Glasgow G4 9SP

*North West*
Navigation Road
Northwich
Cheshire CW8 1BH

*North East*
1 Dock Street
Leeds LS1 1HH

*Midlands & South West*
Peel's Wharf
Lichfield Street
Fazeley
Tamworth
Staffordshire B78 3QZ

*Southern*
Brindley House
Corner Hall
Lawn Lane
Hemel Hempstead
Hertfordshire HP3 9YT

# *Broadcasting Standards Commission*

7 The Sanctuary
London SW1P 3JS

**Tel** 0171 233 0544
**Fax** 0171 233 0397

**status**     Executive body

**founded**    1996

**sponsor**    Department for Culture, Media and Sport (DCMS)

**powers**     Broadcasting Act 1996

**mission**    To maintain standards and fairness in all UK broadcasting (BBC and commercial broadcasters, text, cable, satellite and digital services) while remaining independent of broadcasters and regulators.

**tasks**      Produces codes of conduct; considers and adjudicates on complaints and provides redress; acts as an alternative to a court of law for people who believe they have been unfairly treated by broadcasters or that they have had their privacy unwarrantably infringed. Represents the interests of UK citizens on broadcasting matters: monitors, researches and reports on the portrayal of violence, sexual conduct and matters of taste and decency.

**operations** Management: The Director reports to the Council - an amalgamation of the Broadcasting Standards Council and the Broadcasting Complaints Commission.

Policy: Fairness and Privacy Code produced by the Commission came into force in January 1998.

Trends: Number of complaints is increasing.

*board*     Commissioners appointed by Secretary of State.

| | | |
|---|---|---|
| Chairman | Lady Howe | |
| Deputy Chair | Jane Leighton | |
| Commissioners | Danielle Barr | Robert Kernoban OBE |
| | Rhiannon Bevan | The Very Rev John Lang |
| | David Boulton | Susan Lloyd |
| | Dame Fiona Caldicott DBE | Sally O'Sullivan |
| | Strachan Heppell CB | Matthew Parris |

*staff*

| | |
|---|---|
| Director | Stephen Whittle |
| Deputy Director | Norman McLean |
| Fairness Director | Hillary Bauer |
| Research Director | Andrea Hargrave |
| Communications Director | Andrew Ketteringham |

# Business Development Service (BDS)

Craigantlet Buildings
Stoney Road
Belfast BT4 3SX

**Tel** 01232 527437
**Fax** 01232 527270

| | |
|---|---|
| *status* | Executive agency |
| *founded* | 1996 |
| *sponsor* | Northern Ireland Office |
| *powers* | BDS Framework Document 1996 |
| *mission* | To provide high-quality business support services to NI government, executive agencies and the public sector in telecommunications (voice and data), management services, training, IT and systems services and other central business facilities. |
| *tasks* | Provides business consultancy services; a common communications infrastructure, also identifies and applies new technologies; runs IS services and advice; gives support on personnel issues; runs training courses; operates central print and design unit. |
| *operations* | Management: The Chief Executive is responsible to the Minister for the management and performance of the agency. The senior management team comprises Chief Exeuctive, Head of Management Consultancy & Training Services and Head of Information Systems. |
| | Policy: Moving towards full cost recovery. |
| | Trends: NI public sector under strong pressure to improve services while cutting revenues; demand for BDS services strong. |
| *performance* | Three out of four targets met in 1996/97. |
| *board* | No board. |

| *Accounting Officer* | *Chief Executive* |
|---|---|

*staff*     269

| | |
|---|---|
| Chief Executive | Ken Millar |
| Head of Management Consultancy & Training Services | Derek Orr |
| Head of Information Systems | Des Vincent |

| financial | RECEIPTS & PAYMENTS | |
|---|---|---|
| | Year end: 31 March | **1997** |
| | | **£000** |
| | **RECEIPTS** | |
| | Printing | 800 |
| | Training | 46 |
| | Consultancy | 47 |
| | HRMS | 65 |
| | Telephonist services | 137 |
| | | **1095** |
| | **PAYMENTS** | |
| | Salaries and wages | 5524 |
| | Operating payments | |
| | General administration | 1207 |
| | Printing costs | 64 |
| | Consultancy costs | 50 |
| | Cost of training courses for NICS | 712 |
| | Stationery | 241 |
| | Accommodation payments to DOE | 60 |
| | | **2334** |
| | Other payments | |
| | Computer and machinery capital | 161 |
| | Telecommunications capital | 827 |
| | | 988 |
| | | **8846** |
| | **NET EXPENDITURE FOR YEAR** | **7751** |

# The Buying Agency (TBA)

5th Floor
Royal Liver Building
Pier Head
Liverpool L3 1PE

**Tel** 0151 227 4262     **E-mail** post@tba.gov.uk
**Fax** 0151 227 3315

| | |
|---|---|
| status | Executive agency operating as a trading fund |
| founded | 1991 |
| sponsor | Cabinet Office (Office of Public Services) |
| powers | Government Trading Funds Act 1973. The Buying Agency Trading Fund Order 1991 |
| mission | To provide a centre of procurement excellence, delivering value for money in public sector purchasing. To act purely in the interests of customers, thereby benefiting taxpayers. |
| tasks | To procure, or make arrangements for, the supply of a wide range of products which comply with public purchasing policy and regulations on behalf of its clients in the public sector, a large number of public bodies, and the armed forces at home and overseas. |
| operations | Management: The Chancellor of the Duchy of Lancaster has overall responsibility and determines the policy and financial framework; the Chief Executive reports to him. The TBA Board comprises the Chief Executive and heads of department. Board members have responsibility for finance, sales, procurement and human resources; the Chief Executive has responsibility for marketing as well as being the Accounting Officer. TBA operates through a range of trading methods: direct call-off from the TBA catalogue; third-party trading which allows private sector companies working for public sector clients to access TBA's products and services; spot buying for volume purchases; direct purchasing of one-off acquisitions (usually where the item is difficult to source and involves complex technical or engineering factors); and Pathfinder (a new service offering a customised approach for specific projects, eg large-scale procurement, facilities management and the Public Private Partnerships). Explicit operational principles now include a commitment to customer care, based on its own Customer Charter, development of quality systems and a strengthening of supplier relationships. TBA operates from its Liverpool office and has regional management network of advisers and technical specialists who provide customers with back-up throughout the country. |

Policy: Three key strategic objectives have been identified: to provide customer services which enable customers to achieve their own purchasing objectives and strategies; to offer supply contracts which ensure better value for money than customers would otherwise achieve; to deliver customer support services that add further value to those contracts.

Trends: TBA's annual buying power of £250 million helps get the best deals but increasing public sector financial constraints keep pressure on reviewing its competitiveness.

**performance**  Not all financial targets met, particularly 20% growth target for non-fuel business, but 1996 overall performance good.

**board**  Appointed by the Chancellor of the Duchy of Lancaster.

| | |
|---|---|
| Chief Executive | SP Sage |
| Finance Director | AJ Phillips |
| Human Resources Director | KS Pope |
| Procurement Director | Dr C Poulter |

**staff**  128, majority civil servants

**financial**

| OPERATING ACCOUNT | 1996 | 1995 |
|---|---|---|
| Year end: 31 December | £000 | £000 |
| TURNOVER | 17,557 | 15,760 |
| Cost of sales | (11,560) | (9,773) |
| GROSS SURPLUS | 5,997 | 5,987 |
| Staff costs | (2,749) | (2,860) |
| Depreciation | (154) | (111) |
| Other operating charges | (2,257) | (1,795) |
| | (5,160) | (4,766) |
| OPERATING SURPLUS | 837 | 1,221 |
| Interest payable on short-term loan | - | (7) |
| Interest receivable | 139 | 129 |
| | 139 | 122 |
| SURPLUS ON ORDINARY ACTIVITIES | 976 | 1,343 |
| Interest payable on long-term loan | (34) | (22) |
| SURPLUS FOR THE YEAR | 942 | 1,321 |
| Amount to be surrendered to the Consolidated Fund | (297) | (983) |
| RETAINED SURPLUS | 645 | 338 |
| Retained surplus brought forward | 2,182 | 1,844 |
| RETAINED SURPLUS CARRIED FORWARD | 2,827 | 2,182 |

**advisers**

**Bankers**  Post Master General's Office

**Auditors**  National Audit Office

**Solicitors**  Treasury Solicitor

**publications**  *TBA News, Corporate Brochure, Specialist Procurement Services*

# Cadw (Welsh Historic Monuments)

Crown Building
Cathays Park
Cardiff CF1 3NQ

**Tel** 01222 500200
**Fax** 01222 826375

**status**  Executive agency

**founded**  1984. Executive agency 1991

**sponsor**  Welsh Office

**mission**  To protect, conserve and promote an appreciation of the built heritage of Wales.

**tasks**  Listing buildings of special architectural or historic interest and providing historic building repair grants; advising the Heritage Lottery Fund on relevant applications; scheduling ancient monuments and providing grants; funds Welsh Archaeological Trusts and provides financial support for Architectural Heritage Fund and Civic Trust for

Wales; conservation of the monuments in its care and opening them to the public.

***operations*** Management: The Advisory Committee advises the Secretary of State on agency policy, strategy and performance. The Executive Management Committee reviews policy, finance and other management issues and is headed by the Chief Executive.

Policy: Continuing acceleration of listing survey programme. Extending number of Monument Management Plans.

Trends: Visitor numbers to sites increasing.

***performance*** All 13 targets were achieved or exceeded in 1996/97.

***board*** Advisory Committee appointed by the Secretary of State.

| Members | GCG Craig |
|---|---|
| | Prof RR Davies |
| | C Evans |
| | A Lewis |
| | TOS Lloyd |
| | RA Wallace |
| *Accounting Officer* | *Chief Executive* |

***staff*** 232

| Chief Executive | TJ Cassidy |
|---|---|
| Chief Inspector of Ancient Monuments & Historic Buildings | JR Avent |
| Chief Architect | JD Hogg |
| Head of Presentation | AJ Hood |
| Director of Policy & Administration | RW Hughes |
| Head of Corporate Services | J Jenkins |
| Head of Administration | S Morris |
| National Manager of Cadwraeth Cymru | MBR Watkins |

***financial***

**INCOME & EXPENDITURE**

| Year end: 31 March | 1997 £000 | 1996 £000 |
|---|---|---|
| **INCOME** | | |
| Monument activities | 3,061 | 2,781 |
| National Heritage Memorial Fund income | - | 6 |
| | 3,061 | 2,787 |
| **EXPENDITURE** | | |
| Monument activities | (6,291) | (6,500) |
| Inspectorate expenditure | (415) | (327) |
| Administration expenditure | (398) | (558) |
| Other expenditure | (385) | (497) |
| Staff costs | (2,453) | (1,571) |
| Grants payable | (4,365) | (5,270) |
| | (14,307) | (14,723) |
| **NET COST OF ACTIVITIES** | (11,246) | (11,936) |
| Loss on disposal of fixed asset | (326) | (371) |
| Notional interest on capital | (345) | (12) |
| **NET EXPENDITURE FOR YEAR** | (11,917) | (12,319) |

***advisers*** **Auditors** National Audit Office 157-197 Buckingham Palace Road London SW1W 9SP

***publications*** *Annual Report and Accounts*

# Caledonian MacBrayne Ltd

The Ferry Terminal
Gourock PA19 1QP

**Tel** 01475 650100
**Fax** 01475 637607          **Web** http://www.calmac.co.uk

| | |
|---|---|
| *status* | Nationalised industry |
| *founded* | 1851. Nationalised in 1968 |
| *sponsor* | Scottish Office |
| *powers* | Transport (Scotland) Act 1989 |
| *mission* | To provide car and passenger ferry services to the Scottish islands. |
| *tasks* | Under contract with the Secretary of State to own ferries and run ferry services in both the Clyde and Western Island areas. To operate ferry services outside those approved by the Secretary of State. |
| *operations* | Management: The company runs subsidised and non-subsidised services with different summer and winter schedules. It also receives capital grants. |
| | Policy: To explore ways of improving revenue and reducing subsidy on a stand-alone basis, eg the Ballycastle to Rathin Island service. To work closely with the Transport Authority and tourist bodies at both local and national level to market the islands served for the benefit of islanders and tourists. |
| | Trends: Timely replacement of vessels to ensure growth in carrying and reduction of subsidies; also upgrading of terminal facilities. |
| *performance* | Financial, efficiency and quality targets set by government have been met or exceeded. |
| *board* | Appointed by the Secretary of State for Scotland.The Secretary of State is a Shadow Director in terms of the Companies Acts. |

| | |
|---|---|
| Chairman | Rear Admiral NE Rankin |
| Managing Director | Captain JAB Simkins |
| Commercial Director | KM Duerden |
| Non-Executive Director | Sir Robert Easton |
| Non-Executive Director | AM Gold |
| Non-Executive Director | S Grier |
| Non-Executive Director | GV MacLeod |
| Finance Director | RJ McKay |
| Company Secretary | GW McKenzie |
| Technical Director | TC McNeill |
| Non-Executive Director | PA Ritchie |

*staff*          900

*financial*

| PROFIT & LOSS Year end: 31 March | 1997 £000 | 1996 £000 | 1995 £000 |
|---|---|---|---|
| **TURNOVER** | **46,427** | **42,577** | **39,073** |
| **OPERATING EXPENDITURE** | | | |
| Fuel, power and lubricants | 3,407 | 2,780 | 2,616 |
| Maintenance materials, supplies and services | 6,636 | 6,044 | 5,664 |
| Staff costs: | | | |
| Wages and salaries | 18,059 | 17,486 | 16,448 |
| Social Security costs | 1,518 | 1,470 | 1,373 |
| Other pension costs | 1,107 | 1,036 | 1,070 |
| Depreciation | 5,758 | 4,471 | 3,385 |
| Less: credit for capital grants | (1,694) | (1,451) | (1,044) |
| Other operating charges | 10,761 | 9,248 | 8,808 |
| | 45,552 | 41,084 | 38,620 |
| **OPERATING PROFIT** | **875** | **1,493** | **453** |
| Interest receivable | 354 | 322 | 139 |
| Interest payable | (1,033) | (1,159) | (1,087) |
| **PROFIT ON ORDINARY ACTIVITIES BEFORE TAXATION** | **196** | **656** | **(495)** |
| Taxation on profit on ordinary activities | - | - | - |
| **PROFIT FOR THE FINANCIAL YEAR** | **196** | **656** | **(495)** |
| Retained profits brought forward | 7,280 | 6,624 | 7,119 |
| **RETAINED PROFITS CARRIED FORWARD** | **7,476** | **7,280** | **6,624** |

| advisers | **Bankers** | Royal Bank of Scotland | 8/10 Gordon Street, Glasgow |
|---|---|---|---|
| | **Auditors** | KPMG | 24 Blythswood Square, Glasgow G2 4QS |
| | **Solicitors** | McGrigor Donald | 70 Wellington Street, Glasgow G2 6SB |
| | **Public Relations** | Boathe Media | 18 Glasgow Road, Uddineston G71 7AS |

*publications*  Braynewaves, Calmac Gazette, Ferry Guide

# Cardiff Bay Development Corporation

Baltic House
Mount Stuart Square
Cardiff CF1 6DH

**Tel** 01222 585858
**Fax** 01222 488924

| | |
|---|---|
| *status* | Executive body |
| *founded* | 1987 |
| *sponsor* | Welsh Office |
| *powers* | Local Government, Planning and Land Act 1980 |
| *mission* | To put Cardiff on the international map as an outstanding maritime city which will stand comparison with any such city in the world, thereby enhancing the image and economic well-being of both the city and Wales. |
| *tasks* | The single task is regeneration over a number of years. To that end the Corporation acquires, holds, manages, reclaims and disposes of land; carries out building and other operations; ensures the provision of services; and carries on other activities as necessary. |
| *operations* | Management: The Corporation has set objectives and targets to deliver its mission but no timetable was set. At the outset it was expected that significant progress would have been made within ten years. Currently it is expected that 60% of targets would be met by the end of the century and 85% by 2003. |
| | Policy: Full consultation about Corporation proposals with principal local authorities and also the Welsh Office, quangos and many community organisations and representatives. |
| | Trends: The Secretary of State will decide on the wind-up date and the succession plans. |

*board*

| Chairman | Sir Geoffrey Inkin OBE | |
|---|---|---|
| Deputy Chairman | The Right Hon The Lord Brooks of Tremorfa | |
| Chief Executive | MD Boyce | |
| Members | JA Beveridge | |
| | Sir Alan Cox CBE | JR Phillips |
| | BJ Foday | JP Sainsbury |
| | R Goodway | Prof HR Silverman |
| | GV Houlston KstG | SM Stringer |
| *Accounting Officer* | *Chief Executive* | |

*staff*  99

*financial*

| INCOME & EXPENDITURE Year end: 31 March | 1997 £000 | 1996 £000 |
|---|---|---|
| **OPERATING INCOME** | | |
| Grant-in-aid released | 60,455 | 63,118 |
| European Regional Development Fund Grant | 298 | 2,609 |
| Rentals | 764 | 762 |
| Recoveries of VAT in respect of prior years | - | 486 |
| Other income | 2,000 | - |
| | **63,517** | **66,975** |
| **EXPENDITURE** | | |
| Operating expenditure | | |
| Grants | 1,109 | 5,216 |
| Revenue projects | 8,054 | 4,257 |
| Estate management | 444 | 391 |
| Promotion and publicity | 1,759 | 1,109 |

| | | |
|---|---:|---:|
| Other operating expenses | 1,565 | 1,205 |
| Staff costs | 3,321 | 2,698 |
| Depreciation of operating assets | 124 | 249 |
| | **16,376** | **15,125** |
| Property transactions | | |
| Depreciation of public assets | 45,908 | 51,164 |
| Provision against development assets | 1,164 | 695 |
| (Surplus)/Deficit on disposal of development assets | (1,022) | 331 |
| | **46,050** | **52,190** |
| | **62,426** | **67,315** |
| **OPERATING SURPLUS/(DEFICIT)** | **1,091** | **(340)** |
| Interest receivable | 186 | 270 |
| **SURPLUS/(DEFICIT) BEFORE TAXATION** | **1,277** | **(70)** |
| Taxation | 255 | 261 |
| **SURPLUS/(DEFICIT) AFTER TAXATION** | **1,022** | **(331)** |
| General reserve brought forward | 2,921 | 3,252 |
| **GENERAL RESERVE CARRIED FORWARD** | **3,943** | **2,921** |

| | | | |
|---|---|---|---|
| *advisers* | **Auditors** | Ernst & Young | Cardiff |

# *Castle Vale Housing Action Trust*

Farnborough Road
Birmingham B35 7NL

**Tel** 0121 776 6784
**Fax** 0121 776 6786

**E-mail** @cvhat.org.uk
**Web** http://www.cvhat.org.uk.

**Contact** Tess Randles

| | |
|---|---|
| *status* | Executive body |
| *founded* | 1993 |
| *sponsor* | Department of the Environment, Transport and the Regions (DETR) |
| *powers* | Housing Act 1998 |
| *mission* | To establish, by 2005, a self-sustaining community living in high-quality homes in a pleasant and safe environment on the Castle Vale Estate in Birmingham. Residents should enjoy an improved quality of life and economic opportunity and be able to choose the ownership and management of their homes |
| *tasks* | To work with residents of Castle Vale and others to achieve sustainable physical, economic and community regeneration. More specifically, to secure the repair or improvement of housing held by the Trust, to secure its effective management, to encourage diversity of tenure in Castle Vale, and generally to improve living conditions and the environment in Castle Vale. |
| *operations* | Management: The Trust received confirmation of its life to 2005 and a cash-limited planning target for grant aid of £205 million in December 1996. |
| | Policy: The early priority has been to provide new homes for those affected by clearance. During 1996/97 the head leasehold interest in the shopping centre was secured and its comprehensive development will be the Trust's largest single project. |
| | Trends: In 1997/98 further refurbishment schemes and new housing association developments started; the shopping centre marketed for redevelopment and the first housing-for-sale site facilitated. |
| *board* | Board of 12 members, appointed by the Secretary of State; four of these are residents, appointed following an estate-wide ballot. |

| | | |
|---|---|---|
| Chairman | Richard Temple Cox | |
| Deputy Chairman | Cllr Dennis Minnis | |
| Members | Cllr Stanley Austin | Pat Niner |
| | Joyce Curtis | A David Owen OBE |
| | Gil Gillis | Carole Ann Rafferty |
| | Joan Lawrie | Cllr Paul Tilsley MBE |
| | John Newton | Robert V Wharton |

| staff | 137 |
| ----- | --- |

| | |
| --- | --- |
| Chief Executive | Angus Kennedy |
| Director of Finance | John Williams |
| Director of Economic & Community Development | Rod Griffin |
| Acting Director of Housing | Carole Wildman |
| Director of Development | Pat Parkin |

**financial**

| INCOME & EXPENDITURE | | | |
| --- | --- | --- | --- |
| **Year end: 31 March** | **1997** | **1996** | **1995** |
| | **£000** | **£000** | **£000** |
| **GROSS INCOME/TURNOVER** | | | |
| Grant-in-aid | 11,464 | 11,787 | 6,822 |
| Receipts from land sales | 1,480 | 669 | 748 |
| Rental income | 4,994 | 4,763 | 5,518 |
| Other | 379 | 57 | 19 |
| | 18,317 | 17,276 | 13,107 |
| **EXPENDITURE** | | | |
| Development | 9,395 | 8,825 | 5,225 |
| Economic & Community Development | 598 | 319 | 188 |
| Asset management | 4,266 | 4,785 | 5,614 |
| Administrative | 4,101 | 3,371 | 2,125 |
| | 18,360 | 17,300 | 13,152 |
| **OPERATING RESULT** | **(43)** | **(24)** | **(45)** |
| Interest receivable | 69 | 41 | 51 |
| Interest payable | 0 | (1) | - |
| **RESULT ON ORDINARY ACTIVITIES BEFORE TAXATION** | **26** | **16** | **6** |
| Taxation | (26) | (16) | (6) |
| **RESULT AFTER TAXATION** | **0** | **0** | **0** |
| Retained surplus brought forward | 0 | 0 | 0 |
| **RETAINED SURPLUS CARRIED FORWARD** | **0** | **0** | **0** |

| advisers | **Bankers** | The Co-operative Bank | 118-120 Colmore Row, Birmingham B3 3BA |
| --- | --- | --- | --- |
| | **Auditors** | Neville Russell | Nexia House, The Broadway, Dudley West Midlands DY1 4PA |
| | **Solicitors** | Herbert Wilkes | 41 Church Street, Birmingham B3 2RT |

**publications**   *Castle Vale News, Housing Reviews, Master Programme, Castle Vale Chronicle*

# Central Computer & Telecommunications Agency (CCTA)

Rosebery Court
St Andrews Business Park
Norwich NR7 0HS

**Tel** 01603 704614
**Fax** 01603 704948

| status | Executive agency |
| --- | --- |
| founded | 1972. Executive agency in 1996 |
| sponsor | Cabinet Office. The Office of Public Service (OPS) |
| powers | Framework Document 1996 |
| mission | To help the public services successfully acquire and use information systems to meet their business needs. |
| tasks | Provides impartial guidance and advice to IT teams within the UK public sector, eg commercial intelligence, electronic commerce, good practice, strategic assignment consultancy; runs one of Europe's largest private telephone networks; manages the outsource contracts for the government data and telecoms networks; runs UK public sector Internet website. |
| operations | Management: Self-financing - income derived from selling its services and products. Chief Executive is responsible for day-to-day management with the support of the Directors of the three main business areas: Procure- |

ment Services, Telecommunications Services, Best Practice Consultancy. There is also a small Corporate Services function.

Policy: Taking lead in helping UK public sector in addressing problems relating to date changes in computer systems at the millennium. Increasing use of services by local authorities, health trusts and police forces. Emphasis increasingly on PFI procurements.

Trends: Represents the UK government on international projects and committees.

**performance**  New agency - not available

**board**

| | |
|---|---|
| Chief Executive | Bob Assirati |
| Director Telecommunications Services | George Harrold |
| IT Director | Nic Hopkins |
| Director Corporate Services | Christine Janner-Burgess |
| Director Best Practice Consultancy | John Stewart |
| Director Procurement Services | John Wright |
| *Accounting Officer* | *Chief Executive* |

**staff**  180

| | |
|---|---|
| Senior Customer Relations Manager | Dave Monk |
| Customer Relations Managers | Laurence Barnett |
| | Richard Bond |
| | Neil Croft |
| | Stephanie Minns |
| | Dave Perry |
| | Sue White |
| | Mike Withey |

**financial**  New agency - not available

**publications**  *This is CCTA, Services Catalogue, Publications Catalogue, Annual Report 96/97*

# Central Council for Education & Training in Social Work (CCETSW)

Derbyshire House
St Chad's Street
London WC1H 8AD

**Tel** 0171 278 2455
**Fax** 0171 278 2934

**status**  Executive body

**founded**  1971

**sponsor**  Department of Health (DH)

**powers**  HASSASSA Act 1983

**mission**  Establishing and maintaining a comprehensive, progressive continuum of education and training and qualifications to meet the needs of social work and social care staff across the UK. This includes vocational qualifications (NVQs and SVQs), the Diploma in Social Work (DipSW) as the qualifying award for social workers and a framework for post-qualifying training, specific mental health and practice teaching qualifications.

**tasks**  Ensuring that the training needs of the service are met, maintaining the quality of training, informing and registering candidates, administering the DipSW student bursary scheme and liaising with employers, government and other organisations in the development and promotion of training for the personal social services.

**operations**  Management: In addition to the DH, CCETSW works to four other sponsoring departments - Scottish Office Home Department, Welsh Office, Department of Health and Social Services (NI) and Home Office. The Chief Executive is appointed by its council. She is supported by two Assistant Directors in charge of Education, Training and Support Services and Operations. There are representative committees for England, NI, Scotland and Wales which are serviced by their national offices. Within England there are four regional offices whose work is co-ordinated by the Assistant Director (Operations).

Policy: Ensuring that training and education needs arising from new legislation are recognised and met within the training continuum.

Trends: Steady expansion of number of CCETSW approved programmes, students and awards. In 1996/97, local government reorganisation across Great Britain affected the provision of education and training in the personal social services. By March 1997, they were joint approved assessment centres (including CCETSW/SQA and CCETSW/City & Guilds), 930 CCETSW approved programmes and schemes of various kinds, 18,371 students and candidates registered for CCETSW awards and 8,949 awards achieved.

*board*  Council members appointed by four national Secretaries of State.

| | | |
|---|---|---|
| Chairman | Jeffrey Greenwood | |
| Members | Ziggi Alexander | |
| | Roy Blair | Brendah Malahleka |
| | Sandy Cameron | Kamlesh Patel |
| | Prof Mono Chakrabarti | Rob Pickford |
| | David Chantler | Denise Platt |
| | Anne Cleverly | Prof Cherry Rowlings |
| | Susan Ely | Eleanor Taggart |
| | Gareth Gimblett | John Thompson |
| | Arthur Keefe | Tony Hall |
| *Accounting Officer* | *Chief Executive* | |

*staff*  251 (150 in head office)

*financial*

| RECEIPTS & PAYMENTS Year end: 31 March | 1997 £ | 1996 £ | 1995 £ |
|---|---|---|---|
| **RECEIPTS** | | | |
| HM Grants received | 37,517,718 | 40,709,201 | 43,942,902 |
| Operating receipts | 1,327,140 | 1,084,382 | 1,139,687 |
| | **38,844,858** | **41,793,583** | **45,082,589** |
| **PAYMENTS** | | | |
| Salaries, wages, etc | 5,980,029 | 5,872,965 | 5,878,020 |
| Other operating payments | 32,905,210 | 35,998,139 | 38,661,776 |
| | **38,885,239** | **41,871,104** | **44,539,796** |
| **SURPLUS/(DEFICIT) FROM OPERATIONS** | **(40,381)** | **(77,521)** | **542,793** |
| Capital receipts (payments) net | (17,623) | 228,718 | (72,117) |
| Other receipts (payments) net | (377,141) | (299,711) | (541,569) |
| **EXCESS OF PAYMENTS OVER RECEIPTS** | **(435,145)** | **(148,514)** | **(70,893)** |

*advisers*  **Bankers**  National Westminster Bank

**Auditors**  National Audit Office  157-197 Buckingham Palace Road London SW1W 9SP

**Solicitors**  Beechcroft Stanleys  20 Furnival Street, London EC4A 1BN

*publications*  *Unlocking Care Management, Acceptable Risk?, Keeping Children in Mind, Confronting Ageing, Learning Together, The Mental Health Dimension in Social Work, Alcohol Problems, Living and Working with HIV - Complete Pack, Achieving Competence in Forensic Social Work, Acting Fairly, Setting Quality Standards of Residential Child Care, Reflections, Practising Equality, Cynnal Cof - Denydd Hel Atgofion Gyda Phobl Hyn, Reminiscence Work with Older People, Antiracist Social Work Education Series Complete Set, Perspectives on Discrimination and Social Work in Northern Ireland*

*branches*

*Bursaries*
3rd Floor
Caledonia House
223-231 Pentonville Road
London N1 9NG
Tel 0171 833 2524
Fax 0171 278 8186

*Thames Valley & South West*
21 Prince Street
Bristol BS1 4PH
Tel 0117 973 4137
Fax 0117 923 9883

*Scotland*
78/80 George Street
Edinburgh EH2 3BU
Tel 0131 220 0093
Fax 0131 220 6717

*Wales*
2nd Floor
West Ring
Southgate House
Wood Street
Cardiff CF1 1EW
Tel 01222 226257
Fax 01222 384764

*Northern England*
26 Park Row
Leeds LS1 5QB
Tel 0113 243 1516
Fax 0113 243 9276

*Northern Ireland*
6 Malone Road
Belfast BT9 5BN
Tel 01232 665390
Fax 01232 669469

Central England
Myson House
Railway Terrace
Rugby CV21 3HT
Tel 01788 572 119
Fax 01788 547139

# Central Office of Information (COI)

Hercules Road
London SE1 7DU

**Tel** 0171 928 2345
**Fax** 0171 928 5037

| | |
|---|---|
| **status** | Executive agency |
| **founded** | 1946. Executive agency in 1990, a trading fund in 1991 |
| **sponsor** | Chancellor of the Duchy of Lancaster |
| **powers** | Central Office of Information Trading Fund Order 1991 |
| **mission** | Procuring and providing publicity services for government departments and agencies to help them meet their policy objectives. |
| **tasks** | Providing strategic advice to departments and agencies on achieving their communications objectives. Providing purchasing and project management services. Supplying services which can only be provided by a government organisation (eg COI Regional Network). Adding value to clients' own activities, eg achieving keen prices through aggregate buying, choosing private sector suppliers etc. |
| **operations** | Management: The Chancellor determines the overall policy and financial framework within which COI operates but does not normally become involved in day-to-day management. The new Chief Executive has combined the previous Management Board and the Operations Board into one smaller Management Team of which all members are employees of COI. The directors continue to represent the key craft functions but also act as client service directors. As the government's executive agency for publicity procurement, it acts as an agent between central government and private sector suppliers and does not seek to carry out activities for which a sustainable and effective private sector market exists. |
| | Policy: To strengthen its relationship with its government sector clients where it has the greatest community of interest ie value for money for the taxpayer. |
| | Trends: A major IT upgrading is planned. |
| **board** | Management Team appointed by the Chief Executive from within COI. |

| | |
|---|---|
| Director General & Chief Executive | Tony Douglas |
| Group Director - Marketing Communications | Peter Buchanan |
| Group Director - Films, Radio, Events | Ian Hamilton |
| Group Director - Network | Rob Haslam |
| Group Director - Publications | Jack Murray |
| Secretariat | Viv Rowlands |
| Director, Review Implementation & Staff Development & Welfare | Richard Smith |
| Group Director - New Business | Sally Whetton |
| Principal Establishment & Finance Officer | Keith Williamson |
| Group Director - Business Improvement | Ralph Windsor |
| *Accounting Officer* | *Chief Executive* |

| | |
|---|---|
| **staff** | 305, all civil servants |

*financial*

| INCOME & EXPENDITURE | | |
| --- | --- | --- |
| Year end: 31 March | **1997** | **1996** |
| | **£000** | **£000** |
| **INCOME** | | |
| Turnover | 123,352 | 123,964 |
| Change in stocks of finished goods and work in progress | (1,416) | 287 |
| Other operating income | 2,568 | 1,821 |
| | **124,504** | **126,072** |
| **EXPENDITURE** | | |
| Raw materials and consumables | (1,360) | (1,660) |
| Other external charges | (109,977) | (110,414) |
| Staff costs: | | |
| (a) Wages and salaries | (9,554) | (10,621) |
| (b) Social security costs | (736) | (828) |
| (c) Other pension costs | (1,844) | (2,156) |
| Depreciation and other amounts written-off tangible assets | (620) | (701) |
| Other operating charges: | | |
| Notional insurance | (47) | (45) |
| Loss on disposal of fixed assets | (27) | (23) |
| Interest received | 369 | 480 |
| Short-term interest payable | (31) | (57) |
| **SURPLUS ON ORDINARY ACTIVITIES BEFORE** | | |
| **INTEREST ON LONG-TERM BORROWING** | **677** | **47** |
| Interest on long-term borrowing | (20) | (47) |
| **OPERATING SURPLUS FOR THE PERIOD** | **657** | **0** |

*advisers*

| **Bankers** | Bank of England | |
| --- | --- | --- |
| **Auditors** | National Audit Office | 157-197 Buckingham Palace Road |
| | | London SW1W 9SP |

# Central Rail Users Consultative Committee (CRUCC)

Clements House
14-18 Gresham Street
London EC2V 7NL

**Tel** 0171 505 9090
**Fax** 0171 505 9004

**Contact** Philip Wilks, External Relations and Policy Manager

*status*       Executive body. Statutory consumer body

*founded*     1993

*sponsor*     Office of the Rail Regulator (ORR)

*powers*      1993 Railways Act

*mission*     The statutory watchdog protecting and promoting the interests of rail passengers.

*tasks*       To represent the interests of rail users effectively within the new industry structure. Specifically, to monitor and investigate the policies and performance of train and station operators and to make recommendations for changes; to refer matters to the Regulator where necessary with a view to him exercising his powers; to undertake work commissioned by the Regulator; to co-ordinate the work of the eight (separate profiles) Rail Users Consultative Committees (RUCCs) and to collate information on key issues supplied by them.

*operations*  Management: CRUCC meets regularly, in public. It liaises closely with the industry, Department of the Environment, Transport and Regions, the Rail Regulator and Franchising Director. It expects to be consulted on proposals for change which impact on passengers and encourages co-operation between operators to maintain and enhance the benefits of a national railway. CRUCC works with the media to publicise its own efforts. It receives relatively few public complaints and does not generally handle them to a conclusion, referring them to the RUCCs or direct to an operator.

Policy: This continues to be to put passengers first. As the ORR is transferring more day-to-day management responsibility to CRUCC, more staff will be recruited.

Trends: 1996/97 witnessed the greatest changes to Britain's railways since nationalisation half a century ago. British Rail ceased to operate trains as the remaining 23 operating companies were franchised. The government is likely to press for increased investment to develop the rail network within an integrated transport policy.

**board**
Members of the CRUCC include the Chairmen of the eight RUCCs, which deal with matters affecting rail users locally, and the London Regional Passengers Committee; all are appointed to their various posts by the Secretary for State. Up to six other CRUCC members may be appointed by the Rail Regulator in consultation with the Secretary of State.

| | | |
|---|---|---|
| Chairman | David Bertram | |
| Deputy Chairman | Mrs Helen Millar | Charles Hogg, JP |
| Members | Jim Beale OBE | Miss Angela Hooper, CBE |
| | Stewart Francis | Dr Peris Jones |
| | Sir Alan Greengross | Bob Miller |
| | David Heseldin | Sir Robert Wall, OBE |

**staff**
Secretariat of 12 members of staff recruited through ORR.

**financial**

### EXPENDITURE BY THE CRUCC AND RUCCs

| Year end: 31 March | 1997 |
|---|---|
| | £ |
| **TOTAL EXPENDITURE BY CATEGORY** | |
| Staff travel & subsistence | 18,138 |
| Hospitality | 9,715 |
| Postage and carriage costs | 18,099 |
| Printing, stationery and publications | 41,089 |
| IT current, office machinery and telecommunications | 83,121 |
| Publicity and advertising | 7,103 |
| CRUCC/RUCC expenditure (inc Members' expenses) | 101,774 |
| Agency costs | 21,134 |
| **TOTAL EXPENDITURE** | **300,173** |
| | |
| **TOTAL EXPENDITURE BY CONSULTATIVE COMMITTEE** | |
| CRUCC | 85,640 |
| RUCC for Scotland | 46,438 |
| RUCC for Wales | 26,314 |
| RUCC for Eastern England | 20,591 |
| RUCC for The Midlands | 19,395 |
| RUCC for North Eastern England | 25,407 |
| RUCC for North Western England | 31,806 |
| RUCC for Southern England | 18,615 |
| RUCC for Western England | 25,967 |
| **TOTAL EXPENDITURE** | **300,173** |

Note. T he figures exclude the salaries of Chairmen and permanent staff, office accommodation costs and major capital expenditure, all of which are paid for from budgets held by ORR.

# Central Science Laboratory (CSL)

Sand Hutton
York
YO4 1LZ

**Tel** 01904 462000          **E-mail** science@csl.gov..uk
**Fax** 01904 4622111

**status**     Executive agency
**founded**     1992
**sponsor**     Ministry of Agriculture, Fisheries and Food (MAFF)
**powers**     Framework Document 1994
**mission**     To deliver high-quality advice, technical support and enforcement activities underpinned by the appropriate research and development to enable departmental customers to meet MAFF's aims.
**tasks**     Provides a wide range of scientific services aimed at promoting the safe and efficient production of food and the protection of the environment, mainly for MAFF but also for the private sector on a commercial basis. Services

include: investigating pesticides; establishing food safety; detecting microbiological contamination; validating food quality; safeguarding plant health; evaluating the risk of infestation; managing the control of pests; balancing the needs of agriculture with the environment; using science creatively to promote alternative crops.

**operations**   Management: The Ownership Board advises the Minister on CSL performance and management. Chief Executive (who is responsible to the Minister of Agriculture, Fisheries and Food is supported by Agriculture & Environment Research Director, Business Support Director and Food Research Director. Now consolidated on two sites, York and Norwich. In 1996/97 the CSL relocated from various sites to the purpose-built laboratory complex in York. New Commercial Director appointed to develop customer base.

Policy: To increase international scientific reputation and business.

Trends: Increasing public interest in food safety and consumer protection.

**performance**   Achieved all but one major target.

**board**   Ownership Board consists of five Ministry staff and two independent members, appointed by the Minister of Agriculture Fisheries & Food.

| Accounting Officer | Chief Executive |
|---|---|

**staff**   643

| | |
|---|---|
| Chief Executive | Prof Peter Stanley |
| Food Research Director Prof John Gilbert | |
| Agriculture & Environment Research Director | Prof Tony Hardy |
| Business Support Director | Brian Simmons |
| Plant Health | Prof Stephen Hill |
| Conservation & Environment Protection | Dr Stephen Hunter |
| Pest Management Strategies | Prof Nick Price |
| Infestation Risk Evaluation | Dr Ken Wildey |
| Human Resources & Quality | Mrs Heather Hamilton |
| Facilities & Procurement Jim Hill | |
| Finance | Andrew Simmonite |
| Information Services | Dr Michael Tas |
| Food Microbiology | Dr Lynton Cox |
| Food Safety & Quality | Dr Rob Massey |
| FAPAS | Dr Alan Patey |
| Pesticides | Dr Michael Wilson |

**financial**

**INCOME & EXPENDITURE**

| Year end: 31 March | 1997 £000 | 1996 £000 | 1995 £000 |
|---|---|---|---|
| **TURNOVER** | | | |
| MAFF - Commissioned research & development | 11,612 | 12,857 | 14,148 |
| MAFF - Commissioned policy support | 9,136 | 10,127 | 9,819 |
| MAFF - Other contracts | 571 | 362 | 201 |
| Levy bodies | 92 | 108 | 289 |
| Private sector and other Government Departments | 2,320 | 2,040 | 1,810 |
| | 23,731 | 25,494 | 26,267 |
| **COST OF SALES** | | | |
| Staff costs | 10,337 | 11,152 | 10,682 |
| Consumables | 2,608 | 1,748 | 2,246 |
| Depreciation | 1,034 | 1,363 | 1,284 |
| | 13,979 | 14,263 | 14,212 |
| **GROSS SURPLUS** | **9,752** | **11,231** | **12,055** |
| Administrative expenses | 15,849 | 12,632 | 12,371 |
| **OPERATING DEFICIT** | **(6,097)** | **(1,401)** | **(316)** |
| Interest on capital | 412 | 499 | 494 |
| **DEFICIT FOR THE YEAR TAKEN TO GENERAL FUND** | **(6,509)** | **(1,900)** | **(810)** |

**advisers**   **Auditors**   National Audit Office   157-197 Buckingham Palace Road London SW1W 9SP

**branches**   Norwich Research Park
Colney
Norwich NR4 7UQ
Tel 01603 259350
Fax 01603 501123
E-mail science@csl.gov.uk

# Centre for Environment, Fisheries & Aquaculture Science (CEFAS)

Lowestoft Laboratory
Pakefield Road
Lowestoft
Suffolk NR33 0HT

**Tel** 01502 562 244
**Fax** 01502 513 865

**E-mail** marketing@cefas.co.uk

| | |
|---|---|
| *status* | Executive agency |
| *founded* | 1997 |
| *sponsor* | Ministry of Agriculture, Fisheries and Food (MAFF) |
| *powers* | Framework Document |
| *mission* | To provide scientific and technical support, consultancy and advice, to MAFF and others, in its expert fields of fisheries' science and management, environmental assessment, aquaculture and fish health. |
| *tasks* | Provides a wide range of contract research, consultancy and training services in environmental impact assessment, environmental research and monitoring, aquaculture, health and hygiene, fisheries science and management. Clients include UK and international government departments, the EU, industry, environmental organisations and public bodies. Involved in formulating, implementing and interpreting UK and EU legislation. |
| *operations* | Management: Formerly MAFF's Directorate of Fisheries Research. Four laboratories and two ocean-going research vessels. Chief Executive reports to Ownership Board. Funds from sponsor and competitive tendering for research and service contracts. |
| | Policy: Broadening customer base. |
| | Trends: Towards more competitive tendering. |
| *board* | External members appointments approved by the Minister. Ownership Board: |

| | |
|---|---|
| Permanent Secretary, MAFF | |
| Fisheries Secretary, MAFF | Head of Environment Group, MAFF |
| Chief Scientist, MAFF | Chief Executive, CEFAS |
| Principal Finance Officer, MAFF | Secretariat, MAFF |
| External Science Member | Prof D Georgala |
| External Business Member | H Walker |

*staff*    440

| | |
|---|---|
| Chief Executive | Dr PW Greig-Smith |
| Deputy Chief Executive | Dr JW Horwood |
| Chair, Fisheries Science & Management Group | Dr GP Arnold |
| Chair, Aquaculture & Health Group | Dr BJ Hill |
| Chair, Environment Group | Dr MJ Waldock |
| Head of Establishment Support Unit | JFM Bumpus |
| Head of Business Support Unit | Dr VJ Bye |
| Marine Superintendent   Captain | BJ Kay |
| Finance Director | Mrs M Palmer |
| Head of Business Development Unit | BJ Robinson |
| *Accounting Officer* | *Chief Executive* |

| | | |
|---|---|---|
| *financial* | First income and expenditure accounts available summer 1998. | |
| *advisers* | **Bankers**  Paymaster (1836) Ltd | West Sussex RM10 1UH |
| | **Auditors**  National Audit Office | 157-197 Buckingham Palace Road London SW1P 9SP |
| | **Solicitors**  MAFF Legal Division | |
| *publications* | *Framework Document* | |

| | | |
|---|---|---|
| *branches* | *CEFAS Weymouth Laboratory* | *CEFAS Burham Laboratory* |
| | Barrack Road | Remembrance Avenue |
| | Weymouth | Burnham-on-Crouch |
| | Dorset DT4 8UB | Essex CMO 8HA |
| | Tel 01305 206600 | Tel 01621 787200 |
| | Fax 01305 206601 | |

CEFAS Conwy Laboratory
Bernarth Road
Conwy LL32 8UB
Tel 01492 593883
Fax 01492 592123

# *Centre for Information on Language Teaching & Research (CILT)*

20 Bedfordbury
London WC2N 4LB

**Tel** 0171 379 5101
**Fax** 0171 379 5082

| | |
|---|---|
| *status* | Executive body |
| *founded* | 1966 |
| *sponsor* | Department for Education and Employment (DfEE) |
| *powers* | Trust Deeds 1966 |
| *mission* | To promote a greater UK capability in modern languages, in particular to provide professional support for teachers of languages. |
| *tasks* | Teaching Resources Library contains language teaching materials; provides information and advice on issues relating to language teaching, learning and research; publishes a wide variety of titles; organises conferences and other training events for professionals; in-service teacher training programmes relating to national policy issues. |
| *operations* | Management: Director responsible for day-to-day management, and reports to the Governors. Has a national network of offices in England and separate centres in Wales (NCCW), Scotland (Scottish CILT) and Northern Ireland (NICILT). |
| | Policy: Expanding training programme. |
| | Trends: Cuts in funding to traditional clientele leads to reduction of CILT income (eg from publication sales). |
| *board* | Board of Governors appointed by the Secretaries of State and is widely representative of education in the UK. |

| Chair | Stephen Jones |
|---|---|
| Members | Jim Beale |
| | Ms Hilary Footitt |
| | Ms Jane Halliday |
| | Barry Jones |
| | Ms Janet Little |
| | David Mallen |
| | Dr Rosamond Mitchell |
| | Ms Mary Ryan |
| | Peter Thompson |
| | Richard Townsend |
| | Derek Winslow |
| *Accounting Officer* | *Director* |

*staff* 25

| Director | Dr Lid King |
|---|---|
| Deputy Director | Peter Boaks |
| Head of Finance & Establishment | Tina Thorp |
| Language Teaching Advisers | Eric Brown |
| | Marian Carty |
| | Patricia McLagan |
| | Glenis Shaw |
| | John Thorogood |
| CILT Programme Manager | Teresa Tinsley |
| Head of Information Resources Section | Phillipa Wright |
| Head of Publishing | Nicholas Evans |
| Business Languages Co-ordinator | Penny Rashbrook |

*financial*

| INCOME & EXPENDITURE Year end: 31 March | 1997 £ | 1996 £ |
|---|---|---|
| **INCOMING RESOURCES** | | |
| Grants receivable | 958,500 | 1,094,000 |
| Conferences | 237,789 | 176,752 |
| Projects | 145,562 | 56,194 |
| Contracts and servicing | 208,449 | 96,761 |
| Publications | 105,150 | 113,046 |
| Other income | 5,551 | 9,803 |
| NatBLIS subscriptions | 45,001 | 33,054 |
| | **1,706,002** | **1,579,610** |
| **RESOURCES EXPENDED** | | |
| Direct charitable expenditure | | |
| Information | 314,715 | 322,856 |
| Conferences | 413,812 | 393,677 |
| Publications | 202,504 | 198,066 |
| Contracts | 148,123 | 103,587 |
| Projects | 139,256 | 92,325 |
| Outreach | 74,065 | 56,221 |
| Liaison | 65,089 | 59,142 |
| Library stock | 14,479 | 21,168 |
| CILT Direct | 7,716 | 10,839 |
| Other | - | 7,225 |
| Grants to regional centres | 58,500 | 73,516 |
| NatBLIS | 44,822 | 38,878 |
| Support costs | 68,844 | 67,465 |
| Other expenditure: management and administration of the charity | 151,657 | 147,779 |
| | **1,703,582** | **1,592,744** |
| **NET INCOMING (OUTGOING) RESOURCES** | **2,420** | **(13,134)** |
| Balances brought forward | 15,350 | 28,484 |
| **BALANCES CARRIED FORWARD** | **17,770** | **15,350** |

# Channel Four Television Corporation (Channel 4)

124 Horseferry Road
London SW1P 2TX

**Tel** 0171 396 4444

*status*  Public corporation

*founded*  1982 as limited company, 1993 as public corporation

*sponsor*  Department of Culture, Media and Sport (DCMS)

*powers*  Broadcasting Act 1990. ITC Licence (1993) to broadcast for the ten years 1993 - 2002

*mission*  Public service TV broadcasting.

*tasks*  The Broadcasting Act 1990 requires Channel 4 to provide television programmes which: appeal to tastes and interests not generally catered for by ITV; are distinctive and encourage innovation and experiment; maintain a general high standard and a wide range; provide high quality news and current affairs; include proportions of educational programmes, programmes which are European and a proportion which are supplied by independent producers.

*operations*  Management: The Board consists of 14 members, most non-executive. It is responsible for ensuring that, in a changing broadcasting environment, Channel 4 meets its commitments under its ITC licence. The non-executive members are independent of management and have considerable weight in matters of strategy, performance and resources. The Chairman and five other executive members of the Board have responsibility for the formulation and operation of detailed policy, and for the conduct of Channel 4's affairs within its remit. The key to Channel 4's success is to maintain the virtuous circle of good programmes attracting audiences that advertisers are willing to pay and returning this investment into programming. Advertising revenue accounts for about 95% of revenue. Payments made to ITC should end 1998.

Policy: Channel 4 intends to take up its digital services frequency allocations and has established with ITV a jointly owned company to apply for the second digital multiplex. It will have sufficient digital capacity to offer new services on digital in addition to the wide-screen simulcast of existing services.

*Trends:* Commitment to its remit through many changes in the UK broadcasting industry. Despite speculation about operating as a Trust, Channel 4 sees no benefit in any change from its present constitutional status. Advertising revenue will decline as growth of satellite and cable services erode the terrestrial broadcaster's market share.

**performance**   1996 was an excellent year for steady viewing, rising turnover and profits and an array of awards for films and programmes.

**board**   Non-Executive members are appointed for fixed terms by ITC, after consultation with Channel 4's Chairman and the Secretary of State.

| | |
|---|---|
| Chief Executive & Director of Programmes | Michael Jackson |
| Managing Director & Director of Finance | David Scott |
| Director of Advertising Sales & Marketing | Andy Barnes |
| Director of Strategy & Development | David Brooke |
| Director & General Manager | Frank McGettigan |
| Director of Business Affairs | Janet Walker |
| *Accounting Officer* | *Chief Executive* |

**staff**   603 (511 Channel 4; 92 subsidiary companies)

| | |
|---|---|
| Managing Director | David Scott |
| Director of Advertising Sales & Marketing | Andy Barnes |
| Director of Strategy & Development | David Brooke |
| Deputy Director of Programmes, Daytime/Children & Sport | Karen Brown |
| Creative Director | Ceri Evans |
| Daytime Strategy Director | Julia Lestage |
| Director & General Manager | Frank McGettigan |
| Director of Programmes John Willis | |
| Corporation Secretary & Head of Rights | Andrew Yeates |

**financial**

| PROFIT & LOSS Year end: 31 December | 1996 £m | 1995 £m |
|---|---|---|
| **TURNOVER** | **518.6** | **464.0** |
| Cost of transmissions and sales | (358.1) | (309.0) |
| **GROSS PROFIT** | **160.5** | **155.0** |
| Administrative expenses | (20.6) | (19.1) |
| Depreciation | (7.6) | (7.7) |
| **OPERATING PROFIT** | **132.3** | **128.2** |
| Net interest | 2.0 | (0.1) |
| **PROFIT BEFORE ITV SUBSIDY** | **134.3** | **128.1** |
| Subsidy payable to ITV | (87.1) | (74.0) |
| **RETAINED PROFIT BEFORE TAXATION** | **47.2** | **54.1** |
| Taxation | (17.9) | (19.3) |
| **RETAINED PROFIT FOR THE YEAR** | **29.3** | **34.8** |

**advisers**

| | | |
|---|---|---|
| **Bankers** | Midland Bank | 27/32 Poultry, London EC3P 2BX |
| **Auditors** | Coopers & Lybrand | 1 Embankment Place, London WC2N 6NN |
| **Solicitors** | DJ Freeman | 43 Fetter Lane, London EC4A 1NA |
| | Allen & Overy | 9 Cheapside, London EC2V 6AD |

**branches**   227 Westgeorge Street
Glasgow G2 2ND
Tel 0141 568 7200
Fax 0141 568 7203

# Child Support Agency (CSA)

Pedmore House
The Waterfront
Brierley Hill
Dudley
West Midlands DY5 1XA

**Tel** 0345 131 000

| | |
|---|---|
| *status* | Executive agency |
| *founded* | 1993 |
| *sponsor* | Department of Social Security (DSS) |
| *powers* | Child Support Act 1991 and 1995. Framework Document |
| *mission* | To ensure that parents who live apart maintain their children whenever they can afford to do so, thus minimising the burden on the taxpayer. |
| *tasks* | Contacting absent parents; arranging the resolution of paternity disputes; assessing child maintenance and arranging payment; recovering arrears; preparing and presenting appeals; liaising with the Benefits Agency. |
| *operations* | Management: Chief Executive runs the agency with the support of the Management Board (five directors and two non-executive directors). Six regional offices, with headquarters in Dudley.

Policy: New Charter to try to improve basic customer contact. Trying to clear large backlogs before introduction of new computer system in 1998.

Trends: Expecting case load to double in next five years and staff numbers to decrease by 10%. |
| *performance* | Four out of five targets met in 1996/97 (only cleared 54% of maintenance applications within 26 weeks - target 60%). |
| *board* | Non-executive directors of the Management Board are appointed by the Secretary of State. |

| | |
|---|---|
| Chief Executive | Mrs F Boardman |
| Business Development & Support Director/ Deputy Chief Executive | S Heminsley |
| Finance Director | M Davison |
| Personnel Director | Ms C Francis |
| Operations Director | M Isaac |
| Non-Executive Board Member | J King |
| Quality & Communications Director | Mrs C Peters |
| Non-Executive Board Member | D Thornham |
| *Accounting Officer* | *Chief Executive* |

*staff* 7093

*financial*

**OPERATING ACCOUNT**

| Year end: 31 March | 1997 | 1996 |
|---|---|---|
| | £000 | £000 |
| **TURNOVER** | 0 | 4,063 |
| **EXPENDITURE** | | |
| Staff costs | 142,563 | 114,078 |
| Other operating costs | 81,516 | 88,704 |
| | 224,079 | 202,782 |
| | 224,079 | 198,719 |
| Other income | (13) | (1) |
| **NET COST BEFORE INTEREST** | 224,066 | 198,718 |
| Interest on capital | 459 | 550 |
| **NET COST** | 224,525 | 199,268 |

| CLIENT FUNDS RECEIPTS & PAYMENTS | 1997 | 1996 |
|---|---|---|
| Year end: 31 March | £000 | £000 |
| **RECEIPTS** | | |
| From clients | 214,911 | 133,508 |
| Bank interest | 651 | 69 |
| | **215,562** | **133,577** |
| **PAYMENTS** | | |
| Persons with care | 110,319 | 61,151 |
| Secretary of State (benefits repaid) | 96,462 | 68,195 |
| Agency (CSA fees and court fees) | 109 | 290 |
| Absent parents (refunds) | 5,368 | 2,032 |
| | **212,258** | **131,668** |
| **NET RECEIPTS** | **3,304** | **1,909** |
| Balance brought forward | 8,222 | 6,313 |
| **BALANCE CARRIED FORWARD** | **11,526** | **8,222** |

*advisers* **Auditors** National Audit Office

157-197 Buckingham Palace Road
London SW1W 9SP

*branches*

Parklands
Callendar Business Park
Callendar Road
Falkirk FK98 1SH
Tel 0345 136 000

Clearbrook House
Towerfield Drive
Buckleigh Down Business Park
Plymouth PL95 1SA
Tel 0345 137 000

Great Northern Tower
17 Great Victoria Street
Belfast BT2 7AD
Tel 0345 132 000

Great Western House
Woodside Ferry Approach
Birkenhead
Merseyside L41 6RG
Tel 0345 138 000

Ashdown House
Seddlescombe Road North
St Leonards
East Sussex TN37 7NL
Tel 0345 134 000

# *Civil Aviation Authority (CAA)*

CAA House
45-59 Kingsway
London WC2B 6TE

**Tel** 0171 379 7311
**Fax** 0171 240 1153

*status* Nationalised industry

*founded* 1972

*sponsor* Department of the Environment, Transport and the Regions (DETR)

*powers* Civil Aviation Act 1982

*mission* The safety and economic regulation of British aviation. To provide air traffic services in UK airspace.

*tasks* Air safety - responsible for airworthiness of aircraft and operational aspects including licensing flight crew, aircraft engineers, air traffic controllers and aerodromes; certification of UK airlines and aircraft and maintaining air traffic services standards; economic regulation - licensing of routes, approval of air fares for journeys outside the EU, regulation of certain airport charges, and licensing of air travel organisers; air traffic services - providing air traffic control services and radio and navigational aids through a wholly owned subsidiary company, National Air Traffic Services Ltd (NATS); also advises the government on aviation issues, represents consumer interests, conducts economic and scientific research and produces statistical data.

*operations* Management: New structure: airspace policy and regulatory activities transferred from NATS to an independent Director of Airspace Policy; a new body - the Joint Air Navigation Services Council - ensures effective provision of civil and military air navigation services. NATS has its own Board and a similar role is performed for the Safety and Economic Regulation groups by their respective policy committees. CAA Board focuses on governance, performance, review and approval of major decisions affecting policy, planning and resourcing. Required to set its unit charges at a level sufficient to recover costs of the UK Airspace Traffic Services and for all other activities to make an 8% return.

Policy: Possible privatisation of NATS. Initiation of major contracts for funding NATS's investment programme via the Private Finance initiative.

Trends: Regulatory issues need to be resolved to ensure successful completion of single European air travel market. Volumes of traffic increasing.

**performance**   Showed improvement for some of the performance indicators.

**board**   Appointed by Secretary of State.

| | |
|---|---|
| Chairman | Sir Malcolm Field |
| Deputy Chairman | Malcolm Argent, CBE |
| Part-time Board Member | Bryan Austin |
| Part-time Board Member | Raymond Birdseye |
| Part-time Board Member | Anthony Blackman, OBE |
| Secretary & Legal Adviser | Rupert Britton |
| Part-time Board Member | Ann Burdus |
| Part-time Board Member | Capt Gil Gray |
| Finance Director | Anthony Herron |
| Part-time Board Member | Rod Lynch |
| Chief Executive, National Air Traffic Services | Derek McLauchlan |
| Group Director, Economic Regulation | Cliff Paice |
| Part-time Board Member | Gillian White |
| Group Director, Safety Regulation | Michael Willett |

**staff**   6212

**financial**

| GROUP PROFIT & LOSS | | |
|---|---|---|
| Year end: 31 March | 1997 | 1996 |
| | £000 | £000 |
| TURNOVER | 592,138 | 578,792 |
| OPERATING COSTS | | |
| Staff costs | 291,262 | 275,849 |
| Services and materials | 90,975 | 94,948 |
| Repairs and maintenance | 34,294 | 33,430 |
| External research and development | 8,335 | 11,185 |
| Depreciation | 51,154 | 53,732 |
| Other operating charges | 51,284 | 41,871 |
| Deferred government grants | (5,514) | (6,524) |
| | 521,790 | 504,491 |
| Income equalisation | 13,151 | 5,241 |
| OPERATING PROFIT BEFORE INTEREST AND TAXATION | 57,197 | 69,060 |
| Net interest payable | (42,217) | (43,654) |
| PROFIT ON ORDINARY ACTIVITIES BEFORE TAXATION | 14,980 | 25,406 |
| Tax credit on profit on ordinary activities | 0 | 9 |
| PROFIT FOR YEAR TRANSFERRED TO RESERVES | 14,980 | 25,415 |

# Civil Service College

Sunningdale Park
Larch Avenue
Ascot
Berks SL5 0QE

**Tel** 01344 634000
**Fax** 01344 634233            **Web** http://www.open.gov.uk/college/cschome.htm

**status**   Executive agency
**founded**   1989
**sponsor**   Cabinet Office, Office of Public Service (OPS)

*mission*    To develop managerial and professional skills among civil servants and promote best practice throughout government, both in management and key professional areas.

*tasks*    To provide: management training for civil servants, particularly those at, or aspiring to, relatively senior positions; specialist training in key professional areas or advanced levels; related consultancy and research.

*operations*    Management: The Business Executive comprises the Chief Executive and the executive directors. Individual members of the College Advisory Council, which meets twice each year, contribute separately to the college. During 1996/97, the internal organisation was streamlined into five groups covering: executive and organisational development; government; management development; specialist development; and international training and development. Full costs were covered entirely from earned income, without a central payment from the OPS, for the first time in 1996/97. Both total earnings and costs were much reduced from 1995/96. Training courses are run at Ascot (Sunningdale Park) and London (11 Belgrave Street), and at customers' premises and hotels. In 1996, the College also re-established a presence in Scotland (in association with the Strathclyde Graduate Business School) The Civil Service College in Scotland, with its own Scottish prospectus.

Policy: To retain its competitiveness in terms of value for money to customers.

Trends: Strong competition in many areas has resulted in a strong trend away from open programmes towards single-client business, mainly public sector clients. Consultancy is performing well in gaining international contracts spread over a number of years. The number of people working in the civil service continues to decrease and a separate financial target of £1.5m is now set for consultancy earnings. Other targets for 1997/98 are to break even in actual accounting terms; to attract 1500+ students from the senior civil service and 900 from the private sector; and to earn 88% of course evaluations in the two highest (of six) categories.

*board*    The College Advisory Council is appointed from civil servants, industry and the universities.

| Members | Sir Robin Butler GCB CVO | |
|---|---|---|
| | Jonathan Baume | |
| | DG Bower | Prof A Kalabadse |
| | William Cockburn | Leigh Lewis |
| | Prof Gavin Drewry | S Matheson CB |
| | Sir Russell Hillhouse KCB | R Mottram |
| | Prof J Hunt | R Mountfield CB |
| | Ms J Hunt | Mrs VPM Strachan CB |
| *Business Executive* | | |
| Chief Executive | Stephen Hickey | |
| Director, Management Development | Martin Barnes | |
| Director of International Consulting | Rob Behrens | |
| Director, International Training & Development | Elizabeth Chennells | |
| Director, Specialist Development | Glynn Llewellyn | |
| Non-Executive Director | Linda Oliver | |
| Director, Executive & Organisational Development | Peter Tebby | |
| Director of Finance | Michael Timmis | |
| Director, Government Group | Andrew Wyatt | |

*staff*    261

*financial*

**INCOME & EXPENDITURE**

| Year end: 31 March | 1997 £000 | 1996 £000 |
|---|---|---|
| **INCOME** | | |
| Training and consultancy | 17,731 | - |
| Received from overseas organisations | 520 | - |
| | 18,251 | 19,568 |
| **EXPENDITURE** | | |
| Staff costs | 6,859 | 7,268 |
| Depreciation of tangible fixed assets | 699 | 604 |
| **OTHER OPERATING CHARGES** | | |
| Staff travel, subsistence and hospitality | 480 | 481 |
| Other staff related costs | 275 | 365 |
| External lecturer fees and contracted-out courses | 2,196 | 2,487 |
| Operating leases - hire of plant and machinery | 74 | 62 |
| Operating leases - other | 44 | 39 |
| Supplies and services | 1,979 | 2,821 |
| Accommodation and utilities | 5,755 | 5,769 |
| Notional costs | 34 | 35 |
| Loss on disposal of fixed assets | 123 | 34 |
| | 10,960 | 12,093 |
| | 18,518 | 19,965 |
| Other operating income | 600 | 0 |
| **OPERATING SURPLUS/(DEFICIT)** | 333 | (397) |
| Interest payable | 120 | 93 |
| **SURPLUS/(DEFICIT) FOR THE FINANCIAL YEAR** | 213 | (490) |

# Coal Authority

200 Lichfield Lane
Berry Hill
Mansfield
Nottinghamshire NG18 4RG

**Tel** 01623 427162
**Fax** 01623 62072

| | |
|---|---|
| *status* | Executive body |
| *founded* | 1994 |
| *sponsor* | Department of Trade and Industry (DTI) |
| *powers* | Coal Industry Act 1994 |
| *mission* | Responsible for overseeing the UK coal industry. |
| *tasks* | Licensing coal-mining operations and making available rights in relation to unworked coal; settling subsidence damage claims not falling on coal-mining operators; managing property, including historic liabilities, arising from ownership of the coal reserves and underground workings; providing access to geological data and coal mining plans. |
| *operations* | Management: The Chief Executive reports to the Authority and oversees the management structure with the support of Directors of Licensing, Contracts, Finance/Administration/IT, and the Solicitor/Secretary. The Authority has two committees: Audit and Remuneration, and an Environment Group. Most operational work is carried out by contractors and consultants, in particular the assessment of liability for coal-mining subsidence damage, negotiating settlements with claimants and organising repairs. The Authority's staff direct and monitor the consultant's performance. |

Policy: Adopted formal environmental policy. New IT system starting in 1998.

Trends: Coal output decreasing in line with demand for UK coal.

*board*   Authority members are appointed by the Secretary of State from the coal-mining industry, planning, finance and the law.

| Chairman | Sir David White DL |
|---|---|
| Deputy Chairman | Eric Hassall |
| Members | John Cunliffe |
| | Roy Lynk OBE |
| | Leslie Rendell |
| | Tom Slee |
| | Neville Washington OBE |
| *Accounting Officer* | *Chief Executive* |

*staff*   109

| Solicitor & Secretary | Ian Cartwright |
|---|---|
| Director of Finance, Administration & IT | Malcolm Edwards |
| Director of Licensing | Keith Leighfield |
| Director of Contracts | Albert Schofield |

*financial*

| INCOME & EXPENDITURE | | |
|---|---|---|
| Year end: 31 March | 1997 | 1996 |
| | £000 | £000 |
| **TURNOVER** | | |
| Grant-in-aid | 34,945 | 53,457 |
| Income from revenue-generating activities | 20,862 | 21,377 |
| | 55,807 | 74,834 |
| **ADMINISTRATIVE EXPENSES** | (33,604) | (47,647) |
| **OPERATING SURPLUS** | 22,203 | 27,187 |
| Exceptional item | (6,131) | - |
| **SURPLUS ON ORDINARY ACTIVITIES BEFORE INTEREST** | 16,072 | 27,187 |
| Interest receivable | 975 | 1,165 |
| Interest payable and similar charges | (2,840) | (441) |
| **SURPLUS ON ORDINARY ACTIVITIES BEFORE** | | |
| **AND AFTER TAXATION** | 14,207 | 27,911 |
| Appropriations by government | (15,325) | (13,882) |
| **RETAINED (DEFICIT)/SURPLUS FOR THE YEAR** | (1,118) | 14,029 |

| *advisers* | **Bankers** | Barclays Bank | PO Box 57, Mansfield NG18 1HT |
| | **Auditors** | National Audit Office | 157-197 Buckingham Palace Road London SW1W 9SP |

# Coastguard

Spring Place
105 Commercial Road
Southampton SO15 1EG

**Tel** 01703 329100
**Fax** 01703 329298     **Web** http://www.coastguard.gov.uk

| | |
|---|---|
| *status* | Executive agency |
| *founded* | 1994 |
| *sponsor* | Department of the Environment, Transport and the Regions (DETR) |
| *powers* | Coastguard Act 1925 and Merchant Shipping Act 1995 |
| *mission* | To minimise loss of life among seafarers and coastal users and minimise pollution from ships to sea and coastline, thus meeting the government's commitments under international agreements and conventions. |
| *tasks* | To provide an effective search and rescue service; to initiate and co-ordinate civil maritime search and rescue within the UK Search and Rescue Region; to deal with major spillages of oil and other hazardous substances from ships at sea which threaten UK interests. Coastguard is the national authority responsible for providing 24-hour readiness to deal with marine emergencies. |
| *operations* | Management: There is a Management Board comprising the Chief Executive, the Chief Coastguard, the Director of Administration and the Director Marine Pollution Control Unit (MPCU). There are two operational divisions: HM Coastguard (HMCG) which has a network of six maritime rescue co-ordination centres, 15 subcentres and 92 sectors; and MPCU provides an adequate marine response capability to meet the UK's international obligations. Administration Division provides corporate support services and shares a building with the Marine Safety Agency. |
| | Policy: To develop and implement safety awareness and accident reduction strategies aimed at prevention rather than cure. |
| | Trends: Rising trend of search and rescue incidents halted for the first time in 11 years - from 12,220 in 1995 to 11,291 in 1996. Lives lost fell too - from 232 to 216. Coastguard continues to improve and test its own responses and those of the maritime industry and other emergency services through low-profile exercise and contingency planning. **From 1 April 1998, Coastguard merged with the Marine Safety Agency to form the Maritime & Coastguard Agency (MCA).** |
| *performance* | All key targets met. |
| *board* | Advisory Board appointed by the Secretary of State. |

| Chairman | D Rowlands |
|---|---|
| Members | R Clarke |
| | C Harris |
| | Mrs L Mathieson |
| | A Melville |
| | P Walsh |

| | |
|---|---|
| *staff* | 729, supported by 3100 auxiliary coastguards |

| Chief Executive | C Harris |
|---|---|
| Chief Coastguard | J Astbury |
| Director of Administration | D Cockram |
| Director, Marine Pollution Control Unit | R Gainsford |

**financial**

| INCOME & EXPENDITURE<br>Year end: 31 March | 1997<br>£000 |
|---|---|
| **INCOME** | |
| Income from services supplied | 476 |
| **OPERATING COSTS** | |
| Staff costs | (15,261) |
| Depreciation | (2,851) |
| Other operating costs | (36,382) |
| | **(54,494)** |
| **OPERATING DEFICIT** | **(54,018)** |
| Profit on disposal of fixed assets | 125 |
| **DEFICIT BEFORE INTEREST ON CAPITAL** | **(53,893)** |
| Interest on capital | (1,570) |
| **DEFICIT FOR THE FINANCIAL YEAR** | **(55,463)** |

**advisers**   **Auditors**   National Audit Office   157-197 Buckingham Palace Road
London SW1W 9SP

# Commission for the New Towns (CNT)

414-428 Midsummer Boulevard
Central Milton Keynes
Bucks MK9 2EA

**Tel** 01908 692692
**Fax** 01908 691333

**status**  Executive body

**founded**  1961

**sponsor**  Department of the Environment, Transport and the Regions (DETR)

**powers**  New Towns Act 1959 and 1981. New Towns and Urban Development Corporations Act 1985. Housing Grants, Construction and Regeneration Act 1997.

**mission**  To take over, manage and dispose of the assets and liabilities of 21 New Town Development Corporations in England, once each Corporation has substantially achieved its objective (the last one was wound up in 1992).

**tasks**  Disposing of the assets and liabilities of New Towns, Urban Development Corporations (UDCs) and Housing Action Trusts (HATs) in England.  Achieving the best possible price for the land and buildings.

**operations**  Management: Scheduled for winding up on 31 March 1998, CNT's role was expanded to include UDCs and HATs and its life extended.  Government will review progress in 2000 to determine when to close it. Organisation was restructured and headquarters moved from London to Milton Keynes where corporate functions are being consolidated with the regional offices covering South and Central Regions. Warrington covering the North will be the other main office. Staff numbers are likely to be reduced.

Policy: From April 1998, CNT will concentrate on selling the remaining new towns' land and on disengaging from the residual assets and liabilities of the eight UDCs. It will also take over any residual assets and liabilities of those HATs winding up during its life-time. Liaison with local authorities and regional organisations remains important.

Trends: Since 1962 CNT has secured £2.8 billion from disposals.

**performance**  Cash receipts were £65.7 million against a target of £130 million from disposals of land and buildings.

**board**

| Chairman | Dr JRG Bradfield |
|---|---|
| Deputy Chairman | MH Mallinson |
| Members | FC Graves |
| | Sir Brian Jenkins |
| | Lady Marsh |
| | Mr J Trustam Eve |
| *Accounting Officer* | *Chief Executive* |

**staff**  360

| Chief Executive | NJ Walker |
|---|---|
| Director of Finance | DV Hone |
| Director Marketing | DR Ludford |
| Director of Personnel & Management Services | HS Ruffman |
| Director South | GD Johnston |
| Director West Midlands & North | CJ Mackrell |
| Director Central | J Napleton |

*financial*

**INCOME & EXPENDITURE**

| Year end: 31 March | 1997 | 1996 |
|---|---|---|
| | £000 | £000 |
| **INCOME** | | |
| Surplus on disposal of property assets | 102,614 | 98,919 |
| Rent and other property income | 14,146 | 25,396 |
| Contributions from local authorities | 3,697 | 4,164 |
| Other operating income | 49 | 178 |
| | 120,506 | 128,657 |
| **EXPENDITURE** | | |
| Administration and management | 16,035 | 17,559 |
| Repairs and maintenance | 7,633 | 10,967 |
| Rent of lease-back properties | 7,316 | 11,102 |
| Contributions to water companies and local authorities | 4,668 | 4,703 |
| Civic assets | 16,455 | 14,922 |
| Provisions for disposal of property assets | 479 | 2,202 |
| Provisions for liabilities and charges | 28,369 | 23,430 |
| Other operating expenditure | 4,558 | 1,435 |
| | 85,513 | 86,320 |
| **SURPLUS ON ORDINARY ACTIVITIES BEFORE INTEREST** | **34,993** | **42,337** |
| Interest receivable | 33,370 | 87,061 |
| Interest payable | (24,733) | (78,569) |
| Premium on the premature redemption of loans | (45,482) | (125,929) |
| Discount on the premature redemption of loans | - | (12,797) |
| **SURPLUS/(DEFICIT) ON ALL ACTIVITIES BEFORE TAXATION** | **(1,852)** | **(87,897)** |
| Taxation | 6,578 | (11,600) |
| **SURPLUS/(DEFICIT) FOR THE YEAR** | **4,726** | **(99,497)** |
| Retained surplus brought forward | 264,737 | 364,234 |
| **RETAINED SURPLUS CARRIED FORWARD** | **269,463** | **264,737** |

*advisers*

**Auditors**  Ernst & Young  London

*branches*

| *North* | *West Midlands* |
|---|---|
| New Town House | Jordan House West |
| Buttermarket Street | Hall Court |
| Warrington | Hall Park Way |
| Cheshire WA1 2LF | Telford TF3 4NN |
| Tel 01925 651144 | Tel 01952 293131 |

# *Commission for Racial Equality (CRE)*

Elliot House
10/12 Allington Street
London SW1E 5EH

**Tel** 0171 828 7022
**Fax** 0171 630 7605

*status*  Executive body

*founded*  1976

*sponsor*  Home Office

*powers*  Race Relations Act 1976

*mission*  Working for a just society, which gives everyone an equal chance to work, learn and live free from discrimination and prejudice, and from the fear of racial harassment and violence.

# Q&Q

**tasks** — Assisting complainants; investigating racial discrimination; tackling institutional discrimination; improving opportunities for young people; tackling racial harassment; raising public awareness.

**operations** — Management: Executive Director reports to the Chairman of the Commission. Head office in London, other offices in Birmingham, Leeds, Leicester, Manchester, Edinburgh and Cardiff. Funds 90 racial equality councils jointly with local authorities.

Policy: Continuing with strategy to follow up individual cases.

Trends: Number of complainants slightly increased and average settlement in racial discrimination cases supported by the Commission increased by 21% in 1996. Greater institutional and corporate willingness in UK to eliminate racial discrimination.

**performance** — In 58% of the cases followed up by the CRE in 1996 they achieved all or most of their objectives.

**board**

| Chairman | Herman Ouseley |
|---|---|
| Deputy Chairman | Hugh Harris |
| Deputy Chairman | Zahida Manzoor |
| Commissioners | Dr Raj Chandran |
| | Blondel Cluff |
| | Marie Cunningham |
| | Michael Hastings |
| | Dr Moussa Jogee JP |
| | Dr Zaka Khan OBE JP |
| | Julie Mellor |
| | Dr Dwain Neil |
| | Dame Simone Prendergast |
| | Bob Purkiss |
| | Dr Jaslien Singh |
| | Ray Singh |

**staff** — 203

| Executive Director | Sukhdev Sharma |
|---|---|
| Joint Head of Equality Policy Consultancy | Phillip Barnett |
| Head of Law & Administration | Christopher Boothman |
| Head of Litigation | Khurshid Drabu |
| Head of Strategy | Colin Hann |
| Manager for the Midlands & Wales | Andrew Housley |
| Joint Head of Equality Policy Consultancy | Susan Ollerearnshaw |
| Manager for the North & Scotland | Eric Seward |
| Head of Central Services | Parveen Sharma |
| Manager for London & the South | Clifford Stewart |
| Head of Communications | Marjorie Thompson |

**financial**

### EXPENDITURE

| Year end: 31 March | 1997 £ | 1996 £ |
|---|---|---|
| Commission members' remuneration and advisory services | 294,423 | 209,514 |
| Salaries and wages, national insurance, etc | 6,004,246 | 6,063,126 |
| Commission and secretariat overhead expenses | 2,471,440 | 2,367,023 |
| Staff and commission travel | 263,610 | 216,364 |
| Legal and other professional charges | 599,385 | 899,663 |
| External training | 107,748 | 127,020 |
| Research and Section 45 | 377,174 | 286,304 |
| Grant aid for employment of racial equality officers | 3,620,251 | 3,995,038 |
| Grant aid to racial equalitycouncils | 102,751 | 171,597 |
| Project aid and self-help | 509,682 | 417,753 |
| Information services and publications | 812,762 | 584,924 |
| Conferences | 202,424 | 269,943 |
| New technology | 266,251 | 493,682 |
| | **15,632,147** | **16,101,951** |

# Commissioner for Protection Against Unlawful Industrial Action

1st Floor
Bank Chambers
2a Rylands Street
Warrington
Cheshire WA1 1EN

**Tel** 01925 415771/414128
**Fax** 01925 415772

**Contact** Terry Wafer/Deborah Shaw

| | |
|---|---|
| *status* | Executive body |
| *founded* | 1993 |
| *sponsor* | Department of Trade and Industry (DTI) |
| *powers* | Trade Union and Labour Relations (Consolidation) Act 1992 and as amended by the Trade Union Employment Rights Act 1993 |
| *mission* | To deter trade unions from becoming involved in unlawful industrial action. |
| *tasks* | To grant assistance - including paying the cost of legal advice and representation - to an individual who is an actual or prospective party to proceedings. These proceedings are where an individual claims that a trade union has done or is likely to do an unlawful act, and an effect of that act is to prevent or delay the supply of good or services, or to reduce the quality of the goods or services to be supplied, because of industrial action organised by a trade union. |
| *operations* | Management: The Commissioner is also Commissioner for the Rights of Trade Union Members. Both offices are located in Warrington, and one-third of common costs are allocated to this office. Both are, however, separate organisations and separate entities. The Commissioner is independent and cannot be directed by any minister to assist, or not assist, any particular application. |

Policy: There is some public confusion about the organising of unlawful action by a trade union and other forms of industrial action, particularly unofficial industrial action. The Commissioner cannot assist with the latter. There are now few, if any, instances of unlawful organised industrial action and the Commissioner believes that his office is an effective deterrent.

Trends: 384 people were in touch with the Commissioner's office and two formal applications for assistance were made, one of which resulted in assistance (concerning the threatened withdrawal of teaching to a secondary school pupil). Information on the Commissioner continues to be publicised, both to the general public and to MPs, solicitors, Citizens' Advice Bureaux etc.

| | |
|---|---|
| *board* | The Commissioner is appointed by the Secretary of State. |
| *staff* | Five |

| Commissioner | AG Corless CBE |
|---|---|
| Assistant Commissioner | Terry Wafer |
| Applications Manager | Jill Culling |
| Office Manager | Deborah Shaw |
| Finance Officer | Roselyn Urey |

*financial*

| RECEIPTS & PAYMENTS Year end: 31 March | 1997 £000 | 1996 £000 | 1995 £000 |
|---|---|---|---|
| **RECEIPTS** | | | |
| Grant-in-aid received | 92 | 98 | 103 |
| **PAYMENTS** | | | |
| Salaries and wages etc | 58 | 52 | 57 |
| Other operating expenses | 32 | 39 | 48 |
| | 90 | 91 | 105 |
| **SURPLUS FROM OPERATIONS** | 2 | 7 | (2) |
| Other payments | 1 | 1 | 0 |
| **SURPLUS FOR THE PERIOD** | 1 | 6 | (2) |
| Appropriations to Consolidated Fund | 1 | 2 | - |
| **EXCESS OF RECEIPTS OVER PAYMENTS** | NIL | 4 | (2) |

**advisers**  **Auditors**  National Audit Office  157-197 Buckingham Palace Road
London SW1W 9SP

**publications**  *A Guide to the Commissioner's Role, Annual Reports*

# Commissioner for the Rights of Trade Union Members

1st Floor
Bank Chambers
2a Rylands Street
Warrington
Cheshire WA1 1EN

**Tel** 01925 415771/414128
**Fax** 01925 415772

**Contact** Terry Wafer/Deborah Shaw

| | |
|---|---|
| **status** | Executive body |
| **founded** | 1987 |
| **sponsor** | Department of Trade and Industry (DTI) |
| **powers** | Trade Union and Labour Relations (Consolidation) Act 1992 |
| **mission** | To ensure that trade union members who wish to take legal action to protect specified legal rights are not placed at a disadvantage by their inability to obtain legal advice or pay expenses. |
| **tasks** | Making arrangements for, and paying for, legal advice and representation where union members make a complaint against their union in respect of specified matters (eg improper conduct of a ballot) or that it is failing to comply with its own rulebook. |
| **operations** | Management: The Commissioner is also Commissioner for Protection Against Unlawful Industrial Action. Both offices are located in Warrington and two-thirds of common costs are allocated to this office. Both are, however, separate organisations and separate entities. The Commissioner is independent and cannot be directed by any minister to grant, or not to grant, assistance in response to any application. |
| | Policy: Commissioner's policy is to encourage the use of internal remedies before granting legal assistance. |
| | Trends: The number of enquiries continues to rise and at 2400 in 1996/97 is double the previous highest figure. Half the enquiries arise as a result of trade unions' information to their own members. |
| **board** | The Commissioner is appointed by the Secretary of State. |
| **staff** | Five |

| | |
|---|---|
| Commissioner | AG Corless CBE |
| Assistant Commissioner | Terry Wafer |
| Applications Manager | Jill Culling |
| Office Manager | Deborah Shaw |
| Finance Officer | Roselyn Urey |

**financial**

| RECEIPTS & PAYMENTS | | | |
|---|---|---|---|
| Year end: 31 March | 1997 | 1996 | 1995 |
| | £000 | £000 | £000 |
| **RECEIPTS** | | | |
| Grant-in-aid received | 225 | 338 | 295 |
| Operating receipts | 65 | 84 | 11 |
| | 290 | 422 | 306 |
| **PAYMENTS** | | | |
| Salaries and wages etc | 115 | 105 | 113 |
| Other operating expenses | 108 | 230 | 180 |
| | 223 | 335 | 243 |
| **SURPLUS FROM OPERATIONS** | 67 | 87 | 13 |
| Other payments | 2 | 2 | 1 |
| **SURPLUS FOR THE PERIOD** | 65 | 85 | 12 |
| Appropriations to Consolidated Fund | 65 | 84 | 11 |
| **EXCESS OF RECEIPTS OVER PAYMENTS** | - | 1 | 1 |

| advisers | **Auditors** | National Audit Office | 157-197 Buckingham Palace Road London SW1W 9SP |

*publications*  *A Guide for Trade Union Members, How We Can Help You, The Commissioner's Charter Standard, Annual Report*

# *Commonwealth Development Corporation (CDC)*

1 Bessborough Gardens
London SW1V 2JQ

**Tel** 0171 828 4488          **E-mail** @mail.london.cdc.co.uk
**Fax** 0171 8286505

| | |
|---|---|
| *status* | Public corporation |
| *founded* | 1948 |
| *sponsor* | Department for International Development |
| *powers* | Commonwealth Development Corporation Acts 1978 to 1996. |
| *mission* | To assist overseas countries in the development of their economies by creating long-term self-sustainable businesses. |
| *tasks* | To investigate, formulate and carry out projects for the creation, promotion, expansion, reorganisation or rationalisation in overseas countries of specified classes of enterprise. To invest in the development of resources (not give grants). To maintain close relations with overseas governments through its own overseas offices to ensure that its activities are effective; to pay its way. |
| *operations* | Management: There are three business units - CDC Investments, CDC Industries and CDC Financial Markets - and a new Business Development unit which also handles 'due diligence' for investment proposals. CDC has a London headquarters and 27 CDC overseas offices. It has £1.6 billion invested in 400 projects in 54 countries. CDC staff provide a level of expertise scarce in many countries. In October 1997 the Prime Minister announced that CDC is to become a new partnership for development - a public/private partnership which will allow private investors to invest money in CDC as a public corporation. Legislation will be needed to allow this. |
| | Policy: CDC combines developmental objectives with investing on a commercial basis in the private sector and adopting a hands-on approach. This involves seeking partnerships and adding value - by introducing otherwise unavailable capital and assisting in the structuring of the business or providing management. |
| | Trends: In 1997, new investment levels were £283.7 million. CDC activities continue to be concentrated in the poorer countries. Growth rates in developing countries are expected to improve, driven primarily by private sector capital flows. In 1996 the Commonwealth Private Investment Initiative (CPII) was launched with the Commonwealth Secretariat, which will bring a number of regional equity funds under the CDC umbrella to mobilise additional private finance. So far three funds have been started in Africa, South Asia and the Pacific Islands. |
| *performance* | CDC Industries reported a pre-tax profit of £28 million on a turnover of £216 million. CDC Financial Markets started another six funds in 1996, bring the number of funds to 12 with committed funds of £147 million (£78 million from third parties). |
| *board* | Appointed by the Secretary of State. |

| | |
|---|---|
| Chairman | Earl Cairns CBE |
| Deputy Chairman | Sir William Ryrie KCB |
| Members | Carolyn Hayman |
| | Pen Kent |
| | Jonathan Kydd |
| | Roger Murray |
| | David Pearce |
| | Russell Seal |
| | Hari Shankar Singhania |

| | |
|---|---|
| *staff* | 432 of whom 239 are in the London office, 192 in the overseas offices and one in a CDC consolidated subsidiary. |

| | |
|---|---|
| Chief Executive | Roy Reynolds |
| *CDC Investments* | |
| Managing Director | Nicholas Selbie |
| Regional Director - South Asia | Stephen Cake |
| Regional Director - East/Central/Southern Africa | Tim Davidson |
| Project Director - Specialised Investments | Rod Evison |
| Regional Director - Asia/Pacific | Chris Orman |
| *Business Development* | |
| Managing Director | Paul Jobson |
| Acting Sector Director - Manufacturing & Commerce | David Allwood |
| Sector Director - Minerals, Oils & Gas | John Hodder |
| Sector Director - Infrastructure | Jim Romanos |
| Sector Director - Agribusiness | Geoff Tyler |
| *CDC Industries* | |
| Managing Director | Bob Clark |
| Business Director - New Business & Power | Richard Beacham |
| Business Director - Cement, Citrus & Fish | Justin Braithwaite |
| Business Director - Arable, Coffee & Rubber | Nick Hetherington |
| Business Director - Palm Oil & Forestry | Donald McCallum |
| Business Director - Tea, Sugar & Forestry | Harry Percy |
| Chief Financial Officer | Derek Pierson |
| *CDC Financial Markets* | |
| Managing Director | Robert Binyon |
| Manager, Investment Capital Funds | Richard Hughes |
| Manager, Financial Intermediaries | Paul Nabavi |
| Director of Finance | Nicholas Denniston |
| Treasury & Pensions Director | Ian Black |
| Accounts & IT Director | Godfrey Davies |
| General Counsel | Gavin Wylie |
| Director, Human Resources | Ian Gill |
| Director, Corporate Relations | Sean Magee |

*financial*

**GROUP REVENUE**
**Year end: 31 December**

| | 1996 £000 | 1995 £000 |
|---|---|---|
| **INCOME** | | |
| Loan interest income | 105,000 | 106,400 |
| Loan fee income | 3,500 | 4,100 |
| Income from loan investments | 108,500 | 110,500 |
| Dividend income | 15,300 | 24,400 |
| Share of net pre-tax profits of non-consolidated subsidiaries and associates | 30,600 | 33,300 |
| Less: dividends related to the above | (10,900) | (21,400) |
| Income from equity investments | 35,000 | 36,300 |
| Other operating income | 8,300 | 8,500 |
| | 151,800 | 155,300 |
| Operating expenditure | (22,500) | (20,800) |
| **OPERATING SURPLUS** | **129,300** | **134,500** |
| Net profits on investment realisations | 13,900 | 17,800 |
| Other gains and (losses) | (1,800) | (700) |
| Investment and other provisions | (44,700) | (41,700) |
| Interest payable on borrowings | (200) | (100) |
| | (32,800) | (24,700) |
| **SURPLUS ON ORDINARY ACTIVITIES BEFORE TAX** | 96,500 | 109,800 |
| UK and overseas tax | (28,900) | (24,500) |
| Share of taxation of non-consolidated subsidiaries and associates | (4,900) | (10,200) |
| Tax on surplus on ordinary activities | (33,800) | (34,700) |
| **SURPLUS ON ORDINARY ACTIVITIES AFTER TAX** | 62,700 | 75,100 |
| Interest payable on loans from government | - | (2,800) |
| **SURPLUS FOR THE YEAR TRANSFERRED TO GENERAL RESERVE** | **62,700** | **72,300** |

*advisers*

| | | |
|---|---|---|
| **Bankers** | Barclays Bank | 54 Lombard Street, London EC3V 9EX |
| **Auditors** | Ernst & Young | 7 Rolls Building, Fetter Lane, London EC4A |
| **Solicitors** | Clifford Chance | 200 Aldersgate Street, London EC1A 4JJ |
| | Simmonds & Simmonds | 21 Wilson Street, London EC2M 2TX |
| **Public Relations** | College Hill Associates | 29 Gresham Street, London EC2V 7AH |

*publications*  *Annual Report and Accounts, CDC Magazine*

**branches**

Bolivia
PO Box 7100
Santa Cruz
Bolivia
Tel 591 3 546 900
Fax 591 3 546 901
E-mail bolivia@cdc.co.uk

Cuba
311 Calle 22
Miramar
Havana
Cuba
Tel 537 244468
Fax 537 244460
E-mail cdc@cenial.inf.cu

East Caribbean
PO Box 1392
Bridgetown
St Michael
Barbados
Tel 1 246 4369890
Fax 1 246 4361504
E-mail barbados@mail.barbados.cdc.co.uk

Latin America
Apartado 721-1000
Oficentro Ejecutivo La Sabana
Edificio no.7 Piso no.6
Sabana Sur
San Jose
Costa Rica
Tel 506 290 5510
Fax 506 290 5212
E-mail comdevco@sol.racsa.co.cr

West Caribbean
PO Box 23
Kingston
Jamaica
Tel 1 876 9261164
Fax 1 876 9261166
E-mail jamaica@mail.jamaica.cdc.co.uk

Ghana
PO Box C 1748
Cantonments
Accra
Ghana
Tel 233 21 226677
Fax 233 21 238407

Kenya
PO Box 43233
Nairobi
Kenya
Tel 254 2 219952
Fax 254 1 219744
E-mail kenya@mail.kenya.cdc.co.uk

Malawi
Lilongwe 3
Malawi
Tel 265 780410
Fax 265 780585

Mozambique
PO Box 1657
Maputo
Mozambique
Tel 258 1 421325
Fax 258 1 422150
E-mail mozambique@mail.mozambique.cdc.co.uk

Nigeria
PO Box 51906
Ikoyi
Lagos
Nigeria
Tel 234 1 2624401
Fax 234 1 610023
E-mail nigeria@mail.london.cdc.co.uk

South Africa
PO Box 1072
Johannesburg
South Africa
Tel 27 11 4845061
Fax 27 11 4843023
E-mail safrica@mail.safrica.cdc.co.uk

Swaziland
PO Box 133
Mbabane
Swaziland
Tel 268 42051/4
Fax 268 45185
E-mail swaziland@mail.swaziland.cdc.co.uk

Tanzania
PO Box 2535
Dar es Salaam
Tanzania
Tel 255 51 112926
Fax 255 51 113274
E-mail tanzania@mail.tanzania.cdc.co.uk

Uganda
PO Box 22581
Kampala
Uganda
Tel 256 41 235787
Fax 256 41 235752
E-mail uganda@mail.uganda.cdc.co.uk

West Africa
1st Floor
Immeuble les Harmonies
Abidjan
Ivory Coast
Tel 225 216590
Fax 225 210239
E-mail ivoire@mail.ivoire.cdc.co.uk

Zambia
PO Box 32000
Lusaka
Zambia
Tel 260 1 254285
Fax 260 1 250122
E-mail zambia@mail.zambia.cdc.co.uk

Zimbabwe
PO Box 3758
Harare
Zimbabwe
Tel 263 4 724286
Fax 263 4 705503
E-mail zimbabwe@mail.zimbabwe.cdc.co.uk

Bangladesh
Safura Tower
20 Karmal Ataturk Avenue
Banani
Dhaka 1213
Bangladesh
Tel 880 2 873080
Fax 880 2 881016
E-mail bangladesh@mail.bangladesh.cdc.co.uk

India
11 Golf Links
New Delhi 110 003
India
Tel 91 11 4691691
Fax 91 11 4691693
E-mail india@mail.india.cdc.co.uk

Thapar Niketan
Bangalore 560 025
7/4 Brunton Road
South India
Tel 9180 555 0651
Fax 9180 555 0592
E-mail sindia@mail.sindia.cdc.co.uk

Advanced Business Center
144, Maker Chambers VI
13th Floor
Nairman Point
Mumbai 400 021
India
Tel 91 22 2832924
Fax 91 22 2040211

Pakistan
First Floor
Bahria Complex II
MT Khan Road
Karachi 74000
Pakistan
Tel 92 21 5610091
Fax 92 21 5611891
E-mail pakistan@mail.pakistan.cdc.co.uk

Indonesia
PO Box 4332
Jakarta 12043
Indonesia
Tel 62 21 5254993
Fax 62 21 5254902
E-mail cdc@infoasia.net.id

Malaysia
PO Box 10494
50714 Kuala Lumpur
Malaysia
Tel 60 3 2014088
Fax 60 3 2021162
E-mail malaysia@mail.malaysia.cdc.co.uk

Pacific Islands
PO Box 907
Port Moresby
Granville
Papua New Guinea
Tel 675 321 2944/2881
Fax 675 321 2867/320
E-mail png@mail.png.cdc.co.uk

Philippines
5F
Taipan Place
Emerald Avenue
Ortigas Centre
Pasig City
Metro Manila
Philippines
Tel 63 2 6374701
Fax 63 2 6374704
E-mail philippine@cdc.co.uk

Thailand
PO Box 2653
Bangkok 10501
Thailand
Tel 662 6519200/6
Fax 662 651 9207
E-mail thailand@mail.thailand.cdc.uk

## Commonwealth Institute

Kensington High Street
London W8 6NQ

**Tel** 0171 603 4535
**Fax** 0171 602 7374

**status**  Executive body
**sponsor**  Foreign and Commonwealth Office
**mission**  To increase, throughout Britain, knowledge and understanding of the Commonwealth, its nations and peoples and the principles upon which it is based, and to further education and cultural co-operation.
**tasks**  To provide information and knowledge on the Commonwealth using all available media through the Commonwealth Resource Centre; education - reawaken interest in and awareness amongst young people and in schools eg running teacher training days, producing curriculum pack for secondary schools, outreach programmes; mounting exhibitions and maintaining collections -the Commonwealth Experience opened in 1997 with interactive exhibitions and a heliride.
**operations**  Management: Directorate (Director General and Administrative & Commercial Director) responsible for day-to-day management and reports to Board of Governors.

Policy: Re-establishing Institute as multi-cultural centre for the visual arts. Work starting in 1998 on restoration of main building funded by grant from Heritage Lottery Fund.

Trends: Government grant decreased from £2.7m in 1995/96 to £800,000 in 1997/98.

**board**  Chairman, Vice Chairman and Chair of Education Advisory Committee of Board of Governors are appointed by the Secretary of State. 44 Commonwealth members are appointed as their government's representatives.

| Trustees | The Rt Hon Robin Cook MP |
|---|---|
| | The Rt Hon David Blunkett |
| | Cllr Mrs Joan Hanham |
| | The Rt Hon Lord Braine MP |

**staff**  26

| Director General | David French |
|---|---|
| Administrative & Commercial Director | Paul Kennedy |
| Projects Director, The Commonwealth Experience | Dr John Stevenson |
| Development Director | Mark Lloyd-Fox |
| Head of Library & Information Services | Karen Peters |
| Assistant Conference Centre Manager | Charles Fielder |
| Assistant Conference Centre Manager | Beccy Thorp |
| Head of Education | Fenella White |
| Head of Finance & Personnel | Henry Barbour |
| Head of Central Services | Colin Burkitt |

**financial**

| RECEIPTS & PAYMENTS Year end: 31 March | 1995 £ |
|---|---|
| **HMG GRANT AND OPERATIONS** | |
| HMG grants received | 2,732,000 |
| Operating receipts | 919,774 |
| | **3,651,774** |
| Staff costs | (1,233,837) |
| Other operating payments | (2,366,063) |
| | **(3,599,900)** |
| Surplus from operations | 51,874 |
| Interest on Investments | 2,348 |
| Other receipts/payments (net) | (39,272) |
| **EXCESS OF RECEIPTS OVER PAYMENTS/(PAYMENTS OVER RECEIPTS)** | **14,950** |
| Staff restructuring | |
| HMG grant received | 800,000 |
| Re-structuring costs | (1,326,977) |
| **EXCESS OF RECEIPTS OVER PAYMENTS/(PAYMENTS OVER RECEIPTS)** | **(526,977)** |
| Sponsored operations | |
| Special building works | |
| HMG grants | 150,000 |
| Operating receipts | 320,809 |
| Bank interest | 2,321 |
| | **473,130** |
| Operating payments | (427,459) |
| **EXCESS OF PAYMENTS OVER RECEIPTS** | **45,671** |

# *Commonwealth Scholarship Commission*

The Association of Commonwealth Universities
John Foster House
36 Gordon Square
London WC1H OPF

**Tel** 0171 387 8572
**Fax** 0171 387 2655

**status**  Executive body

**founded**  1959

**sponsor**  Department for International Development

**powers**  Commonwealth Scholarship Act 1959. Overseas Development and Co-operation Act 1980

| | |
|---|---|
| *mission* | To help people achieve better education and, through its awards, to widen opportunities for women as well as men. |
| *tasks* | Broadly, management of UK's responsibilities under the Commonwealth Scholarship and Fellowship Plan (CSFP). These include: selection of scholars and fellows coming to the UK; placing them at appropriate institutions; arranging supervision of their work and selection and nomination of candidates from the UK for CSFP scholarships and fellowships granted by countries outside the UK. |
| *operations* | Management: The Association of Commonwealth Universities provides the secretariat and its Head of Commonwealth Awards is its Executive Secretary. The British Council provides non-academic support for the scholars and fellows - briefing them before departure, making travel arrangements, receiving them on arrival. It also pays for (and accounts for) travel costs, stipends and allowances. In 1996/97 the UK government contributed over £13.7 million; there were 837 award holders in Britain from 50 Commonwealth countries - four out of five from developing countries. Scholarships offered by overseas countries (especially Canada) are in great demand and members of the Commission interview for each country roughly twice as many shortlisted candidates as Britain has been asked to nominate. |
| | Policy: Awards must recognise and promote the highest standards of intellectual achievement or technical and professional performance, while responding to the expressed human resource and development needs of the nominating countries. |
| | Trends: Substantial budget cuts in 1996, and the prospect of further drastic cuts for 1997/98 and 1998/99, mean priorities have changed. The number of undergraduate awards has been restricted and greater emphasis is placed on one-year awards at the expense of three-year (mainly doctoral) higher degrees. |
| *board* | Commission members are appointed by the Secretary of State. |

| Chairman | Sir Michael Caine | |
|---|---|---|
| Deputy Chairman | Prof Berrick Saul CBE | |
| Members | Suhail Aziz | Prof Ian Livingstone |
| | Prof Anthony Diplock | Mrs Anne Lonsdale |
| | Dr David Fussey | Prof David Luscombe |
| | Colin George | Prof Shula Marks OBE |
| | Prof John Ledingham | Dr Bridget Ogilvie |

| *staff* | Executive Secretary | Terry Illsley |
|---|---|---|
| | Assistant Secretary | Mrs Betty Warnock |

# *Community Development Foundation (CDF)*

60 Highbury Grove
London N5 2AG

**Tel** 0171 226 5375  **E-mail** admin@cdf.org.uk
**Fax** 0171 704 0313  **Web** http://www.cdf.org.uk

| | |
|---|---|
| *status* | Executive agency |
| *founded* | 1968 |
| *sponsor* | Home Office |
| *mission* | To strengthen communities throughout the UK by ensuring the effective participation of people in determining the conditions which affect their lives by supporting community initiatives, promoting best practice and informing national and local policy-makers. |
| *tasks* | Community Initiatives Team develops the capacity of local people to take part in local decision-making and local groups to become more active; best practice promoted through conferences, seminars, consultancies, training and publications; community needs assessed (for local authorities etc) through evaluation surveys and community audits. |
| *operations* | Management: CDF receives support from the government's Voluntary and Community Unit, now at the Home Office. CDF's work in Scotland is carried out through the Scottish Community Development Centre, run in partnership with Glasgow University. Northern Ireland was brought within CDF remit in 1996/97. During 1996/97, responsibility for CDF passed to the Department of National Heritage but has now reverted to the Home Office. |

Policy: To work with communities of interest (eg health, leisure pursuits) and communities of place (identified strongly with a geographical area).

Trends: While CDF is a UK agency, concerned with the quality of life of those living in the UK, it is increasingly involved in discussion with the EU on the detail of EU programmes as they apply to the UK. Sums involved in the Euro-programmes are significant. Recognition of the importance of involving the community effectively in new national and local programmes will give CDF an increasingly important role.

**board**

Board of Trustees, one of whom is from NI.

| | | |
|---|---|---|
| President | Lord Houghton of Sowerby | |
| Vice Presidents | Prof Lord Desai | |
| | Sir Robert B Horton | |
| | Sir David Lane | |
| | Hon Sir Charles Morrison | |
| | Baroness Seear | |
| Chairman of Trustees | Sir Alan Haselhurst MP | |
| Trustees | Anita Bhalla | |
| | Amir Bhatia OBE | Diana Maddock MP |
| | Rodney Brooke CBE | Michael Meadowcroft |
| | Ross Flockhart OBE | Eddie O'Hara MP |
| | Dr Ken Ife | A David Owen OBE |
| | Prof Walter James | Gerry Wade |
| | Avila Kilmurray | Kenneth Webster |
| | Janet Lewis-Jones | Colin Williams |

**staff**

31

| | |
|---|---|
| Chief Executive | Alison West |

**financial**

**INCOME & EXPENDITURE**

| Year end: 31 March | 1997 |
|---|---|
| | £ |
| **INCOME** | |
| Department of National Heritage | 902,034 |
| Other government grants | 681,636 |
| Local authority grants | 1,902 |
| Research and evaluation | 25,117 |
| Trusts and business | 122,858 |
| Sales of publications | 27,340 |
| Consultancy, conference, and training fees | 235,949 |
| Donations and sponsorships | 15,871 |
| Interest | 42,282 |
| | **2,054,989** |
| **EXPENDITURE** | |
| Employment | 690,520 |
| Premises | 125,167 |
| Communications and information | 83,152 |
| Research and evaluation | 10,011 |
| Project grants and other costs | 416,227 |
| Consultancies, conferences, and training | 254,072 |
| Travel and meetings | 40,064 |
| Administration and miscellaneous | 88,100 |
| | **1,707,313** |
| **EXCESS OF INCOME OVER EXPENDITURE** | **347,676** |
| Less transfer to reserves | (100,000) |
| **SURPLUS FOR THE YEAR** | **247,676** |

# Companies House (CH)

Crown Way
Maindy
Cardiff CF4 3UZ

**Tel** 01222 388588
**Fax** 01222 380323

| | |
|---|---|
| *status* | Executive agency and trading fund |
| *founded* | 1844; as a Next Steps agency 1988; as trading fund 1991 |
| *sponsor* | Department of Trade and Industry (DTI) |
| *powers* | A range of delegated powers from the centre of DTI relating to finance, personnel and support services |
| *mission* | To hold the public records of over one million companies in Great Britain. |
| *tasks* | Company registration: to register and dissolve companies, to enforce compliance with statutory filing requirements, also to exercise certain discretionary powers on behalf of the Secretary of State. Company information: to provide information on registered companies to customers in a variety of formats, and also in summary form from the CH database. |
| *operations* | Management: CH is implementing the progressive contracting-out programme announced by the President of the Board of Trade (December 1995). It also covers non-core activities (eg cheque processing, postal searches and customer enquiries) carried out from Companies House Cardiff. CH will remain an executive agency and core activities remain with it. |
| | Policy: To continue to develop its business along more commercial lines in partnership with the private sector. |
| | Trends: In partnership with the private sector, customers and suppliers, CH is working to develop and deliver new technology which will ensure that by the year 2000, most information will be distributed electronically and held as a mixture of electronic data and digital images of documents. Microfiche will cease to be the primary means of storing company information. |
| *board* | The CH Steering Board has members from a wide variety of backgrounds and interests. Input from the commercial world provides a wide forum for the discussion of CH policy and its implications for customers. |

| Chairman | Brian Hilton |
|---|---|
| Members | Elaine Brant |
| | John Holden |
| | Michael Jackson |
| | Prof Ian Percy CBE |
| | Hugh Savill |

*staff*    1218, the majority in Cardiff and its satellite offices; 141 in London; 47 in Edinburgh.

| | |
|---|---|
| Chief Executive | John Holden |
| Director Policy & Planning | Liz Carter |
| Director Operations | Tim Lonsdale |
| Director Development | Eddie Tomlin |
| Data Distribution | Ian Baildon-Smith |
| Accounts Image | Steve Cryer |
| Input Systems | Dave Garnett |
| Office Systems | Simon Goman |
| Special Projects | Phil Hopkins |
| Programme Support | Margaret Hornsby |
| Customer Accounts | Ros James |
| MADE | Phil Officer |
| Director Marketing & Sales | Mark Pacey |
| Director Finance | Jack Mansfield |
| Companies Administration | Richard Davies |
| Systems Operations & Support | Ray Gullis |
| Prosecuting Solicitor | Elizabeth Hope |
| Customer Services | Phil Lewis |
| Assistant Director Processing | Graham Price |
| Search Production | Stephen Rolph |
| Compliance | John Spears |
| Project Support | Bob Willis |
| Legal Adviser | Wendy Benjamin |
| Head of Human Resources | John David |
| Overseas Consultancy | David Walke |

| Companies House London | Tim Barnsley |
|---|---|
| Late Filing, Penalties | Paul Coles |
| Companies House Edinburgh | Jim Henderson |
| Incorporations & Changes of Name | Linda Higgins |
| Public Search Room, Certified Copies | Stephen Rolph |

*financial*

**OPERATING ACCOUNT**

| **Year end: 31 March** | **1997** | **1996** | **1995** |
|---|---|---|---|
| | **£000** | **£000** | **£000** |
| **INCOME** | | | |
| Fees and charges | 32,866 | 33,346 | 35,841 |
| Other operating income | 2,263 | 1,112 | 965 |
| | **35,129** | **34,458** | **36,806** |
| **EXPENDITURE** | | | |
| Staff costs | 14,705 | 14,922 | 15,326 |
| Exceptional staff costs | - | 1,215 | - |
| Depreciation | 1,422 | 1,831 | 1,857 |
| Exceptional property costs | - | 2,000 | 3,900 |
| Other operating charges | 15,231 | 11,566 | 12,375 |
| | **31,358** | **31,534** | **33,458** |
| **OPERATING SURPLUS** | **3,771** | **2,924** | **3,348** |
| Loss on disposal of fixed assets | 10 | 523 | - |
| **SURPLUS BEFORE INTEREST** | **3,761** | **2,401** | **3,348** |
| Interest receivable | 1,006 | 690 | 506 |
| Interest payable | 394 | 432 | 469 |
| **SURPLUS ON ORDINARY ACTIVITIES** | **4,373** | **2,659** | **3,385** |
| Dividend payable | 1,000 | 1,000 | 2,000 |
| **RETAINED SURPLUS FOR THE YEAR** | **3,373** | **1,659** | **1,385** |
| Retained surplus brought forward | 2,151 | 492 | (893) |
| **RETAINED SURPLUS CARRIED FORWARD** | **5,524** | **2,151** | **492** |

*advisers*     **Auditors**          National Audit Office          157-197 Buckingham Palace Road
London SW1W 9SP

*publications*     *The Register, Companies House Notes for Guidance*

*branches*

55-71 City Road
London EC1Y 1BB
Tel 0171 253 9393

Central Library
Chamberlain Square
Birmingham B3 3HQ
Tel 0121 233 9047

25 Queen Street
Leeds LS1 2TW
Tel 0113 233 8338

75 Mosley Street
Manchester M2 2HR
Tel 0161 236 7500

37 Castle Terrace
Edinburgh EH1 2EB
Tel 0131 535 5800

7 West George Street
Glasgow G2 1BQ
Tel 0141 221 5513

# *Compensation Agency*

Royston House
34 Upper Queen Street
Belfast BT1 6FD

**Tel** 01232 249944
**Fax** 01232 246956

*status*     Executive agency

*founded*     1992

*sponsor*     Northern Ireland Office

*powers*     Criminal Injuries (Compensation) (NI) Order 1998; Criminal Damage (Compensation) (NI) Order 1997; Northern Ireland (Emergency Provisions) Acts 1991 and 1996

*mission*     To support the victims of violent crime by providing compensation to those who suffer serious injury and financial loss. To sustain the confidence of the community by providing compensation for physical damage and consequential loss arising from criminal damage to property. To provide compensation to those who suffered loss from action taken under emergency provisions legislation.

**tasks**
To receive, process and resolve on their individual merits all claims made under the three compensation schemes operating in NI: the criminal injuries compensation scheme which provides compensation for pain, suffering, financial loss and loss of amenity by the victims of violent crime, including terrorist crime in NI; the criminal damage compensation scheme which provides compensation for malicious damage to property in NI caused by terrorism or unlawful assemblies and for malicious damage to agricultural property; the emergency provisions compensation scheme which provides for compensation to those who suffer loss or damage resulting from action taken under the Northern Ireland (Emergency Provisions) Acts of 1991 and 1996.

**operations**
Management: The Chief Executive is supported by a senior management team and is directly responsible to the Minister. Extensive use is made of external professional advisers such as loss adjusters, motor engineers, barristers and medical consultants.

Policy: To achieve continual improvements in the standard of service provided to applicants.

Trends: The agency anticipated that the downward trend in claims begun in earlier years would continue in 1996/97. In the event 25% more criminal injury claims, 225% more criminal damage claims and 38% more emergency provisions claims were received than had been expected, due to the civil disturbances in 1996.

**performance**
All 11 performance targets were achieved despite the great pressure placed on the staff by increased claims.

**board**
Appointed from administrative and specialist staff.

| | |
|---|---|
| Chief Executive | D Stanley |
| Head of Operations | F Brannigan |
| Head of The Legal Unit | K Ham |
| Senior Quantity Surveyor | M McMath |
| Industrial Accountant | W Scott |
| *Accounting Officer* | *Chief Executive* |

**staff**
123 (all civil servants)

**financial**

| EXPENDITURE Year end: 31 March | 1997 £000 | 1996 £000 |
|---|---|---|
| **EXPENDITURE** | | |
| Staff costs | 2,309 | 2,378 |
| Depreciation | 74 | 113 |
| Other operating costs | 939 | 935 |
| **TOTAL OPERATING COSTS ON CONTINUING ACTIVITIES FOR YEAR, BEFORE INTEREST ON CAPITAL** | **3,322** | **3,426** |
| Interest on capital | 13 | 17 |
| **COST OF OPERATIONS** | **3,335** | **3,443** |

**advisers**   **Auditors**   National Audit Office   157-197 Buckingham Palace Road London SW1W 9SP

# Construction Industry Training Board (CITB)

Bircham Newton
Kings Lynn
Norfolk PE31 6RH

**Tel** 01485 577577
**Fax** 01485 577689

**status**    Executive body
**founded**    1964
**sponsor**    Department for Education and Employment (DfEE)
**powers**    Industrial Training Act 1982
**mission**    To promote and facilitate the training of sufficient people in the skills needed for a world-class construction industry in the UK.

**tasks**  To identify training requirements and to set and monitor occupational standards for craft, operative, technical, supervisory and management staff; to promote recognised qualifications and schemes; to encourage suitable people to enter and stay in the construction industry; to advise and facilitate industry to provide training.

**operations**  Management: Chief Executive is responsible for day-to-day management and reports to the Board. He is assisted by three Directors (Training Operations, Training Standards & Strategy, Finance & Support). It is a National Training Organisation; it is registered as a charity and funded by levies.

Policy: Developing sector training targets.

Trends: Number of young people entering industry falling well below level needed to replace those retiring.

**board**  Appointed by the Secretary of State.

| | | |
|---|---|---|
| Chairman | HW Try | |
| Deputy Chairman | PC Rainbird | |
| Members | H Baggaley | OCG Robbins |
| | AJ Barry | G Snow |
| | MJ Denyer MBE | BG Tierney |
| | AN Duncan | SA Tilley |
| | MJ Fitchett | S Watson |
| | DJ Gleeson | GB Brumwell |
| | IM McAlpine OBE | GP Henderson OBE |
| | DF McGinley | Prof M Romans |
| Government Assessors | MJ Brown | |
| | E Criswick | |
| | JD Kirkwood | |
| *Accounting Officer* | *Chief Executive* | |

**staff**  951

| | |
|---|---|
| Chief Executive | Peter Lobban |
| Director of Finance & Support | Terry Best |
| Director of Training Standards & Strategy | PG Martin |
| Director of Training Operations | H Maylard |
| Board Secretary | PB Castle |

**financial**

**INCOME & EXPENDITURE**

| Year end: 31 December | 1997 | 1996 |
|---|---|---|
| | £000 | £000 |
| **INCOMING RESOURCES** | | |
| Levy | 58,768 | 56,555 |
| Funding for New Entrant Training | 20,669 | 23,733 |
| Grants | 696 | 709 |
| Training services | 12,821 | 12,356 |
| Registrations | 4,298 | 3,642 |
| Other operating income | 366 | 319 |
| Interest receivable | 2,580 | 2,659 |
| | **100,198** | **99,973** |
| **RESOURCES USED** | | |
| Grants, allowances and college fees | | |
| Training grants | 38,344 | 36,172 |
| Trainee allowances & assistance | 6,995 | 7,667 |
| New Entrant Training college fees | 9,827 | 9,252 |
| | **55,166** | **53,091** |
| Training costs | | |
| Direct training operations | 11,320 | 11,207 |
| Field operations | 12,703 | 13,620 |
| Prevocational education | 2,115 | 1,990 |
| Registrations | 2,573 | 2,469 |
| Training development | 2,417 | 2,652 |
| Support costs | 996 | 887 |
| | **32,094** | **32,825** |
| Consultation and communication with industry | | |
| Consultation and committees | 960 | 956 |
| Communications and marketing | 1,544 | 2,223 |
| | **2,504** | **3,179** |
| Other expenditure | | |
| Head office support costs | 6,238 | 6,490 |
| Exceptional items | 2,747 | (98) |
| | **8,985** | **6,392** |
| | **98,749** | **95,487** |
| **NET INCOMING RESOURCES/(RESOURCES USED)** | **1,448** | **4,486** |

| advisers | **Bankers** | Barclays Bank | 17 Market Place, Fakenham<br>Norfolk NR21 9BE |
|---|---|---|---|
| | **Auditors** | BDO Stoy Hayward | 87 Guildhall Street, Bury St Edmunds<br>Suffolk IP33 1PU |
| | **Solicitors** | Frere, Cholmele, Bischoff | 4 John Carpenter Street, London EC4Y 0NH |

**publications**   *Annual Report; 500 training publications for the construction industry*

**branches**

*London*
Hillgate House
8th Floor
26 Old Bailey
London EC4M 7QA
Tel 0171 489 1662
Fax 0171 236 2875

*Wales*
Units 4 & 5
Bridgend Business Centre
David Street
Bridgend Industrial Estate
Bridgend
Mid-Glamorgan CF31 3SH
Tel 01656 655226
Fax 01656 655232

*South West*
2 Kew Court
Pynes Hill
Rydon Lane
Exeter
Devon EX2 5AZ
Tel 01392 444900
Fax 01392 445044

*North*
Wearbank House
Charles Street
Sunderland
Tyne and Wear SR6 0AN
Tel 0191 567 9230
Fax 0191 510 0165

*North West*
10 Waterside Court
St Helens
Technology Campus
Pocket Nook Street
Merseyside WA9 1VA
Tel 01744 616004
Fax 01744 617003

*North East*
Milton House
Queen Street
Morley
Leeds LS27 9EL
Tel 01132 521 966
Fax 01132 531117

*Midlands*
Belton Road Industrial Estate
20 Prince William Road
Loughborough
Leicestershire LE11 5TB
Tel 01509 610266
Fax 01509 210241

*South*
Eastleigh House
Upper Market Street
Eastleigh
Hampshire SO5 4FD
Tel 01703 620505
Fax 01703 612056

*East*
1a Peel Street
Lutton
Bedfordshire LU1 2QR
Tel 01582 727462
Fax 01582 456318

*South East*
Walker House
London Road
Riverhead
Sevenoaks
Kent TN13 2DN
Tel 01732 464520
Fax 01732 460561

*Scotland (North)*
6 Queens Gate
Inverness IV1 1DA
Tel 01463 222893
Fax 01463 230868

*Scotland (East)*
Pritchard House
Grays Mill
32 Inglis Green Road
Edinburgh EH14 2ER
Tel 0131 443 8893
Fax 0131 443 1820

*Scotland (West)*
4 Edison Street
Hillington
Glasgow G52 4XN
Tel 0141 810 3044
Fax 0141 882 1100

*Glasgow Training Centre*
2 Edison Street
Hillington
Glasgow G52 4XN
Tel 0141 8826455
Fax 0141 8103197

*Birmingham Training Centre*
83 Lifford Lane
King's Norton
Birmingham B30 3JE
Tel 0121 459 4262/8000
Fax 0121 459 8330

# *Construction Industry Training Board NI (CITBNI)*

17 Dundrod Road
Crumlin
Co Antrim BT29 4SR

**Tel** 01232 825466
**Fax** 01232 825693

**E-mail** citb@psilink.co.uk
**Web** http://www.citbni.org.uk

| | |
|---|---|
| **status** | Executive body |
| **founded** | 1964 |
| **sponsor** | Northern Ireland Office, Department of Economic Development (DEDNI) |
| **powers** | Industrial Training Orders 1964 and 1984 |
| **mission** | To improve the quality and effectiveness of the workforce in the construction industry in NI through training. |
| **tasks** | Developing training plans; providing information on courses available; providing direct training for courses which are not available elsewhere; providing financial assistance towards the cost of taking part in training; promoting construction as a career; ensuring that training is carried out to industry standards. |
| **operations** | Management: Chief Executive reports to the Board. The three Heads of Divisions (Training Advisory, Finance & Administration and Training) plus the Chief Executive and Board Administrator make up the Senior Management Executive Group. Funds raised through levy on employers. |
| | Policy: Promoting and funding Construction Skills Register. |
| | Trends: New initiatives being developed in partnership with industry. |
| **performance** | 12 out of 13 targets achieved in 1996/97. |
| **board** | Appointed by the Minister of Education and Employment for Northern Ireland, from employers, union and education representatives. |

| Chairman | WF Gillespie OBE | |
|---|---|---|
| Deputy Chairman | D Poole | |
| Members | H Burns | |
| | S Campbell | G Matchett |
| | K Chambers | D McClure |
| | S Cox | Prof B Norton |
| | J Crooks | J Patterson |
| | WA Doran | T Patterson |
| | F Duffyn | P Rogers |
| | N Kerr | A Smith |
| | W Martin | J Stirling |
| *Accounting Officer* | *Chief Executive* | |

**staff** 54

| Chief Executive | Allan McMullen |
|---|---|

**financial**

**INCOME & EXPENDITURE**

| Year end: 31 August | 1997 £ | 1996 £ | 1995 £ |
|---|---|---|---|
| **INCOME** | | | |
| Levy income | 2,333,698 | 2,493,086 | 2,216,361 |
| Income from Department of Economic Development | 3,762 | 117,862 | 311,387 |
| Grants from European Social Fund | 154,267 | 149,209 | 140,259 |
| Sale of services and course income | 512,438 | 506,490 | 656,392 |
| | 3,104,165 | 3,266,647 | 3,324,399 |
| **EXPENDITURE** | | | |
| Training facilities provided by the Board | 1,785,187 | 1,991,726 | 1,935,044 |
| Board direct operating expenses | 1,045,610 | 869,836 | 975,769 |
| | 2,830,797 | 2,861,562 | 2,910,813 |
| **OPERATING SURPLUS** | 273,368 | 405,085 | 413,586 |
| Interest receivable | 102,002 | 100,268 | 65,199 |
| **SURPLUS OF THE YEAR** | 375,370 | 505,353 | 478,785 |
| Accumulated fund brought forward | 2,535,001 | 2,029,648 | 1,550,863 |
| **ACCUMULATED FUND CARRIED FORWARD** | 2,910,371 | 2,535,001 | 2,029,648 |

| **advisers** | **Bankers** | Ulster Bank | 27 Main Street, Crumlin, Co Antrim |
|---|---|---|---|

| | | |
|---|---|---|
| **Auditors** | Jones, Peters & Co | 6 Church Street, Banbridge, Co Down |
| **Solicitors** | J P Hagan & Co | 17/19 Church Street, Portadown, Co Armagh |
| | Babington & Croasdaile | New Row, Coleraine, Co Antrim |
| **Public Relations** | Gordon Corporate Communications | 47 Whiterock Road, Killinchy |

*publications*    Annual Report, Employers Guide, Prospectus

# Construction Service

Churchill House
Victoria Square
Belfast BT1 4QW

**Tel** 01232 250269
**Fax** 01232 250333

| | |
|---|---|
| *status* | Executive agency |
| *founded* | 1996 |
| *sponsor* | Northern Ireland Office, Department of the Environment for NI (DOENI) |
| *powers* | Framework Document 1996 |
| *mission* | Providing a professional design, maintenance and advisory service to government departments, agencies and other public bodies covering a wide range of construction industry disciplines in Northern Ireland |
| *tasks* | Provides a project management and multidisciplinary design service for projects of any size. Full range of maintenance related services and a 24-hour, seven days per week response facility for all building needs. Wide range of specialist services, eg energy conservation, fire safety, furniture and furnishings, etc and advice to housing, education, industry and grants departments. |
| *operations* | Management: The Chief Executive reports to the Minister. Agency is managed by a Management Board consisting of the Chief Executive, the Directors in charge of New Works Division and Estate Maintenance and Advisory Division, and the Assistant Directors in charge of Corporate Services Division and Business and Technical Support Division. The agency is spread across a number of locations. |
| *performance* | Of the 11 measures set, seven were met, three were not and a system was not in place in 1996/97 to measure one. |

*board*

| Chief Executive | Peter Ronaldson |
|---|---|
| *Accounting Officer* | *Chief Executive* |

| | |
|---|---|
| *staff* | 580 |
| *publications* | Framework Document, Corporate and Business Plan, Annual Report, Charter Standard Statement, Corporate Brochure |

# Contributions Agency (CA)

Longbenton
Newcastle upon Tyne NE98 1YX

**Tel** 0191 225 7665
**Fax** 0191 225 4198

| | |
|---|---|
| *status* | Executive agency |
| *founded* | 1991 |
| *sponsor* | Department of Social Security (DSS) |
| *powers* | Framework Document 1994 |

| | |
|---|---|
| *mission* | Protecting the rights of National Insurance (NI) contributors and the interests of the taxpayer through the efficient payment and recording of NI contributions. |
| *tasks* | Operating the NI scheme. This includes maintaining over 62 million customer accounts and further databases covering 1.3 million employers, over 3 million self-employed and 5.6 million personal pension population; also administering the collection of National Insurance, maintaining fund records and countering fraud and abuse. |
| *operations* | Management: The Board of Management is responsible to the Secretary of State for administering the collection of NI contributions, for maintaining NI fund records and for the accounts. It comprises the Chief Executive and five senior Executive Directors and two Non-Executive Directors. A new Chief Executive, George Bertram, was appointed in 1997. Majority of CA staff is based in and around Newcastle upon Tyne, updating individual contribution records and administering contracting-out arrangements for occupational and personal pensions. About 40% work in field offices throughout the country, dealing directly with employers, businesses and contributors. |

Policy: Increasing use of new technology. Developing Newcastle site with private sector finance (PFI).

Trends: Joint working programme with Inland Revenue and Customs & Excise delivering a range of products and services, eg National tripartite Telephone helpline offers advice on income tax, NI contributions and VAT registration (1996); pilot automated Telephone calculation service for employers.

*performance* All the Secretary of State's targets achieved in 1996/97.

*board*

| | |
|---|---|
| Chief Executive | George Bertram |
| Non-Executive Director | Stephen Banyard |
| Cultural Development Director | Keith Elliott |
| Finance Director | Terry Lord |
| Strategy Director | David Slater |
| Non-Executive Director | John Wilson |
| Human Resource Director | Ken Wilson |
| *Accounting Officer* | *Chief Executive* |

*staff*  7210

*financial*

| INCOME & EXPENDITURE Year end: 31 March | 1997 £000 | 1996 £000 | 1995 £000 |
|---|---|---|---|
| **INCOME** | | | |
| Miscellaneous income | 32,124 | 46,052 | 41,582 |
| **EXPENDITURE** | | | |
| Staff costs | 169,342 | 180,345 | 170,140 |
| Other operating costs | 88,724 | 96,167 | 106,665 |
| | **(258,066)** | **(276,512)** | **(276,805)** |
| **NET COST BEFORE INTEREST** | **(225,942)** | **(230,460)** | **(235,223)** |
| Interest receivable and similar income | 168 | 62 | 145 |
| Interest on capital | (1,153) | (792) | (666) |
| **NET COST OF OPERATIONS** | **(226,927)** | **(231,190)** | **(235,744)** |

# Council for Catholic Maintained Schools (CCMS)

160 High Street
Holywood
County Down BT18 9HT

**Tel** 01232 426972
**Fax** 01232 424255

| | |
|---|---|
| *status* | Executive body |
| *founded* | 1990 |
| *sponsor* | Northern Ireland Office, Department of Education NI (DENI) |
| *powers* | Education Reform Order (NI) 1989 |
| *mission* | To promote Catholic education and to help raise and sustain the highest standards in the Catholic maintained sector by providing strategic leadership and direction in keeping with the culture and values of CCMS. |
| *tasks* | For Catholic maintained schools to: employ teachers; promote and co-ordinate the planning of provision; assist and advise on management and control by the Boards of Governors. |

| | |
|---|---|
| *operations* | Management: The Council operates through a system of committees (Education Curricular, Education Provision, Finance & Personnel, Diocesan Education). CCMS is run by the Director, supported by the Deputy Director. |
| | Policy: Increasing number of CCMS staff |
| | Trends: Four new primary schools opened in 1996/97. |
| *board* | Council appointed by Secretary of State from representatives of Trustees, parents, teachers and DENI. |

|  |  |  |
|---|---|---|
| | *Trustee Representatives* | |
| Chairman | The Most Rev M Dallat | |
| Vice Chairperson | Mrs M Pedersen | |
| Members | The Most Rev F Brooks | *Dept of Education Representatives* |
| | The Right Rev Monsignor S Cahill | Mrs MR Cooper |
| | Mrs P Carville | O Corrigan |
| | B Curran | Mrs M McAvoy |
| | S Doherty | J Simpson |
| | The Right Rev Dean E Hamill | JV Simpson |
| | The Most Rev F Lagan | Mrs E Waterson |
| | F Magee | *Parent Representatives* |
| | Sister O McConville | Mrs A Jenkins |
| | The Rt Rev Monsignor L McEntegart | Mrs I McCartan |
| | E McGrade | Mrs C Quinn |
| | The Very Rev I McQuillan | Mrs M Russel |
| | Dr A Moran | *Teacher Representatives* |
| | The Very Rev J Mullin | B Kyne |
| | The Very Rev Canon C O'Byrne | OA McCaffrey |
| | J Smyth | Mrs N McMorrow |
| | The Most Rev P Walsh | Miss M Murray |

| | |
|---|---|
| *staff* | 44 |

| | |
|---|---|
| Director | Donal Flanagan |
| Deputy Director | Eddie McArdle |
| Human Resources Manager | Sean McGuickin |

# Council for the Central Laboratory of the Research Councils (CLRC)

Chilton
Didcot
Oxfordshire OX11 0QX

**Tel** 01235 445789
**Fax** 01235 446665        **Web** http://www.cclrc.ac.uk

| | |
|---|---|
| *status* | Executive body |
| *founded* | 1995 |
| *sponsor* | Department of Trade and Industry (DTI) |
| *powers* | Science and Technology Act 1965. Royal Charter |
| *mission* | To promote high-quality scientific and engineering research by providing research facilities and technical expertise. To support the advancement of knowledge and technology, meeting the needs of research councils and UK and overseas customers. To promote public understanding of science, engineering and technology. |
| *tasks* | Managing the Rutherton Appleton Laboratory, the Daresbury Laboratory and the Chilbolton Observatory. Working in close collaboration with the research councils and undertaking commercial work. |
| *operations* | Management: The Chairman is also the Chief Executive. A new management structure was completed in 1996/97. Implementation of the first corporate plan (published in 1996) began with the development of policies to |

meet its nine objectives in association with the research councils and universities. CLRC facilities are used by over 12,000 researchers each year.

Policy: To align its policies and activities with those of the Foresight exercise and those of the other research councils and to emphasise non-research council programmes, eg from the European Commission, CERN and other European programmes, and also industry.

**board**

| Chairman & Chief Executive | | Dr Paul R Williams CBE |
|---|---|---|
| Members | Prof Julia Higgins CBE | |
| | Prof John Krebs | Dr Geoffrey Robinson |
| | Richard Lawrence-Wilson | Dr Gordon Walker |
| | Dr Allyson Reed | Prof Robin Williams |
| | Sir Derek Roberts CBE | Sir Martin Wood OBE |
| *Accounting Officer* | *Chief Executive* | |

**staff**   1769

| Chairman & Chief Executive | Dr Paul Williams CBE |
|---|---|
| Director, Computation & Information | Brian Davies |
| Director, Administration & Finance | Richard Lawrence-Wilson |
| Commercial Director | Allyson Reed |
| Director, Technology | Peter Sharp |
| Director, Research & Development | Gordon Walker |
| Director, Space Science | Eric Dunford |
| Director, Central Laser Facility | Henry Hutchinson |
| Director, Particle Physics | George Kalmus |
| Director, Synchrotron Radiation | David Norman |
| Director, Applied Science | Hywel Price |
| Director, ISIS | Andrew Taylor |

**financial**

**INCOME & EXPENDITURE**
**Year end: 31 March**

| | 1997 £000 |
|---|---|
| **INCOME** | |
| Income from operating activities | 89,651 |
| Grant-in-aid | 1,454 |
| Release of deferred income | 24,174 |
| | **115,279** |
| **EXPENDITURE** | |
| Staff costs | 45,675 |
| Restructuring costs | 2,654 |
| Equipment and supplies | 14,778 |
| Services | 15,803 |
| Depreciation | 23,593 |
| Notional cost of capital | 16,213 |
| Other operating costs | 12,987 |
| | **131,703** |
| **OPERATING DEFICIT FOR THE YEAR** | **(16,424)** |
| Loss on disposal of fixed assets | (329) |
| Reversal of notional cost of capital | 16,213 |
| | **15,884** |
| **DEFICIT FOR THE YEAR** | **(540)** |
| Accumulated deficit brought forward | (1,310) |
| **ACCUMULATED DEFICIT CARRIED FORWARD** | **(1,850)** |

**advisers**   **Auditors**   National Audit Office   157-197 Buckingham Palace Road London SW1W 9SP

# Countryside Commission

John Dower House
Crescent Place
Cheltenham
Gloucestershire GL50 3RA

**Tel** 01242 521381
**Fax** 01242 228914      **Web** http://www.countryside.gov.ukz

| | |
|---|---|
| *status* | Executive body |
| *founded* | 1968. As executive body 1981 |
| *sponsor* | Department of the Environment, Transport and the Regions (DETR) |
| *powers* | National Parks and Access to the Countryside Act 1949, Countryside Act 1949, Wildlife and Countryside Act 1981 |
| *mission* | To ensure that the English countryside is protected, and can be used and enjoyed now and in the future. |
| *tasks* | Develop countryside policies for England and promote them with local authorities, public agencies, farmers and landowners, conservation organisations, voluntary bodies and individual members of the public. Distributes grants to local authorities, public and non-public bodies, and individuals - also advice on obtaining other funds. |
| *operations* | Management: Divided into eight regions. New corporate strategy in 1996. New concept of programme teams to plan and monitor the delivery of the programme more effectively. |
| | Policy: To provide expertise rather than grants to help others win EU and Lottery funds. |
| | Trends: EU plans to translate CAP into integrated rural policy. |
| *performance* | 83% met. |
| *board* | Commissioners appointed by the Secretary of State from people of all walks of life. |
| *staff* | 249 |

| | |
|---|---|
| Chief Executive | Richard Wakeford |
| Strategic Affairs | David Coleman |
| Information and Support Services | John Huntley |
| Farms & Woodlands | Richard Lloyd |
| Local Identity | Terry Robinson |
| Planning for Sustainable Development | Jeremy Worth Worth |
| Regional Officer, North East | Keith Buchanan |
| Regional Officer, North West | Liz Newton |
| Regional Officer, Yorkshire & The Humber | Sally Bucknall |
| Regional Officer, East & West Midlands | Tim Allen |
| Regional Officer, Eastern | Michael Carroll |
| Regional Officer, South East | Marian Spain |
| Regional Officer, South West | Nick Holliday |
| *Accounting Officer* | *Chief Executive* |

*financial*

| RECEIPTS & EXPENDITURE Year end: 31 March | 1996 £ |
|---|---|
| **RECEIPTS** | |
| Grant-in-aid | 42,124,000 |
| Y. Receipts | 576,674 |
| Decrease in cash at bank and in hand | 88,378 |
| | **42,789,052** |
| **EXPENDITURE** | |
| Running costs | 9,791,755 |
| Research and experiments | 1,977,573 |
| Information and publicity | 853,643 |
| Other expenditure | 496,568 |
| Grants to local authorities and other public bodies | 11,640,972 |
| Grants to private persons and non-public bodies | 3,516,682 |
| Groundwork | 2,175,392 |
| Countryside premium | 228,857 |
| Countryside stewardship | 12,011,563 |
| Subscriptions to international organisations | 50,491 |
| Major capital costs | 45,556 |
| | **42,789,052** |

**publications**  *Countryside, A Living Countryside: our strategy for the next ten years, Annual Report, Catalogue of Publications*

**branches**

*North East*
Warwick House
4th Floor
Grantham Road
Newcastle upon Tyne NE2 1QF
Tel 0191 232 8252
Fax 0191 222 0185

*Yorkshire & The Humber*
2nd Floor
Victoria Wharf
Embankment IV
Sovereign Street
Leeds LS1 4BA
Tel 0113 246 9222
Fax 0113 246 0353

*East & West Midlands*
1st Floor
Vincent House
Tindal Bridge
92-93 Edward Street
Birmingham B1 2RA
Tel 0121 233 9399
Fax 0121 233 9286

*Eastern*
Ortona House
Cambridge CB2 1LQ
Tel 01223 354462
Fax 01223 313850

*North West*
7th Floor
Bridgewater House
Whitworth Street
Manchester M1 6TL
Tel 0161 237 1061
Fax 0161 237 1062

*South East*
4th Floor
71 Kingsway
London WC2B 6ST
Tel 0171 831 3510
Fax 0171 831 1439

*South West*
Bridge House
Sion Place
Clifton Down
Bristol BS8 4AS
Tel 0117 973 9966
Fax 0117 923 8086

# *Countryside Council for Wales (CCW)*

Cyngor Cefn Gwlad Cymru
Plas Penrhos
Ffordd Penrhos
Bangor
Gwynedd LL57 2LQ

**Tel** 01248 385500
**Fax** 01248 355782          **Web** http://www.ccw.gov.uk

**Contact** Public Relations Officer

**status**      Executive body

**founded**     1990

**sponsor**     Welsh Office

**powers**      Environmental Protection Act 1990

**mission**     To advise the government on sustaining natural beauty, wildlife and the opportunity for outdoor enjoyment in Wales and its inshore waters and to conserve wildlife in Wales.

**tasks**       Protecting landscape; conserving habitats and wildlife; developing the experimental Tir Cymen environmentally sensitive scheme of farming; improving access for public enjoyment of the countryside; monitoring the impact of the Sea Empress disaster.

**operations**  Management: The Chief Executive and the Director of Policy and Science and the Director of Conservation are all located in the Bangor headquarters. Operational groups are: natural sciences; landscape and interpretation policy; recreation, access and European affairs; agriculture and forestry, land management and statutory protection and monitoring. There are five area teams (North West, North East, East, West and South) and twelve local offices spread across the whole of Wales.

Policy: Now that the CCW budget has been restored in real terms to its 1994/95 level, operational momentum has been regained and the government's White Paper *A Working Countryside* has confirmed the CCW's importance. The CCW ethos is to be proactive in meeting its objectives.

Trends: CCW works in partnership with a wide range of organisations and individuals. Key partners are the new unitary authorities (April 1996) and voluntary organisations which CCW grant aids. CCW is developing a close relationship with the Environment Agency because of the common interest in safeguarding the environment. Partners can be individuals, eg Tir Cymen farmers, farmers participating in other agri-environment schemes, landowners managing Sites of Special Scientific Interest, and individuals giving their time and skills on the National Nature Reserves.

**board**  Council members appointed by the Secretary of State for Wales from environmental experts.

| | | |
|---|---|---|
| Chairman | Michael Griffith CBE | |
| Vice Chairman | Prof DQ Bowen | |
| Members | Elizabeth Andrews | Roger Lovegrove |
| | Robert Dodgshon | Robin Pratt |
| | Cllr S Essex | Bryan Riddleston |
| | W Allan Evans | Dei Tomos |
| | T Jones OBE | Prof L Warren |
| *Accounting Officer* | *Chief Executive* | |

**staff**  Average 305 permanent and fixed term staff 1996/97

| | |
|---|---|
| Chief Executive | Paul Loveluck CBE, JP |

**financial**

### INCOME & EXPENDITURE

| Year end: 31 March | 1997 £000 | 1996 £000 | 1995 £000 |
|---|---|---|---|
| **INCOME** | | | |
| Grant-in-aid | 21,566 | 18,342 | 20,495 |
| Release of deferred government grant account | 755 | 742 | 700 |
| Release of deferred private capital | - | 1 | - |
| Income from activities | 71 | 52 | 74 |
| Retainable European income | 708 | 1,132 | - |
| Other operating income | - | - | 2 |
| Heritage Lottery grant | 45 | - | 2 |
| | **23,145** | **20,268** | **21,271** |
| **EXPENDITURE** | | | |
| Mananagement of National Nature Reserves | 1,010 | 779 | 670 |
| Management of Sites of Special Scientific Interest | 1,602 | 1,332 | 1,177 |
| Scientific support | 1,630 | 1,210 | 1,547 |
| Annual cost of the JNCC Support Unit | 665 | 502 | 549 |
| Grants payable | 3,476 | 2,821 | 3,625 |
| Tir Cymen grants | 4,884 | 3,418 | 2,944 |
| Staff costs and council members' renumeration | 6,179 | 5,385 | 6,526 |
| Notional charges | 205 | 186 | - |
| Other operating charges | 2,772 | 2,815 | 2,932 |
| Legal costs/public inquiries | 107 | 123 | 179 |
| Depreciation | 835 | 715 | 666 |
| | **23,365** | **19,286** | **20,815** |
| **EXCESS OF EXPENDITURE OVER INCOME ON OPERATING ACTIVITIES** | **(220)** | **982** | **456** |
| Surplus (Deficit) on disposal of fixed assets | 10 | (23) | (29) |
| Interest receivable | 131 | 1 | 3 |
| Non-retainable European income | 1,101 | 878 | 1,158 |
| Adjustment for the notional cost of capital | 180 | 163 | - |
| Share of JNCC notional cost adjustment/income | 6 | - | - |
| Amount surrendered to Welsh Office | (1,203) | (1,221) | (1,246) |
| Transfer from reserves | 15 | 1 | (2) |
| Transfer from/to JNCC provisions and reserves | 7 | (30) | |
| **EXCESS OF INCOME OVER EXPENDITURE** | **27** | **751** | **340** |

**advisers**  **Auditors**   National Audit Office       23-24 Park Place, Cardiff CF1 3BA

# *Court Service*

Southside
105 Victoria Street
London SW1E 6QT

**Tel** 0171 210 2200
**Fax** 0171 210 1797

| | |
|---|---|
| *status* | Executive agency |
| *founded* | 1995 |
| *sponsor* | Lord Chancellor's Department |
| *powers* | Courts and Legal Services Act 1990 |
| *mission* | To enable criminal cases to be heard, civil disputes to be adjudicated, family proceedings to be decided, judgments to be enforced and grants of probate to be issued. |
| *tasks* | To carry out the administrative and support tasks for the following jurisdictions: the Court of Appeal, the High Court, the Crown Court, the county courts, the Probate Service, the Lord Chancellor's Tribunals (seven tribunals covering immigration, social security and child support, pensions, income tax, VAT and duties, land, transport). |
| *operations* | Management: The basis for judicial administration is a partnership between the judges on the one hand and the Court Service and Lord Chancellor's Department on the other. The judiciary have been regularly consulted by the Chief Executive and his staff since the Court Service was created in 1971. After becoming an executive agency in 1995, a radical review of the management began almost immediately and a new management structure was introduced in 1996/97. For operational purposes the Court Service is now divided into eight commands: the Criminal Appeal Office, the Supreme Court Group and the six circuits covering England and Wales. The Director of Tribunal Operations is responsible for the management of the Lord Chancellor's Tribunals across the country; the Civil and Family Operations Director and the Criminal Operations Director are responsible for keeping under review the procedures and systems used to deliver court services to the public, the profession and the judiciary. |

Policy: To improve the quality of service provided to the public in the courts, in particular reducing waiting times for trials and hearings. To counter the continuing shortfall between expenditure on civil business and civil court fee income.

Trends: Despite an increase in workloads, waiting times in the Crown Court have shortened. Information technology is being used increasingly in the courts and an IT future development contract has been awarded under the Private Finance Initiative (PFI) to Electronic Data Systems. This is to develop the rollout system (CaseMan) to replace the county court record system - the first stage in computerising the county courts.

*board* The Court Service Management Board is appointed by the Lord Chancellor from within the service.

| Chief Executive | Michael Huebner CB | |
|---|---|---|
| Members | Graham Calvett | |
| | Bob Clark | John Powell |
| | Charles Everett | Peter Risk |
| | Peter Farmer | Dave Ryan |
| | Peter Handcock | Nick Smedley |
| | Peter Jacob | Paul Stockton |
| | Mike McKenzie QC | Robin Vincent |

*staff* 10,092

| Chief Executive | Michael Huebner CB |
|---|---|
| Head of Information Systems Division | Ian Hyams |
| Head of Personnel & Training Division | Bernadette Kenny |
| Head of Resources & Planning Division | Kevin Pogson |
| Head of Accommodation, Procurement, Libraries & Records Division | Alistair Shaw |

# Covent Garden Market Authority (CGMA)

Covent House
New Covent Garden Market
London SW8 5NX

**Tel** 0171 720 2211
**Fax** 0171 622 5307

**Contact** Helen Evans

| | |
|---|---|
| *status* | Public corporation |
| *founded* | 1961 |
| *sponsor* | Ministry of Agriculture, Fisheries and Food (MAFF) |
| *powers* | Covent Garden Market Act 1961 |
| *mission* | To operate an efficient wholesale market at Nine Elms while ensuring that revenues are sufficient at least to break even. |
| *tasks* | Provides warehouse and office premises, market halls, roads and vehicle parks; also supplies services including cleansing and waste disposal, energy supplies, site security, traffic control, and maintenance of buildings, plant and equipment. |
| *operations* | Management: Run by the General Manager who reports to the Authority. Annual payment to MAFF from profits (£816,000 in 1996/97). |
| | Policy: Continuing campaign to market the vacant space for alternative uses. |
| | Trends: Decline of turnover in the fruit and vegetable wholesale sector, but increase in trade in flower market. |
| *performance* | Met revenue targets in 1996/97. |
| *board* | One Member of the Authority is appointed by the Secretary of State for Environment, Transport and the Regions and the others are appointed by the Minister of Agriculture. |

| | |
|---|---|
| Chairman | L Mills CBE |
| Members | GK Noon MBE |
| | Mrs AM Vinton |
| *Accounting Officer* | *General Manager* |

*staff* 44

| | |
|---|---|
| General Manager | Dr PM Liggins |
| Secretary | CR Farey |
| Assistant Operations Manager | T Anderson |
| Mechanical Engineer | J Ball |
| Assistant Operations Manager | K Dooney |
| Information Officer | Mrs HM Evans |
| Lettings Officer | WJ Kearns |
| Internal Auditor | K Lander |
| Finance Officer | PG Marsden |
| Building Superintendent K Newman | |
| Commercial Manager | M Potter |
| Electrical Engineer | G Taylor |
| Market Operations Manager | A Thomson |

*financial*

| PROFIT & LOSS Year end: 31 March | 1997 £ | 1996 £ | 1995 £ |
|---|---|---|---|
| **INCOME** | | | |
| Rents | 2,423,909 | 3,031,512 | 2,798,492 |
| Recoveries from tenants for services | 2,532,512 | 2,619,187 | 2,617,310 |
| Commercial vehicle charges | 657,465 | 685,144 | 697,117 |
| Car & coach parking charges etc | 99,698 | 87,230 | 66,615 |
| Miscellaneous receipts | 10,677 | 33,977 | 84,522 |
| | **5,724,261** | **6,457,050** | **6,264,056** |

| EXPENDITURE | | | |
|---|---:|---:|---:|
| Emoluments of Members of the Authority | 82,944 | 80,108 | 73,950 |
| Salaries and wages | 794,824 | 791,213 | 761,296 |
| National insurance | 67,275 | 68,898 | 65,971 |
| Pension plan contributions | 57,732 | 56,318 | 71,179 |
| Market security | 593,654 | 626,944 | 614,134 |
| Rates | 272,710 | 332,043 | 265,918 |
| Rates refunded | (82,000) | - | - |
| Maintenance, repairs and renewals | 798,256 | 773,529 | 896,388 |
| Provision for major repairs | 155,000 | 200,000 | 80,000 |
| Cleaning | 621,073 | 643,620 | 673,676 |
| Heat, light and power | 792,977 | 891,564 | 852,864 |
| Insurance | 151,409 | 151,786 | 162,557 |
| Printing, stationery and telephone | 56,987 | 60,632 | 49,644 |
| Professional fees | 128,737 | 103,607 | 57,636 |
| Auditors' remuneration | 18,250 | 18,250 | 17,500 |
| Other fees paid to auditors | 19,635 | 20,500 | 25,950 |
| Bad debt provision | (20,000) | - | - |
| Publicity | 57,409 | 57,659 | 72,011 |
| General expenses | 114,798 | 142,977 | 92,708 |
| Provision for service charge costs | 158,000 | (60,000) | 75,000 |
| Depreciation - buildings | 205,744 | 203,426 | 207,970 |
| Depreciation -other assets | 171,471 | 154,809 | 108,858 |
| | **5,216,885** | **5,317,883** | **5,225,210** |
| **OPERATING SURPLUS** | **507,376** | **1,139,167** | **1,038,846** |
| Interest receivable on market activities | 308,275 | 345,857 | 273,871 |
| Interest receivable on funds invested following the sale of Market Towers | 119,069 | 125,039 | 98,238 |
| **SURPLUS BEFORE TAXATION** | **934,720** | **1,610,063** | **1,410,955** |
| Taxation | (430,000) | (550,000) | 485,000 |
| **SURPLUS FOR THE YEAR** | **504,720** | **1,060,63** | **925,955** |

| *advisers* | **Bankers** | Midland Bank | Albert Embankment, London SE1 |
|---|---|---|---|
| | **Auditors** | Price Waterhouse | 32 London Bridge Street, London SE1 |

# *Crafts Council*

44a Pentonville Road
Islington
London N1 9BY

**Tel** 0171 278 7700
**Fax** 0171 837 6891          **Web** http://www.craftscouncil.org.uk

| *status* | Executive body |
|---|---|
| *founded* | 1971. Royal Charter 1982 |
| *sponsor* | Department of Culture, Media and Sport (DCMS) |
| *powers* | Royal Charter 1982 |
| *mission* | To encourage the creation of works of fine craftsmanship and to promote interest in it, and access to it, in Great Britain. |
| *tasks* | Administers its own grants made to Regional Arts Boards, to individual craftspeople and towards national exhibitions etc. Promotes formal and informal crafts teaching at all levels. Provides exhibitions and displays of national importance, with related publications and events. Runs shops at the V&A Museum and its own gallery and magazine. |
| *operations* | Management: It is organised into five sections: Education, Exhibitions and The Collection, Craft Development, Craft Magazine, and Trading. In Wales, the Arts Council of Wales' Craft Department, supported by the Crafts Council, provides all services. An Index of Selected Makers has been launched to promote commissions. |
| | Policy: Focusing effort on craft education entering the secondary school curriculum and also on tertiary level teaching effectiveness and commercial and industrial links. Improving craftwork marketing. |
| | Trends: The government is encouraging the commissioning of craftwork. |

# Q&Q

**performance** Targets exceeded: crafts business survival and trading; audience development; and education. Efficiency target almost met.

**board** Appointed by the Secretary of State.

| | | |
|---|---|---|
| Chairman | Sir Nigel Broackes | |
| Members | Brian Asquith | |
| | Polly Binns | Luke Hughes |
| | Dr Alan Borg | Prof James More |
| | John Buston | Prof Eric Spiller |
| | Michaela Butter | Janice Tchalenko |
| | Susan Collier | Lucia van der Post |
| | David H Davis | Moira Vincentelli |
| *Accounting Officer* | *Director* | |

**staff** 46

| | |
|---|---|
| Director | Tony Ford |
| Head of Trading | Clare Beck |
| Head of Education | Stephen Burroughs |
| Head of Craft Development | Barclay Price |
| Head of Resources | Penelope Rhodes |
| Publisher Crafts Magazine | Andrew Ryan |
| Head of Exhibitions and the Collection | Louise Taylor |
| Head of Finance | Rona Udall |

**financial**

**FINANCIAL ACTIVITIES**

| Year end: 31 March | 1997 £ | 1996 £ |
|---|---|---|
| **INCOMING RESOURCES** | | |
| Grant-in-aid | 3,250,000 | 3,250,000 |
| Scottish Arts Council | 45,000 | 45,000 |
| National Lottery consultancy | 77,000 | 15,000 |
| Exhibitions - touring & catalogues | 64,141 | 58,737 |
| Education | 43,150 | 31,258 |
| Library and photostore | 12,123 | 5,671 |
| Crafts Magazine | 377,733 | 351,786 |
| Retail trading | 451,639 | 467,854 |
| Development of craft sales | 416,891 | 387,939 |
| Miscellaneous income | 4,745 | 809 |
| Sponsorship & donations | 63,770 | 83,079 |
| Bank interest received | 16,860 | 21,097 |
| | **4,823,052** | **4,718,230** |
| **RESOURCES EXPENDED** | | |
| Direct charitable expenditure | | |
| Regional Arts Boards | 663,200 | 663,200 |
| Welsh Arts Council | 104,400 | 104,400 |
| Other grants and bursaries | 257,103 | 196,100 |
| Grants to individuals | 143,261 | 168,046 |
| Craft development | 186,811 | 198,616 |
| Exhibitions, touring and catalogues | 712,888 | 634,546 |
| Collection maintenance | 95,281 | 111,179 |
| Education | 417,662 | 393,815 |
| Library and photostore | 236,471 | 260,902 |
| Crafts Magazine | 504,517 | 482,652 |
| Retail trading | 530,612 | 544,773 |
| Development of craft sales | 547,529 | 529,444 |
| Other expenditure | | |
| Fundraising and publicity | 205,787 | 222,429 |
| Management and administration | 190,742 | 175,626 |
| Notional costs | | |
| Cost of capital | 74,000 | - |
| Insurance | 8,109 | - |
| | **4,878,373** | **4,685,728** |
| **NET INCOMING RESOURCES BEFORE TRANSFERS** | **(55,321)** | **32,502** |
| Transfer to designated fund | | |
| Reversal of notional costs | 82,109 | - |
| **NET INCOMING RESOURCES** | **26,788** | **32,502** |

**advisers** | **Auditors** | Coopers & Lybrand | London

# *Criminal Cases Review Commission (CCRC)*

Alpha Tower
Suffolk Street Queensway
Birmingham B1 1TT

**Tel** 0121 633 1800
**Fax** 0121 6331804/1823

| | |
|---|---|
| *status* | Executive body |
| *founded* | 1997 |
| *sponsor* | Home Office |
| *powers* | Criminal Appeal Act 1995 |
| *mission* | An independent body responsible for investigating suspected miscarriages of justice in England, Wales and Northern Ireland. |
| *tasks* | Reviews the convictions of those who believe they have either been wrongly found guilty of a criminal offence, or wrongly sentenced, after they have been through the appeal system. Can seek further information relating to a case and carry out its own investigations, or arrange for others to do so. Decides whether or not to refer the case to the appropriate appeal court. |
| *operations* | Management: The Commission's 14 Members are supported by a Chief Executive, Director of Finance and Personnel, two Legal Advisors, and an Investigations Advisor and caseworkers. Over 250 cases were transferred from the Home Office around 31 March 1997, when the Commission took over responsibility for casework. |
| | Policy: Dealing thoroughly and expeditiously with applications. |
| *board* | Commission Members are appointed by HM The Queen. Members are chosen from the legal profession and from those with experience of the criminal justice system; in addition, one-third of the Commission are lay members. |

| | |
|---|---|
| Chairman | Sir Frederick Crawford |
| Commissioners | Barry Capon CBE |
| | Laurence Elks |
| | Tony Foster |
| | Jill Gort |
| | Fiona King |
| | John Knox |
| | David Kyle |
| | John Leckey |
| | Prof Leonard Leigh |
| | James MacKeith |
| | Karamjit Singh |
| | Baden Skitt |
| | Edward Weiss |
| *Accounting Officer* | *Chief Executive* |

| | | |
|---|---|---|
| *staff* | 60 | |
| *advisers* | **Bankers** | Lloyds Bank |
| | **Auditors** | National Audit Office |
| *publications* | *Annual Report, Management Statement* | |

# Criminal Injuries Compensation Authority (CICA)

Morley House
Holborn Viaduct
London EC1A 2JQ

**Tel** 0171 842 6800
**Fax** 0171 436 0804

| | |
|---|---|
| **status** | Executive body |
| **founded** | 1996. As Criminal Injuries Compensation Board, 1934 |
| **sponsor** | Home Office. Scottish Office |
| **powers** | Criminal Injuries Compensation Act 1995 |
| **mission** | Administering the new tariff-based Criminal Injuries Compensation Scheme for victims of violence in Great Britain. |
| **tasks** | A new body administering the new compensation scheme for all applications made after 1 April 1996. The staff also administers the backlog of cases under the old (1990) Common Law Damages Scheme which was the residual responsibility of the Criminal Injuries Compensation Board. |
| **operations** | Management: Formerly the Criminal Injuries Compensation Board, the staff have been constituted as a new body - CICA. 1996/97 involved operating the new tariff-based scheme alongside clearing up claims received under the 1990 Common Law Damages Scheme up to 31 March 1996. Claims officers decide what awards should be make in individual cases, and how they should be paid. Adjudicators are appointed to a panel to administer the appeals system. Clearing the backlog of cases under the old scheme has been a huge but finite task for the staff and Board: at the beginning of 1996/97, there were 109,000 people whose applications were still to be resolved; also some 25,000 cases awaiting resolution on appeal. The senior full-time official of CICA is the Chief Executive who reports to the Home Secretary. CICA administrative costs and payment of compensation awards are financed by a grant-in-aid from the Home Office, with a contribution from the Scottish Office. |

**board**

| Accounting Officer    Chief Executive |
|---|

**staff** 444

| Chief Executive    Peter Spurgeon |
|---|

**financial**

| RECEIPTS & PAYMENTS | |
|---|---|
| **Year end: 31 March** | **1997** |
| | £ |
| **RECEIPTS** | |
| HMG grants received | 26,421,771 |
| Operating receipts | 16,145 |
| | **26,437,916** |
| **PAYMENTS** | |
| Salaries and wages etc | 1,334,483 |
| Other operating payments | 21,762,074 |
| | **23,096,557** |
| **SURPLUS/(DEFICIT) FROM OPERATIONS** | **3,341,359** |
| Other receipts/payments (net) | (675,075) |
| **EXCESS OF RECEIPTS OVER PAYMENTS** | **2,666,284** |

**branches**
Tay House
300 Bath Street
Glasgow G2 4JR
Tel 0141 331 2726
Fax 0141 331 2287

# Crofters' Commission

4-6 Castle Wynd
Inverness IV2 3EQ

**Tel** 01463 663450
**Fax** 01463 711820

| | |
|---|---|
| *status* | Executive body |
| *founded* | 1955 |
| *sponsor* | Scottish Office |
| *powers* | The Crofters (Scotland) Act 1993 |
| *mission* | To promote a thriving crofting community. |

*tasks* To reorganise, develop and administer crofting. More specifically, to rearrange crofting units to the benefit of crofters; to promote development through, for example, the Crofting Counties Agricultural Grants Scheme and the Crofting Township Development Scheme; to encourage young people into crofting through the Croft Entrant Scheme; to encourage forestry schemes and community ownership; and to regulate crofting to the benefit of the crofting community overall.

*operations* Management: The Commission has seven members, a part-time Chairman and a full-time Secretary. The Commissioners are responsible for establishing long term aims and objectives and for setting crofting policy, reaching agreement on regulatory cases, and commenting on local crofting issues. Each commissioner is responsible for, and active in, an assigned area. All crofters are represented by an Area Commissioner who is well placed to identify local trends and opportunities. There is a separate panel of assessors for each of 14 area sections.

Policy: Deeply committed to developing thriving and sustainable crofting communities and to retaining fragile rural populations in the remoter areas of the Highlands and Islands.

Trends: Demand for crofts is rising. The Commission is actively encouraging absent crofters to pass their crofts to young entrants.

*board* Commissioners are appointed by the Secretary of State from people with experience of crofting.

| | |
|---|---|
| Chairman | Iain MacAskill |
| Vice Chairman | Ian MacKinnon |
| Commissioner - East Inverness, East Ross-shire & East Sutherland | Marina Dennis |
| Commissioner - Caithness & Sutherland | Alistair Fraser |
| Commissioner - Argyll, Argyll Islands, the Uists & Barra | Fr John Angus Macdonald |
| Commissioner - Lewis & Harris | Agnes Rennie |
| Commissioner - Shetland & Orkney | Dr Jessie Watt |
| Secretary to the Commission | Mike Grantham |

*staff* 50

| | |
|---|---|
| Information Officer | Brian MacDonald |
| Chief Technical Officer | Sandy Renfrew |
| Legal Officer | Donald Smith |

*financial*

**RECEIPTS & PAYMENTS**

| Year end: 31 March | 1997 £ | 1996 £ |
|---|---|---|
| **RECEIPTS** | | |
| Voted provision | 1,474,000 | 1,444,000 |
| **PAYMENTS** | | |
| Salaries | | |
| Chairman & Members | 127,729 | 138,021 |
| Staff | 706,533 | 718,827 |
| Superannuation | 90,676 | 88,007 |
| Employers ERNIC | 61,866 | 62,767 |
| | 986,804 | 1,007,622 |
| **OPERATING COSTS** | | |
| Running costs | 289,092 | 273,744 |
| Accommodation | 170,754 | 160,344 |
| | 459,846 | 434,088 |
| **TOTAL PAYMENTS** | 1,446,650 | 1,441,710 |
| **EXCESS RECEIPTS OVER PAYMENTS** | 27,350 | 2,290 |

# Crown Agents Foundation (Crown Agents)

St Nicholas House
St Nicholas Road
Sutton SM1 1EL

**Tel** 0181 643 3311
**Fax** 0181 643 8232

| | |
|---|---|
| *status* | Holding company (limited by guarantee) |
| *founded* | 1997 |
| *sponsor* | Department for International Development |
| *powers* | Crown Agents Act 1997. Memorandum and Articles of Association |
| *mission* | An executive body which acts as a holding company for a new operating company, The Crown Agents for Oversea Governments and Administrations Ltd, to which the government transferred all the functions, assets and obligations of the former Crown Agents. Applying the operating company's surplus income to the furtherance of social and developmental objectives. |
| *tasks* | Providing professional, commercial, technical and financial services to 150 governments, international organisations, particularly the World Bank and the European Union, the regional development banks, and a number of bilateral donors, including the British and Japanese governments and other public sector bodies worldwide - from the Caribbean to all parts of Africa and the Far East. Heavily involved in Russia and other former Soviet republics. |
| *operations* | Management: The Council of the Foundation is responsible for managing the Foundation's business and for supervising the operating company. The Foundation has up to 50 permanent and elected members - all are organisations with an interest in Crown Agents' activities and objectives. The Secretary of State is a special member for the time being. |
| | Policy: To operate commercially but in line with the broader interests of social and economic development. |
| | Trends: The International Development Administration will remain a major client and new government capital has been made available to the new operating company in the form of subordinated loans. |
| *board* | The Council of the Foundation is elected by the members. |

| | |
|---|---|
| Chairman & Senior Crown Agent | DH Probert CBE |
| Deputy Chairman | AK Stewart-Roberts |
| Members | JD Andrewes |
| | F Cassell CB |
| | Miss KMH Mortimer |
| | FI Sumner |

*staff*

| | |
|---|---|
| Managing Director & Crown Agent | PF Berry |
| Director Corporate Marketing & Development | DF Cook |
| Managing Director, Crown Agents Financial Services | AH Oxford |
| Director, International Development Group | D Phillips |
| Finance Director | JP Pigott |
| Director, Procurement Services | AM Slater |
| Corporate Secretary | KG White |

*financial*

**CROWN AGENTS FOR OVERSEA GOVERNMENTS & ADMINISTRATIONS PROFIT & LOSS**

| Year end: 31 December | 1996 | 1995 |
|---|---|---|
| | £000 | £000 |
| **TURNOVER** | 57,470 | 63,213 |
| **COST OF SERVICES** | (52,340) | (58,978) |
| **CONTRIBUTION** | 5,130 | 4,235 |
| Administrative expenses | (4,244) | (4,017) |
| **OPERATING PROFIT BEFORE TAXATION** | 886 | 218 |
| Tax charge on profit | (314) | (51) |
| **PROFIT FOR THE YEAR** | 572 | 167 |

*advisers*

| | | |
|---|---|---|
| **Bankers** | Bank of England | |
| **Auditors** | Price Waterhouse | Southwark Towers, 32 London Bridge Street London SE1 9SY |
| **Solicitors** | Norton Rose | |

# Crown Prosecution Service (CPS)

50 Ludgate Hill
London EC4M 7EX

**Tel** 0171 273 8000
**Fax** 0171 329 8167

| | |
|---|---|
| *status* | Government department |
| *founded* | 1986 |
| *sponsor* | Attorney General's Department |
| *powers* | Prosecution of Offences Act 1985 |
| *mission* | To provide a high-quality national prosecution service for England and Wales working in the interests of justice. |
| *tasks* | Advising the police on possible prosecutions; taking over prosecutions begun by the police; preparing cases for court; advocacy at court. Only prosecutes cases when there is sufficient evidence and it is in the public interest to do so. |
| *operations* | Management: Director of Public Prosecutions (DPP) is responsible for overall management of the CPS and is superintended by the Attorney General. 13 geographical areas each headed by a Chief Crown Prosecutor. 93 local branches led by a Branch Crown Prosecutor. Almost all casework carried out in local branches (some complex or specialist cases are dealt with by Central Casework). Headquarters in London and York. |
| | Policy: To bring the right case to the right court at the right time. |
| | Trends: Review underway into organisation of CPs - will be reorganised into 42 teams, coterminous with Police forces. Criminal Justice system continuing to change with new legislation. |
| *performance* | Met nearly all targets in 1996/97. |

| *board* | Director of Public Prosecutions<br>*Accounting Officer* | Dame Barbara Mills<br>*Director of Public Prosecutions* |
|---|---|---|

| | |
|---|---|
| *staff* | 6000 |
| *financial* | 1996/97 Net Expenditure £300 million. |
| *publications* | *Annual Report, Branch Annual Report, Code of Crown Prosecutors* |

# Defence Analytical Services Agency (DASA)

Northumberland House
Northumberland Avenue
London WC2N 5BP

**Tel** 0171 218 1638
**Fax** 0171 218 5203

**E-mail** resources@dasa.mod.uk/dasa/dasahome.htm
**Web** http://www.open.gov.uk

| | |
|---|---|
| *status* | Defence agency |
| *founded* | 1992 |
| *sponsor* | Ministry of Defence (MOD) |
| *powers* | Framework Document 1992 |
| *mission* | To provide MoD with professional statistical and other analytical services for budgetary, personnel and logistics planning and policy formulation. |
| *tasks* | Manpower statistics and planning. Financial and economic advice including prices. Logistics advice including inventory management, vehicle fleet management etc. Defence statistics, also including search and rescue and aircraft accidents. Balance of payments data for Office of National Accounts and MoD and Armed Services numbers for HM Treasury. |

**operations** Management: Formed after an amalgamation of three MoD Statistical Divisions in 1992. The Secretary of State delegates ownership responsibilities to Assistant Under Secretary (General Finance). The owner is responsible for the strategic direction of the agency and for ensuring that services provided meet MoD's wider needs. There is a Chief Executive who is also Chief Statistical Adviser to MoD, and an Advisory Board. There is a heavy reliance on, and investment in, IT systems.

Policy: Continual review of IT systems for technological obsolescence.

Trends: Large investment in development work at request of customers.

**board** Advisory Board

| | | |
|---|---|---|
| Chairman | David Heyhoe | |
| Members | David Adams Jones | |
| | Paul Altobell | Mike Smart |
| | John Baird | Brian Taylor |
| | Fabian Malbon | Alexa Walker |
| | Richard Oliver | Simon Webb |
| | Brian Perowne | Stan Webster |
| *Accounting Officer* | *Chief Executive* | |

**staff** 130

| | |
|---|---|
| Chief Executive | Paul Altobell |
| Director, AS (Manpower & Finance) | Fred Johnson |
| Personnel Manager | Andrew King |
| Director, AS (Information Services & Logistics) | Colin Youngson |

**financial**

| EXPENDITURE | | |
|---|---|---|
| **Year end: 31 March** | **1997** | **1996** |
| | £ | £ |
| **EXPENDITURE** | | |
| Staff costs | 2,854,872 | 2,776,005 |
| Supplies and services consumed | 1,160,809 | 1,234,808 |
| Accommodation and associated costs | 585,906 | 570,514 |
| Other administration costs | 683,774 | 731,098 |
| Interest charge on capital | 26,468 | 18,603 |
| Loss on revaluation of fixed assets | 34,790 | 19,577 |
| **NET EXPENDITURE** | **5,346,619** | **5,350,605** |

**advisers** **Auditors** National Audit Office 157-197 Buckingham Palace Road
London SW1W 9SP

# Defence Animal Centre (DAC)

Welby Lane
Melton Mowbray
Leicestershire LE13 0SL

**Tel** 01664 411811 **E-mail** 113166.712@compuserve.com
**Fax** 01664 410694

**status** Defence agency

**founded** 1993

**sponsor** Ministry of Defence (MOD)

**powers** Framework Document

**mission** To train dogs and handlers, horses and equine managers for ceremonial and operational use throughout MOD sponsored establishments. Specialist dog handler training for Home Office agencies and foreign governments is provided on a repayment basis.

**tasks** Providing military working animals trained for different roles and to varying levels; training personnel to handle, manage and care for animals; providing veterinary health programmes including basic veterinary support. Dogs and handlers are trained for a variety of tasks, including security patrolling and detection of drugs, firearms, explosives and bodies.

| | |
|---|---|
| *operations* | Management: The Director General of the Army Medical Services is Chairman of the Advisory Board and is the Agency Owner. He provides budgetary and management control. The other members of the Advisory Board reflect customer interests and MOD policy. DAC operates under the direction of the DAC Management Board, consisting of Chief Executive, Deputy Commandant, Support and Planning Officer, Operations and Training Officer, and Finance and Budgets Officer. Through Service Level Agreements the DAC provides training and working animals to the three Armed Services, MOD, Customs & Excise, HM Prison Service, Police and Immigration Services, overseas governments and civilian companies at home and overseas. |

Policy: Replacing administrative and staff accommodation with new buildings, under PFI.

Trends: Identifying new business opportunities.

*performance*  Four out of seven targets were met.

*board*  Advisory board appointed by the Secretary of State from relevant organisations.

*staff*  184 (33% civilian)

| | |
|---|---|
| Chief Executive | Julia Kneale |
| Second in Command | Paul Marks |
| Finance and Budgets Officer | Zelda Hall |
| Agency Management Planner | Roly Owers |
| Accounting Officer | Chief Executive |

*financial*

**INCOME & EXPENDITURE**

| Year end: 31 March | 1997 £000 | 1996 £000 | 1995 £000 |
|---|---|---|---|
| **EXPENDITURE** | | | |
| Staff costs | 3,557 | 3,685 | 4,118 |
| Supplies and services consumed | 794 | 828 | 671 |
| Accommodation costs | 1,194 | 1,576 | 1,436 |
| Other administration costs | 876 | 798 | 984 |
| Interest charge on capital | 265 | 240 | 204 |
| | 6,686 | 7,127 | 7,413 |
| **INCOME** | | | |
| Income from non-MOD customers | (344) | (241) | (197) |
| **NET EXPENDITURE** | 6,342 | 6,886 | 7,216 |

*advisers*  **Auditors**   National Audit Office   157-197 Buckingham Palace Road London SW1W 9SP

# *Defence Bills Agency (DBA)*

Mersey House
Drury Lane
Liverpool L2 7PX

**Tel** 0151 242 2519
**Fax** 0151 242 2470

*status*  Defence agency
*founded*  1996
*sponsor*  Ministry of Defence (MOD)
*powers*  Framework document
*mission*  To provide accounting services to MOD and MOD branches.
*tasks*  Authorising and paying MOD supplier and contractor bills. Invoicing and collecting receipts. Providing budget holders and other MOD customers with management and accounting information. Maintaining MOD central ledger accounting records. Developing Project CAPITAL and implementing Project JIGSAW.
*operations*  Management: 1996/97 was the first full year of operating and management concentrated on range of new MOD initiatives but principally on its resource accounting system under Project CAPITAL and its review of purchasing systems under Project JIGSAW. DBA's owner is the Assistant Under Secretary of State (General Finance) and he is advised on service standards by the Advisory Board. DBA operates under a Service Level Agreement with MOD. Day-to-day management is carried out by the Management Board comprising the Chief Executive, the Managing Director and the Heads of Business Operations and Information Technology.

Policy: Staff and IT resources diverted to Project CAPITAL.

Trends: The business process engineering involved in DBA's launch has now been completed and performance will be consolidated and continue to meet MOD's expanding service requirements.

**Performance** 98.7% against MOD targets; 101.9% including debt recovery.

**board** The Advisory Board is appointed by the Secretary of State.

| Members | Mrs SA Beaver |
|---|---|
| | PA Crowther |
| | P Ellis |
| | H Griffiths |
| | MJ Heritage-Owen |
| | P Mabe |
| | NJ McEwan |

**staff** 647

| Chief Executive | Iain S Elrick |
|---|---|
| Managing Director | Trevor R Thurgate |
| Head of Business Operations | Vernon Ashworth |
| Head of Information Technology | Jack Thomas |

**financial**

| NET EXPENDITURE Year end: 31 March | 1997 £000 | 1996 £000 |
|---|---|---|
| **EXPENDITURE** | | |
| Staff costs | 10,633 | 2,592 |
| Supplies and services consumed | 207 | 128 |
| Accommodation costs | 1,597 | 414 |
| Other administration costs | 2,196 | 637 |
| | 14,633 | 3,771 |
| **INCOME** | | |
| Less income from repayment customers | 25 | 28 |
| NET OPERATING EXPENDITURE | 14,608 | 3,743 |
| Interest charge on capital | 97 | 20 |
| NET EXPENDITURE | 14,705 | 3,763 |

**advisers** **Auditors** National Audit Office 157-197 Buckingham Palace Road London SW1W 9SP

**publications** *Annual Report and Accounts*

# *Defence Clothing & Textiles Agency (DCTA)*

Building 25
Skimmingdish Lane
Caversfield
Bicester
Oxon OX6 9TS

**Tel** 01869 875700
**Fax** 01869 875509          **Web** http://www.mod.uk/dcta

**Contact** J Deas, Director of Business Management

**status** Defence agency

**founded** 1994

**sponsor** Ministry of Defence (MOD)

**powers** Framework document

**mission** To provide the clothing and stores its customers need. Primary customers: Royal Navy, Army and Royal Airforce.

**tasks** To procure operational clothing, uniforms and general stores from outside suppliers. Research and development of new products. Also any expert support which may be needed, from original concept, specification and design to manufacturing techniques, quality control and supply scheduling.

**operations**　Management: DCTA replaced separate organisations responsible for uniforms, operational clothing and associated items for the Royal Navy, Army and Royal Air Force. It is owned by the Director General Logistic Support (Army). He reports to the Quartermaster General. It has a Chief Executive and a Management Board comprising the Chief Executive and the Heads of Business Management, Product Management (Clothing and Textiles), Product Management (General Stores), Science & Technology, Quality & Product Support and Contracts.

Policy: To integrate operations on a single site at Caversfield, Oxfordshire, by 1999.

Trends: Collocation and IT developments are key to future operations. Internally integrated Local Area Network has drastically reduced paperwork and in 1998 DCTA Business Support System forms a direct link between finance, contracts, and procurement branches. Externally, interfaces with MOD-wide initiatives (eg Project CAPITAL) will expand.

**performance**　Did not fully meet the target of 80% underlying availability of stock from shelf; Clothing and Textiles achieved 78%, General Stores 89%. The 80% R&D milestones yielded 94% research but only met 75% of the development targets. The expenditure target of 2.5% within budget was not met (mainly due to carry over of £20m which had resulted on underspend the previous year).

**board**　Management Board

| | |
|---|---|
| Chief Executive | Brigadier MJ Roycroft |
| Product Director (General Stores) | Major M Appleton |
| Director Quality & Product Support | A Beattie |
| Product Division (Clothing & Textiles) | Group Captain DC Bernard MBE |
| Director Business Management | J Deas |
| Finance Director | RN Dixson |
| Director (Contracts Division) | W Finch |
| Director, Science & Technology | Prof C Lewis OBE |
| *Accounting Officer* | *2nd PUS RT Jackling* |

**staff**　520

**financial**

| NET EXPENDITURE<br>Year end: 31 March | 1997<br>£000 | 1996<br>£000 | 1995<br>£000 |
|---|---|---|---|
| **EXPENDITURE** | | | |
| Staff costs | 10,904 | 10,279 | 3,378 |
| Supplies and services consumed | 154,945 | 99,034 | 51,647 |
| Accommodation costs | 1,823 | 1,432 | 382 |
| Other administration costs | 4,313 | 3,189 | 1,420 |
| Interest charge on capital | 14,291 | 14,277 | 4,964 |
| | 186,276 | 128,211 | 61,791 |
| **INCOME** | | | |
| Less income from non-MOD customers | (3,919) | (4,109) | (2,459) |
| **NET EXPENDITURE** | **182,357** | **124,102** | **59,332** |

# *Defence Codification Agency (DCA)*

Kentigern House
65 Brown Street
Glasgow G2 8EX

**Tel** 0141 224 2066
**Fax** 0141 224 2148

**status**　Defence agency

**founded**　1996

**sponsor**　Ministry of Defence (MOD)

**powers**　Framework Document 1996

**mission**　To maximise the benefits of the NATO Codification System. To manage the UK codification system, ensuring it is consistent with NATO policy and to promote the benefit of codification throughout the MOD.

**tasks**　Provision, mainly through contractors, of codifying services; training and production of operating instructions; represents the interests of the UK in developing and implementing NATO codification policy; ensures that each item of supply in the MOD UK inventory is identified uniquely and allocated a NATO stock number; maintains an efficient database of codification information.

**operations**  Management: The Owner is Air Officer Communications Information Systems. The Chief Executive reports to the Owner and is responsible for the day-to-day management. Within MOD, the codification process is applied to items ranging from elementary parts, such as nuts and bolts, to complex weapons, systems and their components. Changes in 1998 will lead to new organisational shape - Chief Executive responsible for three divisions: Operations (policy, procedures, codification, quality IT support); Information Management (product development, marketing, IT development); and Business Support (finance, planning, human resources).

Policy: Maximising potential savings by increasing visibility and influence throughout MOD. Replacing computer database system.

Trends: Codification is assuming an increasingly strategic role in defence logistics.

**board**  None.

| Accounting Officer | Chief Executive |
|---|---|

**staff**  100

| Chief Executive | Ken Bradshaw |
|---|---|
| Director Operations Management | John Clark |
| Director Business Management | Alexander B Smith |

**publications**  ISIS-CD, DCA News

# Defence Dental Agency (DDA)

RAF Halton
Aylesbury
Theobalds Road
Buckinghamshire HP22 5PG

**Tel** 01296 623535
**Fax** 01296 623535

**status**  Defence agency
**founded**  1996
**sponsor**  Ministry of Defence (MOD)
**powers**  Framework Document 1996
**mission**  To contribute to the operational effectiveness of the Armed Forces by achieving and maintaining their dental fitness in war, operational situtations other than war, and peace.
**tasks**  Provides primary dental care at 180 locations world-wide for 225,000 Service personnel and their dependants overseas; provides trained dental staff for operational deployment. Trains dental ancillaries and provides postgraduate training for dental officers.
**operations**  Management: One of the first tri-Service agencies. Employs civilian as well as personnel from all three Armed Forces. The Owner is the Surgeon General, who reports to the Deputy Chief of the Defence Staff (Programmes & Personnel). The Chief Executive reports to the Owner and is responsible for day-to-day management, with the support of the Management Board: Director of Clinical Services, Director of Plans & Resources, Director of Dental Services, and Head of Finance & Secretariat.

Policy: Dental teams with portable equipment ready to support personnel on operational deployment (four teams in former Yugoslavia).

Trends: Difficulties in recruiting high-calibre personnel.

**performance**  Met all key targets in 1996/97.
**board**  Appointed by the Secretary of State (through single service secretaries).

| | |
|---|---|
| Chief Executive | Air Vice-Marshal IG McIntyre |
| Director of Clinical Services | Brigadier JA Gamon |
| Director of Plans & Resources | Surgeon Commodore D Hargraves |
| Head of Finance & Secretariat | Mrs T O'Regan |
| Director of Dental Services (RAF) | Air Commodore RM Butler |
| Non-Executive Director | JR Wild |
| *Accounting Officer* | *Chief Executive* |

**staff**  871 (service 703, civilian 168)

**advisers**  **Auditors**  National Audit Office  157-197 Buckingham Palace Road
London SW1W 9SP

# Defence Estates Organisation (DEO)

St George's House
Blakemore Drive
Sutton Coldfield
West Midlands B75 7RL

**Tel** 0121 311 3850
**Fax** 0121 311 2100

**status**  Defence agency

**founded**  1997

**sponsor**  Ministry of Defence (MOD)

**powers**  Framework Document 1997

**mission**  Provides an overview of the defence estate and advises on capital works and property management.

**tasks**  To develop a strategic overview of the MOD estate (225 hectares of freehold land, rights over a further 122,000 and 250,000 buildings on over 3000 sites worldwide) to enable MOD to optimise the size of it and achieve maximum benefit from it; help MOD improve its stewardship and to meet its statutory, conservation, heritage and contractual obligations.

**operations**  Management: The Chief Executive is responsible for the day-to-day management and reports to the Second Permanent Under Secretary, who is the Owner. The Owner sets targets, monitors and assesses performance and approves budgets. The Board of Management consists of the Chief Executive and the Directors of Works, Lands, Contracts, and Corporate Services. The Chief Executive is appointed by open competition. Headquarters in Sutton Coldfield and 28 regional offices; also has staff overseas.

Policy: Exploring PFI, works contracting and partnering methods for new projects.

Trends: Changing military requirements and UK and EU environmental legislation are having great impact.

**performance**  Targets have been set for 1997/98.

**board**  Owner's Advisory Board is appointed by the Secretary of State from DEO's customers and some external representatives.

| *Accounting Officer* | *Permanent Under Secretary* |
|---|---|

**staff**  1400

| | |
|---|---|
| Chief Executive | Brian Hirst |
| Director of Lands | Allan Baillie |
| Director of Contracts | John Hall |
| Director of Works | John Mustow |
| Director of Corporate Services | Stephen Smith |

**branches**  Stirling House
Denny End Road
Waterbeach
Cambridge CB5 9QB
Tel 01223 25 5008

Estate Office
High Street
Durrington
Salisbury
Wilts SP4 8AF
Tel 01980 594553

Blandford House
Farnborough Road
Aldershot
Hants GU11 2HA
Tel 01252 24431 3933

Brunel House
42 The Hard
Portsmouth PO1 3DS
Tel 01705 822341

MOD Victoria House
Military Road
Canterbury
Kent CT1 1JL
Tel 01227 818701

1-13 St Giles High Street
St Giles Court
London WC2H 8LD
Tel 0171 3055555

Gough Road
Catterick Garrison
North Yorkshire DL9 3EJ
Tel 01748 832521

Copthorne Barracks
Shrewsbury SY3 7LT
Tel 01743 262598

The Barracks
Brecon
Powys LD3 7EA
Tel 01874 613 2880

Hilton Road
Rosyth
Fife KY11 2BL
Tel 01383 648022

HMNB
Room 239
Building 1/150 PP19D
Murrays Lane
Portsmouth PO1 3NH
Tel 01705 22721

DRA Farnborough
Q4 Building via Q1
Farnborough
Hants GU14 6TD
Tel 01252 392840

EWSD Building 1207
HMB Clyde Faslane
Helensborough
Dunbartonshire G84 8HL
Tel 01436 674321

Room 726
Metropole Building
Northumberland Avenue
London WS2N 5BL
Tel 0171 2186979

Mount Wise
Devonport
Plymouth
Devon PL1 4JH
Tel 01752 501439

FONA HQ
Yeovilton
Somerset BA22 8HL
Tel 01935 456602

HQ Land Command
Erskine Barracks
Wilton
Salisbury SP2 0AG
Tel 01722 436823

HQ 4 Div
Steeles Road
Aldershot
Hants GU11 2DP
Tel 01252 349115

HQ 3 Div
Bulford Camp
Salisbury
Wilts SP4 9NY
Tel 01980 672645

Flagstaff House
Colchester
Essex CO2 7ST
Tel 01206 78 2144

Craigie Hall
Army HQ Scotland
South Queensferry
West Lothian H30 9TN
Tel 0131 3102313

Elizabeth House
Imphal Barracks
HQ2 Div
Fulford Road
York YO1 4AU
Tel 01904 662334

Building 140a
RAF Benson
Wallingford
Oxon OX10 6AA
Tel 01491 83776

HQ Logistics Command
RAF Brampton
Huntingdon
Cambs PE18 8QL
Tel 01480 52151

HQ P&T Command
Room G123
Building 255
RAF Innsworth
Innsworth Gloucester GL3 1EZ
Tel 01452 712612

# *Defence Evaluation & Research Agency (DERA)*

Ively Road
Farnborough
Hants GU14 OLX

**Tel** 01252 393300
**Fax** 01252 393399

**E-mail** centralenquiries@dera.gov.uk
**Web** http://www.dera.gov.uk

| | |
|---|---|
| *status* | Executive agency. Trading fund |
| *founded* | Executive agency 1991. Trading fund 1993 |
| *sponsor* | Ministry of Defence (MOD) |
| *powers* | Statutory Instrument 1995 No 650. Framework Document |
| *mission* | To harness science and technology to UK defence needs. |
| *tasks* | Supplying scientific and technical services in defence-related technologies. Maintaining an effective capability to protect against the threats from chemical and biological attack. Defence operational analysis and decision support. Technology transfer - through its extramural research programme. About one-third of research budget is contracted out. |

*operations* Management: The Defence Research Agency (DRA) was expanded by 60% in 1996/97 by the addition of 12 MOD science and technology units and renamed. There is a DERA Board and its Executive Members are members of the Management Board - the Operations Committee. DERA is organised into operating divisions with their own Managing Directors. The Chemical and Biological Defence Establishment (CBDE) Division was formed largely from CBDE Porton Down and the Chemical and Electronic Systems Sector. CBDE Porton Down's concerns include detection, hazard assessment, physical protection and medical countermeasures. The Forensic Explosives Laboratory (FEL) provides expert assistance to UK police forces and foreign governments (eg US Oklahoma bombing). Centre for Defence Analysis (CDA) provides impartial advice in support of MOD decision processes across the areas of policy and force structure, procurement of equipment and support for current operations. Technology Transfer Division manages by-products from DERA's primary military research product through the extramural research programme and proactive effort.

Policy: To break even and earn an average of 6% return on capital over a three-year period.

Trends: Defence research funds have declined every year since 1991. Core research programme most affected, but as MOD research programme retreats DERA scientists are finding other government and commercial customers to use their capabilities.

*performance* Seven out of ten key targets achieved in 1996/97.

*board*

| Chief Executive | John Chisholm |
|---|---|
| Members | Ian Andrews |
| | Lieutenant General Edmund Burton |
| | Graham Coley |
| | Prof Sir David Davies |
| | Peter Gershon |
| | Lieutenant General Sir Robert Hayman-Joyce |
| | John Howe |
| | John Mabberley |
| | Stephen Park |
| | Andrew Sleigh |
| | John Weston |
| Company Secretary | Liz Peace |
| *Accounting Officer* | *Chief Executive* |

*staff* 12,549

| Chief Executive | John Chisholm |
|---|---|
| MD Facilities | Ian Andrews |
| MD Science | Graham Coley |
| MD Programmes | John Mabberley |
| Finance Director | Stephen Park |
| MD Analysis | Andrew Sleigh |
| Company Secretary | Liz Peace |
| Commercial Director | Mike Goodfellow |
| Personnel Director | Bill Hedley |
| Technical Director | Adrian Mears |

| Senior Military Officer | Air Cdre Bill Tyack |
| Land Systems | David Anderson |
| Electronics | Norman Apsley |
| Weapons Systems | Bill Clifford |
| T&E Facilities | Ray Gould |
| CIS | Nick Helbren |
| PROMT | Rosemary Lee |
| SMC | John Morton |
| T&E Ranges | Chris Rigden |
| CDA | Frances Saunders |
| Air Systems | Mike Steeden |
| Sea Systems | Chris Stonehouse |
| CBD | Paul Taylor |
| T&E Aircraft | Alan Threadgold |
| CHS | Mary Walker |
| CES | John Widdowson |

**financial**

| PROFIT & LOSS<br>Year end: 31 March | 1997<br>£m | 1996<br>£m |
|---|---|---|
| TURNOVER | 1,047.3 | 1,044.2 |
| Cost of sales | 292.8 | 300.5 |
| GROSS PROFIT | 754.5 | 743.7 |
| Net operating expenses | 678.6 | 670.5 |
| OPERATING PROFIT | 75.9 | 73.2 |
| Restructuring costs | (65.1) | (51.6) |
| Rationalisation funding | 22.1 | 34.9 |
| Surplus on sale of operations | 30.9 | - |
| Loss on disposal of fixed assets | (1.0) | (0.9) |
| PROFIT BEFORE INTEREST | 62.8 | 55.6 |
| Interest receivable | 9.0 | 9.9 |
| Interest payable | (10.1) | (15.9) |
| PROFIT FOR YEAR | 61.7 | 49.6 |
| Proposed dividend | (15.0) | - |
| Proposed appropriation of surplus arising on sale of operations | (8.9) | - |
| RETAINED PROFIT FOR YEAR | 37.8 | 49.6 |

**publications**  *Annual Report*

# Defence Intelligence & Security Centre (DISC)

Chicksands
Shefford
Bedfordshire SG17 5PR

**Tel** 01462 752101
**Fax** 01462 752291

**status**  Defence agency
**founded**  1996
**sponsor**  Ministry of Defence (MOD)
**powers**  DISC Framework Document 1996
**mission**  To train the Armed Forces and other intelligence organisations in security, psychological and intelligence operations while contributing to effective and timely advice on appropriate intelligence and security policy matters and maintaining operational capability.
**tasks**  To train the required number of personnel to agreed standards; to provide the Armed Forces with professional advice on appropriate intelligence and security policy matters, and contribute to the development of military concepts and doctrine; to provide personnel to support military operations and other government departments.
**operations**  Management: DISC has been created by collocating a number of defence intelligence and security training assets spread across the UK into RAF Chicksands in Bedfordshire, and amalgamating them. The Director

General Intelligence and Geographic Resources (DGIGR) is the agency's Owner and is responsible for approving the business plans, setting targets, monitoring performance and approving its cash allocation. The Owner is supported by an Advisory Board; and four other MOD boards also give guidance. The Chief Executive will always be an internal appointment due to security. He is responsible for the day-to-day management, supported by a Management Board, and is directly responsible to the Permanent Under Secretary for its financial control.

Policy: A robust customer-oriented regime to prevail.

**performance** Targets have been set.

**board** Owner's Advisory Board appointed by the Secretary of State.

| Chief Executive | Brigadier Michael Laurie |
|---|---|
| *Accounting Officer* | *Permanent Under Secretary* |

**staff** 484

# Defence Medical Training Organisation (DMTO)

Brunel House
42 The Hard
Portsmouth PO1 3DS

**Tel** 01705 822 341
**Fax** 01705 730 579

**status** Defence agency

**founded** 1997

**sponsor** Ministry of Defence (MOD)

**powers** Framework Document 1997

**mission** Trains individual specialist medical personnel to meet the operational requirements of all three Services.

**tasks** To train personnel to the standard prescribed by customers while reflecting the changing doctrine and best medical practice. To undertake equipment research and development. To run the Royal Defence Medical College (RDMC) and the Defence Medical Services Training Centre (DMSTC). To run the Defence Medical Library Service and the Defence Entomology Service.

**operations** Management: The Director General Medical Training (DGMT) runs the agency and reports to the Secretary of State. Headquarters in Portsmouth. The RDMC, which is responsible for postgraduate medical education and health studies, training all medical officers and nurses, is at HMS Dolphin, Gosport. The DMSTC is at Aldershot and is responsible for most of the other ranks' medical training for all three Services.

Policy: During its second year, focusing on strategic planning and developing sound relationships with customers.

Trends: Rationalisation of DMSTC continues, and instructors and courses are gaining increasing civilian awards and qualifications.

**board**

| DGMT Chairman | Major General CG Callow |
|---|---|
| DDMT (Pol) | Gp Capt PKL Coles |
| DDNE | Capt P Hambling |
| Comdt RDMC | Surg Cdre I Jenkins |
| Comd DMSTC | Brig M Ratcliffe |
| Hd Med Trg (F&S) | P Woolley |

# Defence Postal & Courier Services Agency (DPCSA)

Corporate HQ
Inglis Barracks
Mill Hill
London NW7 1PX

**Tel** 0181 818 6293
**Fax** 0181 818 6309

| | |
|---|---|
| *status* | Defence agency |
| *founded* | 1992 |
| *sponsor* | Ministry of Defence (MOD) |
| *powers* | Framework Document 1992 |
| *mission* | To provide a worldwide mail and secure courier services for Service personnel and the MOD. Also supports Forces Post Offices and provides a transit system for the MOD in the UK. |
| *tasks* | Delivery and collection of mail to and from British Forces Post Offices (BFPOs) around the world; operation of a secure courier service in the UK and worldwide for use by MOD/Service organisations; delivery of mail between MOD/Services establishments within the UK; training of forces postal staff; accounting and financial centre for BFPOs. |
| *operations* | Management: The Owner is Director General Logistic Support (Army). Chief Executive is responsible for management, with support of the Management Board. Wherever it makes economic and operational sense, mail carriage services are contracted out. |
| | Policy: Agency operates in compliance with international regulations governing carriage of mail and in close co-operation with the Post-Office. Most mail carriage services are contracted out. |
| | Trends: Increasing investment in high technology. |
| *performance* | Met all key targets in 1996/97. |
| *board* | Management Board appointed by the Secretary of State. |

| | |
|---|---|
| Chief Executive | Brigadier Tweedie Brown OBE |
| Head of Courier & Corporate Services | Colonel Richard Bugler |
| Head of Finance & Corporate Affairs | Howard Embleton |
| Head of Policy Strategy & BE | Lieutenant Colonel Charles Hillyer |
| Non-Executive Board Member | Malcolm Kitchener |
| Head of Postal Services | Colonel Euan Morrow TD |
| *Accounting Officer* | *Chief Executive* |

| | |
|---|---|
| *staff* | 40% military, 60% civilian |

*financial*

**INCOME & EXPENDITURE**

| Year end: 31 March | 1997 | 1996 | 1995 |
|---|---|---|---|
| | £000 | £000 | £000 |
| **EXPENDITURE** | | | |
| Staff costs | 11,398 | 9,797 | 9,313 |
| Supplies and services consumed | 9,795 | 8,458 | 8,633 |
| Accommodation costs | 2,664 | 2,523 | 2,488 |
| Other administrative expences | 3,980 | 3,801 | 4,115 |
| Loss on disposal of fixed assets | 302 | 0 | - |
| Interest charge on capital | 824 | 580 | 480 |
| | 28,953 | 25,159 | 25,029 |
| **INCOME** | | | |
| Income from non-MOD customers | (2,510) | (2,312) | (2,437) |
| **NET EXPENDITURE** | **26,443** | **22,847** | **22,592** |

| | | | |
|---|---|---|---|
| *advisers* | **Bankers** | Lloyds Bank | |
| | | Giro Bank | |
| | **Auditors** | National Audit Office | 157-197 Buckingham Palace Road |
| | | | London SW1W 9SP |
| | **Solicitors** | Treasury Solicitor | |

# *Defence Secondary Care Agency (DSCA)*

St Giles' Court
1-13 St Giles' High Street
London WC2H 8LD

**Tel** 0171 305 3432
**Fax** 0171 305 3432

**Contact** Mike Blackwell, Communication Officer, extention 2351

| | |
|---|---|
| ***status*** | Defence agency |
| ***founded*** | 1996 |
| ***sponsor*** | Ministry of Defence (MOD) |
| ***powers*** | Framework Document 1996 |
| ***mission*** | To provide trained Service medical staff to the UK Armed Forces Commanders in Chief for operations, deployments and exercises. |
| ***tasks*** | As a tri-Service agency, to manage the Armed Forces hospital system in the UK and overseas (Cyprus, Germany, Gibraltar, the Falkland Islands). Specifically: to provide secondary medical care to both Service and NHS patients in its wholly owned units; to provide a varied and challenging environment for military clinical staff through MOD Hospital Units; to purchase secondary medical care for Service personnel treated in NHS Trust hospitals which host MOD Hospital Units. |
| ***operations*** | Management: DSCA is owned by the Surgeon General who reports to the Secretary of State and in practice formulates policy, sets financial frameworks and delimits the working freedoms of the agency. There is a Chief Executive (recruited by open competition) who, although not Accounting Officer, has analogous accounting responsibilities. He is supported by an Executive Board which comprises the three Headquarters directors plus the Commanding Officers of DSCA units. The creation of DCSA has involved a radical reorganisation of the Armed Service's secondary care services. Two hospitals were closed, new MOD Hospital Units were located in host NHS Trusts and DSCA staff and medical services are provided within civilian hospitals in Northern Ireland, Germany (NHS) Healthcare Alliance and the Falkland Islands. The Royal Hospital Haslar is the core tri-Service hospital which trains uniformed staff in clinical elements of their war role, it also acts as a District General Hospital. |
| | Policy: To expand and renovate the core hospital, Haslar. To review the future of the Duchess of Kent's Hospital, Catterick. |
| | Trends: IT and financial systems are being developed. Staff shortages are a concern. |
| ***performance*** | Seven strategic targets have been set for 1997/98. |
| ***board*** | Executive Board |

| | |
|---|---|
| Chief Executive | Ron Smith |
| Director of Finance and Management Information | Paul James |
| Director of Corporate Development | Maggie Somekh |
| Director of Personnel & Services | Brigadier Peter Lynch |
| Commanding Officer, Royal Naval Hospital, Gibraltar | Surgeon Commander Neil Butterfield |
| Commanding Officer, Ministry of Defence Hospital Unit, Peterborough | Group Captain Simon Dougherty |
| Commanding Officer, Ministry of Defence Hospital Unit, Frimley Park | Colonel Peter Fabricius |
| Defence Services Medical Rehabilitation Centre, Headley Court | Brigadier Robin Garnett |
| Commanding Officer, Ministry of Defence Hospital Unit, Derriford | Surgeon General Charlie Johnston |
| Commanding Officer, Royal Hospital, Haslar | Brigadier Guy Ratcliffe |
| Commanding Officer, Duchess of Kent's Hospital, Catterick | Brigadier Kim Stephens |
| *Accounting Officer* | *Permanent Under Secretary, MOD* |

| | |
|---|---|
| ***staff*** | 2519 |

| financial | **NET EXPENDITURE** | |
|---|---|---|
| | Year end: 31 March | **1997** |
| | | **£000** |
| | **EXPENDITURE** | |
| | Staff costs | 66,475.1 |
| | Supplies and services | 17,516.6 |
| | Accommodation services | 8,154.9 |
| | Other administration | 28,239.7 |
| | | **120,386.3** |
| | **INCOME** | **(677.9)** |
| | **NET EXPENDITURE** | **119,708.4** |

**advisers**    **Auditors**    Audit Office

**Solicitors**    Treasury Solicitor

**publications**    *Framework Document, Annual Report, Suture Self (House Magazine), DSCA Handbook*

**branches**

*Ministry of Defence Hospital Unit*
*Frimley Park Hospital NHS Trust*
Portsmouth Road
Frimley
Camberley
Surrey GU16 5UJ
Tel 01276 604201
Fax 01276 675660

*Ministry of Defence Hospital Unit*
*Derriford Hospital NHS Trust*
Derriford
Plymouth PL6 8DH
Tel 01752 763755
Fax 01752 763755

*Ministry of Defence Hospital Unit*
*Peterborough Hospital NHS Trust*
Thorpe Road
Peterborough PE3 6DA
Tel 01713 3874939
Fax 01713 3874939

*Royal Hospital Haslar*
Haslar Road
Gosport
Hampshire PO12 2AA
Tel 01705 584255 ext 2121
Fax 01705 584255 ext 2519

*Duchess of Kent's Hospital*
Horne Road
Catterick Garrison
North Yorkshire
Tel 01714 887 3024
Fax 01714 887 3011

*Defence Services*
*RAF Headley Court*
Medical Rehabilitation Unit
Epsom
Surrey
Tel 01372 378271 ext 7214
Fax 01372 378271 ext 7276

*The Princess Mary's Hospital*
RAF Akrotiri
Cyprus BFPO 53
Tel 00 357 527 5586
Fax 00 357 527 5606

*The Royal Naval Hospital*
Gibraltar BFPO52
Tel 00 3505 5270
Fax 00 3505 5270

# Defence Transport & Movements Executive (DTMX)

Monxton Road
Andover
Hampshire SP11 8HT

**Tel** 01264 383766

**status**    Defence agency

**founded**    1995

**sponsor**    Ministry of Defence (MOD)

**powers**    Framework Document

**mission**    Providing agreed surface transport and movements services (and operational logistic support) worldwide for all HM Armed Forces, MOD, other government departments and sponsored organisations in peace, crisis, transition to war, and war.

| | |
|---|---|
| *tasks* | Transport and movements support to forces and garrisons around the world, both through DTMX's own port, rail and road assets and, under contract, through commercial shipping, forwarding agents, freight rail and road services. Providing the Army with an unaccompanied baggage service. Managing peacetime business travel contracts including rail passenger agreements and national car hire contracts. Specialised transport and movements services to support the MOD and Central Staffs. |
| *operations* | The Owner is the Director General Logistic Support (Army) (DGLogSp(A)), who chairs the Advisory Board. There is a Board of Directors which comprises the Chief Executive, the three Directors of Operations, Business Support and Finance and other senior staff including Commanders of Marchwood Military Post and 25 Freight Distribution Squador DTMX military units. The Chief Executive reports to DGLogSp(A). |
| | Policy: Commercial Business Adviser appointed as part of DTMX proactive marketing strategy. |
| *performance* | 1996/97 most key targets achieved. |
| *board* | Owner's Advisory Board appointed by the Secretary of State. |
| *staff* | 210 |

| | |
|---|---|
| Chief Executive | Brigadier RE Ratazzi CBE |
| Secretary | Major C Belgum |
| Commanding Officer, 17 Port & Maritime Regiment RLC | Lieutenant Colonel P Bennett |
| Director Business Support | Colonel M Bowles |
| Director Operations | Colonel FA Bush |
| Head of Contracts Branch | M Cox |
| Officer Commanding, 25 Freight Distribution Sqn RLC | Major FAS Martin |
| Director Finance | DA Tysoe |
| *Accounting Officer* | *Chief Executive* |

*financial*

**INCOME & EXPENDITURE**

| Year end: 31 March | 1997 £000 | 1996 £000 |
|---|---|---|
| **EXPENDITURE** | | |
| Staff costs | 5,072 | 5,087 |
| Supplies and services consumed | 82,538 | 70,805 |
| Accommodation costs | 1,450 | 2,811 |
| Other administration costs | 1,057 | 7,612 |
| Interest charge on capital | 5,269 | 4,668 |
| Notional loss on disposal of fixed assets | 233 | - |
| | 95,619 | 90,983 |
| **INCOME** | | |
| Less income from non-MOD customers | (2,976) | (6,429) |
| **NET EXPENDITURE** | **92,643** | **84,554** |

| | | | |
|---|---|---|---|
| *advisers* | **Auditors** | National Audit Office | 157-197 Buckingham Palace Road London SW1W 9SP |
| | **Solicitors** | MOD | |
| *publications* | *Annual Report, Framework Document, Corporate Plan* | | |

# *Defence Vetting Agency (DVA)*

Room 454
Metropole Building
Northumberland Avenue
London WC2N 5BL

**Tel** 0171 218 9000
**Fax** 0171 218 1352

| | |
|---|---|
| *status* | Defence agency |
| *founded* | 1997 |
| *sponsor* | Ministry of Defence (MOD) |
| *powers* | Framework Document 1997 |

| | |
|---|---|
| **mission** | To provide an acceptable level of assurance as to the integrity of defence employees and defence industry staff. Also to undertake vetting work for other government departments on a repayment basis. |
| **tasks** | To undertake investigations and security checks on individuals who will have access to sensitive government information and valuable assets. To investigate and assess cases where there may be some doubts concerning the continued security status of personnel. |
| **operations** | Management: Formed from elements of the Army, Royal Navy and RAF Vetting Units, and part of the Headquarters Directorate of Security responsible for vetting HQ civilians and defence industry personnel. DVA is an entirely civilian organisation under the control of the Chief Executive, a civil servant appointed by open competition. The Chief Executive reports to the Owner (Assistant Under Secretary (Security and Support)), who is responsible to the Secretary of State for Defence for strategic direction, policy, standards cash budget and corporate and business plans. The Chief Executive is assisted by a Management Board comprising senior executives and a non-executive member. Customers - the numerous defence organisations, the 30 other government departments and firms in the defence industry - are responsible for identifying vetting requirements through their Customer Groups and these are built into the DVA corporate and business plans. DVA occupies sites at Portsmouth, Woolwich, RAF Rudloe Manor and in central London. 60% of its Field Investigation Officers work from home.

Policy: To provide a highly responsive vetting service to customers. To improve efficiency and time liners through BER organisation, collocation and the introduction of new IS/IT.

Trends: Work loads likely to go down. |
| **performance** | Launched as an agency (April 1997). No key targets in 1996/97. |
| **board** | Members of DVA's Owner's Advisory Board appointed by the Owner. Includes *ex officio*, the president of the Guild of Services Controllers, as an External Member. |
| **staff** | 350 |

| Chief Executive | Michael PBG Wilson |
|---|---|
| *Accounting Officer* | *Permanent Under Secretary* |

| | | | |
|---|---|---|---|
| **advisers** | **Auditors** | National Audit Office | 157-197 Buckingham Palace Road London SW1W 9SP |
| | **Public Relations** | MOD (PR) | |
| **publications** | Framework Document, Corporate Plan, Business Plan, Quarterly Newsletter | | |

# Design Council

34 Bow Street
London WC2E 7DL

**Tel** 0171 420 5200
**Fax** 0171 420 5300

**E-mail** 100443.1213@compuserv.com
**Web** http://www.design-council.org.uk/

| | |
|---|---|
| **status** | Executive body |
| **founded** | 1944 |
| **sponsor** | Department of Trade and Industry (DTI) |
| **powers** | Royal Charter (revised 1973) and Framework Document |
| **mission** | To enable business and government to make better use of design, to make UK industry more competitive. |
| **tasks** | Works by developing new knowledge, by creating new tools and partnerships and by building new awareness in partnership with business, education and government. |
| **operations** | Management: A registered charity. Chief Executive is accountable to DTI for the performance of the organisation. There is a non-executive Design Council appointed by the President of the Board of Trade. The Chief Executive has a management board of four directors. Millennium Products project is funded by a separate DTI contract and is managed by the Communications Director.

Policy: Launched Millennium Products, a major new initiative to identify the best and most innovative of Britain's products and services for the year 2000. |

Trends: Adapting to changing circumstances ranging from technological innovations to devolution.

**performance**   All performance targets met in 1996/97.

**board**   Up to 15 Non-Executive Council Members, appointed by the President of the Board of Trade.

| Chairman | John Sorrell CBE | |
| Members | Richard Dykes | Alice Rawsthorn |
| | James Dyson | Paul Smith CBE |
| | Dorothy Mackenzie | Ivor Tiefenbrun MBE |
| | Dick Powell | John Towers CBE |
| | Jane Priestman OBE | Roy Williams CB |
| *Accounting Officer* | *Chief Executive* | |

**staff**   40

| Chief Executive | Andrew Summers |
| Director, CommunicationPaul Crake | |
| Director, Design | Sean Blair |
| Director, Education & Training | Moira Fraser Steele |
| Director, Resources | Anthony Land |

**financial**

| INCOME & EXPENDITURE | | | |
| Year end: 31 March | **1997** | **1996** | **1995** |
| | **£000** | **£000** | **£000** |
| **INCOME** | | | |
| Government grants | 7,075 | 6,863 | 10,607 |
| Income from activities | 64 | 426 | 1,427 |
| | **7,139** | **7,289** | **12,034** |
| **EXPENDITURE** | | | |
| Operating costs | 4,324 | 4,808 | 5,667 |
| Staffing costs | 1,275 | 1,201 | 2,018 |
| Depreciation | 28 | 28 | 148 |
| Notional Insurance costs | 1 | - | - |
| | **5,628** | **6,037** | **7,833** |
| Notional cost of capital | 50 | - | - |
| Reorganisation costs | 1,171 | 1,506 | 4,211 |
| | **6,849** | **7,543** | **12,044** |
| **OVERALL SURPLUS/(DEFICIT)** | **290** | **(254)** | **(10)** |

**publications**   *Design*

# Disposal Sales Agency (DSA)

6 Hercules Road
London SE1 7DJ

**Tel** 0171 261 8826
**Fax** 0171 261 8696

**status**   Defence agency

**founded**   1994

**sponsor**   Ministry of Defence (MOD)

**powers**   Framework Document 1994

**mission**   To secure the best return to the tax-payer from sales of surplus equipment and stores and to minimise the cost of holdings by savings in the storage of surplus items.

**tasks**   Selling MOD surplus equipment and stores for the best financial results; minimising storage costs; organising government-to-government sales and operating as an intelligent contracting organisation. A wide range of commodities is sold on behalf of a variety of non-MOD customers - eg the Benefits Agency, the Defence Evaluation and Research Agency (DERA), the Foreign and Commonwealth Office, the Home Office, the Security Services and the US Air Force.

**operations**   Management: The Owner is the Head of Defence Exports, who is responsible for monitoring DSA's strategic direction and setting targets, advised by an Advisory Board. The Chief Executive reports to the Owner and is responsible for the conduct and efficiency of DSA. The strategic direction is agreed and monitored by the Owner's Advisory Board. The organisation is structured on a commodity basis under a Director of Ships, Armaments & Aircraft and a Director of Contracts and Technical Services with a third Director covering finance and planning and administration.

Policy: Placing commercial storage and marketing agreements which require contractors to collect, store, account for, market and sell the equipment or spares on a profit share basis thus reducing DSA costs and increasing the disposal sales return.

Trends: Forecast sales again exceeded 1996/97.

**performance**    1996/97 most targets achieved.

**board**    Appointed by Owner and MOD.

| Owner | Charles Masefield | |
|---|---|---|
| Members | Roger Allen | Richard Jewson |
| | Dr Alan Fox | Bruce Mann |
| | Brigadier Peter Hodson | Malcolm Westgate |
| *Accounting Officer* | *Chief Executive* | |

**staff**    80

| *Management Board* | |
|---|---|
| Chief Executive | Malcolm Westgate |
| Assistant Under Secretary (Export Policy Finance) | Dr Alan Fox |
| Commercial Adviser | Richard Jewson |
| Director (Ships, Aircraft & Armaments) | Michael Robinson |
| Director (Contracts & Technical Services) | Colin MacPhee |
| Director (Finance, Planning & Administration) | Garry Thomas |

**advisers**    **Auditors**    National Audit Office    157-197 Buckingham Palace Road
London SW1W 9SP

**publications**    *Annual Report and Accounts*


# Driver & Vehicle Licensing Agency (DVLA)

Longview Road
Morriston
Swansea SA6 7JL

**Tel** 01792 782341
**Fax** 01792 782472

**Contact** Press Officer - 01792 782070

**status**    Executive agency
**founded**    1990
**sponsor**    Department of the Environment, Transport and the Regions (DETR)
**powers**    Framework document
**mission**    Registers and licences drivers and vehicles and collects Vehicle Excise Duty in Great Britain (NI has its own DVLA) on behalf of the Secretary of State.
**tasks**    Maintain records of drivers and vehicles to meet the needs of law enforcement agencies and others with a legitimate right of access; issuing licences to drivers; issuing registration documents to vehicle keepers; collecting Vehicle Excise Duty; to assist government in meeting its road safety objectives.
**operations**    Management: The Chief Executive is responsible for the overall running of the Agency, supported by a team of Executive Directors. He meets regularly with Ministers, the Permanent Secretary and the Chairman of the DVLA's Advisory Board to assess performance. Management has recently been streamlined. The DVLA Executive Board is chaired by the Chief Executive, and attended by the four Executive Directors and the Head of Executive Agencies Division of DETR (Transport).

The headquarters is in the DVLA Centre at Swansea and there is a network of 40 properties throughout Great Britain. The number of Vehicle Registration Offices (VROs) was reduced from 52 to 40 in 1997; most of the responsibilities for local DVLA services had been merged with central operations in 1996. There are now five area office: Edinburgh (Scotland and North of England); Manchester (North Wales and West of England); Nottingham (Eastern England); Bristol (South Wales and South of England); and Wimbledon (South East of England).

Policy: Major policy changes included inclusion of EU Directives relating to new drivers and photographs in driving licenses and completion of local office network restructuring project.

Trends: EU Directive affecting existing drivers being introduced in 1998. It also involves setting up a register of foreign drivers who come and live in Britain; registration will be voluntary for car drivers, compulsory for bus and lorry drivers. The project work on issuing photocard driving licences will be progressed so that DVLA can start issuing them not later than July 2001. DVLA will extend electronic data interchange links to all magistrates courts in England and Wales.

*board*

| | |
|---|---|
| Chief Executive | Dr SJ Ford |
| Director of Finance | Paul A Houston |
| Director of Personnel | Robin Hancock |
| Director of External & Corporate Services | Trevor J Horton |
| Director of Central Operations | Richard J Verge |
| *Accounting Officer* | *Chief Executive* |

Advisory Board, appointed by the Secretary of State, comprises representatives from DETR's Road and Vehicle Safety Directorate and its Executive Agencies Division, plus three external members with relevant experience.

| | |
|---|---|
| Chairman | Richard Dudding |
| Members | Dr SJ Ford |
| | Mrs AE Hemingway |
| | Miss SJ Lambert |
| | A Melville |
| | AS Orton |

*staff*   3,902

*financial*

| INCOME & EXPENDITURE | | | |
|---|---|---|---|
| Year end: 31 March | **1997** | **1996** | **1995** |
| | **£000** | **£000** | **£000** |
| **GROSS INCOME** | | | |
| Income from activities | 67,977 | 63,796 | 58,298 |
| Income from sale of Cherished Registration Marks | | | |
| (payable directly to the Consolidated Fund) | 35,207 | 26,967 | 26,816 |
| | **103,184** | **90,763** | **85,114** |
| **OPERATING COSTS** | | | |
| Staff costs | 59,862 | 58,490 | 62,702 |
| Other operating costs | 124,210 | 125,448 | 119,192 |
| Pension provision for former local taxation officers | 13,595 | - | - |
| Depreciation and other amounts written off to fixed assets | 4,304 | 2,991 | 2,948 |
| | **201,971** | **186,929** | **184,842** |
| **NET OPERATING EXPENDITURE** | **98,787** | **96,166** | **99,728** |
| Loss on disposal of fixed assets | 107 | 2,109 | 123 |
| Interest on capital | 1,313 | 1,218 | 1,175 |
| Interest payable on the finance lease | 465 | 183 | - |
| **NET EXPENDITURE CHARGED TO GENERAL FUND** | **100,672** | **99,676** | **101,026** |

*advisers*   **Auditors**   National Audit Office   157-197 Buckingham Palace Road
London SW1W 9SP

*publications*   *Annual Report and Accounts*

# Driver & Vehicle Licensing Northern Ireland (DVLNI)

County Hall
Castlerock Road
Coleraine BT51 3HS

**Tel** 01265 41461
**Fax** 01265 41422

| | |
|---|---|
| *status* | Executive agency |
| *founded* | 1993 |
| *sponsor* | Northern Ireland Office, Department of the Environment (DOENI) |
| *powers* | Framework Document |
| *mission* | To promote compliance with the legislation covering the licensing of drivers and vehicles in NI. |
| *tasks* | The registration and licensing of drivers in NI; the registration and licensing of vehicles in NI; the collection of vehicle excise duty in NI. It assists with law enforcement activities, promotes road safety and provides database services to external organisations and the public. |
| *operations* | Management: DVLNI operates from the Vehicle Licensing and Driver Licensing Central Offices in Coleraine and eight local offices around Northern Ireland. |
| | Policy: Major policy developments included the introduction of the Second EU Directive on driver licensing and pursuit of continuous improvement programme, alongside 29 other agencies, with the Cabinet Office. |
| | Trends: This is the second year of the peak renewal period for driving licence renewals (ten year licences replaced three-year licences between 1985 and 1987) and  renewals are still running at three or four times the volume normally expected. 271,000 driving licences were issued.  Provisional licences were in line with forecast at about 28,000. 720,000 vehicle licences were issued and action was taken against 26,000 people for evasion of VED, including prosecution. |
| *board* | The DVLNI Management Board is appointed by the Secretary of State. |

| | |
|---|---|
| Chief Executive | Brendan Magee |
| Director of IT | Bernie Cosgrove |
| Acting Director of Operations | George Dillon |
| Acting Director of Driver Licensing | Jane Hunter |
| Director of Vehicle Licensing | Ann McCabe |
| Director of Finance & Personnel | Lucia O'Connor |

*staff* 273

*financial*

| INCOME & EXPENDITURE Year end: 31 March | 1997 £000 | 1996 £000 | 1995 £000 |
|---|---|---|---|
| **INCOME** | | | |
| Income from activities | 7,068 | 6,769 | 5,315 |
| **EXPENDITURE** | | | |
| Staff costs | 3,800 | 3,614 | 3,354 |
| Depreciation | 253 | 390 | 352 |
| Other operating costs | 2,886 | 2,909 | 2,492 |
| | **6,939** | **6,913** | **6,198** |
| **NET OPERATING INCOME/(EXPENDITURE)** | **129** | **(144)** | **(883)** |
| Loss on disposal of fixed assets | (165) | - | - |
| **NET OPERATING EXPENDITURE BEFORE INTEREST** | **(36)** | **(144)** | **(883)** |
| Interest on capital | (58) | (84) | (76) |
| **NET EXPENDITURE FOR THE YEAR** | **(94)** | **(228)** | **(959)** |

*advisers* **Auditors**  Northern Ireland Audit Office   106 University Street, Belfast BT7 1EU

# Driver & Vehicle Testing Agency

Balmoral Road
Belfast BT12 6QL

**Tel** 01232 681831
**Fax** 01232 665520

| | |
|---|---|
| **status** | Executive body |
| **founded** | 1992. Trading Fund 1996 |
| **sponsor** | Northern Ireland Office, Department of the Environment (DOENI) |
| **powers** | Framework Document 1992 |
| **mission** | To promote and improve road safety in Northern Ireland by providing a fair, independent and efficient testing service for drivers and vehicles. |
| **tasks** | Examines vehicles to ensure roadworthiness; conducts practical and theory driving tests; assesses applicants for registration as approved driving instructors and monitor tuition standards. |
| **operations** | Management: Chief Executive is responsible to the Minister and is supported by the Management Board of five directors. First NI agency to operate as a trading fund. |
| | Policy: Replacing vehicle test equipment under PFI. |
| | Trends: EU directives to harmonise standards of testing and licensing throughout member states. |
| **performance** | Achieved all 11 targets and all but two of its key tasks in 1996/97. |
| **board** | No external board. |

| Accounting Officer | Chief Executive |
|---|---|

**staff** 320

| | |
|---|---|
| Chief Executive | JB Watson |
| Financial Controller | CR Berry |
| Director of Personnel Services | M Cox |
| Director of Driving Test Administration | S Duncan |
| Director of Vehicle Test Administration | G McKenna |
| Director of Operations | A Peoples |

**financial**

**INCOME & EXPENDITURE**

| Year end: 31 March | 1997 £000 | 1996 £000 | 1995 £000 |
|---|---|---|---|
| **INCOME** | | | |
| Test fees and licences | 10,654 | 9,244 | 8,253 |
| **EXPENDITURE** | | | |
| Staff costs | 6,274 | 5,793 | 5,092 |
| Depreciation | 305 | 114 | 54 |
| Other operating costs | 2,941 | 2,686 | 2,528 |
| | 9,520 | 8,593 | 7,674 |
| **OPERATING SURPLUS** | 1,134 | 651 | 579 |
| Interest receivable | 64 | - | - |
| Interest payable and similar charges | (134) | (22) | (16) |
| **NET SURPLUS OF THE YEAR** | 1,064 | 629 | 563 |
| Dividend payable | 120 | - | - |
| **RETAINED SURPLUS FOR THE YEAR** | 944 | 629 | 563 |

| | | | |
|---|---|---|---|
| **advisers** | **Auditors** | Northern Ireland Audit Office | 106 University Street, Belfast BT7 1EU |
| | **Solicitors** | Crown Solicitor | |

**publications** *Annual Report, Business Plan, Customer Charter and Code of Practice*

**branches**

Balmoral Road
Belfast BT12 6QL
Tel 01232 681831

47 Hamiltonsbawn Road
Armagh BT60 1HW
Tel 01861 522699

Pennybridge Industrial Estate
Larne Road
Ballymena BT42 3ER
Tel 10266 656801

2 Loughan Hill Industrial Estate
Gateside Road
Coleraine BT52 2NJ
Tel 01265 43819

Sandholes Road
Cookstown BT80 9AR
Tel 016487 64809

Diviny Drive
Carn Industrial Estate
Craigavon BT63 5RY
Tel 01762 336188

Cloonagh Road
Flying Horse Road
Downpatrick BT30 6DU
Tel 01396 614565

Chanterhill
Enniskillen BT74 6DE
Tel 01365 322871

Ballyboley Road
Ballyloran
Larne BT40 2SY
Tel 01574 278808

Ballinderry Industrial Estate
Ballinderry Road
Lisburn BT28 2SA
Tel 01846 663151

New Buildings Industrial Estate
Victoria Road
Londonderry BT47 2SX
Tel 01504 43674

Commercial Way
Hydepark Industrial Estate
Mallusk BT36 8YY
Tel 01232 842111

51 Rathfriland Road
Newry BT34 1LD
Tel 01693 62853

Jubilee Road
Newtownards BT23 4XP
Tel 01247 813064

Gortrush Industrial Estate
Derry Road
Omagh BT78 5CJ
Tel 01662 242540

55 Broughshane Street
Ballymena

Shields House
19 James Street South
Belfast

20 Strand Road
Londonderry

Granite House
Mary Street
Newry

11b Foundry Lane
Omagh

Unit 11c
Magowan House
West Street
Portadown

## Driving Standards Agency (DSA)

Stanley House
56 Talbot Street
Nottingham NG1 5GU

**Tel** 0115 901 2500

**E-mail** 106027.3210@compuserve.com
**Web** http://www.coi.gov.uk/coi/depts/gds/gds.html

**Contact** Christine Nickles

*status* — Executive agency
*founded* — 1990. Trading Fund, 1997
*sponsor* — Department of the Environment, Transport and the Regions (DETR)
*powers* — Road Traffic Act 1988
*mission* — To promote road safety in Great Britain by testing drivers and driving instructors fairly and efficiently.
*tasks* — To conduct practical and theoretical driving tests for cars, motorcycles, lorries, buses and other vehicles. To control the Register of Approved Driving Instructors (ADI). To supervise Compulsory Basic Training for Motorcyclists.
*operations* — Management: The Chief Executive is appointed by and responsible to the Secretary of State. An Advisory Board advises the Secretary of State on business plans, corporate plans and policy. The Chief Executive appoints the Management Board. In 1996/97 new tests were introduced, implementing the EC Second Directive on Driving Licences.

Policy: Financial flexibility has increased with the introduction of Trading Fund status. Developing the information systems strategy.

Trends: Practical tests being reviewed by DETR and changes will be implemented from 2000. LGV driving instructors voluntary register introduced in 1997. European Commission looking towards harmonisation of theory, practical tests, examiner training and drivers' medical fitness.

**performance** In partnership with DriveSafe Services Ltd, the theory driving tests for cars, motorcycles, lorries and buses were introduced to timetable.

**board** Members of the Advisory Board are appointed by the Secretary of State. Members of the Management Board are appointed by the Chief Executive from senior executives.

| Accounting Officer | Chief Executive |
|---|---|

**staff** 2033

| Chief Executive | Bernard Herdan |
|---|---|
| Chief Driving Examiner | R Cummins |
| Personnel Director | A Evans |
| Operations Director | P Hedley |
| Finance Director | Ms LM Manley |

**financial**

**INCOME & EXPENDITURE**

| Year end: 31 March | 1997 £000 | 1996 £000 | 1995 £000 |
|---|---|---|---|
| **INCOME** | | | |
| Income from activities | 78,952 | 57,759 | 54,243 |
| Other operating Income | 1,684 | 625 | 507 |
| | 80,636 | 58,384 | 54,750 |
| **EXPENDITURE** | | | |
| Staff costs | 41,603 | 35,233 | 34,378 |
| Amortisation | - | 300 | 596 |
| Depreciation | 620 | 439 | 357 |
| Other operating charges | 33,808 | 15,023 | 13,896 |
| | 76,031 | 50,995 | 49,227 |
| **OPERATING SURPLUS** | 4,605 | 7,389 | 5,523 |
| Provision for reorganisation | - | - | 1,350 |
| Surplus on ordinary activities before interest | 4,605 | 7,389 | 4,173 |
| Interest receivable | 480 | 600 | 396 |
| Interest payable | (3) | 0 | (33) |
| **SURPLUS FOR THE FINANCIAL YEAR** | 5,082 | 7,989 | 4,536 |

**advisers** **Auditors** National Audit Office — 157-197 Buckingham Palace Road, London SW1W 9SP

**publications** The Bus and Coach Driving Manual, The Driving Manual - New Issue, The Driving Test, The Goods,, Vehicle Driving Manual, The Motorcycling Manual, The Official Theory Test for Car Drivers and Motorcyclists, The Official Theory Test for Drivers of Large Vehicles, The Theory Test and Beyond CD-ROM, The Theory Test for Large Vehicle Drivers, Theory Test Sample Question Papers, Car/Mc, Theory Test Sample Question Papers, PCV/LGV

# *Duke of York's Royal Military School*

Dover
Kent CT15 5EQ

**Tel** 01304 245029
**Fax** 01304 245019

**E-mail** duke@easynet.co.uk

**status** Defence agency
**founded** 1801, 1992 as Defence agency
**sponsor** Ministry of Defence (MOD)
**powers** Framework Document 1992

| | |
|---|---|
| **mission** | To provide boarding school education for the dependants, aged between 11 and 18 years, of Service personnel. |
| **tasks** | To provide cost-effectively for all pupils, a high standard of secondary education and a full range of extra-curricular sports and activities within a stable, caring, boarding environment. |
| **operations** | Management: HM Board of Commissioners are responsible to the Secretary of State. School run by Headmaster (who is also the Chief Executive). |
| | Policy: To reduce the per capita costs each year. |
| **performance** | Achieved 10 out of 12 targets in 1996/97. |

**board**

| Commissioners | Major-General BM Bowen |
|---|---|
| | Vice Admiral Sir John Cadell KBE |
| | Air Vice Marshal CE Evans CBE |
| | Brigadier Anne Field CB CBE |
| | General Sir John Stibbon KCB OBE |
| | Brigadier MA Atherton CBE JP |
| | Sir John Carter |
| | LC Stephenson |
| | Mrs JBE Wells JP |
| | K Jennings |
| | DH Webb |
| *Accounting Officer* | *Chief Executive* |

**staff**

| Headmaster & Chief Executive | GH Wilson |
|---|---|

**financial**

| NET EXPENDITURE Year end: 31 March | 1997 £000 | 1996 £000 | 1995 £000 |
|---|---|---|---|
| **EXPENDITURE** | | | |
| Staff costs | 2,483 | 2,371 | 2,287 |
| Supplies and services consumed | 530 | 408 | 422 |
| Accommodation costs | 2,518 | 2,138 | 2,200 |
| Other administration costs | 199 | 184 | 178 |
| Permanent diminution in value of tangible fixed assets | 1,976 | - | - |
| | 8,571 | 5,738 | 5,687 |
| **INCOME** | | | |
| Income from non-departmental customers | (481) | (446) | (435) |
| **NET EXPENDITURE** | **8,090** | **5,292** | **5,252** |

| | | |
|---|---|---|
| **advisers** | **Auditors** | National Audit Office |
| | | 157-197 Buckingham Palace Road London SW1W 9SP |

# East of Scotland Water Authority

Pentland Gait
597 Calder Road
Edinburgh EH11 4HJ

**Tel** 0131 453 7500
**Fax** 0131 453 7527

**E-mail** info@esw.co.uk
**Web** http://www.esw.co.uk

**Contact** Information Executive

| | |
|---|---|
| **status** | Public corporation |
| **founded** | 1995 |
| **sponsor** | Scottish Office |
| **powers** | Local Government etc (Scotland) Act 1994 |
| **mission** | To provide water and waste water services to customers in the Borders, Fife, Forth Valley, The Lothians and Edinburgh |
| **tasks** | Maintains and manages water mains, sewers, 86 water treatment works, 289 waste water treatment works and manages 100 reservoirs, lochs, rivers and streams. Maintains rigorous water quality standards while respecting and preserving the environment. |

| | |
|---|---|
| *operations* | Management: The Board meets every six weeks and significant policy matters are referred to it for decision. The Executive team comprises the Chief Executive and five directors. Four regional divisions. |
| | Policy: Substantial capital investment needed to meet environmental standards and improve underground infrastructure (water and wastewater networks). Major initiative to reduce the leakage in water distribution network. |
| | Trends: Increased pace of investment with continue over medium-term. |
| *performance* | Key performance targets have been set for 1998/99 through to 2000/2001, in relation to cost, quality and customer service. |
| *board* | Appointed by the Secretary of State for Scotland. |

| Chairman | Cllr Robert Cairns | |
|---|---|---|
| Chief Executive | Rod Rennet | |
| Members | Disney Barlow OBE | Cllr Jeanette Burness |
| | Robin Bell | Cllr Thomas Dair |
| | Cllr Ian Berry JP | Cllr Ann Dickson JP |
| | David Bleiman | Cllr Ian Galloway |
| | John Broadfoot CBE | Roy Summers |
| *Accounting Officer* | *Chief Executive* | |

*staff* 1940

| Chief Executive | Rod Rennet |
|---|---|
| Director of Operations | Jim Brown |
| Director of Corporate Services | Michael Cunliffe |
| Director of Finance | R Gardner |
| Director of Development | Robin Hamilton |
| Director of Water Quality | Dr Michael Heap |
| Director of Human Resources | Frank Sharp |

*financial*

| INCOME & EXPENDITURE | |
|---|---|
| Year end: 31 March | **1997** |
| | **£000** |
| **TURNOVER** | **161,519** |
| **OPERATING COSTS** | |
| Manpower costs | 44,058 |
| Exceptional item - manpower reorganisation costs | 4,802 |
| Materials and consumables | 8,581 |
| Other operational costs | 53,811 |
| Depreciation | 17,030 |
| Amortisation of grants and contributions | (213) |
| Infrastructure maintenance charge | 20,375 |
| Charge to capital | (10,795) |
| Charge to work in progress | (697) |
| | **136,952** |
| **OPERATING SURPLUS** | **24,567** |
| Surplus on disposal of fixed assets | 0 |
| **OPERATING SURPLUS BEFORE INTEREST** | **24,567** |
| Interest receivable | 503 |
| Interest payable and similar charges | (44,770) |
| **DEFICIT BEFORE TAXATION** | **(19,700)** |
| Taxation | 29 |
| **DEFICIT FOR THE YEAR** | **(19,671)** |

| | | | |
|---|---|---|---|
| *advisers* | **Bankers** | Bank of Scotland | 1 Castle Terrace, Edinburgh EH1 2DP |
| | **Auditors** | KPMG | 20 Castle Terrace, Edinburgh EH1 2EG |
| *publications* | *Annual Report & Accounts: Drinking Water Quality Report, Conservation, Access and Recreation Annual Report, Waste Water Treatment Report, Environment Policy, Policies for Conservation, Access and Recreation, Code of Practice, Scheme of Charges* | | |

*branches*

*Edinburgh Division*
55 Buckstone Terrace
Edinburgh EH10 6XH

*Forth Valley Division*
Woodlands
St Ninians Road
Stirling FK8 2HB

*Fife Division*
Craig Mitchell House
Flemington Road
Glenrothes KY7 5QH

*Lothians & Borders Division*
West Grove
Waverley Road
Melrose TD6 9SJ

# Economic & Social Research Council (ESRC)

Polaris House
North Star Avenue
Swindon SN2 1UJ

**Tel** 01793 413000
**Fax** 01793 413001          **Web** http://www.esrc.ac.uk/home/html

| | |
|---|---|
| *status* | Executive body |
| *founded* | 1965 |
| *sponsor* | Department of Trade and Industry (DTI) |
| *powers* | Science and Technology Act 1965 |
| *mission* | To promote and support high-quality basic, strategic and applied research and related postgraduate training in social sciences. To advance knowledge and provide trained social scientists. To disseminate knowledge and promote public understanding of social sciences. |
| *tasks* | Awarding funds to research centres, programmes and grants. Providing high-quality research on issues of importance to business, the public sector and government. Issues include key social and economic concerns, the effectiveness of public services and policy, and our quality of life. |
| *operations* | Management: Chief Executive and staff are based in Swindon. The Research Priorities Board develops the themes and implements the strategy for the research centres and programmes and is made up primarily of academics but also includes those from business, government and independent institutions.<br><br>Policy: To continue to strengthen its work with the users of the research, through consultation on new developments, involvement in Council's panels, and collaborative ventures with business and industry.<br><br>Trends: Balancing research into wealth creation and research into the quality of life. Greater openness in decision-making. |
| *performance* | New and stronger links have been developed with users. |
| *board* | Council members appointed by President of the Board of Trade from academia, business and the civil service. |

| Chairman | Dr Bruce Smith OBE |
|---|---|
| Chief Executive | Prof Ronald Amann |
| Members | Dr Dorothy Bishop |
| | Prof Robert Burgess |
| | Michael Hughes |
| | Mrs Elizabeth Mills |
| | Ms F Price |
| | Prof David Rhind |
| | Sir James Sharples |
| *Accounting Officer* | *Chief Executive* |

*staff*     94

| | |
|---|---|
| Chairman | Dr Bruce Smith OBE |
| Chief Executive | Prof Ronald Amann |
| Deputy Chief Executive & Director of Resources | Dr Glyn Davies |
| Deputy Director of Research | Adrian Alsop |
| Director of Research | Chris Caswill |
| Head of Computing & Office Services | Andy Gibbs |
| Head of Management, Psychology, Linguistics & Education Research Support | Ms Ros Goldstraw |
| Head of Finance | Brian Hooper |
| Head of Sociology, History, Anthropology & Resources Research Support Team | Martin Kender |
| Head of Policy and Evaluation | Peter Linthwaite |
| Head of Politics, Economics & Geography Research Support Team | Mrs Christine McCulloch |
| Head of Postgraduate Training | Phil Sooben |
| Director of External Relations | Tim Whitaker |

*financial*

| INCOME & EXPENDITURE Year end: 31 March | 1997 £000 | 1996 £000 |
|---|---|---|
| **INCOME** | | |
| Grant-in-aid | 63,615 | 61,334 |
| Other receipts | 1,437 | 1,323 |
| | **65,052** | **62,657** |
| **EXPENDITURE** | | |
| **Research** | | |
| Programmes | 12,407 | 11,516 |
| Centres | 10,187 | 9,889 |
| Grants | 15,013 | 13,519 |
| Resources | 4,527 | 4,976 |
| Central research | 250 | 215 |
| International | 200 | 173 |
| Technology Foresight | 206 | - |
| **Other** | | |
| Postgraduate training | 17,789 | 18,316 |
| Policy and evaluation | 88 | 76 |
| External relations | 526 | 501 |
| Administration | | |
| Running costs | 3,388 | 3,834 |
| Superannuation | 251 | 239 |
| Lease costs | 363 | 556 |
| | **65,195** | **63,810** |
| **OPERATING DEFICIT** | **(143)** | **(1,153)** |
| Loss on disposal of fixed assets | 0 | (5) |
| Interest receivable | 1 | 1 |
| Transfer from revaluation reserve | 8 | 9 |
| Reversal of notional cost of capital | 167 | 200 |
| **SURPLUS/(DEFICIT) FOR THE YEAR** | **33** | **(948)** |

*advisers* **Auditors** National Audit Office 157-197 Buckingham Palace Road London SW1W 9SP

# *Education Assets Board (EAB)*

Capitol House
Bond Court
Leeds LS1 5SS

**Tel** 0113 234 8888
**Fax** 0113 246 0569

*status* Executive body

*founded* 1988

*sponsor* Department for Education and Employment (DfEE)

*powers* Education Reform Act 1988, Further and Higher Education Act 1992, Education Act 1996

*mission* Responsible for the transfer of property, rights and liabilities from local authorities to higher and further education institutions and to governing bodies of grant-maintained schools in England and Wales.

*tasks* Organises property transfer agreements; gives directions determining disagreements between institutions and local authorities (appeals are made to the Secretary of State).

*operations* Management: Chief Executive is responsible for day-to-day management and reports to the Board.

Policy: To complete property transfers efficiently, effectively and economically.

Trends: Decline in new cases in recent years. Reducing staff as workload decreases (284 outstanding cases at March 1997). The School Standards and Framework Bill will change the Board's name to Education Transfer Council.

*performance* Exceeded target number of cases to be completed in 1996/97.

*board* Board appointed by the Secretary of State.

|  |  |
|---|---|
| Chairman | KJ Bridge CBE |
| Chief Executive | HS Hoare |
| Members | BC Arthur CBE |
|  | Ms K Buckley |
|  | HE Couch |
|  | JM Edwards CBE QC |
|  | Miss A Lees OBE |
|  | M Lodge |
|  | Mrs MG Ryding |
|  | Miss JM Schofield |
|  | AN Solomons |
| *Accounting Officer* | *Chief Executive* |

**staff** 10

| Chief Executive | HS Hoare |
|---|---|

**financial**

| RECEIPTS & PAYMENTS Year end: 31 March | 1997 £000 | 1996 £000 | 1995 £000 |
|---|---|---|---|
| **RECEIPTS** |  |  |  |
| HMG grants received | 693 | 826 | 858 |
| **PAYMENTS** |  |  |  |
| Remuneration, fees & salaries | 473 | 533 | 561 |
| **Other operating payments** |  |  |  |
| Travelling & subsistence | 16 | 24 | 33 |
| Accommodation | 115 | 121 | 76 |
| Office expenses | 32 | 39 | 40 |
| Payments to consultants & fees | 36 | 84 | 76 |
| Audit fees | 12 | 13 | 13 |
|  | 211 | 281 | 238 |
|  | 684 | 814 | 799 |
| **SURPLUS/ (DEFICIT) FROM OPERATIONS** | 9 | 12 | 59 |
| Less non-recurring capital costs | 0 | 10 | 69 |
| **SURPLUS/ (DEFICIT) FOR THE FINANCIAL YEAR** | 9 | 2 | (10) |
| Appropriations | 0 | 0 | 0 |
| **EXCESS/ (SHORTFALL) OF RECEIPTS OVER PAYMENTS** | 9 | 2 | (10) |

**advisers**

**Bankers**      HM Paymaster General

**Auditors**      Comptroller and Auditor General

**publications**   *Statement of Accounts*


# Employment Service

Caxton House
Tothill Street
London 9NA

**Tel** 0171 273 6060
**Fax** 0171 273 6098

**E-mail** ert.es.svh@gtnet.gov.uk
**Web** http://www.ert.es.svh@gtnet.gov.uk

**Contact** Paul Carter

**status**    Executive agency

**founded**    1990

**sponsor**    Department for Education and Employment (DfEE)

**powers**    Framework Document 1990

**mission**    To promote a competitive, efficient and flexible labour market by helping unemployed people into work, while ensuring they understand and fulfil the conditions for receipt of Jobseeker's Allowance.

**tasks**    To offer initiatives to help jobseekers back to work eg display job vacancies, arrange interviews, provide advice and guidance, provide training programmes (through Training and Enterprise Councils/Local Enterprise Companies); advise jobseekers of the labour market conditions for receipt of Jobseeker's Allowance and administer claims; help and advise people with disabilities; pay benefit promptly and accura**Tel**y.

**operations**  Management: Led by Chief Executive who is responsible to the Secretary of State for Education and Employment. Employment Service Board consists of Chief Executive and four Directors of Jobcentre Services, Policy & Process Design, Human Resources and Finance. Agency's main services delivered through a network of more than 1,000 Jobcentres. Agency's resources determined annualy as part of Public Expenditure Survey (PES) settlement for the Department for Education & Employment.

Policy: Agency central to Government's overall Welfare to Work programme. Initiatives include New Deal for young unemployed.

Trends: Number of registered unemployed people seeking work decreasing.

**performance**  Four out of 12 targets were achieved in 1996/97.

**board**  The Members of the ES Board are made up of directors who are appointed through their successful application for the advertised posts. The posts are advertised within the Department for Education and Employment.

| | |
|---|---|
| Chief Executive | Leigh Lewis |
| Senior Director of Operations | John Turner |
| Director Finance and Planning | P eter Collis |
| Director Policy and Process Design | Richard Foster |
| Director Human Resources | Kevin White |
| *Accounting Officer* | *DfEE Permanent Secretary and Chief Executive* |

**staff**  33,867

**financial**

| INCOME & EXPENDITURE | | | |
|---|---|---|---|
| Year end: 31 March | 1997 | 1996 | 1995 |
| | £000 | £000 | £000 |
| **EXPENDITURE** | | | |
| Running costs | | | |
| Staff costs | 606,530 | 643,513 | 704,307 |
| General administrative expenditure | 135,073 | 167,400 | 180,804 |
| Accommodation costs | 218,105 | 198,541 | 206,187 |
| | **959,708** | **1,009,454** | **1,091,298** |
| Other costs | | | |
| Depreciation | 25,741 | 22,621 | 15,414 |
| Notional interest | 6,018 | 5,031 | 3,469 |
| Other | 24,346 | 15,113 | 10,754 |
| | **56,105** | **42,765** | **29,637** |
| Programme costs | 271,373 | 351,508 | 373,768 |
| | **1,287,186** | **1,403,727** | **1,494,703** |
| **INCOME** | **(18,884)** | **(584,067)** | **(798,001)** |
| **NET OPERATING COST** | **1,268,302** | **819,660** | **696,702** |

**publications**  *Annual Report and Accounts 1996-1997, The Framework Document, The Annual Performance Agreement, Operational Plan 1998-1999, This is The Employment Service, The Way Ahead.*

**branches**  National network of more than 1,000 Jobcentres supported by 135 District Offices and 9 Regional Offices.

# *Employment Tribunals Service (ETS)*

19-29 Woburn Place
London WC1H 0LU

**Tel** 0171 273 8517
**Fax** 0171 273 8670

**status**  Executive agency

**founded**  1997

**sponsor**  Department of Trade and Industry (DTI)

**powers**  Framework Document 1996

**mission**  Administrative support to enable applications to industrial tribunals throughout Great Britain to be resolved and appeals to the Employment Appeals Tribunal (EAT) to be determined.

**tasks**    Dealing with all paperwork and correspondence; making practical arrangements for hearings including supporting the judiciary in its responsibility for listing cases; supporting the tribunals during hearings; supplying information on procedures to the public; maintaining the national decisions archive and the public register of applications.

**operations**    Management: Formed from three separate organisations within the DTI Industrial Relations Directorate (the Industrial Tribunals Service in England and Wales, the Service in Scotland and the Employment Appeals Tribunal). The Secretary of State determines the agency's policy framework, sets key financial and performance targets and approves the corporate plan. She is not involved in day-to-day management, which is the responsibility of the Chief Executive, whom she appoints. The industrial tribunals are independent judicial bodies which mainly determine disputes relating to individual employment rights established in British and EU law. The Employment Appeal Tribunal (EAT) is a Superior Court of Record and sits in London and Edinburgh. The Steering Board, which includes external members, advises the Secretary of State on the corporate plan, targets and performance. Internally, the agency is organised into five directorates: Operations; Personnel; Estates; IT; and Finance and Planning.

Policy: Training agency staff to meet business objectives.

Trends: Underlying tribunal and EAT workloads continued to rise in 1996/97.

**performance**    No published targets for 1996/97.

**board**    Agency Steering Board appointed by the Secretary of State.

| Chairman | Brian Hilton CB | |
|---|---|---|
| Chief Executive | Ian Jones | |
| Members | Paula Carter | Leif Mills |
| | Mikie Jackson | Hugh Savill |
| | Helen Leiser | Tony Young |
| *Accounting Officer* | *Chief Executive* | |

**staff**    620

**financial**

| EXPENDITURE | |
|---|---|
| Year end: 31 March | **1997** |
| | **£000** |
| **PAT COSTS** | |
| Salaries | 15,350 |
| Superannuation | 1,687 |
| Overtime | 305 |
| | **17,342** |
| **ACCOMMODATION** | |
| Accommodation charges | 4,746 |
| Fuel and utilities | 143 |
| Other accommodation costs | 474 |
| | **5,363** |
| **GAE** | |
| Computers | 256 |
| Conferences | 42 |
| Consultancy | 19 |
| Office machinery | 182 |
| Publications | 377 |
| Publicity | 16 |
| Stationery | 497 |
| Travel and subsistence | 2,240 |
| Agency staff costs | 126 |
| Postage | 382 |
| Security services | 113 |
| Telecoms | 202 |
| Fees | 8,699 |
| Other | 959 |
| | **14,110** |
| **HARD CHARGES** | **154** |
| **TOTAL GROSS RUNNING COSTS** | **36,968** |
| **RECEIPTS FROM FEES AND CHARGES** | **130** |

**advisers**

| **Auditors** | National Audit Office | 157-197 Buckingham Palace Road London SW1W 9SP |
|---|---|---|
| **Solicitors** | DTI | |
| **Public Relations** | DTI Press Office | |

**publications**    *Corporate Plan, Annual Report and Accounts, Citizen's Charter Statements of Standards*

**branches**

*Industrial Tribunal Offices*
19-29 Woburn Place
London WC1H 0LU
Tel 0171 273 8517
Fax 0171 273 8670

Tufton House
Tufton Street
Kent
Ashford TN33 1RJ
Tel 01233 621 346
Fax 01233 624 423

8/10 Howard Street
Bedford MK40 2HS
Tel 01234 351306
Fax 01234 353315

100 Southgate Street
Bury St Edmunds
Suffolk IP33 2AQ
Tel 01284 762171
Fax 01284 706064

Phoenix House
1/3 Newhall Street
Birmingham B3 3NH
Tel 0121 2366051
Fax 0121 2366029

The Crescent Centre
Temple Back
Bristol BS1 6EZ
Tel 0117 929 8261
Fax 0117 925 3452

Caradog House
1/6 St Andrews Place
Cardiff CF1 3BE
Tel 01222 372693
Fax 01222 225906

Renslade House
Bonhay Road
Exeter EX4 3BX
Tel 01392 279 665
Fax 01392 430063

3rd Floor
11 Albion Street
Leeds LS1 5ES
Tel 0113 245 9741
Fax 0113 242 8843

5a New Walk
Leicester LE1 6TE

Montague Court
101 London Road
Croydon CR0 2RF
Tel 0181 667 9131
Fax 0181 649 9470

Cunard Building
Pier Head
Liverpool L3 1TS
Tel 0151 236 9397
Fax 0151 231 1484

Alexandra House
14/22 The Parsonage
Manchester M3 2JA
Tel 0161 833 0581
Fax 0161 832 6249

Quayside House
110 Quayside
Newcastle upon Tyne NE1 3DX
Tel 0191 2328865
Fax 0191 2221880

Byron House
2a Maid Marion Way
Nottingham NG1 6HS
Tel 0115 947 5701
Fax 0115 950 7612

3/31 Friar Street
Reading RG1 1DY
Tel 01734 594 917/9
Fax 01734 568 66

14 East Parade
Sheffield S1 3ET
Tel 0114 276 0348
Fax 0114 276 2551

Prospect House
Belle Vue Road
Shrewsbury SY3 7AR
Tel 01743 358 341
Fax 01743 244 186

Duke's Keep
3rd Floor
Marsh Lane
Southampton SO1 1EX
Tel 01703 639 555
Fax 01703 635 506

44 Broadway
East London
Stratford E15 1HX
Tel 0181 221 0921
Fax 0181 221 0398

Inverlier House
2nd Floor
West North Street
Aberdeen AB24 5ES
Tel 01224 643307
Fax 01224 631 1551

13 Albert Square
Dundee DD1 1DD
Tel 01382 221 578
Fax 01382 227 136

54/56 Melville Street
Edinburgh EH3 7HF
Tel 0131 226 5584
Fax 0131 220 6847

Eagle Building
215 Bothwell Street
Glasgow G2 7TS
Tel 0141 204 0730
Fax 0141 204 0732

*Employment Appeal Tribunals*
Audit House
58 Victoria Embankment
London EC4Y 0DS
Tel 0171 273 1041
Fax 0171 273 1045

52 Melville Street
Edinburgh EH3 7HS
Tel 0131 225 3963
Fax 0131 220 6694

# Engineering Construction Industry Training Board (ECITB)

Blue Court
1 Church Lane
Kings Langley
Hertfordshire WD4 8JP

**Tel** 01923 260000
**Fax** 01923 270969          **Web** http://www.ecitb.org.uk

**Contact** CB Lang, Manager of Strategy & Communications

| | |
|---|---|
| **status** | Executive body |
| **founded** | 1965 |
| **sponsor** | Department for Education and Employment (DfEE) |
| **powers** | Industrial Training Act 1982. The Industrial Training (Engineering Construction Board) Order 1991 |
| **mission** | To help all in-scope companies become more competitive by promoting and encouraging training and development and by supporting their efforts to attract new talent to the engineering construction industry. |
| **tasks** | To identify training and development needs through consultation with the engineering construction industry. To initiate, promote, improve and facilitate training and develop standards for use throughout the industry; to ensure an adequately trained workforce; to establish and enhance national training standards. |
| **operations** | Management: ECITB operates through four committees: Finance & General Purposes; Fellowship Selection and Advisory; Management, Supervisory & Professional Training; Skills Development Training. |
| | Policy: ECITB is funded by a levy on all in-scope establishments. Companies which benefit from the pool of skilled labour contribute to training costs and companies which train are eligible for financial support. |
| | Trends: The special training needs of the engineering construction industry continue - the industry's labour force is highly mobile and there is relatively less opportunity for individual employers to train. ECITB's current remit runs until 2003. |
| **board** | Appointed by Secretary of State from senior members of the engineering and construction industry, trade unions and relevant educational institutions. |

| | |
|---|---|
| Chairman | NNW Dunlop |
| Employer Members | Mike Hockey |
| | John Lee |
| | Peter Miller |
| | Derek Mowforth |
| | David Odling |
| | Hugh Rees |
| | Barbara Rider |
| | Arnold Russel |
| | Kewn Turnbull |
| Employer Association Members | IM Bell |
| | RB Williams |
| Trade Union Members | Jim Egan |
| | Dave Hewitt |
| Client Members | Mike Ashbrook |
| | Tony Probert |
| Education Members | Prof Ron McCaffer |
| | Rae Angus |

**staff** 41

| | |
|---|---|
| Director & Chief Executive | PJ Griffiths |
| Director of Training Operations | NM Bowden |
| Director of Finance & Board Secretary | PJ Johnston |
| Manager, Development Team | R Dodd |
| Area Manager - South | AG Keeling |
| Manager of Strategy & Communications | CB Lang |
| Area Manager - North | J McNeillie |

*financial*

| FINANCIAL ACTIVITIES Year end: 31 December | 1997 £000 | 1996 £000 | 1995 £000 |
|---|---|---|---|
| **INCOMING RESOURCES** | | | |
| Levy receivable | 10,794 | 9,445 | 10,365 |
| Investment income, grant and initiative support and other operating income | 2,509 | 2,833 | 2,709 |
| | **13,303** | **12,278** | **13,074** |
| **OUTGOING RESOURCES** | | | |
| Training grants and initiatives | 12,367 | 11,687 | 11,463 |
| Management and administration | 1,013 | 909 | 841 |
| Redundancy and severance costs | 273 | 34 | 50 |
| Notional cost of capital | 1,219 | 1,217 | - |
| Total resources expended and notional cost of capital | 14,872 | 13,847 | 12,354 |
| **NET (OUTGOING)/INCOMING RESOURCES FOR THE YEAR AFTER NOTIONAL COST OF CAPITAL** | **(1,569)** | **(1,569)** | **720** |
| Notional cost of capital | 1,219 | 1,217 | - |
| Unrealised (losses)/gains on investment assets | 686 | (83) | 415 |
| **NET MOVEMENT IN FUNDS** | **336** | **(435)** | **1,135** |
| Balance brought forward | 15,460 | 15,895 | 14,760 |
| **BALANCE CARRIED FORWARD** | **15,796** | **15,460** | **15,895** |

*advisers*   **Bankers**   Barclays   32 Clarendon Road, Watford WD1 1BZ

**Auditors**   Moores Rowland   Cliffords Inn, Fetter Lane, London EC4 1AS

*publications*   Annual Report

# Engineering & Physical Sciences Research Council (EPSRC)

Polaris House
North Star Avenue
Swindon SN2 1ET

**Tel** 01793 444000
**Fax** 01793 444010

**Web** http://www.epsrc.ac.uk

*status*   Executive body

*founded*   1994

*sponsor*   Department of Trade and Industry (DTI)

*powers*   Science and Technology Act 1965

*mission*   To promote and support high-quality basic, strategic and applied research and related postgraduate training in engineering and the physical sciences. To advance knowledge and technology, and provide trained engineers and scientists. To provide advice, disseminate knowledge and promote public understanding of engineering and physical sciences.

*tasks*   Awarding research grants to individuals, supporting facilities that researchers are able to use, and providing research studentships. Ensuring that its programme of high-quality research and training is of relevance to national needs. Encouraging the broadening of postgraduate skill development.

*operations*   Management: Chief Executive based in London. Separate advisory panels (User Panel, Technical Opportunities Panel, Public Understanding of Science, Engineering and Technology Steering Group, Peer Review Panel Membership) made up of senior industrialists and academics.

Policy: To improve links between universities and small to medium-sized enterprises with new initiative.

Trends: Increased evaluation of EPSRC's research programmes.

*performance*   Substantial savings in administrative costs and good progress made in achieving other objectives.

*board*   Council appointed by Secretary of State from industry, academia and the civil service.

| Chairman | Dr AW Rudge CBE | |
|---|---|---|
| Members | Prof JM Ball | Prof BFG Johnson |
| | Prof AN Broers | Dr A Ledwith CBE |
| | Prof RJ Brook OBE | SC Miller CBE |
| | Prof Sir David Davies CBE | ALC Quigley |
| | Dr WD Evans | Dr DJH Smith |
| | Dr DJ Giachardi | Prof JO Thomas CBE |
| | Prof JS Higgins CBE | Prof DJ Wallace CBE |
| *Accounting Officer* | *Chief Executive* | |

**staff** 299

| Chief Executive | Prof RJ Brook OBE |
|---|---|
| Director Engineering & Science | Dr Tony Hughes |
| Director Finance & Administration | Peter Maxwell |

**financial**

**INCOME & EXPENDITURE**

| Year end: 31 March | 1996 |
|---|---|
| | £000 |
| **INCOME** | |
| Parliamentary grant-in-aid | 368,660 |
| Release of deferred capital grant-in-aid | 870 |
| Other income | 13,858 |
| | **383,388** |
| **EXPENDITURE** | |
| Research grants | 220,119 |
| UK facility costs | 51,129 |
| International subscriptions | 14,324 |
| Decommissioning cost of research facilities | 1,900 |
| Postgraduate awards | 75,864 |
| Staff costs | 9,635 |
| Staff restructuring costs | 1,807 |
| Other operating costs | 11,922 |
| | **(386,700)** |
| **OPERATING DEFICIT** | **(3,312)** |
| Profit on disposal of fixed assets | 3 |
| Transfer from revaluation r eserve | 36 |
| **DEFICIT FOR THE YEAR** | **(3,273)** |

**advisers**  **Auditors**  National Audit Office  157-197 Buckingham Palace Road
London SW1W 9SP

# English Heritage

23 Saville Row
London W1X 1AB

**Tel** 0171 973 3000
**Fax** 0171 973 3001

**status** Executive body

**founded** 1984

**sponsor** Department for Culture, Media and Sport (DCMS)

**powers** National Heritage Act 1983

**mission** Conserving the built environment in England.

**tasks** Management and conservation of over 400 ancient and historic properties in its direct care; awarding conservation grants to assist owners of ancient and historic properties; providing advisory and education services.

**operations** Management: Formerly Historic Buildings and Monuments Commission for England. Chief Executive responsible for day-to-day management and reports to the Chairman. Ten subject advisory committees: Museums and Collections, Ancient Monuments, Cathedrals and Churches, Historic Buildings and Areas, Historic Parks and Gardens, London, Industrial Archaeology, Science and Conservation, Hadrian's Wall, Battlefields.

Policy: Decentralising and going into partnership with others (eg Conservation Area Partnership scheme with local authorities).

Trends: Heritage Lottery Fund providing large contributions.

**board**     Commissioners appointed by the Secretary of State.

| | |
|---|---|
| Chairman | Sir Jocelyn Stevens CVO |
| Commissioners | The Lord Cavendish of Furness |
| | Mrs Bridget Cherry |
| | Andrew Fane |
| | Prof Eric Fernie CBE |
| | Lady Gass |
| | HRH The Duke of Gloucester GCVO |
| | Mrs Candida Lycett Green |
| | Richard MacCormac CBE |
| | Miss Kirsty McLeod |
| | Prof Richard Morris |
| | Julian Seymour |
| | Geoffrey Wilson |
| *Accounting Officer* | *Chief Executive* |

**staff**     1317

| | |
|---|---|
| Chief Executive | Pam Alexander |
| Director, Conservation Department | Oliver Pearcey |
| Director, Major Projects Department | Bob Tranter |
| Acting Director, Historic Properties Department | Jeffrey West |
| Legal Director | Michael Brainsby |
| Human Resources Director | Geoff Le Fevre |
| Finance Director | Tony Sannia |
| Public Affairs Director | Miss Christine Wall OBE |

**financial**

| INCOME & EXPENDITURE | | |
|---|---|---|
| Year end: 31 March | **1997** | **1996** |
| | **£000** | **£000** |
| **INCOME** | | |
| Earned income | 20,484 | 17,530 |
| Other operating income | 3,738 | 126 |
| Income from fixed asset investments | 4 | - |
| Interest receivable | 514 | 454 |
| Government grant-in-aid | 108,919 | 107,671 |
| | **133,659** | **125,781** |
| **EXPENDITURE** | | |
| Conservation | 65,040 | 62,360 |
| Historic properties | 36,374 | 37,085 |
| Promotion, development and research | 20,213 | 18,739 |
| Corporate services | 7,267 | 6,778 |
| Severance costs | 848 | 1,238 |
| Notional cost of capital | 517 | 325 |
| | **130,259** | **126,525** |
| **SURPLUS/(DEFICIT) FOR THE FINANCIAL YEAR** | **3,400** | **(744)** |
| Notional cost of capital | 517 | 325 |
| **ADJUSTED SURPLUS/(DEFICIT) FOR FINANCIAL YEAR** | **3,917** | **(419)** |
| Transfer to the restricted fund | (3,294) | - |
| **INCOME & EXPENDITURE ACCOUNT SURPLUS/(DEFICIT)** | **623** | **(419)** |
| Accumulated deficit at 1 April | (5,266) | (4,847) |
| **ACCUMULATED DEFICIT AT 31 MARCH** | **(4,643)** | **(5,266)** |

**advisers**     **Auditors**          Price Waterhouse

# English National Board for Nursing, Midwifery & Health Visiting (ENB)

Victory House
170 Tottenham Court Road
London W1P 0HA

**Tel** 0171 3916277
**Fax** 0171 383 4031

**E-mail** enblink@easynet.co.uk
**Web** http://www.enb.org.uk

**Contact** The Administrator

| | |
|---|---|
| **status** | Executive body |
| **founded** | 1979 |
| **sponsor** | Department of Health (DOH) |
| **powers** | Nurses, Midwives and Health Visitors Act 1997 |
| **mission** | Quality education for quality care. To facilitate the delivery of high-quality patient care through the development of effective and efficient educational programmes. |
| **tasks** | ENB provides education guidelines for developing flexible programmes to meet local needs. Approves educational institutions that provide relevant teacher education. Works with the purchasers and providers of education and healthcare to ensure development of standards. It also commissions research projects, organises national conferences, runs careers service and issues a wide range of publications. |
| **operations** | Management: Chief Executive and head office based in London and four regional offices (including a London local office). Each local office has a responsibility for a professional specialist focus: London (mental health and learning disability nursing); Bristol (midwifery education and practice); Chester (primary healthcare nursing); York (adult and children's nursing). Local offices work closely with the regional offices of the NHS Executive. |
| | Policy: Developing and advancing nursing, midwifery and health visiting education and practice. Developing high-quality, cost-effective education programmes. |
| | Trends: Increasing availability of professional education. Developing an international strategy. Successful implementation of new government initiatives. |
| **performance** | All six core operational objectives 1996/97 achieved. |
| **board** | Appointed The Secretary of State. |

| | |
|---|---|
| Chairman | Prof R DeWitt |
| Non-Executive Members | Ms Pamela Charlwood |
| | Prof Mel Chevannes |
| | Prof Jacqueline Filkins |
| | Mrs Pat Oakley |
| | Prof Lesley Page |
| | Prof Jeff Thompson CBE |
| Executive Members | Sam Koroma |
| | Mrs Rita Le Var |
| | Tony Smith |
| *Accounting Officer* | *Chief Executive* |

| | |
|---|---|
| **staff** | 133 |

| | |
|---|---|
| Chief Executive | Tony Smith |
| Director of Mental Health & Learning Disability Nursing | Geoff Boume |
| Director of Finance & Administration | Sam Koroma |
| Director, Primary Health Care Nursing | Tom Langlands |
| Director, Educational Policy | Rita Le Var |
| Director of Adult & Children's Nursing | Mrs Jane Marr |
| Director, Human Resources | Mrs P McEvoy-Williams |
| Director, Midwifery Education & Practice | Miss Meryl Thomas |
| Assistant Director, Research & Development | Sonia Crow |
| Assistant Director, Midwifery Supervision & Practice | Glynnis Mayes |
| Assistant Director, Policy Development | Ann Tucker |
| Director, Mental Health & Learning Disability Nursing | Geoff Boume |
| Director, Midwifery Education & Practice | Meryl Thomas |
| Director, Primary Health Care Nursing | Tom Langlands |
| Director, Adult & Children's Nursing | Jane Marr |

*financial*

| INCOME & EXPENDITURE Year end: 31 March | 1997 £000 | 1996 £000 | 1995 £000 |
|---|---|---|---|
| **INCOME** | | | |
| HMG grant | 6,647 | 6,701 | 6,282 |
| Fees | 1,338 | 1,299 | 1,417 |
| Other Income | 742 | 664 | 1,148 |
| | 8,727 | 8,664 | 8,847 |
| **EXPENDITURE** | | | |
| Staff costs | 4,372 | 4,661 | 4,128 |
| Depreciation | 311 | 297 | 250 |
| Other charges | 4,044 | 5,185 | 5,893 |
| | 8,727 | 10,143 | 10,271 |
| OPERATING SURPLUS/(DEFICIT) | 0 | (1,479) | (1,424) |
| Investment income | 94 | 155 | 221 |
| Interest receivable | 9 | 11 | 19 |
| SURPLUS/(DEFICIT) FOR THE YEAR | 103 | (1,313) | (1,184) |
| Retained surplus/(deficit) brought forward | (643) | 670 | 1,854 |
| RETAINED SURPLUS/(DEFICIT) CARRIED FORWARD | (540) | (6430 | 670 |

*advisers*

**Bankers** Lloyds Bank — 32 Oxford Street, London W1A 2LD

**Auditors** District Audit Service — 4th Floor, Millbank Tower, London SW1P 4QP

**Solicitors** Bird & Bird — 90 Fetter Lane, London EC4A 1JP

*publications* 1996/97 Annual Report, ENB Strategic Plan 1997/2001, ENB Factfile

*branches*

Bristol
Goldsmith's House
Broad Plain
Bristol BS2 OJP
Tel 0117 925 9143
Fax 0117 925 1800

York
East Villa
109 Heslington Road
York YO1 5BS
Tel 01904 430505
Fax 01904 430309

Chester
BSP House
Station Road
Chester CH1 3DR
Tel 01244 311393
Fax 01244 321140

# English Nature

Northminster House
Peterborough PE1 1UA

**Tel** 01733 455000
**Fax** 01733 568834

**Web** http://www.english-nature.org.uk

*status* Executive body

*founded* 1991

*sponsor* Department of the Environment, Transport and the Regions (DETR)

*powers* National Parks and Access to the Countryside Act 1949. Countryside Act 1968. Nature Conservancy Council Act 1973. Wildlife and Countryside Act 1981 (amended 1985). Environmental Protection Act 1990

*mission* To sustain and improve the wildlife and natural features of England for everyone.

*tasks* Providing advice and information on nature conservation to government and other organisations; identifying the most important areas for wildlife and natural features as Sites of Special Scientific Interest (SSSIs) and promoting sustainable management of SSSIs; licensing various activities relating to wild animals and plants; establishing and managing Natural Nature Reserves; supporting and conducting research; implementing international conventions and EC Directives on nature conservation; implementing the Biodiversity Action Plan and assisting in the practical application of sustainable development; increasing opportunities for individual action or experience wildlife natural features and offering various types of grants to help others carry out nature conservation.

**operations**  Management: Formerly known as Nature Conservancy Council for England. There are 21 local teams based in 23 offices and 10 national specialist support teams based in Peterborough. Local teams are responsible for working with others to maintain the characteristic wildlife and natural features within a geographical area. Specialist Support Teams assist in delivering nature conservation through provision of specialist services and support - scientific, technical and service-oriented. Most work done through active partnerships, on a national and local scale.

Policy: Boosting marine conservation work through increased grants. Programme of restoration and expansion of lowland heathland, primarily financed by Heritage Lottery Fund. Implementing UK Biodiversity Plan.

Trends: Implementation of measures deriving from EU Directives and global initiatives.

**performance**  English Nature has a wide range of measure and targets at different levels eg wildlife gain (measuring biodiversity and natural features and contextual measures), strategic change and efficiency measures. These are all detailed in English Nature's Work Plan.

**board**  Council Members appointed by the Secretary of State.

| | | |
|---|---|---|
| Chairman | The Earl of Cranbrook | |
| Chairman designate | Baroness Young | |
| Members | Prof JM Anderson | |
| | Ms J Barber | Prof D Norman |
| | Prof DL Hawskworth | Dr DF Shaw MBE |
| | Prof J Kear OBE | MT Thomasin-Foster CBE |
| | Miss J Kelly | SR Tromans |
| | Dr DR Langslow | Prof RCL Wilson |
| | Prof GL Lucas | GN Woolley |
| Chief Executive | Dr Derek Langslow | |
| *Accounting Officer* | *Chief Executive* | |

**staff**  590

| | |
|---|---|
| Directors | Ms Sue Collins |
| | Dr Keith Duff |
| | Eddie Idle |
| | Ms Caroline Wood |
| Corporate Manager | Andy Brown |
| General Managers | Tim Bines |
| | Kevin Charman |
| | Andrew Deadman |
| | Mark Felton |
| | Jenny Heap |
| | Sarah Priest |
| | Deryk Steer |
| Chief Land Agent | Bill Hopkin |
| Team Manager, Human Resource Services Team | Margaret Bull |
| Team Manager, Office Services | Geoff Cooper |
| Team Manager, Information Resources Services Team | John Creedy |
| Team Manager, Private Office | Richard Findon |
| Team Manager, National Partnerships Team | Michael Ford |
| Team Manager, Publicity & Grants Team | Sharon Gunn |
| Team Manager, Conservation Services Team | Wyn Jones |
| Team Manager, Finance Services Team | Keith Little |
| Team Manager, Environmental Impacts Team | Colin Prosser |
| Team Manager, Maritime Team | Geoff Radley |
| Team Manager, Information Systems Team | Alan Williams |
| Team Manager, Uplands Team | Will Williams |
| Team Manager, Lowlands Team | Richard Wright |

**financial**

**INCOME & EXPENDITURE**

| Year end: 31 March | 1997 £000 | 1996 £000 |
|---|---|---|
| **INCOME** | | |
| Grant-in-aid received | 35,076 | 36,017 |
| Ring-fenced grant aid to the JNCC | 2,339 | 2,487 |
| Other government grants | 85 | 40 |
| Income from activities | 867 | 765 |
| Transfer from reserves and provisions | 1,659 | 2,471 |
| Other operating income | 396 | 295 |
| | **40,422** | **42,075** |

| EXPENDITURE | | |
|---|---:|---:|
| Maintenance of Natural Nature Reserves | 1,643 | 2,132 |
| Management agreements | 7,052 | 8,084 |
| Conservation support | 3,195 | 2,521 |
| Information and publicity | 1,000 | 996 |
| Grants | 2,248 | 2,718 |
| Staff costs | 15,910 | 15,478 |
| Other operating costs | 6,716 | 6,732 |
| Depreciation | 1,165 | 1,056 |
| Annual contribution to the JNCC | 2,385 | 2,507 |
| Permanent diminution of fixed assets | 207 | 1,012 |
| Notional costs | 1,150 | 1,311 |
| | **42,671** | **44,547** |
| **(DEFICIT) BEFORE SUPERANNUATION** | **(2,249)** | **(2,472)** |
| Supperannuation receipts | 362 | 310 |
| **(DEFICIT) ON OPERATING ACTIVITIES** | **(1,887)** | **(2,162)** |
| Profit/(loss) on the sale fixed assets | 8 | (105) |
| Interest receivable | 160 | 167 |
| Notional costs of capital | (445) | (432) |
| **(DEFICIT) ON ORDINARY ACTIVITIES** | **(2,164)** | **(2,532)** |
| Add back notional costs | 1,580 | 1,703 |
| Amount surrended to the Department of the Environment | (51) | - |
| Transfer to revaluation reserve | (51) | - |
| **RETAINED (DEFICIT) FOR THE FINANCIAL YEAR** | **(686)** | **(829)** |

***advisers***   **Auditors**        National Audit Office            157-197 Buckingham Palace Road
London SW1W 9SP

***publications***   *Annual Report, Progress, Facts and Figures, Welcome to English Nature, English Nature Magazine*

***branches***

*Northumbria*
Archbold House
Archbold Terrace
Newcastle upon Tyne NE2 1EG
Tel 0191 281 6316
Fax 0191 281 6305

*North West*
Pier House
Wallgate
Wigan
Lancashire WN3 4AL
Tel 01942 820342
Fax 01942 820364

*Leyburn Office*
Thornborough Hall
Leyburn
North Yorkshire DL8 5ST
Tel 01969 623447
Fax 01969 624190

*East Midlands*
The Maltings
Wharf Road
Grantham
Lincolnshire NG31 6BH
Tel 01476 568431
Fax 01476 570927

*West Midlands*
Attingham Park
Shrewsbury
Shropshire SY4 4TW
Tel 01743 709611
Fax 01743 709303

*Three Counties*
Bronsil House
Eastnor
near Ledbury
Herefordshire HR8 1EP
Tel 01531 638500
Fax 01531 638501

*Cumbria*
Juniper House
Murley Moss
Oxenholme Road
Kendal
Cumbria LA9 7RL
Tel 01539 792800
Fax 01593 792830

*North & East Yorkshire*
Genisis Building 1
Science Park
University Road
Heslington
York YO1 5DQ
Tel 01904 435500
Fax 01904 435501

*Humber to Pennines*
Bull Ring House
Northgate
Wakefield
West Yorkshire WF1 1HD
Tel 01924 387010
Fax 01924 201507

*Peak District & Derbyshire*
Manor Barn
Over Haddon
Bakewell
Derbyshire DE45 1JE
Tel 01629 815095
Fax 01629 815091

*Banbury Office*
10/11 Butchers Row
Banbury
Oxfordshire OX16 8JH
Tel 01295 257601
Fax 01295 275180

Norfolk
60 Bracondale
Norwich
Norfolk NR1 2BE
Tel 01603 620558
Fax 01603 762552

Suffolk Team
Norman Town House
1-2 Crown Street
Bury St Edmunds
Suffolk IP33 1QX
Tel 01284 762218
Fax 01284 764318

London Office
26/27 Boswell Street
London WC1N 3JZ
Tel 0171 8316922
Fax 0171 4043369

Sussex & Surrey
Howard House
31 High Street
Lewes
East Sussex BN7 2LU
Tel 01273 476595
Fax 01273 483063

Hampshire & Isle of Wight
1 Southampton Road
Lyndhurst
Hampshire SO43 7BU
Tel 01703 283944
Fax 01703 283834

Dorset
Slepe Farm
Arne
Wareham
Dorset BH20 5BN
Tel 01929 556688
Fax 01929 554752

Devon, Cornwall & Isles of Scilly
The Old Mill House
37 North Street
Okehampton
Devon EX20 1AR
Tel 01837 55045
Fax 01837 55046

Cornwall
Trevint House
Strangways Villas
Truro
Cornwall TR1 2PA
Tel 01872 262550
Fax 01872 262551

Bedfordshire, Cambridgeshire &
Northamptonshire
Ham Lane House
Ham Lane
Nene Park
Orton Waterville
Peterborough
Cambridgeshire PE2 5UR
Tel 01733 391100
Fax 01733 39409

Essex, Hertfordshire & London Team
Harbour House
Hythe Quay
Norman Tower House
Essex CO2 8JF
Tel 01206 796666
Fax 01206 794466

Kent
Coldharbour Farm
Wye
Ashford
Kent TN25 5DB
Tel 01233 812525
Fax 01233 812520

Thames & Chilterns
Foxhold House
Thornford Road
Crookham Common
Thatcham
Berkshire RG19 8EL
Tel 01635 268881
Fax 01635 268940

Wiltshire
Prince Maurice Court
Hambleton Avenue
Devizes
Wiltshire SN10 2RT
Tel 01380 726344
Fax 01380 721411

Somerset
Roughmoor
Bishop's Hull
Taunton
Somerset TA1 5AA
Tel 01823 283211
Fax 01823 272978

# English Partnerships

16-18 Old Queen Street
London SW1H 9HP
**Tel** 0171 976 7070
**Fax** 071 9767740

| | |
|---|---|
| *status* | Executive body |
| *founded* | 1993 |
| *sponsor* | Department of the Environment, Transport and the Regions (DETR) |
| *powers* | Leasehold Reform, Housing and Urban Development Act 1993 |
| *mission* | The regeneration of derelict, vacant and under-used land and buildings throughout England, in partnership with public, private and voluntary sector organisations, and so to transform areas of need into quality places for people to live and work. |
| *tasks* | To deliver regeneration, economic development, job creation and environmental improvement and to obtain best value for money to the taxpayer and to maximise private sector investment. Its programmes address the need for land for a variety of purposes including housing, industrial and commercial premises, the attraction of inward investment, infrastructure, leisure, recreation and environmental improvements. |
| *operations* | Management: The Chairman and Board Members have overall responsibility for all aspects of the business. There is a network of regional offices. |
| | Policy: It recognises that one of the key factors in achieving sustainable regeneration is a long-term commitment to areas of need - decades of economic and social decline cannot normally be reversed in a three to five year time span. A large proportion of the agency's investment fund is concentrated on 20 long-term regeneration projects, investing in concentrated geographic areas that have potential to benefit large urban populations. Each region has its own long-term strategy. |
| | Trends: The development programme is set to grow rapidly over the next three to five years and is fully committed for the next two. There are 2700 projects in hand across the whole country. Since 1994/95, private finance has doubled while government finance has only grown by 6% (excluding Greenwich Peninsula). |
| *board* | Appointed by the Secretary of State and includes local authority, trades union and private sector representatives. |

| | | |
|---|---|---|
| Chairman | Lord Walker of Worcester MBE | |
| Deputy Chairman | Sir Idris Pearce CBE | |
| Members | Michael Carr | Bill Jordan CBE |
| | Anthony Dunnett | Stephen Massey |
| | Paula Hay-Plumb | Dennis Stevenson CBE |
| *Accounting Officer* | *Chief Executive* | |

| | |
|---|---|
| *staff* | 445 |

| | |
|---|---|
| Chief Executive | Anthony Dunnett |
| Managing Director (Operations) | Paula Hay-Plumb |

*financial*

**GROUP INCOME & EXPENDITURE**

| Year end: 31 March | 1997 | 1996 |
|---|---|---|
| | £000 | £000 |
| **INCOME** | | |
| Grant-in-aid released | 164,048 | 183,146 |
| Clawback of grants and contributions | 10,631 | 21,107 |
| European Regional Development Fund | 512 | - |
| Proceeds on disposal of investment assets | 7,837 | 10,080 |
| Proceeds on disposal of development assets | 4,792 | 640 |
| Proceeds on disposal of other assets | 30 | 32 |
| Rents and maintenance charges receivable | 33,984 | 29,907 |
| Contributions from partners | 1,711 | - |
| Other operating income | 3,064 | 2,203 |
| Capital reserve fund released | - | 3,152 |
| | **226,609** | **250,267** |

| EXPENDITURE | | |
|---|---:|---:|
| Staff costs | 11,973 | 10,029 |
| Other administrative costs | 3,358 | 3,245 |
| Promotion and publicity costs | 2,965 | 2,347 |
| Estate management costs | 6,802 | 4,955 |
| Partnership Initiatives | 157,188 | 170,419 |
| Clawback of grant returnable to the Treasury | 6,384 | 19,418 |
| Contribution to the Groundwork Trust | - | 1,000 |
| Feasibility studies | - | 308 |
| Depreciation on tangible fixed assets | 1,071 | 855 |
| Other operating costs | 6,570 | 8,473 |
| Amounts written off investment assets | (4,145) | 6,119 |
| Amounts written off development assets | 26,477 | 16,012 |
| Book value of investment properties sold | 5,425 | 7,696 |
| Book value of development assets sold | 1,566 | 640 |
| Book value of other assets sold | - | 28 |
| Payments to joint investors | 113 | 120 |
| Debts written off/provision for bad debts | 560 | 282 |
| Transfer to capital reserve fund | 31 | - |
| Notional cost of capital | 26,126 | 21,985 |
| | **252,464** | **273,931** |
| **OPERATING DEFICIT** | **(25,855)** | **(23,664)** |
| Share of losses of associated undertakings | (211) | (16) |
| Share of loss of subsidiary undertaking | (122) | (73) |
| Interest receivable | 2,263 | 1,917 |
| Interest payable | - | (3) |
| **DEFICIT BEFORE TAXATION** | **(23,925)** | **(21,839)** |
| Taxation | (2,201) | (146) |
| **DEFICIT AFTER TAXATION** | **(26,126)** | **(21,985)** |
| Notional cost of capital | 26,126 | 21,985 |
| **RETAINED SURPLUS AFTER TAXATION** | **-** | **-** |

*advisers*

**Auditors**    Kidsons Impey

*branches*

***Other Corporate Office***
3 The Parks
Lodge Lane
Newton-le-Willows
Merseyside WA12 0JQ
Tel  01942 296900
Fax  01942 296927

***Regional Offices***
*North East*
St George's House
Kingsway
Team Valley
Gateshead
Tyne & Wear NE11 0NA
Tel  0191 487 8941
Fax  0191 487 5690

*Yorkshire & Humberside*
Hall Cross House
1 South Parade
Doncaster
South Yorkshire DN1 2DY
Tel  01302 366865
Fax  01302 366880

*Midlands*
Osiers Office Park
Braunstone
Leicester LE3 2DX
Tel  0116 282 8400
Fax 0116 282 8440

*North West*
Lancaster House
Mercury Court
Tithebarn Street
Liverpool L2 2QP
Tel  0151 236 3663
Fax  0151 236 3731

*South East*
58-60 St Katharine's Way
London E1 9LB
Tel 0116 680 2000
Fax  0171 680 2040

*South West*
North Quay House
Sutton Harbour
Plymouth PL4 0RA
Tel  01752 251071
Fax  01752 234840

# *English Sports Council (ESC)*

16 Upper Woburn Place
London WC1H 0QP

**Tel** 0171 273 1500
**Fax** 0171 383 5740

| | |
|---|---|
| *status* | Executive body |
| *founded* | 1997 |
| *sponsor* | Department for Culture, Media and Sport (DCMS) |
| *powers* | Royal Charter |
| *mission* | In England, to see more people involved in sport; more places to play sport; higher standards of performance in sport leading to more medals. |
| *tasks* | To lead the development of sport in England by influencing and serving the public, private and commercial sectors. ESC works closely with a network of contacts and partners - including governing bodies of sport, local authorities, national and regional organisations concerned with sport education and the environment and business. ESC is a National Lottery distributing board. |
| *operations* | Management: In January 1997 the ESC took over operational responsibility for the work in England of the defunct GB Sports Council. The Chief Executive reports to the Secretary of State. ESC headquarters are in London and there are ten regional offices. 100 members of ESC staff work on distributing the Lottery Sports Fund. There are advisory panels covering the Lottery, local authorities, women and sport, disability, racial equality and grants. |
| | Trends: Lottery Sports Fund critical - £275 million lottery fund expected to be distributed 1997/98 (£33.75 million government grant). |
| *board* | Council Members appointed by the Secretary of State. |

| | | |
|---|---|---|
| Chairman | Sir Rodney M Walker | |
| Vice-Chairmen | Trevor Brooking MBE | |
| | Gerald Dennis | |
| Members | Mrs Phyllis Avery | |
| | Peter Blake OBE | Jim Munn MBE |
| | Chris Boardman MBE | Keith Oates |
| | Ms Julia Bracewell | David Oxley OBE |
| | Garth Crooks | Jeff Probyn |
| | Cllr Carol Gustafson | Samuel Stoker |
| | Tim Marshall MBE | Geoff Thompson MBE |
| Observer | Malcolm Denton | |
| *Accounting Officer* | *Chief Executive* | |

| | |
|---|---|
| *staff* | 400 |

| | |
|---|---|
| Chief Executive | Derek Casey |
| Director of National Lottery | David Carpenter |
| Director of Corporate Services | Terry Price |
| Director of Development | Dr Anita White |
| Head of Secretariat | Richard Bocock |
| Head of External Affairs | Jonathan O'Neil |
| Regional Director, South West | Paul Chambers |
| Regional Director, South | David Dolman |
| Regional Director, North | Dacre Dunlop |
| Regional Director, East Midlands | Tim Garfield |
| Regional Director, Yorkshire | Dave Heddon |
| Regional Director, East | Jeff Neslen |
| Regional Director, North West | Sheldon Phillips |
| Regional Director, West Midlands | John Roberts |
| Regional Director, Greater London | Andy Sutch |

| | |
|---|---|
| *branches* | *Eastern Region* |

*Eastern Region*
Crescent House
19 The Crescent
Bedford MK40 2QP
Tel 01234 345222
Fax 01234 359046

*East Midlands Region*
Grove House
Bridgford Road
West Bridgford
Nottinghamshire NG2 6AP
Tel 0115 9821887
Fax 0115 9455236

Greater London & South East Regions
Crystal Palace National Sports Centre
Ledrington Road
London SE19 2BQ
Tel 0181 7788600
Fax 0181 6769812

Northern Region
Aykley Heads
Durham DH1 5UU
Tel 0191 3849595
Fax 0191 3845807

North West Region
Astley House
Quay Street
Manchester M3 4AE
Tel 0161 8340338
Fax 0161 8353678

Southern Region
51a Church Street
Reading
Caversham
Berkshire RG4 8AX
Tel 0118 9483311
Fax 0118 9475935

South West Region
Ashlands House
Ashlands
Crewkerne
Somerset TA18 7LQ
Tel 01460 73491
Fax 01460 77263

West Midlands Region
1 Hagley Road
Five Ways
Birmingham B16 8TT
Tel 0121 4563444
Fax 0121 4561583

Yorkshire Region
Coronet House
Queen Street
Leeds LS1 4PW
Tel 0113 2436443
Fax 0113 2422189

# English Tourist Board (ETB)

Thames Tower
Black's Road
London W6 9EL

**Tel** 0181 846 9000
**Fax** 0181 563 0302          **Web** http://www.visitbritain.com

**Contact** Sandie Dawe, Director of Press & PR

*status*      Executive body
*founded*     1969
*sponsor*     Department of Culture, Media and Sport (DCMS)
*powers*      Development of Tourism Act 1969
*mission*     To achieve a prosperous and sustainable tourism industry by counteracting market failure through strategic leadership.
*tasks*       To represent the industry to government, to liaise effectively with the industry through Regional Tourist Boards, and to disseminate strategic research into the domestic holiday market; to identify and communicate strategic changes in consumer demand; to increase competitiveness - training in customer care, service skills; to improve the flow of information between providers and customers - product information, booking, reservations etc; to generate greater trial and repeat purchase eg conversion from overseas to domestic, increased seasonal spread, targeted short breaks activity.
*operations*  Management: A formal funding agreement is made every year between the Secretary of State and the Chairman of the Board. It also summarises the main objectives and targets of the annual business plan. The financial aim is to maximise income generated from the ETB's own activities (including commercial contributions) and thus reduce reliance on government funding. There is a Chief Executive and the ETB management group. Links with the regional boards have been strengthened by the appointment of five members of the ETB management group as regional sponsors, representing the ETB on one or more regional board. The new harmonised accommodation rating and classification schemes announced by the ETB, AA and RAC was implemented in 1997. Commercial partnerships with ABTA and Reeds Exhibitions are being successfully developed.

Policy: ETB has now focused on five key priorities: gaining a better understanding of consumer needs; developing the products that will meet those needs now and in the future; raising quality and value for money to meet customer expectations; reaching consumers in order to bring them better information; working with the industry to harness collective strengths. Following the Agenda 2000 consultation exercise, an action plan for the development of English tourism in the 21st century (ACTION2000) has been developed.

Trends: Holiday making by British people in England has been static for many years as overseas destinations have absorbed the growth in holiday spending.

***board***   Appointed by the Secretary of State for Culture, Media & Sport from a wide range of backgrounds related to the tourism industry.

| | |
|---|---|
| Chairman | David Quarmby |
| Members | Peter Chappelow |
| | John Lee |
| | Peter Moore OBE |
| | Eve Pollard |

***staff***   60

| | |
|---|---|
| Chief Executive | Tim Bartlett |
| Director of ETB Operations | Elaine Noble |
| Director, Press & Public Relations | Sandie Dawe |
| Director, Policy & Legal | Sue Garland |
| Director, Marketing Services | Jonathan Griffin |
| Director, Financial Management & Information | |
| Management Services | Chris Howard |

***financial***

| INCOME & EXPENDITURE Year end: 31 March | 1997 £000 | 1996 £000 | 1995 £000 |
|---|---|---|---|
| **INCOME** | | | |
| HMG grant-in-aid | 10,050 | 10,000 | 11,300 |
| Tourism projects | 695 | 360 | 867 |
| Income from activities | 2,941 | 2,405 | 3,689 |
| Other operating income | 29 | 33 | 58 |
| | 13,715 | 12,798 | 15,914 |
| **EXPENDITURE** | | | |
| Staff costs | 2,066 | 1,810 | 2,610 |
| Other operating charges | 5,349 | 4,866 | 5,010 |
| Regional Tourist Boards | 4,034 | 4,005 | 4,792 |
| Tourism development fund | 1,480 | 1,931 | 2,303 |
| Tourism projects | 695 | 360 | 867 |
| Notional costs | 57 | 52 | - |
| | 13,681 | 13,024 | 15,582 |
| **OPERATING SURPLUS/(DEFICIT) BEFORE TAXATION** | 34 | (226) | 332 |
| Add notional costs | 57 | 52 | - |
| Taxation | (15) | (8) | (15) |
| **SURPLUS/(DEFICIT) FOR THE FINANCIAL YEAR** | 76 | (182) | 317 |
| Retained surplus brought forward | 739 | 921 | 604 |
| **RETAINED SURPLUS CARRIED FORWARD** | 815 | 739 | 921 |

***advisers***

| | | |
|---|---|---|
| **Bankers** | National Westminster Bank | King Street, Hammersmith, London W6 |
| **Auditors** | National Audit Office | 157-197 Buckingham Palace Road London SW1W 9SP |

# Enterprise Ulster

The Close
Ravenhill Reach
Belfast BT6 8RB

**Tel** 01232 736400
**Fax** 01232 736404

**E-mail** eulster@enterpriseulster.co.uk
**Web** http://www.enterpriseulster.co.uk

**Contact** Joe Eagleson, Chief Executive

| | |
|---|---|
| *status* | Executive body |
| *founded* | 1973 |
| *sponsor* | Northern Ireland Office, Department of Economic Development (DEDNI) |
| *powers* | Enterprise Ulster (Northern Ireland) Order 1973 |
| *mission* | To provide training for the unemployed which will expand their work prospects in the spheres to which they are best suited. |
| *tasks* | To provide training for those unemployed longer than three months - principally in the 18-25 age band. Training is provided in its own premises, workshops and sites and outside, eg FE colleges and placements. |
| *operations* | Management: Funded by the Training and Employment Agency which also has general oversight of the corporation, its management and control are vested in the board. Extra funding was obtained from the EU Special Support Programme for Peace and Reconciliation. |
| | Policy: To follow and monitor government equality policy: equality of opportunity and equal treatment of all people in NI irrespective of religion etc; targeting social need, disablement, gender discrimination etc. |
| | Trends: Training and employment activities are limited to the public and voluntary sectors militating against better job placement figures in the expanding private sector. |
| *performance* | Targets generally met except for increase in proportion finding work within three months. |
| *board* | Appointed by the Minister and one member on the nomination of the CBI. |

| | |
|---|---|
| Chairman | J Len O'Hagan OBE |
| Member of Board | Mrs PL Bateson |
| Member of Board | D McAteer |
| Member of Board | Mrs N Whittaker |
| *Nominated by Northern Ireland Committee, Irish Congress of Trade Unions* | |
| Member of Board | Ms P Buchanan |
| Member of Board | E McDaid |
| *Nominated by Confederation of British Industry/Northern Ireland Chamber of Commerce & Industry* | |
| Member of Board | Mrs D Boyd |
| Member of Board | A Broomhead, MBE, JP |
| *Accounting Officer* | *Chief Executive* |

*staff* 150 (plus 1260 trainees)

| | |
|---|---|
| Chief Executive | JH Eagleson |
| Finance Manager | WJ Barbour |
| Operations Manager | HC Martin |
| Human Resource Manager | JW McCall |

*financial*

| INCOME & EXPENDITURE | 1997 | 1996 | 1995 |
|---|---|---|---|
| Year end: 31 March | £ | £ | £ |
| **INCOME** | | | |
| Grant from Training and Employment Agency | 6,472,794 | 6,487,911 | 6,944,955 |
| Project income | 714,693 | 835,255 | 680,430 |
| Sundry income | 42,445 | 47,301 | 66,207 |
| | **7,229,932** | **7,370,467** | **7,691,592** |
| **OPERATING EXPENSES** | | | |
| Projects | 1,473,386 | 1,627,910 | 1,582,506 |
| Training | 4,693,334 | 4,898,656 | 4,845,370 |
| Administration and technical | 1,064,409 | 979,649 | 985,453 |
| Cost of redundancy | 10,186 | 1,974 | 58,411 |
| Pay in lieu of notice | 5,694 | 1,822 | 42,792 |
| Pension buy outs | 7,270 | - | 63,737 |
| | **7,254,279** | **7,510,011** | **7,578,269** |

| (DEFICIT)/ SURPLUS FOR THE YEAR BEFORE NOTIONAL COST OF CAPITAL | **(24,347)** | **(139,544)** | **113,323** |
|---|---|---|---|
| Notional cost of capital | (19,121) | (14,206) | - |
| **(DEFICIT)/ SURPLUS FOR YEAR AFTER NOTIONAL COSTS** | **(43,468)** | **(153,750)** | **113,323** |
| Credit in respect of notional costs | | | |
| -notional administration costs | 27,263 | 24,445 | - |
| -notional cost of capital | 19,121 | 14,206 | - |
| **(DEFICIT)/SURPLUS FOR YEAR BEFORE NOTIONAL COSTS** | **2,916** | **(115,099)** | **113,323** |

| *advisers* | **Bankers** | First Trust | 31-35 High Street, Belfast BT7 1EU |
|---|---|---|---|
| | **Auditors** | Coopers & Lybrand | 108 Great Victoria Street, Belfast BT7 1EU |
| | **Solicitors** | Tugham Company 30 Victoria Street, Belfast | |

*publications*  Annual Report

# Environment Agency

Rio House
Waterside Drive
Aztec West
Almondsbury
Bristol BS12 4UD

**Tel** 01454 624400
**Fax** 01454 624409

| | |
|---|---|
| *status* | Executive body |
| *founded* | 1995 |
| *sponsor* | Department of the Environment, Transport and the Regions (DETR) |
| *powers* | Environment Act 1995 |
| *mission* | To protect and improve the environment in England and Wales by effective regulation, by own actions and by working with and influencing others. |
| *tasks* | To achieve significant and continuous improvement in the quality of air, land and water; to actively encourage the conservation of natural resources, flora and fauna; to maximise the benefits of integrated pollution control and integrated river basin management; provide defence and warning systems against flooding; to achieve significant reductions in waste through minimisation, re-use and recycling and improve standards of disposal; to manage water resources; to improve and develop salmon and freshwater fisheries; to conserve and enhance inland and coastal waters and their use for recreation; to maintain and improve non-marine navigation. |
| *operations* | Management: It is an amalgamation of the National Rivers Authority, Her Majesty's Inspectorate of Pollution, 83 Waste Regulation Authorities and parts of the Department of the Environment. The Board is accountable to Ministers for formulating and delivering the agency's policies. The Chief Executive chairs the Directors Team, which comprises eight Directors who oversee and co-ordinate the development of strategy and formulation of national policies. Head Offices in London and Bristol and eight regional offices. 68% of costs are covered by charges and levies (rest of funding from government grants). |
| | Policy: Local Environment Area Plans (LEAPs) for all of England and Wales to be introduced by 1999. |
| | Trends: European funding of growing importance. Staffing levels likely to be reduced. |
| *board* | Appointed by Secretary of States of Environment, Wales and MAFF. |

| Chairman | Lord De Ramsey | |
|---|---|---|
| Vice Chairman | Sir Richard George | |
| Members | Peter Burnham | |
| | Professor Ron Edwards CBE | Mrs Karen Morgan |
| | Imtiaz Farookhi | John Norris CBE |
| | Ed Gallagher | Derek Osborn CB |
| | Nigel Haigh OBE | Dr Anne Powell |
| | Christopher Hampson CBE | Tony Rodgers |
| | Cllr John Harman | Joan Wykes OBE |

Regional Environment Protection Advisory Committees (REPACs), Regional Fisheries Advisory Committees (RFACs) and Regional Flood Defence Committees (RFDCs)

*Anglian Region*

| | |
|---|---|
| Chairman, REPAC | Mrs Betty Goble |
| Chairman, RFAC | Christopher Penn |
| Chairman, RFDC | John Martin |

*Midlands Region*

| | |
|---|---|
| Chair, REPAC | Mrs Penny Perry |
| Chairman, RFAC | Fred Jennings OBE |
| Chairman, Severn Trent RFDC | J Dainty OBE |

*North East Region*

| | |
|---|---|
| Chairman, REPAC | Ian Bonas |
| Chairman, Yorkshire RFAC | JA Fawcett |
| Chairman, Northumbria RFAC | PL Tennant |
| Chairman, Northumbria RFDC | JP Hackney |
| Chairman, Yorkshire RFDC | TD Collier |

*North West Region*

| | |
|---|---|
| Chairman, REPAC | B Alexander |
| Chairman, RFAC | JR Carr |
| Chairman, RFDC | WM Wannop OBE JP |
| Chairman, REPAC | Dr T Crossett |
| Chairman, RFAC | Dr N Giles |
| Chairman, RFDC | D Monnington |

*South West Region*

| | |
|---|---|
| Chairman, REPAC | D Mitchell CBE |
| Chairman, South West RFAC | Mrs A Voss-Bark MBE |
| Chairman, Wessex RFAC | CR Rothwell |
| Chairman, South West RFDC | GC Manning OBE |
| Chairman, Wessex RFDC | R Willis |

*Thames Region*

| | |
|---|---|
| Chairman, REPAC | J Ferguson OBE |
| Chairman, RFAC | PT McIntosh |
| Chairman, RFDC | Mrs J Venables |
| Vice-Chairman, RFDC | AK Gray |
| Chairman, REPAC | Cllr G Court |
| Chairman, RFAC | WP O'Reilly |
| Chairman, RFDC | J Hughes |

**staff** 9450

| | |
|---|---|
| Chief Executive | Ed Gallagher |
| Director of Personnel | Giles Duncan |
| Director of Water Management | Dr Geoff Mance |
| Director of Legal Services | Ric Navarro |
| Chief Scientist and Director of Environmental Strategy | Dr Jan Pentreath |
| Director of Finance | Nigel Reader |
| Director of Operations | Archie Robertson |
| Director of Pollution Prevention and Control | Dr David Slater CB |
| Director of Corporate Affairs | Miles Wilson |

**financial**

### INCOME & EXPENDITURE
**Year end: 31 March**

| | 1997 £m |
|---|---|
| **INCOME** | |
| Income from activities | 382.4 |
| Government grant-in-aid | 106.4 |
| Capital grants and contributions | 48.6 |
| | **537.4** |
| **EXPENDITURE** | |
| Staff costs | 203.0 |
| Depreciation and expenditure on intangible fixed assets | 183.5 |
| Other operating costs | 194.7 |
| | **581.2** |
| **OPERATING (DEFICIT)/SURPLUS** | **(43.8)** |
| Notional cost of capital | (104.2) |
| Interest receivable | 7.4 |
| **DEFICIT FOR YEAR AFTER NOTIONAL COST OF CAPITAL** | **(140.6)** |
| Reversal of notional cost of capital | 104.2 |
| **(DEFICIT)/SURPLUS BEFORE RESERVE TRANSFERS** | **(36.4)** |
| Capital reserve | 23.3 |
| Special asset replacement fund | 11.3 |
| | (1.8) |
| Balance brought forward | 25.8 |
| **BALANCE CARRIED FORWARD** | **24.0** |

**branches**

Anglian
Kingfisher House
Goldhay Way
Orton Goldhay
Peterborough PE2 5ZR
Tel 01733 371811
Fax 01733 231840

Midlands
Sapphire East
550 Streetsbrook Road
Solihull B91 1QT
Tel 0121 711 2324
Fax 0121 711 5824

North East
Rivers House
21 Park Square South
Leeds LS1 2QG
Tel 0113 244 0191
Fax 0113 246 1889

North West
Richard Fairclough House
Knutsford Road
Warrington WA4 1HG
Tel 01925 653 999
Fax 01925 415 961

Southern
Guildbourne House
Chatsworth Road
Worthing
West Sussex BN11 1LD
Tel 01903 832 000
Fax 01903 821 832

South West
Manley House
Kestrel Way
Exeter EX2 7LQ
Tel 01392 444 000
Fax 01392 444 238

Thames
Kings Meadow House
Kings Meadow Road
Reading RG1 8DQ
Tel 0118 953 5000
Fax 0118 950 0388

Welsh
Rivers House/Plas-yr-Afon
St Mellons
Cardiff CF3 0LT
Tel 01222 770 088
Fax 01222 798 555

# Environment & Heritage Service (EHS)

Commonwealth House
35 Castle Street
Belfast BT1 1GU

**Tel** 01232 251477
**Fax** 01232 546660

**status** Executive agency

**founded** 1996

**sponsor** Northern Ireland Office, Department of the Environment (DOENI)

**mission** To protect and conserve the natural and built environment of Northern Ireland and to promote its appreciation for the benefit of present and future generations.

**tasks** To give high-quality advice within government on all environmental issues. Environmental regulation - preventing air, water and land pollution, protecting historic buildings and monuments and wildlife and natural habitats. Designating and listing - Areas of Special Scientific Interest (ASSIs), Special Protection Areas for Birds (SPAs), Areas of Outstanding Natural Beauty (AONBs), Scheduled Monuments, and Listed Buildings. Partnership development - helping others to conserve the countryside, its wildlife and its heritage and also to provide facilities which help people enjoy the natural and built environment. Conservation and maintenance EHS properties: eight country parks, 45 nature reserves, and 181 historic monuments. Research - by in-house team of habitat surveyors and by contractors. Information and education.

**operations** Management: Four business areas: Natural Heritage, Built Heritage, Environmental Protection and Corporate Affairs.

Policy: Sustainable development: natural resources and built heritage services are being reviewed to take into account biodiversity, climate change, air quality and waste.

Trends: Growing holistic approach to the delivery of EHS services.

**board**

| Chief Executive | Robert C Martin |
|---|---|

*financial*

| PROGRAMME EXPENDITURE BY BUSINESS AREA | |
|---|---|
| Year end: 31 March | **1997** |
| | **£000** |
| **NATURAL HERITAGE** | |
| Conservation science | 754 |
| Conservation designations | 551 |
| Countryside and coast | 1,105 |
| Regional operations | 915 |
| Information and education | 43 |
| | **3,368** |
| **BUILT HERITAGE** | |
| Protecting historic buildings | 2,804 |
| Protecting historic monuments | 1,514 |
| Recording the built heritage | 348 |
| | **4,666** |
| **ENVIRONMENTAL PROTECTION** | |
| Alkali and Radiochemical Inspectorate | 217 |
| Water quality | 3,728 |
| Waste management | 282 |
| Air and environmental quality | 292 |
| Drinking Water Inspectorate | - |
| | **4,519** |
| **CORPORATE AFFAIRS** | |
| IT support | 113 |
| Advisory bodies | 87 |
| Other expenditure | 86 |
| | **286** |
| | **12,839** |
| **INCOME (FEE EARNING ACTIVITIES)** | **557** |
| **TOTAL NET EXPENDITURE** | **12,282** |

# *Equal Opportunities Commission (EOC)*

Overseas House
Quay Street
Manchester M3 3HN

**Tel** 0161 833 9244
**Fax** 0161 835 1657

*status*        Executive body

*founded*      1975

*sponsor*     Department for Education and Employment (DfEE)

*powers*      Sex Discrimination Act 1975. Equal Pay Act 1975

*mission*     To challenge inequalities between women and men in England, Scotland and Wales. More particularly, to work towards the elimination of unlawful sex and marriage discrimination, to promote equality of opportunity between women and men generally and to keep the Sex Discrimination and Equal Pay Acts under review.

*tasks*        To tackle inequality by using: the law to secure compliance and change; communication and promotion to raise awareness and achieve change; research to keep at the leading edge of change.

Legal, promotional and research powers are focused on specific issues, eg equal pay, education, pensions and social security, consumer affairs, employment, part-time work and job segregation.

*operations*  Management: EOC's headquarters are in Manchester with major services also delivered from offices in Glasgow, Cardiff and London. (Northern Ireland has its own Equal Opportunities Commission for Northern Ireland, EOCNI). Its corporate plan (1997-2001) targets equality in employment, the balance between work and family life, gender differences in education and training, structural inequality of income, legal equality in the provision of services etc, support for cases which clarify the law, and building equal opportunities into every part of the activities of government departments and public bodies. The EOC is funded by a grant-in-aid from DfEE.

Policy: EOC sees the development of partnerships as central to making equality a feature of everyday life.

Trends: 1996 saw the first large-scale partnership with the voluntary sector; the National Agenda for Action (with the Women's National Commission and EOCNI); the decision by DfEE to fund Fair Play for a fourth year; the first joint initiative with OFSTED which led to the publication of *The Gender Divide*; and a joint conference with the European Commission on The Economics of Equal Opportunities. The intention is to build on these, focusing on higher education and vocational training, the development of equality exchanges and campaigning on the National Agenda for Action.

**board**  Up to 15 Commissioners appointed by the Secretary of State.

| | | |
|---|---|---|
| Chairwoman | Kamlesh Bahl | |
| Deputy Chairwoman | Elizabeth Hodder | |
| Members | Mary Berg | Teresa Rees |
| | Robert Fleeman | Peter Smith |
| | Anne Gibson | Joan Stringer |
| | Richard Grayson | Elizabeth Symons |
| | Georgina James | Cecilia Wells |

**staff**  167

**financial**

| INCOME & EXPENDITURE Year end: 31 March | 1997 £ | 1996 £ |
|---|---|---|
| **EXPENDITURE** | | |
| Commissioners' salaries | 135,630 | 116,630 |
| Staff salaries | 3,498,583 | 3,467,489 |
| Commissioners' travel expenses | 76,548 | 66,738 |
| Staff travel, training and recruitment | 211,340 | 270,049 |
| Premises, services and equipment | 1,193,525 | 1,852,589 |
| Organisation change | 177,251 | - |
| Audit fee | 10,227 | 9,900 |
| Legal expenses | 317,712 | 338,634 |
| Research and s.54 Grants | 46,686 | 61,744 |
| Communications, information services,etc | 327,376 | 386,289 |
| Equality Exchange | 20,581 | 41,707 |
| European Union projects | 166,547 | 208,807 |
| Fair Play Initiative - Scotland | 37,844 | 8,786 |
| | **6,219,850** | **6,829,362** |
| **INCOME** | | |
| Government grant-in-aid | 5,821,000 | 6,429,533 |
| Equality Exchange | 35,544 | 52,941 |
| European Union projects | 139,250 | 227,380 |
| Fair Play Initiative - Scotland | 10,617 | 44,000 |
| Other income | 150,564 | 126,382 |
| | **6,156,975** | **6,880,236** |
| Opening balance | 249,184 | 198,140 |
| **TOTAL FUNDS AVAILABLE TO COMMISSION** | **6,406,159** | **7,078,546** |
| Total expenditure | 6,219,850 | 6,829,362 |
| **CLOSING BALANCE** | **186,309** | **249,184** |

# Equal Opportunities Commission for Northern Ireland (EOCNI)

22 Great Victoria Street
Belfast BT2 7BA

**Tel** 01232 242752
**Fax** 01232 331047

**status**  Executive body

**founded**  1976

**sponsor**  Northern Ireland Office, Department of Economic Development (DEDNI)

**powers**  Sex Discrimination (NI) Order 1976, Equal Pay Act 1970

**mission**  To work towards the elimination of sex discrimination and to promote equality of opportunity between women and men.

| | |
|---|---|
| **tasks** | To promote equality of opportunity in education and training; to promote the reconciliation of work and family life; to encourage positive action and non-discriminatory employment practices; to promote women's economic independence; to raise awareness of equality issues and the Commission's services; to encourage a strengthening of the legislative framework. |
| **operations** | Management: Chair and Chief Executive responsible for day-to-day management. |
| | Policy: Issued detailed and significant recommendations for changes to legislation in 1997. Continuing to work closely with other agencies. |
| | Trends: Still need for specific positive action and antidiscrimination measures. |
| **board** | Members of the Commission are appointed by the Secretary of State. |

| | | |
|---|---|---|
| Chair & Chief Executive | Joan Smyth | |
| Deputy Chair | Ann Hope | |
| Members | Brenda Callaghan | |
| | Harry Coll OBE | Elizabeth Kearns |
| | Seamus Connolly | Laura Lundy |
| | Judith Eve | Edward Wilson |
| *Accounting Officer* | | *Chief Executive* |

**staff** 31

| | |
|---|---|
| Chief Executive | Joan Smyth |
| Chief Equality Officer | Evelyn Collins |
| Chief Legal Officer (Job Share) | Jennifer Greenfield |
| Chief Investigation Officer | Joan McKiernan |
| Chief Administrative Officer | Sheila Rogers |

**financial**

| RECEIPTS & PAYMENTS<br>Year end: 31 March | 1997<br>£ | 1996<br>£ | 1995<br>£ |
|---|---|---|---|
| **RECEIPTS** | | | |
| Grant received from DEDNI | 1,582,000 | 1,520,000 | 1,485,000 |
| **PAYMENTS** | | | |
| Salaries and members' fees | (749,451) | (733,783) | (721,706) |
| Other operating payments | (763,829) | (769,161) | (738,151) |
| **SURPLUS FROM OPERATIONS** | **68,720** | **17,056** | **25,143** |
| Other payments | (43,397) | (20,172) | (32,658) |
| Other receipts | 13,179 | 5,980 | 7,974 |
| **SURPLUS FOR THE FINANCIAL YEAR** | **38,502** | **2,864** | **459** |
| Appropriations | - | (2,869) | (622) |
| **EXCESS OF RECEIPTS OVER PAYMENTS/(PAYMENTS OVER RECEIPTS) FOR THE FINANCIAL YEAR** | **38,502** | **(5)** | **(163)** |

**publications** Annual Report, Working Towards Equality in the 21st Century: proceedings of the 20th anniversary conference, Thinking About Equality: surveys of attitudes towards equality issues, The Working Lives of Women and Men in N Ireland, Code of Practice on Recruitment and Selection, The Sex Discrimination Legislation: recommendations for change

# Fair Employment Commission for Northern Ireland (FEC)

Andras House
60 Great Victoria Street
Belfast BT2 7BB

**Tel** 01232 240020
**Fax** 01232 331544

| | |
|---|---|
| **status** | Executive body |
| **founded** | 1989 |
| **sponsor** | Northern Ireland Office, Department of Economic Development (DEDNI) |
| **powers** | Fair Employment (Northern Ireland) Act 1989 |

| | |
|---|---|
| ***mission*** | To promote equality of opportunity in NI. To work for the elimination of unlawful discrimination. To promote affirmative action. |
| ***tasks*** | Advice and information generally and for employers, eg on the Fair Employment Code of Practice and promoting affirmative action. Monitoring compliance with the law and registration. Enforcement of the law eg prosecutions. |
| ***operations*** | Management: FEC is organised into five departments: Advice and Information, General Operations, Legal Services, Policy and Planning and Resources. |
| | Policy: To work for proportionate representation of both communities in all employment and the removal of segregation in the labour force. |
| | Trends: Unemployment discrepancy between Protestants and Catholics can only be solved in the context of increasing overall employment which depends on peace and reconciliation. |
| ***board*** | Members of the Commission are appointed by the Secretary of State. |

| Chairman | Robert G Cooper CBE | |
|---|---|---|
| Commissioners | Peter Bloch | Elizabeth Meehan |
| | Ernest McBride | Declan Morgan |
| | Kevin McCabe | Jane O'Dempsey |
| | Jim McCurley | Myrtle Richardson |

***staff*** 89

| Chief Executive | Harry Goodman |
|---|---|
| *Advice & Information* | |
| Director | Keith Brown |
| Manager (Press & Information) | Dennis Godfrey |
| Manager (Advice & Information) | Myran Pollock |
| Manager (Small Business Unit) | Deirdre Vaugh |
| *General Operations* | |
| Director | Mary Bunting |
| Managers, General Operations | Aidan Fitzpatrick |
| | Frank Fleming |
| | Jacqui McKee |
| *Legal Services* | |
| Directors | Anne Balmer |
| | Suzanne Bradley |
| Senior Complaints Officers | Drusilla Hawthorne |
| | Michael McDowell |
| | Eunan McMullan |
| | Margaret Watson |
| *Policy & Planning* | |
| Director | Eileen Lavery |
| Senior Research Officer | John Power |
| *Resources* | |
| Director | Len Murray |
| Manager (Finance, Administration & Management Services) | Terry Craig |
| Manager (Systems Development) | Donal Shiels |

***financial***

| **RECEIPTS & PAYMENTS** | | |
|---|---|---|
| **Year end: 31 March** | **1996** | **1995** |
| | **£** | **£** |
| **RECEIPTS** | | |
| Grants received from DEDNI | 2,957,000 | 2,899,000 |
| **PAYMENTS** | | |
| Salaries and wages | 1,821,560 | 1,740,113 |
| Other operating payments | 1,089,628 | 1,135,695 |
| | 2,911,188 | 2,875,808 |
| **SURPLUS FROM OPERATIONS** | **45,812** | **23,192** |
| Other payments | 45,812 | 23,191 |
| **SURPLUS FOR THE FINANCIAL YEAR** | **-** | **1** |

| ***advisers*** | **Auditors** | Ernst & Young | Belfast |
|---|---|---|---|

# Farming & Rural Conservation Agency (FRCA)

Nobel House
17 Smith Square
London SW1P 3JR

**Tel** 0171 238 5432
**Fax** 0171 238 5588

| | |
|---|---|
| *status* | Executive agency |
| *founded* | 1997 |
| *sponsor* | Ministry of Agriculture, Fisheries and Food (MAFF). Welsh Office |
| *powers* | Framework Document 1997 |
| *mission* | Assisting government on the design, development and implementation of policies on the integration of farming and conservation, environmental protection and the rural economy in England and Wales. |
| *tasks* | Providing professional, scientific and technical services as required by government, particularly in relation to: the rural economy - advice and technical support to MAFF; milk hygiene - FRCA Dairy Hygiene Officers inspect holdings; environmental protection - specialist advice on the prevention of water, air and soil pollution by farms; agri-environment incentive schemes to farmers; wildlife management - advice and control to protect wildlife and act against species causing agricultural damage. |
| *operations* | Management: FRCA took over the residual work of the MAFF Land Use Planning Unit and ADAS after privatisation. It does not compete with the private sector and its customers are MAFF and the Welsh Office. The Minister of Agriculture, Fisheries and Food is responsible for FRCA in England, and the Secretary of State for Wales in Wales. They determine the overall policy and the financial framework. There is an Ownership Board chaired by an official from the sponsoring departments which advises Ministers, monitors performance and supports the Chief Executive who is herself a member. It also advises on unresolved disputes between FRCA and its customers. The Chief Executive is responsible for day-to-day management. |
| *board* | Members of the Ownership Board are appointed jointly by the two Ministers, largely from officials but there are normally two external members. |
| *staff* | 560 |

| Chief Executive | Miss Sarah Nason |
|---|---|
| *Accounting Officer* | *Chief Executive* |

*branches*

Brooklands Avenue
Cambridge CB2 2BL
Tel 01223 462762
Fax 01223 455911

Government Buildings
Otley Road
Lawnswood
Leeds LS16 5QT
Tel 0113 2613333
Fax 0113 2300879

St Agnes Road
Gabalfa
Cardiff CF4 4FR
Tel 01222 586530
Fax 01222 586763

Burghill Road
Westbury-on-Trym
Bristol BS10 6YW
Tel 0117 9591000
Fax 0117 9590463

# *Financial Services Authority (FSA)*

Gravelle House
2-14 Bunhill Row
London EC1Y 8RA

**Tel** 0171 638 1240
**Fax** 0171 382 5900

| | |
|---|---|
| *status* | Executive body |
| *founded* | 1997 |
| *sponsor* | HM Treasury |
| *powers* | Financial Services Act 1986, as to be amended by planned revised legislation |
| *mission* | Aiming to be a world-leading financial regulator, respected for its professionalism and integrity both in the UK and internationally, eg Memorandum of Understanding with the SEC and CFTC of the USA. |
| *tasks* | The FSA is to be given four statutory objectives: working with the Bank of England to sustain confidence in the UK financial sector and markets (as set out in a Memorandum of Understanding between the Bank, the FSA and the Treasury); protecting consumers by ensuring that firms are competent and financially sound, while recognising that consumers must bear some responsibility of their own for their financial decisions; promoting public understanding of the benefits and risks of financial products; monitoring, detecting and preventing financial crime, with other agencies. |

*operations*   Management: FSA involves a merger between nine existing regulatory organisations (SROs): the Building Societies Commission; the Friendly Societies Commission; the Insurance Directorate of the Department of Trade and Industry; the Investment Management Regulatory Organisation (IMRO); the Personal Investment Authority (PIA); the Registry of Friendly Societies; the Securities and Futures Authority (SFA); the former Securities and Investments Board (SIB); and the Supervision and Surveillance Divisions of the Bank of England. The net operating cost of the FSA regulatory system is expected to be £153.9m during 1998/99. This compares with £153.5m in 1997/98. Of this amount £66.8m will be incurred by the FSA itself on its continuing statutory responsibilities and on banking supervision. Transitional costs of restructuring are expected to amount to £13m and these will be recovered once the new legislation has come into operation.

Policy: The fundamental operational characteristic of the FSA is to implement risk-based supervision, with the intensity of regulation related to the risks to consumers, and to the capital base of the business. This is designed to achieve the statutory objectives in a way that is efficient and economic, with the regulatory burden no heavier than is consistent with the likely benefits, and which does not stifle innovation or competition. Competition is regarded as the best guarantee of proper service to consumers.

Trends: Creation of the Financial Services Authority will occur in two stages. It will acquire responsibility for banking supervision following the Bank of England Bill (expected spring 1998). At that point, staff employed by IMRO, the PIA and the SFA will also transfer to the FSA, and then supply services back to the SRO Boards. The second stage will follow the passage of the Regulatory Reform Bill (expected during 1998/99), when responsibility for the regulation of investment business will pass to the FSA, along with the existing responsibilities of the remaining four regulators.

*board*   Members are appointed by the Chancellor of the Exchequer.

| | |
|---|---|
| Chairman | Howard Davies |
| Managing Director & Chief Operating Officer | Richard Farrant |
| Managing Director & Head, Financial Supervision | Michael Foot |
| Managing Director & Head of Authorisation, Enforcement & Consumer Relations | Phillip Thorpe |
| Secretary to the Board | Tim Allen |
| General Counsel to the Board | Michael Blair QC |
| Director, General Policy | Clive Briault |
| Director, Communications & Corporate Affairs | Philip Robinson |
| Director, Pensions Review | Ron Devlin |
| Director, Complex Groups | Oliver Page |
| Director, Insurance & Friendly Societies | Martin Roberts |
| Director, Banking & Building Societies | Carol Sergeant |
| Director, Authorisation | David Kenmir |
| Director, Enforcement | Dan Waters |
| Director, Human Resources | Sandra Jenner |

**SROs**

Building Societies Commission
Victory House
30/34 Kingsway
London WC2 6ES
Tel 0171 663 5000

Registry of Friendly Societies
Victory House
30/34 Kingsway
London WC2 6ES
Tel 0171 663 5000

Friendly Societies Commission
Victory House
30/34 Kingsway
London WC2 6ES
Tel 0171 663 5000

Supervision & Surveillance Division of the Bank of England
Threadneedle Street
London EC2R 8AH
Tel 0171 601 4878

Insurance Directorate of the Department of Trade & Industry
1 Victoria Street
London SW1H 0ET
Tel 0171 215 0200

Investment Management Regulatory Organisation (IMRO)
5th Floor
Lloyds Chambers
1 Portsoken Street
London E1 8BT
Tel 0171 390 5000

Personal Investment Authority (PIA)
1 Canada Square
Canary Wharf
London E14 4AB
Tel 0171 378 9000

Securities & Futures Authority (SFA)
Cottons Centre
Cotton's Lane
London SE1 2QB
Tel 0171 378 9000

# Fire Service College

Moreton-in-Marsh
Gloucestershire GL56 0RH

**Tel** 01608 650 831
**Fax** 01608 651 788

**E-mail** moreton@campus.bt.com

**status**  Executive agency. Trading fund

**founded**  1968. 1992 as executive agency and trading fund

**sponsor**  Home Office

**powers**  Fire Services Act 1947. Framework Document 1992

**mission**  To remain the pre-eminent higher education college for fire-related training and promoting fire safety awareness.

**tasks**  Progressive training for all fire officers in command and leadership skills to prepare them for watch, station, division and brigade leadership. Specialist courses on fire safety and prevention and technical disciplines, eg Airport Fire Service instructors. Finance and management training for fire service personnel. Training for commerce and industry (eg offshore hydrocarbon industry), and for students from overseas fire brigades. Higher education strategic alliances to enhance its own programmes by credit accumulation and to provide specialist contribution to degree courses.

**operations**  Management: The Chief Executive reports to the Secretary of State and is responsible for finance. The Commandant is responsible for College operations. The Executive Board comprises the Chief Executive, the Commandant, the Dean, the Secretary and the Sales and Marketing Director. Management delayered in 1996/97. In 1997 the Home Secretary announced a financial restructuring - a Home Office grant of £13.5 million in 1997/98 used immediaTely to repay the deemed loan element of the originating debt and thus some £1.3 million in annual interest payments, and a separate Home Office grant 1997/98 of £1.3 million, and further annual reducing grants. Rigorous and realistic financial targets were set by the Home Office to prevent College relying on support.

Policy: Steady financial improvement over a five-year period to include full cost recovery from customers, expenditure reduction in both staff and running costs, a review of staff terms and conditions and IT efficiency improvements.

Trends: External factors have been affecting turnover and performance. Since 1994, College unable to reclaim VAT (some £1.2 million pa) on educational services. 1995/96 local government Revenue Support Settlement reduced UK Fire Service course bookings. Financial restructuring (1997/98) should help the College break even under its trading fund status over a five-year period, after which Home Office support will cease. Given Home Office support, the National Audit Office expects the College to continue as a going concern.

**performance**  Financial objectives have never been met. Corporate Plan business volume never achieved.

| board | | |
|---|---|---|
| | Chief Executive | NK Finlayson |
| | Commandant | F David |
| | Dean | Dr R Willis-Lee |
| | College Secretary | JK Burne |
| | Sales & Marketing Manager | PJ Ripley |
| | *Accounting Officer* | *Chief Executive* |

**staff** 251

| | | |
|---|---|---|
| | Chief Executive | NK Finlayson |
| | Commandant | F David |
| | Dean | Dr R Willis-Lee |
| | College Secretary | JK Burne |
| | Sales & Marketing Manager | PJ Ripley |

| financial | | | |
|---|---|---|---|
| | **INCOME & EXPENDITURE** | | |
| | **Year end: 31 March** | **1996** | **1995** |
| | | **£000** | **£000** |
| | **TURNOVER** | 13,324 | 13,968 |
| | **COST OF SALES** | 8,643 | 8,756 |
| | **GROSS PROFIT** | 4,681 | 5,212 |
| | Administrative expenses | 6,210 | 6,069 |
| | | (1,529) | (857) |
| | Other operating income | | |
| | Home Office grant | 2,250 | - |
| | **OPERATING SURPLUS/ (DEFICIT)** | 721 | (857) |
| | Interest receivable and similar income | 33 | 60 |
| | Interest payable and similar charges | (1,755) | (1,751) |
| | **DEFICIT FOR THE FINANCIAL YEAR** | (1,001) | (2,548) |

| advisers | **Auditors** | National Audit Office | 157-197 Buckingham Palace Road |
|---|---|---|---|
| | | | London SW1W 9SP |

# Fisheries Conservancy Board for Northern Ireland (FCB)

1 Mahon Road
Portadown
Co Armagh BT62 3EE

**Tel** 01762 334666
**Fax** 01762 338912

| | |
|---|---|
| **status** | Executive body |
| **founded** | 1966. As an executive body 1983 |
| **sponsor** | Northern Ireland Office, Department of Agriculture NI (DANI) |
| **powers** | Fisheries Act (Northern Ireland) 1966. Fisheries (Amendment) (Northern Ireland) Order 1983 |
| **mission** | To conserve and protect salmon and the inland fisheries of Northern Ireland (other than the fisheries of the Londonderry area). |
| **tasks** | To make byelaws for game angling, coarse angling and commercial fishing. To enforce protection by patrolling and policing. To restock rivers and check fish. Additional tasks are to act as DANI water bailiff in respect of DANI fishing rights, and as agent for Department of the Environment on water pollution investigations, water Act discharge consents, river monitoring and proactive pollution control. |
| **operations** | Management: There is a Chief Executive appointed by the Board with DANI approval. He is secretary of the Board and responsible for management, implementation of the Board's policy and financial and public relations matters. The staff network is divided up into four main geographical areas, which are subdivided into 15 areas controlled by fishery conservation officers. |
| | Policy: To provide a more effective presence at NI fisheries and actively publicise legal requirements. |
| | Trends: DANI has decided to gradually shift executive functions to FCB, starting with public angling estate and |

the fish farm at Movanagher.

**performance**  Targets have been set for 1997.

**board**  Board - not more than 24 members, appointed by the Head of the DANI. Executive Committee of the Board - not less than three or more than six members, appointed by Board.

| | |
|---|---|
| Chairman | Dr J Parsons |
| Deputy Chairman | Mrs C Kennedy |
| Members | |
| *Appointed as representatives of a substantial number of anglers* | |
| | J Haughey |
| | A Kilgore |
| | JS McCreight |
| | J Tisdall |
| *Commercial fishing company representatives* | |
| | FG Conlon |
| | Sir Patrick Macnaghten |
| | F Tennyson |
| *Commercial fishermen's representatives* | |
| | Rev Father OP Kennedy |
| | R Montgomery |
| | R Shaw |
| *Nominated by the Ulster Farmers Union* | |
| | R Farrell |
| | J Mulvenna |
| *Independent anglers* | |
| | A Hanna |
| | J Todd |
| | Mrs A Courtney |
| *Other representatives* | |
| | W Gallagher |
| | D Houston |
| | M McClure |
| | S McGirr |
| *Accounting Officer* | Chief Executive |

**staff**  42

**financial**

**INCOME & EXPENDITURE**

| Year end: 31 March | 1996 £ | 1995 £ |
|---|---|---|
| **INCOME** | | |
| Ordinary income | 711,726 | 745,051 |
| Exceptional item | 42,886 | - |
| | 754,612 | 745,051 |
| **EXPENDITURE** | | |
| Salaries and expenses field staff | 580,339 | 535,825 |
| Administrative expenses | 171,047 | 172,050 |
| Exceptional item | 10,000 | - |
| | 761,386 | 707,875 |
| **OPERATING (DEFICIT)/SURPLUS** | (6,774) | 37,176 |
| Other income | 21,479 | 28,182 |
| **EXCESS OF INCOME OVER EXPENDITURE** | 14,705 | 65,358 |

**advisers**

| **Bankers** | Ulster Bank | High Street, Portadown |
|---|---|---|
| **Auditors** | Witt Thornton | 7 Donegall Square West, Belfast BT1 6BR |
| **Solicitors** | O'Rorke McDonald & Tweed | 37-39 Church Street, Antrim BT41 4BD |

**publications**  *Annual Report*

# *Fisheries Research Services (FRS)*

Marine Laboratory
PO Box 101
Victoria Road
Aberdeen AB11 9DB

**Tel** 01224 878 544
**Fax** 01224 875 511        **Web** http:www.marlab.ac.uk

| | |
|---|---|
| *status* | Executive agency |
| *founded* | 1997 |
| *sponsor* | Scottish Office |
| *powers* | Framework Document 1997 |
| *mission* | To provide expert scientific and technical advice and information on marine and freshwater fisheries, on aquaculture, and on the protection of the aquatic environment and its wildlife in Scotland. |
| *tasks* | To provide for Scotland timely scientific and technical advice and information, much of it to guide policy development and regulatory and statutory activities, in relation to the management and conservation of marine and freshwater fisheries, the protection of the aquatic environment and wildlife; to undertake statutory and regulatory responsibilities including the licensing of marine dumping operations, the inspection of fish farms, the monitoring of shellfish toxins, assessment of the quality of waters from which shellfish are harvested, and the compilation of fisheries statistics; to represent Scottish, and where appropriate UK, interests at national and international meetings. |
| *operations* | Management: Made up of two laboratories: the Scottish Office's Marine Laboratory in Aberdeen and the Freshwater Fisheries Laboratory at Pitlochry. The Director is responsible for management and day-to-day operations and reports to the Secretary of State. |
| | Policy: Principal customer is the Scottish Office, but also provides services to other government departments, UK and international bodies, local government and private companies. |
| | Trends: The FRS programme is expanding as further controls are put in place to protect the marine environment and the sustainable industries of fishing and fish farming. |
| *performance* | As a new agency, first targets have been set for 1997/98. |
| *board* | Strategy board appointed by The Scottish Office. |

| *Accounting Officer* | Director |
|---|---|

| | |
|---|---|
| *staff* | 230 |

| Chief Executive | Prof AD Hawkins |
|---|---|

| | |
|---|---|
| *financial* | First set of accounts to be published in 1998/99. |
| *publications* | *Marine Laboratory Biennial Review, Freshwater Fisheries Biennial Review, Scottish Fisheries Research Report, Scottish Fisheries Information Pamphlet, Scottish Aquaculture Research Report, Scottish Shellfish Farms Annual Production Survey, Scottish Fish Farms Annual Production Survey, Aquaculture Information Series* |
| *branches* | *Freshwater Fisheries Laboratory* Faskally Pitlochry Perthshire PH16 5LB Tel: 01796 472000 Fax: 01796 473523 |

# Fleet Air Arm Museum

Royal Naval Air Station
Yeovilton
Ilchester
Somerset BA22 8HT

**Tel** 01935 840565
**Fax** 01935 840181

| | |
|---|---|
| *status* | Executive body |
| *founded* | 1964 |
| *sponsor* | Ministry of Defence (MOD) |
| *powers* | National Heritage Act 1983 |
| *mission* | To maintain for public display items which are of historical interest concerning the Royal Naval Air Service and the Fleet Air Arm; to demonstrate to Naval personnel and others the evolution of naval aviation; to provide a display which appeals to civilians to keep the Royal Navy in the public eye and act as a recruiting aid. |
| *tasks* | Maintains, develops and preserves the collections; provides educational and research services. |
| *operations* | Management: The Director exercises day-to-day management under the aegis of the Management Committee of the Chairman, Deputy Chairman, Director, Deputy Director and Museum Administrator. The Trustees meet twice a year mainly to review and approve the Strategic Plan. |
| *board* | Six members of the Board of Trustees are *ex officio* (including Chairman and Deputy Chairman) and the remainder are appointed by Board of Trustees on an initial five-year appointment. |

| Trustees | Sir Michael Cobham CBE | |
|---|---|---|
| | Sir Donald Gosling | Jeffrey Smith |
| | Admiral Sir Michael Layard KCB CBE | Dame Margaret Weston DBE |
| | Torquil Norman | Dr Thomas Wright |
| *Accounting Officer* | *Director* | |

*staff* 50

| Director | CG Mottram |
|---|---|
| Deputy Director/Curator | Cdr DA Hobbs MBE |
| Administrator | AP Davies |

*financial*

**INCOME & EXPENDITURE**

| Year end: 31 March | 1996 £ | 1995 £ |
|---|---|---|
| **INCOMING RESOURCES** | | |
| Admissions | 420,592 | 488,521 |
| Other income | 650,420 | 619,412 |
| Carrier exhibition donations | - | 404,315 |
| Other donations | 350,956 | 265,000 |
| Grant-in-aid operating account | 383,419 | 400,617 |
| Grant-in-aid exhibits reserve | 12,475 | 15,301 |
| | **1,817,862** | **2,193,166** |
| **RESOURCES EXPENDED** | | |
| Direct charitable expenditure | 1,311,912 | 1,282,180 |
| Fund raising & publiciy | 432,314 | 502,635 |
| Management & administration support costs | 59,630 | 53,108 |
| | **1,803,856** | **1,837,923** |
| **NET MOVEMENT IN FUNDS** | **14,006** | **355,243** |
| Fund balances brought forward | 393,318 | 406,933 |
| Prior year adjustment | 2,016,260 | 1,647,402 |
| Fund balances brought forward restated | 2,409,578 | 2,054,335 |
| **FUND BALANCES CARRIED FORWARD** | **2,423,584** | **2,409,578** |

| *advisers* | **Bankers** | Barclays Bank | King George Street, Yeovil BA20 1PX |
|---|---|---|---|
| | **Auditors** | Baker Tilly | 49 Princess Street, Yeovil BA20 1EG |
| | **Solicitors** | Porter Dodson | Central House, Church Street, Yeovil BA20 1EG |

# *Food from Britain (FFB)*

123 Buckingham Palace Road
London SW1W 9SA

**Tel** 0171 233 5111
**Fax** 0171 2339515

**E-mail** info@foodfrombritain.co.uk
**Web** www@foodfrombritain.com

| | |
|---|---|
| *status* | Executive body |
| *founded* | 1983 |
| *sponsor* | Ministry of Agriculture, Fisheries and Food (MAFF) |
| *powers* | Agricultural Marketing Act 1983 |
| *mission* | To market and promote British food and drink overseas, working in partnership with companies to achieve export success.  To assist the development of speciality food and drink products in the UK. |
| *tasks* | Helping to identify market opportunities; organising promotions of British products overseas; organising inward and outward missions; assisting companies in researching a market and finding a distributor; running export seminars; organising participation at international trade events; publishing market data; public relations activity. |
| *operations* | Management: FFB is run by the Directorate, consisting of the Chairman, Chief Executive, International Director and Finance & UK Development Director.  53% of income is from the private sector.  Privatised offices in Belgium, France, Germany, Italy, The Netherlands, North America, Spain, Japan and Scandinavia.  Assisted 1000 British companies advance their exports (same number as previous year).  Organises Export Innovation Awards. |
| | Policy: Expanding numbers of offices overseas.  Increasing range of exporter services. |
| | Trends: BSE dominated 1997. |
| *performance* | Mainly met targets as set out in Corporate Plan. |
| *board* | Appointed by the Minister for a fixed term; affiliations invited from the food industry. |

| Chairman | Geoffrey John OBE | |
|---|---|---|
| Members | Stanley Bernard | |
| | Don Curry CBE | Philip Rycroft |
| | Sir Richard George | Prof Susan Shaw |
| | Prof Michael Haines | Caroline Spelman |
| | John Irish CBE | David Thomas |
| | Richard Lazenby | Neil Thornton |
| | Liam McKibben | Lionel Walford |
| | Kirit K Pathak OBE | James Walker |
| | Meurig Raymond | Robert Watson |
| *Accounting Officer* | *Chief Executive* | |

*staff* 23

| *Directorate* | |
|---|---|
| Chairman | Geoffrey John CBE |
| Chief Executive | Patrick Davis |
| Finance & UK Development Director | Mike Callaghan |
| International Director | Simon Waring |
| | |
| *International Offices* | |
| United Kingdom | Simon Waring |
| Belgium | Philip Horemans |
| France | Dominique Mine |
| Germany | Roy Edleston |
| Italy | Paul Garrett |
| Japan | Kei Kurosu |
| | Dan Thomas |
| Netherlands | Eric van Thiel |
| North America | Tony Matthews OBE |
| Scandinavia | Preben Sand |
| | Jakob True |
| Spain | Guillermo Alvarez de Lorenzana |
| Switzerland | Erich Braun |
| Rest of the World | Andrea Ng |

*financial*

| INCOME & EXPENDITURE<br>Year end: 31 March | 1997<br>£ | 1996<br>£ |
|---|---|---|
| **INCOME** | | |
| HMG grant | 5,318,000 | 5,400,000 |
| Less appropriations for capital expenditure | (28,616) | (81,020) |
| (Increase)/decrease in MAFF creditor | (14,906) | 112,430 |
| HMG grants applied to non-capital expenditure | 5,274,478 | 5,431,410 |
| Income from activities | 4,054,232 | 3,647,212 |
| | **9,328,710** | **9,078,622** |
| **EXPENDITURE** | | |
| Operating expenditure | 6,202,656 | 5,734,608 |
| Staff costs | 847,888 | 948,235 |
| Depreciation | 53,145 | 56,027 |
| Less release of capital reserve | (53,145) | (56,027) |
| Administrative expenses | 2,290,656 | 2,404,123 |
| | **9,341,200** | **9,086,966** |
| **OPERATING DEFICIT** | **(12,490)** | **(8,344)** |
| Interest receivable | 16,434 | 11,125 |
| **SURPLUS BEFORE TAX** | **3,944** | **2,781** |
| Taxation | (3,944) | (2,781) |
| **SURPLUS AFTER TAX** | **0** | **0** |

*advisers*

| **Auditors** | Shipleys | 10 Orange Street, London WC2H 7DQ |
|---|---|---|
| **Solicitors** | Wilmett & Co | 27 Sheet Street, Windsor, Berks SL4 1BS |

*branches*

*Belgium*
Rue du Biplan 187
B-1140 Evere - Brussels
Tel 00 32 2 240 7520
Fax 00 32 2 245 8210
E-mail info@foodfrombritain.be

*Germany*
Rossertstrasse 9
60323 Frankfurt/Main
Tel 00 49 69 971 2910
Fax 00 49 69 971 29110
E-mail foodfrombritain_germany@t-onli

*Japan*
Kioicho WITH Bldg 4F
3-32 Kioi-cho
Chiyoda-Ku
Tokyo 102
Tel 00 81 332 396 638
Fax 00 81 332 392 848
E-mail kkurosu@iic.co.jp

*North America*
4700 Magnolia Circle Marietta
Georgia 30067
USA
Tel 00 1 770 955 4074
Fax 00 1 770 952 9792
E-mail foodfrombritain@worldnet.att.

*Spain*
Arroyofresno 19
Bloque A, 2-D Dcha
28035 Madrid
Tel 0034 1 386 07 44
Fax 0034 1 386 68 18
E-mail ffbspain@alc.es

*France*
134 rue du Faubourg St Honore
75008 Paris
St Honore
Tel 00 33 1 5353 0853
Fax 00 33 1 4225 0185
E-mail foodfrombritain@ffb.fr

*Italy*
via Manuzio 17
20124 Milan
Tel 00 39 2 655 5640
Fax 00 39 2 657 0124
E-mail pgarrett@ffb.it

*The Netherlands*
PO Box 280
5240 AG Rosmalen
Tel 00 31 7352 21222
Fax 00 31 7352 10043
E-mail Info@ffb.nl

*Scandinavia*
Nannasgade 28
DK-2200 Copenhagen N
Denmark
Tel 00 45 35 83 35 73
Fax 00 45 35 83 35 72
E-mail ffb.scan@internet.dk

*Switzerland*
Sennweidstrasse 44
6312 Steinhausen (ZG)
Tel 00 41 41 748 7060
Fax 00 41 41 748 7066
E-mail ebraun@ffb.ch

# *Food Standards Agency (FSA)*

Department of Health
Room 634B
Skipton House
80 London Road
London SE1 6LH

**Tel** 0171 972 5087/88

**Contact** Ms Pat Steward

| | |
|---|---|
| *status* | Executive body |
| **founded** | 1998 |
| *sponsor* | Department of Health (DOH) |
| **powers** | Not yet defined but see White Paper CM3830 (14 January 1998) |
| *mission* | Independent protector of consumer interests in every area of food safety in the UK. A strategic view of food safety throughout the complete food chain and open, independent advice to Health and other Ministers. |

*tasks*

The Agency is to be given a strong independent role and powers; able to change government policies if needed; free to make its advice and findings public; and to oversee and influence the work of other organisations. The Agency will: commission scientific research and develop new policies; set standards and monitor the safety and standards of all food for human consumption; issue licences, approvals and authorisations; advise the public, Ministers and the food industry about food safety, nutrition and diet.

The government's proposals are designed to address the key factors identified as contributing to the erosion of public and producer confidence in the current system of food controls: the potential for conflicts of interest within MAFF arising from its dual responsibility for protecting public health and for sponsoring the agriculture and food industries; the fragmentation and lack of coordination between the various government bodies involved in food safety; and the uneven enforcement of food law.

*operations*

Management: Staff to be appointed by the Civil Service Commission with the staff's independence protected. The Agency will be financed in part through transfer of the budgets for those functions becoming its responsibility and in part through charges on the food industry. The government is considering mechanisms for transferring a higher proportion of the costs of food safety and maintaining standards from the taxpayer to the food industry.

Policy: The Agency will be required by law to operate in accordance with clearly defined guiding principles, as follows: assessments of food standards and safety to be unbiased and based on the best available independent scientific advice; decisions and action to be proportionate to the risk (paying due regard to costs as well as benefits to those affected), avoiding over-regulation and independent of specific sectoral interests; the general public to have adequate information, presented clearly and avoiding unjustified alarm, allowing informed choices to be made; decision-making processes to be open, transparent and consultative, in order that interested parties have an opportunity to make their views known, can see the basis on which decisions have been taken and are able to reach an informed judgement about the quality of the Agency's processes and decisions; the Agency to consult widely before taking action unless the need for urgent action to protect public health makes this impossible; clarity and consistency of approach in decisions and actions; full account to be taken of the UK's obligations under domestic and international law; efficiency and economy in delivering an effective operation.

*board*

Yet to be appointed; possibly two bodies modelled on the Health and Safety Commission, responsible for advice to Ministers, and the Health and Safety Executive, responsible for other functions.

# Football Licensing Authority (FLA)

27 Harcourt House
19 Cavendish Square
London W1M 9AD

**Tel** 0171 491 7191
**Fax** 0171 491 1882

| | |
|---|---|
| *status* | Executive body |
| *founded* | 1989 |
| *sponsor* | Department for Culture, Media and Sport (DCMS) |
| *powers* | Football Spectators Act 1989 |
| *mission* | Originally to supervise a national membership scheme; following Hillsborough disaster that was dropped and FLA's function became to implement the recommendations in Lord Justice Taylor's Final Report, in particular those relating to seated accommodation. |
| *tasks* | To operate a licensing scheme for grounds at which designated football matches are played; advise the government on the introduction of all seated accommodation at Premier and First Division grounds and the national stadia; ensure that any terracing which is retained at football league second and third division grounds meets the necessary safety standards; keep under review the discharge by local authorities of their functions under the Safety of Sports Grounds Act. |
| *operations* | Management: Chief Executive reports to the Board. Nine Inspectors responsible for certain clubs and stadia. |
| *board* | Appointed by the Secretary of State. |

| | | |
|---|---|---|
| Chairman | Clive Sherling | |
| Members | Dr Judith Fisher MB | |
| | C Lewis | Prof M Talbot OBE |
| | M Sheldon | Prof S Thorburn OBE |
| *Accounting Officer* | *Chief Executive* | |

*staff* 16

| | | |
|---|---|---|
| Chief Executive | JRK De Quidt | |
| Inspectors | DJ Beaumont | |
| | JA Chalmers | EO Sheridan |
| | JW Froggatt | JS Smith |
| | RH Grainger | A Swales |
| | JG Levison | GB Wilson |

*financial*

**INCOME & EXPENDITURE**

| Year end: 31 March | 1997 £ | 1996 £ | 1995 £ |
|---|---|---|---|
| **INCOME** | | | |
| HMG grant | 896,000 | 896,000 | 870,000 |
| Net movement in deferred grant-in-aid | (11,369) | 14,439 | (4,005) |
| Income from activities | 9,400 | 9,300 | 9,400 |
| Other operating income | 0 | 450 | 71 |
| | 894,031 | 920,189 | 875,466 |
| **EXPENDITURE** | | | |
| Salaries and wages | 597,289 | 615,547 | 601,289 |
| Other operating payments | 299,220 | 262,327 | 261,343 |
| Depreciation | 8,280 | 15,220 | 13,642 |
| | 904,789 | 893,094 | 876,274 |
| **OPERATING SURPLUS/(DEFICIT)** | (10,758) | 27,095 | (808) |
| Deposit account interest | 328 | 3,637 | 2,550 |
| Current account interest | 1,553 | 288 | 0 |
| **(DEFICIT)/SURPLUS FOR THE YEAR** | (8,877) | 31,020 | 1,742 |
| Appropriations | | 9,300 | 9,400 |
| **RETAINED SURPLUS/(DEFICIT) FOR THE YEAR** | (18,910) | 21,080 | (7,658) |
| Retained surplus brought forward | 45,972 | 24,892 | 32,550 |
| **RETAINED SURPLUS CARRIED FORWARD** | **27,062** | **45,972** | **24,892** |

| | | |
|---|---|---|
| *advisers* | **Auditors** Binder Hamlyn | 20 Old Bailey, London EC4M 7BH |
| *publications* | *Guidance on Safety Certificates, Football Club Contingency Planning, Guidance Notes for Drawing up a Statement of Safety Policy for Spectators at Football Grounds, Code of Practice, Annual Reports* | |

# *Forensic Science Agency of Northern Ireland (FSANI)*

151 Belfast Road
Carrickfergus
County Antrim BT38 8PL

**Tel** 01 232 365 744
**Fax** 01 232 365 727

**E-mail** FSANI@NICS,GOV.UK
**Web** http://www.fsani.org

**Contact** Chief Executive

| | |
|---|---|
| *status* | Executive agency |
| *founded* | 1995 (as executive agency) |
| *sponsor* | Northern Ireland Office |
| *powers* | Framework document |
| *mission* | Provide effective scientific advice and support to enhance the delivery of justice. |
| *tasks* | Provide scientific support for police in the investigation of crime; scientific advice for the legal protection and objective expert testimony to the courts; training in the effective and efficient application of Forensic Science Analytical Support for Pathologists. |
| *operations* | Management: The Chief Executive is responsible for the efficient and effective operation of the FSANI and is directly responsible to the Minister. A Ministerial Advisory Board oversees its work. A senior management team, comprising the five business managers and one special project manager supports the Chief Executive. Most of the Agency costs are recovered from the Police Authority for NI as fundholders for the RUC; a small amount of income was generated from private clients. |
| | Policy: To maintain the quality and standards of the science it practises to preserve the confidence of the RUC and the wider justice system. To continue to develop its services on a commercial basis. |
| | Trends: Legislation allowing a National DNA Database of offenders has provided FSANI with an opportunity to develop a major new service. |
| *performance* | 11 key targets were set by the Minister but three were revised. Nine were achieved. |
| *board* | Ministerial Advisory Board appointed by Minister of State. |

| Chief Executive | RW Adams |
|---|---|
| *Accounting Officer* | *Chief Executive* |

*staff*    123

*financial*

| INCOME & EXPENDITURE | | |
|---|---|---|
| Year end: 31 March | **1997** | **1996** |
| | **£000** | **£000** |
| **INCOME** | **4,285** | **3,348** |
| **EXPENDITURE** | | |
| Staff costs | 3,170 | 2,150 |
| Depreciation | 365 | 177 |
| Other operating charges | 1,162 | 798 |
| Capital charges | 160 | 112 |
| | 4,857 | 3,237 |
| **OPERATING SURPLUS/(DEFICIT)** | **(572)** | **111** |
| Transitional costs on move to executive agency status | 0 | 113 |
| **DEFICIT TRANSFERRED FROM THE GENERAL FUND** | **(572)** | **(2)** |

*publications*    *Annual Report and Accounts*

# Forensic Science Service (FSS)

Priory House
Gooch Street North
Birmingham B5 6QQ

**Tel** 0121 607 6800
**Fax** 0121 622 5889

| | |
|---|---|
| *status* | Executive agency |
| *founded* | 1991 |
| *sponsor* | Home Office |
| *powers* | Framework document |
| *mission* | To serve the administration of justice in England and Wales by providing scientific support in the investigation of crime and expert evidence in the courts - to the maximum public benefit and without making profit. |
| *tasks* | To provide a national service to the 43 police forces in England and Wales, Customs and Excise and other law enforcement agencies in the UK and overseas, and to private sector companies. To meet customers' investigative requirements. To work in partnership with customers on projects (not just cases) and take a national view. To undertake research and development. |
| *operations* | Management: During 1996/97, FSS was restructured on a corporate commercial model and became entirely financed by the revenue it earns from customers. Management was restructured. There is now a Main Board chaired by the Chief Executive composed of four non-executive and four executive Directors. There are three committees: the Executive Committee handles day-to-day management; the Corporate Quality Committee is responsible for applying Total Quality; the Audit Committee, chaired by a Non-Executive Director, monitors control systems and audit. The Metropolitan Police Forensic Science Laboratory merged with FSS and the laboratory structure was rationalised with the closure the Aldermaston site. |
| | Policy: Through its research and development work, to remain at the leading edge of the application of scientific advances to the investigative process. |
| | Trends: FSS holds the world's first DNA database and leads the world in the forensic application of DNA. |
| *performance* | Financial - operating surplus up 144% (excepting exceptional items); efficiency up 2%. An arson attack on Wetherby laboratory impacted severely on DNA delivery. |

*board*

| Advisory Board | | |
|---|---|---|
| Chairman | S Boys-Smith | |
| Members | JL Bickers | P Lewis |
| | RTB Dykes | J Lyon |
| | R Fulton | JA Stevens |
| *Management Board* | | |
| Chief Executive | | Dr J Thompson |
| Finance Director | | RJ Anthony |
| Non-Executive Director | | J Botten |
| Non-Executive Director | | P Hobbs |
| Director, Law Enforcement Business | | TH Howitt |
| Operations Director | | MR Loveland |
| Non-Executive Director | | R Pannone |
| Non-Executive Director | | P Riley |
| Director of Research & DNA Services | | Dr DJ Werrett |
| *Accounting Officer* | | *Chief Executive* |

*staff* 1157

| Executive Committee | |
|---|---|
| Chief Executive | Dr J Thompson |
| Finance Director | Rod Anthony |
| Chief Scientist | Dr Bob Bramley |
| Head of Policy Unit | Mrs Deborah Grice |
| Operations Director | Mike Loveland |
| Corporate Communications Manager | Rob Smith |
| Chief Executive | Dr Janet Thompson |
| New Law Enforcement Business Manager | Geoff Vinall |
| Director of Research & DNA Development | Dr Dave Werrett |
| Director, Law Enforcement Business | Trevor Howitt |
| Human Resources Manager | Danny Kavanagh |
| Corporate Marketing Manager | Mrs Andrea Roberts |

*financial*

| INCOME & EXPENDITURE Year end: 31 March | 1997 £000 | 1996 £000 | 1995 £000 |
|---|---|---|---|
| **INCOME** | | | |
| Income from continuing activities | 33,889 | 31,188 | 28,653 |
| Income through Metropolitan laboratory | 16,950 | - | - |
| | 50,839 | 31,188 | 28,653 |
| **EXPENDITURE** | | | |
| Staff costs | 29,159 | 18,180 | 16,525 |
| Depreciation | 3,328 | 2,509 | 2,248 |
| Other operating charges | 17,402 | 7,904 | 7,261 |
| | 49,889 | 28,593 | 26,034 |
| **OPERATING SURPLUS FROM CONTINUING ACTIVITIES** | 196 | 2,595 | 2,619 |
| Operating surplus through Metropolitan laboratory | 754 | - | - |
| **TOTAL OPERATING SURPLUS** | 950 | 2,595 | 2,619 |
| Notional interest | 2,407 | 1,982 | 1,522 |
| **(DEFICIT)/SURPLUS FOR THE YEAR TRANSFERRED (FROM)/TO THE HOME OFFICE GENERAL FUND** | (1,457) | 613 | 769 |

*advisers*

**Auditors** National Audit Office

157-197 Buckingham Palace Road
London SW1W 9SP

*branches*

*Metropolitan Forensic Science Laboratory*
109 Lambeth Road
London SE1 7LP
Tel 0171 230 6700
Fax 0171 230 6253

*Chepstow Forensic Science Laboratory*
Usk Road
Chepstow
Gwent NP6 6YE
Tel 01291 628141
Fax 01291 629482

*Chorley Forensic Science Laboratory*
Washington Hall
Euxton
Chorley
Lancashire PR7 6HJ
Tel 01257 265666
Fax 01257 274752

*Huntingdon Forensic Science Laboratory*
Hinchingbrooke Park
Huntingdon
Cambridgeshire PE18 8NP
Tel 01480 450071
Fax 01480 450079

*Wetherby Forensic Science Laboratory*
Sandbeck Way
Audby Lane
Wetherby
West Yorkshire LS22 7DN
Tel 01937 548100
Fax 01937 587683

*Woodley Local Office*
Suite C
London Vale House
Hurricane Way
Reading RG5 4UX
Tel 0118 9440391
Fax 0118 9440408

# *Forest Enterprise (FE)*

231 Corstorphine Road
Edinburgh EH12 7AT

**Tel** 0131 314 6465
**Fax** 0131 314 4473

**E-mail** info@forestry.gov.uk
**Web** http://www.forestry.gov.uk

*status* Executive agency
*founded* 1996
*sponsor* Forestry Commission
*powers* Forestry Act 1967
*mission* Developing and managing the nation's forests in an efficient and environmentally responsible manner, supplying products and services to customers and making best use of the assets.
*tasks* To market timber and forest products; increase opportunities for public recreation; increase attractiveness and conservation value of its forests and woodlands; market forest holidays; exploit non-timber commercial opportunities.

**operations** Management: Run by Chief Executive with support of Management Board. Head office in Edinburgh, four regions (each in charge of a Regional Director) and 32 Forest Districts (run by Forest District Managers, accountable to a Regional Director). Another executive agency, the Forestry Authority, regulates FE's felling and planting activities.

Policy: Producing the environmental, financial, social and other outputs sought by Ministers and the Forestry Commissioners, meeting international commitments and sustaining environmental quality and productive potential of the forest estate. Environmental programmes to be funded by increasing timber production and marketing. Increasing efficiency through contracting out to private sector contractors.

Trends: Timber prices dictated by imported stock.

**board**

| Management Board | |
|---|---|
| Chief Executive | Dr Bob McIntosh |
| Director of Corporate Services | Keith Gliddon |
| Regional Director | Dr Hugh Insley |
| Head of Forest Operations | Mike Lofthouse |
| Director, Estate Management | Peter Ranken |
| Head of Environment & Communications | Alan Stevenson |
| Regional Director, South of Scotland | Paul Hill-Tout |
| Regional Director Wales | Bob Farmer |
| Regional Director England | vacant |
| Accounting Officer | Chief Executive |

**staff** 2585

**financial**

| INCOME & EXPENDITURE Year end: 31 March | 1997 £m | 1996 £m | 1995 £m |
|---|---|---|---|
| **INCOME** | | | |
| **Forest Estate** | | | |
| Sales of timber | 100.3 | 95.0 | 91.1 |
| Other forest sales | 3.9 | 3.6 | 3.0 |
| | **104.2** | **98.6** | **94.1** |
| Other activities | 13.3 | 13.8 | 13.5 |
| | **117.5** | **112.4** | **107.6** |
| **EXPENDITURE** | | | |
| **Forest Estate** | | | |
| Harvesting and haulage of timber | 44.9 | 44.0 | 44.8 |
| Restocking after felling | 12.8 | 12.2 | 11.7 |
| Forest roads | 11.6 | 12.7 | 13.2 |
| Forest maintenance and protection | 15.0 | 14.9 | 14.1 |
| | **84.3** | **83.8** | **83.8** |
| Other activities | 14.2 | 15.6 | 14.4 |
| | **98.5** | **99.4** | **98.2** |
| **OPERATING PROFIT** | **19.0** | **13.0** | **9.4** |
| Recreation, conservation and heritage income | 5.2 | 4.6 | 3.9 |
| Recreation, conservation and heritage expenditure | 17.8 | 17.9 | 17.0 |
| Recreation, conservation and heritage net expenditure | (12.6) | (13.3) | (13.1) |
| **NET SURPLUS/(DEFICIT)** | **6.4** | **(0.3)** | **(3.7)** |

**advisers** **Bankers** HM Treasury

**Auditors** National Audit Service

**publications** *Corporate Plan, Annual Report and Accounts, Forest Life*

**branches**

*North Scotland*
21 Church Street
Inverness IV1 1EL
Tel 01463 232811
Fax 01463 243846

*South Scotland*
55/57 Moffat Road
Dumfries DG1 1NP
Tel 01387 269171
Fax 01387 251491

*North and East England*
1A Grosvenor Terrace
York YO3 7BD
Tel 01904 620221
Fax 01904 610664

*South and West England*
Avon Fields House
Somerdale
Keynsham
Bristol BS18 2BD
Tel 01179 869481
Fax 01179 861981

*Wales*
Victoria Terrace
Aberystwyth
Ceredigion SY23 2DQ
Tel 01970 612367
Fax 01970 625282

# Forest Research

Northern Research Station
Roslin
Midlothian
Edinburgh EH25 9SY

**Tel** 0131 445 2176
**Fax** 0131 445 5124

| | |
|---|---|
| *status* | Executive agency |
| *founded* | 1997 |
| *sponsor* | Forestry Commission |
| *powers* | Framework Document 1997 |
| *mission* | To provide a capability to conduct research, development and surveys relevant to the forest industry. Also provides authoritative advice to support the development and implementation of the government's forest policy. |
| *tasks* | Improving the understanding of threats to tree health including the effects of changes in climate and atmospheric chemistry; developing environmentally benign and humane methods of controlling pests and diseases; improving understanding of the effects of trees and forest operations on the environment; developing improved methods of managing forests for sustainable benefits including the maintenance of biodiversity; developing cost-effective methods of restocking and establishing trees on sites likely to become available for forestry; increasing the commercial returns from forestry through cost reduction, improved timber quality, increased yield and improved information on the resource. |
| *operations* | Management: The Chief Executive is responsible for the day-to-day management and reports to the Director General of the Forestry Commission. An advisory Committee provides guidance on the quality of its research activities and the direction research should be taking. Operates from two research stations and 11 field stations. |
| | Trends: Government policy is to increase the tree cover of Britain but funding of research is tending to decline. |
| *performance* | Targets have been set for 1997/98. |
| *staff* | 298 |

| | |
|---|---|
| Chief Executive | Jim Dewar |
| Chief Research Officer | Peter Freer-Smith |
| Head of Branch, Woodland Surveys | Graham Bull |
| Head of Branch, Personnel & Administration | Ken Charles |
| Head of Branch, Technical Support South | Dave Elgy |
| Head of Branch, Entomology | Hugh Evans |
| Head of Branch, Pathology | John Gibbs |
| Head of Branch, Woodland Ecology | Simon Hodge |
| Head of Branch, Technical Development | Bill Jones |
| Head of Branch, Silviculture North | Bill Mason |
| Head of Branch, Mensuration | Janet Methley |
| Head of Branch, Environmental Research | Andy Moffat |
| Head of Branch, Finance | Dick Murray |
| Head of Branch, Communications | John Parker |
| Head of Branch, Tree Improvement | Sam Samuel |
| Head of Branch, Technical Support North | Tony Sharpe |
| Head of Branch, Statistics & Computing | Jane Smyth |
| Head of Branch, Silviculture & Seed Research | Paul Tabbush |
| *Accounting Officer* | *Chief Executive* |

| | | |
|---|---|---|
| *advisers* | **Bankers** | Bank of England |
| | **Auditors** | National Audit Office |
| *publications* | *Annual Report on Forest Research 1997* | |
| *branches* | Alice Holt Lodge | |
| | Wrecclesham | |
| | Farnham GU10 4LH | |
| | Surrey | |
| | Tel 01420 22255 | |
| | Fax 01420 23653 | |

# Foyle Fisheries Commission

8 Victoria Road
Londonderry BT47 2AB

**Tel** 01504 342100
**Fax** 01504 342720

| | |
|---|---|
| *status* | Executive body |
| *founded* | 1952 |
| *sponsor* | Northern Ireland Office, Department of Agriculture NI (DANI) |
| *powers* | Foyle Fisheries Act 1952. Foyle Fisheries Act (Northern Ireland) 1952 |
| *mission* | Enforcement of the Fisheries Acts and Regulations. |
| *tasks* | Enforcement with assistance of DANI, the Garda Siochanna, the Irish Naval Service and the RUC. Conservation and licensing. Water quality agency for DOENI. |
| *operations* | Management: Chief Executive supported by an Advisory Council. |
| | Policy: Commission's operations are under review. |
| | Trends: New equipment partly funded by EU Fisheries Surveillance Programme. |

*board*

| | |
|---|---|
| Chairman | JS Allister |
| Senior Commissioner | N McCutchen |
| Junior Commissioners | B Hogan |
| | D Houston |
| Chief Executive | RJD Anderson |

*staff* 24

| | |
|---|---|
| Chief Executive | RJD Anderson |
| Chief Inspector | S Thorpe |
| District Inspectors | P Harkin |
| | C Hegarty |
| | W Kennedy |
| | R Wray |

*financial*

**REVENUE**
**Year end: 30 September**

| | 1996 £ | 1995 £ |
|---|---|---|
| **INCOME** | | |
| Licence duties | 108,996 | 106,492 |
| Permits and rental fees | 1,811 | 1,968 |
| Fish dealers licences | 914 | 923 |
| Fishery rates | 1,041 | 922 |
| Fines and costs recovered | 8,184 | 9,738 |
| Sundry receipts | 2,918 | 2,486 |
| | **123,864** | **122,529** |
| EU and government grants released | - | 51,089 |
| Gain/(loss) on exchange | 464 | 570 |
| | **124,328** | **174,188** |
| **EXPENSES** | | |
| Rent and rates | 4,894 | 5,875 |
| Insurance | 23,115 | 23,866 |
| Wages and salaries | 225,994 | 283,832 |
| Licence distributors commission | 4,116 | 3,845 |
| Research programmes | 364 | 637 |
| Travelling and subsistence | 28,130 | 30,731 |
| Motot vehicle expenses | 3,190 | 9,605 |
| Printing and stationery | 3,507 | 6,510 |
| Advertising | 6,259 | 9,287 |
| Repairs | 23,656 | 14,963 |
| Sundry expenses | 29,551 | 30,601 |
| Contribution to pension scheme and pension gratuities | 63,529 | 60,185 |
| Legal costs | 16,625 | 9,398 |
| Crew hire | - | 28,350 |
| | **432,930** | **517,685** |

| | | |
|---|---|---|
| Depreciation | 10,724 | 58,971 |
| | **443,654** | **576,656** |
| **OPERATING DEFICIT** | **(319,326)** | **(402,468)** |
| Interest received | 12 | - |
| Interest and charges paid | (1,809) | (102,22) |
| **DEFICIT TO ACCUMULATED REVENUE ACCOUNT** | **(321,123)** | **(412,690)** |

# *Funding Agency for Schools (FAS)*

Albion Wharf
25 Skeldergate
York YO1 2XL

**Tel** 01904 661661
**Fax** 01904 661686

| | |
|---|---|
| *status* | Executive body |
| *founded* | 1994 |
| *sponsor* | Department for Education and Employment (DfEE) |
| *powers* | Education Act 1993 and 1996 |
| *mission* | To support grant-maintained (GM) schools in England to enable them to flourish, to produce long-term plans with confidence and to optimise their freedom to produce the best possible educational outcomes for children. |
| *tasks* | For GM schools it carries out the following: calculation and payment of grant; financial monitoring, including value for money studies; provision of sufficient school places; management of the school improvement regime. |
| *operations* | Management: The Chief Executive and management team are based in York. Other offices in Darlington and London. |
| | Policy: New arrangements for funding early years' education. The first new GM schools will open in 1997-98. |
| | Trends: To be dissolved, subject to legislation. |
| *performance* | The performance targets listed in the Corporate Plan for 1996-97 were largely met. |
| *board* | Members are appointed by The Secretary of State from various areas of education and management. |

| | |
|---|---|
| Chairman | Vice-Admiral Sir Anthony Tippet |
| Vice Chairman | Prof David Newton |
| Members | Rev Dr Alan Billings |
| | John Chastney |
| | Stella Earnshaw |
| | Rodney East |
| | Ray Jobson |
| | Prof David Johns |
| | Louise Kidd |
| | Lesley King MBE |
| | Cynthia Lake |
| | Robert Lloyd |
| | George Phipson |
| | Linda Wedgbury |
| | Robin Wendt |
| *Accounting Officer* | *Chief Executive* |

*staff* 328

| | |
|---|---|
| Chief Executive | Michael Collier |
| Finance Director | John Codling |
| Operations Director | David Halladay |
| Planning Director | Robert Lanwarne |
| Board Secretary | Jane Markham |
| Personnel & Services Director | James Walker |

**financial**

| INCOME & EXPENDITURE | | | |
|---|---|---|---|
| Year end: 31 March | 1997 | 1996 | 1995 |
| | £000 | £000 | £000 |
| **INCOME** | | | |
| Grant-in-aid from DfEE | | | |
| Running costs | 12,120 | 11,305 | 9,848 |
| Grants to GM schools | 1,851,655 | 1,701,473 | 1,600,723 |
| | **1,863,775** | **1,712,778** | **1,610,571** |
| Other operating Income | 15 | 69 | - |
| | **1,863,790** | **1,712,847** | **1,610,571** |
| Deferred grant | 366 | 354 | 258 |
| | **1,864,156** | **1,713,201** | **1,610,829** |
| **EXPENDITURE** | | | |
| Grants paid to GM schools | 1,850,100 | 1,715,460 | 1,583,430 |
| **Agency running costs** | | | |
| Staff costs | 6,741 | 5,480 | 4,097 |
| Depreciation | 547 | 576 | 481 |
| Other operating charges | 5,503 | 6,713 | 5,742 |
| | **12,791** | **12,769** | **10,320** |
| | **1,862,891** | **1,728,229** | **1,593,750** |
| **OPERATING SURPLUS/DEFICIT** | **1,265** | **(15,028)** | **17,079** |
| Add back notional interest on cost of capital to surplus | 392 | 619 | 50 |
| **Transfer from reserves** | | | |
| Revaluation reserve | 29 | 18 | - |
| Capital reserve | 152 | 204 | 212 |
| | **181** | **222** | **212** |
| Loan repayments from GM schools | 205 | 108 | 38 |
| **Appropriations to DfEE** | | | |
| Loan recoveries from GM schools | (205) | (108) | (38) |
| Recovery of overpayments from GM schools | (135) | (137) | - |
| Other cash receipts | (7) | (11) | - |
| | **(347)** | **(256)** | **(38)** |
| **RETAINED SURPLUS/DEFICIT CARRIED FORWARD** | **1,696** | **(14,335)** | **17,341** |

**advisers**

| | | |
|---|---|---|
| **Bankers** | HM Paymaster General | Sutherland House, Russel Way, Crawley West Sussex RH10 1UH |
| **Auditors** | National Audit Office | 157-197 Buckingham Palace Road London SW1W 9SP |
| **Solicitors** | Treasury Solicitors | Queen Anne's Chambers 28 Broadway, London SW1H 9JS |

**publications** Annual Report, Corporate Plan, Financial Management in GM Schools, Planning Secondary School Places in London/the New Unitary Authorities

**branches**

Vincent House
2 Woodlands Road
Darlington DL3 7JP
Tel 01904 661661
Fax 01904 661686

13th Floor, Centre Point
103 New Oxford Street
London WC1A 1DU
Tel 0171 379 3750
Fax 0171 240 8047

# Further Education Funding Council (FEFC)

Cheylesmore House
Quinton Road
Coventry CV1 2WT

**Tel** 01203 863000
**Fax** 01203 863100

**status** Executive body

**founded** 1992

**sponsor** Department for Education and Employment (DfEE)

**powers** Further and Higher Education Act 1992

| | |
|---|---|
| *mission* | To secure further education provision which meets the needs and demands of individuals, employers and the requirements of government in respect of the location, nature and quality of provision in England. |
| *tasks* | Funds 800 institutions in England, mostly FE and sixth-form colleges but also independent and local adult education centres and universities which provide FE courses. |
| *operations* | Management:  The Chief Executive sits on the Council. The Council committees are Audit, Remuneration, Capital Programmes, and Widening Participation. There are also six working groups. The Council is split into nine regional offices each with its own regional committee, advisory rather than executive, but their advice is influential to the Council.  There is a FEFC Ombudsman. |
| | Policy:  Putting pressure on government to provide a fair and secure funding base. |
| | Trends:  Further 7% reduction in funding for 1997/98.  Increasing number of colleges in weak financial position. |
| *performance* | Most measures were met in 1996/97. |
| *board* | Members of the Council are appointed by the Secretary of State and include ten heads of FE institutions. |

| Chairman | Lord Davies of Oldham | |
|---|---|---|
| Members | Mary Curnock Cook | |
| | David Eade | Mitchell Hogg |
| | Peter Elliott | Christopher Jonas CBE |
| | Peter Garrod | Nick Lewis |
| | Colin George | Prof David Melville |
| | Colin Harris | Alfred Morris |
| | Margaret Hobrough OBE | Judith Round |

*staff*  387

| Chief Executive | Prof David Melville |
|---|---|

*financial*

**INCOME & EXPENDITURE**

| Year end: 31 March | 1997 £000 | 1996 £000 |
|---|---|---|
| **INCOME** | | |
| Grant-in-aid for revenue purposes | 3,153,706 | 3,023,554 |
| Earmarked grants | 6,040 | 6,040 |
| Transfer from deferred government capital grant | 1,034 | 910 |
| European structural fund grant | 157 | 132 |
| Other operating income | 165 | 124 |
| | 3,161,102 | 3,030,760 |
| **EXPENDITURE** | | |
| Colleges in the further education sector | 2,960,188 | 2,865,918 |
| External institutions | 66,387 | 62,774 |
| Institutions in the higher education sector | 54,369 | 56,369 |
| Purchases of special education needs provision | 35,128 | 33,144 |
| Local authorities | 7,855 | 8,161 |
| Further Education Development Agency (FEDA) | 4,655 | 4,275 |
| Administration costs | 23,365 | 23,579 |
| Notional cost of capital | 963 | 0 |
| | 3,152,910 | 3,054,220 |
| **SURPLUS/(DEFICIT) BEFORE TAX** | 8,192 | (23,460) |

*advisers*

| **Auditors** | National Audit Office | 157-197 Buckingham Palace Road London SW1W 9SP |
|---|---|---|

*branches*

*Eastern Region*
2 Quayside
Bridge Street
Cambridge CB5 8AB
Tel 01223 454500
Fax 01223 454535

*Greater London Region*
Metropolis House
22 Percy Street
London W1P 0LL
Tel 0171 312 4100
Fax 0171 312 4134

*East & West Midlands Region*
Cheylesmore House
Quinton Road
Coventry CV1 2WT
Tel 01203 863000
Fax 01203 863359

*North West Region*
10 Brindley Road
City Park Business Village
Cornbrook
Manchester M16 9HQ
Tel 0161 877 3811
Fax 0161 876 2936

Northern Region
Clough House
Kings Manor
Newcastle upon Tyne
NE1 6PA
Tel 0191 211 2200
Fax 0191 211 2235

South West Region
Kempton House
Blackbrook Park Avenue
Taunton TA1 2PF
Tel 01823 444404
Fax 01823 443815

South East Region
3 Queens Road
Reading RG1 4AR
Tel 01734 554200
Fax 01734 554220

Yorkshire and Humberside Region
1 Blenheim Court
Blenheim Walk
Leeds LS2 9AE
Tel 0113 245 2644
Fax 0113 245 2477

# Further Education Funding Council for Wales (FEFCW)

Linden Court
Orchards
Ty Glas Avenue
Llanishen
Cardiff CF4 5DZ

**Tel** 01222 761861
**Fax** 01222 763163

| | |
|---|---|
| **status** | Executive body |
| **founded** | 1992 |
| **sponsor** | Welsh Office |
| **powers** | Further and Higher Education Act 1992 |
| **mission** | To secure the provision of facilities for further education (FE) and for the administration of funds for FE institutions, higher education institutions and sponsored bodies in Wales. |
| **tasks** | Funds 25 FE colleges, one sixth-form college, one residential college, and teaching provided by two WEA Districts and the YMCA in Wales. Inspects each college's performance and gives quality assessment gradings. |
| **operations** | Management: The Chief Executive is a member of the Council and is accountable to the Secretary of State. The relationship between the FEFCW and the Welsh Office is defined in a Management Statement, including the Financial Memorandum describing the accountability of the Council and the role of the Chief Executive. The Council is supported by an executive established jointly with the Higher Education Funding Council for Wales (HEFCW). |
| | Policy: FEFCW's policies are designed to ensure that the FE sector contributes fully to the economic development, eg providing courses that match employer needs. Developing comprehensive programme of Welsh for Adults. |
| | Trends: Increasing number of institutions merging. An FEFCW priority is ensuring institutions are fully accountable for the public money. |
| **performance** | Targets and objectives are set out in the FEFCW Corporate Plan. |
| **board** | Members of the Council are appointed by the Secretary of State and are drawn from FE institutions and the public and private sector. |

| Chairman | Richard Webster | |
|---|---|---|
| Members | Prof John Andrews | Osborn Jones |
| | Stephen Dunster | Caroline Lewis |
| | Shaun Dyke | Idris Price |
| | H Gareth Jones | Trevor Wilmore |
| *Accounting Officer* | *Chief Executive* | |

| | |
|---|---|
| **staff** | 51 |

| Chief Executive | Prof John Andrews |
|---|---|
| Head of Further Education | Linda Gainsbury |
| Head of Finance & Common Services Division | Richard Hirst |

**financial**

**INCOME & EXPENDITURE**

| Year end: 31 March | 1997 | 1996 |
|---|---|---|
| | £000 | £000 |
| **GROSS INCOME** | | |
| Grant-in-aid | 179,986 | 178,401 |
| Release of deferred government grant | 135 | 148 |
| Operating income | 2 | 4 |
| Other income | 426 | 393 |
| | **180,549** | **178,946** |
| **EXPENDITURE** | | |
| Funding of further education | | |
| Recurrent expenditure | 159,102 | 157,029 |
| Major capital work | 3,646 | 5,370 |
| Minor capital/estates development work | 11,478 | 10,825 |
| Purchase of equipment | 2,199 | 4,952 |
| Other purposes | 426 | 393 |
| | **176,851** | **178,569** |
| **Council expenditure** | | |
| Administration costs | 1,105 | 1,056 |
| Staff costs | 1,163 | 1,080 |
| Depreciation | 133 | 142 |
| **Notional charges** | | |
| -insurance | 5 | 4 |
| -cost of capital | 136 | 158 |
| | **2,542** | **2,440** |
| | **179,393** | **181,009** |
| **SURPLUS/(DEFICIT) ON OPERATING ACTIVITIES** | **1,156** | **(2,063)** |
| (Deficit) on sales of fixed assets | (1) | - |
| Interest receivable | 154 | 178 |
| **SURPLUS/(DEFICIT) FOR THE FINANCIAL YEAR** | **1,309** | **(1,885)** |
| Appropriations | (156) | (182) |
| **SURPLUS/(DEFICIT) TRANSFERRED TO RESERVES** | **1,153** | **(2,067)** |

**advisers**

| **Bankers** | Midland Bank | 114 St Mary Street, Cardiff CF1 1LF |
|---|---|---|
| **Auditors** | National Audit Office | 23/24 Park Place, Cardiff CF1 3BA |
| **Solicitors** | Bevan Ashford | Newport Road, Cardiff CF2 1EL |

**publications** Annual Report, Corporate Plan, Further and Higher Education Statistics in Wales, Statement of Service Standards

# *Gaming Board for Great Britain*

Berkshire House
168/173 High Holborn
London WC1V 7AA

**Tel** 0171 306 6253
**Fax** 0171 306 6267

**status** Executive body

**founded** 1968

**sponsor** Home Office

**powers** Gaming Act 1968. Lotteries and Amusements Act 1976

**mission** Ensuring that gaming and lotteries in Great Britain are only run by those fit and proper to do so, are free from criminal infiltration and are run fairly and lawfully.

**tasks** Regulating casinos, bingo clubs, gaming machines and the larger society and local authority lotteries, including certificating providers of casino and bingo gaming and their management and staff. Advising the Secretary of State on developments.

# Q&Q

| | |
|---|---|
| **operations** | Management: The Board consists of a part-time Chairman and four other part-time members. The Secretary to the Board is the senior full-time official and reports to the Chairman and Board. The Board's Inspectorate supervises licence holders and is organised into five regions covering SE England, SW England and South Wales, North of England and North Wales, Midlands, and Scotland and North England. Secretariat staff organised into separate sections covering casino gaming, bingo, certification of gaming employees, lotteries and machines. The Board is expected to cover its expenditure from fees. |

Policy: Want an independent review of gambling and lotteries regulation because, inter alia, the advance of the National Lottery has challenged its conceptual basis.

Trends: The Gaming Regulators European Forum (GREF) has formed an Internet Gaming Working Party, to asses the Internet's threat to gaming regulation. Piecemeal deregulation by the Home Office.

**performance**  1996/97 target times for regular duties showed some improvement over 1995/96, except for those in the gaming machines section.

**board**  Appointed by the Secretary of State for fixed terms.

| | |
|---|---|
| Chairman | Lady S Littler |
| Members | B Austin |
| | D Elliott CBE |
| | WB Kirkpatrick |
| | R Lockwood |
| Secretary | TJ Kavanagh |
| *Accounting Officer* | *Secretary* |

**staff**  75

| | |
|---|---|
| Chief Inspector | RG White |
| Deputy Chief Inspector | DW Burns |
| Section Head, Casino & Bingo | D Aldridge |
| Section Head, Finance & Management Services | S Birkett |
| Senior Inspector, South West Region | A Carpenter |
| Senior Inspector, Scottish Region | K MacLean |
| Senior Inspector, Midland Region | RG Nicholson |
| Section Head, Lotteries and Machines | Ms S Pearson |
| Senior Inspector, Northern Region | G Smale |
| Senior Inspector, South East Region | T Adams |
| Senior Inspector, Operations | J Hyde |

**financial**

| **RECEIPTS & PAYMENTS** | | |
|---|---|---|
| **Year end: 31 March** | **1997** | **1996** |
| | **£** | **£** |
| **RECEIPTS** | | |
| HMG grants received | 3,367,000 | 3,260,000 |
| Operating receipts | 1,105,611 | 1,486,457 |
| | **4,472,611** | **4,746,457** |
| **PAYMENTS** | | |
| Salaries and wages | 1,995,681 | 1,957,704 |
| Other operating payments | 1,349,214 | 1,290,911 |
| | **3,344,895** | **3,248,615** |
| **SURPLUS FROM OPERATIONS** | **1,127,716** | **1,497,842** |
| Other receipts/other payments (net) | (32,181) | (38,064) |
| **SURPLUS** | **1,095,535** | **1,459,778** |
| Appropriations | 1,078,517 | 1,516,515 |
| **EXCESS OF (PAYMENTS OVER RECEIPTS)/ RECEIPTS** | | |
| **OVER PAYMENTS** | **17,018** | **(56,737)** |

**advisers**

**Bankers**  Barclays

**Auditors**  National Audit Office

**Solicitors**  Gregory, Rowcliffe and Milners

**publications**  *Annual Report*

**branches**

| | |
|---|---|
| *South West Region* | *Midland Region* |
| Unit 16 | Minerva House |
| Apex Court | Spaniel Row |
| Woodlands | Nottingham NG1 6EP |
| Almondsbury | Tel 0115 941 991 |
| Bristol BS12 4XA | Fax 0115 948 4587 |
| Tel 01454 616 687 | |
| Fax 01454 613090 | |

*Northern Region*
Warwickgate House
Warwick Road
Old Trafford
Manchester M16 0QQ
Tel 0161 872 6016
Fax 0161 873 8248

*Scottish Region*
Portcullis House
21 India Street
Glasgow G2 4PZ
Tel 0141 2215537
Fax 0141 2215494

# Gas Consumers' Council (GCC)

6th Floor
Abford House
15 Wilton Road
London SW1V 1LT

**Tel** 0171 931 0977
**Fax** 0171 630 9934

| | |
|---|---|
| *status* | Executive body (consumer consultative body) |
| *founded* | 1986 |
| *sponsor* | Department of Trade and Industry (DTI) |
| *powers* | Gas Acts 1986 and 1995. Competition and Service (Utilities) Act 1992 |
| *mission* | To ensure that consumers benefit from a safe, efficient customer-focused gas industry that offers competitive prices, gas supply and service to customers - whatever their level of income or method of payment. |
| *tasks* | To represent the interests of gas consumers and seek redress on their complaints. To ensure that, as gas competition opens up, all operating companies adopt the best practices to serve all consumers and meet their public service obligations. |
| *operations* | Management: The head office is in London and there are ten regional offices. The Council is financed by a grant-in-aid from the DTI. DTI authorises staff numbers and conditions of service. |
| | Policy: To become more proactive in representing consumer interests within an increasingly fragmented industry. To ensure that business and domestic consumers have a real choice of efficient suppliers. To ensure that the Regulator puts consumer interests at the heart of regulation. |
| | Trends: Government's review of regulation in 1998 could change GCC's vote. |
| *performance* | 1996/97 standards of service not met. |
| *board* | Council has up to 20 members, including a stipendiary Chairman and six salaried members who represent regional gas consumer interests. Others are unsalaried and are from backgrounds and professions appropriate to the Council's work. |

| | |
|---|---|
| Chairman | Jenny Kirkpatrick |
| Member for Wales | John Bellis |
| Member for Scotland | Ken Gilbert MBE |
| Member for the East of England | Nick Ridley JP |
| Specialist Member | Bill Sinden |
| Member for the West of England | Linda Wilhams |
| Member for the North of England | Patricia Wynne CBE |

*staff*     81 (68 in regional offices, 13 head office)

| | |
|---|---|
| Director | Sue Slipman OBE |
| Field Director | Phillip Hamer |
| Finance Officer | Brian Ayres |
| Information Technology Manager | Stephen Greenhalgh |
| Policy Development Adviser | Jacquie Mackenzie-Taylor |
| Administrative Services Manager | Patricia Ormiston |
| Public Affairs Officer | Elizabeth Vaughan |
| Manager, London & South East | Nikki Abraham |
| Manager, East Midlands | Chris Chemney |
| Manager, Eastern | Ray Cope |
| Manager, Southern | Peter Court |
| Deputy Manager, London & South East | Hilary Horley |

| Manager, West Midlands | Janet Marsh |
| Manager, North East | Hilary Putman |
| Manager, Scotland | Euan Robson |
| Manager, North West | David Sidebottom |
| Manager, Northern | Robert Todd |
| Manager, Wales | Helen Wooldridge |

*financial*

**RECEIPTS & PAYMENTS**

| **Year end: 31 March 1996** | **1997** | **1996** |
|---|---|---|
| | £ | £ |
| **RECEIPTS** | | |
| Grant-in-aid received during the year | 2,924,000 | 2,759,057 |
| Grant-in-aid transferred from pension fund account | 15,515 | 44,943 |
| Sundry receipts | 76,805 | 105,906 |
| Net pension receipts | 31,592 | (15,515) |
| | **3,047,912** | **2,894,391** |
| **PAYMENTS** | | |
| **General** | | |
| Salaries | 1,688,771 | 1,599,943 |
| Rent and office expenses | 579,622 | 539,812 |
| Travel and subsistence | 114,026 | 117,812 |
| Other office expenses | 227,742 | 238,002 |
| Sundry expenses | 51,997 | 32,833 |
| Publications | 6,077 | 7,211 |
| Research | 15,218 | 9,294 |
| Communications | 67,967 | 102,530 |
| Training | 15,829 | 31,875 |
| Subscriptions | 2,672 | 2,886 |
| Entertainment | 7,114 | 8,006 |
| Miscellaneous | 2,634 | 3,950 |
| Petty cash | 3,660 | 6,877 |
| New technology | 235,864 | 241,455 |
| | **3,019,193** | **2,942,486** |
| Pension fund account transfer | - | 44,943 |
| | **3,019,193** | **2,987,429** |

*advisers*  **Auditors**   Kingston Smith

*publications*   *Annual Reports, Our Standards of Service, Gas Problems? We Can Help*

*branches*

*Scotland*
86 George Street
Edinburgh EH2 3BU
Tel 0131 2266523
Fax 0131 2203732

*North West*
Boulton House
Chorlton Street
Manchester M1 3HY
Tel 0161 2361926
Fax 0161 2368896

*East Midlands*
Carlton House
Regent Road
Leicester LE1 6YH
Tel 0116 2556611
Fax 0116 2556609

*Wales*
Caradog House
St Andrew's Place
Cardiff CF1 3BE
Tel 01222 226547
Fax 01222 238611

*Southern*
3rd Floor Roddis House
4-12 Old Christchurch Road
Bournemouth BH1 1LG
Tel 01202 556654
Fax 01202 291080

*Northern*
Northumberland House
Princess Square
Newcastle upon Tyne NE1 8ER
Tel 0191 2619561
Fax 0191 2220071

*North East*
No 1 Eastgate
Leeds LS2 7RL
Tel 0113 2439961
Fax 0113 2426935

*West Midlands*
Broadway House
Calthorpe Road
Birmingham B15 1TH
Tel 0121 4550285
Fax 0121 456 2976

*Eastern*
51 Station Road
Letchworth
Herts SG6 3BQ
Tel 01462 685399
Fax 01462 480902

# *Geffrye Museum*

Kingsland Road
London E2 8EA

**Tel** 0171 739 9893
**Fax** 0171 729 5647

**E-mail** geffrye-museum.org.uk
**Web** http://www.lattimore.co.uk/geffrye

**Contact** Nancy Loader

| | |
|---|---|
| *status* | Executive body |
| *founded* | 1990 (as executive body) |
| *sponsor* | Department for Culture, Media and Sport (DCMS) |
| *powers* | Trust deeds |
| *mission* | To encourage people to learn from and enjoy the museum's collections, buildings and gardens. |
| *tasks* | To acquire, preserve, research and manage collections and information relating to the history of English domestic furniture and interiors. To provide services and facilities to the benefit and enjoyment of visitors. |
| *operations* | Management: Twelve Trustees have responsibility for policy, financial accountability and the overall management. The museum's day-to-day management and development is run by the Director, who reports to the Trustees. The museum is organised under three departments (Curatorial, Public Services, Finance and Administration), each led by a senior member of staff, who, with the Director, form the management team. |
| | Policy: To increase visitor numbers and educational services as a result of new extension. |
| | Trends: Collections must be accessible and useful to the public. |
| *performance* | Record number of visitors and high level of satisfaction. Increased earned income as percentage of grant-in-aid income. |
| *board* | The Chairman and three Trustees are appointed by the Secretary of State and the remainder of the Board is self-selecting. |

| Chairman | The Baroness Brigstocke |
|---|---|
| Trustees | Christopher Claxton Stevens |
| | Anna Ford |
| | Daphne Gould OBE |
| | Philip Hedley |
| | Brenda Herbert |
| | Richard Hunting |
| | Martin Landau |
| | Robert Marshall-Andrews QC |
| | Judith Mayhew |
| | Frank Smith |
| | Lady Vaizey |

*staff* 28

| Director | David Dewing |
|---|---|

| *advisers* | **Bankers** | National Westminster Bank |
|---|---|---|
| | **Auditors** | Chantrey Vellacott |
| | **Solicitors** | Payne Hicks Beach |

# General Consumer Council for Northern Ireland

Elizabeth House
116 Holywood Road
Belfast BT4 1NY

**Tel** 01232 672488
**Fax** 01232 657701

**E-mail** gcc@nics.gov.uk

| | |
|---|---|
| *status* | Executive body |
| *founded* | 1985 |
| *sponsor* | Northern Ireland Office, Department of Economic Development (DEDNI) |
| *powers* | General Consumer Council (NI) Order 1984, Gas (NI) Order 1996 |
| *mission* | To give a voice to consumers and ensure that their interests are articulated and defended in NI. |
| *tasks* | Carries out research, publishes reports, seeks to influence both the public and private sectors, and campaigns for a fair deal. Has statutory responsibilities to promote and safeguard the interests of consumers including specific responsibilities for transport, energy, food and natural gas. |
| *operations* | Management: The Director reports to the Council. Works closely with trading standards departments. |
| | Policy: Making consumers aware of their rights is still a top priority. |
| | Trends: Rapid changes in technology, eg the Internet, have implications for consumers. |
| *board* | The Council is appointed following ministerial approval. |

| | | |
|---|---|---|
| Chairman | Mrs Joan Whiteside | |
| Deputy Chairman | David Gray | |
| Members | Ciaran Brolly | Pat Mallon |
| | Ann Collins | Rory McShane |
| | Daniel Corr | Brian Oliphant |
| | Mark Gavin | Denis Smith |
| | Felicity Huston | Jacqueline Weir |
| | Dawn Livingstone | Jane Wilde |
| *Accounting Officer* | *Director* | |

*staff*  9

| | |
|---|---|
| Director | Maeve Bell |
| Assistant Director | Sam Miskelly |
| Consumer Affairs Officer | Lillian Buchanan |
| Consumer Affairs Officer - Education | Carol Edwards |
| Finance & Administration Officer | Alison Hawthorne |
| Consumer Affairs Officer - Research | Wesley Henderson |

*financial*

| RECEIPTS & PAYMENTS Year end: 31 March | 1997 £ | 1996 £ | 1995 £ |
|---|---|---|---|
| **RECEIPTS** | | | |
| Grants received from Department of Economic Development | 462,000 | 439,000 | 420,000 |
| Operating receipts | 1,219 | 5,217 | 209 |
| Independent project income | 15,681 | 16,002 | 16,500 |
| Bank Interest received | 111 | 469 | - |
| | 479,011 | 460,688 | 436,709 |
| **PAYMENTS** | | | |
| Corporate programme | 86,841 | 99,081 | 90,715 |
| Salaries and wages | 253,406 | 238,776 | 218,752 |
| Other operating payments | 111,069 | 112,025 | 119,803 |
| | 451,316 | 449,882 | 429,270 |
| **SURPLUS FROM OPERATIONS** | **27,695** | **10,806** | **7,439** |
| Other Payments | 25,329 | 5,876 | 7,167 |
| **EXCESS OF RECEIPTS OVER PAYMENTS** | **2,366** | **4,930** | **272** |

| *advisers* | **Auditors** | KPMG | |
|---|---|---|---|
| | | Northern Ireland Audit Office | 106 University Street, Belfast BT7 1EU |

*publications*  *Raising Standards - Protection Rights 1985-1990, The General Consumer Council Pack, Charter Standards Statement*

# Government Car & Despatch Agency (GCDA)

46 Ponton Road
London SW8 5AX

**Tel** 0171 217 3838
**Fax** 0171 217 3875

*status*  Executive agency

*founded*  1997

*sponsor*  Cabinet Office, Office of Public Service (OPS)

*powers*  Framework Document 1997

*mission*  To provide secure transport, distribution and mail services to central government, the public sector and other approved customers.

*tasks*  Two separate businesses: Government Car Service provides long- and short-term chauffeur and car hire services to the Prime Minister, government ministers and other public sector customers, taxi booking services, protected security cars and drivers trained in defensive driving techniques, driver training courses; InterDespatch Service provides secure mail services to government departments and the public sector, motorcycle courier services, van and driver hire, special mail delivery services, associated mail services, eg file storage, confidential waste disposal.

*operations*  Management: Chancellor of the Duchy of Lancaster determines policy and financial resources. Operates predominantly in London, but also bases in Cardiff and Bradford. The Minister appoints the Chief Executive and approves the business plans and performance targets. The Chief Executive is responsible to the Minister for day-to-day management.

*performance*  Targets have been set for 1997/98.

*board*  The Minister may appoint an Advisory Board.

| Chief Executive | Nicholas Matheson |
|---|---|
| *Accounting Officer* | *Chief Executive* |

# Government Property Lawyers (GPL)

Riverside Chambers
Castle Street
Taunton
Somerset TA1 4AP

**Tel** 01823 345200
**Fax** 01823 345202

*status*  Executive agency

*founded*  1993

*sponsor*  Treasury Solicitor's Department

*powers*  The Attorney-General has Ministerial responsibility for the Agency

*mission*  To meet its clients' needs; to deliver a quality service that provides best value for money; to recover full operating costs.

*tasks*  To provide a comprehensive and efficient conveyancing and lands advisory service to government departments and other publicly financed bodies in England and Wales. GPL services include Private Finance Initiative projects, purchase of land and buildings, sale of surplus land, negotiation of high-value commercial leases for office accommodation including development and construction contracts and land transactions of all kinds, and advice on all land matters.

**operations**  Management: Established within the Treasury Solicitor's Department, GPL operates under gross running cost control and is subject to market testing. It is one of the largest property law offices in England and Wales. General management is the responsibility of the Chief Executive supported by a Management Board which he chairs. GPL is organised into three conveyancing groups and one advisory group, each headed by a Board director, and one administrative group working directly to the Chief Executive.

Policy: To develop long-term relationships with client government departments, by offering a more comprehensive range of services, and cementing them through service level agreements. Also to remain competitive, a high-priority given to management and employee development, ensuring the highest calibre workforce.

Trends: The period since the creation of GPL has seen falling workloads and increased competition throughout the whole legal profession. GPL has responded by concentrating on the structure of its business which has resulted in a reduction of staff and a transitional phase in which the full effects of market testing have not yet been seen. But the shift from high-volume work to lower-volume but more complex work is a trend likely to continue.

**board**  Management Board appointed from within the agency.

| | |
|---|---|
| Chief Executive | Philip Horner |
| Acting Group Director | David Ager |
| Group Director | Maurice Benmayor |
| Advisory Group Director | Richard Paddock |
| Group Director | Mike Rawlins |
| Group Director | Andrew Scarfe |

**financial**

| INCOME & EXPENDITURE Year end: 31 March | 1997 £000 | 1996 £000 | 1995 £000 |
|---|---|---|---|
| **INCOME** | | | |
| Income from continuing operations | 4,616 | 4,784 | 5,808 |
| **OPERATING COSTS** | | | |
| Staff costs | 3,159 | 3,279 | 3,393 |
| Depreciation | 104 | 108 | 66 |
| Other operating costs | 1,173 | 1,421 | 1,432 |
| Operational costs | - | - | 410 |
| **TOTAL OPERATING EXPENDITURE** | 4,436 | 4,808 | (5,301) |
| **OPERATING SURPLUS/(DEFICIT)** | 180 | (24) | 507 |
| Less: loss on disposal of fixed assets | (1) | (5) | (4) |
| Notional interest payable | (90) | (93) | (25) |
| **SURPLUS (DEFICIT) FOR THE FINANCIAL YEAR** | 89 | (122) | 478 |
| **TRANSFER TO GENERAL FUND** | 89 | (122) | 478 |

**staff**  120

**advisers**

| | |
|---|---|
| **Bankers** | National Westminster Bank Paymaster General |
| **Auditors** | National Audit Office |
| **Solicitors** | Treasury Solicitor |
| **Public Relations** | Central Office of Information |

**publications**  Annual Report

# Government Purchasing Agency (GPA)

Annex 6
Castle Buildings
Upper Newtownards
Belfast BT4 3TP

**Tel** 01232 526391
**Fax** 01232 526564

| | |
|---|---|
| *status* | Executive agency |
| *founded* | 1996 |
| *sponsor* | Northern Ireland Office, Department of Finance and Personnel (DFP) |
| *powers* | Framework Document 1996 |
| *mission* | Ensuring the best use of all the resources available to the Secretary of State in pursuit of government policy and objectives. |
| *tasks* | Establishes effective procurement contracts for goods and services on behalf of customers. Gives professional advice to Ministers and NI public bodies on all procurement matters. Uses its considerable purchasing power to sharpen small companies' competitiveness and to protect the environment. |
| *operations* | Management: The Chief Executive reports to the Secretary of State. He is supported by a Board comprising a Deputy Chief Executive and three Directors. Client organisations have been untied from GPA so it must be a customer-driven organisation delivering value for money. Purchasing on behalf of customers is managed by three Customer Service Managers. GPA's direct and indirect spend in 1996/97 was about £250 million. |
| | Policy: Establishing staff training programme. |
| | Trends: DFP intends to operate the GPA as a trading fund. Significant increase in customers. |
| *performance* | Successful performance in first year, while setting up agency. |

*board*

| | |
|---|---|
| Chief Executive | David Court |
| Acting Deputy Chief Executive | Gerry Murray |
| Finance Director | Brendan O'Neill |
| Director of Capital Works | Paul Snelling |
| Director of Operations | Malcolm Turner |
| *Accounting Officer* | *Chief Executive* |

*staff*  73

*financial*

| INCOME & EXPENDITURE | |
|---|---|
| Year end: 31 March | **1997** |
| | **£000** |
| **OPERATING INCOME** | **88** |
| **EXPENDITURE** | |
| Staff costs | 1511 |
| Depreciation and amortisation | 42 |
| Other operating and administration costs | 596 |
| | **2149** |
| **COST OF OPERATIONS BEFORE FINANCING** | **2061** |
| Interest on capital employed | 15 |
| **NET COST OF OPERATIONS AFTER COST OF CAPITAL** | **2076** |

# Great Britain - China Centre

15 Belgrave Square
London SW1X 8PS

**Tel** 0171 235 6696
**Fax** 0171 245 6885

**E-mail** contact@gbcc.org.uk
**Web** http://www.gbcc.org.uk

**Contact** Katie Lee

| | |
|---|---|
| *status* | Executive body |
| *founded* | 1974 |
| *sponsor* | Foreign and Commonwealth Office (FCO) |
| *powers* | Articles of Association |
| *mission* | To promote closer economic, professional, cultural and academic relations between Britain and China and to encourage mutual knowledge and understanding. |
| *tasks* | Core activities are: the exchange programme (for both British and Chinese professionals and experts) which operates in five main areas - legal development and criminal justice, economic reform, public administration and social policy, environment, arts and humanities; the Information and Advice Service which publishes (eg *China Review* and the *Directory of British Organisations with an Interest in China*), briefs British individuals before departure to China and runs lectures and seminars. |
| *operations* | Management:  The Centre is governed by the Executive Committee and run by a small committed team of Chinese speakers. It is funded primarily by an annual FCO grant but also raises project finance from the private sector. The Centre also administers The Great Britain-China Educational Trust which promotes the education of British and Chinese peoples in the cultures and institutions of each other's country and receives financial support from the Sino-British Fellowship Trust.  The cost of administering grant applications made from China are shared with the Universities' China Committee. |
| | Policy: To reduce the proportion of FCO grant-in-aid in its overall budget. |
| | Trends:  Ways of attracting more corporate members are being sought. |
| *board* | Executive Committee members appointed by Executive Committee. |

| | |
|---|---|
| President | Lord Howe of Aberavon PC QC |
| Vice Presidents | Lord Callaghan of Cardiff KG |
| | Graham Greene CBE |
| | Sir Edward Heath KG MBE MP |
| | Lord MacLehose of Beoch KT GBE KCMG KCVO |
| Chairman | David Brewer |
| Vice Chairmen | Dr Abraham S-T Lue MBE |
| | Lady Youde OBE |
| Treasurer | Michael McIntyre |
| Members | Prof Hugh Baker |
| | Gordon S Barrass CMG |
| | Ben Chapman MP |
| | David Coates |
| | Martin Davidson |
| | Peter Goldsmith QC |
| | Alistair Goodlad MP |
| | Mike Hancock MP |
| | Adrian Johnson |
| | Miao Ling Thompson |
| | D'Arcy Payne |
| | Ian Stewart MP |
| | Jonathan Swire |
| | Elizabeth Wright |
| | Michael Yahuda |

*staff*　　4

| | |
|---|---|
| Director | Katie Lee |
| Deputy Director | Fiona McConnon |

*financial*

| INCOME & EXPENDITURE Year end: 31 March | 1997 £ | 1996 £ |
|---|---|---|
| **INCOME** | | |
| Grant-in-aid | 235,000 | 235,000 |
| Investment income | - | 1,317 |
| Fees and donations | 2,290 | 85 |
| Administration of Trust | 6,000 | 1,546 |
| Subscriptions | 13,569 | 13,717 |
| Grant from GBCET | - | 4,000 |
| Miscellaneous | 438 | 540 |
| Exchange programme ODA grant | 21,462 | 40,908 |
| Exchange programme other | 2,412 | 523 |
| Information services | 39,283 | 39,186 |
| | 324,258 | 336,822 |
| **COST OF ACTIVITIES** | | |
| Exchange programme | 78,084 | 55,266 |
| Information services | 55,003 | 73,969 |
| Membership services | 2,662 | 3,534 |
| | 135,749 | (132,769) |
| **GROSS SURPLUS** | 188,509 | 204,053 |
| Administration expenses | (205,408) | (189,858) |
| **OPERATING SURPLUS/(DEFICIT)** | (16,899) | 14,195 |
| Interest receivable | 2,464 | 1,574 |
| Interest payable | - | 34 |
| **NET SURPLUS/(DEFICIT) FOR THE YEAR** | (14,435) | 15,735 |

*advisers*  **Bankers**    Royal Bank of Scotland

**Auditors**    Keith Vaudrey & Co

*publications*  Annual Report, China Review, Directory of British Organisations with an Interest in China

# *Hannah Research Institute*

Ayr KA6 5HL

**Tel** 01292 674000
**Fax** 01292 674004

**E-mail** username@main.hri.sari.ac.uk
**Web** http://www.hri.sari.ac.uk

*status*        Executive body

*founded*       1928

*sponsor*       Scottish Office, Agricultural, Environment and Fisheries Department (SOAEFD)

*powers*        Articles of Association

*mission*       Research into animal biotechnology and bioscience, ultimately aimed at wealth creation and enhancing the quality of life.

*tasks*         Research in animal sciences concentrates on the biological processes that are important in animal productivity and in enhancing animal welfare. Food research concentrates on the science and technology of making attractive and better tasting food products with improved nutritional value, freshness and convenience. Some research is commissioned by SOAEFD.

*operations*    Management: The Principal of Glasgow University is Chairman of the Council and the Directorship is a joint appointment with the university to the Hannah Chair. Close ties in research and postgraduate studies with Glasgow University. Most public funding is from SOAEFD.

Policy: Increasing information to public and other scientists about the work they do.

Trends: Growth in media interest in science stories to the detriment of the scientific process.

*performance*  Internationally recognised achievements.

*board*         Two members of the Council of the Institute are appointed by the Secretary of State for Scotland, three by the University of Glasgow and three by the Scottish Agricultural College.

| | | |
|---|---|---|
| Chairman | Sir Graeme J Davies | |
| *Nominated by University of Glasgow* | | |
| Members | Prof JR Coggins | |
| | Prof NG Wright | |
| *Nominated by Scottish Agricultural College* | | |
| | A Campbell | |
| | WJ Ferguson | |
| | J McMyn | |
| *Nominated by Secretary of State for Scotland* | | |
| | LP Hamilton CB | |
| | JR Laidlaw | |
| *Nominated by Council* | | |
| | TS Bryson | |

**staff**  140

| | |
|---|---|
| Director | Prof Malcolm Peaker |
| Head, Science Development & Planning | RG Vernon |
| Operations Manager | E Taylor |
| Head, Cell Biochemistry | VA Zammit |
| Head, Cell Physiology Group | CJ Wilde |
| Head, Animal Physiology Group | CH Knight |
| Head, Food Quality | DD Muir |
| Head, Integrative Metabolism | A Faulkner |
| Head, Molecular Homeorhesis | RG Vernon |
| Head, Molecular Recognition | DJ Flint |
| Head, Scientific Liaison, Information & Media Services | E Taylor |
| Information Technology & Computing | TG Parker |
| Institute Secretary | MW Scott |
| Building Services Manager | J McCallum |
| Head, Biological Resources | CH Knight |

# Health Estates

Stoney Road
Dundonald
Belfast BT16 1US

**Tel** 01232  520025
**Fax** 01232 523900

**Contact** Mrs A Toner

| | |
|---|---|
| **status** | Executive agency |
| **founded** | 1995 |
| **sponsor** | Northern Ireland Office, Department of Health and Social Services |
| **powers** | Framework Document |
| **mission** | To provide a centre of specialist professional and technical health and social care estate expertise in contributing to the health and social well being of the people of Northern Ireland. |
| **tasks** | Provides policy, advice, guidance and support on estate matters at strategic and operational levels to the various bodies charged with responsability for the Health and Social Services in Northern Ireland. |

**board**

| | |
|---|---|
| Chief Executive | RH Browne |
| Director, Estate Policy | G McConkey |
| Director, Estates Development | I Spence |
| Director, Consultancy Services | S Blayney |

**financial**  Expenditure £4.179m, 1996/97.

# Health & Safety Commission (HSC)
# Health & Safety Executive (HSE)

Rose Court
2 Southwark Bridge Road
London SE1 9HS

**Tel** 0171 717 6000
**Fax** 0171 717 6616          **Web** http://www.open.gov.uk/hse/hse

| | |
|---|---|
| *status* | Executive bodies |
| *founded* | 1974 |
| *sponsor* | Department of the Environment, Transport and the Regions (DETR) |
| *powers* | Health and Safety at Work Act 1974 |
| *mission* | To ensure that risks to people's health and safety from work activities are properly controlled. |
| *tasks* | To protect the health, safety and welfare of employees, and to safeguard others, principally the public, who may be exposed to risks from industrial activity by: defining standards; promoting and enforcing compliance with legislation; inspecting workplaces; investigating accidents and industrial health problems; provide specific services (eg Employment Medical Advisory Service); provide information to ministers and the public; negotiation and implementation of EU Directives etc. |
| *operations* | Management: The HSC is responsible for policy, HSE for implementation. The HSC is run by the HSE. The HSE is a distinct statutory body consisting of the Director General, Deputy Director General and Chief Executive Offshore Safety, appointed by the Commission. There are seven regional offices and each is responsible for a different industrial national interest group. |
| | Policy: Major reforms of offshore health and safety. Raising profile of HSC with small firms. |
| | Trends: Fatal injuries at work have been decreasing since 1992/93, but 1996/97 figures were slightly higher than the previous year. European Agency for Health and Safety is being set up. |
| *performance* | Exceeded targets for efficiency gains and economies in 1996/97. |
| *board* | Members of the Council are appointed by the Secretary of State from business and unions. |

| Chairman | Frank J Davies CBE, OStJ | |
|---|---|---|
| Members | Cynthia Atwell | |
| | Eddie Carrick | Dr Michael McKiernan |
| | Christopher Chope OBE | Dr Geraldine Schofield |
| | Anne Gibson | Ann Scully OBE |
| | Alan Grant | Rex HM Symons CBE |
| *Health & Safety Executive* | | |
| Director General | | Jenny Bacon CB |
| Deputy Director General | | David Eves CB |
| Chief Executive, Offshore Safety | | Roderick Allison CB |

| | |
|---|---|
| *staff* | 4077 |

| | |
|---|---|
| Director General | Jenny Bacon |
| Deputy Director General | David Eves |
| Director, Safety Policy Directorate | Mark Addison |
| Director, Offshore Safety Division | Roderick Allison |
| Director, Field Operations Directorate | Dr Adrian Ellis |
| Director, Health Directorate | Dr Peter Graham |
| Director Chief Inspector, Nuclear Safety Directorate | Dr Sam Harbison |
| Director, Resources & Planning Directorate | Richard Hillier |
| Chief Scientist | Dr Jim McQuaid |
| Head, Operations Unit | David Ashton |
| Head, Local Authority Unit | Don Barnett |
| Chief Executive, Health & Safety Laboratory | Dr David Buchanan |
| Director, Electrical Equipment Certification Service | Ian Cleare |
| Head, Policy Unit | Richard Clifton |

| Head, Chemicals & Hazardous Installations Division | Dr Paul Davies |
| Solicitor | Barry Ecclestone |
| Chief Inspector, Mines Inspectorate | Brian Langdon |
| Head, Senior Management & Support Unit | Bob Ledsome |
| Chief Inspector, Railway Inspectorate | Stan Robertson |

**financial**

**RECEIPTS & EXPENDITURE**

| Year end: 31 March | 1997 £000 | 1996 £000 | 1995 £000 |
|---|---|---|---|
| **CURRENT EXPENDITURE** | | | |
| Staff-related expenditure | 156,808 | 167,369 | 168,415 |
| Other current expenditure | 52,059 | 34,613 | 31,977 |
| | 208,867 | 201,982 | 200,392 |
| **CAPITAL EXPENDITURE** | | | |
| Capital equipment | 6,239 | 10,075 | 10,024 |
| Capital building | 1,094 | 3,819 | 6,073 |
| | 7,333 | 13,894 | 16,097 |
| **HEALTH & SAFETY LABORATORY** | -2,579 | 0 | - |
| **RECEIPTS** | 35,786 | 38,209 | 40,130 |
| **NET EXPENDITURE** | 179,487 | 177,667 | 176,359 |

**branches**

*Wales & West*
Brunel House
2 Fitzalan Road
Cardiff CF2 1SH
Tel 01222 263000
Fax 01222 263120

Inter City House
Mitchell Lane
Victoria Street
Bristol BS1 6AN
Tel 01179 886000
Fax 01179 262998

The Marches House
Midway
Newcastle under Lyme ST5 1DT
Tel 01782 602300
Fax 01782 602400

*Home Counties Region*
14 Cardiff Road
Luton LU1 1PP
Tel 01582 444200
Fax 01582 444320

Priestley House
Priestley Road
Basingstoke RG24 9NW
Tel 01256 404000
Fax 01256 404100

39 Baddow Road
Chelmsford CM2 0HL
Tel 01245 706200
Fax 01245 706222

*London & South Region*
1 Long Lane
London SE1 4PG
Tel 0171 556 2100
Fax 0171 556 2200

Maritime House
1 Linton Road
Barking IG11 8HF
Tel 0181 235 8000
Fax 0181 235 8001

3 East Grinstead House
London Road
East Grinstead RH19 1RR
Tel 01342 334200
Fax 01342 334222

*Midlands Region*
McLaren Building
35 Dale End
Birmingham B4 7NP
Tel 0121 607 6200
Fax 0121 607 6349

Belgrave House
1 Greyfriars
Northampton NN1 2BS
Tel 01604 738300
Fax 01604 738333

1st Floor
The Pearson Building
55 Upper Parliament Street
Nottingham NG1 6AU
Tel 01159 712800
Fax 01159 712802

*Yorkshire & North East Region*
8 St Paul's Street
Leeds LS1 2LE
Tel 0113 283 4200
Fax 0113 283 4296

Sovereign House
110 Queen Street
Sheffield S1 2ES
Tel 0114 291 2300
Fax 0114 291 2379

Arden House
Regent Centre
Gosforth
Newcastle upon Tyne NE3 3JN
Tel 0191 202 6200
Fax 0191 202 6300

*North West Region*
Quay House
Quay Street
Manchester M3 3JB
Tel 0161 952 8200
Fax 0161 952 8222

Victoria House
Ormskirk Road
Preston PR1 1HH
Tel 01772 836200
Fax 01772 836222

The Triad
Stanley Road
Bootle
Merseyside L20 3PG
Tel 0151 479 2200
Fax 0151 479 2201

*Scotland*
Belford House
59 Belford Road
Edinburgh EH4 3UE
Tel 0131 247 2000
Fax 0131 247 2121

375 West George Street
Glasgow G2 4LW
Tel 0141 275 3000
Fax 0141 275 3100

*Mining*
Room 514
St Anne's House
University Road
Bootle
Merseyside L20 3RA
Tel 0151 951 4136

*Railways*
4th Floor
Rose Court
2 Southwark Bridge
London SE1 9HS
Tel 0171 717 6533

*Nuclear*
St Peter's House
Balliol Road
Bootle
Merseyside L20 2LZ
Tel 0151 951 4103

*Offshore Oil & Gas*
Lord Cullen House
Fraser Place
Aberdeen AB9 1BU
Tel 01224 252652

*Chemicals & Hazardous Installations*
St Anne's House
Stanley Precinct
Bootle
Merseyside L20 3RA
Tel 0151 951 3235

*Explosives*
Magdalen House
Stanley Precinct
Bootle
Merseyside L20 3QZ
Tel 0151 951 4025

*Health & Safety Laboratory*
Broad Lane
Sheffield S3 7HQ
Tel 0114 289 2920

*HSE Books*
PO Box 1999
Sudbury
Suffolk CO10 6FS
Tel 01787 881165
Fax 01787 313995

# *Higher Education Funding Council for England (HEFCE)*

Northavon House
Coldharbour Lane
Bristol BS16 1QD

**Tel** 0117 931 7316
**Fax** 0117 931 7463

**E-mail** hefce@hefce.ac.uk
**Web** http://www.hefce.ac.uk/

**Contact** External Relations Department

| | |
|---|---|
| *status* | Executive body |
| *founded* | 1992 |
| *sponsor* | Department for Education and Employment (DfEE) |
| *powers* | Further Education and Higher Education Acts (FHE) 1992 and 1994 |
| *mission* | Working in partnership, it promotes and funds high-quality, cost-effective teaching and research, meeting the needs of students, the economy and society. |
| *tasks* | Funding over 135 English universities and colleges, each with its own distinctive mission, history and character, and promoting excellence in research through selective research funding. Also specifically: maintaining effective relationships with Higher Education Institutions (HEIs); keeping student numbers approximately within government target numbers; promoting the quality of teaching and research; monitoring the financial health of HEIs; promoting the sector's infrastructure and capital base. |

**operations**   Management: One of the three national councils replacing the University Funding Council and the Polytechnics and Colleges Funding Council.

Policy: To maintain broad policy objectives in teaching and research within government limits on funds and student numbers.

Trends: The age participation rate of young people studying full-time in higher education remains about 30% and there were 1.4 million university and college students funded by the HEFCE, of whom one-third were part time. There was a large reduction in capital grant and HEIs are moving from wafer-thin surplus into deficit and assistance both financial and technical will be offered to HEIs experiencing particular financial difficulty.

**board**   Appointed by the Secretary of State, from universities, the professions and industry

| | | |
|---|---|---|
| Chairman | Sir Michael Checkland | |
| Chief Executive | Prof Brian Fender | |
| Members | Mrs Joan Bingley | |
| | Anthony Booth CBE | David Potter CBE |
| | Prof Marilyn Butler | Prof Sir Gareth Roberts |
| | Prof Sir John Cadogan | Ms Barbara Stephens |
| | Prof Ron Cooke | Prof Sir Stewart Sutherland |
| | Dr David Fussey | Dr Keith Taylor |
| | Ms Caroline Neville | Ms Dorma Urwin |
| Assessor | Roger Dawe CB OBE | |
| Observers | Prof John Andrews | Mike Mercer |
| | Peter Holmes | Prof John Sizer |
| *Accounting Officer* | *Chief Executive* | |

**staff**   165

**financial**

| INCOME & EXPENDITURE Year end: 31 March | 1997 £000 | 1996 £000 | 1995 £000 |
|---|---|---|---|
| **INCOME** | | | |
| Government grants (DfEE) | | | |
| Recurrent and capital | 3,434,808 | 3,601,990 | 3,408,734 |
| Access funds | 21,693 | 21,693 | 21,014 |
| Council administration | 12,478 | 11,761 | 11,041 |
| | **3,468,979** | **3,635,444** | **3,440,789** |
| Transfer from deferred grant account | 399 | 429 | 581 |
| Income from activities | 313 | 362 | 265 |
| Funding from other sources | 4,834 | 4,751 | 3,335 |
| Other operating income | 48 | 30 | 175 |
| | **5,195** | **5,143** | **3,775** |
| | **3,474,573** | **3,641,016** | **3,445,145** |
| **EXPENDITURE** | | | |
| Grants paid to institutions | | | |
| Recurrent and capital | 3,452,652 | 3,593,027 | 3,407,220 |
| Access funds | 21,693 | 21,693 | 21,014 |
| | **3,474,345** | **3,614,720** | **3,428,234** |
| Council administration | 13,594 | 12,910 | 12,032 |
| | **3,487,939** | **3,627,630** | **3,440,266** |
| **OPERATING SURPLUS (DEFICIT)** | **(13,366)** | **13,386** | **4,879** |
| Profit (loss) on sale of fixed assets | 7 | (4) | 5 |
| Appropriations to DfEE | (49) | (398) | (642) |
| **SURPLUS(DEFICIT) FOR THE PERIOD** | **(13,408)** | **12,984** | **4,242** |

**advisers**   
**Bankers**   Bank of England   Threadneedle Street, London

**Auditors**   National Audit Office   157-197 Buckingham Palace Road London SW1W 9SP

**Solicitors**   Beachcroft Stanley   21 Furnival Street, London EC4 1BN

**branches**   28th Floor
Centrepoint
103 New Oxford Street
London WC1A 1DD

# *Higher Education Funding Council for Wales (HEFCW)*

Linden Court
The Orchards
Ty Glas Avenue
Llanishen
Cardiff CF4 5DZ

**Tel** 01222 761861
**Fax** 01222 763163

| | |
|---|---|
| *status* | Executive body |
| *founded* | 1992 |
| *sponsor* | Welsh Office |
| *powers* | Further and Higher Education Act 1992 |
| *mission* | Responsible for the administration of funds in support of the provision of education and undertaking of research by higher education institutions (HEIs) in Wales. Also the funding of teacher training. |
| *tasks* | Allocates funds to 13 HEIs (the University of Glamorgan, four colleges and institutes of HE, and eight colleges of the University of Wales); collaborates with rest of UK in research and teaching quality assessments; carries out reviews and studies; collects, analyses and publishes information and statistics about the sector; represents the needs and aspirations of the sector to the Secretary of State. |
| *operations* | Management: The Chief Executive is a member of the Council and is accountable to the Secretary of State. The relationship between the HEFCW and the Welsh Office is defined in a Management Statement, including the Financial Memorandum describing the accountability of the Council and the role of the Chief Executive. The Council is supported by an executive organisation established jointly with the Further Education Funding Council for Wales (FEFCW). |
| | Policy: Initiatives to develop the contribution that HEIs make in support of wealth creation. To back institutions with high research ratings with greater funds. |
| | Trends: Significant reduction in funding for 1997/99. Improved research ratings in 1996 Research Assessment Exercise (RAE) for Wales. Good teaching assessments for Wales in 1996/97 Quality Assessments. |
| *performance* | There are no targets set for measuring performance. |
| *board* | Members of the Council are appointed by the Secretary of State from HEIs. |

| | |
|---|---|
| Chairman | Sir Philip Jones CB |
| Members | Prof John Andrews |
| | Prof Brian Clarkson |
| | Dr Eleri Edwards |
| | Dr Kenneth Gray CBE |
| | Alfred Morris |
| | Dr Brynley Roberts CBE |
| | Prof Roger Williams |
| *Accounting Officer* | *Chief Executive* |

*staff*  25

| | |
|---|---|
| Chief Executive | Prof John Andrews |
| Head of Finance & Common Services | Richard Hirst |
| Head of Higher Education Division | Dr Rowland Wynne |

*financial*

| **INCOME & EXPENDITURE** | | |
|---|---|---|
| **Year end: 31 March** | **1997** | **1996** |
| | **£000** | **£000** |
| **GROSS INCOME** | | |
| Grant-in-aid | 243,474 | 242,465 |
| Release of deferred government grant | 68 | 74 |
| Operating income | 1 | 2 |
| Other income | 1,312 | 1,275 |
| | **244,855** | **243,816** |

**EXPENDITURE**

| | | |
|---|---:|---:|
| Funding of higher education | | |
| Recurrent expenditure | 229,506 | 214,029 |
| Major capital work | 32 | 204 |
| Minor capital/estates development work | 11,022 | 11,795 |
| Purchase of equipment | - | 15,739 |
| Other purposes | 1,318 | 1,275 |
| | **241,878** | **243,042** |
| **Council expenditure** | | |
| Administration costs | 907 | 901 |
| Staff costs | 681 | 621 |
| Depreciation | 67 | 71 |
| Notional charges | | |
| Insurance | 3 | 2 |
| Cost of capital | 204 | 191 |
| | **1,862** | **1,786** |
| | **243,740** | **244,828** |
| **SURPLUS/(DEFICIT) ON OPERATING ACTIVITIES** | **1,115** | **(1,012)** |
| Interest receivable | 217 | 236 |
| **SURPLUS/(DEFICIT) FOR THE YEAR** | **1,332** | **(776)** |
| Appropriations | (219) | (239) |
| **SURPLUS/(DEFICIT) TRANSFERRED TO RESERVES** | **1,113** | **(1,015)** |

| *advisers* | **Bankers** | Midland Bank | 114 St Mary Street, Cardiff CF1 1LF |
|---|---|---|---|
| | **Auditors** | National Audit Office | 23/24 Park Place, Cardiff CF1 3BA |
| | **Solicitors** | Bevan Ashford | Newport Road, Cardiff CF2 1EL |

*publications* Annual Report, Corporate Plan, Profiles of Higher Education Institutions, Further and Higher Education Statistics in Wales, Statement of Service Standards

# Highlands & Islands Airports

Inverness Airport
Inverness IV1 2JB

**Tel** 01667 462445
**Fax** 01667 462579

| | |
|---|---|
| *status* | Private limited company owned by the Secretary of State for Scotland |
| *founded* | 1986 |
| *sponsor* | Secretary of State for Scotland |
| *powers* | Civil Aviation Act 1982 |
| *mission* | To offer social, business and welfare links to otherwise remote communities by providing an efficient, economical and safe airport infrastructure. |
| *tasks* | To manage and operate ten airports in the Highlands and Islands of Scotland - Barra, Benbecula, Campbeltown, Inverness, Islay, Kirkwall, Stornoway, Sumburgh, Tiree and Wick. |
| *operations* | Management: Head office relocated to purpose-built building adjacent to Inverness Airport. It undertakes legal/regulatory tasks previously undertaken by the CAA. |
| | Policy: The grant of some £6.4 million from the Secretary of State is to enable the company to reduce charges to users - other than oil-related traffic at Sumburgh - and the company's policy is to increase value for money to the communities and airlines served. |
| | Trends: Aircraft movements rose but passenger numbers fell slightly. Sumburgh oil-related traffic and revenue is greatly reduced. Inverness terminal building facilities will be redeveloped through the Public Finance Initiative. |
| *board* | Appointed by the Secretary of State. |

| Chairman | Peter J Grant |
|---|---|
| Directors | W Francis F Hamilton |
| | Robert M McLeod |
| | William K Semple |
| Secretary | A John Burns |

*staff*        194

| Managing Director | Bob McLeod |
|---|---|
| General Manager | Paul Jenkins |
| Fire Service | Roy Cartledge |
| Transport & Engineering | Keith Hodinott |
| Works | George McHollan |
| Personnel | Gordon McPhee |
| Operations | George Stevenson |

*financial*

**PROFIT & LOSS**

| Year end: 31 March | 1997 | 1996 | 1995 |
|---|---|---|---|
| | £000 | £000 | £000 |
| **TURNOVER** | | | |
| Traffic operations and other charges | 10,598 | 11,300 | 10,793 |
| Total grants received | 7,500 | 7,800 | 8,000 |
| Less capital grants carried to deferred income: | | | |
| Scottish Office | 750 | 3,090 | - |
| European Regional Development Fund | 320 | - | - |
| Scottish Office revenue grant | 6,430 | 4,710 | 8,000 |
| | 18,793 | 17,028 | 16,010 |
| Direct operating costs | 16,261 | 16,480 | 14,891 |
| **GROSS PROFIT (LOSS)** | **767** | **(470)** | **3,902** |
| Administrative expenses | 1,772 | 1,630 | 1,426 |
| **OPERATING (LOSS)** | **(1,005)** | **(2,100)** | **2,476** |
| Exceptional item | - | - | 1,170 |
| Interest receivable | 46 | 74 | 325 |
| **(LOSS) ON ORDINARY ACTIVITIES BEFORE TAX** | **(959)** | **(2,026)** | **1,631** |
| Tax on (loss) on ordinary activities | (66) | (475) | 910 |
| **(LOSS) FOR THE FINANCIAL YEAR** | **(893)** | **(1,551)** | **721** |

*advisers*      Auditors          Ernst & Young          Moray House, 16 Bank Street, Inverness IV1 1QY

*publications*  *Annual Report And Accounts 1996-1997*

*branches*

**Barra Airport**
*Manager* Peter Houghton
Tel  01871 890212
Fax  01871 890220

**Benbecula Airport**
*Manager* Mark Lowery
Tel  01870 602051
Fax  01870 602278

**Campbeltown Airport**
*Manager* John Scott
Tel  01586 553797
Fax  01586 555620

**Inverness Airport**
*Manager* James Walton
Tel  01463 232471
Fax  01463 462041

**Islay Airport**
*Manager* Pete Houghton
Tel  01496 302361
Fax  01496 302096

**Kirkwall Airport**
*Manager* Mick Bain
Tel  01856 872421
Fax  01856 875051

**Stornoway Airport**
*Manager* Malcolm Hay
Tel  01851 702256
Fax  01851 703115

**Sumburgh Airport**
*Manager* Amos Amos
Tel  01950 460654
Fax  01950 460218

**Tiree Airport**
*Manager* Pete Houghton
Tel  01879 220456
Fax  01879 220714

**Wick Airport**
*Manager* Angela Donaldson
Tel  01955 602215
Fax  01955 605946

# Highlands & Islands Enterprise (HIE)

Bridge House
20 Bridge Street
Inverness IV1 1QR

**Tel** 01463 234171
**Fax** 01463 244469

**E-mail** hie.general@hient.co.uk
**Web** http://www.hie.co.uk

**Contact** Iain A Robertson

| | |
|---|---|
| *status* | Executive body |
| *founded* | 1991 |
| *sponsor* | Scottish Office |
| *powers* | Enterprise and New Towns (Scotland) Act 1990 |
| *mission* | To enable the people of the area to realise their full potential through a strong and prosperous economy and a high quality of life. |
| *tasks* | Financing business; providing factories and offices; running training programmes; assisting community and cultural projects; furthering environmental improvement. |
| *operations* | Management: The Chief Executive and core body are based in Inverness. Ten Local Enterprise Companies (LECs) are regionally based and led by the private sector. They implement the strategy and provide assistance and advice at local level. The LECs are: Argyll & The Islands Enterprise; Caithness & Sutherland Enterprise; Inverness & Nairn Enterprise; Lochaber Limited; Moray Badenoch & Strathspey Enterprise; Orkney Enterprise; Ross & Cromarty Enterprise; Shetland Enterprise; Skye & Lochalsh Enterprise; Western Isles Enterprise. |
| | Policy: To diversify the area's economic activity: the key areas for growth being food and drink; manufacturing and production; tourism; knowledge, information and telecommunications. |
| | Trends: Continuing to encourage growth of manufactured exports, new businesses and improvements to infrastructure. |
| *performance* | A record number of jobs created or retained in 1996/97. |
| *board* | Members are appointed by Secretary of State. In 1997, the HIE network introduced Appointability through Openness policy to broaden selection. |

| | | |
|---|---|---|
| Chairman | AF Morrison CBE | |
| Chief Executive | IA Robertson CBE | |
| Members | Mrs A Banister | |
| | J Goodlad | JAD Harrison OBE |
| | J Gray | JA Nicolson |
| | S Gray | C Paterson |
| | H Halcro-Johnston | P Timms CBE |
| *Accounting Officer* | *Chief Executive* | |

*staff*    350

| | |
|---|---|
| Chief Executive | Iain A Robertson |
| Director Executive Office | Sandy Brady |
| Director Projects and Marketing | Maurice Cantley |
| Head of European Affairs | Frank Gaskell |
| Head of Communications | Bob Kass |
| Director Network Strategy | Ken MacTaggart |
| Senior Business Development Manager | Gordon Moggach |
| Director, Network Operations | Ralph Palmer |
| Director of Finance and Administration | Alan Price |
| Head of Personnel & Secretariat | Andrew Ross |
| *Argyll & The Islands Enterprise* | |
| Chairman | Hon Mike Shaw |
| Chief Executive | Ken Abernethy |
| *Caithness & Sutherland Enterprise* | |
| Chairman | Jack Watson |
| Chief Executive | Neil Money |
| *Inverness & Nairn Enterprise* | |
| Chairman | Norman Cordiner |
| Chief Executive | Fiona Larg |
| *Lochaber Ltd* | |
| Chairman | Andrew Rogers |
| Chief Executive | Douglas MacDiarmid |

| Moray Badenoch & Strathspey Enterprise | |
|---|---|
| Chairman | George Chesworth OBE |
| Chief Executive | Dick Ruane |
| *Orkney Enterprise* | |
| Chairman | Eric Green |
| Chief Executive | Ken Grant |
| *Ross & Cromarty Enterprise* | |
| Chairman | Alan Whiteford |
| Chief Executive | Sandy Cumming |
| *Shetland Enterprise* | |
| Chairman | Brian Anderson |
| Chief Executive | David Finch |
| *Skye & Lochalsh Enterprise* | |
| Chairman | Jim Hunter |
| Chief Executive | Lorne MacLeod |
| *Western Isles Enterprise* | |
| Chairwoman | Agnes Rennie |
| Chief Executive | Donnie MacAulay |

***financial***

**INCOME & EXPENDITURE**

| Year end: 31 March | 1997 £000 | 1996 £000 |
|---|---|---|
| **INCOME FROM OPERATING ACTIVITIES** | **8,948** | **7,012** |
| **EXPENDITURE ON OPERATING ACTIVITIES** | | |
| Enterprise | 50,447 | 43,065 |
| Environmental renewal | 3,708 | 3,948 |
| Skill-seekers | 6,202 | 5,784 |
| Training for Work | 4,299 | 4,604 |
| Community Action grants | 1,295 | 1,059 |
| | 65,951 | 58,460 |
| Administration and management charges | 12,716 | 13,164 |
| **DEFICIT ON OPERATING ACTIVITIES** | **(69,719)** | **(64,612)** |
| Notional interest charge | 2,417 | 2,718 |
| Investment income | 2,379 | 2,261 |
| Share of profits/(losses) of associated undertakings | 10 | (35) |
| **DEFICIT ON ORDINARY ACTIVITIES BEFORE TAXATION** | **(69,747)** | **(65,104)** |
| Taxation | 622 | 730 |
| Deficit on ordinary activities after taxation | (70,369) | (65,834) |
| Notional interest credit | 2,417 | 2,718 |
| **DEFICIT FOR THE YEAR** | **(67,952)** | **(63,116)** |
| Unrealised surplus/(loss) on revaluation of property | 1,888 | (998) |
| European Regional Development Fund received during the year | 1,677 | 2,855 |
| Grant-in-aid received | 59,099 | 60,249 |
| **TOTAL RECOGNISED GAINS AND LOSSES** | **(5,288)** | **(1,010)** |

***advisers*** **Auditors** National Audit Office 22 Melville Street
Edinburgh EH3 7NS

***publications*** *Annual Report, The Brief, Strategy for Enterprise Development*

***branches***

*Argyll & The Islands Enterprise*
The Enterprise Centre
Kilmory Industrial Estate
Lochgilphead PA31 8SH
Tel 01546 602281
Fax 01546 603964

*Caithness & Sutherland Enterprise*
Scapa House
Castlegreen Road
Thurso
Caithness KW14 7LS
Tel 01847 896115
Fax 01847 893383

*Inverness & Nairn Enterprise*
Castle Wynd
Inverness IV2 3DW
Tel 01463 713504
Fax 01463 712002

*Orkney Enterprise*
14 Queen Street
Kirkwall
Orkney KW15 1JE
Tel 01856 874638
Fax 01856 872915

*Ross & Cromarty Enterprise*
62 High Street
Invergordon
Ross-shire IV18 0AA
Tel 01349 853666
Fax 01349 853833

*Shetland Enterprise*
Toll Clock Shopping Centre
26 North Road
Lerwick
Shetland ZE1 0DE
Tel 01595 693177
Fax 01595 693208

Lochaber Ltd
St Mary's House
Gordon Square
Fort William PH33 6DY
Tel 01397 704326
Fax 01397 705309

Moray Badenoch & Strathspey Enterprise
Elgin Business Centre
Elgin
Moray IV30 1RH
Tel 01343 550567
Fax 01343 550678

Skye & Lochalsh Enterprise
King's House
The Green
Portree
Isle of Skye IV51 9BS
Tel 01478 612841
Fax 01478 612164

Western Isles Enterprise
3 Harbour View
Cromwell
Stornaway
Isle of Lewis HS1 2DF
Tel 01851 703703
Fax 01851 704130

# Highways Agency (HA)

St Christopher House
Southwark Street
London SE1 0TE

**Tel** 0171 921 4443
**Fax** 0171 921 2214

**E-mail** publicrelations@dial.pipex.com
**Web** http://www.highways.gov.uk

| | |
|---|---|
| *status* | Executive agency |
| *founded* | 1994 |
| *sponsor* | Department of the Environment, Transport and the Regions (DETR) |
| *powers* | Framework Document |
| *mission* | To secure an efficient, reliable, safe and environmentally acceptable motorway and trunk road network in England. |
| *tasks* | Managing, maintaining and improving England's 6600 miles of trunk roads and motorways. Contracting and managing agents to carry out the work on their behalf. Overseeing design, procurement and construction of new road schemes, some privately financed. |
| *operations* | Management: Secretary of State sets strategic policy framework and financial resources. Public and private sector contractual agents carry out the maintenance work (number of agents being reduced from 83 to 24). Advisory Board reports on the Agency's performance. Day-to-day operations are run by the Chief Executive and management board. The Chief Executive reports to the Secretary of State. |
| | Policy: Serving the road user and taxpayer, as well as protecting the environment. Growing emphasis on raising the quality of services. |
| | Trends: Increasing demands on the road network will require innovative solutions to be developed, such as sophisticated traffic control systems. |
| *performance* | Met or surpassed 94% of its key targets in 1996-97. |
| *board* | Appointed by Secretary of State. |

| Chairman | Andrew Turnball |
|---|---|
| Members | Chris Brearley |
| | DW Cawthra CBE |
| | L Haynes |
| | Ms W Pritchard |
| | H Wenban-Smith |
| Accounting Officer | Chief Executive |

*staff*  1700

| Chief Executive | L Haynes |
|---|---|
| Quality Services Director | John Kerman |
| Network Customer Services Director | P Nutt |
| Human Resource Services Director | Hazel Parker-Brown |
| Finance Services Director | J Seddon |
| Project Services Director | D York |

*financial*

| EXPENDITURE Year end: 31 March | 1997 £000 |
|---|---|
| **CAPITAL EXPENDITURE** | |
| Preparation and supervision | 136,372 |
| Land | 170,847 |
| Works | 820,491 |
| Compensation | 0 |
| Road maintenance | 226,001 |
| Bridge maintenance | 128,942 |
| Vehicles and equipment | 3,980 |
| | **1,486,633** |
| Receipts that can be used to offset expenditure | (105,479) |
| **Net capital expenditure** | **1,381,136** |
| **CURRENT EXPENDITURE** | |
| Roads and bridges maintenance | 142,563 |
| Motorway communications maintenance | 10,231 |
| Other current expenditure | 34,323 |
| Compensation | 4,348 |
| Research and development | 12,960 |
| Grants to the police for Controlled Motorway Pilot Scheme | 259 |
| | **204,684** |
| Receipts that can be used to offset expenditure | (13,146) |
| **Net current expenditure** | **191,538** |
| **ADMINISTRATION** | |
| Running costs | 75,202 |
| Highways Agency capital administration | 3,835 |
| | **79,037** |
| Receipts that can be used to offset expenditure | (191) |
| **Net administration expenditure** | **78,846** |
| **EUROPEAN REGIONAL DEVELOPMENT FUND (NET)** | |
| Grants and transfers: current | 0 |
| **TRANS-EUROPEAN NETWORKS (TENS) (NET)** | |
| Grants and transfers: current | (619) |
| Grants and transfers: capital | 619 |
| **TOTAL GROSS EXPENDITURE** | **1,770,354** |
| **RECEIPTS** | **(118,834)** |
| **NET EXPENDITURE** | **1,651,520** |

*publications*  Annual Report, Toolkit, Living with Roads

*branches*

Charter Court
Midland Road
Hemel Hempstead HP2 5RL
Tel 0645 556575

Falcon Road
Sowton
Exeter EX2 7LB
Tel 0645 556575

Federated House
London Road
Dorking RH4 1SZ
Tel 0645 556575

Heron House
49/53 Goldington Road
Bedford MK40 3LL
Tel 0645 556575

Jefferson House
27 Park Place
Leeds LS1 2SZ
Tel 0645 556575

City House
New Station Street
Leeds LS1 4UR
Tel 0645 556575

Sunley Tower
Piccadilly Plaza
Manchester M1 4BE
Tel 0645 556575

Tollgate House
Houlton Street
Bristol BS2 9DJ
Tel 0645 556575

5 Broadway
Broad Streeet
Birmingham B15 1BL
Tel 0645 556575

# Historic Royal Palaces

Hampton Court Palace
Surrey KT8 9AU

**Tel** 0181 781 9752
**Fax** 0181 781 9754

**Contact** Chief Executive's Office

| | |
|---|---|
| **status** | Executive agency |
| **founded** | 1989 (as an executive agency) |
| **sponsor** | Department of Culture, Media and Sport (DCMS) |
| **powers** | Royal Charter |
| **mission** | The care, conservation and presentation to the public of five palaces - the Tower of London, Hampton Court Palace, Kensington Palace (State Apartments and Royal Ceremonial Dress Collection), the Banqueting House in Whitehall and Kew Palace with Queen Charlotte's Cottage - all owned by the Queen in right of the Crown. |
| **tasks** | To conserve the palaces and their gardens to a standard reflecting their importance; to meet the highest standards of interpretation and presentation; to provide excellent visitor service - admissions, retailing, functions and events; to run the palaces efficiently and cost-effectively; to generate income to fund future improvements. |
| **operations** | Management: The Secretary of State is advised on the agency's performance by the Board of Trustees, which includes some members of the Royal Household and some professionals from outside the agency and the Royal Household. The Chief Executive and seven executives comprise the Board of Directors. |
| | Policy: To marry commercial activities with the highest possible conservation standards and fund further improvements from successful income generation. |
| | Trends: Has applied for National Lottery funds to improve the environs of the Tower of London. |
| **board** | The Secretary of State appoints five Trustees, the Queen three. The Chairman is appointed by the Secretary of State on the advice of the Queen. |

| Chairman | Earl of Airlie KT GCVO | |
|---|---|---|
| Trustees | Lord Camoys GCVO | Simon Jones LVO |
| | Michael Herbert CBE | Sir Michael Peat KCVO |
| | Angela Heylin OBE | Hugh Roberts CVO |
| | Lord Inge of Richmond GCB | Jane Sharman CBE |
| *Accounting Officer* | *Chief Executive* | |

**staff**    504

| | |
|---|---|
| Chief Executive | David Beeton |
| Tower Environs Scheme | Stephen Bond |
| Finance Director | Tony Cornwell |
| Commercial Director | Robin Evans |
| Governor of the Tower of London | Geoffrey Field |
| Deputy Director of Hampton Court Palace | Dennis McGuinnes |
| Curator & Acting Surveyor of the Fabric | Simon Thurley |

**financial**

| INCOME & EXPENDITURE | | | |
|---|---|---|---|
| Year end: 31 March | **1997** | **1996** | **1995** |
| | **£000** | **£000** | **£000** |
| **INCOME** | | | |
| Admissions | 18,960 | 18,653 | 17,295 |
| Retailing - gross sales | 6,871 | 6,914 | 6,415 |
| Other income | 3,971 | 2,878 | 2,294 |
| | **29,802** | **28,445** | **26,004** |
| **EXPENDITURE** | | | |
| Staff payroll costs | 10,645 | 9,475 | 10,378 |
| Cost of retail sales | 3,414 | 3,462 | 3,277 |
| Maintenance costs | 2,689 | 2,131 | 1,934 |
| Depreciation | 1,605 | 1,417 | 1,176 |
| Other expenditure | 17,352 | 14,948 | 14,380 |
| | 35,705 | 31,433 | 31,145 |
| **OPERATING DEFICIT BEFORE INTEREST** | **(5,903)** | **(2,988)** | **(5,141)** |
| Notional interest on capital employed | (1,631) | (1,558) | (986) |
| **NET OPERATING DEFICIT** | **(7,534)** | **(4,546)** | **(6,127)** |

| *advisers* | **Bankers** | Barclays Bank | Corporate Banking Centre, Watford Herts WD11BZ |
| | **Auditors** | National Audit Office | 157-197 Buckingham Palace Road London SW1W 9SP |
| | **Solicitors** | Farrers | 66 Lincoln's Inn Fields, London WC2A 3LH |

*publications*  Annual Report

# Historic Scotland

Longmore House
Salisbury Place
Edinburgh EH9 1SH

**Tel** 0131 668 8600
**Fax** 0131 668 8741                                        **Web** http://www.historic-scotland.gov.uk

| | |
|---|---|
| *status* | Executive agency |
| *founded* | 1991 |
| *sponsor* | Scottish Office |
| *powers* | Framework document |
| *mission* | To protect, preserve and present Scotland's built heritage for present and future generations. |
| *tasks* | It protects, preserves and presents Scotland's built heritage. Presentation involves admissions, visitor services, retailing and special events. The built heritage includes ancient monuments and archaeological sites; historic buildings (including Holyrood House); parks and gardens; and designed landscapes. |
| *operations* | Management: In 1994 the headquarters moved into Longmore House, Edinburgh, bringing many staff together into one building for the first time. |
| | Organised in six divisions: Ancient Monuments, providing management, advice and financial assistance to owners and occupiers and government departments; Rescue Archaeology excavation often in partnership with universities etc; Listed Buildings, making a systematic listing of buildings by resurveying whole geographic areas, thematic listings by building type or architect; Historic Buildings, awarding grants for the repair of buildings of outstanding architectural or historic interest; Technical Conservation, Research and Education, to raise the standard of conservation practice; Properties in Care, conservation of Historic Scotland properties, using revenue which it generates from visitors and from grants from local government and Europe. (2.9 million visitors to 70 Historic Scotland properties with admissions charges). |
| | Business trends: Conservation and presentation activities will continue in line with government spending plans. |
| | Scottish Office responsibility for property and administrative services transferred in 1994; delegated responsibility for staff, pay policy and bargaining first settlement in 1995. |
| *board* | The agency is headed by a Director and Chief Executive who is accountable to the Secretary of State for Scotland. Directors are drawn from the Senior Management. |

| | |
|---|---|
| Director & Chief Executive | Graeme Munro |
| Director, Heritage Policy | Frank Lawrie |
| Director, Technical Conservation, Research & Education | Ingval Maxwell |
| Director, Properties in Care | Brian Naylor |
| Director of Personnel | Brian O'Neil |
| Director of Finance | Leslie Wilson |
| Chief Inspector of Ancient Monuments | David Breeze |
| Chief Inspector of Historic Buildings | John Hume |
| *Accounting Officer* | *Chief Executive* |

| | |
|---|---|
| *staff* | 666 staff, largely in Longmore House. Staffing levels fluctuate, peaking in summer months. Overall numbers fell by 20 to 720. |

**financial**

| INCOME & EXPENDITURE<br>Year end: 31 March | 1997<br>£000 | 1996<br>£000 | 1995<br>£000 |
|---|---|---|---|
| **INCOME** | | | |
| Income from properties in care | 10,696 | 8,929 | 7,455 |
| Other income | 1,366 | 352 | 210 |
| | **12,062** | **9,281** | **7,665** |
| **EXPENDITURE** | | | |
| Cost of goods sold | 1,564 | 1,260 | 1,103 |
| Grants | 11,980 | 12,048 | 11,323 |
| Archaeology | 2,646 | 1,866 | 1,671 |
| Employment costs | 12,496 | 13,057 | 12,273 |
| Operating activities | 11,132 | 9,829 | 9,225 |
| Other costs | 4,144 | 3,998 | 4,108 |
| Depreciation | 940 | 887 | 964 |
| | **44,902** | **42,945** | **40,667** |
| **OPERATING DEFICIT** | **(32,840)** | **(33,664)** | **(33,002)** |
| Interest on capital | (564) | (493) | (437) |
| **DEFICIT FOR THE FINANCIAL YEAR** | **(33,404)** | **(34,157)** | **(33,439)** |

**advisers**  **Auditors**  National Audit Office  22 Melville Street, Edinburgh EH3 7NS

**publications**  Annual Report, Corporate Plan

# HM Customs & Excise

New King's Beam House
22 Upper Ground
London SE1 9PJ

**Tel** 0171 620 1313  **E-mail** hmce.cmu@gtnet.gov.uk

**status**  Government department operating on Next Steps lines

**founded**  1908, operating on Next Steps lines 1991

**sponsor**  HM Treasury

**mission**  To collect indirect taxes and carry out functions relating to goods and people crossing UK national borders.

**tasks**  Collects and manages VAT, insurance premium tax, landfill tax, excise duties, including air passenger duty; collects EU duties and levies; fights drug trafficking and enforces other import and export prohibitions and restriction; maintains balance between trade facilitation and effective enforcement; compiles and supplies trade statistics; advises government.

**operations**  Management: The department is managed by a Board of Commissioners who take operational decisions. Chairman of the Board is accountable to the Chancellor of the Exchequer. The Financial Secretary has delegated responsibility for the department and gives broad policy direction. There is a small headquarters and 24 Executive Units, made up of 14 Collections (regional organisations) and ten operational or support units. Each has its own framework document and each publishes its own annual report.

Policy: Works closely with overseas agencies to combat drug smuggling. InTelligence work becoming increasingly important.

Trends: Discussing EC proposal for common VAT system.

**performance**  Achieved or exceeded 31 out of 44 targets in 1996/97.

**board**  Commissioners appointed by the Chancellor of the Exchequer.

| Accounting Officer | Chairman |
|---|---|

**staff**

| | |
|---|---|
| Chairman | Valerie Strachan |
| Deputy Chairman | Sandy Russell |
| Director Personnel and Finance | Dennis Battle |
| Director VAT Policy | Martin Brown |
| Director Customs Policy | Mike Eland |
| Director Excise and Central Policy | David Howard |
| Director, Operations (Central) | Ray McAfee |

| Director IS | Alan Paynter |
|---|---|
| Solicitor | David Pickup |
| Director Operations (Prevention) | Tony Sawyer |
| Director Operations (Compliance) | Lis Woods |

*financial*

**RECEIPTS & PAYMENTS COLLECTION OF TAX AND DUTY**

| Year end: 31 March | 1997 | 1996 | 1995 |
|---|---|---|---|
| | £m | £m | £m |
| **RECEIPTS** | | | |
| Net taxes and duties | 82,381 | 76,686 | 72,601 |
| Fines and penalties | 110 | 117 | 113 |
| Proceeds from sale of seized goods | 3 | 3 | 4 |
| Other receipts | 37 | 43 | 34 |
| | 82,531 | 76,849 | 72,542 |
| **PAYMENTS** | | | |
| Payments to the Consolidated Fund | 82,499 | 76,829 | 72,636 |
| Revenue paid to the Isle of Man | 94 | 62 | 57 |
| Other payments | 21 | 4 | 22 |
| | 82,614 | 76,895 | 72,715 |
| SHORTFALL OF RECEIPTS OVER PAYMENTS FOR YEAR | (83) | (46) | 37 |

**RECEIPTS & PAYMENTS ADMINISTRATION**

| Year end: 31 March | 1997 | 1996 | 1995 |
|---|---|---|---|
| | £m | £m | £m |
| **RECEIPTS** | | | |
| Government grant drawn | 851 | 859 | 881 |
| Other receipts | 25 | 18 | 15 |
| | 876 | 877 | 896 |
| **PAYMENTS** | | | |
| Staff costs | 550 | 546 | 552 |
| Personnel overheads | 46 | 46 | 45 |
| Accommodation | 81 | 90 | 93 |
| Office services | 59 | 65 | 55 |
| Other payments | 3 | 3 | 3 |
| Legal, investigative and other costs | 47 | 45 | 45 |
| Capital expenditure | 80 | 80 | 92 |
| | 866 | 875 | 885 |
| **EXCESS OF RECEIPTS OVER PAYMENTS FOR YEAR** | **10** | **2** | **11** |

*advisers*

| **Auditors** | National Audit Office | 157-197 Buckingham Palace Road London SW1W 9SP |
|---|---|---|

# HM Land Registry

32 Lincoln's Inn Fields
London WC2A 3PH

**Tel** 0171 917 8888
**Fax** 0171 955 0110     **Web** http://www.open.gov.uk/landreg/das.htm

*status*     Executive agency

*founded*    1990 as executive agency, 1993 as trading fund

*sponsor*    Lord Chancellor's Department

*powers*     Land Registration Act 1925. Land Charges Act 1972. Agricultural Credits Act 1928

*mission*    To maintain and develop a stable, effective and secure land registration system throughout England and Wales as the cornerstone for the creation and free movement of interests in land.

*tasks*      To guarantee title to registered estates (and interests in land) for the whole of England and Wales. To provide customer access to up-to-date and guaranteed land information in order to facilitate dealing in property and provide security of title.

**operations**    Management: There is a Chief Land Registrar & Chief Executive who reports directly to the Lord Chancellor. There are two departments. The Registration of Title Department, by far the larger, has a London headquarters and 18 District Land Registry Offices in England; the Swansea District Land Registry handles all titles falling within Wales. The Land Charges and Agricultural Credits Department, based in Plymouth, maintains registers of land charges, pending actions, writs etc affecting non-registered properties. 85% of the land register is now computerised (14 million registers). RACAL Network Services Ltd is the private sector partner managing the communications for the Direct Access Service, which allows customers to view the computerised land register from terminals in their own offices. Registrations continued of large-scale applications resulting from the Railway Act 1993 and Local Industry Act 1994 and the Commercial Arrangements Group advised on large-scale securitisation and disposals of married quarters by the Ministry of Defence, in one case involving 25,000 titles.

Policy: To achieve a complete land register for England and Wales at a measured pace through the introduction of fee concessions to encourage voluntary registration. To use projected surplus fee income to help reduce the cost of conveyancing through fee reductions.

Trends: The Land Registration Act 1997 extends compulsory registration to non-sale transactions such as gifts and first mortgages, 'triggers' for compulsory registration representing a major step towards a complete English and Welsh land register. An Internet site was launched in 1996 which includes back issues of the *Residential Property Price Report*. The Land Charges and Agricultural Credits Department handled four million applications, an increase of 11% despite the decrease in unregistered titles.

**performance**    All targets but one met (accuracy just missed).

**board**

| | |
|---|---|
| Chief Land Registrar & Chief Executive | Dr SJ Hill |
| Director of Personnel & Corporate Services | EG Beardsall |
| Director of Operations | GN French |
| Director of Finance | Miss HM Jackson |
| Controller of Management Services | PR Laker |
| Director of Information Technology | PJ Smith |
| Senior Land Registrar | Mrs JG Totty |
| Solicitor to HMLR | CJ West |

**staff**    7859

**financial**

**INCOME & EXPENDITURE**

| Year end: 31 March | 1997 | 1996 |
|---|---|---|
| | £000 | £000 |
| **FEE INCOME** | 235,018 | 210,883 |
| **COST OF SERVICE** | 189,768 | 182,375 |
| **GROSS SURPLUS** | 45,250 | 28,508 |
| Administrative expenses | 11,439 | 11,659 |
| **OPERATING SURPLUS** | 33,811 | 16,849 |
| Loss on disposal of fixed assets | 85 | 553 |
| Interest receivable | 3,193 | 2,851 |
| **SURPLUS FOR THE FINANCIAL YEAR** | 36,919 | 19,147 |
| Dividend payable | 9,202 | 8,560 |
| **RETAINED SURPLUS FOR THE FINANCIAL YEAR** | 27,717 | 10,587 |

**advisers**    **Auditors**    National Audit Office    157-197 Buckingham Palace Road
London SW1W 9SP

**branches**

*Birkenhead*
Old Market House
Hamilton Street
Birkenhead
Merseyside L41 5FL
Tel 0151 4731110

Rosebrae Court
Woodside Ferry Approach
Birkenhead
Merseyside L41 6DU
Tel 0151 473 1110

*Coventry*
Leigh Court
Torrington Avenue
Tile Hill
Coventry CV4 9XZ
Tel 01203 860860

*Croydon*
Sunley House
Bedford Park
Croydon CR9 3LE
Tel 0181 781 9100

*Durham*
Southfield House
Southfield Way
Durham DH1 5TR
Tel 0191 301 2345

Boldon House
Wheatlands Way
Pity Me
Durham DH1 5GJ
Tel 0191 301 2345

*Gloucester*
Twyver House
Bruton Way
Gloucester GL1 1DQ
Tel 01452 51111

*Harrow*
Lyon House
Lyon Road
Harrow
Middlesex HA1 2EU
Tel 0181 235 1181

*Kingstom upon Hull*
Earle House
Portland Street
Hull HU2 8JN
Tel 01482 223244

*Leicester*
Thames Tower
99 Burleys Way
Leicester LE1 3UB
Tel 0116 265 4000

*Lytham*
Birkenhead House
East Beach
Lytham St Annes
Lancs FY8 5AB
Tel 01253 849849

*Nottingham*
Chalfont Drive
Nottingham NG8 3RN
Tel 0115 935 1166

*Peterborough*
Touthill Close
City Road
Peterborough PE1 1XN
Tel 01733 288288

*Plymouth*
Plumer House
Tailyour Road
Crownhill
Plymouth PL6 5HY
Tel 01752 636000

*Portsmouth*
St Andrew's Court
St Michael's Road
Portsmouth
Hampshire PO1 2JH
Tel 01705 768888

*Stevenage*
Brickdale House
Swingate
Stevenage
Herts SG1 1XG
Tel 01438 788888

*Swansea*
Ty Cwm Tawe
Phoenix Way
Llansamlet
Swansea SA7 9FQ
Tel 01792 458877

Ty Bryn Glas
High Street
Swansea SA1 1PW
Tel 01792 458877

*Telford*
Parkside Court
Hall Park Way
Telford TF3 4LR
Tel 01952 290355

*Tunbridge Wells*
Curtis House
Forest Road
Hawkenbury
Tunbridge Wells
Kent TN2 5AQ
Tel 01892 510015

*Weymouth*
Melcombe Court
1 Cumberland Drive
Weymouth
Dorset DT4 9TT
Tel 01305 363636

*York*
James House
James Street
York YO2 3YZ
Tel 01904 450000

*Land Charges*
Drakes Hill Court
Burrington Way
Plymouth P5 3LP
Tel 01752 635600

# HM Prison Service

Cleland House
Page Street
London SW1P 4LN

**Tel** 0171 217 3000
**Fax** 0171 271 8645

| | |
|---|---|
| *status* | Executive agency |
| *founded* | 1993 |
| *sponsor* | Home Office |
| *mission* | To keep in custody those committed by the courts. To look after prisoners with humanity and help them to lead law-abiding and useful lives in custody and after release. |
| *tasks* | Providing prison services in England and Wales, both directly and through contractors. Main goals are to keep prisoners in custody; maintain order, control, discipline and a safe environment; provide decent conditions for prisoners and meet their needs, including healthcare; provide positive regimes which help prisoners address their offending behaviour and allow them as full and responsible a life as possible; help prisoners prepare for their return to the community; deliver prison services using the resources provided by parliament with maximum efficiency. Also to generate income (1996/97 £15.6 million). |
| *operations* | Management: The Director General is supported by an Executive Committee. Individual prisons are run by Governors.<br><br>Policy: Partnership rather than privatisation, thus maximising the number of staff remaining in the Prison Service (up to 10% outsourcing). Plans for emergency accommodation (eg houseblocks and prison ship) and building of new prisons (through PFI).<br><br>Trends: Unprecedented rise in prison population (10% in 1996/97). Substantial increase in funding. Court escorting privatised. |
| *performance* | Achieved the majority of targets. |
| *board* | Management Board appointed by Secretary of State from senior operational management and external appointees. |

| | |
|---|---|
| Director General | Richard Tilt |
| Non-Executive Committee Member | W Bentley |
| Director of Health Care | Dr M Longfield |
| Non-Executive Committee Member | Sir D Nichol |
| Director of Finance | S Norris |
| Member, Executive Committee | A Papps |
| Member, Executive Committee | A Pearson |
| Member, Executive Committee | D Scott |
| Director of Administration & Services | H Taylor |
| Member, Executive Committee | A Walker |
| Member, Executive Committee | P Wheatley |

*staff* 38,212

*financial*

**INCOME & EXPENDITURE**

| Year end: 31 March | 1997 £m | 1996 £m |
|---|---|---|
| **EXPENDITURE** | | |
| Staff costs | 948.7 | 895.7 |
| Accommodation costs | 113.9 | 122.4 |
| Other operating costs | 373.9 | 369.0 |
| Depreciation | 123.6 | 159.3 |
| Charge on capital employed | 225.5 | 211.5 |
| | **1,785.6** | **1,757.9** |
| **INCOME** | | |
| Contribution from industries | (6.6) | (6.4) |
| Other operating income | (5.3) | (4.9) |
| | **(11.9)** | **(11.3)** |
| **NET OPERATING COSTS FOR YEAR** | **1,773.7** | **1,746.6** |

# *Home-Grown Cereals Authority (HGCA)*

Caledonia House
223 Pentonville Road
London N1 9NG

**Tel** 0171 520 3926
**Fax** 0171 713 2030          **Web** http://www.hgca.com

| | |
|---|---|
| *status* | Executive body |
| *founded* | 1965 |
| *sponsor* | Ministry of Agriculture, Fisheries and Food (MAFF) |
| *powers* | Cereals Marketing Act 1965 |
| *mission* | To improve the production and marketing of UK cereals and oilseeds. |
| *tasks* | Funding research and development programmes; providing market information; promoting exports; increasing home and overseas markets; acting as an agent of the Intervention Board (until 1 July 1998). |
| *operations* | Management: The Authority appoints advisory committees from the industry for each of the services it provides. The Executive is led by a small senior management team under the Chief Executive. Income depends upon the size of the UK harvest and the levy rate. |
| | Policy: Increasing research and development. Increasing export drive. |
| | Trends: Reduction in farming profits per acre. Consumers' heightened interest in food safety and quality becoming important. Agricultural proposals in Community Agenda 2000 may mean fundamental changes to the internal market. |
| *performance* | Short-term objectives were met in 1996/97. |
| *board* | Directors of the Board of the Authority appointed by the Agriculture Ministers. Seven represent the interests of cereal and oilseed growers, 7seven the interests of cereal dealers and processors;  the Chairman and Deputy Chairman are independent directors. |

| | |
|---|---|
| Chairman | Brian Nelson CBE |
| Deputy Chairman | Dr Caroline Vaughan |
| *Growers* | |
| Directors | Philip Chamberlain |
| | David George OBE |
| | Julian Gibbons |
| | John Gilliland |
| | Glen Sanderson |
| | Marie Skinner |
| | Peter Stewart |
| *Dealers and processors* | |
| | Christopher Barnes |
| | Noel Bartram |
| | Michael Gutsell |
| | Ken Hairs |
| | Pat Lake |
| | Bill Niven |
| | Tony Reynolds |
| *Accounting Officer* | *Chief Executive* |

| | |
|---|---|
| *staff* | 47 |

| | |
|---|---|
| Chief Executive | Tony Williams |
| Communications & Planning | Ian Aitchison |
| Cereals Marketing | Dr Alan Almond |
| R&D Cereals & Oilseeds | Dr Paul Biscoe |
| Finance & Administration | John Cable |
| Technical Services | Chris Prevett |
| Market Information | Stephen Thornhill |

**financial**

| INCOME & EXPENDITURE<br>Year end: 30 June | 1997<br>£ | 1996<br>£ | 1995<br>£ |
|---|---|---|---|
| **INCOME** | | | |
| Levy income - cereals | 9,858,655 | 6,516,946 | 5,582,124 |
| Levy income - oilseeds | 913,758 | 743,273 | 645,763 |
| Interest less taxation | 320,286 | 300,956 | 273,021 |
| Efficiency saving on IBEA agreement less taxation | 33,992 | 49,413 | - |
| | **11,126,691** | **7,610,588** | **6,500,908** |
| **EXPENDITURE** | | | |
| Administration costs | 3,376,063 | 2,762,809 | 2,972,392 |
| Less: recoveries in respect of agency services for Intervention Board | (409,838) | (461,232) | (666,889) |
| Research and development project expenditure - cereals | 4,125,200 | 4,245,703 | 3,907,645 |
| Research and development project expenditure - oilseeds | 616,410 | 589,406 | 382,136 |
| British Cereal Exports project expenditure | 299,033 | 270,354 | 284,653 |
| Food From Britain project expenditure | 639,529 | 764,475 | 778,198 |
| | **8,565,397** | **8,171,515** | **7,658,135** |
| Less: MAFF payment for marketing information | (105,000) | (105,000) | (100,000) |
| **SURPLUS/(DEFICIT) FOR THE PERIOD** | **2,666,294** | **(455,927)** | **(1,057,227)** |

**advisers**

**Bankers**   Lloyds Bank   Archway, London

**Auditors**   Kidsons Impey   London

**Solicitors**   Stephenson Harwood   London

**Public Relations**   Chamberlain Partnership Ltd   Peterborough

**publications**   Annual Report and Accounts, What It Is, What It Does, Corporate Plan 1998/99-2001/02, Annual Business Plan, Services, Costs and Levies 1997/98, BCE Fact Sheet 1998, BCE Export News, Cereal Product News, R & D - Strategy for Cereals, R & D - Strategy for Oilseeds, MI Weekly Bulletin, MIWeekly Digest, Market Statistics 1997, Cereals Quality Survey 1997

# Horniman Museum

100 London Road
Forest Hill
London SE23 3PQ

**Tel** 0181 699 1872
**Fax** 0181 291 5506

**status**   Executive body

**founded**   1992

**sponsor**   Department for Culture, Media and Sport (DCMS)

**powers**   Articles and Memorandum of Association

**mission**   To provide a public, educational museum and gardens to encourage a wider appreciation of the world, its peoples and their cultures, and its environments.

**tasks**   Collection development, care and management, access and communication (active programme of educational exhibitions, events, activities and publications).

**operations**   Management: The museum is run by the Director, who reports to the Committee of Directors and Trustees. It is a limited company and a registered charity. Collections include musical instruments, ethnographic collections and natural history, including refurbished aquarium.

Policy: Continuing the computerised documentation of the collections.

Trends: Provisional approval of an application to the Lottery Fund, so it is hoped to start rebuilding part of the museum in 1999.

**performance**   Visitor figures were 12% up in 1996/97.

**board**  Four Directors and Trustees are appointed by the Secretary of State and the remainder by the Board.

| | | |
|---|---|---|
| Chairman | Donald Kirkham CBE | |
| Directors & Trustees | Dame Jocelyn Barrow DBE | Michael Horniman |
| | Dr Eileen Buttle CBE | Sir Alistair Hunter KCMG |
| | Richard Foster | Prof Sir Ghillean Prance |
| | His Honour Brian Galpin | Mr Ronald Watts |
| | Dr Eilean Hooper-Greenhill | Michael Wheeler |
| Secretary | Mrs Jennifer Beever | |
| *Accounting Officer* | *Museum Director* | |

**staff**  78

| | |
|---|---|
| Museum Director | Michael Houlihan |

**financial**

| FINANCIAL ACTIVITIES Year end: 31 March | 1997 £ | 1996 £ |
|---|---|---|
| **INCOMING RESOURCES** | | |
| Grant-in-aid | 3,047,000 | 3,348,000 |
| Other grants and donations | 217,465 | 414,566 |
| Interest receivable | 47,250 | 47,475 |
| Merchandising income | 76,542 | 53,808 |
| Other operating income | 41,288 | 37,328 |
| | **3,429,545** | **3,901,177** |
| **RESOURCES EXPENDED** | | |
| Direct charitable expenditure | 2,576,591 | 2,624,953 |
| Other expenditure | 115,351 | 76,788 |
| | **2,691,942** | **2,701,741** |
| Notional costs | 214,972 | 156,855 |
| Net incoming resources after notional costs | 522,631 | 1,042,581 |
| Reversal of notional costs | 214,972 | 156,855 |
| **NET INCOMING RESOURCES - SURPLUS** | **737,603** | **1,199,436** |
| Fund balances brought forward | 848,420 | 719,284 |
| Prior year adjustments | 2,065,555 | 995,255 |
| Fund balances brought forward as adjusted | 2,913,975 | 1,714,539 |
| **FUND BALANCES CARRIED FORWARD** | **3,651,578** | **2,913,975** |

**advisers**

**Bankers**     Clydesdale Bank

**Auditors**    Deloitte & Touche

**Solicitors**  Currey & Co

# *Horserace Betting Levy Board*

52 Grosvenor Gardens
London SW1W 0AU

**Tel** 0171 333 0043
**Fax** 0171 333 0041

**status**    Executive body

**founded**   1963

**sponsor**   Home Office

**powers**    Betting, Gaming and Lotteries Act 1963 (as amended)

**mission**   Improving breeds of horses; advancing and encouraging veterinary science and veterinary education; the improvement of horseracing.

**tasks**     Assessing and collecting the betting levy from bookmakers and the Horserace Totalisator Board (the Tote). Protecting the integrity of racing - by helping racecourses to fund technical security and officials' services (eg high-quality camera patrols, photofinish and starting stalls services) and by drug screening at its subsidiary, the Horseracing Forensic Laboratory (HFL). Implementing new anti-doping scientific advice measures (in cooperation with the Jockey Club) while European harmonisation continues. Supporting improved facilities for racegoers

# Q&Q

through interest-free loans from its capital fund (but no revenue support). Improving breeding by, for example, prize schemes.

**operations**  Management: The Audit Committee controls the revenue budget and the capital fund.

Policy:  Positive action to improve turnover and viability of bookmakers. Increased emphasis on assessing racecourses' business plans, marketing strategies and management initiatives.

Trends: Increased emphasis on racecourses' business plans, marketing strategies and management initiatives in assessing applications for financial assistance.

**board**  The Chairman and Deputy Chairman and a number of independent members are appointed by the Home Secretary. Three members are also appointed by The Jockey Club, two by the Bookmakers' Committee, and one by the Horserace Totalisator Board.

| | |
|---|---|
| Chairman | John Sparrow |
| Deputy Chairman | John Robb |
| Chief Executive | Rodney Brack |
| Members | Angus Crichton-Miller |
| | Norman Miller |
| | David Oldrey |
| | Tristram Ricketts |

**staff**  108 (Board 26, HFL 81)

| | |
|---|---|
| Chief Executive | Rodney Brack |
| Scientific Liaison Executive | Libby Archer |
| Projects Development Executive | Godfrey Ayres |
| Head of Legal Affairs | Lucilla Evers |
| Head of Finance | Roger Haincock |

**financial**

**REVENUE & EXPENDITURE**

| Year end: 31 March | 1997 £000 | 1996 £000 |
|---|---|---|
| **REVENUE** | | |
| **Levy income receivable for:** | | |
| Thirty-fifth levy scheme | 49,000 | - |
| Additional levy following reduction in general betting duty | 5,000 | - |
| Thirty-fourth levy scheme | 96 | 48,000 |
| Previous levy schemes | 7 | (408) |
| | 54,103 | 47,592 |
| Levy income receivable from Horserace Totalisator Board | 2,271 | 2,000 |
| | 56,374 | 49,592 |
| Laboratory third-party services | 1,188 | 1,064 |
| Interest receivable | 1,080 | 1,928 |
| | 58,642 | 52,584 |
| **EXPENDITURE** | | |
| Improvement of horseracing | 50,988 | 51,396 |
| **Improvement of breeds** | | |
| Breeder's prizes scheme | 1,084 | 1,081 |
| Breed societies | 272 | 305 |
| Advancement of veterinary science and education | 1,535 | 1,555 |
| Administration costs | 2,357 | 2,329 |
| Laboratory operating expenses | 1,188 | 1,064 |
| Bookmarkets' committee costs | 175 | 266 |
| Charitable payments | 5 | 5 |
| | 57,604 | 58,001 |
| **SURPLUS/(DEFICIT) BEFORE TAXATION** | 1,038 | (5,417) |
| Taxation | (124) | (266) |
| **SURPLUS/(DEFICIT) TRANSFERRED TO RESERVES** | 914 | (5,683) |

**advisers**

| | | |
|---|---|---|
| **Bankers** | Midland Bank | 89 Buckingham Palace Road London SW1W 0QL |
| **Auditors** | KPMG | 8 Salisbury Square, London EC4Y 8BB |
| **Solicitors** | Harbottle & Lewis | 14 Hanover Square, London WIR 0BE |

# *Horserace Totalisator Board (Tote)*

Tote House
74 Upper Richmond Road
London SW15 2SU

**Tel** 0181 874 6411
**Fax** 0181 875 1882

| | |
|---|---|
| *status* | Executive body |
| *founded* | 1928 |
| *sponsor* | Home Office |
| *powers* | Act 1928. Order 1996. Horserace Totalisator Board Act 1997 |
| *mission* | To provide financial support to horseracing and a full betting service to customers |
| *tasks* | To provide a pool betting service at all 59 UK racecourses. To run 209 high street betting offices - ranking it fifth among the UK's bookmakers. To run the world's largest credit betting operation. To distribute profits to British horseracing. |
| *operations* | Management: The Tote is a commercially managed organisation with medium-term profit objectives of some £25 million a year. The Tote is organised into four divisions: Racecourse Division (Tote bets, at 59 racecourses); Tote Bookmakers (on and off-course); Tote Credit (50,000 customers, offices at all courses); Tote Direct (all Tote bets, football pools, 2700 outlets). Tote Direct is 50% owned by Bass (Coral bookmakers) and in 1997 achieved a major breakthrough when Ladbrokes agreed to install terminals in all its 1900 betting offices. A new (highly cost-effective) computer system has been installed. |
| | Policy: To distribute about two-thirds of its profits to British horseracing. |
| | Trends: In 1996, the Home Office arranged for an Order permitting the Tote to offer bets on Irish Lottery numbers. The Horserace Totalisator Board Act 1997 has enabled the Tote to offer bets on all events whether of a sporting or non-sporting nature. |
| *performance* | Record profits. |

*board*

| | |
|---|---|
| Chairman | Lord Wyatt |
| Chief Executive | John Heaton |
| Member | The Hon Jeremy Deedes |
| Member | Peter Jones |
| Finance Director | Tom Phillips |
| Member | John Sanderson |
| Member | The Hon David Sieff |
| Member | Christopher Sporborg |

*staff* 23

*financial*

**INCOME & EXPENDITURE**

| Year end: 31 March | 1997 | 1996 |
|---|---:|---:|
| | £000 | £000 |
| **TURNOVER** | | |
| **Racecourse Totalisator** | | |
| On-course | 75,819 | 72,591 |
| Tote Direct | 33,190 | 29,063 |
| Tote Credit | 67,563 | 56,445 |
| Tote Bookmakers | 143,463 | 146,091 |
| | **320,035** | **304,190** |
| Amounts payable to winning customers | 251,719 | 238,273 |
| Betting duty | 12,492 | 13,736 |
| Tote Direct commissions | 6,988 | 6,528 |
| | **271,199** | **258,537** |
| **GROSS PROFIT** | **48,836** | **45,653** |
| Operating expenses | 38,301 | 36,906 |
| | **10,535** | **8,747** |
| **OTHER INCOME** | | |
| Fees for authorities | 1,739 | 1,753 |
| Unclaimed dividends | 467 | 439 |
| | **2,206** | **2,192** |

| | | |
|---|---|---|
| **OPERATING PROFIT** | **12,741** | **10,939** |
| Share of profits/(losses) in associated undertaking | 54 | (141) |
| Income from other investments | 401 | 292 |
| Net interest payable | (377) | (484) |
| **PROFIT BEFORE CONTRIBUTION TO RACING** | **12,819** | **10,606** |
| Contribution to racing | 7,916 | 7,574 |
| **PROFIT BEFORE STAFF PROFIT SHARE** | **4,903** | **3,032** |
| Staff profit share | 374 | - |
| **PROFIT BEFORE TAXATION** | **4,529** | **3,032** |
| Taxation | 1,404 | 1,036 |
| **RETAINED PROFIT TRANSFERRED TO RESERVES** | **3,125** | **1,996** |

*advisers* **Auditors** BDO Stoy Hayward     8 Baker Street, London W1M 1DA

          **Solicitors** Simmons & Simmons     14 Dominion Street, London EC2M 2RJ

# *Horticultural Development Council (HDC)*

Bradbourne House
Stable Block
East Malling
Kent ME19 6DZ

**Tel** 01732 848383
**Fax** 01732 848498

*status*     Executive body

*founded*     1986

*sponsor*     Ministry of Agriculture, Fisheries and Food (MAFF), the Scottish Office and Welsh Office

*powers*     Horticultural Development Council Order 1986 (as amended in 1990 and 1992)

*mission*     To provide the horticultural industry with cost-effective research and development information that will be easily assimilated into practice in order to improve individual business performance.

*tasks*     *Technical*: To identify and commission scientific research appropriate to the needs of the industry. To promote or undertake studies on optimum commercial practice within each sector of the industry. To transfer all such findings to the industry. To provide the industry with technical and scientific support to ensure that it can compete successfully with imported products and that export opportunities are fully exploited. To assist the industry with information on pesticides and to obtain off-label approvals which benefit the industry. *Levy:* To collect a levy from all eligible producers, assessed on sales turnover of horticultural produce with the exception of apples, pears and hops; there is a separate mushroom levy.

*operations*     Management: The roles of Chairman and Chief Executive have been combined for a trial period. There are six HDC Sector Panels - Bulbs and Outdoor Flowers, Field Vegetables, Hardy Nursery Stock, Mushrooms, Protected Crops and Soft and Stone Fruits. The research commissioning is an ongoing process and most is initiated by one of these panels; 200 research projects were funded by HDC in 1995/96. HDC has moved office to Kent where the rent is recycled into horticultural research via the East Malling Research Association Trustees.

Policy: HRC is focusing its business on two core activities - research and communication. Changes underway in horticultural research funding will require constant vigilance if the national research base is to be maintained at its current level.

Trends: 1995/96 is the fourth consecutive year with no levy increase. The problem of growers evading the levy is being attacked to enable the HDC to commission more projects requested by growers. Voluntary membership offered to any grower below the levy threshold is proving successful - 115 growers each contributing £75 pa. Access to levy-funded research results has been given to about 40 companies (some of which offer support for the research in the form of equipment, plants or material) and to about 23 consultants, for an annual fee.

*board*     14 Council Members, all appointed jointly by agricultural ministers; 11 are growers, one represents employees, one has expertise in marketing and one (the Chairman) is an independent member.

| Chairman | Mrs Margaret Charrington | |
|---|---|---|
| Members | Charles Bransden | |
| | Peter Brice | Alec Samson |
| | John Evans | Chris Sanders |
| | Bob Hilborn | Pam Smith |
| | Robert Hillier | Bernard Sparkes |
| | Margaret Holmes | Roy Willingham |
| | Andrew May | Peter Woad |

*staff*    10

*financial*

**INCOME & EXPENDITURE**

| Year end: 30 September | 1996 | 1995 |
|---|---|---|
| | £ | £ |
| **GROSS INCOME** | | |
| Levies, voluntary and corporate contributions | 3,025,927 | 2,913,742 |
| Other income | 98,050 | 83,326 |
| | **3,123,977** | **2,997,068** |
| **EXPENDITURE** | | |
| Horticultural research | 2,359,889 | 2,054,258 |
| Operational expenses | 268,166 | 217,987 |
| Administration expenses | 217,038 | 162,867 |
| Council expenses | 39,084 | 40,120 |
| Enforcement costs | 11,705 | 16,235 |
| | **2,895,882** | **2,491,467** |
| **SURPLUS FOR THE YEAR ON ORDINARY ACTIVITIES** | | |
| **BEFORE AND AFTER TAXATION** | **228,095** | **505,601** |
| Retained surplus brought forward | 725,522 | 219,921 |
| **RETAINED SURPLUS CARRIED FORWARD** | **953,617** | **725,522** |

*advisers*

| **Bankers** | Midland Bank | Market Square, Petersfield, Hants GU32 3HQ |
|---|---|---|
| **Auditors** | Barter, Durgan & Muir | 35 Lavant Street, Petersfield, Hants GU32 3EL |
| **Solicitors** | MacDonald Oates & Co | Square House, The Square, Petersfield Hants GU32 3HT |
| | Dundas & Wilson CS | Saltire Court, 20 Castle Terrace Edinburgh EH1 2EN |

# *Horticultural Research International (HRI)*

Wellesbourne
Warwick CV35 9EF

**Tel** 01789 470382
**Fax** 01789 470552

**E-mail** horti.tec@hri.ac.uk
**Web** http://www.hri.ac.uk

*status*    Executive body

*founded*    As private company limited by guarantee

*sponsor*    Ministry of Agriculture, Fisheries and Food (MAFF)

*powers*    Memorandum and Articles of Association

*mission*    Expanding international reputation for multidisciplinary research and development in horticulture.

*tasks*    Providing customers with relevant cost-effective research, development and technology transfer. Meeting the particular needs of the UK horticultural industry and government policy requirements. Advancing plant, animal and microbial science of particular relevance to horticulture.

*operations*    Management: HRI is governed by a Board of Non-Executive Directors whose Chairman reports to ministers. There is a Management Board comprising the Chief Executive and six Executive Directors. The Chief Executive reports to the Minister. Funding is mainly from customers, principally MAFF policy groups; also the Biotechnology and Biological Sciences Research Council (BBSRC) contributes 14% . It is organised into six scientific sites, a Head Office which handles administration and a commercial sales and marketing operation under the brand name HortiTech. HortiTech arranges contract services and products in scientific search and development within the UK and internationally in agriculture/horticulture; Biotechnology and Environmental Management Sectors in which HRI HortiTech work includes Agriculture; Leisure; Food & Drink and Education. In 1996/97, a minority of staff was directly employed (195), the remainder were seconded from BBSRC (349) and MAFF (87).

Trends: In 1997 the government confirmed that it would support HRI for the time being. However private sector commercial income from the UK and internationally is to become a larger source of income in the future.

**board** Six members are appointed by MAFF and three by the Chancellor of the Duchy of Lancaster; Directors come from commerce, the horticultural industry and from higher education.

| | | |
|---|---|---|
| Chairman | Peter Siddal | |
| Directors | Dr AR Burne | |
| | Prof JA Callow | AG Jeffries |
| | Prof TJ Flowers | David Piccaver |
| | Prof JC Gray | Dr Richard Pugh |
| | MG Holmes | MW Rowe |
| *Accounting Officer* | *Chief Executive* | |

**staff** 631

| | |
|---|---|
| Chief Executive | Prof CC Payne |
| Company Secretary & Director of Finance & Administration | TG Heller |
| Site Director - Wellesbourne | Prof Ian Crute |
| Site Director - East Malling | Dr Alwyn Thompson |
| Site Director - Stockbridge House | Malcolm Bradley |
| Site Director - Efford | James Best |
| Director - New Business Development | George Thorburn |

**financial**

**INCOME & EXPENDITURE**

| Year end: 31 March | 1996 £000 | 1995 £000 |
|---|---|---|
| **INCOME** | | |
| Commission from MAFF | 11,747 | 13,247 |
| Grant-in-aid from BBSRC | 3,603 | 3,353 |
| Commercial contracts research income | | |
| MAFF Open and Link contracts | 1,564 | 633 |
| Other | 4,671 | 4,799 |
| Other receipts | 1,323 | 1,516 |
| Amortisation of capital grants | 2,321 | 2,118 |
| | **25,229** | **25,666** |
| **RESOURCES EXPENDED** | | |
| Direct charitable expenditure | 24,015 | 23,723 |
| Other expenditure: management and administration | 1,680 | 1,674 |
| | **25,695** | **25,397** |
| **NET (OUTGOING)/ INCOMING RESOURCES** | **(466)** | **269** |
| Fund Balance brought forward | 1,521 | 1,252 |
| Reserve Fund | 639 | 639 |
| **FUND BALANCES CARRIED FORWARD** | | |
| **RESERVE FUND** | **1,521** | **1,521** |
| **ACCUMULATED SURPLUSES** | **173** | **639** |

**advisers** **Auditors** Robson Rhodes

**publications** *Annual Report, HortiTech Brochures*

**branches**

*HRI HortiTech*
Wellesbourne
Warwick
CV35 9EF
Tel 01789 470382
Fax 01789 470552
E-mail horti.tech@hri.ac.uk

*HRI East and West Malling*
Kent ME19 6BJ
Tel 01732 843833
Fax 01732 849067

*HRI Wye*
Wye College
Wye
Ashford
Kent TN25 5AH
Tel 01233 812179
Fax 01233 813126

*HRI Efford*
Lymington
Hampshire SO41 0LZ
Tel 01590 673341
Fax 01590 671553

*HRI Kirton*
Willington Road
Kirton
Boston
Lincolnshire PE20 1NN
Tel 01205 723477
Fax 01205 724957

*HRI Stockbridge House*
Cawood
Selby
North Yorkshire YO8 0TZ
Tel 01757 268275
Fax 01757 268996

# *Housing Corporation*

149 Tottenham Court Road
London W1P 0BN

**Tel** 0171 393 2000
**Fax** 0171 393 2111          **Web** http://www.open.gov.uk/hcorp

| | |
|---|---|
| *status* | Executive body |
| *founded* | 1964 |
| *sponsor* | Department of the Environment, Transport and the Regions (DETR) |
| *powers* | Housing Act 1996 |
| *mission* | To improve people's quality of life through social housing. More specifically, to secure efficient delivery of new social housing; to promote social tenants' interests and involvement; to protect taxpayers by ensuring the financial and managerial viability of Registered Social Landlords (RSLs); and to encourage innovation and best practice. |
| *tasks* | Funding, regulating and facilitating the proper performance of RSLs. |
| *operations* | Management: Sir Brian Peace retired as Chairman in 1997. The board's remit is to establish the overall strategic role of the corporation within the policy and resources framework agreed with the Secretary of State and oversee the delivery of planned results against performance. The corporation works through its London headquarters and a network of seven regional offices throughout England: London (Noel Street), South East (Croydon), South West (Exeter), East (Leicester), West Midlands (Wolverhampton), Leeds (North Eastern), and North West and Merseyside (Manchester). |

*operations* (cont.)

Policy: Allocation of Approved Development Programme (ADP) capital grants is determined by four factors: local authorities strategic housing plans; value for money offered by bidders; priorities and targets set by ministers.

Trends: Over the past few years between 40,000 and 60,000 homes per year have been developed through ADP, depending on the fluctuating public grants provided. Since 1989, over £11 billion of unguaranteed private sector funds has been invested in RSLs, But the downward spiral of public investment in social housing affects both the Corporation's and local authorities' investment programmes. A first-class working relationship between the Corporation, local authorities, RSLs and private lenders will be developed. Private investment through the Public Finance Initiative is likely to be crucial.

*board*          Chairman and up to 15 members appointed by the Secretary of State.

| | | |
|---|---|---|
| Chairman | Baroness Dean | |
| Members | Eric Armatage | David Kleeman |
| | Sheila Button | Anthony Mayer |
| | George Cracknell | Robin Thompson CBE |
| | Sylvia Denman CBE | Julia Unwin |
| | John Foster OBE | Derek Waddington OBE |
| | Ken Griffin OBE | Dr Peter Williams |
| *Accounting Officer* | *Chief Executive* | |

*staff*

| | |
|---|---|
| Chief Executive | Anthony Mayer |
| Deputy Chief Executive & Chief Operations Officer | Simon Dow |
| Director of Personnel & Administration | Peter Bush |
| Director of Finance & Information Services | John George |
| Director of Investment | Derek King |
| Director of Regulation | Atul Patel |
| Director of Corporate Affairs | Nigel Phethean |
| Director, West Midlands Region | Heather Mytton |
| Director, London Region | Neil Hadden |
| Director, North East Region | Nigel Armstrong |
| Director, South East Region | Marion Franks |
| Director, North West & Merseyside Region | Max Steinberg |
| Director, South West Region | Andrew Wiles |
| Director, East Region | Nick Reed |

*financial*

| INCOME & EXPENDITURE Year end: 31 March | 1997 £000 | 1996 £000 |
|---|---|---|
| **INCOME** | | |
| Grants from the Secretary of State | 1,639,100 | 1,753,400 |
| Interest receivable on loans | 103,000 | 107,100 |
| Premium received on early redemption of loans | 2,100 | 700 |
| Decrease in bad debt provisions | - | 400 |
| | **1,744,200** | **1,861,600** |
| **EXPENDITURE** | | |
| Grants paid to registered social landlords | 1,608,200 | 1,722,600 |
| Interest payable on loans from the National Loans Fund | 100,500 | 103,500 |
| Administrative expenditure | 29,900 | 30,800 |
| Provision for notional insurance | 100 | - |
| Corporation tax | 1,800 | 1,500 |
| | **1,740,500** | **1,858,400** |
| **SURPLUS FOR THE YEAR** | **3,700** | **3,200** |

*branches*

West Midlands
Norwich Union House
Waterloo Road
Wolverhampton WV1 4BP
Tel 01902 795000

London
Waverley House
7-12 Noel Street
London W1V 4BA
Tel 0171 292 4400

North Eastern
St Paul's House
23 Park Square South
Leeds LS1 2ND
Tel 0113 233 7100

South East
Leon House
High Street
Croydon
Surrey CR9 1UH
Tel 0181 253 1400

North West & Merseyside
Elisabeth House
16 St Peter's Square
Manchester M2 3DF
Tel 0161 242 2000

South West
2nd Floor
Beaufort House
51 New North Road
Exeter EX4 4EP
Tel 01392 428200

East
Attenborough House
109-119 Charles Street
Leicester LE1 1FQ
Tel 0116 242 4800

# *Human Fertilisation & Embryology Authority (HFEA)*

Paxton House
30 Artillery Lane
London E1 7LS

**Tel** 0171 377 5077
**Fax** 0171 377 1871          **Web** http://www.hfea.gov.uk

**Contact** Suzanne McCarthy, Chief Executive

*status*   Executive body

*founded*   1990, taking up full powers August 1991

*sponsor*   Department of Health (DOH)

*powers*   Human Fertilisation and Embryology Act (HFE Act) 1990

*mission*   To ensure that treatment and research using human embryos are undertaken with the utmost respect and responsibility and that the vulnerability of infertile patients is not exploited. All relevant interests are considered: patients, children and potential children, licensed clinics and the wider public. Considerations of safety, efficacy and ethics are taken into account.

**tasks**   To regulate the practice of reproductive technologies in human reproduction, principally by licensing and monitoring clinics carrying out *in vitro* fertilisation (IVF), donor insemination (DI) or embryo research, and publishing a Code of Practice. It also regulates storage of gametes and embryos and keeps a register of information about donors, treatments and children born from those treatments so these offspring can trace their genetic background. It advises and informs individual patients and donors; reviews information about embryos, subsequent development of embryos and treatment services governed by the HFE Act. It licences all UK research using human embryos.

**operations**   Management: Organised in five sections: Policy and Finance; Personnel and Resource Management; Communications; Licensing; and the Information Register. It earns about two thirds of its income from licensing clinics for treatment and/or storage of gametes and embryos. Where there is an apparent breach of the HFE Act or Code of Practice, the HFEA investigates and, if need be, the matter is referred to the Director of Public Prosecutions.

Policy: Third revision of Code of Practice now in hand includes consideration of upper age limit of sperm donors and screening of gamete donors for cystic fibrosis. As medical technology advances the HFEA works to achieve a balance between the views of patients, scientists, doctors, ethicists and members of the public. HFEA also reviewing payments to egg and sperm donors and the licensing of pre-implantation genetic diagnosis (PGD). Joint consultation underway with the Human Genetics Advisory Commission (HGAC) on the future of cloning.

**board**   Appointed by UK Health Ministers from those with a broad range of medical, scientific, social, legal and religious knowledge and experience. The Act requires that the Chairman, Deputy Chairman and at least half of the board members are not involved in medical or scientific practice.

| | | |
|---|---|---|
| Chairman | Ruth Deech | |
| Deputy Chairman | Jane Denton | |
| Members | Dr Gulam Bahadur | |
| | Prof David Barlow | Prof Stuart Lewis |
| | Prof Ruth Chambers | Dr Brian Lieberman |
| | Liz Forgan | Dr Anne McLaren |
| | Prof Christine Gosden | Dr Joan Stringer |
| | David Greggains | Prof Allan Templeton |
| | Prof Andrew Grubb | Prof The Rev Canon Anthony Thiselton |
| | Prof Martin Johnson | Julia Tugendhat |
| | Richard Jones | John Williams |
| *Accounting Officer* | *Chief Executive* | |

**staff**   28

| Chief Executive | Suzanne McCarthy |
|---|---|

**financial**

**INCOME & EXPENDITURE**

| Year end: 31 March | 1997 | 1996 | 1995 |
|---|---|---|---|
| | £ | £ | £ |
| **GROSS INCOME** | | | |
| Government grant | 377,609 | 329,130 | 459,078 |
| Income from licensing | 1,453,307 | 1,004,158 | 884,289 |
| Income from other sources | 1,274 | 1,177 | 8,686 |
| | 1,832,190 | 1,334,465 | 1,352,053 |
| Transfer from reserves/deferred government grant | 43,485 | 51,856 | 49,177 |
| | 1,875,675 | 1,386,321 | 1,401,230 |
| **EXPENDITURE** | | | |
| Staff costs | 720,134 | 586,358 | 597,365 |
| Depreciation | 43,485 | 51,856 | 49,177 |
| Other operating charges | 1,014,016 | 752,345 | 676,987 |
| | 1,777,635 | 1,390,559 | 1,322,529 |
| **OPERATING SURPLUS/(DEFICIT)** | 98,040 | (4,238) | 77,701 |
| Notional interest | 25,500 | 18,500 | - |
| **SURPLUS/(DEFICIT) ON ORDINARY ACTIVITIES** | 72,540 | (22,738) | 77,701 |
| Write back of notional interest | 25,500 | 18,500 | - |
| **SURPLUS/(DEFICIT) FOR THE YEAR** | 98,040 | (4,238) | 77,701 |
| Appropriations | - | - | (7,732) |
| Retained surplus brought forward | 44,589 | 48,827 | (21,142) |
| **RETAINED SURPLUS CARRIED FORWARD** | 142,629 | 44,589 | 48,827 |

**advisers**   **Bankers**   Barclays

**Auditors**   Bindler Hamlyn
National Audit Office

**Solicitors**   Morgan Bruce

**publications**   *Annual Reports: 1992-97, Patient's Guide to DI and IVF Clinics (1997 Edition), List of all licensed clinics, List of sperm donor recruitment centre, List of egg donation centres, List of ICSI centres, Code of Practice (Fourth Edition), Code of Practice on Enforcement*

# Imperial War Museum

Lambeth Road
London SE1 6HZ

**Tel** 0171 416 5000
**Fax** 0171 416 5374

| | |
|---|---|
| *status* | Executive body |
| *founded* | 1920 |
| *sponsor* | Department for Culture, Media and Sport (DCMS) |
| *powers* | Imperial War Museum Act 1920 |
| *mission* | To collect, preserve and display material relating to all aspects of warfare, including social, technological, economic, cultural and political ones, as well as the military. |
| *tasks* | Active collecting programme: works of art, posters, photographs, sound recordings, film and videotape, private papers, books and pamphlets, maps, in addition to the extensive collection of three-dimensional objects (from aircraft to cap badges).  Puts on exhibitions and runs large education programme.  Conservation of vast archives. |
| *operations* | Management:  Run by Director-General, supported by three Assistant Directors and nine Keepers.  Main museum at Lambeth Road (London), and major branches at Duxford Airfield (Cambridgeshire), HMS Belfast and the Cabinet War Rooms (both London). Commercial activities produce about half total income.  Imperial War Museum Trust is a charity which administers appeal funds and donations. |
| | Policy: Seeking site for a new branch in the north of England. Technological improvements has resulted in much progress in the conversion of manual records onto computer databases an the establishment of online catalogues available to visitors. |
| | Trends:  Increasing number of visitors. |
| *board* | Trustees appointed by Secretary of State. Seven Trustees are High Commissioners of Commonwealth countries. |

| | |
|---|---|
| President | The Duke of Kent  KG GCMG GCVO |
| Vice-President & Chairman | Field Marshal The Lord Bramall |
| Deputy Chairman | The Right Reverend Michael Mann KCVO |
| Trustees | Admiral Sir Jeremy Black GBE KVB DSO |
| | His Excellency The Hon Neal Blewett |
| | His Excellency John Collinge |
| | General Sir Peter de la Billiere KCB KBE DSO MC |
| | His Excellency Royce Frith QC |
| | His Excellency Wajid Hasan |
| | Mrs Michael Heseltine |
| | His Excellency Mendi Msimang |
| | Prof RJ O'Neill |
| | Sir William Purves CBE DSO |
| | Sir Robin Renwick KCMG |
| | IJ Scott CBE |
| | DRW Silk CBE JP |
| | Major-General George Sinclair CB CBE |
| | His Excellency Dr LM Singhvi |
| | IMH Smart |
| | Sir Moray Stewart KCB |
| | The Lady Vaizey |
| | His Excellency SK Wickremesinghe |
| *Accounting Officer* | *Director-General* |

| | |
|---|---|
| *staff* | 417 |

| | |
|---|---|
| Director-General | RWK Crawford |
| Secretary | JJ Chadwick |

*financial*

| INCOME & EXPENDITURE Year end: 31 March | 1996 £000 | 1995 £000 |
|---|---|---|
| **INCOME** | | |
| Grant-in-aid | 11,007 | 10,920 |
| Other operating income | 8,484 | 7,700 |
| Investment income | 524 | 539 |
| Release from deferrred capital account | 2,175 | 2,017 |
| Release from Collection Purchases Fund | 207 | 287 |
| | **22,397** | **21,463** |
| **EXPENDITURE** | | |
| Staff costs | 9,052 | 8,627 |
| Other operating charges | 7,789 | 7,194 |
| **Depreciation** | | |
| Tangible fixed assets | 2,266 | 2,096 |
| Purchases for the Collection | 207 | 287 |
| | **19,314** | **18,204** |
| **SURPLUS (FUNDING REQUIREMENT)** | **3,083** | **3,259** |

*advisers*    **Auditors**    National Audit Office    157-197 Buckingham Palace Road London SW1W 9SP

## Independent Commission for Police Complaints for Northern Ireland (ICPC)

Chamber of Commerce House
22 Great Victoria Street
Belfast BT2 7LP

**Tel** 01232 244821
**Fax** 01232 248563

*status*    Executive body

*founded*    1987

*sponsor*    Northern Ireland Office

*powers*    Police (Northern Ireland) Order 1987

*mission*    To provide an independent, impartial and effective system for handling complaints made by members of the public against members of the Royal Ulster Constabulary (RUC), and to encourage public confidence in the quality of service provided by the police.

*tasks*    To advise people on how to make a complaint; to inform and educate the public and the police about the work of the Commission; to promote the informal resolution of as many complaints as possible within the confines of the legislation; to maximise the number of investigations supervised by the Commission; to encourage Complaints and Discipline Department, in the discharge of its responsibility, to provide a fair and objective assessment of allegations of police misconduct; to bring information about complaints or other matters, where appropriate, to the attention of police management, the Police Authority for NI and the Secretary of State.

*operations*    Management: All Commissioners, with the exception of one full-time Chairman and one full-time Deputy Chairman, serve on a part-time basis. Chief Executive is responsible for day-to-day management.

     Trends: Police Ombudsman to be established in 1999 which will replace the Commission.

*board*    Commission appointed by the Secretary of State.

| Chairman | Paul Donnelly | |
|---|---|---|
| Deputy Chairman | Brian Reid | |
| Members | Suzanne Bryson | Geralyn McNally |
| | Robin Davidson | Bob Moore |
| | Tom Gillen | David Shillington JP |
| *Accounting Officer* | *Chief Executive* | |

*staff*    18

| Chief Executive | Brian McClelland |
|---|---|
| Deputy Chief Executive | Patricia Russell |

**financial**

| RECEIPTS & PAYMENTS Year end: 31 March | 1997 £ | 1996 £ | 1995 £ |
|---|---|---|---|
| **RECEIPTS** | | | |
| HMG grant-in-aid received | 816,000 | 780,000 | 781,000 |
| **PAYMENTS** | | | |
| Salaries and wages, etc | 607,823 | 581,065 | 535,573 |
| Other operating payments | 206,125 | 199,706 | 248,047 |
| | 813,948 | 780,771 | 783,620 |
| **SURPLUS/(DEFICIT) FROM OPERATIONS** | 2,052 | (771) | (2,620) |
| Other receipts/(payments) - net | 2,289 | 3,410 | 11,289 |
| **EXCESS/(SHORTFALL) OF RECEIPTS OVER PAYMENTS** | (237) | 2,639 | 8,669 |

**advisers**   **Auditors**   National Audit Office   157-197 Buckingham Palace Road
London SW1W 9SP

**publications**   Annual Report, Triennial Report

# Independent Television Commission (ITC)

33 Foley St
London W1P 7LB

**Tel** 0171 255 3000
**Fax** 0171 306 7800

**E-mail** publicaffairs@itc.org.uk
**Web** http:www.itc.org.uk

**status**      Public corporation

**founded**     1990

**sponsor**     Department of Culture, Media and Sport (DCMS)

**powers**      Broadcasting Act 1990 and 1996

**mission**     Licenses and regulates commercial television services in the UK (terrestrial, cable and satellite); protects viewer's interests.

**tasks**       Draws up codes to cover taste, decency, privacy and impartiality; undertakes research to ascertain public opinion; licenses 15 regional ITV companies, GMTV, Channels 4 and 5, teletext and local cable delivery franchises and regulates the quality and diversity of their programmes; publishes and applies codes and rules on the content, amount and distribution of advertising and on programme sponsorship; active in developing and maintaining high technical standards for analogue and digital television, eg manages engineering research projects.

**operations**  Management: The Chief Executive is responsible for day-to-day management and reports to the Commission. Eleven national and regional offices, which form a local focus for monitoring regional programmes and viewers' comments (each has a Viewer Consultative Council). ITC appoints the Gaelic Television Committee, which makes grants to ensure high-quality Gaelic broadcasting. ITC administers the flow of Channel 4 Television Corporation's (C4C's) income - collecting from Channel 3 (C3) levies or redistributing excess C4C income to C3 licensees.

Policy: Continuing to monitor portrayal of violence on television.

Trends: Preparing for digital broadcasting.

**board**       Members of the Commission are wholly non-executive and appointed by the Secretary of State.

| Chairman | Sir Robin Biggam | |
|---|---|---|
| Deputy Chairman | The Earl of Dalkeith | |
| Commissioners | Dr John Beynon | |
| | Roy Goddard | John Ranelagh |
| | Jude Goffe | Dr Michael Shea CVO |
| | Dr Maria Moloney | Eleri Wynne Jones |
| Secretary | Michael Redley | |

**staff**       186

| | |
|---|---|
| Chief Executive | Peter Rogers |
| Deputy Chief Executive | Clare Mulholland |
| Director of Finance | Sheila Cassells |
| Controller of Administration | Don Horn |
| Director of Public Affairs | Paul Smee |
| Director of Programmes & Cable | Sarah Thane |
| Director of Engineering | Gary Tonge |
| Director of Advertising & Sponsorship | Frank Willis |
| Regional Executive | Jean Young |
| Regional Officer | Michael Fay |
| Regional Executive | Louise Bennett |
| Regional Executive | Robert Conlon |
| Officer for Scotland | Brian Marjoribanks |
| Regional Executive | Alan Stewart |
| Regional Executive | Nicholas Bull |
| Officer for Wales & West of England | Stella Mair Thomas |
| Regional Officer | Janet Wootton |
| Regional Executive | Peter Monteith |
| Regional Executive | Sally Laverack |

**financial**

**INCOME & EXPENDITURE**
**Year end: 31 March**

| | 1996 £000 | 1995 £000 |
|---|---|---|
| **INCOME** | | |
| Licence fees | 15,676 | 15,311 |
| Other income | 671 | 1,392 |
| | 16,347 | 16,703 |
| **EXPENDITURE** | | |
| Staff costs | 6,781 | 7,688 |
| BCC contribution | 268 | 302 |
| Other operating costs | 9,811 | 9,223 |
| | 16,860 | 17,213 |
| **OPERATING DEFICIT** | (513) | (510) |
| Interest receivable | 136 | 138 |
| **DEFICIT ON ORDINARY ACTIVITIES BEFORE TAXATION** | (377) | (372) |
| Taxation | 17 | (42) |
| **DEFICIT FOR THE FINANCIAL YEAR** | (360) | (414) |

**advisers**

**Auditors**  Smith and Williamson  Guildford

**branches**

*Winchester*
King's Worthy Court
King's Worthy
Winchester SO23 7QA
Tel 01962 886141
Fax 01962 886141

*North of England*
15 Paternoster Row
Sheffield S1 2BX
Tel 0114 276 9091
Fax 0114 276 9089

Television House
Mount Street
Manchester M2 5WT
Tel 0161 834 2707
Fax 0161 835 3513

3 Collingwood St
Newcastle upon Tyne NE1 1JS
Tel 0191 261 0148
Fax 0191 261 1158

*Scotland*
123 Blythswood St
Glasgow G2 4AN
Tel 0141 226 4436
Fax 0141 226 4682

*South of England*
153 Armada Way
Plymouth PL1 1HY
Tel 01752 663031
Fax 01752 662490

*Wales & West of England*
2nd Floor
Cardiff CF1 1PA
Tel 01222 384541
Fax 01222 223157

*Midlands & East of England*
10-11 Poultry
Nottingham NG1 2HW
Tel 0115 952 7333
Fax 0115 952 7353

24 Castle Meadow
Norwich NR1 3DH
Tel 01603 623533
Fax 01603 633631

62 Hagley Road
Birmingham BI6 8PE
Tel 0121 693 0662
Fax 0121 693 2753

*Northern Ireland*
75 Great Victoria Street
Belfast BT2 7AF
Tel 01232 248733
Fax 01232 322828

# Industrial Research & Technology Unit (IRTU)

17 Antrim Road
Lisburn
Co Antrim BT 28 3AL

**Tel** 01846 623000
**Fax** 01846 623119

**E-mail** info@irtu.dedni.gov.uk
**Web** http://www.nics.gov.uk/irtu

**Contact** Dr Deirdre Griffith

| | |
|---|---|
| *status* | Advisory body |
| *founded* | 1995 |
| *sponsor* | Northern Ireland Office, Department of Economic Development (DEDNI) |
| *powers* | Industrial Development Order (1982). Framework Document 1995 |
| *mission* | To improve the competitiveness of industry and strengthen the economy of Northern Ireland by encouraging innovation, industrially relevant research and development, and technology transfer. |
| *tasks* | Administers regional, national and European R&D financial assistance programmes. Also delivers a sustained innovation awareness campaign and promotes industrial design. Has extensive laboratory facilities offering services to industry and government including technical advice, scientific testing, an information service and programmes for effective environmental management. |
| *operations* | Management: Chief Executive is responsible for the day-to-day operation and performance. Board acts in an advisory and provides a link between industry, academia and IRTU and also monitors the work. |
| | Policy: NI Innovation Awards launched in 1996. |
| | Trends: EU funding vital to support R&D and networking. |
| *board* | Appointed by Minister for the Economy |

| | | |
|---|---|---|
| Chairman | Prof Peter Mckie CBE | |
| Board Members | Prof Ingrid Allen CBE | Dr Tom Little CBE |
| | Prof Eric Beatty MBE | Prof Fabian Monds |
| | Jim Collins | Prof William Morris |
| | Martin Dummingan | Mrs Joan Ruddock OBE |
| | Mrs Gillian Graccy | Peter Schuddeboom |
| | Frank Graham | Prof Ernest Shannon |
| *Accounting Officer* | *Chief Executive* | |

*staff* 150

| | |
|---|---|
| Chief Executive | Greg Connel |
| Director, technology division | David Duncan |
| Director, industrial science | Jim Monaghan |

*financial*

| INCOME & EXPENDITURE | |
|---|---|
| **Year end: 31 March** | **1997** |
| | **£** |
| **INCOME** | **2,257,825** |
| **EXPENDITURE** | |
| Staff costs | 3,645,574 |
| Depreciation | 245,206 |
| Other operating costs | 1,513,259 |
| | (5,404,039) |
| **EXPENDITURE BEFORE INTEREST ON CAPITAL** | **(3,146,214)** |
| Interest on capital employed | (159,105) |
| **NET EXPENDITURE** | **(3,305,319)** |

*publications* Corporate Plan, Framework Document, Annual Report, R&D Capability in NI

# *Information Technology Services Agency (ITSA)*

Blackpool Industrial Estate
Brunel Way
Blackpool FY4 5ES

**Tel** 01253 335039

| | |
|---|---|
| *status* | Executive agency |
| *founded* | 1990 |
| *sponsor* | Department of Social Security (DSS) |
| *mission* | To provide secure and cost-effective computer and communication technology services for the DSS. |
| *tasks* | Delivering the IT systems necessary to support day-to-day social security operations. Setting the IS/IT strategic direction for the DSS. Maximising the cost-effectiveness. Working with external suppliers in the development and provision of IT services. |
| *operations* | Management: Four operational Directorates, backed up by three internal service Directorates. ITSA works for Child Support Agency, Contributions Agency, War Pensions Agency etc. |
| | Policy: Developing and implementing a new IS/IT strategy. Leading Year 2000 project to ensure the current systems are compliant. |
| | Trends: Improvement of customer service. Deliver IS/IT support for New Deal initiatives under Welfare to Work. |
| *performance* | Met or exceeded all targets. |
| *board* | The board is made up of internal management and one non-executive director. |

| | |
|---|---|
| Chief Executive | Ian Magee |
| Strategic Business Manager | Justine Brewood |
| Control IT Supply Director | G Brown |
| Corporate IS/IT Projects Director | N Haighton |
| Customer Director | G Hextall |
| Corporate IS/IT Management & Regulation Director | G Kemp |
| Non-Executive Director | KE Pfotzer |
| IT Provider Director | Pete Sharkey |
| Director of Finance & Audit and Director of Human Resources | J Thomas |
| *Accounting Officer* | *Chief Executive* |

| | |
|---|---|
| *staff* | 2137 |

*financial*

| INCOME & EXPENDITURE | 1997 | 1996 | 1995 |
|---|---|---|---|
| **Year end: 31 March** | **£000** | **£000** | **£000** |
| **INCOME** | | | |
| Benefits Agency | 244,815 | 244,028 | 239,941 |
| Employment Service | 34,653 | 64,686 | 101,957 |
| Contributions Agency | 7,412 | 23,269 | 35,487 |
| Child Support Agency (including Northern Ireland) | 24,663 | 29,480 | 24,501 |
| Northern Ireland Social Security Agency | 6,252 | 6,274 | 7,976 |
| War Pensions Agency | 4,033 | 6,848 | 7,032 |
| DSS headquarters | 2,430 | 3,192 | 6,052 |
| Others | 2,622 | 1,849 | 3,901 |
| | **326,880** | **379,626** | **426,847** |
| **EXPENDITURE** | | | |
| Staff costs | 52,434 | 75,955 | 104,558 |
| Depreciation | 20,404 | 45,280 | 80,316 |
| Contracted personnel costs | 46,623 | 55,038 | 64,744 |
| Consulting costs | 4,094 | 4,441 | 9,658 |
| Computer operational expenses | 158,124 | 117,888 | 70,896 |
| Telecommunications costs | 26,618 | 33,981 | 35,552 |
| Accommodation charges | 9,274 | 11,059 | 10,328 |
| Utilities | 2,317 | 3,485 | 4,624 |
| General expenses | 11,307 | 30,026 | 38,458 |
| Revaluation of computer equipment | 6,568 | 331 | - |
| Audit fee | 74 | 96 | 96 |
| Travel, subsistence and hospitality | 111 | 77 | 54 |
| Employees | 1,532 | 2,524 | 2,829 |
| | **266,642** | **258,946** | **237,239** |

| | | | |
|---|---|---|---|
| **TOTAL OPERATING COSTS** | 339,480 | 380,181 | 422,113 |
| **SURPLUS/(DEFICIT) OF OPERATIONS** | (12,600) | (555) | (4,734) |
| Reorganisation and restructuring costs | 1,504 | 22,103 | 50,652 |
| **NET SURPLUS/(DEFICIT) OF OPERATIONS BEFORE** | | | |
| **INTEREST ON CAPITAL** | (14,104) | (22,658) | (45,918) |
| Interest on capital | 2,536 | 6,429 | 10,900 |
| Interest receivable | (268) | (194) | (217) |
| **NET SURPLUS/(COST OF OPERATIONS)** | (16,372) | (28,893) | (56,601) |

*advisers*   **Auditors**        National Audit Office                157-197 Buckingham Palace Road
London SW1W 9SP

# Inland Revenue (IR)

Somerset House
London WC2R 1LB

**Tel** 0171 438 6420

*status*      Government department operating on Next Steps lines

*founded*     1858

*sponsor*     HM Treasury

*mission*     To provide an efficient, effective and fair tax service to the country and government.

*tasks*       Administering, assessing and collecting income tax, corporation tax, capital gains tax, petroleum revenue tax, inheritance tax and stamp duties; providing valuation services for rating, council tax; providing policy analysis and advice to Ministers; collecting Class 1 and 4 National Insurance contributions for the Contributions Agency.

*operations*  Management: Under the overall direction of Treasury Ministers, the IR is managed by a Board of Commissioners. The Chairman reports directly to the Chancellor of the Exchequer. The Board is assisted by the Departmental Management Board which comprises the Statutory Board members, Directors of Business Operations, Finance, Human Resources, Business and Management Services, Self-Assessment Programme and three non-executive directors. The Chairman is directly accountable to the Chancellor of the Exchequer. There are 24 operational and executive/regional offices, and 96% of staff work in executive offices. The IR has one executive agency, the Valuation Office, which is profiled separately (see index).

Policy: Self-assessment launched in 1997, implementation continues in 1998. Simplifying the tax system and reducing the compliance burden on business

Trends: UK became first country to secure comprehensive tax treaties with 100 countries in 1997. European issues have implications for the direct tax system.

*performance* Met 25 out of 30 key targets for 1996/97.

*board*       Commissioners appointed by Royal Warrant.

| | |
|---|---|
| *Statutory Board* | |
| Chairman | Nick Montagu CB |
| Deputy Chairman | Clive Corlett CB |
| Deputy Chairman | Steve Matheson CB |
| Director General | Geoffrey Bush |
| *Departmental Management Board* | |
| Chairman | Nick Montagu CB |
| Director General | Geoffrey Bush |
| Deputy Chairman | Clive Corlett CB |
| Deputy Chairman | Steve Matheson CB |
| Non-Executive Member | George Cox |
| Director Human Resources | John Gant |
| Director Business Operations | Michael Johns |
| Director Finance | Robin Martin |
| Non-Executive Member | Dame Sheila Masters |
| Director Self-Assessment Programme | Doug Smith |
| Non-Executive Member | Ms Sue Wilson |
| Director Business & Management Services | John Yard |
| *Accounting Officer* | *Chairman* |

*staff*   54,906

| | |
|---|---|
| Chairman | NLJ Montagu CB |
| Deputy Chairman | CW Corlett CB |
| Deputy Chairman | SCT Matheson CB |
| Director General | GH Bush |
| Solicitor | BE Cleave CB |
| Valuation Office Agency, Chief Executive | Mrs V Lowe |
| Personal Taxation, Oil & International, Collection, Criminal Prosecutions, Rating & Employment | RJ Alderman |
| Financial Institutions & Company Tax Divisions | MF Cayley |
| Customer Service Division | TR Evans |
| Human Resources Division | J Gant |
| Compliance & Business Profits Divisions | EJ Gribbon |
| Departmental Planning Division | Miss M Hay |
| Business Operations Division | MA Johns |
| Solicitor (Scotland) | IK Laing |
| Savings & Investment and Capital & Valuation Divisions | BA Mace |
| Finance Division | RR Martin |
| Personal Tax Division | E McGivern CB |
| Tax Law Rewrite Project | NC Munro |
| Head of Profession, Valuation Office Agency | RJ Pawley |
| Legislation, Business Profits, Avoidance, Capital Taxes & Stamp Duty | PL Ridd |
| Self-Assessment Programme | DA Smith |
| International Divison | IR Spence |
| Statistics & Economics Division | RG Ward |
| Business & Management Services Division | JE Yard |
| Head, Inland Revenue London | JF Carling |
| Head, Inland Revenue East | MJ Hodgson |
| Head, Inland Revenue Wales & Midlands | MW Kirk |
| Head, Inland Revenue North | RI Ford |
| Head, Inland Revenue North West | G Lunn |
| Head, Inland Revenue South East | DLS Bean |
| Head, Inland Revenue South West | RS Hurcombe |
| Head, Inland Revenue South Yorkshire | AC Sleeman |
| Head, Inland Revenue Scotland | IS Gerrie |
| Head, Inland Revenue Northern Ireland | RST Ewing |
| Head, Accounts Office (Cumbernauld) | A Geddes OBE |
| Head, Accounts Office (Shipley) | RJ Warner |
| Head, Capital Taxes Office | E McKeegan |
| Head, Enforcement Office | Ms SF Walsh |
| Head, Internal Audit Office | NR Buckley |
| Head, Large Groups Office | Mrs ME Williams |
| Head, Oil Taxation Office | RC Mountain |
| Head, Pension Schemes Office | SJ McManus |
| Head, Solicitor's Office | BE Cleave CB |
| Head, Financial Intermediaries & Claims Office | SW Jones |
| Head, Financial Accounting Office | JD Easey |
| Head, Special Compliance Office | FJ Brannigan |
| Head, The Stamp Office | KS Hodgson OBE |
| Head, Training Office | AW Kuczys |

*financial*

**RECEIPTS & PAYMENTS IN RESPECT OF THE COLLECTION OF TAXES, DUTIES AND OTHER NON-ADMINISTRATIVE ITEMS**

| Year end: 31 March | 1997 £m | 1996 £m |
|---|---:|---:|
| **RECEIPTS** | | |
| Taxes and duties | 121,452.4 | 115,255.1 |
| Other receipts | 46,222.4 | 43,706.4 |
| Parliamentary funding | 269.0 | 318.9 |
| | **167,943.8** | **159,280.4** |
| **PAYMENTS** | | |
| Taxes and duties | 17,707.4 | 18,323.0 |
| Other payments | 46,160.3 | 43,980.7 |
| | **63,867.7** | **62,303.7** |
| **NET RECEIPTS (PAYMENTS)** | **104,076.1** | **96,976.7** |
| Opening balance | 159.8 | 284.3 |
| Less: closing balance | 343.5 | 159.8 |
| **TRANSFERS TO CONSOLIDATED FUND** | **103,892.4** | **97,101.2** |

| RECEIPTS & PAYMENTS FOR THE ADMINISTRATION OF THE DEPARTMENT OF INLAND REVENUE | | |
|---|---|---|
| Year end: 31 March | 1997 | 1996 |
| | £m | £m |
| **RECEIPTS** | | |
| Parliamentary funding | 1,640.9 | 1,633.1 |
| Other receipts | 355.2 | 343.7 |
| | **1,996.1** | **1,976.8** |
| **PAYMENTS** | | |
| Staff costs | 1,164.6 | 1,192.5 |
| Accommodation costs | 254.3 | 234.2 |
| Other current expenditure | 448.2 | 416.2 |
| Total running costs | 1,867.1 | 1,842,9 |
| Capital expenditure | 95.0 | 125.5 |
| Total expenditure | 1,962.1 | 1,968.4 |
| Payments to the Consolidated Fund | 21.3 | 27.0 |
| | **1,983.4** | **1,995.4** |
| **NET RECEIPTS (PAYMENTS) FOR THE YEAR** | **12.7** | **(18.6)** |

**branches**

*London*
New Court
Carey Street
London WC2A 2JE
Tel 0171 324 0229

*East*
Churchgate
New Road
Peterborough PE1 1TD
Tel 01733 754321

*Wales & Midlands*
1st Floor
Ty Glas
Llanishen
Cardiff CF4 5TS
Tel 01222 755789

*North*
100 Russel Street
Middlesborough
Cleveland TS1 2RZ
Tel 01642213214

*North West*
The Triad
Stanley Road
Bootle
Merseyside L20 3PD
Tel 0151 300 3000

*South East*
Dukes Court
Duke Street
Woking
Surrey GU21 5XR
Tel 01483 258600

*South West*
Longbrook House
New North Road
Exeter EX4 4UA
Tel 01392 453210

*South Yorkshire*
Concept House
5 Young Street
Sheffield S1 4LF
Tel 0114 2969696

*Scotland*
80 Lauriston Place
Edinburgh EH3 9SL
Tel 0131 473 4100

*Northern Ireland*
Dorchester House
52/58 Great Victoria Street
Belfast BT2 7QE
Tel 01232 245123

*Accounts Offices*
Cumbernauld
Glasgow G70 5TR
Tel 01236 736121

Shipley
Victoria Street
Shipley
West Yorkshire BD98 8AA
Tel 01274 530750

*Capital Taxes Office*
Ferrers House
Castle Meadow Road
PO Box 38
Nottingham NG2 1BB
Tel 0115 9743043

*Enforcement Office*
Durrington Bridge House
Barrington Road
Worthing BN12 4SE
Tel 01903 700222

*International Audit Office*
5th Floor North West Ring
Bush House
London WC2B 4PP
Tel 0171 438 728

*Large Groups Office*
New Court
Carey Street
London WC2A 2JE
Tel 0171 324 1321

*Oil Taxation Office*
Melbourne House
Aldwych
London WC2B 4LL
Tel 0171 438 6908

*Pension Schemes Office*
Yorke House
Castle Meadow Road
Nottingham NG2 1BG
Tel 0115 9741599

Solicitor's Office
East Wing
Somerset House
London WC2R 1LB
Tel 0171 438 7259

Finacial Intermediaries & Claims Office
St Johns House
Merton Road
Bootle
Merseyside L69 9BB
Tel 0151 472 6000

Financial Accounting Office
South Block
Barrington Road
Worthing BN12 4XH
Tel 01903 700222

Special Compliance Office
Angel Court
199 Borough High Street
London SE1 1HZ
Tel 0171 234 3701

The Stamp Office
South West Wing
Bush House
Strand
London WC2B 4QN
Tel 0171 438 7282

Training Office
Lawress Hall
Riseholme
Lincoln LN2 2BJ
Tel 01522 561761

# Insolvency Service

PO Box 203
21 Bloomsbury Street
London WC1B 3SS

**Tel** 0171 637 1110
**Fax** 0171 291 6713

| | |
|---|---|
| **status** | Executive agency |
| **founded** | 1990 |
| **sponsor** | Department of Trade and Industry (DTI) |
| **powers** | Insolvency Act 1986; Company Directors Disqualification Act 1986; Companies Act 1985. Framework Document |
| **mission** | Maintaining confidence in markets by providing means of dealing with individual and corporate financial failure and tackling fraud and wrong-doing in insolvencies. |
| **tasks** | The remit differs in England and Wales and Scotland. Preliminary investigations and administration of compulsory insolvencies (bankruptcies and companies, including partnerships, wound up by the courts) and acting as interim receiver and provisional liquidation in appropriate cases (England and Wales). Reporting criminal offences in compulsory insolvencies and taking disqualification proceedings against unfit directors or failed companies (Great Britain). Acting as trustee or liquidation in compulsory insolvencies where no private sector insolvency practitioner is appointed (England and Wales). Authorisation and regulation of private sector insolvency practitioners - directly or through professional bodies (England, Scotland, Wales). Providing banking and investment services for bankruptcies and liquidations (England and Wales). Policy advice to ministers on insolvency issues (England Scotland and Wales). |
| **operations** | Management: The Inspector General is also the Chief Executive. There is a Steering Board which comprises the Director General, Corporate and Consumer Affairs, the Chief Executive, two senior DTI officials and three private sector members. It assists the DTI Deputy Secretary to assess the corporate plan and monitor performance. There is a Directing Board which consists entirely of senior management and assists the Inspector General. The Agency works through its official receivers, its HQ Enforcement Units in London, Birmingham and Edinburgh and its Central Accounting Unit in Birmingham. |
| | Trends: There has been a recent fall in case numbers. Operational targets are fixed on an assumption of 25,000 new cases a year. Some work began to be contracted out in 1995/96. |
| **performance** | 1996/97 all key targets met. |
| **board** | Appointed by the Director General, Corporate and Consumer Affairs. |

| | |
|---|---|
| Chairman | Brian Hilton |
| Inspector General & Agency Chief Executive | Peter Joyce |
| Members | Stephen Adamson |
| | Edward Bonner Dignum |
| | Jonathan Phillips |
| *Accounting Officer* | *Inspector General & Agency Chief Executive* |

**staff** 1565 permanent staff

**financial** 1996/97 running costs £56.6 million

**advisers** **Auditors** National Audit Office

**publications** *The Insolvency Service Published Standard, The Insolvency Service Annual Report 1995-96, Insolvency General Annual Report 1996, Framework Document, List of Official Receivers (February 1997), A Guide for Creditors (August 1994), A Guide for Directors (June 1996), Bankruptcy Public Search Room - Information on Bankruptcy Services (March 1996), Company Directors Disqualification Act 1986 and Failed Companies Act (January 1997), Directory of Authorised Insolvency Practitioners (1996), An Insolvency Practitioner's Guide to the Central Accounting Unit (issued to IPs only) (January 1996)*

**branches**

*Official Receivers*
45/6 Stephenson Street
Birmingham B2 4UP
Tel 0121 698 4000
Fax 0121 698 4402

2nd Floor
Abbeygate House
164-167 East Road
Cambridge CB1 1DB
Tel 01223 324480
Fax 01223 464717

Dee Hills Park
Chester CH3 5AR
Tel 01244 321 471/2
Fax 01452 310910

St Clare House
Greyfriars
Ipswich IP1 1LX
Tel 01473 217565
Fax 01473 230430

5th Floor
Haymarket House
Haymarket Centre
Leicester LE1 3YS
Tel 0116 262251/3
Fax 0116 262417

Ground Floor
Scottish Life House
29 St Katherine's Street
Northampton NN1 2QZ
Tel 01604 542400
Fax 01604 542450

2 Covent Road
Norwich NR2 1PA
Tel 01603 628983
Fax 01603 760842

1st Floor
Chaddesden House
77 Talbot Street
Nottingham NG1 5GA
Tel 0115 901 1000
Fax 0115 901 1019

London House
Hide Street
Stoke-on-Trent ST4 1QN
Tel 01782 845256
Fax 01782 844787

Suite J
Anchor House
The Maltins
Silvester Street
Hull HU1 3HA
Tel 01482 323720/323729
Fax 01482 217806

2nd Floor
Savile House
Trinity Street Arcade
Leeds LS1 6QP
Tel 01132 455776
Fax 01132 428031

2nd Floor
Cunard Building
Pier Head
Liverpool L3 1DS
Tel 0151 236 9131
Fax 0151 255 0278

1st Floor
Boulton House
17/21 Chorlton Street
Manchester M1 3HY
Tel 0161 934 5400
Fax 0161 934 5450

3rd Floor
Westgate House
Westgate Road
Newcastle upon Tyne NE1 1TU
Tel 0191 232 11 04
Fax 0191 261 7936

Petros House
St Andrews Road North
Lytham St Anne's FY8 2JB
Tel 01253 784200

6th Floor
Don House
20-22 Hawley Street
Sheffield S1 2EA
Tel 01142 726692/1
Fax 01142 721394

Bayheath House
Prince Regent Street
Stockton-on-Tees TS18 1DF
Tel 01642 617720
Fax 01642 618644

69 Middle Street
East Sussex
Brighton BN1 1BE
Tel 01273 861300
Fax 01273 822239

50 New Dover Road
Canterbury CT1 3DT
Tel 01227 462070
Fax 01227 450537

5th Floor
Sunley House
Bedford Park
Croydon CR9 1TX
Tel 0181 681 5166
Fax 0181 667 8000

1st Floor
47 Friar Street
Reading RG1 1RY
Tel 01189 581931
Fax 01189 504941

Gordon House
15 Star Hill
Rochester ME1 1TX
Tel 01634 815367/842603
Fax 01634 831129

1st Floor
Trident House
42-48 Victoria Street
St Albans AL1 3HR
Tel 01727 832233
Fax 01727 815700

2nd Floor
Tylers House
Tylers Avenue
Southend-on-Sea SS1 2AX
Tel 01702 602570
Fax 0170 2602567

3rd Floor
Bristol & West House
Post Office Road
Bournemouth BH1 1LH
Tel 01202 558208
Fax 01202 297590

3rd & 4th Floors
Intercity House
Mitchell Lane
Bristol BS1 6BD
Tel 01179 279515
Fax 01179 252054

3rd Floor
Hayes House
The Hayes
Cardiff CF1 2UG
Tel 01222 230575/232381
Fax 01222 342148

3rd Floor
Finance House
Barnfield Road
Exeter EX1 1QR
Tel 01392 436886
Fax 01392 422618

21-23 London Road
Gloucester GL1 3HB
Tel 01452 521658/527997

1st Floor
Cobourg House
Mayflower Street
Plymouth PL1 1DJ
Tel 01752 635200
Fax 01752 635222

Western Range
83-85 London Road
Southampton SO15 2SH
Tel 01703 223348
Fax 0173 303177

5th Floor
Sun Aliance House
166-167 St Helens Road
Swansea SA1 5DL
Tel 01792 642 861
Fax 01792 644235

# *Intervention Board (IB)*

Kings House
33 Kings Road
Reading RG1 3BU

**Tel** 0118 958 3626
**Fax** 0118 953 1370

| | |
|---|---|
| *status* | Executive agency. Also government department |
| *founded* | 1990. 1972 as a government department |
| *sponsor* | Ministry of Agriculture, Fisheries and Food (MAFF), the Welsh, Scottish and Northern Ireland Offices (the Agricultural Departments) |
| *powers* | European Communities Act 1972. Framework Document |

**mission**   Administering the Common Agricultural Policy (CAP) in the UK as economically, efficiently and effectively as possible, in accordance with EU and UK law; advising UK Agricultural Ministers (the Minister of Agriculture, Fisheries and Food, and the Secretaries of State for Scotland, Wales and Northern Ireland).

**tasks**   Operating many of the EU schemes to regulate the market in agricultural products. Accounting for these schemes and those administered by the Agricultural Departments. The IB also issues and monitors import and export licences and pays export refunds on agricultural products; buys, stores and sells beef, butter, skimmed milk powder and cereals; supports the production, processing and consumption of a wide range of agricultural products; and is responsible for milk quotas. IB officers visit traders to check their compliance with regulations; submits more than 200 accounts with supporting computerised data to the EU. It is responsible for accounting to the European Commission and the European Court of Auditors. In the UK it reports on spending to parliament, and its accounts are scrutinised by the National Audit Office.

**operations**   Management: Independent Non-Executive Chairman. The Chief Executive reports, through the Board, to Agricultural Ministers. Some IB work is handled by the Agricultural Departments and by HM Customs and Excise which operates import and export controls. IB expenditure on CAP support is funded initially by the UK Exchequer and almost all of it is subsequently recovered from the European Commission. There is a high level of activity against fraud.

Policy: IB does not set agricultural policy but it does advise the Agricultural Departments on practical aspects of any proposals to change CAP.

Trends: Cost of supporting agriculture rising. Support shifting (1994/95) from price support to direct producer payments.

**performance**   In 1994/95 five out of seven key targets met.

**board**   Members of the Board are appointed by the Agricultural Ministers. The Chief Executive is a member, otherwise they are senior officials of the Agricultural Departments excepting the Non-Executive Chairman, who is independent.

**staff**   973

| | |
|---|---|
| Chief Executive | George Trevelyan |
| External Trade Director | Nick Dixon |
| Finance Director | Graham Jenkins |
| Internal Market Director | Hugh MacKinnon |
| Chief Accountant | Robert Bryant |
| Cereal Intervention, All Crop Market Support Schemes | Alan Butler |
| Milk Quotas | Chris Collins |
| Verification Trader Visits | Bob Hill |
| Export/Import Processed Goods, Recipes | Fran Mallin |
| Debts & Guarantees | Sarah McGilway |
| Customer Relations Manager | Gordon Munro |
| Export/Import Milk, Milk Products, Sheepmeat, Sugar, Fruit & Vegetables, Fish | Ivan Parsons |
| Export/Import Cereals, Rice, Oils, Fats & Seeds, Beef & Veal | Paul Rhodes |
| Export/Import Pigmeat, Eggs, Poultry, Community Victualling, Multi-Commodity Claims | John Welsh |
| All Dairy, Beef & Fish Market Support Schemes | David Williams |

**financial**

**OPERATING**
**Year end: 31 March**

| | 1995 |
|---|---|
| | £000 |
| **MARKET SUPPORT OPERATIONS** | |
| Internal market support | |
| Intervention buying and selling | (94,383) |
| Other internal market support | 1,966,244 |
| Cost of internal market support | 1,871,861 |
| Cost of external market support | 445,696 |
| Other payments | 105,356 |
| Cost of CAP market support | 2,422,913 |
| Less other receipts | 13,066 |
| EC contributions | 2,408,307 |
| **NET COST OF CAP MARKET SUPPORT REMAINING WITH THE AGENCY** | **1,540** |
| Administration expenses | 52,590 |
| Interest on capital | 18,545 |
| Change in provisions | 12,460 |
| **COST OF OPERATIONS REMAINING WITH THE AGENCY** | **85,135** |

# Investors in People UK

7-10 Chandos Street
London W1M 9DE

**Tel** 0171 467 1900
**Fax** 0171 636 2386

| | |
|---|---|
| ***status*** | Executive body |
| ***founded*** | 1993 |
| ***sponsor*** | Department for Education and Employment (DfEE) |
| ***powers*** | Memorandum and Articles of Association |
| ***mission*** | To contribute to the increased performance and competitive advantage of UK organisations by establishing, through the Investors in People Standard, the framework for effective training and development for all people in employment to meet business needs. |
| ***tasks*** | Providing advice, support and assessment services to organisations to help them implement improved management and development processes to achieve the Standard. Working with TECs and LECs and other training organisations, and providing publications, workshops and promotional events. |
| ***operations*** | Management: Chief Executive reports to the Board. Runs National Assessment Centre - seven assessors work in partnership with local assessment units - for needs of large multi-sited companies. By December 1997 30% of the workforce were employed in organisations involved with the Standard. |
| | Policy: Increased support activities for participating companies and encouragement to undergo assessment. |
| | Trends: New Investors in People company set up under licence in Australia. More countries may follow. |
| ***performance*** | Number of recognised organisations doubled to over 3500 in 1995/96. Increasing number of organisations committed to achieving the standard. |
| ***board*** | Appointed by Secretary of State from all sectors of business. One appointed from the DfEE, who is the Secretary of State's Board representative. |

| | | |
|---|---|---|
| Chairman | Sir Brian Wolfson | |
| Chief Executive | Ms MM Chapman | |
| Members | DF Beattie | |
| | Anthony Dubbins | NJA Hutton |
| | Sir Tom Farmer CBE | TK Morgan |
| | C Hadley OBE | NW Stuart CB |
| | HJ Hastings | Ms Sue Todd |
| | John Hazlewood CBE | Dr Louise M Wallace |
| | Martin Henry | Derek Wanless |
| *Accounting Officer* | *Chief Executive* | |

***staff*** 30

***financial***

| INCOME & EXPENDITURE | 1997 | 1996 | 1995 |
|---|---|---|---|
| Year end: 31 March | £000 | £000 | £000 |
| **GROSS INCOME** | | | |
| Grant-in-aid | 1,801 | 1,595 | 2,763 |
| Additional funding | 1,000 | 1,000 | - |
| Income from operations | 1,933 | 1,424 | 647 |
| | 4,734 | 4,019 | 3,410 |
| **GROSS EXPENDITURE** | | | |
| Cost of sales | 1,486 | 1,222 | 1,618 |
| Marketing | 1,776 | 1,400 | 561 |
| Development | 316 | 402 | 186 |
| Staff costs | 702 | 546 | 595 |
| Administration | 479 | 446 | 393 |
| Relocation | - | - | 52 |
| Depreciation | 43 | 38 | 18 |
| | 4,802 | 4,054 | 3,423 |
| **OPERATING DEFICIT FOR THE YEAR BEFORE TAXATION** | (68) | (35) | (13) |
| Interest receivable | 22 | 19 | 17 |
| **(DEFICIT)/SURPLUS BEFORE TAX** | (46) | (16) | 4 |
| Tax on (deficit)/surplus | (5) | (5) | (4) |
| **DEFICIT FOR THE YEAR** | (51) | (21) | - |
| Reversal of notional cost of capital | 51 | 21 | - |
| **RETAINED SURPLUS** | - | - | - |

| advisers | Bankers | Yorkshire Bank |
|---|---|---|
| | **Auditors** | Grant Thornton |
| | **Solicitors** | Cameron McKenna |
| | **Public Relations** | Countrywide |

## Joint Air Reconnaissance Intelligence Centre (JARIC)

Royal Air Force Brampton
Huntingdon
Cambridgeshire PE18 8QL

**Tel** 01480 52151

| | |
|---|---|
| *status* | Defence agency |
| *founded* | 1996 |
| *sponsor* | Ministry of Defence (MOD) |
| *mission* | To exploit and analyse imagery from all available sources and produce intelligence products and services to meet MOD and operational command requirements. |
| *tasks* | To produce imagery intelligence reports for defence planning, defence intelligence assessments and support to current operations; to produce illustrative graphics to support operational planning and current operations for all forms of aerial warfare; to detach trained and experienced military personnel of all ranks and trades to headquarters and other military units in support of military operations; to hold and maintain the UK's national military aerial imagery archives; to reproduce archive images in support of planning, security, exercise and other training by military units wordwide and to civilians on repayment; to advise on all aspects of reconnaissance, imagery and photography. |
| *operations* | Management: JARIC is owned by the Director General Intelligence Geographical Resources (MOD). It is managed by a Chief Executive from the RAF, supported by three Service Heads of Department (operations, business support, technical support) and one civilian (science and products). In its first year of operations, substantial progress was made with implementing the five-year action plan, although service level agreements with JARIC suppliers have not yet been completed. A new IT strategy has been approved. The permanent location of JARIC remains unresolved. |
| | 1996/97 saw JARIC tasked by the MOD, government agencies, and operational headquarters in response to a growing number of flashpoints (eg in the former Yugoslavia or locating refugees in Zaire and Rwanda). Over 5000 individual tasks were completed. High-level technical support remained crucial, and JARIC is at the forefront of specialist imagery-related technical services. |
| | Policy: A service delivery survey was conducted, the results of which will be implemented. |
| | Trends: Operationally, JARIC has continued to increase its focus on supporting military operations and has developed a good working relationship with the new PJHQ (Permanent Joint Headquarters) but despite this change in focus most of JARIC's effort is still directed towards answering the tasks of the Defence In**Tel**ligence Staff. |

| board | | |
|---|---|---|
| | Chief Executive | Group Captain Nigel Pearson |
| | Head Operations | Wing Commander Martin Hallam |
| | Head Business Support | Lieutenant Colonel Chris Lawton |
| | Head Science & Projects | John Longbottom |
| | Head Technical Support | Wing Commander Bill McCluggage |

| *staff* | 488 (138 non-industrial, 3 industrial and 347 service) |
|---|---|

*financial*

| INCOME & EXPENDITURE | |
|---|---|
| Year end: 31 March | **1997** |
| | **£000** |
| **EXPENDITURE** | |
| Staff costs | 11,844 |
| Supplies and services consumed | 5,024 |
| Accommodation costs | 1,110 |
| Other administration costs | 1,844 |
| Interest charged on capital | 360 |
| | **20,182** |
| **INCOME** | |
| Less income from non-MOD customers | (11) |
| **NET EXPENDITURE** | **20,171** |

# *Joint Nature Conservation Committee (JNCC)*

Monkstone House
City Road
Peterborough PE1 1JY

**Tel** 01733 866801
**Fax** 01733 555948

*status*  Executive agency

*founded*  1990

*sponsor*  Department of the Environment, Transport and the Regions

*powers*  Environmental Protection Act 1990

*mission*  To deliver the special functions of the three Conservation Councils for England, Scotland and Wales. To coordinate the UK's obligations arising under the Biodiversity Action Plan.

*tasks*  To be responsible for research, data collection and advice on nature conservation at both UK and international levels. To contribute to and report on the UK Biodiversity Action Plan and other obligations arising from the Convention on Biological Diversity. To implement the EC Habitats Directive.  To report to Ministers under the Wildlife & Countryside Act.

*operations*  Management: JNCC is supported by a Chief Officer and officer group, and the Support Unit staffed by specialists assigned to it from the three country agencies. The Support Unit was restructured in 1996/97 to give a publishing function and three main activities: the Advice Service advises government and key partners and is responsible for setting common standards for Great Britain as a whole and internationally; the Biodiversity Information Service is responsible for reporting systems under national, European and global conventions; Projects are undertaken to provide advice or information on nature conservation issues in Great Britain and internationally. Current projects include the Geological Conservation Review, the Marine Nature Conservation Review, Seabirds at Sea, Coastal Directories.

Policy: JNCC establishes a lead agency where a country agency has the appropriate expertise, eg English Nature is the lead agency on toxic chemicals and air pollution.

Trends: Coordination of the country agency effort to develop the candidate list of sites under the EC Habitats Directive (first 211 sites submitted to the European Commission). Partnership with government, statutory agencies, local authorities and industry on the provision of coastal zone information led to publication of the first four regional volumes in the *Coastal Directories* series.

*board*  JNCC is a committee of the Countryside Council for Wales, English Nature and Scottish Natural Heritage together with independent members and representatives of the Countryside Commission of Northern Ireland. The Chairman and three independent members are appointed directly by the Secretary of State.

| | | |
|---|---|---|
| Chairman | Sir Angus Stirling | |
| Members | Prof DQ Bowen | Prof PJ Newbould OBE |
| | The Earl of Cranbrook | Dr DF Shaw |
| | Dr JS Faulkner | R Simmonds |
| | EMW Griffith CBE | Prof TC Smout CBE |
| | M Magnusson KBE | Prof JI Sprent OBE |
| *Accounting Officer* | *Chief Executive* | |

**staff**   104 (all assigned from the country agencies: 59 from English Nature, 33 from Scottish Natural Heritage and 12 from the Countryside Council for Wales)

**financial**

| INCOME & EXPENDITURE Year end: 31 March | 1996 £000 | 1995 £000 |
|---|---|---|
| **GROSS INCOME** | | |
| Grant-in-aid | 4,559 | 4,911 |
| European Union funding | 6 | - |
| Income from activities | 351 | 423 |
| Transferred from deferred government grant account | 148 | 126 |
| Transfer from provisions | 3 | - |
| | **5,067** | **5,460** |
| **EXPENDITURE** | | |
| Conservation support | 2,436 | 2,660 |
| Staff costs | 1,100 | 1,136 |
| Depreciation | 139 | 125 |
| Other operating costs | 1,164 | 1,356 |
| Notional costs | 186 | 181 |
| | **5,025** | **5,458** |
| **SURPLUS ON OPERATING ACTIVITIES** | **42** | **2** |
| Loss on sale of fixed assets | (10) | (1) |
| Interest receivable | 15 | - |
| Notional costs | 182 | 177 |
| **APPROPRIATIONS** | | |
| Amount surrenderable to the country agencies | (226) | - |
| **RETAINED SURPLUS FOR THE FINANCIAL YEAR** | **3** | **178** |

**publications**   *Coastal Directories*

# *Labour Relations Agency (LRA)*

2-8 Gordon Street
Belfast BT1 2LG

**Tel** 01232 321442
**Fax** 01232 330827

| | |
|---|---|
| *status* | Executive body |
| *founded* | 1976 |
| *sponsor* | Northern Ireland Office, Department of Economic Development (DEDNI) |
| *powers* | Industrial Relations (Northern Ireland) Order 1976. Industrial Relations (Northern Ireland) Order 1992 |
| *mission* | To improve industrial relations in Northern Ireland. |
| *tasks* | To provide an effective, impartial and confidential service to people in industry, commerce and the public service. This includes all aspects of industrial relations and employment, comprehensive conciliation and arbitration, and industrial relations research. |
| *operations* | Management: The Chief Executive reports to the Board of the Agency. |
| | Trends: Continuing demand for Agency's services. |
| *board* | Part-time Chairman and nine other members appointed by DEDNI: three after consultation with organisations representative of employees; and three directly by the Department itself. |

| Part-time Chairman | Prof D Rea OBE |
|---|---|
| Members | Ms M Blood |
| | J Collins |
| | R Coughlin |
| | Mrs M Donnelly |
| | Mrs R Johnston |
| | J Lyttle |
| | Ms P Maxwell |
| | Ms Elizabeth May |
| | A Snoddy |
| *Accounting Officer* | *Chief Executive* |

*staff* 49

| Chief Executive | W Patterson |
|---|---|
| Board Secretary | G Crossan |

*financial*

**RECEIPTS & PAYMENTS**

| Year end: 31 March | 1997 | 1996 | 1995 |
|---|---|---|---|
| | £ | £ | £ |
| **RECEIPTS** | | | |
| Grants received from DEDNI | 1,840,000 | 1,692,000 | 1,560,000 |
| Operating receipts | 5,752 | 14,523 | 19,137 |
| | 1,845,752 | 1,706,523 | 1,579,137 |
| **PAYMENTS** | | | |
| Salaries and wages & superannuation | 1,379,624 | 1,253,687 | 1,179,193 |
| Other operating payments | 427,702 | 413,634 | 380,744 |
| | 1,807,326 | 1,667,321 | 1,559,937 |
| **SURPLUS FROM OPERATIONS** | 38,426 | 39,202 | 19,200 |
| Less other payments | 38,428 | 38,970 | 15,069 |
| **SURPLUS FOR THE FINANCIAL YEAR** | (2) | 232 | 4,131 |
| Surrenders to Consolidated Fund | 0 | 230 | 4,137 |
| **EXCESS (DEFICIT) OF RECEIPTS OVER PAYMENTS** | (2) | 2 | (6) |

| | | | |
|---|---|---|---|
| *advisers* | **Auditors** | Deloitte & Touche | 19 Bedford Street, Belfast BT2 7EJ |

*branches*
3 Foyle Street
Londonderry BT48 6AL
Tel 01504 269639
Fax 01504 267729

# Laganside Corporation

15 Clarendon Road
Belfast BT1 3BG

**Tel** 01232 328507
**Fax** 01232 332141

**E-mail** info@laganside.com
**Web** http://www.laganside.com

| | |
|---|---|
| *status* | Executive body |
| *founded* | 1989 |
| *sponsor* | Northern Ireland Office, Department of the Environment for NI (DOENI) |
| *powers* | Laganside Development (NI) Order 1989 |
| *mission* | To regenerate 200 hectares within the boundary of the City of Belfast, including the River Lagan. |
| *tasks* | Bringing land and buildings into effective use, encouraging public and private investment by creating an attractive environment and by ensuring that housing, social and recreational facilities are available to encourage people to live and work in the area. |
| *operations* | Management: The Corporation is funded by DOENI and grants from the European Regional Development Fund (ERDF).<br><br>Policy: To make a major contribution to providing jobs in the area.<br><br>Trends: Designated area extended (1997) to include Northside. |

**board**

| | | |
|---|---|---|
| Chairman | AS Hopkins CBE | |
| Members | E Airey | GR Irwin |
| | Dr L Blakiston-Houston | Ms G McAteer |
| | R Empey | Dr A McDonnell |
| | Mrs R Fairhead | H Smyth |
| Advisors | B Hanna | |
| | P Hunter | |
| | R Warburton | |
| *Accounting Officer* | *Chief Executive* | |

**staff** 32

| | |
|---|---|
| Acting Chief Executive | Mike Smith |
| Director of Finance & Administration | JD McCracken |

**financial**

## INCOME & EXPENDITURE

| Year end: 31 March | 1997 £ | 1996 £ | 1995 £ |
|---|---|---|---|
| **INCOME** | | | |
| Grant-in-aid released | 2,574,995 | 5,516,140 | 6,372,511 |
| ERDF grant release | 4,526,213 | 3,355,465 | 2,197,259 |
| Rental income | 19,236 | 34,942 | 57,329 |
| Other income | 1,210,030 | 500,588 | 938,223 |
| | **8,330,474** | **9,407,135** | **8,565,322** |
| **EXPENDITURE** | | | |
| Infrastructure and community projects | 6,826,848 | 8,117,641 | 6,705,039 |
| Operating costs | 523,516 | 499,322 | 446,577 |
| Staff costs | 720,644 | 620,672 | 648,811 |
| Estate costs | 392,981 | 272,229 | 211,379 |
| Depreciation - operating assets | 48,202 | 60,570 | 68,389 |
| Depreciation - major public assets | 130,873 | 609,512 | 494,946 |
| Reduction in provision for development assets | (421,000) | (277,000) | - |
| **SURPLUS/(DEFICIT) BEFORE INTEREST AND TAXATION** | **108,410** | **(495,811)** | **(9,819)** |
| Notional cost of capital | (628,365) | (395,556) | - |
| Interest receivable | 48,716 | 523,562 | 46,630 |
| Interest payable | - | (100) | (457) |
| Deficit after interest | (471,239) | (367,905) | 36,354 |
| Reversing notional cost of capital | 628,365 | 395,556 | - |
| **SURPLUS BEFORE TAXATION** | **157,126** | **27,651** | **36,354** |
| Taxation payable | (157,126) | (27,651) | (29,706) |
| **SURPLUS OF INCOME OVER EXPENDITURE** | **-** | **-** | **6,646** |

| advisers | **Bankers** | First Trust |
|---|---|---|
| | **Auditors** | Ernst & Young |
| | **Solicitors** | L'Estrange-Brett |
| | **Public Relations** | Future Image |
| *publications* | Annual Report, Corporate Plan, Laganside Guide | |

# Land Registers of Northern Ireland

27-45 Great Victoria Street
Belfast BT2 7SL

**Tel** 01232 251512
**Fax** 01232 251550

| *status* | Executive agency |
|---|---|
| *founded* | 1996 |
| *sponsor* | Northern Ireland Office, Department of the Environment for NI (DOENI) |
| *powers* | Land Registration Act (NI) 1970. Framework Document 1996 |
| *mission* | To be the most customer responsive land registration service in the British Isles. |
| *tasks* | Supporting the conveyancing and property markets in NI by: guaranteeing the validity of title to registered land; protecting the priority of conveyancing transactions for unregistered properties; supplying accurate, reliable and cost-effective information about land ownership and rights; providing a forum for the resolution of disputes regarding registered land. Administers the Land Registry of NI, the Registry of Deeds and the Statutory Charges Register. |
| *operations* | Management: The Minister determines the Agency's policy and financial framework. The Chief Executive, who is also the Registrar of Titles, is responsible for the management of the Agency and reports directly to the Minister. The Agency has a statutory duty to cover its costs from fee income. The business is demand-led and its fee income reflects fluctuations in the property market. |
| | Policy: To invest in IT, preferably with the help of Private Finance Initiative (PFI). |
| | Trends: Introduction of ground rent redemption scheme and phased extension of compulsory first registration will significantly increase workload. |
| *performance* | Key targets met or exceeded in 1996/97. |
| *board* | Appointed by the Minister. |

| Chief Executive/Registrar of Titles | Arthur Moir | |
|---|---|---|

| *staff* | 195 |
|---|---|

# Legal Aid Board (LAB)

85 Gray's Inn Road
London WC1X 8AA

**Tel** 0171 813 1000
**Fax** 0171 813 8638

| *status* | Executive body |
|---|---|
| *founded* | 1988 as a Shadow Board, assumed statutory responsibility in 1989 |
| *sponsor* | Lord Chancellor's Department |
| *powers* | Legal Aid Act 1988 |

| | |
|---|---|
| *mission* | To secure that advice, assistance, mediation and respresentation are available to those of small or moderate means in England and Wales and that it is provided in ways which are effective and give the best value for money. |
| *tasks* | Managing the major elements of the legal aid schemes; civil legal aid, legal advice and assistance, the duty solicitor schemes and some criminal legal aid to pay for them from the legal aid fund, including determining an individual's legal and financial entitlement to legal aid. The Board assists the Lord Chancellor in meeting his aims and objectives for publicly funded legal services; through its quality assurance initiative, franchising in improving and assuring the quality of service provided to the public by suppliers of legal aid. Assists the Lord Chancellor in his various legal aid reform initiatives including the establishment of regional legal services committees, based in each of Board's 13 area offices. Piloting block contracting with firms of solicitors, not-for-profit agencies and the provision of legal aid for mediation services. Working on an implementation plan for the Lord Chancellor for moving towards the delivery of all civil advice and assistance through exclusive contracts by the end of 1999. |
| *operations* | Management: The Chief Executive is responsible to the Board for the exercise of its functions. |
| | Policy: Establishing RLSCs in each of the Board's 13 areas. Franchising expanding. |
| | Trends: Continuing concern over costs per case and the need for cost control. The Lord Chancellor's proposals for reform include contracting for services, means tests and conditional fees. |
| *performance* | The Board has set targets for the delivery of services and details of performance against those targets. These are reviewed annually and will be published in the Board's *Annual Report*. (June 1998). |
| *board* | The Board shall consist of no fewer than 11 and no more than 17 members appointed by the Lord Chancellor. The Board has to include at least two solicitors (appointed after consultation with the Law Society) and two barristers (after consultation with the General's Council of the Bar). Other members include people with expertise in or knowledge of the provision of legal services, the work of the courts and social conditions, and management. |

| Chairman | Sir Tim Chessells | |
|---|---|---|
| Deputy Chairman | Henry Hodge OBE | |
| Members | Diane Charnock | |
| | Jean Dunkley | Steve Orchard |
| | Philip Ely | Diana Payne |
| | Colin George | Jim Shearer |
| | Brian Harvey | David Sinker OBE |
| *Accounting Officer* | *Chief Executive* | |

*staff*     1282

| Chief Executive | Steve Orchard |
|---|---|
| Director of Resources & Supplier Development | Brian Harvey |

*financial*

| EXPENDITURE | | | |
|---|---|---|---|
| **Year end: 31 March** | **1997** | **1996** | **1995** |
| | **£m** | **£m** | **£m** |
| Total amount paid out by the Board | 1,614 | 1,507 | 1,383 |
| Recovered through contributions, the statutory charge and costs | 397 | 350 | 298 |
| Net expenditure | 1,217 | 1,157 | 1,085 |
| Administration | 54 | 52 | 49 |
| Payments out of legal aid fund for legal aid | 1,163 | 1,104 | 1,036 |

*advisers*     **Auditors**     Clarke Whitehill

*branches*

29-37 Red Lion Street
London WC1R 4PP
Tel 0171 813 5300
Fax 0171 813 5812

3rd & 4th Floors
Invicta House
Trafalgar Place
Cheapside
Brighton BN1 4FR
Tel 01273 699622
Fax 01273 670690

80 Kings Road
Reading RG1 4LT
Tel 0118 9581620
Fax 0118 9584056

33-35 Queen Square
Bristol BS1 4LU
Tel 0117 921 4801
Fax 0117 9252584

Marland House
Central Square
Cardiff CF1 1PF
Tel 01222 388971
Fax 01222 238959

Centre City Podium
5 Hill Street
Birmingham B5 4UD
Tel 0121 632 6541
Fax 0121 632 5078

2nd Floor
Elisabeth House
16 St Peter's Square
Manchester M2 3DA
Tel 0161 228 1200
Fax 0161 228 0445

Eagle Star House
Fenkle Street
Newcastle upon Tyne NE1 5RU
Tel 0191 232 3461
Fax 0191 230 0084

City House
New Station Street
Leeds LS1 4IS
Tel 0113 244 2851
Fax 0113 244 9820

1st Floor
Fothergill House
16 King Street
Nottingham NG1 2AS
Tel 0115 9559600
Fax 0115 9560716

Kett House
Station Road
Cambridge CB1 2JT
Tel 01223 366511
Fax 01223 222608

Pepper House
2nd Floor
Pepper Row
Chester CH1 1DW
Tel 01244 315455
Fax 01244 319036

Cavern Walks
8 Mathew Street
Liverpool L2 6RE
Tel 0151 236 8371
Fax 0151 227 2533

# *Liverpool Housing Action Trust (HAT)*

2nd Floor
Cunard Building
Water Street
Liverpool L3 1EG

**Tel** 0151 227 1099
**Fax** 0151 236 5263

**Contact** David Green

| | |
|---|---|
| ***status*** | Executive body |
| ***founded*** | 1993 |
| ***sponsor*** | Department of the Environment, Transport and the Regions (DETR) |
| ***powers*** | Housing Act 1988 |
| ***mission*** | To secure the repair, improvement and effective management of its housing accommodation; to encourage diversity of occupancy, ownership and landlords to improve living conditions, social conditions and the general environment of the area. |
| ***tasks*** | To redevelop and improve its remaining 4626 dwellings in 57 high-rise blocks scattered over 35 sites throughout the city. |
| ***operations*** | Management: It is the largest HAT in the country and is to be wound up in 2005. The Chief Executive is responsible to the HAT board and the Secretary of State. Differs from other regeneration agencies as it has no critical mass in any one area, an increasingly frail and elderly tenant profile and almost exclusively high-rise housing stock - all within a city which lost 23% of its population from 1971-1991.

Policy: To work closely with the main agencies operating in each area, especially the Pathways Partnerships set up by the City Council as part of the EC objectives and the funding agencies like the Housing Corporation, English Partnerships, and the Merseyside Development Corporation.

Trends: Having approved the demolition of 24 blocks, it began a programme of priority catch-up repairs and started a new housing scheme. |
| ***performance*** | 1996/97 targets mostly met. |
| ***board*** | Appointed by the Secretary of State from HAT residents, local council and a range of local voluntary and private sector organisations. |

| | |
|---|---|
| Chair | Paula Ridley OBE, JP |
| Deputy Chairman | Rodney Dykes |
| Members | Eileen Clark |
| | Joe Devaney |
| | Marjorie Gallimore |
| | Charles Hubbard |
| | Sue Last |
| *Accounting Officer* | *Chief Executive* |

|  |  |
|---|---|
| | Edward McGonagle |
| | Joe Power |
| | June Roberts |
| | Jack Sheridan |

**staff** 150

| | |
|---|---|
| Chief Executive | David Green |
| Director of Development & Planning | Tom Clay |
| Director of Finance & Administration | David Houltby |
| Director of Housing Services | Kevin Morrison |
| Director of Community Services | Sue Thomas |

**financial**

**INCOME & EXPENDITURE**

| Year end: 31 March | 1997 £000 | 1996 £000 | 1995 £000 |
|---|---|---|---|
| **GROSS INCOME** | | | |
| Grant-in-aid receivable | 20,666 | 17,339 | 13,153 |
| Income from activities | 4,886 | 5,497 | 5,983 |
| | 25,552 | 22,836 | 19,136 |
| **EXPENDITURE ON ACTIVITIES** | | | |
| Other operating costs | 12,249 | 11,503 | 14,151 |
| Administrative expenses | 3,967 | 3,890 | 4,028 |
| Financial assistance | 9,367 | 7,479 | 1,028 |
| | 25,583 | 22,872 | 19,207 |
| **OPERATING DEFICIT** | (31) | (36) | (71) |
| Interest payable | (15) | - | - |
| Interest receivable | 48 | 48 | 95 |
| **SURPLUS ON ORDINARY ACTIVITIES BEFORE TAX** | 2 | 12 | 24 |
| Taxation | (17) | (12) | (24) |
| **SURPLUS FOR YEAR AFTER NOTIONAL COST OF CAPITAL** | (15) | 0 | 0 |
| Notional charges included above | 15 | 0 | 0 |
| **SURPLUS FOR YEAR BEFORE NOTIONAL COST OF CAPITAL** | 0 | 0 | 0 |

**advisers**

| | | |
|---|---|---|
| **Bankers** | Lloyds Bank | India Buildings, Water Street, Liverpool |
| **Auditors** | Kidsons Impey | Devonshire House, 36 George Street Manchester M1 4HA |
| **Solicitors** | Weightmans | Richmond House, Richmond St, Liverpool |

**publications** *Annual Report and Accounts 1996/97*

# Livestock & Meat Commission for Northern Ireland (LMC)

57 Malone Road
Belfast BT9 6SA

**Tel** 01232 590000
**Fax** 01232 590001

| | |
|---|---|
| **status** | Executive body |
| **founded** | 1967 |
| **sponsor** | Northern Ireland Office, Department of Agriculture NI (DANI) |
| **powers** | Livestock Marketing Commission Act (Northern Ireland) 1967 |
| **mission** | To maximise the return to the NI economy from its beef and sheepmeat industries. To advise DANI on matters relating to these industries and provide services to the industry. |

| | |
|---|---|
| **tasks** | Provision of market information to producers and processors; the representation of the industry in home and export promotion and marketing at a generic level; the operation of the Northern Ireland Farm Quality Assurance Scheme and the development and implementation of marketing initiatives for NI beef and sheepmeat in the home and export markets; provision of beef and sheep carcase classification services; representation of the Intervention Board as its agents within NI. |
| **operations** | Management: Chief Executive reports to the Commission and DANI. No direct government funding; funding is from levies, classification service, intervention board, European promotional fund. |
| | Policy: Has pushed for end of beef export ban for NI. |
| | Trends: BSE has been major preoccupation - 50% of markets disappeared as a result of export ban. LMC concluded that NI merited separate treatment from rest of the UK beef industry because of computer traceability system and lower incidence of BSE and is promoting that message. |
| **performance** | Historically most marketing focus on export activities, but since BSE crisis more focus on home (NI) and GB. |
| **board** | Members of the Commission are appointed by the Minister from the industry. |

| Chairman | Gerry Lowe | |
|---|---|---|
| Members | Bernie Cranfield | Owen McMahon |
| | Ian Mark | Richard Moore |
| | Miceal McCoy | Patricia Smyth |
| *Accounting Officer* | *Chief Executive* | |

**staff** 80

| Chief Executive | David Rutledge |
|---|---|
| Accountant | Suzanne Blain |
| Marketing Manager | Phelim O'Neill |
| Secretary & Economist | David Ritchie |
| Agricultural Manager | Dr Mike Tempest |
| Chief Field Officer | John Wilson |

**financial**

| INCOME & EXPENDITURE Year end: 31 March | 1997 £ | 1996 £ | 1995 £ |
|---|---|---|---|
| **GROSS INCOME** | | | |
| Income from activities | 1,955,810 | 850,884 | 955,041 |
| **NET OPERATING EXPENSES** | | | |
| Staff and related costs | 1,319,764 | 498,875 | 525,752 |
| Depreciation | 26,000 | 25,477 | 24,496 |
| Other operating charges | 356,339 | 385,622 | 327,210 |
| | 1,702,103 | 909,974 | 877,458 |
| **OPERATING SURPLUS/(DEFICIT)** | 253,707 | (59,090) | 77,583 |
| Income from investments | 105,570 | 118,221 | 84,912 |
| **SURPLUS ON ORDINARY ACTIVITIES BEFORE TAXATION** | 359,277 | 59,131 | 162,495 |
| Taxation | 25,201 | 29,555 | 21,228 |
| **SURPLUS FOR THE FINANCIAL YEAR** | 334,076 | 29,576 | 141,267 |

| | | | |
|---|---|---|---|
| **advisers** | **Bankers** | Ulster Bank | |
| | **Auditors** | Coopers & Lybrand | Great Victoria Street, Belfast |
| **publications** | *Bulletin, Meat Trade* | | |

# *Local Enterprise Development Unit (LEDU)*

LEDU House
Upper Galwally
Belfast BT8 6TB

**Tel** 01232 491031  **E-mail** ledu@ledu-ni.gov.uk
**Fax** 01232 691432  **Web** http://www.ledu-ni.gov.uk

| | |
|---|---|
| **status** | Executive body |
| **founded** | 1971 |
| **sponsor** | Northern Ireland Office, Department of Economic Development (DEDNI) |
| **mission** | To encourage the creation and development of small-scale business in Northern Ireland by providing financial and advisory services. |

# Q&Q

| | |
|---|---|
| **tasks** | Provide information, guidance, financial support and a range of programmes and services to help small businesses become more competitive. Encourage exports. |
| **operations** | Management: LEDU is a company limited by guarantee. There is an Executive Management Group comprising the Chief Executive and three Directors (Corporate Services, Business Development and Regional Operations). Head office in Belfast and five regional offices. LEDU's business start-up training is delivered through the Local Enterprise Agency Network. |
| | Policy: Trying to increase number of jobs created in disadvantaged areas. |
| | Trends: Business start-ups increasing. |
| **board** | Appointed by Secretary of State. |

| | | |
|---|---|---|
| Chairman | Paul McWilliams OBE | |
| Members | Michael Black | |
| | Mrs Mary Breslin | Will McKee |
| | The Hon Claire Faulkner | Gerry Mullan |
| | Prof Jim Magowan | Mrs Joan Ruddock, OBE |
| | Dr Bill McCourt | Mrs Teresa Townsley |
| Accounting Officer | Chief Executive | |

**staff**  231

| | |
|---|---|
| Chief Executive | Chris Buckland |
| Business Development Director | Kevin McCann |
| Corporate Services Director | Alan Neville |
| Regional Operations Director | Jim Sayers |
| Manager Administration, Finance & Legal | Danny Adair |
| Manager Business Development Services | Denis Babes |
| Manager Human Resources | Colum Boyle |
| Manager General Manufacturing & Services | Brian Dane |
| Manager Western Regional Office | Joe Doherty |
| Manager North Western Regional Office | Gerard Finnegan |
| Manager Corporate Marketing | Nigel Hardy |
| Manager North Eastern Regional Office | Olive Hill |
| Manager Strategic Planning | Carol Keery |
| Manager Belfast Regional Office | Tim Losty |
| Manager Food | Peter McArdle |
| Manager Marketing & Information Services | Bill McGowan |
| Manager Engineering | Michael Polson |
| Manager Regional Development | Sharon Polson |
| Manager Textiles & Electronics | Michele Shirlow |
| Manager Southern Regional Office | Tom Short |
| Manager Information Systems & Support | Keith Turkington |
| Executive Company Services | Molly Vannan |
| Manager North Western Regional Office | Gerard Finnegan |
| Manager North Eastern Regional Office | Olive Hill |
| Manager Belfast Regional Office | Tim Losty |
| Manager Southern Regional Office | Tom Short |
| Manager Western Regional Office | Joe Doherty |

**financial**

**INCOME & EXPENDITURE**
**Year end: 31 March**

| | 1996 £ | 1995 £ |
|---|---|---|
| DEDNI | 30,341,602 | 32,084,235 |
| From enterprises under contact | 257,432 | 228,834 |
| | **30,599,034** | **32,313,069** |
| Expenditure relating to job creation | (23,403,000) | (24,849,450) |
| Administrative expenses | (7,375,254) | (7,373,056) |
| Other operating income | 274,905 | 245,178 |
| Amount provided and written-off loans and investments | (95,685) | (335,741) |
| Surplus on ordinary activities before taxation | - | - |
| Tax charge on ordinary activities | - | - |
| Result for the financial year | - | - |

**branches**

*North West*
13 Shipquay Street
Londonderry BT48 6DJ
Tel 01504 267257
Fax 01504 266054
E-mail nwro@ledu.binternet.com

*North East*
Clarence House
86 Mill Street
Ballymena BT43 5AF
Tel 01266 49215
Fax 01266 48427
E-mail nero@ledu.binternet.com

*Belfast*
25-27 Franklin Street
Belfast BT2 8DT
Tel 01232 242582
Fax 01232 249730

*South*
6-7 The Mall
Newry BT34 1BX
Tel 01693 62955
Fax 01693 65358
E-mail sro@ledu.btinternet.com

*West*
Kevlin Buildings
47 Kevlin Avenue
Omagh BT78 1ER
Tel 01662 245763
Fax 01662 244291
E-mail wro@ledu.binternet.com

# Logistic Information Systems Agency (LISA)

Monxton Road
Andover
Hants SP11 8HT

**Tel** 01264 382745
**Fax** 01264 382820

| | |
|---|---|
| *status* | Defence agency |
| *founded* | 1994 |
| *sponsor* | Ministry of Defence |
| *powers* | Framework Document |
| *mission* | Enhancing the logistic effectiveness of the Army in peace and war by providing information systems, services and support. |
| *tasks* | LISA provides a 'one-stop shop' for IS within the Quartermaster General's (QMG) area, which is increasingly tri-Service. Core tasks are to define, formulate and maintain IS strategy and implementation policy on behalf of QMG, to regulate IS activity within the QMG area, to provide operational support to Army units, to provide resources for programme management, account management and project management to QMG. |
| *operations* | Management: LISA's Owner is the Chief of Staff QMG. He is responsible for approving the corporate and business plans, and monitoring performance. The Chief Executive reports to the Owner. Non-core activities (defined as those better delivered by the private sector) are usually delivered by its partner Electronic Data Systems (EDS), a commercial company, through a LISA/EDS partnership contract. |
| | Policy: To be the preferred supplier to all customers. |
| | Trends: The QMG agencies have tri-Service commitments and LISA is increasingly exposed to defence-wide considerations. |
| *performance* | Five of the six targets were met for 1996/97. |
| *board* | Owner's Advisory Board appointed by the Owner. |

| Members | | |
|---|---|---|
| | Major General K Donoghue | COS QMG |
| | Brigadier AW Pollard | CE LISA |
| | Brigadier JW Clinter | DQIS |
| | Brigadier MGR Hodson | D Log Sp Pol |
| | Brigadier SG Middleton | DES 1 |
| | P Waring | Prin QMG Fin |
| | Dr C Barnes | DPMP |
| *Accounting Officer* | *Permanent Under Secretary* | |

*staff*      250 (50 military, 200 civilian)

| | |
|---|---|
| Chief Executive | Brigadier Alan W Pollard |
| Director of Equipment Support | Colonel Ian CD Blair-Pilling |
| Director of Corporate and Infrastructure | Ray Neath |
| Director of Finance | Mike Robbins |
| Director, IS Strategy & Policy | John Pearson |
| Director, Contract Management & Support Services | Andy Targett |
| Director, Personnel | Lindsay Milne |
| SO2 Business Plans | Major John A Ensor |

*publications*      *Corporate Plan, Annual Report and Accounts*

# London Pensions Fund Authority (LPFA)

Dexter House
2 Royal Mint Court
London EC3N 4LP

**Tel** 0171 369 6000
**Fax** 0171 369 6111

| | |
|---|---|
| *status* | Executive body |
| *founded* | 1989 |
| *sponsor* | Department of the Environment, Transport and the Regions (DETR) |
| *powers* | LPFA Management Statement |
| *mission* | To administer the Local Government Pension Scheme (LGPS). |
| *tasks* | To manage the investment portfolio; to increase the contributor membership. |

*operations*  Management: The Board is responsible for the proper administration of the LGPS and has a fiduciary duty to the contributors and beneficiaries of the Fund and to the council tax payers of Greater London who finance residual liabilities. The Chief Executive reports to the Board with the Board reporting to the Secretary of State for Environment, Transport and the Regions. The Chairman and Deputy Chairman meet weekly with the executive management on investment matters; the three investment managers report directly to the Board at least twice a year. The Fund is divided into two - a Pensioner Sub-Fund and an Active Sub-Fund for investment strategy purposes.

Policy: To follow an investment strategy which maintains the solvency of the fund, while delivering low and stable contribution rates.

Trends: Continued net expenditure on the Pension Fund, which reflects the maturity of the fund at current membership levels.

*performance*  All financial targets met 1996/97. Won Watson Wyatt Scheme of the Year Award 1996/97 (for service to customers).

*board*  Appointed by Secretary of State, at least half after consultation with London local government representative.

| | | |
|---|---|---|
| Chairman | Cholmeley Messer | |
| Deputy Chairman | Michael Roberts | |
| Members | Sir Nigel Althaus | Cllr Judith Jorsling |
| | Cllr Dennis Barkway CBE | Cllr Serge Lourie |
| | Cllr Steve Bullock | David Mason |
| | Ms Caroline Burton | Maurice Stonefrost |
| *Accounting Officer* | *Permanent Under Secretary* | |

*staff*  67

| | |
|---|---|
| Chief Executive | Peter Scales |
| Director of Development Richard Allen | |
| Director of Resources | Martin Campbell |
| Director of Operations | Phil Goodwin |

*financial*

| INCOME & EXPENDITURE | | |
|---|---|---|
| **Year end: 31 March** | **1997** | **1996** |
| | **£000** | **£000** |
| **INCOME** | | |
| Reimbursement of costs: | | |
| Recoverable benefit payments | 81,876 | 78,328 |
| Management charges | 415 | 446 |
| **Levies receivable** | | |
| Greater London account | 8,446 | 8,367 |
| Inner London account | 15,027 | 14,367 |
| Interest and other charges | 2,504 | 2,480 |
| Expenses charged to the fund | 2,999 | 3,209 |
| | **111,267** | **107,197** |

| EXPENDITURE | | |
|---|---|---|
| **Remuneration and other costs** | | |
| Members | 74 | 66 |
| Employees | 1,902 | 2,000 |
| Premises costs | 1,097 | 1,082 |
| Computing services | 382 | 306 |
| Other services | 486 | 390 |
| Office expenses | 250 | 280 |
| | **4,191** | **4,124** |
| **Recoverable benefit payments** | | |
| Firemen's Pension Scheme | 65,280 | 57,042 |
| **Local government scheme** | | |
| Agency services | 7,966 | 12,709 |
| Non-funded pension benefits | 8,630 | 8,577 |
| | **81,876** | **78,328** |
| **Non-funded benefits chargeable to levy** | | |
| Greater London account | 9,856 | 9,635 |
| Inner London account | 14,623 | 14,442 |
| | **24,479** | **24,077** |
| Loan stock interest and administration | 922 | 923 |
| | **111,468** | **107,452** |
| **NET OPERATING EXPENDITURE** | **(201)** | **(255)** |
| Fixed asset restatement reserve | 12 | 16 |
| Earmarked Reserve | 27 | (110) |
| **DEFICIT FOR THE YEAR** | **(162)** | **(349)** |
| Balance brought forward | 761 | 1,110 |
| **BALANCE CARRIED FORWARD** | **599** | **761** |

*advisers*   **Bankers**     Midland Bank

**Auditors**    The District Audit Service
Coopers & Lybrand

**Solicitors**   Clifford Chance
Eversheds
Nabarro Nathanson
Portner & Jaskell

*publications*   Annual Report and Accounts, Corporate Plan

*branches*   Dexter House
2 Royal Mint Court
London EC3N 4LP

# London Regional Passengers Committee

Clements House
14-18 Gresham Street
London EC2V 7PR

**Tel** 0171 505 9000
**Fax** 0171 505 9003

*status*    Executive body

*founded*    1984

*sponsor*    Department of the Environment, Transport and the Regions (DETR)

*powers*    London Regional Transport Act 1984.   Railways Act 1993.

*mission*    Statutory watchdog protecting, promoting and speaking for the interests of public transport users in and around London.

*tasks*    Protects, promotes and speaks for the users of the national rail network and Eurostar in and around London, together with users of the underground, Docklands Light Railway, London Transport Buses and Victoria Coach Station.  Promotes an integrated public transport network in the London area; represents the interests of passengers; monitors performance and encourages higher standards by the operators.

**operations**  Management:  The Secretariat (led by the Director and two Assistant Directors) runs day-to-day management, reporting to the Committee Chairman.

Policy:  Becoming more proactive in pressing for specific improvements and at the centre of the decision-making process.  4996 representations received from the public in 1996/97 (a 3.8% increase).

Trends:  Size and complexity of new railway industry structure leading to increasing workload.

**board**  Committee members are appointed by the Minister following public advertisement.

| Chairman | Alan Greengross | |
|---|---|---|
| Deputy Chairmen | Delia Buckle | |
| | Suzanne May | |
| Members | Andy Brabin | |
| | Philippa Carling | John Illenden |
| | Doris Colloff | Amanda Ingram |
| | Vidur Dindayal | Anne Jobson |
| | Daniel Dobson-Mouawad | Charles King |
| | Angela Fitzgerald | Cynthia Lake |
| | Stella Fowler | Peter Nichols |
| | Judith Hanna | Peter Noble |
| | Christine Hodgson | Graham Taylor |
| | Andy Holt | Barry Turner |
| | Brian Hord | Mulugeta Yegezu |
| *Accounting Officer* | *Director* | |

**staff**  14

| Director | Rufus Barnes |
|---|---|
| Assistant Director, Policy Development | John Cartledge |
| Assistant Director, Finance & Administration | Christine Evans |

**financial**

| RECEIPTS & PAYMENTS Year end: 31 March | 1997 £ | 1996 £ | 1995 £ |
|---|---|---|---|
| RECEIPTS | | | |
| HMG grants received (Class V Vote 2) | 552,933 | 471,094 | 458,644 |
| PAYMENTS | | | |
| Salaries & wages | (250,446) | (240,522) | (211,950) |
| Other operating expenses | (295,513) | (215,398) | (199,783) |
| IT project expenses | (2,374) | (4,531) | (16,743) |
| | (548,333) | (460,451) | (428,476) |
| SURPLUS FROM OPERATIONS | 4,600 | 10,643 | 30,168 |
| Other payments (net of receipts) | (1,671) | (9,242) | (30,151) |
| SURPLUS FOR THE FINANCIAL YEAR | 2,929 | 1,401 | 17 |

**advisers**  **Bankers**  Royal Bank of Scotland

**Auditors**  National Audit Office

**publications**  *Annual Report*

# London Transport (LT)

55 Broadway
London SW1H 0BD

**Tel** 0171 222 5600
**Fax** 0171 222 5719          **Web** http://www.londontransport.co.uk

**status**  Nationalised Industry

**founded**  1984 in its present form

**sponsor**  Department of the Environment, Transport and the Regions (DETR)

**powers**  London Regional Transport Act 1984

**mission**  To ensure that safe, efficient and economic public transport is provided for those who live in, work in and visit London.

**tasks**      London Underground Ltd (LUL) operates the existing London Underground network and plans and builds extensions to it; LT Buses plans routes, specifies service levels and works with others to extend bus priority measures (private operators provide the buses); LT manages Victoria Coach Station, the LT Museum and a portfolio of commercial property based on London Underground stations.

**operations**  Management: As a nationalised industry, LT consults with government on policy; there are regular meetings on policy and performance. The LT Board (LTB) approved a group budget for 1997/98 which includes a government grant of £760 million. Gross operating margins improved in 1996/97 (the fifth consecutive year) by 30%. London Underground Ltd, the principal operating subsidiary, invested £374 million in existing underground systems, largely in infrastructure projects, and £660 million in the Jubilee Line extension. Since it was formed in 1994, LT Buses has reduced net subsidy per operating kilometre by 80% in real terms. Victoria Coach Station, which handles over 90% of London's long-distance scheduled coach travel, has concentrated on improving customer service and training staff in customer awareness. LT Property manages LT property interests and in 1996/97 over £50 million was generated from commercial letting (£31 million) and development sales (£21 million).

Policy: Sustained investment in underground and bus networks to address the backlog of under-investment is seen as vital and LT is lobbying to ensure that adequate public funds are restored.

Trends: Gross operating margins are now expected to be positive and so make some contribution towards investment. But LT is exploring the possibilities of public/private partnerships, the Public Finance Initiative (PFI), and capital borrowing.

**board**

| **London Regional Transport** | |
|---|---|
| Chairman and Chief Executive | Peter Ford |
| Non-Executive Vice-Chairman | Brian Appleton |
| Non-Executive Director | Sir Alan Bailey KCB |
| Non-Executive Director | Bob Chase |
| Non-Executive Director | Rosemary Day |
| Managing Director, LTB | Clive Hodson CBE |
| Non-Executive Director | Michael Lawrence |
| Non-Executive Director | Sally O'Sullivan |
| Board Member for Finance | Tony Sheppeck |
| Managing Director, LUL | D Tunnicliffe CBE |

| **London Underground** | |
|---|---|
| Chairman | Peter Ford |
| Managing Director | D Tunnicliffe CBE |
| Non-Executive Director | B Appleton |
| Director of Development | D Bailey |
| LT Director of Human Resources | Ms AC Burfutt |
| LT Director of Marketing | NV Cohen |
| Director of Engineering | DJ Hornby |
| LT Director, Group Financial Planning & Control | JJ Hughes |
| Non-Executive Director | Dr R Jeffery |
| LT Board Member for Finance | Tony Sheppeck |
| Director of Passenger Services | HL Sumner |

| **Victoria Coach Station** | |
|---|---|
| Chairman | Clive Hodson CBE |
| Managing Director | WEC Hillman |
| Member of Board | NV Cohen |

| **LT Buses** | |
|---|---|
| Chairman | Peter Ford |
| Deputy Chairman | Sir Alan Bailey KCB |
| Managing Director | Clive Hodson CBE |
| Finance Director | A Brindle |
| LT Marketing Director | NV Cohen |
| Procurement Director | BD Everett |
| Operations & Services Director | MG Heath |
| Managing Director, Victoria Coach Station | WEC Hillman |
| Non-Executive Director | JK Isaac |
| Non-Executive Director | Ms S O'Sullivan |
| LT Board Member for Finance | AJ Sheppeck |
| Planning & Development Director | RS Smith |

| **LT Property** | |
|---|---|
| Chairman | Peter Ford |
| Managing Director | CH Smith |
| Member of Board | Clive Hodson CBE |
| Member of Board | IE King |
| Member of Board | Tony Sheppeck |
| Member of Board | D Tunnicliffe |
| Property Development Manager | M Withers |

**staff** 18,149

**financial**

| GROUP PROFIT & LOSS Year end: 31 March | 1997 £000 | 1996 £000 | 1995 £000 |
|---|---|---|---|
| SALES REVENUE | | | |
| Continuing operations | 1,158,900 | 1,087,700 | 1,012,200 |
| Discontinued operations | - | - | 143,000 |
| | 1,158,900 | 1,087,700 | 1,155,200 |
| COST OF OPERATIONS | (989,500) | (958,000) | 1,114,800 |
| GROSS OPERATING MARGIN | 169,400 | 129,700 | 40,400 |
| Depreciation | (136,800) | (137,300) | (249,200) |
| Renewals | (202,900) | (279,900) | (188,100) |
| OPERATING LOSS BEFORE GRANTS | (170,300) | (287,500) | (396,900) |
| Grants received and released from reserves | 170,900 | 288,700 | 397,800 |
| OPERATING PROFIT AFTER GRANTS | 600 | 1,200 | 900 |
| Profit on disposal of assets | 8,300 | 16,800 | (5,600) |
| Profit on sale of subsidiary companies | - | - | 105,300 |
| PROFIT BEFORE TAXATION | 8,900 | 18,000 | 100,600 |
| Taxation | - | - | - |
| PROFIT FOR THE YEAR | 8,900 | 18,000 | 100,600 |
| Transfer to capital reserve | (8,300) | (16,800) | (99,700) |
| PROFIT AND LOSS ACCOUNT MOVEMENT IN THE YEAR | 600 | 1,200 | 900 |
| Accumulated profit at the beginning of the year | 4,400 | 3,200 | 2,300 |
| ACCUMULATED PROFIT AT THE END OF THE YEAR | 5,000 | 4,400 | 3,200 |

**advisers**  **Auditors**  KPMG

# Macaulay Land Use Research Institute (MLURI)

Craigiebuckler
Aberdeen AB15 8QH

**Tel** 01224 318611
**Fax** 01224 311556

**E-mail** @mluri.sari.ac.uk
**Web** http://www.mluri.sari.ac.uk

**status** Executive body
**founded** 1987
**sponsor** Scottish Office
**mission** To understand how to identify and create sustainable, integrated land use options, that is options which attempt to reconcile the three often conflicting objectives of: producing food, fibre, chemical or energy foodstock; sustaining the social and environmental functions of the countryside; and maintaining the viability of producers.
**tasks** To undertake research, in the context of rural land use and resource management, with the objective of assessing the environmental, economic and social impacts of agriculture and associated land uses, and the consequences of change resulting from factors and influences such as policy, management, effects of climate, and pollution; to find successful ways of using land and other natural resources in creating wealth without compromising environmental quality and the quality of human life, and by increasing the efficiency and minimising the use of non-renewable resources.
**operations** Management: MLURI is funded primarily by the Scottish Office Agriculture and Fisheries Department (SOAFD) and works within the context of UK and EU environmental policy objectives. Its commercial company, Macaulay Research and Consultancy Services, has broadened the funding base, as has the award of research contracts by the European Commission. Current research themes are sustainable integrated land use options, integrated catchment management; sustainable management of soils and of marginal lands.

Policy: To continue to develop collaborative links both locally, in Scotland, and internationally in Europe, South Asia, China, Africa, the USA and Australia.

Trends: The research programme has increasingly focused on issues that have a direct bearing on sustainable land use and sustainable development.
**performance** Prior Options Review concluded MLURI was needed and should retain its separate existence within the public sector.

| board | | |
|---|---|---|
| Chairman | Prof JI Sprent OBE | |
| Vice-Chairman | Prof HM Keir | |
| Members | JR Carr, CBE | I Miller, OBE |
| | JIM Crawford | WH Porter |
| | Mrs MT Dennis | Prof JHD Prescott |
| | JAC Don JP | Prof PA Racey |
| | JFS Gourlay | AK Rae |
| | J Lind | Dr PBH Tinker |
| | DTM Lloyd | Prof WH van Riemsdijk |

**staff**  265

| | |
|---|---|
| Director | Prof T Jeff Maxwell |
| Deputy Director | John A Milne |
| Assistant to the Director Claire | L Howard |
| External Affairs Officer | Sue P Bird |
| Head, Land Use Science Group | Richard V Birnie |
| Programme Unit Manager | J Robert Crabtree |
| Head, Soil Science Group | M Jeffrey Wilson |
| Programme Unit Manager | Robert C Ferrier |
| Programme Unit Manager | Edward Paterson |
| Head, Plant Science Group | Peter Millard |
| Head, Ecology & Animal Science Group | John A Milne |
| Programme Unit Manager | Iain J Gordon |
| Programme Unit Manager | Iain A Wright |
| Head, Analytical Group | Alistair Smith |
| Head, Computing & Information Services Group | Christopher H Osman |
| Head, Research Stations Group | Prof TJ Maxwell |
| Institute Secretary | Robert B Devine |
| Institute Deputy Secretary/Finance Officer | David T Wilkinson |
| Head, Consultancy Division | James H Gauld |

**financial**

| FINANCE STATEMENT | |
|---|---|
| Year end: 31 March | 1996 |
| | £000 |
| **INCOME** | |
| Scottish Office Agriculture and Fisheries Department | 5,842 |
| SOAFD Flexible Research Funding and other SOAFD contracts | 1,325 |
| European Union research contracts | 379 |
| Funding from other government departments, public bodies and agencies | 383 |
| Private research and consultancy contracts | 242 |
| Other income | 143 |
| | **8,314** |
| Less equipment purchased from revenue grants | (67) |
| | **8,247** |
| **EXPENDITURE** | |
| Staff costs | 5,156 |
| Research expenditure including research station costs | 1,574 |
| Other operating costs | 1,202 |
| | **7,932** |
| **SURPLUS (DEFICIT)** | **315** |

# *Marine Safety Agency (MSA)*

Spring Place
105 Commercial Road
Southampton SO15 1EG

**Tel** 01703 329100
**Fax** 01703 329298

| | |
|---|---|
| **status** | Executive agency |
| **founded** | 1994 |
| **sponsor** | Department for the Environment, Transport and the Regions (DETR) |
| **powers** | Framework Document 1994 |

0# Q&Q

| | |
|---|---|
| **mission** | To develop, promote and enforce high standards of marine safety in the UK and to minimise the risk of pollution of the marine environment from ships. |
| **tasks** | Develop and monitor marine safety and pollution prevention policies and standards; implement DETR's Shipping Policy Directorate; inspect UK and foreign ships and enforce standards; provide survey and certification services to the shipping industry; provide examination and certification services to seafarers; provide advice and information to the DETR, shipping industry and public. |
| **operations** | Management: Chief Executive is supported by a Management Board of three divisional Directors and one Non-Executive Director. It reports quarterly to the Advisory Board, which advises the Secretary of State on the plans and performance of the agency. Headquarters in Southampton, with three regional offices, 13 suboffices and Registry of Shipping and Seamen in Cardiff. |
| | Policy: To assist industry to achieve a reduction in the accident rate of UK registered merchant ships and fishing vessels; and to reduce pollution of the marine environment by ships. |
| | Trends: Accident rate for merchant ships decreasing, but increasing for fishing vessels. Emphasis on training seafarers in 1997/98. |
| **note** | **From 1 April 1998, MSA merged with Coastguard to form the Maritime & Coastguard Agency (MCA).** |
| **performance** | Achieved eight out of nine targets for 1996/97. |
| **board** | Advisory Board appointed by the Secretary of State. |

| Accounting Officer | Chief Executive |
|---|---|

| | |
|---|---|
| **staff** | 357 |

| | |
|---|---|
| Chief Executive | Robin Bradley |
| Director, Marine Safety & Standards | Tom Allan |
| Director, Operations & Seafarer Standards | Alan Cubbin |
| External Member | JM (Ian) Fraser |
| Director, Finance & Corporate Services | Roy Padgett |

**financial**

**INCOME & EXPENDITURE**

| Year end: 31 March | 1997 £000 | 1996 £000 |
|---|---|---|
| **EXPENDITURE** | | |
| Operating costs | 16,480 | 16,958 |
| Notional costs | 2,757 | 3,473 |
| Depreciation | 751 | 711 |
| | **19,988** | **21,142** |
| Current grants | 5,908 | 7,298 |
| Other disbursements | 7,840 | 6,079 |
| | **33,736** | **34,519** |
| **INCOME** | | |
| Income from services provided | (4,664) | (4,465) |
| **NET EXPENDITURE** | **29,072** | **30,054** |

**advisers** **Auditors** National Audit Office 157-197 Buckingham Palace Road London SW1W 9SP

**branches**

*North England & Wales*
Crosskill House
Mill Lane
Beverley
East Riding of Yorkshire HU17 9JB
Tel 01482 866606
Fax 01482 869989

*Scotland & Northern Ireland*
Blaikies Quay
Aberdeen AB11 5EZ
Tel 01224 574122
Fax 01224 571920

*Registry of Shipping and Seamen*
Unit 12
Cheviot Close
Parc Ty Glas
Llanishen
Cardiff CF4 5JA
Tel 01222 747333
Fax 01222 747877

# Marshall Aid Commemoration Commission

36 Gordon Square
London WC1H 0PF

**Tel** 0171 3878572
**Fax** 0171 3872655

| | |
|---|---|
| *status* | Executive body |
| *founded* | 1953 |
| *sponsor* | Foreign and Commonwealth Office (FCO) |
| *powers* | Marshall Aid Commemoration Act 1953 |
| *mission* | To award Marshall Aid Scholarships at leading British universities to US citizens and ensure the Marshall Scholars' academic and social welfare for the duration of their study in Britain. |
| *tasks* | Selecting Marshall Scholars, placing them at the British university of their choice, funding them through their British university placements; monitoring their academic progress and social welfare. |
| *operations* | Management: The Marshall Aid Commemoration Commission is housed at the Association of Commonwealth Universities which provides the Secretariat and its Secretary General is the Commission's Executive Secretary. The Commission is responsible for overall funding and for specifying the number of scholarships to be offered each year, but HM Treasury specifies their value. The final selection of scholars is made by the Ambassador's Advisory Council in Washington, chaired by the British Ambassador. In 1995/96 there were 84 Marshall Scholars in residence at British universities and 40 Marshall Scholarships were awarded for 1996/97. |
| | Policy: Achieving better Marshall Scholar gender balance. |
| *board* | Members of the Commission are appointed by the Secretary of State. |

| | | |
|---|---|---|
| Chairman | Dr Robert Stevens | |
| Members | Prof Christine Bolt | |
| | Sir Charles Chadwyck-Healey | Ms Hilary Heilbron QC |
| | Prof Lord Desai | Sir Gordon Jewkes KCMG |
| | Prof Harry Dickinson | Ms Sue MacGregor OBE |
| | Dr Kenneth Edwards | Dr Onora O'Neill CBE |
| Observer | AD Sprake | |

| | |
|---|---|
| *staff* | Executive Secretary | Dr A Christodoulou CBE |

# Meat Hygiene Service (MHS)

Foss House
Kings Pool
1-2 Peasholme Green
York YO1 2PX

**Tel** 01904 455501
**Fax** 01904 455502

| | |
|---|---|
| *status* | Executive agency |
| *founded* | 1995 |
| *sponsor* | Ministry of Agriculture, Fisheries and Food (MAFF) |
| *powers* | Framework Document 1995 |
| *mission* | To safeguard public health and animal welfare through fair, consistent and effective enforcement of hygiene, inspection and welfare regulations and to be a service which has the full confidence of all its customers, including the meat industry, consumers and Ministers, through the achievement of improving standards and increasing efficiency |

**tasks**  To enforce hygiene rules in licensed red and poultry meat premises and in meat products plants (colocated and integrated); to provide meat inspection and health-marking; to enforce welfare at slaughter rules; to collect and dispatch samples for statutory veterinary medicine residue testing; to enforce controls on SBM and other animal by-products; to provide export certification required by EU rules. MHS staff inspect every animal before it is slaughtered and every carcase before it enters the food chain.

**operations**  Management: Ownership Board advises Ministers and provides advice and support to the Chief Executive. It also monitors the Agency's performance against targets. The Chief Executive appointed by open competition. Director of Operations is a vet and has a team of six Regional Directors. Official Veterinary Surgeons (OVSs) are appointed to each fresh meat premise and contracts are awarded through open competitive tender. MHS recovers in full all costs of inspections and health controls from customers (industry and government).

Policy:  Meat hygiene is central to the Agency's mission.

Trends:  MHS will continue to recruit and train quality staff to meet the requirements of  its customers as the work of the Agency continues to expand.

**performance**  All performance targets were met in 1997/98.

**board**  Ownership Board appointed by the Minister, from relevant government departments and business.

| | |
|---|---|
| Chairman | RJD Carden |
| Members | P Elliott |
| | AJ Ellis CBE |
| | JDJ McNeill |
| | AR Pugh |
| | Dr E Rubery |
| | J Scudamore |
| | L Walford |
| | Dr JR Wildgoose |
| Accounting Officer | Chief Executive |

**staff**  1500

| | |
|---|---|
| Chief Executive | Johnston McNeill |
| Director of Finance | Stuart Moore |
| Director of Information Technology | Graham Perry |
| Director of Human Resources | Monica Redmond |
| Director of Operations | Peter Soul |
| Operations Manager | Paul Wandless |
| Business Efficiency Manager | Trevor Yardley |
| Regional Director, Central | Barry Gidman |
| Regional Director, North | Michael Greaves |
| Regional Director, South & West | Paul Jackson |
| Regional Director, South & East | Gifford Lewis |
| Regional Director, Wales | Ivor Pumfrey |
| Regional Director, Scotland | Spencer Dawson |

**financial**

| INCOME & EXPENDITURE | | |
|---|---|---|
| Year end: 31 March | **1997** | **1996** |
| | **£000** | **£000** |
| **INCOME** | **46,788** | **32,701** |
| **EXPENDITURE** | | |
| Staff costs | (28,932) | (21,944) |
| Depreciation | (286) | (242) |
| Other operating charges - ordinary | (17,522) | (12,510) |
| Other operating charges - exceptional | (165) | (7,179) |
| | **(46,905)** | **(41,875)** |
| **OPERATING SURPLUS/(DEFICIT)** | **(117)** | **(9,174)** |
| Net interest charged | (481) | (295) |
| **NET COST OF OPERATIONS SURPLUS/(DEFICIT)** | **(598)** | **(9,469)** |

**advisers**  **Auditors**  National Audit Office  157-197 Buckingham Palace Road
London SW1W 9SP

**publications**  *Annual Reports & Accounts 1995/96, Annual Reports & Accounts 1996/97, Clean Livestock Strategy*

**branches**

| *Central* | *South & East* |
|---|---|
| Block A | Room G9 |
| Wergs Road | Spur B (West) |
| Woodthorne | Block A |
| Tettenhall | Brooklands Avenue |
| Wolverhampton WV6 8TQ | Cambridge CB2 2DD |
| Tel 01902 693396 | Tel 01223 456703 |

South & West
Room 609
Quantock House
Paul Street
Taunton TA1 3NX
Tel 01823 330066

Wales
3rd Floor West
Welsh Office
Cathays Park
Cardiff CF1 3NQ
Tel 01222 825549

Scotland
Room E1/9
Saughton House
Broomhouse Drive
Edinburgh EH11 3XD
Tel 0131 244 8441

# Meat & Livestock Commission (MLC)

Winterhill House
Snowdon Drive
Milton Keynes MK6 1AX

**Tel** 01908 677577
**Fax** 01908 609221

| | |
|---|---|
| **status** | Executive body |
| **founded** | 1967 |
| **sponsor** | Ministry for Agriculture, Fisheries and Food (MAFF) |
| **powers** | Agriculture Act 1967 |
| **mission** | To advise MAFF on matters relating to the beef, sheep and pig meat industries, and provide services to the industry. |
| **tasks** | Development and implementation of marketing initiatives in home and export markets; provision of market information to producers and processors; industry representation in home and export promotion and marketing at a generic level; the operation of Integrated Assurance Initiatives; funding research projects; and the provision of authentication services; operating the Intervention Board scheme. |
| **operations** | Management: Commissioners exercise full and effective control over the Commission. The day-to-day management is exercised by the Director General together with Directors and Senior Managers responsible for the major activities. |
| | Policy: Target to be self-financing. Rebuilding of beef market. Establishment of the 'Assured British Meat' initiative. |
| | Trends: 1996/97 dominated by BSE crisis. Food safety a priority following E-coli outbreaks. |
| **board** | Commissioners appointed by the Minister in conjunction with the Secretaries of State for Wales and Scotland. |

| Chairman | Donald Curry CBE | |
|---|---|---|
| Deputy Chairman | Mike Buswell | |
| Commissioners | John Baker MBE | John Jones |
| | Miss Bridget Bloom OBE | Peter Redshaw |
| | Wilson Ferguson | John Ross CBE |
| | Ralph Green OBE | Richard Sadler |
| | Mrs Elizabeth Hodder | David Walker MBE TD |
| | Colin Jay | John Wilyman |
| *Accounting Officer* | *Director General* | |

**staff**    620

| Director General | Colin Maclean |
|---|---|
| Technical Director | Mike Attenborough |
| Industry Development Director | Bob Bansback |
| Operations Group Manager | Tony Blackburn |
| Marketing Director | Gwyn Howells |

**financial**

| INCOME & EXPENDITURE | | | |
|---|---|---|---|
| Year end: 31 March | 1997 | 1996 | 1995 |
| | £000 | £000 | £000 |
| **INCOME** | | | |
| Gross levy, fee and other income | 48,324 | 41,789 | 40,700 |
| HM government agency and related services | 2,769 | 1,638 | 2,409 |
| | **51,093** | **43,427** | **43,109** |
| **EXPENDITURE** | | | |
| General and species promotion funds | 44,624 | 41,532 | 41,146 |
| Restoring consumer confidence in beef | 4,389 | - | - |
| HM government agency and related services | 2,769 | 1,638 | 2,409 |
| | **51,782** | **43,170** | **43,555** |
| **OPERATING (DEFICIT)/SURPLUS** | **(689)** | **257** | **(446)** |
| Share of profit/(loss) of associated undertaking | 3 | (27) | (5) |
| Exceptional (expenditure)/income | (550) | 3 | 179 |
| **(DEFICIT)/SURPLUS ON ORDINARY ACTIVITIES** | | | |
| **BEFORE INTEREST** | **(1,236)** | **233** | **(272)** |
| Interest receivable less payable | 229 | 212 | 208 |
| **(DEFICIT)/SURPLUS ON ORDINARY ACTIVITIES** | | | |
| **BEFORE TAXATION** | **(1,007)** | **445** | **(64)** |
| Taxation | 61 | 62 | 48 |
| **(DEFICIT)/SURPLUS FOR THE YEAR ON ORDINARY** | | | |
| **ACTIVITIES AFTER TAXATION** | **(1,068)** | **383** | **(112)** |

**advisers**

**Bankers**  Barclays Bank

**Auditors**  Coopers & Lybrand

Oriel House, 55 Sheep Street
Northampton NN1 2NF

**branches**

*Northern*
Copthall Tower House
Station Parade
Harrogate
North Yorkshire HG1 1TL
Tel 01423 560361
Fax 01423 525722

*Scotland*
Rural Centre
West Mains Ingliston
Newbridge
Midlothian EH28 8NZ
Tel 0131 472 4111
Fax 0131 472 4122

*Wales*
21a North Parade
Aberystwyth
Ceredigiona SY23 2JL
Tel 01970 625050
Fax 01970 615148

*Europe Office*
23-25 rue de la Science
Box 18
Bruxelle
Belgium 1040
Tel 00322 2308668
Fax 00 322 2308620

*British Meat*
134 rue du Fauburg
St Honore
Paris
France 75008
Tel 00 331 49539686
Fax 00 331 42254181

# Medical Devices Agency (MDA)

Hannibal House
Elephant and Castle
London SE1 6TQ

**Tel** 0171 972 8000
**Fax** 0171 972 8108

**E-mail** mail@medical-devices.gov.uk
**Web** http://www.medical-devices.gov

**status**  Executive agency
**founded**  1994
**sponsor**  Department of Health (DOH)
**powers**  MDA Framework Document

| mission | To protect the public health and safeguard the interests of patients and users by ensuring that medical devices and equipment meet appropriate standards of safety, quality and performance and that they comply with relevant Directives of the European Union. |
|---|---|
| tasks | Ensure that in the UK medical devices (eg wheelchairs, X-ray equipment) are of safe design, of appropriate quality, perform as intended and are properly used. Maintain post-market surveillance system based on analysis and prompt investigation of adverse incidents. Publish guidance and advisory bulletins. |
| operations | Management: The Advisory Board reports to the Secretary of State. Day-to-day management is carried out by the Senior Management Team led by the Chief Executive, who reports to the Minister. The Chief Executive is appointed by open competition. The Agency's performance is monitored by an Advisory Board which reports to the Secretary of State. |
| | Policy: Levelling off of number of incident reports. |
| | Trends: Increasing number of new medical devices comply with statutory UK Regulations rather than the voluntary controls of the past. |
| performance | Met six out of the seven targets for 1996/97. |

**board**

| Chairman | Dr Jeremy Metters | |
|---|---|---|
| Members | Alan Burton | |
| | Haydn Cook | Martin Staniforth |
| | George Kennedy | Dr Sheila Willatts |
| | Chris O'Donnell | John Wotton |
| *Accounting Officer* | *Chief Executive* | |

**staff**    140

| Chief Executive | Alan Kent |
|---|---|
| Harmonisation & Quality Assurance | Robert Allen |
| Finance Director | Keith Cornelius |
| Device Evaluation Programme & Corporate Services | Tom Crawley |
| Nursing Director | Dr Helen Glenister |
| Device Technology & Safety | Dr Eamonn Hoxey |
| Medical Director | Dr Susanne Ludgate |
| European & Regulatory Affairs | Steve Owen |

**financial**

| NET EXPENDITURE Year end: 31 March | 1997 £000 | 1996 £000 | 1995 £000 |
|---|---|---|---|
| **EXPENDITURE** | | | |
| Staff costs | 4,224 | 4,643 | 4,959 |
| Programme costs | 3,603 | 3,479 | 4,647 |
| Depreciation | 532 | 434 | 431 |
| Other operating charges | 3,472 | 3,357 | 4,147 |
| | 11,831 | 11,913 | 14,184 |
| **INCOME** | (2,556) | (1,537) | (1,221) |
| **NET EXPENDITURE** | 9,275 | 10,376 | 12,963 |

| advisers | **Auditors** | National Audit Office | 157-197 Buckingham Palace Road London SW1W 9SP |
|---|---|---|---|

# Medical Practices Committee (MPC)

1st Floor
Eileen House
80-94 Newington Causeway
London SE1 6EF

**Tel** 0171 972 2930
**Fax** 0171 972 2985

| status | Executive body |
|---|---|
| founded | 1946 |
| sponsor | Department of Health (DOH) |
| powers | NHS Act 1977 |

| | |
|---|---|
| **mission** | To ensure equitable distribution of GPs in England and Wales. |
| **tasks** | Considers all applications for admission to the GP medical list of health authorities; identifies numbers of GPs needed in each area and classifies them according to actual figures; to control distribution it refuses applications on the grounds that the number of GPs in the area is already adequate. |
| **operations** | Management: Chief Executive is responsible for day-to-day management and reports to the Chairman of the Committee. Committee meets 46 times a year. |
| | Policy: Trying to eliminate under-doctored areas (30 out of 1450 areas). |
| | Trends: NHS Primary Care Act 1997 will affect current systems. |
| **board** | Committee appointed by the Secretary of State. |

| | |
|---|---|
| Chairman | Miss Mary Leigh |
| Lay Members | Bob Jewitt JP |
| | Dr Chris Robinson CBE |
| | Geoff Shepherd |
| GP Members | Dr Malcolm Freeth |
| | Dr John Griffiths |
| | Dr Sarah Jarvis |
| | Dr Surendra Kumar |

**staff**   13

| | |
|---|---|
| Secretary & Chief Executive Officer | John Gooderham |

# Medical Research Council (MRC)

20 Park Crescent
London W1N 4AL

**Tel** 0171 636 5422
**Fax** 0171 436 6179

| | |
|---|---|
| **status** | Executive body |
| **founded** | 1913 |
| **sponsor** | Department of Trade and Industry (DTI) |
| **powers** | Royal Charter 1993 |
| **mission** | To promote and support high-quality basic, strategic and applied research and postgraduate training in the biomedical and other sciences with the aim of maintaining and improving human health. To advance knowledge and technology and provide trained researchers. To provide advice, disseminate knowledge and promote public understanding of the biomedical sciences. |
| **tasks** | Supports the science base through its own MRC establishments and through universities. It does this by: large-scale research investment through two MRC institutes; medium-scale research investment through its own MRC units close to universities but independent of them; interdisciplinary research in partnership with universities - within Interdisciplinary Research Centres (IRCs) - in areas of strategic importance; programme grants - the principal mechanism for the renewable support of long-term strategic university research; project grants - single projects, strategic projects and small projects; LINK collaborative projects between universities and industry, funded half by MRC and half by industry; ROPAs (Realising our Potential Awards) for curiosity-driven research to scientists with a proven track-record of collaboration with industry; infrastructure grants - supporting major strategic research facilities in collaboration with universities and industry; training and career development awards to research scientists at all career stages. |
| **operations** | Management: The Council decides overall strategy, determines allocation of resources and the roles of the MRC Advisory Board. The subject area Boards provide expert advice on funding and the management of MRC's resources. The MRC Private Fund is a charity funded by donations. Health Services Research Collaboration (HSRC) was founded in 1997 to provide direct support for health services research. |
| | Policy: Commercial exploitation of MRC-funded research. Consolidation of links with the users of the research. Increasing the budget for training. |
| | Trends: MRC continues to seek collaborative ventures with other research funders (particularly industry and research charities); opened Scottish Collaborative Centre in 1996. |

***performance*** Seven decades of major discoveries with outstanding achievements in the 1990s.

***board*** Council appointed by the Secretary of State.

| Chairman | Sir David Plastow | |
|---|---|---|
| Chief Executive | Prof GK Radda CBE | |
| Members | Prof JI Bell | |
| | Prof LK Borysiewicz | P McLachlan OBE |
| | Prof IAD Bouchier | Rabbi Julia Neuberger |
| | Sir Kenneth Calman | ALC Quigley |
| | Prof A Haines | Dr T Robbins |
| | Prof PA Jacobs | Dr B Ross |
| | Prof E Johnstone | Prof John Swales |
| | Prof AM McGregor | Dr IP Sword |

***staff*** 3018

***financial***

**RECEIPTS & PAYMENTS**

| Year end: 31 March | 1997 £m | 1996 £m | 1995 £m |
|---|---|---|---|
| **RECEIPTS** | | | |
| Parliamentary grant-in-aid | 282.1 | 278.1 | 269.4 |
| Government departments | 8.7 | 7.7 | 6.2 |
| Other UK public sectors | 2.6 | 2.4 | 3.4 |
| Charities | 2.8 | 3.2 | 3.3 |
| Industry | 4.1 | 3.5 | 3.3 |
| International and overseas bodies | 3.7 | 4.6 | 4.4 |
| Commercial fund | 1.6 | 1.0 | 1.1 |
| Private funds | 0.1 | 0.5 | 1.7 |
| Miscellaneous | 5.7 | 3.1 | 3.3 |
| | **311.4** | **304.1** | **296.1** |
| **PAYMENTS** | | | |
| Recurrent and capital expenditure on institutes and units | | | |
| National Institute for Medical Research | 25.0 | 23.8 | 24.9 |
| Laboratory of Molecular Biology | 13.9 | 13.8 | 13.4 |
| Clinical Research Centre | - | 0.2 | 3.4 |
| Clinical Sciences Centre | 11.4 | 14.2 | 10.4 |
| Research units and external staff | 86.3 | 80.9 | 77.1 |
| | **136.6** | **132.9** | **129.2** |
| Expenditure in universities and other institutions | | | |
| Programme and special project/strategic grants | 59.2 | 57.6 | 60.2 |
| Projects grants | 42.3 | 45.7 | 40.2 |
| ROPAs | 4.4 | 2.7 | 0.3 |
| Training awards and fellowships | 27.2 | 25.5 | 21.9 |
| Special contributions | 8.0 | 8.3 | 6.8 |
| International subscriptions | 6.2 | 6.7 | 6.1 |
| | **147.3** | **146.5** | **135.5** |
| Administrative running costs | | | |
| Head office | 10.4 | 10.9 | 11.6 |
| Information systems strategy | 1.8 | 1.5 | 3.6 |
| Central expenses | 1.2 | 1.6 | 3.5 |
| | **13.4** | **14.0** | **18.7** |
| Expenditure on building | | | |
| Capital building projects | 6.2 | 5.1 | - |
| Estates care and maintenance | 5.6 | 6.4 | - |
| | **11.8** | **11.5** | **14.6** |
| | **309.1** | **304.9** | **298.0** |

# Medical Supplies Agency (MSA)

Drummond Barracks
Ludgershall
Nr Andover
Hants SP11 9RU

**Tel** 01980 80524
**Fax** 01980 808676

| | |
|---|---|
| *status* | Defence agency |
| *founded* | 1996 |
| *sponsor* | Ministry of Defence (MOD) |
| *powers* | MSA Framework Document 1996 |
| *mission* | To be the preferred supplier of medical material and associated services to the MOD and other government departments. |
| *tasks* | Provides medical supplies (including blood) to 2000 individual locations worldwide, with 2.5 million issues pa from an inventory of 38,000 items. |
| *operations* | Management: Owned by the Surgeon General, run by Chief Executive (civilian, appointed by open competition). MSA has taken over the functions previously managed by the Defence Medical Equipment Depot, the Army Blood Supply Depot and 16 Medical Distribution Centres, previously Medical Provisioning Points, located throughout the UK and overseas. |
| | Policy: Improving customer service. |
| | Trends: Improving relationships with suppliers. |
| *performance* | Graduate improvement following placement of IT system, with more significant improvement in 1997/98 as electronic trading is introduced. |
| *board* | Management Board. |

| | |
|---|---|
| Chief Executive | BE Nimick |
| *Accounting Officer* | *Chief Executive* |

*staff* 285 (237 civilian, 49 military)

*financial*

| EXPENDITURE | |
|---|---|
| Year end: 31 March | **1997** |
| | **£000** |
| **OPERATING EXPENDITURE** | |
| Staff costs | 5,297 |
| Supplies and services consumed | 485 |
| Procurement for supply to customers | 26,865 |
| Accommodation | 1,367 |
| Other administration charges | 1,647 |
| | **35,661** |
| **INCOME** | |
| Income from repayment customers | (95) |
| **NET OPERATING EXPENDITURE** | **35,566** |
| Interest Charge on Capital | 1,684 |
| **NET EXPENDITURE** | **37,250** |

*advisers* **Bankers** HM Paymaster General

**Auditors** National Audit Office

*publications* Framework Document, Corporate Plan, Annual Report and Accounts

# *Medicines Control Agency (MCA)*

Market Towers
1 Nine Elms Lane
Vauxhall
London SW8 5NQ

**Tel** 0171 273 0000
**Fax** 0171 273 0353          **Web** http://www.open.gov.uk/mca/mcahome.htm

**Contact** Information Centre

| | |
|---|---|
| *status* | Executive agency and Trading Fund |
| *founded* | 1991 as an agency, having been established to take over the duties of the Medicines Division of the Department Health in 1989 |
| *sponsor* | Department of Health (DOH) |
| *powers* | Medicines Act 1968. Framework document |
| *mission* | Controlling medicines for human consumption on behalf of the UK Licensing Authority (the UK Ministers of Health and Agriculture). Issuing single marketing authorisations (licences) valid throughout the EU, as contractor to the European Medicines Evaluation Agency (EMEA). |
| *tasks* | Licensing medicinal products; monitoring the safety of medicines on the market; monitoring standards of manufacture and wholesaling; varying the terms of licences already granted and enforcement of licence requirements and provisions. |

*operations* Management: Chief Executive and Executive Directors comprise MCA Board of Management. Licensing division controls new licences and the *British Pharmacopoeia*. Post-licensing division is responsible for pharmacovigilance and five-yearly licence renewals, reclassification of medicines, regulating medicine promotion and product information. Inspection and enforcement division monitors and enforces the laws and regulations relating to medicines with its own clinical research and toxicology laboratories. Executive support division works with ministers on UK and European medicines regulation, on statutory instruments, Parliamentary Questions, safety of medicines deregulation etc.

Policy: Now that effective EU marketing authorisations procedures have been developed, increased attention has to be paid to post-licensing enforcement and anti-counterfeit measures. Rising numbers of legal challenges, mainly by pharmaceutical companies, means more MCA focus and expenditure on legal work. Worldwide concerns over BSE has led MCA to survey all currently authorised medicines in the UK and audit the safety of all UK medicines.

Trends: From 1999, EU targets will cover an increasingly significant part of MCA's work. Key issues are the increasing complexity of the work, particularly as the proportion of European, as opposed to national, work expands; mutual recognition work is growing; continuing recruitment and retention difficulties; and increasing legal work.

*board* Board of Management appointed by Secretary of State from civil servants and interested parties.

| | |
|---|---|
| Chief Executive | Dr Keith Jones |
| Head of Executive Support | Roy Alder |
| Director of Licensing | Dr David Jefferys |
| Director of Inspection & Enforcement | Dr Gordon Munro |
| Legal Adviser | Ms G Parker |
| Director of Finance | Dr Jim Stockwell |
| Director of Post-Licensing | Dr Susan Wood |
| *Accounting Officer* | *Chief Executive* |

*staff* 373

**financial**

| INCOME & EXPENDITURE Year end: 31 March | 1997 £000 | 1996 £000 | 1995 £000 |
|---|---|---|---|
| **INCOME** | **26,839** | **22,421** | **25,634** |
| **EXPENDITURE** | | | |
| Staff costs | 13,465 | 12,510 | 11,912 |
| Other operating costs | 9,774 | 9,003 | 9,004 |
| Depreciation | 1,749 | 2,166 | 1,564 |
| | 24,988 | 23,679 | 22,480 |
| **OPERATING SURPLUS/(DEFICIT) BEFORE INTEREST** | **1,851** | **(1,258)** | **3,154** |
| Interest receivable | 1,704 | 1,617 | 1,335 |
| **OPERATING SURPLUS** | **3,555** | **359** | **4,489** |
| Interest payable | 121 | 117 | 110 |
| **SURPLUS ON ORDINARY ACTIVITIES** | **3,434** | **242** | **4,379** |
| Dividend payable on public dividend capital | 131 | 136 | 146 |
| **RETAINED SURPLUS FOR THE YEAR** | **3,303** | **106** | **4,233** |
| Retained surplus brought forward | 11,689 | 11,583 | 7,350 |
| **RETAINED SURPLUS CARRIED FORWARD** | **14,992** | **11,689** | **11,583** |

**advisers**      Auditors                National Audit Office                157-197 Buckingham Palace Road
London SW1W 9SP

**publications**   Annual Report And Accounts 1996-1997, Medicines Act 1968: Guidance Notes on Applications for Clinical Trial Exemptions and Clinical Trial Certificates, Rules and Guidance for Pharmaceutical, Manufacturers and Distributors 1997 (Orange Guide), MCA Business Plan, Framework Document Medicines Commission. Annual Report for 1996

# Mental Health Commission for Northern Ireland

Elisabeth House
118 Holywood Road
Belfast BT4 1NY

**Tel** 01232 651157
**Fax** 01232 471180

**status**       Executive body

**founded**      1986

**sponsor**      Northern Ireland Office, Department of Health and Social Services (DHSS)

**powers**       Mental Health (NI) Order 1986

**mission**      To review the care and treatment of persons suffering from mental disorder.

**tasks**        An independent body with investigative, inspectorial and advisory functions. Visits hospitals, nursing homes, residential homes and other facilities where persons suffering from mental disorder are treated (announced and unannounced visits). Secures patients' welfare by preventing ill-treatment, remedying any deficiency in care or treatment, and terminating improper detention in hospital.

**operations**   Management: All the Commission's staff are seconded from the DHSS and handle the administration

**performance**  Eight out of 14 targets met in 1996/97.

**board**        Commissioners are appointed by the Head of DHSS.

| Chairman | Gerard Duffy | |
|---|---|---|
| Commissioners | Dr Grace Campbell | Mrs Sheila Millar |
| | Dr Stephen Compton | Brendan Mullen |
| | Mrs Marie Crothers | Mrs Mary O'Boyle |
| | Michael Dixon | Mrs Marian O'Neill |
| | Dr Ruth Elliot | Ms Clare Quigley |
| | Dr Ronald Galloway | Dr Maurice Russell |
| | Mrs Marjorie Keenan | Dr Oliver Shanks |
| Secretary | Francis Walsh | |
| Accounting Officer | Secretary | |

**staff**        Three

| financial | RECEIPTS & PAYMENTS Year end: 31 March | 1997 £ | 1996 £ | 1995 £ |
|---|---|---|---|---|
| | RECEIPTS | | | |
| | Grant from the DHSS | 314,351 | 345,273 | 311,179 |
| | PAYMENTS | | | |
| | Salaries | 169,379 | 164,344 | 153,755 |
| | Other operating payments | 144,029 | 180,045 | 156,851 |
| | | 313,408 | 344,389 | 310,606 |
| | Other payments | 996 | 884 | 573 |
| | | 314,404 | 345,273 | 311,179 |
| | EXCESS OF PAYMENTS OVER RECEIPTS | 53 | - | - |

**advisers**   **Auditors**      Northern Ireland Audit Office      106, University Street, Belfast

KPMG      17-25 College Square East,Belfast BT1 6DH

**publications**   *Information Leaflet*

# Met Office

London Road
Bracknell RG12 2SZ

**Tel** 01344 420242                    **Web** http://www.met-office.gov.uk

**status**       Executive agency

**founded**      1990 as executive agency, 1996 as trading fund

**sponsor**      Ministry of Defence (MOD)

**powers**       Framework Document 1996

**mission**      To develop capabilities in meteorological forecasting so as to deliver high-quality, cost-effective services to public and commercial customers in the UK and elsewhere.

**tasks**        Defence: to meet the Armed Forces' major requirement for weather information for day-to-day operations in the UK and overseas. Civil Aviation: to provide a wide range of services to civil aviation within the UK and internationally - the National Meteorological Centre in Bracknell is one of only two World Area Forecast Centres. Environment: through the Hadley Centre for Climate Prediction and Research, the Met. Office provides scientific information for UK regulatory policy on greenhouse gas emissions. Public Meteorology Service (PMS): to provide PMS on behalf of the government.

**operations**   Management: The Secretary of State for Defence is owner of The Met Office. He is advised by the Defence Meteorological Board (DMB); DMB members have relevant scientific and commercial expertise. The Chief Executive is advised by the Meteorological Committee on broad matters of Met Office policy and by its research subcommittee; the committee also reviews aspects of the programme and activities with particular emphasis on meeting customers' needs. Day-to-day business is managed by the Management Board. There are five business areas: (1) The Core Customer Group (CCG) is fundamental to the business success of the organisation. It includes the global exchange of weather information, along with the operation and interpretation of sophisticated computer-based weather forecasting systems. (2) Defence, the largest business area; most forecasts for the RAF but all the Armed Services are customers as is the Defence Research and Evaluation Agency and NATO. There are 30 RAF and Army airfields with on-site staff and nine others. (3) Civil Aviation Authority (CAA) and the civil aviation industry. (4) PMS, including severe weather warning and storm tide warning services. (5) Commercial - services to all areas of industry, commerce and the media. (6) Department of Environment, Transport and the Regions - the Hadley Centre for Climate Prediction and Research is contracted to carry out its major Climate Prediction Programme.

Policy: To provide a core capability and meteorological services to customers' agreed requirements with sufficient profit to fund future investment.

Trends: A more commercially oriented scrutiny of major capital expenditure has been introduced.

**performance**  Met the £151 million revenue target and held operating costs below budget. Did not meet two quality and one administrative targets.

**board**

Members of the DMB and the Management Board are appointed by the Secretary of State from people with relevant scientific and business experience.

| Management Board | |
|---|---|
| Chief Executive | Peter Ewins |
| Technical Director | Jim Caughey |
| Business Director | Simon Cross |
| Forecasting Director | Colin Flood |
| Chief Scientist | Paul Mason |
| Finance Director | David Roberts |
| Company Secretary | Ann Tourle |
| *Accounting Officer* | *Chief Executive* |

| Defence Meteorological Board | | |
|---|---|---|
| Members | CM Brendish | |
| | Prof Sir D Davies CBE | Prof BEF Fender CMG |
| | Maj Gen GA Ewer CBE | RT Jackling CB CBE |
| | Peter Ewins | JM Legge CMG |

**staff**

2118

**financial**

| PROFIT & LOSS | |
|---|---|
| **Year end: 31 March** | **1997** |
| | **£000** |
| **TURNOVER** | |
| MOD | 72,263 |
| Other government departments | 29,636 |
| Others | 50,088 |
| | **151,987** |
| **COST OF SALES & OPERATING EXPENSES** | |
| Staff costs | 62,621 |
| Travel and subsistence | 3,456 |
| Equipment and services | 27,715 |
| Accommodation | 8,685 |
| Depreciation | 18,663 |
| International subscriptions | 7,667 |
| Other administrative expenses | 1,432 |
| | **130,239** |
| **OPERATING PROFIT** | **21,748** |
| Profit on disposal of fixed assets | 50 |
| **PROFIT ON ORDINARY ACTIVITIES** | **21,798** |
| Interest receivable | 1,867 |
| Interest payable | (3,265) |
| **RETAINED PROFIT** | **20,400** |

**advisers**

| **Auditors** | National Audit Office | 157-197 Buckingham Palace Road London SW1W 9SP |
|---|---|---|

**publications**

*Handbook of Aviation Meteorology, Marine Observers' Handbook, Ships Code and Decode Book, Images in Weather Forecasting, Met Office Annual Report and Accounts, Forecaster's Reference Book, Forecaster's Source Book*

# Military Survey

Elmwood Avenue
Feltham
Middlesex TW13 7AH

**Tel** 0181 8182247
**Fax** 0181 8182148

**status**    Defence agency

**founded**    1991

**sponsor**    Ministry of Defence (MOD)

**powers**    Framework Document 1991

| | |
|---|---|
| *mission* | To ensure the provision of geographic support to defence planning, training and operations of the Armed Forces. |
| *tasks* | Supply of maps, in-the-field advice, geodetic positioning, terrain analysis and field printing; acquire cartographic and digital products (either contracted out or in-house); manage the Defence Geographic Library, information centres and map supply depots; provide geographic training courses for all Services through the School of Military Survey. |
| *operations* | Management: The Owner is Director General of Intelligence and Geographic Resources and is supported by the Owner's Board. Director of Military Survey is the Chief Executive, who reports to the Owner and is supported by the Management Board. Service personnel are mainly from Corps of Engineers. Two main UK sites at Feltham, Middlesex and Hermitage, Berkshire. Major restructuring of agency in 1995/96. |
| | Policy: High level of deployment in Bosnia. New strategy to meet future requirements. |
| | Trends: Increasing requirements, particularly in the field of digital information. |
| *performance* | 1996/97 all five targets met. |
| *board* | Defence Geographic Board appointed by the Secretary of State. |

| Accounting Officer | Chief Executive |
|---|---|

| | |
|---|---|
| *staff* | 1210 (848 civilian) |

| | |
|---|---|
| Director of Military Survey & Chief Executive | Brigadier Phil Wildman OBE |
| Deputy Chief Executive & Director of Geographic Resources | Martin Sands |
| Director of Geographic Field Support & Commander | |
| 42 Survey Engineer Group | Col C Dorman |
| Director of Finance | S Hall |
| Director of Geographic Information | Stuart Haynes |
| Director of Geographic Information Systems & Development | Dr J Jensen |
| Director of Geographic Production | Tony Painter |
| Colonel Geographic Commitments | Col I Whittington |

*financial*

**INCOME & EXPENDITURE**

| Year end: 31 March | 1996 | 1995 |
|---|---|---|
| | £000 | £000 |
| **EXPENDITURE** | | |
| Staff costs | 29,457 | 26,311 |
| Supplies and services consumed | 16,506 | 14,155 |
| Accommodation costs | 9,266 | 9,479 |
| Other administration costs | 4,611 | 4,310 |
| Interest charge on capital | 4,055 | 3,659 |
| | 63,895 | 57,914 |
| **INCOME** | | |
| Income from non-MOD customers | 1,723 | 885 |
| **NET EXPENDITURE** | 62,172 | 57,029 |

| | | | |
|---|---|---|---|
| *advisers* | **Auditors** | National Audit Office | 157-197 Buckingham Palace Road London SW1W 9SP |

| | |
|---|---|
| *publications* | Annual Report |


# *Milk Development Council (MDC)*

5-7 John Princes Street
London W1M 0AP

**Tel** 0171 629 7262
**Fax** 0171 629 4820

| | |
|---|---|
| *status* | Executive body |
| *founded* | 1995 |
| *sponsor* | Ministry of Agriculture, Fisheries and Food (MAFF) |
| *powers* | Industrial Organisation and Development Act 1947 |
| *mission* | To enhance the technical strength and advance the competitive position of Great Britain's dairy farmers through promoting or undertaking scientific research in the fields of milk production and milk consumption. |

| | |
|---|---|
| **tasks** | Funds research projects (over 50% of budget) and communicates results to farmers; supports the National Dairy Council by funding information to health professionals and educational establishments; funds production of the UK's independent breeding and production statistics. |
| **operations** | Management: Chief Executive responsible for day-to-day management. 11 project managers monitor specified R&D projects. Contracts out most functions (eg public relations). Income is raised as a levy on milk produced and sold. |
| | Policy: Increasing number of projects funded. Strengthening codes on traceability of milk. |
| | Trends: Pressure from farmers for generic advertising of milk but outside MDC's current remit. |
| **board** | Council members appointed by the Minister of Agriculture and the Secretaries of State for Scotland and Wales. |

| Chairman | John Moffitt CBE | |
|---|---|---|
| Members | Ben Boot OBE | |
| | Alex Brown | David Harden |
| | Malcolm Crabtree | Peter Merson |
| | Philippa Foster Back | Martin Stanbury |
| | Chris French | Irene Unsworth |
| | John Gibson | Hugh Wilson MBE |
| *Accounting Officer* | *Chief Executive* | |

**staff** — Five

| Chief Executive | Peter Merson |
|---|---|

**financial**

**INCOME & EXPENDITURE**
Year end: 31 March

| | 1997 £ | 1996 £ |
|---|---|---|
| **INCOME** | | |
| Levy income | 4,857,754 | 5,411,199 |
| Sales of publications | - | 210 |
| Interest receivable | 208,066 | 66,972 |
| | 5,065,820 | 5,478,381 |
| **ADMINISTRATIVE COSTS** | (1,147,263) | (472,661) |
| **EXCESS OF INCOME OVER EXPENDITURE** | 3,918,557 | 5,005,720 |
| Grant to National Dairy Council | (1,038,996) | (935,000) |
| Grant to Animal Data Centre | (378,000) | (179,000) |
| Research and development project expenditure | (1,566,412) | (422,540) |
| | (2,983,408) | (1,536,540) |
| **SURPLUS OF INCOME OVER EXPENDITURE BEFORE TAXATION** | 935,149 | 3,469,180 |
| Provision for taxation | (1,499,029) | - |
| **SURPLUS/(DEFICIT) OF INCOME OVER EXPENDITURE AFTER TAXATION CARRIED FORWARD** | (563,880) | 3,469,180 |

**advisers**

| **Bankers** | Midland Bank | Poultry & Princess Street, London EC2P 2BX |
|---|---|---|
| | Barclays Bank | 54 Lombard Street, London EC3V 9EX |
| **Auditors** | Ernst & Young | 1 Lambeth Palace Road, London SE1 7EU |
| **Solicitors** | Rowe & Maw | 20 Black Friars Lane, London EC4V 6HD |

# Millennium Commission (MC)

Portland House
Stag Place
London SW1E 5EZ

**Tel** 0171 880 2001
**Fax** 0171 880 2000     **Web** http://www.millennium.gov.uk

| | |
|---|---|
| **status** | Executive body |
| **founded** | 1994 |
| **sponsor** | Department of Culture, Media and Sport (DCMS) |
| **powers** | National Lottery Act 1993 |

**mission**  Assisting communities in marking the millennium. Uses money raised by the National Lottery to encourage projects throughout the UK which enjoy public support and which will be lasting monuments. To support programmes of awards to individuals; and to enable the nation to enjoy a festival in the year 2000.

**tasks**  Capital projects (£1 billion): 14 major landmark projects across the UK and many others - funded with partners (eg local authorities, European grants); Millennium Awards (£200 million): awards from £2000 to £15,000 are made to individuals to undertake activities which fulfil personal goals and demonstrate a community benefit - made through grant-making organisations; The Millennium Festival (£20 million) will be national civic and community celebrations with the New Millennium Experience (£200 million) at Greenwich as its centrepiece. It aims to focus on the theme of time and will contain multimedia and interactive exhibits on the environment, society, culture and life in the future.

**operations**  Management: The Owner is the Chancellor of the Duchy of Lancaster. The Commission is run by the Chief Executive supported by three Directors. Funded entirely through the National Lottery (MC's share is 5.6p of every pound spent). The proceeds are invested on receipt and income forecasts are regularly reviewed. UK-wide panel of professional advisers offers expert advice to the Commission on applications. During 1996/97 the MC continued to develop the Millennium Exhibition based at Greenwich. After a government review in summer 1997, The Millennium Experience Co Ltd (TMECL) was set up with new management and a grant memorandum under which MC pays TMECL up to £449 million. The Chancellor of the Duchy of Lancaster transferred ownership of TMECL to the Minister without Portfolio to ensure that there was no conflict of interest between MC and TMECL.

Policy: Investing in Education; encouraging environmental sustainability; revitalising cities; supporting communities; promoting science and technology.

Trends: Wide range of views sought to plan funding strategy.

**board**  Members of the Commission are appointed by HM the Queen.

| | |
|---|---|
| Chairman | Chris Smith |
| Members | Dr Heather Couper |
| | The Earl of Dalkeith |
| | The Lord Glentoran CBE |
| | Sir John Hall |
| | The Rt Hon Michael Heseltine MP |
| | Simon Jenkins |
| | Michael Montague CBE |
| | Miss Patricia Scotland QC |
| *Accounting Officer* | *Chief Executive* |

**staff**  70

| | |
|---|---|
| Chief Executive | Jennifer A Page CBE |
| Director of Policy & Corporate Affairs | Michael O'Connor |
| Director of Finance | Graham Savage |
| Director of Projects | Douglas Weston |

**financial**

**INCOME & EXPENDITURE**

| Year end: 31 March | 1997 £000 | 1996 £000 | 1995 £000 |
|---|---|---|---|
| **INCOME** | | | |
| Proceeds from Lottery | 289,172 | 294,276 | 58,099 |
| Investment income on balances at NLDF | 31,883 | 13,918 | 594 |
| Bank interest received | 71 | 17 | 3 |
| Grant in Aid | - | - | 995 |
| Other income | 1 | - | 4 |
| | **321,127** | **308,211** | **59,695** |
| **EXPENDITURE** | | | |
| Grants to applicants | 354,212 | 171,030 | - |
| Grant in Aid repayable | | - | 1,119 |
| Employee costs | 1,818 | 1,076 | 283 |
| Other operating costs | 16,043 | 3,597 | 1,093 |
| Depreciation: tangible assets | 240 | 172 | 129 |
| Total administrative expenditure | 18,101 | 4,845 | 2,624 |
| Total expenditure | 372,313 | 175,875 | 2,624 |
| **INCREASE IN FUNDS BEFORE TAX** | **(51,186)** | **132,336** | **57,071** |
| Corporation tax due on interest income | (22) | 4 | 1 |
| **INCREASE IN FUNDS AFTER TAX** | **(51,208)** | **132,332** | **57,070** |

# Ministry of Defence Police (MDP)

Wheathersfield
Braintree
Essex CM7 4AZ

**Tel** 01371 854208
**Fax** 01371 854010

| | |
|---|---|
| *status* | Defence agency |
| *founded* | 1971 (1996 as defence agency) |
| *sponsor* | Ministry of Defence (MOD) |
| *powers* | MDP Framework Document 1996 |
| *mission* | To provide both a civil policing service and a security service to MOD. |
| *tasks* | To provide an effective police service to MOD - as a statutory civilian police force, independent of political or departmental influence. To provide a security service to MOD - an armed guarding service for important defence installations - using specially trained dogs for security policing and detecting explosives and drugs. Its marine division escorts nuclear submarines as well as policing waterfronts, dockyards, naval ports and training areas. MDP has certain responsibility for the professional standards and training of the civilian MOD Guard Service (MGS). |
| *operations* | Management: The Chief Executive is the MDP Chief Constable. He ultimately reports to the Secretary of State through the Second Permanent Secretary, and is assisted by the Senior Management Team. Headquarters are collocated with the Police Training Centre at Wethersfield, Essex. The bulk of the force is deployed at defence installations within the UK and organised in 13 Operational Command Units (OCUs). MOD is the principal customer; others include UK Commanders-in-Chief, US Commanders, the Atomic Weapons Establishment and the Royal Mint. |
| | Policy: Implementation of Front Line First recommendations for alternative guarding. |
| | Trends: Run-down of UK defence installations. |
| *performance* | All key targets met in 1996/97. |
| *board* | Members of the MOD Police Committee are appointed by the Secretary of State from serving officers and civil servants. The Agency Management Board (Senior Management Team) is appointed from within DPA by the Secretary of State. The Chief Executive is appointed by open competition. |

| | | |
|---|---|---|
| Chairman | RT Jackling CB CBE | |
| Vice Chairman | ACM Sir John Willis KCB CBE | |
| Members | Capt JS Kelly OBE | AVM TB Sherrington OBE |
| | Rear Admiral RB Lees | Sir William Sutherland QPM |
| | M Legge CMG | Maj Gen PCC Troudsdell |
| | AG Rucker | Sir John Woodcock CBE QPM |
| Accounting Officer | *Permanent Under Secretary (Chief Executive may also be called to account by the Public Accounts Committee)* | |

| | |
|---|---|
| *staff* | 3880 |

| | |
|---|---|
| Chief Constable | Walter Boreham OBE OStJ |
| OCU, CID | Det Ch Supt PW Anderson |
| OCU, Hereford | Supt G Barnett |
| OCU, Corsham | Ch Supt DP Boulter |
| OCU, Stafford | Supt FA Cadden |
| OCU, Portsmouth | Supt WM Grainger |
| OCU, Longtown | Supt JJ Guyan |
| OCU, Aldermaston | Supt W Hammersley |
| OCU, Faslane | Ch Supt W Hatfield |
| OCU, Devonport | Supt GE Heal |
| OCU, Coulport | Supt S Mason |
| OCU, Greenock | Supt W Mason |
| OCU, Aldershot | Supt IG Richards |
| OCU, Burghfield | Supt HM Roddie |
| OCU, PTC | Supt R Russell |
| OCU, Stanmore | Supt TP Sloman |
| OCU, OSU | Ch Inspr D Vaughan |

**financial**

| INCOME & EXPENDITURE | | |
|---|---|---|
| Year end: 31 March | 1997 | 1996 |
| | £000 | £000 |
| **GROSS EXPENDITURE** | | |
| Staff costs | 121,925 | 130,971 |
| Overtime | 13,163 | 10,260 |
| Administration costs | 11,076 | 11,574 |
| Accommodation costs | 3,092 | 3,310 |
| | 149,256 | 156,115 |
| **GROSS INCOME** | | |
| Other government departments/agencies | 10,198 | 12,381 |
| Foreign government customers | 4,422 | 4,517 |
| Defence contractors | 2,509 | 3,913 |
| Other receipts | 1,742 | 1,035 |
| | 18,871 | 21,846 |
| **NET EXPENDITURE** | 130,385 | 134,269 |

# Monopolies & Mergers Commission (MMC)

New Court
48 Carey Street
London WC2A 2JT

**Tel** 0171 324 1467
**Fax** 0171 324 1400

**E-mail** MMC@gtnet.gov.uk
**Web** http://www.open.gov.uk/mmc/mmchome.htm

**Contact** Kim Horwood

**status**  Executive body

**founded**  1948

**sponsor**  Department of Trade and Industry (DTI)

**powers**  Operates within the framework of UK competition legislation, including the Competition Act (1980) and Fair Trading Act (1973)

**mission**  To work in the public interest, independent of government and the referring bodies.

**tasks**  The MMC identifies, assesses and reports on the public interest impact of mergers, monopolies, anti-competitive practices and disputed licence conditions (between utility regulators/licensees) referred to it. MMC has no policy role.

**operations**  Management: Each inquiry is the responsibility of a group (usually between four and six commission members) appointed by the Chairman and chaired and led by himself or one of his deputies. MMC's workload is determined by the references made to it by the Director General of Fair Trading, ministers and utility regulators. MMC aims to produce thorough, accurate and rigorously argued reports within specified deadlines; 21 reports were published in 1997. MCC has no control over the inflow of references. Panels of reference secretaries, accountants and industrial advisers are drawn up to meet peaks of work. Staff teams, which support each inquiry and are responsible to the Group Chairman, usually include one or more from each of the specialist divisions - economists, accountants, industrial advisers and lawyers. MMC reports are subject to judicial review. Ministers take the final executive decisions on them. MMC is financed by a grant-in-aid from the DTI (some £7.6 million in 1996/97).

Policy: MMC insists that members involved in each inquiry approach issues with an open mind and are seen to do so. There is a code of conduct for members, staff and consultants which helps to avoid actual and potential conflicts of interest that could arise from shareholdings, directorships, consultancy or family relationships with those being investigated.

Trends: There is general agreement that the Restrictive Trade Practices Act should be reformed and there is much debate about possible reforms to the whole of UK competition and institutional frameworks. The central issue is the relative merits of a prohibition-based approach (eg to prohibit certain agreements or behaviours; those breaking prohibitions being subject to penalties and liability for damages) or an administrative approach as in the present UK competition law, subject to the overriding need for companies to respect EC Treaty.

**board**  40 Commission members appointed by the President of the Board of Trade, from individuals of stature with a wide range of backgrounds including business, the professions, universities and the trade unions. The Chairman is fulltime and the Deputy Chairmen almost full-time.

| Chairman | Derek Morris | |
|---|---|---|
| Deputy Chairmen | Graham Corbett CBE | |
| | Mrs Denise Kingsmill | |
| Members | Hugh Aldous | |
| | Prof Jack Beatson | Peter Mackay CB |
| | Robert Bertram | Kate Mortimer |
| | Mrs Sarah Brown | Roger Munson |
| | Prof Martin Cave | Prof David Newbery FBA |
| | Anthony Clothier | Dr Gill Owen |
| | Roy Croft CB | Prof John Pickering |
| | Christopher Darke | Richard Prosser |
| | Roger Davies MBE | Arthur Pryor CB |
| | Nicholas Finney OBE | Richard Rawlinson |
| | Sir Archibald Forster | Prof Judith Rees |
| | Prof Paul Geroski | Timothy Richmond MBE |
| | Sir Ronald Halstead CBE | Jonathan Rickford |
| | David Hammond | Dr Ann Robinson |
| | Mrs Judith Hanratty | James Roe |
| | Charles Henderson CB | Mrs Helena Shovelton |
| | Patricia Hodgson CBE | Graham Stacy CBE |
| | David Jenkins MBE | David Stark |
| | Roger Lyons | Prof Anthony Steele |
| *Accounting Officer* | *Secretary* | |

**staff**  Core staff of 74, supplemented by staff on short-term contracts as required. The majority of senior staff are civil servants.

| Secretary | Penny Boys |
|---|---|
| Chief Accountant Adviser | Tim Head |
| Senior Legal Adviser | Jane Richardson |
| Chief Industrial Adviser | Clive Rix |
| Senior Economic Adviser | Geoffrey Sumner |

**publications**  *Role of the MMC, Annual Review and Accounts*

# Museum of London

London Wall
London EC2Y 5HN

**Tel** 0171 600 3699
**Fax** 0171 600 1058

**status**      Executive body

**sponsor**     Department for Culture, Media and Sport (DCMS)

**powers**      Museum of London Act 1986

**mission**     To promote understanding and appreciation of historic and contemporary London and its society and culture.

**tasks**       To care for and add to the objects in the collection. To run temporary exhibitions and provide school services. To manage the Museum in Docklands project at West India Quay. To provide archaeological investigations and research in connection with land in Greater London and the surrounding region.

**operations**  Management: The London Docklands Development Corporation allocated buildings facing Canary Wharf and provided capital for the Museum in Docklands project.

Policy: To obtain lottery funds for the Museum in Docklands.

Trends: Major grant cuts from both DCMS and the Corporation of London.

**board**       Nine members of the Board of Governors are appointed by the Prime Minister and nine by the Corporation of London.

**staff**   295

| | |
|---|---|
| Director | Max Hebditch |

**financial**

**INCOME & EXPENDITURE**
**Year end: 31 March**

| | 1996 £000 | 1995 £000 |
|---|---|---|
| **INCOME** | | |
| Department of National Heritage | 4,446 | 4,359 |
| Corporation of London | 4,446 | 4,359 |
| Archaeological services | 6,078 | 4,419 |
| Customer and client receipts | 1,138 | 945 |
| Other receipts | 481 | 355 |
| | **16,589** | **14,437** |
| **EXPENDITURE** | | |
| Employees | 8,033 | 6,866 |
| Premises | 1,912 | 2,331 |
| Supplies and services | 3,642 | 2,914 |
| Central support services | 372 | 357 |
| Depreciation | 384 | - |
| Provision for tax liability | - | (150) |
| Provision for dilapidations | 7 | (13) |
| | **14,350** | **12,305** |
| **OPERATING SURPLUS FOR YEAR** | **2,239** | **2,132** |
| Interest charges | (1,256) | (1,493) |
| Investment income | 196 | 121 |
| Net gain on disposal of investments | 6 | - |
| **SURPLUS FOR YEAR** | **1,184** | **760** |
| Contributions to reserves | (1,014) | (1,450) |
| Balance brought forward | 321 | 1,011 |
| **BALANCE CARRIED FORWARD** | **491** | **321** |

# Museum of Science & Industry, Manchester (MSIM)

Liverpool Road
Castlefield
Manchester M3 4JP

**Tel** 0161 832 2244
**Fax** 0161 833 2184

**E-mail** all@ mussci.u-net.com
**Web** http://www.edes.co.uk

**status**   Executive body

**founded**   1981. Opened to the public 1983

**sponsor**   Department for Culture, Media and Sport (DCMS)

**powers**   Memorandum and Articles of Association

**mission**   To use its remarkable site (the world's oldest railway station) and its collections to create a museum of international standing which has as its overall theme the industrial city, thereby capitalising on Manchester's unique past, contributing towards its future prosperity and fostering the pleasure of understanding for a broad public.

**tasks**   Preservation, restoration, improvement, enhancement and maintenance of features and objects of industrial, scientific and historical interest in the Manchester area; organising exhibitions, lectures, publications and educational activities.

*operations*  Management: It is a private company limited by guarantee (and a registered charity). The Director runs the museum and reports to the Trustees. MSIM Enterprises Ltd is its profitable trading subsidiary.

Policy: To complete its development plans by 2003. Final phase of development funded by Lottery grant, European Development Fund and the museum itself.

Trends: Cyclical visitor numbers.

*performance*  Best ever year in 1996/97 in terms of visitors numbers and income. Down turn seen in 1997/98.

*board*  Consists of 15 Trustees. 10 Trustees appointed by the other Trustees and 5 (including Chair and Vice-Chair) appointed by the Secretary of State for Culture, Media and Sport.

| | | |
|---|---|---|
| Chairman | John Lee | |
| Vice-Chairman | Virginia Halliwell | |
| Members | Michael Bailey | Peter Salmon |
| | Lou Brennan | Tony Strachan |
| | Joan Brown | Raj Williamson |
| | Michael Dyble | Anthony Wilson |
| | Ben Hurren | Don Wilson |

*staff*  95

| | |
|---|---|
| Life Vice President | Anthony Goldstone |
| Vice President | Col John Timmins |
| Director | Dr J Patrick Greene |
| Deputy Director | Bob Scott |
| Workshop Manager | Les Aylward |
| Shop Manager | Samantha Carleton |
| Visitor Services Manager | Tracey Layne |
| Personnel & Training Manager | Anna Mitchell |
| Curatorial Services Manager | Dr Gaby Porter |
| Education Services Manager | Jacqueline Roberts |
| Marketing Manager | Alison Vincent |
| Design Manager | John Williams |
| Finance Manager | Mike Woodward |

*financial*

**INCOME & EXPENDITURE**

| Year end: 31 March | 1997 £ | 1996 £ |
|---|---:|---:|
| **INCOMING RESOURCES** | | |
| Capital Grants | 1,017,656 | 1,352,149 |
| Revenue Grants | 2,138,712 | 2,177,004 |
| Admissions income | 642,783 | 444,605 |
| Payment under deed of covenant from trading subsidiary | 36,923 | 21,455 |
| Bank interest receivable | 17,344 | 16,136 |
| Donations | 70,000 | - |
| Other income | 73,938 | 64,556 |
| | **3,997,356** | **4,075,905** |
| **RESOURCES EXPENDED** | | |
| Direct charitable expenditure | | |
| Curatorial | 453,371 | 412,593 |
| Technical services | 260,761 | 259,537 |
| Education | 210,257 | 203,979 |
| Temporary exhibitions | 352,456 | - |
| Design | 212,942 | 213,733 |
| Galleries | 1,216,266 | 1,320,192 |
| | **2,706,053** | **2,410,034** |
| **OTHER EXPENDITURE** | | |
| Fundraising and publicity | 244,570 | 278,990 |
| Management and administration | 145,547 | 152,378 |
| | **3,096,170** | **2,841,402** |
| **NET INCOMING RESOURCES** | **901,186** | **1,234,503** |
| Total Funds brought forward | 10,654,960 | 9,420,457 |
| **TOTAL FUNDS CARRIED FORWARD** | **11,556,146** | **10,654,960** |

*advisers*

| **Bankers** | Midland Bank |
|---|---|
| **Auditors** | Delloite & Touche |
| **Solicitors** | Halliwell Landau |

# Museums & Galleries Commission (MGC)

16 Queen Anne's Gate
London SW1H 9AA

**Tel** 0171 233 4200
**Fax** 0171 233 3686

| | |
|---|---|
| *status* | Executive body |
| *founded* | 1931, Royal Charter 1987 |
| *sponsor* | Department for Culture, Media and Sport (DCMS) |
| *powers* | Royal Charter |
| *mission* | To safeguard and promote Britain's 2500 museums and galleries. |
| *tasks* | Government's principal adviser on museum matters; provides expert and impartial advice on conservation and security; raises standards through Registration Scheme which recognises professional standards; acts as an advocate for museums and galleries throughout the UK; administers the Acceptance in Lieu Scheme (works of art accepted in lieu of inheritance taxes); operates grants scheme (over 80% of its funding allocated). |
| *operations* | Management: Director is responsible for running MGC and reports to Commission. Works closely with the ten Area Museum Councils (AMCs) and funds the seven in England. AMCs take a strategic approach to increasing access to museums. Commissioners are unpaid. |
| | Policy: To streamline the work of the AMCs, the Museum Training Institute and the Museum Documentation Association. |
| | Trends: Assessing increasing number of Lottery applications. Cuts in funding for museums and galleries is continuing. |
| *performance* | No targets are set. |
| *board* | Commissioners appointed by the Prime Minister. |

| Chairman | James Joll | |
|---|---|---|
| Vice-Chairman | Robert Smith | |
| Commissioners | Sir Jack Baer | |
| | Prof Patrick Bateson | Loyd Grossman |
| | Baroness Brigstocke | Robert Hiscox |
| | Prof Ronald Buchanan OBE | Admiral Sir John Kerr GCB |
| | Rosemary Butler | Dr Ian Mackenzie Smith |
| | Penelope Viscountess Cobham | Alan Warhurst CBE |
| | Richard Foster | Catherine Wilson OBE |
| *Accounting Officer* | *Director* | |

*staff* 46

*financial*

| INCOME & EXPENDITURE Year end: 31 March | 1997 £ | 1996 £ |
|---|---|---|
| **INCOMING RESOURCES** | | |
| Grant-in-aid | 9,302,500 | 9,195,706 |
| Other grants | 71,674 | 96,388 |
| Other operating income | 189,909 | 112,414 |
| Interest receivable | 62,979 | 71,632 |
| | **9,627,062** | **9,476,140** |
| **RESOURCES EXPENDED** | | |
| **Direct charitable expenditure** | | |
| Grants and other activities | 7,561,211 | 7,799,762 |
| Grant-related costs | 163,023 | 181,262 |
| Advice | 651,143 | 603,000 |
| Standards | 503,183 | 570,825 |
| Advocacy | 192,923 | 179,102 |
| | **9,071,483** | **9,333,951** |
| Management and administration of the charity | 241,785 | 239,281 |
| Notional costs: insurance | 1,702 | 1,656 |
| Notional costs: cost of capital | 64,310 | 57,809 |
| Reversal of notional costs | 66,012 | 59,465 |
| **NET INCOMING/(OUTGOING) RESOURCES** | **313,794** | **(97,092)** |
| Fund balances brought forward | 914,942 | 1,012,034 |
| **FUND BALANCES CARRIED FORWARD** | **1,228,736** | **914,942** |

| advisers | **Auditors** | National Audit Office | 157-197 Buckingham Palace Road<br>London SW1W 9SP |

**publications** Annual Report, National Government Policy 1993-94, Local Authorities and Museums, The MGC and Europe, The Legal Status of Museums Collections in the UK, Fundraising for Museums and the Arts, By Popular Demand: A strategic analysis of the market potential for museums and art galleries in the UK, The Museums Marketing Handbook

## National Army Museum

Royal Hospital Road
Chelsea
London SW3 4HT

**Tel** 0171 730 0717
**Fax** 0171 823 6573

| | |
|---|---|
| **status** | Executive body |
| **founded** | 1960 |
| **sponsor** | Ministry of Defence (MOD) |
| **powers** | Royal Charter |
| **mission** | To tell the story of the soldier in Britain's armies from the 15th century to the present day. |
| **tasks** | To collect, preserve and exhibit objects and records relating to the history and traditions of the Army; to collect, collate and publish information, and carry out and encourage research into, the Army's history and traditions. |
| **operations** | Management: The Director undertakes the direction and management of the museum and is responsible to the Council. There are three divisions of staff: administration, collections and museum services, each headed by an Assistant Director. Core funding is from MOD grant-in-aid. |
| **board** | Nine Council members are appointed by the Army Board and there are three *ex officio* members. |
| **staff** | 83 |

| | |
|---|---|
| Director | Alan Robertson |
| Assistant Director, Administration Division | Major Pater Bateman |
| Assistant Director, Collections Division | Dr Alan Guy |
| Assistant Director, Museum Services Division | David Smurthwaite |

## National Biological Standards Board (NBSB)

Blanche Lane
South Mimms
Potters Bar
Hertfordshire EN6 3QG

**Tel** 1707 654753
**Fax** 1707 646730

**E-mail** enquiries@nibsc.ac.uk
**Web** http://www.nibsc.ac.uk

| | |
|---|---|
| **status** | Executive body |
| **founded** | 1975 |
| **sponsor** | Department of Health (DoH) |
| **powers** | Biological Standards Act 1975. National Biological Standards Board (Functions) Order 1976 (No 917) |
| **mission** | To safeguard and enhance public health by controlling and standardising biological substances used in medicine. |

*tasks*   NBSB manages the National Institute for Biological Standards and Control (NIBSC), which control tests and evaluates biological medicines (including vaccines, products derived from human blood, and hormones); prepares biological standards and reference materials; and conducts research and development relevant to such control and standardisation, and special investigations in coordination with DoH.

*operations*   Management: NBSB is accountable to the Secretary of State for the management of NIBSC. NIBSC is run by the Director, with the support of two Assistant Directors (Scientific and Administration), and he reports to NBSB.

Policy: NIBSC is an Official Medicines Control Laboratory within Europe and tests biological medicines for release into the EU. NIBSC is also the leading World Health Organisation International Laboratory for Biological Standards and prepares and distributes most of the world's International Standards for biological medicines.

Trends: The number and complexity of biologicals used in medicine increasing, and projected to continue to increase over the next 20 years as developments in science in general and biotechnology in particular take effect. NIBSC is also devoting increases to special scientific investigations of the safety of vaccines and blood products.

*performance*   13 out of 14 targets achieved in 1996/97.

*board*   NBSB members are appointed by the Minister of State for Public Health.

| Chairman | Dr NJB Evans CB | |
|---|---|---|
| Members | Prof I Allen CBE | Prof HS Jacobs |
| | Prof SR Bloom | Prof FY Liew |
| | Prof JD Cash CBE | JH Metcalf |
| | Prof DS Davies | Mrs N Morris |
| | Dr M Ferguson | Prof JG Ratcliffe |
| | Prof MPF Girard | AJ Robertson |
| | Prof K Gull | Dr GC Schild CBE |
| *Accounting Officer* | *Director of NIBSC* | |

*staff*   277

| **Senior NIBSC staff** | |
|---|---|
| Director | GC Schild CBE |
| Assistant Director (Scientific) | MM Jordan |
| Assistant Director (Administration) | RA Stewart |
| Head of Retrovirology | N Almond |
| Head of Haematology | TW Barrowcliffe |
| Head of Endocrinology | A Bristow |
| Head of Bacteriology | MJ Corbel |
| Head of Molecular Structure | C Jones |
| Head of Informatics | MM Jordan |
| Head of Virology | PD Minor |
| Head of Standards | PK Phillips |
| Head of Immunobiology R Thorpe | |

*financial*

**NBSB INCOME & EXPENDITURE**

| Year end: 31 March | 1997 £000 | 1996 £000 | 1995 £000 |
|---|---|---|---|
| **INCOME** | | | |
| Government grants | 10,390 | 11,229 | 11,103 |
| Other grants | 1,882 | 1,186 | 1,247 |
| Income from activities | 1,984 | 1,000 | 854 |
| | 14,256 | 13,415 | 13,204 |
| **EXPENDITURE** | | | |
| Consumable laboratory supplies | 2,031 | 2,002 | 1,723 |
| Staff costs | 7,4993 | 6,631 | 6,876 |
| Depreciation | 1,474 | 1,269 | 1,264 |
| Current cost depreciation adjustment | 394 | 336 | 185 |
| Other operating charges | 3,900 | 3,393 | 2,920 |
| Permanent diminution in value of assets | 52 | - | - |
| Provision for early retirement compensation | - | 92 | 656 |
| Provision for loss on grant | - | (46) | 117 |
| | 15,344 | 13,677 | 13,741 |
| **OPERATING DEFICIT** | (1,088) | (262) | (537) |
| Investment income | 66 | 67 | 35 |
| Capital charge | (1,442) | 1,070 | - |
| Write-back of capital charge | 1,442 | 1,070 | - |
| Transfer from revaluation reserve | 382 | 267 | 188 |
| **DEFICIT FOR THE FINANCIAL YEAR** | (640) | 72 | (314) |
| Retained Deficit brought forward | (135) | (207) | 107 |
| **RETAINED DEFICIT CARRIED FORWARD** | (775) | (135) | (207) |

| advisers | Bankers | National Westminster Bank |
|---|---|---|
| | Auditors | National Audit Office |
| | Solicitors | Treasury Solicitor |

**publications**  NIBSC Annual Report & Accounts, NIBSC Corporate Plan, NIBSC Catalogue of Reference Materials

## National Board for Nursing, Midwifery & Health Visiting for Northern Ireland (NBNI)

Centre House
79 Chichester Street
Belfast BT1 4JE

**Tel** 01232 238152
**Fax** 01232 333298

**status**  Executive body

**founded**  1979 (1992, as executive body)

**sponsor**  Northern Ireland Office, Department of Health and Social Services (DHSS)

**powers**  Nurses, Midwives and Health Visitors Act 1979 and subsidiary legislation

**mission**  Contributing to the health and well-being of the public through the approval of educational institutions and courses in nursing, midwifery and health visiting and monitoring them in line with the standards set by the UK Central Council for Nursing, Midwifery and Health Visiting.

**tasks**  Quality assurance - pre-registration and post-registration course approval and improvement. Educational development - professional preparation, specialist practice development, continuing education for teachers. Research and development. Student Bursaries - processing and payment.

**operations**  Management: The Management Team comprises the Chief Executive, the Director of Finance and Administration and other professional and administrative staff who are on the rota for staff cover. Funded largely by DHSS grant and partly by fees for indexing, examinations and assessments.

Trends: During 1997/98 the NBNI ceased to be a provider of nursing and midwifery education. Its role is now that of a statutory body.

**performance**  Satisfactory as per the Annual NBNI/DHSS Accountability Review.

**board**  Members appointed by the Head of DHSS.

| Accounting Officer | Chief Executive |
|---|---|

**staff**  28

| Chief Executive | Prof O Slevin |
|---|---|
| Director of Finance & Administration | EN Thom |
| Midwifery/Paediatrics | Miss L Barrowman |
| Committee Clerk | Mrs H Craig |
| Student Bursary Manager | Mrs L Giles |
| Support Services Manager | Mrs H McBride |
| Higher Education/Community Nursing | Mrs R McCausland |
| Finance Officer | M O'Doherty |
| Mental Nursing/Mental Handicap Nursing | JP Sloan |
| Project Officer | Mrs H Thompson |
| General/Adult Nursing | Mrs MM Watkins |

*financial*

| INCOME & EXPENDITURE Year end: 31 March | 1997 £ | 1996 £ | 1995 £ |
|---|---|---|---|
| **INCOME** | | | |
| Grant from DHSS | 15,712,000 | 16,137,000 | 17,300,000 |
| Fees | 27,818 | 30,563 | 28,496 |
| Other | 414,310 | 423,137 | 373,042 |
| | 16,154,128 | 16,590,700 | 17,701,538 |
| **EXPENDITURE** | | | |
| Staff costs | 7,690,217 | 7,648,664 | 8,267,350 |
| Student bursary costs | 5,753,585 | 6,029,210 | 6,687,577 |
| Other charges | 2,064,012 | 1,894,561 | 2,459,114 |
| Notional charges | 80,000 | - | - |
| Early retirement costs | 118,032 | 1,414,152 | 299,322 |
| Profit/Loss on disposal of fixed assets | - | 1,689 | 1,752 |
| | 15,705,846 | 16,988,276 | 17,715,115 |
| **SURPLUS/(DEFICIT) FOR THE YEAR** | 448,282 | (397,576) | (13,577) |
| Adjustment to add back notional cost of capital | 70,000 | - | - |
| **SURPLUS/(DEFICIT) EXCLUDING NOTIONAL COST** | 518,282 | (397,576) | (13,577) |

*advisers*

**Bankers**    Northern Bank      110 Victoria Street, Blefast

**Auditors**    Price Waterhouse      Royston House, Belfast
            KPMG                Stokes House, Belfast

**Solicitors**    Brangam, Bagnall & Co      Hildon House, 30-34 Hill Street, Belfast

*publications*    Annual Report

# National Board for Nursing, Midwifery & Health Visiting for Scotland (NBS)

22 Queen Street
Edinburgh EH2 1NT

**Tel** 0131 226 7371
**Fax** 0131 225 9970          **Web** http://www.nbs.org.uk

*status*    Executive body

*founded*    1983

*sponsor*    Scottish Office

*powers*    Nurses, Midwives and Health Visitors Act 1997

*mission*    To promote improvement in the standards, quality and effectiveness of professional education in nursing, midwifery and health visiting through the approval of institutions and courses, and through research and development.

*tasks*    Quality assurance - pre-registration and post-registration course approval and improvement. Educational development - professional preparation, specialist practice development, continuing education of teachers. Research and development - small projects funded by the General Nursing Council for Scotland (Education) Fund. Running CATCH - the central automated system for processing applications for diploma courses.

*operations*    Management: The Chief Executive reports to the Chief Executive of the NHS in Scotland

                 Policy: Further extension of research and development work. Partnership development, eg with the Health Service in Scotland, the higher education sector and the Royal Colleges.

*performance*    1996/97 all key targets met.

*board*    Ten members appointed by the Secretary of State. Three Executive members: Chief Executive, Executive Director (Standards) and Executive Director (Resources); seven Non-Executive Members, including the Chairman and at least one registered nurse, one practising midwife and one registered health visitor.

| | |
|---|---|
| Chairman | Mrs Isobel A Mackinlay |
| Deputy Chairman | Miss Linda E Sydie |
| Non-Executive Members | George J Brechin |
| | Mrs Isobel J d'Inverno |
| | Mrs Lorne M Davidson |
| | Miss Lily G Shand |
| | Prof William S Stevely |
| Chief Executive | David C Benton |
| Executive Director (Standards) | Mrs Shiona Monfries |
| Executive Director (Resources) | Peter S Taylor |
| *Accounting Officer* | *Chief Executive* |

**staff**    48

| | |
|---|---|
| Chief Executive | David C Benton |
| Executive Director (Standards) | Mrs Shiona Monfries |
| Professional Officer (Nursing) | Mrs Audrey Cowie |
| Professional Officer (Nursing/Community) | Bill Deans |
| Professional Officer (Nursing) | Mrs Elizabeth Gillies |
| Professional Officer (Midwifery) | Miss Beatrice Grant |
| Professional Officer (Community Health Care) | Mrs Susan Hickie |
| Professional Officer (Nursing) | Ms Helen Mackinnon |
| Executive Director ( Resources) | Peter Taylor |
| Finance Officer | Alan Davidson |
| Corporate Services Manager/Board Secretary | David Ferguson |
| Registry Manager | Ewan Hainey |
| Administrator (Research & Development) | Ms Elizabeth M Harden |
| Careers and CATCH Manager | Mrs Lorna Hendrie |
| Personnel Officer | Mrs Sandra Millar |
| Records Officer | Miss Kathleen Reynolds |
| Information Services Officer | Mrs Christine Waddington |

**financial**

**INCOME & EXPENDITURE**

| Year end: 31 March | 1997 £000 | 1996 £000 | 1995 £000 |
|---|---|---|---|
| **INCOME** | | | |
| Grant from the Scottish Office | 2,647 | 2,488 | 2,678 |
| Fees | 312 | 361 | 540 |
| Other Income | 54 | 58 | 48 |
| | 3,013 | 2,907 | 3,266 |
| **ADMINISTRATIVE EXPENDITURE** | | | |
| Staff costs | 1,123 | 1,096 | 1,057 |
| Depreciation | 35 | 45 | 61 |
| Other charges | 1,860 | 2,085 | 2,119 |
| | 3,018 | 3,226 | 3,237 |
| **OPERATING (DEFICIT)/SURPLUS** | (5) | (319) | 29 |
| Interest receivable | 12 | 17 | 17 |
| **(DEFICIT)/SURPLUS FOR THE YEAR** | 7 | (302) | 46 |
| Transfer to education fund | (12) | (10) | 21 |
| Retained (deficit)/surplus brought forward | (99) | 213 | 146 |
| **RETAINED (DEFICIT)/SURPLUS CARRIED FORWARD** | (104) | (99) | 213 |

**advisers**

| | | |
|---|---|---|
| **Bankers** | The Royal Bank of Scotland |
| **Auditors** | Ernst & Young Chartered Accountants |
| **Solicitors** | W & J Burness |

**publications**   *Annual Report, Corporate Plan, NBS Newsletter, What Can We Do For You?*

# *National Consumer Council (NCC)*

20 Grosvenor Gardens
London SW1W 0DH

**Tel** 0171 730 3469
**Fax** 0171 730 0191

**Contact** Peter Stewart, Consumer Liaison Officer

| | |
|---|---|
| *status* | Executive body |
| *founded* | 1975 |
| *sponsor* | Department of Trade and Industry (DTI) |
| *powers* | Non-statutory, set up following 1974 White Paper, National Consumers' Agency |
| *mission* | To give a vigorous and independent voice to consumers in the UK. More specifically, and taking a UK-wide perspective, to promote action safeguarding consumer interests, to ensure decision-takers can have an authoritative view of consumer interests, and to insist that the interests of consumers, including those who experience disadvantage, are taken into account. |
| *tasks* | Identifying and researching issues which reflect consumer interests, concerns and trends. Developing robust, reliable and persuasive policy analyses of concern to consumers about the provision of goods and services, whether publicly or privately provided. Influencing key decision-makers on the formulation and implementation of policy. Helping consumers speak for themselves through support and development of consumer organisations and networks. |
| *operations* | Management: The NCC represents UK consumers and is funded largely by the DTI but other government departments commission projects. It is divided into three departments: Policy, Public Affairs and Corporate Resources. There are two associate Councils, which are independent in policy, planning and execution but funded by the NCC: the Scottish Consumer Council (SCC) and the Welsh Consumer Council (WCC) represent the particular consumer concerns in Scotland and Wales. Consumers in Europe Group (UK), based in London, serves the needs of UK consumers within the context of the EU and is funded through the NCC. (The General Consumer Council for Northern Ireland (GCCNI) is separately funded.) The Chairmen of SCC, WCC and GCCNI are all members of the NCC. |
| | Policy: Between 1998 and 2001, the policy work will include the utilities, the information society, the quality of public services, financial services, environmental policy, agriculture, access to justice, freedom of information, transport and consumer protection. |
| | Trends: The work of the Councils in the UK, Scotland and Wales will be affected by the government's regulative programme, devolution, technological developments and social and economic trends. |
| *performance* | Six annual and four triennial performance indicators are reported in the *Annual Report*. |
| *board* | Appointed by the President of the Board of Trade. The aim is to include a cross section of skills and experience, eg lawyers, economists, experts in health, trading standards, business, financial services etc. |

| | |
|---|---|
| Chairman | David Hatch CBE, JP |
| Vice Chairman | Deirdre Hutton |
| Members | Loraine Ashton |
| | Paul Ekins |
| | David Gilchrist |
| | Barbara Hicks |
| | Janet Humble OBE |
| | Noel Hunter |
| | Prof George Jones |
| | Stephen Locke |
| | Shamit Saggar |
| | Joan Whiteside |
| | Helena Wiesner |
| | Prof Geoffrey Woodroffe |
| *Accounting Officer* | *Director* |

*staff*  42 (including seven each in SCC and WCC)

| | |
|---|---|
| Director | Ruth Evans |
| Deputy Director | Robin Simpson |

*financial*

| INCOME & EXPENDITURE<br>Year end: 31 March | 1997<br>£ | 1996<br>£ | 1995<br>£ |
|---|---|---|---|
| **INCOME** | | | |
| Government grant-in-aid | 2,650,732 | 2,409,846 | 2,802,606 |
| Other grants | 378,237 | 155,998 | 209,320 |
| Other income | 323,610 | 188,494 | 75,273 |
| | **3,352,579** | **2,754,338** | **3,087,199** |
| **EXPENDITURE** | | | |
| Salaries | 1,398,487 | 1,513,606 | 1,433,961 |
| Pension scheme payments | 104,375 | 74,868 | 68,727 |
| Redundancy payments | 431,723 | - | - |
| Research | 493,002 | 333,010 | 430,905 |
| Cost of occupation of premises | 419,390 | 430,288 | 521,054 |
| Postage and telephone | 62,381 | 65,435 | 72,032 |
| Travelling | 69,665 | 86,023 | 96,964 |
| Administration | 164,556 | 139,167 | 276,886 |
| Equipment | 59,129 | 42,723 | 52,258 |
| Depreciation | 73,732 | 40,369 | 64,614 |
| (Profit)/loss on disposal of fixed assets | - | (463) | 240 |
| Staff recruitment and advertising | 17,268 | 5,724 | 12,927 |
| Audit and accountancy | 12,156 | 11,233 | 14,898 |
| | **3,305,864** | **2,741,983** | **2,992,446** |
| **OPERATING SURPLUS** | **46,715** | **12,355** | **94,753** |
| Interest on bank deposits | 4,975 | 4,977 | 6,283 |
| **SURPLUS BEFORE TAXATION** | **51,690** | **17,332** | **101,036** |
| Taxation | (26,437) | (7,691) | (1,571) |
| **SURPLUS FOR THE YEAR** | **25,253** | **9,641** | **99,465** |

*advisers* **Bankers** Royal Bank of Scotland  26 Grosvenor Place, London SW1X 7HP

**Auditors** Coopers & Lybrand  1 Embankment Place, London WC2N 6NN

*publications* Annual Report and Accounts, Annual Review, Bulletin (quarterly newletter)

*branches*
Scottish Consumer Council
Royal Exchange House
100 Queen Street
Glasgow G1 3DN
Tel 0141 226 5261
Fax 0141 221 0731
E-mail 101346.3164@compuserve.com

Welsh Consumer Council
5th Floor
Longcross Court
47 Newport Road
Cardiff CF2 1WL
Tel 01222 396 056
Fax 01222 238 360

# National Film & Television School

Station Road
Beaconsfield
Bucks HP9 1LJ

**Tel** 01494 671234
**Fax** 01494 674042

*status* Executive body

*founded* 1970

*sponsor* Department for Culture, Media and Sport (DCMS)

*mission* To provide training in the art of film and television programme making.

*tasks* Promotes and provides instruction in the art of making cinematograph and other films and in the production of programmes for television. Provides postgraduate three-year courses and over 100 short course training programmes a year.

*operations* Management: The school is a company limited by guarantee (and a charity), governed by its Trustees who form the Board of Governors. The Director runs the day-to-day management and is appointed by, and reports to, the Board of Governors. National Film School Distribution Co Ltd and NFTS Ealing Studios Ltd are wholly owned subsidiaries.

Policy: European Social Fund provides support for courses. Planning to move to Ealing Studios.

Trends: Increasing amounts of voluntary and discounted support.

*board*  Chairman and Board of Governors appointed by the Secretary of State in consultation with the Secretaries of State of Scotland and Wales.

| Chairman | David Elstein | |
|---|---|---|
| Governors | Andy Allan | |
| | Moira Armstrong | Linda James |
| | Floella Benjamin | Gus Macdonald |
| | Ann Beynon | Frank McGettigan |
| | Roger Bolton | Steve Morrison |
| | Andrea Calderwood | Simon Perry CBE |
| | Viscount Chandos | Marc Samuelson |
| | Robert Devereux | Eric Senat |
| | Jane Drabble | Joyce Taylor |
| | Rupert Gavin | Stewart Till |

*staff*  106

| Director | Henning Camre |
|---|---|
| Secretary | Jim Rodda |

*financial*

| INCOME & EXPENDITURE | | |
|---|---|---|
| Year end: 31 March | 1997 | 1996 |
| | £ | £ |
| **INCOMING RESOURCES** | | |
| Donations and other income | 983,081 | 710,725 |
| Grants receivable | 3,551,346 | 5,372,500 |
| Net income from trading subsidiaries | 428,160 | 499,555 |
| Bank interest received | 2,215 | - |
| | **4,964,802** | **6,582,780** |
| **RESOURCES EXPENDED** | | |
| Direct charitable expenditure | | |
| Curricular activity | 2,539,315 | 2,437,542 |
| National short course training programme | 651,408 | 494,397 |
| Createc multimedia | 166,578 | - |
| Support costs | 551,279 | 565,962 |
| | **3,908,580** | **3,497,901** |
| Other expenditure | | |
| Fundraising and publicity | 229,283 | 163,681 |
| Management and administration | 489,827 | 572,350 |
| Ealing move preparation | 77,069 | - |
| | **796,179** | **736,031** |
| **NET INCOMING/(OUTGOING) RESOURCES** | **260,043** | **2,348,848** |
| Funds brought forward | 2,493,921 | 145,073 |
| **FUNDS CARRIED FORWARD** | **2,753,964** | **2,493,921** |

*advisers*  **Auditors**  BDO Stoy Hayward

# National Forest Company

Enterprise Glade
Bath Lane
Moira
Swadlincote
Derbyshire DE12 6BD

**Tel** 01283 551211
**Fax** 552844

*status*  Executive body
*founded*  1995
*sponsor*  Department of the Environment, Transport and the Regions
*mission*  To create a multi-purpose forest over 200 square miles of the Midlands of England.

**tasks**   Implements, in partnership with others, the National Forest Strategy; buys land and brings land into forest; organises tree-planting (through various means of which Tender Scheme is most important).

**operations**   Management: Chief Executive runs day-to-day management and reports to the Board.

Policy: In creating the Forest, it will promote nature conservation and the cultural heritage; assist provision and opportunities for sport, recreation and tourism; encourage agricultural and rural enterprise; stimulate economic regeneration; and enthuse community and business participation.

Trends: Needs to attract private sector funding if it is to meet targets. Land values rising. Unlikely to meet tree-planting targets in future years.

**board**   Non-executive directors are appointed by the Secretary of State.

| Chairman | Rodney Swarbrick CBE |
|---|---|
| Chief Executive | Susan Bell |

**staff**   13

**financial**

| INCOME & EXPENDITURE Year end: 31 March | 1997 £ | 1996 £ |
|---|---|---|
| **INCOME** | | |
| Grant-in-aid | 2,079,304 | 1,847,119 |
| Donations | 35,460 | 25,707 |
| Gift of assets from Countryside Commission | - | 22,759 |
| Other | 8,964 | 3,490 |
| | 2,079,304 | 1,899,075 |
| **EXPENDITURE** | | |
| Running costs | | |
| Staff costs | 427,436 | 361,538 |
| Administrative expenses | 300,451 | 332,103 |
| Research | 30,283 | 24,270 |
| Tax due | 1,944 | 731 |
| | 760,114 | 718,642 |
| Capital expenditure | 11,958 | 127,182 |
| Programme expenditure | | |
| Tender Scheme | 995,001 | 472,018 |
| Programme Development Fund | 136,412 | 174,571 |
| Land acquisition | 99,975 | 15,625 |
| Special projects | 34,881 | 334,765 |
| | 1,266,269 | 996,979 |
| Donations received expended | 22,549 | - |
| Retained in revenue reserve | 18,414 | 56,272 |
| | 2,079,304 | 1,899,075 |

**advisers**   **Auditors**   Kidsons Impey
Bentley Jennison

**publications**   Annual Report

# National Galleries of Scotland (NGS)

13 Heriot Row
Edinburgh EH3 6HP

**Tel** 0131 556 8921
**Fax** 0131 556 9972

**status**   Executive body
**founded**   1906
**sponsor**   Scottish Office
**powers**   National Galleries of Scotland Act 1906, National Heritage (Scotland) Act 1985
**mission**   To preserve and display Scotland's national collection of works of fine art for the enjoyment and education of the widest possible public and to maintain the National Galleries of Scotland as a centre of excellence.

| tasks | To enhance visitor experience by improving the quality of physical and intellectual access to the collection; heighten awareness and knowledge by a stimulating exhibitions programme; add works of art important to the national collections; continue and improve research and scholarship; look after the collections. Responsible for National Gallery of Scotland, Scottish National Portrait Gallery, Scottish National Gallery of Modern Art, Royal Scottish Academy, Duff House and Paxton House. |
|---|---|

**operations** Management: Run by the Director who reports to the Trustees. Each gallery has its own Keeper, who reports to the Director.

Policy: Lottery funding obtained for new Paolozzi Gallery in Edinburgh. Seeking gallery in Glasgow. Opening Camperdown House in autumn 1998. Trying to increase income from commercial activities.

Trends: Massive reduction in Purchase Grant - trying to increase it.

**board** Trustees appointed by the Secretary of State.

| Chairman | Countess of Airlie | |
|---|---|---|
| Trustees | Mrs Valerie Atkinson | Mrs Anna McCurley |
| | Eric Hagman | Dr Michael Shea |
| | Prof J Ross Harper | Lord Gordon of Strathblane |
| | James Hunter Blair | Giles Weaver |
| | Prof Christina Lodder | Prof Ian Whyte |
| *Accounting Officer* | *Director* | |

**staff** 189

**advisers**

**Bankers** Royal Bank of Scotland

**Auditors** Deloitte & Touche

**Solicitors** Dundas & Wilson
Turcan Connell

**branches**

*National Gallery of Scotland*
The Mound
Edinburgh

*Scottish National Portrait Gallery*
1 Queen Street
Edinburgh

*Scottish National Gallery of Modern Art*
Belford Road
Edinburgh

*Royal Scottish Academy*
Princess Street
Edinburgh

*Paxton House*
Berwick

*Duff House*
Banff

# National Gallery

Trafalgar Square
London WC2N 5DN

**Tel** 0171 839 3321
**Fax** 0171 930 4764

**E-mail** information @ng-London.org.uk
**Web** http://www.nationalgallery.org.uk/

**Contact** Miranda Carrol, Head of Information

**status** Executive body

**founded** 1824

**sponsor** Department for Culture, Media and Sport (DCMS)

**powers** Act of Parliament 1824.

**mission** To house the UK national collection of Western European painting - from the 13th century to the end of the 19th - and to keep it in trust for the people of the UK.

**tasks** To keep the pictures in the collection safe for future generations; to make the collection accessible to the public; to make available to the public the finest possible scholarship about the collection; to add great pictures to the collection for the enjoyment of present and future generations.

**operations**  Management: There is a Director and Board of Trustees, Management Committee. National Gallery Publications Ltd is a wholly owned subsidiary. Virtually the whole collection is on show and admission is free of charge.

Policy: To deploy the national holdings as rationally as possible in collaboration with other galleries so as to increase overall public use and enjoyment, eg transferring works after 1900 to the Tate Gallery. To arrange touring exhibitions, especially in the case of pictures bought with Lottery money. To keep closely involved with the proposed pedestrianisation of Trafalgar Square.

Trends: Major pictures from the collection are exhibited throughout the country as never before - during 1996/97 forming the focal point of exhibitions in Cardiff, Edinburgh, Norwich, Hull, Sheffield, Newcastle and Birmingham. Under a four-year agreement with the Tate, 1900 is taken as the dividing line between the two collections. All pre-1900 continental paintings at the Tate are temporarily lent to the National Gallery and a number of important works have been lent to the Tate.

**board**  The Trustees are appointed by the Secretary of State.

| | | |
|---|---|---|
| Chairman | Philip Hughes CBE | |
| Trustees | Alan Bennett | Lady Monck |
| | Lady Bingham | Sir Mark Richmond |
| | Sir Ewen Fergusson GCMG GCVO | Mrs Paula Ridley |
| | Robert Gavron CBE | Hon Simon Sainsbury |
| | Dr David Landau | Hon Raymond GH Seitz |
| | Christopher Le Brun | Sir Keith Thomas |
| *Accounting Officer* | *Director* | |

**staff**  410

| | |
|---|---|
| Director | Neil MacGregor |
| Director of Administration | John MacAuslan |
| Chief Curator | Christopher Brown |
| Head of Building Department | Peter Fotheringham |
| Chief Restorer | Martin Wyld |
| Head of Design | Herb Gillman |
| Head of Development | Colin McKenzie |
| Head of Education | Kathleen Adler |
| Head of Exhibitions & Display | Michael Wilson |
| Head of Art Handling | Patricia Goddard |
| Head of Finance | Andrew Robson |
| Head of Framing | John England |
| Head of Libraries and Archive | Elspeth Hector |
| Head of Scientific | Ashok Roy |
| Head of Personnel | Margaret Pegler |
| Reception Manager | Michael Dobson |
| Front of House Manager | Martin Wyatt |
| Head of Photographic | Sara Hattrick |
| Head of Press & Public Relations | Jean Liddiard |
| Head of Information | Miranda Carroll |
| Registrar | Rosalie Cass |
| Head of Security | Mike Collings |
| Chief Warder | Mick (Manharlal) Patel |
| **National Gallery Publications** | |
| Managing Director | Geoffrey Matthews |
| Finance Director | Elizabeth Whittaker |
| Direct Marketing Director | John Wallace |
| Merchandise Director | Julie Molloy |
| Picture Library Manager | Belinda Ross |
| Production Manager | Sue Curnow |
| Director of Book Publishing | Patricia Williams |
| Sales Director | James Faichnie |

**financial**

| INCOME & EXPENDITURE | | | |
|---|---|---|---|
| **Year end: 31 March** | **1997** | **1996** | **1995** |
| | **£m** | **£m** | **£m** |
| **INCOME** | | | |
| Grant-in-Aid | 18.7 | 18.3 | 18.2 |
| Other operating income | 3.5 | 4.2 | 4.0 |
| Other income | 11.8 | 13.3 | 1.5 |
| | **34.0** | **35.8** | **23.7** |
| **EXPENDITURE** | | | |
| Operating costs | 18.7 | 18.6 | 18.1 |
| Collections purchases | 14.0 | 14.0 | 4.9 |
| Capital expenditure | 1.3 | 2.7 | 2.9 |
| | **34.0** | **35.3** | **25.9** |

**publications**  *Annual Report*

# National Heritage Memorial Fund (NHMF)

7 Holbein Place
London SW1W 8NR

**Tel** 0171 591 6000
**Fax** 0171 591 6001

| | |
|---|---|
| *status* | Executive body |
| *founded* | 1980 |
| *sponsor* | Department for Culture, Media and Sport (DCMS) |
| *powers* | National Heritage Act 1980 |
| *mission* | To save the most outstanding parts of the national heritage which are at risk. Intended as a memorial to those who gave their lives for the UK. |
| *tasks* | A fund of last resort, which gives financial assistance towards the cost of acquiring, maintaining or preserving land, buildings, works of art and other objects of outstanding interest which are also of importance to the UK heritage. |
| *operations* | Management: NHMF and HLF are run by the same Director and staff and controlled by independent Trustees. |
| | Policy: Has more flexible powers than the HLF. |
| | Trends: Grant funding drastically cut for 1997/98. |

## Heritage Lottery Fund (HLF)

| | |
|---|---|
| *status* | Executive body |
| *founded* | 1995 |
| *sponsor* | Department for Culture, Media and Sport (DCMS) |
| *powers* | National Lottery Act 1993 |
| *mission* | One of the National Lottery distributing agencies, its mission is to safeguard and enhance the heritage of the UK. |
| *tasks* | Distributes lottery funds to a wide range of projects which will provide lasting improvements to the quality of life for people in the UK. By March 1998 distributed £900 million to 1573 projects. |
| *operations* | Management: NHMF and HLF are run by the same Director and staff and controlled by independent Trustees. Expert and Advisory Panels assist with assessment of applications. |
| | Policy: Using money raised by the National Lottery, HLF aims to improve quality of life by safeguarding and enhancing the heritage of buildings, objects and the environment, whether man-made or natural, which have been important in the formation of the character and identity of the United Kingdom; assisting people to appreciate and enjoy their heritage, and allowing them to hand it on in good heart to future generations. |
| | Trends: Money, grant applications and awards increasing beyond expectation. HLF's impact on museums and galleries very great. |

## NHMF & HLF

*board*      Appointed by the Secretary of State

| Chairman | Dr Eric Anderson | |
|---|---|---|
| Trustees | Sir Richard Carew Pole | Patricia Lankester |
| | Lindsay Evans | Prof Palmer Newbould |
| | Sir Alistair Grant | Susan Palmer |
| | Sir Martin Holdgate | Catherine Porteous |
| | Caryl Hubbard | Mary Ann Sieghart |
| | John Keegan | Dame Sue Tinson |
| *Accounting Officer* | *Director* | |

*staff*      142

*financial*

**HERITAGE LOTTERY FUND INCOME & EXPENDITURE**

| Year end: 31 March | 1997 £000 | 1996 £000 | 1995 £000 |
|---|---|---|---|
| **INCOME** | | | |
| Proceeds from the National Lottery | 316,622 | 305,868 | 58,466 |
| Interst receivable and sundry income | 331 | 197 | - |
| **EXPENDITURE** | | | |
| Grants commitments and payments | (235,516) | (70,906) | - |
| Operating costs | (10,739) | (3,895) | (1,299) |
| **INCREASE IN FUNDS BEFORE NOTIONAL COSTS** | **70,148** | **231,264** | **57,167** |
| Notional costs | (550) | (750 | - |
| **INCREASE IN FUNDS AFTER NOTIONAL COSTS** | **70,148** | **231,189** | **57,167** |
| Reserval of notional costs | 550 | 75 | - |
| **INCREASE IN FUNDS** | **70,698** | **231,264** | **57,167** |

**NATIONAL HERITAGE MEMORIAL FUND INCOME & EXPENDITURE**

| Year end: 31 March | 1997 £000 | 1996 £000 | 1995 £000 |
|---|---|---|---|
| **INCOME** | | | |
| HMG grant and other income | 8,016 | 8,881 | 9,262 |
| **EXPENDITURE** | | | |
| Grant paid and heritage property transfer | (10,066) | (12,800) | (9,734) |
| Operating costs | (404) | (585) | (690) |
| **OPERATING DEFICIT** | **(2,454)** | **(4,504)** | **(1,162)** |
| Net investment income | 1,465 | 1,857 | 978 |
| **NET DEFICIT BEFORE NOTIONAL COSTS** | **(989)** | **((2,647)** | **(184)** |
| Notional costs | (1,451) | (1,502) | - |
| **NET DEFICIT AFTER NOTIONAL COSTS** | **(2,440)** | **(4,149)** | **(184)** |
| Reversal of notional costs | 1,451 | 1,502 | - |
| **NET DEFICIT** | **(989)** | **(2,647)** | **(184)** |

*advisers*   **Auditors**     National Audit Office     157-197 Buckingham Palace Road London SW1W 9SP

*publications*   Application Pack, Lottery Update, Heritage Fund News

# National Library of Scotland

George IV Bridge
Edinburgh EH1 IEW

**Tel** 0131 226 4531
**Fax** 0131 220 6662      **Web** http://www.nls.uk

*status*     Executive body

*founded*     1925

*sponsor*     Scottish Office

*powers*     National Library of Scotland Act 1925

*mission*     To preserve the written record of Scotland by building the collections and ensuring that they are safeguarded.

*tasks*     Collection development, preservation and user access. General research library and a world centre for the study of Scotland and the Scots.

**operations** Management: Run by The Librarian who reports to the Board of Trustees. It is a national and legal deposit library. Half of income comes from grant-in-aid, quarter from trust funds and bequests, and quarter from revenue-earning activities.

Policy: Major building works have resulted in suspension of all reader services in main building until September 1998. Further development of the electronic infrastructure and digitisation.

Trends: Library's services being adversely affected by cut in staff numbers, resulting from government constraints on funding.

**board** Some Trustees are *ex officio*, some are appointed by the Crown, the Faculty of Advocates, the Universities, Convention of Scottish Local Authorities and three are coopted.

| | | |
|---|---|---|
| Chairman | Earl of Crawford & Balcarres KT PC | |
| Vice-Chairman | Lord Emslie MBE PC | |
| The Lord President of the Court of Session | | |
| The Lord Advocate | | |
| The Secretary of State for Scotland | | |
| The Dean of the Faculty of Advocates | | |
| The Minister of the High Kirk (St Giles'), Edinburgh | | |
| The Member of Parliament for the Central Division of the city of Edinburgh | | |
| The Crown Agent | | |
| The Lord Provost of Edinburgh | | |
| The Lord Provost of Glasgow | | |
| The Lord Provost of Dundee | | |
| The Lord Provost of Aberdeen | | |
| Trustees | Prof Kathleen J Anderson OBE | |
| | Prof Graham D Caie | Prof A Rennie McElroy |
| | Jack Dale | Colin A McLaren |
| | Lady Dunnett OBE | Ruari McLean CBE |
| | Prof Arthur J Forty CBE | John M Menzies |
| | Prof Josephine A Haythornthwaite | Nigel M P Morrison QC |
| | Bruce Kerr QC | Angus Stewart QC |
| | Ian MacDougall | Michael F Strachan CBE |
| | Cllr Elizabeth Maginnis | MG Thomson QC |
| *Accounting Officer* | *The Librarian* | |

**staff** 243

| | |
|---|---|
| Librarian & Secretary to the Board of Trustees | Ian D McGowan |
| Secretary of the Library | Martin C Graham |
| Keeper of Manuscripts, Maps & Music, and of the Scottish Science Library | Ian C Cunningham |
| Keeper of Printed Books | Ann Matheson |
| Director of Public Services | Alan M Marchbank |

**financial**

| FINANCIAL ACTIVITY | | |
|---|---|---|
| **Year end: 31 March** | **1997** | **1996** |
| | **£000** | **£000** |
| **INCOMING RESOURCES** | | |
| Grant-in-aid | 9,898 | 11,250 |
| Book purchase fund grant | 858 | 858 |
| Income from revenue-earning activities | 93 | 104 |
| Gross income from grant-aided activities | 164 | 131 |
| Endowment income | 15 | 13 |
| Trust fund and bequests | 82 | 72 |
| Release of deferred government grant depreciation | 1,109 | 1,009 |
| | **12,219** | **13,437** |
| **RESOURCES EXPENDED** | | |
| Collection development | 3,882 | 3,895 |
| User-access to collections | 2,559 | 2,521 |
| Preservation | 860 | 822 |
| Buildings | 1,421 | 1,489 |
| Publicity | 227 | 260 |
| Revenue-earning activities | 83 | 98 |
| Administration | 894 | 839 |
| | **9,926** | **9,924** |
| **NET INCOMING/(OUTGOING) RESOURCES** | **2,293** | **3,513** |
| Transfer to deferred government grant account Capital Expenditure | (2,261) | (3,236) |
| Increase in market value of investments | 128 | 233 |
| Net movement in funds | 160 | 510 |
| Fund balances brought forward | 2,483 | 1,973 |
| **FUND BALANCES CARRIED FORWARD** | **2,643** | **2,483** |

| advisers | Bankers | HM Paymaster General |
|---|---|---|
| | Auditors | National Audit Office |
| | Solicitors | Dundas & Wilson WS |
| | | Turcan Connel WS |

## National Library of Wales

Aberystwyth
Ceredigion
SY23 3BU

**Tel** 01970 632800
**Fax** 01970 615709

**Web** http://www.llgc.org.uk

| | |
|---|---|
| *status* | Executive body |
| *founded* | 1907 |
| *sponsor* | Welsh Office |
| *powers* | Royal Charter |
| *mission* | The collection, preservation and maintenance of manuscripts, printed matter, maps, photographs, visual and audio-visual material relating to Wales and the Celtic peoples and similar material which furthers the aims of higher education and literary and scientific research. |
| *tasks* | Provides an effective service to near and remote users by delivery and enquiry services and by the provision of automated and manual catalogues and handlists. Collects materials by legal deposit, purchase, donation, bequest, exchange, and deposit, according to defined collection development policies; preserves and conserves materials in the collections; interprets and publicises the collections by means of guides, publications, printed and online bibliographies, exhibitions, lectures and produces and maintains the national bibliography; provides expert and professional input and collaboration at a Welsh, UK and international level. |
| *operations* | Management: Run by the Librarian who reports to the Council. The Library has private investment fund. |
| | Policy: Reduction in staffing has had detrimental effect, particularly in preservation and conservation section. New computer service being installed. |
| | Trends: Public enquiries increasing significantly, mainly because of electronic mail. Grant-in-aid was increased in 1996/97. |
| *performance* | Most targets in 1996/97 operational plan achieved. |
| *board* | The Court of Governors comprises representatives of various bodies (eg University of Wales, MPs Arts Council of Wales) and a small number appointed by the Secretary of State. The Council is elected by the Court, with a small number appointed by the Secreatry of State and others coopted. |

| **The Council** | | |
|---|---|---|
| President | R Brinley Jones | |
| Vice-President | TA Owen | |
| Treasurer | Conrad L Bryant | |
| | *Appointed by the Secretary of State for Wales* | |
| Members | Miss Katherine Hughes | |
| | Ian C Lovecy | |
| | Roy Luff OBE | |
| | *Elected by the Court of Governors* | |
| | Sandra J Anstey | |
| | Alun Creunant Davies | |
| | Prof Emeritus Ieuan Gwynedd Jones | |
| | J Arfon Hughes | *Coopted by the Council* |
| | Emyr Wyn Jones OBE | John M Lancaster |
| | Prof Derec Llwyd Morgan | Prof Peter H Morgan |
| | Miss Gwerfyl Pierce Jones | Cllr HM Morgan MBE |
| | Prof Emeritus Graham L Rees | Prof Patricia Layzell Ward |
| | Elan Closs Stephens | W Gwyn Williams OBE |
| *Accounting Officer* | *Librarian* | |

*staff*    225

| | |
|---|---|
| Librarian | J Lionel Madden |
| Keeper of Pictures & Maps | D Huw Owen |
| Keeper of Manuscripts & Records | Gwyn Jenkins |
| Keeper of Printed Books | W Rhidian M Griffiths |
| Director of Administration & Technical Services | Mark W Mainwaring |
| Director of Finance | D Kenneth Rees |

*advisers*    **Bankers**    National Westminster Bank

**Auditors**    National Audit Office

**Solicitors**    Allen and Overy

**Public Relations**    Strata

*publications*    Annual Report, Journal


# National Lottery Charities Board

St Vincent House
30 Orange Street
London WC2 7HH

**Tel** 0171 747 5299
**Fax** 0171 747 5347            **Web** http://www.nlcb.org.uk

*status*    Executive body

*founded*    1994

*sponsor*    Department for Culture, Media and Sport (DCMS)

*powers*    National Lottery Act 1993

*mission*    To help those at greatest disadvantage in society and to improve the quality of life in communities across the UK.

*tasks*    Gives grants to charities and voluntary groups throughout the UK.

*operations*    Management: Local decision-making offices in Wales, Scotland and Northern Ireland. Nine regional offices in England; head office in Leicester, and corporate headquarters in London. Advisory committees for each country and UK as whole, plus regional, medical and social research advisory panels. Run by Chief Executive, each region headed by a Director.

Policy: Grant applications now assessed in-house.

Trends: Received 5.6p from every pound spent on the Lottery. Moving towards continuous grant making instead of setting closing dates for applications.

*performance*    Undertaken consultation/survey of public opinion: generally seen as open, accountable and accessible, but bureaucratic.

*board*    Directors and Committee members appointed by the Secretary of State.

| | |
|---|---|
| Chairman | David Sieff |
| Deputy Chairman | Sir Adam Ridley |
| Chair, England Committee | Stella Clarke JP |
| Members of England Committee | Amir Bhatia OBE |
| | Ian Clarke |
| | Julia Kaufmann |
| | Sir Eric Stroud |
| | Chris Woodcock |
| Chair, Wales Committee | Tom Jones OBE |
| Members of Wales Committee | June Churchman OBE |
| | Alan Higgins OstJ OBE |
| | Linda Quinn |
| Chair, Scotland Committee | Graham Bowie CBE |
| Members of Scotland Committee | Philomena de Lima |
| | William Kirkpatrick |
| | Garth Morrison CBE |

| Chair, Northern Ireland Committee and National Lottery Charities | John Simpson OBE |
| Members of Northern Ireland Committee | Aideen McGinley |
| | Monica McWilliams |
| | Noel Stewart OBE |
| Chair, UK Committee | Graham Bowie CBE |
| Members of UK Committee | Tessa Baring |
| | Amir Bhatia OBE |
| | Amanda Jordan |
| | Julia Kaufmann |
| | Linda Quinn |
| | Sir Adam Ridley |
| | John Simpson |
| *Accounting Officer* | *Chief Executive* |

**staff**  148

| Chief Executive | Timothy Hornsby |
| Director of Personnel & Administration | Stephen Bubb |
| Director of Communications | Paul Hensby |
| Director of Finance | Barry MacDonald |
| Director for Northern Ireland | Robin Mullan |
| Director for Wales | Roy Norris |
| Director UK & Corporate Planning | Gerald Oppenheim |
| Director for England | Janet Paraskeva |
| Director for Scotland | John Rafferty |
| Director for Wales | Roy Norris |
| Director for Scotland | John Rafferty |
| Director for Northern Ireland | Robin Mullan |

**financial**

### INCOME & EXPENDITURE

| Year end: 31 March | 1997 | 1996 |
| --- | --- | --- |
| | £m | £m |
| **INCOME** | | |
| Income from the National Lottery | 289 | 293 |
| Investment and other income | 29 | 14 |
| | 318 | 307 |
| **EXPENDITURE** | | |
| Grant commitments made in the year | 319 | 158 |
| Operating expenditure | 18 | 13 |
| | 337 | 171 |
| **NET INCOME /(COST)AFTER TAX AND NOTIONAL CHARGES** | (19) | 136 |

**advisers**

**Auditors**     National Audit Office

157-197 Buckingham Road Palace
London SW1W 9SP

**branches**

Ladywell House
Newtown
Powys SY16 1JB
Tel 01686 621644

Norloch House
36 Kings Stables Road
Edinburgh EH1 2EJ
Tel 0131 221 7110

2nd Floor
30-34 Hill Street
Hildon House
Belfast BT1 2LB
Tel 01232 551455

96-98 Regent Road
Readson House
Leicester LE1 7DZ
Tel 0116 258 7000

# National Maritime Museum

Greenwich
London SE10 9NF

**Tel** 0181 858 4422
**Fax** 0181 3126632                **Web** http://www.nmm.ac.uk

| | |
|---|---|
| *status* | Executive body |
| *founded* | 1937 |
| *sponsor* | Department for Culture, Media and Sport (DCMS) |
| *powers* | National Maritime Museum Act 1934 |
| *mission* | To promote an understanding of the history and future of Britain and the sea, the story of time and the historic sites at Greenwich. |
| *tasks* | To manage, display and preserve the collections. Runs specialist maritime library; puts on exhibitions. Consists of Main Museum, The Old Royal Observatory, The Queen's House, and other outstations (including one at Cotehele in Cornwall with the National Trust). |
| *operations* | Management:: Two operational divisions (Information and Display), a support division (Collections & Museum Services) and the Directorate, spread over different sites. |
| *board* | Appointed by the Secretary of State. |
| *staff* | 353 |

# National Museum of Science & Industry (NMSI)

Exhibition Road
London SW7 2DD

**Tel** 0171 938 8000
**Fax** 0171 938 8118                **Web** http://www.nmsi.ac.uk

| | |
|---|---|
| *status* | Executive body |
| *founded* | 1984 as executive body |
| *sponsor* | Department for Culture, Media and Sport (DCMS) |
| *powers* | National Heritage Act 1983 |
| *mission* | To promote the public's understanding of the history and contemporary practice of science, medicine, technology and industry. |
| *tasks* | NMSI incorporates the Science Museum, the Wellcome Museum of the History of Medicine, London; National Railway Museum (NRM), York; National Museum of Photography, Film & Television (NMPFT), Bradford; Wroughton Airfield and Concorde 002, Yeovilton. Its objectives are to build, research and care for the collections and increase the public's interest. Runs educational programmes and temporary exhibitions. |
| *operations* | Management: Board of Trustees of Science Museum is responsible for the whole of NMSI. The Director is responsible to the Board of Trustees. The Science Museum has four internal divisions: Collections, Science Communication, Public Affairs and Resource Management, each headed by an Assistant Director. NRM and NMPFT are organised on similar lines with Head of Museum responsible to the appropriate Assistant Director and the Science Museum. The main decision-making body is the Executive Management Committee which consists of the Director, the Assistant Director and the Heads of Museum. |
| | Policy: Visitor numbers increasing. Rising profits for NMSI Trading Ltd (a wholly owned subsidiary). |
| | Trends: Lottery Funding applied for at NRM. Increasing level industry sponsorship. |
| *board* | Trustees are appointed by the Prime Minister. |

**staff**  650

| | |
|---|---|
| Director | Sir Neil Cossons |
| Assistant Director | Prof John Durant |
| Assistant Director | Dr Thomas Wright |
| Head of NMPFT | Mrs Amanda Nevill |
| Head of NRM | Andrew Scott |
| Assistant Director, Public Affairs Division | Mark Pemberton |
| Assistant Director, Resource Management Division | Jeffrey Defries |

**financial**

**INCOME & EXPENDITURE**

| Year end: 31 March | 1997 £000 | 1996 £000 |
|---|---|---|
| **INCOMING RESOURCES** | | |
| Grant-in-aid | 20,633 | 21,700 |
| Income from commercial activities | 4,404 | 4,321 |
| Sponsorship, grants and donations | | |
| Lottery income | 2,183 | - |
| Other | 3,663 | 3,015 |
| Admissions | 3,482 | 3,215 |
| Other operating income | 384 | 240 |
| Investment income | 425 | 471 |
| | **35,174** | **32,962** |
| **RESOURCES EXPENDED** | | |
| Direct charitable expenditure | | |
| Collections purchases | 334 | 157 |
| Care for and research into collections | 5,349 | 5,229 |
| Science education and communication | 5,220 | 5,048 |
| Visitor services | 3,359 | 3,231 |
| Support services | 9,755 | 9,633 |
| Other expenditure | | |
| Publicity and fundraising | 187 | 192 |
| Admission costs | 1,208 | 1,108 |
| Commercial costs | 3,733 | 3,596 |
| Management and administration of the charity | 810 | 745 |
| | **29,955** | **28,939** |
| Notional cost of capital | 1,949 | 1,672 |
| Notional cost of insurance | 29 | 28 |
| **NET INCOMING/ (OUTGOING) RESOURCES AFTER NOTIONAL COSTS** | **3,241** | **2,323** |
| Reversal of notional costs | 1,978 | 1,700 |
| **NET INCOMING/ (OUTGOING) RESOURCES** | **5,219** | **4,023** |
| Fund balances brought forward | 29,873 | 25,850 |
| **FUND BALANCES CARRIED FORWARD** | **35,092** | **29,873** |

**advisers**

**Auditors**  National Audit Office  157-197 Buckingham Palace Road
London SW1W 9SP

**branches**

*The National Railway Museum*
Leeman Road
York
Yorkshire Y02 4XJ

*The National Museum of Photography, Film & Television*
Pictureville
Bradford
West Yorkshire BD1 1NQ

*Science Museum Wroughton*
Block D4
Red Barn Gate
Wroughton
Swindon SN4 9NS

# National Museums & Galleries, Merseyside (NMGM)

Liverpool Museum
William Brown St
Liverpool L3 8EN

**Tel** 0151 207 0001
**Fax** 0151 478 4390

| | |
|---|---|
| *status* | Executive body |
| *founded* | 1986 |
| *sponsor* | Department for Culture, Media and Sport (DCMS) |
| *mission* | Caring for collections at Lever Art Gallery, Sudley House, Liverpool Museum, Merseyside Maritime Museum, Museum of Liverpool Life, HM Customs & Excise National Museum. |
| *tasks* | Collection development, care and management, access and communication (active programme of educational exhibitions, events, activities and publications). Displaying and adding to the collections. Documenting, researching and publishing the collection. Caring for the collections by means of an active programme of conservation. Arranging temporary exhibitions. Caring for the buildings. |
| *operations* | Management: Director's office manages IT provision for whole of NMGM. |
| | Policy: NMGM Enterprises is wholly owned trading company, which pays its profit to the Trustees. |
| *performance* | Performance measures and indicators are being developed. |
| *staff* | 466 |

*financial*

**INCOME & EXPENDITURE**
**Year end: 31 March**

| | 1995 £m |
|---|---|
| **INCOME** | |
| Grant-in-aid | 16,411 |
| Restricted income | 2,936 |
| Operating income | 1,003 |
| Collection purchase fund | 0,364 |
| Investment income | 0,232 |
| | **20,946** |
| **EXPENDITURE** | |
| Staff costs | 8,170 |
| Other running costs | 3,312 |
| Building & maintenance costs | 2,106 |
| Purchases for collections | 0,920 |
| Additions to fixed assets | 5,196 |
| | **19,704** |

# National Museums & Galleries of Wales (NMGW)

Cathays Park
Cardiff CF1 3NP

**Tel** 01222 397951
**Fax** 01222 573321

| | |
|---|---|
| *status* | Executive body |
| *founded* | 1907 |
| *sponsor* | Welsh Office |
| *powers* | Royal Charter 1990 |
| *mission* | To promote knowledge and understanding of Wales, its history and culture, through the collection and preservation of objects relating to the story of Wales from the earliest times, including flora, fauna, geology and the artefacts of man. |

# Q&Q

**tasks** Enhancing collections through research, acquisitions, conservation and management; providing exhibitions and educational facilities and events. Main institutions are: National Museum & Gallery Cardiff, Museum of Welsh Life, Welsh Industrial & Maritime Museum, Welsh Slate Museum, Museum of the Welsh Woollen Industry, Turner House Gallery, Roman Legionary Museum.

**operations** Management: The Council is responsible for the management and administration of the finances and property of NMGW. The Director is supported by the Directorate which consists of Assistant Director and Directors of Collections & Research, Education & Interpretation, Public Services, Resource Management, Museums Development.

Policy: Awarded Heritage Lottery Grant for Welsh Slate Museum. Encouraging more private sector support.

Trends: Looking at PFI for funding building projects.

**performance** Attendance figures rose by 14% in 1996/97.

**board** Court of Governors are appointed by the Secretary of State.

**staff** 461

| Director | C Ford CBE |
|---|---|
| Resource Management | THC Arnold |
| Education & Interpretation | I Fell |
| Museums Development | A Southall |
| Public Services | C Thomas |
| Assistant Director, Collections & Research | Dr E Wiliam |
| *Accounting Officer* | *Director* |

**financial**

| FINANCIAL ACTIVITIES<br>Year end: 31 March | 1997<br>£000 | 1996<br>£000 |
|---|---|---|
| **INCOMING RESOURCES** | | |
| Grants receivable | 13,048 | 13,380 |
| Donations and bequests | 48 | 162 |
| Investment income | 40 | 37 |
| Admission income | 908 | 890 |
| Net shop sales | 247 | 177 |
| Other income | 930 | 797 |
| | 15,221 | 15,443 |
| **RESOURCES EXPENDED** | | |
| Direct expenditure | | |
| Charitable expenditure | | |
| Collection & preservation | 4,363 | 5,709 |
| Research | 652 | 785 |
| Exhibition & education | 3,861 | 2,636 |
| Support expenditure | 3,697 | 3,981 |
| Other expenditure | | |
| Fund raising and publicity | 966 | 853 |
| Management and administration | 1,061 | 982 |
| Provision for severance scheme costs | 0 | 924 |
| | 14,600 | 15,870 |
| **NET INCOMING/(OUTGOING) RESOURCES** | 621 | (427) |

# *National Museums of Scotland (NMS)*

Chambers Street
Edinburgh EH1 IJF

**Tel** 0131 225 7532

**status** Executive body

**sponsor** Scottish Office

**mission** To provide Scotland with a national museum service of international standing which preserves and enhances the collections in its care and promotes research on them so that they can be used to communicate and increase knowledge, understanding and enjoyment of human and natural history.

308

*tasks*  Displaying, increasing, documenting, researching and publishing the collections. Caring for the collections by means of an active programme of conservation. Arranging exhibitions and educational events. Responsible for The Royal Museum, Scottish United Services Museum, Scottish Agricultural Museum, Museum of Flight, Museum of Piping, Shambellie House Museum of Costume.

*operations*  Management: Management Team comprises the Director and two Depute Directors.

Policy: New Museum of Scotland opens in November 1998. National Museum of Scottish Country Life, a joint project between NMS and National Trust for Scotland, is to be funded by the Heritage Lottery Fund.

Trends: 22% increase in visitors in 1996/97. Over 50% reduction in Purchase Grant.

*performance*  93% of visitors to the Royal Museum regarded their experience as excellent or good.

*board*

| | |
|---|---|
| Chairman | Robert Smith |
| Trustees | The Countess of Dalkeith |
| | Prof Tom Devine |
| | Lesley Glasser |
| | Alexander Gordon CBE |
| | Sir Alistair Grant |
| | Prof Peter Jones |
| | Allan Massie |
| | Anna Ritchie OBE |
| | The Countess of Rosebery |
| | Sir John Thomson GCMG |
| | Prof Veronica van Heyningen |

*staff*  303

| | |
|---|---|
| Director | Mark Jones |
| Depute Director (Collections) & Keeper of History & Applied Art | Dale Idiens |
| Depute Director (Resources) & Project Director, Museum of Scotland | Ian Hooper |
| Campaign Director, Museum of Scotland | Sheila Brock |
| Head of Public Affairs | Mary Bryden |
| Keeper of Archaeology | David Clarke |
| Head of Buildings & Museum Services | Stephen Elson |
| Keeper of Geology & Zoology | Mark Shaw |
| Keeper of Social & Technological History | Gavin Sprott |
| Head of Administrative Services | Allan Young |

*financial*

**INCOME & EXPENDITURE**

| Year end: 31 March | 1997 £000 | 1996 £000 | 1995 £000 |
|---|---|---|---|
| **INCOME** | | | |
| Running costs grant | 10,714 | 11,126 | 11,460 |
| Major capital grant | 10,175 | 5,626 | 5,940 |
| Purchase grant | 210 | 732 | 947 |
| Self-generated income | 2,293 | 1,547 | 633 |
| Previous year's unspent income brought forward | 654 | 348 | 468 |
| | **24,046** | **19,379** | **19,172** |
| **EXPENDITURE** | | | |
| Museum of Scotland construction | 8,710 | 2,855 | 1,220 |
| Museum of Scotland development | 467 | 449 | 452 |
| Construction of Granton storage facility | 68 | 1,673 | 3,019 |
| Royal Museum of Scotland accommodation | 2,157 | 1,937 | 1,398 |
| Estates and buildings upkeep | 1,595 | 1,610 | 2,673 |
| Exhibitions and galleries | 1,309 | 920 | 662 |
| Salaries | 6,305 | 6,437 | 6,177 |
| Operating costs | 2,487 | 2,768 | 2,223 |
| Collections purchase | 794 | 548 | 706 |
| | **23,892** | **19,197** | **18,530** |
| **FUNDS CARRIED FORWARD** | **154** | **182** | **623** |

# National Portrait Gallery (NPG)

2 St Martin's Place
London WC2H 0HE

**Tel** 0171 306 0055
**Fax** 0171 306 0056          **Web** http://www.npg.org.uk

| | |
|---|---|
| *status* | Executive body |
| *founded* | 1856 |
| *sponsor* | Department for Culture, Media and Sport (DCMS) |
| *powers* | Treasury minute |
| *mission* | To preserve, maintain and acquire paintings, sculpture and photographs of national figures in UK life, past and present. |
| *tasks* | Acquisition and preservation of collection; extensive exhibitions programme. |
| *operations* | Management: The Director reports to the Trustees. |
| | Policy: Staff levels held at minimum, and optimum use made of contracted-out services. Heritage Lottery Fund grant for centenary development scheme. |
| *board* | Trustees appointed by the Prime Minister. |

| Chairman | Henry Keswick | |
|---|---|---|
| Vice-Chairman | Lord Morris of Castle Morris | |
| Trustees | Sir Antony Acland GCMG GCVO | Prof the Earl Russell |
| | Mrs Jane Benson LVO OBE | Sir David Scholey CBE |
| | Sir Philip Dowson CBE | Anne Taylor MP |
| | Max Hastings | Mrs Claire Tomalin |
| | Prof Norbert Lynton | Lady Tumim OBE |
| | Tom Phillips | John Tusa |
| | Dr John Roberts CBE | Baroness Willoughby de Eresby |

*staff*   138

| | |
|---|---|
| Director | Charles Saumarez Smith |
| Chief Curator | Robin Gibson |
| Head of Exhibitions & Collections Management | Kathleen Soriano |
| Head of PR & Development | Pim Baxter |
| Press Officer | Ben Rawlinson Plant |
| Head of Administration | John Wykeham |
| Head of Education | John Cooper |
| Head of Retailing & Publications | Robert Carr-Archer |
| Marketing Manager | Emma Marlow |
| 16th/17th Century Curator | Catharine McLeod |
| 18th Century Curator | Jacob Simon |
| 19th Century Curator | Peter Funnell |
| 20th Century Curator | Honor Clerk |
| Photography Curator | Terence Pepper |

*financial*

| INCOME & EXPENDITURE | | |
|---|---|---|
| **Year end: 31 March** | **1997** | **1996** |
| | **£000** | **£000** |
| **INCOME** | | |
| Grant-in-aid | 4915 | 5065 |
| Sponsorship and donations | 2952 | 862 |
| Trading | 1249 | 1182 |
| Exhibition admissions | 86 | 206 |
| Investment income | 157 | 102 |
| Other income | 177 | 171 |
| | **9536** | **7588** |
| **EXPENDITURE** | | |
| Collection purchases | 338 | 274 |
| Gallery services | 4327 | 3989 |
| Trading | 1127 | 934 |
| Support services | 1248 | 1070 |
| | **7040** | **6267** |

| *advisers* | **Bankers** | National Westminster Bank | |
|---|---|---|---|
| | **Auditors** | National Audit Office | |
| | **Solicitors** | Farrer & Co | 66 Lincoln's Inn Fields,London WC2A 3LH |
| | **Public Relations** | Colman Getty PR | Carrington House, 126-130 Regent Street London W1R 5FE |
| | | Cameron Duncan PR | 56-58 Fitzroy Street,London W1P 5HT |
| *publications* | Exhibition Catalogues, Gallery Collection Guides | | |

# National Radiological Protection Board (NRPD)

Chilton
Didcot
Oxon OX11 0RQ

**Tel** 01235 831600
**Fax** 01235 833891

**E-mail** nrpb@nrpb.org.uk
**Web** http://www.nrpb.org.uk

| | |
|---|---|
| *status* | Executive body |
| *founded* | 1970 |
| *sponsor* | Department of Health (DOH) |
| *powers* | Radiological Protection Act 1970 |
| *mission* | To advance knowledge about the protection of mankind from radiation hazards and non-ionising electro-magnetic radiations. To provide information and advice to those in the UK (including government departments) with responsibilities for protecting the community from radiation hazards and non-ionising electro-magnetic radiations. |
| *tasks* | To conduct radiation research in the environmental, physical and biomedical sciences and also research on non-ionising radiations. To provide technical service to those concerned with radiation hazards. To specify emergency levels of dose. To advise government and statutory bodies on the UK implications of the recommendations of certain international and intergovernmental bodies. |
| *operations* | Management: NRPB interacts with ten UK government departments and four agencies and internationally with at least eleven organisations, ranging from the European Commission and the International Atomic Energy Agency to the UN Scientific Committee on the Effects of Atomic Radiation and the US National Council on Radiation Protection and Measurements and the World Health Organisation. NRPB's government grant is under scrutiny so it is under pressure to seek increased revenue from industry and research funding bodies. NRPB charges for technical services, information and advice. |
| | Policy: National and international relations are crucial to further the cause of radiological protection. |
| | Trends: The adoption of the new Euratom Directive (1996) meets many of NRPB's objectives for protecting workers and the public and it is working closely with the Health and Safety Executive to develop occupational health guidance. |

*performance* All scientific targets met 1996/97.

*board* The Chairman and between seven and twelve other members, all appointed by Health Ministers.

| Chairman | Prof Sir Keith Peters | |
|---|---|---|
| Members | Prof AD Baddeley | Prof JM Harrington CBE |
| | Prof V Beral | Prof RM MacKie |
| | Mrs PM Castle | Prof J McEwen |
| | Prof KE Davies CBE | Hon Mrs S Morrison |
| | Prof EH Grant | Prof GM Roberts |
| | Prof DG Harnden | Dr MF Spittle |

*staff* 342 (32 on fixed term contracts).

| Director | Prof RH Clarke |
|---|---|
| Assistant Director | Miss FA Fry |
| Medical Assistant Director | Dr JR Harrison |
| Senior Assistant Director | Dr JW Stather |
| Assistant Director | Dr AD Wrixon |

| Head of Department, Dose Assessments | Dr MR Bailey |
|---|---|
| Head of Department, Environmental Assessments | Dr JR Cooper |
| Head of Department, Biomedical Effects | Dr R Cox |
| Head of Department, Industrial Operations | JR Croft |
| Head of Department, Population Exposure | Dr GM Kendall |
| Head of Department, Dosimetry & Instrumentation | TO Marshall |
| Head of Department, Non-ionising Radiation | Dr AF McKinlay |
| Head of Department, Medical | Dr C Sharp |
| Head of Department, Administration | DB Talbot |

*financial*

**INCOME & EXPENDITURE**

| Year end: 31 March | 1997 | 1996 |
|---|---|---|
| | £000 | £000 |
| **INCOME** | | |
| Income from activities | 8,033 | 8,082 |
| Government grant | 6,203 | 6,169 |
| Transfer from deferred government grant and reserves | 573 | 543 |
| | **14,809** | **14,794** |
| **EXPENDITURE** | | |
| Staff costs | 8,829 | 8,303 |
| Depreciation | 796 | 854 |
| Other operating charges | 5,604 | 5,400 |
| | **15,229** | **14,557** |
| **OPERATING SURPLUS/(DEFICIT)** | **(420)** | **237** |
| Interest receivable | 13 | - |
| Capital charge | (683) | - |
| Write back of capital charge | 683 | - |
| **SURPLUS/(DEFICIT) FOR THE FINANCIAL YEAR** | **(407)** | **237** |
| Retained surplus brought forward | 2,563 | 2,302 |
| Prior year's adjustment | - | (27) |
| Transfer from reserves | 186 | 51 |
| **RETAINED SURPLUS CARRIED FORWARD** | **2,342** | **2,563** |

*advisers*

| **Auditors** | National Audit Office | 157-197 Buckingham Palace Road London SW1W 9SP |
|---|---|---|

# *National Savings*

Charles House
375 Kensington High Street
London W14 8SD

**Tel** 0171 605 9300
**Fax** 0171 605 9438          **Web** http://www.open.gov.uk/natsav

*status*      Executive agency

*founded*      1996

*sponsor*      HM Treasury

*powers*      Framework Document

*mission*      To provide a cost-effective source of borrowing to help meet the Central Government Borrowing Requirement (CGBR).

*tasks*      Designing, marketing and administering savings and investment products for the retail market (eg Savings Certificates, Income Bonds, Premium Bonds).

*operations*      Management: The Chief Executive reports to the Economic Secretary of the Treasury. Each year they agree what National Savings' contribution to the CGBR is to be and what it will cost, which is set within the cost parameters of borrowing through Gilts. Six Directors, each with clearly defined areas of responsibility. Post offices are active retail outlets.

Policy: To keep competitive in a rapidly changing retail financial services market means both investment in new systems to improve flexibility and service to the huge customer base and reviewing products, marketing and distribution to attract new customers. Press relations very important.

Trends: Continually reviewing products' competitiveness.

**performance** 1996/97 targets met or nearly met.

**board**

| | |
|---|---|
| Chief Executive | Peter Bareau |
| Contracting Director | Kit Chivers |
| Funding Director | Michael Corcoran |
| Operational Services Director | Dan Monaghan |
| Finance Director | Maurice Nicholls |
| Personnel Director | Scott Speedie |
| Non-Executive Director | Roy Heape |
| Secretary | Alasdair Muir |

**financial** 1996/97 running costs £178 million; capital costs £3.7 million; gross receipts £13.4 billion.

**branches**
Boydstone Road
Glasgow G58 1SB
Tel 0141 649 4555

Millburngate House
Durham DH99 1NS
Tel 0191 386 4900

Marton
Blackpool FY3 9YP
Tel 01253 766151

# National Weights & Measures Laboratory (NWML)

Stanton Avenue
Teddington
Middlesex TW11 0JZ

**Tel** 0181 943 7272
**Fax** 0181 943 7270

**status** Executive agency

**founded** 1989

**sponsor** Department of Trade and Industry, (Consumer Affairs and Competition Management Directorate)

**powers** Weights and Measures Act 1985. Regulatory agency within DTI.

**mission** Accurate measurement, fair measurement and legal measurement all within an overall policy framework of consumer protection without unnecessary burdens on business; plus the development of commercial utilisation of its laboratories.

**tasks** Regulates the equipment used for trade weighing and measuring; represents the UK in international discussions of technical requirements for measuring instruments; prepares legislation; approves new measuring instrument design and recalibration; and approves local authority standards. It also provides equipment testing and calibration services to a wide range of customers from its Teddington laboratories.

**operations** Management: Organised into four customer-focused units: Legal metrology policy, handling domestic and international legislation and the free movement of measuring instruments throughout Europe and the world; measuring instruments certification, a service to the measuring instrument industry; metrology and training, high-quality customer calibration service and specialist training; business support, to meet the needs of internal customers.

Policy: Agency moved to a net running cost regime in 1996. A programme budget pays for the statutory and policy work, subject to a service level agreement between NWML and the Consumer Affairs and Competition Policy Division of DTI. Removal of unnecessary regulations and harmonisation with international specifications continues. Deregulation and updating of continues.

Trends: Although fees were increased, income from external work remained at the same level as previous year. Income from type-approval continued to decline from 1993-1994 peak.

**board** Steering Board appointed by the Secretary of State, from within DTI and outside.

| | |
|---|---|
| Chairman | Robert Foster |
| Members | Dr Seton Bennett |
| | Margaret Carmichael |
| | Dr John Cooke |
| | Hugh Savill |
| | Geoff Young |

**staff** 46

| Chief Executive & Director | Dr Seton Bennett |
|---|---|
| Head of Legal Metrology Policy Unit | Peter Badger |
| Head of Measuring Instruments Certification Unit | Mike Koch |
| Head of Business Support Unit | Iain MacGregor |
| Head of Metrology & Training Unit | Chris Rosenberg |

**financial**

**INCOME & EXPENDITURE**

| Year end: 31 March | 1997 £000 | 1996 £000 | 1995 £000 |
|---|---|---|---|
| **INCOME** | | | |
| Income from activities | 2,645* | 679 | 625 |
| **EXPENDITURE** | | | |
| Staff costs | 1,345 | 1,274 | 1,211 |
| Depreciation | 144 | 147 | 111 |
| Other operating costs | 957 | 1,060 | 1,056 |
| Diminution in value of assets | - | - | 15 |
| | **(2,446)** | **(2,481)** | **(2,393)** |
| **NET COST OF OPERATIONS BEFORE INTEREST** | 199 | (1,802) | (1,768) |
| Interest on capital | (78) | (78) | (60) |
| **NET COST OF OPERATIONS** | **121** | **(1,880)** | **(1,828)** |

*Income from DTI included

**advisers**  **Auditors**   National Audit Office    157-197 Buckingham Palace Road
London SW1W 9SP

**publications**  Annual Reports and Accounts

# Natural Environment Research Council (NERC)

Polaris House
North Star Avenue
Swindon SN2 1EU

**Tel** 01793 411500
**Fax** 01793 411501

**status**   Executive body
**founded**  1995
**sponsor**  Department of Trade and Industry (DTI)
**powers**   Royal Charter
**mission**  To foster knowledge, understanding and prediction of the environment and its resources, covering atmospheric, earth, terrestrial and aquatic sciences.

**tasks**   Fostering research and technology development aimed at understanding and predicting environmental processes; educating training and maintaining core excellence in basic and strategic science; collecting curating, interpreting and supplying environmental data; providing objective, independent, expert advice and information; developing and using technologies and maintaining scientific facilities; ensuring linkage with the user community and effective technology transfer; encouraging public understanding of the environment.

**operations**  Management: Management Team consists of Chairman, Chief Executive and the Director Science and Technology. Science and Technology Boards report to the Council. Runs Centre for Ecology and Hydrology, Centre for Coastal and Marine Sciences, British Geological Survey, British Antarctic Survey and Southampton Oceanography Centre, with Southampton University. About half of science budget goes to universities via research grants etc or via contracts with specialist groups located within universities.

Policy: Increasing work on biodiversity, environmental risks and hazards and global change. Expansion of network for the exploitation of science and technology (NEST) on the Internet.

Trends: The Antarctic ozone hole was discovered by British Antarctic Survey. Private sector funding for research is growing.

**board**

| | | |
|---|---|---|
| Chairman | R Malpas CBE | |
| Members | Prof GS Boulton | Prof HE Huppert |
| | Dr DJ Fisk | Prof IA Johnston |
| | Dr IJ Graham-Bryce | Prof JH Lawton |
| | Prof JE Harries | Dr RJ Pentreath |
| | ER Hassall | Prof MJ Pilling |
| | Dr CP Hicks | Prof G Randall |
| | Prof JCR Hunt | Dr DWF Shannon |

**staff**    2664

| | |
|---|---|
| Chief Executive | Prof JR Krebs |
| Deputy Chief Executive | Dr DJ Drewry |
| Awards & Training | Prof JB Ellis |
| Acting Establishment Officer | JG Hansford |
| Scientific Services | Mr BJ Hinde OBE |
| Communications | Dr RKG Paul |
| Finance | CM Read |
| Technology Interaction | Dr MJ Tricker |
| Directors | Dr PJ Cook CBE |
| | Dr BL Bayne |
| | Prof J Shepherd |
| | Dr RB Heywood |
| | Prof WB Wilkinson |
| | BJ Hinde |

**financial**

| PAYMENTS & RECEIPTS | | |
|---|---|---|
| **Year end: 31 March** | **1996** | **1995** |
| | **£000** | **£000** |
| **PAYMENTS** | | |
| Recurrent | 194,574 | 171,045 |
| Capital | 25,718 | 24,516 |
| | **220,292** | **195,561** |
| **RECEIPTS** | | |
| Science budget | 169,493 | 148,725 |
| External receipts for research | 41,448 | 40,814 |
| Other receipts | 9,351 | 6,022 |
| | **220,292** | **195,561** |

**branches**

*British Geological Survey*
Kingsley Dunham Centre
Keyworth
Nottingham NG12 5GG
Tel 0115 936 3100
Fax 0115 9363200

*Centre for Coastal & Marine Sciences*
Plymouth Marine Laboratory
Prospect Place
West Hoe
Plymouth PL1 3DH
Tel 01752 633100
Fax 01752 633101

*Southampton Oceanography Centre*
Empress Dock
Southampton SO14 3ZH
Tel 01703 596888
Fax 01703 595107

*British Antarctic Survey*
High Cross
Madingley Road
Cambridge CB3 0ET
Tel 01223 251400/361188
Fax 01223 362616

*Centre for Ecology & Hydrology*
Maclean Building
Crowmarsh Gifford
Oxon OX10 8BB
Tel 01491 838800
Fax 01491 6922424

*NERC Scientific Services*
Holbrook House
Station Road
Swindon SN1 1DE
Tel 01793 411998
Fax 01793 411910

## Natural History Museum

Cromwell Road
London SW7 5BD

**Tel** 0171 938 9123

| | |
|---|---|
| *status* | Executive body |
| *founded* | 1881 |
| *sponsor* | Department for Culture, Media and Sport (DCMS) |
| *mission* | To maintain and develop its collections and to use them to promote the discovery, understanding and enjoyment of the natural world. |
| *tasks* | Scientific research and scientific advice; maintenance of the Museum's collections of some 68 million specimens; providing public access to the collections for millions of people; providing education for hundreds of thousands of visiting school children; arranging touring exhibitions. |

*operations*

Management: The Museum is headed by a Director. There are six scientific departments (Botany, Entomology, Mineralogy, Palaeontology, Zoology and Library & Information Services) as well as corporate services, marketing, exhibitions and visitor services. During 1993/96 government funding declined and led to increased pressure on the Museum to secure its own funding. The Natural History Museum Development Trust is an independent exempt charity, with its own separate Board of Trustees, established to promote private sector support. It raised £3.1 million during 1993-96. The Natural History Trading Company Ltd was established in 1994.

Science. A world renowned scientific research institution and centre of excellence in taxonomy, its research was restructured during 1993-96. It now addresses six interdisciplinary themes: (1) systematics and evolution - to discover the broad patterns of biodiversity and evolution; (2) faunas and floras - to make known the diversity of the natural world; (3) biomedical science - to record and explain the taxonomy, molecular diversity etc of organisms detrimental to human and animal health; (4) environmental quality - to assess the impact of mineralogical, geochemical and human disturbances; (5) earth materials, history and processes - to study minerals, meteorites, rocks and fossils and enhance understanding of the origin and history of the earth; (6) ecological patterns and processes - to provide a sound scientific basis for conservation and management of biological diversity worldwide.

Policy: To maintain the Museum as a world centre of excellence; to ensure that it is up-to-date, responsive and accessible to its many audiences; to increase self-generated income. But if core grant-in-aid continues to decline the museum will find it increasingly difficult to fulfil its mission effectively.

Trends: Electronic databasing of the Museum's collections is in progress, as part of a global information network. A succession of new permanent exhibitions, including the Wildlife Garden, is presenting life sciences dynamically; the most ambitious is the complete renovation of the Earth Galleries funded from a £6 million Heritage Lottery Fund grant. Scientific research is flourishing and the Museum's expertise is sought worldwide.

*board*

| Chairman | Sir Robert May | |
|---|---|---|
| Trustees | Baroness Tessa Blackstone | Dr Anne McLaren DBE |
| | Mrs Jennifer d'Abo | Prof Keith O'Nions |
| | Prof Sir Brian Follett | Lord Palumbo |
| | Sir Denys Henderson | Sir Richard Sykes |
| | Prof Christopher Leaver | Sir Crispin Tickell GCMG KCVO |

*staff*  698

| | |
|---|---|
| Director | Dr NR Chalmers |
| Director of Science | Prof P Henderson |
| Museum Secretary | CJE Legg |
| Keeper, Botany Department | Prof S Blackmore |
| Acting Keeper, Entomology Department | Dr R Post |
| Keeper, Mineralogy Department | Dr A Fleet |
| Keeper, Palaeontology Department | Dr LRM Cocks |
| Keeper, Zoology Department | Prof P Rainbow |
| Head of Department, Library & Information Services | R Lester |
| Head of Finance, Corporate Services | J Card |
| Head of Personnel, Corporate Services | P Orchard |
| Head of Department, Corporate Services | Sir Ronald Oxburgh |
| Head of Estates Management, Corporate Services | G Pellow |
| Head of Audit & Review, Corporate Services | D Thorpe |
| Head of Department, Development & Marketing | Ms T Burman |
| Head of Department, Exhibitions & Education | Dr GCS Clarke |
| Head of Department, Visitor Services | Mrs B Gullick |

*financial*

| INCOME & EXPENDITURE | | | |
|---|---|---|---|
| Year end: 31 March | **1997** | **1996** | **1995** |
| | **£000** | **£000** | **£000** |
| **SELF-GENERATED INCOME** | | | |
| **Trading income** | | | |
| Admissions | 4,124.9 | 3,230.7 | 3,433.4 |
| Membership | 94.3 | 66.1 | - |
| Brand management/picture library | 252.0 | 253.3 | 287.2 |
| Retail | 1,721.5 | 1,361.6 | 1,471.1 |
| Catering & functions | 1,514.3 | 1,065.4 | 867.8 |
| Exhibitions & education | 328.0 | 390.4 | 328.6 |
| Curation & research | 2,832.8 | 2,622.9 | 2,530.7 |
| Touring exhibitions | 524.8 | 570.4 | 675.8 |
| | 11,392.6 | 9,560.8 | 9,594.6 |
| **Costs** | **5,532.2** | **5,173.4** | **5,241.3** |
| **Profit** | **5,860.4** | **4,387.4** | **4,353.3** |
| **Sponsorship and other income** | | | |
| Income | 4,113.0 | 4,750.2 | 3,274.8 |
| Related expenditure | 2,787.8 | 3,555.3 | 2,307.5 |
| **Contribution** | **1,325.2** | **1,194.9** | **967.3** |
| **Heritage Lottery funding** | **4,064.4** | **-** | **-** |
| **TOTAL PROFIT AND CONTRIBUTION** | **11,250.0** | **5,582.3** | **5,320.6** |
| **GRANT-IN-AID** | **27,449.0** | **28,790.0** | **27,556.0** |
| **EXPENDITURE** | | | |
| **Current** | | | |
| Buildings & rates | 3,912.2 | 3,374.8 | 4,010.0 |
| Development & marketing | 869.0 | 843.2 | 846.3 |
| Visitor services | 3,698.4 | 3,966.7 | 4,212.0 |
| Exhibitions & education | 3,282.5 | 2,960.4 | 3,269.4 |
| Curation & research | 10,178.7 | 9,852.8 | 9,346.8 |
| Libraries & Information systems | 1,838.5 | 1,550.2 | 1,438.8 |
| Directorate | 184.8 | 197.3 | 185.3 |
| Corporate services | 2,567.9 | 2,454.7 | 2,345.9 |
| Restructuring costs | 340.6 | 337.9 | 372.8 |
| | 26,872.6 | 25,538.0 | 26,027.3 |
| **Capital** | | | |
| Buildings | 3,001.0 | 2,774.3 | 2,627.6 |
| New exhibitions | 6,917.3 | 1,680.0 | 100.7 |
| Equipment | 1,049.7 | 480.4 | 791.0 |
| | 10,968.0 | 4,934.7 | 3,519.3 |
| **TOTAL EXPENDITURE** | **37,840.6** | **30,472.7** | **29,546.6** |

# *Naval Aircraft Repair Organisation (NARO)*

NARO Fleetlands Division
Fareham Road
Gosport
Hampshire PO13 OAA

**Tel** 01705 543375
**Fax** 01705 543318

| | |
|---|---|
| *status* | Defence agency |
| *founded* | 1992 |
| *sponsor* | Ministry of Defence (MOD) |
| *powers* | NARO Framework Document |
| *mission* | To maintain position as Europe's number one helicopter repair and overhaul facility. |
| *tasks* | Provides a full range of repair, modification, overhaul and storage services for helicopters, aero engines and mechanical and avionic components for the UK's Armed Forces. Also repair centre for marine gas turbines for the Royal Navy and some European allies. |
| *operations* | Management: Present Chief Executive (CE) is the first civilian appointment and was recruited through open competition. The CE is accountable to the Secretary of State through the Director General Aircraft (Navy), the Owner of the agency with responsibility for the strategic context. The CE is responsible for the management of |

the business and for the propriety of expenditure and for its prudent and economical administration. The Management Board comprises the CE and six Directors. Two operating sites: near Perth, Scotland specialising in hydraulics and transmission components, employing 400; Gosport employing 1200 on the overhaul of aircraft, engines and some components.

Policy: To improve services and offer greater value for money. Upgrading technical facilities. Recently introduced commercial accounting package.

Trends: Shrinking defence budgets. New partnering arrangements with industry.

**performance**  Achieved one out of five performance targets set (reduction in customer complaints).

**board**  Management Board appointed by the Secretary of State.

| | |
|---|---|
| Chief Executive | SR Hill |
| Personnel Director | Ms J Garstang |
| Director of Facilities | G Noad |
| Business Director, Almondbank Division | J Reilly |
| Commercial Director | R Sparshott |
| Operations Director | Cdr S Wiles |
| Finance Director | G Wood |
| *Accounting Officer* | *Chief Executive* |

**staff**  1600 (all civil servants bar eight military personnel)

**financial**

| EXPENDITURE | | |
|---|---|---|
| Year end: 31 March | 1997 | 1996 |
| | £000 | £000 |
| **EXPENDITURE** | | |
| Staff costs | 30,569 | 28,415 |
| Supplies and services consumed | 94,047 | 80,017 |
| Accommodation costs | 5,661 | 4,492 |
| Other administration costs | 6,882 | 6,920 |
| Interest on capital | 5,406 | 2,064 |
| | 142,565 | 121,908 |
| **INCOME** | | |
| Income from fees & charges | (675) | (901) |
| **NET EXPENDITURE** | **141,890** | **121,007** |

**publications**  *Annual Reports and Accounts*

**branches**  *Almondbank Division*
*Almondbank*
*Perth PH1 3NQ*
*Tel 01738 583301*
*Fax 01738 583163*

# Naval Bases & Supply Agency (NBSA)

Room 120 A
D Block
Ensleigh
Bath BA1 5AB

**Tel** 01225 467156
**Fax** 01225 468421

**status**  Defence agency

**founded**  1996

**sponsor**  Ministry of Defence (MOD)

**powers**  Framework Document 1996

**mission**  To provide the Royal Navy and other authorised customers with engineering, supply and naval personnel services in war, crisis and peace.

**tasks**      Provides ships and submarines with Naval Base facilities and depots, and support services including routine maintenance, repairs and equipment update; acquires, stores, maintains and supplies weapons, ammunition, spares, equipment and fuel; reponsible for tri-Service food supply and the production of operational ration packs; maintains infrastructure of Naval Bases.

**operations**      Management: The Chief of Fleet Support (CFS) is the Agency Owner and approves the business plans, sets targets, and monitors budgets. He is advised by an Advisory Board. The Chief Executive is responsible for the day-to-day management and performance of the Agency. Headquarters in Bath, three Naval Bases (Devonport, Portsmouth and Clyde), with regional storage and processing depots.

Policy: Rationalisation of depots continues which may lead to more closures. Major review of Bath HQ continues.

Trends: Providing ongoing support to service personnel in former Yugoslavia. Shortage of service manpower leading to increased contracted-out work.

**performance**      Met targets set for 1996/97.

**board**      Advisory Board appointed by the Secretary of State.

| | |
|---|---|
| Chief Executive | Rear Admiral John Trewby |
| Deputy Chief Executive | DJ Stevens |
| Director of Contracts | AJ Bell |
| Naval Base Commander (Devonport) | Commodore JA Burch CBE |
| Director Fleet Support (Personnel) | B Cooper |
| Director Supply (South) | JA Curran |
| Deputy Director (Finance) | DTF Dick |
| Director (Business Management) | K Earley |
| Naval Base Commander (Portsmouth) | Commodore IR Henderson CBE |
| Flag Officer Scotland, Northern England & Northern Ireland/Naval Base Commander | Rear Admiral JG Tolhurst CB |
| Non-Executive Board Member | J Wilson |
| Naval Base Commander (Portsmouth) | Commodore IR Henderson |
| Naval Base CommanderCommodore | JA Burch CBE |
| Director Supply (South) | JA Curran |
| Naval Base Commander | Rear Admiral JG Tolhurst CB |
| *Accounting Officer* | *Permanent Under Secretary* |

**staff**      13,350 (3150 service, 10,200 civilian)

**financial**

**INCOME & EXPENDITURE**
**Year end: 31 March**

| | 1997 £000 |
|---|---|
| **EXPENDITURE** | |
| Staff costs | 286,184 |
| Accommodation services | 60,480 |
| Estate maintenance | 115,237 |
| Equipment, stores & transport | 18,613 |
| Support services | 90,957 |
| Other administration | 35,667 |
| Miscellaneous expenditure | 2,204 |
| Service food supply | 153,584 |
| Marine fuel | 26,524 |
| | **789,450** |
| **INCOME** | |
| Income from receipts | 138,257 |
| **NET COST OF OUTPUT** | **651,193** |

**branches**

Semaphore Tower
HM Naval Base
Portsmouth
Hants PO1 3LT
Tel 01705 722625

South Office Block
HM Naval Base
Portsmouth
Hants PO1 3LU
Tel 01705 723938

Naval Base Headquarters
Devonport
Plymouth PLI 4SL
Tel 01752 552536

Clyde
HM Naval Base
Faslane
Helensburgh
Dunbartonshire G84 8HL
Tel 01436 674321

# Naval Manning Agency (NMA)

Old Naval Academy
Victory Building
HM Naval Base
Portsmouth
Hampshire PO1 3LS

**Tel** 01705 727340
**Fax** 01705 727413

**status** Defence agency

**founded** 1996

**sponsor** Ministry of Defence (MOD)

**powers** Framework Document 1996

**mission** Ensuring that sufficient manpower is both available and deployed by the Royal Navy and Royal Marines in peace, crisis or war.

**tasks** Appointing sufficient suitable skilled and experienced manpower, both officers and ratings; collating manpower requirement and matching forecast strength to it; planning and developing individuals' careers; advising ministers and parliament.

**operations** Management: The Owner is Second Sea Lord and Commander-in-Chief Naval Home Command. He is responsible for strategic management, corporate and business plans. The Owner's Advisory Board advises him on strategy. The Chief Executive is responsible to the Owner. He is supported by a Management Board (seven Directors, two coopted Directors and one Non-Executive Director) which advises him on plans, budgets and performance.

Policy: Programme of redundancies finished.

Trends: Lack of manpower in some areas and this growing imbalance between strength and requirement continues to prove a problem.

**performance** Eight out of nine key targets met in 1996/97.

**board**

| | |
|---|---|
| Owner | Admiral Sir John Brigstoke |
| Naval Secretary & Chief Executive | Rear Admiral Fabian Malbon |
| Director Naval Officer Appointments | Cdre Chris Beagley |
| Naval Assistant | Cdre Bryan Burns CBE |
| Deputy Director Naval Manning (Development) | Captain RF Cheadle |
| Head of NMA Secretariat | Mrs Dorothy Cox |
| Director Naval Manning | Cdre Richard Hibbert |
| Non-Executive Director | Michael Hoffman |
| Secretary to the Naval Secretary | Commander RR Morris |
| Commodore Naval Drafting | Cdre RA Rowley OBE |
| Management Planner | Lieutenant Commander DE Shinn |
| Chief Staff Officer Personnel, HQRM | Colonel D Wilson OBE |
| *Accounting Officer* | *Chief Executive* |

**staff** 290 (30% civilian)

**financial**

| INCOME & EXPENDITURE | |
|---|---|
| Year end: 31 March | **1997** |
| | **£000** |
| **EXPENDITURE** | |
| Staff costs | 7,580 |
| Supplies and services consumed | 464 |
| Accommodation costs | 132 |
| Other administration costs | 1,322 |
| Interest on capital | 13 |
| Revaluation of fixed assets | 8 |
| Loss on disposal of fixed assets | (2) |
| | 9,517 |
| **INCOME** | - |
| **NET EXPENDITURE** | **9,517** |

# *Naval Recruiting & Training Agency (NRTA)*

HM Naval Base
Portsmouth
Hants PO1 3LS

**Tel** 01705 727716
**Fax** 01705 721613

| | |
|---|---|
| *status* | Defence agency |
| *founded* | 1995 |
| *sponsor* | Ministry of Defence (MOD) |
| *powers* | Framework Document 1995 |
| *mission* | To provide the world's best naval training. |
| *tasks* | To recruit the required number of new entrants and train them to meet the requirements of the Naval Service. To maintain the volunteer Naval Reserves. |
| *operations* | Management: The Chief Executive is the Flag Officer Training and Recruiting (FOTR) who is responsible for day-to-day management. The Secretary of State has ultimate responsibility for determining the policy and resources framework, but in practice these responsibilities are delegated to the Second Sea Lord and Commander-in-Chief Naval Home Command who is the Owner of the Agency. |
| *performance* | Met four out of ten targets in 1996/97 |
| *board* | Executive Management Board. |

| | |
|---|---|
| Chief Executive | Rear Admiral JHS McAnally |
| Chief of Staff/Director Naval Training | Cdre WHJ Kelly |
| Director Naval Recruiting | Brig SP Hill OBE |
| Director Naval Reserves | Capt NR Hodgson |
| Finance Director/Agency Secretary | P Hurst |
| Assistant Director Training Management | Capt CPR Montgomery |
| Assistant Director Plans & Procurement | Capt MJ Potter |
| Non-Executive Director | M Dodson |
| Owner's Representative | Cdre K Day |
| *Accounting Officer* | *Chief Executive* |

*staff*   5050 (3560 Service personnel)

*financial*

| EXPENDITURE | |
|---|---|
| **Year end: 31 March** | **1997** |
| | **£000** |
| **EXPENDITURE** | |
| Staff costs | 153,247 |
| Accommodation services | 18,028 |
| Estate maintenance | 24,181 |
| Supplies and services | 51,207 |
| Administration costs | 69,178 |
| Notional interest | 3,364 |
| | **319,205** |
| **INCOME** | **(3,419)** |
| **NET OPERATING COST** | **315,786** |

*publications*   *Corporate Plan, Annual Report*

# New Millennium Experience Company Ltd (NMEC)

110 Buckingham Palace Road
London SW1W 9SB

**Tel** 0171 808 8200          **E-mail** nmec@newmill.co.uk
**Fax** 0171 808 8222          **Web** http://www.mx2000.com.

**Contact** Jennie Page CBE (CEO)
Terence Gibbons (Press, Media and Parliamentary)

| | |
|---|---|
| **status** | Executive body |
| **founded** | 1997 |
| **sponsor** | Minister without Portfolio |
| **powers** | Financial Memorandum issued by the shareholder. Conditions of grant agreed between the Millennium Commission (MC) and NMEC. |
| **mission** | To create, build, and operate a national Millennium Experience - incorporating the Dome at Greenwich and The Challenge, a linked programme of events and activities throughout the UK - which inspires, entertains, educates and involves visitors and participants with no extra burden on the public purse. |
| **tasks** | To deliver a once-in-a-lifetime, high-quality experience and a country-wide challenge programme to time and to budget. To achieve at least 12 million visits to the Dome at Greenwich. To deliver value for money to the MC, sponsors and paying visitors. To optimise access, to involve, educate and entertain visitors and participants, and to make the best use of British and international creative talent and state-of-the-art technology. To create a world profile for the celebration of the millennium in the UK and leave a lasting legacy for the nation from the Experience. |
| **operations** | Management: Millennium Commission National Lottery funding was extended to December 2001 and responsibility for the exhibition was transferred to the public sector early in 1997. The Exhibition Company, MCL, was relaunched as NMEC in June 1997. The Owner is the Minister Without Portfolio. The Chairman/Chief Executive reports the Minister Without Portfolio. The overall cash budget is £758 million which NMEC expects to recover mainly from MC grant (using National Lottery funds), sponsorship and sales revenue. |
| **performance** | Project milestones set for 1997 were met. |
| **board** | Appointed by the Shareholder and CEO. |

| | |
|---|---|
| Chairman | Robert Ayling |
| Deputy Chairman | Sam Chisholm |
| Non-Executive Directors | Ian Ash |
| | Sir Alan Cockshaw |
| | Cllr Len Duvall |
| | Michael Grade CBE |
| | Sir Brian Jenkins |
| | Ruth MacKenzie OBE |
| | Sara Morrison |
| | David Quarmby |
| *Accounting Officer* | *Chief Executive* |

| | |
|---|---|
| **staff** | 70 |

| | |
|---|---|
| Chief Executive | Jennifer Page CBE |
| Finance & Corporate Services Director | Steve Brown |
| Chief Executive | Jennifer Page CBE |
| Finance & Corporate Services Director | Steve Brown |
| Implementation Director | Jeff Hawkins |
| Commercial Director | Kevin Johnson |
| Operations Director | Ken Robinson CBE |
| Production Director | Claire Sampson |
| Challenge Director | Joe Simpson |
| Site & Structures Director | David Trench |

**financial**

| INCOME & EXPENDITURE BUDGET for lifetime of project (1997/98 - 2001/02) | £m |
|---|---|
| **INCOME** | |
| Millennium Commission Grant (net) | 399 |
| Sponsorship | 150 |
| Commercial revenue (ticket sales, merchandising and licensing) | 194 |
| Disposal proceeds | 15 |
| | **758** |
| **EXPENDITURE** | |
| The Dome | |
| Construction & infrastructure | 260 |
| Exhibition & central attraction | 198 |
| Operations & running costs in year of operation | 95 |
| The Challenge | 54 |
| Central costs | |
| Marketing | 29 |
| Support services | 34 |
| Central Contingency | 88 |
| | **758** |

**advisers**    **Solicitors**         Norton Rose

**branches**    12 regional offices (to be announced)

# NHS Estates

1 Trevelyan Square
Boar Lane
Leeds LS1 6AE

**Tel** 0113 2547000
**Fax** 0113 2547299              **Web** http://www.open.gov.uk/doh/nhsest/hpage.htm

**status**        Executive agency

**founded**       1991

**sponsor**       Department of Health (DOH)

**powers**        Framework Document 1991

**mission**       To encourage effective, efficient and economical management of properties used for healthcare and to promote excellence of design, with value for money, in new buildings.

**tasks**         Core policy function is to advise ministers on the NHS Estates (worth £23 billion); trading activities are providing professional and technical advice in the fields of health estate, capital investment and project management; managing and disposing of the retained estate; publishing technical guidance and best practice (hard copy and electronic).

**operations**    Management: Chief Executive is responsible for direct management of regional teams and reports to the Secretary of State, who is assisted by the Ministerial Advisory Board. The Chief Executive is supported by Head of Policy, Directors of Consultancy & Business Development, and Resources. Fully recovers costs through fees and charges. Eight regional offices, HQ in Leeds.

Policy: There is considerable scope for more efficient use of land and property by healthcare managers. Developing new business opportunities.

Trends: Continuing to work towards eventual privatisation; advising Ministers function could revert to DOH.

**performance**   Achieved eight out of ten targets in 1996/97.

**board**         Ministerial Advisory Board appointed by the Secretary of State from senior members of the NHS and DOH.

| Chairman | Colin Reeves | |
|---|---|---|
| Members | WW Murray OBE | Martin Staniforth |
| | Prof Michael Schofield | Robert Tinston |
| *Accounting Officer* | *Chief Executive* | |

| *staff* | 180 | |
|---|---|---|
| | Chief Executive | Kate Priestley |
| | Acting Director of Consultancy & Business Development | Bob Horner |
| | Head of Policy | Marc Taylor |
| | Director of Resources | John Wardle |
| | Regional Office, North Thames | Pam Castro |
| | Regional Office, Northern & Yorkshire | Nigel Dorman |
| | Regional Office, South Thames | David Gubb |
| | Regional Office, West Midlands | Tom Hayes |
| | Regional Office, Anglia & Oxford | John Holmes |
| | Regional Office, North West | John Kemp |
| | Regional Office, Trent | Eric Liddell |
| | Regional Office, South West | John Orr |

*financial*

| INCOME & EXPENDITURE | | |
|---|---|---|
| Year end: 31 March | 1997 | 1996 |
| | £000 | £000 |
| INCOME | 9,436 | 9,098 |
| EXPENDITURE | | |
| Staff costs | 5,126 | 3,544 |
| Depreciation | 282 | 370 |
| Other operating costs | 3,832 | 4,090 |
| | 9,240 | 8,004 |
| OPERATING SURPLUS BEFORE INTEREST | 196 | 1,094 |
| Notional interest on capital employed | 57 | 33 |
| SURPLUS FOR THE FINANCIAL YEAR | 139 | 1,061 |

| *advisers* | **Bankers** | National Westminster Bank | Boar Lane Branch, 29 Boar Lane Leeds LS1 6DZ |
|---|---|---|---|
| | **Auditors** | National Audit Office | 157-197 Buckingham Palace Road |
| | **Solicitors** | Department of Health Solicitors | Carey Street, London WC2A 2LS |

# NHS Pensions Agency (NHSPA)

200-220 Broadway
Fleetwood
Lancs FY7 8LG

**Tel** 01253 774774

| *status* | Executive agency |
|---|---|
| *founded* | 1992 |
| *sponsor* | Department of Health (DOH) |
| *powers* | NHSPA Framework Document 1992 |
| *mission* | Administers the NHS Occupational Pension Scheme. Also provides information and advice on NHS pension matters. |
| *tasks* | Administers the NHS Pension Scheme, NHS Injury Benefits Scheme and NHS Compensation Scheme for early retirement. Each scheme is separately accounted for by the DOH. Secures the prompt and accurate collection and payment of sums due under the scheme. Calculates new pensions and benefits. |
| *operations* | Management: Chief Executive is responsible to the Secretary of State, who receives independent advice from the ministerial Advisory Board. Eleven client centres. Largest occupational pension scheme in Western Europe. |
| | Policy: Payment of pensions contracted out to private sector (Paymaster Ltd). |
| | Trends: Pensions mis-selling causing a lot of extra work as members are being reinstated onto the scheme. |
| *performance* | Great improvement in 1996/97 over previous year. |
| *board* | Ministerial Advisory Board appointed by Secretary of State. |

| Chairman | Mike Deegan | |
|---|---|---|
| Members | Neil Chapman | |
| | David Jordison | RCN Coombs |
| | George O'Brien | Alec Cowan |
| | Stephen Redmond | Robin Heron |
| | Adrian McNeil | Neil Paterson |
| | Jonathan Stopes-Roe | Ray Szynowski |
| *Accounting Officer* | *Chief Executive* | |

**staff** 372

| Chief Executive | AF Cowan |
|---|---|

**financial**

| INCOME & EXPENDITURE | | |
|---|---|---|
| **Year end: 31 March** | **1997** | **1996** |
| | **£000** | **£000** |
| **EXPENDITURE** | | |
| Staff costs | 6,660 | 7,239 |
| Depreciation and amounts written-off tangible fixed assets | 587 | 341 |
| Other costs | 7,964 | 7,022 |
| Services from other government agencies | 4,340 | 5,568 |
| **LESS: INCOME FROM OPERATIONS** | (183) | - |
| **NET OPERATING EXPENDITURE BEFORE INTEREST** | **19,368** | **20,170** |
| Interest on capital employed | 78 | 82 |
| **NET EXPENDITURE FOR THE YEAR** | **19,446** | **20,252** |

**advisers**    **Auditors**      National Audit Office      157-197 Buckingham Palace Road
London SW1W 9SP

# North of Scotland Water Authority

Cairngorm House
Beechwood Park North
Inverness IV2 3ED

**Tel** 01463 245400
**Fax** 01463 240489

| | |
|---|---|
| **status** | Public corporation |
| **founded** | 1995 |
| **sponsor** | Scottish Office |
| **powers** | Local Government etc (Scotland) Act 1994 |
| **mission** | To provide high-quality water and waste-water services for Grampian, Highland, Tayside, Western Isles, Orkney and Shetland Islands. |
| **tasks** | Maintains and manages water mains, sewers, water and waste water treatment. Maintains water quality standards while respecting and preserving the environment. |
| **operations** | Management: Board reports to the Secretary of State. The Authority structures its operations on a regional basis, with locally delivered services. Financial objective to set charges at actual cost of services. |
| | Policy: PFI contract for two new waste-water treatment facilities. |
| | Trends: Massive capital investment is required to meet UK and EU legislation. |
| **performance** | Quality standards (1996/97). In 1996 just over 62,000 water samples were tested for microbiological compliance, achieving a compliance rate of 98.5% against the faecal coliform standard, a 0.3% rise in compliance compared with 1995. |
| **board** | Appointed by the Secretary of State for Scotland; five are local councillors, including Chairman. |

# Q&Q

| | | |
|---|---|---|
| Chairman | Cllr Colin Rennie | |
| Chief Executive | Alastair Findlay | |
| Members | Cllr Raymond Bisset | Nicolas McAndrew |
| | Cllr Joan Easten | Alasdair MacCallum |
| | Cllr Nigel Graham | Cllr Olwyn Macdonald |
| | Nigel Hawkins | Cllr Donald Nicholson |
| | Andrew Lewis | David Paton OBE |
| *Accounting Officer* | *Chief Executive* | |

**staff** 1947

| | |
|---|---|
| Managing Director - Water Services | JMT Cockburn |
| Managing Director - Finance | GWD Sutherland |
| Director of Personnel | Miss VAS Jack |
| Director of Capital Investment | JMC Johnstone |
| Director of Corporate Affairs | AG Smith |
| Director of Operations (Grampion & Tayside) | Tom Stuart |

**financial**

| INCOME & EXPENDITURE Year end: 31 March | 1997 £000 |
|---|---|
| TURNOVER | 120,203 |
| OPERATING COSTS | |
| Manpower costs | 42,828 |
| Materials and consumables | 5,546 |
| Other operational costs | 42,554 |
| Depreciation | 10,736 |
| Amortisation of grants and contributions | (227) |
| Infrastructure maintenance charge | 7,679 |
| Own work capitalised | (9,376) |
| | 99,740 |
| OPERATING SURPLUS | 20,463 |
| Surplus on disposal of fixed assets | 129 |
| SURPLUS BEFORE INTEREST | 20,592 |
| Interest receivable | 711 |
| Interest payable | (29,127) |
| Refinancing costs | (20,106) |
| DEFICIT BEFORE TAXATION | (27,930) |
| Taxation | 38 |
| DEFICIT FOR YEAR | (27,892) |

**advisers**

**Bankers** Bank of Scotland — 9 High Street, Inverness IV1 1JB

**Auditors** Price Waterhouse — 58 Albany Street, Edinburgh EH1 3QR

**publications** Annual Report and Accounts 1996/97, Annual Water Quality Report, 1996, The Way Forward Code of Practise for Customers, 1998

**branches** Regional/ Islands Offices in Aberdeen, Dundee, Inverness, Kirkwall, Lerwick and Stornway.

# Northern Ireland Child Support Agency (NI CSA)

Great Northern Tower
17 Great Victoria Street
Belfast BT2 7AD

**Tel** 01232 896666
**Fax** 01232 896850

**E-mail** CSA@nics.gov.uk
**Web** http://www.nics.gov.uk/csa/index.htm

**Contact** Doros Michail

**status** Executive agency

**founded** 1993

**sponsor** Northern Ireland Office, Department of Health and Social Services

**powers** Child Support (NI) Order 1991 and Child Support (NI) Order 1995

| | |
|---|---|
| *mission* | To arrange or collect the appropriate child support maintenance on behalf of children whose parents live apart. |
| *tasks* | To assess, collect and, when required, enforce child maintenance payments made under the two Child Support (NI) Orders. |
| *operations* | Management: The Chief Executive and his Management Team make up the Agency Board and have overall responsibility for the Agency. 819 of the staff supply a service under contract to the GB Agency, entirely funded by the GB Agency and so excluded from the NI CSA accounts. There are seven area offices located in Social Security Offices in Antrim, Londonderry, Newry and Omagh and in Belfast in Corporation Street, Falls Road, and Holywood Road. |
| | Policy: To improve the quality of services to new and existing clients while securing even greater efficiencies. |
| | Trends: Starting in 1998/99 funding will be linked to service level agreements which will set out the products staff will deliver. Funding will be based on an agreed price for specific outputs and made on a repayment basis. |
| *board* | Members of the Agency Management Board are all NI civil servants and are appointed by the Minister. |

| | |
|---|---|
| Chief Executive | Pat Devlin |
| Director of Northern Ireland Operations | John Canavan |
| Personnel Officer | Maureen Cullen |
| Director of Resources | David Elwood |
| EBU Manager | John Johnston |
| Director of Quality & Client Services & Business Development | Doros Michail |

| | |
|---|---|
| *staff* | 1155 staff, most of whom are located at the Headquarters and Regional Centre in Belfast; 51 are based in area offices. |

*financial*

| INCOME & EXPENDITURE | | | |
|---|---|---|---|
| Year end: 31 March | 1997 | 1996 | 1995 |
| | £000 | £000 | £000 |
| INCOME | (7) | (27) | 182 |
| EXPENDITURE | | | |
| Staff costs | 4,765 | 3,842 | 3,507 |
| Depreciation | 270 | 313 | 284 |
| Other operating costs | 3,325 | 2,884 | 2,275 |
| | 8,360 | 7,039 | 6,066 |
| NET COST OF OPERATIONS | (8,367) | (7,066) | (5,884) |
| Interest on Capital Employed | 174 | 200 | 193 |
| NET COST OF OPERATIONS | (8,541) | (7,266) | (6,077) |

| | | | |
|---|---|---|---|
| *advisers* | **Auditors** | Northern Ireland Audit Office | 106 University Street,Belfast BT7 1EU |
| | **Solicitors** | Departmental Solicitors | Victoria Halls, May Street,Belfast BT1 4NL |
| | **Public Relations** | DHSS Information Office | Upper Newtownards Road,Belfast BT4 3SF |

| | |
|---|---|
| *publications* | Annual Report 96/97, Business Plan 97/98, Strategic Plan 97-2000 |

# Northern Ireland Commissioner for Protection Against Unlawful Industrial Action

Scottish Legal House
65-67 Chichester Street
Belfast BT1 4JT

**Tel** 01232 233640
**Fax** 01232 237787

**Contact** Debbie Reid

| | |
|---|---|
| *status* | Executive body |
| *founded* | 1995 |
| *sponsor* | Northern Ireland Office, Department of Economic Development (DEDNI) |
| *powers* | Trade Union and Labour Relations (NI) Order 1995 |

| | |
|---|---|
| **mission** | To help individuals take legal action against a trade union which has organised unlawful industrial action. |
| **tasks** | To assist in certain legal proceedings, generally where unlawful industrial action leads to individuals being deprived of goods or services. To pay for legal advice and representation where appropriate. To add the Commissioner's name to legal proceedings although not a party to them. |
| **operations** | Management: Although located in the same office as the NI Commissioner for the Rights of Trade Union Members and having staffing in common, the two organisations are completely separate entities. |
| | Policy: To raise awareness of the assistance available. |
| | Trends: 1995/96, the first year of operations, there were no enquiries. |
| **performance** | Targets not set. |
| **board** | None |

| Accounting Officer | The Commissioner |
|---|---|

**staff**  One

| Commissioner | Mrs Margaret-Ann Dinsmore |
|---|---|

**financial**

| RECEIPTS & PAYMENTS Year end: 31 March | 1997 £ | 1996 £ |
|---|---|---|
| RECEIPTS | | |
| Grant received | 15,000 | 12,000 |
| | 15,000 | 12,000 |
| PAYMENTS | | |
| Salaries & wages etc | 4,218 | 2,047 |
| Other operating costs | 10,703 | 9,727 |
| | 14,921 | 11,774 |
| SURPLUS FROM OPERATIONS | 79 | 226 |
| Other payments | - | 57 |
| EXCESS OF RECEIPTS OVER PAYMENTS | 79 | 169 |

| | | | |
|---|---|---|---|
| **advisers** | **Bankers** | Northern Bank | Donegall Square North, Belfast BT1 5GJ |
| | **Auditors** | Northern Ireland Audit Office | 106 University Street,Belfast BT7 1EU |
| **publications** | A Guide for Trade Union Members | | |

# Northern Ireland Commissioner for the Rights of Trade Union Members

Scottish Legal House
65-67 Chichester Street
Belfast BT1 4JT

**Tel** 01232 233640
**Fax** 01232 237787

**Contact** Debbie Reid

| | |
|---|---|
| **status** | Executive body |
| **founded** | 1992 |
| **sponsor** | Northern Ireland Office, Department of Economic Development (DEDNI) |
| **powers** | Industrial Relations (NI) Order 1992. Trade Union and Labour Relations (NI) Order 1995 |
| **mission** | To help individual members of trade unions take legal action in NI to protect their rights against a union. |
| **tasks** | To consider and where appropriate assist trade union members contemplating or taking legal action against their union. Likewise to assist a member where the union breeches its own rulebook. To ensure that applicants are not placed at a disadvantage by lack of ability to pay for legal advice. To supply public information about the Commissioner's operations. |

| operations | Management: The Commissioner cannot be directed by a minister or anyone else to assist or not assist any particular application. Assistance can be provided where the union's main office is in NI and also where, in certain circumstances, it based outside NI. |
|---|---|
| | Policy: To raise awareness of the assistance available. |
| | Trends: In 1995/96, 17 enquiries were made. |
| **performance** | Targets not set. |
| **board** | None |

| Accounting Officer | The Commissioner |
|---|---|

| staff | One |
|---|---|

| Commissioner | Mrs Margaret-Ann Dinsmore |
|---|---|

**financial**

**RECEIPTS & PAYMENTS**

| Year end: 31 March | 1997 | 1996 | 1995 |
|---|---|---|---|
| | £ | £ | £ |
| **RECEIPTS** | | | |
| Grant received | 26,000 | 38,000 | 40,000 |
| | 26,000 | 38,000 | 40,000 |
| **PAYMENTS** | | | |
| Salaries & wages etc | 7,167 | 6,956 | 6,838 |
| Other operating costs | 18,134 | 30,827 | 31,535 |
| | 25,301 | 37,783 | 38,373 |
| **SURPLUS FROM OPERATIONS** | **699** | **217** | **1,627** |
| Other payments | - | 95 | 1,300 |
| **EXCESS OF RECEIPTS OVER PAYMENTS** | **699** | **122** | **327** |

| advisers | **Bankers** | Northern Bank | Donegall Square North, Belfast BT1 5GJ |
|---|---|---|---|
| | **Auditors** | Northern Ireland Audit Office | 106 University Street, Belfast BT7 1EU |
| **publications** | *A Guide for Trade Union Members* | | |

# Northern Ireland Council for the Curriculum, Examinations & Assessment (NICCEA)

Clarendon Dock
29 Clarendon Road
Belfast BT1 3BG

**Tel** 01232 261200
**Fax** 01232 261234

**E-mail** info@cea.org.uk
**Web** http://www.ccea.org.uk

| status | Executive body |
|---|---|
| **founded** | 1994 |
| **sponsor** | Northern Ireland Office, Department of Education NI (DENI) |
| **powers** | Education and Libraries (NI) order 1993. |
| **mission** | To work in partnership to provide the best possible opportunities for children and young people to reach their potential through learning. |
| **tasks** | To keep all aspects of the curriculum, examinations and assessment under review; publish and disseminate curriculum, examinations and assessment materials; conduct and award certificates for examinations; ensure that standards of the relevant examinations and assessments are recognised and maintained; develop, conduct and mark the transfer tests; develop and produce teaching support materials; advise DENI; develop educational technology and produce multimedia resources. |
| **operations** | Management: Chief Executive is responsible for day-to-day management and reports to the Council. |
| | Policy: Works closely with other partners in the education service. |
| **board** | Council appointed by the Secretary of State. |

| Chairman | Dr Alan Lennon |
|---|---|
| *Accounting Officer* | *Chief Executive* |

**staff** 249

| Chief Executive | Mrs Catherine Coxhead |
|---|---|

**publications** *Annual Report*

# Northern Ireland Council for Postgraduate Medical & Dental Education

5 Annadale Avenue
Belfast BT7 3JH

**Tel** 01232 491731
**Fax** 01232 642279

**status**      Executive body

**founded**      1970 (as Northern Ireland Council for Postgraduate Medical Education). 1994 reconstituted (under present name)

**sponsor**      Northern Ireland Office, Department of Health and Social Services

**powers**      Ministries of Northern Ireland Act 1921, 1974

**mission**      To facilitate the provision of high-quality postgraduate and continuing medical and dental education within Northern Ireland enabling healthcare to be provided which compares favourably with the best of the UK.

**tasks**      Purchase, provide and accredit training. Provision of training by entering into block training contracts with the HSS Trusts. Implementation of Calman training. Regional budgets.

**operations**      Management: Executive Committee is responsible for operational decision-making and taking forward policy initiatives adopted by Council. Subcommittees on Education, Finance, Audit and Remuneration. The Chief Executive/Postgraduate Dean is appointed for Council and is assisted by the Postgraduate Dental Dean, the Director for Postgraduate General Practice Education, Postgraduate Clinical Tutors, Specialty Advisers and the members of specialty training committees.

**board**      Chairman and Vice-Chairman and four other members appointed by the NI Department of Health and Social Services. Four members *ex officio* and up to 25 additional members appointed by the Chairman, who are nominated by relevant bodies to represent a consortium of professional, statutory and academic interests in the medical and dental professions in Northern Ireland.

| | *Appointed by DHSS* | |
|---|---|---|
| Chairman | Prof AHG Love | |
| Vice-Chairman | Dr DAJ Keegan | |
| Members | Dr C Bharucha | *Nominated by NHSSB* |
| | DH Campbell | Dr J Watson |
| | WJN Collins | *Nominated by SHSSB* |
| | Miss MEA Hanna | Dr PC Loughran |
| | Dr J Howe | *Nominated by EHSSB* |
| | Dr O Quigley | Dr C Beattie |
| | *Dean, Medical Faculty, QUB* | *Nominated by WHSSB* |
| | Prof RW Stout | Dr PB Devlin |
| | *Nominated by Medical Faculty, QUB* | *Nominated by Royal College of Physicians (London)* |
| | Prof RJ McClelland | Dr ME Callender |
| | Prof PM Reilly | *Nominated by Royal College of Surgeons* |
| | *Nominated by NI Faculty of RCGPs* | JW Calderwood |
| | Dr C Kenny | *Nominated by Royal College of Pathologists* |
| | Dr A Little | Prof ER Trimble |
| | *Director, Dentistry, QUB* | *Nominated by Royal College of Psychiatrists* |
| | Prof IC Benington | Dr D Patterson |
| | *Nominated by Dental Co-ordinating Committee* | *Nominated by Royal College of Radiologists* |
| | | Dr HK Wilson |
| | JH Gilleece | *Nominated by Royal College of O&G* |
| | Miss M McCabe | Dr H Lamki |

|  |  |  |
|---|---|---|
| | Nominated by Royal College of Anaesthetists | |
| | Dr IW Carson | |
| | Nominated by Faculty of PHM | Nominated by General Medical Services Committee |
| | Dr F Kee | Dr DO Todd |
| | Nominated by Royal College of Physicians (London) Paediatric Division | Nominated by NI Consultants & Specialists Committee |
| | Dr JG Jenkins | Dr JM Dunlop |
| | Nominated by BMA (NI) | Nominated by Hospital Junior Staff Committee (NI) |
| | Dr JAF Beirne | Dr EGJ O'Neill |
| Accounting Officer | Chief Executive/Postgraduate Dean | |

**staff**    45

| | |
|---|---|
| Chief Executive/Postgraduate Dean | Dr JR McCluggage |
| Administrative Director | Ms M Roberts |
| Financial Manager | T Hutchinson |
| Training Coordinator | Ms R Campbell |
| Postgraduate Dental Dean | IDF Saunders |
| Adviser in GDP | K Alexander |
| Adviser in GDP (CE) | J Farmer |
| Associate Adviser in GDP (VT) | DEB Mark |
| Associate Adviser GDP (CE) | Mrs U McKeogh |
| Director of Postgraduate General Practice Education | Dr A McKnight |
| Associate Adviser in Postgraduate General Practice Education | Dr M Crawford |
| Associate Adviser in Postgraduate General Practice Education | Dr T Bradley |
| Associate Adviser in Postgraduate General Practice Education | Dr D Gibson |

**financial**

**REVENUE INCOME & EXPENDITURE**

| Year end: 31 March | 1997 | 1996 |
|---|---|---|
| | £ | £ |
| **INCOME** | | |
| Cash advances from DHSS | 15,038,000 | 14,112,529 |
| Income from other sources | 171,343 | 136,821 |
| | **15,209,343** | **14,249,350** |
| **EXPENDITURE** | | |
| Junior doctors salaries | 12,909,383 | 12,191,332 |
| Education costs | 761,672 | 742,069 |
| Salaries & wages | 857,892 | 705,610 |
| Lecture fees | 151,217 | 130,339 |
| Supernumerary scheme | 124,274 | 201,769 |
| Doctors Retainer scheme | 9,864 | 12,938 |
| Clinical audit | 25,000 | 40,000 |
| Interview panels | 90,603 | - |
| Residentials & conferences | 30,862 | 22,593 |
| Travel & subsistence | 74,735 | 62,614 |
| Locum fees | 12,910 | 11,245 |
| Operational costs | 157,790 | 85,621 |
| Equipment | - | 41,406 |
| | **15,206,202** | **14,247,536** |
| **EXCESS OF INCOME OVER EXPENDITURE** | **3,141** | **1,814** |

**CAPITAL INCOME & EXPENDITURE**

| Year end: 31 March | 1997 |
|---|---|
| | £ |
| **INCOME** | |
| Capital advances from DHSS | 147,000 |
| Other Income | - |
| | **147,000** |
| **EXPENDITURE** | |
| Payments to acquire tangible fixed assets | 138,505 |
| | **138,505** |
| **EXCESS OF INCOME OVER EXPENDITURE** | **8,495** |

**publications**    *Annual Report*

# Northern Ireland Fishery Harbour Authority

3 St Patrick's Avenue
Downpatrick
Co Down BT30 6DW

**Tel** 01396 613844

| | |
|---|---|
| *status* | Executive body |
| *founded* | 1973 |
| *sponsor* | Northern Ireland Office, Department of Agriculture NI (DANI) |
| *powers* | Northern Ireland Fishery Harbour Authority Order (NI) 1973 |
| *tasks* | To improve, manage and maintain the harbours of Ardglass, Kilkeel and Portavogie and to operate facilities provided at the harbours. |
| *operations* | Policy: To improve the entrance to Kilkeel harbour. New fishing centre being constructed at Kilkeel and plans to improve the entrance to the harbour. |
| | Trends: Increased tonnage of fish being landed. |
| *performance* | No targets set. |
| *board* | Appointed by the Secretary of State on three-year terms. |

| Chairperson | RT Ferris |
|---|---|
| Deputy Chairperson | AM Cunningham |
| Members | M Andrews |
| | R Coulter |
| | RG Doyle |
| | D Harding |
| | J Mawhinney |
| | WG Smyth |
| *Accounting Officer* | *Chief Executive* |

*staff* 21

| Chief Executive/Secretary | CM Warnock |
|---|---|

*financial*

**REVENUE**

| Year end: 31 March | 1997 | 1996 |
|---|---|---|
| | £ | £ |
| **INCOME** | | |
| Operating income | 1,165,860 | 937,099 |
| **OPERATING EXPENSES** | | |
| Staff costs | (307,646) | (297,832) |
| Depreciation | (446,752) | (320,610) |
| Other operating charges | (346,242) | (292,252) |
| **OPERATING SURPLUS** | **65,220** | **26,405** |
| Interest payable | (35,731) | (26,469) |
| **SURPLUS/(DEFICIT) BEFORE TAXATION** | **29,489** | **(64)** |
| Taxation | 7,300 | (3,571) |
| **SURPLUS/(DEFICIT) BEFORE NOTIONAL COSTS** | **36,789** | **(3,635)** |
| Notional cost of capital | (658,232) | (643,650) |
| **DEFICIT AFTER NOTIONAL COST OF CAPITAL** | **(621,443)** | **(647,285)** |
| Reversal of notional cost of capital | 658,232 | 643,650 |
| **RESTATED SURPLUS/ (DEFICIT)** | **36,789** | **(3,635)** |

| *advisers* | **Bankers** | First Trust Bank |
|---|---|---|
| | **Auditors** | Price Waterhouse |
| | **Solicitors** | L'Estrange and Brett |
| *publications* | *Annual Report* | |

# Northern Ireland Local Government Officers' Superannuation Committee (NILGOSC)

Templeton House
411 Holywood Road
Belfast BT4 2LP

**Tel** 01232 768025          **E-mail** 100670.733@compuserve.com
**Fax** 01232 768790

| | |
|---|---|
| *status* | Executive body |
| *founded* | 1950 |
| *sponsor* | Northern Ireland Office, Department of the Environment for NI (DOENI) |
| *powers* | Local Government (Superannuation) Regulations (NI) 1992 |
| *mission* | To administer a statutory pension scheme for the 26 local authorities and 137 other admitted bodies in Northern Ireland. |
| *tasks* | Maintain a fund for the payment of current and prospective benefits to members of the scheme. Administer membership events from joining until leaving the scheme. Administer and calculate leavers' benefits. |
| *operations* | Management: The fund is managed by two external Fund Managers and the property portfolio is managed in-house by a property adviser. All report to the Committee. |
| | Policy: To attain the maximum return on fund investments having due regard to the liabilities of the fund and an acceptable level of investment risks. |
| *performance* | The total return, including property, for the year to 31 March 1997 was 9.1% against CAPS median of 11.1%. Over three years to 31 March 1997 the total return was 11.7% against CAPS median of 11.1%. |
| *board* | The Committee is appointed by DOENI and is representative of employee and employer organisations (eight from each). |

| | | |
|---|---|---|
| Chairman | Frank Ledwidge OBE | |
| Deputy Chairperson | Mrs Elizabeth May | |
| Members | Cllr Mary Bradley | |
| | Ken Brown | Gordon Manly |
| | Mrs Marion Cassidy | Eric A McKinley |
| | Brian Delaney | John Miskelly MBE |
| | Fergus E Donnelly | Ald Tom D Robinson JP |
| | Mrs Deirdre Hanna | Trevor Salmon |
| | James Hanna | Mrs Carol Shields |
| | Mrs Linda Leonard | Mrs Maureen Taggart |
| Secretary | R W Nesbitt | |
| *Accounting Officer* | *Secretary* | |

*staff*          25

*financial*

**FUND**

| Year end: 31 March | 1997 | 1996 | 1995 |
|---|---|---|---|
| | £000 | £000 | £000 |
| **CONTRIBUTIONS AND BENEFITS** | | | |
| Contriibutions receivable | 31,879 | 29,759 | 28,993 |
| Transfers in | 3,500 | 2,745 | 3,123 |
| | 35,379 | 32,504 | 32,116 |
| Benefits payable | 48,351 | 43,855 | 40,413 |
| Leavers | 1,777 | 1,714 | 1,567 |
| Administration expenses | 933 | 927 | 896 |
| | 51,061 | 46,496 | 42,876 |
| **NET ADDITIONS (WITHDRAWALS) FROM DEALINGS WITH MEMBERS** | (15,682) | (13,992) | (10,760) |
| **RETURN ON INVESTMENTS** | | | |
| Investment income | 68,282 | 61,968 | 51,775 |
| Change in market value of investments | 80,292 | 259,722 | (19,762) |
| Investment management expenses | (1,901) | (1,759) | (1,399) |
| **NET RETURN ON INVESTMENTS** | 146,673 | 319,931 | 30,614 |
| **NET INCREASE IN THE FUND DURING THE YEAR** | 130,991 | 305,939 | 19,854 |
| **NET ASSETS OF THE SCHEME AT YEAR END** | 1,781,397 | 1,650,406 | 1,344,467 |

| advisers | Bankers | Northern Bank |
|---|---|---|
| | Auditors | Local Government Auditor |
| | Solicitors | Tughan & Co |
| | | Johns Elliot |

# Northern Ireland Museums' Council (NIMC)

66 Donegall Pass
Belfast BT7 1BU

**Tel** 01232 550215
**Fax** 01232 550216

| | |
|---|---|
| status | Executive body |
| founded | 1993 |
| sponsor | Northern Ireland Office, Department of Education NI (DENI) |
| powers | Established by the order of the Minister for Education NI. |
| mission | To support museums in Northern Ireland in maintaining and improving their standards of collections care and service to the public and to promote a coherent framework of museum provision. |
| tasks | Provides grant-in-aid, advice and information, and training to local museums. Ensures maintenance of Museums and Galleries Commission Registration Scheme in NI. |
| operations | Management: NIMC is a private company limited by guarantee and a recognised charity managed by a Board of Directors. Also a membership organisation, with 49 members. Director runs day-to-day management. |
| | Policy: Increase growth of membership. |
| | Trends: By 1999, museums will have to work to Collections Management Plans and grant-in-aid for collections care projects will only be available to those operating within the framework. |
| performance | Exceeded almost all targets set. |
| board | Appointed by Secretary of State. |

| Chairman | Lord O'Neill TD | |
|---|---|---|
| Members of Board | Mrs Joanna McVey | |
| | Cllr Owen Adams | John Gilmour |
| | Cllr Mrs Annie Courtney | Dr Jonathon Bell |
| | Philip Wilson | Marshall McKee |
| | Brian Lacey | Dr Brian Walker |
| | Mrs Helen Lanigan Wood MBE | Robert Rowe |
| | Dr Brian Turner | Rt Hon Roy Bradford |
| Observers | Timothy Mason | Patrick Higgins |
| | Mrs Marie Brown | Mrs Lynda Lister |
| Accounting Officer | Director | |

**staff** 3

| Director & Company Secretary | Aidan Walsh |
|---|---|
| Development Officer | Elizabeth Ritchie |

**financial**

| INCOME & EXPENDITURE Year end: 31 March | 1997 £ | 1996 £ | 1995 £ |
|---|---|---|---|
| GROSS INCOME | 174,333 | 174,380 | 131,533 |
| EXPENDITURE | | | |
| Operating expenses | 79,254 | 91,442 | 49,400 |
| Administration expenses | 97,728 | 77,250 | 57,765 |
| | (176,982) | (168,692) | (107,165) |
| (DEFICIT)/SURPLUS FOR THE YEAR | (2,649) | 5,688 | 24,368 |
| Notional credit cost of capital | 1,777 | - | - |
| (DEFICIT)/SURPLUS TRANSFERRED TO RESERVES | (872) | 5,688 | 24,368 |

| advisers | Auditors | McClure Watters | 14-16 James Street, Belfast BT2 7GA |
|---|---|---|---|

# Northern Ireland Prison Service

Dundonald House
Upper Newtownards Road
Belfast BT4 3SU

**Tel** 01232 520700
**Fax** 01232 525160

**Contact** Alan Shannon

| | |
|---|---|
| *status* | Executive agency |
| *sponsor* | Northern Ireland Office |
| *powers* | Prisons Act (Northern Ireland) 1953. Young Offenders Centres Rules (Northern Ireland) 1995 made under that Act. |
| *mission* | To protect the community through holding securely those committed to its charge; to contribute to peace and stability in Northern Ireland by ensuring prisoners are offered opportunities to develop their physical and mental well-being and are prepared for their release. |
| *tasks* | To keep in custody, with a degree of security and control by staff appropriate to each individual, persons committed to custody by the courts and to produce or release them as required; to provide all prisoners with the necessities of life including accommodation, food, exercise, healthcare, and the freedom to practise their religion; and to provide the opportunity to engage in constructive activities, eg work, education, training, hobbies and sport, to fill at least the working day; to enable prisoners to retain links with their families and to assist sentenced prisoners in their preparation for release into the community; to treat prisoners as individuals regardless of their religious beliefs or political opinions; and to offer them the opportunity to serve their sentences free from paramilitary influence; to manage the resources economically and efficiently and, in particular, to enhance the morale and abilities of staff by providing the appropriate conditions of service, management structures and training. |
| *operations* | Management: Headquarters in Belfast. There are three prisons (HMP Maghaberry, HMP Magilligan, and HMP Maze) and two young offenders centres, Maghaberry (female) and Hydebank Wood. By agreement, Her Majesty's Chief Inspector of Prisons carries out inspections in NI prisons. The NI Prison Service faces challenges very different from the rest of the UK including: the need to contain over 500 paramilitary prisoners in one prison; the challenge posed to security and control by segregated living conditions; the risks to prison staff living within the community; and the close relationship between the climate inside prisons and in the wider community. The average cost of keeping a prisoner in Northern Ireland is more than three times that of Great Britain. |
| | Policy: The Prison Service recognises that costs are too high and need to be reduced and that manpower costs, which account for over 80% of total expenditure, are where there is most potential for making savings. |
| | Trends: The prison population fell for the third year in succession in 1996/97; the number of short-term prisoners received (five years maximum) increased while life-sentence and long-term prisoners decreased. Efficiency measures now being introduced include civilianisation, the manpower review, the competing for quality initiative and contracts with establishments. |
| *performance* | Of the eight main targets, four were met in full and two were not met. The outcome was an improvement over 1995/96 and two targets related to the expansion of prisoners' activities which were constrained by lack of money. |
| *board* | |

| Chief Executive | Alan Shannon |
|---|---|

# Northern Ireland Statistics & Research Agency (NISRA)

The Arches Centre
11-13 Bloomfield Avenue
Belfast BT5 5HD

**Tel** 01232 520400
**Fax** 01232 526948

**E-mail** Pauline.Wilson@dfpni.gov.uk
**Web** http://www.nics.gov.uk/nisra/index.htm

**Contact** Edgar Jardine

| | |
|---|---|
| *status* | Executive agency |
| *founded* | 1996 |
| *sponsor* | Northern Ireland Office, Department of Finance and Personnel |
| *powers* | Framework document 1996 |
| *mission* | To provide statistical, research and registration services for the Northern Ireland government and to disseminate reliable official statistics to parliament and the wider community. To administer the marriage laws and to provide a reliable system for the civil registration of births, marriages, adoptions and deaths in Northern Ireland. |
| *tasks* | To support the Secretary of State as the government's principal advisory body on statistics and social research; to provide and coordinate professional statistics and research services and advise government departments; to collect, analyse and make available official statistics which describe Northern Ireland society, its economy, population and public services; to provide high-quality demographic information; to support the development of interdepartmental social policies; to ensure the quality standards of government statistics and research; to undertake the work of the General Register Office and to run the Census of Population. |
| *operations* | Management: The Chief Executive reports directly to the Minister and is a member of the Department's Planning Group. NISRA is managed by a Management Executive, comprising the Chief Executive and two senior statisticians (including the Registrar General for NI), and a Management Board, chaired by the Chief Executive comprising the 19 heads of individual NISRA branches. Staff are either in direct line management to the Chief Executive (all administrative staff plus some professionals) or on long-term secondment to a NI government department, agency or NDPB (the great majority of professionals) where the Chief Executive is responsible for their deployment and career development. A successful overseas consultancy service is provided by staff seconded to Northern Ireland Public Service Enterprises Ltd. During 1996/97 a drug abuse research programme was initiated and a base-line study for the special Peace and Reconciliation programme was completed; preparation for the 2001 census of population continued and detailed planning of the 1997 Census Test successfully completed. The NI Registration Software System, which computerised the registration of births and deaths in 26 district councils was introduced. |
| | Policy: To make increasing use of developments in IT, in particular using CD-Rom and information superhighways. |
| | Trends: Demand for information and data is expanding across a range of users including government, business, academia and the public. The government's commitment to service improvement, openness and policy review impact significantly on demand for the whole range of NISRA work. |
| *performance* | Met six key targets set by the Minister which applied to the 1996/97 financial year. |
| *board* | Management Executive supported by the Management Board comprising 19 heads of branches. |

| Accounting Officer | Chief Executive |
|---|---|

| | |
|---|---|
| *staff* | 198, all civil servants. Professional staff 109, administrative 89. Also a NISRA fee-paid survey fieldforce of 150. |

| Chief Executive | EF Jardine |
|---|---|

**financial**

| RECEIPTS & PAYMENTS | |
| --- | --- |
| Year end: 31 March | **1997** |
| | £ |
| **PAYMENTS** | |
| Salaries and wages | 2,427,842 |
| **Operating Payments** | |
| Agency charges | 1,160,692 |
| Research (non-DRC) | 1,254,433 |
| Surveys (non-DRC) | 795,208 |
| Surveys (DRC) | 203,617 |
| Computer charges | 113,593 |
| Printing & reprographics | 78,688 |
| General administration | 219,177 |
| | **3,825,408** |
| Capital expenditure | 254,010 |
| | **6,507,260** |
| **RECEIPTS** | |
| Operating receipts | (1,693,889) |
| **OPERATING DEFICIT** | **4,813,371** |

**publications**   *Focus on Northern Ireland 1997, Northern Ireland Annual Abstract of Statistics 1997, Annual Report of the Registrar General 1996*

# Northern Ireland Tourist Board (NITB)

St Anne's Court
59 North Street
Belfast BT1 1NB

**Tel** 01232 231221
**Fax** 01232 240960

**status**   Executive body

**founded**   1948

**sponsor**   Northern Ireland Office, Department of Economic Development NI (DEDNI)

**powers**   Tourism (Northern Ireland) Order 1992

**mission**   To encourage tourism and the provision of good tourist facilities and amenities in Northern Ireland.

**tasks**   Marketing and promoting NI as tourist destination. Sponsoring events. Running accommodation classification scheme. Running capital grant assistance programmes. Inspecting certain catering establishments.

**operations**   Management: Executive team headed by Chief Executive. 24 tourist information offices. European Regional Development Fund monies play major part in development of amenities.

Policy: Major improvements in amenities and facilities. Joint marketing with the Republic of Ireland.

Trends: Increased government funding and EU grants.

**board**   Appointed by the Secretary of State.

| | |
| --- | --- |
| Chairman | Lord Rathcavan |
| Deputy Chairman | Roy Bailie |
| Members | Brian Adgey |
| | Annie Courtney |
| | Tony Hopkins CBE |
| | Alan Lambert |
| | Bill McGinnis |
| | Mary Peters CBE |
| *Accounting Officer* | *Chief Executive* |

**staff**   132

| Chief Executive | Ian Henderson |
|---|---|
| Director, Visitor & Industry Services | John Beattie |
| Director of Development | David Cartmill |
| Director, Communications | Jackie D'Arcy |
| Director, Sales | Sandra Elliott |
| Director, Marketing | Paul Lavery |
| Director, Investment | David McAuley |
| Director, Appraisal | Gillian McKenna |
| Dirctor, Finance & Personnel | Trevor Sturgess |

**financial**

| INCOME & EXPENDITURE Year end: 31 March | 1997 £000 | 1996 £000 | 1995 £000 |
|---|---|---|---|
| TURNOVER | - | 14,562 | 13,779 |
| OPERATING (DEFICIT)/SURPLUS FOR THE YEAR | - | (684) | (52) |
| Net interest receivable | - | 26 | 55 |
| RETAINED (DEFICIT)/SURPLUS | - | (658) | 2 |

**advisers**  **Auditors**  Comptroller and Auditor General for NI

# Northern Ireland Transport Holding Company (NITHC)

Chamber of Commerce House
22 Great Victoria Street
Belfast BT2 7LX

**Tel** 01232 243456
**Fax** 01232 333845

**status**  Public corporation

**founded**  1964

**sponsor**  Northern Ireland Office, Department of the Environment for NI (DOENI)

**mission**  To operate public transport in Northern Ireland and manage associated property within policies specified by Ministers.

**tasks**  Operation of public transport and property management. Trading subsidiaries are: Ulsterbus Ltd, Citybus Ltd, Flexibus Ltd, Northern Ireland Railways Company Ltd, NIR Leasing Ltd, NIR Travel Ltd.

**operations**  Management: New Chief Executive and Senior Management Team recruited for both bus and rail services in previous year now paves the way for the introduction of coordinated public transport services, the implementation of the Private Finance Initiative (PFI) and better value for money for the tax payer.

Policy: NITHC and its operating subsidiaries are committed to providing integrated coordinated public transport systems, implementing PFI, disposing of non-core business and, where appropriate, contracting out services.

Trends: European Community Structural Funds, which have helped to finance the Great Victoria Railway Station project and the Cross Border upgrade, are confidently expected to help fund future rail and bus projects.

**board**  The former boards of the Bus and Rail companies were stood down in December 1995 and the new common membership Board of Directors, comprised largely of senior executives, took over. Nine members of the Board.

| Chairman | I Doherty | |
|---|---|---|
| Managing Director | RS Martin | |
| Directors | J Freeman | |
| | L Hasson | N Stewart |
| | M Moloney | N Whitehead |
| | SR Reed | M Wilson |

**staff**  3776

*financial*

| PROFIT & LOSS Year end: 30 March | 1997 £000 | 1996 £000 | 1995 £000 |
|---|---|---|---|
| **TURNOVER** | 106,103 | 101,499 | 97,932 |
| **OPERATING COSTS** | (94,224) | (89,292) | (84,936) |
| **GROSS OPERATING PROFIT** | 11,879 | 12,207 | 12,996 |
| Administrative expenses | (7,852) | (8,093) | (7,547) |
| Other operating income | 422 | 267 | 278 |
| **OPERATING PROFIT** | 4,449 | 4,381 | 5,727 |
| Restructuring costs | (1,344) | (159) | - |
| Diminution in value of properties | (485) | - | - |
| Profit on sale of properties | 150 | 568 | 799 |
| Income from other fixed asset investments | 453 | 453 | 453 |
| **PROFIT ON ORDINARY ACTIVITIES BEFORE INTEREST** | 3,223 | 5,243 | 6,979 |
| Net interest receivable | 1,284 | 1,685 | 1,248 |
| **PROFIT ON ORDINARY ACTIVITIES BEFORE TAXATION** | 4,507 | 6,928 | 8,227 |
| Taxation on profit on ordinary activities | (1,978) | (2,127) | (1,802) |
| **PROFIT FOR THE FINANCIAL PERIOD** | 2,529 | 4,801 | 6,425 |
| Appropriations - transfer to other reserves | (119) | (606) | (898) |
| **RETAINED PROFIT FOR THE PERIOD** | 2,410 | 4,195 | 5,527 |

*advisers*

| **Bankers** | Northern Bank |
|---|---|
| **Auditors** | Coopers & Lybrand |
| **Solicitors** | Carson & McDowell |

# Northern Lighthouse Board

84 George Street
Edinburgh EH2 3DA

**Tel** 0131 473 3100
**Fax** 0131 220 2093

**E-mail** nlb@dial.pipex.com

| *status* | Executive body |
|---|---|
| *founded* | 1786 |
| *sponsor* | Department of the Environment, Transport and the Regions (DETR) |
| *powers* | Merchant Shipping Act 1894. Merchant Shipping Act 1979 |
| *mission* | Security of navigation and fishing. |
| *tasks* | Managing lighthouses, buoys and beacons throughout Scotland and the adjacent seas and islands and the Isle of Man. |
| *operations* | Management: A General Lighthouse Authority. |

Policy:  The Board supports the 'User Pays'  principle for the provision of marine aids to navigation and its extension to the whole spectrum of marine users - including seagoing leisure craft - within a fair and balanced system.

*Accounting Officer  Chief Executive.*

| *staff* | 247 |
|---|---|

# *Occupational Pensions Regulatory Authority (OPRA)*

Invicta House
Trafalgar Place
Brighton BN1 4DW

**Tel** 01273 627600          **E-mail** Helpdesk@opra.co.uk
**Fax** 01273 627688

| | |
|---|---|
| *status* | Executive body |
| *founded* | 1996 |
| *sponsor* | Department of Social Security (DSS) |
| *powers* | 1995 Pensions Act |
| *mission* | To be a responsive regulator which helps to ensure that occupational pension scheme members' interests are protected and that schemes comply with the law. OPRA's overriding concern is the security of scheme assets to prevent the misuse of funds, to recover any lost scheme assets, to prevent those responsible for misuse from being able to repeat the offence and to impose appropriate penalties on them. |
| *tasks* | To investigate alleged breaches of the law or regulations and to take legal, disciplinary or regulatory action against employers or trustees where breaches are found; to safeguard scheme members' assets where, as a result of possible breaches of the law or regulations, there is a serious threat to them; to monitor scheme compliance by investigating reports of non-compliance and conducting spot checks; to provide scheme members and others with simple means to inform OPRA about incidents and allegations; to maintain a record of pension schemes that can be used to trace individual pension rights; to collect the levies which pay for OPRA, the Pensions Ombudsman, The Pensions Advisory Service and the Pensions Compensation Board (PCB); to keep ministers and officials informed about current events, activities and plans. |
| *operations* | Management: OPRA is an independent and autonomous organisation representing the whole of the UK. The OPRA Board sets the strategic direction and is responsible for deciding individual cases. Nevertheless, the Secretary of State must be satisfied that OPRA's activities are consistent with its functions under the Pensions Act and the government's general aims, including value for money. Board minutes and reports (other than papers concerning individual cases) are sent to DSS, which is consulted on a range of issues. Funding comes from the new general and compensation levies on occupational pension schemes; they are collected by OPRA on behalf of the DSS and PCB and OPRA receives funds monthly from DSS. |
| | The Chief Executive is in charge of day-to-day operations. The Senior Management Team comprises a Resources Director, two Regulatory Directors and the Solicitor to the Board. |
| | Policy: OPRA is committed to communicating its policies, decisions and activities clearly and effectively across the widest range of audiences and media. Over 20 million people have a direct financial interest in some 200,000 occupational pension schemes with assets totalling over £600 billion. |
| | To work in partnership with every one involved in occupational pension schemes - scheme members, employers, employees, trustees and pensions professionals. |
| | Trends: 1996/97 was spent preparing for live operations. |
| *performance* | Live operations started in April 1997. |
| *board* | A full-time Chairman and eight part-time members, all appointed by the Secretary of State as knowledgeable and skilled individuals from different sections of the pensions community. |

| | |
|---|---|
| Chairman | John Hayes CBE |
| Members | Ron Amy OBE |
| | John Bowman |
| | Hugh Brown |
| | Mike Jones |
| | Harriet Maunsell OBE |
| | Joanne Segars |
| | Sue Ward |
| | Anne Wood |

| | |
|---|---|
| *staff* | 140, of whom 70 are at the Brighton headquarters and 70 administrative staff at the Pension Schemes Registry in Newcastle. |

| | |
|---|---|
| Chief Executive | Caroline Johnston |
| Resources Director | Keith Blackburn |
| Personnel Manager | Margaret Cramp |
| IT Manager | Mike Fitzsimons |
| Registry Manager | Tony Richardson |
| Finance Manager | Clive Butler |
| Regulatory Directors | Roger Hills |
| | Joe Robertson |
| Regulatory Managers | Rod Fraser |
| | Rachel Low |
| | David Pullen |
| | Garry Walker |
| Actuary | Wendy Beaver |
| Communications Manager | David Cresswell |
| Secretary to the Board | Marian Jones |
| Solicitor to the Board | Jennie Kreser |

**financial**

| INCOME & EXPENDITURE | |
|---|---|
| Year end: 31 March | **1997** |
| | **£000** |
| **INCOME** | |
| Goverment grants | 2,366 |
| Transfers from deferred capital grants | 167 |
| **EXPENDITURE** | |
| Staff costs | 738 |
| Other operating charges | 1,969 |
| | 2,707 |
| **OPERATING DEFICIT ON ORDINARY ACTIVITIES** | **(174)** |
| Notional interest on capital employed | (32) |
| **DEFICIT FOR YEAR TRANSFERRED TO GENERAL RESERVE** | **(206)** |

**advisers**    **Auditors**       National Audit Office       157-197 Buckingham Palace Road
London SW1W 9SP

**publications**   *Annual Report*

# Office of the Data Protection Registrar

Wycliffe House
Water Lane
Wilmslow
Cheshire SK9 5AF

**Tel** 01625 545745      **E-mail** data@wycliffe.demon.co.uk
**Fax** 01625 524510      **Web** http://www.open.gov.uk/dpr/dpr

**status**      Executive body

**founded**     1984

**sponsor**     Home Office

**powers**      Data Protection Act 1984 (DPA) 1984

**mission**     To promote respect for the private lives of individuals and in particular for the privacy of their information by implementing the DPA (1984) and by influencing national and international thinking on privacy and personal information.

**tasks**       To compile a register of all those processing personal data, who are not exempt from the DPA (1984); take action to enforce the registration provision; to enforce compliance with the eight data protection principles of good practice; to encourage the establishment of codes of practice; to promote understanding of data protection.

**operations**  Management: The position is unusual. The Registar's powers and responsibilities are set out in the DPA (1984) and all decisions are subject to the supervision of the courts and the Data Protection Tribunal. The Registrar is an independent body created by statute and reporting directly to parliament, subject only to Treasury general review of Non-Departmental Public Bodies. However the Home Office may conduct or commission reviews of policy, management or financial management, or staffing, but only after consultation with the Registrar. The last such review, the Quinquennial Review, was completed in 1996/97.

The Office of the Data Protection Registrar has its own statutory basis and this means that it has no Commission or Non-Executive Board members and the staff are the Registrar's employees. The Office is divided into five directorates covering the following broad areas of work: strategic policy and international; legal; operations; marketing; personnel and finance.

Policy: The Registrar's policy is to give priority to streamlining procedures, raising awareness and stimulating debate.

Trends: The new Data User Information Service (DUIS) has sped up registration of applications (which have risen from 300 to 500 per week) and simplified and sped up user registrations. It is now possible to search the register by Internet so that what was a little used public register is now accessible and searchable and the public can check details of personal data processing. The EU Data Protection Directive requires the public declaration of processing by some users. The purposes of processing have to be specified. Neither require use of a public register but use of the Data Protection Register could ensure that the data users are complying with the law. Complaints are increasing as are compliance and enforcement activities

**board** Management Board only, consisting of the Registrar and five executive Heads of Directorates. The Registrar is appointed by Her Majesty by letters patent; staff by the Registrar.

| | |
|---|---|
| Registrar | Elizabeth France |
| Deputy Registrar | Francis Aldhouse |
| Personnel & Finance Director | Mike Duffy |
| Legal Director | Rosemary Jay |
| Marketing & Communications Director | Barrie Kelly |
| Operations Director | John Woulds |

**staff** 109

**financial**

| RECEIPTS & PAYMENTS Year end: 31 March | 1997 £ | 1996 £ | 1995 £ |
|---|---|---|---|
| **RECEIPTS** | | | |
| HMG grants received | 3,972,000 | 3,955,000 | 3,853,000 |
| Operating receipts | 5,057,358 | 6,976,648 | 3,301,572 |
| | 9,029,358 | 10,931,648 | 7,154,572 |
| **PAYMENTS** | | | |
| Salaries & wages | 1,861,248 | 1,851,569 | 1,659,435 |
| Other operating payments | 2,092,485 | 1,951,225 | 1,791,595 |
| | 3,953,733 | 3,802,794 | 3,451,030 |
| **SURPLUS FROM OPERATIONS** | 5,075,625 | 7,128,854 | 3,703,542 |
| Other receipts | 115,250 | 95,777 | 118,210 |
| Other payments | 71,568 | 171,977 | 346,976 |
| | 43,682 | (76,200) | (228,766) |
| **SURPLUS FOR YEAR** | 5,119,307 | 7,052,654 | 3,474,776 |
| Appropriations | 5,191,785 | 7,042,751 | 3,493,736 |
| **EXCESS OF RECEIPTS OVER PAYMENTS/(PAYMENTS OVER RECEIPTS)** | (72,478) | 9,903 | (18,960) |

**advisers**

| | | |
|---|---|---|
| **Bankers** | The Royal Bank of Scotland | |
| **Auditors** | National Audit Office | 157-197 Buckingham Palace Road London SW1W 9SP |
| **Solicitors** | Messrs Baily Gibson | 5 Station Parade, Beaconsfield Bucks HP9 2PG |
| | Messrs Gilchrists | 3rd Floor, 44 Great Malborough Street London W1V 1DB |
| | Woollcombe Beer Watts | 24 Tor Hill Road, Torquay,Devon TQ2 5RD |
| | Messrs Granville-West | 23 Commercial Street, Pontypool Gwent NP4 6XT |
| | Hamiltons Solicitors | 42B Independent Place, Shacklewell Lane London E8 2HE |
| | Swaffields Solicitors | 69 High Street, Corsham,Wiltshire SN13 0HW |
| | Messrs Rutherfords | 6/9 Lady Bank, Tamworth,Staffs B79 7NF |
| | Waller Needham & Green | 72 Broadway, Peterborough PE1 1SU |
| | Messrs Trethowan Woodford | The Director General's House, Rockstone Place, Southampton SO1 2EP |

| Alasdair Watson | 10 Ashfield Road, Whickham Newcastle upon Tyne NE16 4PL |
| Messrs Zermansky & Partners | 10 Butts Court, Leeds LS1 5JS |
| Phillips McDade & Co Solicitors | 3 Brunswick Street, Macclesfield Cheshire SK10 1ER |
| Shepherd & Wedderburn WS | Saltire Court, 20 Castle Terrace Edinburgh EH1 2ET |

# Office of Electricity Regulation (Offer)

Hagley House
Hagley Rd
Edgbaston
Birmingham B16 8QG

**Tel** 0121 456 2100
**Fax** 0121 456 4664

**Contact** Steve Macarthy

| | |
|---|---|
| ***status*** | Regulator |
| ***founded*** | 1989 |
| ***sponsor*** | Department of Trade and Industry (DTI); in Scotland, the Scottish Office |
| ***powers*** | Electricity Act 1989 |
| ***mission*** | Promoting competition in the electricity industry in England, Wales and Scotland and protecting customers' interests by regulating electricity supply, transmission and distribution. |
| ***tasks*** | Consumer affairs - codes of practice, performance standards, complaints and energy efficiency. Business regulation - pooling and settlement, licensing, generation, levy, price control, price discrimination and cross-subsidy, mergers. Supply competition - making arrangements for full competition in 1998. Technical matters - grid code, distribution code, metering and Electricity Meter Examining Service. |
| ***operations*** | Management: Although independent of government, the Director General reports to the Secretary of State for Trade and Industry and, in Scotland, to the Secretary of State for Scotland. The Senior Management Team comprises the Director General, the Deputy Director General and the Deputy Director General for Scotland, plus nine heads of department. 14 regional offices and Consumers' Committees, one for each company. Offer's costs are recovered from the annual licence and it must recover full economic costs.

Policy: Giving highest priority to competition in supply in 1998.

Trends: Only one regional electricity company remains independent, seven becoming subsidiaries of US-based utility companies. |
| ***board*** | None. Director General appointed by the Secretary of State. |

| *Accounting Officer* | *Director General* |
|---|---|

| | |
|---|---|
| ***staff*** | 250 |

| | |
|---|---|
| Director General | Prof Stephen Littlechild |
| Deputy Director General | Peter Carter |
| Legal Adviser | Derek Bevan |
| Director of Supply Competition | Tony Boorman |
| Chief Examiner | John Cooper |
| Director of Consumer Affairs | Dr David Hauser |
| Director of Administration | Howard Jones |
| Director of Public Affairs | Miss Jan Luke |
| Director of Regulation & Business Affairs | John Saunders |
| Director of Regulation & Business Affairs | Andrew Walker |
| Technical Director | Dr Brian Wharmby |
| ***Scotland*** | |
| Deputy Director General for Scotland | David Wilson |

*North of Scotland Consumers' Committee*

| | | |
|---|---|---|
| Chairman | DR Jack Earls | |
| Members | Mrs Fiona Auld | James Matthew |
| | Laurence Brown | Cllr George McMillan |
| | Hugh Duncan | Colin Neilson |
| | James Forsy | Mrs Susan Rhodes |
| | Adam Gilmour | Mrs Mary Scott |
| | John Graham | Graham Strachan |
| | Cllr John Halcro-Johnston | Katherine Wragg |

*Southern Scotland Consumers' Committee*

| | | |
|---|---|---|
| Chairman | Graeme Millar | |
| Members | Rev Joseph Brown | Alan Hutton |
| | Mrs Frances Buchanan | Mrs Caroline Ivins-Whatley |
| | Jim Craigen | Prof David Lidgate |
| | Mrs Jean Douglas | Graeme Marwick |
| | Mrs Elizabeth Futcher | Mrs Margaret McDonald |
| | Peter Gibson | John Weir |

**North East**

| | | |
|---|---|---|
| Regional Manager | Mrs Diane Kirkup | |

*North Eastern Consumers' Committee*

| | | |
|---|---|---|
| Chairman | Mrs Elizabeth Derrington | |
| Members | John Anderson CBE | Stuart Elliott |
| | Jeffrey Bell | Ms Barbara Hawkins |
| | Peter Blacklock | Ms Jennifer Hopper |
| | Mrs Susan Bolam | John Littlefair |
| | Kenneth Brown | Peter Moss |
| | Ronald Campbell | Mrs Brenda Pattison |
| | Mrs Anne-Marie Darke | Leslie Rutherford |
| | Michael Dulieu | David Steckles |

**North West**

| | | |
|---|---|---|
| Regional Manager | Miss Judith O'Leary | |

*North Western Consumers' Committee*

| | | |
|---|---|---|
| Chairman | Prof Lorraine Baric | |
| Members | Riaz Ahmad | |
| | Godfrey Bainbridge | Stanley Handley MBE |
| | Dr Carol Baxter | Bernard Harris |
| | Richard Bragg | Nicholas McNamara |
| | Mrs Judith Byrne | George Osundiya |
| | Mrs Jean Craske | Mrs Sally Steele |

**Yorkshire**

| | | |
|---|---|---|
| Regional Manager | Ms Cathy Jones | |

*Yorkshire Consumers' Committee*

| | | |
|---|---|---|
| Chairman | Mrs Christine Woods | |
| Members | Gerald Atkinson | John Healey |
| | Mrs Carole Barr | Leslie McHugh |
| | Norman Cole | John Mordy |
| | Tim Cole | Mrs Deborah Parry |
| | Mrs Jean Ellerton | Mrs Rosemary Sung |
| | Stuart Grant | Michael Yates |

**Merseyside & North Wales**

| | | |
|---|---|---|
| Regional Manager | Miss Judith O'Leary | |

*Merseyside & North Wales Consumers' Committee*

| | | |
|---|---|---|
| Chairman | David Owen CBE | |
| Members | William Baker | |
| | Peter Burbidge | Elwyn Owens |
| | Dr Shanti Chakravarty | Allan Powell |
| | Jim Davies | Ian Sanderson |
| | John Hooson | Mrs Kay Stacey |
| | Mrs Linda Jones | Ross Thomson |
| | Mrs Vicky MacDonald | Emrys Wynn Jones |

**East Midlands**

| | | |
|---|---|---|
| Regional Manager | Jeff Rush | |

*East Midland Consumers' Committee*

| | | |
|---|---|---|
| Chairman | Mrs Irene Bloor | |
| Members | Mrs Ann Brennan | Mrs Marjorie Lewin |
| | Mrs Ann Button | Finbarr Looney |
| | Uday Dholakia | Tony Lord |
| | Frank Elliott | Mrs Jean Moss |
| | Mrs Jane Field | John Rose |
| | James Gilmour | Nicholas Tate |
| | Stan Godward | Danny Waite |
| | Chris Harrison | Ken Webster |

**Midlands**

| | |
|---|---|
| Regional Manager | Jeff Rush |

*Midlands Consumers' Committee*

| | | |
|---|---|---|
| Chairman | Raymond O'Brien | |
| Members | Keith Batchelor | |
| | Peter Collings | Mrs Eleanor Noble |
| | Mrs Ruth Crofts | Michael Phelan |
| | Stuart Edwards | Neil Roberts |
| | Mrs Marion Forster | Nilendu Roy |
| | Ian Gibson | Ms Sandra Spence |
| | Nicholas Hurst | Mrs Edwina Turner |
| | Mrs Elspeth Metcalfe | Gary Ward |

**South Wales**

| | |
|---|---|
| Regional Manager | Ian Fitzpatrick |

*South Wales Consumers' Committee*

| | | |
|---|---|---|
| Chairman | Mrs Janet Candler | |
| Members | Gwyn Breeze | |
| | Mrs Christine Casseldine | Allen King |
| | Evan Davies | Mrs Dorothy Lees |
| | Norman Griffiths | Mrs Marilyn Mason |
| | David Honeyman | Maldwyn Rees |
| | John Howell | Dr Elizabeth Rhodes |

**East**

| | |
|---|---|
| Regional Manager | Wilson Bowers |

*Eastern Consumers' Committee*

| | | |
|---|---|---|
| Chairman | Malcolm Roberts | |
| Members | Mrs Heather Barrow | |
| | Mrs Esther Challis | Ian Monson |
| | Alan Conway | Kelvin Nel |
| | Mrs Joan Davis | Robin Sadler |
| | Mrs Sheila Edwards | Mrs Kathryn Saward |
| | Stephen King | Arthur Stevens |
| | Gordon Laing | Roy Thompson |

**South**

| | |
|---|---|
| Regional Manager | Brian Rayner |

*Southern Consumers' Committee*

| | | |
|---|---|---|
| Chairman | Kenneth Prior | |
| Members | David Burditt | |
| | Mrs Betty Guyatt | John Partington |
| | Mrs Sonia Lightfoot | Mike Robson |
| | Mrs Anne Mantle | Kevin Senior |
| | Robert Owen | Peter Wyatt |
| | Robert Parson | Mrs Anne Yammaghas |

**London**

| | |
|---|---|
| Regional Manager | Arthur Cooke |

*London Consumers' Committee*

| | | |
|---|---|---|
| Chairman | Mrs Yvonne Constance | |
| Members | Ms Tobe Aleksander | Ms Kristyne Hibbert |
| | Anthony Colman | Ms Cassandra Kent |
| | Stuart Davidson | Mrs Dora Rickford |
| | Bernard Donoghue | John Stocking |

**South East**

| | |
|---|---|
| Regional Manager | Ms Elizabeth Stallibrass |

*South Eastern Consumers' Committee*

| | | |
|---|---|---|
| Chairman | Mrs Pauline Ashley | |
| Members | Mrs Patricia Baldwin | Cllr George Miller |
| | Edward Brickley | Ronald Neath |
| | Alaster Calder | Anthony Parker |
| | Mrs Rosemary Edwards | Bernard Quigg |
| | Mrs Christine Field | Frank Redman |
| | Peter Jarvis | Geoffrey Skinner CBE |

**South West**

| | |
|---|---|
| Regional Manager | Ian Fitzpatrick |

*South Western Consumers' Committee*

| | | |
|---|---|---|
| Chairman | Mr Peter Weston | |
| Members | Michael Apps | |
| | John Bartlett | |
| | Arthur Carden | Albert Kirkham ISO |
| | Mrs Margaret Cook | Graham Parkhouse |
| | Mrs Pamela Gwyther | Mrs Ruth Parnell |
| | Richard Hall | Peter Turner |
| | Arthur Hills | Mrs Teresa Wallace |

*financial*

| INCOME & EXPENDITURE Year end: 31 March | 1996 £000 | 1995 £000 |
|---|---|---|
| **GROSS INCOME** | **12,210** | **10,132** |
| **EXPENDITURE** | | |
| Staff costs | 5,675 | 5,257 |
| Depreciation | 867 | 621 |
| Other operating costs | 5,668 | 4,887 |
| Total expenditure | 12,210 | 10,132 |
| **OPERATING SURPLUS/DEFICIT** | **nil** | **nil** |

*branches*

*Scotland*
70 West Regent Street
Glasgow G2 2QZ
Tel 0141 331 2678

*North East*
1st Floor
St Cuthbert Chambers
35 Nelson Street
Newcastle upon Tyne NE1 5AN
Tel 0191 221 2071

*North West*
5th Floor
Boulton House
17-21 Chorlton Street
Manchester M1 3HY
Tel 0161 236 3484

*Yorkshire*
Symons House
Belgrave Streeet
Leeds LS2 8DD
Tel 0113 234 1866

*Merseyside & North Wales*
4th Floor
Hamilton House
Hamilton Place
Chester CH1 2BH
Tel 01244 320849

*East Midlands*
Suite 3c
Langford House
40 Friar Lane
Nottingham NG1 6DQ
Tel 0115 950 8738

*Midlands*
Hagley House
Hagley Road
Birmingham B16 8QG
Tel 0121 456 4424

*South Wales*
5th Floor
St David's House
West Wing
Wood Street
Cardiff CF1 1ES
Tel 01222 228388

*East*
4th Floor
Waveney House
Handford Road
Ipswich
Suffolk IP1 2BJ
Tel 01473 216101

*South*
30-31 Friar Street
Reading
Berkshire RG1 1DX
Tel 01734 560211

*London*
11 Belgrave Road
London SW1V 1RB
Tel 0171 233 6366

*South East*
1-4 Lambert's Yard
Tonbridge
Kent TN9 1ER
Tel 01732 351356

*South West*
Unit 1
Hide Market
West Street
Bristol BS2 0BH
Tel 0117 954 0934

# *Office of Fair Trading (OFT)*

Field House
15-25 Breams Buildings
London EC4A 1PR

**Tel** 0171 211 8000
**Fax** 0171 211 8800

| | |
|---|---|
| *status* | Non-ministerial government department |
| *founded* | 1973 |
| *sponsor* | Department of Trade and Industry |
| *powers* | Fair Trading Act 1973 |
| *mission* | To promote the economic interests of consumers in the UK by safeguarding effective competition, removing trading malpractices and publishing appropriate guidelines. |
| *tasks* | To identify and put right trading practices which are against the consumer's interests; to regulate the provision of consumer credit; to act directly on the activities of industry and commerce by investigating and remedying anti-competitive practices and abuses of market power, and bringing about market structures which encourage competitive behaviour (can recommend referal to the Monopolies and Mergers Commission); sponsors research and issues advisory publications. |
| *operations* | Management: The Director General reports to the Secretary of State. There are two policy divisions, Consumer Affairs and Competition Policy, each headed by a Director. Consumer Affairs Division is divided into Consumer Policies, Research and Financial Services, Trader Control including Regulation of Consumer Credit, Adjudication Unit. Competition Policy Division is divided into Goods, Services and International, Restrictive Agreements, Broadcasting and other Media, Merger Control, Economic Advisers. Much work done in partnership with trading standards authorities. |
| | Policy: Protection duties have extended to domestic customers of regulated energy markets. |
| | Trends: EU competition law applies within the UK. OFT acts as a Competent Authority in the UK for competition issues and works in close liaison with the EC. Participates in international competition forums. |
| *performance* | In 1996, exceeded targets set for consumer credit licensing and monopolies and anti-competitive practices, but failed to meet all others. |
| *staff* | 402 |

| | |
|---|---|
| Director General of Fair Trading | John Bridgeman TD |
| Deputy Director General | Martin Howe CB |
| Director, Competition Policy | Margaret Bloom |
| Assistant Directors | Peter Bamford |
| | Henry Emden |
| | Andrew White |
| | Edward Whitehorn |
| | Steven Wood |
| Director, Consumer Affairs | Geoffrey Horton |
| Assistant Directors | Peter Casey |
| | Martin Graham |
| | Roger Watson |
| Legal Director | Pat Edwards |
| Assistant Director (Legal) Consumer Affairs | Arif Khan |
| Assistant Director (Legal) Competition Policy | Peter Rostron |
| Principal Establishment & Finance Officer | Caroline Banks |
| Assistant Director (Information) | Dermod Hill |

# Office of Gas Supply (Ofgas)

Stockley House
130 Wilton Road
London SW1V 1LQ

**Tel** 0171 828 0898
**Fax** 0171 932 1600

| | |
|---|---|
| *status* | Regulator |
| *founded* | 1986 |
| *sponsor* | Department of Trade and Industry (DTI) |
| *powers* | Gas Act 1995 |
| *mission* | Securing competition in gas supply to domestic, commercial and industrial users in Great Britain. |
| *tasks* | Setting British Gas prices where it still has a monopoly; securing competition in gas supply to domestic customers; licensing competing companies for the transportation, shipping and supply of gas; protects the interests of gas consumers. Ofgas Technical Directorate enforces regulations on gas quality, approves and stamps meters, and provides technical advice. |
| *operations* | Management: Set up to regulate British Gas, Ofgas now regulates a thoroughly fragmented industry in which companies compete in every sector - gas transport, shipping and supply to customers. The Director General is appointed by the Secretary of State. Funded by licence and other fees. |
| | Policy: By May 1998, all customers throughout Great Britain should have a choice of gas supplier. |
| | Trends: Gas competition has led to lower prices with saving up to 20% on the average domestic gas bill. Competition has also brought down prices in the industrial sector by about 46% since 1990, making the whole economy more competitive. |
| *performance* | No targets set. |
| *board* | None. |

| Director General of Gas Supply | Clare Spottiswoode |
|---|---|
| Accounting Officer | Director General |

| | |
|---|---|
| *staff* | 130 |
| *financial* | Total expenditure 1996/97 £11,699,000. |
| *advisers* | **Auditors**    National Audit Office    157-197 Buckingham Palace Road London SW1W 9SP |
| *publications* | 1997 Price Control Review: British Gas' Transportation and Storage. The Director General's Initial Proposals (May 1996), 1997 Price Control Review: Supply at or Below 2500 Therms a Year - British Gas Trading, The Director General's Initial Proposals (June 1996), 1997 Price Control Review: British Gas' Transportation and Storage, The Director General's Final Proposals (August 1996), Review of the Ofgas Trial of Provision and Installation of Non-domestic Meters by Registered Gas Meter Installers (December 1997), 1997 Competitive Market Review (December 1997), Marketing of Gas to Domestic Customers, Licence Modification - A Decision Document (January 1998), Dual Fuel Offers in the Gas and Electricity Markets - An Offer and Ofgas Joint Decision Document (January 1998) |

# Office of the National Lottery (Oflot)

2 Monck Street
London SW1P 2BQ

**Tel** 0171 227 2030
**Fax** 0171 227 2005

| | |
|---|---|
| *status* | Regulator |
| *founded* | 1993 |
| *sponsor* | Department for Culture, Media and Sport (DCMS) |
| *powers* | National Lottery Act 1993 |
| *mission* | To ensure that the UK National Lottery is properly run and regulated, and players are protected, while maximising the money raised for the Good Causes. |
| *tasks* | Awarded seven-year licence to operating company (Camelot Group plc); licensing each individual game (eg scratchcards) and approving game rules and regulations; ensuring that advertising code of practice is adhered to; dealing with complaints that Camelot have not resolved; ensuring that Camelot meets licence commitments; commissions surveys to monitor players' spending. |
| *operations* | Management: Director General manages day-to-day affairs, supported by three Directors (Operations, Consumer Affairs and Deputy Director General). Oflot imposes no net cost on government funds - funding from operator's licence fees. |
| | Policy: Required Camelot to undertake a new public awareness campaign and other measures to reduce underage sales. Agreement from Camelot to pay interest on the prize target shortfall to the Good Causes. |
| | Trends: Oflot would like powers to impose financial penalties on Camelot for breaches of licence rules. |
| *board* | None. Director General appointed by Secretary of State |

| Accounting Officer | Director General |
|---|---|

| | |
|---|---|
| *staff* | 31 |

| | |
|---|---|
| Acting Director General | John Stoker |
| Director of Operations & Acting Deputy Director General | Kingsley Jones |
| Compliance Manager | Stephen Lawrance |
| Head of Administration | Adrian Reid |
| Finance Manager | Andrew Dobson |
| Head of Business Affairs Alan Chant | |
| Business Affairs Manager | Brian Bade |
| Head of Public Affairs | Karen Wilde |
| Personnel Manager | Kerena Daveridge |
| Head of Licensing & Vetting | Ros Poulson |
| Head of Compliance | Sue Whitehouse |
| Head of IT Operations | Derek Woolley |

*financial*

**GRANT & EXPENDITURE**

| Year end: 31 March | 1997 | 1996 |
|---|---|---|
| | £000 | £000 |
| **Grant** | | |
| Running costs (net of VAT funds) | 2,396 | 2,440 |
| Capital expenditure | 104 | 60 |
| | 2,500 | 2,500 |
| **Expenditure** | | |
| Running costs (net of VAT funds) | 1,875 | 2,061 |
| Capital expenditure | 23 | 205 |
| | **1,898** | **2,266** |

| | | |
|---|---|---|
| *advisers* | **Bankers** | National Westminster Bank |
| | **Auditors** | Deloitte and Touche |
| | **Solicitors** | Treasury Solicitors |
| *publications* | *Section 5 Licences, Section 6 Licences, Annual Reports, Invitation to Apply, A Guide to the National Lottery, Anonymity Review, Rafferty Report, Oflot Social Research 1 & 2, Underage Participation in National Lottery* | |
| *branches* | Tolpits Lane | |
| | Watford WD1 8RN | |

# Office for National Statistics (ONS)

1 Drummond Gate
London SW1V 2QQ

**Tel** 0171 233 9233
**Fax** 0171 533 6261

**E-mail** info@ons.gov.uk
**Web** http//www.ons.gov.uk

| | |
|---|---|
| *status* | Executive agency and government department |
| *founded* | 1996 |
| *sponsor* | HM Treasury |
| *powers* | ONS Framework Document 1996 |
| *mission* | To be an independent supplier of authoritative, timely and high-quality information and services. Provides government, parliament and the wider community with a statistical service to support the formulation and monitoring of economic and social policies. |
| *tasks* | Compiles National Accounts (including GDP and GNP); collects, publishes and disseminates other economic and business statistics (eg Retail Sales Index, Producer Price Index, Average Earnings Index); produces and analyses labour market statistics and a wide range of social, health and population statistics (eg Social and Regional Trends, Family Spending, National Food Survey, Population Trends). Administers the marriage laws and secures the system for registration of births, marriages and deaths. Maintains NHS Central Register (database of all patients registered with a GP in England and Wales). |
| *operations* | Management: Amalgamation of Central Statistical Office and the Office of Population Censuses and Surveys. The Director is directly accountable to the Chancellor of the Exchequer. The Statistical Advisory Committee meets three times a year and provides advice to the Director. The six main business activities are: business statistics; macro-economic statistics and analysis; socio-economic statistics and analysis; census, population and health; survey and statistical services; administration services and registration. |
| | Policy: Improving the coherence and compatibility of statistics. Planning for 2001 Census. |
| | Trends: Criticism of the validity of unemployment statistics based on the claimant count. |
| *performance* | Met eight out of nine targets in 19996/97. |
| *board* | The Management Team consists of the Director, the 6 Group Directors and 2 non-executive Directors. |

| Director | Tim Holt |
|---|---|
| *Accounting Officer* | *Director* |

*staff*    3100

*financial*

| INCOME & EXPENDITURE | |
|---|---|
| Year end: 31 March | **1997** |
| | **£000** |
| **EXPENDITURE** | |
| Running costs | 130,573 |
| Depreciation | 3,280 |
| Notional superannuation | 7,274 |
| Other non-cash costs and services provided from other votes | 158 |
| Notional Interest | 1,558 |
| | **142,843** |
| **INCOME** | |
| Services supplied in year | (30,718) |
| **NET COST OF OUTPUT** | **112,125** |

*publications*    *Business Plan, Annual Report & Accounts*

*branches*

Cardiff Road
Newport
Gwent NP9 1XG
Tel 06633 815696
Fax 01633 815599

East Lane House
East Lane
Halton
Runcorn WA7 2DN
Tel 01928 715151
Fax 01928 792416

The Family Records Centre
1 Myddleton Street
London EC1R 1UW
Tel 0171 233 9233

Segensworth Road
Tichfield
Fareham
Hants PO15 5RR
Tel 01329 842511
Fax 01329 813570

Smedley Hydro
Trafalgar Road
Birkdale
Southport PR8 2HH
Tel 01704 569824
Fax 0151 471522

# *Office of Passenger Rail Franchising (OPRAF)*

Golding's House
2 Hay's Lane
London Bridge
London SE1 2HB

**Tel** 0171 940 4200
**Fax** 0171 940 4210

| | |
|---|---|
| *status* | Regulatory body |
| *founded* | 1994 |
| *sponsor* | Department of the Environment, Transport and the Regions (DETR) |
| *powers* | Railways Act 1993 |
| *mission* | To let the rail franchises and to monitor and manage the performance of the 25 franchisees to improve the overall quality of railway services. |
| *tasks* | Now all franchises have been let, work switched to monitoring, management and enforcement - looks at performance of franchise operators, punctuality and reliability. Implements financial incentive regimes to encourage operators to improve services (OPRAF makes payments if targets exceeded, collects if not). Sets out and monitors Franchise Agreements and Plans which give the rights and obligations of the franchisee - can fine operators or terminate the franchise if serious breaches. |
| *operations* | Management: Franchising Director reports to the Secretary of State. |
| | Policy: Prepared to use its statutory powers to secure the delivery of contracts. |
| | Trends: Too early to say whether franchising has led to improved performance. |
| *performance* | Franchise sales completed on schedule. |

*board*

| *Accounting Officer* | *Franchising Director* |
|---|---|

*staff*    103

| Director of Passenger Rail Franchising | John O'Brien |
|---|---|

*financial*

| EXPENDITURE | |
|---|---|
| **Year end: 31 March** | **1997** |
| | **£000** |
| **EXPENDITURE** | |
| Running costs | 7,048 |
| Other current | 31,303 |
| Capital | 315 |
| Current grants | 1,843,109 |
| | **1,881,775** |
| **RECEIPTS** | |
| Appropriations in aid | -34,435 |
| **NET TOTAL** | **1,847,340** |

| *advisers* | **Auditors** | National Audit Office | 157-197 Buckingham Palace Road London SW1W 9SP |
|---|---|---|---|

## *Office of the Rail Regulator (ORR)*

1 Waterhouse Square
138-142 Holborn
London EC1N 2ST

**Tel** 0171 282 2000
**Fax** 0171 282 2040                          **Web** http://www.rail-reg.gov.uk

| | |
|---|---|
| *status* | Regulator |
| *founded* | 1993 |
| *sponsor* | Department of the Environment, Transport and the Regions (DETR) |
| *powers* | Railways Act 1993. Framework Document |
| *mission* | Working with the industry to create a better railway for passengers and freight customers in Great Britain in UK. |
| *tasks* | Ensuring that Railtrack acts as a responsible and efficient steward of the national rail network and that all parts of the matrix (every regulated contract and licence) fit together to promote a better railway. Representing and supporting passengers and freight users. Ensuring that monopoly is controlled and promoting competitive structures. Controlling terms and conditions on which new undertakings move into the private sector. Cooperating with other railway decision-makers while maintaining independence. |
| *operations* | Management: The Regulator reports to the Secretary of State. The new Regulator's Council is the policy making body, comprising executive and non-executive members. ORR is organised into four groups each headed by a Group Director. Passenger Services Group has two divisions: Licensing and Consumer Protection, and Passenger Operator Relations. Rail Network Group is organised in three divisions: Network Regulation, Freight Regulation and Technical Services which deals with safety. Economic Regulation Group has policy responsibility for mergers, competition policy, finance and property funding. Resources and RUCC Sponsorship deals with RUCC resources and organisation. |
| | Policy: Regulator is guided by the broad public interest set out in 1993 Act - to improve public rail transport, to improve access to it and to get better value for money for the taxpayer. |
| | Trends: Railway structure is built on different kinds of monopoly for Railtrack and the 100 separate trading companies into which BR was divided. 13 companies now own 25 franchises and the acquisition of further franchise could create competition policy problems which will ultimately have to be resolved by the Secretary of State or the EU. |
| *staff* | 86 |

| | |
|---|---|
| The Regulator | John Swift QC |
| Director of Network Regulation | Michael Beswick |
| Group Director, Economic Regulation | Chris Bolt |
| Chief Legal Adviser | Michael Brocklehurst |
| Group Director, Railway Network | Charles Brown |
| Non-Executive Director | Ann Foster |
| Non-Executive Director | Dr Stephen Glaister |
| Director of Resources & RUCC Sponsorship | Peter Murphy |
| Non-Executive Director | Sir Wilfrid Newton CBE |
| Group Director, Passenger Services | John Rhodes |
| Director of Licensing & Consumer Protection | Iryna Terlecky |
| Head of Private Office & Public Affairs | Keith Webb |

# *Office for the Regulation of Electricity & Gas (Ofreg)*

Brookmount Buildings
42 Fountain Street
Belfast BT1 5EE

**Tel** 01232 311575
**Fax** 01232 311740

**E-mail** ofreg@nics.gov.uk
**Web** ofreg.nics.gov.uk

| | |
|---|---|
| *status* | Regulator |
| *founded* | 1992 to support the Director General of Electricity Supply (DGES). Expanded in 1995 to support the Director General of Gas (DGG) for Northern Ireland |
| *sponsor* | Northern Ireland Office, Department of Economic Development (DEDNI) |
| *powers* | Electricity (NI) Order 1992 and Gas (Northern Ireland) Order 1996. |
| *mission* | A multi-regulatory body, promoting an efficient and competitive electricity industry in Northern Ireland and protecting the interests of electricity consumers; developing and maintaining an efficient, economic and coordinated gas industry. |
| *tasks* | Promoting competition in the generation and supply of electricity in NI and protecting the interests of electricity customers in respect of price and quality of supply. Extending natural gas throughout Northern Ireland and monitoring Phoenix Natural Gas' development plans. Granting and modifying licences for the generation, transmission and supply of electricity and the conveyance and supply of gas in NI. |
| *operations* | Management: Ofreg supports DGES and DGG; both are statutory part-time appointments and Mr Molldoon holds both posts. Ofreg's funds are voted by parliament but its costs are recovered from electricity and gas licensees. The DGES has a duty to promote the degree of competition which has been introduced into the NI electricity industry, using as tools the right to vary the terms of licences and the power to control prices. Electricity consumers' interests are protected by Ofreg. The Director General monitors Northern Ireland Electricity's (NIE) standards of performance, approves its codes of practice and supervises its complaints procedures. Ofreg provides resources for the NI Consumer Committee for Electricity, whose agenda has been dominated by electricity prices (standard domestic tariff is 6% more than elsewhere in the UK). The equivalent gas function is carried out by the General Consumer Council for Northern Ireland. |

Policy: To introduce wholesale competition into the NI electricity market where (unlike the rest of the UK) there is no freedom of trade in electricity generation. To extend natural gas throughout the province.

Trends: NI electricity generation remains more expensive than that of Great Britain. In 1997 the MMC reported on the price controls to be applied to the regulated income of NIE and the DGES subsequently published modified price control proposals. NIE rejected his revised proposals and are challenging his decision by judicial review. An interconnector between the north and south of Ireland was recommissioned in 1995; the Moyle interconnector between NI and Scotland is subject to an economic appraisal by the DGES.

DGG has granted licences to Premier Power Ltd and Amoco (UK) Exploration Co for the supply of gas to Ballylumford power station. A 26km pipeline has been constructed to transport gas from Ballylumford to Torytown, where the distribution network starts. Development of the network is expected to extend to North, West and South Belfast during 1998. DGES is dicussing the possibility of extending the gas network outside Greater Belfast.

| | |
|---|---|
| *performance* | Work has continued on setting up a gas regulatory system to suport the DGG. |

| *board* | *Northern Ireland Consumer Committee for Electricity.* | |
|---|---|---|
| | Chairman | Nuala O'Loan |
| | Members | Sheila Fleming |
| | | Jill Girvan |
| | | David Mann |
| | | Michael McGinley |
| | | Maria McGuinness |
| | | Dr Fiona Mulholland |
| | | Desmond Shackleton |
| | | Thomas Stewart |

| | |
|---|---|
| *staff* | 19 |

| | |
|---|---|
| Director General, Electrical Supply/Director General Gas | Douglas Molldoon |
| Head, Consumer & Business Affairs | Leslie Adams |
| Head, Economic Regulation (Electricity) | Mike Archer |
| Deputy Director General, Electricity & Gas | Charles Coulthard |
| Head, Economic Regulation (Gas) | Mary McWilliams |

| *financial* | EXPENDITURE Year end: 31 March | 1997 £000 | 1996 £000 | 1995 £000 |
|---|---|---|---|---|
| | Running costs | 837 | 679 | 648 |
| | Capital expenditure | 10 | 37 | 15 |
| | Publicity and consultancies | 507 | 244 | 234 |
| | | **1,354** | **960** | **897** |

*advisers*

**Bankers** Ulster Bank

**Auditors** Northern Ireland Audit Office

**Solicitors** Denton's/Simmons & Simmons

**Public Relations** GCAS

*publications* Report on Customers Service Standards 1996/97, Director General of Electricity Supply for Northern Ireland & Annual Report 1996, Director General of Gas for Northern Ireland & Annual Report 1996, Northern Ireland Consumer Committee for Electricity: Annual Report 1996/1997

# Office for Standards in Education (OFSTED)

Alexandra House
33 Kingsway
London WC2B 6SE

**Tel** 0171 421 6800
**Fax** 0171 421 6522          **Web** http://www.ofsted.gov.uk

**Contact** Jonathan Lawson, Head of Communications

*status* Independent non-ministerial government department

*founded* 1992

*powers* School Inspections Act 1996. Nursery Education and Grant-Maintained Schools Act 1996. Educational Act 1997.

*mission* Keeping the government and the national educational service informed about the quality of education provided by schools in England; the educational standards achieved in them; the efficiency of their financial management; and the spiritual, moral, social and cultural development of pupils. Inspecting and reporting on the measures taken by Local Education Authorities (LEAs) to improve standards and the quality of education in schools in their areas.

*tasks* Maintaining (in England) the system for regular inspection, by independent inspectors, of all state-funded schools - primary, secondary, special and PRU's and state-funded nursery schools. This involves arranging the training of inspectors; keeping a register of approved inspectors; giving guidance on inspections and report writing; monitoring inspections to ensure high standards. Also inspection of LEAs, teacher training and youth and adult education and independent schools.

*operations* Management: A non-ministerial government department with a regulatory role over the independent school inspectorate. OFSTED is the Office of Her Majesty's Chief Inspector of Schools in England. It is headed by Her Majesty's Chief Inspector (HMCI). Staff include Her Majesty's Inspectors (HMI) who draw on inspection evidence to report on good practice in schools and on a wide range of other educational issues.

Policy: In 1996/97 the framework for inspections was revised; the criteria for grading lessons and the way in which pupils' standards are judged, both changed. In 1997/98 and 1998/99 academic years greater emphasis is being placed on inspection of local educator authorities and on teacher training.

Trends: Additional inspectors recruited temporarily to ensure meeting corporate plan objectives.

*performance* By the end of the academic year 1996/97 all secondary schools had been inspected, and by the end of 1997/98 all primary, nursery and special schools had been inspected.

| | |
|---|---|
| *staff* | 509 |

| | |
|---|---|
| HM Chief Inspector | Chris Woodhead |
| Communications, Media & Public Relations | Jonathan Lawson |
| Director of Inspection | Jim Rose CBE |
| Director of Inspection | Mike Tomlinson CBE |
| Research, Analysis & International | Christine Agambar |
| Contracts | Clive Bramley |
| Subject Adviser, Mathmatics | Nigel Bufton |
| Information Systems | Mike Childs |
| Subject Adviser, PE | Gordon Clay |
| Subject Adviser, Modern Languages | Alan Dobson |
| Administrative Support & Estates Management | Keith Francis |
| Subject Adviser, IT | Gabriel Goldstein |
| Secondary | Cliff Gould |
| Subject Adviser, History | Scott Harrison |
| Subject Adviser, English | John Hertrich |
| Subject Adviser, Design & Technology | Michael Ive |
| Subject Adviser, Art | Peter Jones |
| Nursery & Primary | Keith Lloyd |
| SEN | Chris Marshall |
| Inspection Quality, Monitoring & Development | Peter Matthews |
| Training & Assessment | Brian McCafferty |
| Subject Adviser, Music | Janet Mills |
| School Improvement | Elizabeth Passmore |
| Personnel Management | Chris Payne |
| Strategic Planning & Resources | Judith Phillips CBE |
| Subject Adviser, Science | Bob Ponchaud |
| LEA Reviews, Reorganisation Proposals | David Singleton |
| Subject Adviser, Geography | Peter Smith |
| Teacher Education & Training | David Taylor |
| Post Compulsory | David West |
| Subject Adviser, Religious Education | Barbara Wintersgill |

| | |
|---|---|
| *financial* | Expenditure: £62.96m,1994/95; £82.14m, 1995/96; £121.66m,1996/97.s |
| *publications* | Annual Report of Her Majesty's Chief Inspector of Schools, England: Standards and Quality in Education 1996/97 |

# Office of Telecommunications (OFTEL)

50 Ludgate Hill
London EC4M 7JJ

**Tel** 0171 634 8700
**Fax** 0171 634 8943             **Web** http://www.open.gov.uk/oftel

| | |
|---|---|
| *status* | Regulator |
| *founded* | 1984 |
| *sponsor* | Department of Trade and Industry (DTI) |
| *powers* | Telecommunications Act 1984 |
| *mission* | To promote the interests of consumers by ensuring they get the best possible deal in terms of quality, choice and value for money from the UK telecommunications industry. |
| *tasks* | Licenses all UK telecommunications operators, approves equipment, and administers the telephone numbering system; keeps registers of all licences granted; regulates industry through modifying, monitoring and enforcing the conditions in their licences; deals with customers' complaints about telecommunications services or apparatus if they have been unable to resolve it with the operator; ensures that certain services are provided, eg emergency services, public call boxes, directory information and services in rural areas; encourages major users of telecommunications services located outside the UK to establish businesses here and to enable UK-based companies to compete effectively overseas; ensures that UK policies and decisions reflect international developments. |

# Q&Q

**operations**  Management: OFTEL is independent of ministerial control. Under the Director General (appointed by the Secretary of State) and Deputy Director General, it is divided into ten branches: Network Competition; Consumer Affairs; Licensing; Licence Enforcement and Fair Trading; Technical Affairs; Economics, Accountancy and Statistics Advice; Legal Advice; Administration; Press Relations and Library; Services Competition and International Affairs. The Director General has six Advisory Committees (ACTs): four deal with issues in each of the UK countries and two look at telecommunications from the position of elderly and disabled people, and smaller businesses. The ACTs in Northern Ireland, Scotland and Wales also deal with consumer complaints and enquiries for these countries. Local Telecommunications Advisory Committees (TACs) advise the ACTs on consumer views and handle local issues (eg public call box problems). Cost of running OFTEL is offset almost entirely by the licence fees paid by the operators.

**board**

| | | |
|---|---|---|
| Director General | | Don Cruickshank |
| Deputy Director General | | Anna Walker |
| Policy Adviser | | Fod Barnes |
| Director of Network Competition | | Ann Taylor |
| Consumer Director | | Christine Farnish |
| Director of Licensing Policy | | Sarah Chambers |
| Director of Licence Enforcement & Fair Trading | | Christopher Wright |
| Technical Director | | Peter Walker |
| Economic Director | | Alan Bell |
| Legal Director | | David Ingham |
| Director of Administration | | David Smith |
| Director of Information | | Nick Gammage |
| Director of Services Competition & International Affairs | | Jim Niblett |
| Chairman, BACT | Peter Calver | |
| Members, BACT | Joy Allan | Oliver Makower |
| | Richard Furey | Dawn Penso |
| | Dr Bernard Juby | Margaret Seymour |
| | Robin Kemp | Spencer Wrench |
| Chairman, DIEL | Jean Gaffin | |
| Members, DIEL | John Barnes | |
| | Robin Birch CBE | Brian McGinnis |
| | David Dunsmuir | Kate Nash |
| | Michael Godfrey | Sheila Porter |
| | David Hyslop OBE | Nancy Robertson MBE |
| | David Mann | Dr Eleanor Steiner |
| | Michael Martin OBE | Ross Trotter |
| Chairman, ENACT | Moira Black | |
| Members, ENACT | Sue Bloomfield | Claire Milne |
| | Iain Bryce | John O'Reilly |
| | Bob Little | Douglas Oram |
| | Brian Love | Elizabeth Stanton-Jones |
| Chairman, SACOT | WK Begg OBE | |
| Members, SACOT | Joyce Wood | |
| | DA Gardner | K Murray |
| | CJ Griffith | J Purvis CBE |
| | NM Hope | Mrs CB Watkin |
| | Mrs CJ Jones | Prof H Williams |
| | I McCulloch | P Wilson JP |
| Secretary | RLL King | |
| Chairman, NIACT | JLC Thompson | |
| Members, NIACT | Miss C Aiken | |
| | Mrs CC Corrigan | WJH McPherson |
| | JA Kerr | Dr J Shields |
| | S Magee | Mr JA Stringer |
| Chairman, WACT | Prof MD Tedd | |
| Members, WACT | Mrs PJ Blackwell | |
| | D Dutton | J Maynard |
| | D Evans | L Murphy JP |
| | Mrs D Hammett | Mrs L Tomos |
| | G Jones | Miss G Williams |
| Secretary, WACT | | GJ Mackenzie |

**staff**  160

| financial | INCOME & EXPENDITURE | |
|---|---|---|
| | Year end: 31 March | **1996** |
| | | **£000** |
| | **INCOME** | |
| | Licence fees | 9,761 |
| | Other income | 308 |
| | | **10,069** |
| | **EXPENDITURE** | |
| | Staff related | 5,499 |
| | Accommodation | 1,459 |
| | Office supplies | 188 |
| | Stationery/consumables | 68 |
| | Common services | 438 |
| | Consultancy | 1,153 |
| | Press and publicity | 432 |
| | Library | 59 |
| | Legal | 143 |
| | Advisory committees | 164 |
| | Insurance | 5 |
| | Depreciation | 133 |
| | Interest on capital | 29 |
| | Interest receivable | -293 |
| | | **9,477** |
| | **SURPLUS/(DEFICIT)** | **592** |

*advisers*    **Auditors**      National Audit Office      157-197 Buckingham Palace Road
London Sw1W 9SP

*publications*    *Advisory Committee on Telecommunications for Disabled and Elderly People (DIEL), Business Advisory Committee on Telecommunications (BACT), English Advisory Committee on Telecommunications (ENACT)*

*branches*    *Scottish Advisory Committee on Telecommunications (SACOT)*
2 Greenside Lane
Edinburgh EH1 3AH
Tel 0131 244 5576
Fax 0131 244 5696

*Northern Ireland Advisory Committee
on Telecommunications (NIACT)*
Chamber of Commerce House
7th Floor
22 Great Victoria Street
Belfast BT2 7QA
Tel 01232 244113
Fax 013232 247024

*Welsh Advisory Committee
on Telecommunications (WACT)*
Caradog House
St Andrews Place
Cardiff CF1 3BE
Tel 01222 374028

# *Office of Water Services (Ofwat)*

Centre City Tower
7 Hill Street
Birmingham B5 4UA

**Tel** 0121 625 1300
**Fax** 0121 625 1400

**E-mail** enquiries@ofwat.gtnet.gov.uk
**Web** http://www.open.gov.uk/ofwat

| | |
|---|---|
| *status* | Regulator |
| *founded* | 1989 |
| *sponsor* | Department for the Environment, Transport and the Regions (DETR). Welsh Office (WO) |
| *powers* | Water Industry Act 1991. Environment Act 1995. |
| *mission* | Economic regulation of the water and sewerage industry in England and Wales. Protection of customers. |
| *tasks* | Ensuring that the statutory functions of water companies are properly carried out and that they are properly financed. Secondarily (but shortly expected to made a primary duty by the Government) protecting customers including ensuring that there is no undue preference or discrimination in the way companies fix and recover |

charges. Other duties include promotion of economy, efficiency and competition. Also has a secondary general environmental duty to conserve and enhance flora and fauna.

**operations**
Management: Ofwat is a non-ministerial government department and the Director has full responsibility for it. He makes an annual report to the sponsor Secretaries of State but is not responsible to them (although they can remove him for incapacity or misbehaviour). He has statutory duties and makes his own judgements about how to use them. In consultation with the Secretary of State for Trade and Industry or the Welsh Office, he appoints the Chairman and members of the ten statutory regional Customer Service Committees (CSCs) which identify and represent customers' concerns and investigate their complaints. He allocates each water company to a CSC. He has also established the Ofwat National Customer Council (ONCC) to strengthen customer representation, and recommended that it should become a statutory body. The Government has backed this idea. Meanwhile, he is acting as if he has a duty to have regard to ONCC as well as CSCs. He does not set environmental standards but works closely with the Environment Agency (which regulates and enforces water quality standards in inland, estuarial and coastal waters), the Drinking Water Inspectorate (which regulates drinking water quality) and the Secretaries of State who set drinking water quality standards.

Policy: The Director has called for customer protection to be made his single primary duty. Increasingly he is monitoring capital investment through an output focused regime concentrating on the service customers receive.

Trends: New price limits will be set in 1999 to operate for the years 2000-2005.

**board**
The Director is appointed by the sponsor Secretaries of State.

| Accounting Officer | Director General of Water Services |
|---|---|

**staff**
190

| Director General | Ian Byatt |
|---|---|
| Assistant Director & Head of Operational Resources | Roger Dunshea |
| Assistant Director & Head of Costs & Performance | Bill Emery |
| Assistant Director & Head of Consumer Affairs | Michael Saunders |
| Chief Economist | Tony Ballance |
| Legal Adviser | Allan Merry |
| Head of External Relations | Dilys Plant |
| Corporate Finance Adviser & Head of Financial Affairs | David Rees |
| Head of CSC Appointments and Performance | Roy Wardle |

**financial**
1996/97 Running costs £9.6 million.

**advisers**

| **Bankers** | Midland Bank | 2 The Marlowes Centre, Hemel Hempstead Herts HP1 1DX |
|---|---|---|
| **Auditors** | National Audit Office | 157-197 Buckingham Palace Road London SW1W 9SP |

**publications**
Annual Report, Report on the Financial Performance and Capital Investment of the Water Companies in England and Wales, Report on Leakage and Water Efficiency, Report on Levels of Service for the Water Industry in England and Wales, Report on Tariff Structure and Charges.

# Ofwat Central Customer Service Committee (Central CSC)

Chanelle House
86 New Street
Birmingham B2 4BA

**Tel** 0121 644 5252
**Fax** 0121 644 5256

**E-mail** clcsc@ofwat.gtnet.gov.uk
**Web** http://www.open.gov.uk/ofwat

**Contact** Will Dawson, Regional Manager

**status** Executive body
**founded** 1990
**sponsor** The Director General of Water Services
**powers** Water Industry Act 1991 (Section 28)

| | |
|---|---|
| *mission* | Representing the interests of, and investigating complaints from, customers of the water and sewage companies in Central region - Severn Trent Water Ltd and South Staffordshire Water plc. Advising and supporting the Director in regulating the water industry and securing for customers the combination of service and price that they would have in a competitive market. |
| *tasks* | Identifying and keeping under review matters affecting customers' interests. To ensure that its companies are aware of, and responsive to, concerns about their services and have adequate complaints procedures. To achieve a speedy and appropriate resolution of individual customer complaints where a company has not adequately dealt with the problem. To publicise the existence, functions and work of Ofwat, ONCC, and the CSC in protecting customers' interests. To advise and report to the Director General on particular issues affecting customers. |
| *operations* | Management: The Committee is headed by a Chairman (six days a month), supported by a full-time secretariat. Costs of supporting the Committee are met by the Director General (£191,000 in 1996/97). |
| | Policy: To ensure customers' views are taken into account in the review of water and sewerage prices in 1999. To press companies to use savings to fund investment and improve levels of service. To push for a one-off price cut in 2000 and price increases below the rate of inflation thereafter. |
| | Trends: Bills continue to rise. Number of complaints to the CSC is reducing. |
| *board* | The Committee members are appointed on merit by the Director from the local community. The Chairman is appointed by the Director in consultation with the Secretary of State for Trade and Industry. |

| Chairman | Clive Wilkinson | |
|---|---|---|
| Members | Brian Adams | Jasnbir Jaspal |
| | Shu Awath-Behari | Mrs Mary Milton |
| | Brenda Finnigan | Mrs Sheila Ray |
| | Dr Richard Franceys | Dr Neil Richardson |
| | Carole Gibbs | Francis Scoon |
| | Gerald Godby | Mike Warrander |
| | Clive Hulls | |
| *Accounting Officer* | *Director General of Water Services* | |

| | |
|---|---|
| *staff* | Five |

| Regional Manager & Secretary | Will Dawson |
|---|---|

| | | | |
|---|---|---|---|
| *advisers* | **Bankers** | Midland Bank | 2 The Marlowes Centre, Hemel Hempstead Herts HP1 1DX |
| | **Auditors** | National Audit Office | 157-197 Buckingham Palace Road London SW1W 9SP |

# Ofwat Eastern Customer Service Committee (Eastern CSC)

Carlyle House
Carlyle Road
Cambridge CB4 3DN

**Tel** 01223 323889
**Fax** 01223 323930

**E-mail** encsc@ofwat.gtnet.gov.uk
**Web** http://www.open.gov.uk/ofwat

**Contact** Marisa Johnson

| | |
|---|---|
| *status* | Executive body |
| *founded* | 1990 |
| *sponsor* | The Director General of Water Services |
| *powers* | Water Industry Act 1991 (Section 28) |
| *mission* | Representing the interests of, and investigating complaints, from customers about their water and sewage companies: Anglian Water Services, Cambridge Water, Essex and Suffolk Water and Tendring Hundred Water Services. Representing the interests of the customers of the water and sewage companies in the Eastern region. Advising and supporting the Director in regulating the water industry and securing for customers the combination of service and price that they would have in a competitive market. |

| | |
|---|---|
| **tasks** | Identifying and keeping under review matters affecting customers' interests. To ensure that its companies are aware of, and responsive to, concerns about their services and have adequate complaints procedures. To achieve a speedy and appropriate resolution of individual customer complaints where a company has not adequately dealt with the problem. To publicise the existence, functions and work of Ofwat, ONCC, and the CSC in protecting customers' interests. To advise and report to the Director General on particular issues affecting customers. |
| **operations** | Management: The Committee is headed by a Chairman (five days a month), supported by a full-time secretariat. Costs of supporting the Committee are met by the Director General (£176,000 in 1996/97).<br><br>Policy: To ensure customers' views are taken into account in the review of water and sewerage prices in 1999. To urge companies to promote metering and to make it more attractive to customers.<br><br>Trends: Price limits to be reset by the Director in 1999 for the years 2000-05. |
| **board** | Committee's members appointed on merit by the Director from the local community. Chairman appointed by Director in consultation with Secretary of State for Trade and Industry. |

| Chairman | Dr Roger Corbett | |
|---|---|---|
| Members | David Bishop | |
| | Mrs Valerie Duncan | Dr Suresh Nesaratnam |
| | James Hayward | Mrs Marianne Neuhoff |
| | Miss Helen Hopkins | Kenneth Rowe |
| | Bryan Johnston | Mrs Jane Scott |
| | H Kok | John Tapp |
| | Mrs Linda Laban | Roy Thompson |
| | Lawrence Larkin | Mrs Kathleen Weekes |
| | Robin Logan | Michael Whitehorn |
| *Accounting Officer* | *Director General of Water Services* | |

| | |
|---|---|
| **staff** | Five |

| Regional Manager & Secretary | Marisa Johnson |
|---|---|

| | | | |
|---|---|---|---|
| **advisers** | **Bankers** | Midland Bank | 2 The Marlowes Centre, Hemel Hempstead Herts HP1 1DX |
| | **Auditors** | National Audit Office | 157-197 Buckingham Palace Road London SW1W 9SP |

# Ofwat National Customer Council (ONCC)

Centre City Tower
7 Hill Street
Birmingham B5 4UA

**Tel** 0121 625 1301
**Fax** 0121 625 1444

**E-mail** oncc@ofwat.gtnet.gov.uk
**Web** http://www.open.gov.uk/ofwat

**Contact** Roy Wardle, Secretary

| | |
|---|---|
| **status** | Executive body |
| **founded** | 1993 |
| **sponsor** | Office of Water Services (Ofwat) |
| **powers** | The Director General of Water Services (the Director) has recommended that ONCC becomes a statutory body. In the meantime, the Director will have regard to representations made by ONCC as if it were a statutory body. |
| **mission** | To represent, at national and international levels, the interests of the 22 million domestic and non-domestic customers of the 29 water and sewage companies in England and Wales. |
| **tasks** | To put water customers' views to government, the European Union (particularly in relation to EC Directives) and the Director whose decisions govern prices and standards. To maintain channels of communication with the water indsutry and the other principal regulators. To co-ordinate the work of the ten independent Customer Service Committees (CSCs) which represent the interests of customers of the water and sewage companies in their regions. |

| operations | Management: ONCC brings together the ten CSC chairmen under a Chairman and two Deputy Chairmen. The ONCC secretariat, led by the Secretary to the Council, is based in Ofwat's CSC Appointments and Performance Division. Press, PR, technical and policy support are provided by Ofwat. |

**operations** Management: ONCC brings together the ten CSC chairmen under a Chairman and two Deputy Chairmen. The ONCC secretariat, led by the Secretary to the Council, is based in Ofwat's CSC Appointments and Performance Division. Press, PR, technical and policy support are provided by Ofwat.

Policy: To push for the return of water industry efficiency savings to customers by means of a substantial price cut. To lobby for costs benefits and affordability to be taken into account in EC decisions on higher water quality standards. To protect lower income households.

Trends: Pressure from environmental groups for higher standards in preference to a cut in water bills. Pressure also for water conservation and growth in metering.

**board**

| Chairman | Sheila Reiter | |
|---|---|---|
| Deputy Chairmen | Maurice Terry | |
| | Clive Wilkinson | |
| Members | John Beishon | Herman Scopes |
| | Roger Corbett | Jessica Thomas |
| | Jim Gardner | Eric Wilson |
| | Raymond Roberts | |

**staff** Four

| Secretary to Council | Roy Wardle |
|---|---|

**advisers**

**Bankers** Midland Bank — 2 The Marlowes Centre, Hemel Hempstead Herts HP1 1DX

**Auditors** National Audit Office — 157-197 Buckingham Palace Road London SW1W 9SP

**publications** *Representing Water Customers 1996-97, Ofwat National Customer Council Briefing Note Number 1 - Revision of the Drinking Water Directive, Ofwat National Customer Council Briefing Note Number 2 - Revision of the Bathing Water Directive, Ofwat National Customer Council's Submission to the Government Review of Utility Regulation, Ofwat National Customer Council's Submission to the Government Review of the Water Charging System in England and Wales, Ofwat National Customer Council's Position Paper on the Framework Directive on European Community Water Policy*

## Ofwat North West Customer Service Committee (North West CSC)

Bridgewater House
Whitworth Street
Manchester M1 6LT

**Tel** 0161 236 6112
**Fax** 0161 228 6117

**E-mail** nwcsc@ofwat.gnet.gov.uk
**Web** http://www.open.gov.uk/ofwat

**Contact** Margaret Smith, Regional Manager

**status** Executive body

**founded** 1990

**sponsor** The Director General of Water Services

**powers** Water Industry Act 1991 (Section 28)

**mission** Representing the interests of, and investigating complaints from, the customers of the water and sewage company in the North West region - North West Water. Advising and supporting the Director in regulating the water industry and securing for customers the combination of service and price that they would have in a competitive market.

**tasks** Identifying and keeping under review matters affecting customers' interests. To ensure that their companies are aware of, and responsive to, concerns about their services and have adequate complaints procedures. To achieve a speedy and appropriate resolution of individual customer complaints where the company has not adequately dealt with the problem. To publicise the existence, functions and work of Ofwat, ONCC, and the CSC in protecting customers' interests. To advise and report to the Director General on particular issues affecting customers.

**operations** Management: The committee is headed by a Chairman (seven days a month), supported by a full-time secretariat. Costs of supporting the committee are met by the Director General (£151,000 in 1996-97).

Policy: To ensure customers' views are taken into account in the review of water and sewerage prices in 1999. To continue to be the champion of the customer and to demand faultless standards.

Trends: Price limits to be reset by the Director in 1999 for the years 2000-05.

**board** The Committee's members are appointed on merit by the Director from the local community. The Chairman is appointed by the Director in consultation with the Secretary of State for Trade & Industry.

| Chairman | Maurice Terry | |
|---|---|---|
| Members | Mrs Anne Bradbury | |
| | Dr Ronald Catlow | Richard Long |
| | Mrs Alison Child | Chris Muir OBE |
| | Anthony Flacks | Dr Colin Reynolds |
| | Mrs Lorena Hunt | Mrs Iris Shanahan |
| | James Johnston | |
| Accounting Officer | Director General of Water Services | |

**staff** Four

| Regional Manager & Secretary | Margaret Smith |
|---|---|

**advisers** **Bankers** Midland Bank 2 The Marlowes Centre, Hemel Hempstead Herts HP1 1DX

**Auditors** National Audit Office 157-197 Buckingham Palace Road London SW1W 9SP

# Ofwat Northumbria Customer Service Committee (Northumbria CSC)

St Cuthbert Chambers
35 Nelson Street
Newcastle upon Tyne NE1 5AN

**Tel** 0191 221 0646
**Fax** 0191 221 0650

**E-mail** nbcsc@ofwat.gnet.gov.uk
**Web** http://www.open.gov.uk/ofwat

**Contact** Elaine Finlay, Regional Manager

**status** Executive body
**founded** 1990
**sponsor** The Director General of Water Services
**powers** Water Industry Act 1991 (Section 28)
**mission** Representing the interests of, and investigating complaints from, the customers of the water and sewage companies in the Northumbria region: Northumbrian Water and Hartlepool Water. Advising and supporting the Director in regulating the water industry and securing for customers the combination of service and price that they would have in a competitive market.

**tasks** Identifying and keeping under review matters affecting customers' interests. To ensure that its companies are aware of, and responsive to, concerns about their services and have adequate complaints procedures. To achieve a speedy and appropriate resolution of individual customer complaints where a company has not adequately dealt with the problem. To publicise the existence, functions and work of Ofwat, ONCC, and the CSC in protecting customers' interests. To advise and report to the Director General on particular issues affecting customers.

**operations** Management: The committee is headed by a Chairman (10 days a month including time spent as Ofwat National Customer Council chairman), supported by a full-time secretariat. Cost of supporting the committee are met by the Director General (£140,000 in 1996-97).

Policy: To ensure customers' views are taken into account in the review of water and sewerage prices in 1999. To press companies to use savings to fund investment and improve levels of service rather than relying on customers' bills. To ensure water companies tackle leakage.

Trends: Price limits to be reset by the Director in 1999 for the years 2000-05. The number of complaints to the CSC reducing.

*board*    Committee's members appointed on merit by the Director from local community. Chairman appointed by the Director in consultation with Secretary of State for Trade and Industry.

| Chairman | Jim Gardner CVO CBE | |
|---|---|---|
| Members | Mrs Maggie Bosanquet | |
| | Ian Brown | Dennis Hudson |
| | Stuart Brown | Alex Lee |
| | David Graham | James Simpson |
| | Norman Guffick | Mrs Mary Storer |
| | David Holliday | Douglas Thompson MBE |
| | Patrick Hornor | Mrs Josephine Turnbull |
| *Accounting Officer* | *Director General of Water Services* | |

*staff*    Four

| Regional Manager & Secretary | Elaine Finlay |
|---|---|

*advisers*

**Bankers**    Midland Bank    2 The Marlowes Centre, Hemel Hempstead Herts HP1 1DX

**Auditors**    National Audit Office    157-197 Buckingham Palace Road London SW1W 9SP

# Ofwat South West Customer Service Committee (South West CSC)

First Floor
Broadwalk House
Southernhay West
Exeter EX1 1TS

**Tel** 01392 428028
**Fax** 01392 428010

**E-mail** swcsc@ofwat.gnet.gov.uk
**Web** http://www.open.gov.uk/ofwat

**Contact** Gillian Johnston, Regional Manager

*status*    Executive body

*founded*    1990

*sponsor*    The Director General of Water Services

*powers*    Water Industry Act 1991 (Section 28)

*mission*    Representing the interests of, and investigating complaints from, the customers of the water and sewage company in the South West region - South West Water Services. Advising and supporting the Director in regulating the water industry and securing for customers the combination of service and price that they would have in a competitive market.

*tasks*    Identifying and keeping under review matters affecting customers' interests. To ensure that its company is aware of, and responsive to, concerns about their services and have adequate complaints procedures. To achieve a speedy and appropriate resolution of individual customer complaints where the company has not adequately dealt with the problem. To publicise the existence, functions and work of Ofwat, ONCC, and the CSC in protecting customers' interests. To advise and report to the Director General on particular issues affecting customers.

*operations*    Management: Committee headed by a Chairwoman (8 days a month), supported by a full-time secretariat. Costs of supporting the committee met by the Director General (£170,000 in 1996/97).

Policy: To ensure customers' views taken into account in review of water and sewerage prices in 1999. To ensure that all costs and benefits of imposing higher stanards are taken into account.

Trends: In 1996/97 the water resource problem eased and South West Water's capital programme improved conditions in many areas but customers still pay the highest bills in the country.

*board*    Committee's members appointed on merit by the Director from local community. Chairwoman appointed by the Director in consultation with the Secretary of State for Trade & Industry.

| Chairman | Mrs Jessica Thomas | |
|---|---|---|
| Members | Hugo Barton | |
| | Norman Bancroft MBE | |
| | Aubrey Bourne | Geoffrey Hibbert |
| | Dr Stuart Coverley | Mrs Suzi Leather MBE |
| | Mike Cox | Mrs Anne Mayes |
| | Mrs Jean Curd | Prof Ian Mercer |
| | Michael Hendy | Graham Parish |
| | Adam Giffard | Ms Ruth Stringer |
| Accounting Officer | Director General of Water Services | |

**staff** Four

| Regional Manager & Secretary | Gillian Johnston |
|---|---|

**advisers**

**Bankers** Midland Bank 2 The Marlowes Centre, Hemel Hempstead Herts HP1 1DX

**Auditors** National Audit Office 157-197 Buckingham Palace Road London SW1W 9SP

## Ofwat Southern Customer Service Committee (Southern CSC)

15-17 Ridgmount Street
London WC1E 7AH

**Tel** 0171 636 3656
**Fax** 0171 637 4813

**E-mail** sncsc@ofwat.gnet.gov.uk
**Web** http://www.open.gov.uk/ofwat

**Contact** Karen Gibbs, Regional Manager

**status** Executive body

**founded** 1990

**sponsor** The Director General of Water Services

**powers** Water Industry Act 1991 (Section 28)

**mission** Representing the interests of, and investigating complaints from, the customers of the water and sewage companies in the Southern region - Southern Water Services, Portsmouth Water, Mid Kent Water, Folkestone & Dover Water Services, South East Water and Mid Southern Water. Advising and supporting the Director in regulating the water industry and securing for customers the combination of service and price that they would have in a competitive market.

**tasks** Identifying and keeping under review matters affecting customers' interests. To ensure that its companies are aware of, and responsive to, concerns about their services and have adequate complaints procedures. To achieve a speedy and appropriate resolution of individual customer complaints where a company has not adequately dealt with the problem. To publicise the existence, functions and work of Ofwat, ONCC, and the CSC in protecting customers' interests. To advise and report to the Director General on particular issues affecting customers.

**operations** Management: Committee headed by a Chairman (seven days a month), supported by a full-time secretariat. Costs of supporting committee met by Director General (£183,000 in 1996-97).

Policy: To ensure customers' views taken into account in review of water and sewerage prices in 1999. To press companies to use efficiency savings to fund investment and improve levels of service rather than relying on customers' bills.

Trends: Further environmental and quality obligations may be placed on the companies. Costs for necessary investment will be reflected in price limits for 2000-05, being set by the Director in 1999.

**board** Committee's members appointed on merit by Director from local community. Chairman appointed by Director in consultation with Secretary of State for Trade and Industry.

| | | | |
|---|---|---|---|
| Chairman | Dr John Beishon | | |
| Members | Mrs Gabrielle Edwards | | |
| | Mrs Rosemary Edwards | Dr John Lawrence | |
| | Mrs Margaret Ginman | Dai Liyanage | |
| | Mrs Catherine Hoey | Mike Perfect | |
| | Clive Howard-Luck | Harry Speight | |
| | Mrs Lynn Judge | Mrs Christine Swan | |
| *Accounting Officer* | *Director General of Water Services* | | |

**staff**    Six

| Regional Manager & Secretary | Karen Gibbs |
|---|---|

**advisers**    **Bankers**    Midland Bank    2 The Marlowes Centre, Hemel Hempstead Herts HP1 1DX

**Auditors**    National Audit Office    157-197 Buckingham Palace Road London SW1W 9SP

# Ofwat Thames Customer Service Committee (Thames CSC)

15-17 Ridgmount Street
London WC1E 7AH

**Tel** 0171 636 3656
**Fax** 0171 637 4813

**E-mail** tmcsc@ofwat.gnet.gov.uk
**Web** http://www.open.gov.uk/ofwat

**Contact** Andrew Milne, Regional Manager

**status**    Executive body

**founded**    1990

**sponsor**    The Director General of Water Services

**powers**    Water Industry Act 1991 (Section 28)

**mission**    Representing the interests of, and investigating complaints from, the customers of the water and sewage companies in the Thames region: Thames Water Utilities, Three Valleys Water, Sutton & East Surrey Water and North Surrey Water. Advising and supporting the Director in regulating the water industry and securing for customers the combination of service and price that they would have in a competitive market.

**tasks**    Identifying and keeping under review matters affecting customers' interests. To ensure that its companies are aware of, and responsive to, concerns about their services and have adequate complaints procedures. To achieve a speedy and appropriate resolution of individual customer complaints where a company has not adequately dealt with the problem. To publicise the existence, functions and work of Ofwat, ONCC, and the CSC in protecting customers' interests. To advise and report to the Director General on particular issues affecting customers.

**operations**    Management: Committee headed by a Chairman (seven days a month), supported by a full-time secretariat. Costs of supporting committee are met by the Director General (£272,000 in 1996-97).

Policy: To ensure customers' views are taken into account in review of water and sewerage prices in 1999. To encourage companies to reduce leakage and adopt strategies to increase the amount of water available at point of use and reduce demand for non-essential use while taking into account the potential impact on customers' bills.

Trends: Price limits to be reset by Director in 1999 for years 2000-05. Region has closest balance between supply and demand for water in England and Wales and demand is increasing faster.

**board**    Committee's members appointed on merit by the Director from local community. Chairman appointed by Director in consultation with Secretary of State for Trade and Industry.

| Chairman | Herman Scopes | |
|---|---|---|
| Members | Mrs Susan Blake | William Holland |
| | Kenneth Brown | Mrs Gillian Jenkins |
| | Clive Collier | John Moore MBE |
| | Mrs Barbara Greggains | Miss Hazel Prowse |
| | John Hayzelden | Alexander Ross |
| | John Hills | |
| Accounting Officer | Director General of Water Services | |

**staff** Three

| Regional Manager & Secretary | Andrew Milne |
|---|---|

**advisers**

**Bankers** Midland Bank — 2 The Marlowes Centre, Hemel Hempstead Herts HP1 1DX

**Auditors** National Audit Office — 157-197 Buckingham Palace Road London SW1W 9SP

# Ofwat Wales Customer Service Committee (Wales CSC)

Room 140
Caradog House
1-6 St Andrews Place
Cardiff CF1 3BE

**Tel** 01222 239852
**Fax** 01222 239847

**E-mail** wlcsc@ofwat.gnet.gov.uk
**Web** http://www.open.gov.uk/ofwat

**Contact** Clive Sterl, Regional Manager

**status** Executive body

**founded** 1990

**sponsor** The Director General of Water Services

**powers** Water Industry Act 1991 (Section 28)

**mission** Representing the interests of , and investigating complaints from, the customers of the water and sewage companies in Wales - Dwr Cymru Cyfyngedig and Dee Valley Water. Advising and supporting the Director in regulating the water industry and securing for customers the combination of service and price that they would have in a competitive market.

**tasks** To identify and keep under review matters affecting customers' interests. To ensure that its companies are aware of, and responsive to, concerns about their services and have adequate complaints procedures. To achieve a speedy and appropriate resolution of individual customer complaints where a company has not adequately dealt with the problem. To publicise the existence, functions and work of Ofwat, ONCC, and the CSC in protecting customers' interests. To advise and report to the Director General on particular issues affecting customers.

**operations** Management: Committee headed by a Chairman (8 days a month), supported by a full-time secretariat. Costs of supporting committee met by Director General (£169,000 in 1996-97).

Policy: To ensure that customers' views taken into account in review of water and sewerage prices in 1999 and priority given to a price fall in real terms and water metering.

Trends: Price limits to be reset by Director in 1999 for 2000-05. Further environmental and quality obligations likely to be placed on companies.

**board** Committee's members appointed on merit by the Director from local community. Chairman appointed by Director in consultation with Secretary of State for Wales.

| Chairman | The Venerable Raymond Roberts CB | |
|---|---|---|
| Members | Andrew Bailey | |
| | Mrs Nerys Haf Biddulph | Ian McFarlane |
| | Mrs Alison Cording | Stephen Powell |
| | Clive George | Maldwyn Rees |
| | Paul Hetherington | Mrs Sheila Tristram |
| | Dr Tim Hughes | John Warman |
| | Mrs Heather March | Russell Young |
| *Accounting Officer* | *Director General of Water Services* | |

*staff*     Four

| Regional Manager & Secretary | Clive Sterl |
|---|---|

*advisers*    **Bankers**    Midland Bank    2 The Marlowes Centre, Hemel Hempstead
                                              Herts HP1 1DX

            **Auditors**    National Audit Office    157-197 Buckingham Palace Road
                                                      London SW1W 9SP

# Ofwat Wessex Customer Service Committee (Wessex CSC)

2 The Hide Market
West Street
St Philips
Bristol BS2 0BH

**Tel** 0117 955 7001          **E-mail** wxcsc@ofwat.gnet.gov.uk
**Fax** 0117 955 7037          **Web** http://www.open.gov.uk/ofwat

**Contact** Teresa Evans, Regional Manager

*status*      Executive body

*founded*     1990

*sponsor*     The Director General of Water Services

*powers*      Water Industry Act 1991 (Section 28)

*mission*     Representing the interests of, and investigating complaints from, the customers of the water and sewage companies in Wessex: Wessex Water Services, Bournemouth & West Hampshire Water, Bristol Water and Cholderton & District Water Company. Advising and supporting the Director in regulating the water industry and securing for customers the combination of service and price that they would have in a competitive market.

*tasks*       Identifying and keeping under review matters affecting customers' interests. To ensure that its companies are aware of, and responsive to, concerns about their services and have adequate complaints procedures. To achieve a speedy and appropriate resolution of individual customer complaints where a company has not adequately dealt with the problem. To publicise the existence, functions and work of Ofwat, ONCC, and the CSC in protecting customers' interests. To advise and report to the Director General on particular issues affecting customers.

*operations*  Management: Committee headed by a Chairman (eight days a month), supported by a full-time secretariat. Costs of supporting committee met by the Director General (£189,000 in 1996-97).

              Policy: To ensure customers' views taken into account in review of water and sewerage prices in 1999. To press companies to ensure there is adequate water resources to supply customers' homes and to reduce leakage.

              Trends: Price limits to be reset by Director in 1999 for years 2000-05 taking into account environmental and quality obligations placed on companies.

*board*       Committee's members appointed on merit by the Director from local community. Chairman appointed by Director in consultation with Secretary of State for Trade and Industry.

| Chairman | Mrs Sheila Reiter | |
| Members | Brigadier David Baines MBE | Mrs Brenda Lalonde |
| | John Dornton | Ian Macdonald |
| | Colin Eddleston | Prof Cedric Sandford |
| | Piers Feilden | Mrs Diana Tory |
| | Mrs Ann Hudson | Graham Turner |
| | Leslie Keyte | Mrs Jean Watkins |
| *Accounting Officer* | *Director General of Water Services* | |

**staff**  Five

| Regional Manager & Secretary | Teresa Evans |
| --- | --- |

**advisers**

**Bankers**  Midland Bank  2 The Marlowes Centre, Hemel Hempstead Herts HP1 1DX

**Auditors**  National Audit Office  157-197 Buckingham Palace Road London SW1W 9SP

# Ofwat Yorkshire Customer Service Committee (Yorkshire CSC)

Ground Floor
Symons House
Belgrave Street
Leeds LS2 8DD

**Tel** 0113 234 0874
**Fax** 0113 234 1316

**E-mail** ykcsc@ofwat.gnet.gov.uk
**Web** http://www.open.gov.uk/ofwat

**status**  Executive body

**founded**  1990

**sponsor**  The Director General of Water Services

**powers**  Water Industry Act 1991 (Section 28)

**mission**  Representing the interests of, and investigating complaints from, the customers of the water and sewage companies in Yorkshire - Yorkshire Water Services and York Waterworks. Advising and supporting the Director in regulating the water industry and to secure for customers the combination of service and price that they would have in a competitive market.

**tasks**  Identifying and keeping under review matters affecting customers' interests. To ensure that its companies are aware of, and responsive to, concerns about their services and have adequate complaints procedures. To achieve a speedy and appropriate resolution of individual customer complaints where a company has not adequately dealt with the problem. To publicise the existence, functions and work of Ofwat, ONCC, and the CSC in protecting customers' interests. To advise and report to the Director General on particular issues affecting customers.

**operations**  Management: Committee headed by a Chairman (eight days a month), supported by a full-time secretariat. Costs of supporting committee met by the Director General (£150,000 in 1996-97).

Policy: To ensure customers' views taken into account in review of water and sewerage prices in 1999. To press companies to ensure that there is adequate water resources to supply customers' homes and to stress that standpipes or rota cuts are not acceptable in any circumstances.

Trends: Price limits to be reset by Director in 1999 for years 2000-05 taking into account environmental and quality obligations placed on companies. CSC looking for any increases in charges to be below rate of inflation.

**board**  Committee's members appointed on merit by the Director from local community. Chairman appointed by Director in consultation with Secretary of State for Trade and Industry.

| Chairman | Eric Wilson | |
|---|---|---|
| Members | Ashraf Bismil BEM | |
| | Justin Brogan | Ms Kath Fysh |
| | Alan Coates | Miss Karen Holmes |
| | Mrs Jenny Clarke | Dr Thomas Morris |
| | Miss Ann Dargan | Gordon Polley MBE |
| | Robert Duncalf | Mrs Pauline Thresh |
| *Accounting Officer* | *Director General of Water Services* | |

**staff**  Four

| Regional Manager & Secretary | Paul Taylor |
|---|---|

**advisers**

**Bankers**  Midland Bank  2 The Marlowes Centre, Hemel Hempstead Herts HP1 1DX

**Auditors**  National Audit Office  157-197 Buckingham Palace Road London SW1W 9SP

# Oil & Pipelines Agency (OPA)

35/38 Portman Square
London W1H 0EU

**Tel** 0171 935 2585
**Fax** 0171 935 3510

**status**  Executive body

**founded**  1985

**sponsor**  Ministry of Defence (MOD)

**powers**  Oil and Pipelines Act 1985

**mission**  To provide for the efficient and effective management of the Government Pipeline and Storage System (GPSS), a strategic defence asset.

**tasks**  MOD sponsors OPA as its Managing Agent. Responsible for managing the GPSS: care, maintenance, security, safety. Operations maintenance and engineering activities are put out to competitive tender. The GPSS receives, stores, transports and delivers a full range of white oil petroleum products for both defence and commercial use. Working through contractors, OPA manages the 2,500 km of underground cross-country pipelines, 46 storage depots, salt cavities, pumping stations etc.

**operations**  Management: General Manager responsible for day-to-day running of business.

Policy: Major engineering projects progressing to enhance operational safety of the System.

Trends: Commercial use of the System provide revenue - new aviation fuel road distribution and increased pipeline trade to the major UK airports.

**board**  Members appointed by the Secretary of State.

| Chairman | GA Richards |
|---|---|
| Member | CG Finch |
| Member | H Griffiths |
| *Accounting Officer* | *General Manager* |

**staff**  17

| General Manager | KG Berry |
|---|---|
| Secretary | VA Wadham |

**Q&Q**

*financial*

| PROFIT & LOSS Year end: 31 March | 1997 £000 | 1996 £000 |
|---|---|---|
| TURNOVER | 1,650 | 1,656 |
| OPERATING & ADMINISTRATIVE EXPENSES | (1,688) | (1,712) |
| OPERATING LOSS | (38) | (56) |
| Interest Receivable | 234 | 244 |
| PROFIT ON ORDINARY ACTIVITIES BEFORE TAXATION | 196 | 188 |
| Tax on Profit on Ordinary Activities | (48) | (58) |
| PROFIT ON ORDINARY ACTIVITIES AFTER TAXATION | 148 | 130 |
| Retained Profit at Beginning of Year | 1,221 | 1,091 |
| RETAINED PROFIT AT END OF YEAR | 1,369 | 1,221 |

## Ordnance Survey (OS)

Romsey Road
Maybush
Southampton SO16 4GU

**Tel** 01703 792000
**Fax** 01703 792452          **Web** http://www.ordsvy.gov.uk

*status* Executive agency

*founded* 1990

*sponsor* Department of the Environment , Transport and the Regions

*powers* Operates under legislation dating back to 1841. OS Framework Document

*mission* The official survey and topographical mapping of Great Britain (GB)

*tasks* Core: Providing and marketing topographical data and mapping at scales 1:10000 and larger for the whole of GB, including the geodetic and topographical surveys. OS also provides and markets mapping at scales 1:25000 and 1:50000. These scales regarded as important to the nation; commercial: Production and marketing of mapping and survey information at scales smaller than 1:50,000 - often co-published; also Geographic Information Systems (GIS) contract work for the private and public sectors in GB and overseas.

*operations* Management: The Director General and Chief Executive reports directly to Ministers in the DoE and is supported by a Management Board. Probably 90% of the land area of GB is uncommercial in mapping terms but OS mapping information and data covers every corner of GB. A major public consultation exercise and departmental soundings were undertaken in 1996/97 to determine which services OS should provide in the public interest.

Policy: A National Interest Mapping Service Agreement should be in place by April 1998.

Trends: Technological change has ensured that an increasing proportion of costs are recouped. Customer quality expectations are rising rapidly and globalisation in mapping increases (buying services from overseas and working for other governments and the overseas private sector).

*performance* All key targets achieved; cost recovery target considerably exceeded.

*board* Non-Executive Directors are appointed by the Secretary of State. Executive Directors are OS Business Unit Directors.

| | |
|---|---|
| Director General & Chief Executive | David Rhind |
| Director of Business & Professional Markets | Tony Black |
| Non-Executive Director | Caroline Graham-Brown |
| Non-Executive Director | Christopher Kington |
| Director of Data Collection | Ian Logan |
| Director of Consumer & Education Markets | Michael Mayes |
| Director of Information Management | Bryan Nanson |
| Non-Executive Director | Geoffrey Robinson |
| Director of Business Services | David Willey |
| *Accounting Officer* | *Chief Executive* |

*staff* 1881

| financial | OPERATING TURNOVER & COSTS | | | |
|---|---|---|---|---|
| | Year end: 31 March | 1997 | 1996 | 1995 |
| | | £000 | £000 | £000 |
| | **TOTAL TURNOVER** | **68,806** | **66,548** | **58,585** |
| | OPERATING COSTS | | | |
| | Staff costs | 43,256 | 47,258 | 43,157 |
| | Depreciation of fixed assets | 3,695 | 3,519 | 3,824 |
| | Loss/(profit) on sales of fixed assets | 7 | (34) | 220 |
| | Other operating charges | 24,921 | 33,028 | 25,045 |
| | Total operating costs | 71,879 | 83,771 | 72,246 |
| | **NET OPERATING DEFICIT** | **(3,073)** | **(17,223)** | **13,661** |
| | Interest on capital | (2,042) | (1,892) | 2,249 |
| | **OPERATING DEFICIT FOR THE YEAR** | **(5,115)** | **(19,115)** | **15,910** |

| advisers | **Auditors** | National Audit Office | 157-197 Buckingham Palace Road |
|---|---|---|---|
| | | | London SW1W 9SP |

# *Ordnance Survey of Northern Ireland (OSNI)*

Colby House
Stranmillis Court
Belfast BT9 5BJ

**Tel** 01232 255755                                **E-mail** 100635,2165@compuserve.com
**Fax** 01232 255700

| | |
|---|---|
| **status** | Executive agency |
| **founded** | 1992 |
| **sponsor** | Northern Ireland Office, Department of the Environment for NI (DOENI) |
| **powers** | Framework Document 1997 |
| **mission** | NI's mapping agency. Responsible for providing accurate, comprehensive and up-to-date topographical information for NI. |
| **tasks** | Undertakes all surveys necessary for the maintenance of the archive of trigonometrical levelling and topographical information of NI and provides customers with information from the archive in forms most appropriate to their needs. Produces smallscale maps, town plans and special products from the topographical database on a commercial basis to meet customers' demands. Undertakes special surveys, cartographic and reprographic services and aerial photography under contract for the private sector. |
| **operations** | Management: Chief Executive is responsible for the day-to-day operation and performance of the Agency. He is supported by a Senior Management Board of five. 70 field surveyors operate from regional offices throughout NI. Takes the lead in developing the Northern Ireland Geographic Information System (NIGIS), which is a partnership of government departments, local authorities and public utilities. |
| | Policy: New projects to increase the effectiveness of survey operations - Automated Graphical Field Survey and Digital Stereo Photogrammetry. |
| | Trends: Pressure on resources continuing, further reduction of staff numbers. |
| **performance** | Exceeded all targets set for 1996/97 |
| **board** | Appointed by Minister. |

| *Accounting Officer* | *Chief Executive* |
|---|---|
| | |

| | |
|---|---|
| **staff** | 177 |

| Director & Chief Executive | MJD Brand |
|---|---|
| Deputy Director | WG Mitchell |
| Field Surveys | KA Adams |
| Photogrammetric Surveys | WA Hopkins |
| Head of Map Production | RJ Clements |
| Digital Production | TJD Martin |
| Graphical Production & Sales | M McVeigh |
| Finance, Personnel & Administration | RSA Hughes |
| Head of Information Systems | HG Mahood |
| NIGIS, IT Systems | J McKinley |

*financial*

| INCOME & EXPENDITURE Year end: 31 March | 1997 £000 | 1996 £000 |
|---|---|---|
| **INCOME** | **1,335** | **1,282** |
| **EXPENDITURE** | | |
| Staff costs | 4,214 | 4,146 |
| Depreciation | 298 | 323 |
| **Other operating costs** | | |
| Early departure costs | 134 | - |
| Map production and survey costs | 153 | 227 |
| Travel and subsistence | 115 | 122 |
| Computer operational expenses | 250 | 216 |
| Supplies and services consumed | 271 | 184 |
| Building running costs | 210 | 205 |
| Loss on disposal of fixed assets | 23 | 20 |
| Notional costs | 1,419 | 706 |
| Permanent diminution in value of fixed assets | 65 | 294 |
| | **2,640** | **1,974** |
| **GROSS OPERATING EXPENDITURE** | **7,152** | **6,443** |
| **NET OPERATING EXPENDITURE** | **5,817** | **5,161** |
| Interest on Capital | 127 | 147 |
| **NET EXPENDITURE** | **5,944** | **5,308** |

*advisers* **Auditors**   Northern Ireland Audit Office   106 University Street,Belfast BT7 1EU

*publications* Annual Report and Accounts, Business and Corporate Plan

*branches*

Boaz House
15 Scarffes Entry
Omagh BT78 1JE
Tel 01662 254734

Crown Buildings
10 Alexander Road
Armagh BT6 7JL
Tel 01762 529805

54 Stone Row
Coleraine BT52 1ER
Tel 01265 43622

# Parole Board (for England & Wales)

Abell House
John Islip Street
London SW1P 4LP

**Tel** 0171 217 5314
**Fax** 0171 217 5677/ 5813

*status*      Executive body

*founded*     1967. As executive body 1996

*sponsor*     Home Office

*powers*      Criminal Justice Acts 1967 and 1991. Criminal Justice and Public Order Act 1994. Crime (Sentences) Act 1997

*mission*     Writing parole licences for individual long-term and life sentence prisoners, on the basis of its own risk assessment designed to further reduce the risk of reoffending.

*tasks*       For long-term determinate sentence prisoners - assessing those sentenced to three years and more when they have served five-sixths of their sentence; reviewing their cases annually; making risk assessments, writing parole licences; directing their release. For automatic and discretionary life sentence prisoners and those detained during Her Majesty's Pleasure - assessing risk, writing life licences and directing release.

*operations*  Management: The Chairman reports to the Home Secretary. The Chief Executive reports to the Secretary of State. The Board meets on most weekdays in panels of three or four members to consider cases for parole, release on life licence and recall from licence for both determinate and life sentence prisoners. Also for representations against recall, requests for cancellation of licence conditions and permissions for licensees to travel abroad. The General Purposes Committee carries out the functions of a management board.

Policy: Dealing with all cases in a consistent and equitable manner, taking into account directions given by the Home Secretary. Providing prisoners with sound reasons for decisions and recommendations. Processing all parole and life sentence cases in a timely manner. Managing operations efficiently and cost-effectively.

Trends: Increased workload resulting from the 1997 Act. Increased security making it more difficult for prisoners to demonstrate their trustworthiness on short home leave. Budgetary restraints on the work of the board, eg reduction of probation staff seconded to prisons.

**performance**   1996/97 all key targets met except timeliness.

**board**   Board members appointed by the Home Secretary. Part-time members and the Chairman. Vice Chairman, full-time members and the Chief Executive.

| | | |
|---|---|---|
| Chairman | Lord Belstead LL PC | |
| Vice-Chairman | Justice Alliot | |
| Members | Mrs JL Addyman JP | |
| | Mrs ABC Barker | Judge Mott |
| | A Barrow | S Murphy |
| | Judge Beaumont QC | Miss E Norton OBE |
| | Dr C Berry | Dr RBL Osborn |
| | Dr JJ Bradley | P Palmer JP |
| | Dr I Bronks | G Park CBE |
| | Dr H Bullard | Mrs SM Peach OBE JP |
| | Miss P Buller | Mrs J Pitchers JP |
| | Sir Robert Bunyard CBE | Ms J Pye |
| | Miss I Butcher | Mrs P Rance |
| | Judge Capstick QC | Mrs S Reiter JP |
| | Mrs S Copper | Sir Samuel Roberts Bt |
| | JA Cotton | RP Robson |
| | Mrs J Coward JP | T Russel |
| | H Dillon MBE | J Sadlik JP |
| | J Entwistle | Prof A Sanders |
| | Mrs DJ Fawcett JP | Mrs R Sargent JP |
| | Dr E Gordon | D Scott |
| | Judge Griffiths | Cllr J Shera |
| | Judge Harris QC | Dr G Shetty |
| | Mrs V Horman JP | DAG Smith OBE JP |
| | Miss S Hubbard | Dr DEM Speed |
| | Dr CC Hunter | RS Statham |
| | N Joseph OBE | Judge Stephens QC |
| | Ms M Kane | G Stone |
| | Dr I Keitch | A Stroyan |
| | Dr DD Kothari | Mrs J Summers |
| | Prof RD Mackay | Dr M Swan |
| | Judge Maddison | Dr D Tidmarsh |
| | Mrs L March JP | Mrs WA Towers |
| | P Martin | PJ Trusler |
| | Judge Matthewman QC | Justice Tucker |
| | Dr D Mawson | Mrs J Turnbull JP |
| | Dr H McClelland | Mrs S Turquet JP |
| | T McNicholas | RO West QPM |
| *Accounting Officer* | *Chief Executive* | |

**staff**   51

| | |
|---|---|
| Chief Executive | M Todd |

**financial**

| RECEIPTS & PAYMENTS | |
|---|---|
| **Year end: 31 March** | **1997** |
| | £ |
| **RECEIPTS** | |
| HM Grants received | 1,863,477 |
| **PAYMENTS** | |
| Salaries and wages | 1,590,565 |
| Other operating payments | 272,912 |
| | 1,863,477 |
| **SURPLUS/ (DEFICIT) FROM OPERATIONS** | 0 |
| **EXCESS OF (PAYMENTS OVER RECEIPTS)/ RECEIPTS** | |
| **OVER PAYMENTS** | 0 |

**advisers**   **Auditors**   National Audit Office   157-197 Buckingham Palace Road
London SW1W 9SP

## Parole Board for Scotland

Saughton House
Broomhouse Drive
Edinburgh EH11 3XD

**Tel** 0131 244 8755
**Fax** 0131 244 6974

| | |
|---|---|
| *status* | Executive body |
| *founded* | 1968 |
| *sponsor* | Scottish Office |
| *powers* | Prisoners and Criminal Proceedings Act (Scotland) 1993. Crime and Punishment (Scotland) Act 1997 |
| *mission* | To direct and advise the Secretary of State on the release on licence and recall from licence, of people serving sentences of imprisonment or detention of four years or more, whose cases he has referred to the Board, and on the conditions, variation and cancellation of licences. |
| *tasks* | Assessing the suitability of prisoners for early release. Directing the release, and licence conditions, of determinate sentence prisoners serving four to ten years. Recommending the release of prisoners serving a determinate sentence of ten years or more. Directing the release of discretionary life prisoners. Recommending the recall to custody of determinate sentence prisoners serving four years or more and life sentence prisoners released on parole or licence - where that is in the public interest. Advising the Secretary of State on the release on life licence of prisoners serving mandatory life sentences. |
| *operations* | Management: The Board reports to the Secretary of State. |
| *board* | Appointed by the Secretary of State; minimum of four members including a Lord Commissioner of Justiciary, a registered medical practitioner who is a psychiatrist, someone with knowledge and experience of supervising or the aftercare of discharged prisoners and someone who has studied the causes of delinquency or the treatment of offenders. |

| Chairman | Ian McNee | |
|---|---|---|
| Vice Chairman | Sheriff Gordon Shiach | |
| | Ms Jeane Freeman OBE | |
| Members | Dr John Bayrd | Lord MacLean |
| | Mrs M Casserly | James Milne |
| | Mrs Linda Costelloe Baker | John Muirhead |
| | Dr Judith Greenwood | Lord Ross |
| | Mrs Irene Gudd | Prof Lorraine Waterhouse |
| | Hamish Hyslop | Dr Peter Whatmore |
| | Sheriff Brian Lockhart | Dr Peter Young |
| *Accounting Officer* | *Board Secretary* | |

*staff*    Five

| Secretary | Hugh P Boyle |
|---|---|

# Particle Physics & Astronomy Research Council (PPARC)

North Star Avenue
Swindon
Wiltshire SN2 1SZ

**Tel** 01793 442000
**Fax** 01793 442002

**E-mail** userid@pparc.ac.uk
**Web** http://www.pparc.ac.uk

| | |
|---|---|
| *status* | Executive body |
| *founded* | 1994 |
| *sponsor* | Department of Trade and Industry (DTI) |
| *powers* | Royal Charter |
| *mission* | To pursue a programme of high-quality basic research in astronomy, planetary science and particle physics which furthers understanding of fundamental questions, trains high-quality scientists and engineers, increases industry's competitiveness, attracts future generations of scientists and engineers, and stimulates the public's interest. |
| *tasks* | Supports: large-scale research facilities, provided through the PPARC's Royal Observatories and through subscription to international organisations such as the European Organisation for Nuclear Research (CERN) and the European Space Agency (ESA); research undertaken largely in the UK universities; the education and training of postgraduate studentships and fellowships; and the public understanding of science programmes. |
| *operations* | Management: Ten committees act as advisory bodies to Council and Chief Executive. Principal funding through grant-in-aid, but some income from Dutch and Canadian government departments with whom the PPARC collaborates in supporting facilities for ground-based astronomy, and some from work undertaken by Royal Observatories on a repayment basis. |
| | Policy: Research predominantly international and involves active collaboration with most major scientific nations. Increasing number of research studentships being funded. |
| | Trends: Continued investment in new UK research facilities for astronomy; difficulty in providing adequate funding for UK particle physics. |
| *board* | Council appointed by Secretary of State. |

| | |
|---|---|
| Chairman | Dr Peter Williams CBE |
| Chief Executive | Prof Ken Pounds CBE |
| Members of Council | Prof Len Culhane |
| | John de Fonblanque CMG |
| | Prof John Dowell |
| | Prof John Enderby |
| | Dr David Evans |
| | Dr Brian Eyre CBE |
| | Prof Ian Halliday |
| | Dr Sue Ion |
| | Prof Carole Jordan |
| | Prof Sir Martin Rees |
| | Dr Geoff Robinson |
| *Accounting Officer* | *Chief Executive* |

*staff*     355

| | |
|---|---|
| Chief Executive | Ken Pounds |
| Director of Science | Ian Corbett |
| Head, Corporate Affairs Division | Geoffrey Findlay |
| Director of Administration | John Love |
| Head, Particle Physics Division | Dave Morrell |
| Head, Astronomy Division | Paul Murdin |
| Director, Organisational Development | Jim Sadlier |
| Director | Jasper Wall |
| Director | Stuart Pitt |
| Director | Ian Robson |
| Director, Isaac Newton Group | Steve Unger |
| Director | Derek Davies |

**Q&Q**

**financial**

| INCOME & EXPENDITURE<br>Year end: 31 March | 1996<br>£000 | 1995<br>£000 |
|---|---|---|
| **INCOME** | | |
| Parliamentary grant-in-aid | 199,513 | 176,622 |
| Release of deferred grant-in-aid | 3,299 | 3,879 |
| Other income | 4,427 | 3,857 |
| | **207,239** | **184,358** |
| **EXPENDITURE** | | |
| Staff costs | 10,921 | 10,896 |
| Research grants | 38,918 | 33,016 |
| International subscriptions | 109,651 | 95,515 |
| Other operating costs | 45,609 | 44,901 |
| | **(205,099)** | **(184,328)** |
| **OPERATING SURPLUS** | **2,140** | **30** |
| Loss on disposal of fixed assets | (44) | (439) |
| Interest receivable | 12 | 24 |
| Transfers from reserves | 35 | 122 |
| **SURPLUS/(DEFICIT) FOR THE YEAR** | **2,143** | **(263)** |
| Accumulated deficit brought forward | (2,022) | (1,759) |
| **ACCUMULATED SURPLUS/(DEFICIT) CARRIED FORWARD** | **121** | **(2,022)** |

**advisers**

**Auditors**      National Audit Office      157-197 Buckingham Palace Road
London SW1W 9SP

**branches**

*Royal Greenwich Observatory*
Madingley Road
Cambridge CB3 0EZ
Tel 01223 374000
Fax 01223 374700
E-mail jvw@mail.ast.cam.ac.uk

*Royal Observatory, Edinburgh*
Blackford Hill
Edinburgh EH9 3HJ
Tel 0131 668 8100
Fax 0131 668 8264
E-mail sgp@roe.ac.uk

*Joint Astronomy Centre*
University Park
Hilo
Hawaii (USA) 96720
Tel 001 808 961 3756
Fax 001 808 961 6516
E-mail eir@jach.hawaii.edu

*Observatorio Del Roque De Los Muchachos, La Palma*
Santa Cruz De La Palma
Canary Islands
Tenerife 38770
Tel 00 3422 411048
Fax 00 3422 414203
E-mail swv@1pve.ing.iac.es

*British National Space Centre*
Bridge Place
88/89 Eccleston Square
London SW1V 1PT
Tel 0171 215 5000
Fax 0171 821 5387
E-mail derek_davis@bnsc-hq.ccmail.com

# *Patent Office*

Concept House
Cardiff Rd
Newport NP9 1RH

**Tel** 01633 81400
**Fax** 01633 814444

**E-mail** enquiries@patent.gov.uk

**status**      Executive agency

**founded**      1990, 1991 as trading fund

**sponsor**      Department of Trade and Industry (DTI)

**powers**      Patents Act 1977; Copyright, Designs and Patents Act 1988; Trade Marks Acts 1938, 1986, 1994; Registered Designs Act 1949. Framework Document 1990 and 1996

**mission**      To help stimulate innovation and international competitiveness of British industry through intellectual property rights relating to patents, trade marks, registered designs and copyright.

**tasks** Grants patents and designs and also registers trade marks for goods and services. Represents the UK in international negotiations on intellectual property (eg treaties under World Intellectual Property Organisation (WIPO) and EU directives).

**operations** Management: Organised into six directorates: the two largest (three quarters of staff) deal with patents, designs and trademarks; the others deal with intellectual property policy, copyright policy, finance and common services. Operating surplus made. In pursuit of government's policy to encourage innovation, patent applicants' fees are below actual cost and differences recovered from renewal fees on granted patents.

Policy: Protection of intellectual property rights throughout the world. Continuing efforts to promote an open and competitive international market. Close links with European Patent Office and the EU trade mark office.

Trends: Seeking international harmonisation of rules and procedures and the modernisation and simplification of intellectual property law.

**performance** Backlog in granting patents in 1996 because of increased demand.

**board** Members of the Steering Board appointed by the Chairman.

| Director General, Corporate & Consumer Affairs | Brian Hilton CB |
|---|---|
| Chief Executive | Paul Hartnack |
| Members | TJ Cassidy |
| | DR Fairbairn |
| | JR Fryer |
| | DR McMurtry |
| | J Phillips |
| | BA Wright |
| *Accounting Officer* | *Chief Executive* |

**staff** 727

| Comptroller General & Chief Executive | Paul Hartnack |
|---|---|
| Director (Copyright) | Jonathan Startup |
| Director (IPPD) | Graham Jenkins |
| Assistant Registrar (Trade Marks) | Norman Harkness |
| Secretary (Administration & Resources) | Craig Octon |
| Assistant Comptroller (Patents & Design) | Ron Marchant |
| Director (Finance) | Julian Thompson |

**financial**

**INCOME & EXPENDITURE**

| Year end: 31 March | 1997 £000 | 1996 £000 | 1995 £000 |
|---|---|---|---|
| Turnover | 59,837 | 57,512 | 52,749 |
| Staff cost | (21,250) | (28,534) | (23,267) |
| Depreciation | (1,446) | (1,803) | (1,718) |
| Amortisation of recollocation costs | (919) | (920) | (1,840) |
| Other operating charges | (16,571) | (16,408) | (15,647) |
| Copyright expenses recoverable from DTI | 730 | 689 | 692 |
| **OPERATING SURPLUS BEFORE INTEREST & DIVIDENDS** | **2,381** | **10,536** | **10,969** |
| Interest receivable | 3,579 | 2,912 | 1,616 |
| Interest payable on short-term loans | - | - | (16) |
| **OPERATING SURPLUS ON ORDINARY ACTIVITIES** | **23,960** | **13,448** | **12,569** |
| Transfer of European Patent (UK) excess to special reserve | (9,787) | (7,858) | (5,725) |
| Interest payable on long-term loans | (351) | (367) | (384) |
| **SURPLUS FOR THE YEAR** | **13,822** | **5,223** | **6,460** |
| Dividends | (1,700) | (2,000) | (1,000) |
| **RETAINED SURPLUS FOR THE YEAR** | **12,122** | **3,223** | **5,460** |

**advisers**

**Bankers** Bank of England

**Auditors** National Audit Office

**Solicitors** DTI Solicitors

**Public Relations** Binns Associates

**publications** *Patents and Design Journal, Trademarks Journal, Designs in View,* and an assortment of free information booklets

**branches** 25 Southampton Buildings
Chancery Lane
Holborn
London WC2A 1PW

# Pay & Personnel Agency (PPA)

Block B
Warminster Road
Bath BA1 5AA

**Tel** 01225 828636

| | |
|---|---|
| *status* | Executive agency |
| *founded* | 1996 |
| *sponsor* | Ministry of Defence (MOD) |
| *powers* | Framework Document 1996 |
| *mission* | Provides a full range of civilian payroll, pensions and allowances services, principally to MOD employees but also to Trading Funds and other government departments and agencies. |
| *tasks* | Calculates and pays salaries and wages for industrial and non-industrial employees; a variety of grading performance-related systems; travel and transfer allowances; pension awards; payment of fees and personal payments; administers monies for estates of deceased servicemen or pensioners. |
| *operations* | Management: Secretary of State has ultimate responsibility for policy and revenue. Deputy Under Secretary of State (Civilian Management) is the Owner of the agency and is accountable to the Secretary of State. Chief Executive is appointed through open competition and attends the Owner's Advisory Board. He is responsible for day-to-day management, assisted by Management Board. Two offices in Bath, one in Worcester, one in Cheadle Hulme, and small pensions office in Malta. |
| | Policy: Developing the plans for integrating pay and personnel services. Renewing marketing efforts to gain new customers. |
| | Trends: Declining number of industrial pay accounts due to external contractors winning bids. Looking at partnership with the private sector. |
| *board* | Owner's Advisory Board appointed by the Secretary of State from senior officials of the MOD. |

| | |
|---|---|
| Chief Executive | Mike Rowe |
| Member of Management Board | Tony Breakell |
| Assistant Director, Pensions | Peter Fisher |
| Assistant Director, Civilian Travel Claims | Graham Jones |
| Member of Management Board | Ray Pollard |
| Assistant Director, Corporate Services Group | Norman Swanney |
| Project Manager, Post Occurrences & Personnel | |
| Information System of Information | Dave Wealthall |
| *Accounting Officer* | *Chief Executive* |

*staff* — 895

*financial*

| INCOME & EXPENDITURE | | |
|---|---|---|
| Year end: 31 March | 1997 | 1996 |
| | £000 | £000 |
| **EXPENDITURE** | | |
| Staff costs | 15,798 | 2,447 |
| Supplies and services consumed | 287 | 103 |
| Accommodation costs | 2,328 | 508 |
| Other administration costs | 9,133 | 2,288 |
| | 27,546 | 5,346 |
| **INCOME** | | |
| Less income from repayment customers | (3,009) | 421 |
| NET OPERATING EXPENDITURE | **24,537** | **4,925** |
| Interest charge on capital | 413 | 54 |
| NET EXPENDITURE | **24,950** | **4,979** |

| | | |
|---|---|---|
| *advisers* | **Auditors** National Audit Office | 157-197 Buckingham Palace Road London SW1W 9SP |
| *branches* | PO Box 42 Stockport Cheshire SK1 1ED Tel 0161 440 8888 | Whittington Road Worcester WR5 2LA Tel 01905 361401 |
| | | Pinesgate West Bath BA1 5AB Tel 01225 449156 |

# Pensions Compensation Board (PCB)

Room 501, 5th Floor
11 Belgrave Road
London SW1V 1RB

**Tel** 0171 828 9794
**Fax** 0171 931 7239

| | |
|---|---|
| *status* | Executive body |
| *founded* | 1997 |
| *sponsor* | Department of Social Security (DSS) |
| *powers* | Pensions Act 1995 |
| *mission* | To compensate occupational pension schemes for losses due to dishonesty. |
| *tasks* | Decides if compensation is payable and if so, pays it (must have reasonable grounds to believe a dishonest act has occurred after April 1997, the funds have been reduced by at least 10%, and the employer is insolvent). |
| *operations* | Management: Set up in direct response to the 'Maxwell' situation. Funded by a levy paid by all eligible occupational pensions schemes. The Secretariat runs day-to-day administration. |
| | Policy: Standing fund of £2 million available. |
| | Trends: No applications for compensation have yet been made. |
| *board* | Appointed by the Secretary of State from names suggested by the CBI, the IoD and the TUC. |

| | |
|---|---|
| Chairman | Julian Farrand |
| Member of Board | Mrs Andrea Banner |
| Member of Board | Lord Brooke of Alverthorpe |
| *Accounting Officer* | *Chairman* |

| | |
|---|---|
| *staff* | Two |

*financial*

| INCOME & EXPENDITURE | |
|---|---|
| **Year end: 5 April** | **1997** |
| | **£** |
| **INCOME** | - |
| **EXPENDITURE** | |
| Staff costs | 43,378 |
| Other operating costs | 120,404 |
| | **163,782** |
| **OPERATING DEFICIT** | **163,782** |
| Interest payable | 3,012 |
| **DEFICIT FOR THE PERIOD** | **166,794** |

*publications*  *A Brief Guide to the Occupational Pensions Compensation Scheme, Application (Handling your Application)*

# Pesticides Safety Directorate (PSD)

Kings Pool
3 Peasholme Green
York YO1 2PX

**Tel** 01904 640500
**Fax** 01904 455733

| | |
|---|---|
| *status* | Executive agency |
| *founded* | 1993 |
| *sponsor* | Ministry of Agriculture, Fisheries and Food (MAFF) |

# Q&Q

| | |
|---|---|
| **powers** | Food and Environment Protection Act 1985, Control of Pesticides Regulations 1986, Plant Protection Produces Regulations 1995 |
| **mission** | Protect the health of human beings, creatures and plants. Safeguard the environment. Secure safe, efficient and humane methods of pest control. |
| **tasks** | Regulation of agricultural pesticides in Great Britain on behalf of MAFF, Department of Health, DETR, Scottish Office and Welsh Office. Advises Ministers on the development and implementation of pesticide policy under national and EU legislation. |

**operations** Management: MAFF oversees PSD's overall performance through an Ownership Board which provides a formal link with Ministers and the Ministry. The Chief Executive is a member both of the Ownership Board and the MAFF Management Board. PSD's costs are financed through payment of fees for evaluation of specific pesticide approval applications and an annual levy charged to the agrochemical industry. The cost of policy-related work is met by the Ministry. A substantial amount of PSD's work (eg personnel support, legal advice and monitoring of pesticide residues) is outsourced through service level agreements and contracts.

Policy: PSD is a member of the York Bioscience Initiative.

Trends: European business is a major focus activity - in 1997 secured a contract from The European Commission (in conjunction with the German Regulatory authority) to run a series of expert groups to help develop the European pesticides regime.

**performance** Met all the agreed targets.

**board** Ownership Board is appointed by the Minister.

| | |
|---|---|
| Chairman | Richard Carden |
| Members | Prof Sir Colin Berry |
| | Geoff Bruce |
| | Jon Lowi |
| Accounting Officer | Chief Executive |

**staff** 200

| | |
|---|---|
| Chief Executive | Geoff Bruce |

**financial**

**INCOME & EXPENDITURE**

| Year end: 31 March | 1997 £000 | 1996 £000 | 1995 £000 |
|---|---|---|---|
| INCOME | 11,841 | 11,728 | 11,879 |
| EXPENDITURE | | | |
| Staff costs | 4,920 | 4,528 | 4,364 |
| Depreciation | 270 | 253 | 205 |
| Other operating costs | 6,482 | 7,093 | 6,988 |
| Relocation costs | - | - | 1,725 |
| | 11,672 | 11,874 | 13,282 |
| OPERATING SURPLUS/ (DEFICIT) BEFORE INTEREST | 169 | (146) | (1,403) |
| Interest on capital | 23 | 43 | 92 |
| OPERATING SURPLUS/ (DEFICIT) FOR THE YEAR | 146 | (189) | (1,495) |

**advisers** **Auditors** National Audit Office 157-197 Buckingham Palace Road London SW1W 9SP

**publications** Annual Report & Accounts 1996/97, Corporate Plan 1997-2001, Framework Document (PB 2609), Statement of Our Service Standards (PB 1898)

# *Planning Inspectorate*

Tollgate House
Houlton Street
Bristol BS2 9DJ

**Tel** 0117 987 8000
**Fax** 0117 987 8408          **Web** http://www.open.gov.uk.pi.pihome.htm

| | |
|---|---|
| *status* | Executive agency |
| *founded* | 1992 |
| *sponsor* | Department of the Environment, Transport and the Regions (DETR). Welsh Office (WO) |
| *powers* | Framework Document 1992. Revised Framework Document to be published 1998 |
| *mission* | To be the prime source of impartial expertise for resolving disputes about the use of land, natural resources and the environment. |
| *tasks* | Serving the two Secretaries of State on appeals against the decisions of local authorities and associated casework under planning, housing, environment and allied legislation in England and Wales. |
| *operations* | Management: The Chief Planning Inspector is also the Chief Executive. He reports to the two Secretaries of State and is supported by a Board of Management. During 1996/97 management was restructured so that each Management Board member is responsible for a specific business area. There are six Directorates: Planning & Environmental Protection; Development Plans; Enforcement & Wales; Highways & Transports; Appeals Administration; Finance & Management Services. Lord Chancellor's Panel of Independent Inspectors Operations in Wales are managed from offices in Cardiff. The Inspectorate operates under a gross running costs regime funded by DETR. |
| | Policy: To apply policy consistently and authoritatively and to operate in a user-friendly way. |
| | Trends: Appeal numbers have been steady in recent years. |
| *performance* | Most targets met in 1996/97. |
| *board* | Appointed by the Chief Executive. |

| | |
|---|---|
| Chief Planning Inspector & Chief Executive | C Shepley |
| Deputy Chief Planning Inspector & Director of Planning & Environmental Protection | D Hanchet |
| Director of Finance & Management Services | ML Brasher |
| Director of Enforcement & Wales | S Bruton |
| Director of Highways & Transport | B Dodd |
| Independent Business Advisor | M Jeans |
| Director of Appeals Administration | G Saunders |
| Director of Development Plans | R Wilson |
| *Accounting Officer* | *Chief Planning Inspector* |

*staff*          637

*financial*

| INCOME & EXPENDITURE Year end: 31 March | 1997 £000 | 1996 £000 | 1995 £000 |
|---|---|---|---|
| **GROSS INCOME** | | | |
| Income from activities | | | |
| Development plan enquiries | 6,342 | 3,349 | - |
| Other income | 1,806 | 1,927 | 1,830 |
| | **8,148** | **5,276** | **1,830** |
| Exceptional income | 0 | 8,658 | - |
| | **8,148** | **13,934** | **1,830** |
| **EXPENDITURE** | | | |
| Staff costs | (17,592) | (14,505) | (15,645) |
| Depreciation | (1,136) | (946) | (1,339) |
| Interest on capital | (723) | (586) | (398) |
| Other operating charges | (12,516) | (10,860) | (9,423) |
| | **(31,967)** | **(26,897)** | **(26,805)** |
| **OPERATING DEFICIT** | **(23,819)** | **(12,963)** | **(24,975)** |

| | | | |
|---|---|---|---|
| *advisers* | **Auditors** | National Audit Office | 157-197 Buckingham Palace Road London SW1W 9SP |

**publications**   *The Annual Report and Accounts 1996/97, Statistical Report 1996/97, Business and Corporate Plan 1996/97-1999/2000*

**branches**   Cathays Park
Room 1-004
Cardiff CF1 3NQ
Tel 01222 825670

# Planning Service

Clarence Court
10-18 Adelaide St
Belfast BT2 8GB

**Tel** 01232 540540                          **E-mail** planning.service.hq@nics.gov.uk
**Fax** 01232 540665

**status**   Executive agency

**founded**   1996

**sponsor**   Northern Ireland Office, Department of the Environment for NI (DOENI)

**powers**   To administer most of the Department's functions under the Planning (Northern Ireland) Order 1991.

**mission**   To plan and manage development in ways which will contribute to a quality environment and seek to meet the economic and social aspirations of present and future generations.

**tasks**   As the single planning authority for Northern Ireland, its business is development planning and development control. More specifically it provides: high-quality professional planning decisions, development plans and policy guidance; an accurate and speedy information service to the conveyancing community; and a planning framework for physical regeneration projects (and supports their implementation). It ensures that development planning and control promote orderly and consistent land use and supports the DOENI's Urban Affairs Division.

**operations**   Management: There is a Chief Executive, responsible to the Minister, and a Management Board. Nine offices located throughout NI deliver services. All planning decisions are taken in the name of the Secretary of State, but the consultative role of district councils is a central feature of NI planning and the DOENI consults district councils more widely than the law requires. The agency relies on advice and information from a number of other agencies, often through service level agreements.

Policy: Elected representatives already have a significant input in decision-making but the agency is committed to making consultation more effective.

Trends: Following a report on the planning system by the NI Affairs Committee, the government has undertaken to introduce legislation providing for additional enforcement powers and giving development plans prime importance in determining planning applications. It reiterated its support for the establishment of democratic control of planning processes as soon as a comprehensive NI political settlement allows.

**performance**   In 1996/97, 12 out of 17 key performance targets set by the Minister were successfully achieved. For another two (processing planning applications and the preparation of area plans) success was limited but original aspirations were too optimistic for the first year of operation.

**board**   Management Board.

| | |
|---|---|
| Chief Executive | TW Stewart |
| Director of Corporate Services | John McConnell |
| Professional Services Manager | HS McKay |

**staff**   389

*financial*

| RECEIPTS & EXPENDITURE | |
|---|---|
| Year end: 31 March | **1997** |
| | **£000** |
| **EXPENDITURE** | |
| Advertising of planning applications | 382 |
| Development plans and publications | 238 |
| Planning compensation | 822 |
| Research, bursaries and awards | 12 |
| Purchase notices (nominal) | 0 |
| Payments for Property Certificate System | 441 |
| Grant to Community Technical Aid | 110 |
| Grant to Disability Action | 140 |
| Consultants fees | 612 |
| Payments to Construction Service | 160 |
| Land registry charges | 36 |
| IT capital expenditure | 56 |
| Departmental running costs | 10,653 |
| | **13,662** |
| **RECEIPTS** | |
| Planning application fees receipts | 6,686 |
| Property certificate fees receipts | 1,238 |
| Recovery of planning compensation | 26 |
| | **7,950** |

# Police Authority for Northern Ireland (PANI)

River House
48 High Street
Belfast BT1 2DR

**Tel** 01232 230111
**Fax** 01232 245098

**E-mail** information.pani@nics.gov.uk
**Web** http://www.pani.org.uk

*status*  Executive body

*founded*  1970

*sponsor*  Northern Ireland Office

*powers*  Police Act (Northern Ireland) 1970

*mission*  To secure for the NI community the provision of an acceptable, effective and efficient police service which is accountable to that community through the Authority. To provide a vital link between the community and the Royal Ulster Constabulary (RUC).

*tasks*  To secure the maintenance of an adequate and efficient police service. In particular, determining the size of the RUC; providing and maintaining all police buildings, equipment and supplies; appointing all officers above the rank of Chief Superintendent; keeping itself informed as to the way in which complaints against the police are dealt with and maintaining financial and budgetary control of police service expenditure. It also makes arrangements for obtaining the views of people about policing and for obtaining their cooperation with the police in preventing crime. It aims to restore confidence in the RUC's ability to enforce the law fairly; strengthen the links between local police and local communities; enhance the accountability of the RUC to the community through the introduction of policing plans and reduce the imbalance in the religious make-up of the RUC by ensuring that a career in the police is equally attractive to people from both traditions.

*operations*  Management: The Authority has five subcommittees which deal with specific areas of work (Policy Coordinating Community Relations, Finance and Personnel, General Purposes, Support Services, Audit). White Paper in 1996 clarified PANI's role in establishing policing strategy and funding for the police service.

Policy: New Code on Openness and a Code of Conduct for Members to ensure greater public scrutiny of its work. Policing plans to be introduced. Growing network of Community and Police Liaison Committees (CPLCs).

Trends: If cease-fire lasts then further changes to policing.

*performance*  Financial expenditure directly related to level of terrorism.

*board*  19 members, including the Chairman and Vice-Chairman, appointed by the Secretary of State. Under a new process, vacancies are advertised in local press inviting people to nominate themselves.

| Chairman | Pat Armstrong CBE |
| Vice-Chairman | Prof Herb Wallace OBE |
| *Accounting Officer* | *Chief Executive* |

**staff** 16,154

| Secretary & Chief Executive | Joe Stewart |

**financial**

| RECEIPTS & PAYMENTS Year end: 31 March | 1997 £m | 1996 £m | 1995 £m |
|---|---|---|---|
| **RECEIPTS** | | | |
| HM government grant | 603.6 | 597.4 | 601.2 |
| Operating receipts | 6.6 | 5.4 | 6.2 |
| Employees' pension contributions (include TVs received) | 30.0 | 30.6 | 27.1 |
| Disposal (transfer values) of assets | 0.9 | 0.6 | 0.7 |
| | **641.1** | **634.0** | **635.2** |
| **PAYMENTS** | | | |
| Civilian staff | 51.3 | 48.9 | 46.3 |
| Royal Ulster constabulary | 331.9 | 313.2 | 323.2 |
| RUC Reserve (full-time members) | 101.5 | 96.4 | 103.0 |
| RUC Reserve (part-time members) | 4.2 | 3.8 | 5.3 |
| Superannuation | 47.0 | 48.2 | 38.3 |
| Travelling, subsistence and removal expenses | 16.3 | 15.3 | 15.6 |
| Transport and communications | 13.5 | 13.0 | 12.7 |
| Accommodation services | 19.2 | 21.0 | 18.3 |
| Catering | 1.7 | 3.2 | 2.6 |
| Uniform clothing and equipment | 2.4 | 2.3 | 4.3 |
| Training aids and courses | 1.9 | 1.9 | 1.9 |
| Compensation and grants | 2.5 | 2.7 | 3.4 |
| Forensic Science Service | 4.6 | 4.0 | 4.4 |
| Professional and specialist services | 2.9 | 2.6 | 2.8 |
| Postage and telephones | 4.7 | 5.6 | 4.6 |
| Printing and stationery | 1.8 | 1.8 | 1.8 |
| Miscellaneous | 1.4 | 1.4 | 1.3 |
| | **608.8** | **585.3** | **589.8** |
| Capital payments | 32.4 | 48.8 | 45.3 |
| **TOTAL PAYMENTS** | **641.2** | **634.1** | **635.1** |

# *Police Complaints Authority (PCA)*

10 Great George Street
London SW1P 3AE

**Tel** 0171 273 6450
**Fax** 0171 273 6401

**status** Executive body

**founded** 1984

**sponsor** Home Office

**powers** Police and Criminal Evidence Act 1984

**mission** To safeguard the public and to improve the quality of policing in England and Wales.

**tasks** To supervise the investigation of the most serious complaints against police officers; to supervise investigations into non-complaint matters voluntarily referred by police forces because of their potential gravity; to review the outcome of every investigation, whether supervised or not, and to decide whether disciplinary action should be taken against any-officer.

**operations** Management: The Chairman is the senior full-time official and Accounting Officer. There are two divisions: the Investigation Division (a Deputy Chairman with five members) carries out supervisory functions; the Disciplinary Division (five members) is responsible for disciplinary review and adjudication. Grant-in-aid is being reduced (by 5% in 1997/98 and by 7.5 % and 10% in the subsequent two years) while workloads increased (up 26% in Discipline Division; 33% in Investigation Division). This has led to the loss of one Deputy Chairman and one member - a 15% reduction in operational capacity.

Policy: PCA will continue its pursuit of greater openness and disclosure of evidence, believing that the public has a right to expect officers to account for their actions on duty.

Trends: The breadth and depth of PCA's work is radically changing, although the majority of cases are still complaints by individuals about one-off incidents. Police forces increasingly recognise issues with a public interest element, which demand independent supervision of investigations. In 19967/97, there were 154 voluntary referrals - many involve deaths in custody or deaths and serious injury from road traffic incidents involving police vehicles.

**performance** The PCA is close to being unable to meet its statutory duties, let alone its declared performance objectives, owing to reduction in grant-in-aid.

**board** The Chairman is appointed by HM The Queen and on the advice of the Home Secretary. Authority members are appointed by the Home Secretary. All appointments are publicly advertised.

| | | |
|---|---|---|
| Chairman | Peter Moorhouse | |
| Deputy Chairman | John Cartwright | |
| Members | Mrs Linda Allan | |
| | Ms Josephine Dobry | Allan Potts |
| | James Elliott | Mrs Margaret Scorer |
| | Molly Meacher | Lorna Whyte |
| | Caroline Mitchell | Anthony Williams MBE |

**staff** 59

**financial**

| RECEIPTS & PAYMENTS Year end: 31 March | 1997 £ | 1996 £ | 1995 £ |
|---|---|---|---|
| **RECEIPTS** | | | |
| HMG grant received | 3,732,000 | 3,891,000 | 3,794,000 |
| **PAYMENTS** | | | |
| Salaries and wages etc | 2,131,209 | 2,069,288 | 1,910,735 |
| Other operating payments | 1,552,079 | 1,747,471 | 1,893,455 |
| | 3,683,288 | 3,816,759 | 3,804,190 |
| **SURPLUS FROM OPERATIONS** | 48,712 | 74,241 | (10,190) |
| Other receipts/(payments) (net) | (39,318) | (52,334) | 13,295 |
| **EXCESS OF RECEIPTS OVER PAYMENTS** | 9,394 | 21,907 | 3,105 |

**advisers**

| **Bankers** | Midland Bank | Central Hall, Westminster,London SW1 |
|---|---|---|
| **Auditors** | National Audit Office | 157-197 Buckingham Palace Road London SW1W 9SP |
| **Solicitors** | Treasury Solicitor | London SW1 |

**publications** *1996/97 Annual Report (also summary), PCA 10 Police Complaints Authority - The First Ten Years , The Independent Police Complaints Authority - Making your complaint against the police, Investigating Serious Incidents*

# *Policyholders' Protection Board*

51 Gresham Street
London EC2B 7HQ

**Tel** 0171 600 3333
**Fax** 0171 216 7654

**status** Executive body

**founded** 1975

**sponsor** Department of Trade and Industry (DTI)

**powers** Policyholders Protection Act 1975. Policyholders Protection Act 1997

**mission** To protect policyholders from loss where an authorised insurance company, operating in the UK, cannot meet its liabilities. To collect a levy from the industry to finance policyholder protection.

**tasks** To assist policyholders. The Board administers two categories of assistance where the insolvent insurer is in liquidation: General Insurance - pays up to 90% of the insurer's liabilities to private individuals (and partnerships); 100% for compulsory insurance, mainly employers' and third-party motor insurance. Long-term Insurance (life etc) - tries to transfer ongoing policies to another insurance company, obtaining 90% of future benefits for policyholders; failing that, it pays 90% of the value of the policy for liquidation. For both categories, it can also make interim payments to policyholders; to assist insurers in financial difficulties; to assess and collect the levy.

**operations**   Management: The administrative costs and the costs of providing protection are met from a levy on insurance companies operating in the UK. During 1996/97 the Board made payments to policyholders of 14 general insurance companies and two life assurance companies.

Trends: The Policyholders Protection Act 1997 excludes protection risks and commitments located outside the UK and the rest of the European Economic Area. Its implementation by statutory instrument is awaited.

**board**   Five members at least should be Directors, Chief Executives or Managers of authorised insurance companies and at least one other who must be qualified to represent the interests of policyholders.

| Chairman | RA Gamble | |
|---|---|---|
| Members | RW Whewell | MAH Willett |
| | Ms HM Wiesner | AS Young |

**staff**   180

| Secretary | DE Wright |
|---|---|

**financial**

| INCOME & EXPENDITURE | | |
|---|---|---|
| Year end: 31 March | **1997** | **1996** |
| | **£000** | **£000** |
| **INCOME** | | |
| General business levy | - | 791 |
| Long-term business levy | (5) | 85 |
| Deposit interest | 10,109 | 12,398 |
| Less: Taxation | 3,334 | 4,092 |
| | **6,775** | **8,306** |
| Liquidation/scheme dividends and other recoveries | 6,749 | 2,924 |
| | **13,519** | **12,106** |
| **EXPENDITURE** | | |
| Protection of policyholders | 32,763 | 62,279 |
| Professional fees and costs | 252 | 311 |
| Administration and other expenses | 380 | 412 |
| Auditors' remuneration | 20 | 19 |
| Board members' remuneration | 2 | 3 |
| | **33,417** | **63,024** |
| **NET EXPENDITURE** | **(19,898)** | **(50,918)** |
| Foreign currency translation differences | (150) | - |
| Balance of funds | 175,402 | 226,320 |
| **BALANCE OF FUNDS** | **155,354** | **175,402** |

**advisers**   **Auditors**      Deloitte & Touche          Stonecutter Court, 1 Stonecutter Street
London EC4A 4TR

# *Post Office*

148 Old Street
London EC1V 9HQ

**Tel** 0171 490 2888
**Fax** 0171 250 2632

**status**   Nationalised industry

**founded**   1647

**sponsor**   Department of Trade and Industry (DTI)

**mission**   To provide an easily accessed nationwide distribution service through which customers can send and receive letters, packages and consignments and conduct a wide range of financial and retail services.

**tasks**   Four main operating businesses: Royal Mail - collects, sorts and delivers mail and packets within the UK and overseas; Parcelforce - parcel collection and delivery, UK and overseas; Post Office Counters - operates a network of 19,4000 post offices, offering 170 services from travel insurance to benefit payments; Subscription Services Ltd - telebusiness arm responsible for collecting BBC TV licence fees.

**operations** The Post Office Group accounts consolidate the accounts of The Post Office Corporation and all its subsidiaries. Separate accounts are presented for the main constituent businesses. The Post Office Board has overall responsibility for the Group. The Post Office Executive Committee (POEC) provides day-to-day leadership and direction. Each business is managed separately but makes use of the others' services under annually negotiated interbusiness contracts (there are controls to prevent cross-subsidy between business protected by the postal monopoly and those in direct competition in the marketplace).

Policy: Seeking a more dynamic, flexible and modern commercial framework in which to develop into a major international communications force.

Trends: The European Commission intends to liberalise postal services in the EU.

**performance** 1996/97 Royal Mail and PO Counters targets for return on capital were exceeded. Industrial action adversely affected targets.

**board**

| | |
|---|---|
| Chairman | Sir Michael Heron |
| Chief Executive | John Roberts CBE |
| Non-Executive Director | Peter Allen |
| Managing Director, Finance | Richard Close |
| Non-Executive Director | Dr David Grieves CBE |
| Non-Executive Director | Sir Christopher Harding |
| Secretary | Richard Osmond |

**staff** 166,300

| Post Office Executive Committee | |
|---|---|
| Chief Executive | John Roberts CBE |
| Managing Director Strategy and Personnel | Jerry Cope |
| Managing Director Finance | Richard Close |
| Managing Director Strategy & Personnel | Jerry Cope |
| Managing Director Royal Mail | Richard Dykes |
| Managing Director Post Office Counters | Stuart Sweetman |
| Director of Communications & Corporate Relations | Alan Williams |
| Managing Director Parcelforce | Kevin Williams |

**financial**

**GROUP PROFIT & LOSS**

| Year end: 30 March | 1997 £m | 1996 £m | 1995 £m |
|---|---|---|---|
| TURNOVER | 6,370 | 6,210 | 5,878 |
| COSTS | | | |
| Staff costs | (3,673) | (3,590) | (3,421) |
| Depreciation and other amounts written off tangible fixed assets | (234) | (238) | (184) |
| Other operating charges | (1,986) | (2,031) | (1,839) |
| | (5,893) | (5,859) | (5,444) |
| OPERATING PROFIT | 477 | 351 | 434 |
| Net profit/(loss) on disposal of tangible fixed assets | 7 | (13) | (13) |
| Restructuring provision released | - | - | 2 |
| PROFIT BEFORE INTEREST | 484 | 338 | 423 |
| Net interest receivable | 93 | 84 | 49 |
| PROFIT BEFORE TAXATION | 577 | 422 | 472 |
| Taxation | (216) | (152) | (158) |
| PROFIT FOR THE YEAR | 361 | 270 | 314 |

**ROYAL MAIL PROFIT & LOSS**

| Year end: 30 March | 1997 £m | 1996 £m | 1995 £m |
|---|---|---|---|
| TURNOVER | 5,019 | 4,804 | 4,540 |
| COSTS | | | |
| Staff costs | (3,147) | (2,991) | (2,829) |
| Depreciation and other amounts written off tangible fixed assets | (174) | (156) | (107) |
| Other operating charges | (1,235) | (1,303) | (1,174) |
| | (4,556) | (4,450) | (4,110) |
| OPERATING PROFIT | 463 | 354 | 430 |
| Net profit on disposal of tangible fixed assets | 6 | 6 | (16) |
| Restructuring provision released | - | - | 1 |
| PROFIT BEFORE INTEREST | 469 | 360 | 415 |
| Interest receivable | 49 | 51 | 34 |
| PROFIT BEFORE TAXATION | 518 | 411 | 449 |
| Taxation | (194) | (130) | (147) |
| PROFIT FOR THE YEAR | 324 | 281 | 302 |
| Appropriation to the holding company function | (338) | (184) | (223) |
| TRANSFER (FROM)/TO RESERVES | (14) | 97 | 79 |

**PARCELFORCE PROFIT & LOSS**

| Year end: 30 March | 1997 £m | 1996 £m | 1995 £m |
|---|---|---|---|
| TURNOVER | 457 | 471 | 481 |
| COSTS | | | |
| Staff costs | (228) | (232) | (239) |
| Depreciation and other amounts written off tangible fixed assets | (31) | (24) | (28) |
| Other operating charges | (217) | (246) | (244) |
| | (476) | (502) | (511) |
| OPERATING LOSS | (19) | (31) | (30) |
| Net loss on disposal of tangible fixed assets | - | (19) | 3 |
| Restructuring provision released | - | - | 1 |
| LOSS BEFORE INTEREST | (19) | (50) | (26) |
| Interest payable | (2) | (4) | (3) |
| LOSS BEFORE TAXATION | (21) | (54) | (29) |
| Taxation | 11 | 6 | 10 |
| LOSS FOR THE YEAR | (10) | (48) | (19) |

**POST OFFICE COUNTERS PROFIT & LOSS**

| Year end: 30 March | 1997 £m | 1996 £m | 1995 £m |
|---|---|---|---|
| TURNOVER | 1,161 | 1,195 | 1,118 |
| COSTS | | | |
| Staff costs | (256) | (252) | (242) |
| Depreciation and other amounts written off tangible fixed assets | (27) | (38) | (24) |
| Other operating charges | (844) | (870) | (822) |
| | (1,127) | (1,160) | (1,088) |
| OPERATING PROFIT | 34 | 35 | 30 |
| Taxation | (16) | (17) | (7) |
| PROFIT FOR THE YEAR | 18 | 18 | 23 |
| Dividends | (32) | (35) | (27) |
| TRANSFER FROM RESERVES | (14) | (17) | (4) |

**SUBSCRIPTION SERVICES PROFIT & LOSS**

| Year end: 30 March | 1997 £m | 1996 £m |
|---|---|---|
| TURNOVER | 71 | 65 |
| COSTS | | |
| Staff costs | (26) | (27) |
| Depreciation and other amounts written off tangible fixed assets | (2) | (1) |
| Other operating charges | (36) | (31) |
| | (64) | (59) |
| OPERATING PROFIT | 7 | 6 |
| Interest receivable | 1 | 1 |
| PROFIT BEFORE TAXATION | 8 | 7 |
| Taxation | (3) | (3) |
| PROFIT FOR THE YEAR | 5 | 4 |
| Dividends | (5) | (3) |
| RETAINED PROFIT FOR THE YEAR | - | 1 |

# Post Office Users' Council for Northern Ireland (POUC Northern Ireland)

7th Floor
Chamber of Commerce House
22 Great Victoria Street
Belfast BT2 7PJ

**Tel** 01232 244113
**Fax** 01232 247024

*status* Executive body
*founded* 1969
*sponsor* Department of Trade and Industry (DTI)

| | |
|---|---|
| *powers* | Post Office Act 1969 |
| *mission* | Representing consumer interests in the monopoly services of the Post Office (PO) in Northern Ireland |
| *tasks* | Investigating complaints from NI customers and representing the interests of the public where such customers are dissatisfied with the PO response. Monitoring the performance of the PO business. Considering and reporting on PO and government proposals on behalf of the NI community. |
| *operations* | Management: The Chairman reports to the Secretary of State. The Secretary is responsible for day-to-day administration. Funded by the DTI. |
| | Policy: Ensuring that the quality of service is not affected adversely by any PO drive towards higher productivity |
| | Trends: PO driving to improve efficiency and increase productivity. |
| *board* | Council members are appointed by the Secretary of State |

| Chairman | Gerard Trainer | |
|---|---|---|
| Members | Ralph Bauer | |
| | Roz Goldie | Jim McDonald MBE |
| | Ann Gormley | Albert Sherrard |
| | Olive Marshall | J Thompson |
| | Anne McCann | G Turkington |
| *Accounting Officer* | *Secretary* | |

*staff*

| Secretary | John Stringer |
|---|---|

# Post Office Users' Council for Scotland (POUC Scotland)

2 Greenside Lane
Edinburgh EH1 3AH

**Tel** 0131 244 5576
**Fax** 0131 244 5696

| | |
|---|---|
| *status* | Executive body |
| *founded* | 1969 |
| *sponsor* | Department of Trade and Industry (DTI) |
| *powers* | Post Office Act 1969 |
| *mission* | To represent the interests of postal service users in Scotland. Voice the users' views on standards or quality of the service and the price charged for it to the Post Office (PO). |
| *tasks* | Dealing with complaints and representations from residential and business customers who have initially tried to get satisfaction from the PO, but who are unhappy with the response. Also keeping watch on PO performance as it affects Scotland and make constructive proposals to them. |
| *operations* | Management: Secretariat is run by the Secretary, who reports to the Council. 13 PO Advisory Committees (voluntary, drawn from wide range of local user groups) report on local matters. On UK policy matters, the Post Office Users' National Council consults with the three country councils including POUCS. |
| | Policy: Encouraging improvement of postal service, particularly in rural areas. |
| | Trends: Increasing number of complaints from users about late deliveries or mail going astray. |
| *board* | Council appointed by the Secretary of State from all walks of life, usually in response to advertisements in local papers. |

| Chairman | AO Robertson OBE | |
|---|---|---|
| Members | RJ Ardern | DG Marnoch MBE |
| | Dr TNA Begg OBE JP | Mrs A Packard |
| | Mrs S Bell | AJ Turnbull |
| | PJS Dry | P Wilson JP |
| | Dr SE Hopwood | E Young |
| *Accounting Officer* | *Secretary* | |

| staff | Three | |
|---|---|---|
| | Secretary | RLL King |

**publications** Annual Report

## Post Office Users' Council for Wales (POUC Wales)

Caradog House
St Andrews Place
Cardiff CF1 3BE

**Tel** 01222 374028
**Fax** 01222 668536

**Contact** Gordon Mackenzie

| | |
|---|---|
| **status** | Executive body |
| **founded** | 1969 |
| **sponsor** | Department of Trade and Industry (DTI) |
| **powers** | Post Office Act 1969 |
| **mission** | To protect consumers by considering complaints and suggestions from Post Office users in Wales. To give notice to the PO and the Post Office Users' National Council (POUNC) suggesting what action should be taken. |
| **tasks** | The remit covers recorded delivery, registered post, supply of stamps, counter services, post offices, collections, delivery, private boxes and some aspects of parcels. |
| **operations** | Management: POUC Wales is independent of the PO. There are 14 local PO Advisory Committees spread across Wales. Action is awaited from the DTI on a report received from independent consultants. |
| | Policy: The existence of POUC Wales is of crucial importance to users in Wales and the Marches because it is the only part of the business which has responsibility for the whole of Wales - the Royal Mail and PO Counters having been reorganised so that Wales has been split and become part of larger regions with main offices in England. |
| | Trends: POUC Wales is experiencing difficulty in obtaining reliable information on the operation of the PO in Wales. |
| **board** | Appointed by the Secretary of State for Trade and Industry as individuals, not representative. |

| Chairman | Eifion Pritchard | |
|---|---|---|
| Members of Council | Gordon Donaldson JP | Charles F Hay |
| | Donald R Dutton JP | Margaret M Kerridge |
| | Lee Evans | William A Pritchard |
| | Nerys Fuller-Love | Margaret Rees |
| | Meryl Gravell JP | Neville W Sims MBE |

| staff | | |
|---|---|---|
| | Secretary | Gordon J Mackenzie |
| | Assistant Secretary | Glenda M Rich |

# Post Office Users' National Council (POUNC)

6 Hercules Road
London SE1 7DN

**Tel** 0171 928 9458

| | |
|---|---|
| *status* | Executive body |
| *founded* | 1969 |
| *sponsor* | Department of Trade and Industry (DTI) |
| *powers* | Post Office Act 1969 |
| *mission* | Independent body representing Post Office (PO) user's interests in England and the UK. |

*tasks*
Remit 7 covers both England and matters concerning to the whole of the UK. Most PO services including letters, recorded delivery, registered post, supply of stamps, counter services, PO outlets, collections, deliveries, private boxes and some aspects of parcels. It has the right to make representations to the Secretary of State, to be consulted about proposed tariff changes, to prior consultation about service changes, to deal with complaints and representations from the public and business. Keeps a vigorous watch on PO performance (and undertakes independent research on it and on user requirements) and makes constructive proposals to both the PO and the government and publishes its reports. Coordinates all UK matters raised by the national Post Office Users' Committees (POUCs) of Scotland, Wales and Northern Ireland.

*operations*
Management: The Chairman reports to the Secretary of State. The Secretary is responsible for day-to-day administration.

Policy: Recommend actions include the improvement in PO industrial relations, that the government should stop taking almost all PO profits as well as many improvements in quality of service.

Trends: 86% of 1996/97 PO profit went to government through negative EFL and taxation, this is likely to recur in 1997/98, and if it continues into 1998/99, the result will be increased prices to users and reduced PO investment.

*board*
Members of the Committee are appointed by the Secretary of State. The three Chairmen of the POUC are *ex officio* members.

| | | |
|---|---|---|
| Chairman | John Hackney | |
| Members | Fred Bell | Eifion Pritchard |
| | Eric R Distin | Andrew O Robertson OBE |
| | Roger E Gooding | Stephanie J Stray |
| | Gary R Hepburn | Gerard Trainer |
| | Keith Hitchings | Edward T Vidler |
| | David B Morris | Denis S Wilson MBE JP |
| *Accounting Officer* | *Secretary* | |

*staff*    9

| | |
|---|---|
| Secretary | James Dodds |

*financial*

| EXPENDITURE | | | |
|---|---|---|---|
| Year end: 31 March | 1997 | 1996 | 1995 |
| | £ | £ | £ |
| **OPERATING COSTS** | | | |
| **STAFFING** | | | |
| Salaries and related costs | 230,318 | 232,650 | 228,900 |
| **OTHER COSTS** | | | |
| Council and Secretariat expenses | 37,858 | 34,575 | 33,137 |
| Office costs including postage, computer, photocopying and telephones | 27,006 | 39,236 | 32,869 |
| Printing and publishing | 4,069 | 12,419 | 223 |
| Research | 15,213 | 1,068 | 885 |
| Miscellaneous | 73 | 29 | 46 |
| **EXCEPTIONAL COSTS** | | | |
| Relocating office | - | - | 11,199 |
| **ACCOMMODATION COSTS** | | | |
| Rent, rates and associated services | 71,596 | 58,000 | 97,211 |
| **TOTAL** | **386,133** | **377,977** | **404,470** |

*publications*    *Annual Report*

# Probation Board for Northern Ireland (PBNI)

80-90 North Street
Belfast BT1 1LD

**Tel** 01232 262400
**Fax** 01232 262470

| | |
|---|---|
| *status* | Executive body |
| *founded* | 1982 |
| *sponsor* | Northern Ireland Office |
| *powers* | Probation Board Northern Ireland Order 1982 |
| *mission* | To help prevent reoffending. |
| *tasks* | Runs the probation service. Court reports, community supervision of offenders, working with young offenders - in partnership with social services, Parents' Support Groups, and the voluntary sector. Also working with the community (bail hostels, Peace and Reconciliation projects) and PBNI funded community programmes. Prison social work, individual pre-release plans and work with released prisoners, particularly sex offenders. Employment and training for ex-prisoners. |
| *operations* | Management: The Chairman reports to the Secretary of State and the Chief Probation Officer reports to the Chairman. |
| | Policy: New partnership projects with local communities, eg NI Sports Council. |
| | Trends: During past decade staff have moved from working with minor offenders to supervising complex and sometimes dangerous people. 1997 introduction of the Supervised Licence of sex offenders on release from prison. 1998 introduction of Pre-sentence Reports, Custody Probation Orders (unique in Europe) and Combination Orders. |
| *performance* | Quinquennial review consultants reported that the current structure is the most appropriate for NI and that the main areas of planning and control in place are sound. Achieved two out of four objectives for 1996/97. |
| *board* | Appointed by Secretary of State |

| | | |
|---|---|---|
| Chairman | SC Curran OBE | |
| Deputy Chairman | T Hopkins | |
| Members of Board | Mrs H Bell | CT Hogg MBE UD JP |
| | Mrs C Boyce | D Moloney |
| | Ms F Cassidy | Ms R McDonough |
| | Mrs M Clark-Glass | T Mcgrath |
| | Mrs I Colvin OBE | A Sherrard |
| | J Crozier | J Strain |
| | F Dolaghan | J Stringer |
| *Accounting Officer:* | *Probation Officer* | |

| | |
|---|---|
| *staff* | 343 |

| | |
|---|---|
| Secretary | B Lyttle OBE |
| Chief Probation Officer | Breidge Gadd |

*financial*

| EXPENDITURE | |
|---|---|
| **Year end: 31 March** | **1997** |
| | **£000** |
| Remuneration | 6,641 |
| Other revenue | 2,235 |
| Voluntary organisations | 2,141 |
| Capital | 83 |
| | **11,100** |

| | | |
|---|---|---|
| *advisers* | **Bankers** | Northern Bank |
| | **Auditors** | Northern Ireland Audit Office |
| | **Solicitors** | Crown Solicitor's Office |
| | **Public Relations** | Davidson Cockcroft |
| *publications* | *Annual Report and Business Plan* | |
| *branches* | 40 offices and units around Northern Ireland. | |

# *Property Advisers to the Civil Estate (PACE)*

Trevelyan house
Great Peter Street
London SW1P 2BY

**Tel** 0171 271 2600
**Fax** 0171 271 2693

| | |
|---|---|
| *status* | Executive agency |
| *founded* | 1996 |
| *sponsor* | Cabinet Office, Office of Public Service (OPS) |
| *powers* | Framework Document 1996 |
| *mission* | Coordinates activity of the government's civil estate where wider exchequer savings can be demonstrated. Also provides general property guidance across government, and specific assistance to departments, agencies and NDPBs on a cost recovery basis. |
| *tasks* | To identify and promote opportunities to coordinate departments' market activity; to plan and broker interdepartmental estate rationalisation schemes; to provide central property guidance to departments; to provide departments with property-related intelligent client services; to supply heating and electricity to departments in the Whitehall area. |
| *operations* | Management: The Chancellor of the Duchy of Lancaster determines the overall policy and financial framework, taking into account the advice of the Chief Executive. Organised on a regional basis with head office in London. Chief Executive responsible for day-to-day management, supported by Management Board of Directors (Policy & Planning, Corporate Services, Central Advice Unit and six Regional). |
| | Policy: To dispose of most of PACE vacant space by 2000. |
| | Trends: High growth rates in rental sector in London and south east unlikely to be achieved for majority of government estate, which is poorer quality property. |
| *performance* | Achieved three out of five targets in 1996/97. |
| *board* | Advisory Board appointed by the Secretary of State. |

| | |
|---|---|
| Chairman | Miss E Turton CB |
| Members | Mrs L Baldry |
| | C Brendish |
| | Ms A French |
| | J Mason |
| | J Nickson |
| | E Watts |
| | A White |
| *Accounting Officer* | *Chief Executive* |

| | |
|---|---|
| *staff* | 249 |

| | |
|---|---|
| Chief Executive | John Locke |
| Director, South West & Wales | Richard Barry |
| Director, Policy & Planning | Malcolm Bowles |
| Director, Central Advice Unit | Arnold Butler |
| Director, London & South East | Liam Colgan |
| Director, Midlands | John Hathaway |
| Director, North West | Alan Jones |
| Director, Personnel | John Kingdom |
| Director, North East | John Lewis |
| Director, Corporate Services | Barry Redfern |
| Director, Scotland | Peter Stewart |

*financial*

| INCOME & EXPENDITURE Year end: 31 March | 1997 |
|---|---|
| | £000 |
| **INCOME** | |
| Rental income | 386,621 |
| Release of surplus provision on disposal of leaseholds | 5,360 |
| Profits on disposal of freeholds | 6,879 |
| Other income | 4,756 |
| | **403,616** |
| OCRs for surrender to the consolidated fund | 359,145 |
| **SURPLUS BEFORE OPERATING CHARGES** | **44,471** |
| Staff costs | 7,001 |
| Early retirement costs | 4,512 |
| Other operating costs | 107,376 |
| | **118,889** |
| **OPERATING DEFICIT** | **74,418** |
| Notional interest | 21,378 |
| **DEFICIT FOR THE YEAR** | **53,040** |

# Public Health Laboratory Services Board (PHLS)

61 Colindale Avenue
London NW9 5DF

**Tel** 0181 200 1295
**Fax** 0181 200 7874

| | |
|---|---|
| *status* | Executive body |
| *founded* | 1946 |
| *sponsor* | Department of Health (DOH), Welsh Office (WO) |
| *powers* | National Health Service Act 1977. Public Health Laboratory Service Act 1979 |
| *mission* | To protect the population of England and Wales from infection. |
| *tasks* | To deliver a microbiological service in England and Wales, maintaining a capability for the detection, diagnosis, surveillance, prevention and control of infectious and communicable diseases and conducting research into them. |
| *operations* | Management: The Chief Executive reports to the Secretaries of State. Coordinates a network of 49 Public Health Laboratories (PHLs), organised into nine groups distributed across England and Wales together with the Central Public Health Laboratory and the Communicable Disease Surveillance Centre which are located with its headquarters in Colindale, London. It works in partnership with government departments, health authorities and NHS trusts, local government, universities and research institutions. |
| | Policy: Strengthen public health functions. |
| | Trends: Reduction in funding in 1996/97 and beyond. £1.4 million pa NHS Executive contract to manage its regional epidemiology services in England. |
| *board* | Appointed by the Secretary of State. |

| Director | Dr Diana Walford |
|---|---|
| *Accounting Officer* | *Director* |

*staff* 3486

*financial*

| INCOME & EXPENDITURE Year end: 31 March | 1996 | 1995 |
|---|---|---|
| | £000 | £000 |
| **INCOME** | | |
| Government grants | 56,252 | 57,613 |
| Other grants | 3,371 | 3,653 |
| Income from activities | 52,631 | 47,058 |
| Transfer from reserves | 2,504 | 2,404 |
| | **114,758** | **110,728** |

| EXPENDITURE | | |
|---|---:|---:|
| Staff costs | 69,687 | 67,819 |
| Other operating charges | 43,383 | 41,980 |
| Depreciation | 2,655 | 2,646 |
| Notional cost of capital | 2,727 | 3,159 |
| | **118,452** | **115,604** |
| **OPERATING DEFICIT FOR THE YEAR** | **(3,694)** | **(4,876)** |
| Loss on disposal of assets | (554) | (225) |
| Interest receivable | - | - |
| Transfer from reserves | 3,358 | 3,647 |
| Exceptional costs (establishment of Microbiology Research Authority) | - | (849) |
| **DEFICIT FOR THE YEAR** | **(890)** | **(2,303)** |
| Retained deficit brought forward | (6,760) | (4,457) |
| **RETAINED DEFICIT CARRIED FORWARD** | **(7,650)** | **(6,760)** |

# Public Record Office (PRO)

Ruskin Ave
Kew
Richmond
Surrey TW9 4DU

**Tel** 0181 876 3444
**Fax** 0181 878 8905

| | |
|---|---|
| *status* | Government department and executive agency |
| *founded* | 1838 |
| *sponsor* | Lord Chancellor's Department |
| *powers* | Public Records Acts 1958 and 1967 |
| *mission* | To assist and promote the study of the past through public records in order to inform the present and the future. |
| *tasks* | It is the national archive for England and Wales (as well as the UK as a whole) and supervises the selection, safekeeping and transfer of public records; keeps and conserves the records and provides access to them. It also advises the government and others on public record issues. |
| *operations* | Management: The Keeper of the PRO is its Chief Executive and reports directly to the Lord Chancellor. She is responsible for managing the PRO and for its policy and executive functions. She is assisted by the Management Board comprising eight other senior staff. The Central Management Department oversees planning, performance monitoring and efficiency plans. In 1996 the PRO moved to new site at Kew. There are operational groups: Public Services, Land Government, Information and Corporate Services. There is an Advisory Council on Public Records, chaired by the Master of the Rolls, which advises the Lord Chancellor on public records in general and the PRO in particular, with its own Secretary reporting to the Master of the Rolls.

Policy: To access more records electronically and increase remote access to users via the Internet.

Trends: Concern for growing volume and cost of government records led to joint Cabinet Office/PRO study and PRO's appointment to lead departments towards best practice in records management and contracting out storage. |
| *performance* | 16 out of 18 targets met in 1996/97.  The move to Kew - covering the new building, refurbishment and the movement of 12.5km of records from Hayes and 35km of records from Chancery Lane to Kew - was completed on schedule and to budget. |
| *staff* | 455 |

| | |
|---|---|
| Chief Executive | Mrs Sarah Tyacke |
| Director of Public Services | Dr Elizabeth Hallam Smith |
| Director of Government, Information & Corporate Services | Dr Duncan Simpson |
| Head of Document Services Department | Bryan Betterton |
| Head of Central Management Department | Christopher Cooper |
| Head of Government Services Department | Dr Andrew McDonald |
| Head of Information & Records Department | Dr David Thomas |
| The Head of Reader Services Department | Iain Watt |
| Head of Financial Services Department | Nicholas Worrall |

**financial**

| INCOME & EXPENDITURE Year end: 31 March | 1997 £000 | 1996 £000 | 1995 £000 |
|---|---|---|---|
| **EXPENDITURE** | | | |
| Running costs | 13,440 | 12,751 | 12,015 |
| Running costs - accommodation | 11,644 | 16,934 | 14,757 |
| Depreciation | 1,416 | 916 | 618 |
| Notional charges | 4,679 | 2,088 | 557 |
| | 31,179 | 32,689 | 27,947 |
| **INCOME** | | | |
| Income from services | (2,414) | (2,268) | (1,290) |
| **NET COST OF OUTPUT** | **28,765** | **30,421** | **26,657** |

**advisers**   **Auditors**   National Audit Office   157-197 Buckingham Palace Road
London SW1W 9SP

**publications**   *Keeper's Report 1996, Corporate Plan 1998-99 to 2001-02, Business Plan 1998-99*

**branches**   *Family Records Centre*
*Myddelton Street*
*London EC1R 14W*

# Public Record Office of Northern Ireland (PRONI)

66 Balmoral Avenue
Belfast BT9 6NY

**Tel** 01232 251318
**Fax** 01232 255999

**E-mail** proni@nics.gov.uk
**Web** http://proni.nics.gov.uk/index

**status**   Executive agency

**founded**   1923, as executive agency in 1995

**sponsor**   Northern Ireland Office, Department of Education NI (DOENI)

**mission**   To identify and preserve Northern Ireland's archival heritage and to ensure public access.

**tasks**   Acquiring (through donations and purchase) public and private records; cataloguing and managing records; maintains the Register of Irish Archives (lists archives held outside Ireland); provides easy access to the public; researches and publishes guides and source books.

**operations**   Management: Chief Executive (Deputy Keeper of the Records), appointed by open competition, is responsible for day-to-day management and accountable to the Minister. He is assisted by the Principal Assistant Keeper, who is responsible for the five departments (Acquisition, Preservation, Corporate Services, Access, Reader Services). The Advisory Board comments and advises on the services provided and meets twice a year.

Policy: Planning to put the Public Search Room catalogues online. Moving in 1998 to Crumlin Road Courthouse and Gaol.

Trends: Open government initiative releasing more public records.

**board**   Advisory Board appointed by the Secretary of State from central and local government, private depositors, experienced promotion or marketing people, history researchers, the private sector generally.

**staff**

| | |
|---|---|
| Chief Executive | Dr APW Malcomson |
| Deputy Chief Executive | Dr GJ Slater |
| Preservation | Miss V Adams |
| Corporate Services | Miss P Kernaghan |
| Reader Services | Dr D Lammey |
| Access | Mrs A McClintock |
| Acquisition | Dr R Strong |

# *Public Trust Office (PTO)*

Stewart House
24 Kingsway
London WC2B 6JX

**Tel** 0171 269 7316
**Fax** 0171 664 7707

**E-mail** enquiries@publictrust.gov.uk.
**Web** http://www.publictrust.gov.uk/

| | |
|---|---|
| *status* | Executive agency |
| *founded* | 1987. As executive agency 1994 |
| *sponsor* | Lord Chancellor's Department |
| *powers* | PTO Framework Document. Public Trustee Act 1906. Law Property & Miscellaneous Provisions Act 1994. Public Trustee and Administration of Funds Act 1986. Mental Health Act 1983. Enduring Powers of Attorney Act 1985. Court Funds Administration of Justice Act 1982. Supreme Court Act 1981 |
| *mission* | To ensure the effective management of private assets and financial affairs entrusted to its care by the courts or by, or on behalf of, people unable or unwilling to manage them, in England and Wales. |
| *tasks* | Clients are people suffering from mental incapacity and their administrators; people involved in Trusts where the Public Trustee is executor or trustee; people involved in civil actions in the courts, including children; and people involved in some institutional funds. Protection - overseeing people acting as receiver for a patient's financial affairs and handling applications to the Court of Protection and implementing its orders. Receivership - acting as receiver where the Public Trustee is appointed receiver by the Court of Protection. Trust - acting as the executor or trustee. Court Funds - banking and investment management of funds deposited in court. |
| *operations* | Management: The Chief Executive, who reports to the Lord Chancellor, holds the statutory offices of Public Trustee and Accountant General of the Supreme Court. She is supported by a Management Board comprising herself plus five senior managers. PTO is responsible for some £3.4 billion of clients' funds. PTO is located in London but its caseworkers maintain direct contact with clients throughout England and Wales. |
| | Trends: Caseload volumes increasing in Mental Health Sector, decreasing in Trust area. Prior Options Review - a root-and-branch review of total business in 1999. |
| *board* | Management Board is chaired by the Public Trustee and Chief Executive. |

| | |
|---|---|
| Public Trustee & Chief Executive | Julia Lomas |
| Director of Corporate Services | Eddie Bloomfield |
| Director of Mental Health Services | Helen Bratton |
| Director of Trust & Funds Services | Frank Eddy |
| Head of Legal & Property Division | Stella Hutcheson |
| Chief Investment Manager | Hugh Stevenson |
| *Accounting Officer* | *Permanent Secretary* |

*staff*  600

*financial*

| INCOME & EXPENDITURE | |
|---|---|
| **Year end: 31 March** | **1997** |
| | **£000** |
| **INCOME** | |
| Fees and charges | |
| Court of Protection fees | 11,303 |
| Public Trustee services | 3,596 |
| Court Funds Office charges to NILO | 3,957 |
| Common Investment Funds Scheme | 383 |
| Other income | 39 |
| | **19,278** |
| **EXPENDITURE** | |
| Running costs | |
| Staff costs | 12,544 |
| Judicial staff costs | 78 |
| Accommodation | 2,449 |
| Other running costs | 3,241 |
| | **18,312** |
| Notional and other non-cash costs | 962 |
| | **19,274** |
| **OPERATING SURPLUS** | **4** |

*publications*  *Framework Document, Corporate Plan, Business Plan, Annual Report*

# Qualifications & Curriculum Authority (QCA)

222 Euston Rd
London NW1 2BZ

**Tel** 0171 387 9898
**Fax** 0171 387 0978

| | |
|---|---|
| *status* | Executive body |
| *founded* | 1997 |
| *sponsor* | Department for Education and Employment (DfEE) |
| *powers* | Education Act 1997 |
| *mission* | To promote quality and coherence in education and training, from pre-school to higher vocational levels in England. |
| *tasks* | Reviewing the National Curriculum; developing and managing the assessment system; as the regulatory body for public examinations and publicly funded qualifications, establishing a national framework of qualifications; carrying out research on policy proposals and their effectiveness; advising the Secretary of State on all matters affecting the school curriculum, pupil assessment and publicly funded qualifications offered in schools, colleges and workplaces. |
| *operations* | Management: Amalgamation of the National Council for Vocational Qualifications (NCVQ) and the School Curriculum and Assessment Authority (SCAA). Managed by Chief Executive and Heads of Division. |
| | Policy: Works closely with range of partners (eg awarding bodies, schools, colleges, training and assessment centres, national representative bodies and other regulatory organisations such as OFSTED) in ensuring that required standards are met. |
| | Trends: Overseeing the development and implementation of a coherent national framework of qualifications as recommended by the Dearing Report 1996. |
| *board* | Appointed by the Secretary of State. |

| | |
|---|---|
| Chairman | Sir William Stubbs |
| Deputy Chairman | Sir Dominic Cadbury |
| Members | Prof Robin Alexander |
| | Geoffrey Ashton |
| | Anne Duke |
| | Dr Philip Evans |
| | Dr Philip Hunter |
| | Pat Lee |
| | Ian McAllister |
| | Patricia Morgan-Webb |
| | Sir George Quingley |
| | Heather Rabbats |
| | Dr Nicholas Tate |
| | Prof Ted Wragg |
| Secretary | Tim Cornford |
| *Accounting Officer* | *Secretary* |

| | |
|---|---|
| *staff* | 470 |

| | |
|---|---|
| Chief Executive | Dr Nicholas Tate |
| Head of Vocational Qualifications & Occupational Standards | Alan Bellamy |
| Head of National Curriculum & Assessment | David Hawker |
| Head of Curriculum Review | Chris Jones |
| Head of Corporate Policy | Geoff Lucas |
| Head of Communications | Tony Millns |
| Head of Corporate Services | Bill Scott |
| Head of General & General Vocational Qualifications | Keith Weller |

| | | |
|---|---|---|
| *advisers* | **Bankers** | HM Paymaster General |
| *branches* | Newcombe House 45 Notting Hill Gate London W11 3JB | |

# Qualifications, Curriculum & Assessment Authority for Wales (ACCAC)

Castle Buildings
Womanby Street
Cardiff CF1 9SX

**Tel** 01222 375400          **E-mail** acac.cardiff@campus.bt.com
**Fax** 01222 343612

| | |
|---|---|
| *status* | Executive body |
| *founded* | 1997 |
| *sponsor* | Welsh Office (WO) |
| *powers* | Education Reform Act 1988, Education Act 1993 |
| *mission* | To promote the raising of the overall level of educational and vocational achievementsin Wales. |
| *tasks* | Responsible in Wales for keeping under review all aspects of the school curriculum and statutory assessment arrangements for maintained schools, for external and vocational qualifications; for commissioning classroom materials to support the teaching of Welsh, other subjects through the medium of Welsh and Wales-specific aspects of the curriculum; and for advising the Secretary of State as required. |
| *operations* | Management: In October 1997, ACCAC came into being following an amalgamation of Curriculum and Assessment Authority in Wales and the National Council for Vocational Qualifications. The Chief Executive is supported by three Assistant Chief Executives responsible for Primary Education, Secondary Education, and Finance and Administration. |
| | Policy: Review of the curriculum in Wales has been launched. Welsh and English are treated on the basis of equality. |
| | Trends: Statutory Welsh Language Scheme being finalised. |
| *board* | The Authority members are appointed by the Secretary of State. |

| | |
|---|---|
| Chairman | Rudi Plaut OBE |
| Deputy Chairman | Owen Rees CB |
| Members | Romey Ahmad |
| | Claire Argyle |
| | Alan Boxford |
| | Clive Carthew |
| | Ann Davies |
| | Karin Davies |
| | Keith Davies |
| | Emlyn Jones |
| | Christopher Kipling |
| | Caroline Lewis |
| | Susan Parsons |
| | Peter Thomas |
| *Accounting Ofiicer* | *Chief Executive* |

*staff*          42

| | |
|---|---|
| Chief Executive | John V Williams |
| *Assistant Chief Executives* | |
| Qualifications & Curriculum 14-19 | Linda Badham |
| Curriculum & Assessment 5-14 | Gary Brace |
| Finance & Administration | Huw Davies |
| Vocational Qualifications | Sara Marshall |

# Queen Elizabeth II Conference Centre (QEIICC)

Broad Sanctuary
Westminster
London SW1P 3EE

**Tel** 0171 222 5000          **E-mail** sarahj@qeiicc.co.uk
**Fax** 0171 7984200          **Web** http://www.qeiicc.co.uk

**Contact** Sarah Jones, Reservations Manager

| | |
|---|---|
| *status* | Executive agency |
| *founded* | 1989 as executive agency, 1997 as a trading fund |
| *sponsor* | Department of the Environment, Transport and the Regions (DETR) |
| *powers* | Framework document |
| *mission* | To provide and manage fully secure conference facilities for national and international meetings. |
| *tasks* | To manage and market its facilities commercially for use by government and the private sector to the highest levels. |
| *operations* | Management: There is a Chief Executive, who reports to the Secretary of State. There is also a Management Board. Operations are outsourced where possible. In 1996/97 catering was contracted out to Leith's Ltd under a 15-year contract, security operations to Pinkerton Security Services on a five-year contract. New five-year contracts were also awarded for engineering, cleaning and portering. The increased capacity from the changes made to the interior of the building are largely funded by Leith's Ltd, under a PFI contract. Immediately after the year end (1 April 1997), QEIICC was appointed as Trading Fund which takes it off the government Vote and allows it to control its own budgets and finances. |

*operations* (continued)

Policy: To keep its reputation as the top UK conference centre.

Trends: While the building is still owned by DETR, QEIICC can now fund capital improvements from retained earnings and borrowings. The private sector continued to represent the greater share of QEIICC income (74%).

*performance* Trading results were the best to date, reflecting substantially improved income and efficient use of resources.

*board* Members of the Management Board are appointed by the Secretary of State. Under their new contract, one member is a Leith's Ltd nominee.

| | |
|---|---|
| Chief Executive | Marcus Buck |
| Operations Director | Geoffrey Booth |
| Non-Executive Director | Patrick Harbour |
| Finance Director | Robert Jackson |
| Commercial Director | Gillian Price |

*staff* 56

*financial*

| INCOME & EXPENDITURE | | |
|---|---|---|
| **Year end: 31 March** | **1997** | **1996** |
| | **£000** | **£000** |
| **INCOME FOR OPERATING ACTIVITIES** | 7,164 | 6,418 |
| Staff costs | 1,805 | 1,587 |
| Depreciation | 490 | 516 |
| Occupancy charge | 6,400 | 6,400 |
| Other operating charges | 4,412 | 4,080 |
| | (13,107) | (12,583) |
| **OPERATING DEFICIT** | **(5,943)** | **(6,165)** |
| Interest on capital employed | (137) | (162) |
| **DEFICIT FOR THE FINANCIAL YEAR** | **(6,080)** | **(6,327)** |

*advisers*   **Auditors**        National Audit Office        157-197 Buckingham Palace Road
London SW1W 9SP

# *Queen Victoria School*

Dunblane
Perthshire FK15 0JY

**Tel** 01786 822288

| | |
|---|---|
| *status* | Defence agency |
| *founded* | 1908, 1992 as defence agency |
| *sponsor* | Ministry of Defence (MOD) |
| *powers* | Royal Warrant 1992 and Framework Document |
| *mission* | To provide education (from age 11) in a boarding environment for the sons and daughters of Scottish Service personnel, or any Service personnel who are serving, or have served, in Scotland. |
| *tasks* | Provides courses and teaching to allow pupils to achieve their full academic potential; provides a wide range of physical and creative extracurricular activities; provides a happy boarding environment based upon boarding houses. |
| *operations* | Management: The Headmaster reports to Her Majesty's Commissioners (who are the governing body), who in turn are responsible to the Secretary of State. Tuition and board are free to pupils. |
| | Policy: No academic selection. Girls accepted in 1996. 260 pupils in 1996/97. |
| | Trends: Careers links with services is strong but increasingly pupils move on to higher education. |
| *performance* | Nine out of 11 targets achieved in 1996/97. |
| *board* | Commissioners appointed by the Secretary of State. |

| | |
|---|---|
| Chairman | Air Vice Marshal CE Simpson MB Chb |
| Commissioners | GF Belton OBE |
| | Mrs NH Howe |
| | Major General JD MacDonald CB CBE |
| | Rear Admiral DJ Mackenzie CB |
| | D MacLehose |
| | Lieutenant General Sir John MacMillan KCB CBE |
| | JSB Martin |
| | Dr SE McClelland CBE |
| | W McD Moodie CBE |
| | Air Vice Marshal J Morris CBE |
| | Captain RA Smith |
| | Sir Moray Stewart KCB |
| *Accounting Officer* | *Chief Executive/Headmaster* |

*staff*    75

*financial*

**INCOME & EXPENDITURE**

| Year end: 31 March | 1997 | 1996 |
|---|---|---|
| | £000 | £000 |
| **EXPENDITURE** | | |
| Staff costs | 1,611 | 1,545 |
| Supplies and services consumed | 355 | 275 |
| Accommodation costs | 2,010 | 1,920 |
| Other administration costs | 243 | 142 |
| Interest charge on capital | 430 | 410 |
| Permanent diminution in value of tangible fixed assets | 2,282 | - |
| | 6,931 | 4,292 |
| **INCOME** | | |
| Income from non-departmental customers | (211) | (221) |
| **NET EXPENDITURE** | 6,720 | 4,071 |

| *advisers* | **Auditors** | National Audit Office | 157-197 Buckingham Palace Road London SW1W 9SP |
|---|---|---|---|

*publications*    *The Victorian*

# Radio Authority

Holbrook House
14 Great Queen Street
Holborn
London WC2B 5DG

**Tel** 0171 430 2724
**Fax** 0171 405 7062          **Web** http://www.radioauthority.gov.uk

| | |
|---|---|
| *status* | Public corporation |
| *founded* | 1990. One of the three bodies replacing the Independent Broadcasting Authority (IBA) |
| *sponsor* | Department for Culture, Media and Sport (DCMS) |
| *powers* | Broadcasting Act 1990 and 1996 |
| *mission* | To support the development and growth of a successful UK commercial radio network which offers a wide listening choice. |
| *tasks* | Licences and regulates commercial radio - national, local, cable satellite and national FM subcarrier as well as restricted and highly localised permanent services, eg hospitals, universities. In particular, it plans frequencies, appoints licensees with a view to broadening listening choice and enforcing ownership rules and regulates programming and advertising. It also publishes codes (from engineering to advertising and sponsorship) and enforces them; and plays an active role in the formulation of government policies affecting the industry and its listeners. |
| *operations* | Management: With the conclusion of the re-advertising process for existing licences it became possible to make good progress with offering new local and regional licences. The sole source of the Authority's income remains fees paid by licensees and applicants. Staff workloads have increased owing to new tasks arising from new broadcasting legislation. |
| | Policy: The Broadcasting Act 1990 provided a statutory shape for Digital Audio Broadcasting (DAB) and the ownership rules have been liberalised, although a 15% limit to the ownership of the total commercial radio industry remains and separate public interest tests to protect plurality and diversity have been introduced. |
| | Trends: The Authority's role is changing. Although developmental activities continue, administrative tasks will in the future demand equal attention. 1996 saw the start of a redefinition of programming and advertising rules in order to allow licensees maximum freedom within clear boundaries, while emphasising the importance of public awareness and input. As radio moves to a mixture of analogue and digital transmission the Authority inevitably finds that it is dealing with multiplex programme providers. Broadening services will involve not only licensing new services but enabling existing services to develop which protects what already has been achieved. |
| *board* | Appointed by the Secretary of State for Culture, Media and Sport from a variety of backgrounds, currently broadcasting, law, education, civil service and journalism. |

| Chairman | Sir Peter Gibbings | |
|---|---|---|
| Deputy Chairman | Michael Moriarty CB | |
| Members | Ms Jennifer Francis | Lady Sheil |
| | Andrew Reid | Mrs Helen Tennant |
| | Michael Reupke | |
| *Accounting Officer* | *Chief Executive* | |

*staff*          33

| | |
|---|---|
| Chief Executive | Tony Stoller |
| Head of Development & Deputy Chief Executive | David Vick |
| Head of Programming & Advertising | David Lloyd |
| Secretary to the Authority | Eve Salomon |
| Head of Finance | Neil Romain |
| Head of Engineering | Mark Thomas |

| financial | INCOME & EXPENDITURE | | |
|---|---|---|---|
| | Year end: 31 December | 1996 | 1995 |
| | | £ | £ |
| | **INCOME** | | |
| | Licence fees | 2,678,773 | 2,550,455 |
| | Wireless Telegraphy Act (WTA) fees | 496,985 | 464,840 |
| | Other Income | 188,249 | 107,001 |
| | | **3,364,007** | **3,122,296** |
| | **EXPENDITURE** | | |
| | Staff costs | 1,469,066 | 1,319,189 |
| | Depreciation | 92,689 | 79,122 |
| | Wireless Telegraphy Act (WTA) fees | 496,985 | 464,840 |
| | Other operating costs | 1,353,786 | 1,271,549 |
| | | **3,412,526** | **3,134,700** |
| | **OPERATING DEFICIT** | **(48,519)** | **(12,404)** |
| | Interest receivable | 30,130 | 37,086 |
| | Interest payable | (1,730 | (10,824) |
| | **(DEFICIT)/SURPLUS BEFORE TAXATION** | **(20,119)** | **13,858** |
| | Taxation on ordinary activities | 30,405 | (7,200) |
| | **SURPLUS TRANSFERRED TO RESERVES** | **10,286** | **6,658** |

| advisers | **Bankers** | Lloyds Bank | Knightsbridge Branch<br>79/81 Brompton Road, London SW3 1DD |
|---|---|---|---|
| | **Auditors** | Grant Thornton | Grant Thornton House, Melton Street<br>Euston Square, London NW1 2EP |
| | **Solicitors** | Allen and Overy | One New Change, London EC4M 9QQ |

**publications**    *The Radio Authority: What it is, What it does, Annual Report and Financial Statements for the Year Ended 31 December 1996, The Radio Authority Advertising and Sponsorship Code, The Radio Authority's Notes of Guidance on Ownership, Notes of Guidance: The Cross-Media Public Interest Test*

# *Radiocommunications Agency (RA)*

151 Buckingham Palace Road
London SW1W 9SS

**Tel** 0171 215 1383

| | |
|---|---|
| *status* | Executive agency |
| *founded* | 1990 |
| *sponsor* | Department of Trade and Industry (DTI) |
| *powers* | RA Framework Document 1996 |
| *mission* | Responsible for most civil radio matters (eg aeronautical and aircraft, maritime business radio, private mobile, on-site paging) including ensuring the efficient use of the radio spectrum and that the maximum amount of spectrum is available for civil use. |
| *tasks* | Granting licenses; assigning frequencies; handling interference reports; international negotiations on access to radio spectrum; regional customer seminars; research and development to extend the usable spectrum and improve untilisation of it; publishing information sheets. |
| *operations* | Management: Management Board consists of Chief Executive and heads of the six branches: international work, spectrum management; mobile services; broadcasting, fixed and space services; finance, corporate planning, information services; monitoring/investigation; information, personnel. Regional customer service offices. Steering Board oversees work. Almost all licensing that does not involve frequency assignment is contracted out. |
| | Policy: Unified licensing IT project (RULES) is continuing. |
| | Trends: Demand for radio services still increasing. |
| *board* | Steering Board appointed by the Secretary of State. |

| | | |
|---|---|---|
| Chairman | Alastair Macdonald | |
| Members | Don Cruickshank | |
| | Bill Dennay | |
| | Jim Norton | |
| | Martin Roberts | |
| | Dr Geoff Robinson | |
| | Dr JCJ Thyme CB | |
| *Accounting Officer* | *Chief Executive* | |

**staff** 512

**financial**

| INCOME & EXPENDITURE | | |
|---|---|---|
| Year end: 31 March | **1996** | **1995** |
| | **£000** | **£000** |
| **GROSS INCOME** | **43,230** | **40,621** |
| **EXPENDITURE** | | |
| Staff costs | (15,488) | (14,768) |
| Depreciation | (2,232) | (1,962) |
| Other operating charges | (30,653) | (19,600) |
| **OTHER OPERATING INCOME** | | |
| Exceptional items | 10,392 | 0 |
| **OPERATING SURPLUS** | **5,249** | **4,291** |
| Loss on disposal of fixed assets | (1,175) | (215) |
| **SURPLUS BEFORE INTEREST** | **4,074** | **4,076** |
| Notional interest | (1,093) | (686) |
| **SURPLUS ON ORDINARY ACTIVITIES** | **2,981** | **3,390** |

**advisers**   **Auditors**   National Audit Office   157-197 Buckingham Palace Road
London SW1W 9SP

# RAF Logistics Support Service (RAF LSS)

PO Box 70
Huntingdon
Cambridgeshire PE17 2PY

**Tel** 01480 446961
**Fax** 01480 446747

**E-mail** mackenziek@logistics.org

**status** Defence agency

**founded** 1996

**sponsor** Ministry of Defence (MOD)

**powers** Framework Document 1996

**mission** To strengthen and enhance RAF and MOD operational capability by provision of effective and efficient specialist military aerospace logistics support and logistics consultancy services.

**tasks** Provides specialist advice and logistics consultancy services on a comprehensive range of aerospace and related equipment and procedures, logistics research, statistical analysis, management information, aircraft fatigue and fault data analysis, assistance with major logistics IT programs, and computer stock control and accounting functions to all three Services.

**operations** Management: The Owner is Air Officer Communications, Information Systems and Support Services (AOCSS). He is advised on the business plan, performance and customers by the Owner's Board. The Chief Executive reports to the Owner. There are three strategic business units: Aerospace Maintenance Development and Support, Information and Data Management, and the Logistics Computer Centre. There are also three business managements branches.

**board** Owner's Board appointed by Owner.

| | |
|---|---|
| *Accounting Officer* | *Permanent Under Secretary* |

**staff** 1201(689 service, 512 civilian)

| | |
|---|---|
| *Chief Executive* | *Air Commodore Ian Sloss* |

**financial** Cash budget total for 96/97 of £42 million.

*advisers*  **Auditors**  National Audit Office

*publications*  *Framework Document 1996, Corporate Plan 1996*

# RAF Maintenance Group Defence Agency (RAF MGDA)

RAF Bramton
Huntingdon
Cambs PE18 8QL

**Tel** 01480 52151
**Fax** 01480 431163

*status*  Defence agency

*founded*  1991

*sponsor*  Ministry of Defence (MOD)

*mission*  To strengthen and enhance RAF and MOD operational capability by provision of effective and efficient specialist military aerospace logistics support and consultancy services.

*tasks*  Provides maintenance and support services to the RAF and other UK and foreign armed services including aerosystems and electronics engineering, equipment supply and distribution, gases and cryogenic support, armament support. Commands and controls the RAF Nuclear Accident Response Organisation. Maintains the necessary level of trained personnel to meet its deployment and surge commitments in time of crisis, transition to war and war.

*operations*  Management: It is an integral component of RAF Logistics Command, with its headquarters at RAF Brampton. The Air Officer Commander-in-Chief (AOCinC) RAF Logistics Command is the Agency Owner. Bulk of business is concentrated at three centres (RAF St Athan, RAF Sealand and RAF Stafford). Agency is run by the Management Board, headed by the Chief Executive.

Policy: Staff numbers decreasing (particularly service personnel).

Trends: Closures of stations because of ongoing programme of rationalisation.

*performance*  Achieved seven out of eleven targets.

*board*  Management Board appointed by the Secretary of State.

| | |
|---|---|
| Chief Executive | Air Vice-Marshal RH Kyle |
| Officer Commanding, RAF North Luffenham | Group Captain BG Benstead |
| Officer Commanding, RAF Sealand | Group Captain JE Chandler |
| Director, RAF MGDA Finance & Plans | MJ Heritage-Owen |
| Air Commodore Defence Agency (Maintenance) | Air Commodore KJM Procter |
| Officer Commanding, RAF St Athan | Air Commodore PJ Scott |
| Officer Commanding, RAF Stafford | Group Captain P Whalley |
| *Accounting Officer* | *Chief Executive* |

*staff*  3121 service personnel and 4675 civilians

*financial*

| INCOME & EXPENDITURE | | |
|---|---|---|
| Year end: 31 March | 1997 | 1996 |
| | £000 | £000 |
| **EXPENDITURE** | | |
| Staff costs | 176,378 | 184,792 |
| Accommodation services | 51,159 | 50,364 |
| Estate maintenance | 38,895 | 29,758 |
| Supplies and services | 141,011 | 114,776 |
| Other administration | 24,218 | 20,317 |
| Higher formation costs | 36,859 | 44,837 |
| Notional interest payable | 23,133 | 23,975 |
| | **491,653** | **468,819** |
| **INCOME** | | |
| From non-departmental customers | (3,859) | (2,764) |
| From others | (1,032) | (385) |
| **NET EXPENDITURE** | **486,762** | **465,670** |

# RAF Personnel Management Agency (RAF PMA)

Room 1101
Building 248
RAF Innsworth
Gloucester GL3 1EZ

**Tel** 01452 712612
**Fax** 01452 712612

| | |
|---|---|
| *status* | Defence agency |
| *founded* | 1997 |
| *sponsor* | Ministry of Defence (MOD) |
| *powers* | Framework Document 1997 |
| *mission* | Allocating trained manpower to enable the RAF to meet its operational requirements; implementing and developing personnel policy; providing personnel management of RAF Regular and Reserve trained manpower. |
| *tasks* | Provision and allocation of manpower; personnel policy; management of RAF Reserve; manpower targets; service-wide allowances; common services including human resource IT strategy, military medals, advice to ministers. |
| *operations* | Management: The Owner is the Air Member for Personnel and Commander-in-Chief Personnel and Training Command and is responsible for the strategic direction and management of the Agency and for its corporate plan and corporate risk. He is advised by the Owner's Board. The Chief Executive is responsible for the day-to-day management and reports to the Owner for the majority of functions; but he is also Air Secretary and in this role reports directly to the Chief of Air Staff and is personally responsible for all air rank and group captain career management and appointments. RAF PMA is organised into six main areas: 3 are in Manning and Career Management - Senior Appointments, Officers and Airmen (Aircrew), Ground Trades; other three are Personnel Management Policy, Central Services and Secretariat.<br><br>Trends: Staff reduced on the formation of the Armed Forces Personnel Administration Agency in April 1997. |
| *board* | Members of Owner's Board appointed *ex officio* or by the Chairman (Owner). |

| | |
|---|---|
| Air Secretary/Chief Executive | Air Vice-Marshal Robert O'Brien OBE |
| Director Officers/Airmen Aircrew | Air Commodore BC Laite |
| Director Personnel Management Policy | Air Commodore AJ Burton OBE |
| Director Airmen/Reserves | Air Commodore C Davison MBE |
| Senior Appointments & Careers Executive | Group Captain (Retd) JS Preston |
| Corporate Services | Group Captain PDJ Turner |
| Agency Secretary | A Cowpe |

| | |
|---|---|
| *staff* | 465 |

# RAF Signals Engineering Establishment (RAF SEE)

RAF Henlow
Bedfordshire SG16 6DN

**Tel** 01462 851515 x 7304
**Fax** 01462 851515 x7129

| | |
|---|---|
| *status* | Defence agency |
| *founded* | 1994 |
| *sponsor* | Ministry of Defence (MOD) |
| *powers* | Framework Document 1994 |
| *mission* | To provide a quick-reaction communications and electronics engineering capability in support of UK Armed Forces' military operations worldwide. |
| *tasks* | The design, installation and integration of airborne and ground-based communications and electronics sys- |

tems; the provision of engineering advice.

**operations**   Management: The Air Officer Commanding Support Units is the agency's Owner and formulates the policy and operating framework. The Owner has direct responsibility for the functions and well-being of the agency and is advised by the Chief Executive. The Owner determines the strategic direction of the agency through the Owner's Board, and also receives advice from a Customer Advisory Committee comprising the agency's major customers. The Chief Executive is responsible for the day-to-day management with the support of the Management Board.

Policy: In 1996/97 focus of work was in former Yugoslavia. Restructuring in 1997 introduced new functions: business development, sales and contracts, bid management and portfolio services.

Trends: Non-core activities are put out to competitive tendering.

**performance**   Achieved all targets in 1996/97.

**board**   Owner's Board appointed by the Secretary of State.

| Accounting Officer | Chief Executive |
| --- | --- |

**staff**   1069 (499 are civilian)

| Chief Executive | Air Commodore G Jones MBE |
| --- | --- |
| Group Captain Policy and Services | Group Captain H Britten-Austin |
| Director Project Division | A Palmer |
| OC Administration Wing | Wing Commander CI Roberts |
| Finance Controller | Mrs J Jenkins |

**financial**

**INCOME & EXPENDITURE**

| Year end: 31 March | 1997 | 1996 | 1995 |
| --- | --- | --- | --- |
| | £000 | £000 | £000 |
| **EXPENDITURE** | | | |
| Staff costs | 27,582 | 30,682 | 13,389 |
| Supplies and services consumed | (8,062) | 1,086 | 787 |
| Accommodation costs | 8,339 | 10,844 | 5,171 |
| Other administration costs | 6,848 | 4,673 | 5,210 |
| Notional interest charge on capital | 3,583 | 2,194 | 817 |
| | 38,290 | 49,479 | 25,374 |
| **INCOME** | | | |
| Income from non-MOD customers | (2,354) | (1,987) | (1,353) |
| **NET EXPENDITURE** | **35,936** | **47,492** | **24,021** |

# RAF Training Group Defence Agency (RAF TGDA)

RAF Innsworth
Gloucester GL3 1EZ

**Tel** 01452 712612
**Fax** 01452 510825

**status**   Defence agency

**founded**   1991. As defence organisation, 1994

**sponsor**   Ministry of Defence

**powers**   Framework Document 1997

**mission**   To contribute to the operational effectiveness of the Royal Air Force by the timely provision of military and civilian personnel trained to standards agreed with customers.

**tasks**   Recruiting and selecting Royal Air Force personnel in the required numbers; training aircrew of the three Services; training military personnel and certain categories of civilians to undertake ground appointments; developing non-operational training policy to meet the needs of customers. The principal outputs of the agency are: trained military and civilian personnel for established flying and ground appointments to meet any crisis, transition to war, war and other commitments; trained military personnel in foreign and Commonwealth armed forces as directed by the Ministry of Defence.

**operations**   The Agency comprises seven Royal Air Force stations, together with the flying and ground training units established at those stations and elsewhere. The Agency's headquarters is located at Royal Air Force Innsworth. The Owner of the Agency is the Air Officer Commander-in-Chief Personnel and Training Command.

**performance** 1996/97 targets met.

**board** The Training Group Management Board comprises the serving officers.

| Owner | Air Chief Marshal Sir David Cousins |
|---|---|
| Chief Executive | Air Vice-Marshal AJ Stables |
| Director of Operations | Air Commodore AP Waldron |
| Director of Corporate Development | Air Commodore MJ Gilding |
| *Accounting Officer* | *Chief Executive* |

**staff** 6634

**financial**

| EXPENDITURE Year end: 31 March | 1997 £000 | 1996 £000 |
|---|---|---|
| EXPENDITURE | | |
| Staff costs | 169,062 | 169,304 |
| Supplies & services consumed | 37,787 | 32,028 |
| Accommodation costs | 71,517 | 68,919 |
| Other administration costs | 181,418 | 169,864 |
| Interest charge on capital | 68,761 | 72,647 |
| GROSS EXPENDITURE | 528,545 | 512,762 |
| INCOME | | |
| Less Income from non-MOD customers | 14,507 | 9,903 |
| NET EXPENDITURE | 514,038 | 502,859 |

**advisers** **Auditors** National Audit Office

**publications** *Framework Document, Corporate Plan, Annual Report*

# Rail Users Consultative Committee (RUCC) for Eastern England

Crescent House
46 Priestgate
Peterborough PE1 1LF

**Tel** 01733 312188
**Fax** 01733 891286

**status** Executive body

**founded** 1994

**sponsor** Office of the Rail Regulator (ORR)

**powers** Railways Act 1993

**mission** To protect and promote the interests of rail passengers in Eastern England.

**tasks** Actively seek the views of passengers; represent passengers' interests to the industry and those who regulate or influence it; seek higher standards and performance and monitor their achievement; seek to ensure that network benefits and safety standards are maintained; encourage the use and development of rail passenger services; investigate passengers' complaints which have not been satisfactorily resolved by the industry.

**operations** Management: Secretary runs day-to-day operation and reports to the Committee. Train Operating Companies (TOCs) covered are: Great Eastern Railway; West Anglia Great Northern; LTS Rail; Central Trains; Great North Eastern Railway; Anglia Railways.

Policy: Subcommittees for each TOC meet with members of other relevant RUCCs.

Trends: Some signs of improvement since privatisation.

**board**   Chairman appointed by the Secretary of State for the Environment, Transport and the Regions and the unpaid members are appointed by the ORR from advertisements.

| Chairman | S Francis | |
| Vice Chairman | RE West | |
| Members | PA Bayless | |
| | JB Brodribb | BMW Frost |
| | Mrs MGA Browning | Mrs JM Honisett |
| | AGR Bryson | BJC Moore |
| | BM Cooke | PR Pennington |
| | Miss SC Dex | Dr TJ Rothwell |
| *Accounting Officer* | *Rail Regulator* | |

**staff**   Three

| Secretary | Guy Dangerfield |

**financial**

| EXPENDITURE Year end: 31 March | 1997 £ |
| --- | --- |
| Staff travel & subsistence | 2,698 |
| Hospitality | 834 |
| Postage/carriage | 11,473 |
| Printing, stationery/publications | 1,123 |
| IT & office machinery | 4,934 |
| RUCC expenditure | 8,392 |
| | **19,454** |

**publications**   Annual Report

# Rail Users Consultative Committee (RUCC) for Midlands

77 Paradise Circus
Queensway
Birmingham B1 2DT

**Tel** 0121 212 2133
**Fax** 0121 236 6945

**Contact** Gill James, Secretary

**status**   Executive body
**founded**   1949
**sponsor**   Office of the Rail Regulator (ORR)
**powers**   Railways Act 1993
**mission**   Act as statutory watchdog, protecting and promoting the interests of rail passengers in the Midlands region.
**tasks**   Representing passengers of the eleven Train Operating Companies (TOCs) which come within the Midlands RUCC area: Central Trains, Chiltern Trains, Virgin Cross Country Trains, Virgin West Coast trains, Midland Main Line, Silverlink, North Western Regional Railways, Regional Railways North East, Wales and West Connex South Central and Thames Trains; also of their passengers travelling on Railtrack. Joint Sub-Committees deal with TOCs which operate in more than one RUCC area and Midlands RUCC provides the Chairman and Secretariat for the Central Joint Sub-Committee.
**operations**   Management: The part-time Chairman, who is appointed by the Secretary of State for the Environment, reports to the Regulator and is a member of the Central Rail Users Consultative Committee (CRUCC). The three full time secretariat staff are civil servants.

Policy: TOC and Railtrack performance being scrutinised.

Trends: Complaints from passengers increasing.
**board**   Committee members appointed after application by the Regulator, after consultation with the Secretary of State and Chairman, from rail users from a variety of backgrounds.

| Chairman | Dr PP Jones | |
|---|---|---|
| Deputy Chairman | G Horrocks CBE JP | |
| Members | J Balmforth | A Meredith |
| | Ms S Barker | J Mortell |
| | S Edwards | Mrs J Needham |
| | Mrs GVE Havenhand | B Picken JP |
| | RMS Lincoln | A Street |
| | AER Manners | Mrs J Thornton |
| *Accounting Officer* | *Rail Regulator* | |

**staff**    Three

| Secretary | Gill James |
|---|---|

**financial**

| EXPENDITURE | |
|---|---|
| **Year end: 31 March** | **1997** |
| | **£** |
| Staff Travel and Subsistence | 1,790 |
| Hospitality | 0 |
| Postage / Carriage costs | 847 |
| I.T. & Office Machinery | 2,560 |
| Printing / Stationery | 933 |
| Publicity | 524 |
| Members and Meeting Expenditure | 10,251 |
| | **16,905** |

**publications**    *1996/97 Annual Report, Rail Users' Consultative Committees - At Your Service (Leaflet)*

# Rail Users Consultative Committee (RUCC) for North Eastern England

Hilary House
16 St Saviour's Place
Yorks YO1 2PL

**Tel** 01904 625615
**Fax** 01904 643026

**status**    Executive body

**founded**    1994

**sponsor**    Office of the Rail Regulator (ORR)

**powers**    Railways Act 1993

**mission**    To protect and promote the rail users' interests in North Eastern England.

**tasks**    To monitor the policies and performance of train and station operators in North Eastern England; to make recommendations for changes; to investigate passenger complaints; to actively seek the views of passengers and to represent their interests to the industry.

**operations**    Management: The Chairman is also a member of the Central Rail Users' Consultative Committee (CRUCC), which coordinates the work of the RUCCs. The Secretary runs the day-to-day operation of the RUCC which is funded by ORR. Committee members (other than the Chairman) are unpaid. Two subcommittees (northern and southern) which meet three times a year; main committee meets four times a year; East Coast Main Line Joint Subcommittee draws Members from RUCC (Eastern England), RUCC (Scotland), RUCC (North Eastern) and LRPC. RUCC (North Eastern) provides secretariat. Meets three times a year.

Policy: Continuing allowing members of the public to express their views at meetings.

Trends: All RUCCs are finding a way of working more closely together.

**performance**    No performance targets are set.

**board**    Committee appointed by the Rail Regulator from members of the public who apply.

| Chairman | AJ Beale OBE | |
|---|---|---|
| Members | RG Brown | MG Plumb |
| | Mrs VA Harriott | P Rayner |
| | JG McGorrigan JP | Dr RWJ Sisson |
| | GW Meikle | JA Taylor |
| | JT Middleton, OBE | DM Walsh, OBE JP |
| | ED Pepper | AR White |
| *Accounting Officer* | *Rail Regulator* | |

**staff** Three

| Secretary | E Preston |
|---|---|

**publications** Annual Report

# Rail Users Consultative Committee (RUCC) for North Western England

Boulton House
17-21 Chorlton St
Manchester M1 3HY

**Tel** 0161 228 6247
**Fax** 0161 236 1476

**status** Executive body

**founded** 1994

**sponsor** Office of the Rail Regulator (ORR)

**powers** Railways Act 1993

**mission** To protect rail users' interests in NW England.

**tasks** To monitor the policies and performance of train and station operators in NW England; to make recommendations for changes; to take up complaints and to assess hardship when lines or stations are proposed for closure.

**operations** Management: Much of the RUCC's work is undertaken by its sub-committees - the Metrolink Sub-Committee, the North Western Trains Sub-Committee and the Merseyrail Sub-Committee - each of which has its own Chair, and also by a series of local and national specialist user groups. The Chairman is also a member of the Central Rail Users' Consultative Committee (CRUCC), which co-ordinates the work of the RUCCs.

Policy: To maintain the 'walk on' services for all ticket types against the moves towards a largely pre-booked service.

Trends: Shift of focus from response to external events to a more powerful set of internally generated priorities.

**board** The Chairman is appointed by the Secretary of State for the Environment, Transport and the Regions and the unpaid committee members are appointed by the ORR.

| Chairman | Prof Tom Cannon | |
|---|---|---|
| Deputy Chairman | Paul Fawcett | |
| Members | Ian Barnett | |
| | David Blanchflower | Val Godfrey |
| | Jennifer Borer | John Hart |
| | David Butterworth | Christie Jackson |
| | Geraldine Evans | Andrew McKearnen |
| | Bob Gale | Robin Morris |
| | Nora Gleave | David Sharples |

**staff**

| Secretary | John Moorhouse |
|---|---|

# Q&Q

## Rail Users Consultative Committee (RUCC) for Scotland

249 West George Street
Glasgow G2 4QE

**Tel** 0141 221 7760
**Fax** 0141 221 3393

**Contact** William Ure, Secretary

| | |
|---|---|
| **status** | Executive body |
| **founded** | 1993 |
| **sponsor** | Office of the Rail Regulator (ORR). Scottish Office |
| **powers** | 1993 Railway Act |
| **mission** | To act as the statutory watchdog protecting and promoting the interests of rail passengers in Scotland and users of the Caledonian MacBrayne Ferries. |
| **tasks** | To actively seek passengers' views; represent passenger interests to the industry and regulators; seek higher standards and performance for passenger services and monitor them; seek to ensure that network benefits and safety standards are maintained; actively encourage the use and development of passenger services; investigate passenger complaints that have not been satisfactorily resolved by the industry; ensure that all representations are fully considered when rail closures are proposed. |
| **operations** | Management: Both rail and shipping committees operate through three subcommittees: two functional subcommittees and the Chairman's strategic subcommittees. The systems subcommittees deal with planning, infrastructure and resources; the passenger services subcommittee with delivery of services to passengers. |
| | Policy: Consumer protection is at the heart of policy. Safety, especially of women, comes first. Access, especially for the disabled, and consumer choice and information are priorities. Redress of complaints and representation to the Rail Regulator and Franchise Director are important. |
| | Trends: Passenger's Charter being developed for rail and shipping. 1996/97 was a stand-still year both for the Scottish rail industry and the Committee. |
| **board** | Chairman appointed, after advertisement, by the Secretaries of State for Transport (Environment, Transport and the Regions of Scottish Office), in consultation with the Rail Regulator. Members are appointed by the Regulator after consultation with the Secretaries of State from a wide range of backgrounds and from all parts of Scotland. |

| | | |
|---|---|---|
| Chairman | Mrs Helen Millar | |
| Deputy Chairman | Lawrence Kemp | |
| Members | Callan Anderson | |
| | Dr Stephen Cribb | David Spaven |
| | Christine Davis | James Stobo CBE |
| | Jane Irvine | Robert White |
| | Tom Lister | Richard Wilkinson |
| | Archie Roberts | Dr Douglas Williamson |
| *Accounting Officer* | *Rail Regulator* | |

| | | |
|---|---|---|
| **staff** | Secretary | William Ure |

412

# Rail Users Consultative Committee (RUCC) for Southern England

4th Floor
35 Old Queen Street
London SW1H 9JA

**Tel** 0171 222 0391
**Fax** 0171 222 0392

| | |
|---|---|
| *status* | Executive body |
| *founded* | 1994 |
| *sponsor* | Office of the Rail Regulator (ORR) |
| *powers* | Railways Act 1993 |
| *mission* | To protect rail users' interests in Southern England. |
| *tasks* | To monitor the policies and performance of train and station operators in Southern England; to make recommendations for changes; to take up complaints and to assess hardship when lines or stations are proposed for closure. |
| *operations* | Management: The Chairman is appointed by the Secretary of State for the Environment, Transport and the Regions. Much of the RUCC's work is undertaken by its subcommittees - the Quality of Service Subcommittee, the Timetable Subcommittee and the Passenger Service Subcommittee. The Chairman is also a member of the Central Rail Users' Consultative Committee (CRUCC), which coordinates the work of the RUCCs. |
| | Policy: To support on-train ticket inspections to ensure that paying passengers are not subsidising the non-paying. |
| | Trends: Penalty fares, more impartial retailing, passenger charters. |
| *board* | Chairman appointed by the Secretary of State for the Environment, Transport and the Regions and the unpaid members are appointed by the ORR from advertisements. |

| | |
|---|---|
| Chairman | Miss Angela Hooper CBE |
| Deputy Chairman | Peter Lee |
| Vice Chairman | Mrs Elizabeth MacDonald-Brown |
| Members | John Bigny |
| | John Doctor |
| | Alan Eadie |
| | Mrs Jennie Hinton |
| | Mrs Janet Roskilly |
| | Mrs Fiona Ross |
| | Alan Shotter |
| *Accounting Officer* | *Rail Regulator* |

*staff*  3

| | |
|---|---|
| Secretary | Michael Hewitson |

*financial*

| EXPENDITURE | | |
|---|---|---|
| **Year end: 31 March** | **1997** | **1996** |
| | £ | £ |
| Staff travel and subsistence | 343 | 280 |
| Room hire/ meeting expenses | 1,402 | 1,270 |
| Postage/carriage costs | 1,655 | 1,475 |
| IT & office machinery | 5,539 | 5,260 |
| Printing/stationery | 2,286 | 2,739 |
| Publicity | 303 | 348 |
| Members' expenditure | 7,162 | 6,056 |
| | **18,690** | **17,428** |

*publications*  Annual Report

# Rail Users Consultative Committee (RUCC) for Wales

St David's House
Wood Street
Cardiff CF1 1ES

**Tel** 01222 227247
**Fax** 01222 223992

| | |
|---|---|
| *status* | Executive body |
| *founded* | 1993 |
| *sponsor* | Office of the Rail Regulator (ORR) |
| *powers* | Railways Act 1993 |
| *mission* | To protect rail users' interests in Wales. |
| *tasks* | To monitor the policies and performance of train and station operators in Wales; to make recommendations for changes; to take up complaints and assess hardship when lines or stations are proposed for closure. |
| *operations* | Management: The Chairman is appointed by Secretary of State for the Environment, Transport and the Regions in consultation with the regulator. The RUCC is funded by the ORR and has its own staff and office in Cardiff. It is entirely independent of the rail industry. It monitors the services of all six train operators in Wales: Cardiff Railway Company, Central Trains, Virgin Trains, Great Western Trains, InterCity West Coast, North West Regional Railways and Passenger Wales and West Trains. The RUCC liaises with county councils. |
| | Policy: To discuss strategy with train operators eg future train timetables, station reconstruction. To insist that Passenger Service Requirements specify adequate connections, particularly between separate train operators. |
| | Trends: Railtrack investing £16 billion on infrastructure. |
| *board* | The chairman is appointed by the Secretary of State for the Environment, Transport and the Regions in consultation with the regulator. Unpaid committee members are appointed by the Rail Regulator fr0m advertisements. |

| | |
|---|---|
| Chairman | Charles A Hogg JP |
| Members | Brian Bigwood |
| | Brenda A Cooper |
| | Philip C Evans JP |
| | Andrew Goodwin |
| | Guy RC Hardy |
| | Paul W Harley |
| | Dafydd Hughes |
| | Ian Hume |
| | Mohammad Javed |
| | Kevin Nield |
| | Gillian E Wright |
| | John Warman |
| | John Wildig |
| | Owen P Williams |
| *Accounting officer* | *Rail Regulator* |

| | |
|---|---|
| *staff* | Secretary Clive G Williams |

*publications* Annual Report

# Rail Users Consultative Committee (RUCC) for Western England

13th Floor
Tower House
Fairfax Street
Bristol BS1 3BN

**Tel** 0117 926 5703
**Fax** 0117 929 4140

| | |
|---|---|
| *status* | Executive body |
| *founded* | 1994 |
| *sponsor* | Office of the Rail Regulator (ORR) |
| *powers* | Railways Act 1993 |
| *mission* | To protect rail users' interests in Western England. |
| *tasks* | To monitor the policies and performance of train and station operators in Western England; to make recommendations for changes; to investigate passenger complaints. |
| *operations* | Management: Train operators in Western England are Central Trains, South Wales and West Railway, Virgin CrossCountry, South West Trains, Great Western Trains Company, and Thames Trains. The Chairman is also a member of the Central Rail Users Consultative Committee (CRUCC), which coordinates the work of the RUCCs. The Secretary runs the day-to-day operation of the RUCC. Committee members (other than the Chairman) are unpaid. Meets four times a year at different locations in the region.

Policy: Trying to get improvement in condition of stations.

Trends: Need for new investment remains high priority for railways. |
| *performance* | No performance targets are set. |
| *board* | Committee appointed by the ORR. |

| | |
|---|---|
| Chairman | Sir Robert Wall OBE |
| Vice-Chairman | CC Irwin |
| Deputy Chairman | Cllr JM Chapman |
| Members | PC Blackburn |
| | Ald GJP Browne |
| | JT Caff |
| | PA Eward |
| | Lady Gass |
| | CG Griffin |
| | Rev PR Long |
| | JAK Phillips |
| | Dr RLD Rees |
| | Cllr Mrs EA Smith |
| *Accounting Officer* | *Rail Regulator* |

*staff* Three

| | |
|---|---|
| Secretary | Sean O'Neill |

*publications* *Annual Report*

# Rate Collection Agency (RCA)

Oxford House
49-55 Chichester Street
Belfast BT1 4HH

**Tel** 01232 252252
**Fax** 01232 252113

**E-mail** dennis.millar.doe@nics.gov.uk

**Contact** Carol McClure

| | |
|---|---|
| *status* | Executive agency |
| *founded* | 1991 |
| *sponsor* | Northern Ireland Office, Department of the Environment for NI (DOENI) |
| *powers* | Rates (NI) Order 1977 |
| *mission* | To collect rates and manage the Housing Benefits Scheme for owner-occupiers effectively, efficiently and economically. |
| *tasks* | To levy, collect and recover rates on behalf of the UK central government and the Province's 36 district councils. To administer the Housing Benefit (HB) and Disabled Persons' Allowance Schemes for those ratepayers who are owner-occupiers. |
| *operations* | Management: There is a Chief Executive, responsible for day-to-day management performance supported by a Directorate of four. In 1996/97 the 13 local offices were merged into five regional offices and the new Housing Benefit Central Unit became fully operational. The five regional offices are situated in Belfast (includes HB Central Unit) Omagh, Londonderry, Ballymena and Craigavon |
| | Policy: Quality of customer service is a priority. General matters of policy are dealt with elsewhere - rating policy by the Department of Finance and Personnel; housing benefit by the Department of Health and Social Services; valuation assessment of properties by the Valuation and Lands Agency. |
| | Trends: An IS Strategy Review has recommended improved systems integration, document imaging, workflow and telephone management. A pilot workflow management scheme will be introduced during 1997/98. |
| *performance* | Main rate collection target and its three subsidiary targets all met; Housing Benefit Central Unit operational and quality service targets also met. |

*board*

| | |
|---|---|
| Chief Executive | David Gallagher |
| Director of Administration | Fred Hempton |
| Director of Operations | Anne McKenna |
| Director of Resources | Dennis Millar |
| Director of Finance | Donald Starritt |
| *Accounting Officer* | *Chief Executive* |

*staff* 235 (all civil servants)

| | |
|---|---|
| South Western | Mervyn Beattie |
| Training and Development | Anne Breen |
| Computer Operations | Paul Brennan |
| Belfast and Eastern | Billy Cassidy |
| Investors in People | Vivienne Collins |
| Central Collection | Roger Gordon |
| Southern | Margaret Grew |
| Enforcement and FLAC | Andrew Kennedy |
| Admin and Personnel | Janet Lunn |
| North Western | Sean Maguire |
| Financial Management | Ronnie McAteer |
| North Eastern | Fred McGuigan |
| Housing Benefit | Maureen Mitchell |
| Information Technology | Philip Mulligan |

*financial*

| INCOME & EXPENDITURE Year end: 31 March | 1997 £000 | 1996 £000 | 1995 £000 |
|---|---|---|---|
| **EXPENDITURE** | | | |
| Staff costs | 4,215 | 4,207 | 3,992 |
| Depreciation | 573 | 508 | 878 |
| Other operating costs | 3,226 | 2,652 | 2,957 |
| Less: legal expenses recoverable | (644) | (508) | (434) |
| **EXPENDITURE BEFORE CAPITAL CHARGES** | **7,370** | **6,859** | **7,393** |
| Capital charges | 274 | 287 | 62 |
| **NET EXPENDITURE** | **7,644** | **7,146** | **7,455** |

*advisers*

| | | |
|---|---|---|
| **Auditors** | Northern Ireland Audit Office | 106 University Street,Belfast BT7 1EU |
| **Solicitors** | Crown Solicitors Office | Royal Courts of Justice,Belfast BT1 3JY |
| **Public Relations** | DOE NI Information Office | 10-18 Adelaide Street, Belfast |

# Registers of Scotland

Meadowbank House
153 London Road
Edinburgh EH8 7AU

**Tel** 0131 659 6111
**Fax** 0131 479 3688

*status* Executive agency

*founded* 1990, as trading fund 1996

*sponsor* Scottish Office

*powers* Land Registration (Scotland) Act 1979

*mission* To protect the rights of the individual by allowing open access to important legal information in Scotland.

*tasks* To register, maintain and provide public access to 15 registers of legal documents in Scotland. The largest, the General Register of Sasines, contains deeds, writs and transactions concerning land and property ownership. It is gradually being superseded by the Land Register, a register of title with Land Certificates backed by a State guarantee. The 13 other smaller registers deal with diverse subjects - bankruptcy, debt, wills, foreign court judgments etc. To extend the Land Register to the whole of Scotland by 2003.

*operations* Management: The work is demand led and self-financing, fluctuating in response to levels of activity in the housing and commercial property markets. Structural changes are being made to reflect the new business emphasis, eg the integrated Scottish Land Information Service (ScotLIS) which links public geographically based data and accesses from a single point, and the Direct Access Service for customers. Annual customer surveys are conducted.

Policy: To convert from paper-based work methods to electronic systems. To generate a 6% return on capital over three years. To work in partnership with the private sector.

Trends: Demand for the agency's services is forecast to remain broadly similar to 1996/97 and the extension of the Land Register is planned within existing resources. In 1997/98, conversion of the agency's main processes into IT-based systems should be complete.

*performance* Most turnaround targets were missed. Land Register extension targets were met.

*board*

| | |
|---|---|
| Keeper/Chief Executive Alan W Ramage | |
| Deputy Keeper | Alistair G Rennie |
| Managing Director | Frank W Manson |
| Non-Executive Board Member | Mrs Myra Cameron |
| *Accounting Officer* | *Chief Executive* |

*staff* 1169

*financial*

| INCOME & EXPENDITURE Year end: 31 March | 1997 £000 | 1996 £000 |
|---|---|---|
| **INCOME** | | |
| Turnover - continuing operations | 30,275 | 30,226 |
| Change in stocks an WIP | (2,831) | (342) |
| | **27,444** | **29,884** |
| Other operating income | 1,225 | 645 |
| | **28,669** | **30,529** |
| **EXPENDITURE** | | |
| Net operating expenses - continuing operations | | |
| Staff costs | 21,779 | 19,415 |
| Depreciation | 2,835 | 1,489 |
| Other operating charges | 7,098 | 8,799 |
| | 31,712 | 29,703 |
| **OPERATING (LOSS) SURPLUS - CONTINUING OPERATIONS** | **(3,043)** | **826** |
| Interest receivable | 429 | - |
| Interest payable | 538 | 745 |
| **RETAINED (LOSS) SURPLUS FOR THE FINANCIAL YEAR** | **(3,152)** | **81** |

*advisers*  **Auditors**  National Audit Office  22 Melville Street, Edinburgh EH3 7NS

# Registrar of Public Lending Right

Bayheath House
Prince Regent Street
Stockton-on-Tees TS18 1DF

**Tel** 01642 604699
**Fax** 01642 615641

**E-mail** Registrar@PLR.octacon.co.uk
**Web** http://www.earl.org.uk/partners/plr/index.html

**Contact** Susan Ridge, PA to the Registrar

*status*  Executive body
*founded*  1979
*sponsor*  Department for Culture, Media and Sport (DCMS)
*powers*  Public Lending Right (PLR) Act 1979. PLR Scheme (1982)
*mission*  To manage the PLR Scheme for the benefit of authors.
*tasks*  Registration of authors and each of their books (by ISBN), statistical sampling of public library loans, calculation of annual rate per loan, payment to each registered author - up to £6000pa and remainder to pool which is reallocated to other authors.
*operations*  Management: PLR is administered by a Registrar responsible to the Secretary of State and funded by central government. An Advisory Committee advises the Minister and Registrar on the operation of the PLR Scheme. Over 27,000 authors are registered. There are reciprocal arrangements with Germany.

Policy: EC Directive on Lending and Rental (1992) has internationalised PLR.

Trends: Author registration increases at about 1000 pa.
*performance*  All met, partially or in full
*board*  Advisory Committee appointed by the Secretary of State.

| | |
|---|---|
| Chairman | Michael Holroyd |
| Members | Hilary Mantel |
| | Gillian McClure |
| | Roger Palmer |
| | Jim Parker |
| | John Saumarez Smith |
| | Claire Tomalin |
| *Accounting Officer* | *Registrar* |

*staff*  18

| Registrar | Jim Parker |
|---|---|
| Team Leader, Author Services | Carolyn Gray |
| Team Leader, Corporate Services (job-share post) | Julie Ramsey |
| Team Leader, Corporate Services (job-share post) | Evelyn Relph |

*financial*

| EXPENDITURE Year end: February | 1998 £ | 1997 £ | 1996 £ |
|---|---|---|---|
| Government funding | 4,921,000 | 5,000,000 | 4,936,000 |
| Operating costs | 670,000 | 654,000 | 606,250 |
| Payments to authors | 4,251,000 | 4,346,000 | 4,329,750 |

*advisers*

**Bankers**    Barclays

**Auditors**    National Audit Office

**Solicitors**    Treasury Solicitor

*publications*    Annual Reports on the Public Lending Right Scheme

# Remploy

415 Edgware Road
Cricklewood
London NW2 6LR

**Tel** 0181 235 0500
**Fax** 0181 235 0576

*status*    Executive body

*founded*    1945

*sponsor*    Department for Education and Employment (DfEE)

*powers*    Remploy Government Agreement 1996/97

*mission*    To create good employment opportunities for people with a wide range of disabilities by providing quality products and services to customers.

*tasks*    To employ severely disabled people in its own factories. To support their employment in host companies through its Interworkers placement scheme. To provide employees based in factories with jobs in the local service industry. To provide training and work experience.

*operations*    Management: 1996/97 was the second year of operation within a fixed government funding limit of £94m.

Policy: To increase the number of disabled people employed by the company by developing Interwork and extending the range of factory jobs.

Trends: Interwork job opportunities are growing and a new Contract Operations Group has been created to extend opportunities into local service industry with immediate results in the hotel sector.

*performance*    The average cost of employing each disabled employee has been reduced. The proportion of Interworkers has greatly increased while the severely disabled employees in manufacturing has reduced. Turnover increased by 10% in 1996/97 owing to the success of the Manufacturing Services Group and the Interwork supported placements. Annual grant is now a fixed limit.

*board*    Appointed by the Secretary of State in consultation with the Chairman.

| Chairman | DG Heywood |
|---|---|
| Chief Executive | AGH Withey CBE |
| Non-Executive Director | DA Boothman |
| Operations Director | LJ Boulton |
| Non-Executive Director | SE Brown |
| Personnel Director | RN Fletcher |
| Non-Executive Director | RA Jackson |
| Non-Executive Director | J Ramsay |
| Non-Executive Director | A Roberts |
| Financial Director | K Taylor |
| Non-Executive Director | DS Winterbottom |
| Secretary | GJG Phillips |
| *Accounting Officer* | Chief Executive |

**staff** 11,224

| | |
|---|---|
| Group General Manager, Manufacturing Services | Ron Biggs |
| Business Manager, Contract Operations | Karen Butigan |
| Group General Manager, Textile | Graham Hudson |
| Group General Manager, Interwork | Stuart Knowles |
| Manager, Healthcare | Peter Say |
| Group General Manager, Creative Products | Ray Smees |
| Group General Manager, Amalgamated Packaging | Robert Wilkinson |

**financial**

**INCOME & EXPENDITURE**

| Year end: 31 March | 1997 £000 | 1996 £000 |
|---|---|---|
| **INCOME** | | |
| Turnover | 147,489 | 133,440 |
| Other operating income: funding from the Secretary of State | 94,161 | 94,161 |
| | **241,650** | **227,601** |
| **EXPENDITURE** | | |
| Materials | (79,108) | (68,482) |
| Staff costs of severely disabled employees | (92,659) | (87,470) |
| Staff costs of non-disabled employees | (30,777) | (29,468) |
| Operating charges | (31,297) | (32,346) |
| Costs of restructuring | (2,583) | (3,582) |
| Depreciation | (10,539) | (11,623) |
| **OPERATING RESULT** | **(5,313)** | **(5,370)** |
| Interest receivable | 589 | 977 |
| **RESULT FOR THE YEAR** | **(4,724)** | **(4,393)** |

**advisers**

**Bankers**   National Westminster Bank   15 Bishopsgate, London EC2P 2AP

**Auditors**   Price Waterhouse   Southwark Towers, 32 London Bridge Street London SE1 9SY

**Solicitors**   Treasury Solicitors

**publications**   *Remploy News, Remploy Outlook*

**branches**

*Amalgamated Packaging*
Suite 37
Concourse House
432 Dewsbury Road
Leeds LS11 7DF
Tel 01132 702000

*Creative Products*
Gorse Hill Industrial Estate
1 Boston Road
Beaumont Leys
Leicester LE4 1BB
Tel 01162 364434

*Healthcare, Interwork*
Spencer House
Britannia Road
Banbury
Oxfordshire OX16 8DP
Tel 01295 275333

*Manufacturing Services*
79 Torrington Avenue
Tile Hill
Coventry
West Midlands CV4 9AQ
Tel 01203 462715

*Contract Operations*
Springfield Lane
Salford
Lancashire M3 7JS
Tel 0161 832 3803

*Furniture*
Bruce Road
Swansea West Industrial Park
Fforest-fach, Swansea
West Glamorgan SA5 4HY
Tel 01792 560100

*Textile*
Unit 4
West Float Industrial Estate off Dock Road
Hickmans Road
Birkenhead
Merseyside L4I 1JH
Tel 0151 343 9555

# *Residuary Body for Wales*

Ffynon-Las
Ty Glas Avenue
Llanishen
Cardiff CF4 5DZ

**Tel** 01222 681244
**Fax** 01222 681308

| | |
|---|---|
| *status* | Executive agency |
| *founded* | 1995 |
| *sponsor* | Welsh Office (WO) |
| *powers* | Local Government (Wales) Act 1994 |
| *mission* | Managing and disposing of properties transferred to it from abolished local authorities. |
| *tasks* | Managing, through agents, both vacant and occupied properties and keeping them in good condition to maintain their market value. Disposing of properties through disposal agents. |
| *operations* | Management: The Chairman and members of the Board have collective responsibility to the Secretary of State for overall conduct and performance. Financed through the imposition of levies on Constituent Principal Councils. Works largely through managing and disposal agents. |
| | Trends: Majority of properties transferred have been sold. Residuary Body for Wales will be wound up 31 December 1998 |
| *performance* | All objectives in 1996/97 were achieved. |
| *board* | Appointed by the Secretary of State. |

| Chairman | D Thomas CBE |
|---|---|
| Members | John Davies |
| | Miss D Jones |
| | Brian Williams JP |
| *Accounting Officer* | *Chief Executive* |

*staff*     Five

| Chief Executive | MJ Bruton CBE |
|---|---|

*financial*

**REVENUE INCOME & EXPENDITURE**

| Year end: 31 March | **1997** |
|---|---|
| | **£** |
| **INCOME** | |
| Levies | 1,349,900 |
| Rents | 692,574 |
| Fees and charges | 16,919 |
| Interest receivable | 14,727 |
| Other income | 4,046 |
| | **2,078,166** |
| **EXPENDITURE** | |
| Capitalised administration cost in 1995/96 written off | 255,194 |
| Members' remuneration | 17,814 |
| Members' other costs | 1,777 |
| Employees' remuneration | 150,140 |
| Employees' other costs | 5,099 |
| Depreciation | 7,930 |
| Establishment costs | 214,826 |
| Hospitality | 70 |
| Professional fees | |
| Audit | 10,217 |
| Other | 135,508 |
| Other operating costs | 489,047 |
| Financing costs | |
| Public works loan board interest | 10,996 |
| | 1,298,618 |
| **SURPLUS** | **779,548** |

| *advisers* | **Bankers** | Barclays | 36 Dunraven Place, Bridgend |
| | **Auditors** | District Audit | |
| | **Solicitors** | Berry Smith | St Andrews Crescent, Cardiff |

*publications*    *Operational Plan 1995-96, 1996-97, 1997-98*

# *Rivers Agency*

Hydebank
4 Hospital Road
Belfast BT8 8JP

**Tel** 01232 253440
**Fax** 01232 253455

| | |
|---|---|
| *status* | Executive agency |
| *founded* | 1996 |
| *sponsor* | Northern Ireland Office, Department of Agriculture NI (DANI) |
| *powers* | Drainage (Northern Ireland) Order 1973. Water Act (Northern Ireland) 1972. Much other legislation. Three EC Directives. Framework Document |
| *mission* | Improving NI social conditions and supporting economic development by reducing risk from river and sea flooding, preserving agricultural land and promoting sustainable development of navigation and recreational facilities on inland waterways. |
| *tasks* | Constructing and maintaining flood and sea defences, maintaining designated watercourses, responding to flood incidents, protecting the drainage function of all watercourses, providing facilities for water recreation, maintaining navigation on Lough Erne and the Lower Bann River and regulating water levels on Lough Neagh and Lough Erne. |
| *operations* | Management: The Chief Executive reports to the Minister and is supported by a Management Board. There are two statutory advisory bodies; the Drainage Council gives independent advice on drainage policy and programmes; the Water Council advises on water recreation. Local interests are represented on agency committees. |
| *performance* | Nearly all key performance targets met 1996/97. |

*board*

| | |
|---|---|
| Chief Executive | Daniel McSorley |
| Director of Corporate Services | Hazel Campbell |
| Director of Client Services | John Hagan |
| Director of Engineering Services | Tom McCully |
| *Accounting Officer* | *Chief Executive* |

*staff*    500

*financial*

| EXPENDITURE | |
|---|---|
| **Year: 1/10/96 - 31/03/97** | **1997** |
| | **£000** |
| **EXPENDITURE** | |
| Running costs | |
| Staff costs | 4,185 |
| Other admin costs | 432 |
| | **4,617** |
| Other current costs | |
| Supplies, services and stores | 711 |
| PV&E running costs | 368 |
| Maintenance contracts | 277 |
| Other expenditure | 32 |
| | **1,388** |

| | |
|---|---:|
| Other non-cash costs and services | |
| Insurance | 26 |
| Interest and depreciation | 548 |
| Accommodation | 139 |
| Internal audit | 7 |
| Department of Agriculture core services | 392 |
| Early departure costs | 74 |
| | 1,186 |
| **INCOME** | (87) |
| **NET COST OF OPERATIONS** | 7,104 |

**branches**

*Western Region*
Woodside Avenue
Gortin Road
Omagh
County Tyrone BT79 7BS
Tel 01662 242623
Fax 01662 247 871

*Coleraine Office*
Coleraine
County Londonderry BT51 3RL
Tel 01265 42357
Fax 01265 320628

*Fermanagh Office*
Ballinamallard
Enneskillen
County Fermanagh BT94 2NA
Tel 01365 388529
Fax 01365 388972

*Eastern Region*
Ravarnet House
Altona Road
Lisburn
County Antrim BT27 5QB
Tel 01846 606100
Fax 01846 606111

*Armagh Office*
44 Seagoe Industrial Estate
Craigavon
County Armagh BT63 5QE
Tel 01762 336213
Fax 01762 391779

*Plant Unit*
44 Seagoe Industrial Estate
Craigavon
County Armagh BT63 5QE
Tel 01762 336213
Fax 01762 335901

# Roads Service

Clarence Court
10-18 Adelaide Street
Belfast BT2 8GB

**Tel** 01232 540540
**Fax** 01232 540024

**E-mail** roads.service.dir@nics.gov.uk
**Web** http://www.nics.gov.uk/doeroads

**status** Executive agency

**founded** 1996

**sponsor** Northern Ireland Office, Department of the Environment for NI (DOENI)

**powers** DOENI is the statutory road authority for NI under the provisions of the Roads (NI) Order 1993, the Road Traffic Regulation (NI) Order 1997, the Private Streets (NI) Order 1980. Roads Service acts on DOENI's behalf as the single body responsible for the public road network

**mission** To make sure that a safe and effective road network is provided throughout Northern Ireland.

**tasks** To make sure that: the public road network is maintained and improved; the road network is developed to improve road safety and traffic management and measures are taken to implement the Department's sustainable transportation policy.

**operations** Management: The Minister is responsible for policy and does not normally become involved in day-to-day business. The Chief Executive is directly responsible to the Minister for the Agency's performance and operations. There is a Ministerial Advisory Board which advises the Minister on the strategic direction of the Agency. The Directorate is headed by the Chief Executive and supported by four Directors. The headquarters is in Belfast and the six divisions, each headed by a divisional roads manager, are located in Ballymena, Belfast, Coleraine, Craigavon, Downpatrick and Omagh. Each division is divided into sections which generally correspond with district council areas. Environmental assessments on significant works involve consultation with a wide range of bodies ranging from the Planning Service to the Royal Fine Arts Commission and the RSPB.

Trends: The entire structure has been reviewed to examine the separation of the Agency's purchaser and provider roles; implementation of agreed recommendations will be an Agency priority in 1998/99.

**performance** Majority of targets met.

**board**

| Chief Executive | Billy McCoubrey |
| Director of Finance | Jim Aiken |
| Director of Corporate Services | Jim Carlisle |
| Technical Director | Victor Crawford |
| Director of Operations | Grahame Fraser |
| *Accounting Officer* | *Permanent Secretary* |

**staff** 2325 (all civil servants)

| Organisational Review | John Angus |
| Head of Transportation | Denis O'Hagan |
| Divisional Roads Managers | Sean Price |
| | Joe Drew |
| | Derick McCandless |
| | Douglas Maxwell |
| | Malcolm McKibbin |
| | Geoff Allister |

**financial**

| INCOME & EXPENDITURE Year end: 31 March | 1997 £000 | 1996 £000 |
|---|---|---|
| **INCOME** | | |
| Car parking receipts | 5,100 | 3,600 |
| Strangford ferry receipts | 600 | 600 |
| Sale of land | 1,900 | 600 |
| Other income | 1,400 | 2,000 |
| | 9,000 | 6,800 |
| **EXPENDITURE** | | |
| **PROGRAME EXPENDITURE** | | |
| **Roads and bridges** | | |
| Completion of major capital schemes | 13,700 | 16,300 |
| Minor capital schemes | 12,700 | 13,500 |
| Maintenance | 53,700 | 53,200 |
| | 80,100 | 83,000 |
| **Street lighting** | | |
| Capital schemes | 3,800 | 3,300 |
| Operation and maintenance | 9,700 | 8,600 |
| | 13,500 | 11,900 |
| **Other services** | | |
| Car parking | 3,600 | 2,300 |
| Strangford Ferry | 700 | 700 |
| | 4,300 | 3,000 |
| **Public liability** | 3,300 | 2,800 |
| **Miscellaneous** | | |
| Consultants' fees | 900 | 1,200 |
| Payments to construction service | 200 | 200 |
| Office machinery and computers | 800 | 1,400 |
| Other | 100 | 200 |
| | 2,000 | 3,000 |
| **TOTAL PROGRAMME EXPENDITURE** | 103,200 | 103,700 |
| **RUNNING COSTS** | | |
| Operational manpower | 44,200 | 43,700 |
| Administration and support | 9,900 | 9,400 |
| **TOTAL RUNNING COSTS** | 54,100 | 53,100 |
| **GROSS EXPENDITURE** | 157,300 | 156,800 |
| **NET EXPENDITURE** | 148,300 | 150,000 |

**publications** *Framework Document, Road User's Charter Statement, Annual Report 1996/97, Corporate Plan 1998-2001, Business Plan 1998-99*

**branches**

*Ballymena Division*
County Hall
182 Galgorm Road
Ballymena BT42 1QG
Tel 01266 653333
Fax 01266 662510

*Belfast Division*
Hydebank
4 Hospital Road
Belfast BT8 8JL
Tel 01232 253000
Fax 01232 253220

Coleraine Division
County Hall
Castlerock Road
Coleraine BT51 3HS
Tel 01265 41300
Fax 01265 41430

Downpatrick Division
Rathkeltair House
Market Street
Downpatrick BT30 6AJ
Tel 01396 612211
Fax 01396 618188

Craigavon Division
Marlborough House
Central Way
Craigavon BT64 1AD
Tel 01762 341144
Fax 01762 341867

Omagh Division
County Hall
Drumragh Avenue
Omagh BT79 9AF
Tel 01662 254280
Fax 01662 254010

# Rowett Research Institute

Greenburn Road
Bucksburn
Aberdeen AB21 9SB

**Tel** 01224 712751
**Fax** 01224 715349

**E-mail** rri.sari.ac.uk
**Web** http://www.rri.sari.ac.uk

**Contact** Mrs Hilary Robertson, Communications Manager

| | |
|---|---|
| *status* | Executive body |
| *founded* | 1913 |
| *sponsor* | Scottish Office |
| *powers* | Memorandum and Articles of Association |
| *mission* | To investigate the links between health, food and agriculture. |
| *tasks* | Employing scientists who undertake research into the biochemical and physiological aspects of nutrition. Informing the general public of its research and its significance for the health and economic welfare of the nation. |
| *operations* | Management: The Director reports to the government body and accounts to the Minister at the Scottish Office for Agriculture, Environment and Fisheries. Extensive network of collaborative links which span the globe, including France, Korea and New Zealand. |
| | Policy: New programme of research which encompasses the whole of the food chain. |
| | Trends: Growing interest in the safety and quality of food. |
| *performance* | Measured in ROAME. |
| *board* | Governing body. Three appointed by Secretary of State and 14 from nominating bodies according to Articles of Association. |

| Chairman | J Provan, MEP |
|---|---|
| Members | Prof CA Barth |
| | Prof A Ferguson |
| | JW Gammie |
| | Prof C Kidd |
| | Prof J Lamb |
| | Prof RB Leslie |
| | DSC Levie, BL |
| | Dr M Mackie |
| | Dr CH McMurray |
| | Prof TH Pennington |
| | Prof CD Rice |
| | Dr J Stewart |
| | Dr T Walker |
| | Prof JC Waterlow, CMG |
| | Prof AJF Webster |

| | |
|---|---|
| *staff* | 319 |

| | |
|---|---|
| Director | W Philip T James, CBE |
| Deputy Director (Administration) | David AB Blair |
| Deputy Director (Science) | Ian Bremner |
| Assistant Director (Academic Affairs) | Paul Trayhurn |
| Co-ordinator of Postgraduate Studies | Frances Quirk |
| Public Relations Manager | Hilary Robertson |
| Head, Biomedical Science Division | Paul Trayhurn |
| Head, Molecular Neuroendocrinology Unit | Peter J Morgan |
| Head, Molecular Ecology & Gut Function Division | Andrew Chesson |
| Head, Protein Metabolism Division | John C MacRae |
| Head, Nutrition, Pregnancy & Development Division | Harry J McArdle |
| Head, Micronutrient & Lipid Metabolism Division | John R Arthur |
| Head, Skeletal Research Unit | Simon P Robins |
| Head, Animal Services & Quality Assurance | Ian Bremner |
| Chief Executive, Rowett Research Services Limited | William H Mullen |
| Director, Korean Collaboration Centre | JJ (Matthew) Choung |
| Head, Biomathematics & Statistics Scotland (Bio SS) | Graham Horgan |

*advisers*  **Bankers**  Clydesdale Bank

**Auditors**  Coopers & Lybrand

**Solicitors**  Burnett and Reid  Aberdeen

# *Royal Air Force Museum*

Grahame Park Way
Hendon
London NW9 5LL

**Tel** 0181 205 2266
**Fax** 0181 200 1751

*status*  Executive body

*founded*  1972

*sponsor*  Ministry of Defence (MOD)

*mission*  To manage Britain's National Museum of Aviation.

*tasks*  Preserving, conserving and exhibiting the collection of historic aircraft and associated exhibits, illustrating the story of aviation from its beginnings to the 21st century. Main site at Hendon and Aerospace Museum at Cosford.

*operations*  Management: Director reports to the Trustees and is responsible for day-to-day management. Funded by MOD grant-in-aid and receipts.

Policy: Implementation of a computerised collections management system. Development of Hendon site.

Trends: Aircraft restoration work carried out by outside contractors.

*board*  Trustees appointed by the Secretary of State.

| | |
|---|---|
| Chairman | Sir Michael Beetham GCB CBE |
| Trustees | Sir John Blelloch KCB |
| | Lord Cuckney |
| | Sir Richard Evans CBE |
| | Dr Basil Greenhill CB CMG |
| | Sir Colin Marshall |
| | Rt Hon Sir Hector Monro PC JP MP |
| | Barry Pinson QC |
| | Group Captain Sir Gordon Pirie CVO CBE JP |
| | Sir Thomas Risk |
| | Sir Ralph Robins |
| | Lord Waterpark |
| Air Member for Personnel | Air Marshal David Cousins CB |
| Air Member for Logistics | Air Chief Marshal Sir John Allison KCB CBE |

*staff*  83

*financial*

### RECEIPTS & EXPENDITURE
**Year end: 31 March**

| | 1996 £ | 1995 £ |
|---|---:|---:|
| **RECEIPTS** | | |
| HMG grants | | |
| Operating | 2,578,240 | 2,534,555 |
| Purchase | 109,000 | 109,000 |
| Special maintenance | 250,000 | 250,000 |
| | **2,937,240** | **2,893,555** |
| **OTHER RECEIPTS** | | |
| Admission charges | 436,490 | 417,252 |
| Operating receipts | 174,850 | 43,478 |
| Donations to trustees | 28,460 | 62,100 |
| Income derived from sales | 230,000 | 210,000 |
| Bank interest | 9,080 | 14,318 |
| | **878,880** | **747,148** |
| | **3,816,120** | **3,640,703** |
| **EXPENDITURE** | | |
| Salaries & wages | 2,023,390 | 1,905,629 |
| Superannuation | 204,970 | 199,083 |
| | **2,228,360** | **2,104,712** |
| **OTHER EXPENDITURE** | | |
| Operating | 1,476,810 | 1,424,929 |
| Purchase of exhibits | 109,000 | 67,806 |
| | **1,585,810** | **1,492,735** |
| **TOTAL EXPENDITURE** | **3,814,170** | **3,597,447** |
| **EXCESS OF RECEIPTS OVER PAYMENTS** | **1,950** | **43,256** |

# Royal Armouries

HM Tower of London
London EC3N 4AB

**Tel** 0171 480 6358
**Fax** 0171 481 2922

**E-mail** enquiries@armouries.org.uk
**Web** http://www.armouries.org.uk

**Contact** Nicholas Boole

*status* Executive body

*founded* 15th century; as executive body, 1983

*sponsor* Department for0 Culture, Media and Sport (DCMS)

*powers* National Heritage Act 1983

*mission* To promote in the UK and worldwide the knowledge and appreciation of arms and armour and of the Tower through the collections of the museum and the expertise of the staff.

*tasks* To care for, preserve and add to the objects in its collections, to secure that the objects are exhibited to the public, to secure that the objects are available for study and research, to maintain a record relating to its collections, to arms and armour in general and to the Tower, generally to promote the public's enjoyment and understanding of arms and armour.

*operations* Management: The museum is run by a Board of Trustees and funded by a grant-in-aid from the government. It operates on three site: Royal Armouries HM Tower of London (Tower history), Royal Armouries at Fort Nelson (artillery), and Royal Armouries Museum, Leeds (arms and armour) nationwide. The Royal Armouries has a developing relationship with a different partner at each site: with Historic Palaces Agency which administers HM Tower of London, Hampshire County Council, from which the Royal Armouries leases Fort Nelson, and with the private company, RA(I) plc which manages and administers the museum building in Leeds.

Policy: In 1990, the Board adopted Strategy 2000, now largely implemented. It proposed the re-display of the Royal Armouries collections at the Tower of London (scheduled for completion 1998), the establishment of an arms and armour museum outside the Tower (opened in Leeds in 1996), and the continued development of the Royal Armouries at Fort Nelson. It also proposed the establishment of a self-funding exhibition forum in the USA.

Trends: Unless dependence on grant-in-aid can be reduced it faces the prospect of reviewing and possibly contracting its services across its three sites. The Board, however, believes that it can secure the long-term financial future of the museum.

**performance**   Achieved 1996/97: 19. Ongoing/In Progress 1996/97: 21

**board**   Board of Trustees. One member is appointed by the Sovereign and another, the Constable of the Tower, is a trustee *ex officio*, the remaining being appointed by the Secretary of State.

| | | |
|---|---|---|
| Chairman | Viscount Younger of Leckie KT KCVO TD | |
| Deputy Chairman | Rufus Bond Gunning | |
| Trustees | Prof John Childs | |
| | Lady Cooksey | Geoffrey Lewis |
| | Richard Fortin | Hon Francis Plowden |
| | Michael Gambon CBE | Sir Blair Stewart-Wilson, KCVO |
| | Field Marshall Lord Inge GCB | Richard Whiteley |
| *Accounting Officer* | *Master of the Armouries* | |

**staff**   133

| | |
|---|---|
| Master of the Armouries | GM Wilson |
| Keeper of Fort Nelson | Nicholas Hall |
| Keeper of Tower History | Geoffrey Parnell |
| Head of Administration | Dick Mundell OBE |
| Head of Curatorial Services | Graeme Rimer |
| Head of Collection Care | Robert Smith |
| Head of Museum Services | Paula Turner |
| Head of Interpretation | John Waller |

**financial**

| INCOME & EXPENDITURE | |
|---|---|
| **Year end: 31 March** | **1995** |
| | **£000** |
| **INCOME** | |
| Government revenue - grant-in-aid receivable | 3,474 |
| Income from activities | 513 |
| Other operating income | 2 |
| **Transferred from** | |
| Deferred grant | 346 |
| Vested asset reserve | - |
| | **4,460** |
| **EXPENDITURE** | |
| Staff costs | 2,803 |
| Depreciation | 346 |
| Operational costs | 1,056 |
| Purchase of objects for the collection | 322 |
| | 4,527 |
| **OPERATING SURPLUS/DEFICIT** | (67) |
| Interest Receivable | 13 |
| **SURPLUS/DEFICIT ON ORDINARY ACTIVITIES** | (54) |
| **SURPLUS/DEFICIT TRANSFERRED** | |
| Grant-in-aid | (54) |
| **Armouries' excess receipts** | - |

**advisers**

| | | |
|---|---|---|
| **Bankers** | National Westminster Bank | |
| **Auditors** | National Audit Office | |
| | Deloitte Touche | |
| **Solicitors** | Treasury Solicitor | |
| | Pinsent Curtis | 41 Park Square, Leeds LS1 2NS |

**publications**   *Royal Armouries Triennial Report 1993/1996, The Royal Armouries in Leeds: The Making of a Museum, Royal Armouries Yearbook: Volume 1 1996*

**branches**

Royal Armouries Museum
Armouries Drive
Leeds
Yorkshire LS10 1LT
Tel 0113 220 1999
Fax 0113 220 1955

*Royal Armouries at Fort Nelson*
Portsdown Road
Fareham
Hampshire
PO17 6AN
Tel 01329 233734
Fax 01329 822092

# Royal Botanic Garden Edinburgh (RBGE)

20A Inverleith Row
Edinburgh EH3 5LR

**Tel** 0131 552 7171
**Fax** 0131 552 0382

| | |
|---|---|
| **status** | Executive body |
| **founded** | 1823. Executive body in 1986 |
| **sponsor** | Scottish Office |
| **powers** | National Heritage (Scotland) Act 1985 |
| **mission** | To explore and explain the plant kingdom - past, present and future - and its importance to humanity. To pursue whole plant science, notably through systematics research of the highest quality, on the diversity and relationships of plants, and their significance in the environment. |
| **tasks** | Curating its living and preserved collections of plants and fungi as a basis for research and education; training new professional botanists and horticulturists; maintaining innovative education programmes; promoting the public understanding and appreciation of plant science and conservation; displaying its living collections for the enjoyment of visitors. Main gardens in Edinburgh (30 acres), and three specialist gardens: Younger (Argyll), Logan (Wigtownshire) and Dawyck (Peebleshire) Botanic Gardens. |
| **operations** | Management: Regius Keeper is responsible for the day-to-day management with the Head of Science and Head of Horticulture. In 1996 Development and Communications Division formed to co-ordinate several related activities (publications, external affairs, marketing, exhibitions, events, media relations and business development). Botanics Trading Company Ltd runs shops and other profit-earning activities. |
| | Policy: Establishing Botanics Foundation to act as a focus for fundraising activites. |
| **board** | Trustees appointed by the Secretary of State. |

| | | |
|---|---|---|
| Chairman | Prof Malcolm Wilkins | |
| Trustees | Ms Carole Baxter | Miss Miriam Greenwood |
| | John Blair | John Robb |
| | Lady Fraser | Sir Crispin Tickell GCMG KCVO |
| | Kenneth Garden | Prof MM Yeoman |
| *Accounting Officer* | *Regius Keeper* | |

**staff** 196

| | |
|---|---|
| Regius Keeper | DS Ingram |

*financial*

| INCOME & EXPENDITURE Year end: 31 March | 1997 £000 | 1996 £000 |
|---|---|---|
| **INCOME** | | |
| Grants received for revenue expenditure | 5,574 | 5,737 |
| Income from grant-aided activities | 377 | 321 |
| Board Reserve Fund income | 775 | 647 |
| Income from BTC Ltd | 649 | 550 |
| | 7375 | 7,255 |
| **EXPENDITURE** | | |
| Staff costs | 4,537 | 4,694 |
| Depreciation | 654 | 527 |
| Other operating charges | 2,111 | 1,962 |
| | 7,302 | 7,183 |
| **OPERATING SURPLUS** | 73 | 72 |
| Dividends and interest receivable | 54 | 57 |
| Notional cost of capital | (359) | (317) |
| **DEFICIT FOR THE FINANCIAL YEAR (AFTER NOTIONAL COSTS)** | (232) | (188) |
| Reversal of notional cost of capital | 359 | 317 |
| **SURPLUS TRANSFERRED TO RESERVES** | 127 | 129 |

# *Royal Botanic Gardens Kew (RBG Kew)*

Royal Botanic Gardens Kew
Richmond
Surrey TW9 3AB

**Tel** 0181 332 5000

*status* — Executive body

*founded* — 1983 as executive body

*sponsor* — Ministry of Agriculture, Fisheries and Food (MAFF)

*powers* — National Heritage Act 1983

*mission* — To enable better management of the earth's environment by increasing knowledge and understanding of the plant and fungal kingdoms.

*tasks* — Maintaining and enhancing the collections of plants and fungi, seed, literature, archives and artefacts and making them available for study. Increasing the understanding of floral and fungal diversity through the publication of researched information. Setting and maintaining an integrated conservation research, training and advisory programme. Increasing visitor numbers and revenue. Promoting and disseminating information on the role of RBG Kew and on plants, horticulture, conservation, biodiversity and environmental issues. Plant quarantine. Restoring and maintaining the historic buildings, landscapes and artefacts.

*operations* — Management: Director reports to the Trustees. The trading company, RBG Kew Enterprises Ltd, runs retailing, concerts, licensing, venue hire and commercial publications.

Policy: Ensuring that cuts do not have an impact on scientific work.

Trends: Increasing recognition by nations and governments that plants are the basis of life.

*performance* — Target on visitor income was exceeded.

*board* — One Trustee is appointed by the Queen and the others by the Minister of Agriculture, Fisheries and Food.

| Chairman | Robin A E Herbert CBE | |
|---|---|---|
| Trustees | Robert P Bauman | |
| | The Viscount Blakenham | Anna Ford |
| | Sir Jeffery Bowman | Lady Lennox-Boyd |
| | Prof Michael Crawley | Prof John S Parker |
| | Spencer de Grey | Lady Renfrew |
| | Prof Hugh Dickinson | The Earl of Selborne KBE |
| *Accounting Officer* | *The Director* | |

*staff* — 512

| Director | Prof Sir Ghillean Prance |
|---|---|
| Director of Operations | J Lavin |
| Head of Buildings & Maintenance | T Bailey |
| Keeper of the Jodrell Laboratory | Prof M Bennett OBE |
| Financial Controller | R Bower |
| Joint Head of Education & Marketing | G Bromley |
| Joint Head of Education & Marketing | R Joiner |
| Head of People Planning & Development | M Long |
| Keeper of the Herbarium | Prof S Owens |
| Head of Information Services | A Prior |
| Curator, Living Collections | N Taylor |
| Head of Corporate Services | W Webb |

*financial*

| FINANCIAL ACTIVITIES Year end: 31 March | 1997 £ | 1996 £ |
|---|---|---|
| **INCOMING RESOURCES** | | |
| Grant-in-aid | 18,936,000 | 17,081,000 |
| Income from activities | 8,306,467 | 8,752,505 |
| Investment income | 380,276 | 410,406 |
| | 27,622,743 | 26,243,911 |
| **RESOURCES EXPENDED** | | |
| Direct Charitable Expenditure | | |
| Primary programmes | 17,212,190 | 15,435,956 |
| Property costs | 2,092,371 | 2,617,892 |
| Support costs | 3,516,978 | 4,283,540 |
| Other Expenditure | | |
| Trading | 1,733,301 | 1,690,091 |
| Management & administration | 2,371,354 | 2,785,296 |
| | 26,926,194 | 26,812,775 |
| Notional costs | (509,842) | (447,450) |
| **NET INCOMING/(OUTGOING) RESOURCES AFTER NOTIONAL COSTS** | **186,707** | **(1,016,314)** |
| Reversal of cost of capital | 457,842 | 447,450 |
| **NET INCOMING/(OUTGOING) RESOURCES** | **644,549** | **(568,864)** |
| **Gains on investment assets** | | |
| Unrealised | 18,107 | 16,877 |
| Revaluation of tangible assets | 48,498 | 165,243 |
| **NET MOVEMENT IN RESERVES** | **711,154** | **(386,744)** |
| Reserves at 1 April as previously stated | 7,044,241 | 7,536,510 |
| Prior year adjustment | 219,885 | 114,360 |
| Reserves at 1 April as adjusted | 7,264,126 | 7,650,870 |
| **RESERVES AT 31 MARCH** | **7,975,280** | **7,264,126** |

*advisers*  **Auditors**  National Audit Office  157-197 Buckingham Palace Road London SW1W 9SP

# Royal Commission on Ancient & Historical Monuments of Scotland (RCAHMS)

John Sinclair House
16 Bernard Terrace
Edinburgh EH8 9NX

**Tel** 0131 662 1456
**Fax** 0131 662 1477/99

| | |
|---|---|
| *status* | Executive body |
| *founded* | 1908 |
| *sponsor* | Scottish Office (through Historic Scotland) |
| *powers* | Royal Warrant 1992 |

# Q&Q

**mission** To survey and record the man-made environment of Scotland; to complete and maintain in the National Monuments Record of Scotland (NMRS) a record of the archaeological and historical environment; and to promote an understanding of this information.

**tasks** To collect archeological and architectural materials, to conduct strategic archaeological surveys and to provide a NMRS database and a public information and advisory service to users. To conduct architectural and industrial surveys of buildings. To manage the Scottish Office Air Photograph Collection.

**operations** Management: The Secretary and Director of the NMRS is the Chief Executive of the RCAHMS. He reports to the Chairman of RCAHMS; the survey aspects of RCAHMS are divided under the heads of Archaeology and Architecture while the NMRS is divided into section specialism in the management of its collections, is public services and internal liaison with the Field Survey sections.

Policy: Increased emphasis on the generation of income and on widening public awareness of RCAHMS and access to NMRS.

Trends: Information technology increasingly important , eg archaeological data service, CANMORE (Computer Application for National Monuments Record Enquiries) etc.

**performance** Most 1996/97 targets met or exceeded.

**board**

| Chairman | Sir William Fraser GCB |
|---|---|
| Commissioners | Prof JM Coles |
| | Prof RJ Cramp CBE |
| | Dr BE Crawford |
| | Dr DJ Howard |
| | Dr Margaret Mackay |
| | Prof RA Paxton MBE |
| | Miss AC Riches |
| | JWT Simpson |
| | Prof TC Smout CBE |
| Accounting Officer | Secretary of Scottish Office Development Department |

**staff** 67

| Secretary & Director NMRS | RJ Mercer |
|---|---|

**financial**

| EXPENDITURE Year end: 31 March | 1997 £000 | 1996 £000 | 1995 £000 |
|---|---|---|---|
| **EXPENDITURE** | | | |
| Staff costs | 1,694 | 1,664 | 1,594 |
| Accommodation: office | 266 | 269 | 261 |
| Archival storage | 241 | 244 | 237 |
| Public/common | 193 | 195 | 190 |
| General expenses: fixed | 175 | 161 | 144 |
| | 2,569 | 2,533 | 2,426 |
| General expenses: other | 464 | 547 | 516 |
| | 3,033 | 3,080 | 2,942 |
| Capital expenditure | 91 | 165 | 122 |
| | 3,124 | 3,245 | 3,064 |
| **FUNDED BY** | | | |
| Scottish Office Vote | 3,049 | 3,200 | 3,031 |
| Income | 75 | 45 | 33 |
| **TOTAL GOVERNMENT EXPENDITURE** | **3,124** | **3,245** | **3,064** |

**advisers** **Auditors** National Audit Office

# Royal Commission on Ancient & Historical Monuments in Wales (RCAHMW)

Plas Crug
Aberystwyth
Ceredigion SY23 1NJ

**Tel** 01970 621233
**Fax** 01970 627701

| | |
|---|---|
| *status* | Executive body |
| *founded* | 1908 |
| *sponsor* | Welsh Office |
| *powers* | Royal Warrants 1908 and 1992 |
| *mission* | To make and maintain an inventory and database of ancient and historical monuments in Wales. |
| *tasks* | To survey, record, publish and maintain a database of ancient, historical and maritime sites and structures, and landscapes in Wales. In addition to the National Monuments Record, it is responsible for the supply of archaeological information to the Ordnance Survey for mapping purposes, for the coordination of archaeological aerial photography in Wales, and for the sponsorship of the regional Sites and Monuments Records. |
| *operations* | Management: Departments are Architectural History, Archaeology, Industrial Archaeology, Information Services, Graphics and Photography and the Heads of each report to the Secretary, who is responsible for the day-to-day management. |
| *board* | Commissioners appointed by the Secretary of State. |

| | |
|---|---|
| Chairman | Prof JB Smith |
| Vice-Chairman | Prof RW Brunskill OBE |
| Commissioners | Prof D Evans |
| | Prof RA Griffiths |
| | RM Haslam |
| | D Jones |
| | Prof GDB Jones |
| | Mrs A Nicol |
| | SB Smith |
| | Prof GJ Wainwright MBE |
| | E Wiliam |
| Secretary | PR White |

*staff*  34

| | |
|---|---|
| Secretary | PR White |
| Head, Archaeology | DM Browne |
| Head, Archaeology | SR Hughes |
| Head, Architectural History | AJ Parkinson |
| Head, Graphics & Photography | DJ Roberts |

*financial*

| EXPENDITURE | |
|---|---|
| **Year end: 31 March** | **1995** |
| | **£000** |
| Salaries | 817 |
| Travel and subsistence | 55 |
| Accommodation | 157 |
| Programmed current | 149 |
| Grants | 143 |
| | **1,321** |

# Royal Commission on Historical Manuscripts

Quality House
Quality Court
Chancery Lane
London WC2A 1HP

**Tel** 0171 242 1198
**Fax** 0171 831 3550

**E-mail** nra@hmc.gov.uk
**Web** http://www.hmc.gov.uk

**Contact** The Secretary

| | |
|---|---|
| *status* | Executive body |
| *founded* | 1869 |
| *sponsor* | Department for Culture, Media and Sport (DCMS) |
| *powers* | Royal Warrant 1869 and 1959 |
| *mission* | To promote the preservation of all the nation's records and to improve the standards of care for, and accessibility of, the written heritage. |
| *tasks* | Enquiring into the existence and location of manuscripts and archives of value for the study of British history. Publishing reports on them. Recording particulars of manuscripts in National the Register of Archives and the Manorial Documents Register. Providing advice to researchers, owners and custodians of archives, grant-awarding bodies, other archival organisations. |
| *operations* | Management: The Secretary reports to the Commissioners. The Commissioners have no statutory powers. |
| | Policy: Maintaining an overall view of the nation's archival resources. |
| *board* | The Commissioners are appointed by the Queen on the advice of the Prime Minister. |

| Chairman | Lord Bingham of Cornhill |
|---|---|
| Commissioners | GE Aylmer |
| | Prof RH Campbell OBE |
| | Sir Patrick Cormack MP |
| | Dr S Davies |
| | Mrs A Dundas-Bekker |
| | Lord Egremont and Lichfield |
| | Sir Matthew Farrer |
| | Sir John Sainty |
| | Earl of Scarbrough |
| | Mrs Cynthia Short |
| | The Very Revd HEC Stapleton |
| | Sir Keith Thomas |
| | DG Vaisey CBE |
| Secretary | CJ Kitching |
| *Accounting Officer* | *Secretary of Scottish Office Development Department* |

| | |
|---|---|
| *staff* | 24 |

| Secretary | CJ Kitching |
|---|---|
| Assistant Keepers | Miss SP Anderson |
| | NW James |
| | RJ Olney |
| | RJ Sargent |

*publications*   *Reports and Calendar*

# Royal Commission on Historical Monuments of England (RCHME)

Kemble Drive
Swindon SN2 2GZ

**Tel** 01793 414700
**Fax** 01793 414606          **Web** http://www.rchme.gov.uk

| | |
|---|---|
| **status** | Executive body |
| **sponsor** | Department for Culture, Media and Sport (DCMS) |
| **powers** | Royal Warrant |
| **mission** | To compile and assess, curate and make available the national record of England's ancient monuments and historic buildings for the use of individuals and bodies concerned with understanding, interpreting and managing the historic environment. |
| **tasks** | Providing information and advice (including electronic access and academic publications); running training programmes (with external bodies); surveying and recording sites and buildings (archaeological and architectural), including statutory recording of threatened listed buildings; compiling, curating and providing greater access to its public archive, the National Monuments Record (NMR). |
| **operations** | Management: Secretary of the Commission is also the Chief Executive and is responsible for day-to-day management. Executive Committee consists of the Chief Executive and Directors of seven departments. Head Office in Swindon with four regional offices. |
| | Policy: Partnership agreement with English Heritage. Lottery funding for enhancing computerised index of the 460,000 listed buildings with a defining photographic image. Agreement with Heritage Lottery Fund to provide project advice and monitoring. |
| | Trends: Government funding decreasing so trying to increase revenue from other sources. |
| **performance** | Met two out of six targets in 1996/97. |
| **board** | Commissioners appointed by the Secretary of State. |

| Chairman | The Right Hon Lord Faringdon | |
|---|---|---|
| Commissioners | Dr M Airs | |
| | Ms A Arrowsmith | |
| | Prof R Bradley | TRM Longman |
| | Prof M Fulford | Prof GI Meirion-Jones |
| | Dr RDH Gem | Dr M Palmer |
| | Dr DJ Keene | Miss AC Riches |
| | | RA Yorke |

**staff**   248

| | |
|---|---|
| Secretary & Chief Executive | Tom Hassall |
| Director of the NMR | Nigel Clubb |
| Director of Personnel & Training | David Jones |
| Director of Finance & Administration | Jim Mirabal |
| Director of Architectural Survey | Hugh Richmond |
| Director of Information Services & Development | Jennifer Stewart |
| Director of Archaeological Survey | Humphrey Welfare |
| Director of Corporate Planning | Rowan Whimster |

**financial**

| INCOME & EXPENDITURE | | |
|---|---|---|
| **Year end: 31 March** | **1997** | **1996** |
| | **£000** | **£000** |
| **EXPENDITURE** | | |
| Salary & pension costs | 6,438 | 7,022 |
| Other staff costs | 287 | 379 |
| Travel costs | 432 | 462 |
| Operating costs | 909 | 1,176 |
| Support to outside bodies | 65 | 230 |
| Purchase of equipment | 406 | 367 |
| Ongoing premises costs | 2,186 | 2,038 |
| Once-only premises costs | 445 | 62 |
| Restructuring costs | 403 | 459 |
| | 11,571 | 12,195 |
| **RECEIPTS** | (258) | (287) |
| **TOTAL PUBLICLY FUNDED EXPENDITURE** | 11.313 | 11.908 |

*Q&Q*

| | | |
|---|---|---|
| **branches** | Shelley House<br>Acomb Road<br>York YO2 4HB<br>Tel 01904 784411<br>Fax 01904 795348 | 55 Blandford Street<br>London W1H 3AF<br>Tel 0171 208 8200<br>Fax 0171 224 5333 |
| | Brooklands<br>24 Brooklands Avenue<br>Cambridge CB2 2BU<br>Tel 01223 324010<br>Fax 01223 311203 | 5 Marlborough Court<br>Manaton Close<br>Exeter EX2 8PF<br>Tel 01392 824901<br>Fax 01392 824490 |

## *Royal Marines Museum*

Southsea
Hampshire PO4 9PX

**Tel** 01705 819385
**Fax** 01705 838420

| | |
|---|---|
| *status* | Executive body |
| *sponsor* | Ministry of Defence (MOD) |
| *mission* | To create a modern military museum complex about the Royal Marines. |
| *operations* | Management: The Director reports to the Secretary of State. It is a charity and its trading subsidiary is Royal Marines Museum Ltd. Have to advertise for Trustees. |
| *performance* | New galleries opened on time. |
| *board* | Trustees appointed by the Secretary of State. |

| Chairman | Major General JIH Owen OBE | |
|---|---|---|
| *Ex officio* Trustees | Captain B Gibbs | Lieutenant Colonel AJF Noyes |
| | D Giles | ME Ware |
| | MT Hancock CBE | WN Weston |
| Appointed Trustees | AL Brend | NSE Martin |
| | P Cautley | R Niddrie |
| | BC Johnston OBE | Prof J Purvis |
| | N Jonas OBE | Miss V Reynolds |

| | |
|---|---|
| *staff* | 19 |

| Director | Colonel KN Wilkins OBE |
|---|---|
| Curator | AJ Lane |
| Finance Officer | Miss LJ Coote |
| Marketing Officer | Mrs J Jarvie |
| Estate/Appeal Manager | Commander WG Samways OBE |

**financial**

| FINANCIAL ACTIVITIES | 1997 | 1996 |
|---|---|---|
| **Year end: 31 March** | £ | £ |
| **INCOMING RESOURCES** | | |
| Donations and grants | 1,036,312 | 583,659 |
| Investment income | 1,409 | 13,147 |
| Net gain on sale of investments | - | 16,218 |
| Museum admissions | 29,091 | 34,716 |
| Fundraising events | 76,146 | 95,885 |
| Income from trading company | 11,132 | 3,028 |
| Sundry income | 34,349 | 60,688 |
| | **1,188,439** | **807,341** |
| **RESOURCES EXPENDED** | | |
| Direct charitable expenditure | 383,683 | 404,906 |
| Fundraising and publicity | 173,438 | 183,132 |
| Management and administration | 123,625 | 128,658 |
| | **680,746** | **716,696** |
| **NET INCOMING/(OUTGOING) RESOURCES** | **507,693** | **90,645** |
| Balances brought forward | 959,842 | 869,197 |
| **BALANCES CARRIED FORWARD** | **1,467,535** | **959,842** |

| | | | |
|---|---|---|---|
| *advisers* | **Auditors** | Walton & Co | Venture House, East Street, Titchfield PO14 4AR |

436

# *Royal Mint*

Royal Mint
Llantrisant
Pontyclun
Mid-Glamorgan CF72 8YT

**Tel** 01443 222111
**Fax** 01443 623190

| | |
|---|---|
| *status* | Executive agency |
| *founded* | 1990 as agency, Trading Fund 1975 |
| *sponsor* | HM Treasury |
| *powers* | Trading Funds Act 1973 and Framework Document 1997 |
| *mission* | To provide sufficient coins for circulation in the UK. |
| *tasks* | Manufactures and distributes UK and overseas coins (circulating and commemorative) and medals and seals. |
| *operations* | Management: Master of the Mint is the Chancellor of the Exchequer. The Chief Executive is Deputy Master and Comptroller. The Chancellor of the Exchequer set a rate of return of 14% for 1998/99. Growth in UK coin demand increased by 20% in 1996/97 and under terms of contract with HM Treasury had the effect of reducing the average margin on UK coins. 41% of sales are UK, 59% overseas. |

*operations* Policy: Growth of collector coin business.

Trends: Heavy overseas competition. The implementation of a single European currency.

*performance* Operating profit of £7.6 million for 1996/97 which exceeded forecast.

*board* Appointed by the Chancellor of the Exchequer.

| | |
|---|---|
| Deputy Master & Comptroller (Chief Executive) | Roger Holmes |
| Director, Finance & Corporate Services (Deputy Chief Executive) | David Snell |
| Director of Operations | Robert Burchill |
| Non-Executive Director | Gisela Burg CBE |
| Director of Sales | Keith Cottrell |
| Non-Executive Director | Lyndon Haddon |
| Director, Personnel & Establishment Officer | Allan Pearce |
| Non-Executive Director | Sidney Taylor |
| *Accounting Officer* | *Chief Executive* |

*staff* 1031

*financial*

**OPERATING ACCOUNT**

| Year end: 31 March | 1997 £000 | 1996 £000 | 1995 £000 |
|---|---|---|---|
| **TURNOVER** | **91,566** | **90,842** | **106,477** |
| Change in stocks of finished goods and work in progress | (522) | 4,475 | (3547) |
| Own work capitalised | 424 | 192 | 209 |
| Other operating income | 192 | 186 | 187 |
| Raw materials and consumables | (42,135) | (40,502) | (42,375) |
| Other external charges | (6,361) | (10,633) | (10,210) |
| Staff costs | (23,858) | (23,845) | (21,935) |
| Depreciation and other amounts written off tangible fixed assets | (2,783) | (3,008) | (2,980) |
| Other operating charges | (8,921) | (8,410) | (11,861) |
| | **(83,964)** | **(81,545)** | **(92,512)** |
| **OPERATING PROFIT** | **7,602** | **9,297** | **13,965** |
| Interest receivable and similar income | 413 | 932 | 1149 |
| Interest payable and similar charges | (336) | (280) | (109) |
| **PROFIT FOR THE YEAR** | **7,679** | **9,949** | **15005** |
| Dividend payable to the consolidated fund | (3,000) | (9,500) | (15000) |
| **RETAINED PROFIT FOR THE YEAR** | **4,679** | **449** | **5** |

*advisers* **Auditors** National Audit Office 157-197 Buckingham Palace Road London SW1W 9SP

Coopers & Lybrand

# Royal Naval Museum (RNM)

HM Naval Base
Portsmouth PO1 3LP

**Tel** 01705 733060

| | |
|---|---|
| *status* | Executive body |
| *founded* | 1911, executive body in 1983 |
| *sponsor* | Ministry of Defence (MOD) |
| *powers* | National Heritage Act 1983 |
| *mission* | To provide a museum of the people of the Royal Navy. |
| *tasks* | Acquiring, managing and conserving exhibits relating to the Royal Navy and its people; maintains Oral History Archive; organises temporary exhibitions. |
| *operations* | Management: The Director is responsible for day-to-day management and he reports to the Board of Trustees. RNM is part of Portsmouth's Historic Dockyard (with *HMS Victory*, the *Mary Rose* and *HMS Warrior*) and most visitors come on a discounted passport ticket which gives admission to all sites. Income to the museum falls slightly year on year because of this. |
| | Policy: Millennium Commission funding for environmental and other infrastructure improvements in the Historic Dockyard. Lottery grant for museum development. |
| | Trends: Joint publishing imprint with Alan Sutton Publications enhancing scholarly dimension of work |
| *board* | Board of Trustees appointed by the Secretary of State. |

| | | |
|---|---|---|
| Chairman | | Vice Admiral Sir Barry Wilson |
| Exofficio Trustee | | Commodore Iain Henderson |
| Representative Trustees | | A Aberg |
| | | Cllr D Giles |
| | | Rear Admiral JR Hill |
| | | B Lavery |
| Trustees | RL Dean | |
| | Cllr FAJ Emery-Wallis | Arm Jaffray CB |
| | TW Ferrers-Walker | Rear Admiral R Lees |
| *Accounting Officer* | *Director* | |

| | |
|---|---|
| *staff* | 36 |

| | |
|---|---|
| Director | HC McMurray |

# Royal Navy Submarine Museum

Haslar Jetty Road
Gosport
Hants PO12 2AS

**Tel** 01705 510354          **E-mail** rnsubs@submarine-museum.demon.co.uk
**Fax** 01705 511349

| | |
|---|---|
| *status* | Executive body |
| *sponsor* | Ministry of Defence (MOD) |
| *powers* | Memorandum and Articles of Association |
| *mission* | To provide an effective and accessible repository for the heritage of the Submarine Branch of the Royal Navy and to encourage scholarship and research into its history. |
| *tasks* | Maintains and manages a public museum and library of all aspects of submarine endeavour; educates the public; preserves and displays the collections; acts as keeper of the Regimental Heritage of the Submarine Service; relieves distress or need among past and present members of the Submarine Service and their dependants. |

| | |
|---|---|
| **operations** | Management: Museum Director is responsible for day-to-day running of museum. Submarine Giftshop Ltd is trading subsidiary. |
| | Policy: Computer catalogue of collection is priority. Centennial Appeal Fund has been established. |
| | Trends: Small increase in visitor numbers. Modifying plan to reapply for Lottery funding following rejection of initial application. |
| **board** | Board of Trustees appointed by the Chairman. |

| Chairman | Rear Admiral AJ Whetstone CB | |
|---|---|---|
| Vice Chairman | Rear Admiral JF Perowne OBE | |
| Trustees | Dr R Bud | |
| | Captain R Channon | D Patch |
| | Mrs L Lee | R Webb |
| | Captain TJ Meadows CBE | R Wilson |
| *Accounting Officer* | *Museum Director* | |

| | |
|---|---|
| **staff** | 27 and 16 part-time guides |

| Museum Director | Commander JJ Tall OBE |
|---|---|
| Secretary to the Trustees | Miss Jennifer Moys |

**financial**

| INCOME & EXPENDITURE | |
|---|---|
| **Year end: 31 March** | **1997** |
| | **£** |
| **INCOMING RESOURCES** | |
| Grant-in-aid (operating) | 272,553 |
| Grant-in-aid (purchases) | 12,000 |
| Donations and grants | 17,200 |
| Museum admissions | 128,577 |
| Income from trading company | 10,310 |
| Sundry income | 35,051 |
| | **475,671** |
| **RESOURCES EXPENDED** | |
| Direct charitable expenditure | 400,548 |
| Fundraising and publicity | 39,014 |
| Management and administration | 57,961 |
| Notional charges | 13,689 |
| | 511,212 |
| **NET INCOMING/(OUTGOING) RESOURCES** | |
| **BEFORE TRANSFERS** | **(35,541)** |
| Adjustment for notional charges | 13,689 |
| Transfers between funds | - |
| **NET INCOMING/(OUTGOING) RESOURCES FOR YEAR** | **(21,852)** |

| **advisers** | **Bankers** | Lloyds and NatWest | Gosport |
|---|---|---|---|
| | **Auditors** | Walton & Co | Titchfield, Hants |
| | **Solicitors** | Blake Lapthorn Solicitors | |

# *Royal Parks Agency*

The Old Police House
Hyde Park
London W2 2UH

**Tel** 0171 298 2000
**Fax** 0171 298 2005

| | |
|---|---|
| **status** | Executive agency |
| **founded** | 1993 |
| **sponsor** | Department for Culture, Media and Sport (DCMS) |
| **powers** | Framework Document 1993 |
| **mission** | Manages and polices the Royal Parks in London: St James's Park, The Green Park, Hyde Park, Kensington Gardens, Regent's Park, Primrose Hill, Greenwich Park, Richmond Park and Bushy Park. |

| | |
|---|---|
| *tasks* | To manage the Royal Parks so that they offer peaceful enjoyment, recreation, entertainment and delight to those who use them, and are enhanced, protected and preserved for the future. The Royal Parks Constabulary is responsible for enforcing regulations, maintaining law and order within the parks, and ensuring security at ceremonial events. Also responsible for a number of other areas in London (eg Brompton Cemetery). |
| *operations* | Management:  The Chief Executive, supported by a Management Board, is responsible for the day-to-day management of the Agency.  He is accountable to the Secretary of State, who sets the policy framework and key performance targets. |
| | Policy: Increasing capital resources for repair and restoration of buildings and monuments; applied for Lottery funding for some projects. |
| | Trends: Appointed a marketing partner to increase income.  Supporting proposals to put Park Lane in a tunnel and extend Hyde Park. |
| *performance* | Met or exceeded all key targets in 1996/97. |
| *board* | Ministerial Advisory Board appointed by the Secretary of State. |

| | | |
|---|---|---|
| Chairman | L Wright | |
| Members | Barbara Abensur | Robin Herbert CBE |
| | Frank Constable MBE | Sir Peter Imbert QPM |
| | Lady Goodison | Neville Labovitch LVO MBE |
| | Lady Grosvenor | Giles Shepard CBE |
| Secretary | Gerard Wheeldon | |
| *Accounting Officer* | *Chief Executive* | |

*staff*     246

| | |
|---|---|
| Chief Executive | David Welch |
| Park Manager, Kensington Gardens | Nick Butler |
| Park Manager, Regent's Park and Primrose Hill | David Caselton |
| Park Manager, St James's Park and Green Park | Dennis Clarke |
| Park Manager, Hyde Park | Steve Edwards |
| Park Manager, Bushy Park | Dennis Goddard |
| Contractor, Brompton Cemetery | Murdo Macmillan |
| Park Manager, Richmond Park | Simon Richards |
| Park Manager, Greenwich Park | Joe Woodcock |
| Head of Commerce & Inner Parks | Jennifer Adams |
| Head of Estates & Outer Parks | Mike Fitt |
| Head of Policy | Viviane Robertson |
| RPC Chief Officer | Commander Walter Ross |
| Head of Finance & Information Technology | Sandra Smith |

*financial*

**INCOME & EXPENDITURE**

| Year end: 31 March | 1997 £000 | 1996 £000 |
|---|---|---|
| **EXPENDITURE** | | |
| Staff costs | 7,324 | 7,063 |
| Depreciation | 1,219 | 1,118 |
| Other operating costs | 18,922 | 18,346 |
| Interest on capital | 1,829 | 1,709 |
| Notional charges | 82 | 82 |
| | **29,376** | **28,318** |
| **INCOME** | | |
| Less income from operations | 3,700 | 2,576 |
| **NET EXPENDITURE** | **25,676** | **25,742** |

*branches*

The Storeyard
Horse Guards Approach
St James' Park
London SW1A 2BJ
Tel 0171 930 1793
Fax 0171 839 7639

Ranger's Lodge
Hyde Park
London W2 2UH
Tel 0171 298 2100
Fax 0171 402 3298

The Magazine Storeyard
Magazine Gate
Kensington Gardens
London W2 2UH
Tel 0171 298 2117
Fax 0171 724 2826

The Chapel Office
Brompton Cemetery
Fulham Road
London SW10 9UG
Tel 0171 352 1201

The Storeyard
Inner Circle
Regent's Park
London NW1 4NR
Tel 0171 486 7905
Fax 0171 224 1895

Park Office
Greenwich Park
Blackheath Gate
Greenwich
London SE10 8QY
Tel 0181 858 2608
Fax 0181 293 3782

Holly Lodge
Richmond Park
Richmond
Surrey TW10 5HS
Tel 0181 948 3209
Fax 0181 332 2730

The Stockyard
Bushy Park
Hampton Court Road
Hampton Hill
Middlesex TW12 2EJ
Tel 0181 979 1586
Fax 0181 941 8196

# *Rural Development Commission (RDC)*

141 Castle Street
Salisbury
Wiltshire SP1 3TP

**Tel** 01722 336255
**Fax** 01722 3322769          **Web** http://www.argonet.co.uk/rdc

Dacre House
19 Dacre Street
London SW1H 0DH

**Tel** 0171 340 2900

| | |
|---|---|
| *status* | Executive body |
| *founded* | 1909, 1983 as RDC |
| *sponsor* | Department of the Environment, Transport and the Regions (DETR) |
| *powers* | Development and Road Improvements Act 1909. Miscellaneous Financial Provision Act 1983. |
| *mission* | Promoting jobs and communities in rural England. |
| *tasks* | Advises government; undertakes and funds research projects; regeneration of Rural Development Areas (areas suffering from the greatest economic and social problems) - 60% of budget; encourages the provision and survival of rural services (eg transport, village shops and post offices, affordable housing). |
| *operations* | Management: Headed by Chief Executive, supported by three Directors. Two Advisory Panels, specialising in rural economic and social development, assist the Commission with the identification and analysis of key issues. Headquarters in London and Salisbury and 11 offices, which provide economic, and social advice and assistance to communities in their area. Network of voluntary County Committees, whose members advise on local trends and issues. |
| | Policy: Trying to ensure that a strong rural dimension is built into new government policies. |
| | Trends: EU proposal to change Structural Funds would mean many rural areas losing EU funds. |
| *board* | Commissioners are appointed by the Queen on the recommendation of the DETR. |

| Chairman | Miles Middleton CBE | |
|---|---|---|
| Commissioners | Richard Best OBE | |
| | Jane Bradford | Dame Anne Mueller DCB |
| | David Fletcher MBE | Prof Howard Newby CBE |
| | Dr Barbara Marsh JP | The Rt Rev Anthony Russell |
| *Accounting Officer* | *Chief Executive* | |

*staff*          270

| Chief Executive | Richard Butt |
|---|---|
| Director of Strategy & Planning | Margaret Clark |
| Director of Operations | John Edwards |
| Director of Resources | Keith Walton |

| Regional Managers | Steve Dann | |
|---|---|---|
| | Anne Grindley | Mark Pearce |
| | Rob Hatt | Trevor Stockton |
| | Simon Hodgson | Peter Stovey |

*financial*

### INCOME & EXPENDITURE

| Year end: 31 March | 1997 | 1996 | 1995 |
|---|---|---|---|
| | £000 | £000 | £000 |
| **GROSS INCOME** | | | |
| **Grant-in-aid from** | | | |
| Department of the Environment | 39,355 | 38,413 | 28,440 |
| Department of Transport | 1,250 | 800 | 703 |
| | **40,605** | **39,213** | **29,143** |
| Amounts generated by fully funded factory workspace | 475 | 266 | 8,852 |
| Other operating income | 449 | 578 | 856 |
| Amounts transferred from deferred government | 318 | 276 | 251 |
| Grant account interest receivable from long-term loans | 1,290 | 1,292 | 1,320 |
| Rental income from partnership workspace | 622 | 617 | 569 |
| Income from business service | 642 | 589 | 603 |
| | **3,796** | **3,618** | **12,451** |
| | **44,401** | **42,831** | **41,594** |
| | | | |
| **EXPENDITURE** | | | |
| Staff costs | 7,641 | 7,062 | 7,170 |
| Depreciation on fixed assets | 290 | 298 | 264 |
| Other operating charges | 8,018 | 7,945 | 8,389 |
| Grants paid | 28,174 | 23,365 | 22,283 |
| Loans written off | 667 | 549 | 60 |
| | **44,790** | **39,219** | **38,166** |
| Release of provision against VAT no longer required | - | 1,600 | - |
| **OPERATING (DEFICIT)/SURPLUS** | **(389)** | **5,212** | **3,428** |
| Profit/(loss) on disposal of tangible fixed asset | - | 1 | 8 |
| Share of profit before taxation of associate | - | 43 | 325 |
| Interest receivable on deposit account | 53 | 62 | 64 |
| Notional cost of capital | (1,765) | - | - |
| **NET (DEFICIT)/SURPLUS BEFORE TAXATION** | **(2,101)** | **5,318** | **3,825** |
| Taxation | (729) | (309) | (563) |
| **(DEFICIT)/SURPLUS AFTER TAXATION** | **(2,830)** | **5,009** | **3,262** |

*publications*  Annual Report, Growth and Survival of Small Rural Manufacturing Firms, Innovation and Technology in Small Rural Firms

*branches*

*North*
Haweswater Road
Penrith
Cumbria CA11 7EH
Tel 01768 865752

Morton Road
Yarm Road Industrial Estate
Darlington
County Durham DL1 4PT
Tel 01325 487123

*Yorkshire & Humber*
Spitfire House
Aviator Court
Clifton Moor
York YO3 4UZ
Tel 01904 693335

*West Midlands*
Strickland House
The Lawns
Park Street
Wellington
Telford
Shropshire TF1 3BX
Tel 01952 247161

*East Midlands*
18 Market Place
Bingham
Nottingham NG13 8AP
Tel 01949 876200

*East Anglia*
Lees Smith House
12 Looms Lane
Bury St Edmunds
Suffolk IP33 1HE
Tel 01284 701743

*South West*
2nd Floor
Highshore House
New Bridge Street
Truro
Cornwall TR1 2AA
Tel 01872 273531

27 Victoria Park Road
Devon
Exeter EX2 4NT
Tel 01392 206240

3 Chartfield House
Castle Street
Taunton
Somerset TA1 4AS
Tel 01823 276905

*South East*
Sterling House
7 Ashford House
Maidstone
Kent ME14 5BJ
Tel 01622 765222

The Chanty House
29-31 Pyle Street
Newport
Isle of Wight PO30 1JW
Tel 01983 52019

# S4C (Welsh Fourth Channel Authority)

Parc Ty Glas
Llanishen
Cardiff CT4 5DU

**Tel** 01222 747444          **E-mail** s4c@s4c.co.uk
**Fax** 01222 754444          **Web** http://www.s4c.co.uk

**Contact** David Meredith, Head of Corporate Press and Public Relations

| | |
|---|---|
| ***status*** | Public corporation |
| ***founded*** | 1982 |
| ***sponsor*** | Department of Culture, Media and Sport (DCMS) |
| ***powers*** | Broadcasting Acts 1990 and 1996 |
| ***mission*** | To broadcast high-quality programmes on the Fourth Channel in Wales, including the provision of Welsh language programmes for broadcasting during peak viewing hours. |
| ***tasks*** | Commission its own Welsh language programmes and maintain the quality of peak hours Welsh language service. |
| | Allowing viewers in Wales access to as much Channel 4 service as possible (target 75%). |
| | Using its new digital TV capacity (Broadcasting Act 1996) to provide an extended version of S4C, beginning in mid-1998. |
| | Initiating commercial activity, eg SDN (S4C Digital Networks Ltd). |
| | Acting as an independent statutory broadcasting authority in respect of S4C programme services. |
| ***operations*** | Management: The Chairman is appointed by the DCMS. There has been an internal reorganisation reflecting more varied programming requirements and an increased commercial emphasis - production department has been created responsible for sourcing funds for programme budgets and a commercial operations department will seek to maximise the commercial potential of joint ventures. S4C receives statutory subvention from DCMS, calculated as 3.2% of UK television (fluctuating) advertising revenue. In 1996 this produced £68.4 million - an increase of 7% over the previous year while commercial revenue increased by 22%. S4C Authority is the principal regulatory body in respect of S4C television service, ensuring that, in a public service and commercial environment, the statutory functions are discharged in accordance with its own policies and the Broadcasting Act 1990. |
| | Policy: SDN has won the right to run the digital multiplex (Multiplex A, on which S4C is guaranteed a place) as an entirely commercial activity; S4C public funding will not be diverted from its Welsh language programme purposes. |
| | Trends: A compliance group was formed under the aegis of the Thompson Foundation. |
| ***performance*** | Increased viewing figures of Welsh speakers. |
| ***board*** | Appointed by the DCMS |

| | |
|---|---|
| Chairman | Elan Closs Stephens |
| Members | Gwenllian M Awbery |
| | Peter Davies MBE |
| | Janet A Lewis-Jones |
| | Janice Rowlands |
| *Accounting Officer* | *Chief Executive* |

| | |
|---|---|
| ***staff*** | 140 |

| Management Team | |
|---|---|
| Chief Executive | Huw Jones |
| Director of Corporate Policy & Secretary to the Authority | Emyr Byron Hughes |
| Director of Engineering | Rodger Fuse |
| Director of Animation | Chris Grace |
| Director of Corporate Affairs | Iona Jones |
| Director of Finance | Kathryn Morris |
| Director of Broadcasting | Dafydd Rhys |
| Director of Personnel & Administration | Ifan Roberts |
| Commissioning Editors | |
| Light Entertainment | Huw Chiswell |
| Children & Youth | Meirion Davies |
| Factual | Cenwyn Edwards |
| Music Consultant | Richard Elfyn Jones |
| Drama | Angharad Jones |

*financial*

| INCOME & EXPENDITURE Year end: 31 December | 1996 £000 | 1995 £000 |
|---|---|---|
| £000 | | |
| **INCOME** | | |
| Income | 68,416 | 63,942 |
| Transfer to deferred income | (357) | (2,834) |
| | **68,059** | **61,108** |
| **EXPENDITURE** | | |
| Cost of programmes transmitted | (65,483) | (57,913) |
| Transmission and distribution costs | (4,838) | (4,687) |
| | **(2,262)** | **(1,492)** |
| Operational and administrative expenses | (7,266) | (7,023) |
| Other income less expenditure | 7,758 | 6,360 |
| **OPERATING DEFICIT** | **(1,770)** | **(2,155)** |
| Interest | 1,770 | 2,155 |
| **SURPLUS FOR THE FINANCIAL PERIOD** | - | - |

# Scottish Agricultural Science Agency (SASA)

East Craigs
Edinburgh EH12 8NJ

**Tel** 0131 244 8893
**Fax** 0131 244 8988

*status* Executive agency

*founded* 1992

*sponsor* Scottish Office

*powers* Framework Document 1997

*mission* To provide government with expert scientific information and advice on agricultural and horticultural crops and aspects of the environment, mainly for Scottish interests.

*tasks* Runs Official Seed Testing Station for Scotland (OSTS); undertakes scientific research into crop performance, disease and pesticides; runs training courses. Also performs statutory and regulatory work in relation to national, EU and other international legislation and crop improvement, genetically manipulated organisms (GMOs) and the protection of crops, food and the environment.

*operations* Management: The Management Team consists of the Director and the heads of the three divisions: Pesticides, Plant Varieties & Seeds; Potato, Plant Health & Zoology; Administration & Support Services. SASA's principal customer is Scottish Office Agriculture, Environment and Fisheries Department (SOAEFD).

Policy: Participation in the formulation of the science strategy for the agricultural and biological organisations in Scotland (CHABOS).

Trends: Cuts in funding required SASA to reduce the costs by 10% in 1996/97, which led to loss of staff.

*performance* Four out of five targets met in 1996/97.

**board**  No board.

| Accounting Officer | Director |
|---|---|

**staff**  127

| Director | Dr RKM Hay |
|---|---|
| Deputy Director | SR Cooper |
| Potato & Plant Health | WJ Rennie |
| Administration | Mrs SM Quinn |
| Information Technology | PJ Winfield |

**financial**

| INCOME & EXPENDITURE | | | |
|---|---|---|---|
| Year end: 31 March | **1997** | **1996** | **1995** |
| | **£000** | **£000** | **£000** |
| INCOME | | | |
| Income from activities | 1,280 | 1,317 | 1,300 |
| EXPENDITURE | | | |
| Staff costs | 2,848 | 3,039 | 2,963 |
| Depreciation | 649 | 611 | 562 |
| Other operating charges | 1,596 | 1,582 | 1,748 |
| | 5,093 | 5,232 | 5,273 |
| **NET EXPENDITURE** | **3,813** | **3,915** | **3,973** |
| Interest on capital | 625 | 569 | 530 |
| **EXCESS OF EXPENDITURE OVER INCOME** | **4,438** | **4,484** | **4,503** |

# Scottish Agricultural Wages Board

Pentland House
47 Robb's Lane
Edinburgh EH14 1TY

**Tel** 0131 244 6397
**Fax** 0131 2446551

**status**  Executive body

**founded**  1949

**sponsor**  Scottish Office

**powers**  Agricultural Wages (Scotland) Act 1949. Agriculture Act 1967

**mission**  Fair wages and conditions of employment for agricultural workers in Scotland.

**tasks**  Negotiating and deciding minimum rates of pay and terms and conditions of employment for agricultural, horticultural and fish farm workers in Scotland and issuing legally enforceable Orders specifying rates and terms.

**operations**  Management: The Board is staffed and financed by the Scottish Office which may prosecute employers breaching the Board's Orders. The staff of the Scottish Office Agriculture Environment and Fisheries Department (SOAEFD), check employers; employees considering that they are not properly paid contact the Secretary of the Board directly.

Trends: New style Wages Order devised to make it easier for employers and workers to understand minimum rates of pay and other conditions of service.

**board**  Five members including the Chairman are appointed by the Secretary of State; five employers' representatives are nominate by the National Farmers' Union of Scotland and the Scottish Landowners Federation; and six are employees' representatives nominated by the Agricultural & Allied Workers National Trade Group (Scotland) of the Transport and General Workers' Union.

| Chairman | Christine AM Davis | |
|---|---|---|
| Members | John B Allan | Ian A Melrose |
| | W Barrie Page | Adam Train |
| | Donald G Mackay | Jim Brown |
| | Andrew WJ Thomson | James Currie |
| | Fraser R Evans | Annmaree Mitchell |
| | Maurice Hankey | Len G Morrison |
| | Tom J Howie | David Stark |
| | John McMyn | George Wilmshurst |

**staff**

| Secretary | Miss F Anderson |
|---|---|

# Scottish Arts Council (SAC)

12 Manor Place
Edinburgh EH3 7DD

**Tel** 0131 226 6051
**Fax** 0131 225 9833

**E-mail** help.desk.SAC@artsfb.org.uk
**Web** http://www.sac.org.uk

| | |
|---|---|
| **status** | Executive body |
| **founded** | 1994 |
| **sponsor** | Scottish Office |
| **powers** | Royal Charter 1994 |
| **mission** | To create a climate in which quality arts (crafts, drama, dance, literature, music, visual arts) flourish and are enjoyed by a wide range of people throughout Scotland. |
| **tasks** | Providing funds to Scottish arts and crafts organisations; increasing the availability of, and access to, the arts in Scotland; supporting the indigenous arts; providing an education programme; establishing international links; encouraging innovation. |
| **operations** | Management: 15 panels and committees to allocate grants. Staff increased to handle Lottery funds and new accommodation leased for them. |
| | Policy: Supporting innovation in the arts and widening access and participation. |
| | Trends: Increasing number of applications to SAC (and sums requested) mean that demand for funding far exceeds the available resources. Scottish Office grant (£24 million) at standstill while Lottery funding becoming increasingly important (£30 million). |
| **board** | Council appointed by the Secretary of State. |

| | | |
|---|---|---|
| Chair | Magnus Linklater | |
| Members | Hugh Buchanan | Maud Marshall |
| | Richard Chester | Ann Matheson |
| | Bill English | Janette Richardson |
| | Cllr Keith Geddes | Prof Eric Spiller |
| | Robert Love | Jean Urquhart |

**staff** 87

| | |
|---|---|
| Director | Seona Reid |
| Director, Crafts | Helen Bennett |
| Director, Finance & Administration | Graham Berry |
| Director, Lottery | David Bonnar |
| Director, Literature | Jenny Brown |
| Director, Visual Arts | Susan Daniel-McElroy |
| Director, Music | Ned Knowles |
| Director, Combined Arts | John Murphy |
| Director, Planning & Development | Barclay Price |
| Director, Drama & Dance | David Taylor |

**financial**

**INCOME & EXPENDITURE**

| Year end: 31 March | 1997 £m | 1996 £m |
|---|---|---|
| **INCOME** | | |
| Grant-in-aid | 25.811 | 24.477 |
| NLDF | - | - |
| Other income | 0.320 | 0.255 |
| | **26.131** | **24.732** |
| **EXPENDITURE** | | |
| Grants & guarantees | 24.048 | 22.674 |
| Direct provision | 0.090 | 0.154 |
| | **24.138** | **22.828** |
| Operating costs | 1.987 | 1.889 |
| Notional interest | 0.058 | - |
| Shared costs | (0.289) | (0.042) |
| Total expenditure | 25.894 | 24.675 |
| **OPERATING SURPLUS/DEFICIT** | **0.237** | **0.057** |

| LOTTERY - INCOME & EXPENDITURE | | |
| --- | --- | --- |
| Year end: 31 March | 1997 | 1996 |
| | £m | £m |
| **INCOME** | | |
| Grant-in-aid | - | - |
| NLDF | 25.736 | 26.110 |
| Other income | 2.472 | 1.203 |
| | **28.208** | **27.313** |
| **EXPENDITURE** | | |
| Grants & guarantees | 30.195 | 19.831 |
| Direct provision | - | - |
| | **30.195** | **19.831** |
| Operating costs | 0.898 | 0.410 |
| Notional interest | 0.031 | - |
| Shared costs | 0.289 | 0.042 |
| Total expenditure | 31.413 | 20.283 |
| **OPERATING SURPLUS/DEFICIT** | **(3.205)** | **7.030** |

| *advisers* | **Bankers** | Bank of Scotland |
| --- | --- | --- |
| | **Auditors** | National Audit Office |
| | **Solicitors** | Burness and Co |
| *publications* | Detailed in *SAC Information Directory* | |

# Scottish Children's Reporter Administration (SCRA)

Ochil House
Springkerse Business Park
Stirling FK7 7XE

**Tel** 01786 459500
**Fax** 01786 459532

| *status* | Executive body |
| --- | --- |
| *founded* | 1996 |
| *sponsor* | Scottish Office |
| *powers* | Local Government etc (Scotland) Act 1994 |
| *mission* | To pursue with care and creativity the best interests of children who are or may be referred to the Reporter, within the framework of Scotland's child welfare and justice systems. |
| *tasks* | To facilitate the work of Children's Reporters for children; deploy and manage staff to carry out that work; provide suitable accommodation for children's hearings. |
| *operations* | Management: Principal Reporter is the head of the service and is supported by the Board of part-time members in the management of SCRA. Headquarters in Stirling which provides strategic and central services. 12 regional offices, headed by a Reporter Manager, provide professional, managerial and administrative support and leadership to local authority teams. For each local authority area an Authority Reporter leads the delivery of the service and plays a major role in liaison with other agencies. |
| | Policy: Replacing IT systems through PFI. |
| | Trends: Numbers of children being referred remains fairly constant. |
| *performance* | No targets have been set. |
| *board* | Board appointed by the Secretary of State from people experienced in different parts of the children's hearings system. |

| Chairman | Sally Kuenssberg | |
| --- | --- | --- |
| Deputy Chairman | John Broadfoot CBE | |
| Principal Reporter | Alan Miller | |
| Members | J Allan | |
| | Mary Beckett | Christine Hallett |
| | Joan Catto | Patricia Stevenson OBE |
| *Accounting Officer* | *Principal Reporter* | |

| staff | 308 |
|---|---|

| Principal Reporter | Alan Miller |
|---|---|
| Assistant Principal Reporter (Operations) | Margaret Cox |
| Assistant Principal Reporter (Practice) | Norman Macleod |
| Director of Human Resources | Heather Barnes |
| Director of Support Services | Barry Simpson |

**financial**

| INCOME & EXPENDITURE | |
|---|---|
| Year end: 31 March | **1997** |
| | **£000** |
| **INCOME** | |
| HM government grant-in-aid | 10,681 |
| **EXPENDITURE** | |
| Staff costs | 7,012 |
| Depreciation | 537 |
| Other operating charges | 3,119 |
| | **10,668** |
| **OPERATING SURPLUS** | **13** |
| Interest payable | 328 |
| **RETAINED PROFIT FOR THE YEAR** | **(315)** |

# Scottish Community Education Council (SCEC)

9 Haymarket Terrace
Edinburgh EH12 5EZ

**Tel** 0131 313 2488
**Fax** 0131 313 6800

| | |
|---|---|
| **status** | Executive body |
| **founded** | 1982 |
| **sponsor** | Scottish Office |
| **mission** | To support those active in community education to meet the learning needs of people in communities. |
| **tasks** | To raise the profile of community education, adult education, community work and youth work at national and local level; to promote with providers the development and delivery of effective community education provision; to develop and influence policies, strategies and initiatives that engage non-participants and the disadvantaged; to influence policy and practice through UK and international partnerships; to deliver training and consultancies to meet users' needs. |
| **operations** | Management: Two divisions: Corporate Services, responsible for business development, publications and design, finance and administration; and Operational Services, responsible for policy and research, practice and product development. Eurodesk Office in Brussels. |
| | Policy: Focusing on voluntary sector following reorganisation of local authorities . |
| **board** | Council appointed by the Secretary of State from public, private and voluntary sector backgrounds. There are two Scottish Office Assessors. |

| Chair | Barbara Vaughan OBE | |
|---|---|---|
| Members | Sue Angus | Val MacIver |
| | Dr Alan Barr | Charlie McConnell |
| | Alan Blackie | Ted Milburn |
| | Gordon Craig | Stewart Murdoch |
| | Ian Graham | Jim Stretton |
| Assessors | David Kelso | |
| | Stewart McDonald | |

| staff | 32 |
|---|---|

| Chief Executive | Charlie McConnel |
|---|---|
| Adult Education & Practice Development Director | Fiona Blacke |
| Company Secretary | David Murdoch |

# Scottish Conveyancing & Executry Services Board

Mulberry House
16-22 Picardy Place
Edinburgh EH1 3YT

**Tel** 0131 556 1945
**Fax** 0131 556 8428

**Contact** Robert H Pateson

| | |
|---|---|
| *status* | Executive body |
| *founded* | 1991 |
| *sponsor* | Scottish Office, Home Department |
| *powers* | Law Reform (Miscellaneous Provisions) (Scotland) Act 1990 |
| *mission* | To register and regulate qualified conveyancers and executry practitioners in Scotland. |
| *tasks* | Register practitioners, ensure that they comply with the conduct and practice regulations, excercise a disciplinary function over them, and deal with complaints from clients. |
| *operations* | Management: The Board was suspended from 1992-1995 because of low level of demand in housing market and the difficulties in arranging consumer protection at reasonable cost. It became fully operational in 1997. |
| | Trends: Expected to become self-financing from fees charged to practitioners. |
| *performance* | First year of operation only. |
| *board* | Appointed by the Secretary of State. |

| | |
|---|---|
| Chairman | Alistair C Clark |
| Members | Ian Buchanan |
| | R Gavin Burnett |
| | Margaret Burns |
| | Joyce Simpson |
| | David Smith OBE |
| | Donald Storrie |
| | Duncan White OBE |
| *Accounting Officer* | *Secretary* |

| | |
|---|---|
| *staff* | Two |

| | |
|---|---|
| Secretary | Robert H Paterson OBE |

*financial*

| INCOME & EXPENDITURE Year end: 31 March | 1997 £ | 1996 £ |
|---|---|---|
| **INCOME** | | |
| Grant-in-aid | 88,626 | 17,045 |
| **EXPENDITURE** | | |
| Staff costs | 36,745 | 4,688 |
| Depreciation | 1,345 | 6,393 |
| Loss on disposal of fixed assets | 414 | 630 |
| Other operating costs | 50,624 | 4,571 |
| Notional operating costs | 15,000 | - |
| | 104,128 | 16,282 |
| **OPERATING (DEFICIT)/SURPLUS** | (15,502) | 763 |
| Taxation | - | - |
| **(DEFICIT)/SURPLUS FOR THE YEAR** | (15,502) | 763 |
| Release of notional operating costs | 15,000 | - |
| **RETAINED (DEFICIT)/SURPLUS** | (502) | 763 |

| *advisers* | **Bankers** | Bank of Scotland | 6 Picardy Place, Edinburgh EH1 3JT |
|---|---|---|---|
| | **Auditors** | Geoghegan & Co | 6 St Colme Street, Edinburgh EH3 6AD |
| | **Solicitors** | Shepherd & Weddeburn WS | Saltire Court, 20 Castle Terrace Edinburgh EH1 2ET |

*publications*    *Annual Report 1996-97, Corporate Plan 1997-98 to 2000-01*

# Scottish Council for Educational Technology (SCET)

74 Victoria Crescent Road
Glasgow G12 9JN

**Tel** 0141 337 5001
**Fax** 0141 337 5050

**E-mail** scet@scet.org.uk
**Web** http://www.scet.org.uk

| | |
|---|---|
| *status* | Executive body |
| *founded* | 1974 |
| *sponsor* | Scottish Office |
| *powers* | Framework Document |
| *mission* | The UK's primary provider of technological and training resources for educative purposes. |
| *tasks* | To provide advice, guidance and technological solutions for education and training, mainly to educational authorities, schools, colleges and special educational needs specialists. Sells educational software at reduced prices; markets its software overseas; devises and develops appropriate products, often in partnership with others; runs conferences. |
| *operations* | Management: Chief Executive responsible for day-to-day management and reports to the Governors. |
| | Policy: Investing in equipment and expertise for Internet. Substantial software sales overseas. |
| | Trends: Decline in income from traditional sources plus the financial demands of reskilling for new technologies. Huge increase in training being Internet-oriented. |
| *performance* | Performed below budget for the first time in 1996/97. |
| *board* | Governors appointed by the Secretary of State. |

| Chairman | Alistair Fleming | |
|---|---|---|
| Governors | Prof Lesley Beddie | |
| | Ms Margery Browning HMI | Prof Tom Mccool CBE |
| | Paul Curtis | Ms Maggie Pollard |
| | Cllr Malcolm Green | Harvey Stalker |
| | Prof Stephen Heppell | John Strang |
| | Owen Lynch | Lyn Tett |
| | Stuart MacDonald | Prof T Wilson |

| | | |
|---|---|---|
| *staff* | 87 | |
| | Chief Executive | Nigel Paine |
| *advisers* | **Bankers** Royal Bank of Scotland | 23 Sauchihall Street, Glasgow G2 3AD |
| | **Auditors** Moores Rowland | 25 Bothwell Street, Glasgow G2 6NL |
| | **Solicitors** MacRoberts Solicitors | 152 Bath Street, Glasgow G2 4TB |

# Scottish Court Service (SCS)

Hayweight House
23 Lauriston Street
Edinburgh EH3 9DQ

**Tel** 0131 221 6826
**Fax** 0131 221 6895

**Contact** David Lym

| | |
|---|---|
| *status* | Executive agency |
| *founded* | 1995 |
| *sponsor* | Scottish Office |

**powers**
The independence of the judiciary in Scotland is an essential constitutional principle and the basis of SCS operations lies in cooperation with the judiciary to meet agreed objectives and targets. It reports to parliament in accordance with the Exchequer and Audit Departments Act 1921.

**mission**
To help secure ready access to justice for the people of Scotland

**tasks**
To provide the staff, buildings and services to support the judiciary in the Supreme and Sheriff Courts.

**operations**
Management: A single integrated management structure being introduced, bringing together the headquarter's services previously provided by the Scottish Courts Administration and the operational services of the SCS. Plans to move to an area structure for the management of the Sheriff Courts in which there would be three Area Directors - one in the west (Glasgow, North and South Strathclyde), one in the east (Tayside, Central and Fife, and Lothian and the Borders), and one in the north (Grampian, Highlands and Islands).

Policy: SCS culture is being deliberately changed from one that is traditional to one that is progressive, eg to plan strategically, act corporately, have a bias for action, be innovative.

Trends: To continue to deliver the performance required to achieve output and quality targets within available resources.

Planned building works include completion of the refurbishment of Paisley Sheriff Court House and the extension to the Justiciary Buildings in Glasgow.

**board**
The SCS Strategy Group comprises the Principal Clerk of Session and Justiciary, the Regional Sheriff Clerks/Area Directors the Heads of the four headquarter's service units under the chairmanship of the Chief Executive. The Chief Executive is the Accounting Officer.

| | |
|---|---|
| Chief Executive | Mike Ewart |
| Deputy Chief Executive | Ian Scott |
| Head of Property & Services Unit | Gordon Beaton |
| Head of Operations & Policy Unit | Eric Cumming |
| Secretary | David Lynn |
| Head of Personnel & Development Unit | Alan Swift |
| Head of Resources & Efficiency Unit | Stephen Woodhouse |
| *Accounting Officer* | *Chief Executive* |

**staff**
817 (including 629 in Sheriff Courts and 121 in Supreme Courts)

| | |
|---|---|
| Principal Clerk of Session & Justiciary | John Anderson |
| Area Director, West & Regional Sheriff Clerk, Glasgow | Ian Scott |
| Regional Sheriff Clerk, South Strathclyde, Dumfries and Galloway | Mike Bonar |
| Regional Sheriff Clerk, Tayside, Central and Fife | John Doig |
| Regional Sheriff Clerk, Grampian, Highlands and Islands | John Robertson |
| Acting Regional Sheriff Clerk, Lothian and Borders | John Ross |

**financial**

**INCOME & EXPENDITURE**

| Year end: 31 March | 1997 £000 | 1996 £000 |
|---|---|---|
| **INCOME** | | |
| Income from activities | 13,561 | 14,184 |
| **EXPENDITURE** | | |
| Staff costs | 15,537 | 15,479 |
| Other operating costs | 48,057 | 27,006 |
| Depreciation | 474 | 8,331 |
| Permanent diminution in value of fixed assets | 445 | - |
| | (64,513) | (50,816) |
| **NET COSTS OF OPERATIONS BEFORE INTEREST** | (50,952) | (36,632) |
| Interest on capital | (400) | (16,595) |
| **NET COSTS OF OPERATIONS AFTER INTEREST** | (51,352) | (53,227) |

**publications**
*The Scottish Court Service Annual Report and Accounts, Corporate and Business Plan*

# Scottish Crop Research Institute (SCRI)

Invergowrie
Dundee DD2 5DA

**Tel** 01382 562731
**Fax** 01382 562426

**E-mail** mail@scri.sari.ac.uk
**Web** http://www.scri.sari.ac.uk

**Contact** Dr W H Macfarlane Smith

| | |
|---|---|
| *status* | Executive body |
| *founded* | 1981 |
| *sponsor* | Scottish Office |
| *powers* | Articles of Association |
| *mission* | To sustain excellence and an international reputation for strategic research in crop, plant and related sciences, and to facilitate the application of new knowledge to end-user industries. |
| *tasks* | Provides a centre for multidisciplinary research on agricultural, horticultural and industrial crops important to northern Britain and the rest of the world. Improving crop quality through genetic breeding techniques and improved agronomic practices. Developing more sustainable, environmentally sensitive methods to protect crops. Exploiting advantages and solving the problems of crop production in northern Britain. |
| *operations* | Management: Run by the Director who reports to the Secretary of State. Limited company with charitable status. 65% of funding is grant-in-aid. Mylnefield Research Services Ltd is the commercial arm of the Institute and gains research contracts from public organisations and private companies. |
| | Policy: SCRI is driven by a quest to solve difficult, long-term research problems that will lead to wealth creation. |
| | Trends: Contraction in public sector research set to continue. |
| *board* | Governing body appointed by the Secretary of State from academia, agriculture and commerce. |

| Chairman | AN MacCallum | |
|---|---|---|
| Members | AC Bain | |
| | Prof RJ Cogdell | JM Sime |
| | JM Drysdale | Prof AR Slabas |
| | JE Godfrey | P Whitworth |
| | K Hopkins | Prof PC Young |
| *Accounting Officer* | *Director* | |

*staff* 343

| | |
|---|---|
| Director | Prof JR Hillman |
| Deputy Director | Prof TMA Wilson |
| Head, Cell & Molecular Genetics Department | Prof W Powell |
| Head, Cellular & Environmental Physiology Department | Prof HV Davies |
| Head, Crop Genetics Department | GR Mackay |
| Head, Chemistry Department | WW Christie |
| Head, Fungal & Bacterial Plant Pathology Department | JM Duncan |
| Head, Nematology Department | DL Trudgill |
| Head, Soft Fruit & Perennial Crops Department | RJ McNicol |
| Head, Virology Department | PF Palukaitis |
| Head, Scientific Liaison & Information Services Department | WH Macfarlane Smith |
| Secretary & Financial Manager | RJ Killick |
| Financial Controller | I Harrington |
| Head, Engineering & Maintenance Department | S Petrie |
| Head, Estate, Glasshouse & Field Research Department | G Wood |
| Director, Biomathematics & Statistics Scotland | RA Kempton |

*financial*

**INCOME & EXPENDITURE**

| Year end: 31 March | 1997 £000 | 1996 £000 | 1995 £000 |
|---|---|---|---|
| Income | 11,744 | 11,480 | 10,826 |
| Expenditure | 11,836 | 11,422 | 10,924 |

*advisers*

| **Bankers** | Bank of Scotland | PO Box 9, 2 West Marketgate Dundee DD1 1QN |
|---|---|---|
| **Auditors** | KPMG | Saltire Court, 20 Castle Terrace Edinburgh EH1 2EF |

| Solicitors | Dundas and Wilson CS | Saltire Court, 20 Castle Terrace Edinburgh EH1 2EF |
|---|---|---|

*publications*   Annual Report

# *Scottish Enterprise*

120 Bothwell Street
Glasgow G2 7JP

**Tel** 0141 248 2700
**Fax** 0141 221 3217

**E-mail** scotentcsd@scotent.co.uk
**Web** http://www.scotent.co.uk

**Contact** Customer Service Desk

| | |
|---|---|
| *status* | Executive body |
| *founded* | 1990 |
| *sponsor* | Scottish Office |
| *powers* | Enterprise and New Towns (Scotland) Act 1990 |
| *mission* | To help create jobs and prosperity for Scotland. |
| *tasks* | Strengthening the business base by working with companies to encourage growth and develop critical strengths - provides expert advisers and market intelligence. Encouraging business start-ups - provides access to finance through investment arm (Scottish Development Finance). Improving exports - set up 13 Local Export Partnerships and its export arm (Scottish Trade International) has overseas offices. Promoting inward investment via Locate in Scotland. Improving the physical business infrastructure - provides information and acts as a catalyst for refurbishing, redeveloping and constructing industrial and commercial property. Reducing unemployment and increasing skills and training through locally run programmes. |
| *operations* | Management: Chief Executive reports to the Board; 13 local enterprise agencies run by separate Chief Executives. |
| | Policy: Encouraging the growth of technology-based businesses. |
| | Trends: Increasing international competition for inward investment. |
| *performance* | Record year for inward investment. |
| *board* | Appointed by the Secretary of State. |

| | | |
|---|---|---|
| Chairman | Sir Ian Wood CBE | |
| Deputy Chairman | Cameron McLatchie CBE | |
| Chief Executive | Crawford W Beveridge CBE | |
| Members | Dr Jim G Adamson OBE | |
| | Prof Andrew Bain OBE | Sir John Shaw CBE KStJ |
| | Keith Geddes CBE | Jim Sillars |
| | Michael M Gray OBE | Yvonne Strachan MBE |
| | Ian Robinson | Celia Urquhart |
| *Accounting Officer* | *Chief Executive* | |

*staff*   1387

| | |
|---|---|
| *Scottish Enterprise Network Management Group* | |
| Chief Executive | Crawford Beveridge CBE |
| Director Finance and Planning | Paul Brady |
| Managing Director, Scottish Enterprise Operations | Ray Macfarlane |
| Director, Network Services | Alistair Proctor |
| *Corporate Advisory Team* | |
| Director, Property Development & Funding | Chris Aitken |
| Director, Strategic Futures | Charlie Woods |
| Director, Corporate Affairs | Gerard O'Brien |
| Director, Network Services | Alistair Proctor |
| *Scottish Enterprise Operations* | |
| Managing Director | Ray Macfarlane |
| Director, Scottish Business | Bob Downes |
| Director, Overseas Business Development | Russel Griggs |
| Director, Scottish Development Finance | Brian Kerr |
| Director, Skills Development | Evelyn McCann |

| | |
|---|---|
| Director, Scottish Development Finance | Calum Paterson |
| Director, Scottish Trade International | David Taylor |
| Director, Locate in Scotland | Martin Togneri |
| Company Secretary | Brian Jamieson |
| *Dumfries & Galloway Enterprise* | |
| Chairman | James Neil Stevenson |
| Chief Executive | Irene Walker |
| *Dunbartonshire Enterprise* | |
| Chairman | Alan Thornton MBE |
| Chief Executive | David Anderson |
| *Enterprise Ayrshire* | |
| Chairman | Barry Allen |
| Chief Executive | David Macdonald |
| *Fife Enterprise* | |
| Chairman | Ray E Baker OBE |
| Chief Executive | Robert MacKenzie |
| *Forth Valley Enterprise* | |
| Chairman | Michael B Cantlay |
| Chief Executive | Bill Morton |
| *Glasgow Development Agency* | |
| Chairman | G Michael Lunn |
| Chief Executive | Stuart Gulliver |
| *Grampian Enterprise* | |
| Chairman | Maitland Mackie CBE |
| Chief Executive | Alan Sim |
| *Lanarkshire Development Agency* | |
| Chairman | Ian L Livingstone OBE |
| Chief Executive | Iain Carmichael |
| *Lothian & Edinburgh Enterprise* | |
| Chairman | Mike Walker |
| Chief Executive | Dr Des Bonnar |
| *Moray Badenoch & Strathspey Enterprise* | |
| Chairman | George A Chesworth OBE |
| Chief Executive | Dick Ruane |
| *Renfrewshire Enterprise* | |
| Chairman | John Ashworth OBE |
| Chief Executive | Tony Cassidy |
| *Scottish Borders Enterprise* | |
| Chairman | Tony Taylor |
| Chief Executive | David P Douglas |
| *Scottish Enterprise Tayside* | |
| Chairman | Iain McMillan |
| Chief Executive | Graham McKee |

**branches**

*Dumfries & Galloway Enterprise*
Solway House
Dumfries Enterprise Park
Tinwald Downs Road
Dumfries DG1 3SJ
Tel 01387 245000
Fax 01387 246224

*Dunbartonshire Enterprise*
2nd Floor
Spectrum House
Clydebank Business Park
Clydebank
Glasgow G81 2DR
Tel 0141 951 2121
Fax 0141 951 1907

*Enterprise Ayrshire*
17-19 Hill Street
Kilmarnock KA3 1HA
Tel 01563 526623
Fax 01563 543636

*Fife Enterprise*
Kingdom House
Saltire Centre
Glenrothes
Fife KY6 2AQ
Tel 01592 623000
Fax 01592 623149

*Lanarkshire Development Agency*
New Lanarkshire House
Strathclyde Business Park
Dove Wynd
Bellshill ML4 3AD
Tel 01698 745454
Fax 01698 842211

*Lothian & Edinburgh Enterprise*
99 Haymarket Terrace
Apex House
Edinburgh EH12 5HD
Tel 0131 313 4000
Fax 0131 313 4231

*Moray Badenoch & Strathspey Enterprise*
Elgin Business Centre
Maisondieu Road
Elgin
Morayshire IV30 1RH
Tel 01343 550567
Fax 01343 550678

*Renfrewshire Enterprise*
27 Causeyside Street
Paisley PA1 1UL
Tel 0141 848 0101
Fax 0141 848 6930

---

*Forth Valley Enterprise*
Laurel House
Laurelhill Business Park
Stirling FK7 9JQ
Tel 01786 451919
Fax 01786 478123

*Glasgow Development Agency*
Atrium Court
50 Waterloo Street
Glasgow G2 6HQ
Tel 0141 204 1111
Fax 0141 248 1600

*Grampian Enterprise*
27 Albyn Place
Aberdeen AB10 1DB
Tel 01224 575100
Fax 01224 213417

*Scottish Borders Enterprise*
Bridge Street
Galashiels TD1 1SW
Tel 01896 758991
Fax 01896 758625

*Scottish Enterprise Tayside*
45 North Lindsay Street
Dundee DD1 1HT
Tel 01382 223100
Fax 01382 201319

# Scottish Environment Protection Agency (SEPA)

Erskine Court
The Castle Business Park
Stirling FK9 4TR

**Tel** 01786 457700
**Fax** 01786 446885

**Contact** Monica Straughan

**E-mail** Monica.Straughan@sepa.org.uk
**Web** http://www.sepa.org.uk

| | |
|---|---|
| **status** | Executive body |
| **founded** | 1996 |
| **sponsor** | Scottish Office |
| **powers** | Environment Act 1995 |
| **mission** | To provide an efficient and integrated environmental protection system for Scotland, which will both improve the environment and contribute to the government's goal of sustainable development. |
| **tasks** | Principal functions are enforcing and monitoring environmental regulations which protect the land, air and water (eg issuing and reviewing licences/authorisations, inspecting sites, analysing samples, investigating complaints). Also developing environmental strategies. |
| **operations** | Management: The SEPA Board is responsible for strategy, resources and monetary performance. Head office in Stirling (run by Chief Executive) provides support and policy direction for the three Regions which are responsible for all operations. North Region HQ is in Dingwall (with eight local offices); West Region HQ is in East Kilbride (with five local offices); and East Region HQ is in Edinburgh (with five local offices). Each Region has its own board. 85% of staff are based in the Regions. |
| | Policy: Moving from being seen simply as a monitoring and control organisation to one which influences the pace and direction of environmental improvement. |
| | Trends: Environmental legislation is developing rapidly and SEPA is likely to be given additional duties. |
| **performance** | Performance measures have now been established. |
| **board** | Board is appointed by the Secretary of State. |

| | | |
|---|---|---|
| Chairman | Prof William Turmeau CBE | |
| Deputy Chairman | Alexander Buchan | |
| Chief Executive | Alasdair C Paton | |
| Members | Brian Fitzgerald | Prof Cliff Johnston |
| | Graeme Gordon OBE | Cllr Mrs Alison Magee |
| | David Hughes Hallet | Cllr Cormick McChord |
| | Cllr Alastair Hewat OBE | Cllr Mrs Jennifer Shaw |
| *Accounting Officer* | *Chief Executive* | |

| | |
|---|---|
| **staff** | 650 |

| Chief Executive | Alasdair Paton |
| Regional Director, West Region | John Beveridge |
| Director of Finance | John Ford |
| Director, East Region | William Halcrow |
| Director of Environmental Strategy | Ms Patricia Henton |
| Regional Director, North Region | Prof David Mackay |

*financial*

**INCOME & EXPENDITURE**

| Year end: 31 March | 1997 |
| | £000 |
| **INCOME** | |
| Grant-in-aid received | 23,714 |
| Income from charging schemes | 6,342 |
| Other income | 567 |
| | **30,623** |
| **EXPENDITURE** | |
| Staff costs | (17,084) |
| Depreciation | (2,646) |
| Other operating charges | (10,469) |
| | **(30,199)** |
| **OPERATING SURPLUS** | **424** |
| Interest receivable and similar income | 79 |
| Interest payable and similar charges | (324) |
| | **(245)** |
| **SURPLUS FOR THE FINANCIAL PERIOD** | **179** |

*advisers*  **Bankers**   The Royal Bank of Scotland

**Auditors**   KPMG

*publications*   *The State of Environment Report 1996*

*branches*

North
Graesser House
Fodderty Way
Dingwall Business Park
Dingwall IV15 9XB
Tel 01349 862021
Fax 01349 863987

East
Clearwater House
Heriot-Watt Research Park
Avenue North
Riccarton
Edinburgh EH14 4AP
Tel 0131 449 7296
Fax 0131 449 7277

West
Rivers House
Murray Road
East Kilbride G75 0LA
Tel 01355 574200
Fax 01355 264323

# Scottish Fisheries Protection Agency (SFPA)

Pentland House
47 Robb's Loan
Edinburgh EH14 1TY

**Tel** 0131 244 6093
**Fax** 0131 244 6471

*status*   Executive agency

*founded*   1991

*sponsor*   Scottish Office

*powers*   Framework Document 1991

*mission*   To enforce UK, EU and international fisheries laws and regulations in 185,000 square miles of Scottish waters and ports.

*tasks*   To deter and detect breaches of law and regulations through the effective deployment of ships, aircraft and fisheries inspectorate and the timely presentation of cases of breaches for prosecution. To provide information on fishing activity through a high level of sea and aerial surveillance of fishing grounds. To undertake regular inspections of fishing vessels at sea.

**operations**  Management: The Chief Executive is responsible to the Secretary of State. The Senior Management Board is responsible for the day-to-day operation and performance and is made up of the Chief Executive, the Marine Superintendent, Director of Operations and Director of Corporate Strategy and Resources.  Head office in Edinburgh.  Three Inspectorate District Offices (Northern, Western and Eastern), each with an Area Manager.

Policy: Investigating procuring replacement Fishery Protection Vessels through PFI.  Introduction of satellite monitoring system for fishing activity starting in 1998.

Trends: Larger fishing vessels have led to reductions in quotas.  Growing environmental concerns about the sustainability of current fishing practices.

**performance**  Seven out of ten targets met in 1996/97.

**board**

| Accounting Officer | Chief Executive |
|---|---|

**staff**  275

| Chief Executive | PE Du Vivier |
|---|---|
| Area Manager | Peter McDougall |
| Area Manager | Donald Miller |
| Area Manager | Cephas Ralph |
| Marine Superintendent | Captain R Mill Irving |
| Director of Corporate Strategy and Resources | JB Roddin |
| Director of Operations | RJ Walker |
| Head of Enforcement Policy | J Burns |
| Head of Finance and Procurement | G Craig |
| Engineer Superintendent | C Davis |
| Head of FIN Systems | L Gray |
| Controller, Operations Air and Sea | S McKerracher |
| Head of Personnel and Training | G Smith |
| Controller, Coastal Operations | A Stewart |

**financial**

INCOME & EXPENDITURE

| Year end: 31 March | 1997 £000 | 1996 £000 | 1995 £000 |
|---|---|---|---|
| **EXPENDITURE** | | | |
| Running costs | 12,306 | 11,807 | 11,660 |
| Depreciation and non-cash interest | 2,952 | 2,852 | 3,230 |
| Other non-cash costs and services provided from other votes | 1,034 | 1,065 | 1,105 |
| | 16,292 | 15,724 | 15,995 |
| **INCOME** | | | |
| Less income from services supplied in year | (3) | (5) | 28 |
| **NET COST OF OPERATIONS** | 16,289 | 15,719 | 15,967 |

**advisers**  **Auditors**  National Audit Office  22 Melville Street, Edinburgh EH3 7NS

**branches**
Longman House
Longman Road
Inverness
Tel 01463 713955

Russel House
King Street
Ayr
Tel 01292 610177

5 Albert Quay
Aberdeen
Tel 01224 211446

# Scottish Further Education Unit (SFEU)

Argyll Court
The Castle Business Park
Stirling FK9 4TY

**Tel** 01786 892000        **E-mail** sfeu@sfeu.demon.co.uk
**Fax** 01786 892001

| | |
|---|---|
| *status* | Executive body |
| *founded* | 1991 |
| *sponsor* | The Scottish Office Education and Industry Department. |
| *powers* | Further & Higher Education (Scotland) Act 1992 |
| *mission* | The national centre for the support and development of Scottish further education (FE) and its colleges. |
| *tasks* | Works in partnership with all 43 FE colleges in Scotland; developing an intelligence infrastructure across the sector; organises conferences and provides facilities; develops programmes and pilot schemes; college staff seconded into SFEU and to other vocational education and training organisations. |
| *operations* | Management: Four teams: Curriculum and Student Services, Enterprise and Organisation Development, Information Services, Client Services. |
| | Policy: Shares premises with Association of Scottish Colleges (ASC) and collaborates with them. |
| | Trends: Two new national research reports raising public debate and understanding of FE. |
| *board* | Board appointed by the Secretary of State on a 4 year term. |

| Chairman | Craig Brown OBE |
|---|---|
| Members | Muriel Dunbar |
| | Michael Leech |
| | Janet Lowe |
| | Malcolm MacKenzie |
| | Alison Reid |
| | Alan Tripp |
| | Alistair Tyre |

*staff*        40

| Chief Executive | Alison Reid |
|---|---|

*financial*

| INCOME & EXPENDITURE Year end: 31 March | 1997 £000 | 1996 £000 |
|---|---|---|
| **INCOME** | | |
| Grant-in-aid from SOEID | 720 | 635 |
| Other operating income | 724 | 964 |
| | 1,444 | 1,599 |
| **EXPENDITURE** | | |
| Staff costs | 858 | 900 |
| Other expenditure | 552 | 641 |
| | 1,410 | 1,541 |
| **SURPLUS/(DEFICIT) FOR YEAR** | 34 | 58 |
| Balance brought forward | 71 | 13 |
| **BALANCE CARRIED FORWARD** | 105 | 71 |

| *advisers* | **Bankers** | Bank of Scotland |
|---|---|---|
| | **Auditors** | Deloitte & Touche |
| | **Solicitors** | Maclay Murray & Spens |
| *publications* | *Broadcast* | |

# *Scottish Higher Education Funding Council (SHEFC)*

97 Haymarket Terrace
Edinburgh EH12

**Tel** 0131 313 6500
**Fax** 0131 313 6501          **Web** http://shefc.ac.uk/shefc/welcome.htm

| | |
|---|---|
| *status* | Executive body |
| *founded* | 1992 |
| *sponsor* | Scottish Office |
| *powers* | Further and Higher Education (Scotland) Act 1992 |
| *mission* | To promote the quality and encourage the expansion of teaching and research in Scottish higher education institutions. |
| *tasks* | Providing grants for teaching and research. Assessing the quality of teaching and learning. Providing Secretary of State with information and advice relating to all aspects of higher education in Scotland, including financial needs. |

*operations*  Management: SHEFC funding of £500 million represents around 45% of the income of Scottish higher education institutions and universities and colleges are accountable for ensuring value for money on their expenditure. There are eight Committees of the Council. A guide was published to enable members of governing bodies to perform their roles effectively and within the Nolan Committee recommendations.

Policy: Continuing to streamline the monitoring framework. Promoting the commercialisation of the science base through Technology Ventures initiative.

Trends: Increasing student numbers and decreasing public funding, at the same time as students set to pay towards tuition fees, makes robust standards for teaching and learning more important.

*performance*  Programme to assess the quality of teaching and learning was delayed by industrial action.

*board*  Council members are appointed by the Secretary of State.

| | | |
|---|---|---|
| Chairman | Prof Sir John C Shaw | |
| Members | Dr James G Adamson CBE | Dr Chris Masters |
| | Prof Geoffrey S Boulton | Prof Sheila AM McLean |
| | Prof Vicki Bruce OBE | Stewart Miller |
| | Prof Graeme RD Catto | Prof John Sizer CBE |
| | Sheena MM Cooper | Prof John Spence |
| | Ann Kettle | Dr Ian Sword |
| | Dr Valerie Maehle | James RG Wright |
| *Accounting Officer* | *Chief Executive* | |

*staff*  59

| | |
|---|---|
| Chief Executive | Prof John Sizer CBE |

*financial*

**INCOME & EXPENDITURE**

| Year end: 31 March | 1997 £000 | 1996 £000 | 1995 £000 |
|---|---|---|---|
| **INCOME** | | | |
| **Gross Income** | | | |
| HM government grant-in-aid received for: | | | |
| Distribution to institutions | 535,140 | 544,700 | 508,479 |
| Council running costs | 3,666 | 3,654 | 3,438 |
| | **538,806** | **548,354** | **511,917** |
| Other grants | 353 | 358 | 1,046 |
| Other operating income | 29 | 9 | 18 |
| | **539,188** | **548,721** | **512,981** |
| **EXPENDITURE** | | | |
| Grants paid to institutions | 535,548 | 541,929 | 511,203 |
| Staff costs | 1,597 | 1,591 | 1,717 |
| Depreciation | 162 | 152 | 135 |
| Other operating charges | 1,981 | 1,979 | 1,548 |
| | **539,288** | **545,651** | **514,603** |

| (DEFICIT)/SURPLUS ON OPERATING ACTIVITIES | (100) | 3,070 | (1,622) |
|---|---|---|---|
| Interest receivable | 1 | 2 | 2 |
| Notional interest payable | (49) | - | - |
| (DEFICIT)/SURPLUS ON ORDINARY ACTIVITIES | (148) | 3,072 | (1,620) |
| Reversal of notional interest | 49 | - | - |
| RETAINED (DEFICIT)/SURPLUS FOR THE YEAR | (99) | 3,072 | (1,620) |
| Balance brought forward | 5,773 | 2,701 | 4,321 |
| RETAINED SURPLUS CARRIED FORWARD | 5,674 | 5,773 | 2,701 |

*advisers*  **Auditors**  National Audit Office  22 Melville Street, Edinburgh EH3 7NS

# Scottish Homes

Thistle House
91 Haymarket Terrace
Edinburgh EH12 5HE

**Tel** 0131 313 0044
**Fax** 0131 313 2680

*status*  Executive body

*founded*  1989

*sponsor*  Scottish Office

*powers*  Housing (Scotland) Act 1988

*mission*  To enable the effective provision of good quality housing and stimulate self-motivated communities.

*tasks*  Improving the quality, variety and cost-effectiveness of housing available in Scotland. It promotes home owner-ship and contributes to providing low-cost homes for sale; provides a greater variety of the type and size of homes to rent, from a wider choice of landlord; provides homes for homeless people and for those with special needs. It works with other agencies in the public and private sector to provide appropriate housing for the development of thriving communities.

*operations*  Management: Chief Executive based in Edinburgh but strong local network. Five new regions, each headed by a Managing Director. Since 1989, over £1 billion has been raised from the private sector: now every £1 of public money spent is matched by almost £1 of private investment.

Policy: Sale of their own houses continues in line with policy and will eventually lead to Scottish Homes with-drawing from its existing landlord role.

Trends: Further staff reductions.

*performance*  Met or bettered the set targets in 1996/97.

*board*  All Board members are appointed by the Secretary of State with the exception of the Chief Executive who is appointed by the Board with the approval of the Secretary of State.

| Chairman | John Ward CBE | |
|---|---|---|
| Chief Executive | Peter McKinlay | |
| Members | Ann Clark | Mrs Frances McCall MBE |
| | Alastair Dempster | Mrs Daphne Sleigh |
| | Mrs Pat Greenhill OBE | Prof John Small CBE |
| | Prof Duncan Maclennan CBE | John D Spencely |
| *Accounting Officer* | *Chief Executive* | |

*staff*  948

| Chief Executive | Peter McKinlay |
|---|---|
| Director of Finance | John Breslin |
| Director of Housing Management | Richard Burn |
| Director of Operations | Andrew Fyfe |
| Director of Development Funding | Jim Hastie |
| Head of Public Affairs | Bill Hoy |
| Director of Management Consultancy Services/Chief Policy Advisor | Maud Marshall |
| Director of Strategy, Policy & Planning | Bob Millar |

| | | | |
|---|---|---|---|
| Head of Human Resource Development | Eileen Scott | | |
| Director of Research & Innovation Services | Raymond Young | | |
| Director of Housing Management | Richard Burn | | |
| Director of Development Funding | Jim Hastie | | |

*financial*

### INCOME & EXPENDITURE

| Year end: 31 March | 1997 £000 | 1996 £000 | 1995 £000 |
|---|---|---|---|
| **INCOME** | | | |
| Rents receivable | 66,901 | 76,707 | 85,070 |
| Interest receivable | 11,740 | 12,227 | 12,132 |
| Surplus on disposal of fixed assets | 1,486 | - | 2,447 |
| Other income | 6,986 | 6,174 | 8,134 |
| | 87,113 | 95,108 | 107,783 |
| **EXPENDITURE** | | | |
| Repairs, maintenance and special services | 22,239 | 23,932 | 24,979 |
| Housing association grants | 266,510 | 288,373 | 275,563 |
| Other grants | 40,977 | 39,033 | 44,853 |
| Interest payable | 50,450 | 50,887 | 51,040 |
| Administration | 38,706 | 39,010 | 39,031 |
| Depreciation | 653 | 3,197 | 3,446 |
| Loss on disposal of building division | - | 263 | - |
| Loss on disposal of fixed assets | - | 2,518 | - |
| Revaluation adjustment | 26,749 | 33,826 | 6,361 |
| | 446,284 | 481,039 | 445,273 |
| **EXCESS OF EXPENDITURE OVER INCOME** | (359,171) | (385,931) | (337,490) |

*advisers*

**Auditors**  National Audit Office    22 Melville Street, Edinburgh EH3 7NS

*branches*

*Scottish Homes*
Rosebery House
9 Haymarket Terrace
Edinburgh EH12 5YA
Tel 0131 313 0044

*Scottish Homes*
Carlyle House
Carlyle Road
Kirkcaldy KY1 1DB
Tel 01592 641055

*Scottish Homes*
Mercantile Chambers
53 Bothwell Street
Glasgow G2 6TS
Tel 0141 248 7177

*Highlands, Islands & Grampian*
Urquhart House
Beechwood Park
Inverness IV2 3BW
Tel 01463 711272

*Tayside & Fife*
Nethergate Business Centre
Dundee DD1 4BU
Tel 01382 202211

*Lanarkshire & Central*
Rex House
Bothwell Road
Hamilton ML3 0DW
Tel 01698 420042

*Ayrshire, Dumfries & Galloway*
52/66 Newmarket Street
Ayr KA7 1LR
Tel 01292 611810

*North & South Clyde*
St James House
25 St James Street
Paisley PA3 2HQ
Tel 0141 889 8896

*Glasgow City*
Highlander House
53 Waterloo Street
Glasgow G2 7DA
Tel 0141 226 4611

*North & East District*
147 Fintry Drive
Dundee DD4 9HE
Tel 01382 504317

*Central & South West*
Temperance House
8 Lint Riggs
Falkirk FK1 1DG
Tel 01324 613376

# Scottish Hospital Endowments Research Trust (SHERT)

Saltire Court
20 Castle Terrace
Edinburgh EH1 2EF

**Tel** 0131 228 8111
**Fax** 0131 228 8118

*status*     Executive body

*founded*     1953

*sponsor*     Scottish Office

*powers*     Hospital Endowment (Scotland) Act 1953. NHS (Scotland) Act 1978. NHS & Community Care Act 1990

*mission*     To receive and hold endowments, donations and bequests and to make grants from these funds to support medical research in Scotland.

*tasks*     To administer and invest the funds; make grants to fund high-quality research, equipment, and research scholarships and fellowships for young doctors; engage in fundraising activities; develop and exploit ideas and intellectual property.

*operations*     Management: Administered by the Members (all unpaid), who are advised by the Chief Scientist for Scotland's Acute Healthcare Research Committee. The Corporate Plan is agreed with the Scottish Office. Trust Secretaries run day-to-day administration.

Policy: Giving preference to applications from younger research workers.

Trends: Income from investment and fundraising rising; also public awareness of SHERT.

*performance*     Performance targets and achievements are reported in each *Annual Report*.

*board*     Members of the Trust are appointed by the Secretary of State from Scottish academic, biomedical and business communities. The Trust is administered by its Secretaries.

*staff*     Two

*financial*

| INCOME & EXPENDITURE Year end: 31 March | 1997 £ | 1996 £ | 1995 £ |
|---|---|---|---|
| **INCOME** | | | |
| Investment income | 1,021,743 | 1,118,391 | 887,744 |
| Legacies and donations | 237,008 | 656,796 | 236,454 |
| Royalties | 30,725 | 39,204 | 29,841 |
| | 1,299,476 | 1,814,391 | 1,154,039 |
| **EXPENDITURE** | | | |
| Grants provided, less provisions no longer required | 759,516 | 549,516 | 1,089,591 |
| Expenses of administration | 219,425 | 176,827 | 153,786 |
| | - | - | 1,243,377 |
| **INCOME SURPLUS/(DEFICIT) FOR YEAR** | 320,535 | 1,088,048 | (89,338) |
| Transfer to endowment fund | | 495,739 | - |
| **NET INCOME SURPLUS/(DEFICIT) FOR YEAR** | 320,535 | 592,309 | (89,338) |
| Income balance brought forward | 672,588 | 80,279 | 169,617 |
| **INCOME BALANCE CARRIED FORWARD** | 993,123 | 672,588 | 80,279 |

*advisers*

**Auditors**          Chiene & Tuit          3 Albyn Place, Edinburgh EH2 4NQ

**Secretaries**          Turcan Connell WS          Saltire Court, 20 Castle Terrace Edinburgh EH12EF

**Public Relations**          Fiona Selkirk Public Relations          1 Railway Cottages, Neilston Road Paisley PA2 6QA

*publications*     Annual Reports and Accounts 1996/97

# *Scottish Legal Aid Board*

44 Drumsheugh Gardens
Edinburgh EH3 7SW

**Tel** 0131 226 7061
**Fax** 0131 220 4878

**Contact** Fiona Shaw, Communications Manager

| | |
|---|---|
| *status* | Executive body |
| *founded* | 1987 |
| *sponsor* | Scottish Office, Home Department |
| *powers* | Legal Aid (Scotland) Act 1986. Crime and Punishment (Scotland) Act 1997 |
| *mission* | To make the most effective use of public funds available for legal aid in Scotland. |
| *tasks* | To assess and grant legal aid applications; to scrutinise and pay solicitors' and advocates' legal aid accounts; to advise the Secretary of State for Scotland on legal aid matters. Under Part V of the Crime and Punishment (Scotland) Act 1997, the Board is now responsible for issuing a code of practice on criminal legal aid practitioners, and setting up a pilot public defence solicitors scheme. |

*operations*  Management: the Chief Executive (who is also a Board member) is appointed by the Secretary of State for Scotland and reports to the Board. Board members and staff work closely together on a number of committees and working groups.

Policy: First published corporate plan (1996-1999) states five aims: improve efficient delivery and quality of service; enhance staff's ability to improve service; advise the Secretary of State on ways to achieve better value for money from publicly funded legal services; promote improvement in the legal aid services purchased on behalf of the public; and be open and effective in communications with staff and customers.

Trends: The cost of legal aid continues to rise despite a slight drop in the numbers of applications received in 1996/97. The greatest part of this expenditure is on criminal legal aid: public defence solicitors scheme will help assess whether criminal legal aid can be provided at less cost to the public purse. Information technology and staff training seen as key to future improvements in operational efficiency.

Proposals (1996) to the Secretary of State for standard fees for summary criminal cases; power to employ solicitors in advice agencies to provide more effective first-level advice; right of access to solicitors' offices to investigate any suspicion of abuse; and mounting a pilot public defenders scheme.

*board*  Appointed by the Secretary of State for Scotland. Members come from a broad range of interests, not just the legal profession, and have a diversity of skills and knowledge.

| | | |
|---|---|---|
| Chairman | Christine AM Davis | |
| Members | Kay Blair | Robert J Livingstone |
| | Sheila Campbell | Colin N McEachran QC |
| | Jean Couper | Yvonne Osman |
| | Peter H Grinyer | Margaret Scanlan |
| | Sheriff Alexander Jessop | Richard Scott |
| | Nick Kuenssberg | Alexander F Wylie QC |
| *Accounting Officer* | *Chief Executive* | |

*staff*  268

| | |
|---|---|
| Chief Executive | Richard Scott |
| Director of Audit | Ian G Middleton |
| Director of Operations | Stephen O'Connor |
| Director of Human Resources | Claire Reid |
| Director of Information Systems | Paul Thrustle |
| Director of Legal Services | Elizabeth Watson |

*financial*

**SCOTTISH LEGAL AID FUND RECEIPTS & PAYMENTS**

| Year end: 31 March | 1997 £000 | 1996 £000 | 1995 £000 |
|---|---|---|---|
| **RECEIPTS** | | | |
| HM government grant | 133,648 | 125,658 | 124,800 |
| Operating receipts | 36,753 | 36,760 | 30,458 |
| | **170,401** | **162,418** | **155,258** |
| **PAYMENTS** | | | |
| Operating payments | 169,682 | 158,993 | 154,029 |
| Other payments | 1,414 | 1,403 | 1,462 |
| | 171,096 | 160,396 | 155,491 |
| **(SURPLUS)/DEFICIT OF PAYMENTS OVER RECEIPTS** | (695) | 2,022 | (233) |
| Balance brought forward from previous year | 7,221 | 5,199 | 5,432 |
| **BALANCE CARRIED FORWARD** | **6,526** | **7,221** | **5,199** |

**SCOTTISH LEGAL AID BOARD RECEIPTS & PAYMENTS**

| Year End: 31 March | 1997 £000 | 1996 £000 | 1995 £000 |
|---|---|---|---|
| **RECEIPTS** | | | |
| HM government grant-in-aid | 7,037 | 7,317 | 7,487 |
| Pensions contributions and transfers | 167 | 272 | 212 |
| Less: surrendered as consolidated fund extra receipt | 0 | 102 | 42 |
| | **7,204** | **7,487** | **7,657** |
| **PAYMENTS** | | | |
| Salaries (including payments to reporters) and other related expenses | 4,886 | 4,839 | 5,039 |
| Superannuation | 364 | 243 | 347 |
| Accommodation | 630 | 925 | 851 |
| Computer services | 150 | 182 | 121 |
| Printing, stationery, post and telecommunications | 404 | 418 | 582 |
| Office equipment | 145 | 219 | 149 |
| Audit fees | 22 | 32 | 19 |
| Other expenses | 384 | 290 | 237 |
| Non-recurring costs | 181 | 341 | 312 |
| | **7,166** | **7,489** | **7,657** |
| **SURPLUS/(DEFICIT) OF RECEIPTS OVER PAYMENTS** | 38 | (2) | 0 |
| Balance brought forward from previous year | 4 | 6 | 6 |
| **BALANCE CARRIED FORWARD** | **42** | **4** | **6** |

*advisers* **Bankers** Royal Bank of Scotland
**Auditors** Price Waterhouse

*publications* Annual Report, Corporate Plan, The Scottish Legal Aid Handbook, The Legal Aid Fees and Taxation Guidelines, Guidelines on Repasation Cases, The Recorder (Newsletter), Code of Practice on Criminal Legal Assistance

# Scottish Medical Practices Committee (SMPC)

Trinity Park House
South Trinity Road
Edinburgh EH5 3PY

**Tel** 0131 551 6255
**Fax** 0131 551 4305

*status* Executive body
*founded* 1947
*sponsor* Scottish Office
*powers* NHS (Scotland) Act 1947. (Amended by the 1978 Act and the NHS General Medical Services (Scotland) regulations 1995)
*mission* To ensure an adequate number of general medical practitioners within each health board area in Scotland.
*tasks* Deals with applications to join or withdraw from a health board's GP medical list (also to vary a GPs commitment); clarifies policy issues; approves accounts of inducement practitioners; considers annual reports of health boards to assess the adequacy of general medical services; produces statistics on supply of GPs.

| | | |
|---|---|---|
| *operations* | Management: The Committee meets about 20 times a year. | |
| | Policy: Currently undertaking annual GP Recruitment Survey. | |
| *board* | Committee appointed by the Secretary of State. | |

| Chairman | Dr Graham McIntosh MBE | |
|---|---|---|
| Members | Mrs Evelyn Brunton | Dr Kenneth Harden |
| | Miss Avril Hamilton | Dr Jackie McDonald |

*staff*  Two

| Secretary | Denise M Booth-Alexander |
|---|---|
| Assistant Secretary | Mrs H Whitton |

# Scottish Natural Heritage (SNH)

12 Hope Terrace
Edinburgh EH9 2AS

**Tel** 0131 447 4784
**Fax** 0131 446 2277

| | |
|---|---|
| *status* | Executive body |
| *founded* | 1992 |
| *sponsor* | Scottish Office |
| *powers* | Wildlife and Countryside Act 1981 |
| *mission* | To work with Scotland's people to care for its natural heritage - wildlife, the habitat and the landscape. |
| *tasks* | Safeguarding and enhancing Scotland's natural heritage through conservation, restoration and rehabilitation; provision of financial assistance to a wide range of bodies. Fostering awareness and understanding through environmental education. Promoting the enjoyment of, and responsible public access to, the countryside. Advising the government and others about the management and the use of the natural heritage and encouraging environmental sustainability in all forms of economic activity. |
| *operations* | Management: The Management Team comprises the Chief Executive, the Director of Corporate Services and three Directors of Strategy and Operations, each of whom has responsibility for a number of the 11 regional areas. The regional Area Managers are key decision-makers in SNH. |
| | Policy: SNH aims to secure the management of The Cairngorms, and Loch Lomond & the Trossachs. Policy guidelines on wind farms has been produced. |
| | Trends: Increasing working in partnership with local and national interests and organisations. |
| *performance* | Of the 21 targets set, only one was not met and eight were exceeded. |
| *board* | Main Board appointed by the Secretary of State. Scientific Advisory Committee and four Regional Boards. |

| Chairman | Magnus Magnusson KBE | |
|---|---|---|
| Vice Chairman | Prof Roger Wheater OBE | |
| Members | Seaton Baxter | Ivor Lewis |
| | Nan Burnett OBE | Peter Mackay CB |
| | Barbara Kelly CBE | Peter Peacock |
| | David Laird | Bill Ritchie |
| | Fred Last | Prof Chris Smout |
| Accounting Officer | Chief Executive | |
| | | |
| *North Areas Board* | | |
| Chairman | Bill Ritchie | |
| Members | Amanda Bryan | |
| | Dr Michael Foxley | Dr James Hunter |
| | Simon Fraser | Annie MacDonald |
| | Nigel Graham | Janet Price |
| | Hugh Halcro-Johnston | Michael Scott |
| | Isobel Holborn | Dr Kenneth Swanson |

*East Areas Board*

| | | |
|---|---|---|
| Chairman | Nan Burnett OBE | |
| Members | Andrew Bradford | Robert Kay |
| | Ian Currie | Jim McCarthy |
| | Elizabeth Hay | Prof John McManus |
| | Bill Howatson | Capt Tony Wilks |

*West Areas Board*

| | | |
|---|---|---|
| Chairman | Barbara Kelly CBE | |
| Members | Colin Carnie | Robin Malcolm |
| | Lady Isobel Glasgow | Dr Malcolm Ogilvie |
| | Dr Jim Hansom | Dr Phil Ratcliffe |
| | Dr Ralph Kirkwood | Richard Williamson |

*Scientific Advisory Committee*

| | | |
|---|---|---|
| Chairman | Prof Paul Racey | |
| Members | Ian Currie | |
| | Prof John Davenport | Prof John McManus |
| | Prof Charles Gimingham OBE | Dr Malcolm Ogilvie |
| | Dr Jim Hansom | Dr Phil Ratcliffe |
| | Dr Ralph Kirkwood | Michael Scott |
| | Prof Fred Last | Prof Chris Smout CBE |
| | Prof Jack Matthews | Prof Brian Staines |
| | Prof Jeff Maxwell | Prof Roger Wheater OBE |

**staff**  627

| | |
|---|---|
| Chief Executive | Roger Crofts |
| Director of Strategy & Operations (East) | Dr Ian Jardine |
| Director of Corporate Services | Lindsay Montgomery |
| Director of Strategy & Operations | John Thomson |
| Director of Strategy & Operations | Dr Jeff Watson |
| Head of National Strategy | Jane Dalgleish |
| Head of Advisory Services | Dr Colin Galbraith |
| Head of Press & PR | Audrey Ramsay |
| Chief Scientist | Prof Michael B Usher |
| Area Manager, Argyll & Sterling | Gerard Henry |
| Area Manager, Strathclyde & Ayrshire | Angus Laing |
| Area Manager, Dumfries & Galloway | Dr Marion Hughes |
| Area Manager, Northern Isles | Ruth Briggs |
| Area Manager, East Highland | George Hogg |
| Area Manager, North Highland | Dr Terry Keatinge |
| Area Manager, West Highland | Dr Greg Mudge |
| Area Manager, Western Isles | David Maclennan |
| Area Manager, Grampian | Ron MacDonald |
| Area Manager, Tayside | Philip Gaskell |
| Area Manager, Forth & Borders | John Burlison |

**financial**

| INCOME & EXPENDITURE Year end: 31 March | 1997 £000 | 1996 £000 | 1995 £000 |
|---|---:|---:|---:|
| **INCOME** | | | |
| HM government grant-in-aid | 34,856 | 38,615 | 37,039 |
| Income from activities | 840 | 584 | 532 |
| Other operating income | 17 | 43 | 53 |
| Transferred from deferred government grant account | 1,558 | 1,701 | 1,574 |
| Ring fenced grant-in-aid to JNCC | 1,164 | 1,343 | 1,473 |
| | **38,435** | **42,286** | **40,671** |
| **EXPENDITURE** | | | |
| Maintenance of National Nature Reserves | 485 | 1,282 | 1,101 |
| Management agreements | 4,007 | 5,873 | 4,303 |
| Research and advisory services | 3,109 | 4,685 | 4,589 |
| Grants | 7,796 | 7,894 | 7,781 |
| Loan charges | 471 | 821 | 1,290 |
| Other operating costs | 6,349 | 6,963 | 6,818 |
| Board members and staff costs | 13,170 | 12,928 | 11,278 |
| Depreciation | 1,518 | 1,691 | 1,520 |
| Notional charges | 2,176 | 2,353 | 2,421 |
| Annual JNCC contribution | 1,164 | 1,343 | 1,473 |
| Early retirement provision | 485 | - | - |
| | **40,730** | **45,833** | **42,574** |

| DEFICIT ON OPERATING ACTIVITIES BEFORE | | | |
|---|---|---|---|
| **SUPERANNUATION** | (2,295) | (3,547) | (1,903) |
| Superannuation receipts | 264 | 385 | 491 |
| **DEFICIT ON OPERATING ACTIVITIES** | **(2,031)** | **(3,162)** | **(1,412)** |
| Interest income | 124 | 222 | 114 |
| **DEFICIT ON ORDINARY ACTIVITIES** | **(1,907)** | **(2,940)** | **(1,298)** |
| Notional charges | 2,131 | 2,303 | 2,322 |
| Appropriations: amounts surrendered to the Scottish Office | - | (197) | (490) |
| **RETAINED (DEFICIT)/SURPLUS FOR THE YEAR** | **224** | **(834)** | **534** |

**branches**

*Argyll & Stirling*
The Beta Centre
Innovation Park
University of Stirling
Stirling FK9 4NF
Tel 01786 450362
Fax 01786 451974

*Strathclyde & Ayrshire*
Caspian House
Mariner Court
Clydebank Business Park
Clydebank G81 2NR
Tel 0141 951 4488
Fax 0141 951 8948

*Dumfries & Galloway*
Carmont House
The Crichton
Bankend Road
Dumfries DG1 4ZF
Tel 01387 247010
Fax 01387 259247

*Northern Isles*
Ground Floor
Stewart Building
Alexandra Wharf
Lerwick
Shetland ZE1 OLL
Tel 01595 693345
Fax 01595 692565

*East Highland*
Fodderty Way
Dingwall Business Park
Dingwall IV15 9XB
Tel 01349 865333
Fax 01349 865609

*North Highland*
Main Street
Golspie
Sutherland KW10 6TG
Tel 01408 633602
Fax 01408 633071

*West Highland*
The Governor's House
The Parade
Fort William
Inverness-shire PH33 6BA
Tel 01397 704716
Fax 01397 700303

*Western Isles*
32 Francis Street
Stornoway
Isle of Lewis HS1 2ND
Tel 01851 705258
Fax 01851 704900

*Grampian*
16/17 Rubislaw Terrace
Aberdeen AB1 1XE
Tel 01224 642863
Fax 01224 635020

*Tayside*
Battleby
Redgorton
Perth PH1 3EW
Tel 01738 444177
Fax 01738 442060

*Forth & Borders*
Laundry House
Dalkeith Country Park
Dalkeith
Midlothian EH22 2NA
Tel 0131 654 2466
Fax 0131 654 2477

# Scottish Office Pensions Agency (SOPA)

St Margaret's House
151 London Rd
Edinburgh EH8 7TG

**Tel** 0131 244 3585
**Fax** 0131 244 3334

**E-mail** Derek.Smith@spoi.scottoff.gov.uk
**Web** http://www.scotland.gov.uk

**status** Executive agency
**founded** 1993
**sponsor** Scottish Office

| | |
|---|---|
| **powers** | Exchequer and Audit Departments Act 1921. SOPA Framework Document 1993 |
| **mission** | To provide an efficient and effective service for those who use the pension schemes. |
| **tasks** | Responsible for administrating and regulating the pension arrangements, injury benefit and compensation schemes of over 370,000 people, mainly employees of NHS Scotland and teaching services. It collects and pays the sums due under the schemes. SOPA exercises regulatory and appellate functions in respect of local authority schemes. |
| **operations** | Management: The Chief Executive, who reports directly to the Secretary of State, is supported by three Directors (Policy; Operations; Resources and Customer Services). Business plans, including key targets, and corporate plans covering the following three years are prepared annually and agreed by the Secretary of State. |
| | Policy: New IT system is expected to increase efficiency. |
| | Trends: Reinstatement of rights in mis-selling of pensions cases continues. |
| **performance** | Replacement of IT systems project was a year late but targets for accuracy, quality and output were met. |
| **board** | None. |

| Accounting Officer | Chief Executive |
|---|---|

| | |
|---|---|
| **staff** | 169 |

| | |
|---|---|
| Chief Executive | Ralph Garden |
| Director of Resources and Customer Services | Murray McDermott |
| Director of Policy | Gavin Mowat |
| Director of Operations | Alistair Small |
| Teachers Scheme Manager | Tom Darling |
| IT Services Manager | Malcolm de Lorey |
| NHS Scheme Manager | Gordon Taylor |

**financial**

| EXPENDITURE Year end: 31 March | 1997 £000 | 1996 £000 |
|---|---|---|
| Staff costs | 2897 | 2972 |
| Other operating charges | 2249 | 2394 |
| Depreciation | 101 | 63 |
| Expenditure before interest | 5247 | 5429 |
| Interest | 58 | 55 |
| TOTAL EXPENDITURE | 5305 | 5484 |

| | | | |
|---|---|---|---|
| **advisers** | **Auditors** | National Audit Office | 22 Melville Street Edinburgh EH3 7NS |
| | **Solicitors** | Scottish Office Solicitors | Victoria Quay, Edinburgh EH6 6QQ |
| **publications** | *Annual Report & Accounts* | | |

# Scottish Prison Service (SPS)

Calton House
5 Redheughs Rigg
Edinburgh EH12 9HW

**Tel** 0131 556 8400
**Fax** 0131 244 8476

| | |
|---|---|
| **status** | Executive agency |
| **founded** | 1993 |
| **sponsor** | Scottish Office |
| **powers** | SPS Framework Document 1993 |
| **mission** | To provide a prison service in Scotland. |
| **tasks** | To keep in custody those committed by the courts; to maintain good order in each prison; to care for prisoners with humanity; to provide prisoners with a range of opportunities to exercise personal responsibility and to prepare for release. |

**operations**   Management: The Chief Executive is supported by the Prisons Board, comprising the six Executive Directors and two Non-Executive Directors. Each of the 22 establishments is managed by a Governor-in-Charge. They are grouped into two regional areas under the line management of the Area Directors.

Policy: Suicide prevention strategy has been reviewed. Research continues into drug abuse in prisons. Mandatory drug testing was introduced in 1997.

Trends: Record numbers of prisoners leading to severe pressure on prisons. New prison at Kilmarnock to be designed, Built and operated by private sector.

**performance**   Targets on escapes met but targets regarding prisoners' self-development not met.

**board**   Non-Executive Directors appointed by the Secretary of State.

| | |
|---|---|
| Chief Executive | Edward Frizzell |
| Director of Custody | John Durno |
| Non-Executive Director | Margaret Ford |
| Director of Strategy & Corporate Affairs | Jinny Hutchison |
| Director of Finance & Information Systems | Willie Pretswell |
| Area Director North & East | Peter Russell |
| Area Director South & West | Peter Withers |
| *Accounting Officer* | *Chief Executive* |

**staff**   4750

**financial**

| INCOME & EXPENDITURE | | |
|---|---|---|
| Year end: 31 March | **1997** | **1996** |
| | **£000** | **£000** |
| **INCOME** | | |
| Income from all sources | 5,688 | 2,462 |
| **EXPENDITURE** | | |
| Staff costs | 115,527 | 116,327 |
| Running costs | 53,840 | 50,179 |
| Other current expenditure | 13,334 | 11,620 |
| | **182,701** | **178,126** |
| **OPERATING DEFICIT** | **177,013** | **175,664** |
| Interest on capital | 22,943 | 21,624 |
| Interest payable and similar charges | 12 | 9 |
| **NET COST OF OPERATIONS** | **199,968** | **197,297** |

**advisers**   **Auditors**          National Audit Office

**publications**   *Annual Report*, *Annual Corporate Plan*, *SPS Special* (staff newspaper), *SPS Briefing* (staff briefing document), *The Gallery* (prisoner newsletter)

# Scottish Qualifications Authority (SQA)

Ironmills Road
Dalkeith
Midlothian EH22 ILE

**Tel** 0131 663 6601
**Fax** 0131 654 2664

**status**   Executive body

**founded**   1997

**sponsor**   Scottish Office

**powers**   Education Act 1996

**mission**   Single national body responsible for most types of qualification in Scotland's schools, colleges, workplaces and training centres.

**tasks**   Developing, awarding and accrediting qualifications (Standard Grades, Higher Grades, CSYS, National Certificate Clusters, Skillstarts, GSVQs, SVQs, HNCs and HNDs, and PDAs) and ensures that they are of a high and consistent quality. Also runs training and development courses. Responsible for conducting National Testing of 5-14 year olds.

| | |
|---|---|
| *operations* | Management: A merger of the Scottish Examination Board and the Scottish Vocational Educational Council (SCOTVEC). |
| | Policy: Introducing new system which will unify academic and vocational education. |
| *board* | Members appointed by the Secretary of State. |

| | |
|---|---|
| Chairman | David Miller CBE |
| Chief Executive | Ron Tuck |

| | |
|---|---|
| *staff* | 505 |
| *branches* | Hanover House<br>24 Douglas St<br>Glasgow G2 7NQ<br>Tel 0141 248 7900<br>Fax 0141 242 2244 |

# Scottish Record Office (SRO)

HM General Register House
Edinburgh EH1 3YY

**Tel** 0131 535 1314
**Fax** 0131 535 1360

| | |
|---|---|
| *status* | Executive agency |
| *founded* | 1993 (as agency) |
| *sponsor* | Scottish Office |
| *mission* | To preserve the public records of Scotland and make them available for public inspection. |
| *tasks* | Preserving, cataloguing, acquiring new records (both public and private) and making them easily available to the public. Also promoting the growth and maintenance of proper archive provision and undertaking extensive conservation treatments. Exhibitions and publications form an important part of its work. |
| *operations* | Management: The Keeper of the Records of Scotland is assisted by the Deputy Keeper and by eight Branch Heads. Arrangement with the Scottish Office for electronic formats are well in hand. |
| | Policy: Growth of amount of material in computer catalogue. Scottish National Archives Policy to be established. Application to National Lottery to establish an electronic National Archives network under discussion and further private finance may be needed. |
| | Trends: SRO keeping up pressure on local authorities to establish archives. Continuing reduction in running costs as budget has been cut again. |
| *performance* | Only one target was not met. |
| *board* | Advisory Council appointed by the Secretary of State. |

| Chairman | Prof M Anne Crowther | |
|---|---|---|
| Members | Lord Cameron of Lochbroom | Miss MM Stewart |
| | Dr David Ditchburn | Dr AM Tod |
| | Earl of Dundonald | Mrs JH Webster |
| | MAJ Gossip | Sheriff JF Wheatley |
| | Prof M Lynch | Dr John Womersley |
| | WW Scott | |
| *Accounting Officer* | *Keeper of the Records* | |

| | |
|---|---|
| *staff* | 140 |

| | |
|---|---|
| Keeper of the Records of Scotland | Patrick M Cadell |
| Deputy Keeper | Peter D Anderson |
| Head, Private Records | Ishbel Barnes |
| Head, Publications & Education | Rosemary M Gibson |
| Head, Court & Legal Services | Ian D Grant |
| Head, Private Records | Barbara LH Horn |
| Head, Preservation Services | Alison Horsburgh |
| Head, Government Records | Frances J Shaw |
| Head, Reader Services | John S Shaw |
| Head, General Services | Patricia HB Smith |

| financial | RECEIPTS & PAYMENTS | | |
|---|---|---|---|
| | Year end: 31 March | 1997 | 1996 |
| | | £000 | £000 |
| | **PAYMENTS** | | |
| | **Running costs** | | |
| | Employee expenses | 2,551 | 2,556 |
| | Premises related expenses | 2,104 | 2,200 |
| | Supplies and services | 322 | 396 |
| | | **4,977** | **5,152** |
| | **Capital costs** | | |
| | Land and buildings | 1,265 | 943 |
| | Office equipment | 39 | 34 |
| | Purchase of documents | 1 | 3 |
| | | **1,305** | **980** |
| | Grant payments | 18 | 16 |
| | | **6,300** | **6,148** |
| | **RECEIPTS** | | 722 |
| | Fees and charges | 851 | 722 |
| | Agency work | 6 | 23 |
| | | **857** | **745** |
| | **NET OPERATING COSTS** | **5,443** | **5,403** |

# Scottish Screen

74 Victoria Crescent Road
Glasgow G12 9JN

**Tel** 0141 302 1700
**Fax** 0141 302 1711

**E-mail** info@scottishscreen.demon.co.uk
**Web** www.scottishscreen.demon.co.uk

| | |
|---|---|
| *status* | Executive body |
| *founded* | 1997 |
| *sponsor* | Scottish Office |
| *powers* | Memorandum & Articles of Association |
| *mission* | To provide a one-stop film and television agency for Scotland. |
| *tasks* | Brings together education, training, script development, production finance, locations, marketing, exhibition and archive; provides funding, advice, courses; stimulates debate on film and television matters in Scotland; represents the interests of the industry to government. |
| *operations* | Management: Formed from the merger of the Scottish Film Council, Scottish Screen Locations, Scottish Film Production Fund and Scottish Broadcast & Film Training. Run by board of 12 associated panels. |

*operations* (continued)

Policy: New locations marketing plan to put Scottish Screen at centre of network of film offices around Scotland. Encouraging local authorities to establish film offices for locations and to support film and TV producers. Scottish Film Enterprise unit undertaking a feasibility study for a film studio in Scotland; also for Scottish Film Producer Support Scheme. Scottish Screen Training became the SVQ Assessment Centre for the industry in Scotland and is developing a New Entrant Producer Scheme.

Trends: Government plans to double audiences of British films in British cinemas and an injection of Lottery money is expected to boost Scottish industry's prospects.

| | |
|---|---|
| *performance* | Targets have been set for 1998/99. |
| *board* | Appointed by the Secretary of State. |

| Chairman | *to be announced* | |
|---|---|---|
| Members | Peter Broughan | |
| | Stuart Cosgrove | Scott Meek |
| | Stephen Forster | Mary Picken |
| | Jim Loni | Phillip Schlesinger |
| | Ray Macfarlane | David Strachan |
| | Eileen Mackay | Michael Walker |
| *Accounting Officer* | *Chief Executive* | |

*staff*     36

| | | |
|---|---|---|
| Chief Executive | | John Archer |
| Senior Development Officers | | Kevin Cowle |
| | | Alan Knowles |
| | | Dan MacRae |
| European Information Officer | | Louise Scott |
| Finance Officer | | Isabel Tulloch |

**advisers**

**Bankers** Royal Bank of Scotland

**Auditors** KPMG

# Scottish Sports Council (SSC)

Caledonia House
South Gyle
Edinburgh EH12 9DQ

**Tel** 0131 317 7200
**Fax** 0131 317 7202

**status** Executive body

**founded** 1972

**sponsor** Scottish Office

**mission** To lead the development of sport and physical recreation in Scotland, with the aim of increasing participation and improving standards of performance.

**tasks** Administering grants to national governing bodies and other sports bodies. Investing in quality sporting opportunities for young people. Investing in a comprehensive, integrated excellence programme for Scotland's aspiring and top performers. Gives grants to support top athletes. Assesses projects applying for funds from the Lottery Sports Fund. Runs three sports centres in Scotland. Supports and encourages Scotland's coaches and national governing bodies.

**operations** Management: The Council has five divisions: Executive Office, Planning, Central Services, Operations, and Marketing & Communications, all based in Edinburgh. Partnerships with the national governing bodies of sport are at the heart of all their initiatives.

Policy: Encouraging more children to get involved in sport through Youth Sport Strategy. Has set up Scottish Institute of Sport to assist in achieving and sustaining world class performance.

Trends: Changes in National Lottery guidelines will benefit individual athletes. Establishment of UK Sports Council will give SSC more influence in UK sports policy.

**performance** Standards in customer care were high.

**board** Council members are appointed by the Secretary of State from successful sportspersons, members of sporting governing bodies, business and local authorities.

| | | |
|---|---|---|
| Chairman | Graeme Simmers | |
| Vice Chairman | Alan Grosset | |
| Members | David Arnott | Malcolm Murray |
| | Eamonn Bannon | Fred Nelson |
| | Lesley Grant | Evlyn Raistrick |
| | Jane Heaney | Margaret Seymour |
| | John MacDonald | Neil Stevenson |
| | Ian Mason | George Urquhart |
| Scottish Office Assessor | | Gerald McHugh |

**staff** 150

| | |
|---|---|
| Chief Executive | Allan Alstead |
| Deputy Chief Executive | Jim Breen |
| Director of Scottish National Sports Centres | Andy Anderson |
| Director of Planning & Lottery Sports Fund | Ivor Davies |
| Joint Director of Marketing and Communications | Ann Fairweather |
| Director of Finance & Administration | Iain Robertson |
| Director of Operations | Brian Samson |
| Joint Director of Marketing and Communications | Kate Vincent |
| Principal, Scottish National Sports Centre, Inverclyde | John Kent |
| Principal, Scottish National Sports Centre, Cumbrae | Bob Smith |
| Principal, Scottish National Sports Centre, Glenmore Lodge | Tim Walker |

*financial*

**INCOME & EXPENDITURE**

| Year end: 31 March | 1996 £ | 1995 £ |
|---|---|---|
| **INCOME** | | |
| Grant-in-aid | 8,574,000 | 8,778,000 |
| National Lottery fund | 122,412 | 82,054 |
| Other operating income | 448,118 | 285,399 |
| | **9,144,530** | **9,145,453** |
| **EXPENDITURE** | | |
| Trust company funding | 1,413,466 | 1,223,359 |
| Sports development and capital grants | 4,433,324 | 4,489,300 |
| Staff costs | 2,120,395 | 2,045,865 |
| Other operating charges | 1,335,507 | 1,108,050 |
| | **9,302,692** | **8,866,574** |
| **OPERATING (LOSS)/SURPLUS** | **(158,162)** | **278,879** |
| Interest | 43,137 | 36,017 |
| **(LOSS)/SURPLUS BEFORE TAXATION** | **(115,025)** | **314,896** |
| Corporation tax | 17,612 | 14,131 |
| **(LOSS)/SUPLUS FOR YEAR TRANSFERRED TO GENERAL FUND** | **(132,637)** | **300,765** |

**INCOME & EXPENDITURE: NATIONAL LOTTERY FUND**

| Year end: 31 March | 1996 £ | 1995 £ |
|---|---|---|
| **INCOME** | | |
| National Lottery fund proceeds | 27,265,994 | 5,201,122 |
| Interest receivable | 49,071 | 2,106 |
| Other operating income | 840 | 570 |
| | **27,315,905** | **5,203,798** |
| **EXPENDITURE** | | |
| Grants paid | 1,496,880 | - |
| Net grant commitments | 12,925,045 | - |
| Staff costs: | | |
| -direct | 108,507 | 33,531 |
| -recharges | 102,126 | 73,601 |
| | **210,633** | **107,132** |
| Depreciation | 31,115 | 837 |
| Other operating charges: | | |
| -direct | 86,550 | 44,707 |
| -recharges | 20,286 | 8,453 |
| | **106,836** | **53,160** |
| | **14,770,509** | **161,129** |
| **OPERATING SURPLUS BEFORE TAX** | **12,545,396** | **5,042,669** |
| Corporation tax | 12,268 | 527 |
| **INCREASE IN FUND** | **12,533,128** | **5,042,142** |

*branches*

*The National Sports Centre*
Inverclyde
Burnside Road
Largs
Ayrshire KA30 8RW
Tel 01475 674666
Fax 01475 674720

*Scottish National Sports Centre*
Cumbrae
Isle of Cumbrae
Ayrshire KA28 0HQ
Tel 01475 530757
Fax 01475 530013

*Scottish National Sports Centre*
Glenmore Lodge
Aviemore
Inverness-shire PH22 1QU
Tel 01479 861256
Fax 01479 861212

# Q&Q

## Scottish Tourist Board (STB)

23 Ravelston Terrace
Edinburgh EH4 3EU

**Tel** 0131 332 2433
**Fax** 0131 315 2906

**E-mail** graham.birse@stb.gov.uk
**Web** http://www.holiday.scotland.net

**Contact** Graham Birse

| | |
|---|---|
| *status* | Executive body |
| *founded* | 1969 |
| *sponsor* | Scottish Office |
| *powers* | Development of Tourism Act 1969. The Tourism (Overseas Promotion) Act 1984. |
| *mission* | To generate jobs and wealth for Scotland through the promotion and development of tourism. More specifically, to increase visitor expenditure, to develop all-year-round tourism, to develop tourism outwith the main tourism areas, to promote high quality in all tourism facilities and services. |
| *tasks* | As the lead agency for tourism in Scotland, STB undertakes marketing activities at home and abroad, identifies development needs and opportunities, ensures productive links with the private sector and advises government on Scottish tourism. Within Scotland it funds (£3,586,000 in 1996/97) and co-ordinates the network and activities of the 14 new Area Tourist Boards (ATBs). Overseas, Scotland is promoted in 36 countries, via the British Tourist Authority (BTA), with which it works closely. |
| *operations* | Management: A new Chief Executive was appointed in 1996. Headquarters in Edinburgh, offices in London and Inverness. Within Scotland, the transition from 32 ATBs to the 14 new ones was managed successfully; it was first year of operations for the new ATBs and there were ups and downs. During 1996/97, it was not possible to get complete unity on the proposed STB Quality Assurance Scheme. Overseas, the four prime markets - USA, Germany, France and The Netherlands - were each targeted with highly successful marketing campaigns; globally, BTA supported and advised STB in branding Scotland and implementing its international marketing programme. |
| | Policy: To work with the ATBs to introduce new technology. To introduce a Quality Assurance Scheme. Continuing development of tourism at local level. |
| | Trends: Overseas tourism to Scotland has increased in nine out of the last ten years. The decline in tourists from England has been halted. Funding from the Scottish Office again increased. |
| *performance* | Most targets were achieved or exceeded, with the exception of Quality Assurance Schemes. |
| *board* | Appointed by the Secretary of State. |

| | |
|---|---|
| Chairman | Lord James Gordon of Strathblane |
| Members | Peter Fairlie |
| | Scott Grier OBE |
| | Dr James Hunter |
| | Peter Lederer OBE |
| | Madeleine McPhail |
| *Accounting Officer* | *Chief Executive* |

*staff* 155

| | |
|---|---|
| Chief Executive | Tom Buncle |
| Director, Planning and Development | Gordon Adams |
| Head of Human Resources | Anne Bell |
| Director, Press & Public Relations | Graham Birse |
| Director, UK Marketing | Lorna Easton |
| Director, Finance & Administration | George Inglis |
| Director, Scottish Convention Bureau | Frank Mullen |
| Director, Visitor Services | Tim Oliphant |
| Acting Director, International Marketing | Katie Rutherford |

**financial**

| INCOME & EXPENDITURE | | | |
|---|---|---|---|
| Year end: 31 March | **1997** | **1996** | **1995** |
| | **£000** | **£000** | **£000** |
| **INCOME** | | | |
| HM government grant-in-aid | 17,916 | 16,965 | 16,196 |
| Tourist projects | 277 | 206 | 1,289 |
| Income from activities | 4,634 | 3,980 | 3,720 |
| | **22,827** | **21,151** | **21,205** |
| **EXPENDITURE** | | | |
| Staff costs | 3,386 | 3,497 | 3,537 |
| Advertising, promotion and other operating costs | 15,761 | 14,541 | 13,214 |
| Area Tourist Boards | 3,586 | 3,584 | 2,737 |
| Tourist projects | 277 | 206 | 1,289 |
| | **23,010** | **21,828** | **20,777** |
| **OPERATING SURPLUS/(DEFICIT)** | **(183)** | **(677)** | **428** |
| Corporation tax | (12) | (13) | (11) |
| | **(195)** | **(690)** | **417** |
| Add back notional costs | 65 | - | - |
| **SURPLUS/(DEFICIT) FOR YEAR** | **(130)** | **(690)** | **417** |

**advisers**    **Auditors**    National Audit Office      22 Melville Street, Edinburgh EH3 7NS

**publications**    *Annual Report*

**branches**    Thistle House             19 Cockspur Street
Beechwood Park North      London SW1Y 5BL
Inverness IV2 3ED

# Scottish Water & Sewerage Customers Council

Springk Erse Business Park
Ochil House
Stirling FK7 7XE

**Tel** 01786 430200
**Fax** 01786 462018

**status**    Executive body

**founded**    1995

**sponsor**    Scottish Office

**powers**    Local Government etc (Scotland) Act 1994

**mission**    To look after the interests of customers of the three Scottish water authorities.

**tasks**    Approves the water and sewerage charges; approves and monitors the water authorities' codes of practice; helps customers with complaints about their authority; consults with the public and representative bodies; promotes awareness within the water authorities of the needs of customers.

**operations**    Management: Council meets every six weeks and has three internal committees. Three area committees (each covering an area corresponding to that of one of the water authorities) of 12 members, chaired by a member of the Customers' Council, are 'eyes and ears' at local level. Director runs the day-to-day business and reports to the Council.

Policy: Discussions with each authority on compensation and guaranteed standards in the provision of services.

Trends: Concerned about implication of PFI on charges to customers. Increased contact with EC and regulatory bodies.

**performance**    Met or exceeded 10 out of 16 objectives for 1996/97.

**board**    Council Members appointed by the Secretary of State from a wide range of backgrounds and experience.

| | | |
|---|---|---|
| Chairman | Dick Douglas | |
| Deputy Chairman | Neil Menzies | |
| Members | Prof Tom Anderson | |
| | Lady Ann Calman | Bill Howatson |
| | Cllr John Connolly | Cllr Rhona Kemp |
| | John Goodfellow | Cllr Alexander Scott |
| | Cllr Lynn Groundwater | Ian Stewart OBE |
| *Accounting Officer* | *Director* | |

| staff | 17 | |
|---|---|---|
| | Director | Vicki Nash |
| | Head of Administration | Penny Hobbs |
| | Head of Charges & Codes of Practice | Archie Minto |
| | Head of Customer Services | Tom Young |

**financial**

**INCOME & EXPENDITURE**
Year end: 31 March

| | 1997 |
|---|---|
| | £ |
| **INCOME** | **1,015,740** |
| **EXPENDITURE** | |
| Council members' remuneration | 64,888 |
| Members' travel and subsistence | 28,181 |
| Staff remuneration | 324,408 |
| Staff travel and subsistence | 21,204 |
| Office accommodation | 43,498 |
| General operating costs | 76,730 |
| Customer support and communication | 133,319 |
| Council meetings | 10,065 |
| Area committees | 48,939 |
| | **751,232** |
| Capital equipment and IT | 103,579 |
| Fitting out of offices | 146,962 |
| | **1,001,773** |
| **SURPLUS BEFORE INTEREST & TAX** | **13,967** |
| Interest received less tax | 4,046 |
| **NET SURPLUS FOR YEAR** | **18,013** |

| advisers | | | |
|---|---|---|---|
| | **Bankers** | Royal Bank of Scotland | Edinburgh |
| | **Auditors** | Scott-Moncrieff Downie Wilson | Edinburgh |
| | **Solicitors** | Shepherd & Wedderburn WS | Edinburgh |
| | **Public Relations** | MCL | Grangemouth |

**publications**  Annual Reports 1996/97, The Scottish Water Industry Review: A Response from the Customers Council (1997), Options Informing the Setting of Water and Sewerage Charges (September 1997), Efficiency of the Scottish Water Industry: Ensuring the Customer Interest (September 1997), Scottish Water and Sewerage Charges and Low Income (March 1998)

# Sea Fish Industry Authority (Seafish)

18 Logie Mill
Logie Green Road
Edinburgh EH7 4HG

**Tel** 0131 558 3331          **E-mail** seafish.co.uk
**Fax** 0131 558 1442

**Contact** Maria Limonci

| status | Executive body |
|---|---|
| founded | 1981 |
| sponsor | Ministry of Agriculture, Fisheries and Food (MAFF) |
| powers | Fisheries Act 1981 |

**mission**  Seafish works with the industry to meet consumer demands, to raise standards, to improve efficiency and unity and to secure a prosperous future for all sectors through research and technical development, training, marketing, and financial assistance.

**tasks**  Marketing - to promote the consumption of fish and shellfish throughout the UK. Technology - to help the fish industry to benefit from new ideas developed through practical research; Aquaculture - to pioneer fish and shellfish farming techniques. Training - to develop training opportunities for the workforce at sea and on shore. Marine Safety - Seafish is closely involved with national and EU safety grant schemes, Marine Safety Agency safety standards, construction standards etc. It is also responsible for the administration of UK and EU grants for safety improvement on fishing vessels - sole responsibility for their administration in England and Wales; and in Scotland and NI, in conjunction with the Scottish Office Agriculture, Environment and Fisheries Department and with the Department of Agriculture for NI. Economics and Statistics - provides information to the industry and the public, eg annual surveys of costs and earnings in UK fleets.

**operations**  Management: Under the Fisheries Act 1981, all the rights, obligations and property of the White Fish Authority and the Herring Industry Board were transferred to Seafish. It is funded by levy and operating income, including EU funds for a major advertising campaign. The Fish Industry Forum of top people in the industry has been set up by Seafish to give the industry a united voice.

Policy: There is a growing problem of black fish - illegal landings of over-quota fish - which distorts orderly marketing and adversely affects conservation; the problem needs the urgent attention of government and the industry jointly.

Trends: Farming is an increasingly significant source of fish and shellfish. Seafish is investigating the potential for farmed cod to command premium prices.

**performance** 40 targets met; nine not met.

**board**  Appointed by Ministers. Eight are from the fish industry and four are independent of the industry.

| Chairman | Eric Davey | |
|---|---|---|
| Members | Ms Margaret Andrews | |
| | Arthur Cook | Andrew Pepper |
| | Cecil Finn | Derek Reid |
| | Prof Mike Haines | James Slater |
| | John Kelly | George Traves |
| | Dr Jasper Parsons | Ken Watmough |
| *Accounting Officer* | *Chief Executive* | |

**staff**  153

| Chief Executive | Alasdair Fairbairn |
|---|---|

**financial**

| INCOME & EXPENDITURE | | | |
|---|---|---|---|
| Year end: 31 March | 1997 | 1996 | 1995 |
| | £000 | £000 | £000 |
| **INCOME** | | | |
| Government grants | 400 | 677 | 608 |
| Levy | 7,668 | 6,641 | 6,666 |
| Interest (net) | 168 | 206 | 150 |
| Technical charges | 129 | 291 | 272 |
| Other income | 1,930 | 1,141 | 1,058 |
| | 10,295 | 8,956 | 8,754 |
| **EXPENDITURE** | | | |
| Marketing | 5,051 | 2,509 | 3,586 |
| Research & development | 2,509 | 2,628 | 2,815 |
| Training | 935 | 917 | 928 |
| Administration & provisions | 1,209 | 697 | 896 |
| Policy & economics | 516 | 526 | 443 |
| Grant & loan services | 284 | 299 | 272 |
| Redundancy/relocation costs | 88 | - | - |
| | 10,592 | 7,576 | 8,940 |
| **SURPLUS/(DEFICIT) BEFORE TAXATION** | (297) | 1,380 | (186) |

**advisers**  **Bankers**  Clydesdale Bank  20 Hanover Street, Edinburgh EH2 2QW

**Auditors**  Coopers & Lybrand  Erskine House, 68-73 Queen Street
Edinburgh EH2 4NH

**Solicitors**  W&J Burness WS  16 Hope Street, Charlotte Square
Edinburgh EH2 4DR

Simon Jackson  St Savior's Wharf, London

**Public Relations**  The Rowland Company  67-69 Whitfield Street, London W1P 5RL

**publications**  *Annual Report 1996/97*

# Security Facilities Executive (SAFE)

St Christopher House
Southwark Street
London SE1 0TE

**Tel** 0171 921 4663          **E-mail** ssg-busdev@safe.ndirect.co.uk
**Fax** 0171 921 3802

**Contact** Sarah March D'angelo

| | |
|---|---|
| *status* | Executive agency |
| *founded* | 1993 |
| *sponsor* | Cabinet Office (Office of Public Service) |
| *powers* | Framework Document |
| *mission* | To provide security-related products and services to central government and the wider public sector, across the UK, Europe and other friendly governments. |
| *tasks* | Two units: Special Services Group (SSG) and Custody Services (CS). SSG Consultancy provides an independent advisory, assessment and evaluation service on integrated security systems, equipment, risk assessment, CCTV, explosion protection, IDS etc. SSG Operations provides specialist expertise in integrated security systems, CCTV, IDS, security lighting, windows and doors, perimeter systems, installation and maintenance etc. Custody Services provides 24-hour manned guarding, mobile patrols, keyholding service and trained reception staff. |
| *operations* | Management: Advisory Board advises the Chancellor of the Duchy of Lancaster on the agency's strategies, plans and performance. Management Board, headed by Chief Executive, runs day-to-day business. Required to recover full economic costs through charging for services. Sites in London and Warrington.

Policy: Is becoming more involved in working with the wider public sector and the PFI.

Trends: No longer restricted to central goverment market. |
| *performance* | Five out of eight targets achieved in 1996/97. |
| *board* | Advisory Board appointed by the Parliamentary Secretary, Office of Public Service. |

| Accounting Officer | Chief Executive |
|---|---|

*staff*      600

| | |
|---|---|
| Chief Executive | Malcolm Farrow |
| Special Services Group Consultancy Director | Nigel Custance |
| Special Services Group Operations Director | Colin Frier |
| Custody Services Business Director | Ian Clements |
| Cultural Development Director | Sean Leahy |
| Finance & IT Director | John Tomkins |
| Personnel Director | Laura Zajdlic |

*financial*

| INCOME & EXPENDITURE | | |
|---|---|---|
| Year end: 31 March | 1997 | 1996 |
| | £000 | £000 |
| INCOME FROM OPERATING ACTIVITIES | 41,282 | 44,544 |
| EXPENDITURE | | |
| Staff costs | 24,013 | 26,593 |
| Other operating costs | 16,360 | 17,052 |
| Depreciation | 844 | 839 |
| OPERATING SURPLUS/(DEFICIT) | 65 | 60 |
| Exceptional items | - | - |
| VER/VES restructuring costs | (1,6500 | - |
| Cost of capital | (256) | (229) |
| SURPLUS/(DEFICIT) FOR THE YEAR | (1,841) | (169) |

| *advisers* | **Bankers** | Paymaster General |
|---|---|---|
| | **Auditors** | Bentley Jennison |
| | **Solicitors** | Treasury Solicitor |

**branches**    RAF Burtonwood
PO Box 10
Warrington
Cheshire WA3 3AL

# Serious Fraud Office

Elm House
10-16 Elm Street
London WC1X OB

**Tel** 0171 239 7272
**Fax** 0171 837 1689

**status**    An independent government department under the superintendence of the Attorney General, operating on Next Steps lines

**founded**    1988

**sponsor**    Attorney General's Department

**powers**    Criminal Justice Act 1987. SFO Framework Document 1997

**mission**    To investigate and prosecute serious and complex fraud and so deter fraud and maintain confidence in the probity of business and financial services in the UK.

**tasks**    To investigate each case quickly and efficiently. To ensure that charges reflect the overall seriousness of each case, allowing the court adequate powers of punishment. To prosecute cases fairly and firmly and present them in such a way that enables a jury to understand complex issues. To assist UK and other investigating and prosecuting authorities and obtain evidence of serious and complex fraud on behalf of overseas authorities.

**operations**    Management: The Director exercises her powers under the superintendence of the Attorney General. She maintains contact with government departments and regulators who report allegations of serious fraud to her. The key criterion for accepting a referral is that the suspected fraud is such that the investigation should be in the same hands as the prosecution. Other criteria include the value of the suspected fraud (normally at least £1 million), a significant international dimension, widespread public concern, the need for highly specialised knowledge. When a case has been accepted, SFO appoints a case team of lawyers, accountants, police officers and support staff, led by a case controller, a lawyer. The decision to prosecute requires that there is a realistic chance of securing a conviction and that it is in the public interest.

Trends: Law Commission considering creation of new fraud offence to replace existing laws.

**board**    None.

| Accounting Officer | Director |
| --- | --- |

**staff**
| Director | Mrs Rosalind Wright |
| --- | --- |

**financial**    1996/97 total vote £16.99 million.

**publications**    *Annual Report 1996-97*

# Service Children's Education (SCE)

Wegberg Military Complex
Building 5
BFPO 140

**Tel** 0049 2161 47 x 2414
**Fax** 00 49 2161 47 x 3487

**status**    Defence agency

**founded**    1997

**sponsor**    Ministry of Defence (MOD)

| | |
|---|---|
| **mission** | To provide schooling to dependent children of Armed Forces personnel including children of UK-based civilians serving overseas. |
| **tasks** | The agency directly provides education through running 57 schools around the world (mainly primary). Also provides educational advice and support to Armed Forces parents and children in the UK. |
| **operations** | Management: Adjutant General exercises ownership responsibilities on behalf of the Secretary of State. He is assisted by an Advisory Board. |
| | Policy: Consolidate changes resulting from the Educational Reform Act. |
| | Trends: Reduction in staffing levels in schools due to budget cuts. Changes of Armed Forces strength and positioning in Germany will lead to school closures. |
| **performance** | School examination results slightly above UK average. |
| **board** | The Adjutant General is assisted by an Advisory Board appointed from Armed Forces, Department of Education and Employment and OFSTED. |

| Chairman | General Sir Michael Rose KCB CBE DSO | |
|---|---|---|
| Members | K Anderson | |
| | Lieutenant Colonel BM Atkins | Major General RA Oliver |
| | Colonel BM Gordon-Smith | WA Perry |
| | Group Captain Harris | M Phipps |
| | Brigadier C Horsefall | Colonel I Rees |
| | Colonel CR Langton | Brigadier AD Thompson |
| *Accounting Officer* | *Chief Executive* | |

**staff** 1646

| Chief Executive | DG Wadsworth |
|---|---|
| Assistant Chief Executive (Quality Assurance) | Ian Forrest |
| Assistant Chief Executive (Strategic Direction of Service) | Paul Niedzwiedzki |
| Director, Finance, Personnel & Administration | Mervyn Harvey |

**financial**

**NET EXPENDITURE**

| Year end: 31 March | 1997 £000 | 1996 £000 |
|---|---|---|
| **EXPENDITURE** | | |
| Staff costs | 46,162 | 35,675 |
| Staff support | 2,610 | 1,334 |
| Accommodation | 15,414 | 10,358 |
| Educational supplies and equipment consumed | 1,768 | 1,701 |
| Capital charges | 972 | 520 |
| Other operating charges | 6,890 | 4,901 |
| Exam fees and schools fees | 591 | 489 |
| | 74,407 | 54,978 |
| **INCOME** | | |
| Fee Income | 2,384 | 1,706 |
| Other Income | 970 | 929 |
| | 3,354 | 2,635 |
| **NET EXPENDITURE** | 71,053 | 52,343 |

**advisers** **Auditors** National Audit Office — 157-197 Buckingham Palace Road, London SW1W 9SP

# Ships Support Agency (SSA)

B Block
Foxhill
Bath BA1 5AB

**Tel** 01225 883743
**Fax** 01225 884313

**E-mail** shipsbiscup.mod.fh@gtnet.gov.uk

**Contact** Miss D Thomas

| | |
|---|---|
| **status** | Defence agency |
| **founded** | 1996 |
| **sponsor** | Ministry of Defence (MOD) |

| | |
|---|---|
| *powers* | Framework Document 1996 |
| *mission* | To be the acknowledged centre of excellence in defining and directing material support to the Royal Navy and Royal Fleet Auxiliaries. |
| *tasks* | Directing timely and effective engineering and material support to the Fleet and other defence customers - using both MOD and commercial suppliers; ensuring support and engineering considerations are taken into account when new Naval ships are procured; maintaining the Fleet in specified readiness states. |
| *operations* | Management: SSA is an integral part of the Naval Support Command and is responsible for directing the support of Naval ships, weapons and equipment from the point of transfer from the MOD Procurement Executive (PE) up to and including disposal. Its Owner is the Chief of Fleet Support (CFS). He is responsible to ministers for SSA's strategic direction, corporate and business plans, and monitoring performance and supporting the Chief Executive. He is advised by the Owner's Board. The Chief Executive reports to the Chief of Fleet Support. He is supported by the Agency Board (Chief Executive plus nine senior Directors). |
| | Policy: During 1996/97 new SSA strategies were developed for service delivery, human resources, support, purchasing and technology and SSA began to operate and report progress against them. |
| | Trends: Devonport and Rosyth Royal Dockyards sold to Devonport Management Limited and the Babcock International Group giving significant savings to the taxpayer. All nuclear submarine refitting and refuelling to be at Devonport after it has been upgraded. |
| *performance* | 1996/97 most targets completely achieved or partly achieved except ship refit timeliness. |
| *board* | Owner's Board appointed by the Chief of Fleet Support. Agency Board appointed by the Chief Executive. |

| Accounting Officer | Chief Executive |
|---|---|

| | |
|---|---|
| *staff* | 2698 |

| Chief Executive | John Coles |
|---|---|
| Director Ships Logistics Engineering | Roger Allen |
| Director In-Service Submarines | Commodore David Burns |
| Director Ships Weapon Engineering | Roy Cummings |
| Superintendent Ships (Devonport) | Commodore David Hall |
| Commercial Director | John Hall |
| Director Marine Engineering | Gan Jenkins |
| Director In-Service Ships | Stan Wallace |

*financial*

| INCOME & EXPENDITURE | |
|---|---|
| **Year end: 31 March** | **1997** |
| | **£000** |
| **EXPENDITURE** | |
| Staff costs | 68,381 |
| Capital works including estate maintenance | 83,008 |
| Equipment support | 649,882 |
| Ship refit and repair programme | 488,745 |
| Other running costs | 20,089 |
| | 1,310,105 |
| **INCOME** | 123,151 |
| **NET COST OF OUTPUT** | 1,186,954 |

| | |
|---|---|
| *publications* | *Annual Report* |

# *Simpler Trade Procedures Board (SITPRO)*

151 Buckingham Palace Road
London SW1W 9SS

**Tel** 0171 215 0825
**Fax** 0171 215 0824

**E-mail** sitpro.org.uk
**Web** http://www.sitpro.org.uk

| | |
|---|---|
| *status* | Executive body |
| *founded* | 1970 |
| *sponsor* | Department of Trade and Industry (DTI) |
| *mission* | To make international trade as simple to undertake as its domestic equivalent. |
| *tasks* | Simplifying international trade practices, working with the UN and EUROPRO at EU level; developing the ADEEP project to create electronic equivalents to key UK export documents; helping small and medium- sized compa- |

nies with the new trading environment resulting from the European single currency; streamlining the flow of information through paper documentation and ADEEP; improving the UK movement of goods through inland depots, ports, airports and the Channel Tunnel; providing advisory services.

**operations**  Management: There is a Board and four policy and advisory groups covering commercial and official procedures, international payment practices, port procedure policy and ADEEP. SITPRO's software business was sold in June 1996, following a DTI review. The 1996/97 accounts show a deficit because the receivables relating to SITPRO are not included and the actual trading performance was positive.

Policy: To maintain close working relationships with all those who can help with promoting best trade practice throughout the UK, Europe and the world.

Trends: The cost and complexity of export processes are now surfacing as a major barrier to trade and being addressed by the World Trade Organisation (WTO). EURPRO set up to in Belgium to make recommendations to the EC.

**board**

| | | |
|---|---|---|
| Chairman | JG Davis | |
| Vice Chairman | JM Fetherston OBE JP | |
| Members | NR Boakes | |
| | MJ Booth OBE | BJ Kelleher |
| | Viscount Chelmsford | M Krayenbrink |
| | R Dale | TBC McGuffog |
| | M Eland | Dr DP Walker |
| *Accounting Officer* | *Chief Executive* | |

**staff**  14

| | |
|---|---|
| Chief Executive | Richard Dale |
| Director, Trade Facilitation | Ray Battersby |
| Deputy Director, Trade Facilitation | Gordon Cragge |
| Assistant Director, Payment Procedures | Ian Durban |
| Assistant Director, Information Technology | Christine Mandikian |
| Assistant Director, Official Procedures | Daren Timson-Hunt |
| Assistant Director, Port Procedures | Michelle Waddilove |
| Trade Facilitation Executive | Martine Brewster |
| Manager, Marketing Services & Administration | Joan Nolan |

**financial**

**INCOME & EXPENDITURE**

| Year end: 31 March | 1997 £000 | 1996 £000 |
|---|---|---|
| **INCOME** | | |
| HMG grant-in-aid | 581 | 1,012 |
| Income from activities | 189 | 705 |
| Other operating income | 9 | 8 |
| Income from investment | 7 | - |
| | 786 | 1,725 |
| **EXPENDITURE** | | |
| Staff costs | (381) | (738) |
| Depreciation | (14) | (31) |
| Notional charges | (206) | - |
| Other operating charges | (466) | (946) |
| | 1,067 | 1,715 |
| **OPERATING (DEFICIT)/SURPLUS** | (281) | 10 |
| Notional interest on capital employed | (6) | - |
| Interest receivable | 7 | 4 |
| | (280) | 14 |
| **(DEFICIT)/SURPLUS/ON ORDINARY ACTIVITIES BEFORE TAXATION** | | |
| Corporation tax | (2) | (1) |
| **(DEFICIT)/SURPLUS ON ORDINARY ACTIVITIES AFTER TAXATION** | (282) | 13 |
| Adjustment for notional charges | 212 | - |
| **(DEFICIT)/SURPLUS** | (70) | 13 |
| Retained surplus brought forward | 135 | 122 |
| **RETAINED SURPLUS CARRIED FORWARD** | 65 | 135 |

# Sir John Soane's Museum

13 Lincoln's Inn Fields
London WC2A 3BP

**Tel** 0171 405 2107
**Fax** 0171 831 3957

| | |
|---|---|
| *status* | Executive body |
| *founded* | 1837, as executive body 1947 |
| *sponsor* | Department for Culture, Media and Sport (DCMS) |
| *powers* | Sir John Soane's Museum Act 1833 |
| *mission* | To maintain the fabric of the museum, keeping it as far as possible in the state in which it was left at the time of Soane's death. |
| *tasks* | Allowing the public free access to the museum and its collections; cataloging and conserving the collections; providing educational facilities; presenting exhibitions and publications. |
| *operations* | Management: Curator and curatorial staff. New financial management. Funding agreement signed by Chairman of Trustees. |
| | Policy: No.14 Lincoln's Inn Fields bought in 1996 substantially with Lottery grant money. |
| | Trends: Declining grant-in-aid. Rising visitor numbers. |
| *performance* | Fulfilled all of Soane's general aims. |
| *board* | Four Life Trustees. Others represent Royal Academy, Royal Society and the Museum itself. |

| | | |
|---|---|---|
| Chairman | The Duke of Grafton KG | |
| Trustees | Mrs Bridget Cherry | Sir Walter Bodmer |
| | Richard Griffiths | David Coombs |
| | Sir Philip Powell CH OBE | Edward Cullinan CBE |
| | Ald Gavyn Arthur | Ronald Lightbown |
| *Accounting Officer* | *Curator* | |

**staff**    19

| | |
|---|---|
| Curator | Margaret Richardson |
| Inspectress & Deputy Curator | Helen Dorey |
| Finance Officer | Roderick Smith |
| Archivist | Susan Palmer |
| Assistant Curator (Drawings) | Stephen Astley |
| Assistant Curator (Education) | Christopher Woodward |
| Secretary | Jean Duffield |

**financial**

| FINANCIAL ACTIVITIES Year end: 25 March | 1997 | 1996 |
|---|---|---|
| | £ | £ |
| **INCOMING RESOURCES** | | |
| Grant from Department of National Heritage | 624,500 | 631,000 |
| Sales of publications, postcards and slides | 73,720 | 74,748 |
| Donations received from visitors | 26,440 | 23,800 |
| Group donations | 2,631 | - |
| Investment income and interest | 7,641 | 5,892 |
| Building account interest | 2,832 | 5,717 |
| Bank of England interest | 672 | 868 |
| Reproduction and hire fees receivable | 3,116 | 2,965 |
| Filming museum | 1,026 | 3,200 |
| Rent receivable | 974 | 974 |
| Sundry Income | 1,737 | 4,900 |
| Contributions to conservation fund | 701 | - |
| | **745,990** | **754,064** |

| RESOURCES EXPENDED | | |
|---|---|---|
| **Direct charitable expenditure** | | |
| General museum costs | 352,413 | 341,486 |
| Conservation | 44,493 | 41,881 |
| Education | 16,065 | 12,654 |
| Research | 54,775 | 42,348 |
| Library services | 36,001 | 34,223 |
| Building expenditure | 36,442 | 220,631 |
| Maintenance | 32,630 | 18,450 |
| Trading expenditure | 76,697 | 69,108 |
| | **649,516** | **780,781** |
| **Other Expenditure** | | |
| Management and administration of the charity | 114,627 | 113,989 |
| Taxation | 1,107 | 8,080 |
| | **765,250** | **902,850** |
| **Notional costs** | | |
| Insurance | 553 | 526 |
| Cost of capital | 3,944 | 17,880 |
| **NET INCOMING/(OUTGOING) RESOURCES (AFTER NOTIONAL COSTS** | **(23,757)** | **167,192** |
| Reversal of notional costs | 4,497 | 18,406 |
| **NET INCOMING/(OUTGOING) RESOURCES** | **(19,260)** | **(148,786)** |
| Gains on investment assets | 10,607 | 14,913 |
| Exceptional pension provision | (45,000) | (277,000) |
| **NET MOVEMENT IN FUNDS** | **(53,653)** | **(410,873)** |
| Fund balances brought forward | 92,562 | 503,435 |
| **FUND BALANCES CARRIED FORWARD** | **38,909** | **92,562** |

| | | | |
|---|---|---|---|
| **advisers** | **Bankers** | National Westminster Bank | High Holborn, London |
| | **Auditors** | Pannell Kerr Forster | London |
| | **Solicitors** | Farrer & Co | |
| **publications** | Annual Report, Exhibition catalogues, Guide books | | |

# Social Security Agency (Northern Ireland)

Castle Buildings
Stormont
Belfast BT4 3SJ

**Tel** 01232 520520
**Fax** 01232 523337

**E-mail** ssa@nics.gov.uk
**Web** http://ssa.nics.gov.uk

**status** Executive agency

**founded** 1991

**sponsor** Northern Ireland Office, Department of Health and Social Services (DHSS)

**powers** Framework Document 1997

**mission** To pay the proper social security benefits to the people of NI and collect certain national insurance contributions.

**tasks** Administers social security benefits - assesses and pays benefits, provides advice, processes reviews and appeals, develops policies to combat fraud and investigates and prosecutes offenders; collects national insurance contributions from employers, employed earners and the self-employed; assessing Legal Aid. Provides services in NI and the London area on behalf of the Benefits Agency and provides an accounting, storage, search and retrieval service for the whole of the UK.

**operations** Management: The largest Next Steps agency in NI and one of largest in UK. Chief Executive appointed by open competition. Management Board consists of Chief Executive and Directors of Operations; Personnel, Planning & Information; Finance & Support Services; Projects. Six districts made up of 35 Social Security Offices and 4 Community Benefit offices, with headquarters in various offices in Belfast.

Policy: Payment by benefit card being introduced in 1999.

Trends: Exploring how the private sector might become involved in the delivery of social security benefits.

**performance**  In 1996/97, 24 out of 29 targets were met.

**board**  Chief Executive is appointed by the Secretary of State.

| | |
|---|---|
| Chief Executive | Chris Thompson |
| Director of Finance & Support Services | John Deery |
| Director of Projects | Peter Gray |
| Director of Personnel, Planning & Information | Jim Johnston |
| Director of Operations | Gerry Keenan |
| *Accounting Officer* | *Chief Executive* |

**staff**  5555

**publications**  *Annual Report & Accounts, Strategic & Business Plan*

# *Specialist Procurement Services (SPS)*

Ministry of Defence (PE)
PO Box 702
Bristol BS12 7DU

**Tel** 0117 913 2724
**Fax** 0117 913 2923

**status**  Defence agency

**founded**  1997

**sponsor**  Ministry of Defence (MOD)

**powers**  SPS Framework Document 1997

**mission**  Advises on all aspects of defence procurement and provides quality assurance in support of UK defence procurement.

**tasks**  To seek the best possible price for goods and services supplied to government; to provide a quality assurance surveillance service for MOD procurers; to provide cost forecasts and advice on their interpretation and use; equipment accounting.

**operations**  Management: Chief of Defence Procurement (CDP) is the Owner and is responsible for the strategic direction and management of the agency. The Chief Executive is responsible for the day-to-day management of the agency, and was appointed from within the MOD (in future from open competition). Headquarters in Bristol and 28 regional offices throughout UK.

Policy: Consultancy Services is a new area established to meet demands of new initiatives (eg advice on PPP).

**performance**  Targets have been set for 1997/98.

**board**  The Owner's Board is appointed by the Secretary of State and comprises senior representatives of all areas having business with the Agency.

| | | |
|---|---|---|
| Chairman | CDP | |
| Members | DCDP(Ops) | |
| | DCDP(Support) | AML |
| | DCDS(S) | HDES |
| | DUS(RP&F) | DG Commercial |
| | CFS | DG Resources |
| | QMG | Independent Advisor |
| *Accounting Officer* | *Permanent under Secretary* | |

**staff**  920

| | |
|---|---|
| Chief Executive | Nick Bennett |
| Commercial Director | J Clark |
| Director Pricing | J Griffin |

**advisers**  **Auditors**  National Audit Office  157-159 Buckingham Palace Road London SW1W 9SP

**publications**  *The Specialist*

# Sports Council for Northern Ireland

House of Sport
Upper Malone Road
Belfast BT9 5LA

**Tel** 01232 381222
**Fax** 01232 682757

| | |
|---|---|
| *status* | Executive body |
| *founded* | 1973 |
| *sponsor* | Northern Ireland Office, Department of Education NI (DENI) |
| *powers* | Recreation and Youth Service (Northern Ireland) Orders 1973 and 1986 |
| *mission* | Increasing committed participation in NI sport and physical recreation, especially among young people. Raising NI standards of sporting excellence. Promoting the good reputation and efficient administration of NI sport. |
| *tasks* | Co-operates with and supports the Governing Bodies of sport financially - providing participation opportunities, performer development courses, training for coaches, technical officials and administrators, organising international and representative events at home and abroad and accessing sports science and sports medicine services. Encouraging the provision of adequate facilities and equipment - including managing the House of Sport and the NI Centre for Outdoor Activities. Making grants - disbursing Capital Grant Aid and National Lottery money. |
| *operations* | Management: The Council's principal activities are agreed with DENI, working within the new Strategy for Sport. It works in partnership with the governing bodies of sport; also with local sport, education, health promotion and community relations organisations. There are 13 committees and associated working groups (eg Lottery Committee; NI 'Sport for All' Board). |
| | Policy: New NI strategy for sport, concentrating on opportunities for young people, support for the voluntary sporting sector and developing sporting excellence. |
| | Trends: Sport is making a considerable economic impact in NI (eg 1997 sporting events attracted thousands of visitors) and is also seen as an important driver for lasting change in NI, in line with people's needs. |
| *board* | Council members appointed by the Minister after consultation with representatives of district councils, education and library boards, and participants in sport and physical recreation. |

| Chairman | DF Allen | |
|---|---|---|
| Vice-Chairman | S Hilditch MBE | |
| Members | D Bowen | |
| | M Bradley | PD Robinson |
| | N McConnell | E Saunders |
| | F McGrady | C Shillington CBE |
| | W McIlmoyle | R Stoker |
| | J McKeever | R Trouton |
| | J O'Neill | M Wilson OBE |
| Assessor | R Downey | |
| Assessor | J Palmer | |
| *Accounting Officer* | *Chief Executive* | |

| | |
|---|---|
| *staff* | 39 |

| Chief Executive | E McCartan |
|---|---|
| Deputy Chief Executive | JM Crabbe |
| Senior Development Officer | JQ McL Clarke |
| Senior Technical Officer | CP O'Callagham |
| Director Facilities/Lottery Funding | DG O'Connor |
| Director of Youth Sports | RW Smyth |
| Marketing/Communications Officer | R McCormick |
| Head of Admin/Finance | RF Mitchell |

**financial**

| RECEIPTS & PAYMENTS Year end: 31 March | 1997 £ | 1996 £ | 1995 £ |
|---|---|---|---|
| **RECEIPTS** | | | |
| Recurrent transactions | | | |
| Department grants received | | | |
| -recurrent | 2,482,000 | 2,481,000 | 2,117,000 |
| -operating receipts | 309,335 | 356,491 | 287,446 |
| | 2,791,335 | 2,837,491 | 2,404,446 |
| **PAYMENTS** | | | |
| Salaries and wages | 844,589 | 846,623 | - |
| Other operating payments | 1,919,071 | 1,960,172 | 2,431,750 |
| | 2,763,660 | 2,806,795 | (27,304) |
| SURPLUS /(DEFICIT) ON REVENUE TRANSACTIONS | 27,675 | 30,696 | - |
| Capital Transactions | | | |
| Departmental grants received | 187,781 | 885,594 | - |
| Other receipts | 162,171 | - | - |
| | 349,952 | | |
| Less: capital payments | 320,949 | 895,361 | - |
| Surplus/(Deficit) on capital transactions | 29,003 | (9,767) | (4,843) |
| EXCESS OF (PAYMENTS OVER RECEIPTS)/RECEIPTS | | | |
| OVER PAYMENTS | 56,678 | 20,929 | (32,147) |

# Sports Council for Wales (SCW)

Sophia Gardens
Cardiff CF1 9SW

**Tel** 01222 300500
**Fax** 01222 300600

**status** Executive body

**founded** 1972

**sponsor** Welsh Office (WO)

**powers** Royal Charter

**mission** Developing and promoting sport and recreation in Wales.

**tasks** As a facilitator working through other organisations (eg 58 governing bodies): helping more people take part in sport; helping sportspeople improve their performances and reach high standards; promoting the best use of Wales's man-made and natural sports facilities; supplying advice and information to help people understand the issues and technical matters facing sport. SCW distributes funds from the National Lottery to sport in Wales (through SPORTLOT) and manages the government's business sponsorship scheme (Sportsmatch).

**operations** Management: The Senior Management Team comprises the Chief Executive and the four Directors of Policy Planning, National Development Services, Local Development Services and Support Services.

Policy: A new strategy for Welsh sport will be announced in spring 1998 based on seven SCW published discussion papers.

Trends: Aiming to meet national targets for increasing opportunities for children of school age to take part in sport - nearly halfway there - and to maintain pace of progress in supporting top performers.

**board**

| Chairman | Ossie Wheatley CBE | |
|---|---|---|
| Vice-Chairman | Tom Baxter-Wright | |
| Members | David H Burcher | |
| | Cllr Mrs Rosemary Butler | Cllr Derlwyn Hughes |
| | Gareth Davies | Ron Jones |
| | Harvey Davies | Edgar Lewis |
| | Miss Anne Ellis MBE | Nicky Piper |
| | Cllr Keith Evans | D Robert Turner |
| | Miss Tanni Grey MBE | Mrs Wendy A Williams MBE |

**staff** 148

| | | |
|---|---|---|
| Chief Executive | Linford Tatham | |
| Director of Local Development Services | Mrs Sara Butlin | |
| Director of National Development Services | Graham Davies | |
| Director of Support Services | Tony Holmstrom | |
| Director of Policy Planning | Dr Huw Jones | |

*financial*

### INCOME & EXPENDITURE

| Year end: 31 March | 1997 £000 | 1996 £000 | 1995 £000 |
|---|---|---|---|
| **INCOME** | | | |
| Grant-in-aid | 6,508 | 6,411 | 6,535 |
| National sports centres | 2,387 | 2,296 | 2,285 |
| Other operating income | 133 | 158 | 140 |
| | **9,028** | **8,866** | **8,960** |
| **EXPENDITURE** | | | |
| Sports development (including capital grants) | 3,163 | 3,328 | 3,263 |
| Sportsmatch | 301 | 280 | 257 |
| National sports centres | 2,842 | 2,695 | 2,733 |
| Council members' remuneration | 28 | 26 | 25 |
| Chief Executive's remuneration | 65 | 61 | 58 |
| Other expenditure | 2,662 | 2,784 | 2,524 |
| | **9,061** | **9,174** | **8,860** |
| **OPERATING DEFICIT** | **(32)** | **(308)** | **100** |
| Profit on sale of tangible fixed assets | 13 | 19 | 19 |
| Interest receivable | 17 | 18 | 18 |
| **DEFICIT BEFORE TAXATION** | **(3)** | **(271)** | **137** |
| Taxation | (4) | (5) | (4) |
| Transfer for reserves | 152 | 129 | - |
| Capital charge adjustment | 34 | 49 | - |
| **RETAINED SURPLUS/(DEFICIT) FOR THE FINANCIAL YEAR** | **179** | **(97)** | **-** |

### SPORTLOT INCOME & EXPENDITURE

| Year end: 31 March | 1997 £000 | 1996 £000 | 1995 £000 |
|---|---|---|---|
| **INCOME** | | | |
| Proceeds from Lottery | 15,806 | 15,325 | 2,935 |
| Interest receivable | 18 | 3 | - |
| Other income | 27 | - | - |
| | **15,851** | **15,328** | **2,935** |
| **EXPENDITURE** | | | |
| New grants paid in the year | 6,984 | 1,367 | - |
| Change in provision for Hard Grant Commitments | 2,772 | 3,425 | - |
| Depreciation - tangible assets | 6 | 7 | - |
| Staff costs | 258 | 174 | 113 |
| Other operating costs | 178 | 147 | 125 |
| | **10,198** | **5,120** | **238** |
| **INCREASE IN FUNDS** | **5,653** | **10,208** | **2,697** |
| Loss on fixed asset disposals | - | (1) | - |
| **INCREASE IN FUNDS BEFORE TAXATION** | **5,653** | **10,207** | **2,697** |
| Taxation payable | (4) | (1) | - |
| **INCREASE IN FUNDS AFTER TAXATION** | **5,649** | **10,206** | **2,697** |
| Balance brought forward | 12,903 | 2,697 | - |
| **BALANCE CARRIED FORWARD** | **18,552** | **12,903** | **2,697** |

*advisers*    **Auditors**    National Audit Office    23-24 Park Place, Cardiff CF1 3BA

# *Stonebridge Housing Action Trust (HAT)*

Kassinga House
37-41 Winchelsea Road
London NW10 8UN

**Tel** 0181 961 0278
**Fax** 0181 961 0291

**Contact** Sorrel Brookes

| | |
|---|---|
| *status* | Executive body |
| *founded* | 1994 |
| *sponsor* | Department of Environment, Transport and the Regions (DETR) |
| *powers* | Housing Act 1988. Leasehold Reform, Housing and Urban Development Act 1993 |
| *mission* | The social and economic regeneration of the Stonebridge Estate in north-west London by 2004. |
| *tasks* | To provide new or refurbished homes for tenants. To tackle the social and economic deprivation of the estate - by working in partnership with residents and local agencies to improve access to jobs, training, and community youth and leisure facilities. |

*operations*  Management: The management team aims to maximise the involvement of residents, including children and young people, and to build productive partnerships with employers and other agencies. It comprises the Chief Executive and four operational directors. Six sub-committees focus on specific areas of its work and regulate its activities. In 1996 the HAT took over the management and maintenance of the estate from Brent Council.

Policy: Planning permission for the wholesale redevelopment of Stonebridge was obtained in 1997.

Trends: Since taking over from Brent, all major estate services and maintenance contracts have been tendered and re-let. The estate management services were market tested and the in-house team appointed for four years.

*performance*  1996/97 targets met.

*board*  Appointed by the Secretary of State from residents and external advertisements.

| | | |
|---|---|---|
| Chair | Ivan Weekes | |
| Deputy Chair | Mary Rogers | |
| Members | Clement Bedeau | Tullah Persand |
| | Tina Fahm | Pauline Ponsonby |
| | Ian Ferguson | Caroline Power |
| | Harbinder Kaur | Theresa Quaye |
| | Dorian Leatham | Irwin Van Colle |
| *Accounting Officer* | *Chief Executive* | |

*staff*  54

| | |
|---|---|
| Chief Executive | Sorrel Brookes |
| Director of Housing Management | John Brewster |
| Director of Finance & Administration | Nick Coates |
| Director of Development & Special Initiatives | Ian McDermott |
| Director of Employment & Social Regeneration | Michael Pearce |

*financial*

| INCOME & EXPENDITURE | | |
|---|---|---|
| **Year end: 31 March** | **1997** | **1996** |
| | **£000** | **£000** |
| **INCOME** | | |
| Government Grants | 5,202 | 2,397 |
| Property Income | 4,246 | 2,438 |
| | **9,448** | **4,835** |
| **EXPENDITURE** | | |
| Administrative expenditure | (2,588) | (1,230) |
| Financial assistance | (221) | (26) |
| Operating costs | (6,663) | (3,599) |
| | **(9,472)** | **(4,855)** |

| | | |
|---|---|---|
| **OPERATING DEFICIT** | **(24)** | **(20)** |
| Interest receivable | 32 | 25 |
| Notional cost of capital | (59) | (18) |
| **SURPLUS/(DEFICIT) ON ORDINARY ACTIVITIES BEFORE TAXATION** | **(51)** | **(13)** |
| Taxation on surplus on ordinary activities | (8) | (5) |
| **RESULT OF ORDINARY ACTIVITIES AFTER TAXATION** | **(59)** | **(18)** |

| *advisers* | **Bankers** | Lloyds Bank | 58 High Street, London NW10 4LP |
|---|---|---|---|
| | **Auditors** | Binder Hamlyn | 20 Old Bailey,London EC4 |
| | **Solicitors** | Field Fisher Waterhouse | 41 Vine Street, London EC3N 2AA |
| *publications* | Annual Report | | |

# Student Awards Agency for Scotland (SAAS)

Gyleview House
3 Redheughs Rigg
Edinburgh EH12 9HH

**Tel** 0131 244 5823
**Fax** 0131 244 5887

| | |
|---|---|
| *status* | Executive agency |
| *founded* | 1994 |
| *sponsor* | Scottish Office |
| *powers* | Student Allowances (Scotland) Regulations |
| *mission* | Providing financial support for Scottish students on full-time UK higher education courses. |
| *tasks* | Administering grants to higher education students under the various schemes: Students' Allowance Scheme (undergraduate courses); Postgraduate Students' Allowance Scheme (short professional or vocational course); Scottish Studentship Scheme (higher degrees); Nursing and Midwifery Bursary Scheme. Giving money to the Student Loans Company Ltd for it to arrange Student Loans. Also distributing Access funds to eligible institutions in Scotland for them to distribute to their own students. Keeping a register of educational endowments. |
| *operations* | Management: The Chief Executive reports to the Secretary of State. There is a Management Board comprising the Chief Executive, three Group Managers and a Finance Manager, which determines policies and priorities. The Chief Executive is appointed by open competition. |
| | Policy: Delay in introduction of new IT system resulted in use of labour-intensive mainframe computer system continuing while staff had already been reduced; it will be in place for academic year 1997/98. |
| | Trends: Very tight financial constraints. |
| *performance* | Two out of seven key targets met 1996/97. |
| *board* | Management Board. |

| | |
|---|---|
| Chief Executive | K MacRae |
| Finance Group Manager | SD Blyth |
| Group Manager IT | Alan Bruce |
| Group Manager Undergraduate | CD Crawford |
| Group Manager Agency, Postgraduate, Nursery & Midwifery Bursary | GJG Halford |
| Group Manager Policy | Mrs GJ Thompson |
| *Accounting Officer* | *Chief Executive* |

| | |
|---|---|
| *staff* | 134.5 |

| financial | INCOME & EXPENDITURE | | |
|---|---|---|---|
| | Year end: 31 March | **1997** | **1996** |
| | | **£000** | **£000** |
| | **EXPENDITURE** | | |
| | Staff costs | 2,051 | 2,158 |
| | Depreciation | 82 | 81 |
| | Other operating charges | 1,432 | 1,311 |
| | **EXPENDITURE BEFORE INTEREST** | **3,565** | **3,550** |
| | Interest | 98 | 42 |
| | **TOTAL EXPENDITURE** | **3,663** | **3,592** |

*advisers* **Auditors**      National Audit Office          22 Melville Street, Edinburgh EH3 7NS

*publications*   *1996-97 Annual Report*

# Student Loans Company (SLC)

100 Bothwell St
Glasgow G2 7JD

**Tel** 0141 306 2000
**Fax** 0141 306 2006          **Web** http://www.slc.co.uk

| | |
|---|---|
| *status* | Executive body |
| *founded* | 1990, 1996 as executive body |
| *sponsor* | Department for Education and Employment (DfEE) |
| *powers* | Education (Student Loans) Act 1990, Education (Student Loans) (Northern Ireland) Order 1990 |
| *mission* | To administer the student loan scheme throughout the UK within the policy context and legislative framework laid down. |
| *tasks* | Pays loans to students, notifies students how much they have to repay, collects the monies due, recovers debts. |
| *operations* | Management: SLC's joint shareholders are the Secretary of State for Education and Employment and the Secretary of State for Scotland. The Chief Executive is responsible for overall management and reports to the Board. Two senior civil servants act as Departmental Assessors and attend Board meetings. The company's Management Team has been working closely with DfEE and its professional advisors in relation to selling part of the debt portfolio to the private sector. |
| | Policy: Selling of debt portfolio to private sector (£2 billion in 1998/99). Proposals to contract out the administrative work. |
| | Trends: Continuing changes to loan and grant entitlement are increasing growth in the rate of loan take-up. |
| *performance* | Full performance report in company's *Annual Report*. |
| *board* | Appointed by the joint shareholders, the Secretaries of State for Education and Employment and  Scotland |

| | |
|---|---|
| Non-Executive Chairman | Sir Ronald Norman OBE |
| Chief Executive | Colin Ward |
| Non-Executive Director | Prof Sir Eric Ash CBE |
| Finance & Administration Director | John Morrison |
| Department Assessor | Neil Flint |
| Department Assessor | Kenneth MacRae |
| *Accounting Officer* | *Chief Executive* |

*staff*      410

| | |
|---|---|
| Chief Executive | Colin Ward |
| Finance & Administration Director | John Morrison |
| Company Secretary | Denise McShane |
| Collections Director | Peter Gregory |
| Information Services Director | Bob Jones |
| Loan Services Director | Erik Ostman |

*financial*

| PROFIT & LOSS Year end: 31 March | 1997 £000 | 1996 £000 | 1995 £000 |
|---|---|---|---|
| TURNOVER | 17,007 | 16,243 | 15,846 |
| ADMINISTRATIVE EXPENSES | (17,034) | (16,262) | (15,884) |
| | (27) | (19) | (38) |
| Interest receivable | 36 | 26 | 51 |
| RESULT BEFORE TAXATION | 9 | 7 | 13 |
| Tax | (9) | (7) | (13) |
| RESULT FOR YEAR | - | - | - |

*advisers*

| | | |
|---|---|---|
| **Bankers** | Royal Bank of Scotland | Sauchie Hall Street, Glasgow |
| **Auditors** | KPMG | 21 Blythswood Square, Glasgow |
| **Solicitors** | McGrigor Donald | Queen Street, Edinburgh |

*publications*    *Students Loans: A Guide for Students*


# Tai Cymru (Housing for Wales)

25/30 Lambourne Crescent
Llanishen
Cardiff CF4 5ZJ

**Tel** 01222 741500
**Fax** 01222 741501        **Web** http://www/tc-hfw.gov.uk

*status*    Executive body

*founded*    1989

*sponsor*    Welsh Office

*powers*    Housing Associations Act 1985. The Housing Act 1996

*mission*    Regulation of Registered Social Landlords (RSLs), who currently manage over 50,000 properties in Wales. Funding RSLs by means of grants.

*tasks*    As independent regulator, ensuring that Welsh RSLs consistently attain high standards; planning, funding and supervising the social housing programme being delivered by RSLs.

*operations*    Management: Main office in Cardiff and a small one in north Wales. Chief Executive is supported by three Directors (Operations, Performance Audit and Finance & Administration). Virtually all programmes rely on a private finance component. Sale of loan portfolio was completed in 1997.

Policy: Closer working relationships with local authorities. Low Cost Home Ownership schemes very successful.

Trends: Subject to the Government of Wales Bill receiving Royal Assent, Tai Cymru's functions will be transferred to the Welsh Office on 1 January 1999. A Shadow Housing Division will be in place from October 1998. Funding reduced by 30% for 1997/98.

*performance*    All targets in operational plan were met or exceeded in 1996/97.

*board*    Appointed by the Secretary of State.

| | |
|---|---|
| Chairman | Gerry Corless CBE |
| Chief Executive | Adam Peat |
| Members | Leighton Andrews |
| | John Carr CBE |
| | Philip Pedley |
| | Julia White MBE |
| *Accounting Officer* | *Chief Executive* |

*staff*    68

| | |
|---|---|
| Chief Executive | Adam Peat |
| Director Operations & Deputy Chief Executive | John Bader |
| Director, Finance & Administration Division | Philip Gray |
| Director, Perfomance Audit Division | Peter Lawler |

*financial*

| INCOME & EXPENDITURE Year end: 31 March | 1997 £000 | 1996 £000 | 1995 £000 |
|---|---|---|---|
| Interest receivable | 6,787 | 7,377 | 8,967 |
| Interest payable | (6,200) | (6,946) | (8,815) |
| Net surplus on sale of loan book | 733 | 0 | 0 |
| Grants from the Secretary of State | 108,239 | 117,232 | 131,971 |
| Other receipts | 4,501 | 3,972 | 5,456 |
| Grants paid to housing associations | (112,740) | (121,204) | (137,427) |
| Recoveries of grant on sales and surplus rental income | | | |
| Receivable | 1,626 | 1,326 | 1,721 |
| Payable to the Secretary of State | (1,626) | (1,326) | (1,721) |
| Grant-in-aid receivable | 2,901 | 2,871 | 2,844 |
| Other income | 61 | 62 | 0 |
| Administrative expenditure | (3,068) | (3,005) | (2,844) |
| Diminution in value/depreciation | (70) | (3) | (3) |
| SURPLUS ON ORDINARY ACTIVITIES BEFORE TAX | 1,144 | 356 | 149 |
| Tax on surplus on ordinary activities | (432) | (120) | (33) |
| Adjustment for notional costs | 102 | 68 | 0 |
| SURPLUS FOR YEAR | 814 | 304 | 116 |

*advisers*

**Bankers**  Barclays Bank

**Auditors**  KPMG
Coopers & Lybrand

*publications*  Annual Report

# Tate Gallery

Millbank
London SW1P 4RG

**Tel** 0171 887 8000
**Fax** 0171 887 8007      **Web** http://www.tate.org.uk

**Contact** Sandy Nairne

*status*  Executive body
*founded*  1992 (as independent institution)
*sponsor*  Department for Culture, Media and Sport (DCMS)
*powers*  Museums and Galleries Act 1992
*mission*  To increase public awareness, understanding and appreciation of British art from the 16th century to the present day and of international modern and contemporary art.
*tasks*  Displaying and adding to the collection at the galleries in London, Liverpool and St Ives. Documenting, researching and publishing the collection. Caring for the collection by means of an active programme of conservation. Arranging complementary exhibitions.
*operations*  Management: The Director is assisted by three Directors and two Keepers. Liverpool and St Ives galleries have separate Advisory Councils and are run by individual curators.

Policy: Developing a new gallery of modern art in London and extending the gallery in Liverpool.

Trends: Further cut in public funding. Private sector funding is crucial in carrying out its work.
*performance*  Record annual attendance figures.
*board*  Trustees are appointed by the Prime Minister.

**Tate Gallery Liverpool Advisory Council**
Chairman — Paula Ridley OBE
Members — Tom Bloxam
Mark Blundell — Prof Jennifer Latto
Cllr Joe Davaney — Aileen McEvoy
Mike David — Prof Roger Wilson
Cllr Beatrice Fraenkel — Bill Woodrow
Robert Hopper — Peter Woods

**Tate Gallery St Ives Advisory Council**
Chairman — Sir Richard Carew Pole
Members — Cllr Doris Ansari — Desmond Hosken
Shirley Beck — John Hubbard
Audrey Bott — Tessa Jackson
Giles Clotworthy — Prof Alan Livingston
Chris Cochlin — Jenni Lomax
Caroline Dudley — Michael O'Donnell
John Farmer — Cllr Barbara Spring
Lady Carol Holland MBE — Cllr Joan Vincent

**staff** 573

|  |  |
|---|---|
| Director | Nicholas Serota |
| Assistant to the Director | Suzanne Freeman |
| Director of Finance & Administration | Alex Beard |
| Director, Tate Gallery of British Art | Stephen Deucher |
| Director of Collection Services | James France |
| Director of Collections | Jerermy Lewison |
| Director of Public & Regional Services | Sandy Nairne |
| Projector Director, Tate Gallery of Modern Art | Dawn Austwick |
| Director of Buildings & Gallery Services | Peter Wilson |
| Development Director | Judy Beard |
| Managing Director, Tate Gallery Publishing | Celia Clear |
| Head of Human Resources | John Mockler |
| Secretary to the Board of Trustees | Sharon Page |
| Director, Tate Gallery Restaurant | Nicholas Stanley |
| Head of Communications | Damien Whitmore |

**financial**

**INCOME FROM GRANT-IN-AID AND OTHER SOURCES**
Year end: 31 March

| | 1996 £m | 1995 £m |
|---|---|---|
| **GRANT-IN-AID** | 18.9 | 17.2 |
| **OTHER INCOME** | | |
| Capital & development | 17.4 | 2.8 |
| Collection purchases | 0.5 | 1.2 |
| **OPERATING** | | |
| Admissions | 1.9 | 1.3 |
| Sponsors | 1.3 | 1.2 |
| Donations | 0.3 | 0.7 |
| Trading (net contribution) | 1.5 | 1.1 |
| Other | 1.4 | 1.9 |
| | 6.4 | 6.2 |
| **TOTAL** | 43.2 | 27.4 |

**advisers**
**Bankers** Coutts & Co
**Auditors** National Audit Office
**Solicitors** Allen and Overy
**Public Relations** Bolton and Quinn

**publications** Biennial Report, Concise Guide

**branches**
Tate Gallery Liverpool
Albert Dock
Liverpool L3 4BB
Tel 0151 7093223
Fax 0151 7093122

Tate Gallery St Ives
Porthmeor Beach
Cornwall TR26 1TG
Tel 01736 796226
Fax 01736 794480

# *Teacher Training Agency (TTA)*

Portland House
Stag Place
London SW1E 5TT

**Tel** 0171 925 3700
**Fax** 0171 925 6073

**E-mail** tta@gtnet.gov.uk

| | |
|---|---|
| *status* | Executive body |
| *founded* | 1994 |
| *sponsor* | Department for Education and Employment (DfEE) |
| *powers* | Education Act 1994 |
| *mission* | Raising standards in schools by improving the quality of teacher training, teaching and school leadership, and by raising the status and esteem of the teaching profession. |
| *tasks* | Attracting sufficient high-quality candidates to the profession, increasing the allocation of places to high quality training institutions, raising initial teacher training (ITT) standards, ensuring structured support for first- year teachers, improving professional competence, underpinning the profession with evidence and research, improving school leadership and management, informing and advising the Secretary of State. |
| *operations* | Management: Organised into five departments: Teacher Supply, Finance & Quality, Corporate Management, Funding Allocation & Personnel Management, Teacher Training. |
| | Policy: Outward looking and consultative, working closely with key partners, in particular OFSTED, HEFCE and the new QCA. |
| | Trends: The new government has placed enormous confidence in the TTA's ability to improve teacher training and recruitment. The Secretary of State has made teachers and heads the heart of the government's drive to raise school standards. He has launched the National Professional Qualification for Headship (NPQH). Continuing professional development and research is being targeted to bring the profession into line with others, eg medicine, law and accountancy. |
| *performance* | 1996/97 targets all achieved or on target. |

**board**

| | | |
|---|---|---|
| Chairman | Prof Clive Booth | |
| Chief Executive | Anthea Millett | |
| Members | Waheed Alli | |
| | Keith Anderson CBE | Tricia Pritchard |
| | Paul Ennals | John Steele |
| | Prof John Gray | Lady Stubbs |
| | Dr Peter Knight CBE | Janet Trotter OBE |
| *Accounting Officer* | *Chief Executive* | |

**staff** 42

| | |
|---|---|
| Chief Executive | Anthea Millett |
| Head of Finance & Quality | Sheena Evans |
| Head of Corporate Management | Stephen Hillier |
| Head of Funding Allocation & Personnel Management | Mike Mercer |
| Head of Teacher Training | Frankie Sulke |
| Board Secretariat & Corporate Planning | John Carr |
| Teacher Supply & Recruitment | Monica Farthing |
| Initial Teacher Training | Annie Grant |
| School Leadership | George Gyte |
| Continuing Professional Development & Research | Steve Harrison |
| External Communications | Dorian Jabri |
| Quality Assessment in ITT | Cath Martindale |
| Funding & Allocations In-Service Training | Ron Rampling |
| Funding & Allocations ITT | James Rogers |
| TTA Unit in Wales | Phil Rogers |
| Contracts, Customer Care & Codes of Conduct | Brian Shipton |
| TTA Running Costs | Derek Spencer |
| Initial Teacher Training | Jill Staley |
| TTA Staffing | Heather Stone |
| Financial Control & Property | Ruth Turley |
| Quality Assessment in ITT | Nigel Vivian |
| Continuing Professional Development & Research | Angela Walsh |

*financial*

| INCOME & EXPENDITURE Year end: 31 March | 1997 £000 | 1996 £000 |
|---|---|---|
| **INCOME** | | |
| **Grants received** | | |
| Programme: recurrent | 188,516 | 118,014 |
| Programme: capital | 4,473 | 6,120 |
| Administration costs | 3,041 | 2,309 |
| | **196,030** | **126,443** |
| Transfers from deferred government grant | 320 | 249 |
| Other operating income | 304 | 33 |
| | **196,654** | **126,725** |
| **EXPENDITURE** | | |
| Grants paid under section 4(2) of 1994 Act | 181,345 | 119,645 |
| Research under section 11 of 1994 Act | 267 | 137 |
| Provision of information and advice under section 1(1)(b) of 1988 Act | 9,793 | 2,387 |
| | **191,402** | **122,169** |
| Administration costs | | |
| Staff | 1,797 | 1,201 |
| Other | 1,215 | 1,039 |
| Depreciation | 325 | 249 |
| Loss on revaluation | 16 | 0 |
| Notional costs | 216 | 99 |
| | **3,569** | **2,588** |
| **OPERATING SURPLUS/(DEFICIT)** | **1,684** | **1,968** |
| Transfers to and from reserves | | |
| Appropriations to DfEE | 0 | 0 |
| Reversal of cost of capital | 212 | 96 |
| Retained surplus brought forward | 2,024 | (40) |
| **RETAINED SURPLUS CARRIED FORWARD** | **3,920** | **2,024** |

*branches*

Communication Centre
PO Box 3210
Chelmsford CM1 3WA
Tel 01245 454454
Fax 01245 261668

# *Tower Hamlets Housing Action Trust*

73 Usher Road
Bow
London E3 2HS

**Tel** 0181 983 4698          **E-mail** srands@thhat.demon.co.uk
**Fax** 0171 204 1556

**Contact** Jackie Odunoye, Acting Chief Executive

*status* — Executive body

*founded* — 1993

*sponsor* — Department of the Environment, Transport and the Regions (DETR)

*powers* — Housing Act 1988. Leasehold Reform, Housing and Urban Development Act 1993

*mission* — To breathe new life into the area by 2005.

*tasks* — Build new homes and manage them as efficiently and effectively as possible; encourage community activity; build up residents' employment skills and help them achieve their ambitions; involve residents in the Housing Action Trust's (HAT) decisions.

*operations* — Management: The Chief Executive reports to the Board. Income is from grant-in-aid and rental. Staff structure is currently going through a succession strategy. Housing Management Department has gone over to Old Ford Housing Association. Community & Economic Development Department has gone over to the Bow People's Trust.

Policy: To transfer the work of building and managing new homes to a housing association, Circle 33 Housing Trust. To transfer the community and economic development work to a new Community Development Trust. The HAT will be a much smaller organisation and its role will be much more behind-the- scenes.

Trends: No longer 100% government funding.

**performance** 1996/97 criteria met. Corporate Plan 1998-2001 now being developed.

**board** Appointed by DETR including three residents.

| | | |
|---|---|---|
| Chair | Dr Michael Barraclough | |
| Vice Chair | Sheila Drew-Smith | |
| Members | Cllr John Biggs | Barbara Richardson |
| | Lucinda Bolton | John Rogerson |
| | Jackie Harris | Christopher Toms |
| | Rev Andrew Mawson | Cllr Shahab Uddin |
| | Rory Moore | Tricia Zipfel |
| *Accounting Officer* | *Chief Executive* | |

**staff** 80

| | |
|---|---|
| Acting Chief Executive | Jackie Odunoye |
| Director of Development | Chris Johnson |

**financial**

| INCOME & EXPENDITURE Year end: 31 March | 1997 £ | 1996 £000 | 1995 £000 |
|---|---|---|---|
| **INCOME** | | | |
| Grant-in-aid | 9,800,000 | 10,018 | 10,043 |
| Rental Income and service charges | 2,396,574 | 2,571 | 2,570 |
| | 12,196,574 | 12,589 | 12,614 |
| **EXPENDITURE** | | | |
| Development | 6,145,556 | 5,081 | 5,083 |
| Housing | 2,105,851 | 3,470 | 3,897 |
| Community and economic development | 724,892 | 144 | 235 |
| Administrative services | 3,220,275 | 3,399 | 3,399 |
| | 12,196,574 | 12,094 | 12,614 |

**advisers**

**Bankers** Barclays Bank — Mile End & Bow Business Centre 240 Whitechapel Road, London E1 1BS

**Auditors** Pannell Kerr Forster — New Garden House, 78 Hatton Garden London EC1N 8JA

**Solicitors** Field Fisher Waterhouse — 41 Vine Street, London EC2 2AA

**publications** *Annual Report*

# *Traffic Director for London*

College House
Great Peter Street
London SW1P 3LN

**Tel** 0171 222 4545
**Fax** 0171 976 8640

**E-mail** @tdfl.gov.uk

**Contact** Heather Bolton, Media & PR Officer

**status** Executive body
**founded** 1991
**sponsor** Department of the Environment, Transport and the Regions (DETR)
**powers** Road Traffic Act 1991
**mission** To implement Red Routes and carry out strategic coordination of traffic management in London.
**tasks** Planning, coordinating, introducing, maintaining and monitoring traffic management measures on a network of Red Routes covering 315 miles of London's key roads. Traffic monitoring.

**operations**  Management: Chairman and Chief Executive is the same person, who reports directly to the Secretary of State. Firms of specialist consultants provide technical advice.

Policy: Developing and implementing new technology for traffic management. Now operating new bus lane enforcement camera project having carried out the research and develoment.

Trends: Increased measures to facilitate and encourage use of buses and bicycles and encourage walking.

**performance**  Implementation of Red Routes is slightly ahead of target.

**board**  There is no board.

| Accounting Officer | Traffic Director |
| --- | --- |

**staff**  25

| Traffic Director for London | Derek Turner |
| --- | --- |
| Senior Assistant Director (Finance & Administration) | RA Chapman |
| Senior Assistant Director (Technical) | M Allan |

**financial**

| INCOME & EXPENDITURE Year end: 31 March | 1997 £000 | 1996 £000 | 1995 £000 |
| --- | --- | --- | --- |
| **INCOME** | | | |
| Secretary of State - grant-in-aid | 17,094 | 15,273 | 10,053 |
| Other operating income | 303 | 80 | 46 |
| | **17,397** | **15,353** | **10,099** |
| **EXPENDITURE** | | | |
| Administrative/running costs | (1,679) | (1,294) | (1,416) |
| **Priority route programme:** | | | |
| Design and development | (2,314) | (2,431) | (4,447) |
| Implementation | (11,581) | (9,068) | (1,734) |
| Maintenance | (116) | (13) | (2) |
| Monitoring | (451) | (651) | (488) |
| Advancement of new technology | (1,234) | (1,873) | (2,013) |
| Operational expenditure | (17,375) | (15,330) | (10,100) |
| Depreciation of fixed assets | (227) | (343) | (393) |
| Transfer from deferred income | 233 | 340 | 383 |
| Notional insurance | (3) | - | - |
| Notional cost of capital | (10) | - | - |
| | **(17,382)** | **(15,333)** | **(10,110)** |
| **OPERATING SURPLUS** | **15** | **20** | **(11)** |
| Taxation | (25) | (20) | (11) |
| **RESULT FOR THE YEAR** | **(10)** | **-** | **(22)** |
| Reversal of notional cost of capital | 10 | - | - |
| **TRANSFER TO RESERVES** | **-** | **-** | **-** |

**advisers**

| | | |
| --- | --- | --- |
| **Bankers** | Barclays Bank | 155 Brompton Road, London SW3 1XD |
| **Auditors** | Kidsons Impey | Spectrum House, 20-26 Cursitor Street London EC4A 1HY |
| **Solicitors** | Dibb Lupton Alsop | 117 The Headrow, Leeds LS1 5JX |

**publications**  *Annual Report, Network Plan*

# Training & Employment Agency (T&EA)

39-49 Adelaide Street
Belfast BT2 8FD

**Tel** 01232 257777
**Fax** 01232 257778

**status**  Executive agency
**founded**  1990
**sponsor**  Northern Ireland Office, Department of Economic Development (DEDNI)
**powers**  Framework Document 1990

| | | |
|---|---|---|
| **mission** | As the principal employment organisation in NI, to assist economic development and help people find work through training and employment services delivered on the basis of equality of opportunity. | |

**mission** As the principal employment organisation in NI, to assist economic development and help people find work through training and employment services delivered on the basis of equality of opportunity.

**tasks** Assists companies in NI to increase their international competitiveness by promoting management development and encouraging employers to develop the skills and versatility of those in employment; to support the attraction of inward investment; to enable the unemployed to receive the necessary careers guidance; to help people find jobs and employers find suitable employees. Administers a range of training and development schemes and several EU programmes and initiatives.

**operations** Management: The Management Team consists of the Chief Executive and the Directors of the five divisions. Operates 31 offices and training centres across NI.

Policy: Long-term unemployed remain a priority. Second phase of AMBIT (American Management and Business Internship Training) started - funded by IFI and gives small businesses hands-on experience studying US companies.

Trends: In 1996/97 manufacturing output and employment continued to rise, but slower growth.

**performance** Only achieved two out of six key targets in 1996/97.

**board** Advisory Board members are appointed by the Secretary of State.

| | | |
|---|---|---|
| Chairman | W McGinnis OBE | |
| Members | B Carlin OBE | |
| | K Cleland | A McClure |
| | Mrs S Davidson | J McCusker |
| | Prof JF Fulton | Mrs C McKenna |
| | H Hastings | Ms SG Mercer |
| | J Kirkwood | A Smith |
| *Accounting Officer* | *Chief Executive* | |

**staff** 1217

| | |
|---|---|
| Chief Executive | Ian Walters |
| Director, Business Support Division | Victor Jordan |
| Director, Regional Operations Division | Derek Noble |
| Director, Training Division | Tom Scott |
| Director, Corporate Services Division | Chris Thompson |

**financial**

| INCOME & EXPENDITURE | | |
|---|---|---|
| **Year end: 31 March** | **1997** | **1996** |
| | **£000** | **£000** |
| **INCOME** | **(192)** | **(232)** |
| **EXPENDITURE** | | |
| Staff costs | 26,187 | 25,324 |
| Depreciation | 634 | 625 |
| Other operating charges | 11,458 | 9,628 |
| | 38,279 | 35,577 |
| **COST OF OPERATIONS BEFORE INTEREST** | **38,087** | **35,345** |
| Interest on capital employed | 620 | 597 |
| **NET COST OF OPERATIONS** | **38,707** | **35,942** |

**advisers** **Auditors** Northern Ireland Audit Office 106 University Street, Belfast BT7 1EU

# Treasury Solicitor's Department

Queen Anne's Chambers
28 Broadway
London SW1H 9JS

**Tel** 0171 210 3000

**status** Executive agency

**founded** 1996

**sponsor** Attorney General's Department

**powers** Framework Document 1996

| | |
|---|---|
| **mission** | Providing economic, effective and efficient legal services to government departments and publicly funded bodies in England and Wales. |
| **tasks** | Providing litigation and advisory services to government departments and public bodies in England and Wales; also administering property with no known owner. |
| **operations** | Management: The Ministerial Advisory Board advises the Attorney General on strategic management and the corporate plan, and monitors progress. The Treasury Solicitor is the Chief Executive and reports to the Attorney General, is who is responsible for setting the policy and financial framework. Headquarters are in London and a small number of advisory teams are located in the government departments they advise. |
| | Policy: Recovering full economic cost from clients. |
| | Trends: Chief Executive has unlimited delegated authority for competitive procurement. |
| **board** | Ministerial Advisory Board members appointed by the Attorney General. It is chaired by a Permanent Secretary from a government department and the other members are the Chief Executive and a private sector nominee. |

| Accounting Officer | Chief Executive |
|---|---|

# Trinity House Lighthouse Service (THLS)

Trinity Square
Tower Hill
London EC3N 4DH

**Tel** 0171 480 6601
**Fax** 0171 480 7662

| | |
|---|---|
| **status** | Executive body |
| **founded** | 1514 |
| **sponsor** | Department of the Environment, Transport and the Regions (DETR) |
| **powers** | Merchant Shipping and Maritime Security Act 1997 |
| **mission** | As the General Lighthouse Authority (GLA) for England, Wales, the Channel Islands and Gibraltar: to deliver reliable, efficient and cost-effective aids to navigation; service to assist the safe and expeditious passage of all classes of mariner. |
| **tasks** | To maintain 74 lighthouses (two abroad), 13 major floating aids, 18 beacons, 429 buoys, 14 radiobeacons, 48 radar beacons, 11 Decca Navigation stations. To inspect annually 9000 local aids to navigation. To collect light dues from commercial shipping. |
| **operations** | Management: Although part of The Corporation of Trinity House, THLS is financed separately from the Corporation's pilotage and charitable activities. The Corporation has delegated THLS management to the Lighthouse Board, which works within (32) policy statements provided by the Court of Elder Bretheren. The Chairman of the Lighthouse Board is THLS's Chief Executive. A Committee of Executive Directors meets regularly to review and update policy and targets. THLS works from five strategically located depots and a small administrative headquarters in London. The Examiners Committee (Elder Bretheren with wide marine experience) determines the mix of aids to navigation and gives consent to harbour authority aids. |
| | Policy: Along with the GLAs in Scotland and Ireland, a Joint GLA Marine Navigation Plan will provide an unencrypted and openly available Differential Global Positioning System by 1998. |
| | Trends: It collects money on behalf of all GLAs on behalf of DETR. Lighthouse automation programme nearing completion - only five manned stations left. |
| **performance** | Main measurement is availability of aids to navigation: above targets in all but one. |
| **board** | The Lighthouse Board comprises four Elder Bretheren (three Executive, one Non-Executive), three Associate Members appointed by the Secretary of State and three senior officials of the Corporation who are non-voting Executive Members. |

| Chairman | Rear Admiral PB Rowe |
|---|---|
| Non-Executive Members | K Ashcroft |
| | Captain M Rawlinson |
| | Captain CMC Stewart |
| | WAC Thomson |

| | |
|---|---|
| Director of Administration | DI Brewer |
| Director of Finance | KW Clark |
| Director of Operations | Captain PH King |
| Director of Navigational Requirements | Captain N MacD Turner |
| Director of Engineering | MGB Wannell |

*staff*      465

# UK Atomic Energy Authority (UKAEA)

B.521 Harwell
Didcot
Oxfordshire OX11 ORA

**Tel** 01235 436897
**Fax** 01235 436899

*status*      Executive body

*sponsor*      Department of Trade and Industry (DTI)

*powers*      Framework Document

*mission*      Nuclear liability management - to safely manage and at the appropriate time decommission the nuclear reactors and other R&D facilities that were used to help develop Britain's nuclear industry.

*tasks*      Caring for and safely dismantling active facilities no longer in use; disposing of radioactive waste in an environmentally acceptable way; ensuring the security of nuclear facilities and materials; implementing the UK's contribution to EU nuclear fusion research programme.

*operations*      Management: Sites it owns are: Dounreay, Winscale, Risley, Harwell and Cullham, and Winfrith. UKAEA Constabulary Police Authority (470 officers) under leadership of Chief Constable.

     Policy: Virtually all decommissioning work is carried out by external contractors.

     Trends: Increasing income from sites by leasing or selling non-nuclear licensed land for development or attracting new tenants for buildings.

*performance*      Met or exceeded targets in 1996/97.

*board*

| | |
|---|---|
| Chairman | Admiral Sir Kenneth Eaton GBE KCB |
| Chief Executive | Dr Derek Poley CBE |
| Non-Executive Director | Chris Appleton |
| Director, Nuclear Operations | John Baxter |
| Director, Property Management & Services | James Bretherton |
| Non-Executive Director | Dr Rex Gaisford CBE |
| Non-Executive Director | Trevor Harrison |
| Non-Executive Director | Neil Hirst |
| Director, Dounreay | Dr Roy Nelson OBE |
| Director, Safety | Dr Richard Peckover |
| Non-executive Director | Clive Pickford |
| Director, Fusion | Dr Derek Robinson |
| Director, Finance | Paul White |

*staff*      2030

*financial*

| **REVENUE & EXPENDITURE** | |
|---|---|
| **Year end: 31 March** | **1997** |
| | **£m** |
| **REVENUE** | |
| DTI sourced revenue | |
| DRAWMOPS programme letter | 143 |
| Property PL | 11 |
| UK Fusion Programme PL | 15 |
| Other PLs | 12 |
| | **181** |

| | |
|---|---|
| Other sources | |
| Lease of buildings | 19 |
| Technical services | 31 |
| Policing | 11 |
| Euratom/ JET Fusion Projects | 14 |
| | **75** |
| | **256** |
| | |
| **EXPENDITURE** | |
| Decommissioning and Waste Management Services | 114 |
| Property Services | 34 |
| Special Payments | 13 |
| Routine Purchases | 17 |
| Plant Operations | 17 |
| Policing | 15 |
| Sites and Liabilities Management | 24 |
| UK Fusion Programme | 13 |
| | **247** |

**branches**

*Dounreay*
Nr Thurso
Caithness KW14 7T
Tel 01847804000

*Winscale*
Seascale
Cumbria CA20 1PF
Tel 01235 820220

*Risley*
Warrington
Cheshire WA3 6AT
Tel 01235 820220

*Harwell & Culham*
Harwell International Business Centre for Science
Technology
Didcot
Oxon OX11 0RA
Tel 01235 820220

*Culham Science Centre*
Abingdon
Oxon OX14 3DB
Tel 01235 820220

*Winfrith*
Winfrith Technology Centre
Dorchester
Dorset DT2 8DH
Tel 01235 820220

# UK Ecolabelling Board (UKEB)

Eastbury House
30-34 Albert Embankment
London SE1 7TL

**Tel** 0171 820 1199
**Fax** 0171 820 1104

**E-mail** Info@ukeb.demon.co.uk

**status**   Executive body

**founded**   1992

**sponsor**   Department of the Environment, Transport and the Regions (DETR)

**powers**   European Communities Act 1972. UK Ecolabelling Regulations 1992. Council Regulation (EEC) 880/92 March 1992

**mission**   This is an EU scheme to promote the design, production, marketing and use of products which have a reduced environmental impact during their entire life-cycle and also to provide customers with better information on the environmental impact of products - all without compromising safety or fitness-for-use.

**tasks**   To operate the EU ecolabelling scheme in the UK by promoting it to industry, retailers and consumers and by developing product criteria.

**operations**   Management: The Secretary of State issues the Management Statement and the Financial Memorandum (within which UKEB works) and supplies most of the funds. The European Commission contributes towards the cost of product criteria development and travel. He is responsible for the day-to-day running of UKEB, supported by the senior officers.

Policy: To make a major contribution to the review of European ecolabel regulation - in response to the EC's proposals for an independent European Ecolabel Organisation to oversee the scheme, and a graded ecolabel.

Trends: A consumer study with the National Consumer Council showed that they were interested in green purchasing and would welcome ecolabels when shopping. The ISO (International Standards Organisation) is drafting standards on environmental labelling and life-cycle assessment.

**performance** Of 1996/97 targets, eight achieved or exceeded, five partially achieved, four not achieved.

**board** Members of the Board are Non-Executive, with the exception of the Chief Executive.

| Chairman | Dr Elizabeth Nelson | |
|---|---|---|
| Members | Tim Brown | Kenneth Miles |
| | Tony Burton | Jyoti Munsiff |
| | Prof Roland Clift | Ian Robinson |
| | Anne Daltrop | Peter White |
| | Julia Hailes | Catherine Whitehead |
| | John Longworth | Nigel Whittaker |
| | George Medley | Stella Whittaker |
| *Accounting Officer* | *Chief Executive* | |

**staff** Three

| Chief Executive | Jerry Rendell |
|---|---|
| Product Development Manager | Dr Paul Jackson |
| Finance & Operations Manager | Michael Jones |
| Marketing Manager | James Pearson |

**financial**

| INCOME & EXPENDITURE Year end: 31 March | 1997 £ | 1996 £ | 1995 £ |
|---|---|---|---|
| **INCOME** | | | |
| Grant-in-aid received | 986,000 | 842,000 | 775,355 |
| Deferred Government grant | 6,972 | 4,147 | 4,202 |
| Income from activities | 30,158 | 68,198 | 96,386 |
| | **1,023,130** | **914,345** | **875,943** |
| **EXPENDITURE** | | | |
| Staff costs | 396,797 | 407,225 | 414,892 |
| Other operating costs | 642,926 | 477,560 | 461,368 |
| Depreciation of fixed assets | 15,255 | 15,189 | 14,839 |
| | **1,054,978** | **899,974** | **891,099** |
| **(DEFICIT)/SURPLUS BEFORE NOTIONAL COSTS** | **(31,848)** | **14,371** | **(15,156)** |
| Interest | - | (847) | (1,121) |
| Insurance | (614) | (644) | (669) |
| **(DEFICIT)/SURPLUS AFTER NOTIONAL COSTS** | **(32,462)** | **12,880** | **(16,946)** |
| Removal of notional interest | 0 | 847 | 1,121 |
| **(DEFICIT)/SURPLUS FOR THE FINANCIAL YEAR** | **(32,462)** | **13,727** | **(15,825)** |
| Appropriation | (74,545) | - | - |
| Transfer from revaluation reserve | 9,294 | 9,294 | 9,294 |
| Deficit brought forward | (10,269) | (33,290) | (26,759) |
| **DEFICIT CARRIED FORWARD** | **(107,982)** | **(10,269)** | **(33,290)** |

**advisers** **Auditors** Binder Hamlyn

# UK Hydrographic Office (UKHO)

Admiralty Way
Taunton
Somerset TA1 2DN

**Tel** 01823 337900
**Fax** 01823 284077

**E-mail** @hydro.gov.uk
**Web** http://www.hydro.gov.uk

**status** Defence agency. Trading fund

**founded** 1795. Defence agency 1990, trading fund 1996

**sponsor** Ministry of Defence (MOD)

**powers** Framework Document 1990

**mission** To meet national, defence and civil needs for navigational charts, publications and other hydrographic information.

| | |
|---|---|
| **tasks** | The National Hydrographic Programme - surveying for civil as well as military purposes, including international responsibilities and the Antarctic survey; defence programme - responding to hydrographic, oceanographic and geophysical requirements of the Royal Navy and MOD customers through contractual arrangements; maritime safety information - publicising timely and accurate information through Radio Navigational Warnings and Notices to Mariners; chart production - from traditional paper to digital charts; bilateral arrangements on the exchange of data; digital product development - commercial ARCS (Admiralty Roster Chart Service) and ENC (Electronic Navigational Chart); representing the UK at the International Hydrographic Organisation (IHO). |
| **operations** | Management: The Secretary of State determines policy and the financial framework and delegates responsibility to a minister, the Parliamentary Under Secretary of State for Defence, who chairs the HO Ministerial Advisory Board. The Hydrographer is the Chief Executive and is responsible for day-to-day management. He is appointed by the Chief of Naval Staff but reports directly to the Minister. The Board consists of the Hydrographer, five Executive Directors and a Non-Executive Director. |
| | Policy: Focus on customers and external orientation. Increasing number of products will be held electronically. |
| | Trends: Increasing international partnerships. Half of the 62 IHO member states have now reached exchange of data understandings. |
| **performance** | 95% of Defence Programme targets met; 98% of civil chart availability targets met in 1996/97. |
| **board** | Appointed by the Secretary of State. |

| | |
|---|---|
| Hydrographer of the Navy & Chief Executive | Rear Admiral John Clarke |
| Director of Production | Barbara Bond |
| Director of Defence Requirements | Captain Robert Bradshaw |
| Director of Marketing | Ian Harkness |
| Non-Executive Director | Ron Hughes |
| Director of Corporate Services | Michael Pack |
| Director of Planning | Steve Parnell |
| *Accounting Officer* | *Chief Executive* |

**staff** 844

**financial**

| INCOME & EXPENDITURE | |
|---|---|
| Year end: 31 March | **1997** |
| | **£000** |
| **TURNOVER** | **36,247** |
| **COST OF SALES** | **(20,999)** |
| **GROSS PROFIT** | **15,248** |
| Distribution costs | (929) |
| Administrative expenses | (10,424) |
| | **3,865** |
| Other operating income | 651 |
| **PROFIT ON ORDINARY ACTIVITIES BEFORE INTEREST** | **4,516** |
| Interest receivable and similar income | 525 |
| Interest payable and similar charges | (1,371) |
| **PROFIT FOR THE FINANCIAL YEAR** | **3,670** |
| Retained profit (loss) brought forward | - |
| **RETAINED PROFIT (LOSS) CARRIED FORWARD** | **3,670** |

# UK Passport Agency

Clive House
70-78 Petty France
London SW1H 9HD

**Tel** 0171 271 8508
**Fax** 0171 271 8813          **Web** http://www.open.gov.uk/ukpass

| | |
|---|---|
| **status** | Executive agency |
| **founded** | 1991 |
| **sponsor** | Home Office |
| **mission** | To provide passport services for British nationals in the UK. |
| **tasks** | To issue new and replacement passports and amend existing passports; to arrange for the availability of other travel documents to meet particular needs; to maintain adequate security measures against passport fraud; to advise the Home Secretary on the appropriate level of full-cost fees; to collect the fees. |

**operations**
Management: There is a Management Board comprising the Chief Executive, the Director of Operations and four heads of department. There are six passport offices in Belfast, Glasgow, Liverpool, London, Newport and Peterborough, supported by a headquarters located in London. Partnerships arrangements exist with Post Office Counters, Lloyds Bank and World Choice Travel Agency for the receipt and basic checking of completed application forms and payover of passport fees. There are now 3800 high street outlets where passport applications can be lodged.

Policy: The supply of the passport and the passport personalisation process will be outsourced as the current computerised personalisation equipment comes to the end of its life in 1998.

**board**
Advisory Board appointed by the Home Secretary from business and the Home Office.

| | |
|---|---|
| Chairman | Hike Eland |
| Members | Keith Ackroyd |
| | Malcolm Davidson |
| | Philippa Drew |
| | Robert Fulton |

**staff**
1874, (all civil servants)

| | |
|---|---|
| Chief Executive | David Gatenby |
| Deputy Chief Executive & Director of Operations | Kevin Sheehan |
| Head of Finance | Ally Cook |
| Head of Systems | John Davies |
| Head of Human Resources | Richard Mycroft |
| Project Program Manager | John McColl |

**financial**

**INCOME & EXPENDITURE**

| Year end: 31 March | 1997 £000 | 1996 £000 | 1995 £ |
|---|---|---|---|
| **TURNOVER FROM CONTINUING ACTIVITIES** | | | |
| Standart passport services | 82,917 | 76,912 | 64,363,509 |
| British visitors passports | 0 | 13,214 | 22,980,687 |
| Visa services | 6 | 9 | 9,700 |
| | 82,923 | 90,135 | 87,353,896 |
| **COST OF SALES** | | | |
| Labour costs (inc. movement in work in progress) | 21,896 | 20,081 | 17,515,162 |
| Payments to Post Office Counters Ltd for the issue of BVPs | 0 | 6,611 | 12,663,056 |
| Bank charges | 158 | 141 | 157,546 |
| PIMIS maintenance | 1,243 | 1,216 | 1,104,273 |
| Passport stationery (inc. movement in stock) | 10,974 | 10,001 | 8,337,466 |
| Depreciation | 304 | 868 | 1,052,275 |
| | 34,575 | 38,918 | 40,829,778 |
| **GROSS SURPLUS** | **48,348** | **51,217** | **46,524,118** |
| **DISTRIBUTION COSTS** | | | |
| Postal charge | 2,957 | 2,553 | 1,848,214 |
| Application form distribution | 459 | 591 | 226,371 |
| | 3,416 | 3,144 | 2,074,585 |
| **ADMINISTRATIVE EXPENSES** | | | |
| Staff | 7,242 | 7,031 | 6,488,894 |
| Accommodation | 4,133 | 5,469 | 5,637,918 |
| Other costs | 3,259 | 3,298 | 2,933,543 |
| Depreciation | 101 | 221 | 404,025 |
| **Notional charges:** | | | |
| HO Payroll | 171 | 160 | 708,273 |
| HO Accounts Branch | 20 | 19 | 34,041 |
| HO Internal Audit | 26 | 21 | 20,653 |
| Insurance | 47 | 47 | 42,359 |
| NAO Audit fee | 56 | 55 | 54,900 |
| | 320 | 302 | 860,226 |
| | 15,055 | 16,321 | 16,324,606 |
| Other operating income | 1,204 | 926 | 69,339 |
| **OPERATING SURPLUS** | **31,081** | **32,678** | **28,194,266** |
| Loss on revaluation | 2,656 | 0 | - |
| Loss on disposal of fixed assets | 0 | 917 | - |
| Interest on capital | 14 | 80 | 166,265 |
| **SURPLUS ON ORDINARY ACTIVITIES** | **28,411** | **31,681** | **28,028,001** |

**advisers**  **Auditors**   National Audit Office    157-197 Buckingham Palace Road
London SW1W 9SP

# UK Register of Organic Food Standards (UKROFS)

Nobel House
17 Smith Square
London SW1P 3JR

**Tel** 0171 270 8080

| | |
|---|---|
| *status* | Executive body |
| *founded* | 1987 |
| *sponsor* | Ministry of Agriculture, Fisheries and Food (MAFF) |
| *powers* | Framework Document |
| *mission* | Coordinates the activities of UK organic associations: Biodynamic Agricultural Association, the Irish Organic Farmers and Growers Association, Organic Farmers and Growers Ltd, the Organic Food Federation, the Scottish Organic Producers Association, and the Soil Association. |
| *tasks* | Legal authority to enforce the EC Regulation on organic food; set national standards; inspects the associations and the registered farmers and processors. |
| *operations* | Management: Small secretariat provided by MAFF assists the Board. |
| | Policy: Anyone growing or processing food which is to be sold as organic must by law by registered with UKROFS or a body approved by them and be inspected at least once a year. |
| | Trends: UK market increasing rapidly (but still less than 1% of UK household food sales). EU developing standards for organic animal production. |
| *board* | Independent Board appointed by Agriculture Ministers from producers, retailers, consumers and trading standards interests. |
| *staff* | Two |

# UK Sports Council (UKSC)

16 Upper Woburn Place
London WC1H 0QP

**Tel** 0171 273 1500
**Fax** 0171 383 5740

| | |
|---|---|
| *status* | Executive body |
| *founded* | 1997 |
| *sponsor* | Department of Culture, Media and Sport (DCMS) |
| *powers* | Royal Charter |
| *mission* | To coordinate and deal at a UK level with matters of common interest to the four home country Sports Councils (England, Northern Ireland, Scotland and Wales). |
| *tasks* | Preparing a UK strategy for sport; international relations, including attracting major sports events to the UK, working with the Council for Europe, and marketing UK sports expertise overseas; coordination of the proposed British Academy of Sport; doping control, including services to governing bodies and educational programmes. |
| *operations* | Management: From January 1997, the UKSC took over responsibility for UK affairs from the GB Sports Council. The assets and liabilities of the GB Sports Council were also transferred to the English and UK Sports Councils. |
| | Policy: To concentrate on the elite. |
| | Trends: It has been proposed that the four home Sports Councils, which are the distributors of Lottery Sports Fund, set aside a percentage of their funds to be allocated on the advice of UKPC to the development of the British Academy of Sport. |
| *board* | The Chairmen of the four home Sports Councils currently sit on UKSC. |

| Chairman | Sir Rodney Walker | |
|---|---|---|
| Vice-Chairmen | Trevor Brooking MBE | Gerald Dennis |
| Members | Julia Bracewell | Graeme Simmers OBE |
| | Tim Marshall MBE | Sarah Springman |
| | Keith Oates | Geoff Thompson MBE |
| | Michael Parker | Ossie Wheatley |
| Assessor | Simon Broadley | |
| Observers | Don Allen | |
| | Allan Alstead CBE | Eamonn McCartan |
| | George A Cubitt MBE | Linford Tatham |

*staff*  25

| Chief Executive | Derek Casey |
|---|---|
| Director of National Lottery | David Carpenter |
| Director of Corporate Services | Lew Hodges |
| Director of Development | Dr Anita White |
| Financial Services | Martin Ball |
| Administrative Services | Sandy Blaney |
| Sports Council Secretariat | Richard Bocock |
| Development | Paul Brivio |
| Management Audit | Barry Chivers |
| National Centres | John Davies |
| Information & Research | Arthur Dye |
| Policy | Sally Hart |
| Human Resources | Dawn Herlihy |
| Finance, National Lottery | Ian Holmes |
| Operations, National Lottery | Bob Knowles |
| Regional Services | Mike Lockhart |
| External Affairs | Jonathan O'Neil |
| Facilities Development | David Payne |
| International Affairs | John Scott |
| Public Affairs, National Lottery | Jenny Stokes |
| Doping Control | Michele Verroken |
| Information Technology | Mike Worthy |

*financial*

**INCOME & EXPENDITURE**

| Year end: 31 March | 1996 £000 | 1995 £000 |
|---|---|---|
| **INCOME** | | |
| Grant-in-aid | 47,004 | 47,458 |
| Operating Income | 2,938 | 2,817 |
| National Lottery | 643 | 133 |
| | 50,585 | 50,408 |
| **EXPENDITURE** | | |
| Staff costs | 10,319 | 10,496 |
| Grants and other operating costs | 40,667 | 40,804 |
| Restructuring costs | 2,361 | 0 |
| | 53,347 | 51,300 |
| **SURPLUS/(DEFICIT) FOR THE YEAR** | (2,762) | (892) |

**NATIONAL LOTTERY DISTRIBUTION ACCOUNT**
**INCOME & EXPENDITURE**

| Year end: 31 March | 1996 £000 | 1995 £000 |
|---|---|---|
| **INCOME** | | |
| Share of net operator proceeds | 244,195 | 48,396 |
| Investment returns from National Lottery Distribution Fund | 11,020 | 493 |
| Interest receivable | 193 | 5 |
| | 255,408 | 48,894 |
| **EXPENDITURE** | | |
| New awards paid and payable in the period | 24,428 | - |
| Provision for new award commitments made | 32,532 | - |
| Staff costs | 823 | 296 |
| Other operating costs | 1,685 | 970 |
| | 59,468 | 1,266 |
| **INCREASE/ (DECREASE) FOR YEAR** | 195,940 | 47,628 |

## Ulster Museum

Botanic Gardens
Stranmillis Road
Belfast BT9 5AB

**Tel** 01232 383000
**Fax** 01232 383003

| | |
|---|---|
| *status* | Executive body |
| *founded* | 1961 |
| *sponsor* | Northern Ireland Office, Department of Education NI (DENI) |
| *powers* | Museums (NI) Act 1961 |
| *mission* | To collect and preserve material and information in the fields of art, history and science and, by interpreting these collections, increase public understanding of Ulster's heritage. |
| *tasks* | Development and care of the collections; provision of educational facilities; programme of temporary exhibits. |
| *operations* | Management: Board of Trustees has overall responsibility for policy and planning, control of expenditure and employment of staff. The Director reports to them and is responsible for the progress of work. Reporting to him are the heads of the Divisions (Fine and Applied Art, Human History, Sciences, Collections Services and Museum Services).<br><br>Policy: Planned development of its collection.<br><br>Trends: Merger with the Ulster Folk & Transport Museum in April 1998. |
| *board* | Trustees appointed by the Secretary of State. |

| Accounting Officer | Director |
|---|---|

| | |
|---|---|
| *staff* | 190 |

## Valuation & Lands Agency (VLA)

Queen's Court
56-66 Upper Queen Street
Belfast BT1 6FD

**Tel** 01232 250700
**Fax** 01232 543750          **Web** http://222.nics.gov.uk/vla/

**Contact** R Stranaghan, Senior Personnel Officer

| | |
|---|---|
| *status* | Executive agency |
| *founded* | 1993 |
| *sponsor* | Northern Ireland Office, Department of Finance and Personnel NI (DFPNI) |
| *powers* | VLA Framework Document 1993 |
| *mission* | To provide professional advice on property and be the principal provider of valuation services to the public sector in Northern Ireland. |
| *tasks* | To maintain the Valuation List for rating purposes in NI. To provide valuation, estate management and property data services to the public sector. To provide the DFPNI advice relating to land valuation. |
| *operations* | Management: The Chief Executive, who has the statutory title of Commissioner of Valuation, is responsible to the Minister. VLA is managed by a Board currently comprising the Commissioner and two Assistant Commissioners. Head office is in Belfast and there is a network of eight offices organsised in seven Districts across NI.<br><br>Policy: Cost reduction programme and voluntary redundancies - professional and technical staff were reduced by 15% in 1996/97. |

Trends: In 1996/97 the non-domestic revaluation completed to schedule, the first NI revaluation in 20 years.

**performance** Main output targets achieved or exceeded but not all timeliness targets.

**board** Appointed internally.

| | |
|---|---|
| Commissioner of Valuation | Nigel Woods |
| Assistant Commissioner, Finance, Policy & Planning Division | Leslie Hughes |
| *Accounting Officer* | *Commissioner* |

**staff** 297

| | |
|---|---|
| District Valuer, Central Advisory Unit | David Rainey |
| District Valuer, Belfast | Alex Weise |
| District Valuer, Ballymena | David Weir |
| District Valuer, Bangor | Mike Moore |
| District Valuer, Craigavon | Brian Sparkes |
| District Valuer, Lisburn | Denis Annett |
| District Valuer, Londonderry | Vincent O'Rourke |
| District Valuer, Omagh | Paul McGuckin |

**financial**

| INCOME & EXPENDITURE Year end: 31 March | 1997 £000 | 1996 £000 | 1995 £000 |
|---|---|---|---|
| INCOME | 1,266 | 1,725 | 1,758 |
| EXPENDITURE | | | |
| Staff costs | 7,478 | 7,624 | 7,330 |
| Depreciation | 302 | 301 | 299 |
| Other operating costs | 4,349 | 2,515 | 2,218 |
| | 12,129 | 10,440 | 9,847 |
| COST OF OPERATIONS BEFORE INTEREST | (10,863) | (8,715) | (8,089) |
| Interest on capital employed | (126) | (162) | (219) |
| NET COST OF OPERATIONS | (10,989) | (8,877) | (8,308) |
| Unrealised surplus/(deficit) on revaluation of fixed assets | 49 | 17 | 68 |
| TOTAL RECOGNISED GAINS AND (LOSSES) | (10,940) | (8,860) | (8,240) |

**advisers** **Auditors** Northern Ireland Audit Office 106 University Street, Belfast BT7 1EU

**publications** *Annual Report, Corporate & Business Plan*

**branches**

*Ballymena*
Government Offices
George Street
Ballymena BT43 5AP
Tel 01266 652 866/7
Fax 01266 630293

*Bangor*
Crown Buildings
Hamilton Road
Bangor BT20 4LQ
Tel 01247 279111
Fax 01247 471644

*Craigavon*
Marlborough House
Central Way
Craigavon BT64 1AD
Tel 01762 341144
Fax 01762 341867

*Lisburn*
1 The Sidings
Antrim Road
Lisburn BT28 3AJ
Tel 01846 677527
Fax 01846 603956

*Londonderry*
Waterside House
75 Duke Street
Londonderry BT47 1FP
Tel 01504 319000
Fax 01504 319087

*Omagh*
Boaz House
15 Scarffe's Entry
Omagh BT78 1JG
Tel 01662 254888
Fax 01662 254880

# Valuation Office Agency (VOA)

New Court
Carey Street
London WC2A 2JE

**Tel** 0171 324 1075

| | |
|---|---|
| *status* | Executive agency |
| *founded* | 1991 |
| *sponsor* | Inland Revenue |
| *powers* | Framework Document |
| *mission* | Undertaking valuations of land and buildings for a wide range of public sector clients. |
| *tasks* | Valuations for rating and council tax in England and Wales. Valuing properties for inheritance and capital gains tax purposes for the Inland Revenue. Providing valuation and estate surveying services to government departments, public bodies and local authorities. Making and recovering contributions in lieu of rates (CILOR) in relation to land and buildings occupied by the Crown in the UK. |
| *operations* | Management: The Management Board (comprising the Chief Executive, senior VOA staff and one Non-Executive member) is responsible for the effective management of the business. The Chief Executive reports to the Chairman of the Board of the Inland Revenue (the Board) and through him to the Economic Secretary to the Treasury, who sets out VOA's key targets. Work on rating - appeals and rating lists for some 1.7 million business properties - produces 67% of VOA's turnover; Council Tax - appeals and keeping valuation lists covering some 21.5 million residential property up to date - 13% turnover; Land Services - distributing monies raised from CILOR, collecting rates from foreign missions - 10% turnover; Inland Revenue - inheritance tax and capital gains tax valuation - 9% turnover; and CILOR (administration cost) 1% turnover. |
| | Policy: Raising service standards, particularly for the individual ratepayer or taxpayer. |
| | Trends: Inheritance tax and capital gains tax work declining with progressive raising of thresholds. Also reflect levels of activity in property market. |
| *performance* | Five out of nine key targets met in 1996/97. |

*board*

| | |
|---|---|
| Chief Executive | Mrs VA Lowe |
| Head of Profession | RJ Pawley |
| Non-Executive Member | Mrs R Connel |
| Director of Customers Services | RA Dales |
| Director of Personnel & Information Technology | J Ebdon |
| Director of Change Management | M Jordan |
| Head of Corporate Communications | Mrs A McKenna |
| Director of Finance & Planning | DK Park |
| Director of Operations | P Upton |

*staff*   4563

*financial*

| INCOME & EXPENDITURE Year end: 31 March | 1997 £000 | 1996 £000 |
|---|---|---|
| **INCOME** | | |
| Gross income | 163,816 | 183,446 |
| Change in value of work in progress | (6,926) | 16,804 |
| | 156,890 | 200,250 |
| **EXPENDITURE** | | |
| Staff costs | (103,615) | (113,897) |
| Early departure costs | (8,447) | (17,693) |
| Depreciation | (3,872) | (6,051) |
| Other operating costs | (42,011) | (51,968) |
| | (157,945) | 189,609 |
| **OPERATING (DEFICIT)/SURPLUS BEFORE INTEREST** | (1,055) | 10,641 |
| Loss on disposal of fixed assets | (925) | (21) |
| Interest receivable | 43 | - |
| **OPERATING (DEFICIT)/SURPLUS** | (1,937) | 10,620 |
| Notional interest on capital | (2,941) | (2,359) |
| **(DEFICIT)/SURPLUS FOR YEAR CHARGED TO GENERAL FUND** | (4,878) | 8,261 |

| | | |
|---|---|---|
| *advisers* | **Auditors** | National Audit Office |

# *Vehicle Certification Agency (VCA)*

1 The Eastgate Office Centre
Eastgate Road
Bristol BS5 6XX

**Tel** 0117 951 5151
**Fax** 0117 952 4103

**E-mail** general.vca.eoc@gtnet.gov.uk
**Web** http://www.detr.gov.uk/vca/

**Contact** P Nicholl

| | |
|---|---|
| *status* | Executive agency |
| *founded* | 1990 |
| *sponsor* | Department of Environment, Transport and the Regions (DETR) |
| *powers* | Road Traffic Act 1988 |
| *mission* | To ensure that vehicles and vehicle parts have been designed and constructed to meet internationally agreed standards of safety and environmental protection. |
| *tasks* | As the UK authority, to test and approve vehicles to national and European standards. |

*operations*
Management: The Advisory Board advises the Secretary of State on the corporate and business plans and the Agency's performance. There is a Management Board comprising the Chief Executive and Deputy Chief Executive and the four Managers heading departments. Most staff are based at the Bristol headquarters, with the remainder at the Nuneaton test centre excepting six engineers in Detroit (USA) and one in Nagoya (Japan). Staff shortages restricted work 1996/97. Much work is carried out at manufacturers' or specialised test facilities throughout the world. More agents were appointed and work through agents in UK and Germany increased.

Policy: The aim is to be the best automotive approval service in Europe and the 1997/98 business plan's main priority is responding to customers' certification programmes and information needs of customers.

Trends: The European Community Whole Vehicle Type Approval (ECWVTA) becomes compulsory for all cars in 1998. Captive national work will continue to decline but the Agency offers a full service to customers seeking European approval. An increase in Commission Notice work is expected as changes to the personal import exception for cars take effect and make Commission Notices the more attractive route to register non-ECWVTA vehicles under three years old from the EU.

*board*
Advisory Board appointed by the Secretary of State from mechanical engineering and business communities.

| | | |
|---|---|---|
| Chairman | R Dudding | |
| Members | M Edwards | DW Harvey |
| | M St J Fendick | AC Melville |
| *Accounting Officer* | *Chief Executive* | |

*staff*
85 (all civil servants)

| | |
|---|---|
| Chief Executive | DW Harvey |
| Deputy Chief Executive | PF Nicholl |
| Manager (Finance and Accounts) | A Buckle |
| Manager (System Certification Operations) | T Davies |
| Manager (Planning and Development) | A Grimm |
| Manager (Compliance Systems) | D Porritt |
| Manager (Test Operations) | AW Stenning |

*financial*

**INCOME & EXPENDITURE**

| Year end: 31 March | 1997 £000 | 1996 £000 | 1995 £000 |
|---|---|---|---|
| **TURNOVER** | | | |
| System and component | 1,644 | 1,612 | 1,280 |
| Whole vehicle | 519 | 777 | 791 |
| Quality system certification | 1,101 | 362 | 255 |
| VSE work | 326 | 280 | 269 |
| Other activities | 294 | 412 | 420 |
| | 3,884 | 3,433 | 3,015 |
| | (2,015) | (1,816) | (1,560) |
| **GROSS SURPLUS** | 1,869 | 1,617 | 1,455 |

| ADMINISTRATIVE EXPENSES | | | |
|---|---|---|---|
| Depreciation and asset charges/loss on write off of fixed assets | 122 | 72 | 64 |
| Pay costs | 786 | 686 | 741 |
| Travel and subsistence | 237 | 201 | 192 |
| Legal and consultancy | 140 | 102 | 62 |
| Audit fee | 27 | 25 | 25 |
| Exchange loss/(profit) on consolidation | 14 | (7) | 9 |
| Other administrative expenses | 622 | 319 | 189 |
| | 1,948 | 1,398 | 1,282 |
| OPERATING (DEFICIT)/SURPLUS | (79) | 219 | 173 |
| Notional interest payable | (27) | (8) | 1 |
| (DEFICIT)/SURPLUS FOR THE YEAR | (106) | 211 | 174 |

**advisers** **Auditors** National Audit Office 157-197 Buckingham Palace Road
London SW1W 9SP

**Solicitors** Treasury Solicitors

**publications** Annual Report

# Vehicle Inspectorate (VI)

Berkeley House
Croydon Street
Bristol BS5 0DA

**Tel** 0117 954 3200
**Fax** 0117 954 3212

**E-mail** enquiries.vi@gtnet.gov.uk
**Web** http://www.demon.co.uk/vehinsp/main.htm

**status** Executive agency and trading fund

**founded** 1988 (as trading fund 1991)

**sponsor** Department of the Environment, Transport and the Regions (DETR)

**powers** Framework Document 1988

**mission** To enforce the law on vehicle standards and environmental standards throughout the UK.

**tasks** Road transport enforcement activities covering roadworthiness and enforcement of regulations (eg drivers' hours, load weights). Vehicle testing activities covering statutory testing of, eg Heavy Goods Vehicles (HGVs) and Public Service Vehicles (PSVs).

**operations** Management: The Chief Executive is responsible to the Secretary of State for the day-to-day running and management, performance and future development of the agency within the Framework Document. There is a Directing Board comprising the Chief Executive and Heads of Divisions. There is a Memorandum of Agreement with DETR covering each area of enforcement work, eg HGV, PSV roadworthiness and operator licensing support, MOT standards, vocational driver licensing, vehicle registration support, approved driving instructor enforcement.

Policy: To recover the full cost of fee-earning services through fees.

Trends: Becoming more customer focused. New IS services are being implemented throughout the country.

**performance** Excepting demand-led targets, all targets met or purposefully let slip for business reasons, eg IS project.

**board** The Chief Executive is appointed by open competition.

| | |
|---|---|
| Chief Executive | Ron Oliver |
| Head of Corporate Affairs Division | Jeff Belt |
| Head of Road Transport Enforcement Division | Julian David |
| Head of Vehicle Testing Division | Bob Tatchell |
| Accounting Officer | Chief Executive |

**staff** 1750

| *financial* | INCOME & EXPENDITURE | | | |
|---|---|---|---|---|
| | Year end: 31 March | 1997 | 1996 | 1995 |
| | | £000 | £000 | £000 |
| | **INCOME FROM OPERATIONS** | | | |
| | Income from activities | 50,362 | 47,961 | 47,662 |
| | Other operating income | 3,554 | 2,790 | 2,446 |
| | | **53,916** | **50,751** | **50,108** |
| | **EXPENDITURE** | | | |
| | Staff costs | (31,146) | (29,832) | (30,670) |
| | Early retirement scheme costs | 79 | (1,219) | (4,383) |
| | Depreciation | (3,409) | (3,225) | (3,182) |
| | Other operating charges | (16,242) | (15,072) | (14,258) |
| | | **(50,718)** | **(49,348)** | **(52,493)** |
| | **OPERATING SURPLUS** | **3,198** | **1,403** | **2,385** |
| | Interest receivable and similar income | 464 | 583 | 409 |
| | **NET SURPLUS ON ORDINARY ACTIVITIES** | **3,662** | **1,986** | **1,976** |
| | Interest paid | (1,830) | (1,730) | (1,730) |
| | Dividend payable | (498) | (256) | (1,203) |
| | **RETAINED SURPLUS FOR THE YEAR** | **1,334** | **-** | **(4,909)** |
| | Retained surplus brought forward | 1,331 | 1,331 | 6,240 |
| | **RETAINED SURPLUS CARRIED FORWARD** | **2,665** | **1,331** | **1,331** |

| *advisers* | **Auditors** | National Audit Office | 157-197 Buckingham Palace Road London SW1W 9SP |
|---|---|---|---|

# *Veterinary Laboratories Agency (VLA)*

New Haw
Addlestone
Surrey KT15 3NB

**Tel** 01932 341111
**Fax** 01932 347046

| | |
|---|---|
| *status* | Executive agency |
| *founded* | 1995 |
| *sponsor* | Ministry of Agriculture, Fisheries and Food (MAFF) |
| *powers* | Framework Document 1995 |
| *mission* | To promote animal health and minimise hazard as associated with the environment. |
| *tasks* | Provides comprehensive diagnostic testing, surveillance programme to monitor for notifiable diseases; identifies new and emerging conditions; and detects trends in the incidence of established diseases. |

*operations*  Management: VLA run by Strategy Management Group headed by Chief Executive. Formed from merger between Central Veterinary Laboratory and Veterinary Investigation Service. Four divisions: research, laboratory services, surveillance and business. A regional network of laboratories provides all sectors of the animal health industry with animal disease surveillance, laboratory services and veterinary scientific reasearch. Achieved full cost recovery in 1996/97. Period of great uncertainty about VLA's future ended with 1996/97 Prior Options Review's recommendation that it should remain a MAFF agency.

Policy: To be the primary supplier of specialist veterinary advice to MAFF, based on sound investigation, surveillance, diagnostic testing, research and development. Increasing number of alliances with European research organisations.

Trends: Examining management of VLA and services offered to customers. Increasing amount of commercial income. Increasing amount of research into BSE and scrapie.

*performance*  Met most of its financial and other performance targets in 1996/97.

*board*  Ownership Board appointed by the Minister of Agriculture.

| Chairman | RJ Packer | |
|---|---|---|
| Members | BHB Dickinson | |
| | P Elliot | Dr DW Shannon |
| | B Hoskin | Dr C Vaughan |
| Secretary | C Southgate | |
| *Accounting Officer* | *Permanent Secretary, MAFF* | |

# Q&Q

**staff**   1000

| | |
|---|---|
| Chief Executive | Dr TWA Little |
| Research Director | Dr JA Morris |
| Laboratory Secretary | CR Edwards |
| Director of Laboratory Services Division | Dr S Edwards |
| Finance Director | I Grattidge |
| Director of Veterinary Investigation Division | JW Harkness |

**financial**

| SALES & COSTS | |
|---|---|
| **Year end: 31 March** | **1997** |
| | **£m** |
| **SALES** | |
| Food sciences | 1.021 |
| VMD | 1.755 |
| Other MAFF income | 0.915 |
| Non-MAFF income | 5.275 |
| AHVG | 24.454 |
| CSG | 10.232 |
| | **43.652** |
| **COSTS** | |
| Accommodation and utilities | 5.402 |
| Building maintenance | 2.761 |
| MAFF overheads | 1.216 |
| Depreciation | 2.109 |
| Staff | 22.663 |
| Other | 1.468 |
| Site services and consumables | 8.004 |
| | **43.623** |

**advisers**

**Bankers**   Bank of England

**Auditors**   National Audit Office

**Solicitors**   MAFF Legal Department

**publications**   Annual Review, Annual Report & Accounts

**branches**

Bush State
Penicuik
Midlothian EH26 0SA
Tel 0131 445 5371
Fax 0131 445 5504

Y Buarth
Aberystwith
Ceredigion SY23 1ND
Tel 01970 612374
Fax 01970 612424

Rougham Hill
Bury St Edmunds
Suffolk IP33 2RX
Tel 01284 724499
Fax 01284 724500

Job's Well Road
Johnstown
Carmarthen
Ceredigion SA31 3EZ
Tel 01267 235244
Fax 1267 236549

Langford House
Langford
North Somerset BS18 7DX
Tel 01934 852421
Fax 01934 852981

Luddington
Stratford-upon-Avon
Warwickshire CV37 9SJ
Tel 01789 750212
Fax 01789 750281

Whitley Road
Longbenton
Newcastle upon Tyne NE12 9SE
Tel 0191 2662292
Fax 0191 2663605

Merrythought
Calthwaite
Penrith
Cumbria CA11 9RR
Tel 01768 885295
Fax 01768 8855314

Barton Hall
Garstang Road
Barton
Preston
Lancashire PR3 5HE
Tel 01772 861611
Fax 01772 862026

Kendal Road
Harlescott
Shrewbury
Shropshire SY1 4HD
Tel 01743 467621
Fax 01743 441060

Staplake Mount
Starcross
Devon
Exeter EX6 8PE
Tel 01626 891121
Fax 01626 891766

Polwhele
Truro
Cornwall TR4 9AD
Tel 01872 721150
Fax 01872 223443

The Elms
College Road
Sutton Bonington
Loughborough
Leicestershire LE12 5RB
Tel 01509 670607
Fax 01509 670206

West House
Station Road
Thirsk
North Yorkshire YO7 1PZ
Tel 01845 52265
Fax 01845 525224

Itchen Abbas
Winchester
Hampshire SO21 1BX
Tel 01962 779966
Fax 01962 842492

# *Veterinary Medicines Directorate (VMD)*

Woodham Lane
New Haw
Addlestone
Surrey KT15 3NB

**Tel** 01932 336911
**Fax** 01932 336618          **Web** http://www.open.gov.uk/vmd/vmdhome.htm

| | |
|---|---|
| *status* | Executive agency |
| *founded* | 1990 |
| *sponsor* | Ministry of Agriculture, Fisheries and Food (MAFF) |
| *powers* | Framework Document |
| *mission* | To safeguard public health, animal health and the environment and promote animal welfare by ensuring the safety, quality and efficacy of all veterinary medicines in the UK. |
| *tasks* | Licensing: marketing authorisations for veterinary medicines; control on their manufacture and distribution. Residues: post-authorisation surveillance of suspected adverse reactions and residues of veterinary products in meat and animal products. Policy: advice to the joint licensing authority - the Agriculture and Health Ministers. |
| *operations* | Management: Day-to-day operation of VMD is the Chief Executive's responsibility. There is an Ownership Board which advises the Minister and provides advice, support and assistance to the Chief Executive at his request. VMD works by using its own expertise to assess, interpret and validate written information on veterinary medicine. It seeks independent expert advice from the Veterinary Products Committee and the Medicines Commission. Where physical tests or other procedures are needed, VMD normally subcontracts to, eg the Veterinary Laboratories Agency, Central Science Laboratory, Medicines Control Agency, Meat Hygiene Service.<br><br>Policy: VMD setting up and chairing EU mutual recognition facilitation group for decentralised authorisation procedures.<br><br>Trends: EC consolidating nine veterinary medicine directives into a single directive. |
| *performance* | 1996/97 targets achieved. |
| *board* | The Chief Executive is appointed by open competition. |

| | |
|---|---|
| Chairman | RJD Carden |
| Members | Prof ID Aitken OBE |
| | P Elliott |
| | G Podger |
| | Dr JM Rutter |
| | AM Simon OBE |
| Secretary | C Southgate |
| *Accounting Officer* | *Chief Executive* |

| | |
|---|---|
| *staff* | 106 |

| | |
|---|---|
| Director & Chief Executive | Dr Michael Rutter |
| Director of Policy | Ray Anderson |
| Director of Licensing | Steve Dean |
| VMD Secretary, Head of Business Unit | John FitzGerald |
| Finance | Michael Addison |
| European & Information Policy | Chris Bean |
| Strategic Support | Phil Davies |
| Immunological Products | Dr Duncan Fawthrop |
| Adverse Reactions Surveillance Scheme | Alaistar Gray |
| Licensing Policy | John Horton |
| Pharmaceuticals & Feed Additives | J O'Brien |
| Licensing Administration | Ms Heather Oliver |
| Information Technology | Neil Paterson |
| Residues, Surveillance & R&D | Colin Penny |

**financial**

| INCOME & EXPENDITURE | | | |
|---|---|---|---|
| Year end: 31 March | **1997** | **1996** | **1995** |
| | **£000** | **£000** | **£000** |
| **INCOME** | | | |
| Income from activities | 8,460 | 8,001 | 7,952 |
| Less: direct subcontracting costs | (3,426) | (3,458) | (3,892) |
| **NET INCOME** | **5,034** | **4,543** | **4,060** |
| **OPERATING UNIT EXPENDITURE** | | | |
| Staff costs | (2,883) | (2,592) | (2,450) |
| Depreciation | (182) | (119) | (135) |
| Other operating costs | (1,056) | (1,114) | (870) |
| **VMD OPERATING COSTS FOR YEAR** | **(4,121)** | **(3,825)** | **(3,455)** |
| **OPERATING RESULT BEFORE DEPARTMENTAL CHARGES** | | | |
| **AND OTHER COSTS** | 913 | 718 | 605 |
| **DEPARTMENTAL CHARGES AND OTHER COSTS** | | | |
| Overhead recharges | (568) | (538) | (416) |
| Veterinary Products Committee | (71) | (82) | (83) |
| | | (639) | (620) |
| (499) | | | |
| **OPERATING SURPLUS BEFORE INTEREST ON CAPITAL** | 274 | 98 | 106 |
| Interest on capital | (71) | (78) | (80) |
| **OPERATING SURPLUS FOR THE YEAR** | 203 | 20 | 26 |

**advisers**   **Auditors**         National Audit Office          157-197 Buckingham Palace Road
London SW1W 9SP

**publications**   *Annual Reports and Accounts*

# Victoria & Albert Museum (V&A)

South Kensington
London SW7 2RL

**Tel** 0171 938 8500
**Fax** 0171 938 8379                        **Web** http://www.vam.ac.uk

**status**       Executive body

**founded**      1852, as executive body 1992

**sponsor**      Department of Culture, Media and Sport

**powers**       National Heritage Acts 1983 and 1992

**mission**      To increase the understanding and enjoyment of art, craft and design through its collections and to make the V&A a powerhouse in the cultural life of the UK.

**tasks**        To maintain and enhance the standards of object-based scholarship and research at the V&A; to improve standards of collections management; to improve its accessibility and attractiveness to the visiting public; to make a fuller contribution to public education in art and design.

**operations**   Management:  The Collection Department is organised into eight discrete South Kensington collections: Ceramics and Glass; Far Eastern; Furniture and Woodwork; Indian and South-East Asian; Metalwork, Silver and

Jewellery; Prints, Drawing and Paintings; Sculpture, Textiles and Design. Three small London museums are also part of the V&A: Apsley House, The Wellington Museum; Bethnal Green Museum of Childhood; and the Theatre Museum. In addition there is a research department conducting its own research and facilitating it elsewhere; and public affairs, education and conservation departments and the National Art Library.

Trends: Major programmes of refurbishment are in hand and rising visitor numbers are expected.

**board**  Trustees appointed by the Prime Minister.

| | | |
|---|---|---|
| Chairman | The Lord Armstrong of Ilminster GCB CVO | |
| Deputy Chairman | Jonathan Scott CBE | |
| Trustees | Miss Nina Campbell | Alton Irby III |
| | The Viscountess Cobham DL | Antony Snow |
| | Lady Copisarow | Prof John Steer MA DLITT |
| | Rodney Fitch CBE | Alan Wheatley |
| | Prof Christopher Frayling | Prof Christopher White CVO |
| | Sir Terence Heiser GCB | |
| | Mrs Anne Heseltine | |
| *Accounting Officer: The Director and the Permanent Secretary* | | |

**staff**

| | |
|---|---|
| Director | Dr Alan Borg |
| Assistant Director (Administration) | Jim Close |
| Assistant Director (Collections) | Timothy Stevens |
| Major Projects | Gwyn Miles |
| Curator, Ceramics & Glass Collection | Oliver Watson |
| Acting Curator, Far Eastern Collection | Rupert Faulkner |
| Curator, Furniture & Woodwork Collection | Christopher Wilk |
| Curator, Indian & South-East Asian Collection | Debora Swallow |
| Acting Curator, Metalwork, Silver & Jewellery Collection | Philippa Glanville |
| Curator, Prints, Drawings & Paintings Collection | Susan Lambert |
| Curator, Sculpture Collection | Paul Williamson |
| Curator, Textiles & Dress Collection | Valerie Mendes |
| Chief Librarian | Jan van der Wateren |
| Head of Conservation | Jonathan Ashley-Smith |
| Head of Research | Paul Greenhalgh |
| Head of Public Affairs | Robin Cole-Hamilton |
| Head of Education | David Anderson |
| Head of Buildings & Estate | Richard Whitehouse |
| Head of Finance & Central Services | Rosamund Sykes |
| Head of Personnel | Gillian Henchley |
| Head of Safety & Security | Richard Bland |
| Head of Museum, Bethnal Green Museum of Childhood | Anthony Burton |
| Acting Head, Bethnal Green Museum of Childhood | Sue Lawrence |
| Head of Museum, Theatre Museum | Margaret Benton |
| Curator, Apsley House, The Wellington Museum | Alicia Robinson |
| Managing Director, V&A Enterprises | Michael Cass |
| Development Director | Candida Morley |

**financial**

**COMBINED INCOME & EXPENDITURE**

| Year end: 31 March | 1997 £000 | 1996 £000 |
|---|---|---|
| **INCOMING RESOURCES** | | |
| Grant in aid | 30,762 | 31,554 |
| Entrance donations and admissions charges | 2,153 | 1,626 |
| Publications and images | 530 | 326 |
| Patrons scheme | 129 | 132 |
| Sponsorship and donations | 1,672 | 3,415 |
| Education income | 234 | 319 |
| Investment income | 879 | 1,008 |
| Legacies | 5 | 25 |
| Trading income | 4,815 | 3,724 |
| Other income | 879 | 1,851 |
| | **42,058** | **43,980** |

| RESOURCES EXPENDED | | |
|---|---:|---:|
| Direct charitable expenditure | | |
| Collection purchases | 1,477 | 2,264 |
| Exhibitions | 967 | 1,552 |
| Education | 1,091 | 1,203 |
| Conservation | 2,748 | 3,067 |
| Collections and research | 11,875 | 12,558 |
| Publications and images | 1,140 | 1,109 |
| Security and access | 4,819 | 4,809 |
| Branch Museums | 3,659 | 4,201 |
| National Art Library | 2,167 | 2,469 |
| Museum developments | 1,034 | 3 |
| | **30,977** | **33,235** |
| Other expenditure | | |
| Fund raising and publicity | 1,105 | 1,071 |
| Management and administration | 2,619 | 3,007 |
| Trading costs | 3,899 | 3,220 |
| Tax on profit of trading subsidiary | 11 | 33 |
| | **38,611** | **40,566** |
| **NET INCOMING (OUTGOING) RESOURCES** | **3,447** | **3,414** |

# Wales Tourist Board

Brunel House
2 Fitzalan Road
Cardiff CF2 1UY

**Tel** 01222 499909
**Fax** 01222 485031

**status** Executive body

**sponsor** Welsh Office

**powers** Development of Tourism Act 1969

**mission** To seek growth in tourism through sustainable means by respecting the needs of the environment and local communities and working in partnership with others.

**tasks** To encourage people to visit Wales and people living in Wales to take their holidays there; to encourage the provision and improvement of tourist amenities and facilities in Wales. More specifically, to develop a strategic direction to a fragmented and diverse industry; to stimulate investment through partnership; to improve quality through financial assistance and linked training programmes; to market Wales in the UK and overseas.

**operations** Management: New Chief Executive has begun to restructure the organisation, creating a communications division and reviewing the role of the three Regional Tourism Companies. Although tourism is predominantly a private sector activity, a wide range of public sector organisations is involved and the Board works closely with the local authorities - the 22 Welsh unitary authorities - and many other partners in the private and public sectors.

Policy: Branding Wales, to establish images both in the overseas and home markets, seen to be a crucial role. A substantial part of the investment budget is concentrated on six coastal resorts and seven historic towns, through its Integrated Development Programme where the aim is to work alongside willing partners.

Trends: Visitors increased by 19% but the Board warns that this growth can be easily undone in this highly sensitive and hugely competitive business. Positive opportunities, such as European Summit being held in Cardiff in 1998, and Wales hosting the Rugby World Cup in 1999, need professional planning by the Board and its partners - County Councils, Agencies and Boards.

**performance** The present strategy - Tourism 2000 - was launched in 1994 and set ambitious growth targets. At this interim stage, all targets have been exceeded.

**board** Appointed by the Secretary of State for Wales.

| | | |
|---|---|---|
| Chairman | Tony Lewis | |
| Members | Teleri Bevan | Thomas Lloyd |
| | Nicholas Brown | James McAllister |
| | Lewis Evans | Ian Rutherford |

| staff | 107 |
|---|---|

| | |
|---|---|
| Chief Executive | John P French MBE JP |
| Finance Director & Secretary | John PF Cory |
| Director of Communications & Corporate Affairs | Jonathan Jones |
| Development Director | Jeffrey Pride |
| Marketing Director | Roger Pride |
| Head of Research & Corporate Planning | Steve Webb |

**financial**

| INCOME & EXPENDITURE | | | |
|---|---|---|---|
| Year end: 31 March | **1997** | **1996** | **1995** |
| | **£000** | **£000** | **£000** |
| **INCOME** | **15,863** | **15,778** | **15,916** |
| **OPERATING SURPLUS/(DEFICIT)** | **(244)** | **(128)** | **143** |
| Loss on disposal of fixed assets | (6) | (1) | (22) |
| Interest Receivable | 75 | 90 | 88 |
| Interest Payable | (78) | (90) | (64) |
| **SURPLUS/(DEFICIT) FOR THE YEAR** | **(253)** | **(129)** | **145** |
| Adjustment for cost of capital | 97 | 107 | - |
| **(SURPLUS)/DEFICIT FOR THE YEAR** | **(156)** | **(22)** | **145** |

| advisers | **Auditors** | National Audit Office | Audit House, 23/24 Park Place, Cardiff CF1 3BA |
|---|---|---|---|

# Wallace Collection

Hertford House
Manchester Square
London W1M 6BN

**Tel** 0171 935 0687
**Fax** 0171 224 2155

**E-mail** admin@wallcoll.demon.co.uk

| status | Executive body |
|---|---|
| founded | 1895, 1992 as executive body |
| sponsor | Department for Culture, Media and Sport (DCMS) |
| powers | Museums and Galleries Act 1992 |
| mission | To safeguard the unique Collection, making it accessible for the present and preserving it for future generations. |
| tasks | To promote understanding and enjoyment of the Collection, maintain and improve conservation and display of its works of art, encourage study of 18th century art and 19th century art collecting, maintain Hertford House and its services. |
| operations | Management: The Director reports to Board of Trustees. The Wallace Collection is a museum with absolute restriction on buying, selling, lending or borrowing works of art. This makes it difficult to increase public interest and visitor numbers through exhibitions etc. The Collection is largely dependent on the government's grant-in-aid, sponsor donations and self-generated income. Shop, entrance hall and two galleries improved by a grant from the Museums and Galleries Improvement Fund. An application for Lottery funds to create an improved educational facility has been successful and completion of the project is June 2000. |
| | Policy: To further expand sources of self-generated income. |
| | Trends: Grant-in-aid continually reduced in real terms. |
| performance | All criteria met. |
| board | The Trustees are appointed by the Prime Minister. |

| Chairman | John Lewis |
|---|---|
| Trustees | Sir Geoffrey de Bellaigue |
| | The Lord Egremont |
| | James Joll |
| | Dr Jennifer Montagu |
| | Lady Shaw Stewart |
| *Accounting Officer* | *Director* |

| staff | 67 | | |
|---|---|---|---|

| | |
|---|---|
| Director | Rosalind Savill |
| Head Curator | Peter Hughes |
| Head of Conservation | Paul Tear |
| Head of Administration & Finance | Arthur Houldershaw |
| Head of Security & Building Management | James White |

**financial**

**INCOME & EXPENDITURE**
Year end: 31 March

| | 1995 £000 |
|---|---|
| **INCOME** | |
| Grant-in-aid | 1,571 |
| Other operating income | 236 |
| Investment income | 9 |
| Release from deferred capital accounts | 421 |
| | **2,237** |
| **EXPENDITURE** | |
| Staff costs | 1,255 |
| Other operating costs | 763 |
| Depreciation: fixed assets | 421 |
| | **2,439** |
| **SURPLUS (FUNDING REQUIREMENT)** | **(202)** |
| **(TRANSFER TO)/DRAWING FROM FUNDS** | |
| Restricted funds | 28 |
| General fund | 174 |
| | **202** |

| advisers | **Bankers** | National Westminster Bank |
|---|---|---|
| | **Auditors** | National Audit Office |

**publications** Annual Report, The Wallace Collection Cataloguing Furniture, Sèvres Porcelain, French Eighteenth Century Clocks and Barometers in the Wallace Collection, Catalogue of Illuminated Manuscript Cuttings

# Waltham Forest Housing Action Trust

Kirkdale House
7 Kirkdale Road
Leytonstone
London E11 1HP

**Tel** 0181 539 5533
**Fax** 0181 539 8074

**E-mail** 101317,1175@compuserve.com

**Contact** Deborah Reid, Communications Manager

| status | Executive body |
|---|---|
| **founded** | 1991 |
| **sponsor** | Department of the Environment, Transport and the Regions (DETR) |
| **powers** | Housing Act 1988 |
| **mission** | By 2002, to leave neighbourhoods of high-quality homes, occupied by stable communities who have the power to make choices about their lives and to work with tenants to bring long-lasting improvements in the quality of life. |
| **tasks** | To replace four large system-built high-rise estates, each situated in a different part of the London Borough of Waltham Forest, with quality homes and gardens set in traditional street patterns. Also to promote sustainable community and economic development, provide high-quality housing management and diversify forms of tenure (including a tenant-run housing association). |
| **operations** | Management: The Trust is a limited-life organisation which must wind itself up by March 2002. The Trust has entered into an arrangement with Dearle and Henderson whereby they administer the development programme, trading as DH Regeneration, to which some staff have transferred. |

Policy: The lifetime DETR cost allocation of £227 million presented a funding shortage of £22 million which cannot be met by further economies and the Trust has therefore transferred all redevelopment properties, temporarily, to Waltham Forest Community Based Housing Association so that the capital receipts will enable redevelopment to be completed by March 2002.

Trends: The succession strategy is well ahead of schedule.

**board**    Appointed by the Secretary of State from tenants and experts (tenants also elected by estate residents.

| | | |
|---|---|---|
| Chairman | John Chumrow | |
| Deputy Chairman | Simon Bartlett | |
| Members | Roger Baker | Howard May |
| | Roy Evans | Helen Pettersen |
| | Julie Fawcett | Melinda Phillips |
| | Jacky Flanders | Shahwar Sadeque |
| | Andy Healy | Cllr Eric Sizer |
| *Accounting Officer* | *Chief Executive* | |

**staff**    38

| | |
|---|---|
| Chief Executive | Michael Wilson |
| Director of Development, DH Regeneration | Stephanie Al-Wahid |
| Director of Finance | David Foster |
| Director of Client Services | Steve Moore |
| Director of Community Development | Marilyn Taylor |

**financial**

| INCOME & EXPENDITURE | | | |
|---|---|---|---|
| Year end: 31 March | **1997** | **1996** | **1995** |
| | **£000** | **£000** | **£000** |
| **GROSS INCOME** | | | |
| HMG grants | 23,998 | 23,167 | 41,399 |
| Income from activities | 5,254 | 4,559 | 4,241 |
| | 29,252 | 27,726 | 45,640 |
| **EXPENDITURE** | | | |
| Grants awarded under s71(2) Housing Act 1988 | 3,268 | 429 | 1,312 |
| Trading activities expenditure | 23,408 | 23,380 | 40,328 |
| Administrative expenditure | 2,652 | 4,011 | 4,078 |
| | 29,328 | 27,820 | 45,718 |
| **OPERATING RESULT** | **(76)** | **(94)** | **(78)** |
| Less: notional cost of capital | (41) | (129) | - |
| Interest receivable | 132 | 226 | 83 |
| **SURPLUS ON ORDINARY ACTIVITIES** | **15** | **3** | **5** |
| Add notional cost of capital | 41 | 129 | - |
| | 56 | 132 | 5 |
| Tax on surplus on ordinary activities | (56) | (42) | (5) |
| **SURPLUS ON ORDINARY ACTIVITIES AFTER TAX** | **0** | **90** | **0** |

**advisers**    **Bankers**    National Westminster Bank

**Auditors**    Robson Rhodes

**publications**    *Annual Report & Accounts, Report to Tenants 1996/97, Changing Times, Changing Futures*

# War Pensions Agency (WPA)

Norcross
Blackpool FY5 3WP

**Tel** 01253 858858
**Fax** 01253 330561

**E-mail** wpa-chief-exec-@nx005.dss.gov.uk
**Web** http://www.dss.gov.uk/wpa/index.htm

**Contact** Val Clarke, Customer Service Manager

**status**    Executive agency
**founded**    1994
**sponsor**    Department of Social Security (DSS)
**powers**    Framework Document 1994

| | |
|---|---|
| *mission* | To administer the War Pensions Scheme and provide appropriate welfare support to war disablement pensioners and war widows. |
| *tasks* | To assess entitlement and pay war pensions. To implement new legislation and policies and provide advice. To provide welfare support through the War Pensioners' Welfare Service. To manage the Ilford Park Polish Home. |
| *operations* | Management: There is a Chief Executive who is responsible for managing day-to-day operations and advising Ministers on operational aspects of war pensions. Central Operations are based near Blackpool and are responsible for assessing and paying war pensions etc. War Pensioners' Welfare Service has a network of 30 offices throughout the UK and Eire. Ilford Park Polish Home, a residential care and nursing home for ex-service Poles, is in Devon. The agency has extensive dealings with the DSS, Benefits Agency, voluntary bodies acting on behalf of war disablement pensioners and carers, with other government departments (eg MOD and the Overseas Administration Agency) and, in an advisory role, with some overseas governments. |
| | Policy: DSS has decided not to contract out the War Pensions Welfare Service but WPA will reorganise and refocus it. |
| *performance* | Exceeded in four out of five categories. |
| *board* | Agency Management Team vacancies are filled through open competition. |

| | |
|---|---|
| Acting Chief Executive | Steve Johnson |
| Finance & Personnel Director | Stuart Munslow |
| Operations & Welfare Director | Alan Burnham |
| Medical Director | Paul Kitchen |
| Operations Manager | Malcolm Clydedale |
| Business Development Manager | Lynn Holden |
| Business Assurance & Change Manager | Teresa McHugh |
| Finance & Personnel Manager | Derek Reid |
| *Accounting Officer* | *Chief Executive* |

| | |
|---|---|
| *staff* | 1058 |

*financial*

| INCOME & EXPENDITURE | | |
|---|---|---|
| Year end: 31 March | 1997 | 1996 |
| | £000 | £000 |
| **INCOME** | | |
| Miscellaneous income | 1,105 | 1,000 |
| **EXPENDITURE** | | |
| Staff costs | (22,853) | (23,642) |
| Other operating costs | (18,405) | (26,506) |
| Depreciation | (699) | (774) |
| | **(41,957)** | **(50,922)** |
| **NET COST OF OPERATIONS BEFORE INTEREST** | **(40,852)** | **(49,922)** |
| Interest on capital | (142) | (122) |
| **NET COST OF OPERATIONS** | **(40,994)** | **(50,044)** |

| | | | |
|---|---|---|---|
| *advisers* | **Auditors** | National Audit Office | 157-197 Buckingham Palace Road London SW1W 9SP |
| *publications* | *Annual Report & Accounts, Business Plan, War Pensioners' Report* | | |

# Water Service

Northland House
3 Frederick Street
Belfast BT1 2NR

**Tel** 01232 244711
**Fax** 01232 354888

**E-mail** water.service@nics.gov.uk

| | |
|---|---|
| *status* | Executive agency |
| *founded* | 1973 |
| *sponsor* | Northern Ireland Office, Department of the Environment for NI (DOENI) |
| *powers* | Water and Sewerage Services (NI) Order 1973. Water Service Framework Document 1996 |

| | |
|---|---|
| *mission* | To provide water and sewerage services cost-effectively throughout Northern Ireland and to meet the needs of existing and future customers - thus contributing to the health and well-being of the community and the protection of the environment. |
| *tasks* | To supply and distribute water which, when supplied for domestic or food production purposes, is wholesome at the time of supply. To provide and maintain sewers for draining domestic sewage, surface water and trade effluent. To deal effectively with the contents of its sewers. |
| *operations* | Management: The Chief Executive reports to the Minister who is responsible for the policy framework and resources. The Chief Executive is supported a Management Board comprising five functional Directors. Head office is in Belfast and there are four operational divisions with main offices in Ballymena, Belfast, Craigavon and Londonderry and a number of local offices. |
| | Policy: Consultation on proposal to develop new water source for Belfast. |
| | Trends: Developing water and sewerage infrastructure to meet increased quality and environmental standards. |
| *performance* | 1996/97 seven targets achieved, one target not achieved. |
| *board* | The Water Service Board is appointed by the Minister. The Chief Executive is appointed by open competition. |

| Accounting Officer | Chief Executive |
|---|---|

*staff*  2260. Management Board comprises:

| | |
|---|---|
| Chief Executive | Director of Development |
| Director of Corporate Services | Technical Director |
| Director of Operations | Director of Finance |

*financial*

| INCOME & EXPENDITURE Year end: 31 March | 1997 £000 | 1996 £000 |
|---|---|---|
| **INCOME** | | |
| Income from activities | 164,971 | 160,726 |
| **EXPENDITURE** | | |
| Staff costs | 46,114 | 45,717 |
| Operating costs | 58,521 | 55,844 |
| Depreciation | 31,770 | 33,618 |
| Infrastructure renewals charge | 19,920 | 19,493 |
| | 156,325 | 154,672 |
| **NET OPERATING INCOME BEFORE INTEREST AND COST OF CAPITAL CHARGES** | **8,646** | **6,054** |
| Interest payable on government loans | 909 | 966 |
| Cost of capital charge | - | - |
| **NET INCOME AFTER COST OF CAPITAL AND INTEREST CHARGES** | **7,737** | **5,088** |

| | | | |
|---|---|---|---|
| *advisers* | **Bankers** | Northern Bank | Donegall Square West, Belfast |
| | **Auditors** | Northern Ireland Audit Office | 106 University Street, Belfast BT7 1EU |
| *publications* | Annual Report & Accounts, Drinking Water Quality Report 1996, Corporate/Business Plans 1997-2002, Charter Standard Statement | | |

# Welsh Development Agency (WDA)

Principality House
The Friary
Cardiff CF1 4AE

**Tel** 01443 845500
**Fax** 01443 845589

**E-mail** enquiries@wda.co.uk
**Web** http://www.wda.co.uk

| | |
|---|---|
| *status* | Executive body |
| *founded* | 1976 |
| *sponsor* | Welsh Office |
| *powers* | Welsh Development Agency Act 1975 |

| | |
|---|---|
| **mission** | To further economic development and employment in Wales. To promote industrial efficiency and international competitiveness in Wales. To improve the environment in Wales. |
| **tasks** | Marketing Wales for inward investment; creating and safeguarding jobs; attracting private investment in partnership with projects; land reclamation; attracting associated investment as a result of inward investment, |
| **operations** | Management: WDA activities are partly financed by the Secretary of State and also from borrowings from the National Loans Fund and the European Coal and Steel Community. EU funding for some 50 partnership projects under the Regional Technology Plan has been obtained to speed up implementation of new technology and innovation. WDA operates through three Regional Divisions - North Wales, South Wales and West Wales - each of which has its own Managing Director reporting to the Board through the Chief Executive. Divisional teams specialise in business development, property, urban regeneration, land reclamation and environmental improvement. There is an International Division handling worldwide inward investment.

Policy: To enhance the competitiveness of Welsh indigenous industry.

Trends: Since taking over responsibility (1983) for inward investment, some 1680 new and expansion projects have been attracted to Wales with a total investment of £11 billion. |
| **performance** | 1996/97 all targets exceeded. |

**board**

| Chairman | David S Rowe-Beddoe | |
|---|---|---|
| Deputy Chairman | Robin Lewis OBE | |
| Members | Rhiannon Chapman | William Legge-Bourke |
| | Noel Crowley | Prof Garel Rhys OBE |
| | Graham Hawker | Patsy Woodward |
| | Trefor Jones OBE | George Wright MBE |
| *Accounting Officer* | *Chief Executive* | |

**staff**  328

| Chief Executive | Brian Willott |
|---|---|
| Managing Director, West Division | Elfed Evans |
| Managing Director, South Division | Graham Moore |
| Managing Director, North Division | Enid Rowlands |
| Managing Director, International Division | James Turner |
| Principal Finance Officer | Richard Beaumont |
| Acting Marketing Director | David Davies |
| Director, Agency Coordination | Alan Morgan |
| Legal Director & Agency Secretary | Roy J Thomas |

**financial**

### INCOME & EXPENDITURE

| Year end: 31 March | 1997 £000 | 1996 £000 |
|---|---|---|
| **INCOME** | | |
| Property rents and related income | 19,244 | 25,710 |
| Interest receivable and similar income | 1,740 | 1,962 |
| Other income from fixed asset investments | 761 | 593 |
| Other operating income including grant recoveries | 3,967 | 4,249 |
| | 25,712 | 32,514 |
| **EXPENDITURE** | | |
| Property services | 6,840 | 6,785 |
| Interest payable and similar charges | 681 | 770 |
| Other investment management costs | 347 | 328 |
| Administration expenses | 19,284 | 21,378 |
| Other operating activities | 14,301 | 16,210 |
| Grants administered | 56,069 | 62,289 |
| Deficit on revaluation of investment properties | 35,695 | 22,705 |
| Notional insurance charge | 40 | 40 |
| Notional cost of capital charge | 8,818 | 11,424 |
| | 142,075 | 141,929 |
| **EXCESS OF EXPENDITURE OVER INCOME BEFORE TAXATION** | **(116,363)** | **(109,415)** |
| Taxation | (17) | (20) |
| **EXCESS OF EXPENDITURE OVER INCOME AFTER TAXATION** | **(116,380)** | **(109,435)** |
| Adjustment for the notional cost of capital | 8,818 | 11,424 |
| **EXCESS OF EXPENDITURE OVER INCOME TRANSFERRED TO RESERVES** | **(107,562)** | **(98,011)** |
| Grant-in-aid received during the year | 61,042 | 29,161 |
| European grants receivable | 2,930 | 8,079 |
| Unrealised surplus on revaluation of own use properties | 410 | - |
| **TOTAL RECOGNISED GAINS AND LOSSES** | **(43,180)** | **(60,771)** |
| Prior year adjustment - Notional insurance | (40) | - |
| **TOTAL RECOGNISED GAINS AND LOSSES** | **(43,220)** | **(60,771)** |

| advisers | **Auditors** | National Audit Office | 23-24 Park Place, Cardiff CF1 3BA |

**branches**

*North Wales Division*
Unit 7
St Asaph Business Park
Glascoed Road
St Asaph LL17 0LJ

*West Wales Division*
Llys-y-Ddraig
Penllergaer Business Park
Penllergaer
Swansea SA4 1HL

*South Wales Division*
QED Centre
Main Avenue
Treforest Estate
Treforest CF37 5YR

# *Welsh Language Board (WLB)*

Market Chambers
5-7 St Mary Street
Cardiff CF1 2AT

**Tel** 01222 224744
**Fax** 01222 224577

**E-mail** ymholiadau@bwrdd-yr-iaith.org.uk
**Web** http://www.netwales.co.uk/byig

**Contact** Gwenan Llwyd Evans

| | |
|---|---|
| *status* | Executive body |
| *founded* | 1993 |
| *sponsor* | Welsh Office |
| *powers* | Welsh Language Act 1993 |
| *mission* | To promote the use of Welsh as a self-sustaining and secure medium of communication in Wales. |
| *tasks* | Promoting and facilitating the use of Welsh. Advising on and influencing matters relating to the Welsh language. Stimulating and working on public sector Welsh language schemes. Distributing grants to promote the use of Welsh. Keeping a strategic overview of Welsh-medium education. |
| *operations* | Management: The Board is a facilitator, not a provider of services per se. The Chief Executive reports to the Board. Grant distribution is a new responsibility assumed by the Board in 1996/97 and is seen as an opportunity to nurture relationships with other organisations. Development of public sector partnerships (eg with the Commission for Racial Equality) and voluntary sector partnerships (eg with the Wales Council for Voluntary Action) are an important part of management. Partnerships with private sector companies wishing to develop their use of Welsh are increasing. |
| | Policy: The Board published *A Strategy for the Welsh Language* in 1996 which guides the Board's work. |
| | Trends: Devolution may radically alter the relationship between the Board and the Secretary of State, but the executive function is expected to continue. |
| *performance* | 1996/97 targets for public sector Welsh language schemes exceeded. |
| *board* | Appointed by the Secretary of State on the basis of open competition. |

| | | |
|---|---|---|
| Chairman | Lord Elis-Thomas of Nant Conwy | |
| Vice-Chairman | Mrs Elan Closs Stephens | |
| Members | Prof Colin Baker | Cllr Gareth Winston Roberts |
| | Ms Ann Beynon | The Rev Dr Patrick Thomas |
| | Gwyn Griffiths | Godfrey Williams |
| | Dr Medwin Hughes | Rhodri Williams |
| | Jeffrey Morgan | |
| *Accounting Officer* | *Chief Executive* | |

| | |
|---|---|
| *staff* | 30 |

| Chief Executive | John Walter Jones |
| Deputy Chief Executive and Head of the Policy & Planning Department | Gwyn Jones |
| Head of the Public and Voluntary Sectors Department | Rhys Dafis |
| Chief Administrative Officer | Gareth Jones |
| Chief Finance Officer | Enid Lewis |
| Head of Marketing & Communications | Gwenan Llwyd Evans |
| Head of the Grants & Private Sector Department | Huw Onllwyn Jones |
| Head of the Education & Training Department | Meirion Prys Jones |

*financial*

**INCOME & EXPENDITURE**

| Year end: 31 March | 1997 £ | 1996 £ |
|---|---|---|
| **GROSS INCOME** | | |
| Grant-in-aid | 2,016,975 | 1,902,423 |
| Release of deferred government grant | 54,537 | 44,856 |
| CySill income | 17,405 | 44,504 |
| Other income | 2,207 | - |
| | **2,091,124** | **1,991,783** |
| **EXPENDITURE** | | |
| Grants | 651,444 | 647,715 |
| Staff salaries | 700,116 | 619,230 |
| Members' salaries | 94,194 | 94,471 |
| Administration | 314,610 | 352,465 |
| Depreciation | 52,728 | 45,022 |
| Permanent diminution in value of fixed assets | 7,478 | - |
| CySill | 10,245 | 34,078 |
| Other purposes | 232,438 | 226,719 |
| Notional interest on capital | 15,999 | 17,556 |
| | **(2,079,252)** | **(2,037,256)** |
| **SURPLUS/(DEFICIT) ON OPERATING ACTIVITIES** | **11,872** | **(45,473)** |
| Interest receivable | 242 | 200 |
| Profit on sale of fixed assets | - | 458 |
| Other income | - | 3,275 |
| Transfer from revaluation reserve | - | 86 |
| Amount payable to the Welsh Office for surrender to the Consolidated Fund | - | (13,791) |
| Adjustment for notional interest on capital | 15,999 | 17,556 |
| **RETAINED SURPLUS/(DEFICIT) FOR THE PERIOD** | **28,113** | **(37,689)** |

*advisers*

| **Bankers** | Midland Bank | 114 St Mary Street, Cardiff CF3 1LF |
| **Auditors** | National Audit Office | Audit House, 23/24 Park Place, Cardiff CF1 3BA |
| **Solicitors** | Morgan Bruce | Princess House, Princess Way, Swansea SA1 3LJ |

*publications* Annual Report & Accounts, Guide to Bilingual Design, The Use of Welsh in Business, Directory of Translators, Welsh Language Schemes, A Strategy for the Welsh Language

# Welsh National Board for Nursing, Midwifery Health & Visiting (WNB)

2nd Floor
Golate House
101 St Mary Street
Cardiff CF1 1DX

**Tel** 01222 261400
**Fax** 01222 2611499

*status* Executive body
*founded* 1983
*sponsor* Welsh Office (WO)
*powers* The Nurses, Midwives and Health Visitors Act 1997

| | |
|---|---|
| *mission* | To protect the public by promoting clinical effectiveness through effective education of nurses, midwives and health visitors in Wales. |
| *tasks* | Responsible for the approval and monitoring the education of nurses, midwives and health visitors; providing advice and guidance to local supervising authorities in relation to the statutory supervision of midwives; careers information to the public and the professions; initial and continuing education for teachers of nursing, midwifery and health visiting. |
| *operations* | Management: The Board comprises an appointed Chairman, three Executive Members, (the Chief Executive and two senior Managers), with six additional Non-executive Members. Funded Welsh Office in the main, with a small fee income. |
| | Policy: To work closely with the higher education sector and healthcare providers in Wales. |
| | Trends: Continuously responding to ever changing professional requirements of the NHS and independent sector in Wales. |
| *board* | Appointed by the Secretary of State. |

| Chairman | SW Jones OBE |
|---|---|
| Members | Mrs Barbara Bale |
| | Mrs Ann Davies OBE |
| | Miss Wendy Fawcus |
| | Mrs SE Gregory |
| | Mrs Mary Hodgeon |
| | Susan Kent |
| | Davey Ravey |
| | JV Williams |
| *Accounting Officer* | *Chief Executive* |

*staff*  25

| | |
|---|---|
| Chief Executive | David Ravey |
| Director of Professional Services | Mrs Ann Davies OBE |
| Director of Business Services | Miss Wendy Fawcus |
| Professional Adviser, Mental Illness & Mental Handicap | Mick Fisher |
| Professional Adviser, General & Adult Nursing | Anne Hopkins |
| Professional Adviser, Midwifery | Robyn Phillips |
| Professional Adviser, Primary Health Care | Mrs Eira Rowley |
| Careers Information Manager | Miss Anne Duggan |
| Computer Services Manager | Mrs Gwyneth Hawkes |
| Operational Manager | Mrs Isabel Owen |
| Personnel & Training Manager | Mrs Christina Roberts |
| Finance Manager | John Roderick |
| Examinations & Records Manager | Ms Jennifer Wheten |

*financial*

**INCOME & EXPENDITURE**

| Year end: 31 March | 1996 | 1995 |
|---|---|---|
| | £ | £ |
| **INCOME** | | |
| Grant from Welsh Office | 1,092,072 | 1,134,312 |
| Release of deferred grant | 41,105 | 42,919 |
| | **1,133,177** | **1,177,231** |
| **EXPENDITURE** | | |
| Teacher training costs | 106,086 | 190,380 |
| Headquarters costs | 983,168 | 931,561 |
| Depreciation | 40,583 | 42,919 |
| Notional charges | | |
| Insurance | 2,305 | 2,208 |
| Cost of capital | 8,026 | 9,357 |
| | **1,140,168** | **1,176,425** |
| **SURPLUS/(DEFICIT)** | **(6,991)** | **(806)** |
| Fees and other non-retainable income receivable | 150,235 | 125,715 |
| Income repayable to Welsh Office in year | (139,651) | (128,943) |
| **SURPLUS/(DEFICIT) FOR YEAR** | **(3,593)** | **(2,422)** |
| Retained surplus brought forward | 37,706 | 30,771 |
| Adjustment for notional charges | 8,026 | 9,357 |
| **RETAINED SURPLUS CARRIED FORWARD** | **49,325** | **37,706** |

# West of Scotland Water Authority

419 Balmore Road
Glasgow G22 6NU

**Tel** 0141 355 5333

| | |
|---|---|
| *status* | Public corporation |
| *founded* | 1995 |
| *sponsor* | Scottish Office |
| *powers* | Local Government etc (Scotland) Act 1994 |
| *mission* | To provide water services to the people of the West of Scotland to the standard which they seek at the least possible cost. |
| *tasks* | Responsible for water and sewerage services in the area previously served by Strathclyde and Dumfries and Galloway Regional Councils (47% of Scotland's population). Ensuring continuity of supply and water quality. Complying with UK and EU environmental legislation. |
| *operations* | Management: Accountable to the Secretary of State and must operate within financial objectives (generate a specified rate of return on net operating assets; revenue not less than outgoings; borrowing to remain within set limits). Board maintains overall control for financial, strategic, budgetary and organisational issues. The Executive Management group, headed by the Chief Executive, has responsibility for the day-to-day management of the Authority and reports to the Board. |
| | Policy: Huge level of investment planned for next ten years in plant and equipment - many projects to be financed through PFI. |
| | Trends: Investment programme will lead to large increases in operating and financing costs - making great efforts not to pass these on to customers. |
| *performance* | Met all financial targets in 1996/97. |
| *board* | Appointed by the Secretary of State. |

| Chairman | John Jameson OBE | |
|---|---|---|
| Chief Executive | Ernest Chambers | |
| Members | Norman Berry | Peter NB Kennedy |
| | Mungo Bryson | Jane McKay |
| | Gerald Carroll | Cllr David Munn JP |
| | John Goodwin | Cllr Billy Petrie OBE JP |
| | David Gray | Cllr Leslie Rosin JP |
| Accounting Officer | Chief Executive | |

*staff* 2845

| | |
|---|---|
| Chief Executive | EGW Chambers |
| Director, Support Services | R Birkinshaw |
| Director, Human Resources | C Cornish |
| Director, Operations | D Davidson |
| Director, Business Planning | P Kuzbyt |
| Director, Engineering Services | DI Little |
| Director, Scientific Services | CJ McFadzean |
| Director, Finance | A Park |
| Director, Special Projects | JB Robertson |
| Director, Customer Services | CE Schooling |

*financial*

**INCOME & EXPENDITURE**
**Year end: 31 March**

| | 1997 £000 |
|---|---|
| **TURNOVER** | 243,076 |
| **OPERATING COSTS** | |
| Manpower costs | 59,857 |
| Materials and consumables | 22,921 |
| Other operational costs | 65,823 |
| Depreciation | 16,190 |
| Amortisation of grants and contributions | (312) |
| Infrastructure maintenance charge | 27,623 |
| Own work capitalised | (11,521) |
| | 180,581 |

| | |
|---|---:|
| **OPERATING SURPLUS** | **62,495** |
| Surplus on disposal of fixed assets | 112 |
| **SURPLUS BEFORE INTEREST** | **62,607** |
| Interest receivable | 1,023 |
| Interest payable and similar charges | 63,027 |
| **SURPLUS BEFORE TAXATION** | **603** |
| Taxation credit | 8 |
| **SURPLUS FOR YEAR** | **611** |

*advisers*   **Bankers**      Bank of Scotland

**Auditors**      Coopers & Lybrand

*publications*   Annual Report, Watermark, Water Quality Report

# Westminster Foundation for Democracy

Clutha House
10 Storey's Gate
London SW1P 3AY

**Tel** 0171 976 7565          **E-mail** wfd@wfd.org
**Fax** 0171 976 7464

**Contact** Alexandra Jones, Chief Executive

*status*    Executive body

*founded*   1992

*sponsor*   Foreign and Commonwealth Office (FCO)

*powers*    Memorandum and Articles of Association. Financial Memorandum with the FCO (1992)

*mission*   To provide assistance in building and strengthening pluralistic democratic institutions overseas.

*tasks*     Funding democratic institutions overseas (mainly in Central and Eastern Europe, the former Soviet Union and Anglophone Africa); promoting political party development abroad; funding initiatives which will make a tangible and practical contribution.

*operations*  Management: The Foundation is supervised by a Chairman and Board and managed by a Chief Executive. There are two forms of project: Political Party Projects - run through the Westminster main parties, with politicians and political party staff sharing expertise with parties overseas; and Foundation Projects - run by the Foundation from its office in Westminster.

Policy: Increasing support for independent media, trade unions, human rights organisations, women's groups etc has strengthened new organisations in developing democratic countries.

Trends: Grant-in-aid increased by 8.5% in 1997/98.

*board*     Appointed by the Secretary of State.

| | | |
|---|---|---|
| Chairman | Ernie Ross MP | |
| Governors | Tony Clarke CBE | |
| | Prof Peter Frank | Ralph Land CBE |
| | Timothy Garton Ash | Richard Page MP |
| | Nik Gowing | Dr Michael Pinto-Duschinsky |
| | Sir Archie Hamilton MP | Gary Streeter MP |
| | Mary Kaldor | Ieuan Wyn Jones MP |
| *Accounting Officer* | *Chief Executive* | |

*staff*     6

| | |
|---|---|
| Chief Executive | Alexandra Jones |
| Project Manager, Commonwealth of Independent Sates | Megan Bick |
| Project Manager, Central & Eastern Europe/Company Secretary | Ms Sue Chudleigh |
| Project Manager, Central & Eastern Europe, Public Relations | Jadranka Porter |
| Project Manager, Anglophone Africa, Corporate Relations | Mrs Tracy Tickle |
| PA to Chief Executive | Clare Morris |

*financial*

| INCOME & EXPENDITURE Year end: 31 March | 1997 £ | 1996 £ | 1995 £ |
|---|---|---|---|
| **INCOME - CONTINUING ACTIVITIES** | | | |
| HM Government grants | 2,500,000 | 2,500,000 | 2,200,000 |
| Corporate funding and donations | 80,061 | 30,995 | 12,770 |
| | **2,580,061** | **2,530,995** | **2,212,770** |
| **DIRECT EXPENDITURE** | | | |
| Projects | 2,179,699 | 2,160,999 | 1,908,487 |
| | **400,362** | **369,996** | **304,283** |
| **OTHER EXPENDITURE** | | | |
| Staff costs | 195,978 | 149,852 | 155,208 |
| Depreciation | 9,828 | 16,567 | 19,189 |
| Other operating charges | 153,271 | 166,238 | 131,220 |
| | **359,077** | **332,657** | **305,617** |
| **OPERATING SURPLUS** | **41,285** | **37,339** | **(1,334)** |
| Interest receivable | 17,185 | 4,339 | 1,364 |
| **SURPLUS ON ORDINARY ACTIVITIES BEFORE TAXATION** | **58,470** | **41,678** | **30** |
| Corporation tax | (4,125) | (1,085) | (436) |
| **SURPLUS FOR THE FINANCIAL YEAR** | **54,345** | **40,593** | **(406)** |

*advisers*

**Bankers**    Midland Bank        Victoria Street, London

**Auditors**    Kingston Smith       Devonshire House, 60 Goswell Road
London EC1M 7AD

*publications*    Annual Report, Quarterly Newsletter

# Wilton Park Executive Agency

Wiston House
Steyning
Sussex BN44 3DZ

**Tel** 01903 815020
**Fax** 01903 879647

**Contact** Andrew Hammond, Associate Director for Finance & Marketing

*status*    Executive agency

*founded*    1946, as executive agency 1991

*sponsor*    Foreign and Commonwealth Office (FCO)

*powers*    Framework Document

*mission*    Organising international policy conferences devoted to discussion of international issues, on behalf of the FCO.

*tasks*    FCO conferences planning and delivery. Co-sponsorship of conferences with UK and overseas partners (eg US Mission to NATO). Venue for commercial conferences, weddings and banquets.

*operations*    Management: The Agency is run as an international policy conference organisation (Wilton Park) and as a home for conferences (Wiston House). Wilton Park's academic independence is guaranteed by an Academic Council and by an International Advisory Council. There is an FCO Departmental Board responsible for setting annual targets. The Director who is also Chief Executive reports to the FCO Director for Public Services. He is supported by a Board of Management comprising senior staff. It organises about 45 conferences a year. Although the Agency is supported by the FCO, over 90% of its cash flow derives from its own activities.

Policy: Wilton Park: increasing Asian profile. Wiston House: increasing commercial income.

Trends: Refurbished in 1995/96, with advice of FCO, to enhance the quality of service to conference and commercial customers. Wiston House is reviewing all supplier contracts and increasing its marketing ability.

*board*    Academic Advisory Council members are appointed by the Secretary of State from distinguished Britons. International Advisory Council members are OECD Ambassadors and High Commissioners based in London.

| | |
|---|---|
| *Academic Council* | |
| Chairman | Mrs Liliana Archibald |
| Members | Anthony Bruce |

*Academic Council*
Chairman — Mrs Liliana Archibald
Members — Anthony Bruce

| | |
|---|---|
| Sir Julian Bullard GCMG | Dr Connie Martin |
| Mrs Juliet Campbell CMG | Geoffrey Martin |
| Robin Corbett MP | Gael Ramsey |
| Sir Brian Fall KCMG | Andrew Rowe |
| George Joffé | Prof Helen Wallace |
| Sir John Hanson KCMG CBE | Michael Walsh |
| Lord Holme of Cheltenham CBE | Mrs Suzanne Warner |
| Prof Michael Kaser | Tony Young |

*Departmental Board*
Members — Mike Brown

| | |
|---|---|
| Edward Clay | Mariot Leslie |
| Peter Dun | Carolin Livingstone |
| Anthony Layden | Jeff Sawyer |
| Miss Valerie Le Moignan | Mrs Ruth Watts Davies |

*Accounting Officer* — *Chief Executive*

**staff**    32

| | |
|---|---|
| Chief Executive & Director | CB Jennings |
| Deputy Director | R Latter |
| Senior Associate Director | N Hopkinson |
| Associate Director | V Crowe |
| Associate Director | R Hart |
| Associate Director (Finance & Marketing) | Andrew Hammond |
| Associate Director | Chris Langdon |
| General Manager | Roger Barr |

**financial**

**INCOME & EXPENDITURE**

| Year end: 31 March | 1997 £000 | 1996 £000 | 1995 £000 |
|---|---|---|---|
| **EXPENDITURE** | | | |
| Current expenditure funded by departmental vote and receipts and consumed in the year | | | |
| Running costs | 1,160 | 1,088 | 949 |
| Other current costs | 435 | 428 | 457 |
| Depreciation and non-cash interest | 233 | 51 | 49 |
| Other non-cash costs and services provided from other votes | 26 | 24 | 24 |
| | **1,854** | **1,591** | **1,479** |
| **INCOME** | | | |
| Less income from services supplied in period | 1,339 | 1,313 | 1,149 |
| Rent received | 4 | 4 | 4 |
| Interest received | 8 | 8 | 4 |
| | **1,348** | **1,325** | **1,157** |
| **NET COST OF OUTPUT** | **506** | **266** | **322** |

**advisers**    **Bankers**    Barclays Bank      High Street, Steyning, West Sussex BN44 3ZA

**publications**    *Annual Report and Accounts*

# *Wine Standards Board (of the Vintners' Company)*

Five Kings House
1 Queen Street Place
London EC4R 1QS

**Tel** 0171 236 9512
**Fax** 0171 236 7908

**status**    Executive body

**founded**    1973

**sponsor**    Ministry of Agriculture, Fisheries and Food (MAFF)

**powers**    Common Agricultural Policy (Wine) Regulations 1973. Memorandum of Agreement between MAFF and the Vintners' Company 1973

| | |
|---|---|
| **mission** | To advise and educate wine traders - importers and retailers who are also wholesalers - on the wine regulations. To regulate wine production, vineyards and oenological processes in the UK. |
| **tasks** | Ensuring that UK and EU wine trading regulations are observed throughout the UK by wine traders, irrespective of the country of production of the wine. These include traders' documents and records, the distinction between quality and table wines and the labelling and price listing of all wines, whatever their origin; deterring would-be offenders by spot checks and inspections and to conduct successful prosecutions against persistent or serious offenders in the UK and EU; management of the UK's Vineyard Register as required by EU regulations. |
| **operations** | Management: Responsibility for the enforcement of the wine regulations, which cover the entire market in wine from grape to final sale to the consumer, is divided between the Wine Standards Board (WSB), MAFF, HM Customs & Excise and local authorities. WSB has a Chief Executive, a London office staff and an inspectorate of nine, the majority of whom are retired senior police officers. The inspectors visit traders and vineyards either by pre-arrangement or without warning to check records etc. WSB is funded by the Vintners' Company and MAFF and a new five-year financial agreement between them was signed in 1996. |
| | Policy: WSB considers prevention/deterrence better than cure/war and welcomes opportunities to discuss, advise and assist rather than prosecute. |
| | Trends: There have been numerous convictions in the UK and elsewhere resulting from WSB investigations. |
| **board** | Appointed equally by MAFF and the Vintners' Company. |

| | |
|---|---|
| Chairman | PJ Purton |
| Members | AC Foster |
| | RE Melville |
| | DC Reed |
| | Brigadier M Smythe |
| | Dr AT Woodrow |

**staff** 13

| | |
|---|---|
| Secretary | JM Findlay |

**financial**

| INCOME & EXPENDITURE Year end: 31 March | 1997 £ | 1996 £ |
|---|---|---|
| **INCOME** | | |
| Sums received from the Vintners' Company | 105,000 | 96,000 |
| Sums received from MAFF | 372,890 | 359,950 |
| | **477,890** | **455,950** |
| **EXPENDITURE AND CHARGES** | | |
| Board salaries and expenses (six members) | 10,780 | 8,430 |
| Office salaries (five employees) | 115,657 | 106,204 |
| Inspectors' salaries (nine inspectors) | 155,969 | 147,075 |
| Inspectors' expenses | 66,400 | 63,243 |
| Defined benefit pension scheme | 67,200 | 64,750 |
| Audit fee | 1,750 | 1,050 |
| Accountancy charges | 962 | 794 |
| Rent and rates | 21,691 | 23,504 |
| Office expenses | 44,788 | 29,974 |
| Printing and stationery | 951 | 891 |
| Postage | 818 | 926 |
| Depreciation of office furniture and equipment | 2,711 | 1,692 |
| Legal and professional fees | 4,643 | 248 |
| Pension management costs | 5,352 | 2,500 |
| | **499,672** | **451,281** |
| **(DEFICIT)/SURPLUS FOR THE YEAR** | **(21,782)** | **4,669** |

| **advisers** | **Bankers** | National Westminster Bank | 1 Princes Street, London EC2R 8PA |
|---|---|---|---|
| | **Auditors** | Coulthards MacKenzie | Five Kings House, 1 Queen Street Place London EC4R 1QS |

# Youth Council for Northern Ireland

Lamont House
Purdy's Lane
Belfast BT8 4TA

**Tel** 01232 643882
**Fax** 01232 643874

| | |
|---|---|
| ***status*** | Executive body |
| ***founded*** | 1990 |
| ***sponsor*** | Northern Ireland Office, Department of Education NI (DENI) |
| ***powers*** | Youth Service (NI) Order 1989. |
| ***mission*** | To influence and advance the quality of life for children and young people in Northern Ireland. |
| ***tasks*** | Assesses and pays grants to voluntary youth organisations; advises government departments/agencies on youth policies; encourages cross-community activity by the youth service; encourages the provision of facilities; develops international work; advises on training; coordinates expertise and resources of government agencies and voluntary groups. |
| ***operations*** | Management: Director responsible for day-to-day management. Funds 35 agencies ranging from the Army Cadet Force to Youthnet. |
| ***board*** | Members appointed by the Minister. |

| Accounting Officer | Director |
|---|---|

***staff*** 18

| | |
|---|---|
| Director | David Guilfoyle |
| Professional Adviser | A Dempster |
| Professional Adviser | J McCormick |
| Professional Adviser | F Murphy |
| Professional Officer (Curriculum) | Ms M-T McGivern |
| Professional Officer (International) | C Richardson |
| Training & Development Officer (Eurobureau) | Ms B Sweeney |
| Research & Information Officer | Ms C Harvey |
| Executive Officer (Finance) | Mrs B Clarke |
| Executive Officer (International) | Ms M Cunningham |
| Executive Officer (Training/Curriculum) | Ms T Mulhern |
| Executive Officer (Personnel) | Mrs S Rader |
| Executive Officer (Public Relations) | Ms K Thompson |
| Executive Officer (Finance) | K Traynor |

***financial***

| INCOME & EXPENDITURE Year end: 31 March | 1997 £ | 1996 £ | 1995 £ |
|---|---|---|---|
| **INCOME** | | | |
| Department of Education grants | 2,302,081 | 2,333,445 | 2,222,067 |
| Other operating income | 110,350 | 136,184 | 104,258 |
| Transfer from deferred government grant | 18,338 | 14,596 | 16,421 |
| | **2,430,769** | **2,484,225** | **2,342,746** |
| **EXPENDITURE** | | | |
| Grants and bursaries | 1,775,157 | 1,735,754 | 1,637,272 |
| Miscellaneous grant aid | 40,175 | 127,999 | 80,375 |
| Staff costs | 420,874 | 410,485 | 347,834 |
| Depreciation | 17,670 | 14,596 | 16,421 |
| Other operating charges | 212,396 | 204,052 | 229,107 |
| | **2,466,272** | **2,492,886** | **2,311,009** |
| **OPERATING SURPLUS/(DEFICIT)** | (35,503) | (8,661) | 31,737 |
| Interest payable and similar charges | 5,741 | 6,555 | 1,165 |
| **DEFICIT FOR THE YEAR** | **(41,244)** | **(15,216)** | **30,572** |

***advisers*** | **Bankers** | Ulster Bank | University Road, Belfast |

# *Regional Index*

This index lists the main and branch addresses for each quango under fourteen regional headings - in England these represent the ten Government Office Regions (GORs).

**England**

East Midlands

Eastern

London

Merseyside

North East

North West

South East

South West

West Midlands

Yorkshire & Humberside

**Northern Ireland**
**Scotland**
**Wales**
**Overseas**

## EAST MIDLANDS

ACAS
Anderson House
Clinton Avenue
Nottingham NG5 1AW
Tel 0115 969 3355

Agricultural Wages Board for
England & Wales
Block 7
Government Buildings
Chalfont Drive
Nottingham NG8 3SN
Tel 01602 291191

British Geological Survey
Kingsley Dunham Centre
Keyworth
Nottingham NG12 5GG
Tel 0115 936 3100
Fax 0115 936 3200

British Waterways
Mill Lane
Mill Gate
Newark
Notts NG24 4TT
Tel 01636 704481

British Waterways
Trent Lock
Lock Lane
Long Eaton
Nottingham NG10 2FF
Tel 0115 946 1017

British Waterways
The Stop House
Braunston
Northants NN11 7JQ
Tel 01788 890666

Coal Authority
200 Lichfield Lane
Berry Hill
Mansfield
Nottinghamshire NG18 4RG
Tel 01623 427162
Fax 01623 62072

Construction Industry Training
Board
Belton Road Indusrial Estate
20 Prince William Road
Loughborough
Leicestershire LE11 5TB
Tel 01509 610266
Fax 01509 210241

Defence Animal Centre
Welby Lane
Melton Mowbray
Leicestershire LE13 0SL
Tel 01664 411811
Fax 01664 410694
E-mail
113166.712@compuserve.com

Driving Standards Agency
Stanley House
56 Talbot Street
Nottingham NG1 5GU
Tel 0115 901 2500
E-mail
106027.3210@compuserve.com
Web http://www.coi.gov.uk/coi/
depts/GDS

Employment Tribunals Service
3rd Floor
Byron House
2a Maid Marion Way
Nottingham NG1 6HS
Tel 0115 947 5701
Fax 0115 950 7612

Employment Tribunals Service
5a New Walk
Leicester LE1 6TE

English Nature
Manor Barn
Over Haddon
Bakewell
Derbyshire DE45 1JE
Tel 01629 815095
Fax 01629 815091

English Nature
The Maltings
Wharf Road
Grantham
Lincs NG31 6BH
Tel 01476 568431
Fax 01476 570927

English Sports Council
Grove House
Bridgford Road
West Bridgford
Nottingham NG2 6AP
Tel 0115 982 1887
Fax 0115 945 5236

Gaming Board for Great Britain
Minerva House
Spaniel Row
Nottingham NG1 6EP
Tel 0115 941 991
Fax 0115 948 4587

Gas Consumers' Council
Carlton House
Regent Road
Leicester LE1 6YH
Tel 0116 255 6611
Fax 0116 2556609

The Health & Safety Executive
Belgrave House
1 Greyfriars
Northampton NN1 2BS
Tel 01604 738300
Fax 01604 738333

The Health & Safety Executive
1st Floor
The Pearson Building
55 Upper Parliament Street
Nottingham NG1 6AU
Tel 0115 971 2800
Fax 0115 971 2802

HM Land Registry
Chalfont Drive
Nottingham NG8 3RN
Tel 0115 935 1166

HM Land Registry
Thames Tower
99 Burleys Way
Leicester LE1 3UB
Tel 0116 265 4000

Horticulture Research International
Wellington Road
Kirton
Boston
Lincs PE20 1NN
Tel 01205 723477
Fax 01205 724957

The Housing Corporation
Attenborough House
109-119 Charles Street
Leicester LE1 1FQ
Tel 0116 242 4800

Independent Television
Commission
10-11 Poultry
Nottingham NG1 2HW
Tel 0115 952 7333
Fax 0115 952 7353

Inland Revenue
Lawress Hall
Riseholme
Lincoln LN2 2BJ
Tel 01522 561761

Inland Revenue
Yorke House
Castle Meadow Road
Nottingham NG2 1BG
Tel 0115 974 1599

Insolvency Service
Ground Floor
Scottish Life House
29 St Katherine's Street
Northampton NN1 2QZ
Tel 01604 542400
Fax 01604 542450

Insolvency Service
1st Floor
Chaddesden House
77 Talbot Street
Nottingham NG1 5GA
Tel 0115 901 1000
Fax 0115 901 1019

Insolvency Service
5th Floor
Haymarket House
Haymarket Centre
Leicester LE1 3YS
Tel 0116 2622251/3
Fax 0116 262417

Legal Aid Board
1st Floor
Fothergill House
16 King Street
Nottingham NG1 2AS
Tel 0115 955 9600
Fax 0115 956 0716

National Forest Company
Enterprise Glade
Bath Lane
Moira
Swadlincote
Derbyshire DE12 6BD
Tel 01283 551211
Fax 01283 552844

National Lottery Charities Board
96-98 Regent Road
Readson House
Leicester LE1 7DZ
Tel 0116 258 7000

Office of Electricity Regulation
Langford House
Suite 3c
40 Friar Lane
Nottingham NG1 6DQ
Tel 0115 950 8738

Remploy Limited
Gorse Hill Industrial Estate
1 Boston Road
Beaumont Leys
Leicester LE4 1BB
Tel 0116 236 4434
Fax 0116 236 5864

Rural Development Commission
18 Market Place
Bingham
Nottingham NG13 8AP
Tel 01949 876200

Veterinary Laboratories Agency
The Elms
College Road
Sutton Bonington
Loughborough
Leicestershire LE12 5RB
Tel 01509 672332
Fax 01509 674805

## EASTERN

ACAS
39 King Street
Thetford
Norfolk IP24 2AU

Agricultural Wages Board for
England & Wales
Block B
Government Buildings
Brooklands Avenue
Cambridge CB2 2DR
Tel 01223 462727

Audit Commission
1st Floor
Sheffield House
Lytton Way
Stevenage SG1 3HB

British Antartic Survey
High Cross
Madingley Road
Cambridge CB3 0ET
Tel 01223 251400/361188
Fax 01223 362616

British Board of Agrément
PO Box 195
Bucknalls Lane
Garston
Watford
Herts WD2 7NG
Tel 01923 670844
Fax 01923 662133
E-mail bba@btinternet.com
Web http://www.bbacerts.co.uk

British Waterways
Willow Grange
Church Road
Watford WD1 3QA
Tel 01923 226422
Fax 01923 201300

British Waterways
Brindley House
Corner Hall
Lawn Lane
Hemel Hempstead
Herts HP3 9YT
Tel 01442 235400

British Waterways
Marsworth Junction
Watery Lane
Marsworth
Tring
Herts HP23 4LZ
Tel 01442 825938

CEFAS
Remembrance Avenue
Burnham-on-Crough
Essex CMO 8HA
Tel 01621 787200

Central Computer &
Telecommunications Agency
Rosebery Court
St Andrews Business Park
Norwich NR7 0HS
Tel 01603 704704
Fax 01603 704817

Centre for Environment, Fisheries
& Aquaculture Science
Lowestoft Laboratory
Pakefield Road
Lowestoft
Suffolk NR33 0HT
Tel 01502 562 244
Fax 01502 513 865

Construction Industry Training
Board
1a Peel Street
Luton
Bedfordshire LU1 2QR
Tel 01582 727462
Fax 01582 456318

Construction Industry Training
Board
Bircham Newton
Kings Lynn
Norfolk PE31 6RH
Tel 01485 577577
Fax 01485 577689

Countryside Commission
Ortona House
110 Hills Road
Cambridge CB2 1LQ
Tel 01223 354462
Fax 01223 313850

CSL Food Science Laboratory
Norwich Research Park
Colney
Norwich NR4 7UQ
Tel 01603 259350
Fax 01603 501123
E-mail science@csl.gov.uk

Defence Estates Organisation
HQ Logistics Command
RAF Brampton
Huntingdon
Cambs PE18 8QL
Tel 01480 52151

Defence Estates Organisation
Flagstaff House
Colchester
Essex CO2 7ST
Tel 01206 782144

Defence Estates Organisation
Stirling House
Denny End Road
Waterbeach
Cambridge CB5 9QB
Tel 01223 255008

Defence Intelligence & Security
Centre
Chicksands
Shefford
Bedfordshire SG17 5PR
Tel 01462 752101
Fax 01462 752291

Employment Tribunals Service
100 Southgate Street
Bury St Edmunds
Suffolk IP33 2AQ
Tel 01284 762171
Fax 01284 706064

Employment Tribunals Service
8/10 Howard Street
Bedford MK40 2HS
Tel 01234 351306
Fax 01234 353315

Engineering Construction Industry
Training Board
Blue Court
1 Church Lane
Kings Langley
Herts WD4 8JP
Tel 01923 260000
Fax 01923 270969
Web http://www/ecitb.org.uk

English Nature
Ham Lane House
Ham Lane
Nene Park
Orton Waterville
Peterborough
Cambridgeshire PE2 5UR
Tel 01733 391100
Fax 01733 394093

English Nature
60 Bracondale
Norwich
Norfolk NR1 2BE
Tel 01603 620558
Fax 01603 762552

English Nature
Harbour House
Hythe Quay
Colchester
Essex CO2 8JF
Tel 01206 796666
Fax 01206 794466

English Nature
Norman Tower House
1-2 Crown Street
Bury St Edmunds
Suffolk IP33 1QX
Tel 01284 762218
Fax 01284 764318

English Nature
Northminster House
Peterborough PE1 1UA
Tel 01733 455000
Fax 01733 568834
Web http://www.english-
nature.org.uk

English Sports Council
Crescent House
19 The Crescent
Bedford MK40 2RT
Tel 01234 345222
Fax 01234 359046

The Environment Agency
Kingfisher House
Goldhay Way
Orton Goldhay
Peterborough PE2 5ZR
Tel 01733 371811
Fax 01733 231840

Farming & Rural Conservation
Agency
Brooklands Avenue
Cambridge CB2 2BL
Tel 01223 462762
Fax 01223 455911

Forensic Science Laboratory
Hinchingbrooke Park
Huntingdon
Cambridgeshire PE18 8NP
Tel 01480 450071
Fax 01480 450079

The Further Education Funding
Council
2 Quayside
Bridge Street
Cambridge CB5 8AB
Tel 01223 454500
Fax 01223 454535

Gas Consumers' Council
51 Station Road
Letchworth
Herts SG6 3BQ
Tel 01462 685399
Fax 01462 480902

The Health & Safety Executive
39 Baddow Road
Chelmsford CM2 0HL
Tel 01245 706200
Fax 01245 706222

The Health & Safety Executive
14 Cardiff Road, Luton
Bedfordshire LU1 1PP
Tel 01582 444200
Fax 01582 444320

The Health & Safety Executive
PO Box 1999
Sudbury
Suffolk CO10 6FS
Tel 01787 881165
Fax 01787 313995

Highways Agency
Heron House
49/53 Goldington Road
Bedford MK40 3LL
Tel 0645 556575

Highways Agency
Charter Court
Midland Road
Hemel Hempstead HP2 5RL
Tel 0645 556575

HM Land Registry
Brickdale House
Swingate
Stevenage
Herts SG1 1XG
Tel 01438 788888

HM Land Registry
Touthill Close
City Road
Peterborough PE1 1XN
Tel 01733 288288

Independent Television
Commission
24 Castle Meadow
Norwich NR1 3DH
Tel 01603 623533
Fax 01603 633631

Inland Revenue
Churchgate
New Road
Peterborough PE1 1TD
Tel 01733 754321

Insolvency Service
2nd Floor
Abbeygate House
164/167 East Road
Cambridge CB1 1DB
Tel 01223 324480
Fax 01223 464717

Insolvency Service
Emmanuel House
2 Covent Road
Norwich NR2 1PA
Tel 01603 628983
Fax 01603 760842

Insolvency Service
1st Floor
Trident House
42-48 Victoria Street
St Albans AL1 3HR
Tel 01727 832233
Fax 01727 815700

Insolvency Service
2nd Floor
Tylers House
Tylers Avenue
Southend-on-Sea
Essex SS1 2AX
Tel 01702 602570
Fax 01702 602567

Insolvency Service
St Clare House
Greyfriars
Ipswich IP1 1LX
Tel 01473 217565
Fax 01473 230430

Intervention Board
Block B
Government Buildings
Brooklands Avenue
Cambridge CB2 2DR
Tel 01223 462727
Fax 01223 455787

Joint Air Reconnaissance
Intelligence Centre
RAF Brampton
Huntingdon
Cambridgeshire PE18 8QL
Tel 01480 52151

Joint Nature Conservation
Committee
Monkstone House
City Road
Peterborough PE1 1JY
Tel 01733 866801
Fax 01733 555948

Legal Aid Board
Kett House
Station Road
Cambridge CB1 2JT
Tel 01223 366511
Fax 01223 222608

Meat Hygiene Service
Room G9, Block A
Government Buildings
Brooklands Avenue
Cambridge CB2 2DD
Tel 01223 456703

Ministry of Defence Hospital Unit
Peterborough Hospital NHS Trust
Thorpe Road
Peterborough PE3 6DA
Tel 01733 874939
Fax 01733 874939

Ministry of Defence Police
Wheathersfield
Braintree
Essex CM7 4AZ
Tel 01371 854208
Fax 01371 854010

National Biological Standards
Board
Blanche Lane
South Mimms
Potters Bar
Herts EN6 3QG
Tel 01701 654753
Fax 01701 646730
E-mail enquiries@nibsc.ac.uk
Web http://www.nibsc.ac.uk

The National Lottery
Tolpits Lane
Watford WD1 8RN

Office of Electricity Regulation
4th Floor
Waveney House
Handford Road
Ipswich
Suffolk IP1 2BJ
Tel 01473 216101

Ofwat Eastern Customer Service
Committee
Ground Floor
Carlyle House
Carlyle Road
Cambridge CB4 3DN
Tel 01223 323889
Fax 01223 323930
E-mail encsc@ofwat.gtnet.gov.uk
Web http://www.open.gov.uk/ofwat

RAF Logistics Support Services
PO Box 70
Huntingdon
Cambridgeshire PE17 2PY
Tel 01480 446961
Fax 01480 446747
E-mail mackenziek@logistics.org

RAF Maintenance Group Defence
Agency
RAF Brampton
Huntingdon
Cambs PE18 8QL
Tel 01480 52151
Fax 01480 431163

RAF Signals Engineering
Establishment
RAF Henlow
Bedfordshire SG16 6DN
Tel 01462 851515 x 6071
Fax 01462 851515 x7687

Rail Users Consultative Committee
for Eastern England
Crescent House
46 Priestgate
Peterborough PE1 1LF
Tel 01733 312188
Fax 01733 891286

Royal Commisison on the
Historical Monuments of England
Brooklands
24 Brooklands Avenue
Cambridge CB2 2BU
Tel 01223 324010
Fax 01223 311203

Royal Greenwich Observatory
Madingley Road
Cambridge CB3 0EZ
Tel 01223 374000
Fax 01223 374700
E-mail jvw@mail.ast.cam.ac.uk

Rural Development Commission
Lees Smith House
12 Looms Lane
Bury St Edmunds
Suffolk IP33 1HE
Tel 01284 701743

Teacher Training Agency
Communication Centre
PO Box 3210
Chelmsford CM1 3WA
Tel 01245 454454
Fax 01245 261668

Veterinary Laboratories Agency
Rougham Hill
Bury St Edmunds
Suffolk IP33 2RX
Tel 01284 724499
Fax 01284 724500

# LONDON

ACAS
Clifton House
83-117 Euston Road
London NW1 2RB
Tel 0171 396 5100

Advisory, Conciliation & Arbitration
Service
Brandon House
180 Borough High Street
London SE1 1LW
Tel 0171 210 3613
Fax 0171 210 3645

Agricultural Wages Board for
England & Wales
Nobel House
17 Smith Square
London SW1P 3JR
Tel 0171 238 6540
Fax 0171 238 6553

Alcohol Education & Research
Council
Room 520
Clive House
Petty France
London SW1H 9HD
Tel 0171 271 8379/8337
Fax 0171 271 8877

The Arts Council of England
14 Great Peter Street
London SW1P 3NQ
Tel 0171 333 0100
Fax 0171 973 6590

Audit Commission
1 Vincent Square
London SW1P 2PN
Tel 0171 396 1428
Fax 0171 828 5295

Audit Commission
4th Floor
Millbank Tower
Millbank
London SW1P 4QP

Bank of England
Threadneedle Street
London EC2R 8AH
Tel 0171 601 4444
Fax 0171 601 4771
Web http://
www.bankofengland.co.uk

BFI On The South Bank
South Bank
London SE1 8XT
Tel 0171 928 3535
Fax 0171 633 9323

The Britain-Russia Centre
14 Grosvenor Place
London SW1X 7HW
Tel 0171 235 2116
Fax 0171 259 6254

The British Association for Central
& Eastern Europe
Fourth Floor
50 Hans Crescent
London SW1X 0NA
Tel 0171 584 0766
Fax 0171 584 8831

British Broadcasting Corporation
Broadcasting House
London W1A 1AA
Tel 0171 580 4468
Web http://www.bbc.co.uk

British Council
10 Spring Gardens
London SW1A 2BN
Tel 0171 930 8466
Fax 0171 839 6347
Web http://www.britcoun.org/

British Film Institute
21 Stephen Street
London W1P 2LN
Tel 0171 255 1444
Fax 0171 436 7950

The British Library
96 Euston Road
London NW1 2DB
Tel 0171 412 7111
Fax 0171 412 7268

British Museum
Great Russell Street
London WC1B 3DG
Tel 0171 638 1555
Fax 0171 323 8118
E-mail info@british-museum.ac.uk
Web http://www.british-
museum.ac.uk

British National Space Centre
Bridge Place
88/89 Eccleston Square
London SW1V 1PT
Tel 0171 215 5000
Fax 0171 821 5387
E-mail derek_davis@bnsc-
hq.ccmail.com

British Railways Board
Whittles House
14 Pentonville Road
London N1 9HF
Tel 0171 904 5008
Fax 0171 904 5018

British Tourist Authority
Thames Tower
Black's Road
London W6 9EL
Tel 0181 846 9000
Fax 0181 563 0302
Web http://www.visitbritain.com

British Waterways
The Toll House
Delamere Terrace
Little Venice
London W2 6ND
Tel 0171 286 6101

Broadcasting Standards
Commission
7 The Sanctuary
London SW1P 3JS
Tel 0171 233 0544
Fax 0171 233 0397

Building Societies Commission
Victory House
30/34 Kingsway
London WC2 6ES
Tel 0171 663 5000

Central Council for Education &
Training in Social Work
Derbyshire House
St Chad's Street
London WC1H 8AD
Tel 0171 278 2455
Fax 0171 278 2934

Central Council for Education and
Training in Social Work
3rd Floor
Caledonia House
223-231 Pentonville Road
London N1 9NG
Tel 0171 833 2524
Fax 0171 278 8186

Central Office of Information
Hercules Road
London SE1 7DU
Tel 0171 928 2345
Fax 0171 928 5037

Central Rail Users Consultative
Committee
Clements House
14-18 Gresham Street
London EC2V 7NL
Tel 0171 505 9090
Fax 0171 505 9004

Centre for Information on
Language Teaching & Research
20 Bedfordbury
London WC2N 4LB
Tel 0171 379 5101
Fax 0171 379 5082

Channel Four Television
Corporation
124 Horseferry Road
London SW1P 2TX
Tel 0171 396 4444

Civil Aviation Authority
CAA House
45-59 Kingsway
London WC2B 6TE
Tel 0171 379 7311
Fax 0171 240 1153

Commission for Racial Equality
Elliot House
10/12 Allington Street
London SW1E 5EH
Tel 0171 828 7022
Fax 0171 630 7605

Commonwealth Development
Corporation
1 Bessborough Gardens
London SW1V 2JQ
Tel 0171 828 4488
Fax 0171 8286505
E-mail @mail.london.cdc.co.uk

Commonwealth Institute
Kensington High Street
London W8 6NQ
Tel 0171 603 4535
Fax 0171 602 7374

Commonwealth Scholarship
Commission
The Association of Commonwealth
Universities
John Foster House
36 Gordon Square
London WC1H OPF
Tel 0171 387 8572
Fax 0171 387 2655

Community Development
Foundation
60 Highbury Grove
London N5 2AG
Tel 0171 226 5375
Fax 0171 704 0313

E-mail admin@cdf.org.uk
Web http://www.cdf.org.uk

Companies House
55-71 City Road
London EC1Y 1BB
Tel 0171 253 9393

Construction Industry Training
Board
Hillgate House
8th Floor
26 Old Bailey
London EC4M 7QA
Tel 0171 489 1662
Fax 0171 236 2875

Countryside Commission
4th Floor
71 Kingsway
London WC2B 6ST
Tel 0171 831 3510
Fax 0171 831 1439

The Court Service
Southside
105 Victoria Street
London SW1E 6QT
Tel 0171 210 2200
Fax 0171 210 1797

Covent Garden Market Authority
Covent House
New Covent Garden Market
London SW8 5NX
Tel 0171 720 2211
Fax 0171 622 5307

Crafts Council
44a Pentonville Road
Islington
London N1 9BY
Tel 0171 278 7700
Fax 0171 837 6891
Web http://
www.craftscouncil.org.uk

Criminal Injuries Compensation
Authority
Morley House
26-30 Holborn Viaduct
London EC1A 2JQ
Tel 0171 842 6800
Fax 0171 436 0804

Crown Agents Foundation
St Nicholas House
St Nicholas Road
Sutton SM1 1EL
Tel 0181 643 3311
Fax 0181 643 8232

Crown Prosecution Service
50 Ludgate Hill
London EC4M 7EX
Tel 0171 273 8000
Fax 0171 329 8167

Defence Analytical Services
Agency
Northumberland Avenue
London WC2N 5BP
Tel 0171 218 1638
Fax 0171 218 5203
E-mail resources@dasa.mod.uk
Web http://www.open.gov.uk/dasa/
dasahom

Defence Estates Organisation
St Giles Court
1-13 St Giles High Street
London WC2H 8LD
Tel 0171 3055555

Defence Estates Organisation
Metropole Building
Northumberland Avenue
London WC2N 5BL
Tel 0171 2186979

Defence Postal & Courier Services
Agency
Inglis Barracks, Mill Hill
London NW7 1PX
Tel 0181 818 6417
Fax 0181 818 6309

Defence Secondary Care Agency
Room 543
St Giles Court
1-13 St Giles High Street
London WC2H 8LD
Tel 0171 305 3432
Fax 0171 305 3432

Defence Vetting Agency
Room 454
Metropole Building
Northumberland Avenue
London WC2N 5BL
Tel 0171 218 9000
Fax 0171 218 1352

The Design Council
34 Bow Street
London WC2E 7DL
Tel 0171 420 5200
Fax 0171 420 5300
E-mail
100443.1213@compuserv.com
Web http://www.design-
council.org.uk/

Disposal Sales Agency
6 Hercules Road
London SE1 7DJ
Tel 0171 261 8826
Fax 0171 261 8696

Employment Appeal Tribunal
Audit House
58 Victoria Embankemnt
London EC4Y 0DS
Tel 0171 273 1041
Fax 0171 273 1045

Employment Service
Level 6
Caxton House
Tothill Street
London WC1H 9NA
Tel 0171 273 6060
Fax 0171 273 6099

Employment Tribunals Service
19-29 Woburn Place
London WC1H 0LU
Tel 0171 273 8517
Fax 0171 273 8670

Employment Tribunals Service
Montague Court
101 London Road
Croydon CR0 2RF
Tel 0181 667 9131
Fax 0181 649 9470

Employment Tribunals Service
44 Broadway
Stratford
London E15 1HX
Tel 0181 221 0921
Fax 0181 221 0398

English Advisory Committee on
Telecommunications
50 Ludgate Hill
London EC4M 7JJ
Tel 0171 634 8770

English Heritage
23 Savile Row
London W1X 1AB
Tel 0171 973 3000
Fax 0171 973 3001

English National Board for
Nursing, Midwifery & Health
Visiting
Victory House
170 Tottenham Court Road
London W1P 0HA
Tel 0171 388 3131
Fax 0171 383 4031
E-mail enblink@easynet.co.uk
Web http://www.enb.org.uk

English Nature
26/27 Boswell Street
London WC1N 3JZ
Tel 0171 831 6922
Fax 0171 404 3369

English Partnerships
16-18 Old Queen Street
London SW1H 9HP
Tel 0171 976 7070
Fax 0171 976 7740

English Sports Council
16 Upper Woburn Place
London WC1H 0QP
Tel 0171 273 1500
Fax 0171 383 5740

English Sports Council
Crystal Palace National Sports
Centre
Ledrington Road
London SE19 2BQ
Tel 0181 7788600
Fax 0181 6769812

English Tourist Board
Thames Tower
Black's Road
London W6 9EL
Tel 0181 846 9000
Fax 0181 563 0302
Web http://www.visitbritain.com

Farming & Rural Conservation
Agency
Nobel House
17 Smith Square
London SW1P 3JR
Tel 0171 238 5432
Fax 0171 238 5588

Financial Services Authority
Gravelle House
2-14 Bunhill Row
London EC1Y 8RA
Tel 0171 638 1240
Fax 0171 382 5900

Food from Britain
123 Buckingham Palace Road
London SW1W 9SA
Tel 0171 233 5111
Fax 0171 233 9515
E-mail info@foodfrombritain.co.uk

Food Standards Agency
Room 634B
Skipton House
80 London Road
London SE1 6LH
Tel 0171 972 5087/88

Football Licensing Authority
27 Harcourt House
19 Cavendish Square
London W1M 9AD
Tel 0171 491 7191
Fax 0171 491 1882

Forensic Science Laboratory
109 Lambeth Road
London SE1 7LP
Tel 0171 230 6700
Fax 0171 230 6253

Friendly Societies Commission
Victory House
30/34 Kingsway
London WC2 6ES
Tel 0171 663 5000

Funding Agency for Schools
13th Floor, Centre Point
103 Oxford Street
London WC1A 1DU
Tel 0171 379 3750
Fax 0171 240 8047

The Further Education Funding
Council
Metropolis House
22 Percy Street
London W1P 0LL
Tel 0171 312 4100
Fax 0171 312 4134

Gaming Board for Great Britain
Berkshire House
168/173 High Holborn
London WC1V 7AA
Tel 0171 306 6253
Fax 0171 306 6267

Gas Consumers' Council
6th Floor
Abford House
15 Wilton Road
London SW1V 1LT
Tel 0171 931 0977
Fax 0171 630 9934

Geffrye Museum
Kingsland Road
London E2 8EA
Tel 0171 739 9893
Fax 0171 729 5647

Government Car & Despatch
Agency
46 Ponton Road
London SW8 5AX
Tel 0171 217 3838
Fax 0171 217 3875

The Great Britain-China Centre
15 Belgrave Square
London SW1X 8PS
Tel 0171 235 6696
Fax 0171 245 6885
E-mail contact@gbcc.org.uk
Web http://www.gbcc.org.uk

Health & Safety Commission
Rose Court
2 Southwark Bridge Road
London SE1 9HS
Tel 0171 717 6000

The Health & Safety Executive
Rose Court
2 Southwark Bridge Road
London SE1 9HS
Tel 0171 717 6606
Fax 0171 717 6616
Web http://www.open.gov.uk/hse/
hsehome.

The Health & Safety Executive
1 Long Lane
London SE1 4PG
Tel 0171 556 2100
Fax 0171 556 2200

The Health & Safety Executive
Maritime House
1 Linton Road
Barking
London IG11 8HF
Tel 0181 235 8000
Fax 0181 235 8001

Higher Education Funding Council
for England
28th Floor
Centrepoint
103 New Oxford Street
London WC1A 1DD

Highways Agency
St Christopher House
Southwark Street
London SE1 0TE
Tel 0171 921 4443
Fax 0171 921 2214
E-mail
publicrelations@dial.pipex.com
Web http://www.highways.gov.uk

Historic Royal Palaces
Hampton Court Palace
East Molesey
Surrey KT8 9AU
Tel 0181 781 9752
Fax 0181 781 9754

HM Customs & Excise
New King's Beam House
22 Upper Ground
London SE1 9PJ
Tel 0171 620 1313
E-mail hmce.cmu@gtnet.gov.uk

HM Land Registry
32 Lincoln's Inn Fields
London WC2A 3PH
Tel 0171 917 8888
Fax 0171 955 0110
Web http://www.open.gov.uk/
landreg/das.

HM Land Registry
Sunley House
Bedford Park
Croydon CR9 3LE
Tel 0181 781 9100

HM Land Registry
Lyon House
Lyon Road
Harrow
Middlesex HA1 2EU
Tel 0181 235 1181

HM Prison Service
Cleland House
Page Street
London SW1P 4LN
Tel 0171 217 3000
Fax 0171 271 8645

Home-Grown Cereals Authority
Caledonia House
223 Pentonville Road
London N1 9NG
Tel 0171 520 3926
Fax 0171 713 2030
Web http://www.hgca.com

Horniman Museum
100 London Road
Forest Hill
London SE23 3PQ
Tel 0181 699 1872
Fax 0181 291 5506

Horserace Betting Levy Board
52 Grosvenor Gardens
London SW1W 0AU
Tel 0171 333 0043
Fax 0171 333 0041

Horserace Totalisator Board
Tote House
74 Upper Richmond Road
London SW15 2SU
Tel 0181 874 6411
Fax 0181 875 1882

The Housing Corporation
Waverley House
7-12 Noel Street
London W1V 4BA
Tel 0171 292 4400

The Housing Corporation
149 Tottenham Court Road
London W1P 0BN
Tel 0171 393 2000
Fax 0171 393 2111
Web http://www.open.gov.uk/hcorp

The Housing Corporation
Leon House
High Street
Croydon
Surrey CR9 1UH
Tel 0181 253 1400

Human Fertilisation & Embryology
Authority
Paxton House
30 Artillery Lane
London E1 7LS
Tel 0171 377 5077
Fax 0171 377 1871
Web http://www.hfea.gov.uk

Imperial War Museum
Lambeth Road
London SE1 6HZ
Tel 0171 416 5000
Fax 0171 416 5374

Independent Television
Commission
33 Foley Street
London W1P 7LB
Tel 0171 255 3000
Fax 0171 306 7800
E-mail publicaffairs@itc.org.uk
Web www.itc.org.uk

Inland Revenue
Angel Court
199 Borough High Street
London SE1 1HZ
Tel 0171 234 3701

Inland Revenue
Somerset House
London WC2R 1LB
Tel 0171 438 6420

Inland Revenue
Bush House
Strand
London WC2B 4QN
Tel 0171 438 7282

Inland Revenue
Melbourne House
Aldwych
London WC2B 4LL
Tel 0171 438 6908

Inland Revenue
New Court
Carey Street
London WC2A 2JE
Tel 0171 324 0229

Insolvency Service
5th Floor
Sunley House
Bedford Park
Croydon CR9 1TX
Tel 0181 681 5166
Fax 0181 667 8000

Insolvency Service
PO Box 203
21 Bloomsbury Street
London WC1B 3SS
Tel 0171 637 1110
Fax 0171 291 6713

Insurance Directorate of
Department of Trade & Industry
1 Victoria Street
London SW1H 0ET
Tel 0171 215 0200

Investment Management
Regulatory Organisation (IMRO)
5th Floor
Lloyds Chambers
1 Portsoken Street
London E1 8BT
Tel 0171 390 5000

Investors in People UK
7-10 Chandos Street
London W1M 9DE
Tel 0171 467 1900
Fax 0171 636 2386

Legal Aid Board
85 Gray's Inn Road
London WC1X 8AA
Tel 0171 813 1000
Fax 0171 813 8638

# Q & Q

Legal Aid Board
29-37 Red Lion Street
London WC1R 4PP
Tel 0171 813 5300
Fax 0171 813 5812

London Pensions Fund Authority
Dexter House
2 Royal Mint Court
London EC3N 4LP
Tel 0171 369 6000
Fax 0171 369 6111

London Regional Passengers
Committee
Clements House
14-18 Gresham Street
London EC2V 7PR
Tel 0171 505 9000
Fax 0171 505 9003

London Transport
55 Broadway
London SW1H 0BD
Tel 0171 222 5600
Fax 0171 222 5719

Marshall Aid Commemoration
Commission
36 Gordon Square
London WC1H 0PF
Tel 0171 387 8572
Fax 0171 387 2655

Medical Devices Agency
Hannibal House
Elephant and Castle
London SE1 6TQ
Tel 0171 972 8000
Fax 0171 972 8108
E-mail mail@medical-
devices.gov.uk
Web http://www.medical-
devices.gov.uk

Medical Practices Committee
1st Floor
Eileen House
80-94 Newington Causeway
London SE1 6EF
Tel 0171 972 2930
Fax 0171 972 2985

Medical Research Council
20 Park Crescent
London W1N 4AL
Tel 0171 636 5422
Fax 0171 436 6179

Medicines Control Agency
Market Towers
1 Nine Elms Lane
Vauxhall
London SW8 5NQ
Tel 0171 273 0000
Fax 0171 273 0353
Web http://www.open.gov.uk/mca/
mcahome.

Military Survey
Elmwood Avenue
Feltham
Middlesex TW13 7AH
Tel 0181 8182247
Fax 0181 8182148

Milk Development Council
5-7 John Prince's Street
London W1M 0AP
Tel 0171 629 7262
Fax 0171 629 4820

Millennium Commission
Portland House
Stag Place
London SW1E 5EZ
Tel 0171 880 2001
Fax 0171 880 2000
Web http://www.millennium.gov.uk

Monopolies & Mergers
Commission
New Court
Carey Street
London WC2A 2JT
Tel 0171 324 1467
Fax 0171 324 1400
E-mail MMC@gtnet.gov.uk
Web http://www.open.gov.uk/mmc/
mmchome.

Museum of London
London Wall
London EC2Y 5HN
Tel 0171 600 3699
Fax 0171 600 1058

Museums & Galleries Commission
16 Queen Anne's Gate
London SW1H 9AA
Tel 0171 233 4200
Fax 0171 233 3686

National Army Museum
Royal Hospital Road
Chelsea
London SW3 4HT
Tel 0171 730 0717
Fax 0171 823 6573

National Consumer Council
20 Grosvenor Gardens
London SW1W 0DH
Tel 0171 730 3469
Fax 0171 730 0191

National Gallery
Trafalgar Square
London WC2N 5DN
Tel 0171 839 3321
Fax 0171 930 4764
E-mail information@ng-
london.org.uk
Web http://
www.nationalgallery.org.uk

National Heritage Memorial Fund
7 Holbein Place
London SW1W 8NR
Tel 0171 591 6000
Fax 0171 591 6001

National Lottery Charities Board
St Vincent House
30 Orange Street
London WC2 7HH
Tel 0171 747 5299
Fax 0171 747 5347
Web www.nlcb.org.uk

National Maritime Museum
Greenwich
London SE10 9NF
Tel 0181 858 4422
Fax 0181 312 6632
Web http://www.nmm.ac.uk

National Museum of Science &
Industry
Exhibition Road
London SW7 2DD
Tel 0171 938 8000
Fax 0171 938 8118
Web http://www.nmsi.ac.uk

National Portrait Gallery
2 St Martin's Place
London WC2H 0HE
Tel 0171 306 0055
Fax 0171 306 0056
Web www.npg.org.uk

National Savings
Charles House
375 Kensington High Street
London W14 8SD
Tel 0171 605 9300
Fax 0171 605 9438

National Weights & Measures
Laboratory
Stanton Avenue
Teddington
Middlesex TW11 0JZ
Tel 0181 943 7272
Fax 0181 943 7270

Natural History Museum
Cromwell Road
London SW7 5BD
Tel 0171 938 9123

New Millennium Experience Co Ltd
110 Buckingham Palace Road
London SW1W 9SB
Tel 0171 808 8200
Fax 0171 808 8222
E-mail nmec@newmill.co.uk
Web www.mx2000.com

Office for National Statistics
The Family Records Centre
1 Myddleton Street
London EC1R 1UW
Tel 0171 233 9233

Office for National Statistics
1 Drummond Gate
London SW1V 2QQ
Tel 0171 233 9233
Fax 0171 533 5689
E-mail info@ons.gov.uk
Web http//www.emap.co.uk/ons/

Office for Standards in Education
Alexandra House
Kingsway
London WC2B 6SE
Tel 0171 421 6800
Fax 0171 421 6522

Office of Electricity Regulation
11 Belgrave Road
London SW1V 1RB
Tel 0171 233 6366

Office of Fair Trading
Field House
15-25 Breams Buildings
London EC4A 1PR
Tel 0171 211 8000
Fax 0171 211 8800

Office of Gas Supply
Stockley House
30 Wilton Road
London SW1V 1LQ
Tel 0171 828 0898
Fax 0171 932 1664

Office of Passenger Rail
Franchising
Golding's House
2 Hay's Lane
London Bridge
London SE1 2HB
Tel 0171 940 4200
Fax 0171 940 4210

Office of Telecommunications
50 Ludgate Hill
London EC4M 7JJ
Tel 0171 634 8700
Fax 0171 634 8943
Web http://www.open.gov.uk/of
Office of the National Lottery
2 Monck Street
London SW1P 2BQ
Tel 0171 227 2000
Fax 0171 227 2005

Office of the Rail Regulator
1 Waterhouse Square
138-142 Holborn
London EC1N 2ST
Tel 0171 282 2000
Fax 0171 282 2040
Web http://www.rail-reg.gov.uk/

Ofwat Southern Customer Service
Committee
Third Floor
15-17 Ridgmount Street
London WC1E 7AH
Tel 0171 636 3656
Fax 0171 636 4813
E-mail sncsc@ofwat.gtnet.gov.uk
Web http://www.open.gov.uk/ofwat

Ofwat Thames Customer Service
Committee
Third Floor
15-17 Ridgmount Street
London WC1E 7AH
Tel 0171 636 3656
Fax 0171 636 4813
E-mail tmcsc@ofwat.gtnet.gov.uk
Web http://www.open.gov.uk/ofwat

Oil & Pipelines Agency
35/38 Portman Square
London W1H 0EU
Tel 0171 935 2585
Fax 0171 935 3510

Parole Board
Abell House
John Islip Street
London SW1P 4LH
Tel 0171 217 5314
Fax 0171 217 5677

Patent Office
25 Southampton Buildings
Chancery Lane
London WC2A 1PW

Pensions Compensation Board
Room 501
5th Floor
11 Belgrave Road
London SW1V 1RB
Tel 0171 828 9794
Fax 0171 931 7239

Personal Investment Authority
(PIA)
1 Canada Square
Canary Wharf
London E14 4AB
Tel 0171 378 9000

Police Complaints Authority
10 Great George Street
London SW1P 3AE
Tel 0171 273 6450
Fax 0171 273 6401

Policyholders' Protection Board
51 Gresham Street
London EC2B 7HQ
Tel 0171 600 3333
Fax 0171 216 7654

Post Office
148 Old Street
London EC1V 9HQ
Tel 0171 490 2888
Fax 0171 250 2632

Post Office Users' National Council
6 Hercules Road
London SE1 7DN
Tel 0171 928 9458

Property Advisers to the Civil
Estate
Trevelyan House
Great Peter Street
London SW1P 2BY
Tel 0171 271 2600
Fax 0171 271 2693

Public Health Laboratory Services
Board
61 Colindale Avenue
London NW9 5DF
Tel 0181 200 1295
Fax 0181 200 7874

Public Record Office
Ruskin Avenue
Kew
Richmond
Surrey TW9 4DU
Tel 0181 876 3444
Fax 0181 878 8905

Public Trust Office
Stewart House
24 Kingsway
London WC2B 6JX
Tel 0171 269 7316
Fax 0171 664 7707
E-mail
enquiries@publictrust.gov.uk.
Web http://www.publictrust.gov.uk/

Qualifications & Curriculum
Authority
Newcombe House
45 Notting Hill Gate
London W11 3JB
Tel 0171 229 1234
Fax 0171 229 8526
E-mail info@qca.org.uk

Qualifications & Curriculum
Authority
222 Euston Road
London NW1 2BZ
Tel 0171 387 9898
Fax 0171 387 0978

Queen Elizabeth II Conference
Centre
Broad Sanctuary
Westminster
London SW1P 3EE
Tel 0171 222 5000
Fax 0171 798 4200
E-mail sarahj@qeiicc.co.uk
Web www.qeiicc.co.uk

The Radio Authority
Holbrook House
14 Great Queen Street
London WC2B 5DG
Tel 0171 430 2724
Fax 0171 405 7062
Web www.radioauthority.gov.uk

Radiocommunications Agency
151 Buckingham Palace Road
London SW1W 9SS
Tel 0171 215 1383

Rail Users Consultative Committee
for Southern England
4th Floor
35 Old Queen Street
London SW1H 9JA
Tel 0171 222 0391
Fax 0171 222 0392

Registry of Friendly Societies
Victory House
30/34 Kingsway
London WC2 6ES
Tel 0171 663 5000

Remploy
415 Edgware Road
Cricklewood
London NW2 6LR
Tel 0181 235 0500
Fax 0181 235 0576

Royal Air Force Museum
Grahame Park Way
Hendon
London NW9 5LL
Tel 0181 205 2266
Fax 0181 200 1751

Royal Armouries
HM Tower of London
London EC3N 4AB
Tel 0171 480 6358
Fax 0171 481 2922
E-mail
enquiries@armouries.org.uk
Web http://www.armouries.og.uk

Royal Botanic Gardens Kew
Richmond
Surrey TW9 3AB
Tel 0181 332 5000

The Royal Commission on
Historical Manuscripts
Quality Court
Chancery Lane
London WC2A 1HP
Tel 0171 242 1198
Fax 0171 831 3550
E-mail nra@hmc.gov.uk
Web http://www.hmc.gov.uk

Royal Commission on the
Historical Monuments of England
55 Blandford Street
London W1H 3AF
Tel 0171 208 8200
Fax 0171 224 5333

Royal Parks Agency
The Magazine Storeyard
Magazine Gate
Kensington Gardens
London W2 2UH
Tel 0171 298 2117
Fax 0171 724 2826

Royal Parks Agency
The Storeyard
Inner Circle
Regent's Park
London NW1 4NR
Tel 0171 486 7905
Fax 0171 224 1895

Royal Parks Agency
Park Office
Greenwich Park
Blakheath Gate
Greenwich
London SE10 8QY
Tel 0181 858 2608
Fax 0181 293 3782

Royal Parks Agency
Holly Lodge
Richmond Park
Richmond
Surrey TW10 5HS
Tel 0181 948 3209
Fax 0181 332 2730

Royal Parks Agency
The Stockyard
Bushy Park
Hampton Court Road
Hampton Hill
Middlesex TW12 2EJ
Tel 0181 979 1586
Fax 0181 941 8196

Royal Parks Agency
The Old Police House
Hyde Park
London W2 2UH
Tel 0171 298 2000
Fax 0171 298 2005

Royal Parks Agency
Ranger's Lodge
Hyde Park
London W2 2UH
Tel 0171 298 2100
Fax 0171 402 3298

Royal Parks Agency
The Storeyard
Horse Guards Approach
St James's Park
London SW1A 2BJ
Tel 0171 930 1793
Fax 0171 839 7639

Royal Parks Agency
The Chapel Office
Brompton Cemetery
Fulham Road
London SW10 9UG
Tel 0171 352 1201

Rural Development Commission
Dacre House
19 Dacre Street
London SW1H 0OD
Tel 0171 3402900

Scottish Tourist Board
19 Cockspur Street
London SW1Y 5BL

Securities & Futures
Authority(SFA)
Cottons Centre
Cottons Lane
London SE1 2QB
Tel 0171 378 9000

Security Facilities Executive
St Christopher House
Southwark Street
London SE1 0TE
Tel 0171 921 4663
Fax 0171 921 3802
E-mail ssg-
busdev@safe.ndirect.co.uk

Serious Fraud Office
Elm House
10-16 Elm Street
London WC1X OB
Tel 0171 239 7272
Fax 0171 837 1689

Simpler Trade Procedures Board
151 Buckingham Palace Road
London SW1W 9SS
Tel 0171 215 0825
Fax 0171 215 0824
E-mail sitpro.org.uk
Web http://www.sitpro.org.uk

Sir John Soane's Museum
13 Lincoln's Inn Fields
London WC2A 3BP
Tel 0171 405 2107
Fax 0171 831 3957

Stonebridge Housing Action Trust
Kassinga House
37-41 Winchelsea Road
London NW10 8UN
Tel 0181 961 0278
Fax 0181 961 0291

Supervision & Surveillance
Division of Bank of England
Threadneedle Street
London EC2R 8AH
Tel 0171 601 4878

Tate Gallery
Millbank
London SW1P 4RG
Tel 0171 887 8000
Fax 0171 887 8007
Web http://www.tate.org.uk

Teacher Training Agency
Portland House
Stag Place
London SW1E 5TT
Tel 0171 925 3700
Fax 0171 925 6073
E-mail tta@gtnet.gov.uk

Tower Hamlets Housing Action
Trust
73 Usher Road
Bow
London E3 2HS
Tel 0181 983 4698
Fax 0181 204 1556
E-mail srands@thhat.demon.co.uk

Traffic Director for London
College House
Great Peter Street
London SW1P 3LN
Tel 0171 222 4545
Fax 0171 976 8640
E-mail @tdfl.gov.uk

Treasury Solicitor's Department
Queen Anne's Chambers
28 Broadway
London SW1H 9JS
Tel 0171 210 3000

Trinity House Lighthouse Service
Trinity Square
Tower Hill
London EC3N 4DH
Tel 0171 480 6601
Fax 0171 480 7662

UK Ecolabelling Board
7th Floor
Eastbury House
30-34 Albert Embankment
London SE1 7TL
Tel 0171 820 1199
Fax 0171 820 1104

UK Passport Agency
Clive House
70-78 Petty France
London SW1H 9HD
Tel 0171 271 8508
Fax 0171 271 8813

UK Register of Organic Food
Standards
Nobel House
17 Smith Square
London SW1P 3JR
Tel 0171 270 8080

UK Sports Council
16 Upper Woburn Place
London WC1H 0QP
Tel 0171 273 1500
Fax 0171 383 5740

Valuation Office Agency
New Court
Carey Street
London WC2A 2JE
Tel 0171 324 1075

Victoria & Albert Museum
South Kensington
London SW7 2RL
Tel 0171 938 8500
Fax 0171 938 8379
Web http://www.vam.ac.uk

Wallace Collection
Hertford House
Manchester Square
London W1M 6BN
Tel 0171 935 0687
Fax 0171 224 2155
E-mail
admin@wallcoll.demon.co.uk

Waltham Forest Housing Action
Trust
Kirkdale House
7 Kirkdale Road
Leytonstone
London E11 1HP
Tel 0181 539 5533
Fax 0181 539 8074
E-mail
101317,1175@compuserve.com

Westminster Foundation for
Democracy
Clutha House
10 Storey's Gate
Westminster
London SW1P 3AY
Tel 0171 976 7565
Fax 0171 976 7464

Wine Standards Board
Five Kings House
1 Queen Street Place
London EC4R 1QS
Tel 0171 236 9512
Fax 0171 236 7908

## MERSEYSIDE

ACAS
Cressington House
249 St Mary's Road
Garston
Liverpool L19 0NF
Tel 0151 427 8881

The Buying Agency
5th Floor
Royal Liver Building
Pier Head
Liverpool L3 1PE
Tel 0151 227 4262
Fax 0151 227 3315
E-mail post@tba.gov.uk

Child Support Agency
Great Western House
Woodside Ferry Approach
Birkenhead
Merseyside L41 6RG
Tel 0345 138000

Construction Industry Training
Board
10 Waterside Court
St Helens Technology Campus
Pocket Nook Street
St Helens
Merseyside WA9 1VA
Tel 01744 616004
Fax 01744 617003

Defence Bills Agency
Mersey House
Drury Lane
Liverpool L2 7PX
Tel 0151 242 2519
Fax 0151 242 2470

Employment Tribunals Service
Cunard Building
Pier Head
Liverpool L3 1TS
Tel 0151 236 9397
Fax 0151 231 1484

The Health & Safety Executive
The Triad
Stanley Road
Bootle
Merseyside L20 3PG
Tel 0151 479 2200
Fax 0151 479 2201

The Health & Safety Executive
Magdalen House
Stanley Precinct
Bootle
Merseyside L20 3QZ
Tel 0151 951 4025

The Health & Safety Executive
Room 514
St Anne's House
University Road
Bootle
Merseyside L20 3RA
Tel 0151 951 4136

The Health & Safety Executive
St Peter's House
Balliol Road
Bootle
Merseyside L20 2LZ
Tel 0151 951 4103

HM Land Registry
Rosebrae Court
Woodside Ferry Approach
Birkenhead
Merseyside L41 6DU
Tel 0151 473 1110

HM Land Registry
Old Market House
Hamilton Street
Birkenhead
Merseyside L41 5FL
Tel 0151 4731110

Inland Revenue
St Johns House
Merton Road
Bootle
Merseyside L69 9BB
Tel 0151 472 6000

Inland Revenue
The Triad
Stanley Road
Bootle
Merseyside L20 3PD
Tel 0151 300 3000

Insolvency Service
2nd Floor
Cunard Building
Pier Head
Liverpool L3 1DS
Tel 0151 236 9131
Fax 0151 255 0278

Legal Aid Board
Cavern Walks
8 Mathew Street
Liverpool L2 6RE
Tel 0151 236 8371
Fax 0151 227 2533

Liverpool Housing Action Trust
Cunard Building
Water Street
Liverpool L3 1EG
Tel 0151 227 1099
Fax 0151 236 5263

National Museums & Galleries
Merseyside
Liverpool Museum
William Brown Street
Liverpool L3 8EN
Tel 0151 207 0001
Fax 0151 478 4390

Remploy Limited
West Float Industrial Estate
off Dock Road
Birkenhead
Merseyside L41 1JH
Tel 0151 631 5000
Fax 0151 631 5190

Tate Gallery
Albert Dock
Liverpool L3 4BB
Tel 0151 709 3223
Fax 0151 709 3122

## NORTH EAST

ACAS
Westgate House
Westgate Road
Newcastle upon Tyne NE1 1TJ
Tel 0191 261 2191

Audit Commission
2nd Floor
Nickalls House
Metro Centre
Gateshead NE11 9NH

British Shipbuilders
89 Sandyford Road
Newcastle upon Tyne NE99 1PL
Tel 0191 232 8493

Construction Industry Training
Board
Wearbank House
Charles Street
Sunderland
Tyne and Wear SR6 0AN
Tel 0191 567 9230
Fax 0191 510 0165

Contributions Agency
Longbenton
Newcastle upon Tyne NE98 1YX
Tel 0191 225 7665
Fax 0191 225 4198

Countryside Commission
Warwick House
Grantham Road
Newcastle upon Tyne NE2 1QF
Tel 0191 232 8252
Fax 0191 222 0185

Employment Tribunals Service
Quayside House
110 Quayside
Newcastle upon Tyne NE1 3DX
Tel 0191 232 8865
Fax 0191 222 1880

English Nature
Archbold Terrace
Newcastle upon Tyne NE2 1EG
Tel 0191 281 6316
Fax 0191 281 6305

English Sports Council
Aykley Heads
Durham DH1 5UU
Tel 0191 384 9595
Fax 0191 384 5807

Funding Agency for Schools
Vincent House
2 Woodlands Road
Darlington DL3 7PJ
Tel 01904 661661
Fax 01904 661686

The Further Education Funding
Council
Clough House
Kings Manor
Newcastle upon Tyne NE1 6PA
Tel 0191 211 2200
Fax 0191 211 2235

Gas Consumers' Council
Northumberland House
Princess Square
Newcastle upon Tyne NE1 8ER
Tel 0191 261 9561
Fax 0191 222 0071

The Health & Safety Executive
Arden House
Regent Centre
Regent Farm Road
Gosforth
Newcastle upon Tyne NE3 3JN
Tel 0191 202 6200
Fax 0191 202 6300

HM Land Registry
Southfield House
Southfield Way
Durham DH1 5TR
Tel 0191 301 3500

HM Land Registry
Boldon House
Wheatlands Way
Pity Me
Durham DH1 5GJ
Tel 0191 301 2345

Independent Television
Commission
3 Collingwood St
Newcastle upon Tyne NE1 1JS
Tel 0191 261 0148
Fax 0191 261 1158

Inland Revenue
100 Russel Street
Middlesborough
Cleveland TS1 2RZ
Tel 01642 213214

Insolvency Service
Bayheath House
Prince Regent Street
Stockton-on-Tees TS18 1DF
Tel 01642 617720
Fax 01642 618644

Insolvency Service
3rd Floor
Westgate House
Westgate Road
Newcastle upon Tyne NE1 1TU
Tel 0191 232 1104
Fax 0191 261 7936

Intervention Board
Lancaster House
Hampshire Court
Newcastle upon Tyne NE4 7YE
Tel 0191 273 9696
Fax 0191 226 1839

Legal Aid Board
Eagle Star House
Fenkle Street
Newcastle upon Tyne NE1 5RU
Tel 0191 232 3461
Fax 0191 230 0084

National Savings
Millburngate House
Durham DH99 1NS
Tel 0191 386 4900
Office of Electricity Regulation
1st Floor
St Cuthbert Chambers
35 Nelson Street
Newcastle upon Tyne NE1 5AN
Tel 0191 221 2071

Ofwat Northumbria Customer
Service Committee
2nd Floor
St Cuthbert Chambers
35 Nelson Street
Newcastle upon Tyne NE1 5AN
Tel 0191 221 0646
Fax 0191 221 0650
E-mail nbcsc@ofwat.gtnet.gov.uk
Web http://www.open.gov.uk/ofwat

Registrar of Public Lending Right
Bayheath House
Prince Regent Street
Stockton-on-Tees TS18 1DF
Tel 01642 604699
Fax 01642 615641
Web http://www.earl.org.uk/
partners/plr

Rural Development Commission
Morton Road
Yarm Road Industrial State
Darlington
County Durham DL1 4PT
Tel 01325 487123

Veterinary Laboratories Agency
Whitley Road
Longbenton
Newcastle upon Tyne NE12 9SE
Tel 0191 266 2292
Fax 0191 266 3605

## NORTH WEST

ACAS
Boulton House
17-21 Chorlton Street
Manchester M1 3HY
Tel 0161 228 3222

Agricultural Wages Board for
England & Wales
Berkeley Towers
Nantwich Road
Crewe
Cheshire CW2 6 PT
Tel 01270 69211

Agricultural Wages Board for
England & Wales
Eden Bridge House
Lowther Street
Carlisle
Cumbria CA3 8DX
Tel 01228 234000

Audit Commission
3rd Floor
Sumner House
St Thomas Road
Chorley PR7 1HP

British Nuclear Fuels plc
Risley
Warrington
Cheshire WA3 6AS
Tel 01925 832242
Fax 01925 835619

British Waterways
Pottery Road
Wigan
Lancs WN3 5AA
Tel 01942 242239

British Waterways
Navigation Road
Northwich
Cheshire CW8 1BH
Tel 01606 74321

British Waterways
Canal Office
Birch Road
Ellesmere
Shropshire SY12 9AA
Tel 01691 622549

British Waterways
Top Lock
Church Lane
Marple
Cheshire SK6 6BN
Tel 0161 427 1079

Commission for the New Towns
New Town House
Buttermarket Street
Warrington
Cheshire WA1 2LF
Tel 01925 651144

Commissioner for Protection
Against Unlawful Industrial Action
1st Floor, Bank Chambers
2a Rylands Street
Warrington
Cheshire WA1 1EN
Tel 01925 415771/414128
Fax 01925 415772

Commissioner for the Rights of
Trade Union Members
1st Floor, Bank Chambers
2a Rylands Street
Warrington
Cheshire WA1 1EN
Tel 01925 415771/414128
Fax 01925 415772

Companies House
75 Mosley Street
Manchester M2 2HR
Tel 0161 236 7500

Countryside Commission
7th Floor
Bridgewater House
Whitworth Street
Manchester M1 6TL
Tel 0161 237 1061
Fax 0161 237 1062

Employment Tribunals Service
Alexandra House
14/22 The Parsonage
Manchester M3 2JA
Tel 0161 833 0581
Fax 0161 832 6249

English National Board for
Nursing, Midwifery and Health
Visiting
BSP House
Station Road
Chester CH1 3DR
Tel 01244 311393
Fax 01244 321140

English Nature
Pier House
Wallgate
Wigan
Lancs WN3 4AL
Tel 01942 820342
Fax 01942 820364

English Nature
Juniper House
Murley Moss
Oxenholme Road
Kendal
Cumbria LA9 7RL
Tel 01539 792800
Fax 01593 792830

English Sports Council
Astley House
Quay Street
Manchester M3 4AE
Tel 0161 834 0338
Fax 0161 835 3678

The Environment Agency
Richard Fairclough House
Knutsford Road
Warrington WA4 1HG
Tel 01925 653 999
Fax 01925 415 961

Equal Opportunities Commission
Overseas House
Quay Street
Manchester M3 3HN
Tel 0161 833 9244
Fax 0161 835 1657

Forensic Science Laboratory
Washington Hall
Euxton Chorley
Lancs PR7 6HJ
Tel 01257 265666
Fax 01257 274752

The Further Education Funding
Council
10 Brindley Road
City Park Business Village
Cornbrook
Manchester M16 9HQ
Tel 0161 877 3811
Fax 0161 876 2936

Gaming Board for Great Britain
Warwickgate House
Warwick Road
Old Trafford
Manchester M16 0QQ
Tel 0161 872 6016
Fax 0161 873 8248

Gas Consumers' Council
Boulton House
Chorlton Street
Manchester M1 3HY
Tel 0161 236 1926
Fax 0161 236 8896

The Health & Safety Executive
Victoria House
Ormskirk Road
Preston PR1 1HH
Tel 01772 836200
Fax 01772 836222

The Health & Safety Executive
Quay House
Quay Street
Manchester M3 3JB
Tel 0161 952 8200
Fax 0161 952 8222

Highways Agency
Sunley Tower
Piccadilly Plaza
Manchester M1 4BE
Tel 0645 556575

HM Land Registry
Birkenhead House
East Beach
Lytham St Anne's
Lancs FY8 5AB
Tel 01253 849849

The Housing Corporation
Elisabeth House
16 St Peter's Square
Manchester M2 3DF
Tel 0161 242 2000

Independent Television
Commission
Television House
Mount Street
Manchester M2 5WT
Tel 0161 834 2707
Fax 0161 835 3513

Information Technology Services
Agency
Blackpool Industrial Estate
Brunel Way
Peel Park
Blackpool FY4 5ES
Tel 01253 335039

Insolvency Service
Dee Hills Park
Chester CH3 5AR
Tel 01244 321471/2
Fax 01452 310910

Insolvency Service
1st Floor
Boulton House
17/21 Chorlton Street
Manchester M1 3HY
Tel 0161 934 5400
Fax 0161 934 5450

Insolvency Service
Petros House
St Andrews Road North
Lytham St Anne's FY8 2JB
Tel 01253 784200

Legal Aid Board
2nd Floor
Elisabeth House
16 St Peter's Square
Manchester M2 3DA
Tel 0161 228 1200
Fax 0161 228 0445

Legal Aid Board
Pepper House
2nd Floor
Pepper Row
Chester CH1 1DW
Tel 01244 315455
Fax 01244 319036

Museum of Science & Industry
Manchester
Liverpool Road
Castlefield
Manchester M3 4JP
Tel 0161 832 2244
Fax 0161 833 2184
E-mail all@ missci.u-net.com
Web http://www.edes.co.uk

National Savings
Marton
Blackpool FY3 9YP
Tel 01253 766151

NHS Pensions Agency
200-220 Broadway
Fleetwood
Lancs FY7 8LG
Tel 01253 774774

Office for National Statistics
East Lane House
East Lane
Halton
Runcorn WA7 2DN
Tel 01928 715151
Fax 01928 792416

Office for National Statistics
Smedley Hydro
Trafalgar Road
Birkdale
Southport PR8 2HH
Tel 01704 569824
Fax 0151 471522

Office of Electricity Regulation
4th Floor
Hamilton House
Hamilton Place
Chester CH1 2BH
Tel 01244 320849

Office of Electricity Regulation
5th Floor
Boulton House
17-21 Chorlton Street
Manchester M1 3HY
Tel 0161 236 3484

Office of the Data Protection
Registrar
Water Lane
Wilmslow
Cheshire SK9 5AF
Tel 01625 545745
Fax 01625 524510
E-mail data@wycliffe.demon.co.uk
Web http://www.open.gov.uk/dpr/
dprhome.

Ofwat North West Customer
Service Committee
Suite 902, 9th Floor
Bridgewater House
Whitworth Street
Manchester M1 6LT
Tel 0161 236 6112
Fax 0161 228 6117
E-mail nwcsc@ofwat.gtnet.gov.uk
Web http://www.open.gov.uk/ofwat

Pay & Personnel Agency
PO Box 42
Stockport
Cheshire SK1 1ED
Tel 0161 440 8888

Rail Users Consultative Committee
for North Western England
Boulton House
17-21 Chorlton St
Manchester M1 3HY
Tel 0161 228 6247
Fax 0161 236 1476

Remploy Limited
Ashton Road
Salford
Oldham OL8 3JS
Tel 0161 626 4119
Fax 0161 627 313

Rural Development Commission
Haweswater Road
Penrith
Cumbria CA11 7EH
Tel 01768 865752

UK Atomic Energy Authority
Risley
Warrington
Cheshire WA3 6AT
Tel 01235 820220

UK Atomic Energy Authority
Winscale
Seascale
Cumbria CA20 1PF
Tel 01235 820220

Veterinary Laboratories Agency
Barton Hall
Garstang Road
Barton
Preston
Lancs PR3 5HE
Tel 01772 861611
Fax 01772 862026

Veterinary Laboratories Agency
Merrythought
Calthwaite
Penrith
Cumbria CA11 9RR
Tel 01768 885295
Fax 01768 8855314

War Pensions Agency
Norcross
Blackpool FY5 3WP
Tel 01253 858858
Fax 01253 330561
E-mail WPA-CHIEF-EXEC-
@NX005.DSS.gov.uk
Web www.dss.gov.uk/wpa/
index.htm

# SOUTH EAST

ACAS
Suites 3-5
Business Centre
1-7 Commercial Road
Paddock Wood
Kent TN12 6EN

ACAS
Westminster House
Fleet Road
Fleet
Hants GU13 8PD
Tel 01252 811868

Agricultural Wages Board for
England & Wales
Block A
Government Buildings
Coley Park
Reading
Berks RG1 6DT
Tel 01734 581222

Apple & Pear Research Council
Bradbourne House
Stable Block
East Malling Research Station
Kent ME19 6DZ
Tel 01732 845115
Fax 01732 844828

Army Base Repair Organisation
Monxton Road
Andover
Hants SP11 8HT
Tel 01264 383295
Fax 01264 383144

Army Base Storage & Distribution
Agency
HQ QMG
Portway
Monxton Road
Andover
Hants SP11 8HT
Tel 01264 383633
Fax 01264 383342

Army Technical Support Agency
Portway
Monxton Road
Andover
Hants SP11 8HT
Tel 01264 383753
Fax 01264 383294

Audit Commission
20 St Peter Street
Winchester SO23 8BP

Centre for Ecology & Hydrology
Maclean Building
Crowmarsh Gifford
Oxon OX10 8BB
Tel 01491 838800
Fax 01491 6922424

Child Support Agency
Ashdown House
Seddlescombe Road North
St Leonards
East Sussex TN37 7NL
Tel 0345 134 000

Civil Service College
Sunningdale Park
Larch Avenue
Ascot
Berks SL5 0QE
Tel 01344 634000
Fax 01344 634233

Coastguard
Spring Place
105 Commercial Road
Southampton SO15 1EG
Tel 01703 329100
Fax 01703 329298
Web http://www.coastguard.gov.uk

Commission for the New Towns
414-428 Midsummer Boulevard
Central Milton Keynes
Bucks MK9 2EA
Tel 01908 692692
Fax 01908 691333

Construction Industry Training
Board
Eastleigh House
Upper Market Street
Eastleigh
Hants SO5 4FD
Tel 01703 620505
Fax 01703 612056

Construction Industry Training
Board
Walker House
London Road
Riverhead
Sevenoaks
Kent TN13 2DN
Tel 01732 464520
Fax 01732 460561

Construction Industry Training
Board
Manor Road
Erith
Kent DA8 2DA
Tel 01322 349638
Fax 01332 332358

Council for the Central Laboratory
of the Research Councils
Chilton
Didcot
Oxon OX11 0QX
Tel 01235 445789
Fax 01235 446665
Web http://www.cclrc.ac.uk

Defence Clothing & Textiles
Agency
Building 25
Skimmingdish Lane
Caversfield
Bicester
Oxon OX6 9TS
Tel 01869 875700
Fax 01869 875509

Defence Dental Agency
RAF Halton
Aylesbury
Buckinghamshire HP22 5PG
Tel 01296 623535
Fax 01296 623535

Defence Estates Organisation
Blandford House
Farnborough Road
Aldershot
Hants GU11 2HA
Tel 01252 24431

Defence Estates Organisation
Building 1/150 PP19D
HM Naval Base
Murrays Lane
Portsmouth PO1 3NH
Tel 01705 22721

Defence Estates Organisation
MOD Victoria House
Military Road
Canterbury
Kent CT1 1JL
Tel 01227 818701
Defence Estates Organisation
Q4 Building via Q1
DRA Farnborough
Hants GU14 6TD
Tel 01252 392840

Defence Estates Organisation
HQ 4 Div
Steeles Road
Aldershot
Hants GU11 2DP
Tel 01252 349115

Defence Estates Organisation
Building 140a
RAF Benson
Wallingford
Oxon OX10 6AA
Tel 01491 83776

Defence Estates Organisation
Brunel House
42 The Hard
Portsmouth PO1 3DS
Tel 01705 822341

Defence Evaluation & Research
Agency
Ively Road
Farnborough
Hants GU14 OLX
E-mail
centralenquiries@dera.gov.uk
Web http://www.dera.gov.uk

Defence Medical Training
Organisation
Brunel House
42 The Hard
Portsmouth PO1 3DS
Tel 01705 822341
Fax 01705 730579

Defence Services
Medical Rehabilitation Unit
RAF Headley Court
Epsom
Surrey
Tel 01372378271 ext7214
Fax 01372 378271 ext7276

Defence Transport & Movements
Executive
HQ QMG
Monxton Road
Andover
Hants SP11 8HT
Tel 01264 383766

Duke of York's Royal Military
School
Dover
Kent CT15 5EQ
Tel 01304 245029
Fax 01304 245019
E-mail duke@easynet.co.uk

Employment Tribunals Service
3rd Floor
Duke's Keep
Marsh Lane
Southampton SO1 1EX
Tel 01703 639 555
Fax 01703 635 506

Employment Tribunals Service
Tufton House
Tufton Street
Ashford
Kent TN33 1RJ
Tel 01233 621346
Fax 01233 624423

Employment Tribunals Service
3/31 Friar Street
Reading RG1 1DY
Tel 0118 959 4917/9
Fax 0118 955 6866

English Nature
1 Southampton Road
Lyndhurst
Hants SO43 7BU
Tel 01703 283944
Fax 01703 283834

English Nature
Foxhold House
Thornford Road
Crookham Common
Thatcham
Berks RG19 8EL
Tel 01635 268881
Fax 01635 268940

English Nature
Howard House
31 High Street
Lewes
East Sussex BN7 2LU
Tel 01273 476595
Fax 01273 483063

English Nature
Coldharbour Farm
Wye
Ashford
Kent TN25 5DB
Tel 01233 812525
Fax 01233 812520

English Nature
10/11 Butchers Row
Banbury
Oxon OX16 8JH
Tel 01295 257601
Fax 01295 275180

English Sports Council
51a Church Street
Caversham
Reading
Berks RG4 8AX
Tel 0118 9483311
Fax 0118 9475935

The Environment Agency
Kings Meadow House
Kings Meadow Road
Reading RG1 8DQ
Tel 0118 953 5000
Fax 0118 950 0388

The Environment Agency
Guildbourne House
Chatsworth Road
Worthing
West Sussex BN11 1LD
Tel 01903 832000
Fax 01903 821832

Forensic Science Laboratory
Suit C, London Vale House
Hurricane Way
Woodley
Reading RG5 4UX
Tel 0118 944 0391
Fax 0118 944 0408

Forest Research
Alice Holt Lodge
Wrecclesham
Farnham
Surrey GU10 4LH
Tel 01420 22255
Fax 01420 23653

The Further Education Funding
Council
3 Queens Road
Reading RG1 4AR
Tel 0118 955 4201
Fax 0118 955 4220

The Health & Safety Executive
3 East Grinstead House
London Road
East Grinstead RH19 1RR
Tel 01342 334200
Fax 01342 334222

The Health & Safety Executive
Priestley House
Priestley Road
Basingstoke RG24 9NW
Tel 01256 404000
Fax 01256 404100

Highways Agency
Federated House
London Road
Dorking RH4 1SZ
Tel 0645 556575

HM Land Registry
Curtis House
Forest Road
Hawkenbury
Tunbridge Wells
Kent TN2 5AQ
Tel 01892 510015

HM Land Registry
St Andrew's Court
St Michael's Road
Portsmouth
Hants PO1 2JH
Tel 01705 768888

Horticultural Development Council
Bradbourne House
Stable Block
East Malling
Kent ME19 6DZ
Tel 01732 848383
Fax 01732 848498

Horticulture Research International
East Malling
West Malling
Kent ME19 6BJ
Tel 01732 843833
Fax 01732 849067

Horticulture Research International
Department of Hop Research
Wye College
Wye
Ashford
Kent TN25 5AH
Tel 01233 812179
Fax 01233 813126

Independent Television
Commission
Kings Worthy Court
Kings Worthy
Winchester SO23 7QA
Tel 01962 886141
Fax 01962 886141

# Q & Q

Inland Revenue
South Block
Barrington Road
Worthing BN12 4XH
Tel 01903 700222

Inland Revenue
Dukes Court
Duke Street
Woking
Surrey GU21 5XR
Tel 01483 258600

Insolvency Service
69 Middle Street
East Sussex
Brighton BN1 1BE
Tel 01273 861300
Fax 01273 822239

Insolvency Service
Western Range
83-85 London Road
Southampton SO15 2SH
Tel 01703 223348
Fax 01703 303177

Insolvency Service
Gordon House
15 Star Hill
Rochester ME1 1TX
Tel 01634 815367/842603
Fax 01634 831129

Insolvency Service
1st Floor
47 Friar Street
Reading RG1 1RY
Tel 0118 958 1931
Fax 0118 950 4941

Insolvency Service
50 New Dover Road
Canterbury CT1 3DT
Tel 01227 462070
Fax 01227 450537

Intervention Board
Kings House
33 Kings Road
Reading RG1 3BU
Tel 0118 958 3626
Fax 0118 953 1370

Legal Aid Board
80 Kings Road
Reading RG1 4LT
Tel 0118 958 1620
Fax 0118 958 4056

Legal Aid Board
3rd & 4th Floors
Invicta House
Trafalgar Place
Cheapside
Brighton BN1 4FR
Tel 01273 699622
Fax 01273 670690

Logistic Information Systems
Agency
Monxton Road
Andover
Hants SP11 8HT
Tel 01264 382745
Fax 01264 382820

Logistic Information Systems
Agency
Arncott
Bicester
Oxon OX6 6LP
Tel 01869 256728

Marine Safety Agency
Spring Place
105 Commercial Road
Southampton SO15 1EG
Tel 01703 329100
Fax 01703 329298

Meat & Livestock Commission
Winterhill House
Snowdon Drive
Milton Keynes MK6 1AX
Tel 01908 677577
Fax 01908 609221

Medical Supplies Agency
Drummond Barracks
Ludgershall
Andover
Hants SP11 9RU
Tel 01980 80524
Fax 01980 808676

Met Office
London Road
Bracknell
Berks RG12 2SZ
Tel 01344 420242
Web http://www.met-office.gov.uk

Ministry of Defence Hospital Unit
Frimley Park Hospital NHS Trust
Portsmouth Road
Frimley
Camberley
Surrey GU16 5UJ
Tel 01276 604201
Fax 01276 675660

National Film & Television School
Station Road
Beaconsfield
Bucks HP9 1LJ
Tel 01494 671234
Fax 01494 674042

National Radiological Protection
Board
Chilton
Didcot
Oxon OX11 0RQ
Tel 01235 831600
Fax 01235 833891
E-mail nrpb@nrpb.org.uk
Web http://www.nrpb.org.uk

Naval Aircraft Repair Organisation
Fareham Road
Gosport
Hants PO13 OAA
Tel 01705 543375
Fax 01705 543318

Naval Bases & Supply Agency
South Office Block
HM Naval Base
Portsmouth
Hants PO1 3LU
Tel 01705 723938

Naval Bases & Supply Agency
Semaphore Tower
HM Naval Base
Portsmouth
Hants PO1 3LT
Tel 01705 722625

Naval Manning Agency
Victory Buildings
HM Naval Base
Portsmouth
Hants PO1 3LS
Tel 01705 727340
Fax 01705 727413

Naval Recruiting & Training
Agency
HM Naval Base
Portsmouth
Hants PO1 3LS
Tel 01705 727716
Fax 01705 721613

Occupational Pensions Regulatory
Authority
Invicta House
Trafalgar Place
Cheapside
Brighton BN1 4DW
Tel 01273 627600
Fax 01273 627688
E-mail Helpdesk@opra.co.uk

Office for National Statistics
Segensworth Road
Tichfield
Fareham
Hants PO15 5RR
Tel 01329 842511
Fax 01329 813570

Office of Electricity Regulation
1-4 Lambert's Yard
Tonbridge
Kent TN9 1ER
Tel 01732 351356

Office of Electricity Regulation
30-31 Friar Street
Reading
Berks RG1 1DX
Tel 01734 560211

Ordnance Survey
Romsey Road
Maybush
Southampton SO16 4GU
Tel 01703 792000
Fax 01703 792452

Remploy Limited
Spencer House
Britannia Road
Banbury
Oxon OX16 8DP
Tel 01295 275333
Fax 01295 274900

Royal Armouries
Portsdown Road
Fareham
Hants PO17 6AN
Tel 01329 233734
Fax 01329 822092

Royal Hospital Haslar
Haslar Road
Gosport
Hants PO12 2AA
Tel 01705 584255 ext2121
Fax 01705 584255 ext2519

Royal Marines Museum
Southsea
Hants PO4 9PX
Tel 01705 819385
Fax 01705 838420

Royal Naval Museum
HM Naval Base
Portsmouth PO1 3LP
Tel 01705 733060

Royal Navy Submarine Museum
Haslar Jetty Road
Gosport
Hants PO12 2AS
Tel 01705 510354
Fax 01705 511349
E-mail rnsubs@submarine-
museum.demon.co

Rural Development Commission
Sterling House
7 Ashford House
Maidstone
Kent ME14 5BJ
Tel 01622 765222

Rural Development Commission
The Chanty House
29-31 Pyle Street
Newport
Isle of Wight PO30 1JW
Tel 01983 52019

Southampton Oceanography
Centre
Empress Dock
Southampton SO14 3ZH
Tel 01703 596888
Fax 01703 595107

UK Atomic Energy Authority
Culham Science Centre
Abingdon
Oxon OX14 3DB
Tel 01235 820220

UK Atomic Energy Authority
Harwell International Business
Centre
Didcot
Oxon OX11 0RA
Tel 01235 820220

Veterinary Laboratories Agency
New Haw
Addlestone
Surrey KT15 3NB
Tel 01932 341111
Fax 01932 347046

Veterinary Laboratories Agency
Itchen Abbas
Winchester
Hants SO21 1BX
Tel 01962 779966
Fax 01962 842492

Veterinary Medicines Directorate
Woodham Lane
New Haw
Addlestone
Surrey KT15 3NB
Tel 01932 336911
Fax 01932 336618

Wilton Park Executive Agency
Wiston House Conference Centre
Steyning
Sussex BN44 3DZ
Tel 01903 815020
Fax 01903 879647

# SOUTH WEST

ACAS
Regent House
27a Regent Street
Clifton
Bristol BS8 4HR
Tel 0117 974 4066

Agricultural Wages Board for
England & Wales
Block 3
Government Buildings
Burghill Road
Westbury-on-Trym
Bristol BS10 6NJ
Tel 0117 559 1000

Agricultural Wages Board for
England & Wales
Government Buildings
Alphington Road
Exeter EX2 8NQ
Tel 01392 277951

Armed Forces Personnel
Administration Agency
Building 182
RAF Innsworth
Gloucester GL3 1EZ
Tel 01452 712612
Fax 01452 510814

Army Training & Recruitment
Agency
Trenchard Lines
Upavon
Pewsey
Wilts SN9 6BE
Tel 01980 615010
Fax 01980 615305

Audit Commission
10 Blenheim Court
Matford Business Park
Lustleigh Close
Exeter EX2 8PW

Biotechnology & Biological
Sciences Research Council
Polaris House
North Star Avenue
Swindon SN2 1UH
Tel 01793 413253
Fax 01793 413382
Web http://www.bbsrc.ac.uk/
opennet/

British Waterways
The Locks
Bath Road
Devizes
Wilts SN10 1HB
Tel 01380 722859

British Waterways
Llanthony Warehouse
Gloucester Docks
Gloucester GL1 2EJ
Tel 01452 318000

CEFAS
Barrack Road
The Nothe
Weymouth
Dorset DT4 8UB
Tel 01305 206600
Fax 01305 206601

Central Council for Education and
Training in Social Work
21 Prince Street
Bristol BS1 4PH
Tel 0117 973 4137
Fax 0117 923 9883

Centre for Coastal & Marine
Sciences
Plymouth Marine Laboratory
Prospect Place
West Hoe
Plymouth PL1 3DH
Tel 01752 633100
Fax 01752 633101

Child Support Agency
Clearbrook House
Towerfield Drive
Buckleigh Down Business Pk
Plymouth PL95 1SA
Tel 0345 137000

Construction Industry Training
Board
2 Kew Court
Pynes Hill
Rydon Lane
Exeter
Devon EX2 5AZ
Tel 01392 444900
Fax 01392 445044

Countryside Commission
John Dower House
Crescent Place
Cheltenham
Glos GL50 3RA
Tel 01242 521381
Fax 01242 228914

Countryside Commission
Bridge House
Sion Place
Clifton Down
Bristol BS8 4AS
Tel 0117 973 9966
Fax 0117 923 8086

Defence Estates Organisation
Building 255
HQ P&T Command
RAF Innsworth
Innsworth
Gloucester GL3 1EZ
Tel 01452 712612

Defence Estates Organisation
Estate Office
High Street
Durrington
Salisbury
Wilts SP4 8AF
Tel 01980 594553

Defence Estates Organisation
Mount Wise
Devonport
Plymouth
Devon PL1 4JH
Tel 01752 501439

Defence Estates Organisation
HQ 3 Div(UK)
Bulford Camp
Salisbury
Wilts SP4 9NY
Tel 01980 672645

Defence Estates Organisation
FONA HQ
Yeovilton
Somerset BA22 8HL
Tel 01935 456602

Defence Estates Organisation
HQ Land Command
Erskine Barracks
Wilton
Salisbury SP2 0AG
Tel 01722 436823

Economic & Social Research
Council
Polaris House
North Star Avenue
Swindon SN2 1UJ
Tel 01793 413000
Fax 01793 413001
Web http://www.esrc.ac.uk/home/
html

Employment Tribunals Service
The Crescent Centre
Temple Back
Bristol BS1 6EZ
Tel 0117 929 8261
Fax 0117 925 3452

Employment Tribunals Service
Renslade House
Bonhay Road
Exeter EX4 3BX
Tel 01392 279665
Fax 01392 430063

Engineering & Physical Sciences
Research Council
Polaris House
North Star Avenue
Swindon SN2 1ET
Tel 01793 444000
Fax 01793 444010
Web http://www.epsrc.ac.uk

English National Board for
Nursing, Midwifery and Health
Visiting
Goldsmith's House
Broad Plain
Bristol BS2 0JP
Tel 0117 925 9143
Fax 0117 925 1800

English Nature
Trevint House
Strangways Villas
Truro
Cornwall TR1 2PA
Tel 01872 262550
Fax 01872 262551

English Nature
Slepe Farm
Arne
Wareham
Dorset BH20 5BN
Tel 01929 556688
Fax 01929 554752

English Nature
The Old Mill House
37 North Street
Okehampton
Devon EX20 1AR
Tel 01837 55045
Fax 01837 55046

English Nature
Prince Maurice Court
Hambleton Avenue
Devizes
Wilts SN10 2RT
Tel 01380 726344
Fax 01380 721411

English Nature
Roughmoor
Bishop's Hull
Taunton
Somerset TA1 5AA
Tel 01823 283211
Fax 01823 272978

English Sports Council
Ashlands House
Ashlands
Crewkerne
Somerset TA18 7LQ
Tel 01460 73491
Fax 01460 77263

The Environment Agency
Rio House
Waterside Drive
Aztec West
Almondsbury
Bristol BS12 4UD
Tel 01454 624400
Fax 01454 624409

The Environment Agency
Manley House
Kestrel Way
Exeter EX2 7LQ
Tel 01392 444 000
Fax 01392 444 238

Farming & Rural Conservation
Agency
Burghill Road
Westbury-on-Trym
Bristol BS10 6YW
Tel 0117 959 1000
Fax 0117 959 0463

Fire Service College
Moreton-in-Marsh
Glos GL56 0RH
Tel 01608 650831
Fax 01608 651788
E-mail moreton@campus.bt.com

Fleet Air Arm Museum
Royal Naval Air Station
Yeovilton
Ilchester
Somerset BA22 8HT
Tel 01935 840565
Fax 01935 840181

Forest Enterprise
Avon Fields House
Somerdale
Keynsham
Bristol BS18 2BD
Tel 0117 986 9481
Fax 0117 986 1981

The Further Education Funding
Council
Kempton House
Blackbrook Park Avenue
Taunton TA1 2PF
Tel 01823 444404
Fax 01823 443815

Gaming Board for Great Britain
Unit 16
Apex Court
Woodlands
Almondsbury
Bristol BS12 4XA
Tel 01454 616687
Fax 01454 613090

Gas Consumers' Council
3rd Floor, Roddis House
4-12 Old Christchurch Road
Bournemouth BH1 1LG
Tel 01202 556654
Fax 01202 291080

The Government Property Lawyers
Riverside Chambers
Castle Street
Taunton
Somerset TA1 4AP
Tel 01823 345200
Fax 01823 345202

The Health & Safety Executive
Inter City House
Mitchell Lane
Victoria Street
Bristol BS1 6AN
Tel 0117 988 6000
Fax 0117 926 2998

Higher Education Funding Council
for England
Northavon House
Coldharbour Lane
Bristol BS16 1QD
Tel 0117 931 7317
Fax 0117 931 7463
E-mail hefce@hefce.ac.uk
Web http://www.hefce.ac.uk/

Highways Agency
Falcon Road
Sowton
Exeter EX2 7LB
Tel 0645 556575

Highways Agency
Tollgate House
Houlton Street
Bristol BS2 9DJ
Tel 0645 556575

HM Land Registry
Plumer House
Tailyour Road
Crownhill
Plymouth PL6 5HY
Tel 01752 636000

HM Land Registry
Twyver House
Bruton Way
Gloucester GL1 1DQ
Tel 01452 511111

HM Land Registry
Drakes Hill Court
Burrington Way
Plymouth Pl5 3LP
Tel 01752 635600

HM Land Registry
Melcombe Court
1 Cumberland Drive
Weymouth
Dorset DT4 9TT
Tel 01305 363636

Horticulture Research International
Efford
Lymington
Hants SO41 0LZ
Tel 01590 673341
Fax 01590 671553

The Housing Corporation
2nd Floor
Beaufort House
51 New North Road
Exeter EX4 4EP
Tel 01392 428200

Independent Television
Commission
153 Armada Way
Plymouth PL1 1HY
Tel 01752 663031
Fax 01752 662490

Inland Revenue
Longbrook House
New North Road
Exeter EX4 4UA
Tel 01392 453210

Insolvency Service
21-23 London Road
Gloucester GL1 3HB
Tel 01452 521658/527997

Insolvency Service
3rd Floor
Finance House
Barnfield Road
Exeter EX1 1QR
Tel 01392 436886
Fax 01392 422618

Insolvency Service
1st Floor
Cobourg House
Mayflower Street
Plymouth PL1 1DJ
Tel 01752 635200
Fax 01752 635222

Insolvency Service
3rd Floor
Bristol & West House
Post Office Road
Bournemouth BH1 1LH
Tel 01202 558208
Fax 01202 297590

Insolvency Sevice
3rd & 4th Floors
Intercity House
Mitchell Lane
Bristol BS1 6BD
Tel 0117 927 9515
Fax 0117 925 2054

Intervention Board
Block 2
Government Buildings
Burghill Road
Westbury-on-Trym
Bristol BS10 6NJ
Tel 0117 959 0399
Fax 0117 959 0364

Legal Aid Board
33-35 Queen Square
Bristol BS1 4LU
Tel 0117 921 4801
Fax 0117 925 2584

Meat Hygiene Service
Room 609
Quantock House
Paul Street
Taunton TA1 3NX
Tel 01823 330066

Ministry of Defence Hospital Unit
Derriford Hospital NHS Trust
Derriford
Plymouth PL6 8DH
Tel 01752 763755
Fax 01752 763755

National Portrait Gallery
Montacute House
Montacute
Somerset TA15

Natural Environment Research
Council
Polaris House
North Star Avenue
Swindon SN2 1EU
Tel 01793 411500
Fax 01793 411501

Naval Bases & Supply Agency
D Block
Ensleigh
Bath BA1 5AB
Tel 01225 467156
Fax 01225 468421

Naval Bases & Supply Agency
Naval Base Headquarters
HM Naval Base
Devonport
Plymouth PLI 4SL
Tel 01752 552536

Nerc Scientific Services
Holbrook House
Station Road
Swindon SN1 1DE
Tel 01793 411998
Fax 01793 411910

Office of Electricity Regulation
Unit 1
Hide Market
West Street
Bristol BS2 0BH
Tel 0117 954 0934

Ofwat South West Customer
Service Committee
1st Floor
Broadwalk House
Southernhay West
Exeter EX1 1TS
Tel 01392 428028
Fax 01392 428010
E-mail swcsc@ofwat.gtnet.gov.uk
Web http://www.open.gov.uk/ofwat

Ofwat Wessex Customer Service
Committee
2 The Hide Market
West Street
St Philips
Bristol BS2 0BH
Tel 0117 955 7001
Fax 0117 955 7037
E-mail wxcsc@ofwat.gtnet.gov.uk
Web http://www.open.gov.uk/ofwat

Particle Physics & Astronomy
Research Council
North Star Avenue
Swindon
Wilts SN2 1SZ
Tel 01793 442000
Fax 01793 442002
E-mail userid@pparc.ac.uk
Web http://www.pparc.ac.uk

Pay & Personnel Agency
Pinesgate West
Bath BA1 5AB
Tel 01225 449156

Pay & Personnel Agency
Block B
Warminster Road
Bath BA1 5AA
Tel 01225 828636

The Planning Inspectorate
Tollgate House
Houlton Street
Bristol BS2 9DJ
Tel 0117 987 8000
Fax 0117 987 8408
Web http://www.open.gov.uk/
pi.pihome.ht

RAF Personnel Management
Agency
Building 248
RAF Innsworth
Gloucester GL3 1EZ
Tel 01452 712612
Fax 01452 712612

RAF Training Group Defence
Agency
RAF Innsworth
Gloucester GL3 1EZ
Tel 01452 712612
Fax 01452 510825

Rail Users Consultative Committee
for Western England
13th Floor
Tower House
Fairfax Street
Bristol BS1 3BN
Tel 0117 926 5703
Fax 0117 929 4140

Royal Commission on Historical
Monuments of England
Kemble Drive
Swindon SN2 2GZ
Tel 01793 414700
Fax 01793 414606
Web http://www.rchme.gov.uk

Royal Commission on the
Historical Monuments of England
5 Marlborough Court
Manaton Close
Exeter EX2 8PF
Tel 01392 824901
Fax 01392 824490

Rural Development Commission
141 Castle Street
Salisbury
Wilts SP1 3TP
Tel 01722 336255
Web http://www.argonet.co.uk/rdc

Rural Development Commission
27 Victoria Park Road
Devon
Exeter EX2 4NT
Tel 01392 206240

Rural Development Commission
3 Chartfield House
Castle Street
Taunton
Somerset TA1 4AS
Tel 01823 276905

Rural Development Commission
2nd Floor
Highshore House
New Bridge Street
Truro
Cornwall TR1 2AA
Tel 01872 273531

Science Museum Wroughton
Block D4
Red Barn Gate
Wroughton
Swindon SN4 9NS

Ships Support Agency
B Block
Foxhill
Bath BA1 5AB
Tel 01225 883743
Fax 01225 884313
E-mail
shipsbiscup.mod.fh@gtnet.gov.uk

Specialist Procurement Services
Ministry of Defence (PE)
PO Box 702
Abbey Wood
Bristol BS12 7DU
Tel 0117 913 2724
Fax 0117 913 2925

Tate Gallery
Porthmeor Beach
Cornwall TR26 1TG
Tel 01736 796226
Fax 01736 794480

UK Atomic Energy Authority
Winfrith Technology Centre
Dorchester
Dorset DT2 8DH
Tel 01235 820220

UK Hydrographic Office
Admiralty Way
Taunton
Somerset TA1 2DN
Tel 01823 337900
Fax 01823 284077
E-mail @hydro.gov.uk
Web http://www.hydro.gov.uk

Vehicle Certification Agency
1 The Eastgate Office Centre
Eastgate Road
Bristol BS5 6XX
Tel 0117 951 5151
Fax 0117 952 4103
E-mail
general.vca.eoc@gtnet.gov.uk
Web http://www.detr.gov.uk/vca/

Vehicle Inspectorate
Berkeley House
Croydon Street
Bristol BS5 0DA
Tel 0117 954 3200
Fax 0117 954 3212
E-mail enquiries.vi@gtnet.gov.uk
Web www.demon.co.uk/vehinsp/
main.htm

Veterinary Laboratories Agency
Staplake Mount
Starcross
Devon
Exeter EX6 8PE
Tel 01626 891121
Fax 01626 891766

Veterinary Laboratories Agency
Polwhele
Truro
Cornwall TR4 9AD
Tel 01872 721150
Fax 01872 223443

Veterinary Laboratories Agency
Langford House
Langford
North Somerset BS18 7DX
Tel 01934 852421
Fax 01934 852981

# WEST MIDLANDS

ACAS
Warwick House
6 Highfield Road
Edgbaston
Birmingham B15 3ED
Tel 0121 456 5856

Agricultural Wages Board for
England & Wales
Government Buildings
Whittington Road
Worcester WR5 2LQ
Tel 01905 763355

Audit Commission
2nd Floor
1 Friarsgate
1011 Stratford Road
Solihull B90 4BN

British Educational
Communications & Technology
Agency
Milburn Hill Road
Science Park
Coventry CV4 7JJ
Tel 01203 416994
Fax 01203 411418
E-mail Enquiry_desk@ncet.org.uk
Web http://www.ncet.org.uk

British Hallmarking Council
St Philip's House
St Philip's Place
Birmingham B3 2PP
Tel 0121 200 3300
Fax 0121 200 3330

British Waterways
Norbury Junction
Stafford ST20 0PN
Tel 01785 284 253

British Waterways
Fradley Junction
Alrewas
Burton-on-Trent
Staffs DE13 7DN
Tel 01283 790236

British Waterways
Bradley Lane
Bilston
West Midlands WV14 8DW
Tel 01902 409010

British Waterways
Brome Hall Lane
Lapworth
Solihull
West Midlands B94 5RB
Tel 01564 784634

British Waterways
Peel's Wharf
Lichfield Street
Fazeley
West Midlands B78 3QZ
Tel 01827 252000

Castle Vale Housing Action Trust
Castle Vale School
Farnborough Road
Birmingham B35 7NL
Tel 0121 776 6784
Fax 0121 776 6786
E-mail cvhat.org.uk
Web http://www.cvhat.org.uk

Central Council for Education and
Training in Social Work
Myson House
Railway Terrace
Rugby CV21 3HT
Tel 01788 572 119
Fax 01788 547139

Child Support Agency
Pedmore House
The Waterfront
Brierley Hill
Dudley
West Midlands DY5 1XA
Tel 0345 131 000

Commission for the New Towns
Jordan House West
Hall Court
Hall Park Way
Telford TF3 4NN
Tel 01952 293131

Companies House
Central Library
Chamberlain Square
Birmingham B3 3HQ
Tel 0121 233 9047

Construction Industry Training
Board
83 Lifford Lane
King's Norton
Birmingham B30 3JE
Tel 0121 459 4262/8000
Fax 0121 459 8330

Countryside Commission
1st Floor
Vincent House
Tindal Bridge
92-93 Edward Street
Birmingham B1 2RA
Tel 0121 233 9399
Fax 0121 233 9286

Criminal Cases Review
Commission
Alpha Tower
Suffolk Street Queensway
Birmingham B1 1TT
Tel 0121 633 1800
Fax 0121 633 1804/1823

Defence Estates Organisation
Copthorne Barracks
Shrewsbury SY3 7LT
Tel 01743 262598

Defence Estates Organisation
St George's House
Blakemore Drive
Sutton Coldfield
West Midlands B75 7RL
Tel 0121 311 3850
Fax 0121 311 2100

Employment Tribunals Service
Phoenix House
1/3 Newhall Street
Birmingham B3 3NH
Tel 0121 236 6051
Fax 0121 236 6029

Employment Tribunals Service
Prospect House
Belle Vue Road
Shrewsbury SY3 7AR
Tel 01743 358 341
Fax 01743 244 186

English Nature
Attingham Park
Shrewsbury
Shropshire SY4 4TW
Tel 01743 709611
Fax 01743 709303
Web http://www.english-
nature.org.uk

English Nature
Bronsil House
Eastnor
Ledbury
Herefordshire HR8 1EP
Tel 01531 638500
Fax 01531 638501

English Sports Council
Metropolitan House
1 Hagley Road
Five Ways
Birmingham B16 8TT
Tel 0121 456 3444
Fax 0121 4561583

The Environment Agency
Sapphire East
550 Streetsbrook Road
Solihull B91 1QT
Tel 0121 711 2324
Fax 0121 711 5824

Forensic Science Service
Priory House
Gooch Street North
Birmingham B5 6QQ
Tel 0121 607 6800
Fax 0121 622 5889

The Further Education Funding
Council
Cheylesmore House
Quinton Road
Coventry CV1 2WT
Tel 01203 863000
Fax 01203 863100

Gas Consumers' Council
Broadway House
Calthorpe Road
Birmingham B15 1TH
Tel 0121 455 0285
Fax 0121 456 2976

The Health & Safety Executive
McLaren Building
35 Dale End
Birmingham B4 7NP
Tel 0121 607 6200
Fax 0121 607 6349

The Health & Safety Executive
The Marches House
Midway
Newcastle under Lyme ST5 1DT
Tel 01782 602300
Fax 01782 602400

Highways Agency
5 Broadway
Broad Street
Birmingham B15 1BL
Tel 0645 556575

HM Land Registry
Parkside Court
Hall Park Way
Telford TF3 4LR
Tel 01952 290355

HM Land Registry
Leigh Court
Torrington Avenue
Tile Hill
Coventry CV4 9XZ
Tel 01203 860860

Horticulture Research International
Wellesbourne
Warwick CV35 9EF
Tel 01789 470382
Fax 01789 470552

The Housing Corporation
Norwich Union House
Waterloo Road
Wolverhampton WV1 4BP
Tel 01902 795000

Independent Television
Commission
Lyndon House
62 Hagley Road
Birmingham B16 8PE
Tel 0121 693 0662
Fax 0121 693 2753

Insolvency Service
London House
Hide Street
Stoke-on-Trent ST4 1QN
Tel 01782 845256
Fax 01782 844787

Insolvency Service
1st & 2nd Floors
Ladywood House
45/6 Stephenson Street
Birmingham B2 4UP
Tel 0121 698 4000
Fax 0121 698 4402

Intervention Board
St John's House
St John's Square
Wolverhampton WV2 4AX
Tel 01902 23903
Fax 01902 717046

Legal Aid Board
Centre City Podium
5 Hill Street
Birmingham B5 4UD
Tel 0121 632 6541
Fax 0121 632 5078

Meat Hygiene Service
Block A
Wergs Road
Woodthorne
Tettenhall
Wolverhampton WV6 8TQ
Tel 01902 693396

Office of Electricity Regulation
Hagley House
Hagley Road
Edgbaston
Birmingham B16 8QG
Tel 0121 456 2100
Fax 0121 456 4664

Office of Water Services
Centre City Tower
7 Hill Street
Birmingham B5 4UA
Tel 0121 625 1300
Fax 0121 625 1400
E-mail
enquiries@ofwat.gtnet.gov.uk
Web http://www.open.gov.uk/ofwat

Ofwat Central Customer Service
Committee
First Floor
Chanelle House
86 New Street
Birmingham B2 4BA
Tel 0121 644 5252
Fax 0121 644 5256
E-mail clcsc@ofwat.gtnet.gov.uk
Web http://www.open.gov.uk/ofwat

Ofwat National Customer Council
Centre City Tower
7 Hill Street
Birmingham B5 4UA
Tel 0121 625 1301
Fax 0121 625 1444
E-mail oncc@ofwat.gtnet.gov.uk
Web http://www.open.gov.uk/ofwat

Pay & Personnel Agency
Whittington Road
Worcester WR5 2LA
Tel 01905 361401

Rail Users Consultative Committee
for the Midlands
77 Paradise Circus
Queensway
Birmingham B1 2DT
Tel 0121 212 2133
Fax 0121 236 6945

Remploy Limited
79 Torrington Avenue
Tile Hill
Coventry
West Midlands CV4 9AQ
Tel 01203 462715
Fax 01203 421411

Rural Development Commission
Strickland House
The Lawns
Park Street
Wellington
Telford
Shropshire TF1 3BX
Tel 01952 247161

Veterinary Laboratories Agency
Kendal Road
Harlescott
Shrewsbury
Shropshire SY1 4HD
Tel 01743 467621
Fax 01743 441060

Veterinary Laboratories Agency
Luddington
Stratford-upon-Avon
Warwickshire CV37 9SJ
Tel 01789 750212
Fax 01789 750281

## YORKSHIRE & HUMBERSIDE

ACAS
Commerce House
St Alban's Place
Leeds LS2 8HH
Tel 0113 243 1371

Agricultural Wages Board for
England & Wales
Government Buildings
Crosby Road
Northallerton
North Yorkshire DL6 1AD
Tel 01609 773751

Audit Commission
Lake House
Acorn Business Park
Woodseats Close
Sheffield S8 0TB

Audit Commission
Deacon House
Seacroft Avenue
Seacroft
Leeds LS14 6JD

Benefits Agency
Quarry House
Quarry Hill
Leeds LS2 7UA
Tel 0113 232 4000

British Waterways
Naburn Lock
Naburn
York YO1 4RU
Tel 01904 728229

British Waterways
Lock Lane
Castleford
West Yorks WF10 2LH
Tel 01977 554351

British Waterways
1 Dock Street
Leeds LS1 1HH
Tel 0113 281 6801

British Waterways
Dobson Lock
Apperley Bridge
Bradford
West Yorks BD10 0PY
Tel 01274 611303

Central Council for Education and
Training in Social Work
26 Park Row
Leeds LS1 5QB
Tel 0113 243 1516
Fax 0113 243 9276

Central Science Laboratory
Sand Hutton
York YO4 1LZ
Tel 01904 462000
Fax 01904 462111

Companies House
25 Queen Street
Leeds LS1 2TW
Tel 0113 233 8338

Construction Industry Training
Board
Milton House
Queen Street
Morley
Leeds LS27 9EL
Tel 0113 252 1966
Fax 0113 253 1117

Countryside Commission
2nd Floor
Victoria Wharf
Embankment IV
Sovereign Street
Leeds LS1 4BA
Tel 0113 246 9222
Fax 0113 246 0353

Defence Estates Organisation
Elizabeth House
Imphal Barracks
Fulford Road
York YO1 4AU
Tel 01904 662334

Defence Estates Organisation
Gough Road
Catterick Garrison
North Yorkshire DL9 3EJ
Tel 01748 832521

Duchess of Kent's Hospital
Horne Road
Catterick Garrison
North Yorkshire
Tel 01714 887 3024
Fax 01714 887 3011

Education Assets Board
Capitol House
Bond Court
Leeds LS1 5SS
Tel 0113 234 8888
Fax 0113 246 0569

Employment Tribunals Service
14 East Parade
Sheffield S1 3ET
Tel 0114 276 0348
Fax 0114 276 2551

Employment Tribunals Service
3rd Floor
11 Albion Street
Leeds LS1 5ES
Tel 0113 245 9741
Fax 0113 242 8843

English National Board for
Nursing, Midwifery and Health
Visiting
East Villa
109 Heslington Road
York YO1 5BS
Tel 01904 430505
Fax 01904 430309

English Nature
Genesis Building 1
Science Park
University Road
Heslington
York YO1 5DQ
Tel 01904 435500
Fax 01904 435501

English Nature
Thornborough Hall
Leyburn
North Yorkshire DL8 5ST
Tel 01969 623447
Fax 01969 624190

English Nature
Bull Ring House
Northgate
Wakefield
West Yorks WF1 1HD
Tel 01924 387010
Fax 01924 201507

English Sports Council
Coronet House
Queen Street
Leeds LS1 4PW
Tel 0113 243 6443
Fax 0113 242 2189

The Environment Agency
Rivers House
21 Park Square South
Leeds LS1 2QG
Tel 0113 244 0191
Fax 0113 246 1889

Farming & Rural Conservation
Agency
Government Buildings
Otley Road
Lawnswood
Leeds LS16 5QT
Tel 0113 261 3333
Fax 0113 230 0879

Forensic Science Laboratory
Sandbeck Way
Audby Lane
Wetherby
West Yorks LS22 7DN
Tel 01937 548100
Fax 01937 587683

Forest Enterprise
1A Grosvenor Terrace
York YO3 7BD
Tel 01904 620221
Fax 01904 610664

Funding Agency for Schools
Albion Wharf
25 Skeldergate
York YO1 2XL
Tel 01904 661661
Fax 01904 661686

The Further Education Funding
Council
1 Blenheim Court
Blenheim Walk
Leeds LS2 9AE
Tel 0113 245 2644
Fax 0113 245 2477

Gas Consumers' Council
No 1 Eastgate
Leeds LS2 7RL
Tel 0113 243 9961
Fax 0113 242 6935

The Health & Safety Executive
8 St Paul's Street
Leeds LS1 2LE
Tel 0113 283 4200
Fax 0113 283 4296

The Health & Safety Executive
Sovereign House
110 Queen Street
Sheffield S1 2ES
Tel 0114 291 2300
Fax 0114 291 2379

The Health & Safety Executive
Broad Lane
Sheffield S3 7HQ
Tel 0114 289 2920

Highways Agency
City House
New Station Street
Leeds LS1 4UR
Tel 0645 556575

Highways Agency
Jefferson House
27 Park Place
Leeds LS1 2SZ
Tel 0645 556575

HM Land Registry
Earle House
Portland Street
Hull HU2 8JN
Tel 01482 223244

HM Land Registry
James House
James Street
York YO2 3YZ
Tel 01904 450000

Horticulture Research International
Cawood
Selby
North Yorks YO8 0TZ
Tel 01757 268275
Fax 01757 268996

The Housing Corporation
St Paul's House
23 Park Square South
Leeds LS1 2ND
Tel 0113 233 7100

Independent Television
Commission
15 Paternoster Row
Sheffield S1 2BX
Tel 0114 276 9091
Fax 0114 276 9089

Inland Revenue
Concept House
5 Young Street
Sheffield S1 4LF
Tel 0114 296 9696

Inland Revenue
Victoria Street
Shipley
West Yorks BD98 8AA
Tel 01274 530750

Insolvency Service
2nd Floor
Savile House
Trinity Street Arcade
Leeds LS1 6QP
Tel 0113 245 5776
Fax 0113 242 8031

Insolvency Service
Suite J, Anchor House
The Maltins
Silvester Street
Hull HU1 3HA
Tel 01482 323720/323729
Fax 01482 217806

Insolvency Service
6th Floor
Don House
20-22 Hawley Street
Sheffield S1 2EA
Tel 0114 272 6692/1
Fax 0114 272 1394

Intervention Board
Windsor House
Corwall Road
Harrogate HG1 2PW
Tel 01423 531444
Fax 01423 501576

Legal Aid Board
City House
New Station Street
Leeds LS1 4IS
Tel 0113 244 2851
Fax 0113 244 9820

Marine Safety Agency
Mill Lane
Beverley
Yorkshire HU17 9JB
Tel 01482 866606
Fax 01482 869989

Meat & Livestock Commission
Copthall Tower House
Station Parade
Harrogate
North Yorkshire HG1 1TL
Tel 01423 560361
Fax 01423 525722

Meat Hygiene Service
Foss House
Kings Pool
1-2 Peasholme Green
York YO1 2PX
Tel 01904 455501
Fax 01904 455502

The National Museum of
Photography, Film & Television
Pictureville
Bradford
West Yorks BD1 1NQ

National Portrait Gallery
Benningbrough Hall
York YO6 1DD

The National Railway Museum
Leeman Road
York
Yorkshire Y02 4XJ

NHS Estates
1 Trevelyan Square
Boar Lane
Leeds LS1 6AE
Tel 0113 254 7000
Fax 0113 254 7299

Office of Electricity Regulation
Symons House
Belgrave Streeet
Leeds LS2 8DD
Tel 0113 234 1866

Ofwat Yorkshire Customer Service
Committee
Ground Floor
Symonds House
Belgrave Street
Leeds LS2 8DD
Tel 0113 234 0874
Fax 0113 234 1316
E-mail ykcsc@ofwat.gtnet.gov.uk
Web http://www.open.gov.uk/ofwat

Pesticides Safety Directorate
Mallard House
Kings Pool
3 Peasholme Green
York YO1 2PX
Tel 01904 640500
Fax 01904 455733

Rail Users Consultative Committee
for North Eastern England
Hilary House
16 St Saviour's Place
Yorks YO1 2PL
Tel 01904 625615
Fax 01904 643026

Remploy Limited
Suite 37
Concourse House
432 Dewsbury Road
Leeds LS11 7DF
Tel 0113 270 2000
Fax 0113 242 0979

Royal Armouries
Armouries Drive
Leeds
Yorkshire LS10 1LT
Tel 0113 220 1999
Fax 0113 220 1955

Royal Commission on the
Historical Monuments of England
Shelley House
Acomb Road
York YO2 4HB
Tel 01904 784411
Fax 01904 795348

Rural Development Commission
Spitfire House
Aviator Court
Clifton Moor
York YO3 4UZ
Tel 01904 693335

Veterinary Laboratories Agency
West House
Station Road
Thirsk
North Yorkshire YO7 1PZ
Tel 01845 52265
Fax 01845 525224

## NORTHERN IRELAND

Agricultural Research Institute of
Northern Ireland
Newforge Lane
Belfast BT9 5PX

Agricultural Research Institute of
Northern Ireland
22 Greenmount Road
Antrim BT41 4PU

Agricultural Research Institute of
Northern Ireland
Hillsborough
Co Down BT26 6DR
Tel 01846 682484
Fax 01846 689594

Agricultural Research Institute of
Northern Ireland
Stormont
Belfast BT4 3SD

Agricultural Wages Board for
Northern Ireland
Room 22A
Dundonald House
Upper Newtownards Road
Belfast BT4 3SB
Tel 01232 524521
Fax 01232 524634

Arts Council of Northern Ireland
77 Malone Road
Belfast BT9 6AQ
Tel 01232 385200
Fax 01232 661715

Business Development Service
Craigantlet Buildings
Stoney Road
Belfast BT4 3SX
Tel 01232 527437
Fax 01232 527270

Central Council for Education and
Training in Social Work
6 Malone Road
Belfast BT9 5BN
Tel 01232 665390
Fax 01232 669469

Compensation Agency
Royston House
34 Upper Queen Street
Belfast BT1 6FD
Tel 01232 249944
Fax 01232 246956

Construction Industry Training
Board (NI)
17 Dundrod Road
Crumlin
Co Antrim BT29 4SR
Tel 01232 825466
Fax 01232 825693
E-mail citb@psilink.co.uk
Web http://www.citbni.org.uk

Construction Service
Churchill House
Victoria Square
Belfast BT1 4QW
Tel 01232 250269
Fax 01232 250333

Council for Catholic Maintained
Schools
160 High Street
Holywood
Co Down BT18 9HT
Tel 01232 426972
Fax 01232 424255

Driver & Vehicle Licensing
Northern Ireland
County Hall
Castlerock Road
Coleraine BT51 3HS
Tel 01265 41461
Fax 01265 41422

Driver & Vehicle Testing Agency
47 Hamiltonsbawn Road
Armagh BT60 1HW
Tel 01861 522699

Driver & Vehicle Testing Agency
Balmoral Road
Belfast BT12 6QL
Tel 01232 681831
Fax 01232 665520

Driver & Vehicle Testing Agency
55 Broughshane Street
Ballymena

Driver & Vehicle Testing Agency
Shields House
19 James Street South
Belfast

Driver & Vehicle Testing Agency
Ballinderry Industrial Estate
Ballinderry Road
Lisburn BT28 2SA
Tel 01846 663151

Driver & Vehicle Testing Agency
Diviny Drive
Carn Industrial Estate
Craigavon BT63 5RY
Tel 01762 336188

Driver & Vehicle Testing Agency
20 Strand Road
Londonderry

Driver & Vehicle Testing Agency
Sandholes Road
Cookstown BT80 9AR
Tel 016487 64809

Driver & Vehicle Testing Agency
2 Loughan Hill Industrial Estate
Gateside Road
Coleraine BT52 2NJ
Tel 01265 43819

Driver & Vehicle Testing Agency
Pennybridge Industrial Estate
Larne Road
Ballymena BT42 3ER
Tel 01266 656801

Driver & Vehicle Testing Agency
Gortrush Industrial Estate
Derry Road
Omagh BT78 5CJ
Tel 01662 242540

Driver & Vehicle Testing Agency
Jubilee Road
Newtownards BT23 4XP
Tel 01247 813064

Driver & Vehicle Testing Agency
11b Foundry Lane
Omagh

Driver & Vehicle Testing Agency
Cloonagh Road
Flying Horse Road
Downpatrick BT30 6DU
Tel 01396 614565

Driver & Vehicle Testing Agency
Chanterhill
Enniskillen BT74 6DE
Tel 01365 322871

Driver & Vehicle Testing Agency
51 Rathfriland Road
Newry BT34 1LD
Tel 01693 62853

Driver & Vehicle Testing Agency
Unit 11c
Magowan House
West Street
Portadown

Driver & Vehicle Testing Agency
Commercial Way
Hydepark Industrial Estate
Mallusk BT36 8YY
Tel 01232 842111

Driver & Vehicle Testing Agency
New Buildings Industrial Estate
Victoria Road
Londonderry BT47 2SX
Tel 01504 43674

Driver & Vehicle Testing Agency
Ballyboley Road
Ballyloran
Larne BT40 2SY
Tel 01574 278808
Driver & Vehicle Testing Agency
Granite House
Mary Street
Newry

Enterprise Ulster
The Close
Ravenhill Reach
Belfast BT6 8RB
Tel 01232 736400
Fax 01232 736404

Environment & Heritage Service
Commonwealth House
35 Castle Street
Belfast BT1 1GU
Tel 01232 251477
Fax 01232 546660

Equal Opportunities Commission
for Northern Ireland
22 Great Victoria Street
Belfast BT2 7BA
Tel 01232 242752
Fax 01232 331047

Fair Employment Commission for
Northern Ireland
60 Great Victoria Street
Belfast BT2 7BB
Tel 01232 240020
Fax 01232 331544

Fisheries Conservancy Board for
Northern Ireland
1 Mahon Road
Portadown
Craigavon
Co Armagh BT62 3EE
Tel 01762 334666
Fax 01762 338912

Forensic Science Agency of
Northern Ireland
151 Belfast Road
Carrickfergus
Co Antrim BT38 8PL
Tel 01232 365744
Fax 01232 365727
E-mail FSANI@NICS,GOV.UK
Web www.fsani.org

Foyle Fisheries Commission
8 Victoria Road
Londonderry BT47 2AB
Tel 01504 342100
Fax 01504 342720

General Consumer Council for
Northern Ireland
Elizabeth House
116 Holywood Road
Belfast BT4 1NY
Tel 01232 672488
Fax 01232 657701
E-mail gcc@nics.gov.uk

Government Purchasing Agency
Annex 6
Castle Buildings
Upper Newtownards
Belfast BT4 3TP
Tel 01232 526391
Fax 01232 526564

Health Estates
Stoney Road
Dundonald
Belfast BT16 0US
Tel 01232 520025
Independent Commission for
Police Complaints for Northern
Ireland
Chamber of Commerce House
22 Great Victoria Street
Belfast BT2 7LP
Tel 01232 244821
Fax 01232 248563

Independent Television
Commission
75 Great Victoria Street
Belfast BT2 7AF
Tel 01232 248733
Fax 01232 322828

Industrial Research & Technology
Unit
17 Antrim Road
Lisburn
Co Antrim BT28 3AL
Tel 01846 623000
Fax 01846 623119

Inland Revenue
Dorchester House
52/58 Great Victoria Street
Belfast BT2 7QE
Tel 01232 245123

Labour Relations Agency
3 Foyle Street
Londonderry BT48 6AL
Tel 01504 269639
Fax 01504 267729

Labour Relations Agency
2-8 Gordon Street
Belfast BT1 2LG
Tel 01232 321442
Fax 01232 330827

Laganside Corporation
Clarendon Building
15 Clarendon Road
Belfast BT1 3BG
Tel 01232 328507
Fax 01232 332141
E-mail info@laganside.com
Web http://www.laganside.com

Land Registers of Northern Ireland
27-45 Great Victoria Street
Belfast BT2 7SL
Tel 01232 251512
Fax 01232 251550

Livestock & Meat Commission for
Northern Ireland
57 Malone Road
Belfast BT9 6SA
Tel 01232 590000
Fax 01232 590001

Local Enterprise Development Unit
25-27 Franklin Street
Belfast BT2 8DT
Tel 01232 242582
Fax 01232 249730

Local Enterprise Development Unit
6-7 The Mall
Newry BT34 1BX
Tel 01693 62955
Fax 01693 65358
E-mail sro@ledu.btinternet.com

Local Enterprise Development Unit
Kevlin Buildings
47 Kevin Avenue
Omagh BT78 1ER
Tel 01662 245763
Fax 01662 244291
E-mail wro@ledu.binternet.com

Local Enterprise Development Unit
LEDU House
Upper Galwally
Belfast BT8 6TB
Tel 01232 491031
Fax 01232 691432
E-mail ledu@ledu-ni.gov.uk
Web www.ledu-ni.gov.uk

Local Enterprise Development Unit
13 Shipquay Street
Londonderry BT48 6DJ
Tel 01504 267257
Fax 01504 266054
E-mail nwro@ledu.binternet.com

Local Enterprise Development Unit
Clarence House
86 Mill Street
Ballymena BT43 5AF
Tel 01266 49215
Fax 01266 48427
E-mail nero@ledu.binternet.com

Mental Health Commission for
Northern Ireland
Elizabeth House
118 Holywood Road
Belfast BT4 1NY
Tel 01232 651157
Fax 01232 471180

National Board for Nursing,
Midwifery & Health Visiting for
Northern Ireland
Centre House
79 Chichester Street
Belfast BT1 4JE
Tel 01232 238152
Fax 01232 333298

National Lottery Charities Board
2nd Floor
Hildon House
30-34 Hill Street
Belfast BT1 2LB
Tel 01232 551455

Northern Ireland Child Support
Agency
Great Northern Tower
17 Great Victoria Street
Belfast BT2 7AD
Tel 01232 896666
Fax 01232 896850
E-mail CSA@nics.gov.uk
Web http://www.nics.gov.uk/csa/
index.ht

Northern Ireland Commissioner for
Protection Against Unlawful
Industrial Action
Scottish Legal House
65-67 Chichester Street
Belfast BT1 4JT
Tel 01232 233640
Fax 01232 237787

Northern Ireland Commissioner for
the Rights of Trade Union
Members
Scottish Legal House
65-67 Chichester Street
Belfast BT1 4JT
Tel 01232 233640
Fax 01232 237787

Northern Ireland Committee on
Telecommunications
7th Floor
Chamber of Commerce House
22 Great Victoria Street
Belfast BT2 7QA
Tel 01232 244113
Fax 01232 247024

Northern Ireland Council for
Postgraduate Medical & Dental
Education
5 Annadale Avenue
Belfast BT7 3JH
Tel 01232 491731
Fax 01232 642279

Northern Ireland Council for the
Curriculum, Examinations &
Assessment
Clarendon Dock
29 Clarendon Road
Belfast BT1 3BG
Tel 01232 261200
Fax 01232 261234
E-mail info@ccea.org.uk
Web http://www.ccea.org.uk

Northern Ireland Fishery Harbour
Authority
3 St Patrick's Avenue
Downpatrick
Co Down BT30 6DW
Tel 01396 613844

Northern Ireland Local
Government Officers'
Superannuation Committee
Templeton House
411 Holywood Road
Belfast BT4 2LP
Tel 01232 768025
Fax 01232 768790
E-mail
100670.733@compuserve.com

Northern Ireland Museums'
Council
66 Donegall Pass
Belfast BT7 1BU
Tel 01232 550215
Fax 01232 550216

Northern Ireland Prison Service
Dundonald House
Upper Newtownards Road
Belfast BT4 3SU
Tel 01232 520700
Fax 01232 525160

Northern Ireland Statistics &
Research Agency
The Arches Centre
11-13 Bloomfield Avenue
Belfast BT5 5HD
Tel 01232 520400
Fax 01232 526948
E-mail
pauline.wilson@dfpni.gov.uk
Web www.nics.gov.uk/nisra/
index.htm

Northern Ireland Tourist Board
St Anne's Court
59 North Street
Belfast BT1 1NB
Tel 01232 231221
Fax 01232 240960

Northern Ireland Transport Holding
Company
Chamber of Commerce House
22 Great Victoria Street
Belfast BT2 7LX
Tel 01232 243456
Fax 01232 333845

Office for the Regulation of
Electricity & Gas
Brookmount Buildings
42 Fountain Street
Belfast BT1 5EE
Tel 01232 311575/314212
Fax 01232 311740
E-mail ofreg@nics.gov.uk
Web ofreg.nics.gov.uk

Ordnance Survey of Northern
Ireland
54 Stone Row
Coleraine BT52 1ER
Tel 01265 43622

Ordnance Survey of Northern
Ireland
Crown Buildings
10 Alexander Road
Armagh BT6 7JL
Tel 01762 529805

Ordnance Survey of Northern
Ireland
Colby House
Stranmillis Court
Belfast BT9 5BJ
Tel 01232 255755
Fax 01232 255700
E-mail
100635,2165@compuserve.com

Ordnance Survey of Northern
Ireland
Boaz House
15 Scarffes Entry
Omagh BT78 1JE
Tel 01662 254734

Planning Service
Clarence Court
10-18 Adelaide Street
Belfast BT2 8GB
Tel 01232 540540
Fax 01232 540665
E-mail
planning.service.hq@nics.gov.uk

Police Authority for Northern
Ireland
River House
48 High Street
Belfast BT1 2DR
Tel 01232 230111
Fax 01232 245098
E-mail
information.pani@nics.gov.uk
Web http://www.pani.org.uk

Post Office Users' Council for
Northern Ireland
7th Floor
Chamber of Commerce House
22 Great Victoria Street
Belfast BT2 7PJ
Tel 01232 244113
Fax 01232 247024

Probation Board for Northern
Ireland
80-90 North Street
Belfast BT1 1LD
Tel 01232 262400
Fax 01232 262470

Public Record Office of Northern
Ireland
66 Balmoral Avenue
Belfast BT9 6NY
Tel 01232 251318
Fax 01232 255999
E-mail proni@nics.gov.uk
Web http://proni.nics.gov.uk/
index.htm

Rate Collection Agency
Oxford House
49-55 Chichester Street
Belfast BT1 4HH
Tel 01232 252252
Fax 01232 252113
E-mail
dennis.millar.doe@nics.gov.uk

Rivers Agency
37 Castlerock Road
Coleraine
Co Londonderry BT51 3RL
Tel 01265 42357
Fax 01265 320628

Rivers Agency
Ravarnet House
Altona Road
Lisburn
Co Antrim BT27 5QB
Tel 01846 606100
Fax 01846 606111

Rivers Agency
Ballinamallard
Enneskillen
Co Fermanagh BT94 2NA
Tel 01365 388529
Fax 01365 388972

Rivers Agency
44 Seagoe Industrial Estate
Craigavon
Co Armagh BT63 5QE
Tel 01762 336213
Fax 01762 391779

Rivers Agency
Woodside Avenue
Gortin Road
Omagh
Co Tyrone BT79 7BS
Tel 01662 242623
Fax 01662 247871

Rivers Agency
Hydebank
4 Hospital Road
Belfast BT8 8JP
Tel 01232 253440
Fax 01232 253455

Roads Service
County Hall
Castlerock Road
Coleraine BT51 3HS
Tel 01265 41300
Fax 01265 41430

Roads Service
County Hall
182 Galgorm Road
Ballymena BT42 1QG
Tel 01266 653333
Fax 01266 662510

Roads Service
Rathkeltair House
Market Street
Downpatrick BT30 6AJ
Tel 01396 612211
Fax 01396 618188

Roads Service
Hydebank
4 Hospital Road
Belfast BT8 8JL
Tel 01232 253000
Fax 01232 253220

Roads Service
Marlborough House
Central Way
Craigavon BT64 1AD
Tel 01762 341144
Fax 01762 341867

Roads Service
Clarence Court
10-18 Adelaide Street
Belfast BT2 8GB
Tel 01232 540540
Fax 01232 540024
E-mail
roads.service.dir@nics.gov.uk
Web www.nics.gov.uk/doeroads

Roads Service
County Hall
Drumragh Avenue
Omagh BT79 9RF
Tel 01662 254280
Fax 01662 254010

Social Security Agency (Northern
Ireland)
Castle Buildings
Stormont
Belfast BT4 3SJ
Tel 01232 520520
Fax 01232 523337
E-mail ssa@nics.gov.uk
Web http://ssa.nics.gov.uk

Sports Council for Northern Ireland
House of Sport
Upper Malone Road
Belfast BT9 5LA
Tel 01232 381222
Fax 01232 682757

Training & Employment Agency
(NI)
39-49 Adelaide Street
Belfast BT2 8FD
Tel 01232 257777
Fax 01232 257778

Ulster Museum
Botanic Gardens
Stranmillis Road
Belfast BT9 5AB
Tel 01232 383000
Fax 01232 383003

Valuation & Lands Agency
Boaz House
15 Scarffe's Entry
Omagh BT78 1JG
Tel 01662 254888
Fax 01662 254880

Valuation & Lands Agency
Queen's Court
56-66 Upper Queen Street
Belfast BT1 6FD
Tel 01232 250700
Fax 01232 543750
Web http://222.nics.gov.uk/vla/

Valuation & Lands Agency
Crown Buildings
Hamilton Road
Bangor BT20 4LQ
Tel 01247 279111
Fax 01247 471644

Valuation & Lands Agency
Waterside House
75 Duke Street
Londonderry BT47 1FP
Tel 01504 319000
Fax 01504 319087

Valuation & Lands Agency
Marlborough House
Central Way
Craigavon BT64 1AD
Tel 01762 341144
Fax 01762 341867

Valuation & Lands Agency
1 The Sidings
Antrim Road
Lisburn BT28 3AJ
Tel 01846 677527
Fax 01846 603956

Valuation & Lands Agency
Government Offices
George Street
Ballymena BT43 5AP
Tel 01266 652 866/7
Fax 01266 630293

Water Service
Northland House
3 Frederick Street
Belfast BT1 2NR
Tel 01232 244711
Fax 01232 354888
E-mail water.service@nics.gov.uk

Youth Council for Northern Ireland
Lamont House
Purdy's Lane
Belfast BT8 4TA
Tel 01232 643882
Fax 01232 64374

# SCOTLAND

ACAS
Franborough House
123-157 Bothwell Street
Glasgow G2 7JR
Tel 0141 204 2677

Accounts Commission for Scotland
18 George Street
Edinburgh EH2 2QU
Tel 0131 447 1234
Fax 0131 477 4567
Web htttp://www.scot-ac.gov.uk

Argyll & The Islands Enterprise
The Enterprise Centre
Kilmory Industrial Estate
Lochgilphead PA31 8SH
Tel 01546 602281
Fax 01546 603964

Army Personnel Centre
Kentigern House
65 Brown Street
Glasgow G2 8EX
Tel 0141 224 2070
Fax 0141 224 2144

British Waterways
Canal House
Applecross Street
Glasgow G4 9SP
Tel 0141 332 6936

British Waterways
Canal Office
Seaport Marina
Muirtown Basin
Inverness IV3 5LS
Tel 01463 233140

British Waterways
Pier Square
Ardrishaig
Lochgilphead
Argyll PA30 8DZ
Tel 01546 603210

British Waterways
Station Road
Broxburn
West Lothian EH52 5PG
Tel 01506 852578

Caithness & Sutherland Enterprise
Scapa House
Castlegreen Road
Thurso
Caithness KW14 7LS
Tel 01847 896115
Fax 01847 893383

Caledonian MacBrayne Ltd
Ferry Terminal
The Pier
Gourock PA19 1QP
Tel 01475 650100
Fax 01475 637607
Web http://www.calmac.co.uk

Central Council for Education and
Training in Social Work
78/80 George Street
Edinburgh EH2 3BU
Tel 0131 220 0093
Fax 0131 220 6717

Channel Four Television
Corporation
227 West George Street
Glasgow G2 2ND
Tel 0141 568 7200
Fax 0141 568 7203

Child Support Agency
Parklands
Callendar Business Park
Callendar Road
Falkirk FK98 1SH
Tel 0345 136 000

Companies House
7 West George Street
Glasgow G2 1BQ
Tel 0141 221 5513

Companies House
37 Castle Terrace
Edinburgh EH1 2EB
Tel 0131 535 5800

Construction Industry Training
Board
Pritchard House
Grays Mill
32 Inglis Green Road
Edinburgh EH14 2ER
Tel 0131 443 8893
Fax 0131 443 1820

Construction Industry Training
Board
6 Queens Gate
Inverness IV1 1DA
Tel 01463 222893
Fax 01463 230868

Construction Industry Training
Board
4 Edison Street
Hillington
Glasgow G52 4XN
Tel 0141 810 3044
Fax 0141 882 1100

Criminal Injuries Compensation
Authority
Tay House
300 Bath Street
Glasgow G2 4JR
Tel 0141 331 2726
Fax 0141 331 2287

Crofters' Commission
4-6 Castle Wynd
Inverness IV2 3EQ
Tel 01463 663450
Fax 01463 711820

Defence Codification Agency
Kentigern House
65 Brown Street
Glasgow G2 8EX
Tel 0141 224 2066
Fax 0141 224 2148

Defence Estates Organisation
Hilton Road
Rosyth
Fife KY11 2BL
Tel 01383 648022

Defence Estates Organisation
EWSD Building 1207
HMB Clyde Faslane
Dunbartonshire G84 8HL
Tel 01436 674321

Defence Estates Organisation
Army HQ Scotland
Craigie Hall
South Queensferry
West Lothian H30 9TN
Tel 0131 310 2313

Dumfries & Galloway Enterprise
Solway House
Dumfries Enterprise Park
Tinwald Downs Road
Heathhall
Dumfries DG1 3SJ
Tel 01387 245000
Fax 01387 246224

Dunbartonshire Enterprise
2nd Floor
Spectrum House
Clydebank Business Park
Clydebank
Glasgow G81 2DR
Tel 0141 951 2121
Fax 0141 951 1907

East of Scotland Water
Woodlands
St Ninians Road
Stirling FK8 2HB

East of Scotland Water
West Grove
Waverley Road
Melrose TD6 9SJ

East of Scotland Water
Craig Mitchell House
Flemington Road
Glenrothes KY7 5QH

East of Scotland Water Authority
55 Buckstone Terrace
Edinburgh EH10 6XH

East of Scotland Water Authority
Pentland Gait
597 Calder Road
Edinburgh EH11 4HJ
Tel 0131 453 7500
Fax 0131 453 7527
E-mail info@esw.co.uk
Web http://www.esw.co.uk

Employment Tribunals Service
Inverlier House
2nd Floor
West North Street
Aberdeen AB24 5ES
Tel 01224 643307
Fax 01224 631551

Employment Tribunals Service
54/56 Melville Street
Edinburgh EH3 7HF
Tel 0131 226 5584
Fax 0131 220 6847

Employment Tribunals Service
Eagle Building
215 Bothwell Street
Glasgow G2 7TS
Tel 0141 204 0730
Fax 0141 204 0732

Employment Tribunals Service
13 Albert Square
Dundee DD1 1DD
Tel 01382 221 578
Fax 01382 227 136

Enterprise Ayrshire
17-19 Hill Street
Kilmarnock KA3 1HA
Tel 01563 526623
Fax 01563 543636

Fife Enterprise
Kingdom House
Saltire Centre
Glenrothes
Fife KY6 2AQ
Tel 01592 623000
Fax 01592 623149

Fisheries Research Services
Marine Laboratory
PO Box 101
Victoria Road
Aberdeen AB11 9DB
Tel 01224 878544
Fax 01224 875511
Web http://www.marlab.ac.uk

Forest Enterprise
231 Corstorphine Road
Edinburgh EH12 7AT
Tel 0131 314 6465
Fax 0131 314 4473
E-mail info@forestry.gov.uk
Web http://www.forestry.gov.uk

Forest Enterprise
55/57 Moffat Road
Dumfries DG1 1NP
Tel 01387 269171
Fax 01387 251491

Forest Enterprise
21 Church Street
Inverness IV1 1EL
Tel 01463 232811
Fax 01463 243846

Forest Research
Northern Research Station
Roslin
Midlothian
Midlothian EH25 9SY
Tel 0131 445 2176
Fax 0131 445 5124

Forth Valley Enterprise
Laurel House
Laurelhill Business Park
Stirling FK7 9JQ
Tel 01786 451919
Fax 01786 478123

FRS Freshwater Fisheries
Laboratory
Faskally
Pitlochry
Perthshire PH16 5LB
Tel 01796 472000
Fax 01796 473523

Gaming Board for Great Britain
Portcullis House
21 India Street
Glasgow G2 4PZ
Tel 0141 221 5537
Fax 0141 221 5494

Gas Consumers' Council
86 George Street
Edinburgh EH2 3BU
Tel 0131 226 6523
Fax 0131 220 3732

Glasgow Development Agency
50 Waterloo Street
Atrium Court
Glasgow G2 6HQ
Tel 0141 204 1111
Fax 0141 248 1600

Grampian Enterprise
27 Albyn Place
Aberdeen AB10 1DB
Tel 01224 575100
Fax 01224 213417

Hannah Research Institute
Ayr KA6 5HL
Tel 01292 674000
Fax 01292 674004

The Health & Safety Executive
375 West George Street
Glasgow G2 4LW
Tel 0141 275 3000
Fax 0141 275 3100

The Health & Safety Executive
Belford House
59 Belford Road
Edinburgh EH4 3UE
Tel 0131 247 2000
Fax 0131 247 2121

The Health & Safety Executive
Lord Cullen House
Fraser Place
Aberdeen AB9 1BU
Tel 01224 252652

Highlands & Islands Airports
Inverness Airport
Inverness IV1 2JB
Tel 01667 462445
Fax 01667 462579

Highlands & Islands Enterprise
Bridge House
20 Bridge Street
Inverness IV1 1QR
Tel 01463 234171
Fax 01463 244469
E-mail
HIE.GENERAL@hient.co.uk
Web www.hie.co.uk

Historic Scotland
Longmore House
Salisbury Place
Edinburgh EH9 1SH
Tel 0131 668 8600
Fax 0131 668 8741
Web www.historic-scotland.gov.uk

Independent Television
Commission
123 Blythswood St
Glasgow G2 4AN
Tel 0141 226 4436
Fax 0141 226 4682

Inland Revenue
80 Lauriston Place
Edinburgh EH3 9SL
Tel 0131 473 4100

Inland Revenue
Cumbernauld
Glasgow G70 5TR
Tel 01236 736121

Intervention Board
Room E1/5
Saughton House
Broomhouse Drive
Edinburgh EH11 3XA
Tel 0131 244 8382
Fax 0131 244 8117

Inverness & Nairn Enterprise
Castle Wynd
Inverness IV2 3DW
Tel 01463 713504
Fax 01463 712002

Lanarkshire Development Agency
New Lanarkshire House
Strathclyde Business Park
Willow Drive
Bellshill ML4 3AD
Tel 01698 745454
Fax 01698 842211

Lochaber Limited
St Mary's House
Gordon Square
Fort William PH33 6DY
Tel 01397 704326
Fax 01397 705309

Lothian and Edinburgh Enterprise
99 Haymarket Terrace
Apex House
Edinburgh EH12 5HD
Tel 0131 313 4000
Fax 0131 313 4231

Macaulay Land Use Research
Institute
Craigiebuckler
Aberdeen AB15 8QH
Tel 01224 318611
Fax 01224 311556
E-mail @mluri.sari.ac.uk
Web http://www.mluri.sari.ac.uk

Marine Safety Agency
Blaikies Quay
Aberdeen AB11 5EZ
Tel 01224 574122
Fax 01224 571920

Meat & Livestock Commission
West Mains Ingliston
Newbridge
Rural Centre
Midlothian EH28 8NZ
Tel 0131 472 4111
Fax 0131 472 4122

Meat Hygiene Service
Saughton House
Broomhouse Drive
Edinburgh EH11 3XD
Tel 0131 244 8441

Moray Badenoch & Strathspey
Enterprise
Elgin Business Centre
Elgin
Moray IV30 1RH
Tel 01343 550567
Fax 01343 550678

NARO Almondbank Division
Almondbank
Perth PH1 3NQ
Tel 01738 583301
Fax 01738 583163

National Board for Nursing,
Midwifery & Health Visiting for
Scotland
22 Queen Street
Edinburgh EH2 1NT
Tel 0131 226 7371
Fax 0131 225 9970
Web www.nbs.org.uk

National Galleries of Scotland
13 Heriot Row
Edinburgh EH3 6HP
Tel 0131 556 8921
Fax 0131 556 9972

National Gallery of Scotland
The Mound
Edinburgh

National Library of Scotland
George IV Bridge
Edinburgh EH1 IEW
Tel 0131 226 4531
Fax 0131 220 6662
Web http://www.nls.uk

National Lottery Charities Board
Norloch House
36 Kings Stables Road
Edinburgh EH1 2EJ
Tel 0131 221 7110

National Museums of Scotland
Chambers Street
Edinburgh EH1 IJF
Tel 0131 225 7532

National Savings
Boydstone Road
Glasgow G58 1SB
Tel 0141 649 4555

National Sports Centre
Inverclyde
Burnside
Largs
Ayrshire KA30 8RW
Tel 01475 674666
Fax 01475 674720

Naval Bases & Supply Agency
HM Naval Base
Clyde
Faslane
Helensburgh
Dunbartonshire G84 8HL
Tel 01436 674321

North of Scotland Water Authority
Cairngorm House
Beechwood Park North
Inverness IV2 3ED
Tel 01463 245400
Fax 01463 240489

Northern Lighthouse Board
84 George Street
Edinburgh EH2 3DA
Tel 0131 473 3100
Fax 0131 220 2093
E-mail NLB@dial.pipex.com

Office of Electricity Regulation
70 West Regent Street
Glasgow G2 2QZ
Tel 0141 331 2678

Orkney Enterprise
14 Queen Street
Kirkwall
Orkney KW15 1JE
Tel 01856 874638
Fax 01856 872915

Parole Board for Scotland
Saughton House
Broomhouse Drive
Edinburgh EH11 3XD
Tel 0131 244 8755
Fax 0131 244 6974
Post Office Users' Council for
Scotland
2 Greenside Lane
Edinburgh EH1 3AH
Tel 0131 244 5576
Fax 0131 244 5696

Queen Victoria School
Dunblane
Perthshire FK15 0JY
Tel 01786 822288

Rail Users Consultative Committee
for Scotland
249 West George Street
Glasgow G2 4QE
Tel 0141 221 7760
Fax 0141 221 3393

Registers of Scotland
Meadowbank House
153 London Road
Edinburgh EH8 7AU
Tel 0131 659 6111
Fax 0131 479 3688

Renfrewshire Enterprise
27 Causeyside Street
Paisley PA1 1UL
Tel 0141 848 0101
Fax 0141 848 6930

Ross & Cromarty Enterprise
62 High Street
Invergordon
Ross-shire IV18 0AA
Tel 01349 853666
Fax 01349 853833

Rowett Research Institute
Greenburn Road
Bucksburn
Aberdeen AB21 9SB
Tel 01224 712751
Fax 01224 715349
E-mail @rri.sari.ac.uk
Web http://www.rri.sari.ac.uk/

Royal Botanic Garden Edinburgh
20a Inverleith Row
Edinburgh EH3 5LR
Tel 0131 552 7171
Fax 0131 552  0382

Royal Commission on Ancient &
Historical Monuments of Scotland
John Sinclair House
16 Bernard Terrace
Edinburgh EH8 9NX
Tel 0131 662 1456
Fax 0131 662 1477/99
Web www.rcahms.gov.uk

Royal Observatory, Edinburgh
Blackford Hill
Edinburgh EH9 3HJ
Tel 0131 668 8100
Fax 0131 668 8264
E-mail sgp@roe.ac.uk

Royal Scottish Academy
Princess Street
Edinburgh

Scottish Advisory Committee on
Telecommunications
2 Greenside Lane
Edinburgh EH1 3AH
Tel 0131 244 5576
Fax 0131 244 5696

Scottish Agricultural Science
Agency
East Craigs
Edinburgh EH12 8NJ
Tel 0131 244 8890
Fax 0131 244 8940

Scottish Agricultural Wages Board
Pentland House
47 Robb's Loan
Edinburgh EH14 1TY
Tel 0131 244 6397
Fax 0131 244 6551

Scottish Arts Council
12 Manor Place
Edinburgh EH3 7DD
Tel 0131 226 6051
Fax 0131 225 9833
E-mail
help.desk.SAC@artsfb.org.uk
Web http://www.sac.org.uk

Scottish Borders Enterprise
Bridge Street
Galashiels TD1 1SW
Tel 01896 758991
Fax 01896 758625

Scottish Children's Reporter
Administration
Ochil House
Springkerse Business Park
Stirling FK7 7XE
Tel 01786 459500
Fax 01786 459532

Scottish Community Education
Council
9 Haymarket Terrace
Edinburgh EH12 5EZ
Tel 0131 313 2488
Fax 0131 313 6800

Scottish Consumer Council
Royal Exchange House
100 Queen Street
Glasgow G1 3DN
Tel 0141 226 5261
Fax 0141 221 0731
E-mail
101346.3164@compuserve.com

Scottish Conveyancing & Executry
Services Board
Mulberry House
16-22 Picardy Place
Edinburgh EH1 3YT
Tel 0131 556 1945
Fax 0131 556 8428

Scottish Council for Educational
Technology
74 Victoria Crescent Road
Glasgow G12 9JN
Tel 0141 337 5001
Fax 0141 337 5050
E-mail scet@scet.org.uk
Web http://www.scet.org.uk

Scottish Court Service
Hayweight House
23 Lauriston Street
Edinburgh EH3 9DQ
Tel 0131 221 6823
Fax 0131 221 6895

Scottish Crop Research Institute
Mylnefield
Invergowrie
Dundee DD2 5DA
Tel 01382 562731
Fax 01382 562426
E-mail mail@scri.sari.ac.uk
Web http://www.scri.sari.ac.uk

Scottish Enterprise
120 Bothwell Street
Glasgow G2 7JP
Tel 0141 248 2700
Fax 0141 221 3217
E-mail scotentcsd@scotent.co.uk
Web http://www.scotent.co.uk

Scottish Enterprise Tayside
45 North Lindsay Street
Dundee DD1 1HT
Tel 01382 223100
Fax 01382 201319

Scottish Environment Protection
Agency
Erskine Court
The Castle Business Park
Stirling FK9 4TR
Tel 01786 457700
Fax 01786 446885
E-mail
monica.straughan@sepa.org.uk
Web http://www.sepa.org.uk

Scottish Environment Protection
Agency
Graesser House
Fodderty Way
Dingwall Business Park
Dingwall IV15 9XB
Tel 01349 862021
Fax 01349 863987

Scottish Environment Protection
Agency
Clearwater House
Heriot Watt Research Park
Avenue North
Riccarton
Edinburgh EH14 4AP
Tel 0131 449 7296
Fax 0131 449 7277

Scottish Environment Protection
Agency
Rivers House
MUrray Road
East Kilbride G75 0LA
Tel 01355 574200
Fax 01355 264323

Scottish Fisheries Protection
Agency
Longman House
Longman Road
Inverness
Tel 01463 713955

Scottish Fisheries Protection
Agency
Pentland House
47 Robb's Loan
Edinburgh EH14 1TY
Tel 0131 244 6093
Fax 0131 244 6471

Scottish Fisheries Protection
Agency
Russel House
King Street
Ayr
Tel 01292 610177

Scottish Fisheries Protection
Agency
5 Albert Quay
Aberdeen
Tel 01224 211446

Scottish Further Education Unit
Argyll Court
The Castle Business Park
Stirling FK9 4TY
Tel 01786 892000
Fax 01786 892001
E-mail sfeu@sfeu.demon.co.uk

Scottish Higher Education Funding
Council
97 Haymarket Terrace
Edinburgh EH12
Tel 0131 313 6500

Scottish Homes
Mercantile Chambers
53 Bothwell Street
Glasgow G2 6TS
Tel 0141 248 7177

Scottish Homes
Temperance House
8 Lint Riggs
Falkirk FK1 1DG
Tel 01324 613376

Scottish Homes
Highlander House
53 Waterloo Street
Glasgow G2 7DA
Tel 0141 226 4611

Scottish Homes
St James House
25 St James Street
Paisley PA3 2HQ
Tel 0141 889 8896

Scottish Homes
52/66 Newmarket Street
Ayr KA7 1LR
Tel 01292 611810

Scottish Homes
Rex House
Bothwell Road
Hamilton ML3 0DW
Tel 01698 420042

Scottish Homes
Nethergate Business Centre
Dundee DD1 4BU
Tel 01382 202211

Scottish Homes
Urquhart House
Beechwood Park
Inverness IV2 3BW
Tel 01463 711272

Scottish Homes
Carlyle House
Carlyle Road
Kirkcaldy KY1 1DB
Tel 01592 641055

Scottish Homes
Thistle House
91 Haymarket Terrace
Edinburgh EH12 5HE
Tel 0131 313 0044
Fax 0131 313 2680

Scottish Homes
147 Fintry Drive
Dundee DD4 9HE
Tel 01382 504317

Scottish Homes
Rosebery House
9 Haymarket Terrace
Edinburgh EH12 5YA
Tel 0131 313 0044

Scottish Hospital Endowments
Research Trust
Saltire Court
20 Castle Terrace
Edinburgh EH1 2EF
Tel 0131 228 8111
Fax 0131 228 8118

The Scottish Legal Aid Board
44 Drumsheugh Gardens
Edinburgh EH3 7SW
Tel 0131 226 7061
Fax 0131 220 4878

Scottish Medical Practices
Committee
Trinity Park House
South Trinity Road
Edinburgh EH5 3PY
Tel 0131 551 6255
Fax 0131 551 4305

Scottish National Sports Centre
Cumbrae
Isle of Cumbrae
Ayrshire KA28 0HQ
Tel 01475 530757
Fax 01475 530013

Scottish National Gallery of
ModernArt
Belford Road
Edinburgh

Scottish National Portrait Gallery
1 Queen Street
Edinburgh

Scottish National Sports Centre
Glenmore Lodge
Aviemore
Inverness-shire PH22 1QU
Tel 01479 861256
Fax 01479 861212

Scottish Natural Heritage
Battleby
Redgorton
Perth PH1 3EW
Tel 01738 444177
Fax 01738 442060

Scottish Natural Heritage
Mariner Court
Clydebank Business Park
Caspian House
Clydebank G81 2NR
Tel 0141 951 4488
Fax 0141 951 8948

Scottish Natural Heritage
Bankend Road
Carmont House
The Crichton
Dumfries DG1 4ZF
Tel 01387 247010
Fax 01387 259247

Scottish Natural Heritage
Alexandra Wharf
Lerwick
Ground Floor
Stewart Building
Shetland ZE1 0LL
Tel 01595 693345
Fax 01595 692565

Scottish Natural Heritage
Fodderly Way
Dingwall Business Park
Dingwall IV15 9XB
Tel 01349 865333
Fax 01349 865609

Scottish Natural Heritage
Dalkeith Country Park
Dalkeith
Laundry House
Midlothian EH22 2NA
Tel 0131 654 2466
Fax 0131 654 2477

Scottish Natural Heritage
The Beta Centre
University of Stirling
Innovation Park
Stirling FK9 4NF
Tel 01786 450362
Fax 01786 451974

Scottish Natural Heritage
12 Hope Terrace
Edinburgh EH9 2AS
Tel 0131 447 4784
Fax 0131 446 2277

Scottish Natural Heritage
16/17 Rubislaw Terrace
Aberdeen AB1 1XE
Tel 01224 642863
Fax 01224 635020

Scottish Natural Heritage
Main Street
Golspie
Sutherland KW10 6TG
Tel 01408 633602
Fax 01408 633071

Scottish Natural Heritage
The Parade
Fort William
The Governor's House
Inverness-shire PH33 6BA
Tel 01397 704716
Fax 01397 700303

Scottish Natural Heritage
32 Francis Street
Stornoway
Isle of Lewis HS1 2ND
Tel 01851 705258
Fax 01851 704900

Scottish Office Pensions Agency
St Margaret's House
151 London Road
Edinburgh EH8 7TG
Tel 0131 244 3585
Fax 0131 244 3334
E-mail
Derek.Smith@sopoi.scottoff.gov.u
Web www.scotland.gov.uk

# Q & Q

Scottish Prison Service
Calton House
5 Redheughs Rigg
Edinburgh EH12 9HW
Tel 0131 244 8400
Fax 0131 244 8476

Scottish Qualifications Authority
Hanover House
24 Douglas St
Glasgow G2 7NQ
Tel 0141 248 7900
Fax 0141 242 2244

Scottish Qualifications Authority
Ironmills Road
Dalkeith
Midlothian EH22 ILE
Tel 0131 663 6601
Fax 0131 654 2664

Scottish Record Office
HM General Register House
Edinburgh EH1 3YY
Tel 0131 535 1314
Fax 0131 535 1360

Scottish Screen
74 Victoria Crescent Road
Glasgow G12 9JN
Tel 0141 302 1700
Fax 0141 302 1711
E-mail
info@scottishscreen.demon.co.uk
Web
www.scottishscreen.demon.co.uk

Scottish Sports Council
Caledonia House
South Gyle
Edinburgh EH12 9DQ
Tel 0131 317 7200
Fax 0131 317 7202

Scottish Tourist Board
23 Ravelston Terrace
Edinburgh EH4 3EU
Tel 0131 332 2433
Fax 0131 315 2906
E-mail graham.birse@stb.gov.uk
Web www.holiday.scotland.net

Scottish Tourist Board
Thistle House
Beechwood Park North
Inverness IV2 3ED

Scottish Water & Sewerage
Customers Council
Ochil House
Springkerse Business Park
Stirling FK7 7XE
Tel 01786 430200
Fax 01786 462018

Sea Fish Industry Authority
18 Logie Mill
Logie Green Road
Edinburgh EH7 4HG
Tel 0131 558 3331
Fax 0131 558 1442
E-mail seafish.co.uk

Shetland Enterprise
Toll Clock Shopping Centre
26 North Road
Lerwick
Shetland ZE1 0DE
Tel 01595 693177
Fax 01595 693208

Skye & Lochalsh Enterprise
King's House
The Green
Portree
Isle of Skye IV51 9BS
Tel 01478 612841
Fax 01478 612164

Student Awards Agency for
Scotland
Gyleview House
3 Redheughs Rigg
Edinburgh EH12 9HH
Tel 0131 244 5823
Fax 0131 244 5887

Student Loans Company
100 Bothwell Street
Glasgow G2 7JD
Tel 0141 306 2000
Fax 0141 306 2006
Web http://www.slc.co.uk

UK Atomic Energy Authority
Dounreay
Nr Thurso
Caithness KW14 7T
Tel 01847 804000

Veterinary Laboratories Agency
Bush State
Penicuik
Midlothian EH26 0SA
Tel 0131 445 5371
Fax 0131 445 5504

West of Scotland Water Authority
419 Balmore Road
Glasgow G22 6NU
Tel 0141 355 5333

Western Isles Enterprise
3 Harbour View
Cromwell Street Quay
Stornaway
Isle of Lewis HS1 2DF
Tel 01851 703703
Fax 01851 704130

## WALES

ACAS
3 Purbeck House
Lambourne Crescent
Llanishen
Cardiff CF4 5GJ
Tel 01222 761126

Agricultural Wages Board for
England & Wales
Penrallt
Caernarfon
Gwynedd LL55 1EP
Tel 01286 674144

Agricultural Wages Board for
England & Wales
Government Buildings
Picton Terrace
Carmarthen SA31 3BT
Tel 01267 234545

Agricultural Wages Board for
England & Wales
Government Buildings
Spa Road East
Llandrindod Wells
Powys LD1 5HA
Tel 01597 823777

Arts Council of Wales
Museum Place
Cardiff CF1 3NX
Tel 01222 336500
Fax 01222 221447

Arts Council of Wales
6 Gardd Llydaw
Jackson Lane
Carmarthen SA31 1QD
Tel 01267 234248
Fax 01267 233084

Arts Council of Wales
36 Princes Drive
Colwyn Bay LL29 8LA
Tel 01492 533440
Fax 01492 533677

Audit Commission
2nd Floor
2-4 Park Grove
Cardiff CF1 3PA

British Waterways
The Wharf
Govilon
Abergavenny
Gwent NP7 9NY
Tel 01873 830328

Cadw
Crown Building
Cathays Park
Cardiff CF1 3NQ
Tel 01222 500200
Fax 01222 826375

Cardiff Bay Development
Corporation
Baltic House
Mount Stuart Square
Cardiff CF1 6DH
Tel 01222 585858
Fax 01222 488924

CEFAS
Bernarth Road
Conwi
North Wales LL32 8UB
Tel 01492 593883
Fax 01492 592123

Central Council for Education and
Training in Social Work
2nd Floor
West Ring
Southgate House
Wood Street
Cardiff CF1 1EW
Tel 01222 226257
Fax 01222 384764

Companies House
Crown Way
Maindy
Cardiff CF4 3UZ
Tel 01222 388588
Fax 01222 380323

Construction Industry Training
Board
Units 4 & 5
Bridgend Business Centre
David Street
Bridgend Industrial Estate
Bridgend
Mid-Glamorgan CF31 3SH
Tel 01656 655226
Fax 01656 655232

Countryside Council for Wales
Plas Penrhos
Ffordd Penrhos
Bangor
Gwynedd LL57 2LQ
Tel 01248 385500
Web http://www.ccw.gov.uk

Defence Estates Organisation
The Barrack
Brecon
Powys LD3 7EA
Tel 01874 613 2880

Driver & Vehicle Licensing Agency
Longview Road
Morriston
Swansea SA6 7JL
Tel 01792 782341
Fax 01792 782472

Employment Tribunals Service
Caradog House
1-6 St Andrews Place
Cardiff CF1 3BE
Tel 01222 372693
Fax 01222 225906

The Environment Agency
Rivers House
Plas-yr-Afon
St Mellons
Cardiff CF3 0LT
Tel 01222 770088
Fax 01222 798555

Farming & Rural Conservation
Agency
St Agnes Road
Gabalfa
Cardiff CF4 4FR
Tel 01222 586530
Fax 01222 586763

Forensic Science Laboratory
Usk Road
Chepstow
Gwent NP6 6YE
Tel 01291 628141
Fax 01291 629482

Forest Enterprise
Victoria Terrace
Aberystwyth
Ceredigion SY23 2DQ
Tel 01970 612367
Fax 01970 625282

Further Education Funding Council
for Wales
Linden Court
The Orchards
Ty Glas Avenue
Llanishen
Cardiff CF4 5DZ
Tel 01222 761861
Fax 01222 763163

Gas Consumers' Council
Caradog House
1-6 St Andrew's Place
Cardiff CF1 3BE
Tel 01222 226547
Fax 01222 238611

The Health & Safety Executive
Brunel House
2 Fitzalan Road
Cardiff CF2 1SH
Tel 01222 263000
Fax 01222 263120

Higher Education Funding Council
for Wales
Linden Court
The Orchards
Ty Glas Avenue
Llanishen
Cardiff CF4 5DZ
Tel 01222 761861
Fax 01222 763163

HM Land Registry
Ty Cwm Tawe
Phoenix Way
Llansamlet
Swansea SA7 9FQ
Tel 01792 458877

HM Land Registry
Ty Bryn Glas
High Street
Swansea SA1 1PW
Tel 01792 458877

Independent Television
Commission
2nd Floor
Elgin House
106 St Mary Street
Cardiff CF1 1PA
Tel 01222 384541
Fax 01222 223157

Inland Revenue
Ty Glas
Llanishen
Cardiff CF4 5TS
Tel 01222 755789

Insolvency Service
5th Floor
Sun Aliance House
166-167 St Helens Road
Swansea SA1 5DL
Tel 01792 642861
Fax 01792 644235

Insolvency Service
3rd Floor
Hayes House
The Hayes
Cardiff CF1 2UG
Tel 01222 230575/232381
Fax 01222 342148

Legal Aid Board
Marland House
Central Square
Cardiff CF1 1PF
Tel 01222 388971
Fax 01222 238959

Marine Safety Agency
Parc Ty Glas
Llanishen
Cardiff CF4 5JA
Tel 01222 747333
Fax 01222 747877

Meat & Livestock Commission
21a North Parade
Aberystwyth
Ceredigion SY23 2JL
Tel 01970 625050
Fax 01970 615148

Meat Hygiene Service
3rd Floor West
Welsh Office
Cathays Park
Cardiff CF1 3NQ
Tel 01222 825549

National Library of Wales
Aberystwyth
Ceredigion SY23 3BU
Tel 01970 632800
Fax 01970 615709
Web http://www.llgc.org.uk

National Lottery Charities Board
Ladywell House
Newtown
Powys SY16 1JB
Tel 01686 621644

National Museums & Galleries of
Wales
Cathays Park
Cardiff CF1 3NP
Tel 01222 397951
Fax 01222 573321

National Portrait Gallery
Bodelwyeldam Castle
Bodelwyeldam
Clywd LL18 5YA

Office for National Statistics
Cardiff Road
Newport
Gwent NP9 1XG
Tel 01633 815696
Fax 01633 815599

Office of Electricity Regulation
5th Floor, West Wing
St David's House
Wood Street
Cardiff CF1 1ES
Tel 01222 228388

Ofwat Customer Service
Committee for Wales
Room 140
Caradog House
1-6 St Andrews Place
Cardiff CF1 3BE
Tel 01222 239852
Fax 01222 239847
E-mail wlcsc@ofwat.gtnet.gov.uk
Web http://www.open.gov.uk/ofwat

Patent Office
Concept House
Cardiff Rd
Newport NP9 1RH
Tel 01633 814000
Fax 01633 814444
E-mail enquiries@patent.gov.uk

The Planning Inspectorate
Room 1-004
Cathays Park
Cardiff CF1 3NQ
Tel 01222 825670

Post Office Users' Council for
Wales
Caradog House
1-6 St Andrews Place
Cardiff CF1 3BE
Tel 01222 374028
Fax 01222 668536

Qualifications, Curriculum &
Assessment Authority for Wales
Castle Buildings
Womanby Street
Cardiff CF1 9SX
Tel 01222 375400
Fax 01222 343612
E-mail
acac.cardiff@campus.bt.com

Rail Users Consultative Committee
for Wales
St David's House
Wood Street
Cardiff CF1 1ES
Tel 01222 227247
Fax 01222 223992

Remploy Limited
Bruce Road
Swansea West Industrial Park
Fforestfach
Swansea SA5 4HY
Tel 01792 560100
Fax 01492 560109

Residuary Body for Wales
Ffynon-Las
Ty Glas Avenue
Llanishen
Cardiff CF4 5DZ
Tel 01222 681244
Fax 01222 681308

Royal Commission on Ancient &
Historical Monuments in Wales
Plas Crug
Aberystwyth
Ceredigion SY23 1NJ
Tel 01970 621233
Fax 01970 627701

Royal Mint
Llantrisant
Pontyclun
Mid-Glamorgan CF72 8YT
Tel 01443 222111
Fax 01443 623190

S4C
Parc Ty Glas
Llanishen
Cardiff CT4 5DU
Tel 01222 747444
Fax 01222 754444
E-mail S4C@S4C.co.uk
Web http://www.s4c.co.uk

The Sports Council for Wales
Sophia Gardens
Cardiff CF1 9SW
Tel 01222 300500
Fax 01222 300600

Tai Cymru
25/30 Lambourne Crescent
Llanishen
Cardiff CF4 5ZJ
Tel 01222 741500
Fax 01222 741501
Web http://www/tc-hfw.gov.uk

Veterinary Laboratories Agency
Y Buarth
Aberystwyth
Ceredigion SY23 1ND
Tel 01970 612374
Fax 01970 612424

Veterinary Laboratories Agency
Job's Well Road
Johnstown
Carmarthen SA31 3EZ
Tel 01267 235244
Fax 01267 236549

Wales Tourist Board
Brunel House
2 Fitzalan Road
Cardiff CF2 1UY
Tel 01222 499909
Fax 01222 485031

Welsh Advisory Committee on
Telecommunications
Caradog House
1-6 St Andrews Place
Cardiff CF1 3BE
Tel 01222 374028
Fax 01222 668536

Welsh Consumer Council
5th Floor
Longcross Court
47 Newport Road
Cardiff CF2 1WL
Tel 01222 396 056
Fax 01222 238360

Welsh Development Agency
Llys-y-Ddraig
Penllergaer Business Park
Penllergaer
Swansea SA4 1HL

Welsh Development Agency
QED Centre
Main Avenue
Treforest Estate
Treforest CF37 5YR

Welsh Development Agency
Unit 7
St Asaph Business Park
Glascoed Road
St Asaph LL17 0LJ

Welsh Development Agency
Principality House
The Friary
Cardiff CF1 4AE
Tel 01443 845500
Fax 01443 845589
E-mail enquiries@wda.co.uk
Web http://www.wda.co.uk

Welsh Language Board
Market Chambers
5-7 St Mary Street
Cardiff CF1 2AT
Tel 01222 224744
Fax 01222 224577
E-mail ymholiadau@bwrdd-yr-
iaith.org.uk
Web http://www.netwales.co.uk/
byig

Welsh National Board for Nursing,
Midwifery & Health Visiting
2nd Floor
Golate House
101 St Mary Street
Cardiff CF1 1DX
Tel 01222 261400
Fax 01222 2611499

# OVERSEAS

Commonwealth Development
Corporation
PO Box 4332
Jakarta 12043
Indonesia
Tel 00 62 21 5254993
Fax 00 62 21 5254902
E-mail cdc@infoasia.net.id

Commonwealth Development
Corporation
PO Box 10494
50714 Kuala Lumpur
Malaysia
Tel 00 60 3 2014088
Fax 00 60 3 2021162
E-mail
malaysia@mail.malaysia.cdc.co.uk

Commonwealth Development
Corporation
PO Box 907
Port Moresby
Granville
Papua New Guinea
Tel 00 675 321 2944/2881
Fax 00 675 321 2867/320
E-mail png@mail.png.cdc.co.uk

Commonwealth Development
Corporation
PO Box 43233
Nairobi
Kenya
Tel 00 254 2 219952
Fax 00 254 1 219744
E-mail
kenya@mail.kenya.cdc.co.uk

Commonwealth Development
Corporation
PO Box 2653
Bangkok 10501
Thailand
Tel 00 662 6519200/6
Fax 00 662 651 9207
E-mail
thailand@mail.thailand.cdc.uk

Commonwealth Development
Corporation
Thapar Niketan
Bangalore 560 025
7/4 Brunton Road
South India
Tel 00 9180 555 0651
Fax 00 9180 555 0592
E-mail
sindia@mail.sindia.cdc.co.uk

Commonwealth Development
Corporation
5F Taipan Place
Emerald Avenue
Ortigas Centre
Pasig City
Metro Manila
Philippines
Tel 00 63 2 6374701
Fax 00 63 2 6374704
E-mail philippine@cdc.co.uk

Commonwealth Development
Corporation
Advanced Business Center
144, Maker Chambers VI
Nariman Point
Mumbal 400 021
India
Tel 00 91 22 2832924
Fax 00 91 22 2040211

Commonwealth Development
Corporation
First Floor
Bahria Complex II
MT Khan Road
Karachi 74000
Pakistan
Tel 00 92 21 5610091
Fax 00 92 21 5611891
E-mail
pakistan@mail.pakistan.cdc.co.uk

Commonwealth Development
Corporation
PO Box 23
Kingston
Jamaica
Tel 001 876 9261164
Fax 001 876 9261166
E-mail
jamaica@mail.jamaica.cdc.co.uk

Commonwealth Development
Corporation
PO Box 7100
Santa Cruz
Bolivia
Tel 00 591 3 546 900
Fax 00 591 3 546 901
E-mail bolivia@cdc.co.uk

Commonwealth Development
Corporation
311 Calle 22
Miramar
Havana
Cuba
Tel 00 537 244468
Fax 00 537 244460
E-mail cdc@cenial.inf.cu

Commonwealth Development
Corporation
PO Box 1657
Maputo
Mozambique
Tel 00 258 1 421325
Fax 00 258 1 422150
E-mail
mozambique@mail.mozambique.cdc.c

Commonwealth Development
Corporation
Apartado 721-1000
Oficentro Ejecutivo La Sabana
Edificio no.7 Piso no.6
Sabana Sur
San Jose
Costa Rica
Tel 00 506 290 5510
Fax 00 506 290 5212
E-mail comdevco@sol.racsa.co.cr

Commonwealth Development
Corporation
11 Golf Links
New Delhi 110 003
India
Tel 00 91 11 4691691
Fax 00 91 11 4691693
E-mail india@mail.india.cdc.co.uk

Commonwealth Development
Corporation
PO Box C 1748
Cantonments
Accra
Ghana
Tel 00 233 21 226677
Fax 00 233 21 238407

Commonwealth Development
Corporation
PO Box 30397
Lilongwe 3
Malawi
Tel 00 265 780410
Fax 00 265 780585

Commonwealth Development
Corporation
PO Box 51906
Ikoyi
Lagos
Nigeria
Tel 00 234 1 2624401
Fax 00 234 1 610023
E-mail
nigeria@mail.london.cdc.co.uk

Commonwealth Development
Corporation
6th Floor (North)
Safura Tower
20 Karmal Ataturk Avenue
Banani
Dhaka 1213
Bangladesh
Tel 00 880 2 873080
Fax 00 880 2 881016
E-mail
bangladesh@mail.bangladesh.cdc.c

Commonwealth Development
Corporation
PO Box 133
Mbabane
Swaziland
Tel 00 268 42051/4
Fax 00 268 45185
E-mail
swaziland@mail.swaziland.cdc.co.
Commonwealth Development
Corporation
PO Box 1392
Bridgetown
St Michael
Barbados
Tel 001 246 4369890
Fax 001 246 4361504
E-mail
barbados@mail.barbados.cdc.co.uk

Commonwealth Development
Corporation
PO Box 1072
Johannesburg
South Africa
Tel 00 27 11 4845061
Fax 00 27 11 4843023
E-mail
safrica@mail.safrica.cdc.co.uk

Commonwealth Development
Corporation
PO Box 2535
Dar es Salaam
Tanzania
Tel 00 255 51 112926
Fax 00 255 51 113274
E-mail
tanzania@mail.tanzania.cdc.co.uk

Commonwealth Development
Corporation
PO Box 22581
Kampala
Uganda
Tel 00 256 41 235787
Fax 00 256 41 235752
E-mail
uganda@mail.uganda.cdc.co.uk

Commonwealth Development
Corporation
04 BP 1661
1st Floor
Immeuble les Harmonies
Abidjan
Ivory Coast
Tel 00 225 216590
Fax 00 225 210239
E-mail ivoire@mail.ivoire.cdc.co.uk

Commonwealth Development
Corporation
PO Box 32000
Lusaka
Zambia
Tel 00 260 1 254285
Fax 00 260 1 250122
E-mail
zambia@mail.zambia.cdc.co.uk

Commonwealth Development
Corporation
PO Box 3758
Harare
Zimbabwe
Tel 00 263 4 724286
Fax 00 263 4 705503
E-mail
zimbabwe@mail.zimbabwe.cdc.co.uk

Food from Britain (Belgium) bvba
Rue du Biplan 187
B-1140 Evere
Brussels
Belgium
Tel 00 32 2 240 7520
Fax 00 32 2 245 8210
E-mail info@foodfrombritain.be
Food from Britain (France) SARL
134 rue du Faubourg
St Honore
Paris
France 75008
Tel 00 33 1 5353 0853
Fax 00 33 1 4225 0185
E-mail foodfrombritain@ffb.fr

Food from Britain (Germany)
GmbH
Rossertstrasse 9
60323 Frankfurt/Main
Germany
Tel 00 49 69 971 2910
Fax 00 49 69 971 29110
E-mail
foodfrombritain_germany@t-onli

Food from Britain (Italy), Srl
via Manuzio 17
20124 Milan
Italy
Tel 00 39 2 655 5640
Fax 00 39 2 657 0124
E-mail pgarrett@ffb.it

Food from Britain (Japan)
Kioicho WITH Bldg 4F
3-32 Kioi-cho
Chiyoda-Ku
Tokyo 102
Japan
Tel 00 81 332 396 638
Fax 00 81 332 392 848
E-mail kkurosu@iic.co.jp

Food from Britain (North America)
Inc
4700 Magnolia Circle Marietta
Georgia 30067
USA
Tel 00 1 770 955 4074
Fax 00 1 770 952 9792
E-mail
foodfrombritain@worldnet.att.

Food from Britain (Scandinavia)
Nannasgade 28
DK-2200 Copenhagen N
Denmark
Tel 00 45 35 83 35 73
Fax 00 45 35 83 35 72
E-mail ffb.scan@internet.dk

Food from Britain (Spain) SL
Arroyofresno 19
Bloque A, 2-D Dcha
28035 Madrid
Spain
Tel 0034 1 386 07 44
Fax 0034 1 386 68 18
E-mail ffbspain@alc.es

Food from Britain (Switzerland)
Gmbh
Sennweidstrasse 44
6312 Steinhausen (ZG)
Switzerland
Tel 00 41 41 748 7060
Fax 00 41 41 748 7066
E-mail ebraun@ffb.ch

Food from Britain (The
Netherlands)BV
PO Box 280
5240 AG Rosmalen
Netherlands
Tel 00 31 7352 21222
Fax 00 31 7352 10043
E-mail Info@ffb.nl
Joint Astronomy Centre
University Park
Hilo
Hawaii (USA) 96720
Tel 001 808 961 3756
Fax 001 808 961 6516
E-mail eir@jach.hawaii.edu

Meat & Livestock Commission
23-25 rue de la Science
Box 18
Bruxelle
Belgium 1040
Tel 00322 2308668
Fax 00 322 2308620

Meat & Livestock Commission
134 rue du Fauburg
St Honore
Paris
France 75008
Tel 00 331 49539686
Fax 00 331 42254181

Observatorio Del Roque De Los
Muchachos, La Palma
Santa Cruz De La Palma
Canary Islands
Tenerife 38770
Tel 00 3422 411048
Fax 00 3422 414203
E-mail swv@1pve.ing.iac.es

Princess Mary's Hospital
RAF Akrotiri
Cyprus BFPO 53
Tel 00 357 527 5586
Fax 00 357 527 5606

Royal Naval Hospital
Gibraltar BFPO52
Tel 00 3505 5270
Fax 00 3505 5270

Service Children's Education
Wegberg Military Complex
Building 5
BFPO 140
Tel 0049 2161 47 x 2414
Fax 00 49 2161 47 x 3487

# *Professional Advisers*

## *(and their Quango clients)*

**Bankers**
**Auditors**
**Solicitors**
**Public Relations Advisers**

# BANKERS

### Bank of England
Central Office of Information
Crown Agents Foundation
Forest Research
Higher Education Funding Council for England
Patent Office
Veterinary Laboratories Agency

### Bank of Scotland
East of Scotland Water Authority
North of Scotland Water Authority
Scottish Arts Council
Scottish Conveyancing & Executry Services Board
Scottish Further Education Unit
West of Scotland Water Authority

### Barclays Bank
Engineering Construction Industry Training Board
Gaming Board for Great Britain
Human Fertilisation & Embryology Authority
Apple & Pear Research Council
Coal Authority
Commonwealth Development Corporation
Construction Industry Training Board
Fleet Air Arm Museum
Historic Royal Palaces
Meat & Livestock Commission
Milk Development Council
Registrar of Public Lending Right
Residuary Body for Wales
Tai Cymru
Tower Hamlets Housing Action Trust
Traffic Director for London
Wilton Park Executive Agency

### Clydesdale Bank
Horniman Museum
Rowett Research Institute
Sea Fish Industry Authority

### Co-operative Bank
Arts Council of Wales
Castle Vale Housing Action Trust

### Coutts & Co
Arts Council of England
Tate Gallery

### First Trust Bank
Enterprise Ulster
Laganside Corporation
Northern Ireland Fishery Harbour Authority

### Giro Bank
Defence Postal & Courier Services Agency

### HM Paymaster General
Duke of York's Royal Military School
Education Assets Board
Funding Agency for Schools
Medical Supplies Agency
National Library of Scotland
Qualifications & Curriculum Authority
Advisory, Conciliation & Arbitration Service

### HM Treasury
Forest Enterprise

### Lloyds Bank
Audit Commission
British Film Institute
British Hallmarking Council
Criminal Cases Review Commission
Defence Postal & Courier Services Agency
English National Board for Nursing, Midwifery & Health Visiting
Home-Grown Cereals Authority
Liverpool Housing Action Trust
Radio Authority
Royal Navy Submarine Museum
Stonebridge Housing Action Trust

### Midland Bank
British Council
British Educational Communications & Technology Agency
Channel Four Television Corporation
Covent Garden Market Authority
Further Education Funding Council for Wales
Higher Education Funding Council for Wales
Horserace Betting Levy Board
Horticultural Development Council
London Pensions Fund Authority
Milk Development Council
Museum of Science & Industry Manchester
Ofwat Central Customer Service Committee
Ofwat Eastern Customer Service Committee
Ofwat National Customer Council
Ofwat North West Customer Service Committee
Ofwat Northumbria Customer Service Committee
Ofwat South West Customer Service Committee
Ofwat Southern Customer Service Committee
Ofwat Thames Customer Service Committee
Ofwat Wessex Customer Service Committee
Ofwat Yorkshire Customer Service Committee
Police Complaints Authority
Welsh Language Board
Westminster Foundation for Democracy
Ofwat Customer Service Committee for Wales

### National Westminster Bank
Arts Council of Wales
British Board of Agrément
British Nuclear Fuels plc
British Shipbuilders
British Tourist Authority
Central Council for Education & Training in Social Work
English Tourist Board
Geffrye Museum
Government Property Lawyers
National Biological Standards Board
National Library of Wales
National Portrait Gallery
NHS Estates
Office of the National Lottery
Office of the National Lottery
Remploy
Royal Armouries
Royal Navy Submarine Museum
Sir John Soane's Museum
Wallace Collection

Waltham Forest Housing Action Trust
Wine Standards Board

**Northern Bank**
Agricultural Research Institute of Northern Ireland
National Board for Nursing, Midwifery & Health Visiting for Northern Ireland
Northern Ireland Commissioner for Protection Against Unlawful Industrial Action
Northern Ireland Commissioner for the Rights of Trade Union Members
Northern Ireland Local Government Officers' Superannuation Committee
Northern Ireland Transport Holding Company
Probation Board for Northern Ireland
Water Service

**Paymaster (1836)**
Centre for Environment, Fisheries & Aquaculture Science

**Paymaster General**
The Buying Agency
Security Facilities Executive

**Royal Bank of Scotland**
British Railways Board
Caledonian MacBrayne Ltd
Great Britain-China Centre
London Regional Passengers Committee
Meat Hygiene Service
National Consumer Council
National Galleries of Scotland
Office of the Data Protection Registrar
Scottish Council for Educational Technology
Scottish Crop Research Institute
Scottish Environment Protection Agency
The Scottish Legal Aid Board
Scottish Screen
Scottish Screen
Scottish Water & Sewerage Customers Council
Student Loans Company
National Board for Nursing, Midwifery & Health Visiting for Scotland

**Ulster Bank**
Construction Industry Training Board (NI)
Fisheries Conservancy Board for Northern Ireland
Livestock & Meat Commission for Northern Ireland
Office for the Regulation of Electricity & Gas
Youth Council for Northern Ireland

**Yorkshire Bank**
Investors in People UK

## AUDITORS

**Auditor General for N Ireland**
Northern Ireland Tourist Board

**Baker Tilly**
Fleet Air Arm Museum

**Barter, Durgan & Muir**
Horticultural Development Council

**BDO Binder Hamlyn**
British Board of Agrément

**BDO Stoy Hayward**
British Film Institute
Construction Industry Training Board
Horserace Totalisator Board
National Film & Television School

**Bentley Jennison**
National Forest Company
Security Facilities Executive

**Binder Hamlyn**
British Waterways
Football Licensing Authority
Human Fertilisation & Embryology Authority
Stonebridge Housing Action Trust
UK Eco-Labelling Board

**BM May & Co**
British Broadcasting Corporation

**Chantrey Vellacott**
Geffrye Museum

**Chiene & Tuit**
Scottish Hospital Endowments Research Trust

**Clarke Whitehill**
Legal Aid Board

**Comptroller and Auditor General**
Duke of York's Royal Military School
Education Assets Board

**Coopers & Lybrand**
Bank of England
Channel Four Television Corporation
Crafts Council
Enterprise Ulster
Livestock & Meat Commission for Northern Ireland
London Pensions Fund Authority
Meat & Livestock Commission
National Consumer Council
Northern Ireland Transport Holding Company
Rowett Research Institute
Royal Mint
Sea Fish Industry Authority
Tai Cymru
West of Scotland

**Coulthards Mackenzie**
Wine Standards Board

**Day, Smith & Hunter**
Apple & Pear Research Council

**Delloite & Touche**
Museum of Science & Industry Manchester
British Hallmarking Council
Horniman Museum
Labour Relations Agency
National Galleries of Scotland
Office of the National Lottery
Policyholders' Protection Board
Royal Armouries
Scottish Further Education Unit

**District Audit Service**
English National Board for Nursing, Midwifery & Health Visiting
London Pensions Fund Authority

**Ernst & Young**
British Nuclear Fuels plc
Cardiff Bay Development Corporation
Commission for the New Towns
Commonwealth Development Corporation
Fair Employment Commission for Northern Ireland
Highlands & Islands Airports
Laganside Corporation
Meat Hygiene Service
Milk Development Council
National Board for Nursing, Midwifery & Health Visiting for Scotland

**Geoghegan & Co**
Scottish Conveyancing & Executry Services Board

**Grant Thornton**
British Educational Communications & Technology Agency
Criminal Cases Review Commission
Investors in People UK
The Radio Authority

**Johnston Graham & Co**
Agricultural Research Institute of Northern Ireland

**Jones, Peters & Co**
Construction Industry Training Board (NI)

**Keith Vaudrey & Co**
Great Britain-China Centre

**Kidsons Impey**
British Educational Communications & Technology Agency
English Partnerships
Home-Grown Cereals Authority
Liverpool Housing Action Trust
National Forest Company
Traffic Director for London

**Kingston Smith**
Gas Consumers' Council
Westminster Foundation for Democracy

**KPMG**
British Broadcasting Corporation
Caledonian MacBrayne Ltd
East of Scotland Water Authority

Horserace Betting Levy Board
London Transport
Mental Health Commission for Northern Ireland
National Board for Nursing, Midwifery & Health Visiting for Northern Ireland
Scottish Crop Research Institute
Scottish Environment Protection Agency
Scottish Screen
Student Loans Company
Tai Cymru

**Local Government Auditor**
Northern Ireland Local Government Officers' Superannuation Committee

**McClure Watters**
Northern Ireland Museums' Council

**Moores Rowland**
Engineering Construction Industry Training Board
Scottish Council for Educational Technology

**National Audit Office**
The Accounts Commission for Scotland
Advisory, Conciliation & Arbitration Service
Army Technical Support Agency
The Arts Council of England
Arts Council of Wales
Audit Commission
Benefits Agency
Biotechnology & Biological Sciences Research Council
British Council
British Tourist Authority
The Buying Agency
Cadw
Central Council for Education & Training in Social Work
Central Office of Information
Central Science Laboratory
Centre for Environment, Fisheries & Aquaculture Science
Child Support Agency
Coal Authority
Coastguard
Commissioner for Protection Against Unlawful Industrial Action
Commissioner for the Rights of Trade Union Members
Companies House
Compensation Agency
Council for the Central Laboratory of the Research Councils
Countryside Council for Wales
Criminal Cases Review Commission
Defence Analytical Services Agency
Defence Animal Centre
Defence Bills Agency
Defence Dental Agency
Defence Postal & Courier Services Agency
Defence Secondary Care Agency
Defence Transport & Movements Executive
Defence Vetting Agency
Driver & Vehicle Licensing Agency
Driving Standards Agency
Duke of York's Royal Military School
Economic & Social Research Council
Employment Tribunals Service
Engineering & Physical Sciences Research Council
English Nature
English Tourist Board

Fire Service College
Forensic Science Service
Forest Enterprise
Forest Research
Funding Agency for Schools
Further Education Funding Council
Further Education Funding Council for Wales
Gaming Board for Great Britain
Government Property Lawyers
Higher Education Funding Council for Wales
Higher Education Funding Council for England
Highlands & Islands Enterprise
Historic Royal Palaces
Historic Scotland
HM Customs & Excise
HM Land Registry
Human Fertilisation & Embryology Authority
Imperial War Museum
Independent Commission for Police Complaints for Northern Ireland
Information Technology Services Agency
Insolvency Service
London Regional Passengers Committee
Marine Safety Agency
Meat Hygiene Service
Medical Devices Agency
Medical Supplies Agency
Medicines Control Agency
Met Office
Military Survey
Museums & Galleries Commission
National Biological Standards Board
National Heritage Memorial Fund
National Library of Scotland
National Library of Wales
National Lottery Charities Board
National Museum of Science & Industry
National Portrait Gallery
National Radiological Protection Board
National Weights & Measures Laboratory
NHS Estates
NHS Pensions Agency
Occupational Pensions Regulatory Authority
Office of Gas Supply
Office of Passenger Rail Franchising
Office of Telecommunications
Office of the Data Protection Registrar
Ofwat Central Customer Service Committee
Ofwat Customer Service Committee for Wales
Ofwat Eastern Customer Service Committee
Ofwat National Customer Council
Ofwat North West Customer Service Committee
Ofwat Northumbria Customer Service Committee
Ofwat South West Customer Service Committee
Ofwat Southern Customer Service Committee
Ofwat Thames Customer Service Committee
Ofwat Wessex Customer Service Committee
Ofwat Yorkshire Customer Service Committee
Ordnance Survey
Parole Board
Particle Physics & Astronomy Research Council
Patent Office
Pay & Personnel Agency
Pesticides Safety Directorate
Planning Inspectorate
Police Complaints Authority

Public Record Office
Queen Elizabeth II Conference Centre
Queen Victoria School
Radiocommunications Agency
RAF Logistics Support Services
RAF Training Group Defence Agency
Registers of Scotland
Registrar of Public Lending Right
Royal Armouries
Royal Botanic Gardens Kew
Royal Commission on Ancient & Historical Monuments of Scotland
Royal Mint
Scottish Agricultural Science Agency
Scottish Arts Council
Scottish Fisheries Protection Agency
Scottish Higher Education Funding Council
Scottish Homes
Scottish Office Pensions Agency
Scottish Prison Service
Scottish Tourist Board
Service Children's Education
Specialist Procurement Services
Sports Council for Wales
Student Awards Agency for Scotland
Tate Gallery
UK Passport Agency
Valuation Office Agency
Vehicle Certification Agency
Vehicle Inspectorate
Veterinary Laboratories Agency
Veterinary Medicines Directorate
Wales Tourist Board
Wallace Collection
War Pensions Agency
Welsh Development Agency
Welsh Language Board

### Neville Russell
Castle Vale Housing Action Trust

### Northern Ireland Audit Office
Driver & Vehicle Licensing Northern Ireland
Driver & Vehicle Testing Agency
General Consumer Council for Northern Ireland
Mental Health Commission for Northern Ireland
Northern Ireland Child Support Agency
Northern Ireland Commissioner for Protection Against Unlawful Industrial Action
Northern Ireland Commissioner for the Rights of Trade Union Members
Office for the Regulation of Electricity & Gas
Ordnance Survey of Northern Ireland
Probation Board for Northern Ireland
Rate Collection Agency
Training & Employment Agency (NI)
Valuation & Lands Agency
Water Service
Youth Council for Northern Ireland

### Pannell Kerr Forster
Sir John Soane's Museum
Tower Hamlets Housing Action Trust

**Price Waterhouse**
British Railways Board
British Shipbuilders
Covent Garden Market Authority
Crown Agents Foundation
English Heritage
National Board for Nursing, Midwifery & Health Visiting for Northern Ireland
North of Scotland Water Authority
Northern Ireland Fishery Harbour Authority
Remploy
Scottish Legal Aid Board

**Robson Rhodes**
Horticulture Research International
Waltham Forest Housing Action Trust

**Saffery Champness**
Alcohol Education & Research Council

**Scott-Moncrieff Downie Wilson**
Scottish Water & Sewerage Customers Council

**Shipleys**
Food from Britain

**Smith and Williamson**
Independent Television Commission

**Walton & Co**
Royal Marines Museum
Royal Navy Submarine Museum

**Witt Thornton**
Fisheries Conservancy Board for Northern Ireland

## SOLICITORS

**Alasdair Watson**
Office of the Data Protection Registrar

**Allen & Overy**
Channel Four Television Corporation
National Library of Wales
Radio Authority
Tate Gallery

**Andrew Sim**
British Railways Board

**Babington & Croasdaile**
Construction Industry Training Board (NI)

**Baily Gibson**
Office of the Data Protection Registrar

**Beachcroft Stanley**
Central Council for Education & Training in Social Work
Higher Education Funding Council for England

**Berry Smith**
Residuary Body for Wales

**Bevan Ashford**
Further Education Funding Council for Wales
Higher Education Funding Council for Wales

**Bird & Bird**
Arts Council of England
English National Board for Nursing, Midwifery & Health Visiting

**Blake Lapthorn Solicitors**
Royal Navy Submarine Museum

**Brangam, Bagnall & Co**
National Board for Nursing, Midwifery & Health Visiting for Northern Ireland

**Burness & Co**
Meat Hygiene Service
National Board for Nursing, Midwifery & Health Visiting for Scotland
Scottish Arts Council
Sea Fish Industry Authority

**Burnett & Reid**
Rowett Research Institute

**Cameron McKenna**
Investors in People UK

**Carson & McDowel**
Northern Ireland Transport Holding Company

**Cleaver Fulton & Rankin**
Agricultural Research Institute of Northern Ireland

**Clifford Chance**
Commonwealth Development Corporation
London Pensions Fund Authority

# Q & Q

**Crown Solicitors Office**
Driver & Vehicle Testing Agency
Probation Board for Northern Ireland
Rate Collection Agency

**Currey & Co**
Horniman Museum

**Denton's**
Office for the Regulation of Electricity & Gas

**Department of Health Solicitors**
NHS Estates

**DETR**
Vehicle Certification Agency

**Dibb Lupton Alsop**
Traffic Director for London

**DJ Freeman**
Channel Four Television Corporation

**DTI Solicitors**
Employment Tribunals Service
Insolvency Service
Patent Office

**Dundas & Wilson CS**
Horticultural Development Council
National Galleries of Scotland
National Library of Scotland
Scottish Crop Research Institute

**Edwards Geward**
Arts Council of Wales

**Eversheds**
British Shipbuilders
London Pensions Fund Authority

**Farrer & Co**
Historic Royal Palaces
National Portrait Gallery
Sir John Soane's Museum

**Field Fisher Waterhouse**
Stonebridge Housing Action Trust
Tower Hamlets Housing Action Trust

**Frere, Cholmele, Bischoff**
Construction Industry Training Board

**Freshfields**
Bank of England
British Nuclear Fuels plc

**Gilchrists**
Office of the Data Protection Registrar

**Granville-West**
Office of the Data Protection Registrar

**Gregory, Rowcliffe & Milners**
Gaming Board for Great Britain

**Halliwell Landau**
Museum of Science & Industry Manchester

**Hamiltons Solicitors**
Office of the Data Protection Registrar

**Harbottle & Lewis**
Horserace Betting Levy Board

**Herbert Wilkes**
Castle Vale Housing Action Trust

**Johns Elliot**
Northern Ireland Local Government Officers' Superannuation Committee

**JP Hagan & Co**
Construction Industry Training Board (NI)

**L'Estrange & Brett**
Laganside Corporation
Northern Ireland Fishery Harbour Authority

**MacDonald Oates**
Apple & Pear Research Council
Horticultural Development Council

**Maclay Murray & Spens**
Scottish Further Education Unit

**MacRoberts Solicitors**
Scottish Council for Educational Technology

**MAFF Legal Department**
Centre for Environment, Fisheries & Aquaculture Science
Veterinary Laboratories Agency

**Martineau Johnson**
British Hallmarking Council

**McGrigor Donald**
Caledonian MacBrayne Ltd
Student Loans Company

**MOD**
Defence Transport & Movements Executive

**Morgan Bruce**
Human Fertilisation & Embryology Authority
Welsh Language Board

**Nabarro Nathanson**
London Pensions Fund Authority

**Nicholson Graham & Jones**
British Film Institute

**Norton Rose**
Crown Agents Foundation
New Millenium Experience Co Ltd

**O'Rorke McDonald & Tweed**
Fisheries Conservancy Board for Northern Ireland

**Payne Hicks Beach**
Geffrye Museum

**Phillips McCade & Co**
Office of the Data Protection Registrar

**Pinsent Curtis**
Royal Armouries

**Porter Dodson**
Fleet Air Arm Museum

**Portner & Jaskell**
London Pensions Fund Authority

**Radcliffes**
British Educational Communications & Technology Agency

**Rowe & Maw**
Milk Development Council

**Rutherfords**
Office of the Data Protection Registrar

**Scottish Office Solicitors**
Scottish Office Pensions Agency

**Shepherd & Wedderburn WS**
Office of the Data Protection Registrar
Scottish Water & Sewerage Customers Council

**Simmons & Simmons**
Commonwealth Development Corporation
Horserace Totalisator Board
Office for the Regulation of Electricity & Gas

**Simon Jackson**
Sea Fish Industry Authority

**Stephenson Harwood**
British Board of Agrément
Home-Grown Cereals Authority

**Swaffields Solicitors**
Office of the Data Protection Registrar

**Treasury Solicitor**
The Buying Agency
Defence Postal & Courier Services Agency
Defence Secondary Care Agency
Funding Agency for Schools
Government Property Lawyers
National Biological Standards Board
Office of the National Lottery
Police Complaints Authority
Registrar of Public Lending Right
Remploy
Royal Armouries
Security Facilities Executive
Vehicle Certification Agency

**Trethowan Woodford**
Office of the Data Protection Registrar

**Tugham Company**
Enterprise Ulster
Northern Ireland Local Government Officers'
Superannuation Committee

**Turcan Connel WS**
National Galleries of Scotland
National Library of Scotland
Scottish Hospital Endowments Research Trust

**Waller Needham & Green**
Office of the Data Protection Registrar

**Weightmans**
Liverpool Housing Action Trust

**Wilmett & Co**
Food from Britain

**Woollcombe Beer Watts**
Office of the Data Protection Registrar

**Zermansky & Partners**
Office of the Data Protection Registrar

## PUBLIC RELATIONS

**Binns Associates**
Patent Office

**Bolton & Quinn**
Tate Gallery

**Cameron Duncan PR**
National Portrait Gallery

**Central Office of Information**
The Government Property Lawyers

**Chamberlain Partnership**
Home-Grown Cereals Authority

**College Hill Associates**
Commonwealth Development Corporation

**Colman Getty PR**
National Portrait Gallery

**Countrywide**
Investors in People UK

**Davidson Cockcroft**
Probation Board for Northern Ireland

**DHSS Information Office**
Northern Ireland Child Support Agency

**DOE Information Office**
Rate Collection Agency

**DTI Press Office**
Employment Tribunals Service

**Fiona Selkirk Public Relations**
Scottish Hospital Endowments Research Trust

**Future Image**
Laganside Corporation

**GCAS**
Office for the Regulation of Electricity & Gas

**Gordon Corporate Communications**
Construction Industry Training Board (NI)

**MCL**
Scottish Water & Sewerage Customers Council

**MOD (PR)**
Defence Vetting Agency

**Strata**
National Library of Wales

**The Rowland Company**
Sea Fish Industry Authority

# Business Index

**A search index of quangos under the following 44 activities**

Accounting & finance
Agriculture, horticulture & forestry
Armed Forces support
Arts, crafts & culture
Betting, gambling & lotteries
Building & construction
Business development & enterprise
Collection of taxes, loans etc
Company law & intellectual property
Conservation of natural & built environment
Consumer protection
Development, urban & rural
Driving & vehicles
Economic management & industry regulation
Education
Employment & human resources
Environment
Fish
Food & wine
Funding (support for agriculture, research, sport etc)
Information systems, telecommunications & logistics
Land & property
Legal, courts & prosecuting/compensating authorities
Libraries, archives, statistics & registrars
Manufacturing & repair
Measuring & calibration
Media
Medical, veterinary & health
Museums & galleries
National Lottery distribution funds
Overseas activities
Pensions & investment
Police, prisons & security
Post, courier & distribution
Promotion
Research
Social & welfare
Sport
Survey & meteorology
Tourism & recreation
Trade (buying & selling)
Training & conferences (incl. venues)
Travel (air, rail, road, rivers, sea)
Water & energy (atomic, coal, electricity, gas)

## Accounting & finance
Accounts Commission for Scotland
Audit Commission
Defence Bills Agency
Financial Services Authority
Royal Mint

## Agriculture, horticulture & forestry
Agricultural Research Institute of Northern Ireland
Agricultural Wages Board for England & Wales
Agricultural Wages Board for Northern Ireland
Apple & Pear Research Council
Central Science Laboratory
Farming & Rural Conservation Agency
Forest Enterprise
Forest Research
Home-Grown Cereals Authority
Horticultural Development Council
Horticulture Research International
Intervention Board
Livestock & Meat Commission for Northern Ireland
Macaulay Land Use Research Institute
Meat & Livestock Commission
Milk Development Council
National Forest Company
Pesticides Safety Directorate
Rowett Research Institute
Royal Botanic Garden Edinburgh
Royal Botanic Gardens Kew
Scottish Agricultural Science Agency
Scottish Agricultural Wages Board
Scottish Crop Research Institute
UK Register of Organic Food Standards
Veterinary Laboratories Agency

## Armed Forces support
Armed Forces Personnel Administration Agency
Army Base Repair Organisation
Army Base Storage & Distribution Agency
Army Personnel Centre
Army Technical Support Agency
Army Training & Recruitment Agency
Defence Analytical Services Agency
Defence Animal Centre
Defence Clothing & Textiles Agency
Defence Codification Agency
Defence Dental Agency
Defence Evaluation & Research Agency
Defence Intelligence & Security Centre
Defence Medical Training Organisation
Defence Secondary Care Agency.
Defence Transport & Movements Executive
Defence Vetting Agency
Joint Air Reconnaissance Intelligence Centre
Logistic Information Systems Agency
Met Office
Military Survey
Ministry of Defence Police
Naval Aircraft Repair Organisation
Naval Bases & Supply Agency
Naval Manning Agency
Naval Recruiting & Training Agency
Oil & Pipelines Agency
RAF Logistics Support Services
RAF Maintenance Group Defence Agency
RAF Personnel Management Agency
RAF Signals Engineering Establishment
RAF Training Group Defence Agency
Ships Support Agency

Specialist Procurement Services
UK Hydrographic Office

## Arts, crafts & culture
Arts Council of England
Arts Council of Northern Ireland
Arts Council of Wales
Britain-Russia Centre
British Association for Central & Eastern Europe
British Broadcasting Corporation
British Council
British Library
British Museum
Cadw
Crafts Council
Design Council
English Heritage
Great Britain-China Centre
Historic Royal Palaces
Historic Scotland
Millennium Commission
New Millenium Experience Co Ltd
Royal Armouries
Scottish Arts Council
Victoria & Albert Museum
Welsh Language Board
Westminster Foundation for Democracy

## Betting, gambling & lotteries
Gaming Board for Great Britain
Horserace Betting Levy Board
Horserace Totalisator Board
Office of the National Lottery

## Building & construction
British Board of Agrément
Construction Industry Training Board
Construction Industry Training Board (NI)
Construction Service
Engineering Construction Industry Training Board
Highways Agency
Roads Service

## Business development & enterprise
Castle Vale Housing Action Trust
Crofters' Commission
Enterprise Ulster
Highlands & Islands Enterprise
Laganside Corporation
Liverpool Housing Action Trust
Local Enterprise Development Unit
Scottish Enterprise
Stonebridge Housing Action Trust
Tower Hamlets Housing Action Trust
Training & Employment Agency (NI)
Waltham Forest Housing Action Trust

## Collection of taxes, loans etc
Child Support Agency
Contributions Agency
HM Customs & Excise
Inland Revenue
Northern Ireland Child Support Agency
Rate Collection Agency
Social Security Agency (Northern Ireland)
Student Awards Agency for Scotland
Student Loans Company

## Company law & intellectual property
Companies House
Insolvency Service
Patent Office
Registrar of Public Lending Right

## Conservation of natural & built environment
Cadw
Countryside Commission
Countryside Council for Wales
English Heritage
English Nature
Environment Agency
Environment & Heritage Service
Farming & Rural Conservation Agency
Historic Royal Palaces
Historic Scotland
Joint Nature Conservation Committee
National Heritage Memorial Fund
Royal Commission on Ancient & Historical Monuments of Scotland
Royal Commission on Ancient & Historical Monuments in Wales
Royal Commission on the Historical Monuments of England
Scottish Environment Protection Agency
Scottish Natural Heritage

## Consumer protection
Gas Consumers' Council
General Consumer Council for Northern Ireland
Independent Commission for Police Complaints for Northern Ireland
London Regional Passengers Committee
National Consumer Council
Office of the Data Protection Registrar
Ofwat National Customer Council & CRCs
Police Complaints Authority
Policyholders' Protection Board
Post Office Users Councils
Rail Users Consultative Committees
Scottish Water & Sewerage Customers Council

## Development, urban & rural
Cardiff Bay Development Corporation
Castle Vale Housing Action Trust
Commission for the New Towns
Commonwealth Development Corporation
Community Development Foundation
Countryside Commission
Countryside Council for Wales
Crofters' Commission
English Partnerships
Highlands & Islands Enterprise
Laganside Corporation
Liverpool Housing Action Trust
Planning Service
Rural Development Commission
Stonebridge Housing Action Trust
Tower Hamlets Housing Action Trust
Training & Employment Agency (NI)
Waltham Forest Housing Action Trust
Welsh Development Agency

## Driving & vehicles
Driver & Vehicle Licensing Agency
Driver & Vehicle Licensing Northern Ireland
Driver & Vehicle Testing Agency
Driving Standards Agency
Government Car & Despatch Agency
Vehicle Certification Agency
Vehicle Inspectorate

## Economic management & industry regulation
Bank of England
Monopolies & Mergers Commission
Northern Ireland Statistics and Research Agency
Occupational Pensions Regulatory Authority
Office of Electricity Regulation
Office of Fair Trading
Office of Gas Supply
Office for National Statistics
Office of Passenger Rail Franchising
Office of the Rail Regulator
Office for the Regulation of Electricity & Gas
Office of Telecommunications
Office of Water Services

## Education
British Educational Communications & Technology Agency
Centre for Information on Language Teaching & Research
Commonwealth Institute
Commonwealth Scholarship Commission
Council for Catholic Maintained Schools
Duke of York's Royal Military School
English National Board for Nursing, Midwifery & Health Visiting
Funding Agency for Schools
Further Education Funding Council
Further Education Funding Council for Wales
Higher Education Funding Council for England
Higher Education Funding Council for Wales
Marshall Aid Commemoration Commission
National Board for Nursing, Midwifery & Health Visiting for Northern Ireland
National Board for Nursing, Midwifery & Health Visiting for Scotland
National Film & Television School
Northern Ireland Council for the Curriculum, Examinations & Assessment
Northern Ireland Council for Postgraduate Medical & Dental Education
Office for Standards in Education
Qualifications, Curriculum & Assessment Authority for Wales
Qualifications & Curriculum Authority
Queen Victoria School
Scottish Community Education Council
Scottish Council for Educational Technology
Scottish Further Education Unit
Scottish Higher Education Funding Council
Scottish Qualifications Authority
Service Children's Education
Student Awards Agency for Scotland
Student Loans Company
Teacher Training Agency
Welsh National Board for Nursing, Midwifery & Health Visiting

## Employment & human resources
Advisory, Conciliation & Arbitration Service
Agricultural Wages Board for England & Wales
Agricultural Wages Board for Northern Ireland
Armed Forces Personnel Administration Agency
Army Personnel Centre
Army Training & Recruitment Agency
Commission for Racial Equality
Commissioner for Protection Against Unlawful Industrial Action
Commissioner for the Rights of Trade Union Members
Employment Service
Employment Tribunals Service
Equal Opportunities Commission
Equal Opportunities Commission for Northern Ireland
Fair Employment Commission for Northern Ireland
Health & Safety Commission
Health & Safety Executive

Investors in People UK
Labour Relations Agency
Naval Manning Agency
Naval Recruiting & Training Agency
Northern Ireland Commissioner for Protection against Unlawful Industrial Action
Northern Ireland Commissioner for the Rights of Trade Union Members
Pay & Personnel Agency
RAF Personnel Management Agency
RAF Training Group Defence Agency
Remploy
Scottish Agricultural Wages Board

**Environment**
Centre for Environment, Fisheries & Aquaculture Science
Countryside Commission
Countryside Council for Wales
English Nature
Environment & Heritage Service
Environment Agency
Foyle Fisheries Commission
Joint Nature Conservation Committee
Natural Environment Research Council
Planning Inspectorate
Planning Service
Rivers Agency
Royal Parks Agency
Scottish Environment Protection Agency
Scottish Natural Heritage
UK Ecolabelling Board

**Fish**
Fisheries Conservancy Board for Northern Ireland
Fisheries Research Services
Foyle Fisheries Commission
Northern Ireland Fishery Harbour Authority
Scottish Fisheries Protection Agency
Sea Fish Industry Authority

**Food & wine**
Food from Britain
Food Standards Agency
Livestock & Meat Commission for Northern Ireland
Meat Hygiene Service
Meat & Livestock Commission
Rowett Research Institute
UK Ecolabelling Board
UK Register of Organic Food Standards
Wine Standards Board

**Funding (support for agriculture, research, sport etc)**
Alcohol Education & Research Council
Arts Council of England
Arts Council of Northern Ireland
Arts Council of Wales
Biotechnology & Biological Sciences Reseach Council
British Film Institute
Crafts Council
Economic & Social Research Council
Engineering & Physical Sciences Research Council
English Sports Council
Funding Agency for Schools
Further Education Funding Council
Further Education Funding Council for Wales
Higher Education Funding Council for England
Higher Education Funding Council for Wales
Industrial Research & Technology Unit
Intervention Board
Medical Research Council

Millennium Commission
National Heritage Memorial Fund
National Lottery Charities Board
Natural Environment Research Council
Scottish Arts Council
Scottish Further Education Unit
Scottish Higher Education Funding Council
Scottish Hospital Endowments Research Trust
Scottish Sports Council
Sports Council for Northern Ireland
Sports Council for Wales
UK Sports Council

**Information systems, telecommunications & logistics**
Army Technical Support Agency
British Educational Communications & Technology Agency
Business Development Service
Central Computer & Telecommunications Agency
Defence Analytical Services Agency
Defence Codification Agency
Information Technology Services Agency
Logistic Information Systems Agency
Office of Telecommunications
RAF Logistics Support Services
RAF Maintenance Group Defence Agency
RAF Signals Engineering Establishment
Scottish Council for Educational Technology

**Land & property**
British Railways Board
Castle Vale Housing Action Trust
Commission for the New Towns
Defence Estates Organisation
Education Assets Board
English Partnerships
Government Property Lawyers
Health Estates
HM Land Registry
Housing Corporation
Laganside Corporation
Land Registers of Northern Ireland
Liverpool Housing Action Trust
London Transport
NHS Estates
Northern Ireland Transport Holding Company
Planning Inspectorate
Planning Service
Property Advisers to the Civil Estate
Rate Collection Agency
Registers of Scotland
Residuary Body for Wales
Scottish Homes
Stonebridge Housing Action Trust
Tai Cymru
Tower Hamlets Housing Action Trust
Valuation & Lands Agency
Valuation Office Agency
Waltham Forest Housing Action Trust

**Legal, courts & prosecuting/compensating authorities**
Compensation Agency
Court Service
Criminal Cases Review Commission
Criminal Injuries Compensation Authority
Crown Prosecution Service
Government Property Lawyers
HM Customs & Excise
Inland Revenue
Insolvency Service
Legal Aid Board

Scottish Conveyancing & Executry Services Board
Scottish Court Service
Scottish Legal Aid Board
Serious Fraud Office
Treasury Solicitor's Department

**Libraries, archives, statistics & registrars**
British Library
Companies House
HM Land Registry
Land Registers of Northern Ireland
National Library of Scotland
National Library of Wales
Northern Ireland Statistics and Research Agency
Office of the Data Protection Registrar
Office for National Statistics
Patent Office
Public Record Office
Public Record Office of Northern Ireland
Registers of Scotland
Registrar of Public Lending Right
Royal Commission on Ancient & Historical Monuments of Scotland
Royal Commission on Ancient & Historical Monuments in Wales
Royal Commission on Historical Manuscripts
Royal Commission on the Historical Monuments of England
Scottish Record Office
UK Passport Agency

**Manufacturing & repair**
Army Base Repair Organisation
Army Technical Support Agency
British Shipbuilders
Naval Aircraft Repair Organisation
Naval Bases & Supply Agency
RAF Maintenance Group Defence Agency
Royal Mint
Ships Support Agency

**Measuring & calibration**
British Hallmarking Council
National Weights & Measures Laboratory

**Media**
British Broadcasting Corporation
British Film Institute
Broadcasting Standards Commission
Channel Four Television Corporation
Independent Television Commission
National Film & Television School
Radio Authority
Radiocommunications Agency
S4C
Scottish Screen

**Medical, veterinary & health**
Defence Animal Centre
Defence Dental Agency
Defence Medical Training Organisation
Defence Secondary Care Agency.
English National Board for Nursing, Midwifery & Health Visiting
Health & Safety Commission
Health & Safety Executive
Human Fertilisation & Embryology Authority
Medical Devices Agency
Medical Practices Committee
Medical Research Council
Medical Supplies Agency
Medicines Control Agency

Mental Health Commission for Northern Ireland
National Biological Standards Board
National Board for Nursing, Midwifery & Health Visiting for Northern Ireland
National Board for Nursing, Midwifery & Health Visiting for Scotland
Northern Ireland Council for Postgraduate Medical & Dental Education
Public Health Laboratory Services Board
Rowett Research Institute
Scottish Hospital Endowments Research Trust
Scottish Medical Practices Committee
Veterinary Laboratories Agency
Veterinary Medicines Directorate
Welsh National Board for Nursing, Midwifery & Health Visiting

**Museums & galleries**
British Museum
Fleet Air Arm Museum
Geffrye Museum
Horniman Museum
Imperial War Museum
Museum of London
Museum of Science & Industry Manchester
Museums & Galleries Commission
National Army Museum
National Galleries of Scotland
National Gallery
National Maritime Museum
National Museum of Science & Industry
National Museums & Galleries Merseyside
National Museums & Galleries of Wales
National Museums of Scotland
National Portrait Gallery
Natural History Museum
Northern Ireland Museums' Council
Royal Air Force Museum
Royal Armouries
Royal Marines Museum
Royal Naval Museum
Royal Navy Submarine Museum
Sir John Soane's Museum
Tate Gallery
Ulster Museum
Victoria & Albert Museum
Wallace Collection

**National Lottery distribution funds**
Arts Council of England
Arts Council of Northern Ireland
Arts Council of Wales
English Sports Council
Millennium Commission
National Endowment for Science, Technology & the Arts *
National Heritage Memorial Fund
National Lottery Charities Board
New Opoportunities Fund *
Scottish Arts Council
Scottish Sports Council
Sports Council for Northern Ireland
Sports Council for Wales

**Overseas activities**
Britain-Russia Centre
British Association for Central & Eastern Europe
British Council
Commonwealth Development Corporation
Commonwealth Institute
Commonwealth Scholarship Commission

Crown Agents Foundation
Great Britain-China Centre
Marshall Aid Commemoration Commission
Simpler Trade Procedures Board
Westminster Foundation for Democracy

**Pensions & investment**
Contributions Agency
London Pensions Fund Authority
National Savings
NHS Pensions Agency
Northern Ireland Local Government Officers' Superannuation
Committee
Occupational Pensions Regulatory Authority
Pensions Compensation Board
Policyholders' Protection Board
Public Trust Office
Scottish Office Pensions Agency
War Pensions Agency

**Police, prisons & security**
British Railways Board
Defence Intelligence & Security Centre
Defence Vetting Agency
Forensic Science Agency of Northern Ireland
Forensic Science Service
HM Prison Service
Horserace Betting Levy Board
Independent Commission for Police Complaints for Northern
Ireland
Ministry of Defence Police
Northern Ireland Prison Service
Police Authority for Northern Ireland
Police Complaints Authority
Scottish Prison Service
Security Facilities Executive
UK Atomic Energy Authority
UK Passport Agency

**Post, courier & distribution**
Army Base Storage & Distribution Agency
Defence Postal & Courier Services Agency
Defence Transport & Movements Executive
Government Car & Despatch Agency
Naval Bases & Supply Agency
Oil & Pipelines Agency
Post Office
Post Office Users Councils

**Promotion**
British Council
British Film Institute
British Tourist Authority
British Waterways
Central Office of Information
Crafts Council
Design Council
English Tourist Board
Home-Grown Cereals Authority
Livestock & Meat Commission for Northern Ireland
Meat & Livestock Commission
Milk Development Council
Northern Ireland Tourist Board
Scottish Tourist Board
UK Ecolabelling Board
Wales Tourist Board

**Research**
Agricultural Research Institute of Northern Ireland
Apple & Pear Research Council
Biotechnology & Biological Sciences Reseach Council
Central Science Laboratory
Centre for Environment, Fisheries & Aquaculture Science
Centre for Information on Language Teaching & Research
Council for the Central Laboratory of the Research Councils
Defence Evaluation & Research Agency
Economic & Social Research Council
Engineering & Physical Sciences Research Council
Fisheries Research Services
Forest Research
Hannah Research Institute
Horticultural Development Council
Horticulture Research International
Human Fertilisation & Embryology Authority
Industrial Research & Technology Unit
Joint Nature Conservation Committee
Macaulay Land Use Research Institute
Medical Research Council
National Biological Standards Board
National Radiological Protection Board
Natural Environment Research Council
Particle Physics & Astronomy Research
Rowett Research Institute
Royal Botanic Garden Edinburgh
Royal Botanic Gardens Kew
Scottish Agricultural Science Agency
Scottish Crop Research Institute
Veterinary Laboratories Agency
Veterinary Medicines Directorate
Victoria & Albert Museum

**Social & welfare**
Benefits Agency
Central Council for Education & Training in Social Work
Child Support Agency
Commission for Racial Equality
Community Development Foundation
Compensation Agency
Criminal Cases Review Commission
Criminal Injuries Compensation Authority
Equal Opportunities Commission
Equal Opportunities Commission for Northern Ireland
Marshall Aid Commemoration Commission
Northern Ireland Child Support Agency
Parole Board
Parole Board for Scotland
Pensions Compensation Board
Probation Board for Northern Ireland
Public Record Office
Public Record Office of Northern Ireland
Remploy
Scottish Children's Reporter Administration
Social Security Agency (Northern Ireland)
Student Awards Agency for Scotland
Student Loans Company
War Pensions Agency
Youth Council for Northern Ireland

**Sport**
English Sports Council
Football Licensing Authority
Horserace Betting Levy Board
Horserace Totalisator Board
Scottish Sports Council
Sports Council for Northern Ireland
Sports Council for Wales
UK Sports Council

**Survey & meteorology**
Joint Air Reconnaissance Intelligence Centre
Met Office
Military Survey
Ordnance Survey
Ordnance Survey of Northern Ireland
UK Hydrographic Office

**Tourism & recreation**
British Tourist Authority
British Waterways
English Tourist Board
Historic Royal Palaces
Northern Ireland Tourist Board
Rivers Agency
Royal Botanic Garden Edinburgh
Royal Botanic Gardens Kew
Royal Parks Agency
Scottish Tourist Board
Wales Tourist Board

**Trading (buying & selling)**
Buying Agency
Covent Garden Market Authority
Defence Bills Agency
Defence Clothing & Textiles Agency
Disposal Sales Agency
Education Assets Board
Government Purchasing Agency
Simpler Trade Procedures Board
Specialist Procurement Services

**Training & conferences (incl. venues)**
Army Training & Recruitment Agency
Central Council for Education & Training in Social Work
Civil Service College
Construction Industry Training Board
Construction Industry Training Board (NI)
Defence Medical Training Organisation
Engineering Construction Industry Training Board
English National Board for Nursing, Midwifery & Health Visiting
Enterprise Ulster
Fire Service College
National Board for Nursing, Midwifery & Health Visiting for Northern Ireland
National Board for Nursing, Midwifery & Health Visiting for Scotland
Naval Recruiting & Training Agency
Queen Elizabeth II Conference Centre
RAF Training Group Defence Agency
Remploy
Scottish Enterprise
Teacher Training Agency
Training & Employment Agency (NI)
Welsh National Board for Nursing, Midwifery & Health Visiting
Wilton Park Executive Agency

**Travel (air, rail, road, rivers, sea)**
British Railways Board
British Waterways
Caledonian MacBrayne Ltd
Civil Aviation Authority
Coastguard
Defence Transport & Movements Executive
Highlands & Islands Airports
Highways Agency
London Regional Passengers Committee
London Transport
Marine Safety Agency
Northern Ireland Transport Holding Company

Northern Lighthouse Board
Office of Passenger Rail Franchising
Office of the Rail Regulator
Rail Users Consultative Committees
Rivers Agency
Roads Service
Ships Support Agency
Traffic Director for London
Trinity House Lighthouse Service
UK Hydrographic Office
UK Passport Agency

**Water & energy (atomic, coal, electricity, gas)**
British Nuclear Fuels plc
Coal Authority
East of Scotland Water Authority
Gas Consumers' Council
North of Scotland Water Authority
Office of Electricity Regulation
Office of Gas Supply
Office for the Regulation of Electricity & Gas
Office of Water Services
Ofwat National Customer Councils & CRCs
Oil & Pipelines Agency
Scottish Water & Sewerage Customers Council
UK Atomic Energy Authority
Water Service
West of Scotland Water Authority

\* New funds, not yet constituted at the time of going to press but funded retrospectively; shadow accounting arrangements have been in place since October 1997

# *Expenditure Listings*

## Rough Guide

**Quangos are listed under 11 broad categories of annual expenditure ***

**More than £2000 million**
**£1000 million to £2000 million**
**£500 million to £1000 million**
**£250 million to £500 million**
**£100 million to £250 million**
**£50 million to £100 million**
**£20 million to £50 million**
**£10 million to £20 million**
**£5 million to £10 million**
**£1 million to £5 million**
**Under £1 million**

* Turnover excludes eg general taxation, national savings funds, benefits payments

## More than £2000 million
Benefits Agency
British Broadcasting Corporation
British Railways Board
Further Education Funding Council
Higher Education Funding Council for England
Intervention Board
Post Office

## £1000 million to £2000 million
British Nuclear Fuels plc
Defence Evaluation & Research Agency
Funding Agency for Schools
Highways Agency
HM Prison Service
Housing Corporation
Inland Revenue
Legal Aid Board
London Transport
Office of Passenger Rail Franchising
Ships Support Agency

## £500 million to £1000 million
Arts Council of England
Channel Four Television Corporation
Civil Aviation Authority
Employment Service
Environment Agency
HM Customs & Excise
Naval Bases & Supply Agency
New Millenium Experience Co Ltd
Police Authority for Northern Ireland
RAF Training Group Defence Agency
Scottish Higher Education Funding Council

## £250 million to £500 million
Army Base Repair Organisation
British Council
Child Support Agency
Contributions Agency
Crown Prosecution Service
Engineering & Physical Sciences Research Council
English Partnerships
English Sports Council
Horserace Totalisator Board
Information Technology Services Agency
London Pensions Fund Authority
Medical Research Council
Millennium Commission
National Heritage Memorial Fund
National Lottery Charities Board
Naval Recruiting & Training Agency
RAF Maintenance Group Defence Agency
Scottish Enterprise
Scottish Homes

## £100 million to £250 million
Army Base Storage & Distribution Agency
Bank of England
Biotechnology & Biological Sciences Reseach Council
British Library
Central Office of Information
Commonwealth Development Corporation
Council for the Central Laboratory of the Research Councils
Criminal Injuries Compensation Authority
Defence Clothing & Textiles Agency

Defence Secondary Care Agency.
Driver & Vehicle Licensing Agency
East of Scotland Water Authority
English Heritage
Further Education Funding Council for Wales
Health & Safety Commission and Executive
Higher Education Funding Council for Wales
HM Land Registry
Met Office
Ministry of Defence Police
National Savings
Natural Environment Research Council
Naval Aircraft Repair Organisation
Office for National Statistics
Particle Physics & Astronomy Research
Property Advisers to the Civil Estate
Public Health Laboratory Services Board
Remploy
Roads Service
Scottish Legal Aid Board
Scottish Prison Service
Tai Cymru
Teacher Training Agency
UK Atomic Energy Authority
UK Sports Council
Valuation Office Agency
Water Service
Welsh Development Agency
West of Scotland Water Authority

## £50 million to £100 million
Audit Commission
British Museum
British Tourist Authority
British Waterways
Cardiff Bay Development Corporation
Coal Authority
Coastguard
Commission for the New Towns
Construction Industry Training Board
Crown Agents Foundation
Defence Transport & Movements Executive
Driving Standards Agency
Economic & Social Research Council
Forest Enterprise
Highlands & Islands Enterprise
Horserace Betting Levy Board
Insolvency Service
Meat & Livestock Commission
Military Survey
North of Scotland Water Authority
Northern Ireland Local Government Officers'
Superannuation Committee
Northern Ireland Transport Holding Company
Ordnance Survey
Patent Office
Qualifications & Curriculum Authority
Royal Mint
S4C
Scottish Arts Council
Scottish Court Service
Service Children's Education
UK Passport Agency
Vehicle Inspectorate

## £20 million to £50 million

Advisory, Conciliation & Arbitration Service
Army Technical Support Agency
Arts Council of Wales
British Film Institute
Caledonian MacBrayne Ltd
Central Council for Education & Training in Social Work
Central Science Laboratory
Companies House
Countryside Commission
Countryside Council for Wales
Defence Postal & Courier Services Agency
Employment Tribunals Service
English Nature
Forensic Science Service
Historic Royal Palaces
Historic Scotland
Horticulture Research International
Joint Air Reconnaissance Intelligence Centre
Liverpool Housing Action Trust
Local Enterprise Development Unit
Marine Safety Agency
Meat Hygiene Service
Medical Supplies Agency
Medicines Control Agency
National Gallery
National Museum of Science & Industry
National Museums of Scotland
Natural History Museum
Northern Lighthouse Board
Pay & Personnel Agency
Planning Inspectorate
Policyholders' Protection Board
Public Record Office
Radiocommunications Agency
RAF Logistics Support Services
RAF Signals Engineering Establishment
Registers of Scotland
Royal Botanic Gardens Kew
Royal Parks Agency
Rural Development Commission
Scottish Environment Protection Agency
Scottish Natural Heritage
Scottish Qualifications Authority
Scottish Sports Council
Scottish Tourist Board
Security Facilities Executive
Tate Gallery
Training & Employment Agency (NI)
Trinity House Lighthouse Service
UK Hydrographic Office
Veterinary Laboratories Agency
Victoria & Albert Museum
Waltham Forest Housing Action Trust
War Pensions Agency

## £10 million to £20 million

British Educational Communications & Technology Agency
Buying Agency
Cadw
Castle Vale Housing Action Trust
Civil Service College
Commission for Racial Equality
Construction Service
Defence Bills Agency
Engineering Construction Industry Training Board

English Tourist Board
Environment & Heritage Service
Fire Service College
Highlands & Islands Airports
Imperial War Museum
Independent Television Commission
Medical Devices Agency
Museum of London
National Biological Standards Board
National Board for Nursing, Midwifery & Health Visiting for Northern Ireland
National Maritime Museum
National Museums & Galleries Merseyside
National Museums & Galleries of Wales
National Radiological Protection Board
NHS Pensions Agency
Northern Ireland Council for Postgraduate Medical & Dental Education
Northern Ireland Council for the Curriculum, Examinations & Assessment
Northern Ireland Tourist Board
Office of Electricity Regulation
Office of Gas Supply
Pesticides Safety Directorate
Planning Service
Probation Board for Northern Ireland
Public Trust Office
Qualifications, Curriculum & Assessment Authority for Wales
Queen Elizabeth II Conference Centre
Rowett Research Institute
Royal Commission on the Historical Monuments of England
Scottish Children's Reporter Administration
Scottish Crop Research Institute
Scottish Fisheries Protection Agency
Sea Fish Industry Authority
Serious Fraud Office
Sports Council for Wales
Student Loans Company
Tower Hamlets Housing Action Trust
Traffic Director for London
Valuation & Lands Agency
Wales Tourist Board

## £5 million to £10 million

Accounts Commission for Scotland
Arts Council of Northern Ireland
Business Development Service
Covent Garden Market Authority
Defence Analytical Services Agency
Defence Animal Centre
Defence Codification Agency
Design Council
Driver & Vehicle Licensing Northern Ireland
Driver & Vehicle Testing Agency
Duke of York's Royal Military School
English National Board for Nursing, Midwifery & Health Visiting
Enterprise Ulster
Equal Opportunities Commission
Food from Britain
Home-Grown Cereals Authority
Industrial Research & Technology Unit
Joint Nature Conservation Committee
Laganside Corporation
Macaulay Land Use Research Institute
Monopolies & Mergers Commission

Museums & Galleries Commission
National Galleries of Scotland
National Library of Scotland
National Library of Wales
National Portrait Gallery
Naval Manning Agency
NHS Estates
Northern Ireland Child Support Agency
Northern Ireland Statistics and Research Agency
Office of Telecommunications
Office of Water Services
Ordnance Survey of Northern Ireland
Queen Victoria School
Rate Collection Agency
Rivers Agency
Royal Armouries
Royal Botanic Garden Edinburgh
Scottish Agricultural Science Agency
Scottish Office Pensions Agency
Scottish Record Office
Stonebridge Housing Action Trust
Ulster Museum

**£1 million to £5 million**
Agricultural Research Institute of Northern Ireland
British Board of Agrément
Broadcasting Standards Commission
Centre for Information on Language Teaching & Research
Commonwealth Institute
Community Development Foundation
Compensation Agency
Construction Industry Training Board (NI)
Council for Catholic Maintained Schools
Crafts Council
Crofters' Commission
Equal Opportunities Commission for Northern Ireland
Fair Employment Commission for Northern Ireland
Fleet Air Arm Museum
Forensic Science Agency of Northern Ireland
Gaming Board for Great Britain
Gas Consumers' Council
Geffrye Museum
Government Property Lawyers
Government Purchasing Agency
Hannah Research Institute
Health Estates
Horniman Museum
Horticultural Development Council
Human Fertilisation & Embryology Authority
Investors in People UK
Labour Relations Agency
Livestock & Meat Commission for Northern Ireland
Marshall Aid Commemoration Commission
Milk Development Council
Museum of Science & Industry Manchester
National Army Museum
National Board for Nursing, Midwifery & Health Visiting for Scotland
National Consumer Council
National Film & Television School
National Forest Company
National Weights & Measures Laboratory
Northern Ireland Fishery Harbour Authority
Occupational Pensions Regulatory Authority
Office for the Regulation of Electricity & Gas
Office of the Data Protection Registrar

Office of the National Lottery
Ofwat National Customer Council (and Customer Services Committees)
Oil & Pipelines Agency
Parole Board
Police Complaints Authority
Post Office Users National Council
Radio Authority
Registrar of Public Lending Right
Residuary Body for Wales
Royal Air Force Museum
Royal Commission on Ancient & Historical Monuments in Wales
Royal Commission on Ancient & Historical Monuments of Scotland
Royal Marines Museum
Royal Naval Museum
Scottish Community Education Council
Scottish Council for Educational Technology
Scottish Further Education Unit
Scottish Hospital Endowments Research Trust
Scottish Screen
Scottish Water & Sewerage Customers Council
Simpler Trade Procedures Board
Sports Council for Northern Ireland
Student Awards Agency for Scotland
UK Ecolabelling Board
Vehicle Certification Agency
Veterinary Medicines Directorate
Wallace Collection
Welsh Language Board
Welsh National Board for Nursing, Midwifery & Health Visiting
Westminster Foundation for Democracy
Wilton Park Executive Agency
Youth Council for Northern Ireland

**Under £1 million**
Agricultural Wages Board for England & Wales
Agricultural Wages Board for Northern Ireland
Alcohol Education & Research Council
Apple & Pear Research Council
Britain-Russia Centre
British Association for Central & Eastern Europe
British Hallmarking Council
British Shipbuilders
Central Rail Users Consultative Committee
Commissioner for Protection Against Unlawful Industrial Action
Commissioner for the Rights of Trade Union Members
Commonwealth Scholarship Commission
Criminal Cases Review Commission
Education Assets Board
Fisheries Conservancy Board for Northern Ireland
Football Licensing Authority
Foyle Fisheries Commission
General Consumer Council for Northern Ireland
Great Britain-China Centre
Independent Commission for Police Complaints for Northern Ireland
London Regional Passengers Committee
Medical Practices Committee
Mental Health Commission for Northern Ireland
Northern Ireland Commissioner for Protection against Unlawful Industrial Action

Northern Ireland Commissioner for the Rights of Trade
Union Members
Northern Ireland Museums' Council
Parole Board for Scotland
Pensions Compensation Board
Rail Users Consultative Committees
Royal Navy Submarine Museum
Scottish Conveyancing & Executry Services Board
Sir John Soane's Museum
UK Register of Organic Food Standards
Wine Standards Board

*People*

# A

**Lesley Abdela MBE**
*Member of Board, British Council*
Journalist, consultant and founder of all-Party 300 Group for Women in Politcs and Public Life.

**Barbara Abensur**
*Member, Royal Parks Agency*
Chairman, Friends of Hyde Prk & Kensington Gardens.

**A Aberg**
*Representative Trustee, Royal Naval Museum*
Society of Friends, Royal Naval Museum, Portsmouth.

**Ken Abernethy**
*Chief Executive, Argyll & The Islands Enterprise*

**Nikki Abraham**
*Manager, London & South East, Gas Consumers' Council*

**Keith Ackroyd**
*Member of Board, UK Passport Agency*
Former Managing Director, Boots Retail Division.

**Sir Antony Acland GCMG GCVO**
*Trustee, National Portrait Gallery*

**Danny Adair**
*Manager Administration Finance & Legal, Local Enterprise Development Unit*

**Brian Adams**
*Member, Ofwat Central Customer Service Committee*

**Gordon Adams**
*Director, Planning and Development, Scottish Tourist Board*

**Jennifer Adams**
*Head of Commerce & Inner Parks, Royal Parks Agency*

**KA Adams**
*Field Surveys, Ordnance Survey of Northern Ireland*

**Leslie Adams**
*Head, Consumer & Business Affairs, Office for the Regulation of Electricity & Gas*

**Mark Adams**
*Head of Programme Planning, BFI On The South Bank*

**Cllr Owen Adams**
*Member of Board, Northern Ireland Museums' Council*
Down District Council. Nominated by District Council.

**RW Adams**
*Chief Executive, Forensic Science Agency of Northern Ireland*

**T Adams**
*Senior Inspector, South East Region, Gaming Board for Great Britain*

**Miss V Adams**
*Preservation, Public Record Office of Northern Ireland*

**David Adams Jones**
*Member of Advisory Board, Defence Analytical Services Agency*
Retired from Scottish Health Service.

**Stephen Adamson**
*Member of Steering Board, Insolvency Service*

**Dr James G Adamson OBE**
*Member, Scottish Higher Education Funding Council*
*Member of Board, Scottish Enterprise*
Vice-Chairman, NCR Financial Systems

**Mark Addison**
*Director, Safety Policy Directorate, The Health & Safety Executive*

**Michael Addison**
*Finance, Veterinary Medicines Directorate*

**Mrs JL Addyman JP**
*Member, Parole Board*

**Hon Edward Adeane CVO**
*Board Member, The British Library*
Appointed by HM the Queen.

**Prof Dawn Ades**
*Trustee, Tate Gallery*

**Brian Adgey**
*Member, Northern Ireland Tourist Board*
Chairman, Tourism & Hospitality Council. Director, Positively Belfast, Belfast Development Agency, Task Software and Commercial Union Insurance. Vice Chairman, Northern Ireland Hospice. Trustee, Karen Mortlock Trust. Founder member, Lord's Taverners in Northern Ireland. Manages own business services company.

**Kathleen Adler**
*Head of Education, National Gallery*

**Christine Agambar**
*Research, Analysis & International, Office for Standards in Education*

**David Ager**
*Acting Group Director, The Government Property Lawyers*

**Riaz Ahmad**
*Member, North Western Consumers' Committee, Office of Electricity Regulation*

**Romey Ahmad**
*Member, Qualifications, Curriculum & Assessment Authority for Wales*
Assistant Director of Education, Vale of Glamorgan County Borough Council.

**Miss C Aiken**
*Member, NIACT, Northern Ireland Committee on Telecommunications*
Managing director, public relations consultancy.

**Jim Aiken**
*Director of Finance, Roads Service*

**E Airey**
*Member of Board, Laganside Corporation*
Managing Director - Cheviot Projects.

**Countess of Airlie**
*Chairman, National Galleries of Scotland*

**Earl of Airlie KT GCVO**
*Chairman of Board of Trustees, Historic Royal Palaces*

**Dr M Airs**
*Commissioner, Royal Commission on Historical Mon uments of England*

**Ian Aitchison**
*Communications & Planning, Home-Grown Cereals Authority*

**Chris Aitken**
*Director, Property Development & Funding, Scottish Enterprise*

**Colonel D Aitken**
*Assistant Director, Partnering, Armed Forces Personnel Administration Agency*

**Prof ID Aitken OBE**
*Member of Ownership Board, Veterinary Medicines Directorate*
Independent Member.

**Stephanie Al-Wahid**
*Director of Development, DH Regeneration, Waltham Forest Housing Action Trust*

**Roy Alder**
*Head of Executive Support, Medicines Control Agency*

**RJ Alderman**
*Personal Taxation, Oil & International, Collection, Criminal Prosecutions, Rating & Employment, Inland Revenue*

**Francis Aldhouse**
*Deputy Registrar, Office of the Data Protection Registrar*

**Hugh Aldous**
*Member, Monopolies & Mergers Commission*
Chartered Accountant. Managing Partner, Robson Rhodes. Chairman, RSM International. Director, First Russian Frontiers Trust and Gartmore Venture Capital Trust. Deputy Chairman, Focus.

**D Aldridge**
*Section Head, Casino & Bingo, Gaming Board for Great Britain*

**Ms Tobe Aleksander**
*Member, London Consumers' Committee, Office of Electricity Regulation*

**B Alexander**
*Chairman, REPAC, The Environment Agency*

**K Alexander**
*Adviser in GDP, Northern Ireland Council for Postgraduate Medical & Dental Education*

**Pam Alexander**
*Chief Executive, English Heritage*

**Prof Robin Alexander**
*Board Member, Qualifications & Curriculum Authority*

Professor of Primary Education and Director of the Centre for Research in Elementary & Primary Education, University of Warwick.

**Ziggi Alexander**
*Member, Central Council for Education & Training in Social Work*

**Prof Margaret Alexander CBE**
*Member, Scottish Hospital Endowments Research Trust*

**Andy Allan**
*Governor, National Film & Television School*

**J Allan**
*Member of Board, Scottish Children's Reporter Administration*
Sheriff, Lanark Sheriff Court. Vice-President, Sheriffs' Association.

**John B Allan**
*Member, Scottish Agricultural Wages Board*
Independent member appointed by the Secretary of State for Scotland.

**Joy Allan**
*Member, BACT, Office of Telecommunications*
Managing Director, hotel and catering company.

**Mrs Linda Allan**
*Member, Police Complaints Authority*

**M Allan**
*Senior Assistant Director (Technical), Traffic Director for London*

**Tom Allan**
*Director, Marine Safety & Standards, Marine Safety Agency*

**M Allchin**
*Member of Council, British Hallmarking Council*

**Barry Allen**
*Chairman, Enterprise Ayrshire*

**Bill Allen**
*Deputy Director, Monetary Analysis, Bank of England*

**DF Allen**
*Chairman, Sports Council for Northern Ireland*

**Don Allen**
*Observer, UK Sports Council*
Observer, Sports Council for Northern Ireland

**Peter Allen**
*Non-Executive Director, Post Office*

**Richard Allen**
*Director of Development, London Pensions Fund Authority*

**Robert Allen**
*Harmonisation and Quality Assurance, Medical Devices Agency*

**Roger Allen**
*Director Ships Logistics Engineering, Ships Support Agency*
*Member of Advisory Board, Disposal Sales Agency*

Director of Supply Logistics Engineering (DSLE).

**Tim Allen**
*Regional Officer, Countryside Commission*

**Tim Allen**
*Secretary to the Board, Financial Services Authority*

**Prof Ingrid Allen CBE**
*Member, National Biological Standards Board*
*Member, Industrial Research & Technology Unit*
Head NI Neuropathology Unit, Institute of Pathology, Royal Victoria Hospital.

**Waheed Alli**
*Member of Board, Teacher Training Agency*
Joint Managing Director, Planet 24 and Planet 24 Productions.

**Justice Alliot**
*Vice-Chairman, Parole Board*

**Air Chief Marshal Sir John Allison KCB CBE**
*Air Member for Logistics, Royal Air Force Museum*

**Roderick Allison CB**
*Chief Executive, Offshore Safety, The Health & Safety Executive*

**Geoff Allister**
*Divisional Roads Manager, Roads Service*

**JS Allister**
*Chairman, Foyle Fisheries Commission*

**Christopher Allsopp**
*Member of Court, Bank of England*

**Marjorie Allthorpe-Guyton**
*Director, Visual Arts, The Arts Council of England*

**David Allwood**
*Acting Sector Director - Manufacturing & Commerce, Commonwealth Development Corporation*

**Dr Alan Almond**
*Cereals Marketing, Home-Grown Cereals Authority*

**N Almond**
*Head of Retrovirology, National Biological Standards Board*

**Adrian Alsop**
*Deputy Director of Research, Economic & Social Research Council*

**Allan Alstead CBE**
*Chief Executive, Scottish Sports Council*
Observer, UK Sports Council

**Sir Nigel Althaus**
*Member, London Pensions Fund Authority*
Former Government Broker.

**Paul Altobell**
*Chief Executive, Defence Analytical Services Agency*

**Guillermo Alvarez de Lorenzana**
*Food from Britain (Spain) SL*

**Prof Ronald Amann**
*Chief Executive, Economic & Social Research Council*

**Colin Amery BA**
*Member of Board of Governors, Museum of London*
Appointed by the Prime Minister.

**Amos Amos**
*Manager, Sumburgh Airport, Highlands & Islands Airports*

**Ron Amy OBE**
*Member of Board, Occupational Pensions Regulatory Authority*
Chief Executive, Aon Consulting. Former member of Occupational Pensions Board and former Chairman National Association of Pensions Funds. (Nominated by the NAPF.)

**Andy Anderson**
*Director of Scottish National Sports Centres, Scottish Sports Council*

**Brian Anderson**
*Chairman, Shetland Enterprise*

**Callan Anderson**
*Member, Rail Users Consultative Committee for Scotland*

**David Anderson**
*Head of Education, Victoria & Albert Museum*

**David Anderson**
*Chief Executive, Dunbartonshire Enterprise*

**David Anderson**
*Land Systems, Defence Evaluation & Research Agency*

**Dr Eric Anderson**
*Chairman, National Heritage Memorial Fund*

**Miss F Anderson**
*Secretary, Scottish Agricultural Wages Board*

**Prof JM Anderson**
*Member of Council, English Nature*
Professor of Ecology, University of Exeter. Former Board of Management, IUBS/UNESCO Tropical Soil Biology Programme.

**John Anderson**
*Principal Clerk of Session & Justiciary, Scottish Court Service*

**K Anderson**
*Member of Advisory Board, Service Children's Education*
Chief Education Officer.

**Prof M Anderson**
*Board Member, The British Library*
University of Edinburgh.

**Peter D Anderson**
*Deputy Keeper, Scottish Record Office*

**Det Ch Supt PW Anderson**
*OCU CID, Ministry of Defence Police*

**Dr RGW Anderson**
*Director, British Museum*

**RJ Derick Anderson**
*Chief Executive, Foyle Fisheries Commission*

**Ray Anderson**
*Director of Policy, Veterinary Medicines Directorate*

**Miss SP Anderson**
*Assistant Keeper, The Royal Commission on Historical Manuscripts*

**T Anderson**
*Assistant Operations Manager, Covent Garden Market Authority*

**Prof Tom Anderson**
*Member, Scottish Water & Sewerage Customers Council*
Chairman, West Area Committee.

**John Anderson CBE**
*Member, North Eastern Consumers' Committee, Office of Electricity Regulation*

**Keith Anderson CBE**
*Member of Board, Teacher Training Agency*
Former Chief Education Officer, Gloucestershire County Council.

**Prof Kathleen J Anderson, OBE**
*Trustee, National Library of Scotland*

**JD Andrewes**
*Member of Board, Crown Agents Foundation*

**Elizabeth Andrews**
*Member of Council, Countryside Council for Wales*
Company Chairman. Member, Environment Agency Committee.

**Ian Andrews**
*MD Facilities, Defence Evaluation & Research Agency*

**Prof John Andrews**
*Chief Executive, Higher Education Funding Council for Wales & Further Education Funding Council for Wales Observer, Higher Education Funding Council for England*
Chief Executive, Higher Education Funding Council for Wales.

**Leighton Andrews**
*Member of Board, Tai Cymru*
Former Head of Worldwide Corporate Affairs, BBC. UK Campaign Director for 1987 International Year of Shelter for the Homeless.

**Ms M Andrews**
*Member, Northern Ireland Fishery Harbour Authority*
*Member, Sea Fish Industry Authority*
Ex-Chief Executive, Newry & Mourne Cooperative. Business & Management Consultant.

**John Angus**
*Organisational Review, Roads Service*

**Rae Angus**
*Education member, Engineering Construction Industry Training Board*

**Sue Angus**
*Member, Scottish Community Education Council*

**Denis Annett**
*District Valuer, Valuation & Lands Agency*

**Cllr Doris Ansari**
*Member, Tate Gallery*

**Sandra J Anstey**
*Member, National Library of Wales*
Elected by the Court of Governors.

**Rod Anthony**
*Finance Director, Forensic Science Service*

**Brian Appleton**
*Non-Executive Vice-Chairman, London Transport*
*Non-Executive Director, LUL*
Former Director of ICI Chemicals & Polymers. Assessor to the Piper Alpha Inquiry.

**Chris Appleton**
*Non-Executive Director, UK Atomic Energy Authority*
Partner, Smith & Williamson, Chartered Accountants.

**Major M Appleton**
*Product Director (General Stores), Defence Clothing & Textiles Agency*

**Michael Apps**
*Member, South Western Consumers' Committee, Office of Electricity Regulation*

**Norman Apsley**
*Electronics, Defence Evaluation & Research Agency*

**John Archer**
*Chief Executive, Scottish Screen*

**Libby Archer**
*Scientific Liaison Executive, Horserace Betting Levy Board*

**Dr Mary Archer**
*Member, National Museum of Science & Industry*

**Mike Archer**
*Head, Economic Regulation (Electricity), Office for the Regulation of Electricity & Gas*

**Mrs Liliana Archibald**
*Chairman, Wilton Park Executive Agency*

**RJ Ardern**
*Member, Post Office Users' Council for Scotland*
Principal Information Officer, Business Information Source, Inverness. Chairman, Highland Post Office Advisory Committee. Member, Highland Telecommunications Advisory Committee. Member, Crown (Inverness) Community Council.

**Malcolm Argent, CBE**
*Deputy Chairman, Civil Aviation Authority*
Chairman, National Air Traffic Services. Previously Secretary, Post Office BT Corporation and British Telecommunications. Non-Executive Director, BT, Clerical Medical Investment Group and Westminster Healthcare Holdings.

**Claire Argyle**
*Member, Qualifications, Curriculum & Assessment Authority for Wales*
Head of English, Ysgol Dyffryn Taf.

**Eric Armatage**
*Board Member, The Housing Corporation*

**Moira Armstrong**
*Governor, National Film & Television School*

**Nigel Armstrong**
*Director, North East Region, The Housing Corporation*

**Pat Armstrong CBE**
*Chairman, Police Authority for Northern Ireland*

**Hilary Armstrong MP**
*Vice-Chairman, British Council*
Labour MP for Durham North-West and Minister of State for local government and housing.

**Lord Armstrong of Ilminster GCB CVO**
*Chairman, Victoria & Albert Museum*

**Dr GP Arnold**
*Chair, Fisheries Science & Management Group, Centre for Environment, Fisheries & Aquaculture Science*

**THC Arnold**
*Resource Management, National Museums & Galleries of Wales*

**David Arnott**
*Member, Scottish Sports Council*

**Ms A Arrowsmith**
*Commissioner, Royal Commission on Historical Monuments of England*

**BC Arthur CBE**
*Member of Board, Education Assets Board*

**Ald Gavyn Arthur**
*Trustee, Sir John Soane's Museum*
Representative of the Court of Aldermen of the City of London.

**John R Arthur**
*Head, Micronutrient & Lipid Metabolism Division, Rowett Research Institute*

**Richard Arthur**
*Member, Audit Commission*
Leader, London Borough of Camden. Member, Leader's Committee, Association of London Government and Policy Committee, Association of Metropolitan Authorities. Worked for Commonwealth Development Finance Company. Consultant.

**Ian Ash**
*Non-Executive Director, New Millennium Experience Co Ltd*
Director, Corporate Relations, BT.

**Prof Sir Eric Ash CBE**
*Non-Executive Director, Student Loans Company*
Professor, Department of Physics, University College London. Former Rector, Imperial College of Science & Technology. Former Non-Executive Director, British Telecom.

**Mike Ashbrook**
*Client member, Engineering Construction Industry Training Board*

**K Ashcroft**
*Non-Executive Member of Board, Trinity House Lighthouse Service*

**Mrs Pauline Ashley**
*Chairman, South Eastern Consumers' Committee, Office of Electricity Regulation*

**Jonathan Ashley-Smith**
*Head of Conservation, Victoria & Albert Museum*

**David Ashton**
*Head, Operations Unit, The Health & Safety Executive*

**Geoffrey Ashton**
*Board Member, Qualifications & Curriculum Authority*
Headteacher, Standish Community High School, Wigan.

**Loraine Ashton**
*Member, National Consumer Council*

**Dr JM Ashworth**
*Chairman, The British Library*

**John Ashworth OBE**
*Chairman, Renfrewshire Enterprise*

**Vernon Ashworth**
*Head of Business Operations, Defence Bills Agency*

**Brian Asquith**
*Member of Council, Crafts Council*
Silversmith.

**Bob Assirati**
*Chief Executive, Central Computer & Telecommunications Agency*

**J Astbury**
*Chief Coastguard, Coastguard*

**Stephen Astley**
*Assistant Curator (Drawings), Sir John Soane's Museum*

**Brigadier MA Atherton CBE JP**
*Commissioner, Duke of York's Royal Military School*

**Lieutenant Colonel BM Atkins**
*Member of Advisory Board, Service Children's Education*

**Prof Bernard Atkinson**
*Member, Biotechnology & Biological Sciences Research Council*

**Gerald Atkinson**
*Member, Yorkshire Consumers' Committee, Office of Electricity Regulation*

**PD Atkinson**
*Member of Council, British Hallmarking Council*

**Mrs Valerie Atkinson**
*Trustee, National Galleries of Scotland*

**Sir David Attenborough CH CVO CBE**
*Trustee, British Museum*

**Mike Attenborough**
*Technical Director, Meat & Livestock Commission*

**Cynthia Atwell**
*Member, Health & Safety Commission*
Director of Operations and Chief Nursing Adviser, Occupational Health Care (Railways). Appointed to represent interests of employees. Former Head of Occupational Health & Safety, Birmingham City Council; Esso Lecturer in Occupational Health, Royal College of Nursing Institute; Director, Seltech Engineering Services; and Member, English National Board for Nursing Midwifery & Health Visiting.

**Bryan Austin**
*Member, Gaming Board for Great Britain Part-time Board Member, Civil Aviation Authority*
Former Group Director Business Planning & Development, WH Smith.

**Cllr Stanley Austin**
*Board Member, Castle Vale Housing Action Trust*
Member, Birmingham City Council. Served on Social Services, Education, Housing, West Midlands Police, West Midlands Fire Service Committees.

**Dawn Austwick**
*Projector Director, Tate Gallery of Modern Art, Tate Gallery*

**JR Avent**
*Chief Inspector of Ancient Monuments & Historic Buildings, Cadw*

**Mrs Phyllis Avery**
*Member, English Sports Council*

**Peter Avis**
*Director, British Educational Communications & Technology Agency*

**Shu Awath-Behari**
*Member, Ofwat Central Customer Service Committee*

**Gwenllian M Awbery**
*Member of Authority, S4C*
Lecturer in Welsh, Department for Continuing Education & Professional Development, University of Wales, Cardiff. Research Associate, School of Celtic Studies, Dublin Institute of Advanced Studies.

**Robert Ayling**
*Chairman, New Millennium Experience Co Ltd*
*Member of Board, British Tourist Authority*
Chief Executive, British Airways. Former Under-Secretary (Legal), Dept of Trade & Industry.

**GE Aylmer**
*Commissioner, The Royal Commission on Historical Manuscripts*

**Les Aylward**
*Workshop Manager, Museum of Science & Industry Manchester*

**Brian Ayres**
*Finance Officer, Gas Consumers' Council*

**Godfrey Ayres**
*Projects Development Executive, Horserace Betting Levy Board*

**Suhail Aziz**
*Member, Commonwealth Scholarship Commission*
Chairman & Managing Director, Brettonwood Partnership.

# B

**Denis Babes**
*Manager Business Development Services, Local Enterprise Development Unit*

**Jenny Bacon CB**
*Director General, The Health & Safety Executive*

**Professor AD Baddeley**
*Member, National Radiological Protection Board*
Department of Psychology, University of Bristol.

**Brian Bade**
*Business Affairs Manager, Office of the National Lottery*

**John Bader**
*Director Operations & Deputy Chief Executive, Tai Cymru*

**Peter Badger**
*Head of Legal Metrology Policy Unit, National Weights & Measures Laboratory*

**Linda Badham**
*Assistant Chief Executive (Qualifications & Curriculum 14-19), Qualifications, Curriculum & Assessment Authority for Wales*

**Sir Jack Baer**
*Commissioner, Museums & Galleries Commission*
Former Chairman, Hazlitt, Gooden & Fox Art Gallery. Former Chairman, Society of London Art Dealers. Former President, Fine Art Provident Institution. Member, Government's Fine Arts & Antiques Export Reviewing Committee. Trustee, Burlington Magazine Foundation.

**H Baggaley**
*Member of Board, Construction Industry Training Board*
Herbert Baggaley Construction.

**Dr Gulam Bahadur**
*Member, Human Fertilisation & Embryology Authority*
Clinical Biochemist. Head of Fertility Laboratories, UCLMS/UCLH Trust.

**Kamlesh Bahl**
*Chairwoman, Equal Opportunities Commission*
Solicitor. Member, Council of the Law Society. European Commission's representative, Consultative Commission on Racism & Xenophobia.

**Ian Baildon-Smith**
*Data Distribution, Companies House*

**Sir Alan Bailey KCB**
*Non-Executive Director, London Transport*
Former Permanent Secretary, Department of Transport and Second Permanent Secretary, Treasury.

**Andrew Bailey**
*Member, Ofwat Customer Service Committee for Wales*

**D Bailey**
*Director of Development, LUL, London Transport*

**Commodore KRG Bailey**
*Director, Armed Forces Personnel Administration Agency*

**Michael Bailey**
*Member of Museum Trust, Museum of Science & Industry Manchester*

**Dr MR Bailey**
*Head of Department, Dose Assessments, National Radiological Protection Board*

**T Bailey**
*Head of Buildings & Maintenance, Royal Botanic Gardens Kew*

**Sir Alan Bailey KCB**
*Deputy Chairman, LTB, London Transport*

**Roy Bailie**
*Member of Court, Bank of England*

**Roy Bailie**
*Deputy Chairman, Northern Ireland Tourist Board*
Chairman, W & G Baird Group. Former Chairman, British Printing Industries Federation and CBI (NI). Board member, Industrial Development Board.

**Roy Bailie OBE**
*Member of Board, British Tourist Authority*

**Allan Baillie**
*Director of Lands, Defence Estates Organisation*

**AC Bain**
*Member of Governing Body, Scottish Crop Research Institute*
Soft fruit grower. Former Chairman, Scottish Soft Fruit Discussion Society. Former Director, Scottish Nuclear Stock Association. Currently Member of Committee of Management, Scottish Society for Crop Research.

**Prof Andrew Bain OBE**
*Member of Board, Scottish Enterprise*

**Mick Bain**
*Manager, Kirkwall Airport, Highlands & Islands Airports*

**Godfrey Bainbridge**
*Member, North Western Consumers' Committee, Office of Electricity Regulation*

**Brigadier David Baines MBE**
*Member, Ofwat Wessex Customer Service Committee*

**John Baird**
*Member of Advisory Board, Defence Analytical Services Agency*
Surgeon General.

**Prof Colin Baker**
*Member of Board, Welsh Language Board*
Professor of Education, University College, Bangor.

**Prof Hugh Baker**
*Member, The Great Britain-China Centre*
Head, Department of East Asia, School of Oriental and African Studies, University of London. Chairman, Great Britain-China Educational Trust.

**John Baker MBE**
*Commissioner, Meat & Livestock Commission*
Joint Managing Director, Baker Group of Companies. Also has farming and transport interests. Former President, Federation of Fresh Meat Wholesalers.

**Martyn Baker**
*Member, Biotechnology & Biological Sciences Research Council*

**Michael Baker**
*Director, Artform Development Division, Arts Council of Wales*

**Ray E Baker OBE**
*Chairman, Fife Enterprise*

**Prof Raymond Baker**
*Deputy Chairman & Chief Executive, Biotechnology & Biological Sciences Research Council*

**Roger Baker**
*Member of Board, Waltham Forest Housing Action Trust*
Housing consultant.

**William Baker**
*Member, Merseyside & North Wales Consumers' Committee, Office of Electricity Regulation*

**Joan Bakewell**
*Governor, British Film Institute*

**Mrs L Baldry**
*Member, Property Advisers to the Civil Estate*

Prudential Portfolio Managers.

**Mrs Patricia Baldwin**
*Member, South Eastern Consumers' Committee, Office of Electricity Regulation*

**Mrs Barbara Bale**
*Member, Welsh National Board for Nursing, Midwifery & Health Visiting*
Principal Lecturer, Midwifery, University of Glamorgan.

**Brigadier AD Ball CBE**
*Chief Executive, Army Technical Support Agency*

**J Ball**
*Mechanical Engineer, Covent Garden Market Authority*

**Prof JM Ball**
*Member of Council, Engineering & Physical Sciences Research Council*
Oxford University

**Martin Ball**
*Financial Services, UK Sports Council*

**Tony Ballance**
*Chief Economist, Office of Water Services*

**Anne Balmer**
*Director, Legal Services, Fair Employment Commission for Northern Ireland*

**J Balmforth**
*Member, Rail Users Consultative Committee for the Midlands*

**Peter Bamford**
*Assistant Director, Office of Fair Trading*

**Norman Bancroft MBE**
*Member, Ofwat South West Customer Service Committee*

**Mrs A Banister**
*Member of Board, Highlands & Islands Enterprise*

**Caroline Banks**
*Principal Establishment & Finance Officer, Office of Fair Trading*

**Mrs Andrea Banner**
*Member of Board, Pensions Compensation Board*
Director of Administration, Abbey National Benefit Consultants. Former OPAS advisor. Member, CBI Pensions Panel. Nominated by CBI.

**Eamonn Bannon**
*Member, Scottish Sports Council*

**Bob Bansback**
*Industry Development Director, Meat & Livestock Commission*

**Stephen Banyard**
*Non-Executive Director, Contributions Agency*
Head, Inland Revenue Deregulation Unit.

**B Barber**
*Member of Council, Advisory, Conciliation & Arbitration Service*

**Ms J Barber**
*Member of Council, English Nature*
Independent consultant. Member, Groundwork Foundation Board and Tarmac's Environmental Advisory Panel. Member, Severn Trent Water's Environmental Panel. Trustee, Forum for the Future. Consultant to WWF, DoE, Environment Protection Strategy and European Division and National Lottery Charities' Board.

**Nicholas Barber**
*Trustee, British Museum*

**Henry Barbour**
*Head of Finance & Personnel, Commonwealth Institute*

**WJ Barbour**
*Finance Manager, Enterprise Ulster*

**Peter Bareau**
*Chief Executive, National Savings*

**Prof Lorraine Baric**
*Chairman, North Western Consumers' Committee, Office of Electricity Regulation*

**Tessa Baring**
*Member of UK Committee, National Lottery Charities Board*
Chairman, Association of Charitable Foundations. Part-time Charity Commissioner. Trustee, of Barnardos. Trustee, Baring Foundation. Former DTI Deregulation Task Force for Charities & Voluntary Organisations. Chair, Mental Health Foundation Enquiry into Mental Health of Children & Young People. Member of Council, Charitable Support & NCVO Advisory Council.

**Mrs ABC Barker**
*Member, Parole Board*

**Ms S Barker**
*Member, Rail Users Consultative Committee for the Midlands*

**Cllr Dennis Barkway CBE**
*Member, London Pensions Fund Authority*
Member, Bromley Council. Trustee, Bromley Pension Fund.

**Prof David Barlow**
*Member, Human Fertilisation & Embryology Authority*
Head of IVF Department, John Radcliffe Hospital, Oxford.

**Disney Barlow CBE**
*Member, East of Scotland Water Authority*
Farmer and Chartered Surveyor. Former Head Factor, National Trust for Scotland. Former Convener, Scottish Landowners Federation. Chairman, Rural Practice Division, Royal Institution of Chartered Surveyors. Member SEPA (East Region Board). Member, Earlston Community Council.

**Andy Barnes**
*Director of Advertising Sales & Marketing, Channel Four Television Corporation*

**Dr C Barnes**
*Member, Logistic Information Systems Agency*
DPMP.

**Christopher Barnes**
*Board Director, Home-Grown Cereals Authority*

**Fod Barnes**
*Policy Adviser, Office of Telecommunications*

**Heather Barnes**
*Director of Human Resources, Scottish Children's Reporter Administration*

**Ishbel Barnes**
*Head, Private Records, Scottish Record Office*

**John Barnes**
*Member, DIEL, Office of Telecommunications*
Chartered telecoms engineer.

**Martin Barnes**
*Director, Management Development, Civil Service College*

**Rufus Barnes**
*Director, London Regional Passengers Committee*

**Don Barnett**
*Head, Local Authority Unit, The Health & Safety Executive*

**Supt G Barnett**
*OCU, Hereford, Ministry of Defence Police*

**Ian Barnett**
*Member, Rail Users Consultative Committee for North Western England*

**Laurence Barnett**
*Customer Relations Manager, Central Computer & Telecommunications Agency*

**Phillip Barnett**
*Joint Head of Equality Policy Consultancy, Commission for Racial Equality*

**Tim Barnsley**
*Companies House London, Companies House*

**Dr Alan Barr**
*Member, Scottish Community Education Council*

**Mrs Carole Barr**
*Member, Yorkshire Consumers' Committee, Office of Electricity Regulation*

**Danielle Barr**
*Commissioner, Broadcasting Standards Commission*
Former Chairman and Managing Director, advertising agencies.

**Roger Barr**
*General Manager, Wilton Park Executive Agency*

**Dr Michael Barraclough**
*Chair, Tower Hamlets Housing Action Trust*
Retired Consultant Physician. Director, Inner City Self Development. Trustee, East London Marine Venture, Mudchute Park & Urban Farm Trust, Queen Elizabeth Barge Project Docklands Sailing Centre.

**Gordon S Barrass CMG**
*Member, The Great Britain-China Centre*
Adviser, International Affairs, Coopers & Lybrand International. Former Under Secretary, Cabinet Office and served in HM Charge d'Affaires, Peking.

**W Barrie Page**
*Member, Scottish Agricultural Wages Board*
Independent member appointed by the Secretary of State for Scotland.

**A Barrow**
*Member, Parole Board*

**Mrs Heather Barrow**
*Member, Eastern Consumers' Committee, Office of Electricity Regulation*

**Dame Jocelyn Barrow DBE**
*Governor, British Film Institute*
*Director & Trustee, Horniman Museum*

**TW Barrowcliffe**
*Head of Haematology, National Biological Standards Board*

**Miss L Barrowman**
*Midwifery/Paediatrics, National Board for Nursing, Midwifery & Health Visiting for Northern Ireland*

**AJ Barry**
*Member of Board, Construction Industry Training Board*
Commercial Finishing Contractors Group.

**Richard Barry**
*Director, South West & Wales, Property Advisers to the Civil Estate*

**Prof CA Barth**
*Member of Governing Body, Rowett Research Institute*

**John Bartlett**
*Member, South Western Consumers' Committee, Office of Electricity Regulation*

**Simon Bartlett**
*Deputy Chairman, Waltham Forest Housing Action Trust*
Tenant Board Member of Cathall Road Estate. Community Development Co-ordinator.

**Tim Bartlett**
*Chief Executive, English Tourist Board*

**Hugo Barton**
*Member, Ofwat South West Customer Service Committee*

**Noel Bartram**
*Board Director, Home-Grown Cereals Authority*

**Major Pater Bateman**
*Assistant Director, Administration Division, National Army Museum*

**Prof Patrick Bateson**
*Commissioner, Museums & Galleries Commission*
Professor of Ethology, Cambridge University. Provost, King's College, Cambridge.

**Mrs PL Bateson**
*Member of Board, Enterprise Ulster*

**SL Batiste**
*Member of Council, British Hallmarking Council*

**Ray Battersby**
*Director, Trade Facilitation, Simpler Trade Procedures Board*

**Dennis Battle**
*Director Personnel and Finance, HM Customs & Excise*

**Hillary Bauer**
*Fairness Director, Broadcasting Standards Commission*

**Ralph Bauer**
*Member, Post Office Users' Council for Northern Ireland*

**Robert P Bauman**
*Trustee, Royal Botanic Gardens Kew*

**Jonathan Baume**
*Member of College Advisory Council, Civil Service College*

**Dr Carol Baxter**
*Member, North Western Consumers' Committee, Office of Electricity Regulation*

**Ms Carole Baxter**
*Trustee, Royal Botanic Garden Edinburgh*

**Clive Baxter**
*Member, Apple & Pear Research Council*
Fruit farmer. Member, ENFRU Variety, NFU Top Fruit and HRI East Malling Advisory Committees.

**John Baxter**
*Director, Nuclear Operations, UK Atomic Energy Authority*
Joined UKAEA in 1980. Former nuclear submarine Engineer Officer in Royal Navy. Former Director of Engineering , AEA Technology and Director Dounreay.

**Pim Baxter**
*Head of PR & Development, National Portrait Gallery*

**Seaton Baxter**
*Member of Board, Scottish Natural Heritage*

**Tom Baxter-Wright**
*Vice-Chairman, The Sports Council for Wales*

**PA Bayless**
*Member, Rail Users Consultative Committee for Eastern England*

**Dr BL Bayne**
*Director, Centre for Coastal & Marine Sciences*

**Dr John Bayrd**
*Member, Parole Board for Scotland*

**Richard Beacham**
*Business Director - New Business & Power, Commonwealth Development Corporation*

**Cdre Chris Beagley**
*Director Naval Officer Appointments, Naval Manning Agency*

**Jim Beale**
*Member, Centre for Information on Language Teaching & Research*
Project Manager, Languages Lead Body. Independent Marketing Consultant.

**Jim Beale OBE**
*Chairman, Rail Users Consultative Committee for North Eastern England*
*Member, Central Rail Users Consultative Committee*
Former commissioned service in The Royal Scots, brand management with Procter & Gamble, and management consultancy with PA Consulting Group. Non-Executive Directorships and Chairmanships of a Pension Fund, a Registered Charity and a Benevolent Fund.

**Chris Bean**
*European & Information Policy, Veterinary Medicines Directorate*

**DLS Bean**
*Head, Inland Revenue South East, Inland Revenue*

**Alex Beard**
*Director of Finance and Administration, Tate Gallery*

**Judy Beard**
*Development Director, Tate Gallery*

**EG Beardsall**
*Director of Personnel & Corporate Services, HM Land Registry*

**Gordon Beaton**
*Head of Property & Services Unit, Scottish Court Service*

**Prof Jack Beatson**
*Member, Monopolies & Mergers Commission*
Rouse Ball Professor of English Law, Cambridge University and Fellow, St John's College. A Recorder of the Crown Court.

**A Beattie**
*Director Quality & Product Support, Defence Clothing & Textiles Agency*

**Dr C Beattie**
*Member, Northern Ireland Council for Postgraduate Medical & Dental Education*
Nominated by EHSSB.

**DF Beattie**
*Member of Board, Investors in People UK*
Chief Executive, Personnel, The BOC Group.

**Prof Eric Beatty MBE**
*Member, Industrial Research & Technology Unit*
Director, Northern Ireland Technology Centre, Queen's University of Belfast.

**John Beattie**
*Director, Visitor & Industry Services, Northern Ireland Tourist Board*

**Mervyn Beattie**
*South Western, Rate Collection Agency*

**DJ Beaumont**
*Inspector, Football Licensing Authority*

**Judge Beaumont QC**
*Member, Parole Board*

**Richard Beaumont**
*Principal Finance Officer, Welsh Development Agency*

**Mrs SA Beaver**
*Member of Advisory Board, Defence Bills Agency*
Director of Procurement Finance.

**Wendy Beaver**
*Actuary, Occupational Pensions Regulatory Authority*

**Clare Beck**
*Head of Trading, Crafts Council*

**Jean Beck**
*Director, British Educational Communications & Technology Agency*

**Shirley Beck**
*Member, Tate Gallery*

**Mary Beckett**
*Member of Board, Scottish Children's Reporter Administration*
Member, Glasgow City Council. Nominated to SCRA by COSLA.

**Prof Lesley Beddie**
*Governor, Scottish Council for Educational Technology*
Napier University.

**Clement Bedeau**
*Member of Board, Stonebridge Housing Action Trust*
Resident Board Member.

**Prof Gillian Beer**
*Trustee, British Museum*

**Sir Michael Beetham GCB CBE**
*Chairman, Royal Air Force Museum*
Marshal of the Royal Air Force.

**David Beeton**
*Chief Executive, Historic Royal Palaces*

**Mrs Jennifer Beever**
*Secretary, Horniman Museum*

**Prof David Begg**
*Part-time Member, British Railways Board*
Professor, Robert Gordon University. Convenor of Transport, City of Edinburgh Council.

**Dr TNA Begg OBE JP**
*Member, Post Office Users' Council for Scotland*
Lecturer, Department of Applied

Consumer Studies, Queen Margaret College, Edinburgh.

**WK Begg OBE**
*Chairman, SACOT, Northern Ireland Committee on Telecommunications*
Chairman engineering group.

**Rob Behrens**
*Director of International Consulting, Civil Service College*

**Dr JAF Beirne**
*Member, Northern Ireland Council for Postgraduate Medical & Dental Education*
Nominated by BMA (NI).

**John Beishon**
*Chairman, Ofwat Southern Customer Service Committee*
*Member, Ofwat National Customer Council*

**Major C Belgum**
*Secretary, Defence Transport & Movements Executive*

**AJ Bell**
*Director of Contracts, Naval Bases & Supply Agency*

**Alan Bell**
*Economic Director, Office of Telecommunications*

**Anne Bell**
*Head of Human Resources, Scottish Tourist Board*

**Fred Bell**
*Member, Post Office Users' National Council*
Former Divisional Manager, Midlands Electricity. Non-Executive Director, Walsall Community NHS Trust. Industrial Tribunals Panel Member. Chairman, Walsall POAC and TAC.

**Mrs H Bell**
*Member of Board, Probation Board for Northern Ireland*

**IM Bell**
*Employer Association Member, Engineering Construction Industry Training Board*
Chief Executive, Offshore Contractors' Association

**Jeffrey Bell**
*Member, North Eastern Consumers' Committee, Office of Electricity Regulation*

**Prof JI Bell**
*Member of Council, Medical Research Council*
University of Oxford.

**Dr Jonathon Bell**
*Member of Board, Northern Ireland Museums' Council*
Acting Director, Ulster Folk & Transport Museum. Nominated by Ulster Folk & Transport Museum.

**Maeve Bell**
*Director, General Consumer Council for Northern Ireland*

**Margaret Bell**
*Chief Executive, British Educational Communications & Technology Agency*

**Robin Bell**
*Member, East of Scotland Water Authority*
Lawyer. Former Chairman, Tods Murray WS Management Board. Former Director, Edinburgh Financial Trust and Upton & Southern Holdings. Director, Citizens Advice Scotland. Vice-Chairman, Edinburgh Central Citizens Advice Bureau. Scottish Charities Nominee. Member, Scottish Council, Salmon & Trout Association.

**Mrs S Bell**
*Member, Post Office Users' Council for Scotland*
Retired hotelier. Member, Dumfries & District Posts & Telecommunications Advisory Committees.

**Susan Bell**
*Chief Executive, National Forest Company*

**Alan Bellamy**
*Head of Vocational Qualifications & Occupational Standards, Qualifications & Curriculum Authority*

**John Bellis**
*Member for Wales, Gas Consumers' Council*

**Lord Belstead LL PC**
*Chairman, Parole Board*

**Jeff Belt**
*Head of Corporate Affairs Division, Vehicle Inspectorate*

**GF Belton OBE**
*Member of Board, Queen Victoria School*

**Prof IC Benington**
*Member, Northern Ireland Council for Postgraduate Medical & Dental Education*
Director, Dentistry, QUB.

**Floella Benjamin**
*Governor, National Film & Television School*

**G Benjamin**
*Director, ABRO Land Command Support Group, Army Base Repair Organisation*

**Wendy Benjamin**
*Legal Adviser, Companies House*

**Maurice Benmayor**
*Group Director, The Government Property Lawyers*

**Alan Bennett**
*Trustee, National Gallery*

**Helen Bennett**
*Director, Crafts, Scottish Arts Council*

**Louise Bennett**
*Regional Executive, Independent Television Commission*

**Nick Bennett**
*Chief Executive, Specialist Procurement Services*

**Lieutenant Colonel P Bennett**
*Commanding Officer, 17 Port & Maritime Regiment RLC, Defence Transport & Movements Executive*

**Dr Seton Bennett**
*Chief Executive & Director, National Weights & Measures Laboratory*

**Prof M Bennett OBE**
*Keeper of the Jodrell Laboratory, Royal Botanic Gardens Kew*

**Mrs Jane Benson LVO OBE**
*Trustee, National Portrait Gallery*

**Group Captain BG Benstead**
*Officer Commanding, RAF North Luffenham, RAF Maintenance Group Defence Agency*

**W Bentley**
*Non-Executive Committee Member, HM Prison Service*

**David C Benton**
*Chief Executive, National Board for Nursing, Midwifery & Health Visiting for Scotland*

**Margaret Benton**
*Head of Museum, Theatre Museum, Victoria & Albert Museum*

**Professor V Beral**
*Member, National Radiological Protection Board*
ICRF Cancer Epidemiology Unit, University of Oxford.

**Mary Berg**
*Member, Equal Opportunities Commission*
Independent consultant. Chairman, Scandinavian Financial Communications. Non-Executive Member, Policy Board of the Office for National Statistics.

**Len Berkowitz**
*Head, Legal Unit, Bank of England*

**Group Captain DC Bernard MBE**
*Product Division (Clothing & Textiles), Defence Clothing & Textiles Agency*

**Stanley Bernard**
*Member of Council, Food from Britain*
Managing Director, Sco-Fro Foods.

**Dr C Berry**
*Member, Parole Board*

**Prof Sir Colin Berry**
*Member, Pesticides Safety Directorate*
Professor of Morbid Anatomy & Histopathology, Royal London Hospital. Chairman, Advisory Committee on Pesticides (ACP).

**CR Berry**
*Financial Controller, Driver & Vehicle Testing Agency*

**Graham Berry**
*Director, Finance & Administration, Scottish Arts Council*

**Cllr Ian Berry JP**
*Member, East of Scotland Water Authority*
City of Edinburgh Councillor. Former

Member, Central Scotland Water Development Board and Forth River Purification Board. Former chairman, Lothian Regional Council Water and Drainage Committee. Former Vice-Convener, Lothian Regional Council and Member, Edinburgh District Council.

**KG Berry**
*General Manager, Oil & Pipelines Agency*

**Norman Berry**
*Member of Board, West of Scotland Water Authority*
Senior Consultant, Babtie Group.

**PF Berry**
*Managing Director & Crown Agent, Crown Agents Foundation*

**David Bertram**
*Chairman, Central Rail Users Consultative Committee*
Chairman, Doncaster Healthcare NHS Trust. Past Director of Total Quality, Rockware Glass. Member of the British Transport Police Committee.

**George Bertram**
*Chief Executive, Contributions Agency*
Joined Civil Service in 1964. Joined Contributions Unit in 1989.

**Robert Bertram**
*Member, Monopolies & Mergers Commission*
Solicitor. Former Partner, Shepherd & Wedderburn WS. Former Member, Scottish Law Commission, Edinburgh VAT Tribunal and Technical Committee of Chartered Institute of Taxation. Non-Executive Director, Weir Group.

**James Best**
*Site Director - Efford, Horticulture Research International*

**Richard Best OBE**
*Commissioner, Rural Development Commission*
Director, Joseph Rowntree Foundation & Joseph Rowntree Housing Trust. Committee Member, Hastoe Housing Association. Vice-President, ACRE. Member, Council for Charitable Support.

**Terry Best**
*Director of Finance & Support, Construction Industry Training Board*

**Michael Beswick**
*Director of Network Regulation, Office of the Rail Regulator*

**Bryan Betterton**
*Head of Document Services Department, Public Record Office*

**JR Bettinson**
*Member of Council, British Hallmarking Council*

**Derek Bevan**
*Legal Adviser, Office of Electricity Regulation*

**Rhiannon Bevan**
*Commissioner, Broadcasting Standards Commission*

Head, National Federation of Women's Institutes in Wales. Former Chairman of Welsh Consumer Council.

**Teleri Bevan**
*Member of Board, Wales Tourist Board*

**JA Beveridge**
*Member, Cardiff Bay Development Corporation*

**John Beveridge**
*Regional Director, West, Scottish Environment Protection Agency*

**Crawford Beveridge CBE**
*Chief Executive, Scottish Enterprise*

**Ms Ann Beynon**
*Member of Board, Welsh Language Board*
Director of Business Development, Cardiff Bay Development Corporation.

**Ann Beynon**
*Governor, National Film & Television School*

**JDE Beynon**
*Member, The British Library*
Royal Academy of Engineering.

**Dr John Beynon**
*Member of Commission, Independent Television Commission*

**Anita Bhalla**
*Trustee, Community Development Foundation*

**Dr C Bharucha**
*Member, Northern Ireland Council for Postgraduate Medical & Dental Education*
Appointed by DHSS.

**Amir Bhatia OBE**
*Trustee, Community Development Foundation*
*Member of England Committee, National Lottery Charities Board*
*Member of UK Committee, National Lottery Charities Board*
Chair, Forbes Trust, Hospice Arts and Project Fullemploy. Trustee, Oxfam, St Christopher's Hospice and Local Investment Fund.

**Tony Bianchi**
*Senior Literature Officer, Arts Council of Wales*

**Michael Bichard**
*Member of Board, British Council*
Permanent Secretary, Department for Education & Employment.

**Megan Bick**
*Project Manager, Commonwealth of Independent Sates, Westminster Foundation for Democracy*

**JL Bickers**
*Member of Advisory Board, Forensic Science Service*
Former Director, Cookson Group.

**Mrs Nerys Haf Biddulph**
*Member, Ofwat Customer Service Committee for Wales*

**Sir Robin Biggam**
*Chairman, Independent Television Commission*

**Cllr John Biggs**
*Member of Board, Tower Hamlets Housing Action Trust*
Councillor for St Dunstans Ward. Member of Council's Planning & Environmental, and Housing Committees. Council representative on ALG Environmental Committee, London Planning Advisory Committee, Parking Committee for London, London Borough's Transport Committee. Nominal shareholder with Bethnal Green and Victoria Park Housing Association.

**Ron Biggs**
*Group General Manager, Manufacturing Services, Remploy*

**John Bigny**
*Member, Rail Users Consultative Committee for Southern England*

**Brian Bigwood**
*Member of Committee, Rail Users Consultative Committee for Wales*
Member, Disabled Persons Transport Advisory Committee. Employed by Conwy County Borough Council.

**Rev Dr Alan Billings**
*Member of Board, Funding Agency for Schools*
Former Deputy Leader, Sheffield City Council.

**Tim Bines**
*General Manager, English Nature*

**Lady Bingham**
*Trustee, National Gallery*

**Lord Bingham of Cornhill**
*Chairman, The Royal Commission on Historical Manuscripts*

**Mrs Joan Bingley**
*Member of Board, Higher Education Funding Council for England*
Chartered Secretary in public practice.

**Polly Binns**
*Member of Council, Crafts Council*
Textile artist.

**Robert Binyon**
*Managing Director, CDC Financial Markets, Commonwealth Development Corporation*

**Sir John Birch**
*Director, The British Association for Central & Eastern Europe*

**Robin Birch CBE**
*Member, DIEL, Office of Telecommunications*
Chairman, Age Concern England.

**Sue P Bird**
*External Affairs Officer, Macaulay Land Use Research Institute*

**Raymond Birdseye**
*Part-time Board Member, Civil Aviation Authority*

Former US President, Corporate Banking Division, Barclays Bank.

**S Birkett**
*Section Head, Finance & Management Services, Gaming Board for Great Britain*

**R Birkinshaw**
*Director, Support Services, West of Scotland Water Authority*

**Richard V Birnie**
*Head, Land Use Science Group, Macaulay Land Use Research Institute*

**Graham Birse**
*Director, Press & Public Relations, Scottish Tourist Board*

**John Birt**
*Director-General, British Broadcasting Corporation*
Former Director of Programmes, London Weekend Television.

**Dr Paul Biscoe**
*R&D Cereals & Oilseeds, Home-Grown Cereals Authority*

**David Bishop**
*Member, Ofwat Eastern Customer Service Committee*

**Dr Dorothy Bishop**
*Member of Council, Economic & Social Research Council*
MRC Applied Psychology Unit, University of Cambridge.

**Ashraf Bismil BEM**
*Member, Ofwat Yorkshire Customer Service Committee*

**Cllr Raymond Bisset**
*Member, North of Scotland Water Authority*
Independent Councillor, South Inverurie. Vice Convenor, Aberdeenshire Council. Director, Gordon Enterprise Trust and Aberdeen Exhibition & Conference Centre. Member, Don District Salmon Fishery Board. Chairman, Gordon Fishings Management Committee. Former Convenor of Environmental Health, Gordon District Council.

**Ian Black**
*Treasury & Pensions Director, Commonwealth Development Corporation*

**Admiral Sir Jeremy Black GBE KVB DSO**
*Trustee, Imperial War Museum*

**Michael Black**
*Member of Board, Local Enterprise Development Unit*
Managing Director, Campsie Real and Steelstown Developments (NI). Vice Chairman, North West International (Derry Boston Venture). Director, Northern Ireland Innovation Programme. Commissioner, Londonderry Port & Harbour Board. Director, Weyhill and Treehaven.

**Moira Black**
*Chairman, ENACT, Office of Telecommunications*
Chairmam, Riverside Community Healthcare NHS Trust. London.

**Robert Black**
*Controller of Audit, The Accounts Commission for Scotland*

**Tony Black**
*Director of Business & Professional Markets, Ordnance Survey*

**Keith Blackburn**
*Resources Director, Occupational Pensions Regulatory Authority*

**PC Blackburn**
*Member, Rail Users Consultative Committee for Western England*

**Tony Blackburn**
*Operations Group Manager, Meat & Livestock Commission*

**Fiona Blacke**
*Adult Education & Practice Development Director, Scottish Community Education Council*

**Alan Blackie**
*Member, Scottish Community Education Council*

**Peter Blacklock**
*Member, North Eastern Consumers' Committee, Office of Electricity Regulation*

**Anthony Blackman OBE**
*Part-time Board Member, Civil Aviation Authority*
Former Special Projects Director, Smiths Industries. Previously Chief Test Pilot, Hawker Siddeley Aviation.

**Prof S Blackmore**
*Keeper, Botany Department, Natural History Museum*

**A Blackstock**
*Director of Finance & Resources, British Museum*

**Baroness Tessa Blackstone**
*Trustee, Natural History Museum*

**Mrs PJ Blackwell**
*Member, WACT, Welsh Advisory Committee on Telecommunications*
Chairmam, Builth Wells Community Support.

**Suzanne Blain**
*Accountant, Livestock & Meat Commission for Northern Ireland*

**David AB Blair**
*Deputy Director (Administration), Rowett Research Institute*

**Frank Blair**
*Director, Scotland, Advisory, Conciliation & Arbitration Service*

**John Blair**
*Trustee, Royal Botanic Garden Edinburgh*

**Kay Blair**
*Member, The Scottish Legal Aid Board*
Marketing consultant, business journalist

and *Scotsman* columnist. Non-Executive Director, Edinburgh Sick Children's NHS Trust.

**Michael Blair QC**
*General Counsel to the Board, Financial Services Authority*
Currently Deputy Chief Executive & General Counsel, SIB. Called to bar in 1965. Twenty years in Lord Chancellor's Department including Head of Courts & Legal Services Group. Treasurer, General Council of the Bar.

**Roy Blair**
*Member, Central Council for Education & Training in Social Work*

**Sean Blair**
*Director, Design, The Design Council*

**Colonel Ian CD Blair-Pilling**
*Director of Equipment Support, Logistic Information Systems Agency*

**Peter Blake OBE**
*Member, English Sports Council*

**Mrs Susan Blake**
*Member, Ofwat Thames Customer Service Committee*

**The Viscount Blakenham**
*Trustee, Royal Botanic Gardens Kew*

**Dr L Blakiston-Houston**
*Member of Board, Laganside Corporation*

**David Blanchflower**
*Member, Rail Users Consultative Committee for North Western England*

**Sir Christopher Bland**
*Chairman, British Broadcasting Corporation*
Member of Board, British Council Chairman, NFC. Former Deputy Chairman, Independent Broadcasting Authority and London Weekend Television.

**Richard Bland**
*Head of Safety & Security, Victoria & Albert Museum*

**Sandy Blaney**
*Administrative Services, UK Sports Council*

**S Blayley**
*Director, Consultancy Services, Health Estates*

**David Bleiman**
*Member, East of Scotland Water Authority*

**Sir John Blelloch KCB**
*Trustee, Royal Air Force Museum*

**His Excellency The Hon Neal Blewett**
*Trustee, Imperial War Museum*

**Peter Bloch**
*Commissioner, Fair Employment Commission for Northern Ireland*

**Ms M Blood**
*Member of Board, Labour Relations Agency*

**A Bloom**
*Board Member, The British Library*
Director, RIT Capital Partners.

**Miss Bridget Bloom OBE**
*Commissioner, Meat & Livestock Commission*
Former Agriculture Correspondent, Financial Times. Non-executive Forestry Commissioner and Director, National Forest Company.

**Margaret Bloom**
*Director, Competition Policy, Office of Fair Trading*

**Prof SR Bloom**
*Member, National Biological Standards Board*

**Eddie Bloomfield**
*Director of Corporate Services, Public Trust Office*

**Sir Kenneth Bloomfield KCB**
*Governor, British Broadcasting Corporation*
National Governor for Northern Ireland. Former Head of Northern Ireland Civil Service.

**Sue Bloomfield**
*Member, ENACT, Office of Telecommunications*
Independent consumer affairs specialist.

**Mrs Irene Bloor**
*Chairman, East Midland Consumers' Committee, Office of Electricity Regulation*

**Tom Bloxam**
*Member, Tate Gallery*

**Mark Blundell**
*Member, Tate Gallery*

**The Rt Hon David Blunkett**
*Trustee, Commonwealth Institute*
Secretary of State for Education.

**SD Blyth**
*Finance Group Manager, Student Awards Agency for Scotland*

**Brigadier Tom Blyth**
*Commandant Defence School of Transport, Army Training & Recruitment Agency*

**NR Boakes**
*Member of Board, Simpler Trade Procedures Board*
Chairman, Europower Management. Non-Executive Director, Tate Freight Forms. Past National Chairman, Chartered Institute of Marketing. Past Master, Marketors Company.

**Peter Boaks**
*Deputy Director, Centre for Information on Language Teaching & Research*

**Davina Boakye**
*Head of Personnel, British Film Institute*

**Chris Boardman MBE**
*Member, English Sports Council*

**Mrs F Boardman**
*Chief Executive, Child Support Agency*

**Richard Bocock**
*Sports Council Secretariat, UK Sports Council*
*Head of Secretariat, English Sports Council*

**Sir Walter Bodmer**
*Trustee, Sir John Soane's Museum*
Representative of the Royal Society.

**Mrs Susan Bolam**
*Member, North Eastern Consumers' Committee, Office of Electricity Regulation*

**Chris Bolt**
*Group Director, Economic Regulation, Office of the Rail Regulator*

**Prof Christine Bolt**
*Member, Marshall Aid Commemoration Commission*

**Lucinda Bolton**
*Member of Board, Tower Hamlets Housing Action Trust*
Director, Best Peninsular Homes and Croxden Financial Services.

**Roger Bolton**
*Governor, National Film & Television School*

**Mike Bonar**
*Regional Sheriff Clerk, South Strathclyde, Dumfries and Galloway, Scottish Court Service*

**Ian Bonas**
*Chairman, REPAC, The Environment Agency*

**Barbara Bond**
*Director of Production, UK Hydrographic Office*

**Richard Bond**
*Customer Relations Manager, Central Computer & Telecommunications Agency*

**Stephen Bond**
*Tower Environs Scheme, Historic Royal Palaces*

**Rufus Bond Gunning**
*Deputy Chairman, Royal Armouries*

**David Bonnar**
*Director, Lottery, Scottish Arts Council*

**Dr Des Bonnar**
*Chief Executive, Lothian and Edinburgh Enterprise*

**Tony Boorman**
*Director of Supply Competition, Office of Electricity Regulation*

**Ben Boot OBE**
*Member, Milk Development Council*
Milk Producer. Former Chairman, NFU Milk Committee. Chairman, European Commission Consultative Committee for Milk & Milk Products.

**Anthony Booth CBE**
*Member of Board, Higher Education Funding Council for England*
Non-Executive Chairman, Ericsson UK.

**Prof Clive Booth**
*Chairman, Teacher Training Agency*
Senior Adviser, Higher Education, British Council. Former Vice-Chancellor, Oxford Brookes University.

**Geoffrey Booth**
*Operations Director, Queen Elizabeth II Conference Centre*

**MJ Booth OBE**
*Member of Board, Simpler Trade Procedures Board*
Director, Customs & International Trade Practice, & Lybrand. Chairman, CBI Customs Panel.

**Denise M Booth-Alexander**
*Secretary, Scottish Medical Practices Committee*

**Christopher Boothman**
*Head of Law & Administration, Commission for Racial Equality*

**DA Boothman**
*Non-Executive Director, Remploy*
Former President, Institute of Chartered Accountants in England & Wales and a Senior Partner, Binder Hamlyn.

**Walter Boreham OBE OStJ**
*Chief Constable, Ministry of Defence Police*

**Jennifer Borer**
*Member, Rail Users Consultative Committee for North Western England*

**Dr Alan Borg**
*Director, Victoria & Albert Museum*
*Member of Council, Crafts Council*

**Prof LK Borysiewicz**
*Member of Council, Medical Research Council*
University of Wales College of Medicine.

**Mrs Maggie Bosanquet**
*Member, Ofwat Northumbria Customer Service Committee*

**Sandra Bosanquet**
*Craft Officer, Arts Council of Wales*

**Audrey Bott**
*Member, Tate Gallery*

**Valerie Bott**
*Deputy Director, Museums & Galleries Commission*

**J Botten**
*Non-Executive Director, Forensic Science Service*
Director, IBM UK.

**Prof Robert Boucher**
*Member of Board, British Council*
Vice-Chancellor and Principal UMIST.

**Prof IAD Bouchier**
*Member of Council, Medical Research Council*
Scottish Office Home & Health Department.

**Ch Supt DP Boulter**
*OCU, Corsham, Ministry of Defence Police*

# Q&Q

**David Boulton**
*Commissioner, Broadcasting Standards Commission*
Author and broadcaster. Former head of news, current affairs, arts and drama documentaries, Granada Television.

**Prof Geoffrey S Boulton**
*Member, Scottish Higher Education Funding Council*
*Member, Natural Environment Research Council*
Dean, Faculty of Science & Engineering, University of Edinburgh.

**LJ Boulton**
*Operations Director, Remploy*
Joined Company in 1988. Former Director, Dunlop Beaufort.

**Geoff Boume**
*Director of Mental Health & Learning Disability Nursing, English National Board for Nursing, Midwifery & Health Visiting*

**Aubrey Bourne**
*Member, Ofwat South West Customer Service Committee*

**NM Bowden**
*Director Training Operations, Engineering Construction Industry Training Board*

**Major-General BM Bowen**
*Chairman, Duke of York's Royal Military School*

**D Bowen**
*Member, Sports Council for Northern Ireland*

**Prof DQ Bowen**
*Vice Chairman, Countryside Council for Wales*
*Member, Joint Nature Conservation Committee*
Professor of Geology, University of Wales, Cardiff.

**DG Bower**
*Member of College Advisory Council, Civil Service College*
Personnel Director, Rover Group

**R Bower**
*Financial Controller, Royal Botanic Gardens Kew*

**Wilson Bowers**
*Regional Manager, Office of Electricity Regulation*

**Graham Bowie CBE**
*Chair, UK & Scotland Committees, National Lottery Charities Board*
Former Chief Executive, Lothian Regional Council. Trustee, Waverley Care Trust. Member of Court, Napier University and Convocation of Heriot-Watt University.

**Colonel M Bowles**
*Director Business Support, Defence Transport & Movements Executive*

**Malcolm Bowles**
*Director, Policy & Planning, Property Advisers to the Civil Estate*

**Sir Jeffery Bowman**
*Trustee, Royal Botanic Gardens Kew*

**John Bowman**
*Member of Board, Occupational Pensions Regulatory Authority*
Director, Commercial Union. Chairman, Pensions Committee of the Association of British Insurers and former member of OPB. (Nominated by the ABI.)

**Dr SGE Bowman**
*Keeper, Scientific Research, British Museum*

**Prof William Bowman**
*Member, Scottish Hospital Endowments Research Trust*

**Jeremy Boxall**
*Member, Apple & Pear Research Council*
Farm Manager, Alan Firmin (Linton). Committee Member, East Kent Fruit Society. Member, steering group, NFU Top Fruit Protocol.

**Alan Boxford**
*Member, Qualifications, Curriculum & Assessment Authority for Wales*
Headteacher, Llanishen High School.

**Mrs C Boyce**
*Member of Board, Probation Board for Northern Ireland*

**MD Boyce**
*Chief Executive, Cardiff Bay Development Corporation*
Board Member, Welsh College of Music & Drama and South East Wales Community Foundation.

**Mrs D Boyd**
*Member of Board, Enterprise Ulster*
Nominated by Confederation of British Industry/Northern Ireland Chamber of Commerce & Industry.

**Sir John Boyd KCMG**
*Non-Executive Director, British Nuclear Fuels plc*
Master of Churchill College, Cambridge. Career diplomat with appointments in Washington, Peking, Bonn, Hong Kong and Japan. Currently Trustee, British Museum; Governor, Royal Shakespeare Company; Vice Chairman, Menuhin Prize; Chairman, Cambridge Union Trustees and Trustee, Wordsworth Trust.

**CJ Boyle**
*Director of Personnel & Finance, Armed Forces Personnel Administration Agency*

**Colum Boyle**
*Manager Human Resources, Local Enterprise Development Unit*

**Hugh P Boyle**
*Secretary, Parole Board for Scotland*

**Penny Boys**
*Secretary, Monopolies & Mergers Commission*

**S Boys-Smith**
*Chairman, Forensic Science Service*
Director, Policy, Home Office.

**Andy Brabin**
*Member, London Regional Passengers Committee*

**Gary Brace**
*Assistant Chief Executive (Curriculum & Assessment 5-14), Qualifications, Curriculum & Assessment Authority for Wales*

**Julia Bracewell**
*Member, UK & English Sports Councils*
Former international and Olympic fencer.

**Rodney Brack**
*Chief Executive, Horserace Betting Levy Board*

**Mrs Anne Bradbury**
*Member, Ofwat North West Customer Service Committee*

**DAG Bradbury**
*Director General, Collections & Services, The British Library*

**Dr JRG Bradfield**
*Chairman, Commission for the New Towns*
Chairman, Abbotstone Agricultural Property Unit Trust. Chairman, Cambridge University Property Unit Trust. Deputy Chairman, Biotechnology Investments. Fellow, Trinity College Cambridge. Board Member, Anglia & Oxford Regional Health Authority Property Board.

**Andrew Bradford**
*Member, East Areas Board, Scottish Natural Heritage*

**Jane Bradford**
*Commissioner, Rural Development Commission*
Regional Managing Director, Westminster Bank. Member of Council, University of Derby.

**Rt Hon Roy Bradford**
*Member of Board, Northern Ireland Museums' Council*
North Down Borough Council. Coopted by Board.

**Dr JJ Bradley**
*Member, Parole Board*

**M Bradley**
*Member, Sports Council for Northern Ireland*

**Malcolm Bradley**
*Site Director - Stockbridge House, Horticulture Research International*

**Cllr Martin Bradley**
*Member, Arts Council of Northern Ireland*
Derry City Councillor.

**Cllr Mary Bradley**
*Member, Northern Ireland Local Government Officers' Superannuation Committee*

**Prof R Bradley**
*Commissioner, Royal Commission on Historical Monuments of England*

602

**Robin Bradley**
*Chief Executive, Marine Safety Agency*

**Suzanne Bradley**
*Director, Legal Services, Fair Employment Commission for Northern Ireland*

**Dr T Bradley**
*Associate Adviser in Postgraduate General Practice Education, Northern Ireland Council for Postgraduate Medical & Dental Education*

**Ken Bradshaw**
*Chief Executive, Defence Codification Agency*

**Captain Robert Bradshaw**
*Director of Defence Requirements, UK Hydrographic Office*

**Paul Brady**
*Director Finance and Planning, Scottish Enterprise*

**Sandy Brady**
*Director Executive Office, Highlands & Islands Enterprise*

**Richard Bragg**
*Member, North Western Consumers' Committee, Office of Electricity Regulation*

**The Rt Hon Lord Braine DL MP**
*Trustee, Commonwealth Institute*

**Michael Brainsby**
*Legal Director, English Heritage*

**Justin Braithwaite**
*Business Director - Cement, Citrus & Fish, Commonwealth Development Corporation*

**Sir Rodric Braithwaite GCMG**
*Chairman, The Britain-Russia Centre*

**Sir Ashley Bramall**
*Deputy Chairman, Museum of London*

**Field Marshal Lord Bramall**
*Vice-President & Chairman, Imperial War Museum*

**Dr Bob Bramley**
*Chief Scientist, Forensic Science Service*

**Clive Bramley**
*Contracts, Office for Standards in Education*

**MJD Brand**
*Director & Chief Executive, Ordnance Survey of Northern Ireland*

**Vanessa Brand**
*Secretary to the Trustees & Head of Corporate Policy, National Heritage Memorial Fund*

**F Brannigan**
*Head of Operations, Compensation Agency*

**FJ Brannigan**
*Head, Special Compliance Office, Inland Revenue*

**Charles Bransden**
*Member, Horticultural Development Council*
Managing Director, B Bransden & Sons.

**Elaine Brant**
*Member of Steering Board, Companies House*
Management Consultant.

**ML Brasher**
*Director of Finance & Management Services, The Planning Inspectorate*

**Helen Bratton**
*Director of Mental Health Services, Public Trust Office*

**Erich Braun**
*Food from Britain (Switzerland) Gmbh*

**Tony Breakell**
*Member of Management Board, Pay & Personnel Agency*

**Chris Brearley**
*Member of Advisory Board, Highways Agency*

**George J Brechin**
*Non-Executive Member of Board, National Board for Nursing, Midwifery & Health Visiting for Scotland*
Chief Executive, Fife Healthcare NHS Trust, Leven.

**Anne Breen**
*Training and Development, Rate Collection Agency*

**Jim Breen**
*Deputy Chief Executive, Scottish Sports Council*

**David Breeze**
*Chief Inspector of Ancient Monuments, Historic Scotland*

**Gwyn Breeze**
*Member, South Wales Consumers' Committee, Office of Electricity Regulation*

**Ian Bremner**
*Deputy Director (Science), Rowett Research Institute*

**AL Brend**
*Appointed Trustee, Royal Marines Museum*

**C Brendish**
*Member, Property Advisers to the Civil Estate*
Ministerial Adviser.

**CM Brendish**
*Member, Met Office*
Chairman & Chief Executive, Admiral.

**Mrs Ann Brennan**
*Member, East Midland Consumers' Committee, Office of Electricity Regulation*

**Lou Brennan**
*Member of Museum Trust, Museum of Science & Industry, Manchester*

**Paul Brennan**
*Computer Operations, Rate Collection Agency*

**Ursula Brennan**
*Change Management Director, Benefits Agency*

**John Breslin**
*Director of Finance, Scottish Homes*

**Mrs Mary Breslin**
*Member of Board, Local Enterprise Development Unit*
Partner, Total Engineering. Chairman, North West Panel of Northern Ireland Branch, Institute of Mechanical Engineers. Harbour Commissioner, Londonderry Port.

**James Bretherton**
*Director, Property Management & Services, UK Atomic Energy Authority*
Joined UKAEA in 1986. Former career Civil Service including appointments at International Energy Agency in Paris and Department of Energy.

**Sir Charles Brett CBE**
*Vice-Chairman, Arts Council of Northern Ireland*

**DI Brewer**
*Director of Administration, Trinity House Lighthouse Service*

**David Brewer**
*Chairman, The Great Britain-China Centre*

**Justine Brewood**
*Strategic Business Manager, Information Technology Services Agency*

**John Brewster**
*Director of Housing Management, Stonebridge Housing Action Trust*

**Martine Brewster**
*Trade Facilitation Executive, Simpler Trade Procedures Board*

**Clive Briault**
*Director, General Policy, Financial Services Authority*
Currently Head, Capital & Wholesale Markets Division, Bank of England.

**Peter Brice**
*Member, Horticultural Development Council*
Managing Director, W Brice & Son.

**Mrs Penny Brickle**
*Member, Ofwat Customer Service Committee for Wales*

**Edward Brickley**
*Member, South Eastern Consumers' Committee, Office of Electricity Regulation*

**KJ Bridge CBE**
*Chairman, Education Assets Board*

**John Bridgeman TD**
*Director General of Fair Trading, Office of Fair Trading*

**Balcolm Bridget**
*Director of Human Resources, Historic Royal Palaces*

**David Brierley**
*Member, The Arts Council of England*

**Ruth Briggs**
*Area Manager, Scottish Natural Heritage*

**The Baroness Brigstocke**
*Chairman, Geffrye Museum*
*Commissioner, Museums & Galleries*
*Commission*
Chairman, English Speaking Union of the Commonwealth. Commissioner, Museums & Galleries Commission. Former High Mistress, St Paul's Girls' Schools. Former Trustee, National Gallery. Former Member of Council, City University. Former Trustee, Kennedy Memorial Trust. President, Bishop Creighton House Settlement. Governor, Imperial College.

**Admiral Sir John Brigstoke**
*Owner, Naval Manning Agency*
Second Sea Lord/Commander in Chief Naval Home Command.

**A Brindle**
*Finance Director, LTB, London Transport*

**A Bristow**
*Head of Endocrinology, National Biological Standards Board*

**Group Captain H Britten-Austin**
*Group Captain Policy and Services, RAF Signals Engineering Establishment*

**Rupert Britton**
*Secretary & Legal Adviser, Civil Aviation Authority*

**Paul Brivio**
*Development, UK Sports Council*

**Sir Nigel Broackes**
*Chairman, Crafts Council*

**John Broadfoot CBE**
*Deputy Chairman, Scottish Children's Reporter Administration*
Former Controller of Audit, The Accounts Commission. Former Chief Executive, Central Regional Council.

**John Broadfoot CBE**
*Member, East of Scotland Water Authority*

**Simon Broadley**
*Assessor, UK Sports Council*
Assessor, Department of National Heritage

**Sheila Brock**
*Campaign Director, Museum of Scotland, National Museums of Scotland*

**Michael Brocklehurst**
*Chief Legal Adviser, Office of the Rail Regulator*

**JB Brodribb**
*Member, Rail Users Consultative Committee for Eastern England*

**Prof AN Broers**
*Member of Council, Engineering & Physical Sciences Research Council*
Cambridge University

**Justin Brogan**
*Member, Ofwat Yorkshire Customer Service Committee*

**Ciaran Brolly**
*Member, General Consumer Council for Northern Ireland*
Senior Lecturer, Human Resource Management & Trade Union Studies, North West Institute of Further & Higher Education, Londonderry. Director of a local engineering firm.

**G Bromley**
*Joint Head of Education & Marketing, Royal Botanic Gardens Kew*

**Dr I Bronks**
*Member, Parole Board*

**David Brooke**
*Director of Strategy & Development, Channel Four Television Corporation*

**Lord Brooke of Alverthorpe**
*Member of Board, Pensions Compensation Board*
Former Joint General Secretary, Public Services, Tax & Commerce Union (PTC). Former member, TUC General Council. Chairman, Civil Service Housing Association. Executive member, Fabian Society. Trustee, Community Service Volunteers and Duke of Edinburgh Study Conference. Nominated by TUC.

**Prof RJ Brook OBE**
*Chief Executive, Engineering & Physical Sciences Research Council*

**Rodney Brooke CBE**
*Trustee, Community Development Foundation*

**Roger Brooke**
*Chairman, Audit Commission*
Chairman, Candover Investments. Member, Economic Affairs Committee, CBI; Council of City University Business School; and Finance & General Purposes Board, Royal College of Physicians. Former Councillor, Royal Borough of Kensington & Chelsea.

**Sorrel Brookes**
*Chief Executive, Stonebridge Housing Action Trust*

**Trevor Brooking MBE**
*Vice-Chairman, UK & English Sports Councils*
Former professional footballer for West Ham United and England.

**The Most Rev F Brooks**
*Member of Council, Council for Catholic Maintained Schools*
Trustee Representative.

**Lord Brooks of Tremorfa**
*Deputy Chairman, Cardiff Bay Development Corporation*
British Boxing Board of Control. Dormerstein. Sportsmatch Wales. STAR Recreation & Community Trust.

**A Broomhead MBE JP**
*Member of Board, Enterprise Ulster*
Nominated by Confederation of British Industry/Northern Ireland Chamber of Commerce & Industry.

**Peter Broughan**
*Member of Board, Scottish Screen*

**Alex Brown**
*Member, Milk Development Council*
Dairy farmer. Former Convener, SNFU Milk Committee. Chairman, DairyScot.

**Andy Brown**
*Corporate Manager, English Nature*

**Charles Brown**
*Group Director, Railway Network, Office of the Rail Regulator*

**Christopher Brown**
*Chief Curator, National Gallery*

**Craig Brown OBE**
*Chairman, Scottish Further Education Unit*
Former Principal, Dundee College.

**Eric Brown**
*Language Teaching Adviser, Centre for Information on Language Teaching & Research*

**G Brown**
*Control IT Supply Director, Information Technology Services Agency*

**Hugh Brown**
*Member of Board, Occupational Pensions Regulatory Authority*
Group Pensions Manager, ICI. (Nominated by CBI.)

**Ian Brown**
*Member, Ofwat Northumbria Customer Service Committee*

**Jenny Brown**
*Director, Literature, Scottish Arts Council*

**Jim Brown**
*Member, Scottish Agricultural Wages Board*
Employees' representative member nominated by the Rural, Agricultural & Allied Workers National Trade Group (Scotland) of the Transport & General Workers' Union.

**Jim Brown**
*Director of Operations, East of Scotland Water Authority*
President, Institution of Water Officers (Scotland).

**Joan Brown**
*Member of Museum Trust, Museum of Science & Industry, Manchester*

**John Brown**
*Director, British Educational Communications & Technology Agency*

**Karen Brown**
*Deputy Director of Programmes, Daytime/Children & Sport, Channel Four Television Corporation*

**Keith Brown**
*Director, Advice & Information, Fair Employment Commission for Northern Ireland*

**Ken Brown**
*Member, Northern Ireland Local Government Officers' Superannuation Committee*

**Kenneth Brown**
*Member, Ofwat Thames Customer Service Committee*

**Kenneth Brown**
*Member, North Eastern Consumers' Committee, Office of Electricity Regulation*

**MJ Brown**
*Government Assessor, Construction Industry Training Board*
The Scottish Office Education & Industry Department.

**Mrs Marie Brown**
*Observer, Northern Ireland Museums' Council*
Arts, Libraries & Museums Branch, Department of Education (NI).

**Martin Brown**
*Director VAT Policy, HM Customs & Excise*

**Mike Brown**
*Member, Departmental Board, Wilton Park Executive Agency*

**Muir Brown**
*Projects Manager, The Britain-Russia Centre*

**Nicholas Brown**
*Member of Board, Wales Tourist Board*

**RG Brown**
*Member, Rail Users Consultative Committee for North Eastern England*

**Mrs Sarah Brown**
*Member, Monopolies & Mergers Commission*
Non-Executive Director, Remploy Former Civil Servant. Member, Friendly Societies Commission. Associate Member, Kensington & Chelsea Health Authority.

**Steve Brown**
*Finance & Corporate Services Director, New Millennium Experience Co Ltd*
Former Deputy MD and FD of Center Parcs.

**Stuart Brown**
*Member, Ofwat Northumbria Customer Service Committee*

**Tim Brown**
*Member of Board, UK Eco-Labelling Board*
Development Officer, National Society for Clean Air & Environmental Protection (NSCA).

**Brigadier Tweedie Brown OBE**
*Chief Executive, Defence Postal & Courier Services Agency*

**Colin Browne**
*Director of Corporate Affairs, British Broadcasting Corporation*
Former Director of Corporate Relations, British Telecom.

**DM Browne**
*Head, Archaeology, Royal Commission on Ancient & Historical Monuments in Wales*

**Ald GJP Browne**
*Member, Rail Users Consultative Committee for Western England*

**John Browne**
*Trustee, British Museum*

**RH Browne**
*Chief Executive, Health Estates*

**Ms Margery Browning**
*Governor, Scottish Council for Educational Technology*
SOEID (Assessor).

**Mrs MGA Browning**
*Member, Rail Users Consultative Committee for Eastern England*

**Alan Bruce**
*Group Manager IT, Student Awards Agency for Scotland*

**Anthony Bruce**
*Member, Academic Council, Wilton Park Executive Agency*

**Geoff Bruce**
*Chief Executive, Pesticides Safety Directorate*

**Prof Vicki Bruce OBE**
*Member, Scottish Higher Education Funding Council*
Deputy Principal, Research, University of Stirling.

**GB Brumwell**
*Member of Board, Construction Industry Training Board*
Union of Construction, Allied Trades & Technicians.

**Prof RW Brunskill OBE**
*Vice-Chairman, Royal Commission on Ancient & Historical Monuments in Wales*

**Mrs Evelyn Brunton**
*Member, Scottish Medical Practices Committee*

**S Bruton**
*Director of Enforcement & Wales, The Planning Inspectorate*

**MJ Bruton CBE**
*Chief Executive, Residuary Body for Wales*

**Amanda Bryan**
*Member, North Areas Board, Scottish Natural Heritage*

**Conrad L Bryant**
*Treasurer, National Library of Wales*

**Robert Bryant**
*Chief Accountant, Intervention Board*

**Iain Bryce**
*Member, ENACT, Office of Telecommunications*
Retired professional accountant.

**Mary Bryden**
*Head of Public Affairs, National Museums of Scotland*

**AGR Bryson**
*Member, Rail Users Consultative Committee for Eastern England*

**Mungo Bryson**
*Member of Board, West of Scotland Water Authority*
Farmer. Former Independent Councillor, Dumfries and Galloway Regional Council. Managing Director, Loch Ken Holiday Centre.

**Suzanne Bryson**
*Member of Commission, Independent Commission for Police Complaints for Northern Ireland*
Solicitor. Deputy Secretary, Law Society of Northern Ireland. Occasional lecturer at Institute of Professional Legal Studies.

**TS Bryson**
*Member of Council, Hannah Research Institute*

**Stephen Bubb**
*Director of Personnel & Administration, National Lottery Charities Board*
Former Assistant Secretary of Personnel, Association of Metropolitan Authorities. Youth Court Magistrate in London. Founded Landmark in South London.

**Alexander Buchan**
*Deputy Chairman, Scottish Environment Protection Agency*

**Dr David Buchanan**
*Chief Executive, Health & Safety Laboratory, The Health & Safety Executive*

**Hugh Buchanan**
*Member of Council, Scottish Arts Council*

**Ian Buchanan**
*Member, Scottish Conveyancing & Executry Services Board*

**Keith Buchanan**
*Regional Officer, Countryside Commission*

**Lillian Buchanan**
*Consumer Affairs Officer, General Consumer Council for Northern Ireland*

**Ms P Buchanan**
*Member of Board, Enterprise Ulster*
Nominated by of the Northern Ireland Committee. Irish Congress of Trade Unions.

**Peter Buchanan**
*Group Director - Marketing Communications, Central Office of Information*

**Prof Ronald Buchanan OBE**
*Commissioner, Museums & Galleries Commission*
Professor Emeritus of Geography, Queen's University Belfast. Member of Council and Executive, National Trust. Member, Advisory Committee of Armagh County Museum. Chairman, Advisory Committee, Down County Museum. Trustee, Ulster Folk & Transport Museum.

**RD Buchanan-Dunlop**
*Member of Council, British Hallmarking Council*

**Marcus Buck**
*Chief Executive, Queen Elizabeth II Conference Centre*

**Chris Buckland**
*Chief Executive, Local Enterprise Development Unit*

**A Buckle**
*Manager (Finance and Accounts), Vehicle Certification Agency*

**Delia Buckle**
*Deputy Chairman, London Regional Passengers Committee*

**Ms K Buckley**
*Member of Board, Education Assets Board*

**NR Buckley**
*Head, Internal Audit Office, Inland Revenue*

**Sally Bucknall**
*Regional Officer, Countryside Commission*

**Dr R Bud**
*Trustee, Royal Navy Submarine Museum*
The Science Museum.

**Nigel Bufton**
*Subject Adviser, Mathmatics, Office for Standards in Education*

**Colonel Richard Bugler**
*Head of Courier & Corporate Services, Defence Postal & Courier Services A gency*

**Graham Bull**
*Head of Branch, Woodland Surveys, Forest Research .*

**Margaret Bull**
*Team Manager, Human Resource Services Team, English Nature*

**Nicholas Bull**
*Regional Executive, Independent Television Commission*

**Dr H Bullard**
*Member, Parole Board*

**Sir Julian Bullard GCMG**
*Member, Academic Council, Wilton Park Executive Agency*

**Miss P Buller**
*Member, Parole Board*

**Cllr Steve Bullock**
*Member, London Pensions Fund Authority*
Member, Lewisham Council. Former Chairman, Local Government Management Board and Association of London Authorities. Member, Lewisham Hospital NHS Trust and Commission for Local Democracy. Consultant with Capita group.

**JFM Bumpus**
*Head of Establishment Support Unit, Centre for Environment, Fisheries & Aquaculture Science*

**Tom Buncle**
*Chief Executive, Scottish Tourist Board*

**Mary Bunting**
*Director, General Operations, Fair Employment Commission for Northern Ireland*

**Sir Robert Bunyard CBE**
*Member, Parole Board*

**Peter Burbidge**
*Member, Merseyside & North Wales Consumers' Committee, Office of Electricity Regulation*

**Alan Burbridge**
*Member, Apple & Pear Research Council*
Director, Herbert Payne Farms. Member, British Independent Fruit Growers Association General Committee.

**Commodore JA Burch CBE**
*Naval Base Commander, Naval Bases & Supply Agency*

**David H Burcher**
*Member of Council, The Sports Council for Wales*

**Robert Burchill**
*Director of Operations, Royal Mint*

**Major General DL Burden CB CBE**
*Chief Executive, Army Personnel Centre*

**David Burditt**
*Member, Southern Consumers' Committee, Office of Electricity Regulation*

**Ann Burdus**
*Part-time Board Member, Civil Aviation Authority*
Former Member, Senior Salaries Review Board. Non-Executive director, Safeway, Dawson International, Next and Prudential Corporation. Committee Member, Automobile Association.

**Ms AC Burfutt**
*LT Director of Human Resources, London Transport*

**Gisela Burg CBE**
*Non-Executive Director, Royal Mint*

**Mrs Averil Burgess OBE**
*Member of Board of Governors, Museum of London*
Appointed by the Prime Minister.

**Prof Robert Burgess**
*Member of Council, Economic & Social Research Council*
Pro-vice Chancellor, University of Warwick.

**Colin Burkitt**
*Head of Central Services,Commonwealth Institute*

**John Burlison**
*Area Manager, Scottish Natural Heritage*

**RS Burman**
*Member of Council, British Hallmarking Council*

**Ms T Burman**
*Head of Department, Development & Marketing, Natural History Museum*

**Richard Burn**
*Director of Housing Management, Scottish Homes*

**Dr AR Burne**
*Director, Horticulture Research International*

**JK Burne**
*College Secretary, Fire Service College*

**Cllr Jeanette Burness**
*Member, East of Scotland Water Authority*

**Dr AM Burnett**
*Keeper, Coins & Medals, British Museum*

**R Gavin Burnett**
*Member, Scottish Conveyancing & Executry Services Board*

**Nan Burnett OBE**
*Chairman, East Areas Board, Scottish Natural Heritage*
*Member of Board, Scottish Natural Heritage*

**Alan Burnham**
*Operations & Welfare Director, War Pensions Agency*

**Peter Burnham**
*Member of Board, The Environment Agency*
Former Senior Partner, Coopers & Lybrand. Former Director of London East TEC, Satellite Observing Systems and Council of Computing Development. Founder Commission Member English Heritage.

**A John Burns**
*Secretary, Highlands & Islands Airports*

**Cdre Bryan Burns CBE**
*Naval Assistant, Naval Manning Agency*

**Commodore David Burns**
*Director In-Service Submarines, Ships Support Agency*

**DW Burns**
*Deputy Chief Inspector, Gaming Board for Great Britain*

**H Burns**
*Member of Board, Construction Industry Training Board (NI)*
ATGWU. Employee representative.

**J Burns**
*Head of Enforcement Policy, Scottish Fisheries Protection Agency*

**Margaret Burns**
*Member, Scottish Conveyancing & Executry Services Board*

**Brigadier Robbie Burns**
*Commandant Royal School of Military Engineering, Army Training & Recruitment Agency*

**William Burns**
*Member, Arts Council of Northern Ireland*
Principal, Olderfleet PS, Larne.

**Sam Burnside**
*Member, Arts Council of Northern Ireland*
Director, Verbal Arts Centre, Derry.

**Stephen Burroughs**
*Head of Education, Crafts Council*

**G Burt**
*Procurement Director, Army Base Repair Organisation*

**Air Commodore AJ Burton OBE**
*Director Personnel Management Policy, RAF Personnel Management Agency*

**Alan Burton**
*Member of Advisory Board, Medical Devices Agency*
Head of Resource Management & Finance Division, Department of Health.

**Anthony Burton**
*Head of Museum, Bethnal Green Museum of Childhood, Victoria & Albert Museum*

**Ms Caroline Burton**
*Member, London Pensions Fund Authority*
Executive Director - Investments, Guardian Royal Exchange. Non-executive Director, Scottish Metropolitan Property.

**Lieutenant General Edmund Burton**
*Member of Board, Defence Evaluation & Research Agency*
DCDS (Systems).

**Tony Burton**
*Member of Board, UK Eco-Labelling Board*
Director, The Planning Exchange, Glasgow.

**Colonel FA Bush**
*Director Operations, Defence Transport & Movements Executive*

**Geoffrey Bush**
*Director General, Inland Revenue*

**Peter Bush**
*Director of Personnel & Administration, The Housing Corporation*

**John Buston**
*Member of Council, Crafts Council*
Chief Executive, East Midlands Arts Board.

**Mike Buswell**
*Deputy Chairman, Meat & Livestock Commission*
Former Director, Dalgety UK, Chief Executive of Dalgety Meat, and Director, Hillsdown Holdings.

**Miss I Butcher**
*Member, Parole Board*

**Karen Butigan**
*Business Manager, Contract Operations, Remploy*

**Sir Adam Butler**
*Member of Council, British Hallmarking Council*

**Alan Butler**
*Cereal Intervention, All Crop Market Support Schemes, Intervention Board*

**Arnold Butler**
*Director, Central Advice Unit, Property Advisers to the Civil Estate*

**Clive Butler**
*Finance Manager, Occupational Pensions Regulatory Authority*

**Prof Marilyn Butler**
*Member of Board, Higher Education Funding Council for England*
Rector, Exeter College, Oxford.

**Nick Butler**
*Park Manager, Kensington Gardens, Royal Parks Agency*

**Air Commodore RM Butler**
*Director of Dental Services (RAF), Defence Dental Agency*

**Sir Robin Butler GCB CVO**
*Member of College Advisory Council, Civil Service College*
Secretary of the Cabinet and Head of the Home Civil Service.

**Cllr Mrs Rosemary Butler**
*Member of Council, The Sports Council for Wales*

**Rosemary Butler**
*Commissioner, Museums & Galleries Commission*

**Mrs Sara Butlin**
*Director of Local Development Services, The Sports Council for Wales*

**Richard Butt**
*Chief Executive, Rural Development Commission*

**Michaela Butter**
*Member of Council, Crafts Council*
Development & Public Services Manager, Nottingham City Museums.

**Surgeon Commander Neil Butterfield**
*Commanding Officer, Royal Naval Hospital, Gibraltar, Defence Secondary Care Agency*

**David Butterworth**
*Member, Rail Users Consultative Committee for North Western England*

**Dr Eileen Buttle CBE**
*Director & Trustee, Horniman Museum*
Nominated by Secretary of State for Culture, Media & Sport.

**Mrs Ann Button**
*Member, East Midland Consumers' Committee, Office of Electricity Regulation*

**Sheila Button**
*Board Member, The Housing Corporation*

**Andrew Buxton**
*Member of Court, Bank of England*
Group Chairman, Barclays.

**Mrs AS Byatt CBE**
*Member of Board, British Council*
Writer.

**Ian Byatt**
*Director General, Office of Water Services*

**Dr VJ Bye**
*Head of Business Support Unit, Centre for Environment, Fisheries & Aquaculture Science*

**Dr A Byrne**
*Corporate Operations Director & Deputy Chief Executive, Army Base Repair Organisation*

**Mrs Judith Byrne**
*Member, North Western Consumers' Committee, Office of Electricity Regulation*

**Emyr Byron Hughes**
*Director of Corporate Policy & Secretary to the Authority, S4C*

# C

**John Cable**
*Finance & Administration, Home-Grown Cereals Authority*

**Sir Dominic Cadbury**
*Deputy Chairman, Qualifications & Curriculum Authority*
Chairman, Cadbury Schweppes

**Supt FA Cadden**
*OCU, Stafford, Ministry of Defence Police*

**Vice Admiral Sir John Cadell KBE**
*Commissioner, Duke of York's Royal Military School*

**Patrick M Cadell**
*Keeper of the Records of Scotland, Scottish Record Office*

**Prof Sir John Cadogan**
*Member of Board, Higher Education Funding Council for England*
Director General, Research Councils.

**JT Caff**
*Member, Rail Users Consultative Committee for Western England*

**The Right Rev Monsignor S Cahill**
*Member of Council, Council for Catholic Maintained Schools*

**Prof Graham D Caie**
*Trustee, National Library of Scotland*

**Sir Michael Caine**
*Chairman, Commonwealth Scholarship Commission*
Former Chairman of Booker.

**Michael Cairns**
*Member of Board, British Waterways*
Chief Operating Officer - Hotels, Queens Moat Houses plc.

**Earl Cairns CBE**
*Chairman, Commonwealth Development Corporation*
Chairman, BAT Industries. Chairman, Overseas Development Institute and Receiver General of the Duchy of Cornwall.

**Cllr Robert Cairns**
*Chairman, East of Scotland Water Authority*
Councillor, City of Edinburgh. Former teacher. Board, member, Historic Buildings Council and Edinburgh Old Town Renewal Trust. Chairman, Shawfair.

**Stephen Cake**
*Regional Director - South Asia, Commonwealth Development Corporation*

**Alaster Calder**
*Member, South Eastern Consumers' Committee, Office of Electricity Regulation*

**Andrea Calderwood**
*Governor, National Film & Television School*

**JW Calderwood**
*Member, Northern Ireland Council for Postgraduate Medical & Dental Education*
Nominated by Royal Colleges of Surgeons.

**Dame Fiona Caldicott DBE**
*Commissioner, Broadcasting Standards Commission*
Principal, Somerville College, Oxford. Consultant psychiatrist.

**Brenda Callaghan**
*Member of Commission, Equal Opportunities Commission for Northern Ireland*
Nominated by Northern Ireland Committee of Irish Congress of Trade Unions. Industrial Official employed by SIPTU.

**Lord Callaghan of Cardiff KG**
*Vice President, The Great Britain-China Centre*
Former Secretary of State for Foreign & Commonwealth Affairs and Prime Minister.

**Mike Callaghan**
*Finance & UK Development Director, Food from Britain*

**Dr ME Callender**
*Member, Northern Ireland Council for Postgraduate Medical & Dental Education*
Nominated by Royal College of Physicians (London).

**Major General CG Callow**
*DGMT Chairman, Defence Medical Training Organisation*

**Prof JA Callow**
*Director, Horticulture Research International*
Appointed by Chancellor of Duchy of Lancaster.

**Lady Ann Calman**
*Member, Scottish Water & Sewerage Customers Council*

**Sir Kenneth Calman**
*Member of Council, Medical Research Council*
Department of Health.

**Peter Calver**
*Chairman, BACT, Office of Telecommunications*
Managing Director, sports simulation software company.

**Graham Calvett**
*Member of Management Board, The Court Service*
Director of the Supreme Court Group.

**Lord Cameron of Lochbroom**
*Member of Advisory Council, Scottish Record Office*

**Mrs Myra Cameron**
*Non-Executive Board Member, Registers of Scotland*

**Sandy Cameron**
*Member, Central Council for Education & Training in Social Work*

**Lord Camoys GCVO**
*Member of Board of Trustees, Historic Royal Palaces*
Lord Chamberlain of the Queen's Household. Former Deputy Chairman, Barclays de Zoete Wedd and Sothebys. Appointed by the Queen.

**A Campbell**
*Member of Council, Hannah Research Institute*

**DH Campbell**
*Member, Northern Ireland Council for Postgraduate Medical & Dental Education*
Appointed by DHSS.

**Dr Grace Campbell**
*Commissioner, Mental Health Commission for Northern Ireland*
General Medical Practitioner, Health Centre, Bangor.

**Hazel Campbell**
*Director of Corporate Services, Rivers Agency*

**Mrs Juliet Campbell CMG**
*Member, Academic Council, Wilton Park Executive Agency*

**Mrs M Campbell**
*Member, The Accounts Commission for Scotland*
General Manager, Standard Life Assurance Company.

**Martin Campbell**
*Director of Resources, London Pensions Fund Authority*

**Miss Nina Campbell**
*Trustee, Victoria & Albert Museum*

**Ms R Campbell**
*Training Coordinator, Northern Ireland Council for Postgraduate Medical & Dental Education*

**Prof RH Campbell OBE**
*Commissioner, The Royal Commission on Historical Manuscripts*

**Ronald Campbell**
*Member, North Eastern Consumers' Committee, Office of Electricity Regulation*

**S Campbell**
*Member of Board, Construction Industry Training Board (NI)*
H&P Campbell. Employer representative.

**Sheila Campbell**
*Member, The Scottish Legal Aid Board*
Justice of the Peace. Member, Justices of the Peace Advisory Committee.

**Henning Camre**
*Director, National Film & Television School*

**John Canavan**
*Director of Northern Ireland Operations, Northern Ireland Child Support Agency*

**Mrs Janet Candler**
*Chairman, South Wales Consumers' Committee, Office of Electricity Regulation*

**Prof Tom Cannon**
*Chairman, Rail Users Consultative Committee for North Western England*

**Hazel Canter**
*Director Resources, Advisory, Conciliation & Arbitration Service*

**Michael B Cantlay**
*Chairman, Forth Valley Enterprise*

**Maurice Cantley**
*Director Projects and Marketing, Highlands & Islands Enterprise*

**Barry Capon CBE**
*Commissioner, Criminal Cases Review Commission*
Fomer Chief Executive, Norfolk Country Council. Assessor, Local Government Commission for England. Director, Waveney Housing Association. Deputy Lieutenant, Country of Norfolk.

**Colonel M Capper**
*Director Engineering, Army Technical Support Agency*

**Judge Capstick QC**
*Member, Parole Board*

**J Card**
*Head of Finance, Corporate Services, Natural History Museum*

**Arthur Carden**
*Member, South Western Consumers' Committee, Office of Electricity Regulation*

**Richard Carden**
*Chairman, Pesticides Safety Directorate Chairman, Meat Hygiene Service Chairman of Ownership Board, Veterinary Medicines Directorate Deputy Secretary, Food Safety & Environment Directorate (MAFF).*

**Sir Richard Carew Pole**
*Chairman, Tate Gallery Trustee, National Heritage Memorial Fund*

**Samantha Carleton**
*Shop Manager, Museum of Science & Industry Manchester*

**B Carlin OBE**
*Member, Training & Employment Agency (NI) Former Executive Vice-President, Organisation Development, Short Brothers.*

**JF Carling**
*Head, Inland Revenue London, Inland Revenue*

**Philippa Carling**
*Member, London Regional Passengers Committee*

**Jim Carlisle**
*Director of Corporate Services, Roads Service*

**Iain Carmichael**
*Chief Executive, Lanarkshire Development Agency*

**Margaret Carmichael**
*Member, National Weights & Measures Laboratory Trading Policy Director, British Retail Consortium.*

**Colin Carnie**
*Member, West Areas Board, Scottish Natural Heritage*

**A Carpenter**
*Senior Inspector, South West Region, Gaming Board for Great Britain*

**David Carpenter**
*Director of National Lottery, UK & English Sports Councils*

**GR Carr**
*Member of Council, British Hallmarking Council*

**JR Carr**
*Chairman, RFAC, The Environment Agency*

**JR Carr, CBE**
*Member of Board of Governors, Macaulay Land Use Research Institute*

**Jane Carr**
*Director, Public Affairs, The British Library*

**John Carr**
*Board Secretariat & Corporate Planning, Teacher Training Agency*

**John Carr CBE**
*Member of Board, Tai Cymru Former Chief Executive, CADW. Consultant on heritage, tourism and marketing. Hon Chairman, Makers of Wales' Millennium Festival campaign. Non-Executive director, Glan-y-Mor NHS Trust. Trustee, United Kingdom Buildings Preservation Trust (The Phoenix Trust).*

**Michael Carr**
*Member of Board, English Partnerships Member, Middlesbrough Borough Council, Member Board of Teesside Development Corporation.*

**Robert Carr-Archer**
*Head of Retailing & Publications, National Portrait Gallery*

**Eddie Carrick**
*Member, Health & Safety Commission Former Councillor, Stirling District Council. Runs retail business in Edinburgh.*

**Gerald Carroll**
*Member of Board, West of Scotland Water Authority Advocate. Labour Councillor for Glasgow City Council. Past President, Glasgow Bar Assocaition.*

**Michael Carroll**
*Regional Officer, Countryside Commission*

**Miranda Carroll**
*Head of Information, National Gallery*

**AF Carson**
*Sheep Production & Heifer Rearing, Agricultural Research Institute of Northern Ireland*

**Dr IW Carson**
*Member, Northern Ireland Council for Postgraduate Medical & Dental Education Nominated by Royal College of Anaesthetists.*

**Sir John Carter**
*Commissioner, Duke of York's Royal Military School*

**Liz Carter**
*Director Policy & Planning, Companies House*

**Paula Carter**
*Member, Employment Tribunals Service Resources Secretary, BBC.*

**Peter Carter**
*Deputy Director General, Office of Electricity Regulation*

**Clive Carthew**
*Member, Qualifications, Curriculum & Assessment Authority for Wales Education Management Consultant.*

**John Cartledge**
*Assistant Director, Policy Development, London Regional Passengers Committee*

**Roy Cartledge**
*Fire Service, Highlands & Islands Airports*

**David Cartmill**
*Director of Development, Northern Ireland Tourist Board*

**Ian Cartwright**
*Solicitor & Secretary, Coal Authority*

**John Cartwright**
*Deputy Chairman, Police Complaints Authority Former Labour and Social Democrat MP.*

**Hilary Carty**
*Director, Dance, The Arts Council of England*

**Marian Carty**
*Language Teaching Adviser, Centre for Information on Language Teaching & Research*

**Mrs P Carville**
*Member of Council, Council for Catholic Maintained Schools*

**Anthea Case**
*Director, National Heritage Memorial Fund*

**David Caselton**
*Park Manager, Regent's Park and Primrose Hill, Royal Parks Agency*

**Derek Casey**
*Chief Executive, UK & English Sports Councils*

**Peter Casey**
*Assistant Director, Office of Fair Trading*

**Prof JD Cash CBE**
*Member, National Biological Standards Board*

**Michael Cass**
*Managing Director, V&A Enterprises, Victoria & Albert Museum*

**Rosalie Cass**
*Registrar, National Gallery*

**Mrs Christine Casseldine**
*Member, South Wales Consumers' Committee, Office of Electricity Regulation*

**F Cassell CB**
*Member of Board, Crown Agents Foundation*

**Sheila Cassells**
*Director of Finance, Independent Television Commission*

**Mrs M Casserly**
*Member, Parole Board for Scotland Principal Officer, Social Work Department, North Lanarkshire Council.*

**Billy Cassidy**
*Belfast and Eastern, Rate Collection Agency*

**Ms F Cassidy**
Member of Board, Probation Board for Northern Ireland

**Mrs Marion Cassidy**
Member, Northern Ireland Local Government Officers' Superannuation Committee

**TJ Cassidy**
Member of Steering Board, Patent Office

**TJ Cassidy**
Chief Executive, Cadw

**Tony Cassidy**
Chief Executive, Renfrewshire Enterprise

**PB Castle**
Board Secretary, Construction Industry Training Board

**Mrs PM Castle**
Member, National Radiological Protection Board
McKenna & Co Solicitors, London.

**Pam Castro**
Regional Office, North Thames, NHS Estates

**Chris Caswill**
Director of Research, Economic & Social Research Council

**Dr Ronald Catlow**
Member, Ofwat North West Customer Service Committee

**Professor Graeme RD Catto**
Member, Scottish Higher Education Funding Council
Vice-Principal & Dean, Faculty of Medicine & Medical Sciences, University of Aberdeen.

**Joan Catto**
Member of Board, Scottish Children's Reporter Administration

**Jim Caughey**
Technical Director, Met Office

**P Cautley**
Appointed Trustee, Royal Marines Museum

**Prof Martin Cave**
Member, Monopolies & Mergers Commission
Vice-Principal and Professor of Economics, Brunel University.

**Lord Cavendish of Furness**
Commissioner, English Heritage

**DW Cawthra CBE**
Member of Advisory Board, Highways Agency
External member.

**MF Cayley**
Financial Institutions & Company Tax Divisions, Inland Revenue

**JJ Chadwick**
Secretary, Imperial War Museum

**Sir Charles Chadwyck-Healey**
Member, Marshall Aid Commemoration Commission

**Prof Mono Chakrabarti**
Member, Central Council for Education & Training in Social Work

**Dr Shanti Chakravarty**
Member, Merseyside & North Wales Consumers' Committee, Office of Electricity Regulation

**Mrs Esther Challis**
Member, Eastern Consumers' Committee, Office of Electricity Regulation

**JA Chalmers**
Inspector, Football Licensing Authority

**Dr NR Chalmers**
Director, Natural History Museum

**Neville Chamberlain CBE**
Deputy Chairman, British Nuclear Fuels plc
Non-Executive Director of Trinity Holdings.

**Philip Chamberlain**
Board Director, Home-Grown Cereals Authority

**Ernest Chambers**
Chief Executive, West of Scotland Water Authority
Formerly employed by East of Scotland Water Board, Lower Clyde Water Board and Strathclyde Regional Council. Former Director, Strathclyde Water and Strathclyde Water Services.

**K Chambers**
Member of Board, Construction Industry Training Board (NI)
Belfast Institute of Further & Higher Education.

**Paul Chambers**
Regional Director, South West, English Sports Council

**Prof Ruth Chambers**
Member, Human Fertilisation & Embryology Authority
GP and Professor of Health Commissioning, Primary Care Development Unit, School of Health, Staffordshire University.

**Sarah Chambers**
Director of Licensing Policy, Office of Telecommunications

**Group Captain JE Chandler**
Officer Commanding, RAF Sealand, RAF Maintenance Group Defence Agency

**Viscount Chandos**
Governor, National Film & Television School

**Dr Raj Chandran**
Member, Commission for Racial Equality
Principal general practitioner. Vice Chairman, Conservative Medical Society. Former chairman and Hon Sec, North Notts Division, BMA. President, Mansfield Medical Society. Former joint national secretary, Overseas Doctors Association. Comprehensive school governor. District Councillor. Chairman,

Asian Sports & Arts Foundation. Chairman, One Nation Forum.

**Captain R Channon**
Trustee, Royal Navy Submarine Museum

**Alan Chant**
Head of Business Affairs, Office of the National Lottery

**David Chantler**
Member, Central Council for Education & Training in Social Work

**Ben Chapman MP**
Member, The Great Britain-China Centre

**Cllr JM Chapman**
Deputy Chairman, Rail Users Consultative Committee for Western England

**Ms MM Chapman**
Chief Executive, Investors in People UK

**Neil Chapman**
Member Advisory Board, NHS Pensions Agency
Finance Director, St James' University Hospital NHS Trust.

**RA Chapman**
Senior Assistant Director (Finance & Administration), Traffic Director for London

**Rhiannon Chapman**
Member of Board, Welsh Development Agency
SR Gent, Plaudit, Policy Studies Institute, Employment Appeal Tribunal.

**Peter Chappelow**
Member, English Tourist Board
MD, Holiday Cottages Group. Board Thomson Travel Group.

**Ken Charles**
Head of Branch, Personnel & Administration, Forest Research

**Ms Pamela Charlwood**
Non-Executive Member, English National Board for Nursing, Midwifery & Health Visiting
Chief Executive, Avon Health Commission.

**Kevin Charman**
General Manager, English Nature

**Diane Charnock**
Member, Legal Aid Board
Magistrate. Former Chairman, NHS community trust. Chair, St Helen's & Knowsley Hospitals Trust. Chair, Mersey Consortium for Non-Medical Education & Training.

**Mrs Margaret Charrington**
Chairman, Horticultural Development Council
Director, Invest in Britain Campaign. Consultant to the British Standards Institution and Governor, University of Westminster. Previously member Apple & Pear Development Council and a founding member of the Women's Farming Union.

**Bob Chase**
*Non-Executive Director, London Transport*
Former Group Managing Director, Automobile Association. Former senior appointments with Orient Overseas Holdings and GEC Hong Kong.

**John Chastney**
*Member of Board, Funding Agency for Schools*
Accountant.

**Captain RF Cheadle**
*Deputy Director Naval Manning (Development), Naval Manning Agency*

**Sir Michael Checkland**
*Chairman, Higher Education Funding Council for England*
Former Director General, BBC.

**Viscount Chelmsford**
*Member of Board, Simpler Trade Procedures Board*
Director, EURIM (European Informatics Market). Council Member, PITCOM (Parliamentary Information Technology Committee). Management Committee, UK Confederation for EDI Standards. President, ITS Focus (Intelligent Transport Systems), IDPM (Institute of Data Processing Management) and ECA (Electronic Commerce Association). Past Director, Willis Faber.

**Chris Chemney**
*Manager, East Midlands, Gas Consumers' Council*

**Elizabeth Chennells**
*Director, International Training & Development, Civil Service College*

**Mrs Bridget Cherry**
*Trustee, Sir John Soane's Museum Commissioner, English Heritage*

**Sir J Cherry**
*Keeper, Medieval & Later Antiquities, British Museum*

**Sir Tim Chessells**
*Chairman, Legal Aid Board*
Former Chairman, London Implementation Group. Former Chairman, North East Thames Regional Health Authority. Chairman, Special Trustees, Guy's and St Thomas's Hospitals and Advisory Board, University College School of Public Policy. Non-Executive Director, Dixons Group and Care UK.

**Andrew Chesson**
*Head, Molecular Ecology & Gut Function Division, Rowett Research Institute*

**Richard Chester**
*Member of Council, Scottish Arts Council*

**George Chesworth OBE**
*Chairman, Moray Badenoch & Strathspey Enterprise*

**Prof Mel Chevannes**
*Non-Executive Member, English National Board for Nursing, Midwifery & Health Visiting*
Head of Department of Nursing & Midwifery Studies, De Montfort University.

**Ross Chiese**
*Group Finance Director, British Nuclear Fuels plc*

**Mrs Alison Child**
*Member, Ofwat North West Customer Service Committee*

**Prof John Childs**
*Trustee, Royal Armouries*

**Mike Childs**
*Information Systems, Office for Standards in Education*

**John Chisholm**
*Chief Executive, Defence Evaluation & Research Agency*

**Sam Chisholm**
*Deputy Chairman, New Millennium Experience Co Ltd*
Former Chief Executive & MD, Sky Broadcasting Group.

**Huw Chiswell**
*Commissioning Editor - Light Entertainment, S4C*

**Barry Chivers**
*Management Audit, UK Sports Council*

**Kit Chivers**
*Contracting Director, National Savings*

**Christopher Chope OBE**
*Member, Health & Safety Commission*
Consultant, Ernst & Young. Former MP for Southampton Itchen and Minister at the Departments of Environment and Transport. Former Member, Local Government Commission for England. Former Leader, Wandsworth Borough Council and member, London Boroughs' Association, Association of Metropolitan Authorities and Inner London Education Authority.

**Lord Chorley**
*Deputy Chairman, British Council*
Former Chairman, The National Trust.

**JJ (Matthew) Choung**
*Director, Korean Collaboration Centre, Rowett Research Institute*

**WW Christie**
*Head, Chemistry Department, Scottish Crop Research Institute*

**Dr A Christodoulou, CBE**
*Executive Secretary, Marshall Aid Commemoration Commission*

**Ms Sue Chudleigh**
*Project Manager, Central and Eastern Europe/Company Secretary, Westminster Foundation for Democracy*

**John Chumrow**
*Chairman, Waltham Forest Housing Action Trust*
Former Director of Wiggins Teape Group. Trustee of Philharmonia Orchestra.

**June Churchman OBE**
*Member of Wales Committee, National Lottery Charities Board*
Vice-President, Guide Association. Deputy Lieutenant, Clwyd. Vice-President, Council for Wales Voluntary Youth Services. Vice-Chair, Wales Assembly of Women, North East Wales branch.

**Alistair Clark**
*Member of Court & Executive Director, Financial Stability, Bank of England*

**Alistair C Clark**
*Chairman, Scottish Conveyancing & Executry Services Board*

**Ann Clark**
*Member of Board, Scottish Homes*
Executive Director, Highland Community Care Forum. Director, Highland Brook Advisory Centre.

**Bill Clark**
*Head of Plans and Resources, Army Training & Recruitment Agency*

**Bob Clark**
*Managing Director, CDC Industries, Commonwealth Development Corporation*

**Bob Clark**
*Member of Management Board, The Court Service*
South Eastern Circuit Administrator.

**Eileen Clark**
*Member of Board, Liverpool Housing Action Trust*
Resident of Buckingham House and founder member of the Tenants' Association.

**J Clark**
*Commercial Director, Specialist Procurement Services*

**John Clark**
*Dir Operations Management, Defence Codification Agency*

**KW Clark**
*Director of Finance, Trinity House Lighthouse Service*

**Margaret Clark**
*Director of Strategy & Planning, Rural Development Commission*

**Mrs M Clark-Glass**
*Member of Board, Probation Board for Northern Ireland*

**Mrs B Clarke**
*Executive Officer (Finance), Youth Council for Northern Ireland*

**David Clarke**
*Keeper of Archaeology, National Museums of Scotland*

**Dennis Clarke**
*Park Manager, St James's Park and Green Park, Royal Parks Agency*

**Dr GCS Clarke**
*Head of Department, Exhibitions & Education, Natural History Museum*

**Ian Clarke**
*Member of England Committee, National Lottery Charities Board*
Former Agent of Bank of England, Newcastle upon Tyne. Council Member, University of Newcastle upon Tyne. Chairman, University Development Trust. Non-Executive Director, Northgate & Prudhoe Hospital NHS Trust. Trustee, Catherine Cookson Foundation.

**Mrs Jenny Clarke**
*Member, Ofwat Yorkshire Customer Service Committee*

**Rear Admiral John Clarke**
*Hydrographer of the Navy & Chief Executive, UK Hydrographic Office*

**PA Clarke**
*Assistant Director, Personnel & Secretariat, Armed Forces Personnel Administration Agency*

**R Clarke**
*Member of Advisory Board, Coastguard*
Director of Shipping Policy

**Prof RH Clarke**
*Director, National Radiological Protection Board*

**Stella Clarke JP**
*Chair, England Committee, National Lottery Charities Board*
Deputy Lieutenant of Bristol. Chair of Council, Bristol University.

**Tony Clarke CBE**
*Governor, Westminster Foundation for Democracy*

**Prof Brian Clarkson**
*Member, Higher Education Funding Council for Wales*
Former Principal, University College of Swansea.

**Christopher Claxton Stevens**
*Trustee, Geffrye Museum*
Member of Court, Worshipful Company of Furniture Makers.

**Edward Clay**
*Member, Departmental Board, Wilton Park Executive Agency*

**Gordon Clay**
*Subject Adviser, PE, Office for Standards in Education*

**Tom Clay**
*Director of Development & Planning, Liverpool Housing Action Trust*

**Celia Clear**
*Managing Director, Tate Gallery Publishing, Tate Gallery*

**Ian Cleare**
*Director, Electrical Equipment Certification Service, The Health & Safety Executive*

**BE Cleave CB**
*Solicitor, Inland Revenue*

**K Cleland**
*Member, Training & Employment Agency (NI)*
Chief Executive, Graham & Heslip.

**David Clementi**
*Deputy Governor, Bank of England*

**Ian Clements**
*Custody Services Business Director, Security Facilities Executive*

**RJ Clements**
*Head of Map Production, Ordnance Survey of Northern Ireland*

**Honor Clerk**
*20th Century Curator, National Portrait Gallery*

**Alexis Cleveland**
*Operations Support Director, Benefits Agency*

**Anne Cleverly**
*Member, Central Council for Education & Training in Social Work*

**Bill Clifford**
*Weapons Systems, Defence Evaluation & Research Agency*

**Prof Roland Clift**
*Member of Board, UK Ecolabelling Board*
Professor of environmental technology, University of Surrey.

**Richard Clifton**
*Head, Policy Unit, The Health & Safety Executive*

**Judith Cligman**
*Deputy Director of Operations, National Heritage Memorial Fund*

**Brigadier JW Clinter**
*Member, Logistic Information Systems Agency*
DQIS.

**Dr Alan Clinton**
*Member of Board of Governors, Museum of London*
Appointed by the Corporation of London.

**Jim Close**
*Assistant Director (Administration), Victoria & Albert Museum*

**Richard Close**
*Managing Director Finance, Post Office*

**Elan Closs Stephens**
*Chairman, S4C*

**Anthony Clothier**
*Member, Monopolies & Mergers Commission*
Independent consultant. Formerly Chairman, Ofwat Wessex Customer Service Committee. Former President, British Footwear Manufacturers Federation and European Shoe Federation.

**Sir Cecil Clothier KCB QC**
*Member, The British Library*

**Giles Clotworthy**
*Member, Tate Gallery*

**Nigel Clubb**
*Director of the NMR, Royal Commission on Historical Monuments of England*

**Blondel Cluff**
*Member, Commission for Racial Equality*
Assistant Director & Head of Legal Department, Lazard Brothers & Co. Consultant legal adviser to the London Stock Exchange and Bank of England on stock exchange money broking. Senior partner, Cluff, Hodge & Co. Legal adviser to Cluff Mining.

**Malcolm Clydedale**
*Operations Manager, War Pensions Agency*

**Alan Coates**
*Member, Ofwat Yorkshire Customer Service Committee*

**C Coates**
*Member, The British Library*
Trades Union Congress.

**David Coates**
*Member, The Great Britain-China Centre*
Foreign & Commonwealth Office representative on the Executive Committee.

**Nick Coates**
*Director of Finance & Administration, Stonebridge Housing Action Trust*

**Cllr Fred Cobain**
*Member, Arts Council of Northern Ireland*
Former Lord Mayor of Belfast.

**Sir Michael Cobham CBE**
*Trustee, Fleet Air Arm Museum*

**Penelope Viscountess Cobham**
*Commissioner, Museums & Galleries Commission*
*Trustee, Victoria & Albert Museum*
Board Member, London Docklands Development Corporation and BTA British Heritage Committee. Member, Historic Royal Palaces Advisory Group. Trustee, Victoria & Albert Museum. Former Commissioner, English Heritage and Countryside Commission.

**Chris Cochlin**
*Member, Tate Gallery*

**JMT Cockburn**
*Managing Director - Water Services, North of Scotland Water Authority*

**William Cockburn**
*Member of College Advisory Council, Civil Service College*

**D Cockram**
*Director of Administration, Coastguard*

**Prof R Cocks**
*Keeper, Palaeontology Department, Natural History Museum*

**Lord Cocks of Hartcliffe**
*Vice-Chairman, British Broadcasting Corporation*
Former Government Chief Whip. Deputy Chairman, Docklands Development Corporation.

**Sir Alan Cockshaw**
*Non-Executive Director, New Millennium Experience Co Ltd*
Former Chairman, AMEC. President, Institute of Civil Engineers.

**John Codling**
*Finance Director, Funding Agency for Schools*

**Prof RJ Cogdell**
*Member of Governing Body, Scottish Crop Research Institute*
Hooker Chair of Botany, Institute of Biomedical & Life Sciences, Glasgow University.

**Prof JR Coggins**
*Member of Council, Hannah Research Institute*

**Janet Cohen**
*Governor, British Broadcasting Corporation*
Director, Charterhouse Bank. Board Member, Sheffield Development Corporation.

**NV Cohen**
*LT Director of Marketing & Member, Victoria Coach Station Board, London Transport*

**Norman Cole**
*Member, Yorkshire Consumers' Committee, Office of Electricity Regulation*

**Tim Cole**
*Member, Yorkshire Consumers' Committee, Office of Electricity Regulation*

**Robin Cole-Hamilton**
*Head of Public Affairs, Victoria & Albert Museum*

**David Coleman**
*Strategic Affairs, Countryside Commission*

**Prof JM Coles**
*Commissioner, Royal Commission on Ancient & Historical Monuments of Scotland*

**John Coles**
*Chief Executive, Ships Support Agency*

**Sir John Coles GCMG**
*Member of Board, British Council*
Permanent Under-Secretary of State, Foreign and Commonwealth Office.

**Gp Capt PKL Coles**
*DDMT (Pol), Defence Medical Training Organisation*

**Paul Coles**
*Late Filing, Penalties, Companies House*

**Frank Coley**
*Director, South & West Region, Advisory, Conciliation & Arbitration Service*

**Graham Coley**
*MD Science, Defence Evaluation & Research Agency*

**Liam Colgan**
*Director, London & South East, Property Advisers to the Civil Estate*

**Harry Coll OBE**
*Member of Commission, Equal Opportunities Commission for Northern Ireland*
Solicitor. Founding Chairman, Springvale Training Ltd.

**Prof Gerald Collee CBE**
*Member, Scottish Hospital Endowments Research Trust*

**Clive Collier**
*Member, Ofwat Thames Customer Service Committee*

**Michael Collier**
*Chief Executive, Funding Agency for Schools*

**Susan Collier**
*Member of Council, Crafts Council*
Designer and businesswoman.

**TD Collier**
*Chairman, Yorkshire RFDC, The Environment Agency*

**His Excellency John Collinge**
*Trustee, Imperial War Museum*

**Mike Collings**
*Head of Security, National Gallery*

**Ann Collins**
*Member, General Consumer Council for Northern Ireland*
Member, Transport Advisory Committe of Disability Action. Coordinator, Shopmobility Belfast. Secretary, Belfast & District Group, Disabled Drivers' Association.

**Chris Collins**
*Milk Quotas, Intervention Board*

**Evelyn Collins**
*Chief Equality Officer, Equal Opportunities Commission for Northern Ireland*

**J Collins**
*Member of Board, Labour Relations Agency*

**Jim Collins**
*Member, Industrial Research & Technology Unit*
Plant Manager, Ford Motor Co.

**Ms Sue Collins**
*Director, English Nature*

**Vivienne Collins**
*Investors in People, Rate Collection Agency*

**WJN Collins**
*Member, Northern Ireland Council for Postgraduate Medical & Dental Education*
Appointed by DHSS.

**Peter Collis**
*Director, Finance and Planning, Employment Service*

**Doris Colloff**
*Member, London Regional Passengers Committee*

**Anthony Colman**
*Member, London Consumers' Committee, Office of Electricity Regulation*

**Mrs I Colvin OBE**
*Member of Board, Probation Board for Northern Ireland*

**Ruth Coman**
*Director, St Pancras Operations & Estates, The British Library*

**Dr Stephen Compton**
*Commissioner, Mental Health Commission for Northern Ireland*
Consultant Psychiatrist, Homefirst Community Health & Social Services Trust.

**FG Conlon**
*Member of Board, Fisheries Conservancy Board for Northern Ireland*
Commercial fishing company representative.

**Robert Conlon**
*Regional Executive, Independent Television Commission*

**Mrs R Connel**
*Non-Executive Member, Valuation Office Agency*

**Cllr John Connolly**
*Member, Scottish Water & Sewerage Customers Council*
Chairman, East Area Committee.

**Seamus Connolly**
*Member of Commission, Equal Opportunities Commission for Northern Ireland*
Chairman & Managing Director, local manufacturing export company.

**Frank Constable MBE**
*Member, Royal Parks Agency*
Former City Parks & Recreation Officer, Derby.

**Mrs Yvonne Constance**
*Chairman, London Consumers' Committee, Office of Electricity Regulation*

**Alan Conway**
*Member, Eastern Consumers' Committee, Office of Electricity Regulation*

**Ally Cook**
*Head of Finance, UK Passport Agency*

**Arthur Cook**
*Member of Board, Sea Fish Industry Authority*
Director, Hull Fish Merchants' Protection Association and Vice-Chairman, Yorkshire & Anglia Fish Producers' Organisation. Past Chairman, Federation of British Port Wholesale Fish Merchants' Associations and North East Sea Fisheries Committee.

**DF Cook**
*Director Corporate Marketing & Development, Crown Agents Foundation*

**Haydn Cook**
*Member of Advisory Board, Medical Devices Agency*
Chief Executive, Calderdale Healthcare NHS Trust.

**Mrs Margaret Cook**
*Member, South Western Consumers' Committee, Office of Electricity Regulation*

**Mary Curnock Cook**
*Member, The Further Education Funding Council*
Director, British Institute of Innkeeping. Former acting Chief Executive, Food from Britain.

**Dr PJ Cook CBE**
*Director, British Geological Survey*

**The Rt Hon Robin Cook MP**
*Trustee, Commonwealth Institute*
Secretary of State for Foreign & Commonwealth Affairs.

**Arthur Cooke**
*Regional Manager, Office of Electricity Regulation*

**BM Cooke**
*Member, Rail Users Consultative Committee for Eastern England*

**Dr John Cooke**
*Member, National Weights & Measures Laboratory*
Managing Director, TESA Metrology.

**Prof Ron Cooke**
*Member of Board, Higher Education Funding Council for England*
Vice-Chancellor, University of York.

**Sir David Cooksey**
*Member of Court, Bank of England*
Chairman, Advent.

**Lady Cooksey**
*Trustee, Royal Armouries*

**David Coombs**
*Trustee, Sir John Soane's Museum*
Representative of the Royal Society of Arts.

**RCN Coombs**
*Member Advisory Board, NHS Pensions Agency*
Health Management Division, Welsh Office

**B Cooper**
*Director Fleet Support ( Personnel), Naval Bases & Supply Agency*

**Brenda Cooper**
*Member of Committee, Rail Users Consultative Committee for Wales*

**Christopher Cooper**
*Head of Central Management Department, Public Record Office*

**Geoff Cooper**
*Team Manager, Office Services, English Nature*

**Dr JR Cooper**
*Head of Dept, Environmental Assessments, National Radiological Protection Board*

**John Cooper**
*Chief Examiner, Office of Electricity Regulation*

**John Cooper**
*Head of Education, National Portrait Gallery*

**Mrs MR Cooper**
*Member of Council, Council for Catholic Maintained Schools*
Department of Education Representative.

**Moss Cooper**
*Director of Operations, Lottery Operations, The Arts Council of England*

**Robert G Cooper CBE**
*Chairman, Fair Employment Commission for Northern Ireland*

**Sheena MM Cooper**
*Member, Scottish Higher Education Funding Council*
Rector, Aboyne Academy.

**Miss LJ Coote**
*Finance Officer, Royal Marines Museum*

**Jerry Cope**
*Managing Director, Strategy and Personnel, Post Office*

**Ray Cope**
*Manager, Eastern, Gas Consumers' Council*

**Nigel Copeland**
*Director of Finance & Resources, The Arts Council of England*

**Lady Copisarow**
*Trustee, Victoria & Albert Museum*

**Mrs S Copper**
*Member, Parole Board*

**MJ Corbel**
*Head of Bacteriology, National Biological Standards Board*

**Ian Corbett**
*Director of Science, Particle Physics & Astronomy Research Council*

**Graham Corbett CBE**
*Deputy Chairman, Monopolies & Mergers Commission*
Former, Chief Financial Officer, Eurotunnel.

**Robin Corbett MP**
*Member, Academic Council, Wilton Park Executive Agency*

**Dr Roger Corbett**
*Chairman, Ofwat Eastern Customer Service Committee*
*Member, Ofwat National Customer Council*

**Michael Corcoran**
*Funding Director, National Savings*

**Norman Cordiner**
*Chairman, Inverness & Nairn Enterprise*

**Mrs Alison Cording**
*Member, Ofwat Customer Service Committee for Wales*

**Richard Cork**
*Member, The Arts Council of England*
Chief Art Critic, *The Times*. Editor, broadcaster, historian, exhibition, organiser. Former Henry Moore Foundation Senior Fellow at the Courtauld Institute. Slade Professor of Fine Art at Cambridge University.

**AG Corless CBE**
*Commissioner, Commission for the Rights of Trade Union Members & Commission for Protection Against Unlawful Industrial Action*
*Chairman, Tai Cymru*
Former Chief Executive, West Glamorgan County Council and London Borough of Southwark.

**Clive Corlett CB**
*Deputy Chairman, Inland Revenue*

**Sir Patrick Cormack MP**
*Commissioner, The Royal Commission on Historical Manuscripts*

**Keith Cornelius**
*Finance Director, Medical Devices Agency*

**Tim Cornford**
*Secretary to the Board, Qualifications & Curriculum Authority*

**C Cornish**
*Director, Human Resources, West of Scotland Water Authority*

**Daniel Corr**
*Member, General Consumer Council for Northern Ireland*
Northern Ireland Manager, Nationwide Building Society. Chairman, Building Societies Association and Council of Mortage Lenders, Northern Ireland. Board Member, Northern Ireland Co-ownership Housing Association and Belfast Common Purpose.

**Mrs CC Corrigan**
*Member, NIACT, Northern Ireland Committee on Telecommunications*
Chartered accountant and registered auditor.

**O Corrigan**
*Member of Council, Council for Catholic Maintained Schools*
Department of Education Representative.

**John PF Cory**
*Finance Director & Secretary, Wales Tourist Board*

**Bernie Cosgrove**
*Director of IT, Driver & Vehicle Licensing Northern Ireland*

**Stuart Cosgrove**
*Member of Board, Scottish Screen*

**Sir Neil Cossons**
*Director, National Museum of Science & Industry*
*Member of Board, British Waterways*

English Heritage Commissioner; Member of Council of Royal College of Art.

**Mrs Linda Costelloe Baker**
*Member, Parole Board for Scotland*
Management Consultant. Chairman, South Lanarkshire Children's Panel Advisory Committee. Member, Criminal Injuries Compensation Appeals Panel.

**JA Cotton**
*Member, Parole Board*

**Keith Cottrell**
*Director of Sales, Royal Mint*

**HE Couch**
*Member of Board, Education Assets Board*

**R Coughlin**
*Member of Board, Labour Relations Agency*

**R Coulter**
*Member, Northern Ireland Fishery Harbour Authority*

**Charles Coulthard**
*Deputy Director General Electricity & Gas, Office for the Regulation of Electricity & Gas*

**Dr Heather Couper**
*Member, Millennium Commission*
Broadcaster and writer. Runs a leading factual television company.

**Jean Couper**
*Member, The Scottish Legal Aid Board*
Non-Executive Director, Health Education Board for Scotland. Principal, Catalyst Consulting.

**David Court**
*Chief Executive, Government Purchasing Agency*

**Cllr G Court**
*Chairman, REPAC, The Environment Agency*

**Peter Court**
*Manager, Southern, Gas Consumers' Council*

**Cllr Mrs A Courtney**
*Member of Board, Fisheries Conservancy Board for Northern Ireland*
*Member of Board, Northern Ireland Museums' Council*
*Member, Northern Ireland Tourist Board*
Member, Derry City Council. Former Member, Western Health & Social Services Board. Member, Board of Council for Nature Conservation and the Countryside (CNCC). Health Promotion Coordinator, Altnagelvin Hospital.

**Air Chief Marshal Sir David Cousins CB**
*Owner, RAF Training Group Defence Agency*
*Air Member for Personnel, Royal Air Force Museum*

**Dr Stuart Coverley**
*Member, Ofwat South West Customer Service Committee*

**AF Cowan**
*Chief Executive, NHS Pensions Agency*

**Mrs J Coward JP**
*Member, Parole Board*

**Prof Ray Cowell**
*Member, The Arts Council of England*
Chairman of East Midlands Arts Board. Vice-Chancellor, Nottingham Trent University. Deputy Lieutenant of County of Nottinghamshire.

**Captain DM Cowell (Isle of Man)**
*Commissioner, Northern Lighthouse Board*

**Mrs Audrey Cowie**
*Professional Officer (Nursing), National Board for Nursing, Midwifery & Health Visiting for Scotland*

**Kevin Cowle**
*Senior Development Officer, Scottish Screen*

**A Cowpe**
*Agency Secretary, RAF Personnel Management Agency*

**Sir Alan Cox CBE**
*Member, Cardiff Bay Development Corporation*
Wales Millenium Centre. Meggitt. Morgan Crucible Company. UK Round Table on Sustainable Development.

**Prof Brian Cox CBE**
*Member, The Arts Council of England*
Chairman of North West Arts Board. Retired Professor of English and Pro-Vice-Chancellor, Manchester University. Former Chair, National Curriculum English Working Group. Honorary Fellow of Westminster College Oxford, and Visiting Professor at Sheffield Hallam University.

**Mrs Dorothy Cox**
*Head of NMA Secretariat, Naval Manning Agency*

**George Cox**
*Non-Executive Member, Inland Revenue*
UNISYS, Former Quality & Personnel Director, Vickers Defence Systems.

**Dr Lynton Cox**
*Food Microbiology, Central Science Laboratory*
Former Head of Food Safety Microbiology, Nestle research centre in Switzerland.

**M Cox**
*Head of Contracts Branch, Defence Transport & Movements Executive*

**M Cox**
*Director of Personnel Services, Driver & Vehicle Testing Agency*

**Margaret Cox**
*Assistant Principal Reporter (Operations), Scottish Children's Reporter Administration*

**Mike Cox**
*Member, Ofwat South West Customer Service Committee*

**Dr R Cox**
*Head of Dept, Biomedical Effects, National Radiological Protection Board*

**Richard Cox**
*Arts Officer, Arts Council of Wales*

**S Cox**
*Member of Board, Construction Industry Training Board (NI)*
North West Institute of Further & Higher Education.

**Mrs Catherine Coxhead**
*Chief Executive, Northern Ireland Council for the Curriculum, Examinations & Assessment*

**JM Crabbe**
*Deputy Chief Executive, Sports Council for Northern Ireland*

**J Robert Crabtree**
*Programme Unit Manager, Macaulay Land Use Research Institute*

**Malcolm Crabtree**
*Member, Milk Development Council*
Managing Director, Leckford Estates, Hampshire. Previously with ADAS.

**George Cracknell**
*Member of Board, The Housing Corporation*
Formerly, Deputy Managing Director, Banking Division, Barclays Bank. Currently, Director of Ivory & Sime Baronsmead, Chairman of ASK Central and Chairman of Glaziers Hall.

**Gordon Cragge**
*Deputy Director, Trade Facilitation, Simpler Trade Procedures Board*

**Brigadier Andy Craig**
*Commander Recruiting, Army Training & Recruitment Agency*

**G Craig**
*Head of Finance and Procurement, Scottish Fisheries Protection Agency*

**GCG Craig**
*Member of Advisory Committee, Cadw*
Head of Transport, Planning & Environment Group, Welsh Office.

**Gordon Craig**
*Member, Scottish Community Education Council*

**Mrs H Craig**
*Committee Clerk, National Board for Nursing, Midwifery & Health Visiting for Northern Ireland*

**Sqn Ldr RF Craig**
*Museum Secretary, Royal Air Force Museum*

**Terry Craig**
*Manager (Finance, Administration & Management Services), Fair Employment Commission for Northern Ireland*

**Michael Craig-Martin**
*Trustee, Tate Gallery*

**Paul Crake**
*Director, Communication, The Design Council*

**Margaret Cramp**
*Personnel Manager, Occupational Pensions Regulatory Authority*

**Prof Rosemary J Cramp CBE**
*Commissioner, Royal Commission on Ancient & Historical Monuments of Scotland*
*Trustee, British Museum*

**Earl of Cranbrook**
*Chairman, English Nature*
*Member, Joint Nature Conservation Committee*
Biologist and farmer. Member, Broads Authority and Harwich Haven Authority. Non-executive director, Anglian Water. Chairman, Environmental Advisory Board of Shanks & McEwan. Chairman, ENTRUST. President, Suffolk Wildlife Trust. Member, UK Roundtable on Sustainable Development.

**Bernie Cranfield**
*Member, Livestock & Meat Commission for Northern Ireland*
Franchisee, McDonalds Restaurant, Donegall Place.

**Mrs Jean Craske**
*Member, North Western Consumers' Committee, Office of Electricity Regulation*

**Dr BE Crawford**
*Commissioner, Royal Commission on Ancient & Historical Monuments of Scotland*

**CD Crawford**
*Group Manager Undergraduate, Student Awards Agency for Scotland*

**Sir Frederick Crawford**
*Chairman, Criminal Cases Review Commission*
Former Vice-Chancellor, Aston University. Deputy Lieutenant, West Midlands.

**JIM Crawford**
*Member of Board of Governors, Macaulay Land Use Research Institute*

**Dr M Crawford**
*Associate Adviser in Postgraduate General Practice Education, Northern Ireland Council for Postgraduate Medical & Dental Education*

**RWK Crawford**
*Director-General, Imperial War Museum*

**Victor Crawford**
*Technical Director, Roads Service*

**Earl of Crawford & Balcarres KT PC**
*Chairman, National Library of Scotland*
*Trustee, National Library of Scotland*

**Prof Michael Crawley**
*Trustee, Royal Botanic Gardens Kew*

**Tom Crawley**
*Device Evaluation Programme & Corporate Services, Medical Devices Agency*

**John Creedy**
*Team Manager, Information Resources Services Team, English Nature*

**David Cresswell**
*Communications Manager, Occupational Pensions Regulatory Authority*

**Dr Stephen Cribb**
*Member, Rail Users Consultative Committee for Scotland*
Consultant geologist and author.

**Angus Crichton-Miller**
*Member, Horserace Betting Levy Board*

**E Criswick**
*Government Assessor, Construction Industry Training Board*
Department of the Environment.

**JR Croft**
*Head of Dept, Industrial Operations, National Radiological Protection Board*

**Neil Croft**
*Customer Relations Manager, Central Computer & Telecommunications Agency*

**Roy Croft CB**
*Member, Monopolies & Mergers Commission*
Non-Executive Director, Countrywide Independent Advisers. Formerly Chief Executive, Securities & Investments Board and Deputy Secretary, Department of Trade & Industry.

**Roger Crofts**
*Chief Executive, Scottish Natural Heritage*

**Garth Crooks**
*Member, English Sports Council*

**J Crooks**
*Member of Board, Construction Industry Training Board (NI)*
UCATT. Employee representative.

**J Cropley**
*Member, The British Library*
Library Association.

**Simon Cross**
*Business Director, Met Office*

**G Crossan**
*Board Secretary, Labour Relations Agency*

**Dr T Crossett**
*Chairman, REPAC, The Environment Agency*

**Mrs Marie Crothers**
*Commissioner, Mental Health Commission for Northern Ireland*
Senior Social Worker, Foyle Health & Social Services Trust, Londonberry.

**N Crouch**
*Member, The British Library*
Confederation of British Industry.

**Sonia Crow**
*Assistant Director, Research & Development, English National Board for Nursing, Midwifery & Health Visiting*

**V Crowe**
*Associate Director, Wilton Park Executive Agency*

**Noel Crowley**
*Member of Board, Welsh Development Agency*
Leader, Neath Port Talbot County Borough Council. Iechyd Morgannwg Health.

**Prof M Anne Crowther**
*Chairman, Scottish Record Office*

**PA Crowther**
*Member of Advisory Board, Defence Bills Agency*
Head of General Finance.

**J Crozier**
*Member of Board, Probation Board for Northern Ireland*

**Don Cruickshank**
*Director General, Office of Telecommunications*
*Member, Radiocommunications Agency*

**Mike Crump**
*Director, Reader Services & Collection Development, The British Library*

**Prof Ian Crute**
*Site Director - Wellesbourne, Horticulture Research International*

**Steve Cryer**
*Accounts Image, Companies House*

**Prof David Crystal OBE**
*Member of Board, British Council*
Author, lecturer, reference books editor, broadcaster on language and linguistics and Hon Professorial Fellow University of Wales, Bangor.

**Alan Cubbin**
*Director, Operations & Seafarer Standards, Marine Safety Agency*

**George A Cubitt MBE**
*Observer, UK Sports Council*
Central Council of Physical Recreation

**Lord Cuckney**
*Trustee, Royal Air Force Museum*

**Prof Len Culhane**
*Member of Council, Particle Physics & Astronomy Research Council*
Mullard Space Science Laboratory

**Maureen Cullen**
*Personnel Officer, Northern Ireland Child Support Agency*

**Edward Cullinan CBE**
*Trustee, Sir John Soane's Museum*
Representative of the Royal Academy.

**Jill Culling**
*Applications Manager, Commissioner for Protection Against Unlawful Industrial Action & Commissioner for the Rights of Trade Union Members*

**Brigadier Andrew Cumming**
*Commander Initial Training Group, Army Training & Recruitment Agency*

**Eric Cumming**
*Head of Operations & Policy Unit, Scottish Court Service*

**Sandy Cumming**
*Chief Executive, Ross & Cromarty Enterprise*

**Roy Cummings**
*Director Ships Weapon Engineering, Ships Support Agency*

**R Cummins**
*Chief Driving Examiner, Driving Standards Agency*

**Prof Barry Cunliffe CBE**
*Member of Board of Governors, Museum of London*
Appointed by the Prime Minister.

**John Cunliffe**
*Member, Coal Authority*
Barrister

**Michael Cunliffe**
*Director of Corporate Services, East of Scotland Water Authority*

**AM Cunningham**
*Deputy Chairperson, Northern Ireland Fishery Harbour Authority*

**Ian C Cunningham**
*Keeper of Manuscripts, Maps & Music, and of the Scottish Science Library, National Library of Scotland*

**Ms M Cunningham**
*Executive Officer (International), Youth Council for Northern Ireland*

**Marie Cunningham**
*Member, Commission for Racial Equality*
Senior Partner, CPW Associates. Equal opportunities adviser, British Railways Board. Associate Member, Enfield Mental Health Trust. Member, British Caribbean Association. Corporate consultant, and former Managing Director, Voice Communications.

**Mrs Jean Curd**
*Member, Ofwat South West Customer Service Committee*

**Sue Curnow**
*Production Manager, National Gallery Publications, National Gallery*

**B Curran**
*Member of Council, Council for Catholic Maintained Schools*

**JA Curran**
*Director Supply (South), Naval Bases & Supply Agency*

**Sean Curran OBE**
*Chairman, Probation Board for Northern Ireland*

**Ian Currie**
*Member, East Areas Board & Scientific Advisory Committee, Scottish Natural Heritage*

**James Currie**
*Member, Scottish Agricultural Wages Board*
Employees' representative member nominated by the Rural, Agricultural & Allied Workers National Trade Group (Scotland) of the Transport & General Workers' Union.

**Donald Curry CBE**
*Chairman, Meat & Livestock Commission*
*Member of Council, Food from Britain*
Farms in Northumberland. Chairman, North Country Primestock. FfB Pension Scheme Trustee. Founder and Chairman, At Home in the Community.

**Dr JE Curtis**
*Keeper, Western Asiatic Antiquities, British Museum*

**Joyce Curtis**
*Board Member, Castle Vale Housing Action Trust*
Helped set up, in Birmingham, Age Concern's first day-care centre for elderly people with Alzheimer's Disease.

**Paul Curtis**
*Governor, Scottish Council for Educational Technology*
PNC Associates.

**Nigel Custance**
*Special Services Group Consultancy Director, Security Facilities Executive*

# D

**Mrs Jennifer d'Abo**
*Trustee, Natural History Museum*

**Jackie D'Arcy**
*Director, Communications, Northern Ireland Tourist Board*

**Mrs Isobel J d'Inverno**
*Non-Executive Member of Board, National Board for Nursing, Midwifery & Health Visiting for Scotland*

**Rhys Dafis**
*Head of the Public and Voluntary Sectors Department, Welsh Language Board*

**J Dainty OBE**
*Chairman, Severn Trent RFDC, The Environment Agency*

**Cllr Thomas Dair**
*Member, East of Scotland Water Authority*

**Brigadier Tony Dalby-Walsh**
*Commander Royal Logistic Corps Training Group, Army Training & Recruitment Agency*

**Jack Dale**
*Trustee, National Library of Scotland*

**Richard Dale**
*Chief Executive, Simpler Trade Procedures Board*

**RA Dales**
*Director of Customers Services, Valuation Office Agency*

**Heather Daley**
*Director, Human Resources, The Arts Council of England*

**Jane Dalgleish**
*Head of National Strategy, Scottish Natural Heritage*

**The Countess of Dalkeith**
*Trustee, National Museums of Scotland*

**The Earl of Dalkeith**
*Deputy Chairman, Independent Television Commission*
*Member, Millennium Commission*
Rural land manager and conservationist.

**The Most Rev M Dallat**
*Chairman, Council for Catholic Maintained Schools*

**Anne Daltrop**
*Member of Board, UK Ecolabelling Board*
Member, National Consumer Council. Past Chairman, Consumers in Europe Group.

**Fred Daly**
*Director, British Educational Communications & Technology Agency*

**Brian Dane**
*Manager General Manufacturing & Services, Local Enterprise Development Unit*

**Guy Dangerfield**
*Secretary, Rail Users Consultative Committee for Eastern England*

**Susan Daniel-McElroy**
*Director, Visual Arts, Scottish Arts Council*

**Steve Dann**
*Regional Manager, Rural Development Commission*

**Miss Ann Dargan**
*Member, Ofwat Yorkshire Customer Service Committee*

**Mrs Anne-Marie Darke**
*Member, North Eastern Consumers' Committee, Office of Electricity Regulation*

**Christopher Darke**
*Member, Monopolies & Mergers Commission*
General Secretary, British Airline Pilots Association.

**Tom Darling**
*Teachers Scheme Manager, Scottish Office Pensions Agency*

**Dr EC Dart CBE**
*Member, Biotechnology & Biological Sciences Research Council*
Research Director, Zeneca Seeds. Member, DTI/MAFF Agro Food Quality Link Committee. Former Chairman, SERC Biotechnology Directorate.

**Cllr Joe Davaney**
*Member, Tate Gallery*

**Carol Davenport**
*Director, Midlands Region, Advisory, Conciliation & Arbitration Service*

**Prof John Davenport**
*Member, Scientific Advisory Committee, Scottish Natural Heritage*

**Kerena Daveridge**
*Personnel Manager, Office of the
National Lottery*

**Eric Davey**
*Chairman, Sea Fish Industry Authority*
Deputy Chairman, Newcastle Building
Society.

**F David**
*Commandant, Fire Service College*

**John David**
*Head of Human Resources, Companies
House*

**Julian David**
*Head of Road Transport Enforcement
Division, Vehicle Inspectorate*

**Mike David**
*Member, Tate Gallery*

**Alan Davidson**
*Finance Officer, National Board for
Nursing, Midwifery & Health Visiting for
Scotland*

**D Davidson**
*Director, Operations, West of Scotland
Water Authority*

**Mrs Lorne M Davidson**
*Non-Executive Member of Board,
National Board for Nursing, Midwifery &
Health Visiting for Scotland*
Matron/Clinical Services Director, Albyn
Hospital, Aberdeen.

**Malcolm Davidson**
*Member of Board, UK Passport Agency*
Former Managing Director, Littlewoods
Pools.

**Martin Davidson**
*Member, The Great Britain-China Centre*
Cultural Counsellor in Beijing. British
Council representative on the Executive
Committee.

**Robert Davidson**
*Surveyor of the Fabric, Historic Royal
Palaces*

**Robin Davidson**
*Member of Commission, Independent
Commission for Police Complaints for
Northern Ireland*
Area Clinical Psychologist, Northern
Health and Social Services Board.
Honorary lecturer, Queen's University,
Belfast. Vice-Chairman of Board of
Governors, Templepatrick School.
Formerly member of Mental Health
Commission.

**Mrs S Davidson**
*Member, Training & Employment Agency
(NI)*
Davidson Cockcroft Partnership.

**Stuart Davidson**
*Member, London Consumers' Committee,
Office of Electricity Regulation*

**Tim Davidson**
*Regional Director - East/Central/
Southern Africa, Commonwealth
Development Corporation*

**AP Davies**
*Administrator, Fleet Air Arm Museum*

**Alun Creunant Davies**
*Member, National Library of Wales*
Elected by the Court of Governors.

**Ann Davies**
*Member, Qualifications, Curriculum &
Assessment Authority for Wales*
Headteacher, Ysgol y Deri.

**Mrs Ann Davies OBE**
*Director of Professional Services, Welsh
National Board for Nursing, Midwifery &
Health Visiting*

**Brian Davies**
*Director, Computation & Information,
Council for the Central Laboratory of the
Research Councils*

**Prof DS Davies**
*Member, National Biological Standards
Board*

**Prof Sir David Davies CBE**
*Member of Council, Engineering &
Physical Sciences Research Council
Member, Met Office
Member of Board, Defence Evaluation &
Research Agency*
MOD Chief Scientific Advisor.

**David Davies**
*Acting Marketing Director, Welsh
Development Agency*

**Derek Davies**
*Director, British National Space Centre*

**Evan Davies**
*Member, South Wales Consumers'
Committee, Office of Electricity
Regulation*

**Frank J Davies CBE, OStJ**
*Chairman, Health & Safety Commission*
Former Chief Executive, Rockware
Group. Past-president, European Glass
Federation (FEVE). Chairman, Nuffield
Orthopaedic Centre NHS Trust.
Chairman, Bardon Group. Non-Executive
Director, Saltire.

**Gareth Davies**
*Member of Council, The Sports Council
for Wales*

**Dr Glyn Davies**
*Deputy Chief Executive & Director of
Resources, Economic & Social Research
Council*

**Godfrey Davies**
*Accounts & IT Director, Commonwealth
Development Corporation*

**Sir Graeme J Davies**
*Chairman, Hannah Research Institute*

**Graham Davies**
*Director of National Development
Services, The Sports Council for Wales*

**Harvey Davies**
*Member of Council, The Sports Council
for Wales*

**Howard Davies**
*Chairman, Financial Services Authority
Member of Court, Bank of England*
Formerly Deputy Governor, Bank of
England.

**Prof HV Davies**
*Head, Cellular & Environmental
Physiology Department, Scottish Crop
Research Institute*

**Huw Davies**
*Assistant Chief Executive (Finance &
Administration), Qualifications,
Curriculum & Assessment Authority for
Wales*

**Ivor Davies**
*Director of Planning & Lottery Sports
Fund, Scottish Sports Council*

**Jim Davies**
*Member, Merseyside & North Wales
Consumers' Committee, Office of
Electricity Regulation*

**John Davies**
*Head of Systems, UK Passport Agency*

**John Davies**
*National Centres, UK Sports Council*

**John Davies**
*Member, Residuary Body for Wales*
Former Chief Executive, Aberconwy
Borough Council.

**Prof KE Davies CBE**
*Member, National Radiological Protection
Board*
Professor of Genetics, University of
Oxford.

**Karin Davies**
*Member, Qualifications, Curriculum &
Assessment Authority for Wales*
Parent, Chair of Governors, Cwm Tawe
Comprehensive School, Pontardawe.

**Keith Davies**
*Member, Qualifications, Curriculum &
Assessment Authority for Wales*
Director of Education, Carmarthenshire
County Council.

**Lord Davies of Oldham**
*Chairman, The Further Education
Funding Council*

**Lyn Davies**
*Senior Officer: Music, Arts Council of
Wales*

**Meirion Davies**
*Commissioning Editor - Children & Youth,
S4C*

**Dr Paul Davies**
*Head, Chemicals & Hazardous
Installations Division, The Health &
Safety Executive*

**Peter Davies MBE**
*Member of Authority, S4C*
Employed by Farmers' Union of Wales.
Non-Executive director, Carmarthen &
District NHS Trust. Chairman, Tai Cantref
Housing Association. Treasurer, Antur
Teifi. Chairman & Treasurer, Llandysul

FC. Treasurer, Dyfed Commonwealth Games Appeal.

**Phil Davies**
*Strategic Support, Veterinary Medicines Directorate*

**Prof RR Davies**
*Member of Advisory Committee, Cadw*
Chairman, Ancient Monuments Board for Wales.

**Richard Davies**
*Companies Administration, Companies House*

**Roger Davies MBE**
*Member, Monopolies & Mergers Commission*
Director, Airtours and Chairman, Going Places. Former Chairman, Thomson Travel Group.

**Mrs Ruth Davies**
*Member, Departmental Board, Wilton Park Executive Agency*

**Dr S Davies**
*Commissioner, The Royal Commission on Historical Manuscripts*

**T Davies**
*Manager (System Certification Operations), Vehicle Certification Agency*

**WV Davies**
*Keeper, Egyptian Antiquities, British Museum*

**Prof Wendy Davies**
*Member of Board of Governors, Museum of London*
Appointed by the Prime Minister.

**C Davis**
*Engineer Superintendent, Scottish Fisheries Protection Agency*

**Christine Davis**
*Member, Rail Users Consultative Committee for Scotland*

**Christine AM Davis**
*Chairman, The Scottish Legal Aid Board*
*Chairman, Scottish Agricultural Wages Board*
Chairman, Scottish Agricultural Wages Board. Teacher. Former member, Scottish Committee of the Council on Tribunals and of the Scottish Economic Council. Trustee, Joseph Rowntree Charitable Trust.

**David H Davis**
*Member of Council, Crafts Council*
Media consultant.

**JG Davis**
*Chairman, Simpler Trade Procedures Board*
Chairman, IMIF (International Maritime Industries Forum). President, Institute of Export. Past President, Chartered Institute Transport (CIT), Institute of Chartered Shipbrokers (ICS) and Institute of Freight Forwarders (now BIFA). Chairman/Director of a number of public companies.

**Mrs Joan Davis**
*Member, Eastern Consumers' Committee, Office of Electricity Regulation*

**Patrick Davis**
*Chief Executive, Food from Britain*

**Air Commodore C Davison MBE**
*Director Airmen/Reserves, RAF Personnel Management Agency*

**M Davison**
*Finance Director, Child Support Agency*

**Roger Dawe CB OBE**
*Assessor, Higher Education Funding Council for England*
Director General, Further & Higher Education & Youth Training, DfEE.

**Sandie Dawe**
*Director, Press & Public Relations, English Tourist Board & British Tourist Authority*

**Spencer Dawson**
*Regional Director, Scotland, Meat Hygiene Service*

**Will Dawson**
*Regional Manager & Secretary, Ofwat Central Customer Service Committee*

**Colonel Chris Day**
*Commander Royal Armoured Corps Centre, Army Training & Recruitment Agency*

**Cdre K Day**
*Owner's Representative, Naval Recruiting & Training Agency*

**Rosemary Day**
*Non-Executive Director, London Transport*
Former Director of Administration, LT. Chairman, London Ambulance NHS Trust. Member, Senior Salaries Review Body.

**Sir Geoffrey de Bellaigue**
*Trustee, Wallace Collection*

**General Sir Peter de la Billiere KCB KBE DSO MC**
*Trustee, Imperial War Museum*

**Hon Mrs Janet de Botton**
*Trustee, Tate Gallery*

**John de Fonblanque CMG**
*Member of Council, Particle Physics & Astronomy Research Council*
Foreign & Commonwealth Office

**Spencer de Grey**
*Trustee, Royal Botanic Gardens Kew*

**Philomena de Lima**
*Member of Scotland Committee, National Lottery Charities Board*
Programme Area Manager, Social Services & Languages, Inverness College of Further & Higher Education. Former Member, Scottish Advisory Panel for Community Development Foundation and Training Advisory Committee for Volunteer Development Scotland. Member, Highland Community Care Forum.

**Malcolm de Lorey**
*IT Services Manager, Scottish Office Pensions Agency*

**JRK De Quidt**
*Chief Executive, Football Licensing Authority*

**Lord De Ramsey**
*Chairman, The Environment Agency*
Chairman of family farming and property business. Lieutenant of Cambridgeshire. Fellow, Royal Agricultural Societies. Crown Estate Commissioner. Former Director of Cambridge Water Company, President, Association of Drainage Authorities and President of Country Landowners Association.

**Andrew Deadman**
*General Manager, English Nature*

**Ray Deahl**
*Governor, British Film Institute*

**Baroness Dean**
*Chairman, The Housing Corporation*
Former General Secretary, SOGAT. Chairman, Independent Committee for the Supervision of Standards of Telephone Information Services (ICSTIS). Member, Press Complaints Commission. Former Member, Broadcasting Complaints Commission. Member, Opportunity 2000 Target Team. President, College of Occupational Therapists. Deputy Chairman, University College London Hospital's NHS Trust Board.

**RL Dean**
*Trustee, Royal Naval Museum*

**Steve Dean**
*Director of Licensing, Veterinary Medicines Directorate*

**Bill Deans**
*Professional Officer (Nursing/ Community), National Board for Nursing, Midwifery & Health Visiting for Scotland*

**J Deas**
*Director Business Management, Defence Clothing & Textiles Agency*

**Ruth Deech**
*Chairman, Human Fertilisation & Embryology Authority*
Principal, St Anne's College, Oxford

**Hon Jeremy Deedes**
*Member, Horserace Totalisator Board*
Managing Director, Telegraph Group.

**Mike Deegan**
*Chairman, NHS Pensions Agency*
HRD, NHS Executive

**Donnel Deeny QC**
*Chairman, Arts Council of Northern Ireland*

**John Deery**
*Director of Finance & Support Services, Social Security Agency (Northern Ireland)*

**Jeffrey Defries**
*Assistant Director, Resource Management Division, National Museum*

of Science & Industry

**B Delaney**
Financial Director, Northern Ireland
Transport Holding Company

**Brian Delaney**
Member, Northern Ireland Local
Government Officers' Superannuation
Committee

**Stephen Dell**
Senior Administrative Officer, British Film
Institute

**A Dempster**
Professional Adviser, Youth Council for
Northern Ireland

**Alastair Dempster**
Member of Board, Scottish Homes
Chief Executive, TSB Bank Scotland.

**Major General Arthur Denaro**
Commandant Royal Military Academy
Sandhurst, Army Training & Recruitment
Agency

**Sylvia Denman CBE**
Member of Board, The Housing
Corporation
Chairman, Camden & Islington Health
Authority. Governor, Oxford Brookes
University. Former Member of Lord
Chancellor's Advisory Committee on
Legal Aid, of the Race Relations Board
and Equal Opportunities Commission.

**Bill Dennay**
Member, Radiocommunications Agency
External Member, Quantel.

**Gerald Dennis**
Vice-Chairman, UK Sports Council &
English Sports Council
Member, Central Arbitration Committee,
Police Arbitration Tribunal, and
Adjudication & Appeals Committee of the
Law Society.

**Mrs MT Dennis**
Member of Board of Governors,
Macaulay Land Use Research Institute

**Marina Dennis**
Commissioner - East Inverness, East
Ross-shire & East Sutherland, Crofters'
Commission

**Nicholas Denniston**
Director of Finance, Commonwealth
Development Corporation

**Charles Denton**
Governor, British Film Institute
Member, The Arts Council of England
Former Head of Television Drama, BBC.
First elected Chairman, PACT (The
Producers Alliance for Cinema and
Television). Sat on Sir Peter Middleton's
Advisory Committee on Film Finance.

**Jane Denton**
Deputy Chairman, Human Fertilisation &
Embryology Authority
Nursing Director, Multiple Births
Foundation, Queen Charlotte's & Chelsea
Hospital, London.

**Malcolm Denton**
Observer, English Sports Council
CCPR.

**JR Denyer**
Director Technical Services, Army
Technical Support Agency

**MJ Denyer MBE**
Member of Board, Construction Industry
Training Board
Fowler Bros (Cowfold).

**Mrs Elizabeth Derrington**
Chairman, North Eastern Consumers'
Committee, Office of Electricity
Regulation

**Prof Lord Desai**
Vice President, Community Development
Foundation
Member, Marshall Aid Commemoration
Commission

**Stephen Deucher**
Director, Tate Gallery of British Art, Tate
Gallery

**Joe Devaney**
Member of Board, Liverpool Housing
Action Trust
Liverpool City Councillor for Gillmoss
Ward.

**Robert Devereux**
Governor, National Film & Television
School

**Kate Devey**
Director, Touring, The Arts Council of
England

**Robert B Devine**
Institute Secretary, Macaulay Land Use
Research Institute

**Prof Tom Devine**
Trustee, National Museums of Scotland

**Graham Devlin**
Deputy Secretary-General, The Arts
Council of England

**Dr PB Devlin**
Member, Northern Ireland Council for
Postgraduate Medical & Dental
Education
Nominated by WHSSB.

**Pat Devlin**
Chief Executive, Northern Ireland Child
Support Agency

**Ron Devlin**
Director, Pensions Review, Financial
Services Authority
Joined SIB in 1988. Currently Head of
Supervision & Standards for Regulated
Businesses. Former Assistant Registrar,
Friendly Societies and Commissioner,
Building Societies Commission.

**Jim Dewar**
Chief Executive, Forest Research

**David Dewing**
Director, Geffrye Museum

**Prof R DeWitt**
Chairman, English National Board for
Nursing, Midwifery & Health Visiting

**Miss SC Dex**
Member, Rail Users Consultative
Committee for Eastern England

**Uday Dholakia**
Member, East Midland Consumers'
Committee, Office of Electricity
Regulation

**DTF Dick**
Deputy Director (Finance), Naval Bases
& Supply Agency

**BHB Dickinson**
Member of Ownership Board, Veterinary
Laboratories Agency
Under Secretary, Animal Health
Veterinary Group, MAFF.

**Prof Harry Dickinson**
Member, Marshall Aid Commemoration
Commission

**Prof Hugh Dickinson**
Trustee, Royal Botanic Gardens Kew

**Cllr Ann Dickson JP**
Member, East of Scotland Water
Authority
Councillor, Stirling Council. Former
Councillor, Stirling District Council.

**Edward Bonner Dignum**
Member of Steering Board, Insolvency
Service

**George Dillon**
Acting Director of Operations, Driver &
Vehicle Licensing Northern Ireland

**H Dillon MBE**
Member, Parole Board

**Vidur Dindayal**
Member, London Regional Passengers
Committee

**Margaret-Ann Dinsmore**
Commissioner, Northern Ireland
Commissioner for the Rights of Trade
Union Members

**Professor Anthony Diplock**
Member, Commonwealth Scholarship
Commission
Chairman, Division of Biochemistry,
United Medical & Dental Schools, Guy's
Hospital.

**Eric R Distin**
Member, Post Office Users' National
Council
Chairman, Plymouth & District POAC and
TAC. Chairman, Saltash District Cancer
Campaign. Chairman, Abbeyfield,
Saltash & Cornwall Society. Member,
Tamar Extra Care. Member, Plymouth
Community Services NHS Trust. Director,
Enterprise Tamar. Chairman, Saltash
Junior & Infants Schools.

**Dr David Ditchburn**
Member of Advisory Council, Scottish
Record Office
Department of History, University of
Aberdeen.

**Michael Dixon**
*Commissioner, Mental Health Commission for Northern Ireland*

**Nick Dixon**
*External Trade Director, Intervention Board*

**RN Dixson**
*Finance Director, Defence Clothing & Textiles Agency*

**Ms Josephine Dobry**
*Member, Police Complaints Authority*
Barrister and journalist. Formerly worked for Consumers' Association and BBC Radio.

**Alan Dobson**
*Subject Adviser, Modern Languages, Office for Standards in Education*

**Andrew Dobson**
*Finance Manager, Office of the National Lottery*

**Michael Dobson**
*Reception Manager, National Gallery*

**Daniel Dobson-Mouawad**
*Member, London Regional Passengers Committee*

**Paul Docherty**
*Secretary of the Council*

**John Doctor**
*Member, Rail Users Consultative Committee for Southern England*

**B Dodd**
*Director of Highways & Transport, The Planning Inspectorate*

**R Dodd**
*Manager, Development Team, Engineering Construction Industry Training Board*

**James Dodds**
*Secretary, Post Office Users' National Council*

**Robert Dodgshon**
*Member of Council, Countryside Council for Wales*
Professor of Human Geography, University of Wales, Aberystwyth.

**M Dodson**
*Non-Executive Director, Naval Recruiting & Training Agency*
Eastern Group.

**I Doherty**
*Chairman, Northern Ireland Transport Holding Company*

**Joe Doherty**
*Manager Western Regional Office, Local Enterprise Development Unit*

**S Doherty**
*Member of Council, Council for Catholic Maintained Schools*

**John Doig**
*Regional Sheriff Clerk, Tayside, Central & Fife, Scottish Court Service*

**Peter Doig**
*Trustee, Tate Gallery*

**F Dolaghan**
*Member of Board, Probation Board for Northern Ireland*

**David Dolman**
*Regional Director, South, English Sports Council*

**JAC Don, JP**
*Member of Board of Governors, Macaulay Land Use Research Institute*

**Angela Donaldson**
*Manager, Wick Airport, Highlands & Islands Airports*

**Gordon Donaldson, JP**
*Member of Council, Post Office Users' Council for Wales*
Retired Mathematics teacher. Clwyd County Secretary, National Union of Teachers. Magistrate, Mold Bench. Industrial Tribunals, Employees' Panel.

**Fergus E Donnelly**
*Member, Northern Ireland Local Government Officers' Superannuation Committee*

**Mrs M Donnelly**
*Member of Board, Labour Relations Agency*

**Patrick Donnelly**
*Member, Arts Council of Northern Ireland*
Solicitor.

**Paul Donnelly**
*Chairman, Independent Commission for Police Complaints for Northern Ireland*

**Bernard Donoghue**
*Member, London Consumers' Committee, Office of Electricity Regulation*

**Major General K Donoghue**
*Member, Logistic Information Systems Agency*
COS QMG.

**K Dooney**
*Assistant Operations Manager, Covent Garden Market Authority*

**WA Doran**
*Member of Board, Construction Industry Training Board (NI)*
Construction Employers Federation. Employer representative.

**Helen Dorey**
*Inspectress & Deputy Curator, Sir John Soane's Museum*

**Colonel C Dorman**
*Director of Geographic Field Support & Commander 42 Survey Engineer Group, Military Survey*

**Gerald Dorman**
*Accountant, The Britain-Russia Centre*

**Nigel Dorman**
*Regional Office, Northern & Yorkshire, NHS Estates*

**John Dornton**
*Member, Ofwat Wessex Customer Service Committee*

**Group Captain Simon Dougherty**

*Commanding Officer, Ministry of Defence Hospital Unit, Peterborough, Defence Secondary Care Agency.*

**David P Douglas**
*Chief Executive, Scottish Borders Enterprise*

**Dick Douglas**
*Chairman, Scottish Water & Sewerage Customers Council*

**Tony Douglas**
*Chief Executive, Central Office of Information*

**Simon Dow**
*Deputy Chief Executive & Chief Operations Officer, The Housing Corporation*

**Prof John Dowell**
*Member of Council, Particle Physics & Astronomy Research Council*
University of Birmingham

**Bob Downes**
*Director, Scottish Business, Scottish Enterprise*

**R Downey**
*Assessor, Sports Council for Northern Ireland*
Department of Education.

**Sir Philip Dowson CBE**
*Trustee, National Portrait Gallery*

**RG Doyle**
*Member, Northern Ireland Fishery Harbour Authority*

**Jane Drabble**
*Governor, National Film & Television School*

**Khurshid Drabu**
*Head of Litigation, Commission for Racial Equality*

**Joe Drew**
*Divisional Roads Manager, Roads Service*

**Philippa Drew**
*Member of Board, UK Passport Agency*
Director Corporate Resources, Home Office.

**JR Drew CBE**
*Chief Executive, Army Base Repair Organisation*

**Peter Drew OBE**
*Member of Board of Governors, Museum of London*
Appointed by the Prime Minister.

**Sheila Drew-Smith**
*Vice Chair, Tower Hamlets Housing Action Trust*
Former Economist, HM Treasury and DHSS. Executive Committee, Centre for Economic Policy & Research. Chair, Broadmoor Hospital Authority. Member, Department of Environment's Audit Committee.

**Dr DJ Drewry**
*Deputy Chief Executive, Natural Environment Research Council*

**David Drewry**
*Director-General, British Council*

**Prof Gavin Drewry**
*Member of College Advisory Council, Civil Service College*

**The Rev Norman Drummond**
*Governor, British Broadcasting Corporation*
National Governor for Scotland. Former Headmaster, Loretto.

**PJS Dry**
*Member, Post Office Users' Council for Scotland*
Member, Council of Law Society of Scotland.

**JM Drysdale**
*Member of Governing Body, Scottish Crop Research Institute*
Specialist cereal grower and contract farmer. Chairman, Tayforth Marketing Group. Director, United Oilseeds.

**Heather Du Quesnay CBE**
*Chairman, British Educational Communications & Technology Agency*
Executive Director of Education, Lambeth.

**PE Du Vivier**
*Chief Executive, Scottish Fisheries Protection Agency*

**Anthony Dubbins**
*Member of Board, Investors in People UK*
General Secretary, Graphical, Paper & Media Union.

**JM Ducker**
*Member, The British Library*
Institute of Information Scientists.

**Richard Dudding**
*Chairman of Advisory Boards, Vehicle Certification Agency & Driver & Vehicle Licensing Agency*
DETR.

**Caroline Dudley**
*Member, Tate Gallery*

**KM Duerden**
*Commercial Director, Caledonian MacBrayne Ltd*

**Dr Keith Duff**
*Director, English Nature*

**Jean Duffield**
*Secretary, Sir John Soane's Museum*

**Gerard Duffy**
*Chairman, Mental Health Commission for Northern Ireland*
Solicitor.

**Jeremy Duffy**
*Director of Corporate Services, British Waterways*

**Mike Duffy**
*Personnel & Finance Director, Office of the Data Protection Registrar*

**F Duffyn**
*Member of Board, Construction Industry Training Board (NI)*
Training & Employment Agency Assessor.

**Robert Dufton**
*Deputy Director of Operations, National Heritage Memorial Fund*

**Miss Anne Duggan**
*Careers Information Manager, Welsh National Board for Nursing, Midwifery & Health Visiting*

**Anne Duke**
*Board Member, Qualifications & Curriculum Authority*
Headteacher, Southwater County Infant School, West Sussex.

**Michael Dulieu**
*Member, North Eastern Consumers' Committee, Office of Electricity Regulation*

**Martin Dummingan**
*Member, Industrial Research & Technology Unit*
Management Consultant.

**Peter Dun**
*Member, Departmental Board, Wilton Park Executive Agency*

**Muriel Dunbar**
*Member of Board, Scottish Further Education Unit*
Former Assistant Director, SCOTVEC. Former Member of Board of Management, Scottish Council for Research in Education.

**Robert Duncalf**
*Member, Ofwat Yorkshire Customer Service Committee*

**AN Duncan**
*Member of Board, Construction Industry Training Board*
The Duncan Group (Scotland).

**David Duncan**
*Director, Technology Division, Industrial Research & Technology Unit*

**Giles Duncan**
*Director of Personnel, The Environment Agency*

**JM Duncan**
*Head, Fungal & Bacterial Plant Pathology Department, Scottish Crop Research Institute*

**S Duncan**
*Director of Driving Test Administration, Driver & Vehicle Testing Agency*

**Mrs Valerie Duncan**
*Member, Ofwat Eastern Customer Service Committee*

**Mrs A Dundas-Bekker**
*Commissioner, The Royal Commission on Historical Manuscripts*

**Earl of Dundonald**
*Member of Advisory Council, Scottish Record Office*

**Eric Dunford**
*Director, Space Science, Council for the Central Laboratory of the Research Councils*

**Jean Dunkley**
*Member, Legal Aid Board*
Former South West Area Officer, National Association of Citizens' Advice Bureaux. Former Chair, South West Viewers Consultative Council for the Independent Television Commission. Former Non-Executive Director, of a health authority and NHS trust. Part-time Consumer Services & Public Affairs Director, NHS.

**Dacre Dunlop**
*Regional Director, North, English Sports Council*

**Dr JM Dunlop**
*Member, Northern Ireland Council for Postgraduate Medical & Dental Education*
Nominated by NI Consultants & Specialists Committee.

**NNW Dunlop**
*Chairman, Engineering Construction Industry Training Board*
Former Director, Foster Wheeler Energy.

**Anthony Dunnett**
*Chief Executive, English Partnerships*

**Lady Dunnett, OBE**
*Trustee, National Library of Scotland*

**Roger Dunshea**
*Assistant Director & Head of Operational Resources, Office of Water Services*

**David Dunsmuir**
*Member, DIEL, Office of Telecommunications*
Former Director, Disability Scotland.

**Stephen Dunster**
*Member, Further Education Funding Council for Wales*
Head of Finance, Welsh Local Government Association.

**Sir Anthony Durant MP**
*Governor, British Film Institute*

**Prof John Durant**
*Assistant Director, National Museum of Science & Industry*

**Ian Durban**
*Assistant Director, Payment Procedures, Simpler Trade Procedures Board*

**John Durno**
*Director of Custody, Scottish Prison Service*

**D Dutton**
*Member, WACT, Welsh Advisory Committee on Telecommunications*
Retired businessman.

**Donald R Dutton, JP**
*Member of Council, Post Office Users' Council for Wales*
Retired Company Director. Hon Secretary, Wrexham National Trust Association. Member, Welsh Advisory Committee on Telecommunications.

**Cllr Len Duvall**
*Non-Executive Director, New Millennium Experience Co Ltd*
Leader, Greenwich Council.

**Michael Dyble**
*Member of Museum Trust, Museum of Science & Industry Manchester*

**Arthur Dye**
*Information & Research, UK Sports Council*

**Greg Dyke**
*Member, National Museum of Science & Industry*

**Shaun Dyke**
*Member, Further Education Funding Council for Wales*
Former Director and General Manager, British Aerospace Airbus, Broughton.

**Richard Dykes**
*Member, The Design Council*

**Richard Dykes**
*Managing Director Royal Mail, Post Office*
*Member of Advisory Board, Forensic Science Service*

**Rodney Dykes**
*Deputy Chairman, Liverpool Housing Action Trust*
Managing Director, Rodney Dykes Housing Services. Former Deputy Chief Executive, Merseyside Improved Houses and North British Housing Association.

**James Dyson**
*Member, The Design Council*


# E

**David Eade**
*Member, The Further Education Funding Council*
Principal, Barnsley College.

**AG Eadie**
*Member, Alcohol Education & Research Council*

**Alan Eadie**
*Member, Rail Users Consultative Committee for Southern England*

**JH Eagleson**
*Chief Executive, Enterprise Ulster*

**K Earley**
*Director (Business Management), Naval Bases & Supply Agency*

**Stella Earnshaw**
*Member of Board, Funding Agency for Schools*
Former Head of Regional Finance Unit, Shell International.

**JD Easey**
*Head, Financial Accounting Office, Inland Revenue*

**DL Easson**
*Crop Production, Agricultural Research Institute of Northern Ireland*

**Rodney East**
*Member of Board, Funding Agency for Schools*
Chartered Accountant. Experience in high street retailing, property, banking, shipping and transport.

**Cllr Joan Easten**
*Member, North of Scotland Water Authority*
Independent Councillor, Unst, Shetland Islands Council. Member, KIMO International Board. Member, Sullon Voe Oil Terminal Advisory Group.

**Lorna Easton**
*Director, UK Marketing, Scottish Tourist Board*

**Sir Robert Easton**
*Non-Executive Director, Caledonian MacBrayne Ltd*

**Admiral Sir Kenneth Eaton GBE KCB**
*Chairman, UK Atomic Energy Authority*

**J Ebdon**
*Director of Personnel & Information Technology, Valuation Office Agency*

**Barry Ecclestone**
*Solicitor, The Health & Safety Executive*

**Frank Eddy**
*Director of Trust & Funds Services, Public Trust Office*

**Stuart Ede**
*Director, Acquisitions Processing and Cataloguing, The British Library*

**Robert Edge**
*Acting Director, Lottery Division, Arts Council of Wales*

**Tony Edge**
*Director of Field Operations (Wales, Midlands & South), Benefits Agency*

**Roy Edleston**
*Food from Britain (Germany) GmbH*

**J Edmonds**
*Member of Council, Advisory, Conciliation & Arbitration Service*

**CR Edwards**
*Laboratory Secretary, Veterinary Laboratories Agency*

**Carol Edwards**
*Consumer Affairs Officer - Education, General Consumer Council for Northern Ireland*

**Cenwyn Edwards**
*Commissioning Editor - Factual, S4C*

**Dr Eleri Edwards**
*Member, Higher Education Funding Council for Wales*
Consultant Anaesthetist, Wrexham Maelor Hospital.

**Mrs Gabrielle Edwards**
*Member, Ofwat Southern Customer Service Committee*

**JM Edwards CBE QC**
*Member of Board, Education Assets Board*

**John Edwards**
*Director of Operations, Rural Development Commission*

**Dr Kenneth Edwards**
*Member, Marshall Aid Commemoration Commission*

**M Edwards**
*Member of Advisory Board, Vehicle Certification Agency*
*Director of Direct Line Insurance*

**Malcolm Edwards**
*Director of Finance, Administration & IT, Coal Authority*

**Pat Edwards**
*Legal Director, Office of Fair Trading*

**Mrs Rosemary Edwards**
*Member, Ofwat Southern Customer Service Committee*

**Mrs Rosemary Edwards**
*Member, South Eastern Consumers' Committee, Office of Electricity Regulation*

**Dr S Edwards**
*Director of Laboratory Services Division, Veterinary Laboratories Agency*

**S Edwards**
*Member, Rail Users Consultative Committee for Midlands*

**Mrs Sheila Edwards**
*Member, Eastern Consumers' Committee, Office of Electricity Regulation*

**Steve Edwards**
*Park Manager, Hyde Park, Royal Parks Agency*

**Prof Ron Edwards CBE**
*Member of Board, The Environment Agency*
Professor Emeritus, University of Wales. Chairman, National Parks Review. Member, Natural Environmental Research Council. Environmental Consultant, Aspinwall & Co. Overseas Lecturer, Middlesex University. Former Member of NRA Board and Chairman of Welsh Regional Advisory Board. Former Deputy Chairman of Welsh Water Authority and Council Member of RSPB.

**JP Egan**
*Trade Union Member, Engineering Construction Industry Training Board*
National Secretary - PMES, AEEU (EETPU Section).

**Lord Egremont & Lichfield**
*Trustee, Wallace Collection*
*Commissioner, The Royal Commission on Historical Manuscripts*
*Trustee, British Museum*

**Paul Ekins**
*Member, National Consumer Council*

**Mike Eland**
*Director Customs Policy, HM Customs & Excise*
*Member of Board, Simpler Trade Procedures Board*

**Richard Elfyn Jones**
*Music Consultant, S4C*

**Dave Elgy**
*Head of Branch, Technical Support South, Forest Research*

**Lord Elis-Thomas of Nant Conwy**
*Chairman, Welsh Language Board*

**Laurence Elks**
*Commissioner, Criminal Cases Review Commission*
Solicitor.

**Mrs Jean Ellerton**
*Member, Yorkshire Consumers' Committee, Office of Electricity Regulation*

**P Elliot**
*Member of Ownership Board, Veterinary Laboratories Agency*
Principal Finance Officer, MAFF.

**Dr Ruth Elliot**
*Commissioner, Mental Health Commission for Northern Ireland*
Consultant Psychologist, Belfast City Hospital Trust.

**Major General Christopher Elliott**
*Director General Training & Recruiting, Army Training & Recruitment Agency*

**D Elliott CBE**
*Member, Gaming Board for Great Britain*

**DCR Elliott OBE**
*Senior Keeper, Department of Design, Display & Conservation, Royal Air Force Museum*

**Frank Elliott**
*Member, East Midland Consumers' Committee, Office of Electricity Regulation*

**Dr Iain Elliott**
*Director, The Britain-Russia Centre*

**James Elliott**
*Member, Police Complaints Authority*
Former Divisional Director of Housing, London Borough of Brent.

**Keith Elliott**
*Cultural Development Director, Contributions Agency*
Joined Department in 1964. Appointed Cultural Development Director in 1996.

**P Elliott**
*Member of Ownership Boards, Meat Hygiene Service & Veterinary Medicines Directorate*
Principal Finance Officer, MAFF.

**PJV Elliott**
*Keeper, Department of Research & Information Services, Royal Air Force Museum*

**Peter Elliott**
*Member, The Further Education Funding Council*
Chairman of Governors, Northumberland College. Chief Executive, SHAW. Chairman, Northumbria Branch, Institute of Management.

**Sir Roger Elliott**
*Member of Board, British Council*
Professor of Physics, Oxford University.

**Sandra Elliott**
*Director, Sales, Northern Ireland Tourist Board*

**Stuart Elliott**
*Member, North Eastern Consumers' Committee, Office of Electricity Regulation*

**Dr Adrian Ellis**
*Director, Field Operations Directorate, The Health & Safety Executive*

**Prof JB Ellis**
*Awards & Training, Natural Environment Research Council*

**P Ellis**
*Member of Advisory Board, Defence Bills Agency*
Deputy Command Secretary, HQ Land Command.

**AJ Ellis CBE**
*Member of Ownership Board, Meat Hygiene Service*
External member with business experience.

**Miss Anne Ellis MBE**
*Member of Council, The Sports Council for Wales*

**Iain S Elrick**
*Chief Executive, Defence Bills Agency*

**Stephen Elson**
*Head of Buildings & Museum Services, National Museums of Scotland*

**David Elstein**
*Chairman, National Film & Television School*

**Jane Elvy**
*Member of Board, British Waterways*
Leisure business interests including fishing, conservation and heritage.

**David Elwood**
*Director of Resources, Northern Ireland Child Support Agency*

**Philip Ely**
*Member, Legal Aid Board*
Solicitor. Senior partner, Paris Smith & Randall. Former President, Law Society. Member of Council, Southampton University. Chairman, Police Disciplinary Appeals Tribunal.

**Susan Ely**
*Member, Central Council for Education & Training in Social Work*

**Howard Embleton**
*Head of Finance & Corporate Affairs, Defence Postal & Courier Services Agency*

**Henry Emden**
*Assistant Director, Office of Fair Trading*

**Bill Emery**
*Assistant Director & Head of Costs & Performance, Office of Water Services*

**Cllr FAJ Emery-Wallis**
*Trustee, Royal Naval Museum*

**R Empey**
*Member of Board, Laganside Corporation*
Belfast City Councillor.

**Lord Emslie MBE PC**
*Vice-Chairman, National Library of Scotland*
Trustee, National Library of Scotland

**Prof John Enderby**
*Member of Council, Particle Physics & Astronomy Research Council*
University of Bristol.

**John England**
*Head of Framing, National Gallery*

**Bill English**
*Member of Council, Scottish Arts Council*

**Sir Terence English**
*Member, Audit Commission*
Master, St Catharine's College, Cambridge. Former President, British Medical Association and Royal College of Surgeons of England.

**Paul Ennals**
*Member of Board, Teacher Training Agency*
Director, Education & Employment, Royal National Institute for the Blind.

**Major John A Ensor**
*SO2 Business Plans, Logistic Information Systems Agency*

**J Entwistle**
*Member, Parole Board*

**Cllr S Essex**
*Member of Council, Countryside Council for Wales*
Lecturer, Town & Country Planning, University of Wales, Cardiff. Member, Cardiff City Council.

**A Evans**
*Personnel Director, Driving Standards Agency*

**C Evans**
*Member of Advisory Committee, Cadw*
President, Wallace Evans & Partners.

**Air Vice Marshal CE Evans CBE**
*Commissioner, Duke of York's Royal Military School*

**Ceri Evans**
*Creative Director, Channel Four Television Corporation*

**Christine Evans**
*Assistant Director, Finance & Administration, London Regional Passengers Committee*

**D Evans**
*Member, WACT, Welsh Advisory Committee on Telecommunications*
Businessman.

**Prof D Evans**
*Commissioner, Royal Commission on Ancient & Historical Monuments in Wales*

**Dr David Evans**
*Member of Council, Particle Physics & Astronomy Research Council*
Department of Trade & Industry.

**Derek Evans**
*Chief Conciliator, Advisory, Conciliation & Arbitration Service*

**Elfed Evans**
*Managing Director, West Division, Welsh Development Agency*

**Fraser R Evans**
*Member, Scottish Agricultural Wages Board*
Employers' representative member nominated by the National Farmers' Union of Scotland and the Scottish Landowners' Federation.

**Geraldine Evans**
*Member, Rail Users Consultative Committee for North Western England*

**Mrs HM Evans**
*Information Officer, Covent Garden Market Authority*

**Hugh Evans**
*Head of Branch, Entomology, Forest Research*

**JG Evans**
*Member of Council, British Hallmarking Council*

**John Evans**
*Member, Horticultural Development Council*
Chairman & Managing Director, H. Evans, H Evans (Europe) and Ruxley Manor Garden Centre.

**Cllr Keith Evans**
*Member of Council, The Sports Council for Wales*

**Lee Evans**
*Member of Council, Post Office Users' Council for Wales*
Presiding officer, local government and Parliamentary elections.

**Lewis Evans**
*Member of Board, Wales Tourist Board*

**Lindsay Evans**
*Trustee, National Heritage Memorial Fund*

**Matthew Evans**
*Governor, British Film Institute*

**Dr NJB Evans CB**
*Chairman, National Biological Standards Board*

**Nicholas Evans**
*Head of Publishing, Centre for Information on Language Teaching & Research*

**Dr Philip Evans**
*Board Member, Qualifications & Curriculum Authority*
Head Master, Bedford School.

**Philip C Evans JP**
*Member of Committee, Rail Users Consultative Committee for Wales*

Member of Aberconwy Borough and Lladudno Town Councils. Planning Liaison Officer and Heritage Officer, Northern Division, Dwr Cymru Welsh Water. Member, Council of Museums of Wales.

**Sir Richard Evans CBE**
*Trustee, Royal Air Force Museum*

**Robin Evans**
*Director of the Palaces Group, Historic Royal Palaces*

**Roy Evans**
*Member of Board, Waltham Forest Housing Action Trust*
Consultant.

**Ruth Evans**
*Director, National Consumer Council*

**Sheena Evans**
*Head of Finance & Quality, Teacher Training Agency*

**Steve Evans**
*Director of Value for Money Studies (Local Government), The Accounts Commission for Scotland*

**TR Evans**
*Customer Service Division, Inland Revenue*

**Teresa Evans**
*Regional Manager & Secretary, Ofwat Wessex Customer Service Committee*

**W Allan Evans**
*Member of Council, Countryside Council for Wales*
Headmaster, Queen Elizabeth Cambria School, Carmarthen.

**Dr WD Evans**
*Member of Council, Engineering & Physical Sciences Research Council*
Department of Trade & Industry.

**Judith Eve**
*Member of Commission, Equal Opportunities Commission for Northern Ireland*
International Liaison Officer, Queen's University of Belfast.

**BD Everett**
*Procurement Director, LTB, London Transport*

**Charles Everett**
*Member of Management Board, The Court Service*
Director of Resources & Support Services.

**Lucilla Evers**
*Head of Legal Affairs, Horserace Betting Levy Board*

**David Eves CB**
*Deputy Director General, The Health & Safety Executive*

**Rod Evison**
*Project Director - Specialised Investments, Commonwealth Development Corporation*

**PA Eward**
*Member, Rail Users Consultative Committee for Western England*

**Mike Ewart**
*Chief Executive, Scottish Court Service*

**Maj Gen GA Ewer CBE**
*Member, Met Office*
Assistant Chief Defence Staff (Logistics), MoD.

**RST Ewing**
*Head, Inland Revenue Northern Ireland, Inland Revenue*

**Peter Ewins**
*Chief Executive, Met Office*

**Dr Brian Eyre CBE**
*Member of Council, Particle Physics & Astronomy Research Council*
AEA Technology

**Sir Richard Eyre CBE**
*Governor, British Broadcasting Corporation*
Director, Royal National Theatre. Former BBC television drama producer.

# F

**Colonel Peter Fabricius**
*Commanding Officer, Ministry of Defence Hospital Unit, Frimley Park, Defence Secondary Care Agency.*

**Tina Fahm**
*Member of Board, Stonebridge Housing Action Trust*

**James Faichnie**
*Sales Director, National Gallery Publications, National Gallery*

**Alasdair Fairbairn**
*Chief Executive, Sea Fish Industry Authority*

**DR Fairbairn**
*Member of Steering Board, Patent Office*

**Mrs R Fairhead**
*Member of Board, Laganside Corporation*
Executive Vice President - Strategy Public Affairs & Communications, ICI.

**Peter Fairlie**
*Member, Scottish Tourist Board*
Sales Director, Macallan-Glenlivet. Former Vice Chairman, Association of Scottish Visitor Attractions. Governor, Strathallan School in Perthshire.

**Ann Fairweather**
*Joint Director of Marketing and Communications, Scottish Sports Council*

**Sir Brian Fall KCMG**
*Member, Academic Council, Wilton Park Executive Agency*
Principal, Lady Margaret Hall, Oxford.

# Q&Q

**Andrew Fane**
*Commissioner, English Heritage*

**CR Farey**
*Secretary, Covent Garden Market Authority*

**Lord Faringdon**
*Chairman, Royal Commission on Historical Monuments of England*

**Bob Farmer**
*Regional Director Wales, Forest Enterprise*

**J Farmer**
*Adviser in GDP (CE), Northern Ireland Council for Postgraduate Medical & Dental Education*

**John Farmer**
*Member, Tate Gallery*

**Peter Farmer**
*Member of Management Board, The Court Service*
North Eastern Circuit Administrator.

**Sir Tom Farmer CBE**
*Member of Board, Investors in People UK*
Chairman & Chief Executive, Kwik-Fit Holdings.

**Christine Farnish**
*Consumer Director, Office of Telecommunications*

**Imtiaz Farookhi**
*Member of Board, The Environment Agency*
Chief Executive, National House Building Council. Member, Queen Mary & Westfield College Public Policy Advisory Board. Member, DEMOS Advisory Council. Former Chief Executive, Leicester City Council. Director, Leicestershire Training & Enterprise Council, Leicestershire Businesslink, Leicestershire Training & Enterprise Council and East Midlands Development.

**Julian Farrand**
*Chairman, Pensions Compensation Board*

**Richard Farrant**
*Managing Director & Chief Operating Officer, Financial Services Authority*
Currently Chief Executive, Securities & Futures Authority (SFA). Will chair Management Committee and be directly responsible for Operations, including Human Resources, Finance and IT. Joined Bank of England, 1967. Worked as economist in Central Banking Service, International Monetary Fund in Washington.

**R Farrell**
*Member of Board, Fisheries Conservancy Board for Northern Ireland*
Nominated by the Ulster Farmers Union.

**Sir Matthew Farrer GCVO**
*Commissioner, The Royal Commission on Historical Manuscripts*
*Board Member, The British Library*
*Trustee, British Museum*

**Malcolm Farrow**
*Chief Executive, Security Facilities Executive*

**Monica Farthing**
*Teacher Supply & Recruitment, Teacher Training Agency*

**A Faulkner**
*Head, Integrative Metabolism, Hannah Research Institute*

**The Hon Claire Faulkner**
*Member of Board, Local Enterprise Development Unit*
Managing Director, Project Planning International. Chairman, ABSA.

**Dr JS Faulkner**
*Member, Joint Nature Conservation Committee*
Environment & Heritage Service, Northern Ireland.

**Rupert Faulkner**
*Acting Curator, Far Eastern Collection, Victoria & Albert Museum*

**Mrs DJ Fawcett JP**
*Member, Parole Board*

**JA Fawcett**
*Chairman, Yorkshire RFAC, The Environment Agency*

**Julie Fawcett**
*Member of Board, Waltham Forest Housing Action Trust*
Chair, Stockwell Park Tenant's Association and Stockwell Park Community Trust.

**Paul Fawcett**
*Deputy Chairman, Rail Users Consultative Committee for North Western England*

**Miss Wendy Fawcus**
*Director of Business Services, Welsh National Board for Nursing, Midwifery & Health Visiting*

**Dr Duncan Fawthrop**
*Immunological Products, Veterinary Medicines Directorate*

**Michael Fay**
*Regional Officer, Independent Television Commission*

**Piers Feilden**
*Member, Ofwat Wessex Customer Service Committee*

**I Fell**
*Education & Interpretation, National Museums & Galleries of Wales*

**Mark Felton**
*General Manager, English Nature*

**Prof Brian Fender CMG**
*Chief Executive, Higher Education Funding Council for England*
*Member, Met Office*

**M St J Fendick**
*Member of Advisory Board, Vehicle Certification Agency*
Chief Mechanical Engineer

**Prof A Ferguson**
*Member of Governing Body, Rowett Research Institute*

**David Ferguson**
*Corporate Services Manager/Board Secretary, National Board for Nursing, Midwifery & Health Visiting for Scotland*

**Ian Ferguson**
*Member of Board, Stonebridge Housing Action Trust*
Resident Board Member

**J Ferguson OBE**
*Chairman, REPAC, The Environment Agency*

**Dr M Ferguson**
*Member, National Biological Standards Board*

**WJ Ferguson**
*Member of Council, Hannah Research Institute*

**Wilson Ferguson**
*Commissioner, Meat & Livestock Commission*
Independent butcher (Fergusons of Airdrie). Past President, Lanarkshire Butchers' Association and Scottish Federation of Meat Traders' Associations.

**Sir Ewen Fergusson GCMG GCVO**
*Trustee, National Gallery*

**Prof Eric Fernie CBE**
*Commissioner, English Heritage*

**Brian Ferran**
*Chief Executive, Arts Council of Northern Ireland*

**TW Ferrers-Walker**
*Trustee, Royal Naval Museum*

**Robert C Ferrier**
*Programme Unit Manager, Macaulay Land Use Research Institute*

**RT Ferris**
*Chairperson, Northern Ireland Fishery Harbour Authority*

**JM Fetherston OBE, JP**
*Vice Chairman, Simpler Trade Procedures Board*
Past National Chairman, Institute of Freight Forwarders (now BIFA).

**Brigadier Anne Field CB CBE**
*Commissioner, Duke of York's Royal Military School*

**Mrs Christine Field**
*Member, South Eastern Consumers' Committee, Office of Electricity Regulation*

**Geoffrey Field**
*Governor of the Tower of London, Historic Royal Palaces*

**Mrs Jane Field**
*Member, East Midland Consumers' Committee, Office of Electricity Regulation*

**Sir Malcolm Field**
*Chairman, Civil Aviation Authority*

Former Group Managing Director, WH Smith. Non-Executive director, MEPC, Scottish & Newcastle, Phoenix Securities and The Stationery Office.

**Charles Fielder**
*Assistant Conference Centre Manager, Commonwealth Institute*

**Prof Jacqueline Filkins**
*Non-Executive Member, English National Board for Nursing, Midwifery & Health Visiting*
Dean, Faculty of Health, St Martins College, Durham.

**CG Finch**
*Member, Oil & Pipelines Agency*

**David Finch**
*Chief Executive, Shetland Enterprise*

**W Finch**
*Director (Contracts Division), Defence Clothing & Textiles Agency*

**Alastair Findlay**
*Chief Executive, North of Scotland Water Authority*
Formerly with The Scottish Office.

**Geoffrey Findlay**
*Head, Corporate Affairs Division, Particle Physics & Astronomy Research Council*

**JM Findlay**
*Secretary, Wine Standards Board*

**Richard Findon**
*Team Manager, Private Office, English Nature*

**Elaine Finlay**
*Regional Manager & Secretary, Ofwat Northumbria Customer Service Committee*

**NK Finlayson**
*Chief Executive, Fire Service College*

**Cecil Finn**
*Member of Board, Sea Fish Industry Authority*
President, Scottish Fishermen's Federation

**Gerard Finnegan**
*Manager North Western Regional Office, Local Enterprise Development Unit*

**Nicholas Finney OBE**
*Member, Monopolies & Mergers Commission*
Chairman, The Waterfront Partnership. Former Director, British Ports Federation and National Association of Ports Employers. Fellow, Chartered Institute of Transport.

**Brenda Finnigan**
*Member, Ofwat Central Customer Service Committee*

**Dr Judith Fisher MB**
*Member of Board, Football Licensing Authority*

**Mick Fisher**
*Professional Adviser, Mental Illness & Mental Handicap, Welsh National Board for Nursing, Midwifery & Health Visiting*

**Peter Fisher**
*Assistant Director Pensions, Pay & Personnel Agency*

**Dr DJ Fisk**
*Member, Natural Environment Research Council*
Department of the Environment

**Rodney Fitch CBE**
*Trustee, Victoria & Albert Museum*

**MJ Fitchett**
*Member of Board, Construction Industry Training Board*
MG Services Group.

**Mike Fitt**
*Head of Estates & Outer Parks, Royal Parks Agency*

**Angela Fitzgerald**
*Member, London Regional Passengers Committee*

**Brian Fitzgerald**
*Member of Board, Scottish Environment Protection Agency*

**John FitzGerald**
*VMD Secretary, Head of Business Unit, Veterinary Medicines Directorate*

**Aidan Fitzpatrick**
*Manager, General Operations, Fair Employment Commission for Northern Ireland*

**Ian Fitzpatrick**
*Regional Manager, Office of Electricity Regulation*

**Mike Fitzsimons**
*IT Manager, Occupational Pensions Regulatory Authority*

**Anthony Flacks**
*Member, Ofwat North West Customer Service Committee*

**Donal Flanagan**
*Director, Council for Catholic Maintained Schools*

**Jacky Flanders**
*Member of Board, Waltham Forest Housing Action Trust*
Tenant Board Member of Chingford Hall Estate. Chair of Waltham Forest Community Based Housing Association. Community Development Officer.

**Baroness Flather JP**
*Chairman, Alcohol Education & Research Council*

**Robert Fleeman**
*Member, Equal Opportunities Commission*
Director, Fleeman Cooper and Smaller Businesses Advisory Services. Member, Institute of Directors Employment Committee. Industrial Tribunal member.

**Dr A Fleet**
*Keeper, Mineralogy Department, Natural History Museum*

**Alistair Fleming**
*Chairman, Scottish Council for Educational Technology*
Chief Executive, Forth Ports.

**Frank Fleming**
*Manager, General Operations, Fair Employment Commission for Northern Ireland*

**Sheila Fleming**
*Member, Northern Ireland Consumer Committee for Electricity, Office for the Regulation of Electricity & Gas*
Business Executive, LEDU.

**Dr David Fletcher**
*Chief Executive, British Waterways*

**David Fletcher MBE**
*Commissioner, Rural Development Commission*
Consultant. Chairman, Pennine Heritage. Director, Transpennine.

**RN Fletcher**
*Personnel Director, Remploy*
Joined Company in 1995. Formerly Personnel & Logistics Director, H&R Johnson Tiles.

**Steve Fletcher**
*Director, Northern Region, Advisory, Conciliation & Arbitration Service*

**DJ Flint**
*Head, Molecular Recognition, Hannah Research Institute*

**Neil Flint**
*Student Loans Company*
Divisional Manager, Department for Education & Employment.

**Ross Flockhart OBE**
*Trustee, Community Development Foundation*

**Colin Flood**
*Forecasting Director, Met Office*

**Prof TJ Flowers**
*Director, Horticulture Research International*
Appointed by Chancellor of Duchy of Lancaster.

**BJ Foday**
*Member, Cardiff Bay Development Corporation*
Councillor, Cardiff County Council. Cardiff Film Commission. Cardiff & Vale Enterprise Group. ITEC. Newemploy Wales. Cardiff Business Technology Centre.

**Prof Sir Brian Follett**
*Trustee, Natural History Museum*
*Member, Biotechnology & Biological Sciences Research Council*
Vice-Chancellor, University of Warwick. Former member, SERC Biological Sciences Committee and AFRC Council. Former Biology Secretary and Vice-President, Royal Society.

**Dr Michael Foop**
*Director, Royal Air Force Museum*

**Michael Foot**
*Managing Director & Head, Financial Supervision, Financial Services Authority*
Currently Executive Director, Bank of England, responsible for Banking Supervision. Will be responsilble for ongoing supervision of all financial institutions authorised under FSAs powers and financial market supervision. Joined Bank of England in 1969.

**Mirjam Foot**
*Director, Collections & Preservation, The British Library*

**Ms Hilary Footitt**
*Member, Centre for Information on Language Teaching & Research*
Head of School Languages, University of Westminster.

**John Footman**
*Deputy Director, Financial Structure, Bank of England*

**Anna Ford**
*Trustee, Geffrye Museum*
*Trustee, Royal Botanic Gardens Kew*
Broadcaster.

**C Ford CBE**
*Director, National Museums & Galleries of Wales*

**G Ford**
*Member, The British Library*
Standing Conference of National and University Libraries.

**John Ford**
*Director of Finance, Scottish Environment Protection Agency*

**Margaret Ford**
*Non-Executive Director, Scottish Prison Service*

**Michael Ford**
*Team Manager, National Partnerships Team, English Nature*

**Peter Ford**
*Chairman and Chief Executive, London Transport*
Former Chairman, P&O European Ferries. Governor, Kingston University.

**RI Ford**
*Head, Inland Revenue North*

**Dr SJ Ford**
*Chief Executive, Driver & Vehicle Licensing Agency*

**Tony Ford**
*Director, Crafts Council*

**Liz Forgan**
*Member, Human Fertilisation & Embryology Authority*
Broadcaster, journalist and media consultant.

**Ian Forrest**
*Assistant Chief Executive (Quality Assurance), Service Children's Education*

**Sir Archibald Forster**
*Member, Monopolies & Mergers Commission*
Former Chairman, Esso UK. Director, Midland Bank, Engen and HSBC Private Equity.

**Stephen Forster**
*Member of Board, Scottish Screen*

**Richard Fortin**
*Trustee, Royal Armouries*

**Prof Arthur J Forty, CBE**
*Trustee, National Library of Scotland*

**Prof George Forwell OBE**
*Member, Scottish Hospital Endowments Research Trust*

**AC Foster**
*Member, Wine Standards Board*

**Andrew Foster**
*Controller, Audit Commission*

**Ann Foster**
*Non-Executive Director, Office of the Rail Regulator*

**David Foster**
*Director of Finance, Waltham Forest Housing Action Trust*

**John Foster OBE**
*Member of Board, The Housing Corporation*
*Member, Audit Commission*
Former Chief Executive of Middlesbrough Borough Council. Currently, Deputy Chairman of Teesside Tomorrow, Non-Executive Director of South Tees Hospital Trust and Member of Boards of Botanic Centre, Middlesbrough and Teesside University. Member of Department of National Heritage Volunteering Forum for England. Trustee of Cleveland Community Foundation.

**Martin Foster**
*Head, Special Investigations Unit, Bank of England*

**Richard Foster**
*Director, Policy & Process Design, Employment Service*

**Richard Foster**
*Director & Trustee, Horniman Museum*

**Richard Foster**
*Commissioner, Museums & Galleries Commission*
Director, National Museums & Galleries on Merseyside. Former Director, Merseyside County Museum, Oxford City & County Museum and Oxfordshire County Museum Service. Deputy Lieutenant for Merseyside.

**Robert Foster**
*Chairman, National Weights & Measures Laboratory*
Head of Consumer Affairs Division, DTI.

**Tony Foster**
*Commissioner, Criminal Cases Review Commission*
Former Chief Executive, ICI Chlorochemicals.

**Philippa Foster Back**
*Member, Milk Development Council*
Group Treasurer, EMI Group. Previously Group Finance Director, DC Gardner Group and Group Treasurer, Bowater. Chairman, Council of Advisers, Society of International Treasurers. General Commissioner of Tax. Independent member, Defence Audit Committee, Ministry of Defence.

**Peter Fotheringham**
*Head of Building Department, National Gallery*

**Stella Fowler**
*Member, London Regional Passengers Committee*

**Dr Alan Fox**
*Member of Advisory Board, Disposal Sales Agency*
Assistant Under Secretary (Export & Policy Finance).

**Dr Michael Foxley**
*Member, North Areas Board, Scottish Natural Heritage*

**Cllr Beatrice Fraenkel**
*Member, Tate Gallery*

**Elizabeth France**
*Registrar, Office of the Data Protection Registrar*

**James France**
*Director of Collection Services, Tate Gallery*

**Dr Richard Franceys**
*Member, Ofwat Central Customer Service Committee*

**Ms C Francis**
*Personnel Director, Child Support Agency*

**JA Francis**
*Manager, Aerospace Museum, Cosford, Royal Air Force Museum*

**Ms Jennifer Francis**
*Member of Authority, The Radio Authority*

**Keith Francis**
*Administrative Support & Estates Management, Office for Standards in Education*

**S Francis**
*Chairman, Rail Users Consultative Committee for Eastern England*
*Member, Central Rail Users Consultative Committee*
Non-Executive Director and Chairman of various broadcasting companies. Past Chairman, Commercial Radio Companies Association. Past Managing Director, Mid-Anglia Radio.

**Professor Peter Frank**
*Governor, Westminster Foundation for Democracy*

**Robert Franklin**
*General Manager Asia, Pacific, Middle East & Africa, British Tourist Authority*

**Marion Franks**
*Director, South East Region, The Housing Corporation*

**Alistair Fraser**
*Commissioner - Caithness & Sutherland, Crofters' Commission*

**Grahame Fraser**
*Director of Operations, Roads Service*

**JM (Ian) Fraser**
*External Member, Marine Safety Agency*
Former Chairman & Managing Director, British Aerospace Enterprises.

**Lady Fraser**
*Trustee, Royal Botanic Garden Edinburgh*

**Rod Fraser**
*Regulatory Manager, Occupational Pensions Regulatory Authority*

**Simon Fraser**
*Member, North Areas Board, Scottish Natural Heritage*

**Sir William Fraser GCB**
*Chairman, Royal Commission on Ancient & Historical Monuments of Scotland*

**Moira Fraser Steele**
*Director, Education & Training, The Design Council*

**Prof Christopher Frayling**
*Member, The Arts Council of England*
*Trustee, Victoria & Albert Museum*
Rector, Royal College of Art. Former Governor, British Film Institute, Member, Crafts Council and Chairman, Freeform Arts Trust. Chairman, Crafts Study Centre in Bath.

**JD Freeborn**
*Deputy Director, Royal Air Force Museum*

**J Freeman**
*Director, Northern Ireland Transport Holding Company*

**O Freeman**
*Member, The British Library*
Aslib.

**Suzanne Freeman**
*Assistant to the Director, Tate Gallery*

**Ms Jeane Freeman OBE**
*Member, Parole Board for Scotland*
Director, APEX Scotland.

**Peter Freer-Smith**
*Chief Research Officer, Forest Research*

**Dr Malcolm Freeth**
*GP Member, Medical Practices Committee*
Dorset.

**Ms A French**
*Member, Property Advisers to the Civil Estate*
HM Customs & Excise.

**Chris French**
*Member, Milk Development Council*
Farmer. Former NFU Office holder. Governor, Royal Agricultural College, Cirencester. Chairs Board of Management, National Federation of Young Farmers Clubs. Trustee, Game

Conservancy. Former member BBC's Advisory Committtee on Agriculture & Rural Affairs. Director, Royal Association of British Dairy Farmers.

**David French**
*Director General, Commonwealth Institute*

**GN French**
*Director of Operations, HM Land Registry*

**John P French MBE JP**
*Chief Executive, Wales Tourist Board*

**Ralph French OBE**
*Hon Treasurer, The Britain-Russia Centre*

**Adrienne Fresko**
*Member, Audit Commission*
Chairman, Croydon Health Authority. Former Non-Executive Director, London Ambulance Service and Director of Human Resources, Citibank. Human resources consultant.

**Colin Frier**
*Special Services Group Operations Director, Security Facilities Executive*

**His Excellency Royce Frith QC**
*Trustee, Imperial War Museum*

**Edward Frizzell**
*Chief Executive, Scottish Prison Service*

**JW Froggatt**
*Inspector, Football Licensing Authority*

**BMW Frost**
*Member, Rail Users Consultative Committee for Eastern England*

**JP Frost**
*Farm Mechanisation, Agricultural Research Institute ofNorthern Ireland*

**Miss FA Fry**
*Assistant Director, National Radiological Protection Board*

**JR Fryer**
*Member of Steering Board, Patent Office*

**Prof M Fulford**
*Commissioner, Royal Commission on Historical Monuments of England*

**PEM Fuller**
*Member of Council, British Hallmarking Council*

**Nerys Fuller-Love**
*Member of Council, Post Office Users' Council for Wales*
Director, Centre for Business Studies, University of Wales, Aberystwyth. Vice-Chairman, Dyfed Agricultural Wages Committee.

**Prof JF Fulton**
*Member, Training & Employment Agency (NI)*
Provost, Legal, Social & Educational Sciences, Queen's University Belfast.

**R Fulton**
*Member of Advisory Board, Forensic Science Service*
*Member of Board, UK Passport Agency*
Director, Planning & Finance, Home Office.

**Peter Funnell**
*19th Century Curator, National Portrait Gallery*

**Richard Furey**
*Member, BACT, Office of Telecommunications*
Managing Director, electronic systems design company.

**Rodger Fuse**
*Director of Engineering, S4C*

**Dr David Fussey**
*Member of Board, Higher Education Funding Council for England*
*Member, Commonwealth Scholarship Commission*
Vice-Chancellor, University of Greenwich.

**Andrew Fyfe**
*Director of Operations, Scottish Homes*

**Ms Kath Fysh**
*Member, Ofwat Yorkshire Customer Service Committee*

# G

**Breidge Gadd**
*Chief Probation Officer, Probation Board for Northern Ireland*

**Jean Gaffin**
*Chairman, DIEL, Office of Telecommunications*
Executive Director, National Council for Hospice & Specialist Palliative Care Services.

**Linda Gainsbury**
*Head of Further Education, Further Education Funding Council for Wales*

**R Gainsford**
*Director, Marine Pollution Control Unit, Coastguard*

**Dr Rex Gaisford CBE**
*Non-Executive Director, UK Atomic Energy Authority*
Director, Worldwide Development, Amerada Hess.

**Dr Colin Galbraith**
*Head of Advisory Services, Scottish Natural Heritage*

**Bob Gale**
*Member, Rail Users Consultative Committee for North Western England*

**David Gallagher**
*Chief Executive, Rate Collection Agency*

**Ed Gallagher**
*Chief Executive, The Environment Agency*
Former, Chief Executive and Board Member, NRA. Governor, Chairman of Audit Committee and Visiting Professor, Middlesex University. Member of Council and Finance Advisory Group, Bristol

University. Vice President, Council for Environmental Education. Member, Living Again Trust. Formerly with Amersham International and Black & Decker.

**W Gallagher**
*Member of Board, Fisheries Conservancy Board for Northern Ireland*
Representative of CBI.

**Marjorie Gallimore**
*Member of Board, Liverpool Housing Action Trust*
Founder member, High Rise Tenants' Group. Former member, Government Advisory Committee on Housing Benefits.

**Cllr Ian Galloway**
*Member, East of Scotland Water Authority*
Member, Scottish Borders Council. Former Chairman, Borders Region Water & Drainage Committee.

**Dr Ronald Galloway**
*Commissioner, Mental Health Commission for Northern Ireland*
Consultant Psychiatrist, Craigavon & Bambridge Community Trust.

**His Honour Brian Galpin**
*Director & Trustee, Horniman Museum*

**RA Gamble**
*Chairman, Policyholders' Protection Board*
Group Chief Executive, Royal & Sun Alliance Insurance Group.

**Michael Gambon CBE**
*Trustee, Royal Armouries*

**Nick Gammage**
*Director of Information, Office of Telecommunications*

**JW Gammie**
*Member of Governing Body, Rowett Research Institute*

**Brigadier JA Gamon**
*Director of Clinical Services, Defence Dental Agency*

**John Gant**
*Director, Human Resources, Inland Revenue*

**Kenneth Garden**
*Trustee, Royal Botanic Garden Edinburgh*

**Ralph Garden**
*Chief Executive, Scottish Office Pensions Agency*

**Caroline Gardner**
*Director of Health & Social Work Studies, The Accounts Commission for Scotland*

**DA Gardner**
*Member, SACOT, Scottish Advisory Committee on Telecommunications*
Director/broadcaster, commercial radio.

**Jim Gardner CVO CBE**
*Chairman, Ofwat Northumbria Customer Service Committee*
*Member, Ofwat National Customer Council*

**R Gardner**
*Director of Finance, East of Scotland Water Authority*
Chairman, Jackton & Thorntonhall Community Council.

**Tim Garfield**
*Regional Director, East Midlands, English Sports Council*

**Sue Garland**
*Director, Policy & Legal, British Tourist Authority & English Tourist Board*

**Dave Garnett**
*Input Systems, Companies House*

**Brigadier Robin Garnett**
*Defence Services Medical Rehabilitation Centre, Headley Court, Defence Secondary Care Agency.*

**Prof MK Garrett**
*Member of Board of Trustees, Agricultural Research Institute ofNorthern Ireland*
Representing the Queen's University of Belfast.

**Paul Garrett**
*Food from Britain (Italy), Srl*

**Peter Garrod**
*Member, The Further Education Funding Council*
Principal, The Adult College, Lancaster. Former Adult Education Manager, Birmingham City Council.

**Ms J Garstang**
*Personnel Director, Naval Aircraft Repair Organisation*

**Timothy Garton Ash**
*Governor, Westminster Foundation for Democracy*

**Frank Gaskell**
*Head of European Affairs, Highlands & Islands Enterprise*

**Philip Gaskell**
*Area Manager, Scottish Natural Heritage*

**Lady Gass**
*Member, Rail Users Consultative Committee for Western England*
*Commissioner, English Heritage*

**David Gatenby**
*Chief Executive, UK Passport Agency*

**James H Gauld**
*Head, Consultancy Division, Macaulay Land Use Research Institute*

**Mark Gavin**
*Member, General Consumer Council for Northern Ireland*
Head, Information & Social Policy Unit, Northern Ireland Association of Citizens' Advice Bureaux. Member, Northern Ireland Secretariat of the Buttle Trust.

**Rupert Gavin**
*Governor, National Film & Television School*

**Robert Gavron CBE**
*Trustee, National Gallery*

**Mrs JM Gaymer**
*Member of Council, Advisory, Conciliation & Arbitration Service*

**A Geddes OBE**
*Head, Accounts Office (Cumbernauld), Inland Revenue*

**Cllr Keith Geddes CBE**
*Member of Council, Scottish Arts Council*
*Member of Board, Scottish Enterprise*
Leader, City of Edinburgh Council. President, COSLA. Board member, Lothian & Edinburgh Enterprise. Livingston Development Corporation and Edinburgh Old Town Renewal Trust.

**Dr RDH Gem**
*Commissioner, Royal Commission on Historical Monuments of England*

**Clive George**
*Member, Ofwat Customer Service Committee for Wales*

**Colin George**
*Member, The Further Education Funding Council*
*Member, Commonwealth Scholarship Commission*
*Member, Legal Aid Board*
Chairman, The Open College. Former Group Personnel Director, Guinness.

**David George OBE**
*Board Director, Home-Grown Cereals Authority*

**Eddie George**
*Governor, Bank of England*

**John George**
*Director of Finance & Information Services, The Housing Corporation*

**Sir Richard George**
*Vice Chairman, The Environment Agency*
*Member of Council, Food from Britain*
Chairman & Managing Director, Weetabix. Chairman, Whitworths. Former President, Food & Drink Federation. Member, Executive Committee, Association of Cereal Food Manufacturers. Chairman, Advisory Board, Institute of Food Research. Member, Prince's Trust Management Board.

**Prof Paul Geroski**
*Member, Monopolies & Mergers Commission*
Dean, MBA Programme, London Business School.

**IS Gerrie**
*Head, Inland Revenue Scotland, Inland Revenue*

**Peter Gershon**
*Member of Board, Defence Evaluation & Research Agency*
MD, GEC Marconi.

**D Gesua**
*Director, Planning & Resources, The British Library*

**Dr DJ Giachardi**
*Member of Council, Engineering & Physical Sciences Research Council*
Courtaulds

**Sir Peter Gibbings**
*Chairman, The Radio Authority*

**Julian Gibbons**
*Board Member, Home-Grown Cereals Authority*

**Andy Gibbs**
*Head of Computing & Office Services, Economic & Social Research Council*

**Captain B Gibbs**
*Ex-Officio Trustee, Royal Marines Museum*

**Carole Gibbs**
*Member, Ofwat Central Customer Service Committee*

**John Gibbs**
*Head of Branch, Pathology, Forest Research*

**Karen Gibbs**
*Regional Manager & Secretary, Ofwat Southern Customer Service Committee*

**Anne Gibson**
*Member, Equal Opportunities Commission*
National Secretary, Manufacturing Science Finance Union (MSF). Member, TUC General Council. Health & Safety Commissioner. Member, Labour Party NEC Women's Committee.

**Anne Gibson**
*Member, Health & Safety Commission*
National Secretary, Manufacturing Science & Finance Union. Member, TUC General Council. Serves on Department for Education & Employment's Advisory Group on Older Workers. Equal Opportunities Commissioner. Former member, Women's National Commission.

**Dr D Gibson**
*Associate Adviser in Postgraduate General Practice Education, Northern Ireland Council for Postgraduate Medical & Dental Education*

**John Gibson**
*Member, Milk Development Council*
Chief Executive, Muller (UK). Former Managing Director, Unigate Dairies. Dairy Industry Federation Council member.

**Robin Gibson**
*Chief Curator, National Portrait Gallery*

**Rosemary M Gibson**
*Head, Publications & Education, Scottish Record Office*

**Barry Gidman**
*Regional Director, Central, Meat Hygiene Service*

**Balram Gidoomal CBE**
*Member, Apple & Pear Research Council*
Chairman, Winning Communication Partnership, Business Link London South and Christmas Cracker Trust. Ethnic Advisor to Princes Youth Business Trust.

**Adam Giffard**
*Member, Ofwat South West Customer Service Committee*

**Prof John Gilbert**
*Food Research Director, Central Science Laboratory*
Joined MAFF in 1973. Former Director, Food Science Laboratory (Norwich). Vice-Chair, IUPAC Food Chemistry Commission. Chair, ILSI Food Packaging Task Force. UK representative on CEN Working Groups on packaging and mycotoxins.

**R Gilbert**
*Member of Council, Advisory, Conciliation & Arbitration Service*

**Dr Roger Gilbert**
*Non-Executive Member, Army Training & Recruitment Agency*

**Ken Gilbert MBE**
*Member for Scotland, Gas Consumers' Council*
Past branch Citizens Advice Bureau Chairman. Past Member, Scottish Consumer Council. Member, Edinburgh Airport Consultative Committee and Independent Tribunal Service. High Constable, City of Edinburgh. President, Edinburgh West Patrons' Club.

**David Gilchrist**
*Member, National Consumer Council*

**Air Commodore MJ Gilding**
*Director of Corporate Development, RAF Training Group Defence Agency*

**Cllr D Giles**
*Representative Trustee, Royal Naval Museum*
*Ex-Officio Trustee, Royal Marines Museum*
City Council of Portsmouth.

**Mrs L Giles**
*Student Bursary Manager, National Board for Nursing, Midwifery & Health Visiting for Northern Ireland*

**Dr N Giles**
*Chairman, RFAC, The Environment Agency*

**Ian Gill**
*Director, Human Resources, Commonwealth Development Corporation*

**JH Gilleece**
*Member, Northern Ireland Council for Postgraduate Medical & Dental Education*
Nominated by Dental Co-ord Committee.

**Tom Gillen**
*Member of Commission, Independent Commission for Police Complaints for Northern Ireland*

**WF Gillespie OBE**
*Chairman, Construction Industry Training Board (NI)*
John Sinton.

**Terry Gilliam**
*Governor, British Film Institute*

**Mrs Elizabeth Gillies**
*Professional Officer (Nursing), National Board for Nursing, Midwifery & Health Visiting for Scotland*

**John Gilliland**
*Board Director, Home-Grown Cereals Authority*

**Gil Gillis**
*Board Member, Castle Vale Housing Action Trust*
Former Managing Director, Nat West Home Loans, Former Deputy Chairman, Council of Mortgage Lenders.

**Herb Gillman**
*Head of Design, National Gallery*

**James Gilmour**
*Member, East Midland Consumers' Committee, Office of Electricity Regulation*

**John Gilmour**
*Member of Board, Northern Ireland Museums' Council*
Director, Ulster American Folk Park. Nominated by Ulster American Folk Park.

**Dr E Gilvarry**
*Member, Alcohol Education & Research Council*

**Gareth Gimblett**
*Member, Central Council for Education & Training in Social Work*

**Prof Charles Gimingham OBE**
*Member, Scientific Advisory Committee, Scottish Natural Heritage*

**Mrs Margaret Ginman**
*Member, Ofwat Southern Customer Service Committee*

**Prof MPF Girard**
*Member, National Biological Standards Board*

**Jill Girvan**
*Member, Northern Ireland Consumer Committee for Electricity, Office for the Regulation of Electricity & Gas*
Law Centre, Belfast.

**Dr Stephen Glaister**
*Non-Executive Director, Office of the Rail Regulator*

**Philippa Glanville**
*Acting Curator, Metalwork, Silver & Jewellery Collection, Victoria & Albert Museum*

**Lady Isobel Glasgow**
*Member, West Areas Board, Scottish Natural Heritage*

**Lesley Glasser**
*Trustee, National Museums of Scotland*

**Nora Gleave**
*Member, Rail Users Consultative Committee for North Western England*

**DJ Gleeson**
*Member of Board, Construction Industry Training Board*
MJ Gleeson Group

**Dr Helen Glenister**
*Nursing Director, Medical Devices Agency*

**The Lord Glentoran CBE**
*Member, Millennium Commission*
Chairman, Redland Tile & Brick Ltd. President, Institute of Roofing. Chairman, Northern Ireland Classic Golf Promotions.

**Keith Gliddon**
*Director of Corporate Services, Forest Enterprise*

**HRH The Duke of Gloucester KG GCVO**
*Commissioner, English Heritage Trustee, British Museum*

**Colonel David Glyn-Owen**
*Commandant Infantry Training Centre Warminster, Army Training & Recruitment Agency*

**Mrs Betty Goble**
*Chairman, REPAC, The Environment Agency*

**Gerald Godby**
*Member, Ofwat Central Customer Service Committee*

**Dennis Goddard**
*Park Manager, Bushy Park, Royal Parks Agency*

**Michael Goddard**
*Director, International Regulation & Spectrum Policy, Radiocommunications Agency*

**Patricia Goddard**
*Head of Art Handling, National Gallery*

**Roy Goddard**
*Member of Commission, Independent Television Commission*

**Dennis Godfrey**
*Manager (Press & Information), Fair Employment Commission for Northern Ireland*

**JE Godfrey**
*Member of Governing Body, Scottish Crop Research Institute*
Director, family farming companies. Former Chairman, Potato Marketing Board. Member or adviser to numerous agricultural committees, including Bishop Burton Agricultural College; The Centre for Agricultural Strategy, University of Reading; The Royal Agricultural Society of England; Food Chain Group of the Foresight Programme; and Humberside Training & Enterprise Council.

**Michael Godfrey**
*Member, DIEL, Office of Telecommunications*
Manager, Friends of the Royal Botanical Gardens, Kew.

**Val Godfrey**
*Member, Rail Users Consultative Committee for North Western England*

**Stan Godward**
*Member, East Midland Consumers' Committee, Office of Electricity Regulation*

**Jude Goffe**
*Member of Commission, Independent Television Commission*

**AM Gold**
*Non-Executive Director, Caledonian MacBrayne Ltd*

**Roz Goldie**
*Member, Post Office Users' Council for Northern Ireland*

**Peter Goldsmith QC**
*Member, The Great Britain-China Centre*

**Gabriel Goldstein**
*Subject Adviser, IT, Office for Standards in Education*

**Anthony Goldstone**
*Life Vice President, Museum of Science & Industry Manchester*

**Ms Ros Goldstraw**
*Head of Management, Psychology, Linguistics & Education Research Support, Economic & Social Research Council*

**Mrs W Goldstraw**
*Member, The Accounts Commission for Scotland*
General Manager (Scotland & Northern Ireland), Post Office Counters.

**Simon Goman**
*Office Systems, Companies House*

**Alan Gomersall**
*Director, Science Reference & Information Service, The British Library*

**J Goodall**
*Member of Council, British Hallmarking Council*

**John Gooderham**
*Secretary & Chief Executive Officer, Medical Practices Committee*

**John Goodfellow**
*Member, Scottish Water & Sewerage Customers Council*

**Prof Julia Goodfellow**
*Member, Biotechnology & Biological Sciences Research Council*

**Mike Goodfellow**
*Commercial Director, Defence Evaluation & Research Agency*

**Roger E Gooding**
*Member, Post Office Users' National Council*
Chairman, Banbury & District POAC and TAC. Office Services Manager, Cherwell District Council. Member, Association of Electoral Administrators.

**Lady Goodison**
*Member of Board of Governors, Museum of London*
*Member, Royal Parks Agency*

**Alistair Goodlad MP**
*Member, The Great Britain-China Centre*

**J Goodlad**
*Member of Board, Highlands & Islands Enterprise*

**Harry Goodman**
*Chief Executive, Fair Employment Commission for Northern Ireland*

**Prof JFB Goodman CBE**
*Member of Council, Advisory, Conciliation & Arbitration Service*

**R Goodway**
*Member, Cardiff Bay Development Corporation*
Councillor, Cardiff County Council. Millennium Stadium.

**Andrew Goodwin**
*Member of Committee, Rail Users Consultative Committee for Wales*
Director of Music, Bangor Cathedral. Vice-President, Bangor Hospitals League of Friends. Chairman, Chester & North Wales Rail Users Association.

**John Goodwin**
*Member of Board, West of Scotland Water Authority*
Chairman, Highland Distilleries Company. Director, Orpar, Robertson & Baxter and AG Barr.

**Phil Goodwin**
*Director of Operations, London Pensions Fund Authority*

**Alexander Gordon CBE**
*Trustee, National Museums of Scotland*

**Charles Gordon**
*Deputy Chief Executive, Army Training & Recruitment Agency*

**David Gordon**
*Member, Tate Gallery*

**Dr E Gordon**
*Member, Parole Board*

**Prof FJ Gordon**
*Director, Agricultural Research Institute of Northern Ireland*
Representing the Queen's University of Belfast.

**Graeme Gordon OBE**
*Member of Board, Scottish Environment Protection Agency*

**Iain J Gordon**
*Programme Unit Manager, Macaulay Land Use Research Institute*

**Lord James Gordon of Strathblane**
*Chairman, Scottish Tourist Board Trustee, National Galleries of Scotland*

**John Gordon**
*Member of Board, British Waterways*
Director, Beeson Gregory Ltd; Chairman, British Waterways Pensions Trustees Ltd.

**Roger Gordon**
*Central Collection, Rate Collection Agency*

**Colonel BM Gordon-Smith**
*Member of Advisory Board, Service Children's Education*

**Ann Gormley**
*Member, Post Office Users' Council for Northern Ireland*

**Jill Gort**
*Commissioner, Criminal Cases Review Commission*
Barrister. Chair, Value Added Tax tribunal. Immigration Adjudicator.

**Prof Christine Gosden**
*Member, Human Fertilisation & Embryology Authority*
Professor of Medical Genetics, University of Liverpool, Liverpool Women's Hospital.

**Sir Donald Gosling**
*Trustee, Fleet Air Arm Museum*

**MAJ Gossip**
*Member of Advisory Council, Scottish Record Office*

**Cliff Gould**
*Secondary, Office for Standards in Education*

**Daphne Gould, OBE**
*Trustee, Geffrye Museum*
Former Head of Mulberry School, Tower Hamlets. Former Chairman, ILEA Headteacher Consultative Committee. Former Member, CBI Committee for the Regeneration of the Inner City. Former Member, National Curriculum Council. Trustee, Citizenship Foundation. Education Consultant to Hackney Education Authority.

**Ray Gould**
*T&E Facilities, Defence Evaluation & Research Agency*

**JFS Gourlay**
*Member of Board of Governors, Macaulay Land Use Research Institute*

**Nik Gowing**
*Governor, Westminster Foundation for Democracy*

**P Gowing**
*Director Business Development, Army Technical Support Agency*

**Chris Grace**
*Director of Animation, S4C*

**Mrs Gillian Gracey**
*Member, Industrial Research & Technology Unit*
Former Senior Pharmacist, Ivex Pharmaceuticals.

**Michael Grade CBE**
*Non-Executive Director, New Millennium Experience Co Ltd*
Chairman, First Leisure Corporation.

**The Duke of Grafton, KG**
*Chairman, Sir John Soane's Museum*

**David Graham**
*Member, Ofwat Northumbria Customer Service Committee*

**Frank Graham**
*Member, Industrial Research & Technology Unit*
Managing Director, Kainos Software.

**Ian Graham**
*Member, Scottish Community Education Council*

**Martin Graham**
*Assistant Director, Office of Fair Trading*

**Martin C Graham**
*Secretary of the Library, National Library of Scotland*

**Nigel Graham**
*Member, North Areas Board, Scottish Natural Heritage*

**Cllr Nigel Graham**
*Member, North of Scotland Water Authority*
Councillor for Nairn. Member, Highland Council. Provost of Nairn. Convener, Northern Joint Police Board. Chairman, Water & Sewerage Committee, Highland Regional Council.

**Dr Peter Graham**
*Director, Health Directorate, The Health & Safety Executive*

**Caroline Graham-Brown**
*Non-Executive Director, Ordnance Survey*
The Royal Institution of Great Britain.

**Dr IJ Graham-Bryce**
*Member, Natural Environment Research Council*
University of Dundee

**RH Grainger**
*Inspector, Football Licensing Authority*

**Supt WM Grainger**
*OCU, Portsmouth, Ministry of Defence Police*

**Alan Grant**
*Member, Health & Safety Commission*
Head, TUC Organisation & Services Department. Formerly worked in printing industry.

**Sir Alistair Grant**
*Trustee, National Museums of Scotland Trustee, National Heritage Memorial Fund*

**Annie Grant**
*Initial Teacher Training, Teacher Training Agency*

**Miss Beatrice Grant**
*Professional Officer (Midwifery), National Board for Nursing, Midwifery & Health Visiting for Scotland*

**Prof EH Grant**
*Member, National Radiological Protection Board*
Department of Chemistry, Imperial College, London.

**Ian D Grant**
*Head, Court & Legal Services, Scottish Record Office*

**Ian D Grant CBE**
*Member of Board, British Tourist Authority*
Chairman, Scottish Tourist Board. Former President, National Farmers Union of Scotland. Non-Executive Director, Clydesdale Bank, Scottish Hydro Electric and National Farmers Union Mutual Insurance Society. Former Member, CBI Scottish Council. Crown Estate Commissioner.

**Ken Grant**
*Chief Executive, Orkney Enterprise*

**Lesley Grant**
*Member, Scottish Sports Council*

**Peter J Grant**
*Chairman, Highlands & Islands Airports*
Deputy Chairman, London Merchant Securities. Former Chairman, Sun Life Assurance Society and former Director, Scottish Hydro Electric.

**S Grant**
*Director, Northern Ireland Transport Holding Company*

**Stuart Grant**
*Member, Yorkshire Consumers' Committee, Office of Electricity Regulation*

**Mike Grantham**
*Secretary to the Commission, Crofters' Commission*

**I Grattidge**
*Finance Director, Veterinary Laboratories Agency*

**Meryl Gravell, JP**
*Member of Council, Post Office Users' Council for Wales*
County Councillor. Member, Social Security Tribunal.

**FC Graves**
*Member of Board, Commission for the New Towns*
Chairman, Francis Graves. Chairman, Ironbridge Heritage Foundation. Advisor, Home Office (Prison Building Board).

**AK Gray**
*Vice-Chairman, RFDC, The Environment Agency*

**Alaistar Gray**
*Adverse Reactions Surveillance Scheme, Veterinary Medicines Directorate*

**Carolyn Gray**
*Team Leader, Author Services, Registrar of Public Lending Right*

**David Gray**
*Deputy Chairman, General Consumer Council for Northern Ireland*
Partner with a Belfast firm of solicitors. Wheelchair user. Deputy Chairman, Northern Ireland Disability Council.

# Q&Q

**David Gray**
*Member of Board, West of Scotland Water Authority*
Managing Director, Caledonian Paper. Previously Partner, KMG Thomson McLintock. Director, Paper Federation of Great Britain. Member, Executive, Scottish Council Development & Industry. Chairman, Institute of Directors, Glasgow & West of Scotland.

**Capt Gil Gray**
*Part-time Board Member, Civil Aviation Authority*
Former Chief Pilot, British Airways' 757 and 767 fleets.

**J Gray**
*Member of Board, Highlands & Islands Enterprise*

**Prof JC Gray**
*Director, Horticulture Research International*

**Prof John Gray**
*Member of Board, Teacher Training Agency*
Director of Research, Homerton College, Cambridge. Former Professor of Education, Sheffield University.

**Dr Kenneth Gray CBE**
*Member, Higher Education Funding Council for Wales*
Technical Director, Thorn EMI. Managing Director, Thorn Transaction.

**L Gray**
*Head of FIN Systems, Scottish Fisheries Protection Agency*

**Michael M Gray OBE**
*Member of Board, Scottish Enterprise*

**Peter Gray**
*Director of Projects, Social Security Agency (Northern Ireland)*

**Philip Gray**
*Director, Finance & Administration Division, Tai Cymru*

**S Gray**
*Member of Board, Highlands & Islands Enterprise*

**Richard Grayson**
*Member, Equal Opportunities Commission*
Solicitor. Former Company Secretary, British Petroleum Company. Member, CBI's Equal Opportunities Forum.

**Michael Greaves**
*Regional Director, North, Meat Hygiene Service*

**Arthur Green**
*Member of Board, British Council*
Former Under-Secretary, Department of Education for Northern Ireland.

**David Green**
*Chief Executive, Liverpool Housing Action Trust*

**Eric Green**
*Chairman, Orkney Enterprise*

**Cllr Malcolm Green**
*Governor, Scottish Council for Educational Technology*
Convenor of Education, Glasgow City Council.

**Ralph Green OBE**
*Commissioner, Meat & Livestock Commission*
Managing Director, McIntosh Donald. Past Member, MLC's Meat Export Council and Board Member, Scotch Quality Beef & Lamb Association. Past President, Scottish Association of Meat Wholesalers.

**Bill Greenaway**
*Director, London, Eastern & Southern Areas, Advisory, Conciliation & Arbitration Service*

**Dr J Patrick Greene**
*Director, Museum of Science & Industry Manchester*

**Graham Greene CBE**
*Chairman, British Museum*
*Vice President, The Great Britain-China Centre*

**Jennifer Greenfield**
*Chief Legal Officer (Job Share), Equal Opportunities Commission for Northern Ireland*

**Tanya Greenfield**
*Lottery Officer, Arts Council of Northern Ireland*

**Sir Alan Greengross**
*Chairman, London Regional Passengers Committee*
*Member, Central Rail Users Consultative Committee*
Chairman of the Institute for Metropolitan Studies, University College London. Chairman, Policy Committee of the Built Environment. Director, London First Centre. Past Deputy Traffic Commissioner and Director, Port of London Authority.

**Paul Greenhalgh**
*Head of Research, Victoria & Albert Museum*

**Stephen Greenhalgh**
*Information Technology Manager, Gas Consumers' Council*

**Dr Basil Greenhill CB CMG**
*Trustee, Royal Air Force Museum*

**Mrs Pat Greenhill OBE**
*Member of Board, Scottish Homes*
Former Member, Stirling District Council. Trustee, Dunblane Fund and Chairman, Dunblane Help Fund.

**Jeffrey Greenwood**
*Chairman, Central Council for Education & Training in Social Work*

**Dr Judith Greenwood**
*Member, Parole Board for Scotland*

**Miss Miriam Greenwood**
*Trustee, Royal Botanic Garden Edinburgh*

**Mrs Barbara Greggains**
*Member, Ofwat Thames Customer Service Committee*

**David Greggains**
*Member, Human Fertilisation & Embryology Authority*
Director, Gorham Partners.

**Prof Kenneth Gregory**
*Director & Trustee, British Educational Communications & Technology Agency*

**Peter Gregory**
*Collections Director, Student Loans Company*

**Prof RL Gregory CBE**
*Member, The British Library*
Royal Society.

**Mrs SE Gregory**
*Member, Welsh National Board for Nursing, Midwifery & Health Visiting*
Director, Gwent Community Health NHS Tust

**Dr PW Greig-Smith**
*Chief Executive, Centre for Environment, Fisheries & Aquaculture Science*

**Margaret Grew**
*Southern, Rate Collection Agency*

**Miss Tanni Grey MBE**
*Member of Council, The Sports Council for Wales*

**EJ Gribbon**
*Compliance & Business Profits Divisions, Inland Revenue*

**Mrs Deborah Grice**
*Head of Policy Unit, Forensic Science Service*

**S Grier**
*Non-Executive Director, Caledonian MacBrayne Ltd*

**Scott Grier OBE**
*Member, Scottish Tourist Board*
Managing Director, Loganair. Director, Glasgow Chamber of Commerce.

**Dr David Grieves CBE**
*Non-Executive Director, Post Office*

**CG Griffin**
*Member, Rail Users Consultative Committee for Western England*

**J Griffin**
*Director Pricing, Specialist Procurement Services*

**Jonathan Griffin**
*Director, Marketing Services, British Tourist Authority & English Tourist Board*

**Ken Griffin OBE**
*Member of Board, The Housing Corporation*
Former Deputy Chairman of Ugland International Holdings, Deputy Chairman of British Ship Builders and Industrial Adviser to Department of Trade & Industry. Member of Law Society's Solicitors Disciplinary Tribunal.

**Rod Griffin**
*Director of Economic & Community Development, Castle Vale Housing Action Trust*

**CJ Griffith**
*Member, SACOT, Scottish Advisory Committee on Telecommunications*
Catering manager.

**EMW Griffith CBE**
*Member, Joint Nature Conservation Committee*
Countryside Council for Wales.

**Michael Griffith CBE**
*Chairman, Countryside Council for Wales*
Farmer. Chairman, Glan Clwyd NHS Tust

**AV Griffiths**
*Keeper, Prints & Drawings, British Museum*

**Gwyn Griffiths**
*Member of Board, Welsh Language Board*
Solicitor.

**H Griffiths**
*Member of Advisory Board, Defence Bills Agency*
Command Secretary, HQ RAF Logistics Command.

**H Griffiths**
*Member, Oil & Pipelines Agency*

**Dr John Griffiths**
*GP Member, Medical Practices Committee*
North Wales.

**Judge Griffiths**
*Member, Parole Board*

**Norman Griffiths**
*Member, South Wales Consumers' Committee, Office of Electricity Regulation*

**PJ Griffiths**
*Director & Chief Executive, Engineering Construction Industry Training Board*

**Prof Peter Griffiths CBE**
*Member, Scottish Hospital Endowments Research Trust*

**Prof RA Griffiths**
*Commissioner, Royal Commission on Ancient & Historical Monuments in Wales*

**Richard Griffiths**
*Trustee, Sir John Soane's Museum*

**W Rhidian M Griffiths**
*Keeper of Printed Books, National Library of Wales*

**Russel Griggs**
*Director, Overseas Business Development, Scottish Enterprise*

**A Grimm**
*Manager (Planning and Development), Vehicle Certification Agency*

**Anne Grindley**
*Regional Manager, Rural Development Commission*

**Peter H Grinyer**
*Member, The Scottish Legal Aid Board*
Emeritus Professor and Professorial Fellow, University of St Andrews. Visiting professor, Stern School of Business, University of New York. Senior Executive (part-time), St Andrews Strategic Management.

**Dr Anne Grocock**
*Member, National Museum of Science & Industry*

**Alan Grosset**
*Vice Chairman, Scottish Sports Council*

**Loyd Grossman**
*Commissioner, Museums & Galleries Commission*
Journalist and broadcaster. Governor, London School of Economics. Chairman, Young Friends of the British Museum.

**Lady Grosvenor**
*Member, Royal Parks Agency*

**Cllr Lynn Groundwater**
*Member, Scottish Water & Sewerage Customers Council*

**Prof Andrew Grubb**
*Member, Human Fertilisation & Embryology Authority*
Professor of Law, King's College, London.

**Nia Gruffydd**
*Literature Officer, Arts Council of Wales*

**David Gubb**
*Regional Office, South Thames, NHS Estates*

**Mrs Irene Gudd**
*Member, Parole Board for Scotland*

**Norman Guffick**
*Member, Ofwat Northumbria Customer Service Committee*

**David Guilfoyle**
*Director, Youth Council for Northern Ireland*

**John Guinness CB**
*Chairman, British Nuclear Fuels plc*
Trustee, Prince's Youth Business Trust. Non-Executive Director, Guinness Mahon Holdings, Ocean Group and Mithras Investment Trust.

**Prof K Gull**
*Member, National Biological Standards Board*

**Mrs B Gullick**
*Head of Department, Visitor Services, Natural History Museum*

**Ray Gullis**
*Systems Operations & Support, Companies House*

**Stuart Gulliver**
*Chief Executive, Glasgow Development Agency*

**Sharon Gunn**
*Team Manager, Publicity & Grants Team, English Nature*

**Cllr Carol Gustafson**
*Member, English Sports Council*

**Michael Gutsell**
*Board Director, Home-Grown Cereals Authority*

**Dr Alan Guy**
*Assistant Director, Collections Division, National Army Museum*

**Supt JJ Guyan**
*OCU, Longtown, Ministry of Defence Police*

**Mrs Betty Guyatt**
*Member, Southern Consumers' Committee, Office of Electricity Regulation*

**Prof Emeritus Ieuan Gwynedd Jones**
*Member, National Library of Wales*
Elected by the Court of Governors.

**Mrs Pamela Gwyther**
*Member, South Western Consumers' Committee, Office of Electricity Regulation*

**George Gyte**
*School Leadership, Teacher Training Agency*

# H

**John Hackney**
*Chairman, Post Office Users' National Council*
*Chairman, Northumbria RFDC, The Environment Agency*
Former Chief Executive, Tees & Hartlepool Port Authority. Director, University of Teesside. Director, Tees Health Authority.

**Neil Hadden**
*Director, London Region, The Housing Corporation*

**Lyndon Haddon**
*Non-Executive Director, Royal Mint*

**C Hadley OBE**
*Member of Board, Investors in People UK*
Former Managing Director, British Aluminium Wire & Conductor.

**John Hagan**
*Director of Client Services, Rivers Agency*

**Eric Hagman**
*Trustee, National Galleries of Scotland*

**Nigel Haigh OBE**
*Member of Board, The Environment Agency*
Director and Company Secretary, Institute of European Environment Policy. Chairmam, Green Alliance and Green Alliance Trust. Consultant, NPI. Visiting Research Fellow, Imperial College Centre for Environmental Technology.

**N Haighton**
*Corporate IS/IT Projects Director, Information Technology Services Agency*

**Julia Hailes**
*Member of Board, UK Ecolabelling Board*
Independent environmental consultant and author.

**Roger Haincock**
*Head of Finance, Horserace Betting Levy Board*

**Prof A Haines**
*Member of Council, Medical Research Council*
Royal Free Hospital School of Medicine, London.

**Prof Michael Haines**
*Member of Council, Food from Britain*
*Member of Board, Sea Fish Industry Authority*
Professor of Agricultural Marketing & Business, University of Wales Director, Welsh Food Promotions and Independent Adviser to Northern Milk Partnership. Member of Council of Food From Britain.

**Ewan Hainey**
*Registry Manager, National Board for Nursing, Midwifery & Health Visiting for Scotland*

**Ken Hairs**
*Board Director, Home-Grown Cereals Authority*

**Hugh Halcro-Johnston**
*Member of Board, Highlands & Islands Enterprise*
*Member, North Areas Board, Scottish Natural Heritage*

**William Halcrow**
*Director, East Region, Scottish Environment Protection Agency*

**GJG Halford**
*Group Manager Agency, Postgraduate, Nursing & Midwifery Bursery, Student Awards Agency for Scotland*

**Commodore David Hall**
*Superintendent Ships (Devonport), Ships Support Agency*

**Sir John Hall**
*Member, Millennium Commission*
Chairman, Newcastle United Football Club. Property developer and former North East Businessman of the Year.

**John Hall**
*Commercial Director, Ships Support Agency*

**John Hall**
*Director of Contracts, Defence Estates Organisation*

**Nicholas Hall**
*Keeper of Fort Nelson, Royal Armouries*

**Richard Hall**
*Member, South Western Consumers' Committee, Office of Electricity Regulation*

**S Hall**
*Director of Finance, Military Survey*

**Tony Hall**
*Director, Central Council for Education & Training in Social Work*

**Tony Hall**
*Chief Executive, BBC News, British Broadcasting Corporation*

**Zelda Hall**
*Finance and Budgets Officer, Defence Animal Centre*

**David Halladay**
*Operations Director, Funding Agency for Schools*

**Wing Commander Martin Hallam**
*Head Operations, Joint Air Reconnaissance Intelligence Centre*

**Dr Elizabeth Hallam Smith**
*Director of Public Services, Public Record Office*

**David Hughes Hallet**
*Member of Board, Scottish Environment Protection Agency*

**Christine Hallett**
*Member of Board, Scottish Children's Reporter Administration*
Professor of Social Policy, Stirling University. Past Chairman, Central Region Child Protection Committee.

**Prof Ian Halliday**
*Member of Council, Particle Physics & Astronomy Research Council*
University of Wales, Swansea

**Ms Jane Halliday**
*Member, Centre for Information on Language Teaching & Research*
General Education Adviser, Modern Languages, London Borough of Harrow.

**Virginia Halliwell**
*Vice-Chairman, Museum of Science & Industry Manchester*

**Sir Ronald Halstead CBE**
*Member, Monopolies & Mergers Commission*
Former Chairman, Beecham Group and Deputy Chairman, British Steel. Former Chairman, Industrial Development Advisory Board, DTI. Member of Council, Reading University. Deputy Chairman, Technology Colleges Trust.

**K Ham**
*Head of The Legal Unit, Compensation Agency*

**John Hambley**
*Visual Arts Officer, Arts Council of Wales*

**Jeff Hamblin**
*General Manager, The Americas, British Tourist Authority*

**Capt P Hambling**
*DDNE, Defence Medical Training Organisation*

**Phillip Hamer**
*Field Director, Gas Consumers' Council*

**The Right Rev Dean E Hamill**
*Member of Council, Council for Catholic Maintained Schools*

**AE Hamilton**
*Head of Press & Public Relations, British Museum*

**Sir Archie Hamilton MP**
*Governor, Westminster Foundation for Democracy*

**Miss Avril Hamilton**
*Member, Scottish Medical Practices Committee*

**Mrs Heather Hamilton**
*Human Resources & Quality, Central Science Laboratory*
Joined MAFF in 1975.

**Ian Hamilton**
*Group Director - Films, Radio, Events, Central Office of Information*

**Robin Hamilton**
*Director of Development, East of Scotland Water Authority*

**W Francis F Hamilton**
*Director, Highlands & Islands Airports*
Chairman & Managing Director, Macrae & Dick.

**LP Hamilton CB**
*Member of Council, Hannah Research Institute*

**Supt W Hammersley**
*OCU, Aldermaston, Ministry of Defence Police*

**Mrs D Hammett**
*Member, WACT, Welsh Advisory Committee on Telecommunications*
Teacher.

**Andrew Hammond**
*Associate Director (Finance & Marketing), Wilton Park Executive Agency*

**David Hammond**
*Member, Monopolies & Mergers Commission*
Chairman, Integrated Transport Systems. Trustee, Crimestoppers Trust. Former Deputy Chairman, ADT.

**Philip Hammond**
*Director, Performing Arts Department, Arts Council of Northern Ireland*

**Christopher Hampson CBE**
*Member of Board, The Environment Agency*
Chairman, Yorkshire Electricity Group. Chairman, RMC Group. Non-Executive Director, SNC Lavalin Inc and Transalta Corp. Vice President, Combined Heat & Power Association. Former Director, Costain Group and Executive Director, ICI.

**D Hanchet**
*Deputy Chief Planning Inspector & Director of Planning & Environmental Protection, The Planning Inspectorate*

**MT Hancock CBE**
*Ex-Officio Trustee, Royal Marines Museum*

**Mike Hancock MP**
*Member, The Great Britain-China Centre*

**Robin Hancock**
*Director of Personnel, Driver & Vehicle Licensing Agency*

**Peter Handcock**
*Member of Management Board, The Court Service*
Midland & Oxford Circuit Administrator.

**Stanley Handley MBE**
*Member, North Western Consumers' Committee, Office of Electricity Regulation*

**Cllr Mrs Joan Hanham**
*Trustee, Commonwealth Institute*
Leader of Council, Royal Borough of Kensington & Chelsea.

**Maurice Hankey**
*Member, Scottish Agricultural Wages Board*
Employers' representative member nominated by the National Farmers' Union of Scotland and the Scottish Landowners' Federation.

**Colin Hann**
*Head of Strategy, Commission for Racial Equality*

**A Hanna**
*Member of Board, Fisheries Conservancy Board for Northern Ireland*
Independent angler.

**B Hanna**
*Advisor to the Board, Laganside Corporation*
Chief Executive - Belfast City Council.

**Mrs Deirdre Hanna**
*Member, Northern Ireland Local Government Officers' Superannuation Committee*

**James Hanna**
*Member, Northern Ireland Local Government Officers' Superannuation Committee*

**Judith Hanna**
*Member, London Regional Passengers Committee*

**Miss MEA Hanna**
*Member, Northern Ireland Council for Postgraduate Medical & Dental Education*
Appointed by DHSS.

**Mrs Judith Hanratty**
*Member, Monopolies & Mergers Commission*
Company Secretary, BP.

**JG Hansford**
*Acting Establishment Officer, Natural Environment Research Council*

**Dr Jim Hansom**
*Member, West Areas Board & Scientific Advisory Committee, Scottish Natural Heritage*

**Sir John Hanson KCMG CBE**
*Member, Academic Council, Wilton Park Executive Agency*

**Dr Sam Harbison**
*Director Chief Inspector, Nuclear Safety Directorate, The Health & Safety Executive*

**Patrick Harbour**
*Non-Executive Director, Queen Elizabeth II Conference Centre*
Managing Director, Leith's.

**David Harden**
*Member, Milk Development Council*
Landowner and farmer. Country Landowners' Association Chairman, Wales and Anglesey & Caernarfon. Council Member, Oxford Farming Conference.

**Ms Elizabeth M Harden**
*Administrator (Research & Developments), National Board for Nursing, Midwifery & Health Visiting for Scotland*

**Dr Kenneth Harden**
*Member, Scottish Medical Practices Committee*

**Sir Christopher Harding**
*Non-Executive Director, Post Office*

**D Harding**
*Member, Northern Ireland Fishery Harbour Authority*

**Guy Hardy**
*Member of Committee, Rail Users Consultative Committee for Wales*

**Nigel Hardy**
*Manager Corporate Marketing, Local Enterprise Development Unit*

**Prof Tony Hardy**
*Agriculture & Environment Research Director, Central Science Laboratory*
Joined MAFF in 1976. Former Research Director, MAFF Slough Laboratory.

**Andrea Hargrave**
*Research Director, Broadcasting Standards Commission*

**Surgeon Commodore D Hargraves**
*Director of Plans & Resources, Defence Dental Agency*

**P Harkin**
*District Inspector, Foyle Fisheries Commission*

**Ian Harkness**
*Director of Marketing, UK Hydrographic Office*

**JW Harkness**
*Director of Veterinary Investigation Division, Veterinary Laboratories Agency*

**Norman Harkness**
*Assistant Registrar (Trade Marks), Patent Office*

**Paul Harley**
*Member of Committee, Rail Users Consultative Committee for Wales*

**Cllr John Harman**
*Member of Board, The Environment Agency*
Leader, Kirklees Metropolitan Council. Lecturer, Barnsley College. Director, Going for Green, Yorkshire Enterprise, AMA (Properties), Kirklees Henry Boot Partnership, Honley Land, Kirklees Metropolitan Development Co, Kirklees Theatre Trust, Kirklees Stadium Development, Local Government International Bureau, Calderdale & Kirklees Training & Enterprise Council.

**Sarah Harman**
*Development Officer, Arts Council of Wales*

**Prof DG Harnden**
*Member, National Radiological Protection Board*
Paterson Institute for Cancer Research, Christie Hospital NHS Trust, Manchester.

**Prof J Harper**
*Trustee, National Galleries of Scotland*

**Lieutenant Commander Stuart Harper**
*Officer Commanding Defence Explosive Ordnance Disposal School, Army Training & Recruitment Agency*

**Prof JE Harries**
*Member, Natural Environment Research Council*
Imperial College, London.

**I Harrington**
*Financial Controller, Scottish Crop Research Institute*

**Prof JM Harrington CBE**
*Member, National Radiological Protection Board*
Professor of Occupational Health, University of Birmingham.

**Mrs VA Harriott**
*Member, Rail Users Consultative Committee for North Eastern England*

**Bernard Harris**
*Member, North Western Consumers' Committee, Office of Electricity Regulation*

**C Harris**
*Chief Executive, Coastguard*

**Colin Harris**
*Member, The Further Education Funding Council*
Managing Director, Legal & General Financial Services.

**Group Captain Harris**
*Member of Advisory Board, Service Children's Education*

**Hugh Harris**
*Deputy Chairman, Commission for Racial Equality*
Director of Operations, London First. Member, Business Leaders Team, Race for Opportunity campaign, Business in the Community. Former Associate Director responsible for Corporate Services, Bank of England. Former

special adviser, Board of the City & Inner London North Training & Enterprise Council (CILNTEC). Former member, Windsor Fellowship Advisory Council.

**Jackie Harris**
*Resident Board Member, Tower Hamlets Housing Action Trust*
Resident of Tredegar Estate. Former Chair, Tenants Association.

**Judge Harris QC**
*Member, Parole Board*

**Vanessa Harris**
*Head of Finance & Administration, Museums & Galleries Commission*

**Sir VT Harris**
*Keeper, Japanese Antiquities, British Museum*

**Chris Harrison**
*Member, East Midland Consumers' Committee, Office of Electricity Regulation*

**Sir David Harrison CBE**
*Member, The Arts Council of England*
Chairman of Eastern Arts Board. Master, Selwyn College, Cambridge. Pro-Vice-Chancellor, University of Cambridge. Former Chairman, Committee of Vice-Chancellors and Principals. Former Vice-Chancellor, Exeter University. Former Chairman, Board of Northcott Theatre, Exeter. Chairman, Board of Trustees, Homerton College, Cambridge.

**JAD Harrison OBE**
*Member of Board, Highlands & Islands Enterprise*

**Dr JR Harrison**
*Medical Assistant Director, National Radiological Protection Board*

**Scott Harrison**
*Subject Adviser, History, Office for Standards in Education*

**Steve Harrison**
*Continuing Professional Development & Research, Teacher Training Agency*

**Trevor Harrison**
*Non-Executive Director, UK Atomic Energy Authority*
Former Senior Executive, ICI. Principal, LEK Management Consultants.

**Dr Victoria Harrison**
*Director of Science Policy, Scientific Audit & International Group, Biotechnology & Biological Sciences Research Council*

**George Harrold**
*Director Telecommunications Services, Central Computer & Telecommunications Agency*

**Sir Peter Harrop KCB**
*Trustee, British Museum*

**John Hart**
*Member, Rail Users Consultative Committee for North Western England*

**R Hart**
*Associate Director, Wilton Park Executive Agency*

**Sally Hart**
*Policy, UK Sports Council*

**Paul Hartnack**
*Comptroller General & Chief Executive, Patent Office*

**Brian Harvey**
*Director of Resources & Supplier Development, Legal Aid Board*

**Ms C Harvey**
*Research & Information Officer, Youth Council for Northern Ireland*

**DW Harvey**
*Chief Executive, Vehicle Certification Agency*

**Martin Harvey**
*Complex Services Manager, BFI On The South Bank*

**Mervyn Harvey**
*Director, Finance, Personnel & Administration, Service Children's Education*

**His Excellency Wajid Hasan**
*Trustee, Imperial War Museum*

**Sir Alan Haselhurst MP**
*Chairman of Trustees, Community Development Foundation*

**RM Haslam**
*Commissioner, Royal Commission on Ancient & Historical Monuments in Wales*

**Rob Haslam**
*Group Director - Network, Central Office of Information*

**Eric Hassall**
*Member, Natural Environment Research Council*
Deputy Chairman, Coal Authority Chairman, British Geological Survey Board. Director, Keele University Science Park. Deputy Chairman, Keele University. Council President, Institution of Mining Engineers.

**Tom Hassall**
*Secretary & Chief Executive, Royal Commission on Historical Monuments of England*

**L Hasson**
*Director, Northern Ireland Transport Holding Company*

**Jim Hastie**
*Director of Development Funding, Scottish Homes*

**HJ Hastings**
*Member, Training & Employment Agency (NI)*
Member of Board, Investors in People UK Managing Director, Hastings Hotel Group.

**Max Hastings**
*Trustee, National Portrait Gallery*

**Michael Hastings**
*Member, Commission for Racial Equality*
BBC Public Affairs Executive. Chairman, Crime Concern. Former member, Social Security Advisory Committee. Member, MetropolitanPolice Committee. Founder, Cities in Schools 'Anti-truancy schemes'. Former adviser to Downing Street Policy Unit on Race, Urban & Community Affairs.

**David Hatch CBE, JP**
*Chairman, National Consumer Council*

**Ch Supt W Hatfield**
*OCU, Faslane, Ministry of Defence Police*

**John Hathaway**
*Director, Midlands, Property Advisers to the Civil Estate*

**Rob Hatt**
*Regional Manager, Rural Development Commission*

**Sara Hattrick**
*Head of Photographic, National Gallery*

**J Haughey**
*Member of Board, Fisheries Conservancy Board for Northern Ireland*
Appointed as representative of a substantial number of anglers.

**Dr David Hauser**
*Director of Consumer Affairs, Office of Electricity Regulation*

**Mrs GVE Havenhand**
*Member, Rail Users Consultative Committee for Midlands*

**David Hawker**
*Head of National Curriculum & Assessment, Qualifications & Curriculum Authority*

**Graham Hawker**
*Member of Board, Welsh Development Agency*
Hyder, Welsh Water, SWALEC, Business in the Community, Water Training International.

**Mrs Gwyneth Hawkes**
*Computer Services Manager, Welsh National Board for Nursing, Midwifery & Health Visiting*

**Prof AD Hawkins**
*Chief Executive, Fisheries Research Services*

**Ms Barbara Hawkins**
*Member, North Eastern Consumers' Committee, Office of Electricity Regulation*

**Jeff Hawkins**
*Implementation Director, New Millenium Experience Co Ltd*
Former Consulting Director, Sema Group and Partner, PA Consulting Group.

**Nigel Hawkins**
*Member, North of Scotland Water Authority*
Chairman, Prospect PR. Principal founder and director, John Muir Trust.

Director, JMT Trading Company, Knoydart Foundation; Discovery FM. President, Dundee & Tayside Chamber of Commerce & Industry.

**Prof DL Hawskworth**
*Member of Council, English Nature*
Director, International Mycological Institute. President, International Union of Biological Sciences. Chairman, Institute of Biology, Biodiversity Committee. Visiting Professor of Botany, University of Reading. Visiting Professor of Biology, University of Kent. Visiting Professor of Mycology, Royal Holloway, University of London.

**Alison Hawthorne**
*Finance & Administration Officer, General Consumer Council for Northern Ireland*

**Drusilla Hawthorne**
*Senior Complaints Officer, Fair Employment Commission for Northern Ireland*

**Bill Hay**
*Director of Audit Services, The Accounts Commission for Scotland*

**Charles F Hay**
*Member of Council, Post Office Users' Council for Wales*
Secretary, Montgomeryshire & Powys TUC.

**Elizabeth Hay**
*Member, East Areas Board, Scottish Natural Heritage*

**Leonard Hay**
*Secretary, Alcohol Education & Research Council*

**Miss M Hay**
*Departmental Planning Division, Inland Revenue*

**Malcolm Hay**
*Manager, Stornoway Airport, Highlands & Islands Airports*

**Dr RKM Hay**
*Director, Scottish Agricultural Science Agency*

**WF Hay CBE**
*Commissioner, Northern Lighthouse Board*

**Paula Hay-Plumb**
*Managing Director (Operations), English Partnerships*

**John Hayes CBE**
*Chairman, Occupational Pensions Regulatory Authority*
Solicitor. Previously Secretary General of the Law Society. Former Chief Executive of Warwickshire County Council.

**Tom Hayes**
*Regional Office, West Midlands, NHS Estates*

**Carolyn Hayman**
*Member, Commonwealth Development Corporation*
*Member, Industrial Research & Technology Unit*
Investor in young technology companies. Chairman, Atraverda Chief Executive, Foyer Federation for Youth. Executive Director, Rutherford Ventures.

**Lieutenant General Sir Robert Hayman-Joyce**
*Member of Board, Defence Evaluation & Research Agency*
DCDP (Operations).

**L Haynes**
*Chief Executive, Highways Agency*

**Stuart Haynes**
*Director Geographic Information, Military Survey*

**Prof Josephine A Haythornthwaite**
*Trustee, National Library of Scotland*

**James Hayward**
*Member, Ofwat Eastern Customer Service Committee*

**John Hayzelden**
*Member, Ofwat Thames Customer Service Committee*

**John Hazlewood CBE**
*Member of Board, Investors in People UK*
Former General Manager, Birds Eye Wall's, Gloucester.

**Supt GE Heal**
*OCU, Devonport, Ministry of Defence Police*

**John Healey**
*Member, Yorkshire Consumers' Committee, Office of Electricity Regulation*

**Andy Healy**
*Member of Board, Waltham Forest Housing Action Trust*
Tenant Board Member for Oliver Close Estate. Site negotiator.

**Jane Heaney**
*Member, Scottish Sports Council*

**Jenny Heap**
*General Manager, English Nature*

**Dr Michael Heap**
*Director of Water Quality, East of Scotland Water Authority*

**Roy Heape**
*Non-Executive Director, National Savings*

**Colonel Shane Hearn**
*Head of Corporate Strategy, Army Training & Recruitment Agency*

**Sir Edward Heath KG MBE MP**
*Vice President, The Great Britain-China Centre*
Former Prime Minister.

**MG Heath**
*Operations & Services Director, LTB, London Transport*

**Frances Heaton**
*Member of Court, Bank of England*
Director, Lazard Brothers & Co.

**John Heaton**
*Chief Executive, Horserace Totalisator Board*
Solicitor. Joined Tote in 1983 as Board Secretary.

**Diane Hebb**
*Senior Development Officer, Arts Council of Wales*

**Max Hebditch**
*Director, Museum of London*

**Elspeth Hector**
*Head of Libraries and Archive, National Gallery*

**Dave Heddon**
*Regional Director, Yorkshire, English Sports Council*

**Bill Hedley**
*Personnel Director, Defence Evaluation & Research Agency*

**P Hedley**
*Operations Director, Driving Standards Agency*

**Philip Hedley**
*Trustee, Geffrye Museum*

**C Hegarty**
*District Inspector, Foyle Fisheries Commission*

**Ms Hilary Heilbron QC**
*Member, Marshall Aid Commemoration Commission*

**Sir Terence Heiser GCB**
*Trustee, Victoria & Albert Museum*

**Nick Helbren**
*CIS, Defence Evaluation & Research Agency*

**TG Heller**
*Company Secretary & Director of Finance & Administration, Horticulture Research International*

**Mrs AE Hemingway**
*Member of Advisory Board, Driver & Vehicle Licensing Agency*
Head of Sales (Home Energy) British Gas Trading.

**S Heminsley**
*Business Development & Support Director/ Deputy Chief Executive, Child Support Agency*

**Dr John Hemming CMG**
*Member of Board, British Council*
Former Director and Secretary Royal Geographical Society.

**Fred Hempton**
*Director of Administration, Rate Collection Agency*

**Gillian Henchley**
*Head of Personnel, Victoria & Albert Museum*

**Bernard Henderson CBE**
*Chairman, British Waterways*
Formerly Chairman of Anglian Water plc and Director, Water Research Centre.

**Charles Henderson CB**
*Member, Monopolies & Mergers Commission*
Former Civil Servant.

**Sir Denys Henderson**
*Trustee, Natural History Museum*

**GP Henderson OBE**
*Member of Board, Construction Industry Training Board*
Transport & General Workers Union.

**Gavin Henderson**
*Member, The Arts Council of England*
Principal, Trinity College of Music. Artistic Director, Dartington International Summer School. Former Director, Brighton Festival. Former Chief Executive, the Philharmonia. Chairman, British Arts Festivals Association. Vice-President, European Festivals Association. President, National Piers Society. Governor, University of Brighton and Chethams School, Manchester. Chairman, Arts

**Commodore Iain Henderson CBE**
*Naval Base Commander (Portsmouth), Naval Bases & Supply Agency*
Ex-officio Trustee, Royal Naval Museum

**Ian Henderson**
*Chief Executive, Northern Ireland Tourist Board*

**Jim Henderson**
*Companies House Edinburgh, Companies House*

**Prof P Henderson**
*Director of Science, Natural History Museum*

**Wesley Henderson**
*Consumer Affairs Officer - Research, General Consumer Council for Northern Ireland*

**Group Captain I F Hendley**
*Director, Armed Forces Personnel Administration Agency*

**Mrs Lorna Hendrie**
*Careers and CATCH Manager, National Board for Nursing, Midwifery & Health Visiting for Scotland*

**Michael Hendy**
*Member, Ofwat South West Customer Service Committee*

**Gerard Henry**
*Area Manager, Scottish Natural Heritage*

**Martin Henry**
*Member of Board, Investors in People UK*
Chairman, Lastolite.

**Paul Hensby**
*Director of Communications, National Lottery Charities Board*
Formerly Head of Press & Public Affairs Local Government Management Board.

**Ms Patricia Henton**
*Director of Environmental Strategy, Scottish Environment Protection Agency*

**Gary R Hepburn**
*Member, Post Office Users' National Council*
Safety & Security Officer, Procord, Winfrith Technology Centre. Former, Quality & Computer Systems Manager, AEA Technology EPM. Secretary, Weymouth & Portland POAC and TAC. Member, Wessex Occupational Safety Association. Trustee, Weymouth Town Charities.

**Prof Stephen Heppell**
*Governor, Scottish Council for Educational Technology*
Anglia Polytechnic University.

**Strachan Heppell CB**
*Commissioner, Broadcasting Standards Commission*
Former Deputy Secretary, Department of Health. Chairman, Management Board, European Medicines Evaluation Agency. Chairman, Family Fund Trust. Visiting Fellow, LSE.

**Brenda Herbert**
*Trustee, Geffrye Museum*
Co-founder, The Herbert Press.

**Michael Herbert CBE**
*Member of Board of Trustees, Historic Royal Palaces*
Former Chairman & Chief Executive, Madame Tussauds Group. Appointed by the Secretary of State.

**Robin AE Herbert CBE**
*Chairman, Royal Botanic Gardens Kew Member, Royal Parks Agency*
Former President, Royal Horticultural Society.

**Stephen Herbert**
*Head of Technical Services, BFI On The South Bank*

**Bernard Herdan**
*Chief Executive, Driving Standards Agency*

**MJ Heritage-Owen**
*Director, RAF MGDA Finance & Plans, RAF Maintenance Group Defence Agency*
*Member of Advisory Board, Defence Bills Agency*

**Dawn Herlihy**
*Human Resources, UK Sports Council*

**Sir Michael Heron**
*Chairman, Post Office*

**Robin Heron**
*Member Advisory Board, NHS Pensions Agency*
NHS Executive.

**Anthony Herron**
*Finance Director, Civil Aviation Authority*
Former Corporate Finance Partner, Touche Ross & Co. NATS Board Member. Non-Executive Director of one public and three private companies.

**John Hertrich**
*Subject Adviser, English, Office for Standards in Education*

**David Heseldin**
*Member, Central Rail Users Consultative Committee*
Head of Business School, York College of Further & Higher Education. Former member, RUCC for North Eastern England.

**Mrs Anne Heseltine**
*Trustee, Victoria & Albert Museum*

**Mrs Michael Heseltine**
*Trustee, Imperial War Museum*

**The Rt Hon Michael Heseltine MP**
*Member, Millennium Commission*
Former Deputy Prime Minister.

**E Hesketh**
*Managing Director (Group Operations), Northern Ireland Transport Holding Company*

**Nick Hetherington**
*Business Director - Arable, Coffee & Rubber, Commonwealth Development Corporation*

**Paul Hetherington**
*Member, Ofwat Customer Service Committee for Wales*

**Cllr Alastair Hewat OBE**
*Member of Board, Scottish Environment Protection Agency*

**Michael Hewitson**
*Secretary, Rail Users Consultative Committee for Southern England*

**D Hewitt**
*Trade Union Member, Engineering Construction Industry Training Board*
National Secretary, GMB-TCS

**PC Hewlett**
*Director, British Board of Agrément*

**Peter Hewitt**
*Secretary-General, The Arts Council of England*

**G Hextall**
*Customer Director, Information Technology Services Agency*

**David Heyhoe**
*Owner, Defence Bills Agency*
*Chairman, Defence Analytical Services Agency*
Assistant Under Secretary of State (General Finance).

**Angela Heylin OBE**
*Member of Board of Trustees, Historic Royal Palaces*
Chairman, Charles Barker. Appointed by the Secretary of State.

**DG Heywood**
*Chairman, Remploy*
Chairman, QS Holdings and Nestor Healthcare. Formerly Deputy Chairmanm, British-American Tobacco Company.

**Dr RB Heywood**
*Director, British Antarctic Survey*

**Geoffrey Hibbert**
*Member, Ofwat South West Customer Service Committee*

**Ms Kristyne Hibbert**
*Member, London Consumers' Committee, Office of Electricity Regulation*

**Cdre Richard Hibbert**
*Director Naval Manning, Naval Manning Agency*

**Stephen Hickey**
*Chief Executive, Civil Service College*

**Mrs Susan Hickie**
*Professional Officer (Community Health Care), National Board for Nursing, Midwifery & Health Visiting for Scotland*

**Nicola Hickman**
*Projects Assistant, The Britain-Russia Centre*

**Barbara Hicks**
*Member, National Consumer Council*

**Dr CP Hicks**
*Member, Natural Environment Research Council*
Department of Trade and Industry

**Alan Higgins OstJ OBE**
*Member of Wales Committee, National Lottery Charities Board*
Retired teacher and HM Inspector of Schools. President, Youth Events Wales. Chair, Welsh Association of Youth Clubs. Vice President, Scout Association. Vice President, YMCA (Wales). Hon Research Fellow, University of Wales College, Cardiff.

**Prof Chris Higgins**
*Member, Biotechnology & Biological Sciences Research Council*

**Prof Julia Higgins CBE**
*Member, Council for the Central Laboratory of the Research Councils Member of Council, Engineering & Physical Sciences Research Council*
Imperial College, London.

**Linda Higgins**
*Incorporations & Changes of Name, Companies House*

**Patrick Higgins**
*Observer, Northern Ireland Museums' Council*
Arts, Libraries & Museums Branch, Department of Education (NI).

**Mrs Anita Higham**
*Member, National Museum of Science & Industry*

**Bob Hilborn**
*Member, Horticultural Development Council*
Chief Food Technologist, J Sainsbury. Member, Council of NIAB.

**S Hilditch MBE**
*Vice-Chairman, Sports Council for Northern Ireland*

**Dr BJ Hill**
*Chair, Aquaculture & Health Group, Centre for Environment, Fisheries & Aquaculture Science*

**Bob Hill**
*Verification Trader Visits, Intervention Board*

**Dermod Hill**
*Assistant Director (Information), Office of Fair Trading*

**Rear Admiral JR Hill**
*Representative Trustee, Royal Naval Museum*
The Society for Nautical Research.

**Jim Hill**
*Facilities & Procurement, Central Science Laboratory*
Architect. Worked in MAFF's Building and Estates Management Division.

**Dr John Hill**
*Governor, British Film Institute*

**Olive Hill**
*Manager North Eastern Regional Office, Local Enterprise Development Unit*

**Dr SJ Hill**
*Chief Land Registrar & Chief Executive, HM Land Registry*

**Brig SP Hill OBE**
*Director Naval Recruiting, Naval Recruiting & Training Agency*

**SR Hill**
*Chief Executive, Naval Aircraft Repair Organisation*

**Prof Stephen Hill**
*Plant Health, Central Science Laboratory*
Formerly responsible for Plant Pathology at Plant Pathology Laboratory. Previously National ADAS specialist in plant virology working at Cambridge, Jersey and Bristol. Currently visiting Professor at Leeds University.

**Paul Hill-Tout**
*Regional Director, South of Scotland, Forest Enterprise*

**Sir Russell Hillhouse KCB**
*Member of College Advisory Council, Civil Service College*
Permanent Under Secretary, Scottish Office.

**Richard Hillier**
*Director, Resources & Planning Directorate, The Health & Safety Executive*

**Robert Hillier**
*Member, Horticultural Development Council*
Managing Director, Hillier Nurseries.

**Stephen Hillier**
*Head of Corporate Management, Teacher Training Agency*

**Prof JR Hillman**
*Director, Scottish Crop Research Institute*

**WEC Hillman**
*Managing Director, Victoria Coach Station, London Transport*

**Arthur Hills**
*Member, South Western Consumers' Committee, Office of Electricity Regulation*

**John Hills**
*Member, Ofwat Thames Customer Service Committee*

**Roger Hills**
*Regulatory Director, Occupational Pensions Regulatory Authority*

**Lieutenant Colonel Charles Hillyer**
*Head of Policy Strategy & BE, Defence Postal & Courier Services Agency*

**Brian Hilton CB**
*Chairman of Steering Board, Companies House*
*Chairman, Insolvency Service*
*Chairman of Steering Board, Patent Office*
*Chairman, Employment Tribunals Service*
DTI Director-General, Corporate & Consumer Affairs.

**BJ Hinde OBE**
*Director, Scientific Services, Natural Environment Research Council*

**Mrs Jennie Hinton**
*Member, Rail Users Consultative Committee for Southern England*

**Brian Hirst**
*Chief Executive, Defence Estates Organisation*

**Neil Hirst**
*Non-Executive Director, UK Atomic Energy Authority*
Head, Nuclear Industries Directorate, Department of Trade & Industry.

**Richard Hirst**
*Head of Finance & Common Services Division, Further Education Funding Council for Wales & Higher Education Funding Council for Wales*

**Robert Hiscox**
*Commissioner, Museums & Galleries Commission*
Chairman, Hiscox. Member, Corporate Development Committee, National Portrait Gallery. Former member, Council of the Friends of the Tate Gallery.

**Graham Hitchen**
*Director, Policy, Research & Planning, The Arts Council of England*

**Keith Hitchings**
*Member, Post Office Users' National Council*
Transport Manager. Chairman, Mail Order Traders' Transport Committee. Member, Merseyside POAC and TAC.

**Isabel Hitchman**
*Senior Visual Arts & Craft Officer, Arts Council of Wales*

**HS Hoare**
*Chief Executive, Education Assets Board*

**Cdr DA Hobbs MBE**
*Deputy Director/Curator, Fleet Air Arm Museum*

**P Hobbs**
*Non-executive Director, Forensic Science Service*
Former Group Personnel Director, Wellcome.

**Penny Hobbs**
*Head of Administration, Scottish Water & Sewerage Customers Council*

**Margaret Hobrough OBE**
*Member, The Further Education Funding Council*
Principal, Godalming Sixth Form College.

**Mike Hockey**
*Employer member, Engineering Construction Industry Training Board*

**Mrs Elizabeth Hodder**
*Deputy Chairwoman, Equal Opportunities Commission*
*Commissioner, Meat & Livestock Commission*
Member, Lifespan Healthcare NHS Trust, Chair, Consumers' Committee, Meat Livestock Commission.
Founder and Honorary President, National Stepfamily Association. Consumer Representative on number of bodies, including Building Societies Ombudsman Council, Code of Banking Practice Review Committee, Eastern Region Milk & Dairies Tribunal and Data Protection Tribunal.

**John Hodder**
*Sector Director - Minerals, Oils & Gas, Commonwealth Development Corporation*

**Henry Hodge OBE**
*Deputy Chairman, Legal Aid Board*
Solicitor. Senior partner, Hodge Jones & Allen. A Recorder, South Eastern Circuit. Former Deputy Vice-President, Law Society. Vice Chairman, Society of Labour Lawyers. Governor, College of Law and Middlesex University.

**Simon Hodge**
*Head of Branch, Woodland Ecology, Forest Research*

**Mrs Mary Hodgeon**
*Member, Welsh National Board for Nursing, Midwifery & Health Visiting*
Director of Nursing & Human Resources, Pembrokeshire NHS Trust.

**Lew Hodges**
*Director of Corporate Services, UK Sports Council*

**Christine Hodgson**
*Member, London Regional Passengers Committee*

**KS Hodgson OBE**
*Head, The Stamp Office, Inland Revenue*

**MJ Hodgson**
*Head, Inland Revenue East, Inland Revenue*

**Capt NR Hodgson**
*Director Naval Reseves, Naval Recruiting & Training Agency*

**Patricia Hodgson CBE**
*Member, Monopolies & Mergers Commission*
*Director of Policy & Planning, British Broadcasting Corporation*
Associate Fellow, Newnham College.
Member, Advisory Body, Judge Institute.

**Prof R Hodgson**
*Scientific Officer, Alcohol Education & Research Council*

**Simon Hodgson**
*Regional Manager, Rural Development Commission*

**Keith Hodinott**
*Transport & Engineering, Highlands & Islands Airports*

**Clive Hodson CBE**
*Chairman, Victoria Coach Station, Managing Director, LTB, Member, LT Property Board*
*London Transport*

**Denys Hodson CBE**
*Observer, The Arts Council of England*

**Brigadier MGR Hodson**
*Member, Logistic Information Systems Agency*
D Log Sp Pol.

**Peter Hodson**
*Member of Advisory Board, Disposal Sales Agency*
Logistic Support and Policy DLSP

**Mrs Catherine Hoey**
*Member, Ofwat Southern Customer Service Committee*

**Michael Hoffman**
*Non-Executive Director, Naval Manning Agency*

**B Hogan**
*Junior Commissioner, Foyle Fisheries Commission*

**CT Hogg MBE JP**
*Member of Board, Probation Board for Northern Ireland*

**Charles A Hogg JP**
*Chairman, Rail Users Consultative Committee for Wales*
*Member, Central Rail Users Consultative Committee*
President, Wrexham Association of Local Councils. Past Director, North East Wales Council of Voluntary Organisations.

**George Hogg**
*Area Manager, Scottish Natural Heritage*

**JD Hogg**
*Chief Architect, Cadw*

**Mitchell Hogg**
*Member, The Further Education Funding Council*
Partner, Financial Services Audit & Investigation Division, Coopers & Lybrand.

**Isobel Holbourn**
*Member, North Areas Board, Scottish Natural Heritage*

**John Holden**
*Chief Executive, Companies House*

**Lynn Holden**
*Business Development Manager, War Pensions Agency*

**Sir Martin Holdgate**
*Trustee, National Heritage Memorial Fund*

**Lady Carol Holland MBE**
*Member, Tate Gallery*

**William Holland**
*Member, Ofwat Thames Customer Service Committee*

**David Holliday**
*Member, Ofwat Northumbria Customer Service Committee*

**Nick Holliday**
*Regional Officer, Countryside Commission*

**Lord Holme of Cheltenham CBE**
*Member, Academic Council, Wilton Park Executive Agency*

**Anna Holmes**
*Senior Officer, Dance & Drama, Arts Council of Wales*

**Ian Holmes**
*Finance, National Lottery, UK Sports Council*

**John Holmes**
*Regional Office, Anglia & Oxford, NHS Estates*

**Miss Karen Holmes**
*Member, Ofwat Yorkshire Customer Service Committee*

**MG Holmes**
*Director, Horticulture Research International*

**Margaret Holmes**
*Member, Horticultural Development Council*
District Officer, Transport & General Workers Union based in Norwich.

**Peter Holmes**
*Observer, Higher Education Funding Council for England*
Under Secretary, Department of Education Northern Ireland.

**Roger Holmes**
*Deputy Master & Comptroller (Chief Executive), Royal Mint*

**Tony Holmstrom**
*Director of Support Services, The Sports Council for Wales*

**Michael Holroyd**
*Chairman, Registrar of Public Lending Right*
Author.

**Andy Holt**
*Member, London Regional Passengers Committee*

**Thelma Holt CBE**
*Member, The Arts Council of England*
Founder, Open Space Theatre. Former
Director, The Round House. Former
Head of Touring & Commercial
Exploitation, Royal National Theatre.
Member, Board of Governors, Middlesex
University.

**Tim Holt**
*Director, Office for National Statistics*

**DV Hone**
*Director of Finance, Commission for the
New Towns*

**David Honeyman**
*Member, South Wales Consumers'
Committee, Office of Electricity
Regulation*

**Mrs JM Honisett**
*Member, Rail Users Consultative
Committee for Eastern England*

**AJ Hood**
*Head of Presentation, Cadw*

**Geoff Hoon MP**
*Governor, British Film Institute*

**Miss Angela Hooper CBE**
*Chairman, Rail Users Consultative
Committee for Southern England
Member, Central Rail Users Consultative
Committee*
Consumer protection work in the public
sector and Local Government.

**Brian Hooper**
*Head of Finance, Economic & Social
Research Council*

**Ian Hooper**
*Depute Director (Resources) & Project
Director, Museum of Scotland, National
Museums of Scotland*

**Dr Eilean Hooper-Greenhill**
*Director & Trustee, Horniman Museum*

**John Hooson**
*Member, Merseyside & North Wales
Consumers' Committee, Office of
Electricity Regulation*

**Ann Hope**
*Deputy Chair, Equal Opportunities
Commission for Northern Ireland*
Advisory Services Officer, Irish Congress
of Trade Unions.

**Elizabeth Hope**
*Prosecuting Solicitor, Companies House*

**NM Hope**
*Member, SACOT, Scottish Advisory
Committee on Telecommunications*
Retired telecommunications engineer.

**Bill Hopkin**
*Chief Land Agent, English Nature*

**AS Hopkins CBE**
*Chairman, Laganside Corporation*
Senior Partner - Deloitte & Touche.

**Anne Hopkins**
*Professional Adviser, General & Adult
Nursing, Welsh National Board for
Nursing, Midwifery & Health Visiting*

**Miss Helen Hopkins**
*Member, Ofwat Eastern Customer
Service Committee*

**K Hopkins**
*Member of Governing Body, Scottish
Crop Research Institute*
Partner, The Scottish Partnership.
Treasurer, District 1010 of Rotary.
Treasurer, Strathmore Cricket Club.
Chairman, Childlink Scotland.

**Sir Michael Hopkins CBE**
*Trustee, British Museum*

**Nic Hopkins**
*IT Director, Central Computer &
Telecommunications Agency*

**Phil Hopkins**
*Special Projects, Companies House*

**T Hopkins**
*Deputy Chairman, Probation Board for
Northern Ireland*

**Tony Hopkins CBE**
*Member, Northern Ireland Tourist Board*
Formerly chief executive, Industrial
Development Board. Managing Partner,
Deloitte & Touche. Regional chairman,
Institute of Management. Deputy
Chairman, Laganside Corporation.
Member of Board, Ulster Business
School.

**WA Hopkins**
*Photogrammetric Surveys, Ordnance
Survey of Northern Ireland*

**N Hopkinson**
*Senior Associate Director, Wilton Park
Executive Agency*

**Ms Jennifer Hopper**
*Member, North Eastern Consumers'
Committee, Office of Electricity
Regulation*

**Robert Hopper**
*Member, Tate Gallery*

**Mererid Hopwood**
*Head of Mid & West Wales Office/
Planning Officer, Arts Council of Wales*

**Dr SE Hopwood**
*Member, Post Office Users' Council for
Scotland*
Psychiatrist, Dundee Healthcare NHS
Trust. Honorary Lecturer, University of
Dundee. Chairman, Gowrie Housing
Association. Member, Tayside Posts &
Telecommunications Advisory
Committees.

**Brian Hord**
*Member, London Regional Passengers
Committee*

**The Rt Hon Sir Peter Hordern MP**
*Board Member, The British Library*

**Philip Horemans**
*Food from Britain (Belgium) bvba*

**Graham Horgan**
*Head, Biomathematics & Statistics
Scotland (Bio SS), Rowett Research
Institute*

**Hilary Horley**
*Deputy Manager, Gas Consumers'
Council*

**Mrs V Horman JP**
*Member, Parole Board*

**Barbara LH Horn**
*Head, Private Records, Scottish Record
Office*

**Don Horn**
*Controller of Administration, Independent
Television Commission*

**DJ Hornby**
*Director of Engineering, LUL, London
Transport*

**Bob Horner**
*Acting Director of Consultancy &
Business Development, NHS Estates*

**Philip Horner**
*Chief Executive, The Government
Property Lawyers*

**Michael Horniman**
*Director & Trustee, Horniman Museum*

**Patrick Hornor**
*Member, Ofwat Northumbria Customer
Service Committee*

**Margaret Hornsby**
*Programme Support, Companies House*

**Timothy Hornsby**
*Chief Executive, National Lottery
Charities Board*
Former Chief Executive, Royal Borough
of Kingston upon Thames Previously
Director General, Nature Conservancy
Council and several posts in the Treasury
and Department of Environment.

**G Horrocks CBE JP**
*Deputy Chairman, Rail Users
Consultative Committee for the Midlands*

**Alison Horsburgh**
*Head, Preservation Services, Scottish
Record Office*

**Brigadier C Horsefall**
*Member of Advisory Board, Service
Children's Education*
Comd ETS Land Command.

**David Horton**
*Member, Ofwat Thames Customer
Service Committee*

**Geoffrey Horton**
*Director, Consumer Affairs, Office of Fair
Trading*

**John Horton**
*Licensing Policy, Veterinary Medicines
Directorate*

**Sir Robert B Horton**
*Vice President, Community Development
Foundation*

**Trevor J Horton**
*Director of External & Corporate
Services, Driver & Vehicle Licensing
Agency*

# Q&Q

**Dr JW Horwood**
*Deputy Chief Executive, Centre for Environment, Fisheries & Aquaculture Science*

**Desmond Hosken**
*Member, Tate Gallery*

**B Hoskin**
*Member of Ownership Board, Veterinary Laboratories Agency*
External Member.

**Sir Joseph Hotung**
*Trustee, British Museum*

**John Hougham CBE**
*Chairman, Advisory, Conciliation & Arbitration Service*

**Pete Houghton**
*Manager, Barra, Islay & Tiree Airports, Highlands & Islands Airports*

**Lord Houghton of Sowerby**
*President, Community Development Foundation*

**Arthur Houldershaw**
*Head of Administration & Finance, Wallace Collection*

**Michael Houlihan**
*Museum Director, Horniman Museum*

**GV Houlston KstG**
*Member, Cardiff Bay Development Corporation*
Councillor, Cardiff County Council.

**David Houltby**
*Director of Finance & Administration, Liverpool Housing Action Trust*

**GAL House**
*Head of Public Services, British Museum*

**Andrew Housley**
*Manager for the Midlands & Wales, Commission for Racial Equality*

**D Houston**
*Member of Board, Fisheries Conservancy Board for Northern Ireland Junior Commissioner, Foyle Fisheries Commission*
Representative of DANI.

**Paul A Houston**
*Director of Finance, Driver & Vehicle Licensing Agency*

**Chris Howard**
*Director, Financial Management & Information Management Services, British Tourist Authority & English Tourist Board*

**Claire L Howard**
*Assistant to the Director, Macaulay Land Use Research Institute*

**Dr DJ Howard**
*Commissioner, Royal Commission on Ancient & Historical Monuments of Scotland*

**David Howard**
*Director Excise and Central Policy, HM Customs & Excise*

**Clive Howard-Luck**
*Member, Ofwat Southern Customer Service Committee*

**Bill Howatson**
*Member, East Areas Board, Scottish Natural Heritage Member, Scottish Water & Sewerage Customers Council*

**Alan Howden**
*Governor, British Film Institute*

**Dr J Howe**
*Member, Northern Ireland Council for Postgraduate Medical & Dental Education*
Appointed by DHSS.

**John Howe**
*Member of Board, Defence Evaluation & Research Agency*
DCDP (Support).

**Lady Howe**
*Chairman, Broadcasting Standards Commission*
Former Chairman, Broadcasting Standards Council. Chairman, BOC Foundation for the Environment. Board Member, Business in the Community. Chair Opportunity 2000. Non-Executive Director, Kingfisher Group. President, UK Committee of UNICEF.

**Lord Howe of Aberavon PC QC**
*President, The Great Britain-China Centre*
Former Secretary of State for Foreign & Commonwealth Affairs.

**Martin Howe CB**
*Deputy Director General, Office of Fair Trading*

**Mrs NH Howe**
*Member of Board, Queen Victoria School*

**John Howell**
*Member, South Wales Consumers' Committee, Office of Electricity Regulation*

**Gwyn Howells**
*Marketing Director, Meat & Livestock Commission*

**Tom J Howie**
*Member, Scottish Agricultural Wages Board*
Employers' representative member nominated by the National Farmers' Union of Scotland and the Scottish Landowners' Federation.

**Trevor Howitt**
*Director, Law Enforcement Business, Forensic Science Service*

**Dr Eamonn Hoxey**
*Device Technology & Safety, Medical Devices Agency*

**Bill Hoy**
*Head of Public Affairs, Scottish Homes*

**Caryl Hubbard**
*Trustee, National Heritage Memorial Fund*

**Charles Hubbard**
*Member of Board, Liverpool Housing Action Trust*
Chartered Surveyor. Partner, Edmund Kirby. Professor of Surveying, Liverpool John Moores University. Chairman, RICS Education and Membership Committee. Past Chairman, Liverpool Everyman Theatre.

**John Hubbard**
*Member, Tate Gallery*

**Miss S Hubbard**
*Member, Parole Board*

**Mrs Ann Hudson**
*Member, Ofwat Wessex Customer Service Committee*

**Dennis Hudson**
*Member, Ofwat Northumbria Customer Service Committee*

**Graham Hudson**
*Group General Manager, Textile, Remploy*

**Michael Huebner CB**
*Chief Executive, The Court Service*

**Dafydd Hughes**
*Member of Committee, Rail Users Consultative Committee for Wales*
Chartered Town Planner. Chief Executive, Teledwyr Annibynnol Cymru (Welsh Independent Producers). Governor, Ysgol David Hughes. Member of Council, University of Wales, Bangor.

**Cllr Derlwyn Hughes**
*Member of Council, The Sports Council for Wales*

**J Hughes**
*Chairman, RFDC, The Environment Agency*

**J Arfon Hughes**
*Member, National Library of Wales*

**JJ Hughes**
*LT Director - Group Financial Planning & Control, London Transport*

**John Hughes**
*Part-time Member, British Railways Board*
Consultant to Trade Union Research Unit. Former Principal, Ruskin College, Oxford.

**Miss Katherine Hughes**
*Member, National Library of Wales*
Appointed by the Secretary of State for Wales

**Leslie Hughes**
*Assistant Commissioner, Finance, Policy & Planning Division, Valuation & Lands Agency*

**Luke Hughes**
*Member of Council, Crafts Council*
Furniture maker and designer.

**Dr Marion Hughes**
*Area Manager, Scottish Natural Heritage*

**Dr Medwin Hughes**
*Member of Board, Welsh Language Board*

Assistant Principal, Trinity College, Carmarthen.

**Michael Hughes**
*Member of Council, Economic & Social Research Council*
Managing Director, BZW Economics & Strategy.

**Peter Hughes**
*Head Curator, Wallace Collection*

**Philip Hughes CBE**
*Chairman, National Gallery*

**RSA Hughes**
*Finance, Personnel & Administration, Ordnance Survey of Northern Ireland*

**RW Hughes**
*Director of Policy & Administration, Cadw*

**Richard Hughes**
*Manager, Investment Capital Funds, Commonwealth Development Corporation*

**Ron Hughes**
*Non-Executive Director, UK Hydrographic Office*

**SR Hughes**
*Head, Archaeology, Royal Commission on Ancient & Historical Monuments in Wales*

**Dr Tim Hughes**
*Member, Ofwat Customer Service Committee for Wales*

**Dr Tony Hughes**
*Director Engineering & Science, Engineering & Physical Sciences Research Council*

**Clive Hulls**
*Member, Ofwat Central Customer Service Committee*

**Janet Humble OBE**
*Member, National Consumer Council*

**Ian Hume**
*Member of Committee, Rail Users Consultative Committee for Wales*
Chief Executive, Welsh Joint Education Committee.

**John Hume**
*Chief Inspector of Historic Buildings, Historic Scotland*

**Dr KW Humphreys CBE**
*Member, Biotechnology & Biological Sciences Research Council*
Former Chairman & Managing Director, Rhone Poulenc. Consultant. Former Managing Director, Ciba-Geigy (UK).

**BJ Hunt OBE**
*Director, ABRO Bovington, Army Base Repair Organisation*

**Ms J Hunt**
*Member of College Advisory Council, Civil Service College*
Chief Executive, Local Government Management Unit.

**Prof J Hunt**
*Member of College Advisory Council, Civil Service College*
Professor and Head of Organisational Behaviour at London Business School.

**Prof JCR Hunt**
*Member, Natural Environment Research Council*
Meteorological Office.

**Mrs Lorena Hunt**
*Member, Ofwat North West Customer Service Committee*

**Sir Alistair Hunter KCMG**
*Director & Trustee, Horniman Museum*

**Dr CC Hunter**
*Member, Parole Board*

**Dr James Hunter**
*Member, Scottish Tourist Board*
*Chairman, Skye & Lochalsh Enterprise*
*Member, North Areas Board, Scottish Natural Heritage*
Member Forestry Commission's Advisory Panel and University of the Highlands & Islands steering group. Founding Director, Scottish Crofters Union.

**Jane Hunter**
*Acting Director of Driver Licensing, Driver & Vehicle Licensing Northern Ireland*

**Noel Hunter**
*Member, National Consumer Council*

**P Hunter**
*Advisor to the Board, Laganside Corporation*
Architectural Advisor.

**Dr Philip Hunter**
*Board Member, Qualifications & Curriculum Authority*
Chief Education Officer, Staffordshire County Council.

**Dr Stephen Hunter**
*Conservation & Environment Protection, Central Science Laboratory*
Carried out seabird research with British Antarctic Survey and University of Cape Town 1978 to 1987. Joined MAFF and then transferred to CSL.

**James Hunter Blair**
*Trustee, National Galleries of Scotland*

**Richard Hunting**
*Trustee, Geffrye Museum*
Former Master, Worshipful Company of Ironmongers. Chairman, Hunting. Presentation Governor, Christ's Hospital. Member of Council, Confederation of British Industry. Life member, Chelsea Society.

**John Huntley**
*Information and Support Services, Countryside Commission*

**Professor HE Huppert**
*Member, Natural Environment Research Council*
University of Cambridge

**RS Hurcombe**
*Head, Inland Revenue South West, Inland Revenue*

**Ben Hurren**
*Member of Museum Trust, Museum of Science & Industry Manchester*

**Dr Tess Hurson**
*Member, Arts Council of Northern Ireland*
Deputy to the Director, Queen's University at Armagh.

**P Hurst**
*Finance Director/Agency Secretary, Naval Recruiting & Training Agency*

**Felicity Huston**
*Member, General Consumer Council for Northern Ireland*
Partner, Huston & Co, Tax Consultants and Accountants, Belfast. Member, Post Office Users Council of Northern Ireland and Personal Investment Authority's Consumer Panel. Member of Board, Clifton House.

**Stella Hutcheson**
*Head of Legal & Property Division, Public Trust Office*

**Henry Hutchinson**
*Director, Central Laser Facility, Council for the Central Laboratory of the Research Councils*

**T Hutchinson**
*Financial Manager, Northern Ireland Council for Postgraduate Medical & Dental Education*

**Jinny Hutchison**
*Director of Strategy & Corporate Affairs, Scottish Prison Service*

**Sir Peter Hutchison Bt CBE**
*Vice Chairman, British Waterways*

**Deirdre Hutton**
*Vice Chairman, National Consumer Council*

**NJA Hutton**
*Member of Board, Investors in People UK*
Chairman & Chief Executive, Greenup & Thompson

**Ian Hyams**
*Head of Information Systems Division, The Court Service*

**J Hyde**
*Member, The British Library*
Confederation of British Industry.

**J Hyde**
*Senior Inspector, Operations, Gaming Board for Great Britain*

**Hamish Hyslop**
*Member, Parole Board for Scotland*

**David Hyslop OBE**
*Member, DIEL, Office of Telecommunications*
Former Director, Breakthrough Trust.

# I

**Dale Idiens**
*Depute Director (Collections) & Keeper of History & Applied Art, National Museums of Scotland*

**Eddie Idle**
*Director, English Nature*

**Dr Ken Ife**
*Trustee, Community Development Foundation*

**John Illenden**
*Member, London Regional Passengers Committee*

**Terry Illsley**
*Executive Secretary, Commonwealth Scholarship Commission*

**Sir Peter Imbert QPM**
*Member, Royal Parks Agency*
Retired Commissioner, Metropolitan Police.

**Edward Impey**
*Curator, Historic Royal Palaces*

**Field Marshall Lord Inge of Richmond GCB**
*Trustee, Royal Armouries*
*Member of Board of Trustees, Historic Royal Palaces*
Former Head of Armed Services. Appointed by Secretary of State.

**David Ingham**
*Legal Director, Office of Telecommunications*

**George Inglis**
*Director, Finance & Administration, Scottish Tourist Board*

**Amanda Ingram**
*Member, London Regional Passengers Committee*

**DS Ingram**
*Regius Keeper, Royal Botanic Garden Edinburgh*

**Sir Geoffrey Inkin OBE**
*Chairman, Cardiff Bay Development Corporation*
Land Authority for Wales. University of Wales, Cardiff.

**Dr Hugh Insley**
*Regional Director, Forest Enterprise*

**Dr Sue Ion**
*Member of Council, Particle Physics & Astronomy Research Council*
British Nuclear Fuels.

**Alton Irby III**
*Trustee, Victoria & Albert Museum*

**John Irish CBE**
*Member of Council, Food from Britain*

**Jane Irvine**
*Member, Rail Users Consultative Committee for Scotland*

**CC Irwin**
*Vice-Chairman, Rail Users Consultative Committee for Western England*

**GR Irwin**
*Member of Board, Laganside Corporation*
Chief Executive - Belfast Harbour Commissioners.

**JK Isaac**
*Non-Executive Director, LTB, London Transport*

**M Isaac**
*Operations Director, Child Support Agency*

**Michael Ive**
*Subject Adviser, Design & Technology, Office for Standards in Education*

# J

**Dorian Jabri**
*External Communications, Teacher Training Agency*

**Miss VAS Jack**
*Director of Personnel, North of Scotland Water Authority*

**RT Jackling CB CBE**
*Chairman, Ministry of Defence Police*
*Member, Met Office*
Second Permanent Under Secretary, MOD.

**Christie Jackson**
*Member, Rail Users Consultative Committee for North Western England*

**Miss HM Jackson**
*Director of Finance, HM Land Registry*

**Michael Jackson**
*Member of Steering Board, Companies House*
General Manager, Strategic Relationships, British Airways.

**Michael Jackson**
*Chief Executive & Director of Programmes, Channel Four Television Corporation*

**Mikie Jackson**
*Member, Employment Tribunals Service*
Chief Executive, Birmingham Midshires Building Society.

**Dr Paul Jackson**
*Product Development Manager, UK Ecolabelling Board*

**Paul Jackson**
*Regional Director, South & West, Meat Hygiene Service*

**RA Jackson**
*Non-Executive Director, Remploy*
Former Assistant General Secretary, Trades Union Congress. Member, Employment Appeals Tribunal.

**Robert Jackson**
*Finance Director, Queen Elizabeth II Conference Centre*

**Tessa Jackson**
*Member, Tate Gallery*

**Peter Jacob**
*Member of Management Board, The Court Service*
Director of Civil & Family Operations.

**Prof HS Jacobs**
*Member, National Biological Standards Board*

**Prof PA Jacobs**
*Member of Council, Medical Research Council*
Salisbury General Hospital.

**Sir Martin Jacomb**
*Chairman, British Council*
Chairman, Prudential Assurance Company.

**Arm Jaffray CB**
*Trustee, Royal Naval Museum*

**Sqn Ldr Bruce James**
*Manager & Deputy Keeper, Reserve Collection & Restoration Centre, Cardington, Royal Air Force Museum*

**Georgina James**
*Member, Equal Opportunities Commission*
Managing Director, de Ritter. Retail Chairwoman, British Chambers of Commerce. Member, European Commission Commerce Committee. Governor, Anglia Polytechnic University.

**Gill James**
*Secretary, Rail Users Consultative Committee for Midlands*

**Linda James**
*Governor, National Film & Television School*

**NW James**
*Assistant Keeper, The Royal Commission on Historical Manuscripts*

**Paul James**
*Director of Finance and Management Information, Defence Secondary Care Agency.*

**Ros James**
*Customer Accounts, Companies House*

**Prof Walter James**
*Trustee, Community Development Foundation*

**W Philip T James, CBE**
*Director, Rowett Research Institute*

**John Jameson OBE**
*Chairman, West of Scotland Water Authority*
Senior Partner, GM Thomson & Co. Convener, Dumfries & Galloway Regional Council and Vice President, Convention of Scottish Local Authorities (COSLA).

**Brian Jamieson**
*Company Secretary, Scottish Enterprise*

**Christine Janner-Burgess**
*Director Corporate Services, Central Computer & Telecommunications Agency*

**EF Jardine**
*Chief Executive, Northern Ireland Statistics & Research Agency*

**Dr Ian Jardine**
*Director of Strategy & Operations (East), Scottish Natural Heritage*

**Mrs J Jarvie**
*Marketing Officer, Royal Marines Museum*

**John F Jarvis CBE**
*Member of Board, British Tourist Authority*
Former Interim Chairman, ETB. Chairman & Chief Executive, Jarvis Hotels. Former Chairman & Chief Executive, Hilton International. Former Chairman & Chief Executive, Ladbroke Hotels, Holidays & Entertainments. Chairman, Prince's Trust.

**Peter Jarvis**
*Member, South Eastern Consumers' Committee, Office of Electricity Regulation*

**Dr Sarah Jarvis**
*GP Member, Medical Practices Committee*

**Jasnbir Jaspal**
*Member, Ofwat Central Customer Service Committee*

**Mohammad Javed**
*Member, Rail Users Consultative Committee for Wales*
Member, Industrial Tribunal, Cardiff. Chairman, New Employ, Wales. Chairman, Pakistan Welsh Association, Wales. Vice-President, Welsh Asians Council. Vice-Chairman, Wales Anti-Racist Alliance. Assessor appointed to sit with County Court Judges in Race Relations cases.

**Colin Jay**
*Commissioner, Meat & Livestock Commission*
Former Group Managing Director, C&T Harries (Calne) and Chief Executive, FMC. Consultant. Chairman, Pension Fund Trustees and Hillsdown Holdings.

**Rosemary Jay**
*Legal Director, Office of the Data Protection Registrar*

**M Jeans**
*Independent Business Advisor, The Planning Inspectorate*

**Dr R Jeffery**
*Non-Executive Director, LUL, London Transport*
Deputy Chairman, British Energy. Chairman & Chief Executive, Scottish Nuclear. Visiting Professor at Strathclyde University.

**Dr David Jefferys**
*Director of Licensing, Medicines Control Agency*

**AG Jeffries**
*Director, Horticulture Research International*

**Mrs A Jenkins**
*Member of Council, Council for Catholic Maintained Schools*
Parent Representative.

**Sir Brian Jenkins**
*Member of Board, Commission for the New Towns*
*Non-executive Director, New Millennium Experience Co Ltd*
Chairman, Woolwich. President, London Chamber of Commerce & Industry. Director, Automobile Association. Director, London First. Trustee, Charities Aid Foundation. Trustee, New Towns Pension Fund.

**David Jenkins MBE**
*Member, Monopolies & Mergers Commission*
General Secretary, Wales TUC. Member, Employment Appeals Tribunal.

**Gan Jenkins**
*Director Marine Engineering, Ships Support Agency*

**Mrs Gillian Jenkins**
*Member of Council, Ofwat Thames Customer Service Committee*

**Graham Jenkins**
*Director (IPPD), Patent Office*

**Graham Jenkins**
*Finance Director, Intervention Board*

**Gwyn Jenkins**
*Keeper of Manuscripts & Records, National Library of Wales*

**Surg Cdre I Jenkins**
*Comdt RDMC, Defence Medical Training Organisation*

**Mrs J Jenkins**
*Finance Controller, RAF Signals Engineering Establishment*

**J Jenkins**
*Head of Corporate Services, Cadw*

**Dr JG Jenkins**
*Member, Northern Ireland Council for Postgraduate Medical & Dental Education*
Nominated by Royal College of Physicians (London) Paediatric Division.

**Kate Jenkins**
*Member, Audit Commission*
Independent consultant. Governor, London School of Economics. Director, London & Manchester. Previously Head Efficiency Unit and Non-Executive Member, NHS Policy Board.

**Paul Jenkins**
*General Manager, Highlands & Islands Airports*

**Simon Jenkins**
*Member, Millennium Commission*
Former Editor of *The Times*. Former Deputy Chairman, English Heritage.

**Sandra Jenner**
*Director, Human Resources, Financial Services Authority*
Currently Head of Finance & Operational Services, PIA. Formerly Head of Personnel, PIA and FIMBRA.

**CB Jennings**
*Chief Executive & Director, Wilton Park Executive Agency*

**K Jennings**
*Commissioner, Duke of York's Royal Military School*
Nominated by Kent County Council.

**Dr J Jensen**
*Director of Geographic Information Systems & Development, Military Survey*

**James Jerram CBE**
*Vice-Chairman, British Railways Board*

**Sheriff Alexander Jessop**
*Member, The Scottish Legal Aid Board*
Former Procurator Fiscal for Glasgow. Sheriff of Grampian, Highland and Islands at Aberdeen.

**Bob Jewitt JP**
*Lay Member, Medical Practices Committee*
Former Chief Officer, Isle of Wight CHC.

**Sir Gordon Jewkes, KCMG**
*Member, Marshall Aid Commemoration Commission*

**Richard Jewson**
*Commercial Adviser, Disposal Sales Agency*

**Anne Jobson**
*Member, London Regional Passengers Committee*

**Paul Jobson**
*Managing Director, Business Development, Commonwealth Development Corporation*

**Ray Jobson**
*Member of Board, Funding Agency for Schools*
Chief Education Officer, Manchester City Council.

**George Joff,**
*Member, Academic Council, Wilton Park Executive Agency*
Director of Studies, Royal Institute of International Affairs.

**Dr Moussa Jogee JP**
*Member, Commission for Racial Equality*
President, Edinburgh Indian Association. Member, Citizens' Advice Council, Scotland. Former chairman, Lothian Community Relations Council. Member, Policy Committee, Scottish Council for Voluntary Organisations. Patron, Positive Action in Housing. Director, Edinburgh MELA. Member, Board of Directors, Ethnic Enterprise Centre. Vice-Convenor, Children in Scotland.

**Geoffrey John CBE**
*Chairman, Food from Britain*

# Q&Q

**Prof David Johns**
*Member of Board, Funding Agency for Schools*
*Vice Chancellor & Principal, University of Bradford.*

**Michael A Johns**
*Director Business Operations, Inland Revenue*

**Adrian Johnson**
*Member, The Great Britain-China Centre*

**Prof BFG Johnson**
*Member of Council, Engineering & Physical Sciences Research Council*
*Cambridge University.*

**Chris Johnson**
*Director of Development, Tower Hamlets Housing Action Trust*

**Fred Johnson**
*Director, AS (Manpower & Finance), Defence Analytical Services Agency*

**Kevin Johnson**
*Commercial Director, New Millennium Experience Co Ltd*
*Former Vice President, Client Development, ISL. Former Marketing Director, British Tourist Authority and National Garden Festival, Wales.*

**Prof Martin Johnson**
*Member, Human Fertilisation & Embryology Authority*
*Professor of Reproductive Sciences, University of Cambridge.*

**Roger Johnson**
*General Manager, Europe, British Tourist Authority*

**Stephen Johnson**
*Director of Operations, National Heritage Memorial Fund*

**Steve Johnson**
*Acting Chief Executive, War Pensions Agency*

**BC Johnston OBE**
*Appointed Trustee, Royal Marines Museum*

**Bryan Johnston**
*Member, Ofwat Eastern Customer Service Committee*

**Caroline Johnston**
*Chief Executive, Occupational Pensions Regulatory Authority*

**Surgeon General Charlie Johnston**
*Commanding Officer, Ministry of Defence Hospital Unit, Derriford, Defence Secondary Care Agency.*

**Prof Cliff Johnston**
*Member of Board, Scottish Environment Protection Agency*

**GD Johnston**
*Director South, Commission for the New Towns*

**Gillian Johnston**
*Regional Manager & Secretary, Ofwat South West Customer Service Committee*

**Prof IA Johnston**
*Member, Natural Environment Research Council*
*University of St Andrews.*

**James Johnston**
*Member, Ofwat North West Customer Service Committee*

**Jim Johnston**
*Director of Personnel, Planning & Information, Social Security Agency (Northern Ireland)*

**John Johnston**
*EBU Manager, Northern Ireland Child Support Agency*

**PJ Johnston**
*Director of Finance & Board Secretary, Engineering Construction Industry Training Board*

**Mrs R Johnston**
*Member of Board, Labour Relations Agency*

**Sir Russell Johnston MP**
*Vice-Chairman, The Britain-Russia Centre*

**Prof E Johnstone**
*Member of Council, Medical Research Council*
*Royal Edinburgh Hospital.*

**JMC Johnstone**
*Director of Capital Investment, North of Scotland Water Authority*

**R Joiner**
*Joint Head of Education & Marketing, Royal Botanic Gardens Kew*

**James Joll**
*Chairman, Museums & Galleries Commission*
*Trustee, Wallace Collection*
*Trustee, Design Museum. Director, Sir John Soane's Museum Society.*

**Christopher Jonas CBE**
*Member, The Further Education Funding Council*
*Adviser on property strategy to boards of a number of major corporations. Past President, Royal Institution of Chartered Surveyors.*

**N Jonas OBE**
*Appointed Trustee, Royal Marines Museum*

**Alan Jones**
*Director, North West, Property Advisers to the Civil Estate*

**Alexandra Jones**
*Chief Executive, Westminster Foundation for Democracy*

**Allen Jones**
*Trustee, British Museum*

**Angharad Jones**
*Commissioning Editor - Drama, S4C*

**Barry Jones**
*Member, Centre for Information on Language Teaching & Research*
*Principal Lecturer, Homerton College.*

**Bill Jones**
*Head of Branch, Technical Development, Forest Research*

**Bob Jones**
*Information Services Director, Student Loans Company*

**C Jones**
*Head of Molecular Structure, National Biological Standards Board*

**CEI Jones**
*Head of Administration, British Museum*

**Ms Cathy Jones**
*Regional Manager, Office of Electricity Regulation*

**Catrin Jones**
*'Arts for All' Officer, Arts Council of Wales*

**Chris Jones**
*Head of Curriculum Review, Qualifications & Curriculum Authority*

**Mrs CJ Jones**
*Member, SACOT, Scottish Advisory Committee on Telecommunications*
*Oil exploration geoscientist.*

**Clifford Jones**
*Head of North Wales Office/Planning Officer, Arts Council of Wales*

**D Jones**
*Commissioner, Royal Commission on Ancient & Historical Monuments in Wales*

**Miss D Jones**
*Member, Residuary Body for Wales*
*Former Director, Social Services, City of Birmingham.*

**David Jones**
*Director of Personnel & Training, Royal Commission on Historical Mon uments of England*

**Emlyn Jones**
*Member, Qualifications, Curriculum & Assessment Authority for Wales*
*Principal, Yale College, Wrexham.*

**Emyr Wyn Jones OBE**
*Member, National Library of Wales*
*Appointed by the Secretary of State for Wales.*

**G Jones**
*Member, WACT, Welsh Advisory Committee on Telecommunications*
*Engineer.*

**Air Commodore G Jones MBE**
*Chief Executive, RAF Signals Engineering Establishment*

**Prof GDB Jones**
*Commissioner, Royal Commission on Ancient & Historical Monuments in Wales*

**Gareth Jones**
*Chief Administrative Officer, Welsh Language Board*

**Prof George Jones**
*Member, National Consumer Council*

**Graham Jones**
*Assistant Director Civilian Travel Claims, Pay & Personnel Agency*

**Gwyn Jones**
*Deputy Chief Executive and Head of the Policy and Planning Department, Welsh Language Board*

**H Gareth Jones**
*Member, Further Education Funding Council for Wales*
Former Director of Education, West Glamorgan County Council.

**Howard Jones**
*Director of Administration, Office of Electricity Regulation*

**Dr Huw Jones**
*Director of Policy Planning, The Sports Council for Wales*

**Huw Jones**
*Chief Executive, S4C*

**Ian Jones**
*Chief Executive, Employment Tribunals Service*

**Iona Jones**
*Director of Corporate Affairs, S4C*

**John Jones**
*Commissioner, Meat & Livestock Commission*
Auctioneer. Partner, Norman R Lloyd & Co. Director, Animal Disease Research Association.

**John Walter Jones**
*Chief Executive, Welsh Language Board*

**Jonathan Jones**
*Director of Communications & Corporate Affairs, Wales Tourist Board*

**Dr Keith Jones**
*Chief Executive, Medicines Control Agency*

**Kingsley Jones**
*Director of Operations & Acting Deputy Director Deneral, Office of the National Lottery*

**Mrs Linda Jones**
*Member, Merseyside & North Wales Consumers' Committee, Office of Electricity Regulation*

**Marian Jones**
*Secretary to the Board, Occupational Pensions Regulatory Authority*

**Mark Jones**
*Director, National Museums of Scotland*

**Michael Jones**
*Finance & Operations Manager, UK Ecolabelling Board*

**Mike Jones**
*Member of Board, Occupational Pensions Regulatory Authority*
Partner, Bacon & Woodrow. (Nominated by Institute & Faculty of Actuaries.)

**Osborn Jones**
*Member, Further Education Funding Council for Wales*
Chief Executive, Snowdonia BIC, Bangor.

**Dr PP Jones**
*Chairman, Rail Users Consultative Committee for Midlands*

**Dr Peris Jones**
*Member, Central Rail Users Consultative Committee*
Chairman, Rail Users' Consultative Committee for the Midlands. Examiner in Chemistry, Open University tutor. Chairman, Evaluation Tribunal. Past Director Welsh National Opera. Past Chairman, West Midlands Passenger Transport Authority. Past Governor, University of Aston.

**Peter Jones**
*Member, Horserace Totalisator Board*
Director, British Horseracing Board. Member of Council, Racehorse Owners' Association.

**Peter Jones**
*Subject Adviser, Art, Office for Standards in Education*

**Prof Peter Jones**
*Trustee, National Museums of Scotland*

**Sir Philip Jones CB**
*Chairman, Higher Education Funding Council for Wales*
Chairman, Total Oil Holdings.

**R Brinley Jones**
*President, National Library of Wales*

**Richard Jones**
*Member, Human Fertilisation & Embryology Authority*
Legal Consultant.

**Roger Jones OBE**
*Governor, British Broadcasting Corporation*
National Governor for Wales. Managing Director of a pharmaceuticals company. Member, Powys Health Care Trust. Chairman, Council of Welsh Training & Enterprise Councils.

**Ron Jones**
*Member of Council, The Sports Council for Wales*

**SW Jones**
*Head, Financial Intermediaries & Claims Office, Inland Revenue*

**SW Jones OBE**
*Chairman, Welsh National Board for Nursing, Midwifery & Health Visiting*

**Simon Jones LVO**
*Member of Board of Trustees, Historic Royal Palaces*
Managing Director, Gardiner & Theobald. Appointed by the Secretary of State.

**Stephen Jones**
*Chair, Centre for Information on Language Teaching & Research*

**Tom Jones OBE**
*Chair, Wales Committee, National Lottery Charities Board*
*Member of Council, Countryside Council for Wales*
Farmer. Past President, Young Farmers Clubs of Wales. Former member, S4C television authority.

**Trefor Jones OBE**
*Member of Board, Welsh Development Agency*
Pilkington Optronics, CBI Wales Council, CELTEC, Glan Clwyd District General Hospital NHS Trust.

**Wyn Jones**
*Team Manager, Conservation Services Team, English Nature*

**Amanda Jordan**
*Member of UK Committee, National Lottery Charities Board*
Senior Executive, Public & Community Affairs NatWest Group. Trustee, NatWest Group Charitable Trust. Former Head of Policy & Communications, NCVO. Head of Campaigns, Scope. Parliamentary officer, Age Concern. Member of Board, Corporate Responsibility Group, Council for Charitable Support. Fellow of RSA and School Governor.

**Bill Jordan CBE**
*Member of Board, English Partnerships*
*Governor, British Broadcasting Corporation*
Former President, Amalgamated Engineering Union. Currently General Secretary of International Confederation of Free Trade Unions. Council Member, Industrial Society and a Governor, London School of Economics.

**Prof Carole Jordan**
*Member of Council, Particle Physics & Astronomy Research Council*
University of Oxford.

**M Jordan**
*Director of Change Management, Valuation Office Agency*

**MM Jordan**
*Head of Informatics, National Biological Standards Board*

**Victor Jordan**
*Director, Business Support Division, Training & Employment Agency (NI)*

**David Jordison**
*Member Advisory Board, NHS Pensions Agency*
Chief Executive, Lancaster Priority Services NHS Trust.

**Cllr Judith Jorsling**
*Member, London Pensions Fund Authority*
Member, Newham Council. Former Chair, London Fire & Civil Defence Authority.

**N Joseph OBE**
*Member, Parole Board*

**Peter Joyce**
*Inspector General & Agency Chief Executive, Insolvency Service*

**Dr Bernard Juby**
*Member, BACT, Office of Telecommunications*
Chairman, publishing, tourism and medical supplies company.

**Mrs Lynn Judge**
*Member, Ofwat Southern Customer Service Committee*

# K

**Prof A Kalabadse**
*Member of College Advisory Council, Civil Service College*
Professor of Management Development, Cranfield School of Management.

**Mary Kaldor**
*Governor, Westminster Foundation for Democracy*

**George Kalmus**
*Director, Particle Physics, Council for the Central Laboratory of the Research Councils*

**Ms M Kane**
*Member, Parole Board*

**Kazimiera Kantor**
*Part-time Member, British Railways Board*
Director Somerfield Holdings. Director Manchester Business School.

**Prof Michael Kaser**
*Member, Academic Council, Wilton Park Executive Agency*

**Bob Kass**
*Head of Communications, Highlands & Islands Enterprise*

**Julia Kaufmann**
*Member of UK & England Committees, National Lottery Charities Board*
Director, BBC Children in Need Appeal. Executive Committee Member, Association of Charitable Foundations. Member, Institute of Charity Fundraising Managers. Former Director, Gingerbread and Association for One Parent Families

**Harbinder Kaur**
*Member of Board, Stonebridge Housing Action Trust*
Director, Islington Age Concern.

**Danny Kavanagh**
*Human Resources Manager, Forensic Science Service*

**TJ Kavanagh**
*Secretary, Gaming Board for Great Britain*

**Captain BJ Kay**
*Marine Superintendent, Centre for Environment, Fisheries & Aquaculture Science*

**Robert Kay**
*Member, East Areas Board, Scottish Natural Heritage*

**Prof J Kear OBE**
*Member of Council, English Nature*
Editor, Wildfowl. Former President, British

Ornithologists Union. Council Member, Jersey Wildlife Preservation Trust, and Royal Society for the Protection of Birds. President, Devon Birdwatching & Preservation Society.

**Elizabeth Kearns**
*Member of Commission, Equal Opportunities Commission for Northern Ireland*
Ten years' experience of human resources in retail and manufacturing.

**WJ Kearns**
*Lettings Officer, Covent Garden Market Authority*

**Dr Terry Keatinge**
*Area Manager, Scottish Natural Heritage*

**Dr F Kee**
*Member, Northern Ireland Council for Postgraduate Medical & Dental Education*
Nominated by Faculty of PHM.

**Sir Curtis Keeble GCMG**
*Vice-President, The Britain-Russia Centre*

**Arthur Keefe**
*Member, Central Council for Education & Training in Social Work*

**Dr DAJ Keegan**
*Vice-Chairman, Northern Ireland Council for Postgraduate Medical & Dental Education*
Appointed by DHSS.

**John Keegan**
*Trustee, National Heritage Memorial Fund*

**AG Keeling**
*Area Manager - South, Engineering Construction Industry Training Board*

**Gerry Keenan**
*Director of Operations, Social Security Agency (Northern Ireland)*

**Mrs Marjorie Keenan**
*Commissioner, Mental Health Commission for Northern Ireland*
Project Manager, Learning Disability Services, Foyle Health & Social Services Trust.

**Dr DJ Keene**
*Commissioner, Royal Commission on Historical Monuments of England*

**Carol Keery**
*Manager Strategic Planning, Local Enterprise Development Unit*

**Prof HM Keir**
*Vice-Chairman, Macaulay Land Use Research Institute*

**Dr I Keitch**
*Member, Parole Board*

**BJ Kelleher**
*Member of Board, Simpler Trade Procedures Board*
President, FIATA. Vice President and previous National Chairman, BIFA.

**Barbara Kelly CBE**
*Chairman, West Areas Board, Scottish Natural Heritage*

**Barrie Kelly**
*Marketing & Communications Director, Office of the Data Protection Registrar*

**Miss J Kelly**
*Member of Council, English Nature*
Independent management consultant. Chairman, West Middlesex University Hospital NHS Trust. Lay Member, General Council and Register of Osteopaths. Trustee, Lifecare Charitable Trust. Member, Council of the National Trust. Visiting Fellow, Department of Health Studies, University of York.

**Capt JS Kelly OBE**
*Member of Committee, Ministry of Defence Police*
Directorate of Security Policy.

**John Kelly**
*Member of Board, Sea Fish Industry Authority*
Director, Nor Sea Foods. Past Chairman of Scottish Fish Merchants' Federation, Aberdeen Fish Curers' and Merchants' Association and Scottish Fish Merchants' Group Training Association.

**Cdre WHJ Kelly**
*Chief of Staff/Director Naval Training, Naval Recruiting & Training Agency*

**David Kelso**
*Assessor, Scottish Community Education Council*
Scottish Office Education & Industry Department.

**G Kemp**
*Corporate IS/IT Management & Regulation Director, Information Technology Services Agency*

**John Kemp**
*Regional Office, North West, NHS Estates*

**Lawrence Kemp**
*Deputy Chairman, Rail Users Consultative Committee for Scotland*
Accountant, Fife Council.

**Prof Martin Kemp**
*Trustee, British Museum*

**Sir Peter Kemp**
*Member, Audit Commission*
Executive, Foundation for Accountancy & Financial Management. Former Second Permanent Secretary, Cabinet Office and Deputy Secretary at the Treasury.

**Cllr Rhona Kemp**
*Member, Scottish Water & Sewerage Customers Council*
Chairman, North Area Committee.

**Robin Kemp**
*Member, BACT, Office of Telecommunications*
Former Managing Director, flooring, ceiling and insulation products company.

**RA Kempton**
*Director, Biomathematics & Statistics Scotland, Scottish Crop Research Institute*

**Dr GM Kendall**
*Head of Dept, Population Exposure, National Radiological Protection Board*

**Martin Kender**
*Head of Sociology, History, Anthropology & Resources Research Support Team, Economic & Social Research Council*

**David Kenmir**
*Director, Auhtorisation, Financial Services Authority*
Currently Executive Director responsible for authorisation, discipline, policy, legal and regulatory information, SFA.

**Andrew Kennedy**
*Enforcement and FLAC, Rate Collection Agency*

**Angus Kennedy**
*Chief Executive, Castle Vale Housing Action Trust*

**Mrs C Kennedy**
*Deputy Chairman, Fisheries Conservancy Board for Northern Ireland*

**George Kennedy**
*Member of Advisory Board, Medical Devices Agency*
Chairman, Smiths Industries Medical Systems.

**Rev Father OP Kennedy**
*Member of Board, Fisheries Conservancy Board for Northern Ireland*
Commercial fishermen's representative.

**Paul Kennedy**
*Administrative & Commercial Director, Commonwealth Institute*

**Peter NB Kennedy**
*Member of Board, West of Scotland Water Authority*
Former Managing Director, Gartmore Scotland. Director, Ivory & Sime Optimum Income Trust. Chairman, River Doon Fishery Board.

**Ron Kennedy**
*Part-time Member, British Railways Board*
Chairman, Essex County Council.

**W Kennedy**
*District Inspector, Foyle Fisheries Commission*

**Bernadette Kenny**
*Head of Personnel & Training Division, The Court Service*

**Dr C Kenny**
*Member, Northern Ireland Council for Postgraduate Medical & Dental Education*
Nominated by NI Faculty of RCGPs.

**Alan Kent**
*Chief Executive, Medical Devices Agency*

**Ms Cassandra Kent**
*Member, London Consumers' Committee, Office of Electricity Regulation*

**John Kent**
*Principal, National Sports Centre*

**Pen Kent**
*Member, Commonwealth Development Corporation*
Former Director, Bank of England. Former Member, Private Finance Panel. Former Alternate Executive Director, IMF.

**Susan Kent**
*Member, Welsh National Board for Nursing, Midwifery & Health Visiting*
Chief Executive, Neville Hall & District NHS Trust.

**HRH The Duke of Kent KG GCMG GCVO ADC**
*President, Imperial War Museum*
*Member, National Museum of Science & Industry*

**Graham Kentfield**
*Deputy Director, Banking and Market Services, Bank of England*

**John Kerman**
*Quality Services Director, Highways Agency*

**Miss P Kernaghan**
*Corporate Services, Public Record Office of Northern Ireland*

**Robert Kernoban OBE**
*Commissioner, Broadcasting Standards Commission*
Freelance writer and broadcaster. Member, newspaper panel of the Monopolies and Mergers Commission.

**Brian Kerr**
*Director, Scottish Development Finance, Scottish Enterprise*

**Bruce Kerr, QC**
*Trustee, National Library of Scotland*

**JA Kerr**
*Member, NIACT, Northern Ireland Committee on Telecommunications*
Communications Manager, Royal Group of Hospitals.

**Admiral Sir John Kerr GCB**
*Commissioner, Museums & Galleries Commission*
Chairman of Committee, Manchester Museum. Chairman of Audit Committee and Member of Council, Lancaster University. Member, Commonwealth War Graves Commission. Member, Central Committee of Management, Royal National Lifeboat Institute. Former Trustee, Royal Naval Museum. Deputy Lieutenant for Lancashire.

**N Kerr**
*Member of Board, Construction Industry Training Board (NI)*
Training & Employment Agency Assessor.

**Margaret M Kerridge**
*Member of Council, Post Office Users' Council for Wales*
Former Sub-Post Mistress.

**N Kershaw**
*Member, The British Library*
Standing Conference of National and University Libraries.

**Sir Chips Keswick**
*Member of Court, Bank of England*
Chairman, Hambros Bank.

**Henry Keswick**
*Chairman, Trustees, National Portrait Gallery*

**Simon Keswick**
*Trustee, British Museum*

**Andrew Ketteringham**
*Communications Director, Broadcasting Standards Commission*

**Ann Kettle**
*Member, Scottish Higher Education Funding Council*
Senior Lecturer in Mediaeval History, University of St Andrews.

**Leslie Keyte**
*Member, Ofwat Wessex Customer Service Committee*

**Arif Khan**
*Assistant Director (Legal) Consumer Affairs, Office of Fair Trading*

**Dr Zaka Khan OBE JP**
*Member, Commission for Racial Equality*
Director in scientific research. Visiting Professor. Chairman, Harmondsworth Board. Chairman, Confederation of Asian Organisations in the UK & Europe. Chairman, Pakistan Welfare Association UK. Former Member, Home Secretary's Advisory Council on Race Relations, Lord Chancellor's Advisory Committee, Regional Health Authority, Higher Education Council, Police Consultative Committee,

**Prof C Kidd**
*Member of Governing Body, Rowett Research Institute*

**Louise Kidd**
*Member of Board, Funding Agency for Schools*
Former Principal/Chief Executive, Rutland College.

**A Kilgore**
*Member of Board, Fisheries Conservancy Board for Northern Ireland*
Appointed as representative of a substantial number of anglers.

**RJ Killick**
*Secretary & Financial Manager, Scottish Crop Research Institute*

**Avila Kilmurray**
*Trustee, Community Development Foundation*

**Lord Kilpatrick of Kincraig CBE**
*Chairman, Scottish Hospital Endowments Research Trust*

**Allen King**
*Member, South Wales Consumers' Committee, Office of Electricity Regulation*

**Andrew King**
*Personnel Manager, Defence Analytical Services Agency*

**Charles King**
*Member, London Regional Passengers Committee*

**Derek King**
*Director of Investment, The Housing Corporation*

**Fiona King**
*Commissioner, Criminal Cases Review Commission*
Solicitor. Former Assistant Chief Crown Prosecutor for London.

**IE King**
*Member, LT Property Board, London Transport*

**J King**
*Non-Executive Board Member, Child Support Agency*

**Lesley King MBE**
*Member of Board, Funding Agency for Schools*
Headteacher, St Joseph's RC GM Primary School, Aldershot.

**Dr Lid King**
*Director, Centre for Information on Language Teaching & Research*

**Mervyn King**
*Executive Director, Monetary Stability, Bank of England*

**Captain PH King**
*Director of Operations, Trinity House Lighthouse Service*

**RLL King**
*Secretary, Scottish Advisory Committee on Telecommunications*
*Secretary, Post Office Users' Council for Scotland*

**Stephen King**
*Member, Eastern Consumers' Committee, Office of Electricity Regulation*

**John Kingdom**
*Director, Personnel, Property Advisers to the Civil Estate*

**Mrs Denise Kingsmill**
*Deputy Chairman, Monopolies & Mergers Commission*
Consultant, Denton Hall. Chairman, Optimum Health Services NHS Trust. Governor, College of Law.

**Christopher Kington**
*Non-Executive Director, Ordnance Survey*
Chris Kington Publishing.

**Christopher Kipling**
*Member, Qualifications, Curriculum & Assessment Authority for Wales*
Training Manager, Sony Manufacturing Co UK.

**MW Kirk**
*Head, Inland Revenue Wales & Midlands, Inland Revenue*

**Albert Kirkham ISO**
*Member, South Western Consumers' Committee, Office of Electricity Regulation*

**Donald Kirkham CBE**
*Chairman, Horniman Museum*

**HR Kirkpatrick**
*Member of Board of Trustees, Agricultural Research Institute ofNorthern Ireland*
Appointed by the Department of Agriculture.

**Jenny Kirkpatrick**
*Chairman, Gas Consumers' Council*
Director, LS Research. Director, the Strategic Partnership (London). Principal, Jenny Kirkpatrick Communications; Chairman, Oxfordshire Community Health NHS Trust; Trustee of the Foundation for Manufacturing & Industry and RICA.

**William B Kirkpatrick**
*Member, Gaming Board for Great Britain*
*Member of Scotland Committee, National Lottery Charities Board*
Former Executive with 3i, Non-Executive Director and JP.

**Mrs Diane Kirkup**
*Regional Manager, Office of Electricity Regulation*

**J Kirkwood**
*Member, Training & Employment Agency (NI)*
Former National Officer, Amalgamated Engineering & Electrical Union.

**JD Kirkwood**
*Government Assessor, Construction Industry Training Board*
Department for Education & Employment.

**Dr Ralph Kirkwood**
*Member, West Areas Board & Scientific Advisory Committee, Scottish Natural Heritage*

**Frank Kirwan**
*Member, The Accounts Commission for Scotland*
Former Director, UK Retail Banking, The Royal Bank of Scotland.

**Paul Kitchen**
*Medical Director, War Pensions Agency*

**Malcolm Kitchener**
*Non Executive Board Member, Defence Postal & Courier Services A gency*
Finance Director, Royal Mail.

**CJ Kitching**
*Secretary, The Royal Commission on Historical Manuscripts*

**David Kleeman**
*Member of Board, The Housing Corporation*
Managing Director of a financial services company and Non-Executive Director of a number of public and private companies. Non-Executive Member of NHS Supplies Authority. Former Chairman of New River Health Authority.

**C Knapman**
*Director Administration, Army Technical Support Agency*

**Julia Kneale**
*Chief Executive, Defence Animal Centre*

**CH Knight**
*Head, Animal Physiology Group & Biological Resources, Hannah Research Institute*

**Dr Peter Knight CBE**
*Member of Board, Teacher Training Agency*
Vice Chancellor, University of Central England.

**Alan Knowles**
*Senior Development Officer, Scottish Screen*

**Bob Knowles**
*Operations, National Lottery, UK Sports Council*

**Ned Knowles**
*Director, Music, Scottish Arts Council*

**Stuart Knowles**
*Group General Manager, Interwork, Remploy*

**JR Knox**
*Keeper, Oriental Antiquities, British Museum*

**John Knox**
*Commissioner, Criminal Cases Review Commission*
Consultant, litigation support division, Pannell Kerr Foster. Former Deputy Director, Serious Fraud Office (SFO).

**WJ Knox**
*Member of Council, Advisory, Conciliation & Arbitration Service*

**Mike Koch**
*Head of Measuring Instruments Certification Unit, National Weights & Measures Laboratory*

**H Kok**
*Regional Manager & Secretary, Ofwat Eastern Customer Service Committee*

**Sam Koroma**
*Director of Finance & Administration, English National Board for Nursing, Midwifery & Health Visiting*

**CJ Koster**
*Member, The British Library*
Society of Local Chief Librarians.

**Dr DD Kothari**
*Member, Parole Board*

**M Krayenbrink**
*Member of Board, Simpler Trade Procedures Board*
General Manager, Ferries, Dover Harbour Board.

**Prof JR Krebs**
*Chief Executive, Natural Environment Research Council*
*Member, Council for the Central Laboratory of the Research Councils*

**Jennie Kreser**
*Solicitor to the Board, Occupational Pensions Regulatory Authority*

**AW Kuczys**
*Head, Training Office, Inland Revenue*

**Nick Kuenssberg**
*Member, The Scottish Legal Aid Board*
Chairman, Halls of Broxburn and GAP Group. Non-Executive Director, Scottish Power and Standard Life Assurance Company. Chairman Association for Management Education & Training in Scotland. Member, Advisory Group of Secretary of State on Sustainable Development. Chairman, Institute of Directors, Scottish Division.

**Sally Kuenssberg**
*Chairman, Scottish Children's Reporter Administration*
Former Member, Strathclyde Children's Panel, Glasgow and Children's Panel Training Organiser, Glasgow University.

**Dr Surendra Kumar**
*GP Member, Medical Practices Committee*

**Kei Kurosu**
*Food from Britain (Japan)*

**P Kuzbyt**
*Director, Business Planning, West of Scotland Water Authority*

**Jonathan Kydd**
*Member, Commonwealth Development Corporation*
Head of Agrarian Development Unit and of Continuing Professional Development Wye College. Board Member, Natural Resources International.

**David Kyle**
*Commissioner, Criminal Cases Review Commission*
Barrister. Former Chief Crown Prosecutor, Central Casework Area, Crown Prosecution Service.

**Air Vice-Marshal RH Kyle**
*Chief Executive, RAF Maintenance Group Defence Agency*

**B Kyne**
*Member of Council, Council for Catholic Maintained Schools*
Teacher Representative.

# L

**Neville Labovitch LVO MBE**
*Member, Royal Parks Agency*
Chairman, Knightsbridge Association & Prince of Wales Royal Parks Tree Appeal Fund.

**Brian Lacey**
*Member of Board, Northern Ireland Museums' Council*
Director, Derry City Council Heritage & Museum Service. Nominated by Northern Ireland Regional Curators Group.

**The Most Rev F Lagan**
*Member of Council, Council for Catholic Maintained Schools*

**JR Laidlaw**
*Member of Council, Hannah Research Institute*

**Angus Laing**
*Area Manager, Scottish Natural Heritage*

**Gordon Laing**
*Member, Eastern Consumers' Committee, Office of Electricity Regulation*

**IK Laing**
*Solicitor (Scotland), Inland Revenue*

**David Laird**
*Member of Board, Scottish Natural Heritage*

**Air Commodore BC Laite**
*Director Officers/Airmen Aircrew, RAF Personnel Management Agency*

**Captain Lake**
*Member of Advisory Board, Service Children's Education*

**Cynthia Lake**
*Member of Board, Funding Agency for Schools*
Chairman of Governors, Queenswell Infants & Junior Schools, Whetstone.

**Cynthia Lake**
*Member, London Regional Passengers Committee*

**Pat Lake**
*Board Director, Home-Grown Cereals Authority*

**PR Laker**
*Controller of Management Services, HM Land Registry*

**Mrs Brenda Lalonde**
*Member, Ofwat Wessex Customer Service Committee*

**Prof J Lamb**
*Member of Governing Body, Rowett Research Institute*

**Alan Lambert**
*Member, Northern Ireland Tourist Board*
Divisional Director, Marks & Spencer.

**Carolyn Lambert**
*Director, Lottery Film Unit, The Arts Council of England*

**Miss SJ Lambert**
*Member of Advisory Board, Driver & Vehicle Licensing Agency*
DETR Road and Vehicle Safety Directorate.

**Susan Lambert**
*Curator, Prints, Drawings & Paintings Collection, Victoria & Albert Museum*

**Dr H Lamki**
*Member, Northern Ireland Council for Postgraduate Medical & Dental Education*
Nominated by Royal College of O&G.

**Dr D Lammey**
*Reader Services, Public Record Office of Northern Ireland*

**John M Lancaster**
*Member, National Library of Wales*
Co-opted by the Council.

**Anthony Land**
*Director, Resources, The Design Council*

**Ralph Land CBE**
*Governor, Westminster Foundation for Democracy*

**Dr David Landau**
*Trustee, National Gallery*

**Martin Landau**
*Trustee, Geffrye Museum*
Deputy Chairman, Development Securities. Non-Executive Director, Wilson (Connolly) Holdings. Managing Director, Conest Corp BV. Former Director, Guiness Mahon & Co. Former Managing Director, Guiness Peat Properties. Former Chief Executive and founder, City Merchant Developers. Former Executive Deputy Chairman, City Merchant Developments and Imry International.

**K Lander**
*Internal Auditor, Covent Garden Market Authority*

**AJ Lane**
*Curator, Royal Marines Museum*

**Sir David Lane**
*Vice President, Community Development Foundation*

**Louise Lane**
*Head of Communications, National Heritage Memorial Fund*

**Dr BA Lang**
*Deputy Chairman & Chief Executive, The British Library*

**CB Lang**
*Manager of Strategy & Communications, Engineering Construction Industry Training Board*

**The Very Rev John Lang**
*Commissioner, Broadcasting Standards Commission*
Dean Emeritus, Lichfield. Former Head of Religious Broadcasting, BBC.

**Brian Langdon**
*Chief Inspector, Mines Inspectorate, The Health & Safety Executive*

**Chris Langdon**
*Associate Director, Wilton Park Executive Agency*

**Tom Langlands**
*Director, Primary Health Care Nursing, English National Board for Nursing, Midwifery & Health Visiting*

**Dr Derek Langslow**
*Chief Executive, English Nature*
Chairman, Asian Wetlands Bureau.
Council Member, Wetlands International -
Asia Pacific and Wetland International -
The Americas.

**Colonel CR Langton**
*Member of Advisory Board, Service
Children's Education*

**Mrs Helen Lanigan Wood, MBE**
*Member of Board, Northern Ireland
Museums' Council*
Curator, Fermanagh County Museum.
Nominated by Northern Ireland Regional
Curators Group.

**Patricia Lankester**
*Trustee, National Heritage Memorial
Fund*

**Sir Tim Lankester KCB**
*Member of Board, British Council*
Director, School of Oriental and African
Studies, University of London.

**Robert Lanwarne**
*Planning Director, Funding Agency for
Schools*

**Fiona Larg**
*Chief Executive, Inverness & Nairn
Enterprise*

**Lawrence Larkin**
*Member, Ofwat Eastern Customer
Service Committee*

**Prof Fred Last**
*Member of Board & Scientific Advisory
Committee, Scottish Natural Heritage*

**Sue Last**
*Member of Board, Liverpool Housing
Action Trust*
Continuing Care Manager, Liverpool
Health Authority. Past Chair, Liverpool
Festival Trust.

**R Latter**
*Deputy Director, Wilton Park Executive
Agency*

**Prof Jennifer Latto**
*Member, Tate Gallery*

**Brigadier Michael Laurie**
*Chief Executive, Defence Intelligence &
Security Centre*

**Sally Laverack**
*Regional Executive, Independent
Television Commission*

**B Lavery**
*Representative Trustee, Royal Naval
Museum*
National Maritime Museum.

**Eileen Lavery**
*Director, Policy & Planning, Fair
Employment Commission for Northern
Ireland*

**Paul Lavery**
*Director, Marketing, Northern Ireland
Tourist Board*

**J Lavin**
*Director of Operations, Royal Botanic
Gardens Kew*

**Peter Lawler**
*Director, Perfomance Audit Division, Tai
Cymru*

**Stephen Lawrance**
*Compliance Manager, Office of the
National Lottery*

**Air Cdre DF Lawrence CBE**
*Keeper, Department of Aircraft &
Exhibits, Royal Air Force Museum*

**Dr John Lawrence**
*Member, Ofwat Southern Customer
Service Committee*

**Sir John Lawrence Bt OBE**
*Vice-President, The Britain-Russia
Centre*

**Michael Lawrence**
*Non-Executive Director, London
Transport*
Former Chief Executive, Stock Exchange.
Former Group Finance Director,
Prudential Corporation and Chairman,
Hundred Group of Finance Directors.

**Sue Lawrence**
*Acting Head, Bethnal Green Museum,
Victoria & Albert Museum*

**Richard Lawrence-Wilson**
*Director, Administration & Finance,
Council for the Central Laboratory of the
Research Councils*

**Frank Lawrie**
*Director, Heritage Policy, Historic
Scotland*

**Joan Lawrie**
*Board Member, Castle Vale Housing
Action Trust*
Former Member, Community Action
Team. Member, Farnborough Road Flats
Tenants Association. Founder member,
Autumn Years Holiday Group. Chair,
Visiting Panel for Age Concern at Castle
Vale.

**Jonathan Lawson**
*Communications, Media & Public
Relations, Office for Standards in
Education*

**Lieutenant Colonel Chris Lawton**
*Head Business Support, Joint Air
Reconnaissance Intelligence Centre*

**Prof JH Lawton**
*Member, Natural Environment Research
Council*
NERC Centre for Population Biology

**Admiral Sir Michael Layard KCB CBE**
*Trustee, Fleet Air Arm Museum*

**Anthony Layden**
*Member, Departmental Board, Wilton
Park Executive Agency*

**Tracey Layne**
*Visitor Services Manager, Museum of
Science & Industry Manchester*

**Richard Lazenby**
*Member of Council, Food from Britain*
Chairman, Mr Lazenby Traditional
Sausages.

**Christopher Le Brun**
*Trustee, National Gallery*

**Geoff Le Fevre**
*Human Resources Director, English
Heritage*

**Colonel Charles Le Gallais**
*Commander Royal School of Signals,
Army Training & Recruitment Agency*

**Miss Valerie Le Moignan**
*Member, Departmental Board, Wilton
Park Executive Agency*

**Rita Le Var**
*Director, Educational Policy, English
National Board for Nursing, Midwifery &
Health Visiting*

**CGR Leach**
*Board Member, The British Library*
Chairman, JIB Group.

**Sean Leahy**
*Cultural Development Director, Security
Facilities Executive*

**Dorian Leatham**
*Member of Board, Stonebridge Housing
Action Trust*
Chief Executive, London Borough of
Hillingdon.

**Mrs Suzi Leather MBE**
*Member, Ofwat South West Customer
Service Committee*

**Prof Christopher Leaver**
*Trustee, Natural History Museum*

**John Leckey**
*Commissioner, Criminal Cases Review
Commission*
Solicitor. HM Coroner, Greater Belfast.

**Peter Lederer OBE**
*Member, Scottish Tourist Board*
MD, Gleneagles Hotel. Member,
Secretary of State for Scotland's
Advisory Scottish Council for Education
and Training Targets. Board member,
Connoisseurs Scotland. Chairman,
Tourism Training Scotland.

**Prof John Ledingham**
*Member, Commonwealth Scholarship
Commission*
Formerly Director, Clinical Studies, John
Radcliffe Hospital.

**Bob Ledsome**
*Head, Senior Management & Support
Unit, The Health & Safety Executive*

**Frank Ledwidge OBE**
*Chairman, Northern Ireland Local
Government Officers' Superannuation
Committee*

**Dr A Ledwith CBE**
*Member of Council, Engineering &
Physical Sciences Research Council*
Pilkington.

**Alex Lee**
*Member, Ofwat Northumbria Customer Service Committee*

**J Lee**
*Employer member, Engineering Construction Industry Training Board*
Director-Contract Support Services, Wood Group Engineering.

**John Lee**
*Chairman, Museum of Science & Industry Manchester*
*Member, English Tourist Board*
Former MP for Nelson & Colne then Pendle. Former Minister for Tourism. Chairman, Association of Leading Visitor Attractions and Christie Hospitals NHS Trust.

**Katie Lee**
*Director, The Great Britain-China Centre*

**Mrs L Lee**
*Trustee, Royal Navy Submarine Museum*
Principal, St. Vincent College.

**Pat Lee**
*Board Member, Qualifications & Curriculum Authority*
Head of Retail Training, Tesco.

**Peter Lee**
*Deputy Chairman, Rail Users Consultative Committee for Southern England*

**Rosemary Lee**
*PROMT, Defence Evaluation & Research Agency*

**Michael Leech**
*Member of Board, Scottish Further Education Unit*
Principal, Stevenson College, Edinburgh. Member of Court Heriot-Watt University. External Examiner in Post-school Education Management, University of Strathclyde. Member, Scottish Committee, British Council.

**Miss A Lees OBE**
*Member of Board, Education Assets Board*

**Sir David Lees**
*Member of Court, Bank of England*
Chairman, Courtaulds and GKN.

**Mrs Dorothy Lees**
*Member, South Wales Consumers' Committee, Office of Electricity Regulation*

**Rear Admiral RB Lees**
*Trustee, Royal Naval Museum*
*Member of Committee, Ministry of Defence Police*
Chief of Staff to the Second Sea Lord and Commander-in-Chief Naval Home Command.

**CJE Legg**
*Museum Secretary, Natural History Museum*

**JM Legge CMG**
*Member, Met Office*
*Member of Committee, Ministry of Defence Police*
Deputy Under Secretary (Civilian Management), MOD.

**William Legge-Bourke**
*Member of Board, Welsh Development Agency*
Kleinwort Benson, Kleinwort Benson Securities. Chairman, Equity Rules Committee, London Stock Exchange. President, Welsh Scout Council.

**Prof Leonard Leigh**
*Commissioner, Criminal Cases Review Commission*
Former Convenor, Law Department, London School of Economics. UK council member, International Penal & Penitentiary Foundation.

**Miss Mary Leigh**
*Chairman, Medical Practices Committee*
Solicitor.

**Keith Leighfield**
*Director of Licensing, Coal Authority*

**Jane Leighton**
*Deputy Chair, Broadcasting Standards Commission*
Former Chair, Broadcasting Complaints Commission. Head of Organisational Development, Tate Gallery. Formerly Head of Public Affairs and Producer of current affair programmes, Granada Television.

**Helen Leiser**
*Member, Employment Tribunals Service*
DTI Director of Employment Rights.

**Colonel MD Lemon**
*Military Director (ABRO Land Command Support), Army Base Repair Organisation*

**Dr Alan Lennon**
*Chairman, Northern Ireland Council for the Curriculum, Examinations & Assessment*

**Lord Nicholas Gordon Lennox KCMG KCVO**
*Governor, British Broadcasting Corporation*
Former diplomat with postings in Washington, Santiago and Paris. Former, Ambassador to Spain.

**Lady Lennox-Boyd**
*Trustee, Royal Botanic Gardens Kew*

**Mrs Linda Leonard**
*Member, Northern Ireland Local Government Officers' Superannuation Committee*

**Mariot Leslie**
*Member, Departmental Board, Wilton Park Executive Agency*

**Prof RB Leslie**
*Member of Governing Body, Rowett Research Institute*

**Julia Lestage**
*Daytime Strategy Director, Channel Four Television Corporation*

**R Lester**
*Head of Department, Library & Information Services, Natural History Museum*

**DSC Levie, BL**
*Member of Governing Body, Rowett Research Institute*

**JG Levison**
*Inspector, Football Licensing Authority*

**Mrs Marjorie Lewin**
*Member, East Midland Consumers' Committee, Office of Electricity Regulation*

**A Lewis**
*Contracts Director, Army Base Repair Organisation*

**A Lewis**
*Member of Advisory Committee, Cadw*
Chairman, Wales Tourist Board.

**Andrew Lewis**
*Member, North of Scotland Water Authority*
Managing Director, Goldcrest Company (UK). President, Aberdeen Chamber of Commerce. Governor, Robert Gordon University. Non-Executive Chairman and founder, Northsound Radio. Honorary German Consul, Aberdeen.

**C Lewis**
*Member of Board, Football Licensing Authority*

**Prof C Lewis OBE**
*Director, Science & Technology, Defence Clothing & Textiles Agency*

**Caroline Lewis**
*Member, Qualifications, Curriculum & Assessment Authority for Wales*
*Member, Further Education Funding Council for Wales*
Deputy Principal, Coleg Menai, Bangor.

**Edgar Lewis**
*Member of Council, The Sports Council for Wales*

**End Lewis**
*Chief Finance Officer, Welsh Language Board*

**Geoffrey Lewis**
*Trustee, Royal Armouries*

**Gifford Lewis**
*Regional Director, South & East, Meat Hygiene Service*

**Ivor Lewis**
*Member of Board, Scottish Natural Heritage*

**John Lewis**
*Chairman, Wallace Collection*

**John Lewis**
*Director, North East, Property Advisers to the Civil Estate*

**Leigh Lewis**
*Chief Executive, Employment Service*

**Leigh Lewis**
*Member of College Advisory Council, Civil Service College*

**Nick Lewis**
*Member, The Further Education Funding Council*
Principal & Chief Executive, Broxtowe College, Nottingham. Board Member, Nottingham Partnership Forum.

**P Lewis**
*Member of Advisory Board, Forensic Science Service*
Crown Prosecution Service.

**Phil Lewis**
*Customer Services, Companies House*

**Robin Lewis OBE**
*Deputy Chairman, Welsh Development Agency*
Magstim, National Trust, The Prince's Trust-Bro. Court of Governors, University of Wales, Swansea. The Fleming Fledgeling Investment Trust.

**Prof Stuart Lewis**
*Member, Human Fertilisation & Embryology Authority*
Professor of Psychology Applied to Medicine, Queen's University, Belfast.

**Tony Lewis**
*Chairman, Wales Tourist Board*
*Member of Board, British Tourist Authority*
Writer and broadcaster. Former Captain of Glamorgan CCC and Captain of England. Former member, Sports Council for Wales. Former Chairman, Association of Business Sponsorship of the Arts (Wales). Consultant, Windsor Insurance Company and Alan Pascoe International (API).

**Janet A Lewis-Jones**
*Member of Board, British Waterways*
*Trustee, Community Development Foundation*
*Member of Authority, S4C*
Barrister and former civil servant. Independent consultant.

**Jerermy Lewison**
*Director of Collections, Tate Gallery*

**Eric Liddell**
*Regional Office, Trent, NHS Estates*

**Jean Liddiard**
*Head of Press & Public Relations, National Gallery*

**Dr Brian Lieberman**
*Member, Human Fertilisation & Embryology Authority*
Medical Director, Regional IVF and DI Unit, St Mary's Hospital, Manchester.

**Prof FY Liew**
*Member, National Biological Standards Board*

**Dr PM Liggins**
*General Manager, Covent Garden Market Authority*

**Ronald Lightbown**
*Trustee, Sir John Soane's Museum*
Representative of the Society of Antiquaries.

**Mrs Sonia Lightfoot**
*Member, Southern Consumers' Committee, Office of Electricity Regulation*

**Lieutenant Colonel Barry Lillywhite**
*Commandant Physical & Adventurous Training Group, Army Training & Recruitment Agency*

**RMS Lincoln**
*Member, Rail Users Consultative Committee for Midlands*

**J Lind**
*Member of Board of Governors, Macaulay Land Use Research Institute*

**The Lady Amabel Lindsay**
*Member of Board of Governors, Museum of London*
Appointed by the Prime Minister.

**F Lines**
*Member, The British Library*
Association of County Councils.

**Miao Ling Thompson**
*Member, The Great Britain-China Centre*
Under Secretary, Royal Society.

**Magnus Linklater**
*Chair, Scottish Arts Council*

**Peter Linthwaite**
*Head of Policy and Evaluation, Economic & Social Research Council*

**Mrs Lynda Lister**
*Observer, Northern Ireland Museums' Council*
Arts, Libraries & Museums Branch, Department of Education (NI).

**Tom Lister**
*Member, Rail Users Consultative Committee for Scotland*

**Colonel Nigel Lithgow**
*Commandant Infantry Training Centre Catterick, Army Training & Recruitment Agency*

**Dr A Little**
*Member, Northern Ireland Council for Postgraduate Medical & Dental Education*
Nominated by NI Faculty of RCGPs.

**Bob Little**
*Member, ENACT, Office of Telecommunications*
Past Director, telecommunications equipment manufacturing company.

**DI Little**
*Director, Engineering Services, West of Scotland Water Authority*

**Ms Janet Little**
*Member, Centre for Information on Language Teaching & Research*
Registered FE Inspector, Further Education Funding Council.

**Keith Little**
*Team Manager, Finance Services Team, English Nature*

**Dr TWA Little**
*Chief Executive, Veterinary Laboratories Agency*

**Dr Tom Little CBE**
*Member, Industrial Research & Technology Unit*
Former Director, Colworth Laboratory Unilever.

**Prof Stephen Littlechild**
*Director General, Office of Electricity Regulation*

**John Littlefair**
*Member, North Eastern Consumers' Committee, Office of Electricity Regulation*

**Lady S Littler**
*Chairman, Gaming Board for Great Britain*

**Mike Littlewood**
*Director, British Educational Communications & Technology Agency*

**PM Lively**
*Board Member, The British Library*
Writer.

**Admiral Sir Michael Livesay KCB**
*Commissioner, Northern Lighthouse Board*

**Prof Alan Livingston**
*Member, Tate Gallery*

**Nick Livingston**
*Director, Strategic Development Department, Arts Council of Northern Ireland*

**Dawn Livingstone**
*Member, General Consumer Council for Northern Ireland*
Director, Share Centre, Fermanagh. Northern Ireland Trustee, Family Fund Trust.

**Ian L Livingstone OBE**
*Chairman, Lanarkshire Development Agency*

**Prof Ian Livingstone**
*Member, Commonwealth Scholarship Commission*
Professor of Development Studies, University of East Anglia.

**Robert J Livingstone**
*Member, The Scottish Legal Aid Board*
Practising solicitor advocate. Temporary sheriff. Secretary, Marcel Properties and Investments Glasgow.

**Dai Liyanage**
*Member, Ofwat Southern Customer Service Committee*

**Glynn Llewellyn**
*Director, Specialist Development, Civil Service College*

**DTM Lloyd**
*Member of Board of Governors, Macaulay Land Use Research Institute*

**David Lloyd**
*Head of Programming & Advertising, The Radio Authority*

**Keith Lloyd**
*Nursery & Primary, Office for Standards in Education*

**Richard Lloyd**
*Farms & Woodlands, Countryside Commission*

**Robert Lloyd**
*Member of Board, Funding Agency for Schools*
Headteacher, Hendon GM School.

**Susan Lloyd**
*Commissioner, Broadcasting Standards Commission*
Barrister. President, London Rent Assessment Panel.

**TOS Lloyd**
*Member of Advisory Committee, Cadw*
Chairman, Historic Buildings Council for Wales.

**Thomas Lloyd**
*Member of Board, Wales Tourist Board*

**Mark Lloyd-Fox**
*Development Director, Commonwealth Institute*

**Gwenan Llwyd Evans**
*Head of Marketing & Communications, Welsh Language Board*

**Peter Lobban**
*Chief Executive, Construction Industry Training Board*

**John Locke**
*Chief Executive, Property Advisers to the Civil Estate*

**Stephen Locke**
*Member, National Consumer Council*

**Sheriff Brian Lockhart**
*Member, Parole Board for Scotland*

**Mike Lockhart**
*Regional Services, UK Sports Council*

**R Lockwood**
*Member, Gaming Board for Great Britain*

**Prof Christina Lodder**
*Trustee, National Galleries of Scotland*

**M Lodge**
*Member of Board, Education Assets Board*

**Mike Lofthouse**
*Head of Forest Operations, Forest Enterprise*

**Ian Logan**
*Director of Data Collection, Ordnance Survey*

**Robin Logan**
*Member, Ofwat Eastern Customer Service Committee*

**Julia Lomas**
*Public Trustee & Chief Executive, Public Trust Office*

**Jenni Lomax**
*Member, Tate Gallery*

**M Long**
*Head of People Planning & Development, Royal Botanic Gardens Kew*

**Rev PR Long**
*Member, Rail Users Consultative Committee for Western England*

**Richard Long**
*Member, Ofwat North West Customer Service Committee*

**John Longbottom**
*Head Science & Projects, Joint Air Reconnaissance Intelligence Centre*

**Colonel Jim Longfield**
*Commandant Royal School of Artillery, Army Training & Recruitment Agency*

**Dr M Longfield**
*Director of Health Care, HM Prison Service*

**TRM Longman**
*Commissioner, Royal Commission on Historical Monuments of England*

**John Longworth**
*Member of Board, UK Ecolabelling Board*
Divisonal Director, Consumer Protection, Tesco Stores.

**Jim Loni**
*Member of Board, Scottish Screen*
Scottish Office.

**Mrs Anne Lonsdale**
*Member, Commonwealth Scholarship Commission*
President, New Hall, University of Cambridge.

**Tim Lonsdale**
*Director Operations, Companies House*

**Finbarr Looney**
*Member, East Midland Consumers' Committee, Office of Electricity Regulation*

**Amanda Loosemore**
*Development Officer, Arts Council of Wales*

**Terry Lord**
*Finance Director, Contributions Agency*
Joined Royal Ordnance in 1969. Became Financial Controller, Inland Revenue's Information Technology Office in 1993. Appointed Director of Finance in 1995.

**Tony Lord**
*Member, East Midland Consumers' Committee, Office of Electricity Regulation*

**Tim Losty**
*Manager Belfast Regional Office, Local Enterprise Development Unit*

**Dr PC Loughran**
*Member, Northern Ireland Council for Postgraduate Medical & Dental Education*
Nominated by SHSSB.

**Cllr Serge Lourie**
*Member, London Pensions Fund Authority*
Member, Richmond Council. Member of Board, London Tourist Board and BTA Pension Fund.

**Roger Louth**
*Director, Mobile Services, Radiocommunications Agency*

**Prof AHG Love**
*Chairman, Northern Ireland Council for Postgraduate Medical & Dental Education*
Appointed by DHSS.

**Brian Love**
*Member, ENACT, Office of Telecommunications*
Consultant, specialising in business telecommunications.

**John Love**
*Director of Administration, Particle Physics & Astronomy Research Council*

**Robert Love**
*Member of Council, Scottish Arts Council*
Chair, Drama Committee. Controller of Drama, Scottish Television.

**Ian C Lovecy**
*Member, National Library of Wales*
Appointed by the Secretary of State for Wales.

**Roger Lovegrove**
*Member of Council, Countryside Council for Wales*
Chairman, Montgomeryshire Wildlife Trust and Environment Training Organisation (Cymru).

**Mike R Loveland**
*Operations Director, Forensic Science Service*

**Paul Loveluck CBE JP**
*Chief Executive, Countryside Council for Wales*

**Rachel Low**
*Regulatory Manager, Occupational Pensions Regulatory Authority*

**Gerry Lowe**
*Chairman, Livestock & Meat Commission for Northern Ireland*
Chief Executive, Lowe Refrigeration Group. Member, British Food Export Council. Member, Netherlands Council for Trade Promotion. Chairman, Castlereagh Economic Development Partnership. Member, Northern Ireland Small Business Institute. Committee Member, CBI SME Group. Director, Laurel Inn Restaurant & Guest House.

**Janet Lowe**
*Member of Board, Scottish Further Education Unit*
Principal, Lauder College. Member, Scottish Consultative Council on the Curriculum. Member, IiP Recognition Panel. Director, Scottish Campaign for Learning Chair, SWAP-East Consortium. Member, Scottish Committee, Dearing Inquiry into Higher Education.

**Rosalynde Lowe**
*Member, Audit Commission*
Director of Operational Services, Hillingdon Hospital Trust.

**Mrs VA Lowe**
*Chief Executive, Valuation Office Agency*

**Mark Lowery**
*Manager, Benbecula Airport, Highlands & Islands Airports*

**Jon Lowi**
*Member, Pesticides Safety Directorate*
Head of Financial Management Division (MAFF).

**Pat Lowrie**
*Member of Council, British Educational Communications & Technology Agency*
Associate Dean, Craigie Campus, Ayrshire.

**Merlyn Lowther**
*Personnel Director, Bank of England*

**Prof GL Lucas**
*Member of Council, English Nature*
Retired Keeper, Herbarium and Library, Royal Botanic Gardens Kew. Chairman, Wyldcourt Rainforest. Vice-Chairman, National Council for the Conservation of Plants & Gardens. Adviser, Friends of Kew. Treasurer, Linnean Society of London. Vice-President, Flora & Fauna International, Surrey Naturalists Trust, BTCV and Royal Geographical Society.

**Geoff Lucas**
*Head of Corporate Policy, Qualifications & Curriculum Authority*

**DR Ludford**
*Director Marketing, Commission for the New Towns*

**Dr Susanne Ludgate**
*Medical Director, Medical Devices Agency*

**Dr Abraham S-T Lue MBE**
*Vice Chairman, The Great Britain-China Centre*
Fellow and former Assistant Principal, King's College, University of London. Chairman, China British Institute. Senior Adviser to the Guangdong Provincial Higher Education Commission.

**Roy Luff OBE**
*Member, National Library of Wales*
Appointed by the Secretary of State for Wales.

**Miss Jan Luke**
*Director of Public Affairs, Office of Electricity Regulation*

**Laura Lundy**
*Member of Commission, Equal Opportunities Commission for Northern Ireland*
Lecturer in Law, Queens University, Belfast.

**G Lunn**
*Head, Inland Revenue North West, Inland Revenue*

**G Michael Lunn**
*Chairman, Glasgow Development Agency*

**Janet Lunn**
*Admin and Personnel, Rate Collection Agency*

**Prof David Luscombe**
*Member, Commonwealth Scholarship Commission*
Professor of Medieval History, University of Sheffield.

**John Lutton**
*Director of Field Operations (Scotland & North), Benefits Agency*

**Mrs Candida Lycett Green**
*Commissioner, English Heritage*

**Prof M Lynch**
*Member of Advisory Council, Scottish Record Office*

**Owen Lynch**
*Governor, Scottish Council for Educational Technology*
Observer. Acting Chief Executive, NCET (Observer).

**Brigadier Peter Lynch**
*Director of Personnel & Services, Defence Secondary Care Agency.*

**R Lynch**
*Chief Executive, BBC Resources, British Broadcasting Corporation*
*Part-time Board Member, Civil Aviation Authority*
Chief Executive Resources, British Broadcasting Corporation. Previously Sales and Marketing Director, Forte Hotels; Managing Director, Air Europe; Head of Customer Service, British Airways; Managing Director, British Airtours.

**Roy Lynk OBE**
*Member, Coal Authority*
Consultant, IMCL.

**David Lynn**
*Secretary, Scottish Court Service*

**Prof Norbert Lynton**
*Trustee, National Portrait Gallery*

**J Lyon**
*Member of Advisory Board, Forensic Science Service*
Deputy Director, Criminal Policy, Home Office.

**Alistair Lyons**
*Non-Executive Director, Benefits Agency*
Non-Executive Director, Managing Director, Insurance Division, Abbey National.

**Roger Lyons**
*Member, Monopolies & Mergers Commission*
General Secretary, Manufacturing, Science and Finance Union. Member, TUC's General Council Executive Committee. Executive member, European Metalworkers Federation and Confederation of Shipbuilding and Engineering Unions. Trustee, Charities Aid Foundation.

**B Lyttle OBE**
*Secretary, Probation Board for Northern Ireland*

**Billy Lyttle**
*Director, Finance, Personnel & Administration Department, Arts Council of Northern Ireland*

**J Lyttle**
*Member of Board, Labour Relations Agency*


# M

**John Mabberley**
*MD Programmes, Defence Evaluation & Research Agency*

**P Mabe**
*Member of Advisory Board, Defence Bills Agency*
Programme Director, Project CAPITAL.

**Mrs Judy MacArthur Clark**
*Member, Biotechnology & Biological Sciences Research Council*

**Nigel Macartney**
*Director, Reseach & Innovation Centre, The British Library*

**Iain MacAskill**
*Chairman, Crofters' Commission*

**Donnie MacAulay**
*Chief Executive, Western Isles Enterprise*

**John MacAuslan**
*Director of Administration, National Gallery*

**Alasdair N MacCallum**
*Member, North of Scotland Water Authority*
*Chairman, Scottish Crop Research Institute*
Chief Executive, Don & Low Holdings. Former Chairman, CBI Scotland. Chairman, Montrose Harbour Trust.

**Richard MacCormac CBE**
*Commissioner, English Heritage*

**Douglas MacDiarmid**
*Chief Executive, Lochaber Limited*

**Alastair Macdonald**
*Chairman, Radiocommunications Agency*
Director General, Industry, DTI.

**Annie MacDonald**
*Member, North Areas Board, Scottish Natural Heritage*

**Barry MacDonald**
*Director of Finance, National Lottery Charities Board*
Former Director of Finance, Spastiss Society. Previously Finance Director, Reuters Television and Financial Controller (Europe), P&O Containers.

**Brian MacDonald**
*Information Officer, Crofters' Commission*

**David Macdonald**
*Chief Executive, Enterprise Ayrshire*

**Gus Macdonald**
*Governor, National Film & Television School*

**Ian Macdonald**
*Member, Ofwat Wessex Customer Service Committee*

**Major General JD MacDonald CB CBE**
*Member of Board, Queen Victoria School*

**John MacDonald**
*Member, Scottish Sports Council*

**Fr John Angus Macdonald**
*Commissioner - Argyll, Argyll Islands, the Uists & Barra, Crofters' Commission*

**Cllr Olwyn Macdonald**
*Member, North of Scotland Water Authority*
Independent Councillor, Caol, Highland Council.

**Ron MacDonald**
*Area Manager, Scottish Natural Heritage*

**Mrs Vicky MacDonald**
*Member, Merseyside & North Wales Consumers' Committee, Office of Electricity Regulation*

**Mrs Elizabeth MacDonald-Brown**
*Vice Chairman, Rail Users Consultative Committee for Southern England*

**Ian MacDougall**
*Trustee, National Library of Scotland*

**BA Mace**
*Savings & Investment and Capital & Valuation Divisions, Inland Revenue*

**Ray Macfarlane**
*Member of Board, Scottish Screen*

**Ray Macfarlane**
*Managing Director, Scottish Enterprise*

**Prof AGJ MacFarlane CBE**
*Member, The British Library*
Scottish Library and Information Council.

**Prof Alistair MacFarlane CBE**
*Non-executive Director, British Nuclear Fuels plc*
Former Vice-Chancellor, Heriot-Watt University. Academic Adviser to the University of Highlands & Islands Project. Member, BT's Scottish Advisory Forum.

**WH Macfarlane Smith**
*Head, Scientific Liaison & Information Services Department, Scottish Crop Research Institute*

**Iain MacGregor**
*Head of Business Support Unit, National Weights & Measures Laboratory*

**Neil MacGregor**
*Director, National Gallery*

**Ms Sue MacGregor OBE**
*Member, Marshall Aid Commemoration Commission*

**Val MacIver**
*Member, Scottish Community Education Council*

**Dr BJ Mack**
*Keeper, Ethnography, British Museum*

**Prof David Mackay**
*Regional Director, North, Scottish Environment Protection Agency*

**Donald G Mackay**
*Member, Scottish Agricultural Wages Board*
Independent member appointed by the Secretary of State for Scotland.

**Eileen Mackay**
*Member of Board, Scottish Screen*

**GR Mackay**
*Head, Crop Genetics Department, Scottish Crop Research Institute*

**Dr Margaret Mackay**
*Commissioner, Royal Commission on Ancient & Historical Monuments of Scotland*

**Peter Mackay CB**
*Member, Monopolies & Mergers Commission*
*Member of Board, Scottish Natural Heritage*
Former Secretary, Scottish Office Industry Department. Visiting Professor, Strathclyde Graduate Business School.

**Prof RD Mackay**
*Member, Parole Board*

**Mrs Teresa Mackay**
*Member, Apple & Pear Research Council*
Member, Transport & General Workers Union. Secretary, Ipswich and District Trades Union Council. Elected East Anglian Representative on TUC's Joint Consultative Committee.

**James MacKeith**
*Commissioner, Criminal Cases Review Commission*
Consultant Forensic Psychiatrist.

**Rear Admiral DJ Mackenzie CB**
*Member of Board, Queen Victoria School*

**Dorothy Mackenzie**
*Member, The Design Council*

**Mrs G Mackenzie**
*Member, Alcohol Education & Research Council*

**Gordon J Mackenzie**
*Secretary, Post Office Users' Council for Wales*
*Secretary, WACT, Welsh Advisory Committee on Telecommunications*

**I Mackenzie**
*Member, Alcohol Education & Research Council*

**Malcolm MacKenzie**
*Member of Board, Scottish Further Education Unit*
Senior Lecturer in Education, University of Glasgow. Former Member, Scottish Consultative Council on the Curriculum and Education Committee, CBI (Scotland).

**Robert MacKenzie**
*Chief Executive, Fife Enterprise*

**Ruth MacKenzie OBE**
*Non-Executive Director, New Millennium Experience Co Ltd*
General Director, Scottish Opera.

**Dr Ian Mackenzie Smith**
*Commissioner, Museums & Galleries Commission*

**Jacquie Mackenzie-Taylor**
*Policy Development Adviser, Gas Consumers' Council*

**Dr M Mackie**
*Member of Governing Body, Rowett Research Institute*

**Prof RM MacKie**
*Member, National Radiological Protection Board*
Professor of Dermatology, University of Glasgow.

**Maitland Mackie CBE**
*Chairman, Grampian Enterprise*

**Mrs Isobel A Mackinlay**
*Chairman, National Board for Nursing, Midwifery & Health Visiting for Scotland*
Retired NHS Trust Nursing Director, Glasgow.

**Ms Helen Mackinnon**
*Professional Officer (Nursing), National Board for Nursing, Midwifery & Health Visiting for Scotland*

**Hugh MacKinnon**
*Internal Market Director, Intervention Board*

**Ian MacKinnon**
*Vice Chairman, Crofters' Commission*

**Lawrence Mackintosh**
*Head of Secretariat, The Arts Council of England*

**CJ Mackrell**
*Director West Midlands & North, Commission for the New Towns*

**Lord Maclay**
*Commissioner, Northern Lighthouse Board*

**Colin Maclean**
*Director General, Meat & Livestock Commission*

**K MacLean**
*Senior Inspector, Scottish Region,*
*Gaming Board for Great Britain*

**Lord MacLean**
*Member, Parole Board for Scotland*

**D MacLehose**
*Member of Board, Queen Victoria School*

**Lord MacLehose of Beoch KT GBE**
**KCMG KCVO**
*Vice President, The Great Britain-China*
*Centre*
Former Governor of Hong Kong.

**David Maclennan**
*Area Manager, Scottish Natural Heritage*

**Prof Duncan Maclennan CBE**
*Member of Board, Scottish Homes*
Mactaggart Chair of Land Economics &
Finance and Co-Director, Centre for
Housing Research & Urban Studies,
University of Glasgow. Past Director,
Rowntree Foundation's Research
Programmes and Academic Advisor to
HRH The Duke of Edinburgh's Inquiry
into British Housing. Member, Scottish
Advisory Committee of Shelter.

**GV MacLeod**
*Non-Executive Director, Caledonian*
*MacBrayne Ltd*

**Lorne MacLeod**
*Chief Executive, Skye & Lochalsh*
*Enterprise*

**Norman Macleod**
*Assistant Principal Reporter (Practice),*
*Scottish Children's Reporter*
*Administration*

**Lieutenant General Sir John MacMillan**
**KCB CBE**
*Member of Board, Queen Victoria School*

**Lady MacMillan**
*Member, The Arts Council of England*
Painter. Former Trustee, Royal Opera
House. Former Chairman, Friends of
Covent Garden.

**Murdo Macmillan**
*Contractor, Brompton Cemetery, Royal*
*Parks Agency*

**Sir Patrick Macnaghten**
*Member of Board, Fisheries*
*Conservancy Board for Northern Ireland*
Commercial fishing company
representative.

**Colin MacPhee**
*Director (Contracts & Technical*
*Services), Disposal Sales Agency*

**Dan MacRae**
*Senior Development Officer, Scottish*
*Screen*

**John C MacRae**
*Head, Protein Metabolism Division,*
*Rowett Research Institute*

**Kenneth MacRae**
*Chief Executive, Student Awards Agency*
*for Scotland*
*Department Assessor, Student Loans*
*Company*

**Prof Enid MacRobbie**
*Member, Biotechnology & Biological*
*Sciences Research Council*

**Ken MacTaggart**
*Director Network Strategy, Highlands &*
*Islands Enterprise*

**J Lionel Madden**
*Librarian, National Library of Wales*
*Member, The British Library*

**Judge Maddison**
*Member, Parole Board*

**Diana Maddock MP**
*Trustee, Community Development*
*Foundation*

**Dr Valerie Maehle**
*Member, Scottish Higher Education*
*Funding Council*
Head of School of Health Sciences, The
Robert Gordon University.

**Cllr Mrs Alison Magee**
*Member of Board, Scottish Environment*
*Protection Agency*

**Bill Magee**
*Secretary to the Commission, The*
*Accounts Commission for Scotland*

**Brendan Magee**
*Chief Executive, Driver & Vehicle*
*Licensing Northern Ireland*

**F Magee**
*Member of Council, Council for Catholic*
*Maintained Schools*

**Ian Magee**
*Chief Executive, Information Technology*
*Services Agency*

**S Magee**
*Member, NIACT, Northern Ireland*
*Committee on Telecommunications*
Chief Officer, Southern Health & Social
Services Council.

**Sean Magee**
*Director, Corporate Relations,*
*Commonwealth Development*
*Corporation*

**Cllr Elizabeth Maginnis**
*Trustee, National Library of Scotland*

**Magnus Magnusson KBE**
*Chairman, Scottish Natural Heritage*
*Member, Joint Nature Conservation*
*Committee*

**Prof Jim Magowan**
*Member of Board, Local Enterprise*
*Development Unit*
Founding partner, Medical Scientific
Computer Services.

**Sean Maguire**
*North Western, Rate Collection Agency*

**John Mahoney**
*Director, Information Systems, The*
*British Library*

**HG Mahood**
*Head of Information Systems, Ordnance*
*Survey of Northern Ireland*

**Robert M Maiden**
*Member, The Accounts Commission for*
*Scotland*
Chairman, Lothian & Edinburgh
Enterprise. Former Managing Director,
Royal Bank of Scotland and Vice
Chairman, CC-Bank AG (Germany).
Member, Court of Napier University.

**Mark W Mainwaring**
*Director of Administration & Technical*
*Services, National Library of Wales*

**Stella Mair Thomas**
*Officer for Wales & West of England,*
*Independent Television Commission*

**Oliver Makower**
*Member, BACT, Office of*
*Telecommunications*
Former Chairman, textile business.

**Brendah Malahleka**
*Member, Central Council for Education &*
*Training in Social Work*

**Rear Admiral Fabian Malbon**
*Naval Secretary & Chief Executive, Naval*
*Manning Agency*
*Member of Advisory Board, Defence*
*Analytical Services Agency*

**Robin Malcolm**
*Member, West Areas Board, Scottish*
*Natural Heritage*

**Dr APW Malcomson**
*Chief Executive, Public Record Office of*
*Northern Ireland*

**Andrew Malin**
*Director, Finance & Resources Division,*
*Arts Council of Wales*

**Sir Christopher Mallaby GCMG, GCVO**
*Member, Tate Gallery*

**David Mallen**
*Member, Centre for Information on*
*Language Teaching & Research*
Senior Adviser, Secondary and Further
Education Borders Regional Council,
Scotland.

**Fran Mallin**
*Export/ Import Processed Goods,*
*Recipes, Intervention Board*

**MH Mallinson**
*Deputy Chairman, Commission for the*
*New Towns*
Chairman, London Small Business
Property (Investment). Director, South
Bank University. Trustee, New Towns
Pension Fund.

**J Mallon**
*Member of Board of Trustees, Agricultural*
*Research Institute ofNorthern Ireland*
Northern Ireland Agricultural Producers'
Association.

**Pat Mallon**
*Member, General Consumer Council for*
*Northern Ireland*
Member, Craigavon Borough Council.
Health Support worker. Chairperson,
Board of Governors, St Peter's Primary

School, Lurgan. Member, NI Housing Executive Southern Region Consumer Panel.

**R Malpas CBE**
*Chairman, Natural Environment Research Council*

**Dr Geoff Mance**
*Director of Water Management, The Environment Agency*

**Christine Mandikian**
*Assistant Director, Information Technology, Simpler Trade Procedures Board*

**Ms LM Manley**
*Finance Director, Driving Standards Agency*

**Gordon Manly**
*Member, Northern Ireland Local Government Officers' Superannuation Committee*

**Bruce Mann**
*Member of Advisory Board, Disposal Sales Agency*

**Prof CNJ Mann**
*Member, The British Library*
British Academy.

**David Mann**
*Member, DIEL, Office of Telecommunications*
*Member, Northern Ireland Consumer Committee for Electricity, Office for the Regulation of Electricity & Gas*
Former Manager, Support for Independent Living RNIB. Self employed. Registered blind.

**The Right Reverend Michael Mann KCVO**
*Deputy Chairman, Imperial War Museum*

**AER Manners**
*Member, Rail Users Consultative Committee for Midlands*

**GC Manning OBE**
*Chairman, South West RFDC, The Environment Agency*

**Jack Mansfield**
*Director Finance, Companies House*

**Frank W Manson**
*Managing Director, Registers of Scotland*

**Hilary Mantel**
*Member of Advisory Committee, Registrar of Public Lending Right*

**Mrs Anne Mantle**
*Member, Southern Consumers' Committee, Office of Electricity Regulation*

**Zahida Manzoor**
*Deputy Chairman, Commission for Racial Equality*
Co-founder & Marketing Director, Intelliysis. Chairman, Bradford Health Authority. Trustee, West Yorkshire Police Community Trust. Member, Bradford Congress. Court Member, University of Bradford. Former Director, NE Regional

Programme, Common Purpose Educational Charitable Trust. Former Member, National NHS Task Group on Open Governance & Corporate Governance.

**Mrs Heather March**
*Member, Ofwat Customer Service Committee for Wales*

**Mrs L March JP**
*Member, Parole Board*

**Ron Marchant**
*Assistant Comptroller (Patents & Design), Patent Office*

**Alan M Marchbank**
*Director of Public Services, National Library of Scotland*

**Brian Marjoribanks**
*Officer for Scotland, Independent Television Commission*

**DEB Mark**
*Associate Adviser in GDP (VT), Northern Ireland Council for Postgraduate Medical & Dental Education*

**Ian Mark**
*Member, Livestock & Meat Commission for Northern Ireland*
Director. Lean & Easy lamb processing company. Chairman, Cattle & Sheep Committee, UFU Member, UFU Executive.

**Jane Markham**
*Board Secretary, Funding Agency for Schools*

**Paul Marks**
*Second in Command, Defence Animal Centre*

**Prof Shula Marks OBE**
*Member, Commonwealth Scholarship Commission*
Professor of South African History, School of Oriental & African Studies.

**Emma Marlow**
*Marketing Manager, National Portrait Gallery*

**DG Marnoch MBE**
*Member, Post Office Users' Council for Scotland*
Chief Executive, Aberdeen Chamber of Commerce. Chairman, Aberdeen & District Posts & Telecommunications Advisory Committees. Member, Scottish Exports Forum. Member, Court of University of Aberdeen.

**Mrs Jane Marr**
*Director of Adult & Children's Nursing, English National Board for Nursing, Midwifery & Health Visiting*

**Edmund Marsden**
*Director Corporate Policy, British Council*

**PG Marsden**
*Finance Officer, Covent Garden Market Authority*

**Dr Barbara Marsh JP**
*Commissioner, Rural Development Commission*
Chairman, Royal Shrewsbury Hospitals NHS Trust. County Councillor, Shropshire. Member of Industrial Tribunal. Magistrate.

**Janet Marsh**
*Manager, West Midlands, Gas Consumers' Council*

**Lady Marsh**
*Member of Board, Commission for the New Towns*
Director, Mannington Management Services.

**Mary Marsh**
*Member of Council, British Educational Communications & Technology Agency*

**Chris Marshall**
*SEN, Office for Standards in Education*

**Sir Colin Marshall**
*Trustee, Royal Air Force Museum*

**Maud Marshall**
*Director of Management Consultancy Services/Chief Policy Advisor, Scottish Homes*
*Member of Council, Scottish Arts Council*

**Olive Marshall**
*Member, Post Office Users' Council for Northern Ireland*

**Ms R Marshall**
*Member, The Accounts Commission for Scotland*
Vice Principal (Strategic Planning & Development), Queen Margaret College, Edinburgh.

**Sara Marshall**
*Assistant Chief Executive (Vocational Qualifications), Qualifications, Curriculum & Assessment Authority for Wales*

**TO Marshall**
*Head of Dept, Dosimetry & Instrumentation, National Radiological Protection Board*

**Tim Marshall MBE**
*Member, UK & English Sports Councils*
Senior Lecturer, Public Health & Epidemiology, University of Birmingham.

**Robert Marshall-Andrews, QC**
*Trustee, Geffrye Museum*
Chair of Governors, Grey Court School. Trustee, George Adamson Wildlife Trust. Author.

**The Hon Mrs Marten OBE**
*Trustee, British Museum*

**Dr Connie Martin**
*Member, Academic Council, Wilton Park Executive Agency*

**Major FAS Martin**
*Officer Commanding, 25 Freight Distribution Sqn RLC, Defence Transport & Movements Executive*

**Geoffrey Martin**
*Member, Academic Council, Wilton Park Executive Agency*

**HC Martin**
*Operations Manager, Enterprise Ulster*

**John Martin**
*Chairman, RFDC, The Environment Agency*

**JSB Martin**
*Member of Board, Queen Victoria School*

**Michael Martin OBE**
*Member, DIEL, Office of Telecommunications*
Consultant in the speech and hearing field.

**NSE Martin**
*Appointed Trustee, Royal Marines Museum*

**P Martin**
*Member, Parole Board*

**PG Martin**
*Director of Training Standards & Strategy, Construction Industry Training Board*

**RR Martin**
*Finance Division, Inland Revenue*

**RS Martin**
*Managing Director, Northern Ireland Transport Holding Company*

**Robert C Martin**
*Chief Executive, Environment & Heritage Service*

**Robin Martin**
*Director Finance, Inland Revenue*

**TJD Martin**
*Digital Production, Ordnance Survey of Northern Ireland*

**W Martin**
*Member of Board, Construction Industry Training Board (NI)*
CIOB. Employee representative.

**Cath Martindale**
*Quality Assessment in ITT, Teacher Training Agency*

**Charles Masefield**
*Member of Advisory Board, Disposal Sales Agency*
Head of Defence Export Services - Owner.

**Bill Mason**
*Head of Branch, Silviculture North, Forest Research*

**David Mason**
*Member, London Pensions Fund Authority*
Chartered Accountant. Former, Finance Director, The Sports Council.

**Ian Mason**
*Member, Scottish Sports Council*

**J Mason**
*Member, Property Advisers to the Civil Estate*
Benefits Agency Estates.

**Mrs Marilyn Mason**
*Member, South Wales Consumers' Committee, Office of Electricity Regulation*

**Paul Mason**
*Chief Scientist, Met Office*

**Supt S Mason**
*OCU, Coulport, Ministry of Defence Police*

**Timothy Mason**
*Director, Museums & Galleries Commission*
*Observer, Northern Ireland Museums' Council*

**Supt W Mason**
*OCU, Greenock, Ministry of Defence Police*

**Dr Rob Massey**
*Food Safety & Quality, Central Science Laboratory*
Joined Food Science Laboratory in 1975.

**Stephen Massey**
*Member of Board, English Partnerships*
Chairman and Chief Executive, Prudential-Bache International (UK). Non-executive Director of Harvington Properties.

**Allan Massie**
*Trustee, National Museums of Scotland*

**Dr Chris Masters**
*Member, Scottish Higher Education Funding Council*
Chief Executive, Christian Salvesen.

**Dame Sheila Masters DBE**
*Non-Executive Member, Inland Revenue*
*Member of Court, Bank of England*
Partner, KPMG, Former Quality & Personnel Director, Vickers Defence Systems.

**G Matchett**
*Member of Board, Construction Industry Training Board (NI)*
GMB. Employee representative.

**Ann Matheson**
*Keeper of Printed Books, National Library of Scotland*
*Member of Council, Scottish Arts Council*

**Nicholas Matheson**
*Chief Executive, Government Car & Despatch Agency*

**Steve CT Matheson CB**
*Deputy Chairman, Inland Revenue*
*Member of College Advisory Council, Civil Service College*

**Lieutenant Colonel T Mathew**
*Director Aircraft Branch, Army Technical Support Agency*

**P Mathias CBE**
*Member, The British Library*
Chairman.

**Mrs L Mathieson**
*Member of Advisory Board, Coastguard*
External member.

**Peter Mathison**
*Chief Executive, Benefits Agency*

**Judge Matthewman QC**
*Member, Parole Board*

**Geoffrey Matthews**
*Managing Director, National Gallery Publications, National Gallery*

**Prof Jack Matthews**
*Member, Scientific Advisory Committee, Scottish Natural Heritage*

**Peter Matthews**
*Inspection Quality, Monitoring & Development, Office for Standards in Education*

**Tony Matthews OBE**
*Food from Britain (North America) Inc*

**Harriet Maunsell OBE**
*Member of Board, Occupational Pensions Regulatory Authority*
Retired Partner, Lovell White Durrant. Former Deputy Chairman, Occupational Pensions Board. (Nominated by Association of Pension Lawyers.)

**J Mawhinney**
*Member, Northern Ireland Fishery Harbour Authority*

**Rev Andrew Mawson**
*Member of Board, Tower Hamlets Housing Action Trust*
Director, Bromley by Bow Centre and McCabe Educational Trust.

**Dr D Mawson**
*Member, Parole Board*

**Barry Maxwell**
*Director, Local Customer Services, Radio Investigation Service, Monitoring & Quality Assurance, Radiocommunications Agency*

**Douglas Maxwell**
*Divisional Roads Manager, Roads Service*

**Ingval Maxwell**
*Director, Technical Conservation, Research & Education, Historic Scotland*

**Prof Jeff Maxwell**
*Member, Scientific Advisory Committee, Scottish Natural Heritage*

**Ms P Maxwell**
*Member of Board, Labour Relations Agency*

**Peter Maxwell**
*Director Finance & Administration, Engineering & Physical Sciences Research Council*

**Prof T Jeff Maxwell**
*Director, Macaulay Land Use Research Institute*

**Andrew May**
*Member, Horticultural Development Council*
Narcissus grower in Isles of Scilly.

**Mrs Elizabeth May**
*Deputy Chairperson, Northern Ireland Local Government Officers' Superannuation Committee*

**Ms Elizabeth May**
*Member of Board, Labour Relations Agency*

**Howard May**
*Member of Board, Waltham Forest Housing Action Trust*
Tenant Board Member of Boundary Road Estate. Local government employee.

**Sir Robert May**
*Chairman, Natural History Museum*

**Suzanne May**
*Deputy Chairman, London Regional Passengers Committee*

**Anthony Mayer**
*Chief Executive, The Housing Corporation*

**Mrs Anne Mayes**
*Member, Ofwat South West Customer Service Committee*

**Glynnis Mayes**
*Assistant Director, Midwifery Supervision & Practice, English National Board for Nursing, Midwifery & Health Visiting*

**Michael Mayes**
*Director of Consumer & Education Markets, Ordnance Survey*

**Judith Mayhew**
*Trustee, Geffrye Museum*
Employment Lawyer, Wilde Sapte. Member, Court of Common Council, Corporation of London. Chairman, Education Committee, Corporation of London. Deputy Chairman, Policy & Resources Committee, Corporation of London. Member, Gresham Committee, Mercers Company. Governor, Birkbeck College. Governor, London Guildhall University. Governor, City of London Girls' School.

**H Maylard**
*Director of Training Operations, Construction Industry Training Board*

**J Maynard**
*Member, WACT, Welsh Advisory Committee on Telecommunications*
IT manager.

**Ray McAfee**
*Director, operations (Central), HM Customs & Excise*

**Ian McAllister**
*Board Member, Qualifications & Curriculum Authority*
Chairman, Chief Executive and Managing Director, Ford Motor Company.

**James McAllister**
*Member of Board, Wales Tourist Board*

**IM McAlpine OBE**
*Member of Board, Construction Industry Training Board*
Sir Robert McAlpine.

**Rear Admiral JHS McAnally**
*Chief Executive, Naval Recruiting & Training Agency*

**Nicolas McAndrew**
*Member, North of Scotland Water Authority*
Chairman, Murray Johnstone. Board Member, Highlands & Islands Enterprise.

Director, Burn Stewart Distillers and Liverpool Victoria Friendly Society.

**Eddie McArdle**
*Deputy Director, Council for Catholic Maintained Schools*

**Harry J McArdle**
*Head, Nutrition, Pregnancy & Development Division, Rowett Research Institute*

**Peter McArdle**
*Manager Food, Local Enterprise Development Unit*

**D McAteer**
*Member of Board, Enterprise Ulster*

**Ms G McAteer**
*Member of Board, Laganside Corporation*
Manager - Upper Springfield Development Trust.

**Ronnie McAteer**
*Financial Management, Rate Collection Agency*

**David McAuley**
*Director, Investment, Northern Ireland Tourist Board*

**Mrs M McAvoy**
*Member of Council, Council for Catholic Maintained Schools*
Department of Education Representative.

**Ernest McBride**
*Commissioner, Fair Employment Commission for Northern Ireland*

**Mrs H McBride**
*Support Services Manager, National Board for Nursing, Midwifery & Health Visiting for Northern Ireland*

**Ann McCabe**
*Director of Vehicle Licensing, Driver & Vehicle Licensing Northern Ireland*

**Kevin McCabe**
*Commissioner, Fair Employment Commission for Northern Ireland*

**Miss M McCabe**
*Member, Northern Ireland Council for Postgraduate Medical & Dental Education*
Nominated by Dental Co-ord Committee.

**Prof Ron McCaffer**
*Education Member, Engineering Construction Industry Training Board*

**Brian McCafferty**
*Training & Assessment, Office for Standards in Education*

**OA McCaffrey**
*Member of Council, Council for Catholic Maintained Schools*
Teacher Representative.

**Mrs Frances McCall MBE**
*Member of Board, Scottish Homes*
Chairperson of Calvay Co-operative. Member Calvay Co-operative Housing Committee. Past Chairperson, Confederation of Scottish Housing Co-operatives.

**JW McCall**
*Human Resource Manager, Enterprise Ulster*

**Donald McCallum**
*Business Director - Palm Oil & Forestry, Commonwealth Development Corporation*

**J McCallum**
*Building Services Manager, Hannah Research Institute*

**Derick McCandless**
*Divisional Roads Manager, Roads Service*

**Anne McCann**
*Member, Post Office Users' Council for Northern Ireland*

**Evelyn McCann**
*Director, Skills Development, Scottish Enterprise*

**Kevin McCann**
*Business Development Director, Local Enterprise Development Unit*

**E McCartan**
*Chief Executive, Sports Council for Northern Ireland*
*Observer, UK Sports Council*

**Mrs I McCartan**
*Member of Council, Council for Catholic Maintained Schools*
Parent Representative.

**Jim McCarthy**
*Member, East Areas Board, Scottish Natural Heritage*

**Suzanne McCarthy**
*Chief Executive, Human Fertilisation & Embryology Authority*

**Mrs R McCausland**
*Higher Education/Community Nursing, National Board for Nursing, Midwifery & Health Visiting for Northern Ireland*

**Cllr Cormick McChord**
*Member of Board, Scottish Environment Protection Agency*

**Brian McClelland**
*Chief Executive, Independent Commission for Police Complaints for Northern Ireland*

**Dr H McClelland**
*Member, Parole Board*

**Prof RJ McClelland**
*Member, Northern Ireland Council for Postgraduate Medical & Dental Education*
Nominated by Medical Faculty, QUB.

**Dr SE McClelland CBE**
*Member of Board, Queen Victoria School*

**Mrs A McClintock**
*Access, Public Record Office of Northern Ireland*

**Wing Commander Bill McCluggage**
*Head Technical Support, Joint Air Reconnaissance Intelligence Centre*

**Dr JR McCluggage**
*Chief Executive/Postgraduate Dean, Northern Ireland Council for Postgraduate Medical & Dental Education*

**A McClure**
*Member, Training & Employment Agency (NI)*
President & Chief Executive Officer, Perfecseal Inc.

**D McClure**
*Member of Board, Construction Industry Training Board (NI)*
Farran Construction. Employer representative.

**Gillian McClure**
*Member of Advisory Committee, Registrar of Public Lending Right*
Author/Illustrator.

**M McClure**
*Member of Board, Fisheries Conservancy Board for Northern Ireland*
Sport & Recreation Representative.

**John McColl**
*Project Program Manager, UK Passport Agency*

**G McConkey**
*Director, Estate Policy, Health Estates*

**Charlie McConnel**
*Chief Executive, Scottish Community Education Council*

**Greg McConnell**
*Chief Executive, Industrial Research & Technology Unit*

**John McConnell**
*Director of Corporate Services, Planning Service*

**N McConnell**
*Member, Sports Council for Northern Ireland*

**Fiona McConnon**
*Deputy Director, The Great Britain-China Centre*

**Sister O McConville**
*Member of Council, Council for Catholic Maintained Schools*

**Prof Tom McCool CBE**
*Governor, Scottish Council for Educational Technology*

**George McCorkell**
*Projects Director, Benefits Agency*

**J McCormick**
*Professional Adviser, Youth Council for Northern Ireland*

**R McCormick**
*Marketing/Communications Officer, Sports Council for Northern Ireland*

**Billy McCoubrey**
*Chief Executive, Roads Service*

**Dr Bill McCourt**
*Member of Board, Local Enterprise Development Unit*
Director, Unibooks (Ulster) and International Net & Twine. President,

Northern Ireland Partnership. Council Member, University of Ulster. Member of CBI. Director, Andras House.

**Miceal McCoy**
*Member, Livestock & Meat Commission for Northern Ireland*
Farmer Manager, South Down/South Armagh LEADER company. Vice Chairman, Northern Ireland Agricultural Producers' Association (NIAPA). Governor, Armagh College of Further Education. Treasurer, Northern Ireland LEADER Network. Founder Member, Regeneration of South Armagh (ROSA) and Rural Community Network for Northern Ireland (RCN).

**JD McCracken**
*Director of Finance & Administration, Laganside Corporation*

**JS McCreight**
*Member of Board, Fisheries Conservancy Board for Northern Ireland*
Appointed as representative of a substantial number of anglers.

**Mrs Christine McCulloch**
*Head of the Politics, Economics & Geography Research Support Team, Economic & Social Research Council*

**I McCulloch**
*Member, SACOT, Scottish Advisory Committee on Telecommunications*
Business Development Manager, eletronics company.

**Tom McCully**
*Director of Engineering Services, Rivers Agency*

**Mrs Anna McCurley**
*Trustee, National Galleries of Scotland*

**Jim McCurley**
*Commissioner, Fair Employment Commission for Northern Ireland*

**J McCusker**
*Member, Training & Employment Agency (NI)*
General Secretary, Northern Ireland Public Service Alliance (NIPSA).

**N McCutchen**
*Senior Commissioner, Foyle Fisheries Commission*

**W McD Moodie CBE**
*Member of Board, Queen Victoria School*

**E McDaid**
*Member of Board, Enterprise Ulster*
Nominated by Northern Ireland Committee. Irish Congress of Trade Unions.

**Ian McDermott**
*Director of Development & Special Initiatives, Stonebridge Housing Action Trust*

**Murray McDermott**
*Director of Resources and Customer Services, Scottish Office Pensions Agency*

**Dr Andrew McDonald**
*Head of Government Services Department, Public Record Office*

**Dr Jackie McDonald**
*Member, Scottish Medical Practices Committee*

**Stewat McDonald**
*Assessor, Scottish Community Education Council*
Assistant Secretary, Scottish Office Education & Industry Department.

**Jim McDonald MBE**
*Member, Post Office Users' Council for Northern Ireland*

**Dr A McDonnell**
*Member of Board, Laganside Corporation*
Belfast City Councillor.

**Ms R McDonough**
*Member of Board, Probation Board for Northern Ireland*

**Peter McDougall**
*Area Manager, Scottish Fisheries Protection Agency*

**Kathryn McDowell**
*Director, Music, The Arts Council of England*

**Michael McDowell**
*Senior Complaints Officer, Fair Employment Commission for Northern Ireland*

**Colin N McEachran, QC**
*Member, The Scottish Legal Aid Board*
President, Pension Appeal Tribunal for Scotland; Chairman, Commonwealth Games Council for Scotland.

**Prof A Rennie McElroy**
*Trustee, National Library of Scotland*

**The Rt Rev Monsignor L McEntegart**
*Member of Council, Council for Catholic Maintained Schools*

**Aileen McEvoy**
*Member, Tate Gallery*

**Mrs P McEvoy-Williams**
*Director, Human Resources, English National Board for Nursing, Midwifery & Health Visiting*

**NJ McEwan**
*Member of Advisory Board, Defence Bills Agency*
Directorate General Ships, Corporate Finance and Accounting.

**Prof J McEwen**
*Member, National Radiological Protection Board*
Professor of Public Health, University of Glasgow.

**CJ McFadzean**
*Director, Scientific Services, West of Scotland Water Authority*

**Ian McFarlane**
*Member, Ofwat Customer Service Committee for Wales*

**Frank McGettigan**
*Director & General Manager, Channel Four Television Corporation*
*Governor, National Film & Television School*

**B McGhee**
*Member, The Accounts Commission for Scotland*
Chairman, Magnum Power. Director, City Site Estates, Thorburn Colquhoun Holdings and Supply Chain Logistics.

**Sarah McGilway**
*Debts & Guarantees, Intervention Board*

**Aideen McGinley**
*Member of Northern Ireland Committee, National Lottery Charities Board*
Chief Executive, Fermanagh District Council. Trustee, Northern Ireland Voluntary Trust. Chair, Northern Ireland Appeals Advisory Committee. Chair, Fermanagh Local Action Group. Chair, Northern Ireland Local Government Training Group. Former Director, Rural Development Council for Northern Ireland. Former Member, Community Development Review Group.

**DF McGinley**
*Member of Board, Construction Industry Training Board*
McGinley Recruitment Services.

**Michael McGinley**
*Member, Northern Ireland Consumer Committee for Electricity, Office for the Regulation of Electricity & Gas*
Community worker.

**Bill McGinnis**
*Member, Northern Ireland Tourist Board*
Former President, Northern Ireland Chamber of Commerce & Industry. Managing Director, Sperrin Metal Products, Draperstown. Chairman designate, Training & Employment Agency.

**Brian McGinnis**
*Member, DIEL, Office of Telecommunications*
Special adviser, Mencap.

**W McGinnis OBE**
*Chairman, Training & Employment Agency (NI)*
Managing Director, Sperrin Metal Products.

**S McGirr**
*Member of Board, Fisheries Conservancy Board for Northern Ireland*
Representative of District Councils.

**E McGivern CB**
*Personal Tax Division, Inland Revenue*

**Ms M-T McGivern**
*Professional Officer (Curriculum), Youth Council for Northern Ireland*

**Edward McGonagle**
*Member of Board, Liverpool Housing Action Trust*
Former Regional Executive Director, National Westminster Bank in Liverpool.

Member of Board, Merseyside Development Corporation. Director Merseyside Special Investment Fund.

**JG McGorrigan JP**
*Member, Rail Users Consultative Committee for North Eastern England*
Magistrate on Kingston upon Hull Bench. Member. Humberside Magistrates Court Committee. Former Chief Nursing Officer, Yorkshire Region. Former General Manager of a Health Trust. Chairman, Hull Victim & Witness Support Scheme and BBC Radio Humberside Local Radio Advisory Committee. Member, BBC Yorkshire & Humberside Regional Advisory Committee.

**Bill McGowan**
*Manager Marketing & Information Services, Local Enterprise Development Unit*

**Ian D McGowan**
*Librarian & Secretary to the Board of Trustees, National Library of Scotland*
*Member, The British Library*

**E McGrade**
*Member of Council, Council for Catholic Maintained Schools*

**F McGrady**
*Member, Sports Council for Northern Ireland*

**Dr T Mcgrath**
*Member of Board, Probation Board for Northern Ireland*

**Prof AM McGregor**
*Member of Council, Medical Research Council*
King's College School of Medicine, London.

**Paul McGuckin**
*District Valuer, Valuation & Lands Agency*

**TBC McGuffog**
*Member of Board, Simpler Trade Procedures Board*
Director, Planning & Logistcs, Nestle UK. Member of Council, Article Number Association. Chairman, UK Confederation for EDI Standards.

**Sean McGuickin**
*Human Resources Manager, Council for Catholic Maintained Schools*

**Fred McGuigan**
*North Eastern, Rate Collection Agency*

**Maria McGuinness**
*Member, Northern Ireland Consumer Committee for Electricity, Office for the Regulation of Electricity & Gas*
Pharmacist.

**George McHollan**
*Works, Highlands & Islands Airports*

**Gerald McHugh**
*Scottish Office Assessor, Scottish Sports Council*

**Leslie McHugh**
*Member, Yorkshire Consumers' Committee, Office of Electricity Regulation*

**Teresa McHugh**
*Business Assurance & Change Manager, War Pensions Agency*

**W McIlmoyle**
*Member, Sports Council for Northern Ireland*

**Dr Bob McIntosh**
*Chief Executive, Forest Enterprise*

**Dr Graham McIntosh MBE**
*Chairman, Scottish Medical Practices Committee*

**PT McIntosh**
*Chairman, RFAC, The Environment Agency*

**Air Vice-Marshal IG McIntyre**
*Chief Executive, Defence Dental Agency*

**Michael McIntyre**
*Treasurer, The Great Britain-China Centre*
Senior Executive, HSBC Private Banking International.

**Malcolm McIver**
*Deputy Chairman, The Accounts Commission for Scotland*
Senior Partner, Bird Semple Solicitors. Chairman Rodime. Director Croft Oil & Gas, Thomson Litho Holdings and other companies. Chairman, Royal Scottish Academy of Music & Drama and Scottish Musicians' Benevolent Fund. Member, Company Law Committee of Law Society of Scotland.

**HS McKay**
*Professional Services Manager, Planning Service*

**Jane McKay**
*Member of Board, West of Scotland Water Authority*
Secretary, Glasgow Trades Union Council. Member, STUC General Council. Member, Glasgow City Council Economic & Industrial Development Committee, Govan Initiative, Scottish Women's Co-ordination Group, Scottish Constitutional Convention and Scottish Family Policy Campaign Group.

**RJ McKay**
*Finance Director, Caledonian MacBrayne Ltd*

**Gary McKeane**
*Director, Literature, The Arts Council of England*

**Andrew McKearnen**
*Member, Rail Users Consultative Committee for North Western England*

**Sheila McKechnie**
*Member of Court, Bank of England*

**Graham McKee**
*Chief Executive, Scottish Enterprise Tayside*

**Jacqui McKee**
*Manager, General Operations, Fair Employment Commission for Northern Ireland*

**Marshall McKee**
*Member of Board, Northern Ireland Museums' Council*
Acting Director, Ulster Museum. Nominated by the Ulster Museum.

**RA McKee**
*Member, The British Library*
Association of Metropolitan Authorities.

**Will McKee**
*Member of Board, Local Enterprise Development Unit*
Director, Broomhill Group, Euroventure Group, Euroventure (Executive Placement), Euroventure Consulting, NIWEB Internet Marketing, Euroventure Executive & Corporate Development, Yellowbrick Training & Development, Euroventure (BG), Stately Homes & Developments and Northern Ireland Innovation Programme.

**J McKeever**
*Member, Sports Council for Northern Ireland*

**Mrs A McKenna**
*Head of Corporate Communications, Valuation Office Agency*

**Anne McKenna**
*Director of Operations, Rate Collection Agency*

**Mrs C McKenna**
*Member, Training & Employment Agency (NI)*
Vice Principal, St Mary's High School, Limavady.

**G McKenna**
*Director of Vehicle Test Administration, Driver & Vehicle Testing Agency*

**Gillian McKenna**
*Director, Appraisal, Northern Ireland Tourist Board*

**Patrick McKenna**
*Member of Board, British Tourist Authority*
Chairman & Chief Executive, The Really Useful Group. Former Partner, Deloitte & Touche.

**Colin McKenzie**
*Head of Development, National Gallery*

**GW McKenzie**
*Company Secretary, Caledonian MacBrayne Ltd*

**Mike McKenzie QC**
*Member of Management Board, The Court Service*
Registrar of Criminal Appeals & Master of the Crown Office.

**Mrs U McKeogh**
*Associate Adviser GDP (CE), Northern Ireland Council for Postgraduate Medical & Dental Education*

**S McKerracher**
*Controller, Operations Air and Sea, Scottish Fisheries Protection Agency*

**Liam McKibben**
*Member of Council, Food from Britain*
Department of Agriculture for Northern Ireland.

**Malcolm McKibbin**
*Divisional Roads Manager, Roads Service*

**Prof Peter McKie CBE**
*Chairman, Industrial Research & Technology Unit*
Health & Safety Consultant.

**Joan McKiernan**
*Chief Investigation Officer, Equal Opportunities Commission for Northern Ireland*

**Dr Michael McKiernan**
*Member, Health & Safety Commission*
Director of Health, Safety & Environment, Lucas Industries. Appointed to represent interests of employers. Member, Health, Safety & Environmental Policy Committee, Engineering Employers Federation (EEF).

**M McKillen**
*Secretary, Agricultural Wages Board for Northern Ireland*

**Dr AF McKinlay**
*Head of Department, Non-ionising Radiation, National Radiological Protection Board*

**Peter McKinlay**
*Chief Executive, Scottish Homes*
Previously career civil servant in The Scottish Office, including Director, Scottish Prison Service. Chairman, Bute Beyond 2000. Board member, Wise Group. Director, St Mary's Cathedral Workshop.

**Eric A McKinley**
*Member, Northern Ireland Local Government Officers' Superannuation Committee*

**J McKinley**
*NIGIS, IT Systems, Ordnance Survey of Northern Ireland*

**Noirin McKinney**
*Director, Creative Arts Department, Arts Council of Northern Ireland*

**Dr A McKnight**
*Director of Postgraduate General Practice Education, Northern Ireland Council for Postgraduate Medical & Dental Education*

**JQ McL Clarke**
*Senior Development Officer, Sports Council for Northern Ireland*

**P McLachlan OBE**
*Member of Council, Medical Research Council*
Bryson House.

**Patricia McLagan**
*Language Teaching Adviser, Centre for Information on Language Teaching & Research*

**Dr Anne McLaren DBE**
*Member, Human Fertilisation & Embryology Authority*
*Trustee, Natural History Museum*
Principal Research Associate, Wellcome CRC Institute.

**Colin A McLaren**
*Trustee, National Library of Scotland*

**Cameron McLatchie CBE**
*Deputy Chairman, Scottish Enterprise*

**Derek McLauchlan**
*Chief Executive, National Air Traffic Services, Civil Aviation Authority*
Former Managing Director, Renishaw Research. Former Director of Technology & Engineering, International Computers. Previously with Marconi, European Space Research Organisation and British Aircraft Corporation.

**Miss Elizabeth K McLean OBE**
*Member, The Accounts Commission for Scotland*
Former Chief Area Nursing Officer, Lothian Health.

**Norman McLean**
*Deputy Director, Broadcasting Standards Commission*

**Ruari McLean, CBE**
*Trustee, National Library of Scotland*

**Prof Sheila AM McLean**
*Member, Scottish Higher Education Funding Council*
Professor of Law & Ethics in Medicine, University of Glasgow.

**Aileen McLeish**
*Director of Finance, Historic Royal Palaces*

**Joyce McLellan**
*Deputy Director, The British Association for Central & Eastern Europe*

**Bob McLeod**
*Managing Director, Highlands & Islands Airports*

**Catharine McLeod**
*16th/17th Century Curator, National Portrait Gallery*

**Miss Kirsty McLeod**
*Commissioner, English Heritage*

**Robert M McLeod**
*Director, Highlands & Islands Airports*

**Owen McMahon**
*Member, Livestock & Meat Commission for Northern Ireland*
Former President, Northern Ireland Master Butchers' Association. Member, Department of Health Advisory Panel (London).

**Prof John McManus**
*Member, East Areas Board & Scientific Advisory Committee, Scottish Natural Heritage*

**SJ McManus**
*Head, Pension Schemes Office, Inland Revenue*

**M McMath**
*Senior Quantity Surveyor, Compensation Agency*

**Iain McMillan**
*Chairman, Scottish Enterprise Tayside*

**Mrs N McMorrow**
*Member of Council, Council for Catholic Maintained Schools*
Teacher Representative.

**Eunan McMullan**
*Senior Complaints Officer, Fair Employment Commission for Northern Ireland*

**Mrs Rosaleen McMullan**
*Member, Arts Council of Northern Ireland*
Arts Development Officer, Craigavon Borough Council.

**Tom McMullan**
*Member of Council, British Educational Communications & Technology Agency*
Director, CLASS Project, Northern Ireland.

**Allan McMullen**
*Chief Executive, Construction Industry Training Board (NI)*

**CH McMurray**
*Member of Board of Trustees, Agricultural Research Institute of Northern Ireland*
Appointed by the Department of Agriculture.

**Dr CH McMurray**
*Member of Governing Body, Rowett Research Institute*

**HC McMurray**
*Director, Royal Naval Museum*

**DR McMurtry**
*Member of Steering Board, Patent Office*

**J McMyn**
*Member of Council, Hannah Research Institute*

**John McMyn**
*Member, Scottish Agricultural Wages Board*
Employers' representative member nominated by the National Farmers' Union of Scotland and the Scottish Landowners' Federation.

**Geralyn McNally**
*Member of Commission, Independent Commission for Police Complaints for Northern Ireland*

**Nicholas McNamara**
*Member, North Western Consumers' Committee, Office of Electricity Regulation*

**Ian McNee**
*Chairman, Parole Board for Scotland*
Chairman, MacDonald Lindsay Pindar. Former Chairman, Lothian Region Children's Panel.

**Adrian McNeil**
*Member Advisory Board, NHS Pensions Agency*
Department of Health.

**Donald McNeil OBE**
*Member, The Accounts Commission for Scotland*
Former Chief Executive, South Ayrshire Hospitals NHS Trust.

**Ian McNeil**
*Member of Board of Governors, Museum of London*
Appointed by the Corporation of London.

**Johnston McNeill**
*Chief Executive, Meat Hygiene Service*
*Member of Ownership Board, Meat Hygiene Service*

**TC McNeill**
*Technical Director, Caledonian MacBrayne Ltd*

**J McNeillie**
*Area Manager - North, Engineering Construction Industry Training Board*

**T McNicholas**
*Member, Parole Board*

**RJ McNicol**
*Head, Soft Fruit & Perennial Crops Department, Scottish Crop Research Institute*

**Madeleine McPhail**
*Member, Scottish Tourist Board*

**Gordon McPhee**
*Personnel, Highlands & Islands Airports*

**Group Captain Ian McPhee**
*Commandant Defence Nuclear Biological & Chemical Centre, Army Training & Recruitment Agency*

**WJH McPherson**
*Member, NIACT, Northern Ireland Advisory Committee on Telecommunications*
Fellow of the Institute of Bankers in Ireland.

**Dr Jim McQuaid**
*Chief Scientist, The Health & Safety Executive*

**The Very Rev I McQuillan**
*Member of Council, Council for Catholic Maintained Schools*

**Denise McShane**
*Company Secretary, Student Loans Company*

**Rory McShane**
*Member, General Consumer Council for Northern Ireland*
Solicitor.

**Daniel McSorley**
*Chief Executive, Rivers Agency*

**M McVeigh**
*Graphical Production & Sales, Ordnance Survey of Northern Ireland*

**Mrs Joanna McVey**
*Member of Board, Northern Ireland Museums' Council*

Businesswoman. Nominee of the Minister for Education.

**Mary McWilliams**
*Head, Economic Regulation (Gas), Office for the Regulation of Electricity & Gas*

**Monica McWilliams**
*Member of Northern Ireland Committee, National Lottery Charities Board*
Senior Lecturer, Social & Community Sciences, University of Ulster. Vice Chair, Northern Ireland European Women's Platform. Elected representative, Northern Ireland Women's Coalition, to the Northern Ireland Forum & Peace Talks.

**Paul McWilliams, OBE**
*Chairman, Local Enterprise Development Unit*
Chairman, Parity Solutions (Ireland), COMPEN Mgmt Cons and Royal Hospitals. Board member, Irish American Partnership. Chairman, CCC Technology and Airports (Europe).

**Molly Meacher**
*Member, Police Complaints Authority*
Former Adviser to Chairman, Russian Federal Employment Service and Mental Health Act Commissioner.

**Michael Meadowcroft**
*Trustee, Community Development Foundation*

**Captain TJ Meadows CBE**
*Trustee, Royal Navy Submarine Museum*

**Adrian Mears**
*Technical Director, Defence Evaluation & Research Agency*

**George Medley**
*Member of Board, UK Ecolabelling Board*
Former Director, World Wide Fund for Nature UK.

**Elizabeth Meehan**
*Commissioner, Fair Employment Commission for Northern Ireland*

**Scott Meek**
*Member of Board, Scottish Screen*

**GW Meikle**
*Member, Rail Users Consultative Committee for North Eastern England*
Former senior partner, Dickinson Dees. Under Sherriff, City of Newcastle. Deputy Lieutenant, County Tyne & Wear.

**Prof GI Meirion-Jones**
*Commissioner, Royal Commission on Historical Mon uments of England*

**Julie Mellor**
*Member, Commission for Racial Equality*
Consultant in equality and diversity. Former Board Member, Employers Forum on Disability. Member, CBI Equal Opportunities Panel. Former Member, National Advisory Council on the Employment of People with Disabilities. Founder and Steering Group Member, Race for Opportunity campaign, Business in the Community.

**Ian A Melrose**
*Member, Scottish Agricultural Wages Board*
Employers' representative member nominated by the National Farmers' Union of Scotland and the Scottish Landowners' Federation.

**A Melville**
*Member of Advisory Board, Driver & Vehicle Licensing Agency*
*Member of Advisory Board, Coastguard*
*Member of Advisory Board, Vehicle Certification Agency*
DETR Executive Agencies Division.

**Prof David Melville**
*Chief Executive, The Further Education Funding Council*

**RE Melville**
*Member, Wine Standards Board*

**Valerie Mendes**
*Curator, Textiles & Dress Collection, Victoria & Albert Museum*

**John M Menzies**
*Trustee, National Library of Scotland*

**Neil Menzies**
*Deputy Chairman, Scottish Water & Sewerage Customers Council*

**A Mercer**
*Human Resources Director, Northern Ireland Transport Holding Company*

**Prof Ian Mercer**
*Member, Ofwat South West Customer Service Committee*

**Mike Mercer**
*Head of Funding Allocation & Personnel Management, Teacher Training Agency*
Observer, Higher Education Funding Council for England

**RJ Mercer**
*Secretary & Director, NMRS, Royal Commission on Ancient & Historical Monuments of Scotland*

**Ms SG Mercer**
*Member, Training & Employment Agency (NI)*
Personnel Manager, FII Footwear Management.

**Bruce A Merchant OBE**
*Member, The Accounts Commission for Scotland*
Partner, South Forrest, Solicitors, Inverness. Dean of Faculty of Solicitors of Highlands. Former Member, Council of Law Society of Scotland. Former Vice Chairman, Highland Health Board.

**A Meredith**
*Member, Rail Users Consultative Committee for Midlands*

**Allan Merry**
*Legal Adviser, Office of Water Services*

**Peter Merson**
*Chief Executive, Milk Development Council*
Former Managing Veterinary Surgeon, Genus.

**Cholmeley Messer**
*Chairman, London Pensions Fund Authority*
Solicitor. Former Chairman, Save & Prosper Group. Director, Bank. Chairman, Hamilton Life Insurance Co and Hamilton Assurance Co. Former Chairman, Code of Advertising Practice Committee of the Advertising Standards Authority and the Unit Trust Association. Former Member, Disciplinary Panel, Life Assurance & Unit Trust Regulatory Organisation.

**JH Metcalf**
*Member, National Biological Standards Board*

**Janet Methley**
*Head of Branch, Mensuration, Forest Research*

**Dr Jeremy Metters**
*Chairman of Advisory Board, Medical Devices Agency*
Deputy Chief Medical Officer, Department of Health.

**Doros Michail**
*Director of Quality & Client Services & Business Development, Northern Ireland Child Support Agency*

**Ian G Middleton**
*Director of Audit, The Scottish Legal Aid Board*

**JT Middleton, OBE**
*Member, Rail Users Consultative Committee for North Eastern England*
Former Sub-Postmaster. Former elected Member, Gateshead Metropolitan Borough Council.

**Miles Middleton CBE**
*Chairman, Rural Development Commission*
Chartered Accountant. Director, North West Chambers of Commerce. Chairman, Northern Enterprise. Trustee, Northumberland Red Cross.

**Brigadier SG Middleton**
*Member, Logistic Information Systems Agency*
DES 1.

**Gordon Midgley**
*Deputy Director, Finance and Resources, Bank of England*

**Ted Milburn**
*Member, Scottish Community Education Council*

**Gwyn Miles**
*Major Projects, Victoria & Albert Museum*

**Kenneth Miles**
*Member of Board, UK Ecolabelling Board*
Former Director General, Incorporated Society of British Advertisers.

**Captain R Mill Irving**
*Marine Superintendent, Scottish Fisheries Protection Agency*

**Bob Millar**
*Director of Strategy, Policy & Planning, Scottish Homes*

**Dennis Millar**
*Director of Resources, Rate Collection Agency*

**Geoffrey T Millar**
*Member, The Accounts Commission for Scotland*
Consultant Ophthalmologist, Royal Infirmary & Western General Hospitals, Edinburgh and St John's Hospital, Livingston.

**Mrs Helen Millar**
*Chairman, Rail Users Consultative Committee for Scotland*
*Deputy Chairman, Central Rail Users Consultative Committee*
Lecturer, Department of Adult Education, Glasgow University. Twenty years' experience in the voluntary consumer movement in Scotland, UK and Europe.

**Ken Millar**
*Chief Executive, Business Development Service*

**Mrs Sandra Millar**
*Personnel Officer, National Board for Nursing, Midwifery & Health Visiting for Scotland*

**Mrs Sheila Millar**
*Commissioner, Mental Health Commission for Northern Ireland*
Company Director.

**Peter Millard**
*Head, Plant Science Group, Macaulay Land Use Research Institute*

**Alan Miller**
*Principal Reporter, Scottish Children's Reporter Administration*
Former Reporter, Glasgow and Regional Reporter, Dumfries & Galloway.

**Bob Miller**
*Member, Central Rail Users Consultative Committee*
Wheelchair user, with a particular interest in the needs of passengers with disabilities.

**David Miller CBE**
*Chairman, Scottish Qualifications Authority*

**Donald Miller**
*Area Manager, Scottish Fisheries Protection Agency*

**Cllr George Miller**
*Member, South Eastern Consumers' Committee, Office of Electricity Regulation*

**I Miller, OBE**
*Member of Board of Governors, Macaulay Land Use Research Institute*

**Norman Miller**
*Member, Horserace Betting Levy Board*

**P Miller**
*Employer member, Engineering Construction Industry Training Board*
Construction Manager, Watson Steel

**SC Miller CBE**
*Member of Council, Engineering & Physical Sciences Research Council*
Rolls-Royce

**Simon Miller**
*Member, Scottish Hospital Endowments Research Trust*

**Stewart Miller**
*Member, Scottish Higher Education Funding Council*
Chairman of Council Loughborough University.

**Anthea Millett**
*Chief Executive, Teacher Training Agency*

**Tony Millns**
*Head of Communications, Qualifications & Curriculum Authority*

**Dame Barbara Mills**
*Director of Public Prosecutions, Crown Prosecution Service*

**Mrs Elizabeth Mills**
*Member of Council, Economic & Social Research Council*
Director, Research into Ageing.

**Janet Mills**
*Subject Adviser, Music, Office for Standards in Education*

**Leif Mills CBE**
*Chairman, Covent Garden Market Authority*
*Member, Employment Tribunals Service*
Former General Secretary, Banking, Insurance & Finance Union. Former Member, TUC General Council. Member, Employment Tribunals Service Board, Personal Investment Authority, Ombudsman Council and Consumers' Association Council.

**Andrew Milne**
*Regional Manager & Secretary, Ofwat Thames Customer Service Committee*

**Claire Milne**
*Member, ENACT, Office of Telecommunications*
Consultant, specialising in social aspects of telecommunications.

**James Milne**
*Member, Parole Board for Scotland*

**John A Milne**
*Deputy Director & Head, Ecology & Animal Science Group, Macaulay Land Use Research Institute*

**Lindsay Milne**
*Director Personnel, Logistic Information Systems Agency*

**Carole Milner**
*Head of Conservation & Collection Care, Museums & Galleries Commission*

**Mrs Mary Milton**
*Member, Ofwat Central Customer Service Committee*

**Dominique Mine**
*Food from Britain (France) SARL*

**Cllr Dennis Minnis**
*Deputy Chairman, Castle Vale Housing Action Trust*
Member Birmingham City Council. Member, Housing, Urban Renewal & Community Affairs Committees.

**Stephanie Minns**
*Customer Relations Manager, Central Computer & Telecommunications Agency*

**PD Minor**
*Head of Virology, National Biological Standards Board*

**Archie Minto**
*Head of Charges & Codes of Practice, Scottish Water & Sewerage Customers Council*

**Jim Mirabal**
*Director of Finance & Administration, Royal Commission on Historical Monuments of England*

**John Miskelly MBE**
*Member, Northern Ireland Local Government Officers' Superannuation Committee*

**Sam Miskelly**
*Assistant Director, General Consumer Council for Northern Ireland*

**Anna Mitchell**
*Personnel & Training Manager, Museum of Science & Industry Manchester*

**Annmaree Mitchell**
*Member, Scottish Agricultural Wages Board*
Employees' Representative Member nominated by the Rural, Agricultural & Allied Workers National Trade Group (Scotland) of the Transport & General Workers' Union.

**Caroline Mitchell**
*Member, Police Complaints Authority*
Solicitor. Former Senior Assistant to Insurance Ombudsman.

**D Mitchell CBE**
*Chairman, REPAC, The Environment Agency*

**Maureen Mitchell**
*Housing Benefit, Rate Collection Agency*

**RF Mitchell**
*Head of Admin/Finance, Sports Council for Northern Ireland*

**Robert Mitchell**
*Member, Apple & Pear Research Council*
Member, MAFF Regional Horticultural Crop Intelligence Committee. Director, Concordia (YSV). Trustee, East Malling Trust.

**Dr Rosamond Mitchell**
*Member, Centre for Information on Language Teaching & Research*
School of Education, University of Southampton.

**WG Mitchell**
*Deputy Director, Ordnance Survey of Northern Ireland*

**John Mockler**
*Head of Human Resources, Tate Gallery*

**Andy Moffat**
*Head of Branch, Environmental Research, Forest Research*

**John Moffitt CBE**
*Chairman, Milk Development Council*
Retired dairy farmer. Member of advisory committees of Edinburgh University research farms Langhill, Roslin Institute. Newcastle University, and Centre for Genome Research, Edinburgh University.

**Gordon Moggach**
*Senior Business Development Manager, Highlands & Islands Enterprise*

**Douglas Molldoon**
*Director General Electrical Supply/ Director General of Gas, Office for the Regulation of Electricity & Gas*

**Arthur Moir**
*Chief Executive/Registrar of Titles, Land Registers of Northern Ireland*

**Bob Mole**
*Development Officer, Arts Council of Wales*

**Julie Molloy**
*Merchandise Director, National Gallery Publications, National Gallery*

**D Moloney**
*Member of Board, Probation Board for Northern Ireland*

**M Moloney**
*Director, Northern Ireland Transport Holding Company*

**Dr Maria Moloney**
*Member of Commission, Independent Television Commission*
Member for Northern Ireland.

**Helena Molyneux**
*Director Corporate Personnel, British Council*

**Dan Monaghan**
*Operational Services Director, National Savings*

**Jim Monaghan**
*Director, Industrial Science Centre, Industrial Research & Technology Unit*

**Lady Monck**
*Trustee, National Gallery*

**Prof Fabian Monds**
*Member, Industrial Research & Technology Unit*
Provost & Pro-Vice Chancellor, Planning & Research, University of Ulster.

**Neil Money**
*Chief Executive, Caithness & Sutherland Enterprise*

**Mrs Shiona Monfries**
*Executive Director (Standards), National Board for Nursing, Midwifery & Health Visiting for Scotland*

**Dave Monk**
*Senior Customer Relations Manager, Central Computer & Telecommunications Agency*

**Mrs SG Monk**
*Member of Council, Advisory, Conciliation & Arbitration Service*

**D Monnington**
*Chairman, RFDC, The Environment Agency*

**Rt Hon Sir Hector Monro PC JP MP**
*Trustee, Royal Air Force Museum*

**Ian Monson**
*Member, Eastern Consumers' Committee, Office of Electricity Regulation*

**Dr Jennifer Montagu**
*Trustee, British Museum*
*Trustee, Wallace Collection*

**Nick LJ Montagu CB**
*Chairman, Inland Revenue*

**Michael Montague CBE**
*Member, Millennium Commission*
Businessman. Former Chairman, English Tourist Board and National Consumer Council.

**Peter Monteith**
*Regional Executive, Independent Television Commission*

**Capt CPR Montgomery**
*Assistant Director Training Management, Naval Recruiting & Training Agency*

**Lindsay Montgomery**
*Director of Corporate Services, Scottish Natural Heritage*

**R Montgomery**
*Member of Board, Fisheries Conservancy Board for Northern Ireland*
Commercial fishermen's representative.

**BJC Moore**
*Member, Rail Users Consultative Committee for Eastern England*

**Bob Moore**
*Member of Commission, Independent Commission for Police Complaints for Northern Ireland*

**Graham Moore**
*Managing Director, South Division, Welsh Development Agency*

**John Moore MBE**
*Member, Ofwat Thames Customer Service Committee*

**Mike Moore**
*District Valuer, Valuation & Lands Agency*

**Peter Moore OBE**
*Member, English Tourist Board*
MD, Center Parcs UK. Board Member, North Nottinghamshire TEC. Member, CBI Tourism Action Group and UK Round Table on Sustainable Development.

**Richard Moore**
*Member, Livestock & Meat Commission for Northern Ireland*

Member, DANI's Research and Development Committee.

**Rory Moore**
*Resident Board Member, Tower Hamlets Housing Action Trust*
Resident on Lefevre Walk Estate. Company Secretary, CAPA (East London) and CASE. Sub-Committee Member, Toynbee Housing Association. Trustee Member, Bow Community Trust.

**Stephen Moore**
*Governor, British Film Institute*

**Steve Moore**
*Director of Client Services, Waltham Forest Housing Action Trust*

**Stuart Moore**
*Director of Finance, Meat Hygiene Service*

**John Moorhouse**
*Secretary, Rail Users Consultative Committee for North Western England*

**Peter Moorhouse**
*Chairman, Police Complaints Authority*
Former Director of a multinational company. Chairman, local review committee of the Parole HMP Wormwood Scrubs.

**Dr A Moran**
*Member of Council, Council for Catholic Maintained Schools*

**John Mordy**
*Member, Yorkshire Consumers' Committee, Office of Electricity Regulation*

**Prof James More**
*Member of Council, Crafts Council*
Head of Design, University of Northumbria.

**Alan Morgan**
*Director, Agency Coordination, Welsh Development Agency*

**Declan Morgan**
*Commissioner, Fair Employment Commission for Northern Ireland*

**Prof Derec Llwyd Morgan**
*Member, National Library of Wales*
Elected by the Court of Governors.

**Dr Janet Morgan**
*Member, Scottish Hospital Endowments Research Trust*

**Jeff Morgan**
*Director, British Educational Communications & Technology Agency*

**Jeffrey Morgan**
*Member of Board, Welsh Language Board*
Managing Director, Hyder Services.

**Cllr HM Morgan MBE**
*Member, National Library of Wales*
Coopted by the Council.

**Dr Janet P Morgan**
*Member of Board, British Council*
Writer and consultant.

**Sir John Morgan KCMG**
*Trustee, British Museum*

**Mrs Karen Morgan**
*Member of Board, The Environment Agency*
Vice Chairman and Member of Board of Governors, University of West of England. Trustee and Director, Bristol Polytechnic Charitable Trust. Trustee and Director, Wallscourt Foundation. Member of Council and Director, WaterAid. Trustee and Director, Bath Festivals Trust and Music Space Trust. Former Board Member, National Rivers Authority.

**Prof Peter H Morgan**
*Member, National Library of Wales*
Co-opted by the Council.

**Peter J Morgan**
*Head, Molecular Neuroendocrinology Unit, Rowett Research Institute*

**TK Morgan**
*Member of Board, Investors in People UK*
Director of Personnel, British Aerospace.

**Patricia Morgan-Webb**
*Board Member, Qualifications & Curriculum Authority*
Principal and Chief Executive, Clarendon College, Nottingham.

**Michael Moriarty CB**
*Deputy Chairman, The Radio Authority*

**Candida Morley**
*Development Director, Victoria & Albert Museum*

**Dave Morrell**
*Head, Particle Physics Division, Particle Physics & Astronomy Research Council*

**Alfred Morris**
*Member, The Further Education Funding Council*
*Member, Higher Education Funding Council for Wales*
Vice-Chancellor, University of the West of England. Non-Executive Director, Bristol & West Building Society.

**Bill Morris**
*Member of Court, Bank of England*

**Clare Morris**
*PA to Chief Executive, Westminster Foundation for Democracy*

**David B Morris**
*Member, Post Office Users' National Council*
Solicitor. Chairman, London South West POAC.

**Derek Morris**
*Chairman, Monopolies & Mergers Commission*
Former Fellow & Tutor in Economics, Oriel College, Oxford and Reader in Economics, Oxford University.

**Air Vice Marshal J Morris CBE**
*Member of Board, Queen Victoria School*

**Dr JA Morris**
*Research Director, Veterinary Laboratories Agency*

**Kathryn Morris**
*Director of Finance, S4C*

**Lisa Morris**
*Capital Officer, Arts Council of Wales*

**Lord Morris of Castle Morris**
*Vice-Chairman, Trustees, National Portrait Gallery*

**Marion Morris**
*Capital Officer, Arts Council of Wales*

**Mrs N Morris**
*Member, National Biological Standards Board*

**Commander RR Morris**
*Secretary to the Naval Secretary, Naval Manning Agency*

**Prof Richard Morris**
*Commissioner, English Heritage*

**Robin Morris**
*Member, Rail Users Consultative Committee for North Western England*

**S Morris**
*Head of Administration, Cadw*

**Dr Thomas Morris**
*Member, Ofwat Yorkshire Customer Service Committee*

**W Morris**
*Member of Council, Advisory, Conciliation & Arbitration Service*

**Prof William Morris**
*Member, Industrial Research & Technology Unit*
Professor of Aerospace Engineering, Queen's University of Belfast.

**AF Morrison CBE**
*Chairman, Highlands & Islands Enterprise*

**Hon Sir Charles Morrison**
*Vice President, Community Development Foundation*

**Garth Morrison CBE**
*Member of Scotland Committee, National Lottery Charities Board*
Farmer in East Lothian. Former Chief Scout of the UK and Member of World Scout Committee. Honorary Fellow, Scottish Community Education Council. Chair, East & Midlothian NHS Trust. Vice Chair, South East Committee of Scottish Landowners' Federation. Trustee, Lamp of Lothian Collegiate Trust. Vice President, Commonwealth Youth Exchange Council.

**John Morrison**
*Finance & Administration Director, Student Loans Company*

**Kevin Morrison**
*Director of Housing Services, Liverpool Housing Action Trust*

**Len G Morrison**
*Member, Scottish Agricultural Wages Board*
Employees' Representative Member nominated by the Rural, Agricultural & Allied Workers National Trade Group

(Scotland) of the Transport & General Workers' Union.

**Nigel M P Morrison, QC**
*Trustee, National Library of Scotland*

**Hon Mrs Sara Morrison**
*Member, National Radiological Protection Board*
*Non-Executive Director, New Millennium Experience Co Ltd*
Executive Director, General Electric Company.

**Steve Morrison**
*Governor, British Film Institute*
*Governor, National Film & Television School*

**Colonel Euan Morrow TD**
*Head of Postal Services, Defence Postal & Courier Services Agency*

**J Mortell**
*Member, Rail Users Consultative Committee for Midlands*

**Miss Kate Mortimer**
*Non-Executive Director, British Nuclear Fuels plc*
*Member, Monopolies & Mergers Commission*
*Member of Board, Crown Agents Foundation*
Independent consultant and financial adviser to UK Know How funds for Eastern and Central Europe and the former Soviet Union.

**Bill Morton**
*Chief Executive, Forth Valley Enterprise*

**John Morton**
*SMC, Defence Evaluation & Research Agency*

**Sir Claus Moser KCB CBE**
*Trustee, British Museum*

**Anthony D Moss**
*Member of Board of Governors, Museum of London*
Appointed by the Corporation of London.

**Mrs Jean Moss**
*Member, East Midland Consumers' Committee, Office of Electricity Regulation*

**Peter Moss**
*Member, North Eastern Consumers' Committee, Office of Electricity Regulation*

**Prof Andrew Motion**
*Member, The Arts Council of England*
Professor of Creative Writing, University of East Anglia.

**Judge Mott**
*Member, Parole Board*

**CG Mottram**
*Director, Fleet Air Arm Museum*
Flag Officer Naval Aviation, RNAS Yeovilton.

**R Mottram**
*Member of College Advisory Council, Civil Service College*
Permanent Under Secretary of State, Ministry of Defence.

**RC Mountain**
*Head, Oil Taxation Office, Inland Revenue*

**R Mountfield CB**
*Member of College Advisory Council, Civil Service College*
Permanent Secretary, Office of Public Service, Cabinet Office.

**Gavin Mowat**
*Director of Policy, Scottish Office Pensions Agency*

**DD Mowforth**
*Employer Member, Engineering Construction Industry Training Board*
IR & Training Manager, UK Construction & Engineering Co.

**Miss Jennifer Moys**
*Secretary to the Trustees, Royal Navy Submarine Museum*

**His Excellency Mendi Msimang**
*Trustee, Imperial War Museum*

**Dr Greg Mudge**
*Area Manager, Scottish Natural Heritage*

**Dame Anne Mueller DCB**
*Commissioner, Rural Development Commission*
Retired Second Permanent Secretary to the Treasury. Company Director.

**Alasdair Muir**
*Secretary, National Savings*

**Chris Muir OBE**
*Member, Ofwat North West Customer Service Committee*

**DD Muir**
*Head, Food Quality, Hannah Research Institute*

**Mrs Dawn Muirhead**
*Member of Board of Governors, Museum of London*
Appointed by the Prime Minister.

**John Muirhead**
*Member, Parole Board for Scotland*
District Officer, Criminal Justice, Social Work Department, Glasgow South.

**Ms T Mulhern**
*Executive Officer (Training/Curriculum), Youth Council for Northern Ireland*

**Clare Mulholland**
*Deputy Chief Executive, Independent Television Commission*

**Dr Fiona Mulholland**
*Member, Northern Ireland Consumer Committee for Electricity, Office for the Regulation of Electricity & Gas*
Research scientist, Department of Agriculture.

**Gerry Mullan**
*Member of Board, Local Enterprise Development Unit*
Director, Laser Therapy, Weyhill Investments, Graham Hunter Shirts and PMH Electronics.

**Robin Mullan**
*Director for Northern Ireland, National Lottery Charities Board*
Formerly Chief Executive, Western Isles Health Board. Chief Executive, Disability Action.

**Brendan Mullen**
*Commissioner, Mental Health Commission for Northern Ireland*
Acting Director of Operations, North Down & Ards Community Health & Social Services Trust.

**Frank Mullen**
*Director, Scottish Convention Bureau, Scottish Tourist Board*

**William H Mullen**
*Chief Executive, Rowett Research Services Limited, Rowett Research Institute*

**Philip Mulligan**
*Information Technology, Rate Collection Agency*

**The Very Rev J Mullin**
*Member of Council, Council for Catholic Maintained Schools*

**John G Mullin**
*Member, The Accounts Commission for Scotland*
Director of Public Affairs, Tait & McLay Communications Group.

**JB Mulvenna**
*Member of Board, Fisheries Conservancy Board for Northern Ireland Member of Board of Trustees, Agricultural Research Institute ofNorthern Ireland*
Appointed by the Ulster Farmers' Union.

**Dick Mundell OBE**
*Head of Administration, Royal Armouries*

**Cllr David Munn JP**
*Member of Board, West of Scotland Water Authority*
Councillor for North Ayrshire. Former Senior Technician, BT. Member, National Society for Clean Air (Scottish Division) and Hunterston Nuclear Liaison Committee.

**Jim Munn MBE**
*Member, English Sports Council*

**Dr Gordon Munro**
*Director of Inspection & Enforcement, Medicines Control Agency*

**Gordon Munro**
*Customer Relations Manager, Intervention Board*

**Graeme Munro**
*Director & Chief Executive, Historic Scotland*

**NC Munro**
*Tax Law Rewrite Project, Inland Revenue*

**Jyoti Munsiff**
*Member of Board, UK Ecolabelling Board*
Company Secretary, Shell Transport & Trading.

**Stuart Munslow**
*Finance & Personnel Director, War Pensions Agency*

**Roger Munson**
*Member, Monopolies & Mergers Commission*
Chartered Accountant. Former Partner, Coopers & Lybrand and Member, Accounting Standards Board.

**Paul Murdin**
*Head, Astronomy Division, Particle Physics & Astronomy Research Council*

**David Murdoch**
*Company Secretary, Scottish Community Education Council*

**Stewart Murdoch**
*Member, Scottish Community Education Council*

**F Murphy**
*Professional Adviser, Youth Council for Northern Ireland*

**John Murphy**
*Director, Combined Arts, Scottish Arts Council*

**L Murphy JP**
*Member, WACT, Welsh Advisory Committee on Telecommunications*
Local Councillor.

**Paul Murphy**
*Personnel & Communications Director, Benefits Agency*

**Peter Murphy**
*Director of Resources & RUCC Sponsorship, Office of the Rail Regulator*

**S Murphy**
*Member, Parole Board*

**Dick Murray**
*Head of Branch, Finance, Forest Research*

**Gerry Murray**
*Acting Deputy Chief Executive, Government Purchasing Agency*

**IC Murray**
*Member of Board of Trustees, Agricultural Research Institute of Northern Ireland*
Appointed by the Ulster Agricultural Organisation Society.

**Jack Murray**
*Group Director - Publications, Central Office of Information*

**K Murray**
*Member, SACOT, Scottish Advisory Committee on Telecommunications*
Director, textile manufacturer.

**Len Murray**
*Director, Resources, Fair Employment Commission for Northern Ireland*

**Miss M Murray**
*Member of Council, Council for Catholic Maintained Schools*
Teacher Representative.

**Malcolm Murray**
*Member, Scottish Sports Council*

**Prof N Murray**
*Member, Biotechnology & Biological Sciences Research Council*
Professor of Molecular Genetics, Institute of Cell & Molecular Biology, University of Edinburgh. Member, European Molecular Biology Organisation and USA Genetics Society. Former President, Genetical Society.

**Roger Murray**
*Member, Commonwealth Development Corporation*
President, Cargill Europe. Director, Fleming Emerging Markets and of Fuerst Day Lawson.

**TK Murray**
*Member of Council, British Hallmarking Council*

**WW Murray OBE**
*Member of Advisory Board, NHS Estates*
Chief Executive, South Tees Acute Hospitals NHS Trust.

**John Mustow**
*Director of Works, Defence Estates Organisation*

**Richard Mycroft**
*Head of Human Resources, UK Passport Agency*

**Heather Mytton**
*Director, West Midlands Region, The Housing Corporation*

# N

**Paul Nabavi**
*Manager, Financial Intermediaries, Commonwealth Development Corporation*

**Sandy Nairne**
*Director of Public and Regional Services, Tate Gallery*

**Bryan Nanson**
*Director of Information Management, Ordnance Survey*

**J Napleton**
*Director Central, Commission for the New Towns*

**Kate Nash**
*Member, DIEL, Office of Telecommunications*
Director, Leadership Consortium, Prince of Wales' Advisory Group on Disability.

**Vicki Nash**
*Director, Scottish Water & Sewerage Customers Council*

**Miss Sarah Nason**
*Chief Executive, Farming & Rural Conservation Agency*

**Rod Natkiel**
*Member, The Arts Council of England*

**Ric Navarro**
*Director of Legal Services, The Environment Agency*

**B Naylor**
*Board Member, The British Library*
Librarian, Southampton University.

**Brian Naylor**
*Director, Properties in Care, Historic Scotland*

**Christopher Neale**
*Finance Director, British Waterways*

**Ray Neath**
*Director of Corporate and Infrastructure, Logistic Information Systems Agency*

**Ronald Neath**
*Member, South Eastern Consumers' Committee, Office of Electricity Regulation*

**Mrs J Needham**
*Member, Rail Users Consultative Committee for Midlands*

**Dr Dwain Neil**
*Member, Commission for Racial Equality*
Global Accounts Manager, for oilfield chemicals, Shell Additives International. Member, Home Secretary's Advisory Council on Race Relations. Former Chairman, Parents' Association for Educational Advance. Founder and first President, British Caribbean Junior Chamber of Commerce.

**Ronald Neil**
*Chief Executive, BBC Production, British Broadcasting Corporation*

**John Neill, CBE**
*Member of Court, Bank of England*
Deputy Chairman & Group Chief Executive, Unipart Group of Companies.

**Alan Neilson**
*Head of Management Studies, The Accounts Commission for Scotland*

**Kelvin Nel**
*Member, Eastern Consumers' Committee, Office of Electricity Regulation*

**Brian Nelson CBE**
*Chairman, Home-Grown Cereals Authority*

**Dr Elizabeth Nelson**
*Chairman, UK Ecolabelling Board*
Formerly of Taylor Nelson AGB.

**Fred Nelson**
*Member, Scottish Sports Council*

**Ian Nelson**
*Head of Finance, British Film Institute*

**Dr Roy Nelson OBE**
*Director, Dounreay, UK Atomic Energy Authority*
Joined UKAEA in 1961. Former Research Director and Assistant Director, Culham/Harwell. Former Director responsible, DRAWMOPS.

**R W Nesbitt**
*Secretary, Northern Ireland Local Government Officers' Superannuation Committee*

**Jeff Neslen**
*Regional Director, East, English Sports Council*

**Rabbi Julia Neuberger**
*Member of Council, Medical Research Council*
Camden & Islington Community Health Services NHS Trust.

**Mrs Marianne Neuhoff**
*Member, Ofwat Eastern Customer Service Committee*

**Mrs Amanda Nevill**
*Head of NMPFT, National Museum of Science & Industry*

**Alan Neville**
*Corporate Services Director, Local Enterprise Development Unit*

**Ms Caroline Neville**
*Member of Board, Higher Education Funding Council for England*
Principal, Norwich City College of Further & Higher Education.

**Prof David Newbery**
*Member, Monopolies & Mergers Commission*
Professor of Applied Economics, University of Cambridge. Fellow, Centre for Economic Policy Research. Member, Environmental Economics Panel at the Department of the Environment.

**Prof Palmer Newbould**
*Trustee, National Heritage Memorial Fund*

**Prof PJ Newbould OBE**
*Member, Joint Nature Conservation Committee*
Council for Nature Conservation & the Countryside (NI).

**Prof Howard Newby CBE**
*Commissioner, Rural Development Commission*
Vice-Chancellor, Southampton University. Chairman and Trustee, Centre for Exploitation of Science & Technology. Trustee, Wessex Medical Trust. Consultant, Unilever Research.

**Mrs Barbara Newman**
*Member of Board of Governors, Museum of London*
Appointed by the Corporation of London.

**K Newman**
*Building Superintendent, Covent Garden Market Authority*

**Prof David Newton**

*Vice Chairman, Funding Agency for Schools*
Education and Management Development Consultant. Governor and Chairman of the Finance Committee, Deer Park GM School, Cirencester. Former Vice-Principal of the Royal Agricultural College.

**Jeremy Newton**
*Director, National Lottery, The Arts Council of England*

**John Newton**
*Board Member, Castle Vale Housing Action Trust*
Member, Area Regeneration Initiative Steering Group, Board Member, Castle Vale Community Housing Association. Board Director, Castle Vale Sports & Community Partnership.

**Liz Newton**
*Regional Officer, Countryside Commission*

**Sir Wilfrid Newton CBE**
*Non-Executive Director, Office of the Rail Regulator*

**Jim Niblett**
*Director of Services Competition & International Affairs, Office of Telecommunications*

**Sir D Nichol**
*Non-Executive Committee Member, HM Prison Service*

**PF Nicholl**
*Deputy Chief Executive, Vehicle Certification Agency*

**Maurice Nicholls**
*Finance Director, National Savings*

**Peter Nicholls**
*Member of Council, British Educational Communications & Technology Agency*
Consultant.

**Peter Nichols**
*Member, London Regional Passengers Committee*

**Adèle Nicholson**
*Membership Secretary, The Britain-Russia Centre*

**Cllr Donald Nicholson**
*Member, North of Scotland Water Authority*
Independent Councillor, Sandwick, Western Isles.

**RG Nicholson**
*Senior Inspector, Midland Region, Gaming Board for Great Britain*

**J Nickson**
*Member, Property Advisers to the Civil Estate*

**Mrs A Nicol**
*Commissioner, Royal Commission on Ancient & Historical Monuments in Wales*

**JA Nicolson**
*Member of Board, Highlands & Islands Enterprise*

**R Niddrie**
*Appointed Trustee, Royal Marines Museum*

**Paul Niedzwiedzki**
*Assistant Chief Executive (Strategic Direction of Service), Service Children's Education*

**Kevin Nield**
*Member, Rail Users Consultative Committee for Wales*

**BE Nimick**
*Chief Executive, Medical Supplies Agency*

**Pat Niner**
*Board Member, Castle Vale Housing Action Trust*
Senior Lecturer Centre for Urban & Regional Studies, University of Birmingham. Former Research Secretary to the Inquiry into British Housing. Member, Bromford Carinthia Housing Association. Trustee, Base Trust. Board Member, Castle Vale Community Housing Association.

**Bill Niven**
*Board Director, Home-Grown Cereals Authority*

**G Noad**
*Director Facilities, Naval Aircraft Repair Organisation*

**Derek Noble**
*Director, Regional Operations Division, Training & Employment Agency (NI)*

**Elaine Noble**
*Director of ETB Operations, English Tourist Board*

**Peter Noble**
*Member, London Regional Passengers Committee*

**Joan Nolan**
*Manager, Marketing Services & Administration, Simpler Trade Procedures Board*

**GK Noon MBE**
*Member of Authority, Covent Garden Market Authority*
Chairman, Noon Products. Director, Taj International Hotels and West London Training & Enterprise Council. Member, Prince's Youth Business Trust Advisory Board. Founder Chairman, Asian Business Association. Governor, Ealing Tertiary College.

**Francis Noonan**
*Director, Operational Policy, Advisory, Conciliation & Arbitration Service*

**Barry Norman**
*Governor, British Film Institute*

**Prof D Norman**
*Director, Synchrotron Radiation, Council for the Central Laboratory of the Research Councils*
*Member of Council, English Nature*
Visiting Professor in Surface Science, University of Liverpool. Chairman,

Merseyside Ringing Group and Mersey Estuary Conservation Group.

**Torquil Norman**
*Trustee, Fleet Air Arm Museum*

**Sir Ronald Norman OBE**
*Non-Executive Chairman, Student Loans Company*
Chairman, Teesside Development Corporation.

**John Norris CBE**
*Member of Board, The Environment Agency*
Farmer. Crown Estates Commissioner. Fellow, Royal Agricultural Societes. Director, Bottesford (Glenelq). Consultant, Ham Dredging. Trustee, Davy Down Trust, Ford of Britain Trust, D E Norris Trust (Holding Property) and Round 1969 Settlement. Vice Lord Lieutenant of Essex. Former NRA Board Member and President of Country Landowners Association.

**Roy Norris**
*Director for Wales, National Lottery Charities Board*
Previously Head, Voluntary Sector Branch, Welsh Office.

**S Norris**
*Director of Finance, HM Prison Service*

**Prof B Norton**
*Member of Board, Construction Industry Training Board (NI)*
University of Ulster.

**Miss E Norton OBE**
*Member, Parole Board*

**Jim Norton**
*Chief Executive, Radiocommunications Agency*

**Lieutenant Colonel AJF Noyes**
*Ex-Officio Trustee, Royal Marines Museum*

**Colonel Maurice Nugent**
*Commandant Adjutant General's Corps Training Group, Army Training & Recruitment Agency*

**RL Nunn**
*Director, ABRO Donnington, Army Base Repair Organisation*

**P Nutt**
*Network Customer Services Director, Highways Agency*

# O

**Mrs Mary O'Boyle**
*Commissioner, Mental Health Commission for Northern Ireland*
Assistant Principal Social Worker, Homefirst Community Health & Social Services Trust.

**George O'Brien**
*Member Advisory Board, NHS Pensions Agency*

**Gerard O'Brien**
*Director, Corporate Affairs, Scottish Enterprise*

**J O'Brien**
*Pharmaceuticals and Feed Additives, Veterinary Medicines Directorate*

**John O'Brien**
*Director of Passenger Rail Franchising, Office of Passenger Rail Franchising*

**Air Vice-Marshal Robert O'Brien OBE**
*Air Secretary/Chief Executive, RAF Personnel Management Agency*

**The Very Rev Canon C O'Byrne**
*Member of Council, Council for Catholic Maintained Schools*

**CP O'Callagham**
*Senior Technical Officer, Sports Council for Northern Ireland*

**DG O'Connor**
*Director Facilities/ Lottery Funding, Sports Council for Northern Ireland*

**Helen O'Connor**
*Librarian and Editor of British East-West Journal, The Britain-Russia Centre*

**Lucia O'Connor**
*Director of Finance & Personnel, Driver & Vehicle Licensing Northern Ireland*

**Michael O'Connor**
*Director of Policy & Corporate Affairs, Millennium Commission*

**Stephen O'Connor**
*Director of Operations, The Scottish Legal Aid Board*

**Jane O'Dempsey**
*Commissioner, Fair Employment Commission for Northern Ireland*

**G O'Doherty**
*Director, Northern Ireland Transport Holding Company*

**M O'Doherty**
*Finance Officer, National Board for Nursing, Midwifery & Health Visiting for Northern Ireland*

**Chris O'Donnell**
*Member of Advisory Board, Medical Devices Agency*
Group Director Medical Products, Smith & Nephew.

**Michael O'Donnell**
*Member, Tate Gallery*

**Denis O'Hagan**
*Head of Transportation, Roads Service*

**J Len O'Hagan OBE**
*Chairman, Enterprise Ulster*

**Eddie O'Hara MP**
*Trustee, Community Development Foundation*

**Miss Judith O'Leary**
*Regional Manager, Office of Electricity Regulation*

**Nuala O'Loan**
*Chairman, Northern Ireland Consumer Coomittee for Electricity, Office for the Regulation of Electricity & Gas*

**Brian O'Neil**
*Director of Personnel, Historic Scotland*

**Jonathan O'Neil**
*External Affairs, UK & English Sports Councils*

**Brendan O'Neill**
*Finance Director, Government Purchasing Agency*

**Dr EGJ O'Neill**
*Member, Northern Ireland Council for Postgraduate Medical & Dental Education*
Nominated by Hospital Junior Staff Com (NI).

**J O'Neill**
*Member, Sports Council for Northern Ireland*

**Lord O'Neill TD**
*Chairman, Northern Ireland Museums' Council*
Nominee of the Minister for Education.

**Mrs Marian O'Neill**
*Commissioner, Mental Health Commission for Northern Ireland*
Solicitor.

**Ms Marnie O'Neill**
*Member, Arts Council of Northern Ireland*
Chair, Old Museum Arts Centre, Belfast.

**Dr Onora O'Neill CBE**
*Member, Marshall Aid Commemoration Commission*

**Phelim O'Neill**
*Marketing Manager, Livestock & Meat Commission for Northern Ireland*

**Prof RJ O'Neill**
*Trustee, Imperial War Museum*

**Sean O'Neill**
*Secretary, Rail Users Consultative Committee for Western England*

**Prof Keith O'Nions**
*Trustee, Natural History Museum*

**Mrs T O'Regan**
*Head of Finance & Secretariat, Defence Dental Agency*

**John O'Reilly**
*Member, ENACT, Office of Telecommunications*
Professor of Telecommunications.

**WP O'Reilly**
*Chairman, RFAC, The Environment Agency*

**Vincent O'Rourke**
*District Valuer, Valuation & Lands Agency*

**Sally O'Sullivan**
*Non-Executive Director, London Transport*
*Commissioner, Broadcasting Standards Commission*
Editor-in-Chief, Home Interest Group,

IPC Magazines. Member, Advisory Council on the Misuse of Drugs.

**Jennifer Oakley**
*Financial Controller, The Arts Council of England*

**Mrs Pat Oakley**
*Non-Executive Member, English National Board for Nursing, Midwifery & Health Visiting*
Senior Consultant/Director, Practices Made Perfect.

**Keith Oates**
*Member, UK & English Sports Councils*
Deputy Chairman, Marks & Spencer. Non-Executive Director, British Telecommunications and Guinness Member, Confederation of British Industry Council.

**Craig Octon**
*Secretary (Administration & Resources), Patent Office*

**Dr WA Oddy**
*Keeper, Conservation, British Museum*

**DN Odling**
*Employer member, Engineering Construction Industry Training Board*
Commercial & HR Director, AOC International

**Jackie Odunoye**
*Acting Chief Executive, Tower Hamlets Housing Action Trust*
Co-opted Member, Finance Sub-Committee, Stratford Development Partnership.

**Phil Officer**
*MADE, Companies House*

**Dr Bridget Ogilvie**
*Member, Commonwealth Scholarship Commission*
Director, The Wellcome Trust.

**Dr Malcolm Ogilvie**
*Member, West Areas Board & Scientific Advisory Committee, Scottish Natural Heritage*

**David Oldrey**
*Member, Horserace Betting Levy Board*

**Brian Oliphant**
*Member, General Consumer Council for Northern Ireland*
Group Chief Environmental Health Officer, Western Group Environmental Health Committee. Chairman, Board of Governors, Rainey Endowed School.

**Tim Oliphant**
*Director, Visitor Services, Scottish Tourist Board*

**Ms Heather Oliver**
*Licensing Administration, Veterinary Medicines Directorate*

**Linda Oliver**
*Non-Executive Director, Civil Service College*

**Paul Oliver**
*Director, North West Region, Advisory, Conciliation & Arbitration Service*

**Major General Richard A Oliver**
*Member of Advisory Board, Service Children's Education*
*Member of Advisory Board, Defence Analytical Services Agency*
Chief of Staff (Adjutant General).

**Ron Oliver**
*Chief Executive, Vehicle Inspectorate*

**Susan Ollerearnshaw**
*Joint Head of Equality Policy Consultancy, Commission for Racial Equality*

**RJ Olney**
*Assistant Keeper, The Royal Commission on Historical Manuscripts*

**Huw Onllwyn Jones**
*Head of the Grants and Private Sector Department, Welsh Language Board*

**Gerald Oppenheim**
*Director UK & Corporate Planning, National Lottery Charities Board*
Formerly Director, London Borough Grants Unit.

**Douglas Oram**
*Member, ENACT, Office of Telecommunications*
Consultant, Former hotel group telecommunications manager.

**P Orchard**
*Head of Personnel, Corporate Services, Natural History Museum*

**Steve Orchard**
*Chief Executive, Legal Aid Board*

**Chris Orman**
*Regional Director - Asia/Pacific, Commonwealth Development Corporation*

**Jeremy Orme**
*Deputy Chairman, Audit Commission*
Head of Enforcement & Legal Services, Securities & Investments Board. Previously managing partner, Robson Rhodes.

**Patricia Ormiston**
*Administrative Services Manager, Gas Consumers' Council*

**Derek Orr**
*Head of Management Consultancy & Training Services, Business Development Service*

**John Orr**
*Regional Office, South West, NHS Estates*

**AS Orton**
*Member of Advisory Board, Driver & Vehicle Licensing Agency*
Formerly, Executive Director, Marks & Spencer.

**Dr RBL Osborn**
*Member, Parole Board*

**Derek Osborn CB**
*Member of Board, The Environment Agency*
UK representative, Management Board, European Environment Agency. Chairman, Advisory Committee, ERM CVS. Chairman, Council of Management, Earth Centre. Visiting Fellow, Green College, Oxford. Former Director-General, Environmental Protection, Department of the Environment.

**Peter Osbourne**
*Museum Security Adviser, Museums & Galleries Commission*

**Christopher H Osman**
*Head, Computing & Information Services Group, Macaulay Land Use Research Institute*

**Yvonne Osman**
*Member, The Scottish Legal Aid Board*
Citizens' Advice Bureau manager. Member, Dumfries & Galloway Health Council and Scottish Consumer Council.

**Richard Osmond**
*Secretary, Post Office*

**Erik Ostman**
*Loan Services Director, Student Loans Company*

**George Osundiya**
*Member, North Western Consumers' Committee, Office of Electricity Regulation*

**Herman Ouseley**
*Chairman, Commission for Racial Equality*
Former Chief Executive, London Borough of Lambeth. Former Chief Executive ILEA. Council Member, Institute of Race Relations. Council Member, Policy Studies Institute. Chairman, Presentation Educational Charitable Trust. Council member, Institute of Education, University of London. Chairman, Uniting Britain Trust.

**A David Owen OBE**
*Board Member, Castle Vale Housing Action Trust*
*Trustee, Community Development Foundation*
Chairman, Rubery Owen Group. Member, Advisory Committee of the National Council for Voluntary Organisations.

**D Huw Owen**
*Keeper of Pictures & Maps, National Library of Wales*

**David Owen CBE**
*Chairman, Merseyside & North Wales Consumers' Committee, Office of Electricity Regulation*

**Dr Gill Owen**
*Member, Monopolies & Mergers Commission*
Energy and environmental policy consultant. Chair, Public Utilities Access Forum. Member, Bedfordshire Police Authority.

**Mrs Isabel Owen**
*Operational Manager, Welsh National Board for Nursing, Midwifery & Health Visiting*

**Major General JIH Owen OBE**
*Chairman, Royal Marines Museum*

**Robert Owen**
*Member, Southern Consumers' Committee, Office of Electricity Regulation*

**Steve Owen**
*European & Regulatory Affairs, Medical Devices Agency*

**TA Owen**
*Vice-President, National Library of Wales*

**Elwyn Owens**
*Member, Merseyside & North Wales Consumers' Committee, Office of Electricity Regulation*

**Prof S Owens**
*Keeper of the Herbarium, Royal Botanic Gardens Kew*

**Roly Owers**
*Agency Management Planner, Defence Animal Centre*

**Sir Ronald Oxburgh**
*Trustee, Natural History Museum*

**AH Oxford**
*Managing Director, Crown Agents Financial Services, Crown Agents Foundation*

**David Oxley OBE**
*Member, English Sports Council*

# P

**Mark Pacey**
*Director Marketing & Sales, Companies House*

**G Pachent**
*Member, The British Library*
Library Association.

**Michael Pack**
*Director of Corporate Services, UK Hydrographic Office*

**Mrs A Packard**
*Member, Post Office Users' Council for Scotland*
Director, The ADAPT (Access for Disabled People to Arts Premises Today) Trust. Former Public Relations Manager, Forth Ports. Former Member, Scottish Advisory Committee, Independent Broadcasting Authority.

**RJ Packer**
*Chairman, Veterinary Laboratories Agency*
Permanent Secretary, MAFF.

**Richard Paddock**
*Advisory Group Director, The Government Property Lawyers*

**Roy Padgett**
*Director, Finance & Corporate Services, Marine Safety Agency*

**Jennifer Page CBE**
*Chief Executive, New Millennium Experience Co Ltd*
*Chief Executive, Millennium Commission*
Former Chief Executive, English Heritage. Former Chief Executive, Millennium Commission. Formerly employed in Departments of the Environment & Transport, BNOC, London Docklands Development Corporation, and Pallas Group. Non-Executive Director, Railtrack Group and Equitable Life Assurance Society.

**Prof Lesley Page**
*Non-Executive Member, English National Board for Nursing, Midwifery & Health Visiting*
Head of Midwifery & Women's Health Studies, Queen Charlotte's College, Thames Valley University.

**Oliver Page**
*Director, Complex Groups, Financial Services Authority*
Currently Deputy Director, Bank of England, responsible for banking supervision.

**Richard Page MP**
*Governor, Westminster Foundation for Democracy*

**Sharon Page**
*Secretary to the Board of Trustees, Tate Gallery*

**Cliff Paice**
*Group Director, Economic Regulation, Civil Aviation Authority*

**Tony Painter**
*Director of Geographic Production, Military Survey*

**A Palmer**
*Director Project Division, RAF Signals Engineering Establishment*

**J Palmer**
*Assessor, Sports Council for Northern Ireland*
Department of Education.

**Mrs M Palmer**
*Finance Director, Centre for Environment, Fisheries & Aquaculture Science*

**Dr M Palmer**
*Commissioner, Royal Commission on Historical Mon uments of England*

**Ralph Palmer**
*Director, Network Operations, Highlands & Islands Enterprise*

**Roger Palmer**
*Member of Advisory Committee, Registrar of Public Lending Right*
Publishing Consultant.

**Susan Palmer**
*Archivist, Sir John Soane's Museum*
*Trustee, National Heritage Memorial*
*Fund*

**P Palmer JP**
*Member, Parole Board*

**PF Palukaitis**
*Head, Virology Department, Scottish*
*Crop Research Institute*

**Lord Palumbo**
*Trustee, Natural History Museum*

**R Pannone**
*Non-executive Director, Forensic Science*
*Service*
Pannone & Partners, Solicitors.

**A Papps**
*Member, Executive Committee, HM*
*Prison Service*

**Janet Paraskeva**
*Director for England, National Lottery*
*Charities Board*
Former Director and Founding Chief
Executive, National Youth Agency. Non-
Executive Director of an NHS Trust and a
JP.

**Graham Parish**
*Member, Ofwat South West Customer*
*Service Committee*

**A Park**
*Director, Finance, West of Scotland*
*Water Authority*

**DK Park**
*Director of Finance & Planning, Valuation*
*Office Agency*

**G Park CBE**
*Member, Parole Board*

**Stephen Park**
*Finance Director, Defence Evaluation &*
*Research Agency*

**Alan Parker**
*Chairman, British Film Institute*

**Anthony Parker**
*Member, South Eastern Consumers'*
*Committee, Office of Electricity*
*Regulation*

**Mrs CN Parker**
*Secretary, British Museum*

**Ms G Parker**
*Legal Adviser, Medicines Control Agency*

**Jim Parker**
*Registrar, Registrar of Public Lending*
*Right*

**John Parker**
*Head of Branch, Communications, Forest*
*Research*

**Prof John S Parker**
*Trustee, Royal Botanic Gardens Kew*

**Michael Parker**
*Member, UK Sports Council*
Deputy Managing Director, Saatchi &
Saatchi Advertising.

**TG Parker**
*Information Technology & Computing,*
*Hannah Research Institute*

**Hazel Parker-Brown**
*Human Resource Services Director,*
*Highways Agency*

**Graham Parkhouse**
*Member, South Western Consumers'*
*Committee, Office of Electricity*
*Regulation*

**Pat Parkin**
*Director of Development, Castle Vale*
*Housing Action Trust*

**AJ Parkinson**
*Head, Architectural History, Royal*
*Commission on Ancient & Historical*
*Monuments in Wales*

**Geoffrey Parnell**
*Keeper of Tower History, Royal Armouries*

**Mrs Ruth Parnell**
*Member, South Western Consumers'*
*Committee, Office of Electricity*
*Regulation*

**Steve Parnell**
*Director of Planning, UK Hydrographic*
*Office*

**Matthew Parris**
*Commissioner, Broadcasting Standards*
*Commission*
Parliamentary sketch writer, *The Times*.
Former Conservative MP and presenter
for London Weekend Television.

**Mrs Deborah Parry**
*Member, Yorkshire Consumers'*
*Committee, Office of Electricity*
*Regulation*

**Prof P Parsloe**
*Member, Alcohol Education & Research*
*Council*

**Robert Parson**
*Member, Southern Consumers'*
*Committee, Office of Electricity*
*Regulation*

**Ivan Parsons**
*Export/ Import Milk, Milk Products,*
*Sheepmeat, Sugar, Fruit & Vegetables,*
*Fish, Wine, Tobacco, Floriculture,*
*Intervention Board*

**Dr Jasper Parsons**
*Chairman, Fisheries Conservancy Board*
*for Northern Ireland*
*Member of Board, Sea Fish Industry*
*Authority*
Managing Director, Cuan Sea Fisheries.
Board Member, A Taste of Ulster.

**Susan Parsons**
*Member, Qualifications, Curriculum &*
*Assessment Authority for Wales*
Headteacher, Llanfihangel Rhydithon CP
School.

**John Partington**
*Member, Southern Consumers'*
*Committee, Office of Electricity*
*Regulation*

**Elizabeth Passmore**
*School Improvement, Office for*
*Standards in Education*

**D Patch**
*Trustee, Royal Navy Submarine Museum*
Nominated by the Submarine Old
Comrades Association.

**Atul Patel**
*Director of Regulation, The Housing*
*Corporation*

**Kamlesh Patel**
*Member, Central Council for Education &*
*Training in Social Work*

**Mick (Manharlal) Patel**
*Chief Warder, National Gallery*

**Calum Paterson**
*Director, Scottish Development Finance,*
*Scottish Enterprise*

**Edward Paterson**
*Programme Unit Manager, Macaulay*
*Land Use Research Institute*

**Neil Paterson**
*Information Technology, Veterinary*
*Medicines Directorate*

**Neil Paterson**
*Member Advisory Board, NHS Pensions*
*Agency*
Department of Health.

**Robert H Paterson**
*Secretary, Scottish Conveyancing &*
*Executry Services Board*

**Dr Alan Patey**
*FAPAS, Central Science Laboratory*

**Kirit K Pathak OBE**
*Member of Council, Food from Britain*
Chairman, Patak Spices.

**Alasdair C Paton**
*Chief Executive, Scottish Environment*
*Protection Agency*

**David Paton OBE**
*Member, North of Scotland Water*
*Authority*
Former Chairman, Scottish Chambers of
Commerce. Chairman, Scottish Council
Development & Industry. Chair, Don
District Salmon Fishery Board, Aberdeen
Harbour and North East Scotland
Preservation Trust.

**Dr D Patterson**
*Member, Northern Ireland Council for*
*Postgraduate Medical & Dental*
*Education*
Nominated by Royal College of
Psychiatrists.

**Glenn Patterson**
*Member, Arts Council of Northern Ireland*
Writer-in-Residence, QUB.

**J Patterson**
*Member of Board, Construction Industry*
*Training Board (NI)*
AEEU. Employee representative.

**T Patterson**
*Member of Board, Construction Industry Training Board (NI)*
Charles Brand. Employer representative.

**W Patterson**
*Chief Executive, Labour Relations Agency*

**Mrs Brenda Pattison**
*Member, North Eastern Consumers' Committee, Office of Electricity Regulation*

**JA Patton CBE**
*Member of Board of Trustees, Agricultural Research Institute of Northern Ireland*
Appointed by the Ulster Farmers' Union.

**Dr RKG Paul**
*Communications, Natural Environment Research Council*

**RJ Pawley**
*Head of Profession, Valuation Office Agency*

**Prof RA Paxton MBE**
*Commissioner, Royal Commission on Ancient & Historical Monuments of Scotland*

**Prof CC Payne**
*Chief Executive, Horticulture Research International*

**Chris Payne**
*Personnel Management, Office for Standards in Education*

**D'Arcy Payne**
*Member, The Great Britain-China Centre*
Director, Corporate Services, Rolls-Royce.

**David Payne**
*Facilities Development, UK Sports Council*

**Diana Payne**
*Member, Legal Aid Board*
Manager, not-for-profit sector franchise pilot unit based in Milton Keynes Citizens' Advice Bureau. Magistrate. Member, Police Area Advisory Committee. Management Committee Member, of a Neighbour Dispute Mediation Service.

**Rodney Payne**
*Governor, British Film Institute*

**Mrs SP Payne**
*Member of Council, British Hallmarking Council*

**Alan Paynter**
*Director IS, HM Customs & Excise*

**Liz Peace**
*Company Secretary, Defence Evaluation & Research Agency*

**Mrs SM Peach OBE JP**
*Member, Parole Board*

**Peter Peacock**
*Member of Board, Scottish Natural Heritage*

**Prof Malcolm Peaker**
*Director, Hannah Research Institute*

**Allan Pearce**
*Director, Personnel & Establishment Officer, Royal Mint*

**David Pearce**
*Member, Commonwealth Development Corporation*
Professor of Environmental Economics, University College London. Associate Director, Centre for Social Economic Research on the Global Environment, Member, UN Secretary General's Advisory Board on Sustainable Development.

**Sir Idris Pearce CBE**
*Deputy Chairman, English Partnerships*
Former Chairman, English Estates. Past President, Royal Institution of Chartered Surveyors. Director, Swan Hill Group, NMB Group and Millennium & Copthorne Hotels. Governor, Peabody Trust.

**Mark Pearce**
*Regional Manager, Rural Development Commission*

**Michael Pearce**
*Director of Employment & Social Regeneration, Stonebridge Housing Action Trust*

**Oliver Pearcey**
*Director, Conservation Department, English Heritage*

**A Pearson**
*Member, Executive Committee, HM Prison Service*

**James Pearson**
*Marketing Manager, UK Ecolabelling Board*

**John Pearson**
*Director, IS Strategy & Policy, Logistic Information Systems Agency*

**Group Captain Nigel Pearson**
*Chief Executive, Joint Air Reconnaissance Intelligence Centre*

**Ms S Pearson**
*Section Head, Lotteries and Machines, Gaming Board for Great Britain*

**Adam Peat**
*Chief Executive, Tai Cymru*
Former civil servant, Welsh Office.

**Sir Michael Peat KCVO**
*Member of Board of Trustees, Historic Royal Palaces*
Keeper of the Privy Purse. Queen's Household's Director of Finance & Property. Appointed by the Queen.

**Dr Richard Peckover**
*Director, Safety, UK Atomic Energy Authority*
Joined UKAEA in 1969. Former Director, Winfrith.

**Mrs M Pedersen**
*Vice Chairperson, Council for Catholic Maintained Schools*

**Philip Pedley**
*Member of Board, Tai Cymru*

Marketing Consultant, Ford Motor company. Former Member, Wirral Borough Council, British Youth Council and Joint Committee Against Racism.

**Margaret Pegler**
*Head of Personnel, National Gallery*

**G Pellow**
*Head of Estates Management, Corporate Services, Natural History Museum*

**Mark Pemberton**
*Assistant Director, Public Affairs Division, National Museum of Science & Industry*

**Piers Pendred**
*Director Educational Enterprises*

**Christopher Penn**
*Chairman, RFAC, The Environment Agency*

**Nicole Penn-Symons**
*Director, Lottery Projects, The Arts Council of England*

**PR Pennington**
*Member, Rail Users Consultative Committee for Eastern England*

**Prof TH Pennington**
*Member of Governing Body, Rowett Research Institute*

**Colin Penny**
*Residues, Surveillance & R&D, Veterinary Medicines Directorate*

**Dawn Penso**
*Member, BACT, Office of Telecommunications*
Partner, training and employment consultancy.

**Dr Jan Pentreath**
*Chief Scientist and Director of Environmental Strategy, The Environment Agency*
*Member, Natural Environment Research Council*

**A Peoples**
*Director of Operations, Driver & Vehicle Testing Agency*

**Andrew Pepper**
*Member of Board, Sea Fish Industry Authority*
Head of Fish Buying, Tesco.

**ED Pepper**
*Member, Rail Users Consultative Committee for North Eastern England*

**Terence Pepper**
*Photography Curator, National Portrait Gallery*

**Harry Percy**
*Business Director - Tea, Sugar & Forestry, Commonwealth Development Corporation*

**Prof Ian Percy CBE**
*Chairman, The Accounts Commission for Scotland*
*Member of Steering Board, Companies House*
Deputy Chairman, Scottish Provident Institution and Scottish Water &

Sewerage Customers Council. Chairman, MacDonald Orr. Non-Executive Director, Morgan Grenfell (Scotland), William Wilson Holdings, The Weir Group and Beale Dobie (Scotland). Member, Steering Board of Companies House. Former Senior Partner, Grant Thornton. Deputy Chairman, Auditing Practices Board.

**Mike Perfect**
*Member, Ofwat Southern Customer Service Committee*

**Brian Perowne**
*Member of Advisory Board, Defence Analytical Services Agency*
Director General Fleet Support (Operations & Plans).

**Rear Admiral JF Perowne OBE**
*Vice Chairman, Royal Navy Submarine Museum*

**Dave Perry**
*Customer Relations Manager, Central Computer & Telecommunications Agency*

**Graham Perry**
*Director of Information Technology, Meat Hygiene Service*

**Mrs Penny Perry**
*Chair, REPAC, The Environment Agency*

**Simon Perry CBE**
*Governor, National Film & Television School*

**WA Perry**
*Member of Advisory Board, Service Children's Education*
Command Secretary (Adjutant General).

**Tullah Persand**
*Member of Board, Stonebridge Housing Action Trust*
Brent Council Labour Group Nominee.

**Mrs C Peters**
*Quality & Communications Director, Child Support Agency*

**Karen Peters**
*Head of Library & Information Services, Commonwealth Institute*

**Prof Sir Keith Peters**
*Chairman, National Radiological Protection Board*
Regius Professor of Physics, University of Cambridge.

**Mary Peters CBE**
*Member, Northern Ireland Tourist Board*
Olympic gold medallist. Manager, Mary Peters Ltd. Member, Women's Committee, International Amateur Athletics Federation. President, British Athletics Federation.

**Cllr Billy Petrie OBE JP**
*Member of Board, West of Scotland Water Authority*
Independent Councillor, Argyll & Bute Council. Former Provost, Dumbarton District. Deputy Lieutenant, Dunbartonshire. Chairman, Argyll & the Isles, Locah Lomond, Stirling & Trossachs Tourist Board.

**Sir Peter Petrie**
*European and Parliamentary Affairs, Bank of England*

**S Petrie**
*Head, Engineering & Maintenance Department, Scottish Crop Research Institute*

**Helen Pettersen**
*Member of Board, Waltham Forest Housing Action Trust*
NHS Manager. Director, Redbridge Community Housing.

**KE Pfotzer**
*Non-Executive Director, Information Technology Services Agency*

**Nigel Phethean**
*Director of Corporate Affairs, The Housing Corporation*

**AJ Phillips**
*Finance Director, The Buying Agency*

**D Phillips**
*Director, International Development Group, Crown Agents Foundation*

**GJG Phillips**
*Secretary, Remploy*
Joined Company in 1994. Previous positions with John Mowlem, American Express and Investment Management Regulatory Organisation.

**J Phillips**
*Member of Steering Board, Patent Office*

**JAK Phillips**
*Member, Rail Users Consultative Committee for Western England*

**JR Phillips**
*Member, Cardiff Bay Development Corporation*
Councillor, Cardiff County Council.

**Jonathan Phillips**
*Member of Steering Board, Insolvency Service*

**PK Phillips**
*Head of Standards, National Biological Standards Board*

**Robyn Phillips**
*Professional Adviser, Midwifery, Welsh National Board for Nursing, Midwifery & Health Visiting*

**Sheldon Phillips**
*Regional Director, North West, English Sports Council*

**Stephen Phillips**
*Member, The Arts Council of England*
Writer, broadcaster and producer. Consultant to Meridian Broadcasting.

**Tom Phillips**
*Finance Director, Horserace Totalisator Board*
Chartered accountant. Joined Board in 1991.

**Tom Phillips**
*Trustee, National Portrait Gallery*

**Trevor Phillips**
*Member, The Arts Council of England*

**Judith Phillips CBE**
*Strategic Planning & Resources, Office for Standards in Education*

**Bob Phillis**
*Deputy Director-General, British Broadcasting Corporation*
Former Chief Executive, ITN.

**Lieutenant Colonel A Phipps**
*Chief of Staff/Planner, Army Technical Support Agency*

**M Phipps**
*Member of Advisory Board, Service Children's Education*
Department for Education and Employment.

**George Phipson**
*Member of Board, Funding Agency for Schools*
Headteacher, West Hatch High School.

**David Piccaver**
*Director, Horticulture Research International*

**Mary Picken**
*Member of Board, Scottish Screen*

**B Picken JP**
*Member, Rail Users Consultative Committee for Midlands*

**Prof John Pickering**
*Member, Monopolies & Mergers Commission*
Economic and educational consultant. Visiting Professor, Durham University Business School. Formerly Deputy Vice-Chancellor, University of Portsmouth and Chairman, University of Portsmouth Enterprise.

**Clive Pickford**
*Non-Executive Director, UK Atomic Energy Authority*
Chairman, London Partnership, Jones Lang Wootton.

**Rob Pickford**
*Member, Central Council for Education & Training in Social Work*

**David Pickup**
*Solicitor, HM Customs & Excise*

**Richard Pierce**
*Member, Arts Council of Northern Ireland*
Architect.

**Miss Gwerfyl Pierce Jones**
*Member, National Library of Wales*
Elected by the Court of Governors.

**Derek Pierson**
*Chief Financial Officer, Commonwealth Development Corporation*

**JP Pigott**
*Finance Director, Crown Agents Foundation*

**Prof MJ Pilling**
*Member, Natural Environment Research Council*
University of Leeds.

**Barry Pinson QC**
*Trustee, Royal Air Force Museum*

**Dr Michael Pinto-Duschinsky**
*Governor, Westminster Foundation for Democracy*

**Nicky Piper**
*Member of Council, The Sports Council for Wales*

**Group Captain Sir Gordon Pirie CVO CBE JP**
*Trustee, Royal Air Force Museum*

**Mrs J Pitchers JP**
*Member, Parole Board*

**Stuart Pitt**
*Director, Royal Observatory, Edinburgh*

**Dilys Plant**
*Head of External Relations, Office of Water Services*

**Sir David Plastow**
*Chairman, Medical Research Council*

**Denise Platt**
*Member, Central Council for Education & Training in Social Work*

**Rudi Plaut OBE**
*Chairman, Qualifications, Curriculum & Assessment Authority for Wales*
Northmace and Techniquest.

**Ian Plenderleith**
*Executive Director, Monetary Stability, Bank of England*

**Hon Francis Plowden**
*Trustee, Royal Armouries*

**MG Plumb**
*Member, Rail Users Consultative Committee for North Eastern England*

**G Podger**
*Member of Ownership Board, Veterinary Medicines Directorate*
Head of Food Safety & Science Group

**Kevin Pogson**
*Head of Resources & Planning Division, The Court Service*

**Prof AJ Pointon**
*Member of Council, Advisory, Conciliation & Arbitration Service*

**Dr Derek Poley CBE**
*Chief Executive, UK Atomic Energy Authority*
Joined UKAEA in 1962. Former Director, Winfrith and Managing Director, Nuclear Business Group, AEA Technology. Appointed Chief Executive, UKAEA (GD) in 1994 and of UKAEA in 1996.

**Brigadier Alan W Pollard**
*Chief Executive, Logistic Information Systems Agency*

**Eve Pollard**
*Member, English Tourist Board*
Former Editor, *Sunday Express* and *Sunday Express Magazine*. Chairwoman Women in Journalism.

**Ms Maggie Pollard**
*Governor, Scottish Council for Educational Technology*
Headteacher, Richmond Park School.

**Ray Pollard**
*Member of Management Board, Pay & Personnel Agency*

**Tony Pollard**
*Director, Personnel, Training, Information Services, General Administration, Radiocommunications Agency*

**Gordon Polley MBE**
*Member, Ofwat Yorkshire Customer Service Committee*

**Myran Pollock**
*Manager (Advice & Information), Fair Employment Commission for Northern Ireland*

**Michael Polson**
*Manager Engineering, Local Enterprise Development Unit*

**Sharon Polson**
*Manager Regional Development, Local Enterprise Development Unit*

**Bob Ponchaud**
*Subject Adviser, Science, Office for Standards in Education*

**Pauline Ponsonby**
*Member of Board, Stonebridge Housing Action Trust*
Resident Board Member.

**D Poole**
*Deputy Chairman, Construction Industry Training Board (NI)*
Craigavon Heating Centre.

**KS Pope**
*Human Resources Director, The Buying Agency*

**D Porritt**
*Manager (Compliance Systems), Vehicle Certification Agency*

**Catherine Porteous**
*Trustee, National Heritage Memorial Fund*

**Dr Gaby Porter**
*Curatorial Services Manager, Museum of Science & Industry Manchester*

**Jadranka Porter**
*Project Manager, Central and Eastern Europe, Public Relations, Westminster Foundation for Democracy*

**Sheila Porter**
*Member, DIEL, Office of Telecommunications*
Principal Social Services Officer, Neath Port Talbot County Borough Council.

**WH Porter**
*Member of Board of Governors, Macaulay Land Use Research Institute*

**Dr R Post**
*Acting Keeper, Entomology Department, Natural History Museum*

**David Potter CBE**
*Member of Board, Higher Education Funding Council for England*
Chairman & Chief Executive, Psion.

**M Potter**
*Commercial Manager, Covent Garden Market Authority*

**Capt MJ Potter**
*Assistant Director Plans & Procurement, Naval Recruiting & Training Agency*

**Dr TW Potter**
*Keeper, Prehistoric & Romano-British Antiquities, British Museum*

**Allan Potts**
*Member, Police Complaints Authority*
Former local authority Chief Executive.

**Ros Poulson**
*Head of Licensing & Vetting, Office of the National Lottery*

**Dr C Poulter**
*Procurement Director, The Buying Agency*

**Ms Chrissie Poulter**
*Member, Arts Council of Northern Ireland*
Lecturer in Drama Studies, TCD.

**Prof Ken Pounds CBE**
*Chief Executive, Particle Physics & Astronomy Research Council*

**Allan Powell**
*Member, Merseyside & North Wales Consumers' Committee, Office of Electricity Regulation*

**Dr Anne Powell**
*Member of Board, The Environment Agency*
Partner, The Hamlet Partnership. Director, Pond Action. Company Secretary, River Restoration Project, Silsoe College. Trustee and Director, Berkshire, Buckinghamshire & Oxfordshire Naturalists Trust. Trustee World Wildlife Fund UK and Thames Salmon Trust. Chairman, Conservation Committee of the Worldwide Fund for Nature UK. Chairman, Agenda 21 Steering Group, Oxfordshire.

**Dick Powell**
*Member, The Design Council*

**John Powell**
*Member of Management Board, The Court Service*
South Eastern Provincial Administrator.

**Sir Philip Powell, CH, OBE**
*Trustee, Sir John Soane's Museum*

**Stephen Powell**
*Member, Ofwat Customer Service Committee for Wales*

**Prof W Powell**
*Head, Cell & Molecular Genetics Department, Scottish Crop Research Institute*

**Caroline Power**
*Member of Board, Stonebridge Housing Action Trust*
Resident Board Member.

**Joe Power**
*Member of Board, Liverpool Housing Action Trust*
Retired from printing industry. Resident of Storrington Heys. Member, High Rise Tenants' Group.

**John Power**
*Senior Research Officer, Fair Employment Commission for Northern Ireland*

**Prof Sir Ghillean Prance**
*Director & Trustee, Horniman Museum Director, Royal Botanic Gardens Kew*

**Robin Pratt**
*Member of Council, Countryside Council for Wales*
Farmer. Former Chairman, Pembrokeshire Coast National Park Authority.

**Dame Simone Prendergast**
*Member, Commission for Racial Equality*
Presiding Justice. Former Member, Lord Chancellor's Advisory Panel. Former Chairman, Jewish Refugees Committee. Chairman, East Grinstead Medical Research Trust. Vice-Chairman, Age Concern, Westminster. Lay Member, Solicitors' Disciplinary Tribunal. Commandant, Jewish Lads & Girls Brigade. Former Chairman, Westminster Children's Society.

**Prof JHD Prescott**
*Member of Board of Governors, Macaulay Land Use Research Institute*

**Michael Prescott**
*Assistant Director, British Film Institute*

**E Preston**
*Secretary, Rail Users Consultative Committee for North Eastern England*

**Group Captain (Retd) JS Preston**
*Senior Appointments & Careers Executive, RAF Personnel Management Agency*

**Willie Pretswell**
*Director of Finance and Information Systems, Scottish Prison Service*

**Chris Prevett**
*Technical Services, Home-Grown Cereals Authority*

**Alan Price**
*Director of Finance and Administration, Highlands & Islands Enterprise*

**Barclay Price**
*Director, Planning & Development, Scottish Arts Council*

**Bob Price**
*Director of Human & Corporate Resources Group, Biotechnology & Biological Sciences Research Council*

**Christopher Price**
*Member, The Arts Council of England*

**Ms F Price**
*Member of Council, Economic & Social Research Council*
Office of Science & Technology.

**Gillian Price**
*Commercial Director, Queen Elizabeth II Conference Centre*

**Graham Price**
*Assistant Director Processing, Companies House*

**Hywel Price**
*Director, Applied Science, Council for the Central Laboratory of the Research Councils*

**Idris Price**
*Member, Further Education Funding Council for Wales*
Managing Director, E&L Instruments, Wrexham.

**Janet Price**
*Member, North Areas Board, Scottish Natural Heritage*

**Prof Nick Price**
*Pest Management Strategies, Central Science Laboratory*
Honorary Chair in Applied Biology, University of Leeds. Honorary Fellowship in Chemistry at University of York.

**Sean Price**
*Divisional Roads Manager, Roads Service*

**Terry Price**
*Director of Corporate Services, English Sports Council*

**Jeffrey Pride**
*Development Director, Wales Tourist Board*

**Roger Pride**
*Marketing Director, Wales Tourist Board*

**Sarah Priest**
*General Manager, English Nature*

**Kate Priestley**
*Chief Executive, NHS Estates*

**Jane Priestman OBE**
*Member, The Design Council*

**A Prior**
*Head of Information Services, Royal Botanic Gardens Kew*

**John Prior**
*Community Touring Manager, Arts Council of Wales*

**Kenneth Prior**
*Chairman, Southern Consumers' Committee, Office of Electricity Regulation*

**Eifion Pritchard**
*Chairman, Post Office Users' Council for Wales*
*Member, Post Office Users' National Council*
Former Deputy Chief Constable, Dyfed Powys Police.

**Tricia Pritchard**
*Member of Board, Teacher Training Agency*
Head, Botley County Primary School, Botley, Oxford.

**Ms W Pritchard**
*Member of Advisory Board, Highways Agency*
External Member.

**William A Pritchard**
*Member of Council, Post Office Users' Council for Wales*
Journalist.

**DH Probert CBE**
*Chairman & Senior Crown Agent, Crown Agents Foundation*

**Tony Probert**
*Client member, Engineering Construction Industry Training Board*

**Jeff Probyn**
*Member, English Sports Council*

**Alice Prochaska**
*Director, Special Collections, The British Library*

**Air Commodore KJM Procter**
*Air Commodore Defence Agency (Maintenance), RAF Maintenance Group Defence Agency*

**Alistair Proctor**
*Director, Network Services, Scottish Enterprise*

**Colin Prosser**
*Team Manager, Environmental Impacts Team, English Nature*

**Richard Prosser**
*Member, Monopolies & Mergers Commission*
Director, Aluminium Products. Director, WQC. Managing Director, Hurley Hall Farms. Director of Blythe Mill (Coleshill). MAFF appointee to the Midland region Environment Agency Flood Defence Committee.

**J Provan, MEP**
*Chairman, Rowett Research Institute*

**Miss Hazel Prowse**
*Member, Ofwat Thames Customer Service Committee*

**Arthur Pryor CB**
*Member, Monopolies & Mergers Commission*
Former Civil Servant.

**Meirion Prys Jones**
*Head of the Education and Training Department, Welsh Language Board*

**AR Pugh**
*Member of Ownership Board, Meat Hygiene Service*
External Member, representing industry.

**Dr RF Pugh**
*Director, Horticulture Research International*

**David Pullen**
*Regulatory Manager, Occupational Pensions Regulatory Authority*

**Ivor Pumfrey**
*Regional Director, Wales, Meat Hygiene Service*

**Bob Purkiss**
*Member, Commission for Racial Equality*
*TGWU National Secretary for Equalities.*
*Member, TUC General Council. Chair,*
*TUC Race Committee. Chair,*
*Southampton Community School*
*Governors. Former Treasurer, Labour*
*Party Black Socialist Society. Former*
*Member, Department of Employment*
*Race Committee. Former National*
*Officer, Jamaican National Workers*
*Union.*

**PJ Purton**
*Chairman, Wine Standards Board*

**Sir William Purves CBE DSO**
*Trustee, Imperial War Museum*

**Prof J Purvis**
*Appointed Trustee, Royal Marines*
*Museum*

**J Purvis CBE**
*Member, SACOT, Scottish Advisory*
*Committee on Telecommunications*
*International business consultant.*

**Hilary Putman**
*Manager, North East, Gas Consumers'*
*Council*

**Sir David Puttman CBE**
*Member, National Museum of Science &*
*Industry*

**Ms J Pye**
*Member, Parole Board*

**JS Pyke**
*Member of Council, British Hallmarking*
*Council*

# Q

**David Quarmby**
*Chairman, British Tourist Authority &*
*English Tourist Board*
*Non-executive Director, New Millennium*
*Experience Co Ltd*
*Former joint Managing Director, J*
*Sainsbury. Former Economic Advisor,*
*Ministry of Transport. Former Managing*
*Director Buses, London Transport*
*Executive/London Regional Transport.*
*Non-executive Director, Management*
*Board, Department of the Environment,*
*Transport and the Regions. President,*
*Institute of Logistics. Chairman, South*
*London Business Partnership.*

**Theresa Quaye**
*Member of Board, Stonebridge Housing*
*Action Trust*
*Resident Board Member*

**Bernard Quigg**
*Member, South Eastern Consumers'*
*Committee, Office of Electricity*
*Regulation*

**ALC Quigley**
*Member of Council, Medical Research*
*Council*
*Member of Council, Engineering &*
*Physical Sciences Research Council*
*Office of Science & Technology.*

**Ms Clare Quigley**
*Member of Board, Mental Health*
*Commission for Northern Ireland*

**Dr O Quigley**
*Member, Northern Ireland Council for*
*Postgraduate Medical & Dental*
*Education*
*Appointed by DHSS.*

**Sir George Quingley**
*Board Member, Qualifications &*
*Curriculum Authority*
*Chairman, Ulster Bank.*

**Mrs C Quinn**
*Member of Council, Council for Catholic*
*Maintained Schools*
*Parent Representative.*

**Linda Quinn**
*Member of UK & Wales Committees,*
*National Lottery Charities Board*
*Drug Misuse Consultant, Researcher and*
*Writer. Member, Independent Tribunal*
*Service. School Governor. Former*
*County and City Councillor. Former*
*Member, South Glamorgan Health*
*Authority and Board of Visitors H.M.*
*Prison & Remand Centre, Cardiff.*

**Mrs SM Quinn**
*Administration, Scottish Agricultural*
*Science Agency*

**Frances Quirk**
*Co-ordinator of Postgraduate Studies,*
*Rowett Research Institute*

# R

**Heather Rabbats**
*Board Member, Qualifications &*
*Curriculum Authority*
*Chief Executive, London Borough of*
*Lambeth.*

**Prof PA Racey**
*Member of Board of Governors,*
*Macaulay Land Use Research Institute*

**Prof Paul Racey**
*Chairman, Scientific Advisory*
*Committee, Scottish Natural Heritage*

**Sarah Radclyffe**
*Governor, British Film Institute*

**Prof GK Radda CBE**
*Chief Executive, Medical Research*
*Council*

**Mrs S Rader**
*Executive Officer (Personnel), Youth*
*Council for Northern Ireland*

**Geoff Radley**
*Team Manager, Maritime Team, English*
*Nature*

**AK Rae**
*Member of Board of Governors,*
*Macaulay Land Use Research Institute*

**Carole Ann Rafferty**
*Board Member, Castle Vale Housing*
*Action Trust*
*Former Chair, Community Action Team.*
*Board Member, Castle Vale Community*
*Housing Association.*

**John Rafferty**
*Director for Scotland, National Lottery*
*Charities Board*
*Former Head of Business Development*
*Strategy, Archdiocese of Glasgow.*
*Previously Chief Executive, Scottish*
*Foundation for Social & Economic*
*Development, and Director, Volunteer*
*Centre, Strathclyde.*

**PC Rainbird**
*Deputy Chairman, Construction Industry*
*Training Board*

**Prof P Rainbow**
*Keeper, Zoology Department, Natural*
*History Museum*

**David Rainey**
*District Valuer, Central Advisory Unit,*
*Valuation & Lands Agency*

**The Rt Hon Sir Timothy Raison PC**
*Trustee, British Museum*

**Evlyn Raistrick**
*Member, Scottish Sports Council*

**Cephas Ralph**
*Area Manager, Scottish Fisheries*
*Protection Agency*

**Alan W Ramage**
*Keeper/Chief Executive, Registers of*
*Scotland*

**Ron Rampling**
*Funding & Allocations In-service Training,*
*Teacher Training Agency*

**Audrey Ramsay**
*Head of Press & PR, Scottish Natural*
*Heritage*

**J Ramsay**
*Non-Executive Director, Remploy*
*Independent management consultant*
*with Chelsworth Partnership. Previously*
*Partner and Director, Strategic*
*Consultancy, Ernst & Young,*
*Management Consultants.*

**Gael Ramsey**
*Member, Academic Council, Wilton Park*
*Executive Agency*
*Chief Executive, British Executive*
*Services Overseas.*

**Julie Ramsey**
*Team Leader, Corporate Services (job-*
*share post), Registrar of Public Lending*
*Right*

**Mrs P Rance**
*Member, Parole Board*

**Prof G Randall**
*Member, Natural Environment Research Council*
Brixham Environmental Laboratory.

**John Ranelagh**
*Member of Commission, Independent Television Commission*

**Peter Ranken**
*Director, Estate Management, Forest Enterprise*

**JA Rankin**
*Member of Board of Trustees, Agricultural Research Institute of Northern Ireland*
Appointed by the Ulster Farmers' Union.

**Rear Admiral NE Rankin**
*Chairman, Caledonian MacBrayne Ltd*

**Penny Rashbrook**
*Business Languages Co-ordinator, Centre for Information on Language Teaching & Research*

**Brigadier RE Ratazzi CBE**
*Chief Executive, Defence Transport & Movements Executive*

**Brigadier Guy Ratcliffe**
*Commanding Officer, Royal Hospital, Haslar, Defence Secondary Care Agency.*

**Prof JG Ratcliffe**
*Member, National Biological Standards Board*

**Brig M Ratcliffe**
*Comd DMSTC, Defence Medical Training Organisation*

**Dr Phil Ratcliffe**
*Member, West Areas Board & Scientific Advisory Committee, Scottish Natural Heritage*

**Lord Rathcavan**
*Chairman, Northern Ireland Tourist Board*
*Member of Board, British Tourist Authority*
Director, Lamont Holdings, Northern Bank, Old Bushmills Distillery, Berkeley Hotel and FRX International.

**David Ravey**
*Chief Executive, Welsh National Board for Nursing, Midwifery & Health Visiting*

**Mike Rawlins**
*Group Director, The Government Property Lawyers*

**Captain M Rawlinson**
*Non-Executive Member of Board, Trinity House Lighthouse Service*

**Richard Rawlinson**
*Member, Monopolies & Mergers Commission*
Director, Monitor Company.

**Ben Rawlinson Plant**
*Press Officer, National Portrait Gallery*

**Alice Rawsthorn**
*Member, The Design Council*

**Tony Rawsthorne**
*Chairman, UK Passport Agency*
Deputy Director General, Home Office.

**Mrs Sheila Ray**
*Member, Ofwat Central Customer Service Committee*

**Meurig Raymond**
*Member of Council, Food from Britain*
HGCA.

**Brian Rayner**
*Regional Manager, Office of Electricity Regulation*

**David Rayner CBE**
*Member, National Museum of Science & Industry*

**P Rayner**
*Member, Rail Users Consultative Committee for North Eastern England*

**Prof D Rea OBE**
*Part-time Chairman, Labour Relations Agency*

**CM Read**
*Finance, Natural Environment Research Council*

**Nigel Reader**
*Director of Finance, The Environment Agency*

**Barry Redfern**
*Director, Corporate Services, Property Advisers to the Civil Estate*

**Michael Redley**
*Secretary to the Commission, Independent Television Commission*

**Frank Redman**
*Member, South Eastern Consumers' Committee, Office of Electricity Regulation*

**Monica Redmond**
*Director of Human Resources, Meat Hygiene Service*

**Stephen Redmond**
*Member Advisory Board, NHS Pensions Agency*
Director of Human Resources, Plymouth Hospitals NHSTrust.

**Peter Redshaw**
*Commissioner, Meat & Livestock Commission*
Farmer. Member, South East Pigs Committee, National Farmers' Union of England & Wales. Deputy Chairman, Western Quality Pigs.

**Dr Allyson Reed**
*Commercial Director, Council for the Central Laboratory of the Research Councils*

**DC Reed**
*Member, Wine Standards Board*

**David Reed**
*Director, Finance, Information Technology Services & Corporate Planning, Radiocommunications Agency*

**Nick Reed**
*Director, East Region, The Housing Corporation*

**Roger Reed**
*Member, The Arts Council of England*
Chairman of South East Arts Board. Chartered Secretary and farmer. Former Director of a Training & Enterprise Council. Fellow, Woodard Foundation. Former Trustee, Brighton Festival Trust and Director, Brighton Festival Society. Chairman, Arts Trust of Brighton & Hove.

**SR Reed**
*Director, Northern Ireland Transport Holding Company*

**D Kenneth Rees**
*Director of Finance, National Library of Wales*

**David Rees**
*Corporate Finance Adviser & Head of Financial Affairs, Office of Water Services*

**Prof Emeritus Graham L Rees**
*Member, National Library of Wales*
Elected by the Court of Governors.

**Hugh Rees**
*Employer member, Engineering Construction Industry Training Board*

**Colonel I Rees**
*Member of Advisory Board, Service Children's Education*

**Prof Judith Rees**
*Member, Monopolies & Mergers Commission*
Professor of Environmental & Resources Management, London School of Economics.

**Maldwyn Rees**
*Member, Ofwat Customer Service Committee for Wales*
*Member, South Wales Consumers' Committee, Office of Electricity Regulation*

**Margaret Rees**
*Member of Council, Post Office Users' Council for Wales*
Nursing Sister, University Hospital of Wales, Cardiff.

**Prof Sir Martin Rees**
*Member of Council, Particle Physics & Astronomy Research Council*
Royal Society Research Professor

**Sir Martin Rees**
*Trustee, British Museum*

**Dr RLD Rees**
*Member, Rail Users Consultative Committee for Western England*

**Teresa Rees**
*Member, Equal Opportunities Commission*
Professor of Labour Market Studies, School for Policy Studies, University of Bristol. Consultant to European Commission.

**Owen Rees CB**
*Deputy Chairman, Qualifications, Curriculum & Assessment Authority for Wales*
Former Under-Secretary, Welsh Office.

**Colin Reeves**
*Chairman, NHS Estates*

**Adrian Reid**
*Head of Administration, Office of the National Lottery*

**Alison Reid**
*Chief Executive, Scottish Further Education Unit*
Member of Board of Management, Scottish Council for Research in Education, General Teaching Council and Chartered Institute of Marketing.

**Andrew Reid**
*Member of Authority, The Radio Authority*

**Brian Reid**
*Deputy Chairman, Independent Commission for Police Complaints for Northern Ireland*
Formerly Personnel & Purchasing Manager for a synthetic fibre company, Member of Board of Labour Relations Agency and Member of Industrial Tribunals Panel for Northern Ireland.

**Claire Reid**
*Director of Human Resources, The Scottish Legal Aid Board*

**David Reid**
*Deputy Chairman, The Arts Council of England*
Chairman of Southern Arts Board. Former Director, IBM UK. Former Member, Scottish Economic Council and Scottish Business in the Community. Former Chairman, Scottish Committee of ABSA. Chairman, Business in the Arts South. Trustee, Arts Foundation.

**Derek Reid**
*Member of Board, Sea Fish Industry Authority*
Former Chief Executive, Scottish Tourist Board.

**Derek Reid**
*Finance & Personnel Manager, War Pensions Agency*

**Iain Reid**
*Director, Combined Arts, The Arts Council of England*

**Seona Reid**
*Director, Scottish Arts Council*

**J Reilly**
*Business Director, Almondbank Division, Naval Aircraft Repair Organisation*

**Prof PM Reilly**
*Member, Northern Ireland Council for Postgraduate Medical & Dental Education*
Nominated by Medical Faculty, QUB.

**Sheila Reiter**
*Chairman, Ofwat National Customer Council*

*Chairman, Ofwat Wessex Customer Service Committee*

**Mrs S Reiter JP**
*Member, Parole Board*

**Evelyn Relph**
*Team Leader, Corporate Services (job-share post), Registrar of Public Lending Right*

**Simon Relph**
*Governor, British Film Institute*

**Jerry Rendell**
*Chief Executive, UK Ecolabelling Board*

**Leslie Rendell**
*Member, Coal Authority*

**Lady Renfrew**
*Trustee, Royal Botanic Gardens Kew*

**The Lord Renfrew of Kaimsthorn**
*Trustee, British Museum*

**Sandy Renfrew**
*Chief Technical Officer, Crofters' Commission*

**Rod Rennet**
*Chief Executive, East of Scotland Water Authority*
Former Director of Water Services, Tayside Regional Council.

**Agnes Rennie**
*Commissioner - Lewis & Harris, Crofters' Commission*
*Chairwoman, Western Isles Enterprise*

**Alistair G Rennie**
*Deputy Keeper, Registers of Scotland*

**Mrs Brenda Rennie**
*Member, Scottish Hospital Endowments Research Trust*

**Cllr Colin Rennie**
*Chairman, North of Scotland Water Authority*
Former member, North Scotland Water Authority. Labour councillor, Dundee City. Former member, Scottish Water & Sewerage Customers Council. Member, Scottish Enterprise, Tayside; Angus & District Tourist Board; Cosla Convention; Cosla Development Services Forum.

**WJ Rennie**
*Potato & Plant Health*

**Lord Renton**
*Vice-Chairman, British Council*

**Sir Robin Renwick KCMG**
*Trustee, Imperial War Museum*

**Michael Reupke**
*Member of Authority, The Radio Authority*

**Peter Revell-Smith CBE**
*Chairman, Museum of London*
Appointed by the Corporation of London.

**Dr Colin Reynolds**
*Member, Ofwat North West Customer Service Committee*

**Miss Kathleen Reynolds**
*Records Officer, National Board for Nursing, Midwifery & Health Visiting for Scotland*

**Roy Reynolds**
*Chief Executive, Commonwealth Development Corporation*

**Tony Reynolds**
*Board Director, Home-Grown Cereals Authority*

**Miss V Reynolds**
*Appointed Trustee, Royal Marines Museum*

**David Rhind**
*Director General & Chief Executive, Ordnance Survey*
*Member of Council, Economic & Social Research Council*

**Dr Elizabeth Rhodes**
*Member, South Wales Consumers' Committee, Office of Electricity Regulation*

**John Rhodes**
*Group Director, Passenger Services, Office of the Rail Regulator*

**Paul Rhodes**
*Export/ Import Cereals, Rice, Oils, Fats & Seeds, Beef & Veal, Intervention Board*

**Penelope Rhodes**
*Head of Resources, Crafts Council*

**Dafydd Rhys**
*Director of Broadcasting, S4C*

**Prof Garel Rhys OBE**
*Member of Board, Welsh Development Agency*
University of Wales, Cardiff. Innovative Manufacturing Initiative, EPSRC. UK Round Table on Sustainable Development. EMAP Automotive. Howle Holdings.

**Prof CD Rice**
*Member of Governing Body, Rowett Research Institute*

**Glenda M Rich**
*Assistant Secretary, Post Office Users' Council for Wales*

**Sir Brian Richards CBE**
*Member, Biotechnology & Biological Sciences Research Council*
Executive Chairman, Peptide Therapeutics Group. Non-Executive Director, British Biotechnology Group. Member, Department of Health Gene Therapy Advisory Committee. Former Specialist Adviser to House of Lords Select Committee II on Biotechnology Regulation.

**GA Richards**
*Chairman, Oil & Pipelines Agency*

**Supt IG Richards**
*OCU Aldershot, Ministry of Defence Police*

**Lieutenant Colonel John Richards**
*Head of Management Information Systems, Army Training & Recruitment Agency*

**Peter Richards**
*Director, Wales, Advisory, Conciliation & Arbitration Service*

**Simon Richards**
*Park Manager, Richmond Park, Royal Parks Agency*

**Sue Richards**
*Member, Audit Commission*

**C Richardson**
*Professional Officer (International), Youth Council for Northern Ireland*

**J Richardson**
*Member, The British Library*
Trades Union Congress.

**Janette Richardson**
*Member of Council, Scottish Arts Council*
Former Councillor, Annandale & Eskdale District Council. Former Chair, Dumfries & Galloway Arts Association.

**Margaret Richardson**
*Curator, Sir John Soane's Museum*

**Myrtle Richardson**
*Commissioner, Fair Employment Commission for Northern Ireland*

**Dr Neil Richardson**
*Member, Ofwat Central Customer Service Committee*

**Colonel Tom Richardson**
*Head of Operations, Army Training & Recruitment Agency*

**Tony Richardson**
*Registry Manager, Occupational Pensions Regulatory Authority*

**Miss AC Riches**
*Commissioner, Royal Commission on Ancient & Historical Monuments of Scotland*
*Commissioner, Royal Commission on Historical Mon uments of England*

**Hugh Richmond**
*Director of Architectural Survey, Royal Commission on Historical Mon uments of England*

**Sir Mark Richmond**
*Trustee, Tate Gallery*
*Trustee, National Gallery*

**Timothy Richmond MBE**
*Member, Monopolies & Mergers Commission*
Chartered Accountant. International Chairman, Pannell Kerr Forster.

**Tristram Ricketts**
*Member, Horserace Betting Levy Board*

**Mrs Dora Rickford**
*Member, London Consumers' Committee, Office of Electricity Regulation*

**Jonathan Rickford**
*Member, Monopolies & Mergers Commission*
Former Director of Corporate Strategy, BT.

**PL Ridd**
*Legislation, Business Profits, Avoidance, Capital Taxes & Stamp Duty, Inland Revenue*

**Bryan Riddleston**
*Member of Council, Countryside Council for Wales*
Former Chief Executive, Celtic Group. Member, Environment Agency Advisory Committee.

**Barbara Rider**
*Employer member, Engineering Construction Industry Training Board*

**Sir Adam Ridley**
*Deputy Chairman, National Lottery Charities Board*

**Nick Ridley JP**
*Member for the East of England, Gas Consumers' Council*
Non-Executive Director, Suffolk Health Authority; Deputy Lieutenant, JP. Member, Suffolk Courts Committee and Management Committee of the Central Council Magistrates Courts Committees

**Mrs Paula Ridley OBE, JP**
*Chairman, Tate Gallery*
*Trustee, National Gallery*
*Chair, Liverpool Housing Action Trust*
Former presenter of Granada Television's. This is Your Right and Granada Action. Member, Board of Merseyside Development Corporation. Former Chair, Merseyside Civic Society. Magistrate and Deputy Lieutenant, County of Merseyside.

**Chris Rigden**
*T&E Ranges, Defence Evaluation & Research Agency*

**David Riggs**
*Finance Director, Benefits Agency*

**P Riley**
*Non-Executive Director, Forensic Science Service*
Former Senior Manager, Zeneca.

**Graeme Rimer**
*Head of Curatorial Services, Royal Armouries*

**PJ Ripley**
*Sales & Marketing Manager, Fire Service College*

**Peter Risk**
*Member of Management Board, The Court Service*
Wales & Chester Circuit Administrator.

**Sir Thomas Risk**
*Trustee, Royal Air Force Museum*

**J Ritblat**
*Board Member, The British Library*
Chairman, British Land Company.

**Anna Ritchie OBE**
*Trustee, National Museums of Scotland*

**Bill Ritchie**
*Chairman, North Areas Board, Scottish Natural Heritage*

**David Ritchie**
*Secretary & Economist, Livestock & Meat Commission for Northern Ireland*

**Elizabeth Ritchie**
*Development Officer, Northern Ireland Museums' Council*

**PA Ritchie**
*Non-Executive Director, Caledonian MacBrayne Ltd*

**Dr B Ritson**
*Member, Alcohol Education & Research Council*

**Timothy Rix CBE**
*Member of Board, British Council*
Former Chairman and Chief Executive, Longman Group.

**John Robb**
*Trustee, Royal Botanic Garden Edinburgh*

**John Robb**
*Deputy Chairman, Horserace Betting Levy Board*

**Mike Robbins**
*Director of Finance, Logistic Information Systems Agency*

**OCG Robbins**
*Member of Board, Construction Industry Training Board*
Cambuslang College.

**Dr T Robbins**
*Member of Council, Medical Research Council*
University of Cambridge.

**A Roberts**
*Non-Executive Director, Remploy*
Director, Country Manor Hotels. Non-Executive Director, SCT Enterprises.

**Mrs Andrea Roberts**
*Corporate Marketing Manager, Forensic Science Service*

**Archie Roberts**
*Member, Rail Users Consultative Committee for Scotland*
Principal Transport Officer, Highland Regional Council.

**Dr Brynley Roberts CBE**
*Member, Higher Education Funding Council for Wales*
Former Librarian, National Library of Wales.

**Mrs Christina Roberts**
*Personnel & Training Manager, Welsh National Board for Nursing, Midwifery & Health Visiting*

**Wing Commander CI Roberts**
*OC Administration Wing, RAF Signals Engineering Establishment*

**DJ Roberts**
*Head, Graphics & Photography, Royal Commission on Ancient & Historical Monuments in Wales*

**David Roberts**
*Finance Director, Met Office*

**Sir Derek Roberts CBE**
*Member, Council for the Central Laboratory of the Research Councils*
University College London.

**Sir Frank Roberts GCMG GCVO**
*Vice-President, The Britain-Russia Centre*

**Prof GM Roberts**
*Member, National Radiological Protection Board*
Professor of Medical Imaging, University of Wales College of Medicine.

**Prof Sir Gareth Roberts**
*Member of Board, Higher Education Funding Council for England*
Vice-Chancellor, University of Sheffield.

**Cllr Gareth Winston Roberts**
*Member of Board, Welsh Language Board*
Leader & Chairman, Isle of Anglesey County Council.

**Hugh Roberts CVO**
*Member of Board of Trustees, Historic Royal Palaces*
Director of the Royal Collection. Surveyor of the Queen's Works of Art. Appointed by the Queen.

**Ifan Roberts**
*Director of Personnel & Administration, S4C*

**Jacqueline Roberts**
*Education Services Manager, Museum of Science & Industry Manchester*

**John Roberts**
*Regional Director, West Midlands, English Sports Council*

**John Roberts CBE**
*Chief Executive, Post Office*

**Dr John Roberts CBE**
*Member of Board, British Council*
Former Warden, Merton College, Oxford.

**Dr John Roberts CBE**
*Trustee, National Portrait Gallery*

**June Roberts**
*Member of Board, Liverpool Housing Action Trust*
Former Chief Executive, Age Concern Liverpool. Conciliator, Liverpool Health Authority, counsellor and yoga teacher.

**Ms M Roberts**
*Administrative Director, Northern Ireland Council for Postgraduate Medical & Dental Education*

**Malcolm Roberts**
*Chairman, Eastern Consumers' Committee, Office of Electricity Regulation*

**Martin Roberts**
*Director, Insurance & Friendly Societies, Financial Services Authority*
*Member, Radiocommunications Agency*
Former Director, Finance & Resource Management, DTI.

**Michael Roberts**
*Deputy Chairman, London Pensions Fund Authority*
Previously Member of Board, London Residuary Body. Deputy Chairman, St Albans & Hemel Hempstead NHS Trust. Director, Milk Marketing Board. Non-Executive Director, Full Circle Industries.

**The Venerable Raymond Roberts CB**
*Chairman, Ofwat Customer Service Committee for Wales*
*Member, Ofwat National Customer Council*

**Sir Samuel Roberts Bt**
*Member, Parole Board*

**AJ Robertson**
*Member, National Biological Standards Board*

**Andrew O Robertson OBE**
*Chairman, Post Office Users' Council for Scotland*
*Member, Post Office Users' National Council*
Solicitor. Secretary, Princess Louise Scottish Hospital (Erskine Hospital). Chairman, Greater Glasgow Community & Mental Health Services NHS Trust. Non-Executive Director, Scottish Building Society.

**Archie Robertson**
*Director of Operations, The Environment Agency*

**George Robertson MP**
*Vice-Chairman, The Britain-Russia Centre*

**Hilary Robertson**
*Public Relations Manager, Rowett Research Institute*

**Iain Robertson**
*Director of Finance & Administration, Scottish Sports Council*

**Iain A Robertson CBE**
*Chief Executive, Highlands & Islands Enterprise*

**Ian Robertson**
*Director, National Army Museum*

**JB Robertson**
*Director, Special Projects, West of Scotland Water Authority*

**Joe Robertson**
*Regulatory Director, Occupational Pensions Regulatory Authority*

**John Robertson**
*Regional Sheriff Clerk, Grampian, Highland and Islands, Scottish Court Service*

**Nancy Robertson MBE**
*Member, DIEL, Office of Telecommunications*
Consultant in the disability field.

**Stan Robertson**
*Chief Inspector, Railway Inspectorate, The Health & Safety Executive*

**Viviane Robertson**
*Head of Policy, Royal Parks Agency*

**Sir Ralph Robins**
*Trustee, Royal Air Force Museum*

**Simon P Robins**
*Head, Skeletal Research Unit, Rowett Research Institute*

**Alicia Robinson**
*Curator, Apsley House, The Wellington Museum, Victoria & Albert Museum*

**Dr Ann Robinson**
*Member, Monopolies & Mergers Commission*
Director General, National Association of Pension Funds.

**BJ Robinson**
*Head of Business Development Unit, Centre for Environment, Fisheries & Aquaculture Science*

**Dr Chris Robinson CBE**
*Lay Member, Medical Practices Committee*
Senior lecturer, University of Newcastle.

**Dr Derek Robinson**
*Director, Fusion, UK Atomic Energy Authority*
Joined UKAEA in 1965. UK Member to Joint European Torus (JET).

**Dr Geoffrey Robinson**
*Member of Council, Particle Physics & Astronomy Research Council*
*Member, Radiocommunications Agency*
*Non-Executive Director, Ordnance Survey*
*Member, Council for the Central Laboratory of the Research Councils*
Director of Technology, IBM UK.

**Gerry Robinson**
*Chairman, The Arts Council of England*

**Ian Robinson**
*Member of Board, Scottish Enterprise*

**Ian Robinson**
*Member of Board, UK Ecolabelling Board*
Technical & Environment Services, Autobar Industries.

**Ken Robinson CBE**
*Operations Director, New Millennium Experience Co Ltd*
MD Leisure Recreation and Tourism, VCL. Chairman, Tourism Society.

**Michael Robinson**
*Director (Ships, Aircraft & Armaments), Disposal Sales Agency*

**PD Robinson**
*Member, Sports Council for Northern Ireland*

**Phillip Robinson**
*Director, Communications & Corporate Affairs, Financial Services Authority*
Currently Executive Director and Chief Operating Officer, IMRO. Former senior management positions at SFA, AFBD, Metallgesellschaft and ICCH.

**Stella Robinson**
*Member, The Arts Council of England*
Chairman of Northern Arts Board. Labour Councillor in Darlington and County Durham. Vice-Chairman, North of England Open Air Museum at Beamish. Member, Council of the Museums Service.

**Terry Robinson**
*Local Identity, Countryside Commission*

**Ald Tom D Robinson JP**
*Member, Northern Ireland Local Government Officers' Superannuation Committee*

**Andrew Robson**
*Head of Finance, National Gallery*

**Euan Robson**
*Manager, Scotland, Gas Consumers' Council*

**Ian Robson**
*Director, Joint Astronomy Centre*

**Mike Robson**
*Member, Southern Consumers' Committee, Office of Electricity Regulation*

**RP Robson**
*Member, Parole Board*

**Tony Roche**
*Member, British Railways Board*

**Jim Rodda**
*Secretary, National Film & Television School*

**Supt HM Roddie**
*OCU, Burghfield, Ministry of Defence Police*

**JB Roddin**
*Director of Corporate Strategy and Resources, Scottish Fisheries Protection Agency*

**John Roderick**
*Finance Manager, Welsh National Board for Nursing, Midwifery & Health Visiting*

**Tony Rodgers**
*Member of Board, The Environment Agency*
Director, Shroeders Asia Pacific Trust and Civic Trust. Chairman, Rodgerss & Rodgers. Owner, Yeoman's Stud. Former Executive Director, ICI and Zeneca Group.

**James Roe**
*Member, Monopolies & Mergers Commission*
Former Director, N M Rothschild & Sons. Director, Jupiter International Group.

**Andrew Rogers**
*Chairman, Lochaber Limited*

**J Rogers**
*Finance Director, Army Base Repair Organisation*

**James Rogers**
*Funding & Allocations ITT, Teacher Training Agency*

**Mary Rogers**
*Deputy Chair, Stonebridge Housing Action Trust*
Director of consultancy specialising in urban regeneration. Former Joint Chief Executive, Greater London Enterprise.

**P Rogers**
*Member of Board, Construction Industry Training Board (NI)*
John Frackleton & Sons. Employer representative.

**Peter Rogers**
*Chief Executive, Independent Television Commission*

**Phil Rogers**
*TTA Unit in Wales, Teacher Training Agency*

**Sheila Rogers**
*Chief Administrative Officer, Equal Opportunities Commission for Northern Ireland*

**John Rogerson**
*Member of Board, Tower Hamlets Housing Action Trust*
Director of Consultancy & Professional Services, National Westminster Bank. Member, Council of Management of Stonham Housing Association.

**Stephen Rolph**
*Public Search Room, Certified Copies, Search Production, Companies House*

**Neil Romain**
*Head of Finance, The Radio Authority*

**Jim Romanos**
*Sector Director - Infrastructure, Commonwealth Development Corporation*

**Prof M Romans**
*Member of Board, Construction Industry Training Board*
University of Westminster.

**Malcolm Ronald**
*Secretary, Apple & Pear Research Council*

**Peter Ronaldson**
*Chief Executive, Construction Service*

**John Roques**
*Non-Executive Director, British Nuclear Fuels plc*
Senior Partner & Chief Executive, Deloitte & Touche. Non-Executive Director, Portman Building Society.

**Jim Rose CBE**
*Director of Inspection, Office for Standards in Education*

**John Rose**
*Member, East Midland Consumers' Committee, Office of Electricity Regulation*

**Sue Rose**
*Head of Press & Public Affairs, The Arts Council of England*

**General Sir Michael Rose KCB CBE DSO**
*Chairman, Service Children's Education*

**The Countess of Rosebery**
*Trustee, National Museums of Scotland*

**Chris Rosenberg**
*Head of Metrology & Training Unit, National Weights & Measures Laboratory*

**Cllr Leslie Rosin JP**
*Member of Board, West of Scotland Water Authority*
Councillor, East Renfrewshire Council. Former Provost, Eastwood District Council. Member, Music Committee, Scottish Arts Council. Director, Scottish Chamber Orchestra. Board Member, Scottish Opera. Director, Scottish Rights of Way Society.

**Mrs Janet Roskilly**
*Member, Rail Users Consultative Committee for Southern England*

**Alexander Ross**
*Member of Council, Ofwat Thames Customer Service Committee*

**Andrew Ross**
*Head of Personnel & Secretariat, Highlands & Islands Enterprise*

**Dr B Ross**
*Member of Council, Medical Research Council*
Glaxo Research & Development.

**Belinda Ross**
*Picture Library Manager, National Gallery Publications, National Gallery*

**Mrs Fiona Ross**
*Member, Rail Users Consultative Committee for Southern England*

**John Ross**
*Acting Regional Sheriff Clerk, Lothian and Borders, Scottish Court Service*

**John Ross CBE**
*Commissioner, Meat & Livestock Commission*
Former President, National Farmers' Union of Scotland. Farmer. Chairman, Scotch Quality Beef & Lamb Association. Director, NFU Mutual Insurance Society. Director, Moredun Research Institute. Chairman, Dumfries & Galloway Health Board.

**Ernie Ross MP**
*Chairman, Westminster Foundation for Democracy*

**Lord Ross**
*Member, Parole Board for Scotland*

**Commander Walter Ross**
*RPC Chief Officer, Royal Parks Agency*

**Peter Rostron**
*Assistant Director (Legal) Competition Policy, Office of Fair Trading*

**Emma Rothschild**
*Member of Board, British Council*
Economist, economic historian and
Fellow, King's College University of
Cambridge.

**CR Rothwell**
*Chairman, Wessex RFAC, The
Environment Agency*

**Dr TJ Rothwell**
*Member, Rail Users Consultative
Committee for Eastern England*

**Judith Round**
*Member, The Further Education Funding
Council*
Principal, Highbury College, Portsmouth.

**Andrew Rowe**
*Member, Academic Council, Wilton Park
Executive Agency*
Conservative Party Member of
Parliament.

**Kenneth Rowe**
*Member, Ofwat Eastern Customer
Service Committee*

**MW Rowe**
*Director, Horticulture Research
International*

**Mike Rowe**
*Chief Executive, Pay & Personnel Agency*

**Rear Admiral PB Rowe**
*Chairman, Trinity House Lighthouse
Service*

**Robert Rowe**
*Member of Board, Northern Ireland
Museums' Council*
Museum of the Royal Irish Regiment.
Nominated by the independent and
service museums.

**David S Rowe-Beddoe**
*Chairman, Welsh Development Agency*
Development Board for Rural Wales,
American Banknote Corporation,
Cavendish Services Group, Development
Securities, GFTA Trendanalysen, The
Prince's Trust-Bro, Welsh College of
Music & Drama.

**Hilary Rowland**
*Member, Audit Commission*
Chief Executive, Royal Liverpool
Children's Trust, Alder Hey Hospital
Liverpool.

**D Rowlands**
*Chairman of Advisory Board, Coastguard*

**Enid Rowlands**
*Managing Director, North Division, Welsh
Development Agency*

**Janice Rowlands**
*Member of Authority, S4C*
Director, Merthyr Institute of the Blind.
Board Member, Victim Support.
Governor, Ysgol Santes Tudful. Former
Chairman, Urdd National Eisteddfod.
Former Member, IBA Welsh Viewers'
Panel. Former Chairman, ITC Viewers'
Panel. Vice-President, Merthyr AFC.

**Viv Rowlands**
*Secretariat, Central Office of Information*

**Mrs Eira Rowley**
*Professional Adviser, Primary Health
Care, Welsh National Board for Nursing,
Midwifery & Health Visiting*

**Cdre RA Rowley OBE**
*Commodore Naval Drafting, Naval
Manning Agency*

**Prof Cherry Rowlings**
*Member, Central Council for Education &
Training in Social Work*

**Ashok Roy**
*Head of Scientific, National Gallery*

**Brigadier MJ Roycroft**
*Chief Executive, Defence Clothing &
Textiles Agency*

**Dick Ruane**
*Chief Executive, Moray Badenoch &
Strathspey Enterprise*

**Dr E Rubery**
*Member of Ownership Board, Meat
Hygiene Service*
Head of Health Aspects, Environment &
Food Division, Department of Health.

**AG Rucker**
*Member of Committee, Ministry of
Defence Police*
Security and Support. Clerk to the
Committee.

**Mrs Joan Ruddock OBE**
*Member, Industrial Research &
Technology Unit*
*Member of Board, Local Enterprise
Development Unit*
Managing Director, EDCO.

**Dr AW Rudge CBE**
*Chairman, Engineering & Physical
Sciences Research Council*

**HS Ruffman**
*Director of Personnel & Management
Services, Commission for the New Towns*

**Lord Runcie MC**
*Vice-President, The Britain-Russia
Centre*

**Jeff Rush**
*Regional Manager, Office of Electricity
Regulation*

**Mrs M Russel**
*Member of Council, Council for Catholic
Maintained Schools*
Parent Representative.

**Muir Russel**
*Member, Biotechnology & Biological
Sciences Research Council*
Secretary of The Scottish Office
Agriculture, Environment & Fisheries
Department.

**NJ Russel**
*Member, The British Library*
Library and Information Services Council
(Northern Ireland).

**T Russel**
*Member, Parole Board*

**A Russell**
*Employer Member, Engineering
Construction Industry Training Board*
Personnel Director, Atlantic Power & Gas.

**Rt Rev Anthony Russell**
*Commissioner, Rural Development
Commission*
Bishop of Dorchester. Member,
Archbishops' Commission on Rural Areas
(1988-91). Trustee, Rural Housing Trust.
Vice-President, ACRE. Vice-President,
Oxfordshire Rural Community Council.

**Prof Earl Russell**
*Trustee, National Portrait Gallery*

**Dr Maurice Russell**
*Commissioner, Mental Health
Commission for Northern Ireland*
Former General Medical Practitioner.

**Patricia Russell**
*Deputy Chief Executive, Independent
Commission for Police Complaints for
Northern Ireland*

**Peter Russell**
*Area Director North & East, Scottish
Prison Service*

**Supt R Russell**
*OCU PTC., Ministry of Defence Police*

**Sandy Russell**
*Deputy Chairman, HM Customs & Excise*

**D Russon**
*Deputy Chief Executive, The British
Library*

**Ian Rutherford**
*Member of Board, Wales Tourist Board*

**Katie Rutherford**
*Acting Director, International Marketing,
Scottish Tourist Board*

**Leslie Rutherford**
*Member, North Eastern Consumers'
Committee, Office of Electricity
Regulation*

**Peter Rutland**
*Head of Computing, British Film Institute*

**David Rutledge**
*Chief Executive, Livestock & Meat
Commission for Northern Ireland*

**Dr Michael Rutter**
*Director & Chief Executive, Veterinary
Medicines Directorate*

**Andrew Ryan**
*Publisher Crafts Magazine, Crafts
Council*

**Dave Ryan**
*Member of Management Board, The
Court Service*
Western Circuit Administrator.

**Ms Mary Ryan**
*Member, Centre for Information on
Language Teaching & Research*
Adviser for Modern Languages, Avon
Advisory Centre, Bristol.

**Philip Rycroft**
*Member of Council, Food from Britain*
Scottish Office of Agriculture, Fisheries & Food.

**Mrs MG Ryding**
*Member of Board, Education Assets Board*

**Sir William Ryrie KCB**
*Deputy Chairman, Commonwealth Development Corporation*
Former Executive Vice President & Chief Executive, International Finance Corporation.


# S

**Shahwar Sadeque**
*Member of Board, Waltham Forest Housing Action Trust*
Education and IT consultant.

**Richard Sadler**
*Commissioner, Meat & Livestock Commission*
Head of Buying for Meat, Poultry & Fish, Waitrose.

**Robin Sadler**
*Member, Eastern Consumers' Committee, Office of Electricity Regulation*

**Jim Sadlier**
*Director, Organisational Development, Particle Physics & Astronomy Research Council*

**J Sadlik JP**
*Member, Parole Board*

**SP Sage**
*Chief Executive, The Buying Agency*

**Shamit Saggar**
*Member, National Consumer Council*

**JP Sainsbury**
*Member, Cardiff Bay Development Corporation*
South Glamorgan TEC. Welsh Sports Aid Foundation. Exchange Registrars. Carrer Paths (Cardiff & Vale). Druidstone House Management. Cardiff & Vale Enterprise Group. Welsh College of Music & Drama. STAR Recreation and Community Trust.

**The Hon. Simon Sainsbury**
*Trustee, National Gallery*

**Sir John Sainty**
*Commissioner, The Royal Commission on Historical Manuscripts*

**Margaret Salmon**
*Director of Personnel, British Broadcasting Corporation*
Former Group Personnel Director, Burton Group.

**Peter Salmon**
*Member of Museum Trust, Museum of Science & Industry Manchester*

**Trevor Salmon**
*Member, Northern Ireland Local Government Officers' Superannuation Committee*

**Eve Salomon**
*Secretary to the Authority, The Radio Authority*

**Claire Sampson**
*Production Director, New Millenium Experience Co Ltd*
Former Head of Exhibition & Festival Unit, Millennium Commission.

**Alec Samson**
*Member, Horticultural Development Council*
Director, Kettle Produce.

**Brian Samson**
*Director of Operations, Scottish Sports Council*

**Sam Samuel**
*Head of Branch, Tree Improvement, Forest Research*

**Marc Samuelson**
*Governor, National Film & Television School*

**Commander WG Samways OBE**
*Estate/Appeal Manager, Royal Marines Museum*

**Preben Sand**
*Food from Britain (Scandinavia)*

**Prof A Sanders**
*Member, Parole Board*

**Chris Sanders**
*Member, Horticultural Development Council*
Production Director, Bridgemere Nurseries.

**Glen Sanderson**
*Board Director, Home-Grown Cereals Authority*

**Ian Sanderson**
*Member, Merseyside & North Wales Consumers' Committee, Office of Electricity Regulation*

**John Sanderson**
*Member, Horserace Totalisator Board*
Chief Executive, International Racing Management. Chairman, Wetherby Racecourse. Director, Thirsk Racecourse. Director, British Horseracing Board, Racecourse Association and Televised Racing.

**Prof Cedric Sandford**
*Member, Ofwat Wessex Customer Service Committee*

**Miss Irene Sandford**
*Member, Arts Council of Northern Ireland*
Soprano.

**Martin Sands**
*Deputy Chief Executive & Director of Geographic Resources, Military Survey*

**Tony Sannia**
*Finance Director, English Heritage*

**Mrs R Sargent JP**
*Member, Parole Board*

**RJ Sargent**
*Assistant Keeper, The Royal Commission on Historical Manuscripts*

**Prof Berrick Saul CBE**
*Deputy Chairman, Commonwealth Scholarship Commission*
Formerly Vice-Chancellor, University of York.

**Charles Saumarez Smith**
*Director, National Portrait Gallery*

**John Saumarez Smith**
*Member of Advisory Committee, Registrar of Public Lending Right*
Bookseller.

**E Saunders**
*Member, Sports Council for Northern Ireland*

**Frances Saunders**
*CDA, Defence Evaluation & Research Agency*

**G Saunders**
*Director of Appeals Administration, The Planning Inspectorate*

**IDF Saunders**
*Postgraduate Dental Dean, Northern Ireland Council for Postgraduate Medical & Dental Education*

**John Saunders**
*Director of Regulation & Business Affairs, Office of Electricity Regulation*

**Michael Saunders**
*Assistant Director & Head of Consumer Affairs, Office of Water Services*

**Dominic Savage**
*Member of Council, British Educational Communications & Technology Agency*
British Education Software Association.

**Graham Savage**
*Director of Finance, Millennium Commission*

**Hugh Savill**
*Member of Steering Board, Companies House*
Member, National Weights & Measures Laboratory
Member, Employment Tribunals Service
DTI Director of Resources

**Rosalind Savill**
*Director, Wallace Collection*

**Mrs Kathryn Saward**
*Member, Eastern Consumers' Committee, Office of Electricity Regulation*

**Jeff Sawyer**
*Member, Departmental Board, Wilton Park Executive Agency*

**Tony Sawyer**
*Director Operations (Prevention), HM Customs & Excise*

**Peter Say**
*Manager, Healthcare, Remploy*

**Jim Sayers**
*Regional Operations Director, Local Enterprise Development Unit*

**Peter Scales**
*Chief Executive, London Pensions Fund Authority*

**Margaret Scanlan**
*Member, The Scottish Legal Aid Board*
Solicitor. Member, Sheriff Ruels Council. Director, Legal Defence Union.

**Earl of Scarbrough**
*Commissioner, The Royal Commission on Historical Manuscripts*

**Andrew Scarfe**
*Group Director, The Government Property Lawyers*

**P Scherer**
*Board Member, The British Library*
Director, Transworld Publishers.

**GC Schild CBE**
*Director, National Biological Standards Board*

**Phillip Schlesinger**
*Member of Board, Scottish Screen*

**Albert Schofield**
*Director of Contracts, Coal Authority*

**Dr Geraldine Schofield**
*Member, Health & Safety Commission*
Senior microbiologist, Unilever Research. Deputy Chairman, CBI's Biotechnology Strategy Group. Chairman, Food & Drink Federation's Novel Foods & Biotechnology Committee. Member, Biotechnology Government Regulatory Advisory Group. Non-Executive Director, Bedford Hospital NHS Trust. Former Member, Government's Advisory Committee on Genetic Manipulation.

**Miss JM Schofield**
*Member of Board, Education Assets Board*

**Prof Michael Schofield**
*Member of Advisory Board, NHS Estates*
Chairman, Dorset Community NHS Trust Director, Health Services Management Unit (Manchester). Chairman, NHS Confederation.

**Sir David Scholey CBE**
*Trustee, National Portrait Gallery*
*Governor, British Broadcasting Corporation*
Former Chairman, SG Warburg Group.

**CE Schooling**
*Director, Customer Services, West of Scotland Water Authority*

**Peter Schuddeboom**
*Member, Industrial Research & Technology Unit*
Director, Northern Ireland Telecommunications Engineering Centre (NORTEL).

**Francis Scoon**
*Member, Ofwat Central Customer Service Committee*

**Herman Scopes**
*Chairman, Ofwat Thames Customer Service Committee*
*Member, Ofwat National Customer Council*

**Mrs Margaret Scorer**
*Member, Police Complaints Authority*
Former Inspector, HM Magistrates Courts' Inspectorate and law lecturer.

**Miss Patricia Scotland QC**
*Member, Millennium Commission*
Barrister. Former Member, Race Relations Committee of the General Council of the Bar.

**Cllr Alexander Scott**
*Member, Scottish Water & Sewerage Customers Council*

**Andrew Scott**
*Head of NRM, National Museum of Science & Industry*

**Bill Scott**
*Head of Corporate Services, Qualifications & Curriculum Authority*

**D Scott**
*Member, Executive Committee, HM Prison Service*

**D Scott**
*Member, Parole Board*

**David Scott**
*Managing Director & Director of Finance, Channel Four Television Corporation*

**Eileen Scott**
*Head of Human Resource Development, Scottish Homes*

**IJ Scott CBE**
*Trustee, Imperial War Museum*

**Ian Scott**
*Deputy Chief Executive, Scottish Court Service*
Area Director, Glasgow & North Strathclyde.

**Mrs Jane Scott**
*Member, Ofwat Eastern Customer Service Committee*

**John Scott**
*International Affairs, UK Sports Council*

**John Scott**
*Manager, Campbeltown Airport, Highlands & Islands Airports*

**Jonathan Scott CBE**
*Deputy Chairman, Victoria & Albert Museum*

**Louise Scott**
*European Information Officer, Scottish Screen*

**MW Scott**
*Institute Secretary, Hannah Research Institute*

**Michael Scott**
*Member, North Areas Board & Scientific Advisory Committee, Scottish Natural Heritage*

**Air Commodore PJ Scott**
*Officer Commanding, RAF St Athan, RAF Maintenance Group Defence Agency*

**Richard Scott**
*Member, The Scottish Legal Aid Board*
Chief Executive

**Tom Scott**
*Director, Training Division, Training & Employment Agency (NI)*

**W Scott**
*Industrial Accountant, Compensation Agency*

**WW Scott**
*Member of Advisory Council, Scottish Record Office*

**Miss Sue Scott-Curtis**
*Head of Personnel, Army Training & Recruitment Agency*

**J Scudamore**
*Member of Ownership Board, Meat Hygiene Service*
Chief Veterinary Officer, MAFF.

**Ann Scully OBE**
*Member, Health & Safety Commission*
Vice Chairman, National Consumer Council. Former Chairman, Domestic Coal Consumers Council. Council Member, Banking Ombudsman. Member, Code of Banking Practice Review Committee. Member, European Coal & Steel Consultative Committee. Past Member, British Standards Institute Consumer Policy Committee. Board Member, Investment Management Regulatory Organisation (IMRO) and Mid Cheshire

**Russell Seal**
*Member, Commonwealth Development Corporation*
Non-Executive Director, Blue Circle Industries.

**J Seddon**
*Finance Services Director, Highways Agency*

**Joanne Segars**
*Member of Board, Occupational Pensions Regulatory Authority*
Pensions Officer, Trades Union Congress and trustee of TUC's superannuation fund. (Nominated by the TUC.)

**The Hon Raymond GH Seitz**
*Trustee, National Gallery*

**Nicholas Selbie**
*Managing Director, CDC Investments, Commonwealth Development Corporation*

**The Earl of Selborne KBE**
*Trustee, Royal Botanic Gardens Kew*

**Anthony Sell**
*Chief Executive, British Tourist Authority*

**William K Semple**
*Director, Highlands & Islands Airports*
Chief Operating Officer, National Air
Traffic Services.

**Eric Senat**
*Governor, National Film & Television
School*

**Kevin Senior**
*Member, Southern Consumers'
Committee, Office of Electricity
Regulation*

**Carol Sergeant**
*Director, Banking and Building Societies,
Financial Services Authority*
Head of Major UK Banks Division, Bank
of England. Joined Bank in 1974. Former
Senior Manager, Gilt Edged & Money
Markets Division.

**Nicholas Serota**
*Director, Tate Gallery*

**Eric Seward**
*Manager for the North & Scotland,
Commission for Racial Equality*

**Julian Seymour**
*Commissioner, English Heritage*

**Margaret Seymour**
*Member, Scottish Sports Council*

**Margaret Seymour**
*Member, BACT, Office of
Telecommunications*
Managing Director, swimming pool
design and construction company.

**Desmond Shackleton**
*Member, Northern Ireland Consumer
Committee for Electricity, Office for the
Regulation of Electricity & Gas*
Energy engineer.

**Mrs Iris Shanahan**
*Member, Ofwat North West Customer
Service Committee*

**Miss Lily G Shand**
*Non-Executive Member of Board,
National Board for Nursing, Midwifery &
Health Visiting for Scotland*
Senior Midwifery Lecturer, University of
Paisley.

**Dr Oliver Shanks**
*Commissioner, Mental Health
Commission for Northern Ireland*
Consultant Psychiatrist, North & West
Belfast Health & Social Services Trust.

**Alan Shannon**
*Chief Executive, Northern Ireland Prison
Service*

**Dr David Shannon**
*Member, Biotechnology & Biological
Sciences Research Council*
*Member of Ownership Board, Veterinary
Laboratories Agency*
*Member, Natural Environment Research
Council*
Chief Scientist, MAFF. Former Member,
AFRC Council. Former UK President,
World's Poultry Science Association.

Former Chairman, CAB International
Executive Council.

**Prof Ernest Shannon**
*Member, Industrial Research &
Technology Unit*
Former Director of Special Projects,
British Gas.

**Pete Sharkey**
*IT Provider Director, Information
Technology Services Agency*

**Parveen Sharma**
*Head of Central Services, Commission
for Racial Equality*

**Sukhdev Sharma**
*Executive Director, Commission for
Racial Equality*

**Jane Sharman CBE**
*Member of Board of Trustees, Historic
Royal Palaces*
Former Acting Chief Executive, English
Heritage. Appointed by the Secretary of
State.

**Dr C Sharp**
*Head of Dept, Medical, National
Radiological Protection Board*

**Frank Sharp**
*Director of Human Resources, East of
Scotland Water Authority*
Chairman, Quality Scotland Personal
Development Programmes Working Party.

**Peter Sharp**
*Director Technology, Council for the
Central Laboratory of the Research
Councils*

**Tony Sharpe**
*Head of Branch, Technical Support
North, Forest Research*

**David Sharples**
*Member, Rail Users Consultative
Committee for North Western England*

**Sir James Sharples**
*Member of Council, Economic & Social
Research Council*
Chief Constable, Merseyside Police.

**Alistair Shaw**
*Head of Accommodation, Procurement,
Libraries & Records Division, The Court
Service*

**Dr DF Shaw MBE**
*Member of Council, English Nature*
*Member, Joint Nature Conservation
Committee*
Chemist. Founder and Chairman, Irish
Sea Forum. Governor, University College,
Chester.

**Deborah Shaw**
*Office Manager, Commissioner for
Protection Against Unlawful Industrial
Action & Commissioner for the Rights of
Trade Union Members*

**Frances J Shaw**
*Head, Government Records, Scottish
Record Office*

**Glenis Shaw**
*Language Teaching Adviser, Centre for
Information on Language Teaching &
Research*

**Cllr Mrs Jennifer Shaw**
*Member of Board, Scottish Environment
Protection Agency*

**Sir John C Shaw CBE KStJ**
*Chairman, Scottish Higher Education
Funding Council*
*Member of Board, Scottish Enterprise*

**John S Shaw**
*Head, Reader Services, Scottish Record
Office*

**Mark Shaw**
*Keeper of Geology & Zoology, National
Museums of Scotland*

**Hon Mike Shaw**
*Chairman, Argyll & The Islands
Enterprise*

**R Shaw**
*Member of Board, Fisheries
Conservancy Board for Northern Ireland*
Commercial fishermen's representative.

**Prof Susan Shaw**
*Member of Council, Food from Britain*
University of Strathclyde.

**Lady Shaw Stewart**
*Trustee, Wallace Collection*

**Dr Michael Shea CVO**
*Member, Independent Television
Commission*
*Trustee, National Galleries of Scotland*

**Jim Shearer**
*Member, Legal Aid Board*
Former Head of Commercial Services,
British Coal. Trustee, Coal Industry
Social Welfare Organisation. Magistrate.
Member, Leicestershire Community
Health Council and East Midlands
Advisory Committee of the Further
Education Funding Council.

**Kevin Sheehan**
*Deputy Chief Executive & Director of
Operations, UK Passport Agency*

**Lady Sheil**
*Member of Authority, The Radio Authority*

**M Sheldon**
*Member of Board, Football Licensing
Authority*

**Giles Shepard CBE**
*Member, Royal Parks Agency*

**Geoff Shepherd**
*Lay Member, Medical Practices
Committee*
Director, Kensington & Chelsea &
Westminster HA.

**Prof J Shepherd**
*Director, Southampton Oceanography
Centre*

**C Shepley**
*Chief Planning Inspector & Chief
Executive, The Planning Inspectorate*

**Tony Sheppeck**
*Board Member for Finance, London Transport*

**Cllr J Shera**
*Member, Parole Board*

**EO Sheridan**
*Inspector, Football Licensing Authority*

**Jack Sheridan**
*Member of Board, Liverpool Housing Action Trust*
High-rise tenant. Former Personnel Manager with large multinational company.

**Clive Sherling**
*Chairman, Football Licensing Authority*

**A Sherrard**
*Member of Board, Probation Board for Northern Ireland*

**Albert Sherrard**
*Member, Post Office Users' Council for Northern Ireland*

**AVM TB Sherrington OBE**
*Member of Committee, Ministry of Defence Police*
Air Officer Administration.

**Dr G Shetty**
*Member, Parole Board*

**Allan Shiach**
*Governor, British Film Institute*

**Sheriff Gordon Shiach**
*Vice Chairman, Parole Board for Scotland*
Sheriff, Edinburgh.

**Mrs Carol Shields**
*Member, Northern Ireland Local Government Officers' Superannuation Committee*

**Dr J Shields**
*Member, NIACT, Northern Ireland Committee on Telecommunications*
Senior Manager, electronics and telecoms equipment group.

**Donal Shiels**
*Manager (Systems Development), Fair Employment Commission for Northern Ireland*

**C Shillington CBE**
*Member, Sports Council for Northern Ireland*

**David Shillington JP**
*Member of Commission, Independent Commission for Police Complaints for Northern Ireland*
Former Marketing/Sales Manager of a drinks company. Chairman of South Ulster Trust for Integrated Education. Member of Board of Governors of St Colman's Primary School, Dromore. Chairman of Downpatrick Racecourse.

**R Shimmon**
*Member, The British Library*
Library Association.

**Lieutenant Commander DE Shinn**
*Management Planner, Naval Manning Agency*

**Brian Shipton**
*Contracts, Customer Care & Codes of Conduct, Teacher Training Agency*

**Michele Shirlow**
*Manager Textiles & Electronics, Local Enterprise Development Unit*

**Mrs Cynthia Short**
*Commissioner, The Royal Commission on Historical Manuscripts*

**Tom Short**
*Manager Southern Regional Office, Local Enterprise Development Unit*

**Aidan Shortt**
*Member, Arts Council of Northern Ireland*
Chair of Open Arts.

**Alan Shotter**
*Member, Rail Users Consultative Committee for Southern England*

**Helena Shovelton**
*Member, Audit Commission*
*Member, Monopolies & Mergers Commission*
Chair, National Association of Citizens' Advice Bureaux. Member, Local Government Commission. Chair, Continuing Care Review Panel, East Sussex Brighton & Hove Health Authority.

**AJ Shuttleworth**
*Secretary, British Nuclear Fuels plc*

**Lady Shuttleworth**
*Non-Executive Director, British Nuclear Fuels plc*
Former Chairman, Community Council of Lancashire. Former Chairman, Lune Valley Rural Housing Association. Chairman of Governors, Wennington Hall Special State School.

**Peter Siddal**
*Chairman, Horticulture Research International*

**David Sidebottom**
*Manager, North West, Gas Consumers' Council*

**The Hon David Sieff**
*Chairman, National Lottery Charities Board*
*Member, Horserace Totalisator Board*
Non-Executive Director, Marks & Spencer. Non-Executive Chair, FIBI (UK). Director, British Retail Consortium, Newbury Racecourse and Horserace Totalisator Board. Founder member, Business in the Community. Member of Council, Prince's Youth Business Trust. Chair, Racing Welfare Charities.

**Mary Ann Sieghart**
*Trustee, National Heritage Memorial Fund*

**DRW Silk CBE JP**
*Trustee, Imperial War Museum*

**Jim Sillars**
*Member of Board, Scottish Enterprise*

**Prof HR Silverman**
*Member, Cardiff Bay Development Corporation*
Assessor, Arts Council of Wales, Lottery Unit.

**Alan Sim**
*Chief Executive, Grampian Enterprise*

**Andrew Sim**
*Solicitor, British Railways Board*

**Stewart Sim**
*Director of Operations, British Waterways*

**JM Sime**
*Member of Governing Body, Scottish Crop Research Institute*
Chief Executive, BioIndustry Association, Held R&D, general management, and strategic marketing positions with Beecham and then SmithKline Beecham. Member, CBI Biostrategy Committee. Member of Management Board, Advanced Centre for Biochemical Engineering, University College, London.

**Captain JAB Simkins**
*Managing Director, Caledonian MacBrayne Ltd*

**Graeme Simmers OBE**
*Chairman, Scottish Sports Council*
*Member, UK Sports Council*

**R Simmonds**
*Member, Joint Nature Conservation Committee*
Countryside Commission.

**Andrew Simmonite**
*Finance, Central Science Laboratory*

**Brian Simmons**
*Business Support Director, Central Science Laboratory*
Joined CSL in 1991. Previously worked for Property Services Agency.

**Sir Neville Simms**
*Member of Court, Bank of England*
Deputy Chairman & Group Chief Executive, Tarmac.

**Jacob Simon**
*18th Century Curator, National Portrait Gallery*

**AM Simon OBE**
*Member of Ownership Board, Veterinary Medicines Directorate*
Independent Member.

**Barry Simpson**
*Director of Support Services, Scottish Children's Reporter Administration*

**Dr Duncan Simpson**
*Director of Government, Information & Corporate Services, Public Record Office*

**JV Simpson**
*Member of Council, Council for Catholic Maintained Schools*
Department of Education Representative.

**JWT Simpson**
*Commissioner, Royal Commission on Ancient & Historical Monuments of Scotland*

**James Simpson**
*Member, Ofwat Northumbria Customer Service Committee*

**Joe Simpson**
*Challenge Director, New Millennium Experience Co Ltd*
Former MD, The Knowledge Network, Digital Television Network. Former Chief Officer, ITV Telethon.

**John Simpson OBE**
*Chair, Northern Ireland Committee and National Lottery Charities, National Lottery Charities Board*
Economist. Former Senior Lecturer, Queen's University. Member, Economic & Social Committee, European Union. Part-time lecturer, University of Ulster. Chairman, Emerging Business Trust. Former Chair, Probation Board of Northern Ireland. Former Chair, Eastern Health & Social Services Board.

**Joyce Simpson**
*Member, Scottish Conveyancing & Executry Services Board*

**Robin Simpson**
*Deputy Director, National Consumer Council*

**Miss ZC Simpson**
*Member of Council, British Hallmarking Council*

**Air Vice Marshal CE Simpson MB Chb**
*Chairman, Queen Victoria School*

**Neville W Sims MBE**
*Member of Council, Post Office Users' Council for Wales*
Chartered Accountant. Member Council of Institute of Chartered Accountants in England & Wales.

**Major-General George Sinclair CB CBE**
*Trustee, Imperial War Museum*

**Bill Sinden**
*Specialist Member, Gas Consumers' Council*
Former Director, Society of British Gas Industries. Member, Witney Citizens Advice Bureau Management Committee.

**Dr Jaslien Singh**
*Member, Commission for Racial Equality*
Partner, Gitanjli-Mayfair Restaurant Group. Founder, the Preventative Initiative. Business adviser, PYBT. Chief Executive, Peter Sellers Foundation.

**Karamjit Singh**
*Commissioner, Criminal Cases Review Commission*
Civil Service Commissioner. Vice-Chairman, Ethnic Minorities Advisory Committee, Judicial Studies Board.

**Ray Singh**
*Member, Commission for Racial Equality*
Barrister. Deputy District Judge. Part-time Chairman, Child Support Appeals Tribunal. Member, Welsh Advisory Committee on Drug & Alcohol Misuse. Member, Race Relations Committee, General Council of the Bar. Member, Family Court Services Committee. Member, Bar Council. Member, Society of Middle Temple, Family Law Bar Association, Criminal Law Bar Association.

**Hari Shankar Singhania**
*Member, Commonwealth Development Corporation*
President, JK Organisation, India. Chairman, Atlas Copco (India). Past President, International Chamber of Commerce, Paris

**His Excellency Dr LM Singhvi**
*Trustee, Imperial War Museum*

**David Singleton**
*LEA Reviews, Reorganisation Proposals, Office for Standards in Education*
*Member of Advisory Board, Service Children's Education*

**David Sinker OBE**
*Member, Legal Aid Board*
Chartered accountant and magistrate. Former adviser to National Board of Prices & Incomes. Former Member, Department of the Environment committee of enquiry. Non-Executive Director, East & North Hertfordshire District Health Authority. Non-Executive Director of group of companies which covers professional photofinishing, printing and graphic arts.

**Dr RWJ Sisson**
*Member, Rail Users Consultative Committee for North Eastern England*
English Teacher, Bradford Grammar School.

**Cllr Eric Sizer**
*Member of Board, Waltham Forest Housing Action Trust*
Labour Ward Councillor, London Borough of Waltham Forest.

**Prof John Sizer CBE**
*Chief Executive, Scottish Higher Education Funding Council*
*Observer, Higher Education Funding Council for England*

**Prudence Skene**
*Member, The Arts Council of England*
Former Executive Director, Ballet Rambert and Executive Producer, English Shakespeare Company. Director, Arts Foundation. Former President, Theatrical Management Association and Chairman and Vice-Chairman respectively, Dancers' Resettlement Trust and Fund.

**Roger Skiffins**
*Director, Broadcasting, Fixed & Space Services, Radiocommunications Agency*

**Geoffrey Skinner CBE**
*Member, South Eastern Consumers' Committee, Office of Electricity Regulation*

**Marie Skinner**
*Board Director, Home-Grown Cereals Authority*

**Baden Skitt**
*Commissioner, Criminal Cases Review Commission*
Former Assistant Commissioner, Metropolitan Police.

**Prof AR Slabas**
*Member of Governing Body, Scottish Crop Research Institute*
Director of Research, Department of Biological Sciences, University of Durham. Member, UK Foresight Programme Panel Committee on Health & Life Sciences. Member Agricultural Systems Directorate Management Committee, the Eukaryotic Cell Link Management Committee and BBSRC Innovative Manufacturing Committee.

**AM Slater**
*Director, Procurement Services, Crown Agents Foundation*

**David Slater**
*Strategy Director, Contributions Agency*
Seconded from Department of Education & Employment.

**Dr David Slater CB**
*Director of Pollution Prevention and Control, The Environment Agency*

**Dr GJ Slater**
*Deputy Chief Executive, Public Record Office of Northern Ireland*

**James Slater**
*Member of Board, Sea Fish Industry Authority*
Vice-Chairman, Scottish Pelagic Fishermen's Association. Director, Scottish Fishermen's Federation. Member, Ullapool and Fraserburgh Harbour Trusts.

**Tom Slee**
*Member, Coal Authority*
Director, Royal London Mutual Insurance Society.

**AC Sleeman**
*Head, Inland Revenue South Yorkshire, Inland Revenue*

**Andrew Sleigh**
*MD Analysis, Defence Evaluation & Research Agency*

**Mrs Daphne Sleigh**
*Member of Board, Scottish Homes*
Conservative Group Leader, City of Edinburgh Council. Member, Salvation Army Advisory Board and Lothian Home's Trust.

**Prof O Slevin**
*Chief Executive, National Board for Nursing, Midwifery & Health Visiting for Northern Ireland*

**Sue Slipman OBE**
*Director, Gas Consumers' Council*

**JP Sloan**
*Mental Nursing/Mental Handicap Nursing, National Board for Nursing, Midwifery & Health Visiting for Northern Ireland*

**Supt TP Sloman**
*OCU, Stanmore, Ministry of Defence Police*

**Air Commodore Ian Sloss**
*Chief Executive, RAF Logistics Support Services*

**G Smale**
*Senior Inspector, Northern Region, Gaming Board for Great Britain*

**Alistair Small**
*Director of Operations, Scottish Office Pensions Agency*

**Prof John Small CBE**
*Member of Board, Scottish Homes Professor of Accountancy & Finance, Heriot-Watt University. Former Chairman, Accounts Commission.*

**IMH Smart**
*Trustee, Imperial War Museum*

**Mike Smart**
*Member of Advisory Board, Defence Analytical Services Agency Chief of Staff, Personnel & Training Command.*

**Nick Smedley**
*Member of Management Board, The Court Service Director of Criminal Operations.*

**Paul Smee**
*Director of Public Affairs, Independent Television Commission*

**Ray Smees**
*Group General Manager, Creative Products, Remploy*

**A Smith**
*Member, Training & Employment Agency (NI) Executive with responsibility for Marks & Spencer in Belgium and France.*

**A Smith**
*Member of Board, Construction Industry Training Board (NI) Department of Education for NI Assessor.*

**AG Smith**
*Director of Corporate Affairs, North of Scotland Water Authority*

**Alexander B Smith**
*Dir Business Management, Defence Codification Agency*

**Alistair Smith**
*Head, Analytical Group, Macaulay Land Use Research Institute*

**Bob Smith**
*Principal, Scottish National Sports Centre*

**Dr Bruce Smith OBE**
*Chairman, Economic & Social Research Council*

**CH Smith**
*Managing Director, LT Property, London Transport*

**Chris Smith**
*Chairman, Millennium Commission Secretary of State for Culture, Media & Sport.*

**DA Smith**
*Self Assessment Programme, Inland Revenue*

**DAG Smith OBE JP**
*Member, Parole Board*

**Dr DJH Smith**
*Member of Council, Engineering & Physical Sciences Research Council*

**David Smith**
*Director of Administration, Office of Telecommunications*

**David Smith OBE**
*Member, Scottish Conveyancing & Executry S ervices Board*

**Denis Smith**
*Member, General Consumer Council for Northern Ireland Chairman, Belfast Development Agency. Member, Fair Employment Tribunal. Governor, Belfast Institute of Higher & Further Education. Chairman, Portview Trade Centre.*

**Donald Smith**
*Legal Officer, Crofters' Commission*

**Doug Smith**
*Director Self Assessment Programme, Inland Revenue*

**Cllr Mrs EA Smith**
*Member, Rail Users Consultative Committee for Western England*

**Frank Smith**
*Trustee, Geffrye Museum Head, International Department, RSM Salustro Reydel, Paris. Former Member, London Chamber of Commerce Tax Committee. Former Member, Chartered Accountants' Tax Legislation Committee. Former Member, Otter Housing Society Committee of Management. Former Governor, Brooklands Primary School.*

**G Smith**
*Head of Personnel and Training, Scottish Fisheries Protection Agency*

**GM Smith**
*Member of Council, British Hallmarking Council*

**Grahame Smith**
*Director Magnox Group, British Nuclear Fuels plc*

**Prof JB Smith**
*Chairman, Royal Commission on Ancient & Historical Monuments in Wales*

**JS Smith**
*Inspector, Football Licensing Authority*

**Jeffrey Smith**
*Trustee, Fleet Air Arm Museum*

**John Smith**
*Director of Finance, British Broadcasting Corporation*

**Malcolm Smith**
*Director, Bibliographic Services & Document Supply, The British Library*

**Margaret Smith**
*Regional Manager & Secretary, Ofwat North West Customer Service Committee*

**Mike Smith**
*Acting Chief Executive, Laganside Corporation*

**PJ Smith**
*Director of Information Technology, HM Land Registry*

**Pam Smith**
*Member, Horticultural Development Council Produce of flowers, bedding plants and dried flowers.*

**Patricia HB Smith**
*Head, General Services, Scottish Record Office*

**Paul Smith CBE**
*Member, The Design Council*

**Peter Smith**
*Member, Equal Opportunities Commission General Secretary, Association of Teachers & Lecturers (ATL).*

**Peter Smith**
*Subject Adviser, Geography, Office for Standards in Education*

**Captain RA Smith**
*Member of Board, Queen Victoria School*

**RS Smith**
*Planning & Development Director, LTB, London Transport*

**Richard Smith**
*Director, Review Implementation & Staff Development & Welfare, Central Office of Information*

**Rob Smith**
*Corporate Communications Manager, Forensic Science Service*

**Robert Smith**
*Chairman, National Museums of Scotland Vice-Chairman, Museums & Galleries Commission Chief Executive, Morgan Grenfell Asset Management. President, British Association of Friends of Museums. Former Treasurer, and Director, Sussex Heritage Trust.*

**Robert Smith**
*Head of Collection Care, Royal Armouries*

**Roderick Smith**
*Finance Officer, Sir John Soane's Museum*

**Ron Smith**
*Chief Executive, Defence Secondary Care Agency.*

**SB Smith**
*Commissioner, Royal Commission on Ancient & Historical Monuments in Wales*

**Sandra Smith**
*Head of Finance & Information Technology, Royal Parks Agency*

**Stephen Smith**
*Director of Corporate Services, Defence Estates Organisation*

**Tony Smith**
*Chief Executive, English National Board for Nursing, Midwifery & Health Visiting*

**Prof Chris Smout CBE**
*Member of Board & Scientific Advisory Committee, Scottish Natural Heritage*
*Commissioner, Royal Commission on Ancient & Historical Monuments of Scotland*
*Member, Joint Nature Conservation Committee*

**David Smurthwaite**
*Assistant Director, Museum Services Division, National Army Museum*

**Damian Smyth**
*Public Affairs Officer, Arts Council of Northern Ireland*

**H Smyth**
*Member of Board, Laganside Corporation*
Belfast City Councillor. Representative of BCC.

**J Smyth**
*Member of Council, Council for Catholic Maintained Schools*

**Jane Smyth**
*Head of Branch, Statistics & Computing, Forest Research*

**Joan Smyth**
*Chair & Chief Executive, Equal Opportunities Commission for Northern Ireland*
One of founders of Equality Forum. Member, European Union's Advisory Committee on Equal Opportunities between Women and Men and Northern Ireland Monitoring Committee for European Commission's Employment-Now programme. Member, Northern Ireland's Standing Advisory Committee on Human Rights (SACHR).

**Patricia Smyth**
*Member, Livestock & Meat Commission for Northern Ireland*
Financial Director, Eurostock Meat Marketing. Member of Board, Southern Group Enterprise.

**RW Smyth**
*Director of Youth Sports, Sports Council for Northern Ireland*

**WG Smyth OBE**
*Chairman of Board of Trustees, Agricultural Research Institute of Northern Ireland*
Appointed by the Department of Agriculture.

**WG Smyth**
*Member, Northern Ireland Fishery Harbour Authority*

**Brigadier M Smythe**
*Member, Wine Standards Board*

**David Snell**
*Director, Finance & Corporate Services (Deputy Chief Executive), Royal Mint*

**Paul Snelling**
*Director of Capital Works, Government Purchasing Agency*

**A Snoddy**
*Member of Board, Labour Relations Agency*

**Antony Snow**
*Trustee, Victoria & Albert Museum*

**G Snow**
*Member of Board, Construction Industry Training Board*
Snows Construction.

**AN Solomons**
*Member of Board, Education Assets Board*

**Maggie Somekh**
*Director of Corporate Development, Defence Secondary Care Agency.*

**Phil Sooben**
*Head of Postgraduate Training, Economic & Social Research Council*

**Kathleen Soriano**
*Head of Exhibitions & Collections Management, National Portrait Gallery*

**John Sorrell CBE**
*Chairman, The Design Council*

**Peter Soul**
*Director of Operations, Meat Hygiene Service*

**Peter Soulsby**
*Member, Audit Commission*
Councillor and Leader, Leicester City Council. Teacher of children with special needs. Chairman, Leicester City Challenge.

**A Southall**
*Museums Development, National Museums & Galleries of Wales*

**C Southgate**
*Secretary, Veterinary Laboratories Agency*
Financial Management Division, MAFF.

**Sir Colin Southgate**
*Member of Court, Bank of England*
Chairman, EMI Group.

**Marian Spain**
*Regional Officer, Countryside Commission*

**Bernard Sparkes**
*Member, Horticultural Development Council*
Executive Manager, English Village Nurseries.

**Brian Sparkes**
*District Valuer, Valuation & Lands Agency*

**Sir John Sparrow**
*Chairman, Horserace Betting Levy Board*

**R Sparshott**
*Commercial Director, Naval Aircraft Repair Organisation*

**David Spaven**
*Member, Rail Users Consultative Committee for Scotland*
Freight Transport Consultant.

**John Spearman**
*Member, The Arts Council of England*
Deputy Chairman, Classic FM. Member, Government Lead Body for Design. Patron Director, Royal Institute of British Architects. Trustee, World Monument Fund. Director, South Bank Foundation.

**John Spears**
*Compliance, Companies House*

**Dr DEM Speed**
*Member, Parole Board*

**Scott Speedie**
*Personnel Director, National Savings*

**Harry Speight**
*Member, Ofwat Southern Customer Service Committee*

**Caroline Spelman**
*Member of Council, Food from Britain*
Spelman, Cormack & Associates.

**I Spence**
*Director, Estates Development, Health Estates*

**IR Spence**
*International Divison, Inland Revenue*

**ProfJohn Spence**
*Member, Scottish Higher Education Funding Council*
Pro-Vice Principal, University of Strathclyde.

**John D Spencely**
*Member of Board, Scottish Homes*
Chairman, Reiach & Hall Architects and Buildings Investigation Centre. Past President, Royal Incorporation of Architects in Scotland. Member, Advisory Committee on Arbitration to the Scottish Law Commission, NHBC Committee and Glasgow 1999 Festival Company.

**Derek Spencer**
*TTA Running Costs, Teacher Training Agency*

**Prof Eric Spiller**
*Member of Council, Crafts Council*
*Member of Council, Scottish Arts Council*
Chair, Crafts Committee. Assistant Principal, Robert Gordon University, Aberdeen. Jewellery designer.

**Dr MF Spittle**
*Member, National Radiological Protection Board*
Meyerstein Institute of Radiotherapy & Oncology, Middlesex Hospital, London.

**Christopher Sporborg**
*Member, Horserace Totalisator Board*
Finance Steward, Jockey Club. Director, Racecourse Holdings Trust and British Horseracing Board. Deputy Chairman, Hambros.

**Clare Spottiswoode**
*Director General of Gas Supply, Office of Gas Supply*

**AD Sprake**
*Observer, Marshall Aid Commemoration Commission*
Cultural Relations Department, Foreign & Commonwealth Office.

**Prof JI Sprent OBE**
*Chairman, Macaulay Land Use Research Institute*
*Member, Joint Nature Conservation Committee*
Trustee, Macaulay Trust. Chairman, Board of Directors, Macaulay Research Consultancy Services. Member, Advisory Group to the Secretary of State for Scotland on Sustainable Development. Member, Advisory Committee, ODA Forestry Research Programme. Consultant, Norsk Hydro.

**Cllr Barbara Spring**
*Member, Tate Gallery*

**Sarah Springman**
*Member, UK Sports Council*
International triathlete. Lecturer in Engineering, Cambridge University.

**Gavin Sprott**
*Keeper of Social & Technological History, National Museums of Scotland*

**Peter Spurgeon**
*Chief Executive, Criminal Injuries Compensation Authority*

**Margaret Spurr OBE**
*Governor, British Broadcasting Corporation*
Chairman, English National Forum. Former Headmistress, Bolton School Girls' Division.

**Air Vice-Marshal AJ Stables**
*Chief Executive, RAF Training Group Defence Agency*

**Mrs Kay Stacey**
*Member, Merseyside & North Wales Consumers' Committee, Office of Electricity Regulation*

**Graham Stacy CBE**
*Member, Monopolies & Mergers Commission*
Chartered Accountant. Formerly Partner, Price Waterhouse. Treasurer, United Reformed Church and Sanctuary Housing Association.

**Prof Brian Staines**
*Member, Scientific Advisory Committee, Scottish Natural Heritage*

**Jill Staley**
*Initial Teacher Training, Teacher Training Agency*

**Harvey Stalker**
*Governor, Scottish Council for Educational Technology*
SOEID (Assessor).

**Ms Elizabeth Stallibrass**
*Regional Manager, Office of Electricity Regulation*

**Prof J Stallworthy**
*Member, The British Library*
British Academy.

**Martin Stanbury**
*Member, Milk Development Council*
Farmer. Past National Chairman, National Federation of Young Farmers Clubs. Member NFU Council & Milk Committee.

**Martin Staniforth**
*Member of Advisory Board, Medical Devices Agency*
*Member of Advisory Board, NHS Estates*
Head of Corporate Affairs NHS Executive, Department of Health.

**D Stanley**
*Chief Executive, Compensation Agency*

**Nicholas Stanley**
*Director, Tate Gallery Restaurant, Tate Gallery*

**Prof Peter Stanley**
*Chief Executive, Central Science Laboratory*
With MAFF since 1970.

**Elizabeth Stanton-Jones**
*Member, ENACT, Office of Telecommunications*
Director, Retail Credit Group.

**Anna Stapleton**
*Director, Drama, The Arts Council of England*

**The Very Revd HEC Stapleton**
*Commissioner, The Royal Commission on Historical Manuscripts*

**David Stark**
*Member, Scottish Agricultural Wages Board*
Employees' Representative Member nominated by the Rural, Agricultural & Allied Workers National Trade Group (Scotland) of the Transport & General Workers' Union.

**David Stark**
*Member, Monopolies & Mergers Commission*
Former Director, Tomkins.

**Donald Starritt**
*Director of Finance, Rate Collection Agency*

**Jonathan Startup**
*Director (Copyright), Patent Office*

**RS Statham**
*Member, Parole Board*

**Dr JW Stather**
*Senior Assistant Director, National Radiological Protection Board*

**David Steckles**
*Member, North Eastern Consumers' Committee, Office of Electricity Regulation*

**Mike Steeden**
*Air Systems, Defence Evaluation & Research Agency*

**Prof Anthony Steele**
*Member, Monopolies & Mergers Commission*
Chartered Accountant. Professor of Accounting, Warwick Business School.

**John Steele**
*Member of Board, Teacher Training Agency*
Group Personnel Director, British Telecom.

**Mrs Sally Steele**
*Member, North Western Consumers' Committee, Office of Electricity Regulation*

**RWJ Steen**
*Milk & Beef Production, Agricultural Research Institute of Northern Ireland*

**Deryk Steer**
*General Manager, English Nature*

**Prof John Steer**
*Trustee, Victoria & Albert Museum*

**Max Steinberg**
*Director, North West & Merseyside Region, The Housing Corporation*

**Dr Eleanor Steiner**
*Member, DIEL, Office of Telecommunications*
General Practioner.

**AW Stenning**
*Manager (Test Operations), Vehicle Certification Agency*

**Ms Barbara Stephens**
*Member of Board, Higher Education Funding Council for England*
Chief Executive, West Cumbria Development Agency.

**Mrs Elan Closs Stephens**
*Vice-Chairman, Welsh Language Board*
*Member, National Library of Wales*
Senior Lecturer, Department of Theatre, Film & Television Studies, University College, Aberystwyth.

**Judge Stephens QC**
*Member, Parole Board*

**Brigadier Kim Stephens**
*Commanding Officer, Duchess of Kent's Hospital, Catterick, Defence Secondary Care Agency.*

**LC Stephenson**
*Commissioner, Duke of York's Royal Military School*

**Clive Sterl**
*Regional Manager & Secretary, Ofwat Customer Service Committee for Wales*

**Prof William S Stevely**
*Non-Executive Member of Board,
National Board for Nursing, Midwifery &
Health Visiting for Scotland*
Vice Principal, University of Paisley.

**Arthur Stevens**
*Member, Eastern Consumers'
Committee, Office of Electricity
Regulation*

**DJ Stevens**
*Deputy Chief Executive, Naval Bases &
Supply Agency*

**JA Stevens**
*Member of Advisory Board, Forensic
Science Service*
HM Inspector of Constabulary.

**Sir Jocelyn Stevens CVO**
*Chairman, English Heritage*

**Dr Robert Stevens**
*Chairman, Marshall Aid Commemoration
Commission*

**Timothy Stevens**
*Assistant Director (Collections), Victoria
& Albert Museum*

**Alan Stevenson**
*Head of Environment & Communications,
Forest Enterprise*

**Dennis Stevenson CBE**
*Chairman, Tate Gallery
Member of Board, British Council
Member of Board, English Partnerships*
Chairman, Pearson GPA Group. Director,
J. Rothchild Assurance, Cloaca Maxima,
BSkyB Group and Manpower Inc.

**George Stevenson**
*Operations, Highlands & Islands Airports*

**Hugh Stevenson**
*Chief Investment Manager, Public Trust
Office*

**James Neil Stevenson**
*Chairman, Dumfries & Galloway
Enterprise*

**Dr John Stevenson**
*Projects Director, The Commonwealth
Experience, Commonwealth Institute*

**Neil Stevenson**
*Member, Scottish Sports Council*

**Patricia Stevenson OBE**
*Member of Board, Scottish Children's
Reporter Administration*
Past Depute Chairman, Tayside
Children's Panel and Chairman, Tayside
Children's Panel Advisory Committee.

**Wilf Stevenson**
*Director, British Film Institute*

**A Stewart**
*Controller, Coastal Operations, Scottish
Fisheries Protection Agency*

**AK Stewart-Roberts**
*Deputy Chairman, Crown Agents
Foundation*

**Alan Stewart**
*Regional Executive, Independent
Television Commission*

**Angus Stewart, QC**
*Trustee, National Library of Scotland*

**Captain CMC Stewart**
*Non-Executive Member of Board, Trinity
House Lighthouse Service*

**Clifford Stewart**
*Manager for London & the South,
Commission for Racial Equality*

**Dr J Stewart**
*Member of Governing Body, Rowett
Research Institute*

**Jennifer Stewart**
*Director of Information Services &
Development, Royal Commission on
Historical Monuments of England*

**Joe Stewart**
*Secretaty & Chief Executive, Police
Authority for Northern Ireland*

**John Stewart**
*Director Best Practice Consultancy,
Central Computer & Telecommunications
Agency*

**Miss MM Stewart**
*Member of Advisory Council, Scottish
Record Office*

**Sir Moray Stewart KCB**
*Trustee, Imperial War Museum
Member of Board, Queen Victoria School*

**N Stewart**
*Director, Northern Ireland Transport
Holding Company*

**Peter Stewart**
*Board Director, Home-Grown Cereals
Authority*

**Peter Stewart**
*Director, Scotland, Property Advisers to
the Civil Estate*

**RA Stewart**
*Assistant Director (Administration),
National Biological Standards Board*

**TW Stewart**
*Chief Executive, Planning Service*

**Thomas Stewart**
*Member, Northern Ireland Consumer
Coomittee for Electricity, Office for the
Regulation of Electricity & Gas*
Retired civil servant.

**Ian Stewart MP**
*Member, The Great Britain-China Centre*

**Ian Stewart OBE**
*Member, Scottish Water & Sewerage
Customers Council*

**John C (Ian) Stewart OBE**
*Member, The Accounts Commission for
Scotland*
Former Director of Finance & Depute
Chief Executive, Dumfries & Galloway
Regional Council.

**Noel Stewart OBE**
*Member of Northern Ireland Committee,
National Lottery Charities Board*
Chartered Accountant. Director,
Northern Ireland Transport Holding

Company. Director, Progressive Building
Society. Retired Regional Partner in
Charge, Coopers & Lybrand (Northern
Ireland). Chair, Craigavon Hospital Trust.
Honorary Treasurer, Queen's University,
Belfast.

**Sir Blair Stewart-Wilson KCVO**
*Trustee, Royal Armouries*
HM Queen's Representative.

**General Sir John Stibbon KCB OBE**
*Commissioner, Duke of York's Royal
Military School*

**Sir Angus Stirling**
*Chairman, Joint Nature Conservation
Committee*

**J Stirling**
*Member of Board, Construction Industry
Training Board (NI)*
North Down & Ards Trade Council.
Employee representative.

**James Stobo CBE**
*Member, Rail Users Consultative
Committee for Scotland*
Farmer. Chairman, Moredun Foundation
for Animal Health & Welfare. Chairman,
Longridge Towers School. Chairman,
Pentland Science Park.

**M Stockbridge**
*Director PFI, Army Technical Support
Agency*

**John Stocking**
*Member, London Consumers' Committee,
Office of Electricity Regulation*

**Paul Stockton**
*Member of Management Board, The
Court Service*
Director of Tribunal Operations.

**Trevor Stockton**
*Regional Manager, Rural Development
Commission*

**Dr Jim Stockwell**
*Director of Finance, Medicines Control
Agency*

**John Stoker**
*Acting Director General, Office of the
National Lottery*

**R Stoker**
*Member, Sports Council for Northern
Ireland*

**Samuel Stoker**
*Member, English Sports Council*

**Jenny Stokes**
*Public Affairs, National Lottery, UK
Sports Council*

**Tony Stoller**
*Chief Executive, The Radio Authority*

**Carol Stone**
*Head of Unit, Lottery Interim Unit, The
Arts Council of England*

**G Stone**
*Member, Parole Board*

**Heather Stone**
*TTA Staffing, Teacher Training Agency*

**Maurice Stonefrost**
*Member, London Pensions Fund Authority*
Former Director General, GLC. Deputy Pro-Chancellor, City University. Chairman, CLF (Municipal) Bank and Dolphin Square Trust. Vice Chairman, Architectural Heritage Fund Committee of Management.

**Chris Stonehouse**
*Sea Systems, Defence Evaluation & Research Agency*

**Jonathan Stopes-Roe**
*Member Advisory Board, NHS Pensions Agency*
Department of Health.

**Mrs Mary Storer**
*Member, Ofwat Northumbria Customer Service Committee*

**Donald Storrie**
*Member, Scottish Conveyancing & Executry Services Board*

**Prof RW Stout**
*Member, Northern Ireland Council for Postgraduate Medical & Dental Education*
Dean, Medical Faculty, QUB.

**Peter Stovey**
*Regional Manager, Rural Development Commission*

**David Strachan**
*Member of Board, Scottish Screen*

**Michael F Strachan CBE**
*Trustee, National Library of Scotland*

**Tony Strachan**
*Member of Museum Trust, Museum of Science & Industry Manchester*

**Valerie Strachan CB**
*Chairman, HM Customs & Excise*
*Member of College Advisory Council, Civil Service College*

**Yvonne Strachan MBE**
*Member of Board, Scottish Enterprise*

**J Strain**
*Member of Board, Probation Board for Northern Ireland*

**John Strang**
*Governor, Scottish Council for Educational Technology*
Headteacher, Renfrew High School.

**Stephanie J Stray**
*Member, Post Office Users' National Council*
Lecturer, University of Warwick.

**A Street**
*Member, Rail Users Consultative Committee for Midlands*

**Gary Streeter MP**
*Governor, Westminster Foundation for Democracy*

**Jim Stretton**
*Member, Scottish Community Education Council*

**Jim Stretton**
*Member of Court, Bank of England*

**J Stringer**
*Member of Board, Probation Board for Northern Ireland*

**JA Stringer**
*Member, NIACT, Northern Ireland Committee on Telecommunications*

**Dr Joan Stringer**
*Member, Human Fertilisation & Embryology Authority*
*Member, Equal Opportunities Commission*
Principal and Vice Patron, Queen Margaret College, Edinburgh. Commissioner for Scotland. Member, Scottish Committee of National Committee of Enquiry into Higher Education.

**John Stringer**
*Secretary, Post Office Users' Council for Northern Ireland*

**Ms Ruth Stringer**
*Member, Ofwat South West Customer Service Committee*

**SM Stringer**
*Member, Cardiff Bay Development Corporation*
Councillor, Vale of Glamorgan Council. Holm View Leisure Centre.

**Dr R Strong**
*Acquisition, Public Record Office of Northern Ireland*

**Sir Eric Stroud**
*Member of England Committee, National Lottery Charities Board*
Director, Overseas Department, Royal College of Physicians. Senior Research Fellow, Department of Paediatrics, Guy's Hospital. Medical adviser, Variety Club of Great Britain.

**A Stroyan**
*Member, Parole Board*

**AJ Struthers OBE**
*Commissioner, Northern Lighthouse Board*

**Tom Stuart**
*Director of Operations (Grampion & Tayside), North of Scotland Water Authority*

**NW Stuart CB**
*Member of Board, Investors in People UK*
Director General, Employment & Lifetime Learning, Department for Education & Employment.

**Lady Stubbs**
*Member of Board, Teacher Training Agency*
Head, Douay Martyrs School, Ickenham, Middlesex. School Governor, Henry Compton School.

**Sir William Stubbs**
*Chairman, Qualifications & Curriculum Authority*
Rector, The London Institute.

**Trevor Sturgess**
*Dirctor, Finance & Personnel, Northern Ireland Tourist Board*

**Frankie Sulke**
*Head of Teacher Training, Teacher Training Agency*

**Andrew Summers**
*Chief Executive, The Design Council*

**Mrs J Summers**
*Member, Parole Board*

**Dr Roy Summers**
*Member, East of Scotland Water Authority*

**FI Sumner**
*Member of Board, Crown Agents Foundation*

**HL Sumner**
*Director of Passenger Services, LUL, London Transport*

**Prof Eric Sunderland**
*Member of Board, British Council*
Lately Principal, University College of North Wales and Vice-Chancellor, University of Wales.

**Mrs Rosemary Sung**
*Member, Yorkshire Consumers' Committee, Office of Electricity Regulation*

**Andy Sutch**
*Regional Director, Greater London, English Sports Council*

**Capt G Sutherland**
*Commissioner, Northern Lighthouse Board*

**GWD Sutherland**
*Managing Director - Finance, North of Scotland Water Authority*

**Prof Sir Stewart Sutherland**
*Member of Board, Higher Education Funding Council for England*
Principal & Vice-Chancellor, University of Edinburgh.

**Sir William Sutherland QPM**
*Member of Committee, Ministry of Defence Police*
HM Chief Inspector of Constabulary (Scotland). Adviser to Police Committee.

**A Swales**
*Inspector, Football Licensing Authority*

**Prof John Swales**
*Member of Council, Medical Research Council*
Department of Health.

**Debora Swallow**
*Curator, Indian & South-East Asian Collection, Victoria & Albert Museum*

**Mrs Christine Swan**
*Member, Ofwat Southern Customer Service Committee*

**Dr M Swan**
*Member, Parole Board*

**Norman Swanney**
*Assistant Director Corporate Services Group, Pay & Personnel Agency*

**Dr Kenneth Swanson**
*Member, North Areas Board, Scottish Natural Heritage*

**Rodney Swarbrick CBE**
*Chairman, National Forest Company*

**Ms B Sweeney**
*Training & Development Officer (Eurobueau), Youth Council for Northern Ireland*

**Stuart Sweetman**
*Managing Director Post Office Counters, Post Office*

**Alan Swift**
*Head of Personnel and Development Unit, Scottish Court Service*

**John Swift QC**
*The Regulator, Office of the Rail Regulator*

**Prof Ian Swingland**
*Chairman, Apple & Pear Research Council*
Chair in Conservation Biology, Kent University. Visiting Professorships at Florence, Auckland and Manchester Metropolitan Universities.

**Jonathan Swire**
*Member, The Great Britain-China Centre*

**Dr Ian Sword**
*Member, Scottish Higher Education Funding Council*
*Member of Council, Medical Research Council*
Chairman, Inveresk Research International.

**Miss Linda E Sydie**
*Deputy Chairman, National Board for Nursing, Midwifery & Health Visiting for Scotland*
Head of Department, Health & Nursing, Queen Margaret College, Edinburgh.

**Sir Richard Sykes**
*Trustee, Natural History Museum*

**Rosamund Sykes**
*Head of Finance & Central Services, Victoria & Albert Museum*

**Elizabeth Symons**
*Member, Equal Opportunities Commission*
Former General Secretary, First Division Association. Member, Employment Appeal Tribunal and Council of the Industrial Society, Open University. Trustee, the IPPR. Member, Hansard Society Council.

**Rex HM Symons CBE**
*Member, Health & Safety Commission*
Health & Safety Consultant, CBI. Chairman, Occupational Health & Safety Lead Body, Dorset Training & Enterprise Agency and Poole Hospital NHS Trust. Chairman, Bournemouth Transport and Dorset Travel. Former Deputy Chairman,

Merck Holdings and Managing Director, British Drug Houses.

**Peter Syson**
*Director, Strategy, Advisory, Conciliation & Arbitration Service*

**Ray Szynowski**
*Member Advisory Board, NHS Pensions Agency*
Department of Health.

# T

**Paul Tabbush**
*Head of Branch, Silviculture & Seed Research, Forest Research*

**Eleanor Taggart**
*Member, Central Council for Education & Training in Social Work*

**Mrs Maureen Taggart**
*Member, Northern Ireland Local Government Officers' Superannuation Committee*

**DB Talbot**
*Head of Dept, Administration, National Radiological Protection Board*

**Prof M Talbot OBE**
*Member of Board, Football Licensing Authority*

**Commander JJ Tall OBE**
*Museum Director, Royal Navy Submarine Museum*

**Pauline Tambling**
*Director, Education & Training, The Arts Council of England*

**John Tapp**
*Member, Ofwat Eastern Customer Service Committee*

**Andy Targett**
*Director Contract Management & Support Services, Logistic Information Systems Agency*

**Tancred Tarkowski**
*Director of Resources & Planning, National Heritage Memorial Fund*

**Iris Tarry**
*Member, Audit Commission*
Chairman, Hertfordshire County Council. Chairman, Hertfordshire Police Authority. Former member, North West Herts Health Authority.

**Dr Michael Tas**
*Information Services, Central Science Laboratory*

**Bob Tatchell**
*Head of Vehicle Testing Division, Vehicle Inspectorate*

**Nicholas Tate**
*Member, East Midland Consumers' Committee, Office of Electricity Regulation*

**Dr Nicholas Tate**
*Chief Executive, Qualifications & Curriculum Authority*

**Linford Tatham**
*Chief Executive, The Sports Council for Wales*
*Observer, UK Sports Council*

**Andrew Taylor**
*Director, ISIS, Council for the Central Laboratory of the Research Councils*

**Ann Taylor**
*Director of Network Competition, Office of Telecommunications*

**Anne Taylor MP**
*Trustee, National Portrait Gallery*

**Brian Taylor**
*Member of Advisory Board, Defence Analytical Services Agency*
AUS (Civilian Management).

**David Taylor**
*Director, Scottish Trade International, Scottish Enterprise*

**David Taylor**
*Director, Drama & Dance, Scottish Arts Council*

**David Taylor**
*Teacher Education & Training, Office for Standards in Education*

**E Taylor**
*Head, Scientific Liaison, Information & Media Services & Operations Manager, Hannah Research Institute*

**G Taylor**
*Electrical Engineer, Covent Garden Market Authority*

**Gordon Taylor**
*NHS Scheme Manager, Scottish Office Pensions Agency*

**Graham Taylor**
*Member, London Regional Passengers Committee*

**H Taylor**
*Director of Administration & Services, HM Prison Service*

**JA Taylor**
*Member, Rail Users Consultative Committee for North Eastern England*
Retired farmer and agricultural management consultant. Independent Member, Alnwick District Council. Vice-Chairman, Northumberland Community Health Council. Clerk of Course, Alnwick amateur Point-to-Point meetings.

**John Taylor**
*Chief Executive, British Nuclear Fuels plc*

**Joyce Taylor**
*Governor, National Film & Television School*

**Julie Taylor**
*Head of Public Affairs, Museums & Galleries Commission*

**K Taylor**
*Financial Director, Remploy*
Joined Remploy Board in 1992. Former Managing Director, RMG Group and John Blackwood Hodge.

**Dr Keith Taylor**
*Member of Board, Higher Education Funding Council for England*
Chairman & Chief Executive, Esso UK.

**Louise Taylor**
*Head of Exhibitions and the Collection, Crafts Council*

**M Taylor**
*Secretary, The British Library*

**Marc Taylor**
*Head of Policy, NHS Estates*

**Marilyn Taylor**
*Director of Community Development, Waltham Forest Housing Action Trust*

**N Taylor**
*Curator, Living Collections, Royal Botanic Gardens Kew*

**Paul Taylor**
*Regional Manager & Secretary, Ofwat Yorkshire Customer Service Committee*

**Paul Taylor**
*CBD, Defence Evaluation & Research Agency*

**Peter S Taylor**
*Executive Director (Resources), National Board for Nursing, Midwifery & Health Visiting for Scotland*

**Sidney Taylor**
*Non-Executive Director, Royal Mint*

**Tony Taylor**
*Chairman, Scottish Borders Enterprise*

**Janice Tchalenko**
*Member of Council, Crafts Council*
Ceramicist.

**Paul Tear**
*Head of Conservation, Wallace Collection*

**Peter Tebby**
*Director, Executive & Organisational Development, Civil Service College*

**Prof MD Tedd**
*Chairman, WACT, Welsh Advisory Committee on Telecommunications*
Professor of Computer Science, University of Wales.

**Dr Mike Tempest**
*Agricultural Manager, Livestock & Meat Commission for Northern Ireland*

**Ian Temple**
*Head of Marketing, BFI On The South Bank*

**Richard Temple Cox**
*Chairman, Castle Vale Housing Action Trust*
Architect. Chairman, Temple Cox Nicholls. Former Chairman, Birmingham Institute for the Deaf. Member, City Pride Board of Birmingham.

**Peter Temple-Morris MP**
*Vice-Chairman, The Britain-Russia Centre*

**Prof Allan Templeton**
*Member, Human Fertilisation & Embryology Authority*
Professor of Obstetrics & Gynaecology, Unversity of Aberdeen.

**Mrs Helen Tennant**
*Member of Authority, The Radio Authority*

**PL Tennant**
*Chairman, Northumbria RFAC, The Environment Agency*

**F Tennyson**
*Member of Board, Fisheries Conservancy Board for Northern Ireland*
Commercial fishing company representative.

**Iryna Terlecky**
*Director of Licensing & Consumer Protection, Office of the Rail Regulator*

**Maurice Terry**
*Chairman, Ofwat North West Customer Service Committee*
Deputy Chairman, Ofwat National Customer Council

**Lyn Tett**
*Governor, Scottish Council for Educational Technology*
Head, Community Education, Moray House College of Education.

**Annie Thackeray**
*Information Services Manager, The Arts Council of England*

**Sarah Thane**
*Director of Programmes & Cable, Independent Television Commission*

**Simon Thirkell**
*Member, Apple & Pear Research Council*
Technical Manager (Fruit), J Sainsbury.

**Prof the Rev Canon Anthony Thiselton**
*Member, Human Fertilisation & Embryology Authority*
Head, Department of Theology, University of Nottingham. Canon Theologian, Leicester Cathedral.

**EN Thom**
*Director of Finance & Administration, National Board for Nursing, Midwifery & Health Visiting for Northern Ireland*

**C Thomas**
*Public Services, National Museums & Galleries of Wales*

**D Thomas CBE**
*Chairman, Residuary Body for Wales*
Former Chief Executive, Mid Glamorgan County Council. Chairman, Morgannwg Health Authority.

**Dan Thomas**
*Food from Britain (Japan)*

**Dr David Thomas**
*Head of Information & Records Department, Public Record Office*

**David Thomas**
*Member of Council, Food from Britain*
Chief Executive, Whitbread.

**Garry Thomas**
*Director (Finance, Planning & Administration), Disposal Sales Agency*

**J Thomas**
*Director of Finance & Audit, and Director of Human Resources, Information Technology Services Agency*

**Prof JO Thomas CBE**
*Member of Council, Engineering & Physical Sciences Research Council*
Cambridge University.

**Jack Thomas**
*Head of Information Technology, Defence Bills Agency*

**Prof Jean Thomas CBE**
*Trustee, British Museum*

**Mrs Jessica Thomas**
*Chairman, Ofwat South West Customer Service Committee*
Member, Ofwat National Customer Council

**Sir Keith Thomas**
*Commissioner, The Royal Commission on Historical Manuscripts*
Trustee, National Gallery

**Mark Thomas**
*Head of Engineering, The Radio Authority*

**Miss Meryl Thomas**
*Director, Midwifery Education & Practice, English National Board for Nursing, Midwifery & Health Visiting*

**The Rev Dr Patrick Thomas**
*Member of Board, Welsh Language Board*
Rector, Brechfa.

**Peter Thomas**
*Member, Qualifications, Curriculum & Assessment Authority for Wales*
Former Senior Inspector, OHMCI.

**Roy J Thomas**
*Legal Director & Agency Secretary, Welsh Development Agency*

**Sue Thomas**
*Director of Community Services, Liverpool Housing Action Trust*

**MT Thomasin-Foster CBE**
*Member of Council, English Nature*
Farmer. Former Chairman, Essex Branch, Country Landowners Association. Chairman, MAFF's Consultative Panel on Badgers and Tuberculosis. Chairman, Hawk and Owl Trust. Member, UK Round Table on Sustainable Development. Member, Agricultural Land Tribunal.

**Brigadier AD Thompson**
*Member of Advisory Board, Service Children's Education*

**Dr Alwyn Thompson**
*Site Director - East Malling, Horticulture Research International*

**Chris Thompson**
*Director, Corporate Services Division, Training & Employment Agency (NI)*

**Chris Thompson**
*Chief Executive, Social Security Agency (Northern Ireland)*

**Douglas Thompson MBE**
*Member, Ofwat Northumbria Customer Service Committee*

**Mrs GJ Thompson**
*Group Manager Policy, Student Awards Agency for Scotland*

**Geoff Thompson MBE**
Member, UK & English Sports Councils Former World Heavyweight Karate Champion. Chairman, Youth Charter for Sport.

**Mrs H Thompson**
*Project Officer, National Board for Nursing, Midwifery & Health Visiting for Northern Ireland*

**J Thompson**
*Member, Post Office Users' Council for Northern Ireland*

**JLC Thompson**
*Chairman, NIACT, Northern Ireland Committee on Telecommunications*
Company Director, President, Royal Ulster Agricultural Society.

**Dr Janet Thompson**
*Chief Executive, Forensic Science Service*

**Prof Jeff Thompson CBE**
*Non-Executive Member, English National Board for Nursing, Midwifery & Health Visiting*
Professor of Education, University of Bath.

**John Thompson**
*Member, Central Council for Education & Training in Social Work*

**Julian Thompson**
*Director (Finance), Patent Office*

**Ms K Thompson**
*Executive Officer (Public Relations), Youth Council for Northern Ireland*

**Marjorie Thompson**
*Head of Communications, Commission for Racial Equality*

**Peter Thompson**
*Member, Centre for Information on Language Teaching & Research*
Head of Education Services, BT.

**Robin Thompson CBE**
*Member of Board, The Housing Corporation*
Farmer. Chairman of South Shropshire Housing Association and President of Rural Community of Shropshire.

**Roy Thompson**
*Member, Ofwat Eastern Customer Service Committee*
*Member, Eastern Consumers' Committee, Office of Electricity Regulation*

**A Thomson**
*Market Operations Manager, Covent Garden Market Authority*

**Andrew WJ Thomson**
*Member, Scottish Agricultural Wages Board*
Independent member appointed by the Secretary for Scotland.

**John Thomson**
*Director of Strategy & Operations, Scottish Natural Heritage*

**Sir John Thomson GCMG**
*Trustee, National Museums of Scotland*

**MG Thomson, QC**
*Trustee, National Library of Scotland*

**Miss Margaret C Thomson**
*Member, The Accounts Commission for Scotland*
Former District Administrator, Renfrew District Council.

**Ross Thomson**
*Member, Merseyside & North Wales Consumers' Committee, Office of Electricity Regulation*

**WAC Thomson**
*Non-Executive Member of Board, Trinity House Lighthouse Service*

**George Thorburn**
*Director - New Business Development, Horticulture Research International*

**Prof S Thorburn OBE**
*Member of Board, Football Licensing Authority*

**D Thornham**
*Non-Executive Board Member, Child Support Agency*

**Stephen Thornhill**
*Market Information, Home-Grown Cereals Authority*

**Alan Thornton MBE**
*Chairman, Dunbartonshire Enterprise*

**Mrs J Thornton**
*Member, Rail Users Consultative Committee for Midlands*

**Neil Thornton**
*Member of Council, Food from Britain MAFF.*

**John Thorogood**
*Language Teaching Adviser, Centre for Information on Language Teaching & Research*

**Beccy Thorp**
*Assistant Conference Centre Manager, Commonwealth Institute*

**Tina Thorp**
*Head of Finance & Establishment, Centre for Information on Language Teaching & Research*

**D Thorpe**
*Head of Audit & Review, Corporate Services, Natural History Museum*

**Phillip Thorpe**
*Managing Director & Head of Authorisation, Enforcement & Consumer Relations, Financial Services Authority*
Currently Chief Executive, Investment Management Regulatory Organisation (IMRO). Will be responsible for industry training and competence, and investor education. New Zealander. Former CEO of Hong Kong Futures Exchange. CEO of Association of Futures Brokers & Dealers, Executive Director of Securities & Futures Authority and seconded CEO of London Commodity Exchange.

**R Thorpe**
*Head of Immunobiology, National Biological Standards Board*

**S Thorpe**
*Chief Inspector, Foyle Fisheries Commission*

**Alan Threadgold**
*T&E Aircraft, Defence Evaluation & Research Agency*

**Mrs Pauline Thresh**
*Member, Ofwat Yorkshire Customer Service Committee*

**Paul Thrustle**
*Director of Information Systems, The Scottish Legal Aid Board*

**Trevor R Thurgate**
*Managing Director, Defence Bills Agency*

**Colonel Nigel Thursby**
*Commandant School of Army Aviation, Army Training & Recruitment Agency*

**Dr JCJ Thyme CB**
*Member, Radiocommunications Agency*
Director & Executive Council Member, Newbridge Networks Corporation.

**Sir Crispin Tickell GCMG KCVO**
*Trustee, Natural History Museum*
*Trustee, Royal Botanic Garden Edinburgh*

**Mrs Tracy Tickle**
*Project Manager, Anglophone Africa, Corporate Relations, Westminster Foundation for Democracy*

**Dr D Tidmarsh**
*Member, Parole Board*

**Ivor Tiefenbrun MBE**
*Member, The Design Council*

**BG Tierney**
*Member of Board, Construction Industry Training Board*
RF Peachey & Sons.

**Stewart Till**
*Governor, National Film & Television School*

**SA Tilley**
*Member of Board, Construction Industry Training Board*
Clugston Construction.

**Cllr Paul Tilsley MBE**
*Board Member, Castle Vale Housing Action Trust*
Member, Birmingham City Council. Former Lord Mayor of Birmingham. Director, Newtown/South Aston City Challenge, National Exhibition Centre and Symphony Hall.

**Richard Tilt**
*Director General, HM Prison Service*

**Col John Timmins**
*Vice President, Museum of Science & Industry Manchester*

**Michael Timmis**
*Director of Finance, Civil Service College*

**P Timms CBE**
*Member of Board, Highlands & Islands Enterprise*

**Daren Timson-Hunt**
*Assistant Director, Official Procedures, Simpler Trade Procedures Board*

**Dr PBH Tinker**
*Member of Board of Governors, Macaulay Land Use Research Institute*

**Teresa Tinsley**
*CILT Programme Manager, Centre for Information on Language Teaching & Research*

**Dame Sue Tinson**
*Trustee, National Heritage Memorial Fund*

**Robert Tinston**
*Member of Advisory Board, NHS Estates*
Regional Director, NHS Executive North West.

**Vice-Admiral Sir Anthony Tippet**
*Chairman, Funding Agency for Schools*

**J Tisdall**
*Member of Board, Fisheries Conservancy Board for Northern Ireland*
Appointed as representative of a substantial number of anglers.

**Dr AM Tod**
*Member of Advisory Council, Scottish Record Office*

**Dr DO Todd**
*Member, Northern Ireland Council for Postgraduate Medical & Dental Education*
Nominated by General Medical Services Committee.

**J Todd**
*Member of Board, Fisheries Conservancy Board for Northern Ireland*
Independent angler.

**M Todd**
*Chief Executive, Parole Board*

**Robert Todd**
*Manager, Northern, Gas Consumers' Council*

**Ms Sue Todd**
*Member of Board, Investors in People UK*
Managing Director, Polymedia.

**Martin Togneri**
*Director, Locate in Scotland, Scottish Enterprise*

**Rear Admiral JG Tolhurst CB**
*Naval Base Commander, Naval Bases & Supply Agency*
Flag Officer Scotland.

**Mrs Claire Tomalin**
*Trustee, National Portrait Gallery*
Member of Advisory Committee, Registrar of Public Lending Right Author.

**John Tomkins**
*Finance & IT Director, Security Facilities Executive*

**Eddie Tomlin**
*Director Development, Companies House*

**Mike Tomlinson CBE**
*Director of Inspection, Office for Standards in Education*

**Dei Tomos**
*Member of Council, Countryside Council for Wales*
Journalist and broadcaster. Vice President, Council for National Parks.

**Mrs L Tomos**
*Member, WACT, Welsh Advisory Committee on Telecommunications*
Librarian service. Director, Wales Information Network.

**Sian Tomos**
*Senior Capital Officer, Arts Council of Wales*

**Christopher Toms**
*Resident Board Member, Tower Hamlets Housing Action Trust*
Resident of Monteith Estate.

**Gary Tonge**
*Director of Engineering, Independent Television Commission*

**Mrs Diana Tory**
*Member, Ofwat Wessex Customer Service Committee*

**Mrs JG Totty**
*Senior Land Registrar, HM Land Registry*

**Ann Tourle**
*Company Secretary, Met Office*

**John Towers CBE**
*Member, The Design Council*

**Mrs WA Towers**
*Member, Parole Board*

**John Townend**
*Deputy Director, Market Operations, Bank of England*

**Richard Townsend**
*Member, Centre for Information on Language Teaching & Research*
Headteacher, Dunraven School.

**Mrs Teresa Townsley**
*Member of Board, Local Enterprise Development Unit*
Joint MD, MTF Employment Services. Director, Management Training & Finance

(NI) and MFT Training & Technology. Vice Chairman, LiveWIRE (NI). Director, Dalradian Leisure Developments, NISBI and Agraton.

**Adam Train**
*Member, Scottish Agricultural Wages Board*
Employers' Representative Member nominated by the National Farmers' Union of Scotland and the Scottish Landowners' Federation.

**Gerard Trainer**
*Chairman, Post Office Users' Council for Northern Ireland*
Member, Post Office Users' National Council
Solicitor.

**Bob Tranter**
*Director, Major Projects Department, English Heritage*

**George Traves**
*Member of Board, Sea Fish Industry Authority*
Former President, National Federation of Fishermen's Organisations. Chairman, Bridlington Flamborough Fishermen's Society. A Bridlington Harbour Commissioner. Chairman, North Eastern Sea Fisheries Committee Chairman, Independent Shellfishermen's Co-operative (Bridlington).

**Paul Trayhurn**
*Assistant Director (Academic Affairs) & Head, Biomedical Science Division, Rowett Research Institute*

**K Traynor**
*Executive Officer (Finance), Youth Council for Northern Ireland*

**Prof GH Treitel DCL QC**
*Trustee, British Museum*

**David Trench**
*Site & Structures Director, New Millenium Experience Co Ltd*
Chairman & founder, Trench Farrow Partners. Formerly at Taylor Woodrow.

**George Trevelyan**
*Chief Executive, Intervention Board*

**Vanessa Trevelyan**
*Head of Public Services & Registration, Museums & Galleries Commission*

**Rear Admiral John Trewby**
*Chief Executive, Naval Bases & Supply Agency*

**Peter Trewin**
*Secretary, British Railways Board*

**Dr MJ Tricker**
*Technology Interaction, Natural Environment Research Council*

**Michael Trickey**
*Director, Planning & Public Affairs Division, Arts Council of Wales*

**Prof ER Trimble**
*Member, Northern Ireland Council for Postgraduate Medical & Dental Education*
Nominated by Royal College Pathologists.

**Alan Tripp**
*Member of Board, Scottish Further Education Unit*
Managing Director, McQueen's global Manufacturing & Fulfilment Services. Member of Board, SCRE. Member, Scottish Economic Council.

**Mrs Sheila Tristram**
*Member, Ofwat Customer Service Committee for Wales*

**SR Tromans**
*Member of Council, English Nature*
Solicitor. Partner, Simmons & Simmons. Member, Environment Development and Advisory Panel (EDAP), National Grid Company.

**Ross Trotter**
*Member, DIEL, Office of Telecommunications*
Secretary, Telecommunication Action Group (for deaf, deafened, hard of hearing and deaf-blind people).

**Janet Trotter OBE**
*Member of Board, Teacher Training Agency*
Director, Cheltenham & Gloucester College of Higher Education. Chair, South West NHS Executive.

**Maj Gen PCC Troudsdell**
*Member of Committee, Ministry of Defence Police*
Chief of Staff HQ Land Command.

**GWC Troughton**
*Secretary to the Board of Trustees, Agricultural Research Institute of Northern Ireland*

**R Trouton**
*Member, Sports Council for Northern Ireland*

**DL Trudgill**
*Head, Nematology Department, Scottish Crop Research Institute*

**Jakob True**
*Food from Britain (Scandinavia)*

**PJ Trusler**
*Member, Parole Board*

**Mr J Trustam Eve**
*Member of Board, Commission for the New Towns*
Chairman, Partnership International. Property Adviser, John Trustam Eve & Partners. Trustee, Worshipful Company of Chartered Surveyors Youth Training Trust. Consultant, Grimley International Property Advisers.

**HW Try**
*Chairman, Construction Industry Training Board*
Try Group.

**Ron Tuck**
*Chief Executive, Scottish Qualifications Authority*

**Ann Tucker**
*Assistant Director, Policy Development, English National Board for Nursing, Midwifery & Health Visiting*

**Justice Tucker**
*Member, Parole Board*

**Julia Tugendhat**
*Member, Human Fertilisation & Embryology Authority*
Family therapist.

**Isabel Tulloch**
*Finance Officer, Scottish Screen*

**Lady Tumim OBE**
*Trustee, National Portrait Gallery*

**Denis Tunnicliffe CBE**
*Managing Director, LUL, London Transport*
Former senior positions with British Airways and Chief Executive, Aviation Division, International Leisure Group.

**G Turkington**
*Member, Post Office Users' Council for Northern Ireland*

**Keith Turkington**
*Manager Information Systems & Support, Local Enterprise Development Unit*

**Ruth Turley**
*Financial Control & Property, Teacher Training Agency*

**Prof William Turmeau CBE**
*Chairman, Scottish Environment Protection Agency*

**AJ Turnbull**
*Member, Post Office Users' Council for Scotland*
Solicitor. Member, Lothians and Borders Posts & Telecommunications Advisory Committees. Secretary, Borders Members Group, National Trust for Scotland. Treasurer, Yetholm Community Council. Secretary, Scottish Ice Rinks Association.

**Andrew Turnball**
*Chairman, Highways Agency*

**David Turnbull**
*Director Finance, British Council*

**Mrs J Turnbull JP**
*Member, Parole Board*

**Mrs Josephine Turnbull**
*Member, Ofwat Northumbria Customer Service Committee*

**K Turnbull**
*Employer member, Engineering Construction Industry Training Board*
Senior Vice-President, Bechtel.

**Barry Turner**
*Member, London Regional Passengers Committee*

**Dr Brian Turner**
*Member of Board, Northern Ireland Museums' Council*
Director, Down County Museum. Nominated by Northern Ireland Regional Curators Group.

**D Robert Turner**
*Member of Council, The Sports Council for Wales*

**Derek Turner**
*Traffic Director for London, Traffic Director for London*

**Graham Turner**
*Member, Ofwat Wessex Customer Service Committee*

**James Turner**
*Managing Director, International Division, Welsh Development Agency*

**John Turner**
*Senior Director of Operations, Employment Service*

**Malcolm Turner**
*Director of Operations, Government Purchasing Agency*

**Captain N MacD Turner**
*Director of Navigational Requirements, Trinity House Lighthouse Service*

**Group Captain PDJ Turner**
*Corporate Services, RAF Personnel Management Agency*

**Paula Turner**
*Head of Museum Services, Royal Armouries*

**Peter Turner**
*Member, South Western Consumers' Committee, Office of Electricity Regulation*

**Richard Turner**
*Senior Arts for All Officer, Arts Council of Wales*

**Sam Turner**
*Property & Services Manager, The Arts Council of England*

**Mrs S Turquet JP**
*Member, Parole Board*

**Miss E Turton CB**
*Chairman, Property Advisers to the Civil Estate*

**John Tusa**
*Trustee, National Portrait Gallery*

**Air Cdre Bill Tyack**
*Senior Military Officer, Defence Evaluation & Research Agency*

**Mrs Sarah Tyacke**
*Chief Executive, Public Record Office*

**Geoff Tyler**
*Sector Director - Agribusiness, Commonwealth Development Corporation*

**Brigadier Tim Tyler**
*Commander Royal Electrical & Mechanical Engineers Training Group, Army Training & Recruitment Agency*

**Alistair Tyre**
*Member of Board, Scottish Further
Education Unit*
Principal, Langside College, Glasgow.
Member of Board, Association of Scottish
Colleges. Director, West of Scotland
Partnership.

**DA Tysoe**
*Director Finance, Defence Transport &
Movements Executive*

# U

**Rona Udall**
*Head of Finance, Crafts Council*

**Cllr Shahab Uddin**
*Member of Board, Tower Hamlets
Housing Action Trust*
Represents St Dunstan's Ward. Director,
Stepney Housing & Development Agency
(SHADA).

**Steve Unger**
*Director, Isaac Newton Group,
Observatorio Del Roque De Los
Muchachos, La Palma*

**Irene Unsworth**
*Member, Milk Development Council*
Farmer. Founder member and past
Chairman, Lincolnshire Women's
Farming Union. Member, WFU National
Dairy Committee. Regional Committee
Member.

**Julia Unwin**
*Member of Board, The Housing
Corporation*
Visiting Fellow at Office for Public
Management and Chair of British
Refugee Council.

**Group Captain JA Upham**
*Assistant Director, Service
Requirements, Armed Forces Personnel
Administration Agency*

**P Upton**
*Director of Operations, Valuation Office
Agency*

**Willian Ure**
*Secretary, Rail Users Consultative
Committee for Scotland*

**Roselyn Urey**
*Finance Officer, Commissioner for the
Rights of Trade Union Members &
Commissioner for Protection Against
Unlawful Industrial Action*

**Celia Urquhart**
*Member of Board, Scottish Enterprise*

**George Urquhart**
*Member, Scottish Sports Council*

**Jean Urquhart**
*Member of Council, Scottish Arts Council*

**Ms Dorma Urwin**
*Member of Board, Higher Education
Funding Council for England*
Principal, Worcester College of Higher
Education.

**Prof Michael B Usher**
*Chief Scientist, Scottish Natural Heritage*

# V

**DG Vaisey CBE**
*Commissioner, The Royal Commission
on Historical Manuscripts*

**Lady Vaizey**
*Trustee, Geffrye Museum
Trustee, Imperial War Museum*
Committee Member, 20th Century
Society. Member, South Bank Board.
Former Member, Arts Council. Former
Member, Advisory Committee, DOE.
Member, British Council Visual Arts
Advisory Committee. Former Member,
Crafts Council. Trustee, National
Museums & Galleries in Merseyside.
Former Governor, Camberwell College of
Arts & Crafts.

**Ian Valder**
*Commercial Director, British Waterways*

**Irwin Van Colle**
*Member of Board, Stonebridge Housing
Action Trust*
Brent Council Conservative Group
nominee.

**Lucia van der Post**
*Member of Council, Crafts Council*
Journalist.

**Jan Van der Wateren**
*Chief Librarian, Victoria & Albert Museum*

**Prof Veronica van Heyningen**
*Trustee, National Museums of Scotland*

**Prof WH van Riemsdijk**
*Member of Board of Governors,
Macaulay Land Use Research Institute*

**Eric van Thiel**
*Food from Britain (The Netherlands)BV*

**Molly Vannan**
*Executive Company Services, Local
Enterprise Development Unit*

**Deirdre Vaugh**
*Manager (Small Business Unit), Fair
Employment Commission for Northern
Ireland*

**Barbara Vaughan OBE**
*Chair, Scottish Community Education
Council*

**Dr C Vaughan**
*Member of Ownership Board, Veterinary
Laboratories Agency*
External Member.

**Dr Caroline Vaughan**
*Deputy Chairman, Home-Grown Cereals
Authority*

**Ch Inspr D Vaughan**
*OCU, OSU, Ministry of Defence Police*

**Elizabeth Vaughan**
*Public Affairs Officer, Gas Consumers'
Council*

**Yvette Vaughan Jones**
*International Manager, Arts Council of
Wales*

**Mrs J Venables**
*Chairman, RFDC, The Environment
Agency*

**John Vereker CB**
*Member of Board, British Council*
Permanent Secretary, Department For
International Development.

**David Verey**
*Trustee, Tate Gallery*

**Richard J Verge**
*Director of Central Operations, Driver &
Vehicle Licensing Agency*

**RG Vernon**
*Head, Molecular Homeorhesis & Science
Development & Planning, Hannah
Research Institute*

**Michele Verroken**
*Doping Control, UK Sports Council*

**David Vick**
*Head of Development & Deputy Chief
Executive, The Radio Authority*

**Edward T Vidler**
*Member, Post Office Users' National
Council*
General Manager, Schlumberger
Industries Metflex. Past President,
Blackburn & District Chamber of
Commerce & Industry. Director,
Hyndburn Enterprise Trust. Member,
East Lancashire POAC. Vice Chairman
of Governors, Accrington & Rossendale
College. Director, ELTEC. Director,
Lancashire Manufacturing Partnership.

**Geoff Vinall**
*New Law Enforcement Business
Manager, Forensic Science Service*

**Alison Vincent**
*Marketing Manager, Museum of Science
& Industry Manchester*

**Des Vincent**
*Head of Information Systems, Business
Development Service*

**Cllr Joan Vincent**
*Member, Tate Gallery*

**Kate Vincent**
*Joint Director of Marketing and
Communications, Scottish Sports Council*

**Robin Vincent**
*Member of Management Board, The
Court Service*
Northern Circuit Administrator.

**Moira Vincentelli**
*Member of Council, Crafts Council*
Art historian.

**Mrs AM Vinton**
*Member of Authority, Covent Garden Market Authority*
Co-founder and former joint Chairman, The Reject Shop. Non-Executive Director, Cadbury Schweppes, Courtaulds Textiles, Thomas Jourdan and WEW. Chairman, Saxon Foods and RAP. Trustee, Marie Curie Cancer Care. Recently a member, School Teachers Pay Review Body.

**SH Visscher**
*Director of Finance Group, Biotechnology & Biological Sciences Research Council*

**Nigel Vivian**
*Quality Assessment in ITT, Teacher Training Agency*

**Mrs A Voss-Bark MBE**
*Chairman, South West RFAC, The Environment Agency*

# W

**Michelle Waddilove**
*Assistant Director, Port Procedures, Simpler Trade Procedures Board*

**Mrs Christine Waddington**
*Information Services Officer, National Board for Nursing, Midwifery & Health Visiting for Scotland*

**Derek Waddington OBE**
*Member of Board, The Housing Corporation*
Former Director of Housing, Birmingham City Council. Former Adviser to Association of Metroplolitan Authorities. Member of Duke of Edinburgh's Inquiry into British Housing. Past President of Chartered Institute of Housing. Currently, Vice Chair, Board of Good Practice Unit, Chartered Institute of Housing.

**Gerry Wade**
*Trustee, Community Development Foundation*

**VA Wadham**
*Secretary, Oil & Pipelines Agency*

**DG Wadsworth**
*Chief Executive, Service Children's Education*

**Terry Wafer**
*Assistant Commissioner, Commissioner for Protection Against Unlawful Industrial Action & Commissioner for the Rights of Trade Union Members*

**Prof GJ Wainwright MBE**
*Commissioner, Royal Commission on Ancient & Historical Monuments in Wales*

**Danny Waite**
*Member, East Midland Consumers' Committee, Office of Electricity Regulation*

**Nicholas Wakefield**
*Part-time Member, British Railways Board*
Former Deputy Chief Executive, London & Continental Railway.

**Richard Wakeford**
*Chief Executive, Countryside Commission*

**Dr MJ Waldock**
*Chair, Environment Group, Centre for Environment, Fisheries & Aquaculture Science*

**Air Commodore AP Waldron**
*Director of Operations, RAF Training Group Defence Agency*

**Dr Diana Walford**
*Director, Public Health Laboratory Services Board*
Former Deputy Chief Medical Officer, Department of Health and Director of Health Care, NHS Management Executive.

**Lionel Walford**
*Member of Ownership Board, Meat Hygiene Service*
*Member of Council, Food from Britain*
Group Director, Welsh Office Agriculture Department.

**David Walke**
*Overseas Consultancy, Companies House*

**A Walker**
*Member, Executive Committee, HM Prison Service*

**Alexa Walker**
*Member of Advisory Board, Defence Analytical Services Agency*
AUS (Service Personnel Policy).

**Andrew Walker**
*Director of Regulation & Bussiness Affairs, Office of Electricity Regulation*

**Anna Walker**
*Deputy Director General, Office of Telecommunications*

**Dr Brian Walker**
*Member of Board, Northern Ireland Museums' Council*
*Member, Arts Council of Northern Ireland*
Institute of Irish Studies, Queen's University Belfast. Jointly nominated by the universities in Northern Ireland.

**Dr DP Walker**
*Member of Board, Simpler Trade Procedures Board*
Director, DTI/FCO Joint Export Promotion Directorate. Secretary, British Overseas Trade Board (BOTB).

**David Walker MBE TD**
*Commissioner, Meat & Livestock Commission*
Chairman and Chief Executive Officer,

McKey Holdings (Europe). President, British Meat Manufacturers' Association. Executive member, Food & Drink Federation.

**Garry Walker**
*Regulatory Manager, Occupational Pensions Regulatory Authority*

**Dr Gordon Walker**
*Director, Research & Development, Council for the Central Laboratory of the Research Councils*

**Guy Walker CBE**
*Member, Biotechnology & Biological Sciences Research Council*

**Irene Walker**
*Chief Executive, Dumfries & Galloway Enterprise*

**James Walker**
*Personnel & Services Director, Funding Agency for Schools*

**James Walker**
*Member of Council, Food from Britain*
Director, Walkers Shortbread.

**Janet Walker**
*Director of Business Affairs, Channel Four Television Corporation*

**Lord Walker of Worcester MBE**
*Chairman, English Partnerships*
Member of all Conservative Cabinets between 1970 and 1990. Chairman, Kleinwort Benson. Chairman, Cornhill Insurance Company. Director, London Financial Futures Exchange. Director, Tate & Lyle.

**Mary Walker**
*CHS, Defence Evaluation & Research Agency*

**Michael Walker**
*Member of Board, Scottish Screen*

**Mike Walker**
*Chairman, Lothian & Edinburgh Enterprise*

**NJ Walker**
*Chief Executive, Commission for the New Towns*

**Peter Walker**
*Technical Director, Office of Telecommunications*

**RJ Walker**
*Director of Operations, Scottish Fisheries Protection Agency*

**Sir Rodney Walker**
*Chairman, UK Sports Council & English Sports Council*
Businessman, President, NHS Trust Federation.

**Dr T Walker**
*Member of Governing Body, Rowett Research Institute*

**Tim Walker**
*Principal, Scottish National Sports Centre*

**Miss Christine Wall OBE**
*Public Affairs Director, English Heritage*

**Jasper Wall**
*Director, Royal Greenwich Observatory*

**Sir Robert Wall OBE**
*Chairman, Rail Users Consultative Committee for Western England*
*Member, Central Rail Users Consultative Committee*
Pro-Chancellor, University of Bristol.

**Prof DJ Wallace CBE**
*Member of Council, Engineering & Physical Sciences Research Council*
Loughborough University.

**Prof Helen Wallace**
*Member, Academic Council, Wilton Park Executive Agency*

**Prof Herb Wallace OBE**
*Vice-Chairman, Police Authority for Northern Ireland*

**John Wallace**
*Direct Marketing Director, National Gallery Publications, National Gallery*

**Dr Louise M Wallace**
*Member of Board, Investors in People UK*

**RA Wallace**
*Member of Advisory Committee, Cadw*
Principal Finance Officer, Welsh Office.

**Stan Wallace**
*Director In-Service Ships, Ships Support Agency*

**Mrs Teresa Wallace**
*Member, South Western Consumers' Committee, Office of Electricity Regulation*

**John Waller**
*Head of Interpretation, Royal Armouries*

**Aidan Walsh**
*Director & Company Secretary, Northern Ireland Museums' Council*

**Angela Walsh**
*Continuing Professional Development & Research, Teacher Training Agency*

**Francis Walsh**
*Secretary, Mental Health Commission for Northern Ireland*

**Michael Walsh**
*Member, Academic Council, Wilton Park Executive Agency*

**P Walsh**
*Member of Advisory Board, Coastguard*
External Member.

**The Most Rev P Walsh**
*Member of Council, Council for Catholic Maintained Schools*

**DM Walsh OBE JP**
*Member, Rail Users Consultative Committee for North Eastern England*
Consultant advising commercial firms on air travel arrangements. Previously ran own travel agency. Past Chairman, Association of British Travel Agents. Founder President, National Association of Independent Travel Agents. Member of a Hospital Management Committee. College Governor. Former President and Member, Bradford Chamber of Commerce.

**Ian Walters**
*Chief Executive, Training & Employment Agency (NI)*

**James Walton**
*Manager, Inverness Airport, Highlands & Islands Airports*

**Keith Walton**
*Director of Resources, Rural Development Commission*

**Paul Wandless**
*Operations Manager, Meat Hygiene Service*

**Derek Wanless**
*Member of Board, Investors in People UK*
Group Chief Executive, NatWest Group.

**MGB Wannell**
*Director of Engineering, Trinity House Lighthouse Service*

**WM Wannop OBE JP**
*Chairman, RFDC, The Environment Agency*

**R Warburton**
*Advisor to the Board, Laganside Corporation*
Belfast Regeneration Office - Department of the Environment for Northern Ireland.

**Colin Ward**
*Chief Executive, Student Loans Company*

**John Ward CBE**
*Chairman, Scottish Homes*
Past Chairman, CBI Scotland and Director for Scotland and Northern England, IBM UK. Currently Chairman, Advisory Scottish Council for Education and Training Targets (ASCETT), Quality Scotland Foundation. Scottish Post Office Board. Member, Scottish Economic Council. Non Executive Director, Dunfermline Building Society.

**Brigadier ML Ward**
*Director, Armed Forces Personnel Administration Agency*

**Prof Patricia Layzell Ward**
*Member, National Library of Wales*
Co-opted by the Council.

**RG Ward**
*Statistics & Economics Division, Inland Revenue*

**Sue Ward**
*Member of Board, Occupational Pensions Regulatory Authority*
Researcher, author and journalist. Secretary, Northern Pensions Resource Group and the Independent Pensions Research Group. A Social Security Appeal Tribunal Member. Former Member of OPB and Pension Law Review Committee. (Nominated by the Northern Pensions Resource Group.)

**John Wardle**
*Director of Resources, NHS Estates*

**Roy Wardle**
*Secretary to Council, Ofwat National Customer Council*
*Head of CSC Appointments and Performance, Office of Water Services*

**ME Ware**
*Ex-Officio Trustee, Royal Marines Museum*

**Alan Warhurst CBE**
*Commissioner, Museums & Galleries Commission*
Chairman, North West Museums Service. Former Director, Manchester Museum, Ulster Museum and Bristol City Museum. Former President, South West Federation of Museums & Art Galleries, Museums Association and North West Federation of Museums & Art Galleries.

**P Waring**
*Member, Logistic Information Systems Agency*
Prin QMG Fin.

**Simon Waring**
*International Director, Food from Britain*

**BM Warman**
*Member of Council, Advisory, Conciliation & Arbitration Service*

**John Warman**
*Member, Ofwat Customer Service Committee for Wales*
*Member, Rail Users Consultative Committee for Wales*
Neath Port Talbot County Councillor. Member, Lord Chancellor's Advisory Committee for the Commission of Peace. Former Member, Press Council. Employee of British Steel, Port Talbot.

**M Warner**
*Member, The British Library*
Independent.

**RJ Warner**
*Head, Accounts Office (Shipley), Inland Revenue*

**Mrs Suzanne Warner**
*Member, Academic Council, Wilton Park Executive Agency*

**Mrs Betty Warnock**
*Assistant Secretary, Commonwealth Scholarship Commission*

**CM Warnock**
*Chief Executive/Secretary, Northern Ireland Fishery Harbour Authority*
Master Mariner.

**Mr Mike Warrander**
*Member, Ofwat Central Customer Service Committee*

**Jeremy Warren**
*Assistant Director, Museums & Galleries Commission*

**Prof L Warren**
*Member of Council, Countryside Council for Wales*

Professor of Environmental Law, University of Wales, Aberystwyth.

**Neville Washington OBE**
*Member, Coal Authority*

**Prof Lorraine Waterhouse**
*Member, Parole Board for Scotland*
Professor of Social Work, University of Edinburgh.

**Prof JC Waterlow, CMG**
*Member of Governing Body, Rowett Research Institute*

**Lord Waterpark**
*Trustee, Royal Air Force Museum*

**Dan Waters**
*Director, Enforcement, Financial Services Authority*
Joined IMRO in 1993 as Director responsible for Enforcement. Subsequently also responsible for Monitoring. Eleven years at CFTC in US.

**Mrs E Waterson**
*Member of Council, Council for Catholic Maintained Schools*
Department of Education Representative.

**Sir Christopher Wates**
*Member, National Museum of Science & Industry*

**Mrs CB Watkin**
*Member, SACOT, Scottish Advisory Committee on Telecommunications*
Home economics adviser.

**Mrs Jean Watkins**
*Member, Ofwat Wessex Customer Service Committee*

**MBR Watkins**
*National Manager of Cadwraeth Cymru, Cadw*

**Mrs MM Watkins**
*General/Adult Nursing, National Board for Nursing, Midwifery & Health Visiting for Northern Ireland*

**Paul Watkinson**
*Member, British Railways Board*

**Ken Watmough**
*Member of Board, Sea Fish Industry Authority*
Fishmonger from Aberdeen. Vice President, National Federation of Fishmongers.

**Elizabeth Watson**
*Director of Legal Services, The Scottish Legal Aid Board*

**Dr J Watson**
*Member, Northern Ireland Council for Postgraduate Medical & Dental Education*
Nominated by NHSSB.

**JB Watson**
*Chief Executive, Driver & Vehicle Testing Agency*

**Jack Watson**
*Chairman, Caithness & Sutherland Enterprise*

**Dr Jeff Watson**
*Director of Strategy & Operations, Scottish Natural Heritage*

**Margaret Watson**
*Senior Complaints Officer, Fair Employment Commission for Northern Ireland*

**Oliver Watson**
*Curator, Ceramics & Glass Collection, Victoria & Albert Museum*

**Robert Watson**
*Member of Council, Food from Britain*
Chief Executive, Foyle Meats.

**Roger Watson**
*Assistant Director, Office of Fair Trading*

**Sir Ron Watson**
*Member, Audit Commission*
Sefton Councillor. Leader, Conservative Group, Association of Metropolitan Authorities. Non-Executive Director and Vice Chairman, Sefton Health Authority. Director, Liverpool Airport and Merseyside Partnership.

**S Watson**
*Member of Board, Construction Industry Training Board*
Kinder Roofing.

**A Watt**
*Operations Director, Northern Ireland Transport Holding Company*

**Iain Watt**
*The Head of Reader Services Department, Public Record Office*

**Dr Jessie Watt**
*Commissioner - Shetland & Orkney, Crofters' Commission*

**E Watts**
*Member, Property Advisers to the Civil Estate*
Watts & Partners.

**Graham Watts**
*Commercial Director, British Nuclear Fuels plc*

**Mr Ronald Watts**
*Director & Trustee, Horniman Museum*

**Dave Wealthall**
*Project Manager, Post Occurrences & Personnel Information System of Information, Pay & Personnel Agency*

**Giles Weaver**
*Trustee, National Galleries of Scotland*

**DH Webb**
*Commissioner, Duke of York's Royal Military School*

**Keith Webb**
*Head of Private Office & Public Affairs, Office of the Rail Regulator*

**R Webb**
*Trustee, Royal Navy Submarine Museum*
Managing Director, Robb Webb.

**Simon Webb**
*Member of Advisory Board, Defence Analytical Services Agency*
Director General Finance.

**Steve Webb**
*Head of Research & Corporate Planning, Wales Tourist Board*

**W Webb**
*Head of Corporate Services, Royal Botanic Gardens Kew*

**Prof AJF Webster**
*Member of Governing Body, Rowett Research Institute*

**Alen Webster**
*Director Development and Training Services, British Council*

**Mrs JH Webster**
*Member of Advisory Council, Scottish Record Office*

**Ken Webster**
*Member, East Midland Consumers' Committee, Office of Electricity Regulation*

**Kenneth Webster**
*Trustee, Community Development Foundation*

**Richard Webster**
*Chairman, Further Education Funding Council for Wales*
Director, Midcast Engineering (Wales), Maesteg.

**Stan Webster**
*Member of Advisory Board, Defence Analytical Services Agency*
Coopers & Lybrand.

**Linda Wedgbury**
*Member of Board, Funding Agency for Schools*
Business Consultant.

**Ivan Weekes**
*Chair, Stonebridge Housing Action Trust*

**Mrs Kathleen Weekes**
*Member, Ofwat Eastern Customer Service Committee*

**Colonel Tim Weeks**
*Commandant Infantry Training Centre Wales, Army Training & Recruitment Agency*

**David Weir**
*District Valuer, Valuation & Lands Agency*

**Jacqueline Weir**
*Member, General Consumer Council for Northern Ireland*
Headmistress, Wellington College. Member, Amnesty International and the Admiralty Interview Board.

**Alex Weise**
*District Valuer, Valuation & Lands Agency*

**Edward Weiss**
*Commissioner, Criminal Cases Review Commission*
Former Finance Director, Chubb Security.

**David Welch**
*Chief Executive, Royal Parks Agency*

**Humphrey Welfare**
*Director of Archaeological Survey, Royal Commission on Historical Monuments of England*

**Keith Weller**
*Head of General & General Vocational Qualifications, Qualifications & Curriculum Authority*

**Cecilia Wells OBE**
*Member of Council, Advisory, Conciliation & Arbitration Service Member, Equal Opportunities Commission*
Human Resource Management Consultant, MaST Organisation. Non-Executive Director, an NHS Trust. Vice-Chair, Centrepoint.

**Harris Wells**
*Director of Audit Strategy, The Accounts Commission for Scotland*

**Mrs JBE Wells JP**
*Commissioner, Duke of York's Royal Military School*

**Keith Wells**
*Member of Board of Governors, Museum of London*
Appointed by the Corporation of London.

**John Welsby CBE**
*Chairman, British Railways Board*

**John Welsh**
*Export/Import Pigmeat, Eggs, Poultry, Community Victualling, Multi-Commodity Claims, Intervention Board*

**Michael Wemms**
*Non-Executive Director, Benefits Agency*
Retail Director, Tesco Stores.

**H Wenban-Smith**
*Member of Advisory Board, Highways Agency*
Director, National Roads Policy.

**Robin Wendt**
*Member of Board, Funding Agency for Schools*
Former Secretary, Assocaition of County Councils. Former Chief Executive, Cheshire County Council.

**Dr DJ Werrett**
*Director of Research & DNA Services, Forensic Science Service*

**Alison West**
*Chief Executive, Community Development Foundation*

**CJ West**
*Solicitor to HMLR, HM Land Registry*

**David West**
*Post Compulsory, Office for Standards in Education*

**Jeffrey West**
*Acting Director, Historic Properties Department, English Heritage*

**RE West**
*Vice Chairman, Rail Users Consultative Committee for Eastern England*

**RO West QPM**
*Member, Parole Board*

**Malcolm Westgate**
*Chief Executive, Disposal Sales Agency*

**Douglas Weston**
*Director of Projects, Millennium Commission*

**Joanna Weston**
*Chief Executive, Arts Council of Wales*

**Dame Margaret Weston DBE**
*Trustee, Fleet Air Arm Museum*

**John Weston**
*Member of Board, Defence Evaluation & Research Agency*
Group MD, British Aerospace.

**Mr Peter Weston**
*Chairman, South Western Consumers' Committee, Office of Electricity Regulation*

**WN Weston**
*Ex-Officio Trustee, Royal Marines Museum*

**Group Captain P Whalley**
*Officer Commanding, RAF Stafford, RAF Maintenance Group Defence Agency*

**Dr Brian Wharmby**
*Technical Director, Office of Electricity Regulation*

**Robert V Wharton**
*Board Member, Castle Vale Housing Action Trust*
Founder Member, High Point. Chairman, Ways Consulting. Past President, Chartered Institute of Building. Member, Birmingham Chamber of Commerce Council.

**Dr Peter Whatmore**
*Member, Parole Board for Scotland*
Former Consultant Psychiatrist.

**Prof Roger Wheater OBE**
*Vice Chairman & Member, Scientific Advisory Committee, Scottish Natural Heritage*

**Alan Wheatley**
*Trustee, Victoria & Albert Museum*

**Sheriff JF Wheatley**
*Member of Advisory Council, Scottish Record Office*

**Ossie Wheatley CBE**
*Chairman, The Sports Council for Wales Member, UK Sports Council*

**P Wheatley**
*Member, Executive Committee, HM Prison Service*

**Gerard Wheeldon**
*Secretary, Royal Parks Agency*
Buildings, Monuments & Sites Division, Department of National Heritage.

**Michael Wheeler**
*Director & Trustee, Horniman Museum*
Nominated by Secretary of State for Culture, Media & Sport.

**Michael J Wheeler**
*Member of Board of Governors, Museum of London*
Appointed by the Prime Minister.

**Andrew Wheldon**
*Member, Apple & Pear Research Council*
Director, Peter Wheldon. Trustee, East Malling Research Association. Member, Brogdale New Varieties Panel. Director, ENFRU.

**Ms Jennifer Wheten**
*Examinations & Records Manager, Welsh National Board for Nursing, Midwifery & Health Visiting*

**Rear Admiral AJ Whetstone CB**
*Chairman, Royal Navy Submarine Museum*

**Sally Whetton**
*Group Director - New Business, Central Office of Information*

**RW Whewell**
*Member, Policyholders' Protection Board*
Consultant, KPMG.

**Rowan Whimster**
*Director of Corporate Planning, Royal Commission on Historical Mon uments of England*

**Tim Whitaker**
*Director of External Relations, Economic & Social Research Council*

**A White**
*Member, Property Advisers to the Civil Estate*
BT Group Property.

**AR White**
*Member, Rail Users Consultative Committee for North Eastern England*

**Adrian White CBE**
*Governor, British Broadcasting Corporation*
Chairman, Biwater. Former Chairman, Epsom Health Care NHS Trust. Chairman, British Water.

**Andrew White**
*Assistant Director, Office of Fair Trading*

**Dr Anita White**
*Director of Development, UK & English Sports Councils*

**Prof Christopher White CVO**
*Trustee, Victoria & Albert Museum*

**Prof David White**
*Director of Science & Technology Group, Biotechnology & Biological Sciences Research Council*

**Sir David White**
*Chairman, Coal Authority*
Chairman, NFC Pension Fund Trustees, Mansfield Brewery, Nottingham Health Authority, Board of Nottingham Trent University and Whitehaven Consultants. Trustee, Djanogly City Technology College. Director, Hilda Hanson. Chairman EPS. Governor, Nottingham High School. President, Nottingham and Notts RSPCA.

**Duncan White OBE**
*Member, Scottish Conveyancing & Executry S ervices Board*

**Fenella White**
*Head of Education, Commonwealth Institute*

**Gillian White**
*Part-time Board Member, Civil Aviation Authority*
Former Secretary and Legal Adviser, CAA

**James White**
*Head of Security & Building Management, Wallace Collection*

**Julia White MBE**
*Member of Board, Tai Cymru*
Chartered Librarian and retired Director of a family business. Former Chairman, Torch Theatre, Milford Haven. Former Chairman, Dance Committee of the Welsh Arts Council. Member, WRVS. Former Emergency Services Organiser for Pembrokeshire.

**Kevin White**
*Director, Human Resources, Employment Service*

**KG White**
*Corporate Secretary, Crown Agents Foundation*

**Paul White**
*Director, Finance, UK Atomic Energy Authority*
Joined UKAEA (GD) in 1994. Former Financial Director, Marconi Radar & Control Systems.

**Peter White**
*Member of Board, UK Ecolabelling Board*
Chairman, British Apparel & Textiles Confederation Technical Committee.

**PR White**
*Secretary, Royal Commission on Ancient & Historical Monuments in Wales*

**RG White**
*Chief Inspector, Gaming Board for Great Britain*

**Robert White**
*Member, Rail Users Consultative Committee for Scotland*
Ship's Master, Stena Line.

**Sue White**
*Customer Relations Manager, Central Computer & Telecommunications Agency*

**Alan Whiteford**
*Chairman, Ross & Cromarty Enterprise*

**Catherine Whitehead**
*Member of Board, UK Eco-Labelling Board*
Staffordshire County Trading Standards Officer.

**N Whitehead**
*Chairman, Northern Ireland Transport Holding Company*

**Edward Whitehorn**
*Assistant Director, Office of Fair Trading*

**Michael Whitehorn**
*Member, Ofwat Eastern Customer Service Committee*

**Richard Whitehouse**
*Head of Buildings & Estate, Victoria & Albert Museum*

**Sue Whitehouse**
*Head of Compliance, Office of the National Lottery*

**Richard Whiteley**
*Trustee, Royal Armouries*

**Joan Whiteside**
*Member, National Consumer Council*

**Mrs Joan Whiteside**
*Chairman, General Consumer Council for Northern Ireland*
Chairman, Northern Ireland Consumer Committee for Eletricity. Former lecturer in consumer law, North Down College of Further Education. Member, Lord Chancellor's Advisory Committee on Legal Aid. General Commissioner for Income Tax.

**Damien Whitmore**
*Head of Communications, Tate Gallery*

**Elizabeth Whittaker**
*Finance Director, National Gallery Publications, National Gallery*

**Mrs N Whittaker**
*Member of Board, Enterprise Ulster*

**Nigel Whittaker**
*Member of Board, UK Ecolabelling Board*
Business Consultant.

**Stella Whittaker**
*Member of Board, UK Ecolabelling Board*
Environmental Scientist, Senior Lecturer, Edge Hill College, Lancs.

**Colonel I Whittington**
*Colonel Geographic Commitments, Military Survey*

**Stephen Whittle**
*Director, Broadcasting Standards Commission*

**Mrs H Whitton**
*Assistant Secretary, Scottish Medical Practices Committee*

**P Whitworth**
*Member of Governing Body, Scottish Crop Research Institute*
Former Technical Director, Snacks, from United Biscuits. Former President, European Snacks Association (ESA). Founder Member of Board, ECSA Research.

**Prof Iain Whyte**
*Trustee, National Galleries of Scotland*

**Lorna Whyte**
*Member, Police Complaints Authority*

**His Excellency SK Wickremesinghe**
*Trustee, Imperial War Museum*

**John Widdowson**
*CES, Defence Evaluation & Research Agency*

**Helena M Wiesner**
*Member, National Consumer Council*
*Member, Policyholders' Protection Board*
Independent Consumer Affairs Consultant.

**JR Wild**
*Non-Executive Director, Defence Dental Agency*
Chief Dental Officer for England.

**CJ Wilde**
*Head, Cell Physiology Group, Hannah Research Institute*

**Jane Wilde**
*Member, General Consumer Council for Northern Ireland*
Public health doctor. Former Executive Director, Health Promotion Agency.

**Karen Wilde**
*Head of Public Affairs, Office of the National Lottery*

**Dr Ken Wildey**
*Infestation Risk Evaluation, Central Science Laboratory*
10 years in stored product research in Slough. Headed Wildlife & Storage Biology Department in ADAS.

**Dr JR Wildgoose**
*Member of Ownership Board, Meat Hygiene Service*
Head of Food Safety & Animal Health Division, Scottish Office Agriculture, Environment & Fisheries Department.

**John Wildig**
*Member, Rail Users Consultative Committee for Wales*
Research Consultant, ADAS, Pwllpeiran.

**Carole Wildman**
*Acting Director of Housing, Castle Vale Housing Action Trust*

**Brigadier Phil Wildman OBE**
*Director of Military Survey & Chief Executive, Military Survey*

**Andrew Wiles**
*Director, South West Region, The Housing Corporation*

**Cdr S Wiles**
*Operations Director, Naval Aircraft Repair Organisation*

**Linda Wilhams**
*Member for the West of England, Gas Consumers' Council*

**Dr E Wiliam**
*Assistant Director, Collections & Research, National Museums & Galleries of Wales*
*Commissioner, Royal Commission on Ancient & Historical Monuments in Wales*

**Christopher Wilk**
*Curator, Furniture & Woodwork Collection, Victoria & Albert Museum*

**Colonel KN Wilkins OBE**
*Director, Royal Marines Museum*

**Prof Malcolm Wilkins**
*Chairman, Royal Botanic Garden Edinburgh*

**Clive Wilkinson**
*Chairman, Ofwat Central Customer
Service Committee
Deputy Chairman, Ofwat National
Customer Council*

**David T Wilkinson**
*Institute Deputy Secretary/Finance
Officer, Macaulay Land Use Research
Institute*

**Richard Wilkinson**
*Member, Rail Users Consultative
Committee for Scotland*
Development Manager, Hansel Village,
Ayrshire. Secretary of Scottish
Representatives Committee, Action
Research. Member of European
Movement (Scottish Council).

**Robert Wilkinson**
*Group General Manager, Amalgamated
Packaging, Remploy*

**Prof WB Wilkinson**
*Director, Centre for Ecology & Hydrology*

**Capt Tony Wilks**
*Member, East Areas Board, Scottish
Natural Heritage*

**Dr Sheila Willatts**
*Member of Advisory Board, Medical
Devices Agency*
Consultant Anaesthetist, Bristol Royal
Infirmary.

**Prof F Willet**
*Member, The British Library*
Royal Society of Edinburgh.

**MAH Willett**
*Member, Policyholders' Protection Board*
Deputy Chairman, Methodist Insurance.

**Michael Willett**
*Group Director, Safety Regulation, Civil
Aviation Authority*
Former Chairman, European Joint
Aviation Authorities. Previously, a pilot
with Laker Airways.

**David Willey**
*Director of Business Services, Ordnance
Survey*

**Alan Williams**
*Team Manager, Information Systems
Team, English Nature*

**Alan Williams**
*Director of Communications & Corporate
Relations, Post Office*

**Anthony Williams MBE**
*Member, Police Complaints Authority*
Former Lieutenant Colonel.

**Baroness Williams of Crosby**
*President, The Britain-Russia Centre*

**Betsan Williams**
*Dance & Drama Officer, Arts Council of
Wales*

**Brian Williams JP**
*Member, Residuary Body for Wales*

**Clive G Williams**
*Secretary, Rail Users Consultative
Committee for Wales*

**Colin Williams**
*Trustee, Community Development
Foundation*

**Dr DJR Williams**
*Keeper, Greek & Roman Antiquities,
British Museum*

**David Williams**
*Member, Audit Commission*

**David Williams**
*All Dairy, Beef & Fish Market Support
Schemes, Intervention Board*

**Miss G Williams**
*Member, WACT, Welsh Advisory
Committee on Telecommunications*
Accountant.

**Godfrey Williams**
*Member of Board, Welsh Language
Board*
Managing Director, Marcher Sound.

**Prof H Williams**
*Member, SACOT, Scottish Advisory
Committee on Telecommunications*
Professor of Business Computing.

**John Williams**
*Director of Finance, Castle Vale Housing
Action Trust*

**John Williams**
*Member, Human Fertilisation &
Embryology Authority*
Dean, Faculty of Economic & Social
Studies, University of Wales,
Aberystwyth.

**John Williams**
*Design Manager, Museum of Science &
Industry, Manchester*

**John V Williams**
*Chief Executive, Qualifications,
Curriculum & Assessment Authority for
Wales
Member, Welsh National Board for
Nursing, Midwifery & Health Visiting*

**Kevin Williams**
*Managing Director Parcelforce, Post
Office*

**Owen P Williams**
*Member, Rail Users Consultative
Committee for Wales*
Head of Civil Engineering, First Hydro
Company, Dinorwig & Ffestiniog Power
Stations, Gwynedd.

**Patricia Williams**
*Director of Book Publishing, National
Gallery Publications, National Gallery*

**Dr Paul R Williams CBE**
*Chairman & Chief Executive, Council for
the Central Laboratory of the Research
Councils*

**Dr Peter Williams**
*Member of Board, The Housing
Corporation*
Deputy Director General of Council of
Mortgage Lenders. Former Deputy
Director of Chartered Institute of
Housing, Board Member of Housing for

Wales and Chairman of Welsh Secretary
of State's Housing Management Advisory
Panel.

**Dr Peter Williams CBE**
*Chairman, Particle Physics & Astronomy
Research Council*
Oxford Instruments.

**Dr Peter Williams CBE**
*Chairman, National Museum of Science
& Industry*

**RB Williams**
*Employer Association Member,
Engineering Construction Industry
Training Board*
Chief Executive, Engineering
Construction Industry Association.

**Rhodri Williams**
*Member of Board, Welsh Language
Board*
Producer, Agenda television company.

**Prof Robin Williams**
*Member, Council for the Central
Laboratory of the Research Councils*
University of Wales, Swansea.

**Prof Roger Williams**
*Member, Higher Education Funding
Council for Wales*
Vice Chancellor, University of Reading.

**Roy Williams CB**
*Member, The Design Council*

**Tony Williams**
*Chief Executive, Home-Grown Cereals
Authority*

**WG Williams**
*Member, The British Library*
Library and Information Services Council
(Wales).

**W Gwyn Williams OBE**
*Member, National Library of Wales*
Co-opted by the Council.

**Mrs Wendy A Williams MBE**
*Member of Council, The Sports Council
for Wales*

**Will Williams**
*Team Manager, Uplands Team, English
Nature*

**Dr Douglas Williamson**
*Member, Rail Users Consultative
Committee for Scotland*
Senior Lecturer in chemistry, University
of Aberdeen. Former Vice Chairman,
Scottish Consumer Council.

**Keith Williamson**
*Principal Establishment & Finance
Officer, Central Office of Information*

**Paul Williamson**
*Curator, Sculpture Collection, Victoria &
Albert Museum*

**Raj Williamson**
*Member of Museum Trust, Museum of
Science & Industry Manchester*

**Richard Williamson**
*Member, West Areas Board, Scottish
Natural Heritage*

**Roy Willingham**
*Member, Horticultural Development Council*
Managing Director, F Dring & Sons.

**Bob Willis**
*Project Support, Companies House*

**Frank Willis**
*Director of Advertising & Sponsorship, Independent Television Commission*

**John Willis**
*Director of Programmes, Channel Four Television Corporation*

**ACM Sir John Willis KCB CBE**
*Vice Chairman, Ministry of Defence Police*
Vice Chief of Defence Staff.

**R Willis**
*Chairman, Wessex RFDC, The Environment Agency*

**Dr R Willis-Lee**
*Dean, Fire Service College*

**Brian Willott**
*Chief Executive, Welsh Development Agency*

**Baroness Willoughby de Eresby**
*Trustee, National Portrait Gallery*

**Trevor Wilmore**
*Member, Further Education Funding Council for Wales*
Former Chief Executive, Barry College. Member, Glamorgan TEC.

**George Wilmshurst**
*Member, Scottish Agricultural Wages Board*
Employees' representative member nominated by the Rural, Agricultural & Allied Workers National Trade Group (Scotland) of the Transport & General Workers' Union.

**Anthony Wilson**
*Member of Museum Trust, Museum of Science & Industry Manchester*

**Vice Admiral Sir Barry Wilson**
*Chairman, Royal Naval Museum*

**Catherine Wilson OBE**
*Commissioner, Museums & Galleries Commission*
Director, Norfolk Museums Service. Fellow, Museums Association. Board member, Museum Training Institute. Personal Member, Association of Independent Museums.

**Colonel D Wilson OBE**
*Chief Staff Officer Personnel, HQRM, Naval Manning Agency*

**David Wilson**
*Deputy Director General for Scotland, Office of Electricity Regulation*

**Denis S Wilson MBE, JP**
*Member, Post Office Users' National Council*
Executive Director, Lincoln Enterprise Agency. Past President, Lincoln Incorporated Chamber of Commerce.

Former Chairman, Lincoln POAC and TAC. Board Member, Lincolnshire Prince's Youth Business Trust. Chairman, Lincoln Sheltered Workshop Trust.

**Don Wilson**
*Member of Museum Trust, Museum of Science & Industry Manchester*

**Edward Wilson**
*Member of Commission, Equal Opportunities Commission for Northern Ireland*
Chairman, Ulster Carpet Mills.

**Eric Wilson**
*Chairman, Ofwat Yorkshire Customer Service Committee*
*Member, Ofwat National Customer Council*

**GB Wilson**
*Inspector, Football Licensing Authority*

**GH Wilson**
*Headmaster and Chief Executive, Duke of York's Royal Military School*

**GM Wilson**
*Master of the Armouries, Royal Armouries*

**Geoffrey Wilson**
*Commissioner, English Heritage*

**Heather Wilson**
*Capital Taxes Officer, Museums & Galleries Commission*

**Dr HK Wilson**
*Member, Northern Ireland Council for Postgraduate Medical & Dental Education*
Nominated by Royal College of Radiologists.

**Hugh Wilson MBE**
*Member, Milk Development Council*
Retired trade unionist. Formerly with agricultural section of T&GW in Scotland.

**J Wilson**
*Non-Executive Board Member, Naval Bases & Supply Agency*

**John Wilson**
*Chief Field Officer, Livestock & Meat Commission for Northern Ireland*

**John Wilson**
*Non-Executive Director, Contributions Agency*
Former Chairman, Midland Electricity and London Electricity Board.

**Ken Wilson**
*Human Resource Director, Contributions Agency*

**Leslie Wilson**
*Director of Finance, Historic Scotland*

**Lord Wilson of Tillyorn GCMG**
*Member of Board, British Council*
Chairman, Scottish Hydro-Electric.

**M Wilson**
*Director, Northern Ireland Transport Holding Company*

**M Wilson OBE**
*Member, Sports Council for Northern Ireland*

**M Jeffrey Wilson**
*Head, Soil Science Group, Macaulay Land Use Research Institute*

**Michael Wilson**
*Chief Executive, Waltham Forest Housing Action Trust*

**Michael Wilson**
*Head of Exhibitions & Display, National Gallery*

**Dr Michael Wilson**
*Pesticides, Central Science Laboratory*
Joined MAFF in 1981. Former Commercial Manager, MAFF Slough Laboratory.

**Michael PBG Wilson**
*Chief Executive, Defence Vetting Agency*

**Miles Wilson**
*Director of Corporate Affairs, The Environment Agency*

**P Wilson JP**
*Member, SACOT, Scottish Advisory Committee on Telecommunications*
*Member, Post Office Users' Council for Scotland*
Former Councillor and past Convenor, Lothian Regional Council. Chairman, Lothian and Borders Posts & Telecommunications Advisory Committees.

**Peter Wilson**
*Director of Buildings & Gallery Services, Tate Gallery*

**Peter Wilson**
*Agency Secretary, Army Training & Recruitment Agency*

**Philip Wilson**
*Member of Board, Northern Ireland Museums' Council*
Craigavon Borough Council. Nominated by District Council.

**R Wilson**
*Trustee, Royal Navy Submarine Museum*
Nominated by Gosport Borough Council.

**R Wilson**
*Director of Development Plans, The Planning Inspectorate*

**Prof RCL Wilson**
*Member of Council, English Nature*
Professor of Earth Sciences, Open University. Consultant to petroleum exploration industry.

**Rodney Wilson**
*Director, Film, Video & Broadcasting, The Arts Council of England*

**Prof Roger Wilson**
*Member, Tate Gallery*

**Ms Sue Wilson**
*Non-Executive Member, Inland Revenue*
Former Quality & Personnel Director, Vickers Defence Systems.

**Prof T Wilson**
*Governor, Scottish Council for Educational Technology*
Principal, Glasgow College of Building & Printing.

**Prof TMA Wilson**
*Deputy Director, Scottish Crop Research Institute*

**John Wilyman**
*Commissioner, Meat & Livestock Commission*
Farmer.

**Ralph Windsor**
*Group Director - Business Improvement, Central Office of Information*

**PJ Winfield**
*Information Technology, Scottish Agricultural Science Agency*

**Air Commodore Chris Winsland**
*Chief Executive, Armed Forces Personnel Administration Agency*

**Derek Winslow**
*Member, Centre for Information on Language Teaching & Research*
Chief Executive and Director, Cardiff Institute of Higher Education.

**Brian Winston**
*Governor, British Film Institute*

**DS Winterbottom**
*Non-Executive Director, Remploy*
Chairman, Barr & Wallace Arnold Trust. Non-Executive Chairman, Wightlink Group, Crompton Lighting Holdings and Coal Products Holdings.

**Barbara Wintersgill**
*Subject Adviser, Religious Education, Office for Standards in Education*

**MR Winwood**
*Secretary, British Hallmarking Council*

**M Withers**
*Property Development Manager, LT Property, London Transport*

**Peter Withers**
*Area Director South & West, Scottish Prison Service*

**AGH Withey CBE**
*Chief Executive, Remploy*
Formerly Chief Executive, Polymers Division, Evered Holdings. Non-executive Director, Linx Printing Technologies.

**Mike Withey**
*Customer Relations Manager, Central Computer & Telecommunications Agency*

**Gordon Wixley CBE TD**
*Member of Board of Governors, Museum of London*
Appointed by the Corporation of London.

**Peter Woad**
*Member, Horticultural Development Council*
Managing Director, Blue Prince Mushrooms.

**Prof Alison Wolf**
*Member of Council, British Educational Communications & Technology Agency*
International Centre for Research on Assessment, Institute of Education, University of London.

**Sir Brian Wolfson**
*Chairman, Investors in People UK*
Global Health Alternatives.

**Dr John Womersley**
*Member of Advisory Council, Scottish Record Office*
Greater Glasgow Health Board.

**Anne Wood**
*Member of Board, Occupational Pensions Regulatory Authority*
Group Pensions Manager, Storehouse. Former Vice-President Pensions Management Institute and former chairman of PMI's Education Committee. (Nominated by the PMI.)

**Ms Caroline Wood**
*Director, English Nature*

**G Wood**
*Finance Director, Naval Aircraft Repair Organisation*

**G Wood**
*Head, Estate, Glasshouse & Field Research Department, Scottish Crop Research Institute*

**Sir Ian Wood CBE**
*Chairman, Scottish Enterprise*

**Joyce Wood**
*Member, ENACT, Office of Telecommunications*
US regulatory lawyer, specialising in telecommunications.

**Sir Martin Wood OBE**
*Member, Council for the Central Laboratory of the Research Councils*
Oxford Instruments.

**Steven Wood**
*Assistant Director, Office of Fair Trading*

**Dr Susan Wood**
*Director of Post-Licensing, Medicines Control Agency*

**Chris Woodcock**
*Member of England Committee, National Lottery Charities Board*
Head of Corporate Affairs, Kellogg's. Board Member, Moss Side & Hulme Community Development Trust, Groundwork Salford & Trafford, and Corporate Responsibility Group. School Governor.

**Joe Woodcock**
*Park Manager, Greenwich Park, Royal Parks Agency*

**Sir John Woodcock CBE QPM**
*Member of Committee, Ministry of Defence Police*
Adviser to Police Committee.

**HM Chris Woodhead**
*Chief Inspector, Office for Standards in Education*

**Stephen Woodhouse**
*Head of Resources and Efficiency Unit, Scottish Court Service*

**Sir Norman Wooding CBE**
*Non-Executive Director, British Nuclear Fuels plc*
Chairman, East European Trade Council. President, Russo-British Chamber of Commerce. Chairman, EIS Group, BEARR Trust, and Council, SSEES, University of London.

**Prof Geoffrey Woodroffe**
*Member, National Consumer Council*

**Dr AT Woodrow**
*Member, Wine Standards Board*

**Bill Woodrow**
*Member, Tate Gallery*

**Charlie Woods**
*Director, Strategic Futures, Scottish Enterprise*

**Mrs Christine Woods**
*Chairman, Yorkshire Consumers' Committee, Office of Electricity Regulation*

**Lis Woods**
*Director Operations (Compliance), HM Customs & Excise*

**Nigel Woods**
*Commissioner of Valuation, Valuation & Lands Agency*

**Peter Woods**
*Member, Tate Gallery*

**Christopher Woodward**
*Assistant Curator (Education), Sir John Soane's Museum*

**Diana Woodward**
*Arts for AllOfficer, Arts Council of Wales*

**C Douglas Woodward CBE**
*Member of Board of Governors, Museum of London*
Appointed by the Corporation of London.

**Mike Woodward**
*Finance Manager, Museum of Science & Industry Manchester*

**Patsy Woodward**
*Member of Board, Welsh Development Agency*
North Wales Newspapers, British Telecom Advisory Forum for Wales, Robert Jones & Agnes Hunt Orthopaedic Hospital, Institute of Directors - Wales, CBI Wales Council. North Wales Board, Arts Council for Wales, Governor, Ellesmere College.

**Helen Wooldridge**
*Manager, Wales, Gas Consumers' Council*

**Derek Woolley**
*Head of IT Operations, Office of the National Lottery*

**GN Woolley**
*Member of Council, English Nature*
Managing Director, Woolley & Company. Director, Beaver Securities. Member,

Environment and Water Committee, and Council of Country Landowners Association. Member, Council, Scottish Landowners' Federation.

**P Woolley**
*Hd Med Trg (F&S), Defence Medical Training Organisation*

**Adrian Wootton**
*Controller, BFI On The South Bank*

**Janet Wootton**
*Regional Officer, Independent Television Commission*

**Nicholas Worrall**
*Head of Financial Services Department, Public Record Office*

**Jeremy Worth**
*Planning for Sustainable Development, Countryside Commission*

**Mike Worthy**
*Information Technology, UK Sports Council*

**John Wotton**
*Member of Advisory Board, Medical Devices Agency*
Non-Executive Director, Huntleigh Technology.

**John Woulds**
*Operations Director, Office of the Data Protection Registrar*

**Prof Ted Wragg**
*Board Member, Qualifications & Curriculum Authority*
Professor of Education, University of Exeter.

**R Wray**
*District Inspector, Foyle Fisheries Commission*

**Spencer Wrench**
*Member, BACT, Office of Telecommunications*
Managing Director, greeting cards, car retail, cable consultation and installation company.

**Alan Wright**
*Security Manager, Royal Air Force Museum*

**BA Wright**
*Member of Steering Board, Patent Office*

**Christopher Wright**
*Director of Licence Enforcement & Fair Trading, Office of Telecommunications*

**DE Wright**
*Secretary, Policyholders' Protection Board*

**Elizabeth Wright**
*Member, The Great Britain-China Centre*
Head, Asia Pacific Region, BBC World Service. Former Director, Great Britain-China Centre.

**George Wright MBE**
*Member of Board, Welsh Development Agency*
Transport & General Workers' Union, Central Arbitration Committee,

Employment Appeal Tribunal, Wales Co-operative Centre, South Wales Police Authority, European Economic & Social Committee.

**Gillian Wright**
*Member, Rail Users Consultative Committee for Wales*

**Iain A Wright**
*Programme Unit Manager, Macaulay Land Use Research Institute*

**James RG Wright**
*Member, Scottish Higher Education Funding Council*
Vice-Chancellor, University of Newcastle upon Tyne.

**John Wright**
*Director Procurement Services, Central Computer & Telecommunications Agency*

**L Wright**
*Chairman, Royal Parks Agency*
Head of Buildings, Art & Millennium Group, Department of National Heritage.

**Prof NG Wright**
*Member of Council, Hannah Research Institute*

**Phillipa Wright**
*Head of Information Resources Section, Centre for Information on Language Teaching & Research*

**Richard Wright**
*Team Manager, Lowlands Team, English Nature*

**Mrs Rosalind Wright**
*Director, Serious Fraud Office*

**Dr Thomas Wright**
*Assistant Director, National Museum of Science & Industry*
*Trustee, Fleet Air Arm Museum*

**Dr AD Wrixon**
*Assistant Director, National Radiological Protection Board*

**Andrew Wyatt**
*Director, Government Group, Civil Service College*

**Lord Wyatt**
*Chairman, Horserace Totalisator Board*
Member, Horserace Betting Levy Board. Director, Satellite Information Services (Holdings).

**Martin Wyatt**
*Front of House Manager, National Gallery*

**Peter Wyatt**
*Member, Southern Consumers' Committee, Office of Electricity Regulation*

**Will Wyatt**
*Chief Executive, BBC Broadcast, British Broadcasting Corporation*

**John Wykeham**
*Head of Administration, National Portrait Gallery*

**Joan Wykes OBE**
*Member of Board, The Environment Agency*
Member, London Borough of Bromley Council. Former Non-Executive Director, Thames Water Authority. Former Member, National Rivers Authority - Thames Regional Board. Former Member, Industrial Tribunals, Central London. Former GLC Member and Chairman, London Waste Regulation Authority.

**Martin Wyld**
*Chief Restorer, National Gallery*

**Alexander F Wylie QC**
*Member, The Scottish Legal Aid Board*
Former Standing Junior Counsel to Accountant of Court. Part-time Chairman, Discipline Committee of the Institute of Chartered Accountants of Scotland.

**Gavin Wylie**
*General Counsel, Commonwealth Development Corporation*

**Ieuan Wyn Jones MP**
*Governor, Westminster Foundation for Democracy*

**Emrys Wynn Jones**
*Member, Merseyside & North Wales Consumers' Committee, Office of Electricity Regulation*

**Dr Rowland Wynne**
*Head of Higher Education Division, Higher Education Funding Council for Wales*

**Sandra Wynne**
*Director, Access Development Division, Arts Council of Wales*

**Patricia Wynne CBE**
*Member for the North of England, Gas Consumers' Council*
Chairman, Durham County Ambulance Service NHS Trust. Vice President, Age Concern Newcastle. Vice President, St Clare's Hospice, South Tyneside. Trustee, Hospital of St Mary the Virgin.

**Eleri Wynne Jones**
*Member of Commission, Independent Television Commission*
Member for Wales.

# Y

**Michael Yahuda**
*Member, The Great Britain-China Centre*
Reader in International Relations, London School of Economics & Political Science.

**Mrs Anne Yammaghas**
*Member, Southern Consumers'
Committee, Office of Electricity
Regulation*

**John E Yard**
*Director Business & Management
Services, Inland Revenue*

**Trevor Yardley**
*Business Efficiency Manager, Meat
Hygiene Service*

**Dr Doug Yarrow**
*Director of Business, Innovation &
International Group, Biotechnology &
Biological Sciences Research Council*

**Michael Yates**
*Member, Yorkshire Consumers'
Committee, Office of Electricity
Regulation*

**Andrew Yeates**
*Corporation Secretary & Head of Rights,
Channel Four Television Corporation*

**Mulugeta Yegezu**
*Member, London Regional Passengers
Committee*

**Prof MM Yeoman**
*Trustee, Royal Botanic Garden Edinburgh*

**D York**
*Project Services Director, Highways
Agency*

**David Yorke CBE**
*Member of Board, British Waterways*
Member of Bristol Urban Development
Corporation.

**RA Yorke**
*Commissioner, Royal Commission on
Historical Monuments of England*

**Lady Youde OBE**
*Vice Chairman, The Great Britain-China
Centre*
Former Chairman, Great Britain-China
Scholars Emergency Fund. Trustee,
Great Britain-China Educational Trust.

**AS Young**
*Member, Policyholders' Protection Board*
Managing Director, NFU Mutual & Avon
Group.

**Allan Young**
*Head of Administrative Services, National
Museums of Scotland*

**Baroness Young**
*Chairman Designate, English Nature*
Patron, Institute of Ecology &
Environmental Management. Member,
UK Round Table for Sustainable
Development. Member, Minister for
Agriculture's Agricultural Advisory Group.

**E Young**
*Member, Post Office Users' Council for
Scotland*
Chairman, Western Isles Posts &
Telecommunications Advisory
Committees.

**Geoff Young**
*Member, National Weights & Measures
Laboratory*
Chief Executive, The Gambica
Association.

**Jean Young**
*Governor, British Film Institute
Regional Executive, Independent
Television Commission*

**Prof PC Young**
*Member of Governing Body, Scottish
Crop Research Institute*
Centre for Research on Environmental
Systems & Statistics, Lancaster
University. Former Member of Council,
Freshwater Biological Association.

**Dr Peter Young**
*Member, Parole Board for Scotland*
Director, Centre for Criminology,
University of Edinburgh.

**Raymond Young**
*Director of Research & Innovation
Services, Scottish Homes*

**Russell Young**
*Member, Ofwat Customer Service
Committee for Wales*

**Tom Young**
*Head of Customer Services, Scottish
Water & Sewerage Customers Council*

**Tony Young**
*Member, Academic Council, Wilton Park
Executive Agency*

**Tony Young**
*Member, Employment Tribunals Service*
Joint General Secretary,
Communications Workers' Union.

**Viscount Younger of Leckie KT KCVO
TD**
*Chairman, Royal Armouries*

**Colin Youngson**
*Director, AS (Information Services &
Logistics), Defence Analytical Services
Agency*

# Z

**Laura Zajdlic**
*Personnel Director, Security Facilities
Executive*

**VA Zammit**
*Head, Cell Biochemistry, Hannah
Research Institute*

**Tricia Zipfel**
*Member of Board, Tower Hamlets
Housing Action Trust*
Founding Director, Priority Estates
Project.

# *Index*

*See also the search indexes and listings on pages 535 to 588*

Seafish *see* Sea Fish Industry Authority
Secondary Care Agency *see* Defence Secondary Care Agency
Securities & Futures Authority *see* Financial Services Authority
Security Facilities Executive 478
SEPA *see* Scottish Environment Protection Agency
Serious Fraud Office 479
Service Children's Education 479
SFEU *see* Scottish Further Education Unit
SFO *see* Serious Fraud Office
SFPA *see* Scottish Fisheries Protection Agency
SHEFC *see* Scottish Higher Education Funding Council
SHERT *see* Scottish Hospital Endowments Research Trust
Shetland Enterprise *see* Highlands & Islands Enterprise
Ships Support Agency 480
Sianel Pedwar Cymru *see* S4C
Signals Engineering Establishment *see* RAF Signals Engineering Establishment
Simpler Trade Procedures Board 481
Sir John Soane's Museum 483
SITPRO *see* Simpler Trade Procedures Board
Skye & Lochalsh Enterprise *see* Highlands & Islands Enterprise
SLC *see* Student Loans Company
SMPC *see* Scottish Medical Practices Committee
SNH *see* Scottish Natural Heritage
Social Security Agency (Northern Ireland) 484
Social Security Child Support Agency *see* Child Support Agency
Social Security Contributions Agency *see* Contributions Agency
Social Work Training *see* Central Council for Education & Training in Social Work
SOPA *see* Scottish Office Pensions Agency
Southampton Oceanography Centre *see* Natural Environment Research Council
Special Services Group *see* Security Facilities Executive
Specialist Procurement Services 485
Sports Council for Northern Ireland 486
Sports Council for Wales 487   (*see also* English, Scottish and UK Sports Councils)
SPS *see* Specialist Procurement Services or Scottish Prison Service
SQA *see* Scottish Qualifications Authority
SRO *see* Scottish Record Office
SSA *see* Ships Support Agency
SSC *see* Scottish Sports Council
STB *see* Scottish Tourist Board
Stonebridge Housing Action Trust 489
Student Awards Agency for Scotland 490
Student Loans Company 491
Submarine Museum *see* Royal Navy Submarine Museum
Tai Cymru 492
Tate Gallery 493
TBA *see* (The) Buying Agency
T&EA *see* Training & Employment Agency (NI)
Teacher Training Agency 495
Technical Support Agency *see* Army Technical Support Agency
Telecommunications Regulator *see* Office of Telecommunications
The Buying Agency *see* Buying Agency
THLS *see* Trinity House Lighthouse Service
Tote *see* Horserace Totalisator Board
Tower Hamlets Housing Action Trust 496
Tower of London *see* Historic Royal Palaces, Royal Armouries
Trade Union Members *see* Commissioner for the Rights of Trade Union Members
Traffic Director for London 497
Training & Employment Agency (NI) 498
Training & Recruiting Agency *see* Army Training & Recruiting Agency
Training Group Defence Agency *see* RAF Training Group Defence Agency
Transport & Movements Executive *see* Defence Transport & Movements Executive
Treasury Solicitor's Department 499
Tribunals Service *see* Employment Tribunals Service
Trinity House Lighthouse Service 500
TTA *see* Teacher Training Agency
UK Atomic Energy Authority 501
UK Ecolabelling Board 502
UK Hydrographic Office 503
UK Passport Agency 504
UK Register of Organic Food Standards 506
UK Sports Council 506
Ulster Folk & Transport Museum *see* Ulster Museum
Ulster Museum 508
Urban Regeneration Agency *see* English Partnerships

V&A *see* Victoria & Albert Museum
Valuation & Lands Agency 508
Valuation Office Agency 510
VCA *see* Vehicle Certification Agency
Vehicle Certification Agency 511
Vehicle Inspectorate 512
Vehicle Licensing *see* Driver & Vehicle Licensing Agency
Veterinary Laboratories Agency 513
Veterinary Medicines Directorate 515
Vetting Agency *see* Defence Vetting Agency
VI *see* Vehicle Inspectorate
Victoria & Albert Museum 516
VLA *see* Valuation & Lands Agency or Veterinary Laboratories Agency
VMD *see* Veterinary Medicines Directorate
VOA *see* Valuation Office Agency
Wales *see also* main title eg Arts Council of Wales
Wales Tourist Board 518
Wallace Collection 519
Waltham Forest Housing Action Trust 520
War Museum *see* Imperial War Museum
War Pensions Agency 521
Water Service 522
Water *see also* Office of the Water Regulator, Ofwat, Scottish Water,
WCC *see* National Consumer Council
WDA *see* Welsh Development Agency
Weights & Measures Laboratory *see* National Weights & Measures Laboratory
Welsh Advisory Committee on Telecommunications *see* Office of Telecommunications
Welsh Consumer Council *see* National Consumer Council
Welsh Development Agency 523
Welsh Fourth Channel Authority *see* S4C
Welsh Funding Councils *see* Further Education Funding Council for Wales, Higher Education Funding Council for Wales
Welsh Historic Monuments *see* Cadw
Welsh Language Board 525
Welsh National Board for Nursing, Midwifery & Health Visiting 526
West of Scotland Water Authority 528
Western Isles Enterprise *see* Highlands & Islands Enterprise
Westminster Foundation for Democracy 529
Wilton Park Executive Agency 530
Wine Standards Board 531
WLB *see* Welsh Language Board
WNB *see* Welsh National Board for Nursing
WPA *see* War Pensions Agency
WSB *see* Wine Standards Board
Youth Council for Northern Ireland 533